Credit Discrimination

With CD-Rom

*The Consumer
Credit and Sales
Legal Practice
Series*

Third Edition

Deanne Loonin
Chi Chi Wu

Contributing Author: Anthony Rodriguez

National Consumer Law Center

77 Summer Street, Boston, MA 02110

www.consumerlaw.org

About NCLC — The National Consumer Law Center, a nonprofit corporation founded in 1969, assists consumers, advocates, and public policy makers nationwide who use the powerful and complex tools of consumer law to ensure justice and fair treatment for all, particularly those whose poverty renders them powerless to demand accountability from the economic marketplace. For more information, go to www.ConsumerLaw.org.

Ordering NCLC Publications — Publications Department, National Consumer Law Center, 77 Summer Street, Boston, MA 02110, www.consumerlaw.org, (617) 542-9595, FAX (617) 542-8028, e-mail publications@nclc.org.

Training and Conferences — NCLC participates in numerous national, regional, and local consumer law trainings. Its annual conference is a forum for consumer rights attorneys from legal services programs, private practice, government, and nonprofit organizations to share insights into common problems and explore novel and tested approaches that promote consumer justice in the marketplace. Contact NCLC for more information or see our web site.

Case Consulting — Case analysis and consulting for lawyers representing consumers are among NCLC's important activities. Administration on Aging funds allow us to provide free consulting to legal services advocates representing elderly consumers on many types of cases. The Massachusetts Legal Assistance Corporation and other funds permit case assistance to advocates representing low-income Massachusetts and California consumers. Other funding may allow NCLC to provide very brief consultations to other advocates without charge. More comprehensive case analysis and research is available for a reasonable fee. See our web site for more information at www.ConsumerLaw.org

Charitable Donations and Cy Pres Awards — NCLC's work depends in part on the support of private donors. Tax deductible donations should be made payable to National Consumer Law Center, Inc. For more information, contact NCLC's Development Office at (617) 542-8010 or scutler@nclc.org. NCLC has also received generous court-approved *cy pres* awards arising from consumer class actions to advance the interests of class members. For more information, contact Robert Hobbs (rhobbs@nclc.org) or Rich Dubois (rdubois@nclc.org) at the same number.

Comments and Corrections — Write to the above address to the attention of the Editorial Department or e-mail consumerlaw@nclc.org.

About This Volume — This is a Third Edition to *Credit Discrimination* with a Cumulative 2002 CD-Rom. The Third Edition and CD-Rom supersede all prior editions, supplements, CD-Roms, and disks, which should all be discarded. Continuing developments can be found in periodic supplements to this volume and in NCLC REPORTS, *Consumer Credit & Usury Edition*.

Cite This Volume As — National Consumer Law Center, Credit Discrimination (3d ed. 2002).

ISBN 1-931697-20-5 (this volume)
ISBN 0-943116-10-4 (Series)

Library of Congress Control Number 2002108713

About the Authors

Deanne Loonin is an NCLC staff attorney specializing in credit discrimination and consumer credit law, with a special emphasis on consumer issues affecting the elderly and immigrants. She is author of *Student Loan Law* (2001) and co-author of *Surviving Debt* (1999, 2002). She was formerly a legal services lawyer in Los Angeles, specializing in consumer fraud cases.

Chi Chi Wu is an NCLC staff attorney specializing in credit discrimination and consumer credit law, with an emphasis on consumer issues affecting domestic violence victims and immigrants. She was formerly an Assistant Attorney General with the Consumer Protection Division of the Massachusetts Attorney General's Office, and an attorney with the Asian Outreach Unit of Greater Boston Legal Services.

Anthony Rodriguez is an NCLC staff attorney, and previously served as the Director of the Massachusetts Attorney General's Disability Rights Project, and also worked as an Assistant Attorney General in the Consumer Protection and Civil Rights Divisions, where he litigated UDAP, telemarketing, credit repair, housing discrimination and public accommodations cases.

Acknowledgments: We want to thank David Aleksic, Allen Agnitti, and Amy Marshall for legal research; Ira Rheingold, Nina Simon, Nina Vinik, Stuart Rossman for providing sample pleadings; and Jon Sheldon for doing the arbitration section.

We are grateful to Eric Secoy for editorial supervision; Dorothy Tan for editorial assistance; Shirlron Williams for assistance with cite checking; Mary McLean for indexing; Xylutions for typesetting services; and Neil Fogarty of Law Disks for preparing the CD-Rom. Finally, this volume builds on the prior two editions, and we want to thank all those who worked on those volumes, particularly the authors, Jonathan Sheldon and Rita Gordon Pereira, and the contributing authors Richard DuBois and Joanne Faulkner.

What Your Library Should Contain

The Consumer Credit and Sales Legal Practice Series contains 16 titles, updated annually, arranged into four libraries, and designed to be an attorney's primary practice guide and legal resource in all 50 states. Each manual includes a CD-Rom allowing information to be copied onto a word processor.

Debtor Rights Library

2000 Sixth Edition, 2001 Supplement, and 2001 Cumulative CD-Rom, Including Law Disk's Bankruptcy Forms

Consumer Bankruptcy Law and Practice: the definitive personal bankruptcy manual, with step-by-step instructions from initial interview to final discharge, and including consumers' rights as creditors when a merchant or landlord files for bankruptcy. Appendices and CD-Rom contain over 130 annotated pleadings, bankruptcy statutes, rules and fee schedules, an interview questionnaire, a client handout, and software to complete petitions and schedules.

2000 Fourth Edition, 2002 Cumulative Supplement, and 2002 Cumulative CD-Rom

Fair Debt Collection: the basic reference in the field, covering the Fair Debt Collection Practices Act and common law, state statutory and other federal debt collection protections. Appendices and companion CD-Rom contain sample pleadings and discovery, the FTC's Official Staff Commentary, *all* FTC staff opinion letters, and summaries of reported and unreported cases.

1999 Fourth Edition, 2001 Cumulative Supplement, and 2001 Cumulative CD-Rom

Repossessions and Foreclosures: unique guide to home foreclosures, car and mobile home repossessions, threatened seizures of household goods, tax and other statutory liens, and automobile lease and rent-to-own default remedies. Appendices and CD-Rom reprint relevant UCC provisions, summarize state foreclosure and right-to-cure laws, and present various sample pleadings.

2001 First Edition with CD-Rom

Student Loan Law: student loan debt collection and collection fees; discharges based on closed school, false certification, failure to refund, disability, and bankruptcy; tax intercepts, wage garnishment, and offset of social security benefits; repayment plans, consolidation loans, deferments, and non-payment of loan based on school fraud. CD-Rom and appendices contain numerous forms, pleadings, interpretation letters and regulations.

2001 Second Edition with CD-Rom

Access to Utility Service: the only examination of consumer rights when dealing with regulated, de-regulated, and unregulated utilities, including telecommunications, terminations, billing errors, low-income payment plans, fuel allowances in subsidized housing, LIHEAP, and weatherization. Includes summaries of state utility regulations.

Credit and Banking Library

1999 Fourth Edition, 2001 Cumulative Supplement, and 2001 Cumulative CD-Rom

Truth in Lending: detailed analysis of *all* aspects of TILA, the Consumer Leasing Act, and the Home Ownership and Equity Protection Act. Appendices and the CD-Rom contain the Acts, Reg. Z, Reg. M, and their Official Staff Commentaries, sample pleadings and rescission notice, and a program to compute APRs.

National Consumer Law Center ■ **77 Summer Street** ■ **10th Floor** ■ **Boston MA** ■ **02110**
(617) 542-9595 ■ **FAX (617) 542-8028** ■ **E-mail: publications@nclc.org** ■ **www.consumerlaw.org**

1998 Fourth Edition, 2001 Cumulative Supplement, and 2001 Cumulative CD-Rom	**Fair Credit Reporting Act**: the key resource for handling any type of credit reporting issue, from cleaning up blemished credit records to suing reporting agencies and creditors for inaccurate reports. Covers the FCRA, the Credit Repair Organizations Act, state credit reporting and repair statutes and common law claims.
2002 Second Edition with CD-Rom	**Consumer Banking and Payments Law**: unique analysis of consumer law as to checks, money orders, credit, debit, and stored value cards, and banker's right of set off. Also extensive treatment of electronic records and signatures, electronic transfer of food stamps, and direct deposits of federal payments. The CD-Rom and appendices reprint relevant agency interpretations and pleadings.
2000 Second Edition, 2002 Cumulative Supplement, and 2002 Cumulative CD-Rom	**The Cost of Credit: Regulation and Legal Challenges**: a one-of-a-kind resource detailing state and federal regulation of consumer credit in all fifty states, federal usury preemption, explaining credit math, and how to challenge excessive credit charges and credit insurance. The CD-Rom includes a credit math program and hard-to-find agency interpretations.
2002 Third Edition with CD-Rom	**Credit Discrimination**: analysis of the Equal Credit Opportunity Act, Fair Housing Act, Civil Rights Acts, and state credit discrimination statutes, including reprints of all relevant federal interpretations, government enforcement actions, and numerous sample pleadings.

Consumer Litigation Library

2002 Second Edition with CD-Rom	**Consumer Arbitration Agreements**: numerous successful approaches to challenge the enforceability of a binding arbitration agreement, the interrelation of the Federal Arbitration Act and state law, class actions in arbitration, the right to discovery, and other topics. Appendices and CD-Rom include sample discovery, numerous briefs, arbitration service provider rules and affidavits as to arbitrator costs.
2002 Fifth Edition with CD-Rom	**Consumer Class Actions: A Practical Litigation Guide**: makes class action litigation manageable even for small offices, including numerous sample pleadings, class certification memoranda, discovery, class notices, settlement materials, and much more. Includes contributions from seven of the most experienced consumer class action litigators around the country.
2001 Cumulative CD-Rom with Index Guide: ALL pleadings from ALL NCLC Manuals, including Consumer Law Pleadings Numbers One through Seven	**Consumer Law Pleadings on CD-Rom**: Over 600 notable recent pleadings from all types of consumer cases, including landlord-tenant, mobile homes, car cases, debt collection, fair credit reporting, home improvement fraud, fringe lending, rent to own, student loans, and lender liability. Finding aids pinpoint the desired pleading in seconds, ready to paste into a word processing program.

Deception and Warranties Library

2001 Fifth Edition with 2002 Supplement and 2002 Cumulative CD-Rom	**Unfair and Deceptive Acts and Practices**: the only practice manual covering all aspects of a deceptive practices case in every state. Special sections on automobile sales, the federal racketeering (RICO) statute, unfair insurance practices, and the FTC Holder Rule.
1998 First Edition, 2001 Cumulative Supplement, and 2001 Cumulative CD-Rom	**Automobile Fraud:** examination of odometer tampering, lemon laundering, sale of salvage and wrecked cars, undisclosed prior use, prior damage to new cars, numerous sample pleadings, and title search techniques.
2001 Second Edition and 2002 Supplement and 2002 Cumulative CD-Rom	**Consumer Warranty Law**: comprehensive treatment of new and used car lemon laws, the Magnuson-Moss Warranty Act, UCC Articles 2 and 2A, mobile home and new home warranty laws, FTC Used Car Rule, tort theories, car repair and home improvement statutes, service contract and lease laws, with numerous sample pleadings.

NCLC's CD-Roms

Every NCLC manual comes with a CD-Rom featuring pop-up menus, PDF format, Internet-style navigation of appendices, indices, and bonus pleadings, hard-to-find agency interpretations and other practice aids. Documents can be copied into a word processing program. Of special note is *Consumer Law in a Box*:

August 2002 CD-Rom

Consumer Law in a Box: a CD-Rom combining *all* documents and software from 16 other NCLC CD-Roms. Quickly pinpoint the document from thousands found on the CD through key word searches and Internet-style navigation, links, bookmarks, and other finding aids.

Other NCLC Publications for Lawyers

issued 24 times a year

NCLC REPORTS covers the latest developments and ideas in the practice of consumer law.

2002 First Edition with CD Rom

STOP Predatory Lending: A Guide for Legal Advocates: provides a roadmap and practical legal strategy for litigating predatory lending abuses, from small loans to mortgage loans. The CD-Rom contains a credit math program, pleadings, legislative and administrative materials, and underwriting guidelines.

Released Annually

Sourcebook of the Annual National Consumer Rights Litigation Conference: once a year, the nation's top consumer law practitioners share what works for them, with practical advice, sample pleadings, new legal developments, novel theories, and key cases.

National Consumer Law Center Guide Series are books designed for consumers, counselors, and attorneys new to consumer law:

2002 Edition

NCLC Guide to Surviving Debt A great overview of consumer law. Everything a paralegal, new attorney, or client needs to know about debt collectors, managing credit card debt, whether to refinance, credit card problems, home foreclosures, evictions, repossessions, credit reporting, utility terminations, student loans, budgeting, and bankruptcy.

2002 Edition

NCLC Guide to Mobile Homes: what consumers and their advocates need to know about mobile home dealer sales practices and an in-depth look at mobile home quality and defects, with 35 photographs and construction details.

2002 Edition

NCLC Guide to Consumer Rights for Immigrants: an introduction to many of the most critical consumer issues faced by immigrants, including international wires, check cashing and banking, *notario* and immigration consultant fraud, affidavits of support, telephones, utilities, credit history discrimination, high-cost credit, used car fraud, student loans and more.

2000 Edition

Return to Sender: Getting a Refund or Replacement for Your Lemon Car: Find how lemon laws work, what consumers and their lawyers should know to evaluate each other, investigative techniques and discovery tips, how to handle both informal dispute resolution and trials, and more.

Summary Contents

Contents

Chapter 2   Scope

Chapter 3   Prohibited Bases for Discrimination

| Chapter 4 | Proving Credit Discrimination |

| Chapter 5 | Discrimination in Pre-Application and Application Procedures |

Contents

Chapter 7   Redlining

Chapter 8   Reverse Redlining to Price Gouging: Discrimination in Credit Terms
and Pricing

Chapter 9   Discrimination Subsequent to the Granting of Credit

Chapter 10   ECOA Procedural Requirements

Chapter 11

Litigating a Credit Discrimination Case

Chapter 12

Government Enforcement

Chapter 1   Introduction and First Considerations

1.1 Credit Discrimination Laws—A Powerful Answer to a Pervasive Problem

1.1.1 Credit Discrimination Is a Widespread and Growing Problem

Credit discrimination permeates American society. Minorities and other protected groups face difficulties obtaining market-rate first and second mortgages; many banks do not even maintain branches in minority neighborhoods. The enormous disparity in mortgage approval rates between whites and nonwhites is evidence that discrimination in the marketplace persists.[1]

Credit discrimination is not limited to home mortgages. Car dealers, utilities, and credit card companies have all engaged in credit discrimination. The practice is also not limited to racial discrimination. Creditors often discriminate on the basis of an applicant's national origin, sex, marital status, familial status, sexual orientation, disability, age, religion, or receipt of public assistance.

Creditors discriminate at every stage of the credit transaction process, including which customers they solicit for business, to whom they grant credit, and how their customers are treated in subsequent stages of the credit transaction, such as in loan servicing and debt collection. Many consumers do not understand why they are turned down for credit.

One direct consequence of credit discrimination is lost opportunity—lost opportunity for home ownership, lost opportunity for a college education, and denial of access to medical care and other essential services. Another consequence of credit discrimination is the emergence of predatory lending in underserved communities.

Predatory lending is a direct and measurable cost of credit discrimination. Subprime, high-interest-rate first and second mortgage lenders target the very groups discriminated against by traditional lenders. These lenders often offer loans with high interest rates, outrageous fees, and onerous terms. This type of predatory lending, targeting minority or other protected groups, itself constitutes a form of credit discrimination.[2]

Credit discrimination starts many families into a downward spiral. Deprived of market-rate unsecured credit, the family may turn to a high-interest finance company which may flip the loan continuously until a small, unsecured loan becomes a large, unaffordable obligation secured by the family home, leading to foreclosure. Another consequence for consumers of being forced to borrow from high-rate creditors is that these creditors are quicker to call in loans when the borrower is delinquent and more likely to engage in aggressive collection tactics and seizure of property.

Outside of mortgages and other home loans, those discriminated against often resort to fringe lenders as their only alternative. These consumers end up paying interest rates of several hundred percent for payday loans, rent-to-own goods, tax refund anticipation loans and, in some states, auto title pawns.[3] Pawnbrokers, loan brokers charging unconscionable commissions, and car dealers selling overpriced used cars on credit with astronomical interest rates, flourish where market-rate lenders refuse to tread.

The adverse impact of credit discrimination on individuals, families and entire communities cannot be overstated. Advocates who fight against such discriminatory practices play an important role in ensuring equal credit opportunities for all.

---

1 For example, in 2000, mortgage lenders rejected nearly half of all African-American applicants and more than one-third of Hispanic applicants for conventional mortgages, as compared to less than one-quarter of white applicants. Ass'n of Community Organizations for Reform Now (ACORN), The Great Divide: An Analysis of Racial and Economic Disparities in Home Purchase Mortgage Lending Nationally and in Sixty Metropolitan Areas 1 (2001), *available at* http://www.acorn.org.

2 See Chapter 8 for a discussion on this form of credit discrimination, called reverse redlining.

3 For more information about non-mortgage predatory lending, see National Consumer Law Center, The Cost of Credit (2d ed. 2000 and Supp.); Lynn Drysdale & Kathleen Keest, *The Two-Tiered Consumer Financial Services Marketplace: The Fringe Banking System and its Challenge to Current Thinking About the Role of Usury Laws in Today's Society*, 51 S.C. L. Rev. 589 (2000).

1.1.2 Credit Discrimination and Other Discrimination Statutes Provide Far-Reaching Remedies

A series of federal and state statutes provide significant remedies to victims of credit discrimination. Violations of the Equal Credit Opportunity Act (ECOA), the Fair Housing Act (FHA), and 42 U.S.C. §§ 1981 and 1982 (hereinafter referred to as the federal Civil Rights Acts) can result not only in recovery of out-of-pocket damages but in recovery for such intangible injuries as humiliation, deprivation of rights, and damage to credit rating. These statutes also provide for punitive damages, equitable relief, and attorney fees.

Certain state credit discrimination statutes also provide for minimum statutory damages; state unfair or deceptive acts and practices statutes sometimes provide for treble damages or minimum statutory damages. The Fair Housing Act and certain state discrimination laws provide consumers with relief pursuant to an administrative proceeding in which the consumer need not pay attorney fees, filing fees or investigational costs. As a result, victims of credit discrimination have an impressive array of remedies available to them.

These statutes prohibit credit discrimination when a creditor treats individuals differently because of certain specified factors which are referred to as "prohibited bases." While the prohibited bases for discrimination vary by statute, one or more of the credit discrimination statutes prohibit discrimination on the basis of race, color, religion, national origin, sex, marital status, familial status, age, disability, public assistance status, and exercise of rights under federal consumer credit statutes. Other bases for discrimination, such as sexual orientation or location of a residence, are also actionable under certain state discrimination statutes, and can sometimes be actionable under the federal statutes.

There are two types of discrimination on a prohibited basis. Any time the discrimination is based directly on a prohibited basis this constitutes illegal disparate treatment, regardless of any business justification the creditor later tries to assert as grounds for its actions. The second type of illegal discrimination occurs when a practice has a disproportional impact or effect on the same classes protected by the statutes, e.g., minorities, women, the disabled, public assistance recipients, the elderly, and other protected groups. Such a practice in appropriate circumstances is still illegal even when a creditor has a legitimate business reason for its action and is not acting because of a prohibited reason.

To bring an action, the plaintiff need not even be a member of the group discriminated against, as long as the discrimination affects the plaintiff. For example, a white woman who was refused credit because she lived in a African-American neighborhood has an action under the credit discrimination statutes. Under the Fair Housing Act and federal Civil Rights Acts, the plaintiff need not even have sought credit, but could be a housing organization, neighbor, or other person affected by the discrimination against a credit applicant.

The credit discrimination statutes prohibit discrimination at all stages of a credit transaction, including differential treatment pre-application, during the application process, or concerning credit evaluation, credit terms, cosigners, price of related goods and insurance, loan servicing, loan collection, and at every other stage of the credit transaction. Credit discrimination statutes reach more than just transactions with stated interest charges, but apply to leases, utility service, certain medical treatment, and other transactions in which the consumer's obligation to pay is deferred until after receipt of the goods or services. Credit discrimination laws may even apply to differential treatment as to the cash price of the goods or services related to the credit.

Finally, the Equal Credit Opportunity Act lists certain specific consumer rights and creditor obligations. If a creditor violates any of these provisions, the creditor is liable for actual damages, a limited amount of punitive damages, and attorney fees. The ECOA also significantly restricts when a creditor may seek a spouse's cosignature on a loan, contains rules as to reporting information to credit reporting agencies, and restricts what information a creditor may request from applicants and what methods the creditor may utilize to evaluate applications.

1.1.3 Growth in the Utilization of Credit Discrimination Laws

Despite these far-reaching remedies, credit discrimination laws were not utilized significantly until the 1990s, and there is still room for growth. Throughout the 1980s, only a small number of ECOA cases were brought each year. The Fair Housing Act, the federal Civil Rights Acts, and even state credit discrimination statutes were rarely applied to credit discrimination.

In the 1990s, more credit discrimination cases were brought, particularly after Congress eliminated weaknesses in the FHA in the 1988 amendments. In addition, several restrictive Supreme Court decisions in the employment discrimination area (which affected the interpretation of the credit discrimination laws) were overturned by the passage of the Civil Rights Act of 1991.

Federal agencies began to take a leadership role in the 1990s by bringing credit discrimination cases. The Department of Justice, as well as the Federal Trade Commission and the Department of Housing and Urban Development, settled major cases against lenders' discriminatory credit practices. The Federal Reserve Bank of Boston issued a seminal report defining for the first time the exact nature of banks' racial discrimination in mortgage lending.[4] Enforcement agencies, including the Comptroller of the Currency, also used paired testers to investigate possible discriminatory practices. It remains to be seen how much of this heightened activity will continue in this decade.

Public awareness also increased in the 1990s concerning the existence of widespread credit discrimination and the consequences of that discrimination. More housing and other nonprofit community organizations began to challenge credit discrimination.

Perhaps most importantly, consumer attorneys started to understand that credit discrimination statutes are a promising avenue of attack in many different types of credit cases. Particularly attractive are the significant opportunities to recover large damages for intangible injuries, punitive damages, and attorney fees, as well as the option to bring cases in federal or state court and as individual or class actions. Consumer attorneys began utilizing credit discrimination statutes to challenge a multitude of abusive credit practices, including predatory lending and hidden broker kickbacks disproportionately charged to minority customers.

1.1.4 Effective Uses of Credit Discrimination Statutes

Listed below are some effective ways to use credit discrimination statutes. These statutes may be used to attack common discriminatory practices and to challenge many different types of creditor practices. They may be used by individuals, groups or in class actions. The statutes also include procedural requirements that apply even when discrimination is not alleged. When their provisions are violated practitioners should carefully evaluate whether to proceed with a case seeking equitable relief, actual out-of-pocket damages, actual damages for intangible losses (such as humiliation, affront, deprivation of rights, damage to credit rating), punitive damages (even when the violation merely relates to defects in a required notice), and attorney fees.

- *Discrimination against a wide variety of groups.* Credit discrimination laws prohibit discrimination on a number of bases in addition to race, national origin, sex, and religion. Creditors violate credit discrimination statutes if they discriminate:
  —against single parents, divorced women, pregnant women, or those taking in foster children;

—against noncitizens;
—on the basis of disability, including AIDS/HIV status;
—on the basis of sexual orientation, but only in a few states or under certain very limited circumstances;
—on the basis of old age.

- *Discrimination based on source of income.* Credit discrimination statutes protect applicants whose income is derived from:
  —public assistance;
  —part-time employment;
  —alimony or child support;
  —retirement benefits.

- *Denying or restricting credit to residents of certain geographic areas, known as redlining.* The practice of redlining is one of the most common and devastating forms of credit discrimination. Redlining can be challenged under the ECOA and the Fair Housing Act under a disparate impact theory when racial or ethnic minorities are being denied credit in disproportionate numbers (redlining is also challengeable as disparate treatment if the reason a creditor excludes certain areas is racial or ethnic). A few state credit discrimination laws explicitly prohibit geographic redlining.

- *Banks discouraging minority applications.* It is illegal credit discrimination for a bank to avoid having branches in minority communities, to target marketing to non-minorities, and to otherwise discourage minority applications.

- *Preferential treatment or coaching for non-minorities in the application process.* Discrimination in the lending process often does not consistent of blatant racism or hostility against protected class members, but rather in subtle forms of preference given to white applicants. Paired testers may be able to uncover creditors who treat individuals differently in the application process by helping only certain applicants overcome blemishes in their credit record. Seemingly identical applicants will consequently have very different looking files which the creditor (and the secondary market) use to determine creditworthiness.

- *Differential treatment of Native Americans, particularly those living on reservations.* Redlining can specifically affect Native Americans when creditors refuse credit to those living on reservations, or treat them differently. Even if a creditor has a legitimate business reason for such conduct it will have a disparate impact on Native Americans, and thus may be illegal if the same business consideration may be met using another factor that has a less disparate impact.

- *Reverse redlining.* Credit discrimination statutes should not only cover creditors denying credit, but also high interest rate lenders preying on minorities. It is clearly illegal for a lender to offer low interest loans to whites and high interest loans to African-Americans; it is also illegal for a lender only offering predatory terms to seek

---

4 Alicia Munnell et al., Mortgage Lending in Boston: Interpreting HMDA Data (Fed. Reserve Bank of Boston, Working Paper Series No. 92-7, 1992) (available from Federal Reserve Bank of Boston, Research Library-D, P.O. Box 2076, Boston, MA 02016-2076, 617-973-3397) (also available as Clearinghouse No. 47,967); *see* Ch. 12, *infra* (full discussion of government agency activities in addressing credit discrimination).

out primarily African-American or other minority borrowers.

- *Car dealers, brokers, or others steering minorities to different creditors or charging them higher prices and fees.* Arrangers of credit are covered by the credit discrimination statutes, and it is illegal for them to steer minorities and non-minorities to different creditors or to different credit programs, or to charge minorities more for credit and services.

- *Discrimination by all kinds of creditors.* Too often practitioners think only of discrimination for bank credit, credit cards, or similar market-rate credit. All creditors are subject to credit discrimination statutes, and actions can be brought against finance companies, loan brokers, car dealers, pawnbrokers, and others. Insurance companies are liable under the Fair Housing Act for discriminating in the provision of insurance for homes.

- *Discrimination by appraisers.* Appraisers may not use different standards or measures to appraise property if those standards or measures are derived on a prohibited basis.

- *Discrimination by eventual loan purchaser.* It is a violation of the credit discrimination laws for an institution that will purchase a loan to discriminate on a prohibited basis in the way it pre-approves or otherwise participates in the credit determinations of an originating lender.

- *Discrimination by utilities.* Every aspect of a utility transaction is subject to the ECOA, so that there cannot be differences in deposit requirements or disconnection procedures based on race, public assistance status, or other prohibited bases. Utilities may not be able to deny service because of outstanding balances owed by a present or former spouse.

- *Discrimination in medical service.* The ECOA applies to medical providers' discrimination against those on Medicare and Medicaid.

- *Differing standards as to when a merchant requires cash up-front.* Many sellers require cash up-front or even pre-payment, while others will bill the consumer and expect one lump sum payment (without any finance charges) within approximately thirty days. The ECOA prohibits sellers from requiring cash up-front from minorities, public assistance recipients, single mothers, or other protected groups if the same seller allows deferral of payment for others.

- *Discrimination in leases.* Different lease terms for public assistance recipients or minorities are illegal.

- *Different requirements as to collateral, cosigners, down payments, guarantors.* A creditor may seek whatever reasonable protection it wants against a consumer's potential default, but it may not discriminate in the type of protection it seeks if the reason for this difference is the applicant's race, public assistance status, or some other prohibited basis.

- *Requiring cosigners.* The ECOA has detailed rules as to when a creditor may and may not seek a spouse's cosignature. A successful ECOA challenge to a creditor's violation of these rules may void the spouse's improperly induced signature, and would certainly provide the spouse with an action for damages equal to the full extent of any obligation resulting from the improper signature.

- *Organizations concerned with home mortgage discrimination can bring actions in their own name.* Although the ECOA requires the plaintiff to be an applicant or someone obligated to pay a loan, the Fair Housing Act allows housing organizations and others to institute suit as long as they are in any way aggrieved.

- *Defects in notice of reasons for credit denial.* The ECOA requires that creditors provide a specific notice to all applicants when taking an adverse action. The creditor may be liable for actual damages, punitive damages, and attorney fees if it fails to provide this notice, if the reason stated for the adverse action is not specific enough or if it is not the creditor's real reason.

- *Home improvement contractor reneging on promised credit or changing credit terms.* Home improvement contractors may promise favorable credit terms, but then renege after the work has been done, often saying that the application has not been approved. This behavior is an ECOA violation if the contractor does not notify the applicant of the adverse action within thirty days of the credit application.

- *Termination or denial of credit because of a Truth In Lending (TIL) or other consumer credit claim.* Creditors may not discriminate against applicants because the applicant has exercised his or her rights under various federal consumer protection laws. Thus, even though a consumer has sued a creditor under such a law, the creditor may not use the suit as the basis of terminating the consumer's credit or lease. This applies also to the denial of new credit by the creditor being sued and also by other creditors.

- *Bad credit record because of TIL or other federal consumer credit claim.* It is an ECOA violation for a creditor to differentiate in the information about a customer it reports to a reporting agency because that individual is pursuing a consumer credit claim against the creditor. Thus the creditor should not represent an account as written off after a TIL settlement when the balance due was forgiven as part of a settlement.

1.2 How to Use This Manual

1.2.1 Abbreviations

This manual commonly uses the following abbreviations and shorthand:

- ECOA for the Equal Credit Opportunity Act;
- FRB for the Federal Reserve Board;
- HUD for the United States Department of Housing and Urban Development;
- DOJ for the United States Department of Justice;
- Federal Civil Rights Acts for 42 U.S.C. §§ 1981 and 1982;
- UDAP for general state statutes that prohibit unfair and deceptive acts and practices;
- HMDA for the Home Mortgage Disclosure Act;
- ADA for the Americans with Disabilities Act.

1.2.2 Overview of Chapters

The first three chapters of this book cover preliminary issues in credit discrimination cases. Chapter 1 of this manual introduces the reader to the issue of credit discrimination and to the various statutes that can be used to address it. It contains an overview and history of the ECOA and the FHA, as well as descriptions of other statutes that are useful in challenging credit discrimination. Chapter 2 details the scope and coverage of the credit discrimination statutes, including who is covered and what types of actions are covered. It discusses the definitions of credit, applicant, and creditor for purposes of the ECOA. This chapter should always be consulted if the practitioner is considering filing an action under the ECOA or the FHA, to ensure that the statute covers the transaction at issue.

Chapter 3 contains an in-depth description of the prohibited bases under both the ECOA and the FHA, the ECOA alone, the FHA alone, the federal Civil Rights Acts, and the ADA. It also notes additional prohibited bases that appear solely in state credit discrimination statues. A practice cannot be found discriminatory unless it discriminates on one of these prohibited bases. Chapter 4 examines the two major forms of credit discrimination, disparate treatment and disparate impact. It also discusses the analyses necessary to prove each form of discrimination.

Chapters 5 and 6 enumerate specific types of discrimination at different stages of a credit transaction. Chapter 5 focuses on discrimination prior to and during the credit application process, including prohibited requests for information and cosignatures. Chapter 6 focuses on discrimination during the credit evaluation process. It includes sections on the topics of credit scoring and discrimination based upon source of income.

Chapters 7 and 8 discuss the practices of redlining and reverse redlining. Chapter 7 examines redlining, the practice of separating out certain neighborhoods for disparate treatment in the granting of credit. Historically, redlining explicitly targeted communities of color for worse treatment. While no longer explicit for the most part, redlining still disproportionately affects neighborhoods of color. Chapter 7 includes a separate section on insurance redlining. Chapter 8 examines "reverse redlining," a form of predatory lending targeting communities of color. In reverse redlining, lenders predominately offer high cost, subprime loans to such communities while offering better loan products and terms in white communities. Chapter 8 explains why reverse redlining is a form of credit discrimination.

Chapter 9 focuses on discrimination during the latter stages of the credit transaction, after credit has been granted. This includes discrimination in loan servicing, in debt collection after default, in adverse actions taken on existing accounts, and in credit reporting.

Chapter 10 focuses on the ECOA's procedural requirements, including its notice and record retention requirements. The ECOA's notification requirements are very specific, and apply in every case—whether or not discrimination is suspected. Chapter 10 gives examples of how practitioners have used the ECOA's notification requirements to challenge abusive credit practices.

Finally, Chapters 11 and 12 cover private and governmental actions against credit discrimination. Chapter 11 discusses the issues involved in litigating a credit discrimination case, including standing, deciding who to sue, forum selection, private remedies, and creditor defenses. Chapter 12 focuses on the various efforts taken by government agencies, including both lawsuits and regulatory action, to challenge credit discrimination.

1.2.3 Violation of the General Prohibition Against Discrimination Versus Violation of Specific ECOA Rules

A useful way to approach this manual and a credit discrimination case in general is to determine if a case involves the general prohibition against discrimination, or whether it involves a specific ECOA requirement. Each type of case will require practitioners to focus on different chapters of this manual. In both types of cases, however, practitioners are advised always to consult Chapter 2 (scope) and Chapter 11 (private remedies and litigation strategies).

A case involving the general prohibition against discrimination will require practitioners to prove their case under either a disparate treatment or a disparate impact theory. The practitioner will need to focus on Chapter 3 (prohibited bases) and Chapter 4 (disparate treatment and disparate impact). Chapter 7 (redlining) and Chapter 8 (reverse redlining) may also need to be consulted if a particular community or geographic neighborhood is excluded or targeted.

The ECOA has a number of specific rules concerning a variety of topics, such as requests for information on a prohibited basis, cosignor requirements, and notification requirements. The chapters which describe these requirements are Chapters 5, 6, and 9 (discrimination at various stages of a credit transaction) and Chapter 10 (notification requirements).

1.2.4 This Manual Analyzes Several Different Statutes

This manual analyzes a number of different credit discrimination statutes. The ECOA is the primary statute discussed, in part because it has the broadest application and the most detailed standards. The Fair Housing Act is also given extensive consideration because it includes several prohibited bases not found in the ECOA (familial and handicap status), because any aggrieved party (even a tester, a neighbor, or housing organization) can bring an action, because punitive damages are not limited to $10,000, and because the Fair Housing Act more directly prohibits discrimination in residential leases and in the sale of residences. Although the FHA only applies to credit relating to a dwelling, it applies to first and second mortgages and to unsecured loans used to improve or maintain a dwelling. The FHA also provides critical remedies in predatory lending cases.

42 U.S.C. §§ 1981 and 1982, the federal Civil Rights Acts, are also analyzed but in less detail. These statutes, like the Fair Housing Act, are broader in some respects than the ECOA. Under these statutes any aggrieved party (not just an applicant) may bring an action; they clearly apply to all types of leases and even to sales not involving credit; and they are not limited in the amount of punitive damages available. These advantages make these statutes important in certain situations, particularly when the Fair Housing Act does not apply—that is, when the transaction is not related to a dwelling. The federal Civil Rights Acts may also be useful when the two-year ECOA and Fair Housing Act limitations period has run because the federal Civil Rights Act limitations period will be based on the analogous state law limitations period, which may be greater than two years.

The Americans with Disabilities Act[5] (ADA) is also briefly discussed in this manual. Title III of the ADA[6], prohibits discrimination on the basis of disability by places of public accommodation, which includes banks, retailers, and other service establishments.[7] The ADA may be especially useful in non-housing financing cases, because the ECOA does not include disability as a prohibited basis. However, the ADA's remedies are not as comprehensive as those under the ECOA, FHA or federal Civil Rights Acts, as the ADA does not provide a monetary damages remedy in its private right of action.

The manual also briefly covers state credit discrimination laws, particularly pointing out when using such laws may be helpful. The state laws themselves are summarized in Appendix E, *infra*. These statutes are particularly important when the plaintiff wants to stay in state court or when the state statute contains a prohibited basis not covered by the federal laws—such as sexual orientation. State discrimination laws also sometimes provide minimum statutory damages which are not found in the federal statutes.

A final category of laws mentioned in this manual are state UDAP statutes, that is, state statutes of general applicability prohibiting unfair and deceptive practices. These statutes are treated in detail in another NCLC manual,[8] and are only referred to in this manual when they are uniquely helpful in a credit discrimination case. They may offer longer limitations periods, better remedies (multiple damages or minimum statutory damages), and they may prohibit unfair discrimination even if the discriminatory basis is not covered by the credit discrimination statutes.

Actions may generally be brought under multiple theories of liability; however, there are certain exceptions. ECOA actions can not include state law theories, and if an action is brought under the ECOA and the Fair Housing Act, recovery may only be had under one or the other statute. But in all other cases, multiple theories may be used in the same suit.

If a practitioner is uncertain which statute to utilize, the discussion in each chapter will explain the relative merits of the various statutes. Once the relevant statutes are selected, the manual clearly indicates which sections of each chapter are relevant to those statutes.

1.2.5 Source Materials Found in This Manual

This manual contains the basic source materials for a credit discrimination case. Appendix A contains the relevant federal statutes, Appendix B contains the Federal Reserve Board's Regulation B under the ECOA, and Appendix C contains the FRB Commentary on Regulation B.

Appendix D contains important excerpts from HUD's fair housing regulations. Appendix E summarizes state discrimination laws; practitioners should supplement this appendix by consulting their own statutes for any recent amendments and for a careful reading of the law.

Other appendices include sample complaints (Appx. F), discovery materials (Appx. G), and a client handout about credit discrimination laws (Appx. H). This manual is accompanied by a CD-Rom that includes additional sample pleadings, consent judgments from credit discrimination

---

5 42 U.S.C. §§ 12101–12213.
6 42 U.S.C. § 12182(a).
7 42 U.S.C. § 12181(7)(F).

---

8 National Consumer Law Center, Unfair and Deceptive Acts and Practices (5th ed. 2001).

cases brought by government agencies, selected sections of other relevant federal statues and accompanying regulations (the Home Mortgage Disclosure Statute, the Community Reinvestment Act, and the Americans with Disabilities Act), and the Federal Reserve Board's proposed revisions to Regulation B, which were issued in August 1999.

Many unreported cases and certain other documents are cited in this manual using a "Clearinghouse" number. These documents are available through the National Center on Poverty Law (formerly the National Clearinghouse for Legal Services). These documents may be ordered from the National Center on Poverty Law by mail at 205 W. Monroe St., 2d Floor, Chicago, IL 60606-5013, via telephone at 800-621-3256 or 312-263-3830, via fax at 312-263-3846, or via e-mail at admin@povertylaw.org. Many documents are also available on their website: http://www.povertylaw.org. There is a $60.00 annual access charge plus $10.00 per copy plus a shipping charge for hard copies. Non-subscribers can order individual documents for $10.00 plus a shipping charge.

This manual should be used in conjunction with its most current cumulative supplement: NCLC typically releases annual cumulative supplements. NCLC REPORTS, *Consumer Credit & Usury* edition provides even more current credit discrimination developments six times a year.[9] Contact the National Consumer Law Center's Publications Department by mail at 77 Summer St., Boston, MA 02110, or by telephone at 617-542-9595, or by fax at 617-542-8028, or by e-mail at publications@nclc.org for more information.

1.3 The ECOA

1.3.1 Overview

The ECOA has two important aspects. First, it sets out a general rule that creditors cannot discriminate in any way against any applicant in any stage of a credit transaction on any of the following bases:

- Race;
- Color;
- Religion;
- National origin;
- Sex;
- Marital status;
- Age;
- Public assistance income; and

- Exercise of rights under the Consumer Credit Protection Act.[10]

Second, the ECOA sets out various specific actions that creditors must, or must not, take.[11] Examples are a required notice as to action taken on an application, a required notice as to an applicant's right to a copy of any appraisal of the value of the applicant's home, restrictions on what information can be sought in the application process, and restrictions on when a spouse can be required to be a cosigner. Other restrictions involve factors that may not be considered in determining creditworthiness (such as the types of income an applicant receives), when an existing account may be closed, and ways in which information is reported to credit reporting agencies concerning spouses.

Both the general rule against discrimination and the more specific requirements have a broad scope (with certain itemized exceptions).[12] Any individual applying for credit or obligated to pay on a loan may bring an action against any creditor, which includes those arranging and participating in loans. The ECOA applies not only to transactions involving multiple installments and to those involving a finance charge but to any deferral of payment, such as payment for services a week after the services are provided. The ECOA also applies not just to consumer credit but to business and other forms of credit. Special purpose credit programs are largely exempt, and exceptions narrow the requirements which apply to incidental consumer credit, utility credit, business credit, and securities credit.

ECOA remedies are actual damages, punitive damages (up to a maximum of $10,000 in an individual action), equitable relief, and attorney fees.[13] Actions may be brought in federal or state court, and may be brought on an individual or class basis.[14] Creditor defenses are limited.[15] Various federal agencies also have enforcement authority over ECOA violations.[16]

1.3.2 History

1.3.2.1 1974 ECOA Version Targeted Sex and Marital Status Discrimination

An important impetus for the ECOA's passage were hearings held by the National Commission on Consumer Finance[17] in 1972 documenting the difficulties women face in obtaining consumer credit:

---

9 Available from the National Consumer Law Center's Publications Department for $55. The other three editions of NCLC REPORTS are titled *Deceptive Practices & Warranties, Bankruptcy & Foreclosures*, and *Debt Collection & Repossession* ($10 for binder, $160 for all six issues of all four editions and binder).

10 42 U.S.C. § 1691; *see also* Reg. B, 12 C.F.R. §§ 202.2(z), 202.4.
11 *See generally* Chs. 5, 6, 9, 10, *infra*.
12 *See* § 2.2, *infra*.
13 *See* § 11.6, *infra*.
14 *See* § 11.4, *infra*.
15 *See* § 11.8, *infra*.
16 *See* Ch. 12, *infra*.
17 *See* National Comm'n on Consumer Fin., Report on Consumer Credit in the United States (1972).

- Single women found it more difficult to obtain credit than did single men in the same financial circumstances, especially in the area of mortgage credit;
- Married women often could not obtain credit in their own names;
- Women frequently were asked to reapply for credit in their husbands' names when they married;
- Creditors refused to consider part or all of the wife's income when a married couple applied for credit, even if she provided the primary or only source of income;
- Married women often were required to offer assurances that they employed birth control or, in extreme circumstances, to provide medical certification that they were no longer capable of bearing children; and
- Divorced or widowed women found it extremely difficult to obtain credit because credit previously obtained in their husbands' names was not taken into consideration when they attempted to apply for credit in their own names.

Responding to these concerns, in 1973 the United States Senate passed S. 2101 by a vote of ninety to zero.[18] The bill died in the House. The Senate Report accompanying S. 2101 is instructive in that it contains examples of the types of discriminatory practices on the basis of sex and marital status which the bill was designed to eliminate.[19]

The ECOA was not enacted until 1974, when a House-Senate Conference Committee reconciled two later bills, S. 3492 and H.R. 14856.[20] The House conferees acceded to the Senate in limiting coverage of the final ECOA only to sex and marital status discrimination (and not to race, color, religion, national origin or age as covered by the House bill), but the enacted version of the ECOA included several other provisions from H.R. 14856.[21]

This first version of the ECOA[22] was enacted on October 28, 1974, and became effective on October 28, 1975. The ECOA amended the Consumer Credit Protection Act[23] by adding a new Title VII, making it unlawful for any creditor to discriminate on the basis of sex or marital status with respect to any aspect of a credit transaction.[24]

1.3.2.2 1976 Amendments Broaden ECOA's Scope

A 1975 hearing before the House Committee on Banking, Currency and Housing gave special attention to age dis-

crimination, finding that creditors often established arbitrary age limits (usually around sixty-five years of age) after which credit would not be granted and existing credit would be revoked. Empirical data supplied to the Committee proved that senior citizens were often better than average credit risks.[25] In response, the Committee reported out H.R. 6516, prohibiting discrimination on the basis of race, color, religion, national origin and age.

Senate hearings in the same year before the Consumer Affairs Subcommittee[26] reached the same conclusion on age discrimination and also focused on discrimination against racial minorities; for example, studies indicated a strong probability of race discrimination in mortgage credit.[27] The Department of Justice urged inclusion of race, color, religion, and national origin as prohibited bases to parallel other civil rights legislation.[28]

The Senate hearings led to a revised bill which was eventually enacted by the Senate on February 2, 1976. The bill added the following prohibited bases for discrimination to the ECOA: age, race, color, religion, national origin, receipt of public assistance benefits, and the exercise of rights under the Consumer Credit Protection Act. The bill also added the ECOA's present remedial scheme, supplementing and expanding on that found in the 1974 statute.[29]

On March 9, 1976, the House and Senate approved the Conference Report. President Ford signed the Equal Credit Opportunity Act Amendments into law on March 23, 1976, effective one year from that date.[30]

In January, 1977, the Federal Reserve Board (FRB), pursuant to its statutory responsibility to implement regulations effectuating the ECOA's purposes,[31] adopted a new version of the implementing regulation called Regulation B.[32] This regulation interpreted both the 1974 statute and the 1976 amendments.

1.3.2.3 1985 Revision of Regulation B and Issuance of FRB Commentary

In 1985, the Federal Reserve Board (FRB) issued an

---

18 S. 2101, 93d Cong. (1973).

19 S. Rep. No. 93-278, at 3 (1973).

20 The ECOA was actually offered as an amendment in the Senate to H.R. 11221.

21 S. Rep. No. 93-902, at 4 (1974), *reprinted in* 1974 U.S.C.C.A.N. 6152.

22 15 U.S.C. §§ 1691 to 1691f (1974).

23 15 U.S.C. §§ 1601 to 1681t (1970).

24 15 U.S.C. § 1691(a) (1974).

25 H.R. Rep. No. 94-210, at 3–4 (1975) (accompanying H.R. 6516).

26 *Equal Credit Opportunity Act Amendments and Consumer Leasing Act—1975: Hearings on S. 483, S. 1900, S. 1927, S. 1961 and H.R. 6516 Before the Subcomm. on Consumer Affairs of the Senate Comm. on Banking, Hous. and Urban Affairs,* 94th Cong. (1975).

27 *Id.* at 39.

28 *Id.* at 317–19.

29 *See* S. Rep. No. 94-589, at 1 (1976), *reprinted in* 1976 U.S.C.C.A.N. 403. The text of the revised Senate bill was substituted for H.R. 6516.

30 Pub. L. No. 94-239, 90 Stat. 251 (1976) (enacted as amendments to 15 U.S.C. §§ 1691 to 1691f).

31 15 U.S.C. § 1691(b) (1976).

32 42 Fed. Reg. 1242 (1977). Regulation B is codified at 12 C.F.R. § 202.

overall revision of Regulation B.[33] At the same time, the FRB issued an Official Staff Commentary to Regulation B which supersedes all previous FRB Board and Staff Interpretations and letters.[34] This Commentary is sometimes referred to as "Supplement 1 to Regulation B" or as "ECO-1." The 1985 revision of Regulation B included (as appendices B and C) model application and notification forms which replaced all previous model forms released by the FRB.[35] The Regulation and Commentary are periodically updated, and the current versions are found at Appendices B and C, *infra*.

In August 1999, the FRB issued an extensive set of proposed revisions to Regulation B and the Official Staff Commentary.[36] The text of these proposed revisions can be found on the CD-Rom accompanying this manual. During the last three years and up until the printing of this edition, the FRB had not finalized these proposed rules. Major proposed revisions include removing the general prohibition against noting information about applicant's characteristics, such as national origin or sex, although such information still generally would not be allowed to be considered in extending credit, and also include requiring creditors to retain records for certain prescreened credit solicitations. Throughout this manual other key changes are noted that would be made by the proposed revisions.

1.3.2.4 Women's Business Ownership Act of 1988

The Women's Business Ownership Act of 1988[37] contained amendments to the ECOA chiefly relating to the Federal Reserve Board's treatment of business credit, but also applying to other FRB-created exclusions from the ECOA. The legislative history in the House Report expresses concern about the continued discrimination against women in business credit transactions.[38] Of particular interest is the House Report's criticism of the exemption allowed by the FRB under the ECOA for certain aspects of business and commercial credit, which led to an erroneous perception that the ECOA was not intended to apply to business credit.[39]

The ECOA was amended to clarify that it applied to business and commercial loans, and to preclude the FRB from making regulatory exceptions to the Act's coverage unless it expressly finds that applying the ECOA to the type of transaction exempted would not substantially effect the ECOA's purposes. As a result of the Women's Business

Ownership Act, the FRB issued revisions to Regulation B in 1989[40] and to the Official Staff Commentary in 1990.[41]

1.3.2.5 1991 Amendments

In 1991, the ECOA was amended as part of the Federal Deposit Insurance Corporation Improvement Act of 1991.[42] The most significant change for consumers was the amendment to section 1691 which mandated that the creditor provide, upon the applicant's request, a copy of its appraisal report on residential real property offered as security for a loan. The amendments also broaden public agencies' enforcement powers in relation to branches of foreign banks, create additional requirements that federal enforcement agencies refer cases to the Department of Justice for prosecution, create additional requirements that federal enforcement agencies refer Fair Housing Act violations to the Department of Housing and Urban Development (HUD), and clarify the Department of Justice's ability to seek monetary damages.

1.3.2.6 1996 Amendments

In 1996, the ECOA was amended as part of the Omnibus Consolidated Appropriations Act of 1996.[43] Incentives for self-testing and self-correcting were added, providing that reports or results of self-tests are privileged information under specified conditions. The FRB (in consultation with HUD) promulgated regulations dealing with these issues effective January 1998.[44]

1.3.3 Sources of ECOA Precedent and Authority

1.3.3.1 The Statute, Regulation, and Commentary

Any ECOA analysis begins with the statute, FRB Regulation B, and the FRB Official Staff Commentary. The statute is found at 15 U.S.C. §§ 1691 to 1691f, and is reprinted as Appendix A.1, *infra*. The ECOA requires the FRB to issue regulations to carry out the statute's purposes,[45] and the FRB has done that through enactment of its Regulation B, 12 C.F.R. §§ 202 to 202.15, reprinted as Appendix B, *infra*. The FRB issued a set of proposed revisions to Regulation B in August 1999, but has not yet

---

33 50 Fed. Reg. 48,018 (Nov. 20, 1985).

34 50 Fed. Reg. 48,018 (Nov. 20, 1985).

35 Reg. B, 12 C.F.R. app. B (Model Application Forms), app. C (Sample Notification Forms).

36 64 Fed. Reg. 44,581 (Aug. 16, 1999).

37 Pub. L. No. 100-533, 102 Stat. 2689, 2692–93.

38 H.R. Rep. No. 100-955, at 7 (1988), *reprinted in* 1988 U.S.C.C.A.N. 3535.

39 *Id.* at 15; *see also id.* at 26.

40 54 Fed. Reg. 50,482 (Dec. 7, 1989) (effective Dec. 8, 1989, compliance optional until Apr. 1, 1990).

41 55 Fed. Reg. 12,471 (Apr. 4, 1990).

42 Pub. L. No. 102-242, 105 Stat. 2300.

43 Pub. L. No. 104-208, 110 Stat. 3009 (1996).

44 Final regulations were published at 62 Fed. Reg. 66,412 (Dec. 18, 1997).

45 15 U.S.C. § 1691b(a)(1).

issued final rules.[46] The text of these proposed revisions can be found on the CD-Rom accompanying this manual.

In 1985, the Federal Reserve Board replaced all of its existing Board and Staff Interpretations and staff letters with an FRB Official Staff Commentary.[47] The FRB plans to incorporate all future Regulation B interpretations into this Commentary, rather than continuing to release individual interpretations.[48] The Commentary is reprinted as Appendix C, *infra*.

1.3.3.2 Case Law

The best sources of cases are: West's Federal Digest (keynote: Consumer Credit); the Consumer Credit Guide (CCH) (index heading: Equal Credit Opportunity); *Clearinghouse Review* (topic: Consumer Case Developments); and Westlaw and Lexis. Some ECOA cases are brought in state court, so state or regional reporters should be searched as well. Federal Trade Commission and Justice Department proceedings often are reported in the Consumer Credit Guide (CCH).

1.3.3.3 Legislative History

Both the 1974 and 1976 versions of the ECOA were accompanied by extensive hearings and congressional reports. The ECOA's legislative history is discussed in § 1.3.2, *supra*. In summary (and in chronological order), the legislative history is found in the following sources:

- S. Rep. No. 93-278 (1973) [to accompany S. 2101].
- *Credit Discrimination: Hearings on H.R. 14856 and H.R. 14908 Before the Subcomm. on Consumer Affairs of the House Comm. on Banking and Currency*, 93d Cong. (1974).
- S. Rep. No. 93-902 (1974), *reprinted in* 1974 U.S.C.C.A.N. 6119, 6152–53.
- H.R. Rep. No. 94-210 (1975).
- *To Amend the Equal Credit Opportunity Act of 1974: Hearings on H.R. 3386 Before the Subcomm. on Consumer Affairs of the House Comm. on Banking, Currency and Housing*, 94th Cong. (1975).
- *Equal Credit Opportunity Act Amendments and Consumer Leasing Act—1975: Hearings on S. 483, S. 1900, S. 1927, S. 1961, and H.R. 6516 Before the Subcomm. on Consumer Affairs of the Senate Comm. on Banking, Housing and Urban Affairs*, 94th Cong. (1975).
- S. Rep. No. 94-589 (1976), *reprinted in* 1976 U.S.C.C.A.N. 403.
- *Credit Card Redlining: Hearings on S. 15 Before the Subcomm. on Consumer Affairs of the Senate Comm. on*

Banking, Housing and Urban Affairs, 96th Cong. (1979).[49]
- H.R. Rep. No. 100-955 (1988), *reprinted in* 1988 U.S.C.C.A.N. 3535.
- H. Rep. No. 102-330 (1991), *reprinted in* 1991 U.S.C.C.A.N. 1901.

1.3.3.4 Other Sources of Authority

Other federal agencies, such as the Federal Trade Commission, have enforcement power under the ECOA.[50] Several of these agencies occasionally issue official interpretations or "informal" correspondence addressing specific credit situations under their jurisdiction. In addition, some state attorney generals have issued advisory opinions concerning the ECOA's relationship to state law. Law review articles are another useful source.

1.4 The Fair Housing Act

1.4.1 Overview

The Fair Housing Act (FHA) contains two different provisions dealing with credit discrimination. The more important of the two prohibits discrimination in residential real estate-related transactions.[51] The other provision focuses more on housing discrimination, in that it prohibits discrimination in the rental or sale of real estate.[52]

Section 3605 of the FHA bars discrimination in residential real estate-related transactions. This includes not only loans to purchase a dwelling but also loans in which a dwelling is taken as collateral, or when the proceeds will go to improve or maintain residential property.[53] This section is the one generally most useful in a credit discrimination case involving housing financing.

Section 3604 of the FHA bars discrimination in the terms or conditions of a sale or lease of any dwelling, as well as discrimination in the services or privileges associated with such a sale or rental, and discrimination in the advertising of any dwelling. Section 3604 also forbids the misrepresentation of the availability of any dwelling based on a discriminatory category and mandates that reasonable modifications for handicapped tenants must be allowed.[54]

There are two other provisions in the FHA which may be useful in a credit discrimination action. Section 3606 bars real estate brokers from discriminating in the provision of

---

46 64 Fed. Reg. 44,581 (Aug. 16, 1999).
47 *See* Official Staff Commentary, 12 C.F.R. § 202 Introduction-3.
48 Official Staff Commentary, 12 C.F.R. § 202 Introduction-2.

49 No legislation was enacted in response to these hearings.
50 *See* Reg. B, 12 C.F.R. app. A (Federal Enforcement Agencies) [reprinted as Appx. B, *infra*].
51 42 U.S.C. § 3605.
52 42 U.S.C. § 3604.
53 *See* § 2.3.2, *infra*.
54 See § 2.3.3.1.2 for a discussion of when section 3604 can be used in predatory lending cases.

their services. Additionally, section 3617 provides that it is unlawful to coerce, intimidate, threaten, or interfere with the exercise or enjoyment of various rights granted or protected by the Fair Housing Act, including the rights set forth in sections 3603, 3604, 3605 and 3606.[55]

Both sections 3604 and 3605 prohibit discrimination on the basis of race, color, religion, national origin, sex, familial status, and handicap. Thus there is considerable overlap with the ECOA; however, only the Fair Housing Act prohibits familial status and handicap discrimination, while only the ECOA prohibits discrimination based on age, marital status, public assistance status, and exercise of rights under the Consumer Credit Protection Act. The FHA also does not impose any specific credit requirements such as those found throughout the ECOA.

Remedies under the FHA include actual damages, punitive damages (unlike the ECOA there is no limit on the size of punitive damages awards), equitable relief, and attorney fees. The Fair Housing Act provides for both administrative and judicial proceedings for redress of violations. Plaintiffs can pursue either approach or both simultaneously (up until the time one or the other goes to actual trial).

Any party aggrieved by discrimination can bring an action, and the Act generally applies to most entities that might be involved in credit discrimination. There are few explicit exemptions from the Act's requirements.

1.4.2 History

The Fair Housing Act was originally passed as Title VIII to the Civil Rights Act of 1968.[56] The Civil Rights Act was enacted pursuant to the Thirteenth Amendment's grant of power to Congress to implement laws eliminating the badges and incidents of slavery,[57] and declares that "it is the policy of the United States to provide, within constitutional limitations, for fair housing throughout the United States."[58]

The Fair Housing Amendments of 1988 significantly amended the Act.[59] While the Fair Housing Act has always included a prohibition against discrimination in the financing of housing, the 1988 Amendments significantly ex-

tended the reach of the statute in this area. The Amendments also expanded the Act to cover discrimination based on disability and familial status, and not just race, color, religion, national origin and sex. The limit on the amount of punitive damages was also removed, meaning Fair Housing Act claims—whether brought on an individual or class basis—have no statutory cap as to the amount of punitive damages that may be awarded.

In addition to the above changes to the prior law, the Amendments also provide for liberal recovery of attorney fees, an expansive definition of an "aggrieved" party and a two year statute of limitations for private actions. Taken together, these Amendments make the Fair Housing Act a powerful tool in credit discrimination cases, as a companion or an alternative to the ECOA.[60]

In January, 1989, the Department of Housing and Urban Development (HUD) issued regulations interpreting the Act, as amended by the 1988 Amendments.[61] Accompanying those regulations was an important preamble, published on January 23, 1989.[62] However, the preamble was withdrawn from 24 C.F.R. part 100 on July 29, 1996 as part of the streamlining of regulations.[63]

On September 30, 1996, the FHA was amended as part of the Omnibus Consolidated Appropriations Act of 1996.[64] Incentives for self-testing and self-correcting were added, providing that reports or results of self-tests are privileged information under specified conditions. HUD (in cooperation with the FRB) promulgated regulations dealing with these issues effective January 1998.[65]

1.5 The Federal Civil Rights Acts: Sections 1981 and 1982

This manual also briefly treats two other federal statutes with some importance to credit discrimination. These two statutes, 42 U.S.C. §§ 1981 and 1982, are referred to throughout this manual as the federal Civil Rights Acts. These are recodifications of statutes enacted after the Civil War.

Section 1981, among other things, guarantees to all persons within the jurisdiction of the United States the same right as white citizens to make and enforce contracts. Section 1982 provides all citizens with the same right as is enjoyed by white citizens to purchase, lease, sell, hold and convey real and personal property.

55 *See* United States v. Am. Inst. of Real Estate Appraisers, 442 F. Supp. 1072, 1079 (N.D. Ill. 1977) (the promulgation of standards which cause real estate appraisers and lenders to treat race and national origin as negative factors in determining the value of dwellings and in evaluating the soundness of home loans may "interfere" with persons in the exercise and enjoyment of rights guaranteed by the Fair Housing Act in contravention of § 3617); Laufman v. Oakley Bldg. & Loan Co., 408 F. Supp. 489, 498 (S.D. Ohio 1976) (mortgage redlining "interferes" with the exercise of one's right to voluntary interracial association in contravention of § 3617).
56 42 U.S.C. §§ 3601–3619.
57 Williams v. Matthews Co., 499 F.2d 819, 825 (8th Cir. 1974); United States v. Hunter, 459 F.2d 205, 214 (4th Cir. 1972).
58 42 U.S.C. § 3601.
59 Pub. L. No. 100-430, 102 Stat. 1636.
60 For a detailed discussion of the provisions of the Amendments, see James A. Kushner, Fair Housing: Discrimination in Real Estate, Community Development, and Revitalization § 1.05 (1992 Supp.); Joseph G. Cook & John L. Sobieski, 3 Civil Rights Actions ch. 19 (1992).
61 24 C.F.R. subtit. B, §§ 100–125.
62 24 C.F.R. subtit. B, ch. I, subch. A, app. I.
63 61 Fed. Reg. 41,282 (Aug. 7, 1996).
64 Pub. L. No. 104-208, 110 Stat. 3009 (1996).
65 62 Fed. Reg. 66,423 (Dec. 18, 1997).

These statutes clearly apply to many aspects of credit transactions,[66] and also apply to many transactions beyond the scope of the ECOA and the Fair Housing Act. They are particularly useful in challenging discrimination in the leasing and sale of personal property.

The federal Civil Rights Acts generally apply only to racial discrimination, but the Supreme Court has expanded the scope of the Acts to include certain types of ethnic discrimination.[67] In addition, section 1981 should reach discrimination against noncitizens.[68] On the other hand, section 1982 does not provide rights to noncitizens.

The federal Civil Rights Acts provide for actual and punitive damages, equitable relief and attorney fees. Like the Fair Housing Act, but unlike the ECOA, there is no statutory cap on the size of punitive damages awards. Unlike the Fair Housing Act and the ECOA, the federal Civil Rights Acts only apply to cases of intentional discrimination, and do not apply to cases of disparate impact—that is, the "effects test" is not available to prove violations of the federal Civil Rights Acts. The limitations period for the federal Civil Rights Acts are determined by state law, so the period may be longer or shorter than the Fair Housing Act and the ECOA's two-year limitations periods.

The Civil Rights Act of 1991 amended section 1981 significantly. It added two new subsections, (b) and (c), and re-designated the prior text as subsection (a).[69] Subsection (b) added a definition of the phrase "make and enforce contracts," stating that it extends to both the "making, performance, modification, and termination of contracts" as well as to the "enjoyment of all benefits, privileges, terms, and conditions of the contractual relationship."[70] Subsection (c) added a provision making clear that section 1981 pro-

hibits discrimination by both private and governmental entities.[71]

1.6 The Americans With Disabilities Act

Another potentially useful tool for addressing credit discrimination is the Americans with Disabilities Act (ADA). The purpose of the ADA includes the "elimination of discrimination against individuals with disabilities" and the regulation of "commerce in order to address the major areas of discrimination faced day to day by people with disabilities."[72] The ADA may be especially useful in non-housing financing cases, because the ECOA does not include disability as a prohibited basis.

Title III of the ADA[73] prohibits discrimination on the basis of disability by places of public accommodations.[74] Public accommodation is defined to include banks, retailers, and other service establishments.[75] One significant and explicit prohibition under Title III of the ADA is the imposition or application of eligibility criteria that screen out or tend to screen out individuals with disabilities or any class of individuals with disabilities from fully and equally enjoying any goods, services, facilities, privileges, advantages, or accommodations, unless such criteria can be shown to be necessary for the provision of the goods, services, facilities, privileges, advantages, or accommodations being offered.[76]

There is virtually no case law under the ADA with respect to credit discrimination. The remedies under the ADA may not be as comprehensive as those found in the other discrimination statutes, because it does not provide for monetary damages in its private right of action.

1.7 State Credit Discrimination Laws

State laws dealing with credit discrimination are of several different types. State equal credit laws are generally patterned after the ECOA. State fair housing laws are generally patterned after the FHA. In the wake of the 1988 Amendments to the FHA, many states amended their fair housing statutes to add familial status and disability to the list of protected classes, to increase the statute of limitations from one to two years, and to eliminate the ceilings for punitive damages awards. States occasionally amend their credit discrimination laws, often to add protected classes. Consequently, the analysis of state housing laws found in

---

66 *See, e.g.*, Johnson v. Equicredit Corp., 2002 U.S. Dist. LEXIS 4817 (N.D. Ill. Mar. 22, 2002) (predatory lending/reserve redlining case brought pursuant to § 1981); Hargraves v. Capital City Mortgage Corp., 140 F. Supp. 2d 7 (2000) (predatory lending/reverse redlining case brought under both §§ 1981 and 1982), *reconsideration granted in part, denied in part*, 147 F. Supp. 2d 1 (D.D.C. 2001) (§ 1981 claim dismissed for lack of standing, but not § 1982 claim); Doane v. Nat'l Westminster Bank, 938 F. Supp. 149 (E.D.N.Y. 1996) (mortgage redlining case brought under §§ 1981 and 1982); Fairman v. Schaumberg Toyota, Inc., 1996 U.S. Dist. LEXIS 9669 (N.D. Ill. July 10, 1996) (§ 1981 suit over allegedly predatory credit scheme targeting African-Americans and Hispanics); Steptoe v. Sav. of Am., 800 F. Supp. 1542 (N.D. Ohio 1992) (mortgage redlining case brought under §§ 1981 and 1982 and the Fair Housing Act); Evans v. First Fed. Sav. Bank of Ind., 669 F. Supp. 915 (N.D. Ind. 1987) (§ 1982 can be used in mortgage lending discrimination case); Associates Home Equity Services v. Troup, 778 A.2d 529 (N.J. 2001) (predatory lending/reverse redlining case brought pursuant to § 1981).

67 *See* § 3.6.1, *infra*.

68 *See* § 3.6.3, *infra*.

69 Pub. L. No. 102-166, 105 Stat. 1071 (1991).

70 42 U.S.C. § 1981(b).

71 42 U.S.C. § 1981(c).

72 42 U.S.C. § 12101(b)(1), (4).

73 42 U.S.C. §§ 12181–12189.

74 42 U.S.C. § 12182(a).

75 42 U.S.C. § 12181(7)(F).

76 42 U.S.C. § 12182(b)(2)(A)(i).

Appendix E, *infra*, should be updated with the most current state amendments.

Sometimes recent amendments to the state fair housing acts offer broader protections than are found in the federal statutes. For example, several states explicitly prohibit discrimination based upon sexual orientation, political affiliation, or geographic boundaries.

1.8 State UDAP Statutes

Every state has a general statute prohibiting deceptive and unfair marketplace conduct. This manual adopts the typical term commonly used to refer to these statutes: UDAP (an acronym for Unfair and Deceptive Acts and Practices). UDAP statutes are treated in detail in another NCLC manual, *Unfair and Deceptive Acts and Practices* (5th ed. 2001).

UDAP statutes are important in that they provide excellent remedies, and because they apply to any kind of deceptive and unfair conduct. Thus, violations of a credit discrimination statute can also violate a state UDAP statute, providing treble damages and/or minimum statutory damages and a relatively long limitations periods in some states. More importantly, credit discrimination on a basis not prohibited by a credit discrimination statute could still be an unfair practice under a state UDAP statute.

1.9 The Community Reinvestment Act (CRA)

The Community Reinvestment Act (CRA) requires federal bank supervisors to monitor and evaluate how banks serve the credit needs of entire communities, including low and moderate-income neighborhoods.[77] It is distinct from the Fair Housing Act (FHA) and the Equal Credit Opportunity Act (ECOA) in that it addresses inequalities in the distribution of credit among geographic areas rather than discrimination against particular protected groups. It applies to all institutions whose deposits are covered by federal deposit insurance.

The basic premise of the CRA is that banks and savings institutions, although privately capitalized, have an underlying obligation to serve their local communities. This obligation is generally considered to be in exchange for government backing such as federal deposit insurance that banks need to survive. Although it does not provide a civil cause of action, the CRA does require regulatory agencies to publicly disclose certain findings and conclusions regarding lending institutions, including whether an institution is meeting community needs.[78] Most importantly for advocates, banks have a strong incentive to maintain a positive CRA rating as federal bank regulatory agencies may deny merger or expansion applications from institutions with low ratings. The CRA in a sense grants implicit standing to neighborhood groups and other advocates to intervene in lender expansion application proceedings.[79] In addition, regulators are permitted to impose sanctions on lenders with weak records.[80]

In general, the CRA is not aggressively enforced by regulatory agencies, although some advocates have been able to use it effectively to address unfair and discriminatory lending practices.[81] Without a civil right of action, it may not be directly relevant for individual litigation.[82] However, as part of an overall advocacy plan, it can be an effective tool for change.

1.10 Other Sources of Precedent

1.10.1 Housing Law in the Non-Credit Discrimination Context

There is an extensive body of cases brought under the Fair Housing Act in the rental, zoning, and other non-credit contexts. Much of this case law is used by courts as a source of precedent in credit discrimination cases brought under both the FHA and the ECOA, even in non-housing finance cases.[83] Some of these cases are discussed in this manual when relevant. However, for a more extensive discussion of fair housing case law, advocates are advised to consult available fair housing treatises and other resources.[84]

---

77 12 U.S.C. § 2903.

78 12 U.S.C. § 2906(b)(2).

79 *See generally* Allen Fishbein, *The Community Reinvestment Act After Fifteen Years: It Works, but Strengthened Federal Enforcement Is Needed*, 20 Fordham Urb. L.J. 293 (1993).

80 12 U.S.C. § 2903.

81 *See generally* Allen Fishbein, *The Community Reinvestment Act After Fifteen Years: It Works, but Strengthened Federal Enforcement Is Needed*, 20 Fordham Urb. L.J. 293 (1993) (it is not the lack of laws but rather the lackluster enforcement of the CRA that has contributed to the continuance of neighborhood disinvestments and lending discrimination); Frank Lopez, *Using the Fair Housing Act to Combat Predatory Lending*, 6 Geo. J. on Poverty L. & Pol'y 73 (1999).

82 One credit discrimination litigant was unsuccessful in his attempt to use negative CRA findings in his individual lawsuit. Stuart v. First Sec. Bank, 15 P.3d 1198 (Mont. 2000) (holding that a negative CRA report by the FRB and subsequent "Notice of Adverse Action Taken" were not sufficient to create a genuine issue of material fact whether the real reason for a loan denial was racial bias).

83 *See, e.g.*, Coleman v. Gen. Motors Acceptance Corp., 196 F.R.D. 315, 325 n.21 (M.D. Tenn. 2000) (applying FHA case law in a non-housing finance ECOA case).

84 *See, e.g.*, James A. Kushner, Fair Housing: Discrimination in Real Estate, Community Development, and Revitalization (2d ed. 1995); John P. Relman, Housing Discrimination Practice Manual (2000 Supp.); Robert G. Schwemm, Housing Discrimination: Law and Litigation (1990).

1.10.2 Employment Discrimination Law

In addition to housing discrimination cases, many courts have relied on the extensive body of law in the employment discrimination area as a source of precedent in credit discrimination cases.[85] For example, courts often turn to employment discrimination law when analyzing disparate impact claims in credit discrimination cases.[86] In addition some, but not all, federal courts have used the three-part, burden-shifting analysis developed by the Supreme Court for employment law cases in the *McDonnell-Douglas* case in credit discrimination cases.[87] Advocates might consider using employment discrimination law theories to develop novel legal theories in credit discrimination cases. For example, one commentator has suggested tackling the problem of discrimination by creditors when issuing pre-screened credit offers by using the analysis developed in cases challenging discrimination in employment recruitment.[88]

However, there are some differences between the two areas of law. For example, the ECOA prohibits creditors from favoring married couples over unmarried couples by only allowing the former to open joint accounts.[89] In contrast, several courts have held that state employment laws which forbid marital status discrimination do not prohibit employers from discriminating against unmarried couples.[90]

---

85 The Equal Employment Opportunity Commission's website is a good resource on federal employment anti-discrimination law, and includes relevant statutes, regulations and the EEOC's enforcement guidance, which is its interpretation of current issues in the law. *See* http://www.eeoc.gov. Other employment anti-discrimination law resources include Barbara Lindemann & Paul Grossman, Employment Discrimination Law (3d ed. 1996).

86 *See, e.g.*, Bhandari v. First Nat'l Bank of Commerce, 808 F.2d 1082, 1101 (5th Cir. 1987), *rev'd in part on other grounds*, 829 F.2d 1343 (5th Cir. 1987) (en banc), *vacated and remanded*, 492 U.S. 901, *reinstated*, 887 F.2d 609 (5th Cir. 1989); Coleman v. Gen. Motors Acceptance Corp., 196 F.R.D. 315, 325–26 (M.D. Tenn. 2000); Buycks-Roberson v. Citibank, 162 F.R.D. 332 (N.D. Ill. 1995); Gross v. United States Small Bus. Admin., 669 F. Supp. 50 (N.D.N.Y. 1987), *aff'd*, 867 F.2d 1423 (2d Cir. 1988); Williams v. First Fed. Sav. & Loan Ass'n, 554 F. Supp. 447 (N.D.N.Y. 1981), *aff'd*, 697 F.2d 302 (2d Cir. 1982); Cherry v. Amoco Oil Co., 490 F. Supp. 1026 (N.D. Ga. 1980).

87 *See* § 4.2.3.2, *infra* (description of the *McDonnell-Douglas* test and of the split among federal courts as to whether it should be applied in credit discrimination cases).

88 Timothy J. Lambert, *Fair Marketing: Challenging Pre-Application Lending Practices*, 87 Geo. L.J. 2181 (1999).

89 Official Staff Commentary, 12 C.F.R. § 202.6(b)(1)-1; Markham v. Colonial Mortgage Serv. Co., 605 F.2d 566 (D.C. Cir. 1979); Diaz v. Va. Hous. Dev. Auth., 101 F. Supp. 2d 415, 419–420 (E.D. Va. 2000).

90 *See* Parker-Bigback v. St. Labre School, 7 P.3d 361 (Mont. 2000), *cert. denied*, 531 U.S. 1076 (2001); Waggoner v. Ace Hardware Corp., 953 P.2d 88 (Wash. 1998). Note that Title VII of the federal Civil Rights Act, which is the federal anti-discrimination employment law, does not prohibit marital status discrimination. 42 U.S.C. § 2000e-2(a)(1). Several states have enacted fair employment and fair housing laws prohibiting marital status discrimination. These states are split as to whether such provisions also protect unmarried couples. *See* John C. Beattie, *Prohibiting Marital Status Discrimination: A Proposal for the Protection of Unmarried Couples*, 42 Hastings L.J. 1415 (1991).

Chapter 2   Scope

2.1 Introduction

Credit discrimination statutes apply broadly to a wide range of credit-related activities. In addition, the statutes cover a wide range of credit actors, including lenders, brokers, assignees and even secondary market purchasers.

This chapter deals specifically with who is covered and what types of actions are covered. Subsequent chapters address the various stages of the credit process at which discrimination might occur and when this discrimination might be illegal. As requirements are different under the different statutes, each statute is treated separately in this chapter.

2.2 Scope of the ECOA

2.2.1 Introduction

Before bringing an ECOA action, an advocate must consider three preliminary questions:

- Has there been an extension of "credit" covered by the ECOA? If so, is the transaction fully subject to the requirements of the ECOA, or has the Federal Reserve Board exempted the transaction from certain Regulation B requirements?
- Is the client an "applicant" who can invoke the statute's protection and recover under its remedy provisions?
- Is the party being sued a "creditor" under the ECOA definition, and therefore subject to the statute's requirements and liable for damages?

All three of these initial issues must be affirmatively resolved before the advocate can begin to consider specific ECOA violations which may have been committed in the client's transaction.

2.2.2 The ECOA Applies to "Credit" Transactions

2.2.2.1 Definition of Credit

2.2.2.1.1 General

The ECOA generally only applies to credit transactions.[1] For ECOA purposes, the definition of credit is quite broad. Credit is the right granted by a creditor to:

- Defer payment of a debt;
- Incur debt and defer its payment; or
- Purchase property or services and defer payment.[2]

The ECOA's definition is intentionally broader than that found under the federal Truth in Lending Act (TILA).[3] In contrast to ECOA, TILA requires that a transaction involve either a finance charge or at least five installment payments.[4] In addition, the ECOA's coverage (unlike TILA's) includes not only consumer, but also commercial credit, such as credit for business, agricultural or investment purposes.[5]

The ECOA explicitly applies to any purchase in which payment is deferred.[6] This obligation can arise by contract, by oral agreement, or by conduct.[7] Common examples are doctor and hospital bills, bills from repair people and other workers, and even a local store where a customer runs up a tab.

---

1 *See* Reg. B, 12 C.F.R. § 202.4 (general rule prohibiting discrimination).

2 15 U.S.C. § 1691a(d); Reg. B, 12 C.F.R. § 202.2(j).

3 Official Staff Commentary, 12 C.F.R. § 202.1(a)-1.

4 *Compare* 15 U.S.C. § 1691a(e) (ECOA) *with* 15 U.S.C. § 1602(f) (TILA). *See* Official Staff Commentary, 12 C.F.R. § 202.2(j)-1; National Consumer Law Center, Truth in Lending § 2.3.4 (4th ed. 1999 and Supp.).

5 Official Staff Commentary, 12 C.F.R. § 202.1(a)-1; *see also* Official Staff Commentary, 12 C.F.R. § 202.2(j)-1.

6 *See* Official Staff Commentary, 12 C.F.R. § 202.2(j)-1 ("Regulation B covers a wider range of credit transactions than Regulation Z. . . . [A] transaction is credit if there is a right to defer payment of a debt. . . .").

7 *See, e.g.,* Mick v. Level Propane Gases, Inc., 183 F. Supp. 2d 1014 (S.D. Ohio 2000) (in finding propane supplier to be creditor court stated that it is the nature of the service transaction, not the creditor's characterization, that is most important).

Although the ECOA's definition of credit is broader than TILA's, not all transactions are covered. The ECOA only applies to transactions that involve deferred payments. Not all transactions meet this broad definition. For example, courts have held that the ECOA does not cover applications for teller cards and savings accounts because they did not qualify as deferred payment arrangements.[8] In addition, the mere charging of interest without other indications that the transaction involves a deferral of payment has been held insufficient to meet the definition of credit.[9]

2.2.2.1.2 Is "debt" required to meet the ECOA definition of credit?

All three elements of the ECOA definition of credit require deferment of payment. However, the third category, the right granted by a creditor to "purchase property or services and defer payment," is distinguishable from the first two in that it does not refer specifically to debt. Some courts have held that this means that the existence of debt is not a prerequisite to an ECOA credit transaction.[10]

For example, a credit transaction was found when a propane gas delivery company gave a twenty-day deferred payment option to its customers.[11] The customers did not owe the company anything during the twenty days and therefore were not in debt. However, because there was a deferral of payment, there was a credit transaction under the third category of the ECOA definition of credit.[12]

The definition of credit in Regulation B lends further support to this interpretation. Regulation B replaces the term debtor used in the statutory definition of credit in § 1691a(d) with the term applicant.[13] At least one court noted that the Federal Reserve Board's definition makes it clear that applicants who have yet to be granted credit and who therefore may not be debtors are nonetheless covered by the ECOA.[14]

The critical issue, therefore, is whether a deferred payment arrangement exists. However, even if such an arrangement exists, the creditor may still be exempted from complying with some of the procedural requirements of the ECOA if the transaction is considered to be "incidental credit."[15]

Incidental credit is defined as credit:

- Primarily for personal, family, or household purposes;
- Not involving public utilities or securities credit;
- Not made pursuant to the terms of a credit card account;
- Not subject to any finance charge or interest; and
- Not payable by agreement in more than four installments.[16]

Examples may include deferment of payment by doctors, lawyers, hospitals, and some small retailers.

2.2.2.2 Do Leases Involve Credit?

2.2.2.2.1 Overview

There are four primary types of consumer leases: 1) leases involving residences (such as apartments and mobile home park space), 2) automobile and other durable goods leases covered by the federal Consumer Leasing Act,[17] 3) credit sales disguised as leases, and 4) rent-to-own leases (terminable at will subject to forfeiture of any built-up equity) of electronic entertainment equipment, appliances, and other consumer items. The arguments to support the application of the ECOA to leases differ depending on the type of lease involved.

2.2.2.2.2 Disguised credit sales

If a lease is really a disguised credit sale, it should certainly fall within the ECOA's definition of credit. Statutes utilize various standards to determine if a transaction is a disguised credit sale. Under the Truth in Lending Act, a lease is "credit" if the customer contracts to pay a sum substantially equivalent to, or in excess of, the value of the property or services involved and will become the owner for no extra cost, or for a nominal consideration, upon full

---

8 *See, e.g.,* Butler v. Capitol Fed. Sav., 904 F. Supp. 1230, 1234 (D. Kan. 1993) (plaintiff's application to open a savings account is not a credit transaction because it is not a right to defer payment of a debt); Dunn v. Am. Express Co., 529 F. Supp. 633, 634 (D. Colo. 1982) (application for a teller card did not involve a credit transaction because no evidence that application gave plaintiff right to defer the payment of any debt).

9 Riethman v. Berry, 113 F. Supp. 2d 765, 769 (E.D. Pa. 2000) (the imposition of an interest charge on any outstanding balance does not constitute the extension of credit under ECOA because it does not grant the debtor the right to defer payment of debt; court also characterized charges by attorneys on clients' unpaid balances as a penalty rather than interest).

10 *See, e.g.,* Barney v. Holzer Clinic, Ltd., 110 F.3d 1207 (6th Cir. 1997); Mick v. Level Propane Gases, Inc., 183 F. Supp. 2d 1014 (S.D. Ohio 2000).

11 Mick v. Level Propane Gases, Inc., 183 F. Supp. 2d 1014 (S.D. Ohio 2000).

12 *Id.*

13 12 C.F.R. § 202.2(j).

14 Barney v. Holzer Clinic, Ltd., 110 F.3d 1207, 1209 (6th Cir. 1997) (applicants who have yet to be granted credit and who

therefore may not be debtors are nonetheless covered by the ECOA; however, the court held that the Medicaid recipient plaintiffs did not meet the definition of applicant under the ECOA and therefore were not covered by the ECOA).

15 *See* Williams v. AT & T Wireless Services, Inc., 5 F. Supp. 3d 1142 (W. D. Wash. 1998) (application for cellular phone service held to be credit, but creditor exempted from notice requirements because considered to be incidental credit). *See generally* § 2.2.6.3, *infra.*

16 Reg. B., 12 C.F.R. § 202.3(c); *see* § 2.2.6.3, *infra.*

17 15 U.S.C. § 1667.

compliance with the lease's terms.[18]

UCC § 1-201(37) provides a more detailed standard as to whether a transaction is a lease or whether it involves a security interest (and thus should be treated as a credit sale).[19]

2.2.2.2.3 Personal property leases covered by the Consumer Leasing Act

The leading case, *Brothers v. First Leasing*,[20] a Ninth Circuit opinion, holds that the ECOA applies to personal property leases covered by the Consumer Leasing Act (CLA). While the decision details numerous reasons for this result, there are two major grounds for the holding. First, in the lease at issue (and most other leases covered by the CLA), the consumer is obligated for a total payment over the lease term and payment is deferred through monthly installment payments. This deferred payment arrangement meets the ECOA's definition of credit.[21]

The second ground for the Ninth Circuit holding stems from the fact that the ECOA and the CLA are both part of the federal Consumer Credit Protection Act (CCPA). A review of the CCPA's structure indicates that Congress intended the ECOA to apply to all transactions regulated by the CCPA. Congress also did not intend that lessors engage in otherwise illegal discrimination.[22]

At least one court, however, has declined to follow *Brothers*, holding that an equipment lease under which contemporaneous payments were made in exchange for possession of the leased equipment was not a credit transaction within the scope of the ECOA.[23] The court concluded that the lessee had not necessarily incurred a debt for which payment was deferred, because a mitigation clause in the agreement provided that the lessee's financial obligation would be extinguished upon surrender of possession of the equipment. The court's reasoning is dubious, as the lessee would not be released from its obligations under the lease unless the lessor succeeded in mitigating its damages. It is always true that one party's obligation under a contract *could* be extinguished if the other party were to mitigate its damages. This contingency is not, however, a sound basis for concluding that no obligation existed in the first place.

This same court also found it significant that in 1985 the Federal Reserve Board of Governors responded to the *Brothers* case by stating in supplemental information to Regulation B that the ECOA should not be construed to cover leases.[24] This reliance appears to overstate the significance of the 1985 interpretation. Since the 1985 Official Staff Interpretation, the Board has declined to make any conforming changes to Regulation B or to the Official Staff Commentary. On the contrary, since 1985, the Board has reasserted its broad definition of credit.[25]

2.2.2.2.4 Residential leases

The *Brothers* holding is explicitly limited to personal property leases covered by the Consumer Leasing Act (CLA). Apartment leases, leases of mobile home park space, and other real estate-related leases are not covered by the CLA, and thus do not fall under the precise *Brothers* court's holding. Moreover, the *Brothers* reasoning concerning the CLA and ECOA being part of the same statute is inapplicable to residential leases.

Nevertheless, the ECOA may apply to residential leases in certain circumstances. The key question is whether a residential lease transaction is considered an extension of credit as defined by the ECOA.[26] Regulation B defines credit as the "right granted by a creditor to an applicant to defer payment of a debt, incur debt and defer its payment, or purchase property or services and defer payment therefor."[27] Even though a lease may not primarily provide credit, any deferral of payment is arguably sufficient to qualify a lease as credit.

18 Regulation Z, 12 C.F.R. § 226.2(a)(16), uses this definition of credit sale. *See, e.g.*, Waldron v. Best T.V. & Stereo Rentals, 485 F. Supp. 718 (D. Md. 1979); Johnson v. McNamara, 1979 U.S. Dist. LEXIS 13081 (D. Conn. Apr. 12, 1979).

19 *See* National Consumer Law Center, Truth in Lending § 9.2.3 (4th ed. 1999 and Supp.); National Consumer Law Center, Repossessions and Foreclosures § 19.1.2 (4th ed. 1999 and Supp.). Note that the U.C.C. § 1-201(37) definition of security interest was significantly amended in conjunction with the enactment of Article 2A on leases in 1987 and 1990. Subsequently, most jurisdictions have adopted the new version of section 1-201(37).

20 724 F.2d 789 (9th Cir. 1984); *see also* Bo Foods, Inc. v. Bojangles of Am., Inc., 1987 U.S. Dist. LEXIS 531 (N.D. Ill. Jan. 23, 1987). *Contra* Liberty Leasing Co. v. Machamer, 6 F. Supp. 2d 714 (S.D. Ohio 1998) (relevant inquiry to determine whether a lease is considered credit under ECOA is whether the incremental payments constitute a contemporaneous exchange of consideration for the possession of the leased goods; in finding car lease not to be credit under the ECOA, court explicitly rejected *Brothers*'s holding that a lease obligation is credit under ECOA as a matter of law).

21 Brothers v. First Leasing, 724 F.2d 789, 792 (9th Cir. 1984).

22 *See id.* at 794.

23 Liberty Leasing Co. v. Machamar, 6 F. Supp. 2d 714 (S.D. Ohio 1998).

24 12 C.F.R. § 202 supp. info. (1985); *see* Liberty Leasing Co. v. Machamer, 6 F. Supp. 2d 714 (S.D. Ohio 1998). *But see* Williams v. AT & T Wireless Services, Inc., 5 F. Supp. 2d 1142 (W.D. Wash. 1998); Ferguson v. Park City Mobile Homes, 1989 U.S. Dist. LEXIS 11010 (N.D. Ill Sept. 15, 1989).

25 Official Staff Interpretations should be accorded less weight than the Official Staff Commentary. The Federal Reserve Board, in fact, notes that the Official Staff Commentary (OSC) replaces all previous Board interpretations of the ECOA. Notably, the OSC does not adopt the 1985 interpretation regarding leasing. *See* Reg. B., 12 C.F.R. § 202 app. D (the commentary is the means by which the Board issues official staff interpretations of Reg. B). *See generally* Brian S. Prestes, *Application of the Equal Credit Opportunity Act to Housing Leases*, 67 U. Chi. L. Rev. 865 (2000).

26 *See* § 2.2.2.1, *supra*.

27 12 C.F.R. § 202.2(j).

There is no clear nationwide rule on this issue and no Supreme Court ruling to date. The key case holding that a real property lease constitutes deferred payment and therefore credit is *Ferguson v. Park City Mobile Homes.*[28] The *Ferguson* court stated that any lease to be paid in installments is a credit transaction, because the willingness of the lessor to defer payments over the life of the lease depends upon the perceived creditworthiness of the lessee.[29] The broad ruling in *Ferguson* would allow nearly all leases to be considered credit transactions, as most leases require periodic payments throughout the lease term. Usually, the lease is for a specified term, such as a year, and payments are made monthly.

According to at least one commentator, the determination of whether a lease is covered by the ECOA depends on a close reading of the terms of the lease and of landlord-tenant law in the particular jurisdiction.[30] The key issue is whether relevant laws mandatorily permit or require the lease to take on the characteristic of deferred payment. For example, from the landlord's perspective, a lease is not an extension of credit so long as the landlord can terminate the lease immediately upon non-payment by the tenant. In contrast, if the landlord cannot force the tenant to surrender possession upon non-payment, the lease more closely resembles credit because the tenant can continue in possession beyond the period for which she has paid.

In cases involving discrimination on the basis of race, national origin, religion, or sex, it may not matter whether the ECOA applies to residential leases, because the Fair Housing Act clearly applies.[31] Nevertheless, ECOA coverage is important if rental discrimination is based on the tenant's age, marital status, receipt of public assistance, or exercise of Consumer Credit Protection Act rights, as these bases are not covered by the Fair Housing Act.[32]

Whether or not the ECOA applies to residential leases is particularly important when a landlord denies a rental application because of problems with the prospective tenant's credit report. Under the Fair Credit Reporting Act, a landlord rejecting a prospective tenant's application based on a credit report is only required to inform the applicant that the application was denied based on the report and provide information on how to obtain a copy of the report.[33] These limited requirements may allow landlords to use applicants' credit reports to hide discriminatory decisions based on prohibited grounds. Application of the ECOA to residential leases would force landlords to provide prospective tenants with the specific reasons why their credit reports were inadequate, presumably providing some additional protection from illegal discrimination.[34]

2.2.2.2.5 *Rent-to-own and other terminable leases*

Rent-to-own transactions (such as those involving televisions, stereos, and appliances) are structured so that the consumer can terminate the lease at any time. Termination of the lease results in the forfeiting of any built up equity from past lease payments, but the consumer owes no other early termination penalty. Typically, payments are made weekly or monthly, and the consumer has the option to keep the property after a stipulated number of payments.

Because they are terminable at will without penalty, rent-to-own transactions are not covered by the Consumer Leasing Act.[35] Consequently, the holding in *Brothers* does not explicitly apply, and the coverage under the ECOA is unclear. Moreover, rent-to-own companies may claim that there is no deferral of payment, because each payment is due in advance. They will claim that, in effect, the transaction is a series of weekly or monthly transactions, each paid in cash, in advance, thus involving no credit.

There are several arguments why a rent-to-own transaction is covered by the ECOA. If the transaction is viewed as a disguised credit sale (and this is the result that a significant number of cases reach), the ECOA clearly applies.[36] Nevertheless, to determine if a rent-to-own transaction is a disguised credit sale requires a careful reading of any special state statute dealing with rent-to-own leases, the state's retail installment sales act, and that state's version of the Uniform Commercial Code, particularly its version of UCC § 1-201(37).[37]

Alternatively, the rent-to-own transaction may still involve a deferral of payment. This may turn on whether the

---

28   1989 U.S. Dist. LEXIS 11010 (N.D. Ill. Sept. 15, 1989) (while not following the reasoning of *Brothers*, the court nevertheless denied creditor's motion to dismiss claim that the ECOA applies to lease of mobile home lot).

29   *Id.* at *8. Some courts have dismissed the *Ferguson* holding because it failed to take into account the 1985 Official Staff Interpretation by the Federal Reserve Board of Governors which stated that leases should not be covered by the ECOA. *See, e.g.,* Liberty Leasing Co. v. Machamer, 6 F. Supp. 2d 714 (S.D. Ohio 1998).

30   *See generally* Brian S. Prestes, *Application of the Equal Credit Opportunity Act to Housing Leases,* 67 U. Chi. L. Rev. 865 (2000).

31   *See* 2.3, *infra.*

32   *See* 3.4, *infra.*

33   15 U.S.C. § 1681m(a). *See generally* National Consumer Law Center, Fair Credit Reporting Act § 5.4.1 (4th ed. 1998 and Supp.).

34   *See* § 10.2.7.2, *infra. See generally* Brian S. Prestes, *Application of the Equal Credit Opportunity Act to Housing Leases,* 67 U. Chi. L. Rev. 865 (2000).

35   National Consumer Law Center, Truth in Lending § 9.2.1 (4th ed. 1999 and Supp.).

36   Fogie v. Thorn Americas, Inc., 95 F.3d 645 (8th Cir. 1996), *aff'd,* 190 F.3d 889 (8th Cir. 1999); Miller v. Colortyme, Inc., 518 N.W.2d 544 (Minn. 1994); Green v. Continental Rentals, 292 N.J. Super. 241, 678 A.2d 759, 30 U.C.C. Rep. 2d 1039 (Super. Ct. Law Div. 1994); *see also* National Consumer Law Center, Unfair and Deceptive Acts and Practices § 5.7.4 (5th ed. 2001).

37   National Consumer Law Center, Repossessions and Foreclosures § 19.3 (4th ed. 1999 and Supp.).

first payment is viewed as a refundable security deposit and whether payments are always made before the weekly or monthly rental period, and never a few days late.

If rent-to-own transactions are covered by the ECOA, preliminary data exists which suggests a pattern of differential treatment of customers that may be attributable to race. A legal services attorney in Minneapolis examined court replevin filings by Rent-A-Center, the nation's largest rent-to-own company.[38] Survey results showed that of the 68 customers subject to replevin in Minnesota in the period covered, 60% were African-American and 12% were white. (African-Americans made up about 35% of Rent-A-Center's customer base, while whites made up 57%; both groups had similar income levels.) In addition, court records revealed that, on average, African-Americans and other nonwhite consumers were in default for a shorter period of time before repossession than whites, even though whites tended to be further along in the contract than the other minority groups—a factor which is not inconsistent with being provided a longer default period prior to repossession.

The implications of data of this nature, coupled with recent state rulings declaring rent-to-own transactions to be credit sales, provides an opportunity for the application of the ECOA to practices by an industry that has already become notorious for abusive pricing and repossession policies.

2.2.2.3 Utility Service

There is no question that utility service involves credit for the purposes of the ECOA. The Commentary states that a utility company is a creditor when it supplies utility service and bills the user after the service has been provided.[39] Virtually all utility service is provided in this manner. Service is received, a monthly bill is sent, and some time after that payment is expected.

The Federal Reserve Board has exempted most forms of government-regulated utility service from a few particular ECOA provisions, but otherwise the ECOA generally applies to utility service, and no utility service is exempt from the general rule against discrimination.[40] Thus every aspect of a utility transaction, from the initial security deposit and connection, to collection procedures and disconnection practices, must comply with the general rule against discrimination on a prohibited basis. In addition, many utilities that might have been exempted from other ECOA provisions in the past may no longer be exempted if the industry has been deregulated (e.g., telephone, natural gas, electricity).[41]

2.2.2.4 Check-Cashing and ATM Cards

Denial of an automated teller card which merely accessed a savings account, without providing any accompanying overdraft privileges, has been found not to involve the right to defer payment of a debt and therefore not to involve "credit."[42] Another court also found a store's check-cashing service to be a customer accommodation rather than an extension of credit.[43] Accepting payment by check, rather than cash, does not involve credit.[44]

2.2.2.5 "Pay as You Go" Is Not Credit

For credit to be involved, there must be a deferral of payment of money owed. Thus a court has found no credit involved when a home improvement contract's schedule of payments substantially coincided with completion of the work, and there was no right given by the creditor to defer payment of the obligation.[45] Similarly, when payment is made immediately upon the service being provided, there is no extension of credit.[46]

The line between "pay as you go" and a deferred payment transaction is not always clear. For example, a cellular telephone service company argued that it was not covered by the ECOA because it billed customers on a monthly basis and payment was due each month. Customers could not defer payment of amounts owed.[47] The court disagreed with this argument, focusing on the fact that the transaction involved was an application for cellular services in which the customer sought to use the service and pay for it later.[48]

2.2.2.6 Medical Treatment

Medical care is another area in which denial of credit is almost equivalent to denial of service. Although some routine services may be offered only on a cash basis, more typically medical care involves deferred payment, to which the ECOA applies.

The fact that the medical provider does not assess a finance charge and requires eventual payment in one installment does not exclude this transaction from ECOA cover-

38 *Hearing Before Senate Banking Comm.*, 103d Cong. (May 13, 1994) (statement of David Ramp, Legal Aid Society of Minneapolis) (available as Clearinghouse No. 49,965).
39 Official Staff Commentary, 12 C.F.R. § 202.3(a)-2.
40 Official Staff Commentary, 12 C.F.R. § 202.3(a); *see* § 2.2.6.2, *infra*.
41 *See generally* National Consumer Law Center, Access to Utility Service (2d ed. 2001).
42 *See* Butler v. Capitol Fed. Sav., 904 F. Supp. 1230 (D. Kan. 1995) (opening a savings account is not a credit transaction because it is not a right to defer payment of a debt); Dunn v. Am. Express Co., 529 F. Supp. 633 (D. Colo. 1982).
43 Bailey v. Jewel Companies, Inc., 1979 U.S. Dist. LEXIS 9193 (N.D. Ill. Oct. 12, 1979).
44 Roberts v. Walmart Stores, Inc., 736 F. Supp. 1527 (E.D. Mo. 1990).
45 Shaumyan v. Sidetex Co., 900 F.2d 16 (2d Cir. 1990).
46 Universal Bonding Ins. Co. v. Esko & Young, Inc., 1991 U.S. Dist. LEXIS 2359 (N.D. Ill. Feb. 28, 1991).
47 *See* Williams v. AT & T Wireless Services, Inc., 5 F. Supp. 2d 1142 (W.D. Wash. 1998).
48 *Id.* (distinguishing *Shaumyan* because plaintiffs in that case prepaid a substantial portion of the amount due).

age.[49] Instead, the transaction becomes one involving incidental consumer credit, to which several ECOA provisions do not apply, but to which the general rule against discrimination does apply.[50]

In fact, the Commentary specifically refers to one area of potential discrimination involving medical providers. Medicare and Medicaid payments are defined as public assistance benefits for purposes of considering the actions of doctors, hospitals or any other entity to whom such benefits are payable.[51] Thus, medical providers, nursing homes, and others who receive Medicare or Medicaid benefits may not discriminate between patients on Medicare or Medicaid and those with private insurance. Of course, under various federal and state laws including the ECOA, medical providers also may not treat patients differently based on the other prohibited bases: race, religion, national origin, sex, and marital status.

At least one court has held, however, that Medicaid patients were not applicants for credit within the meaning of the ECOA and were therefore not protected by the ECOA.[52] The court ruled that Medicaid recipients under Ohio's Medicaid payment scheme were merely third-party beneficiaries of a reimbursement agreement between state and medical care givers and, as such, had neither the right to "purchase" services nor the right to defer payment for services. The court also observed that the Medicaid system "allows states to pay either the provider or, in some circumstances, the patient,"[53] but did not discuss whether a patient who directly received Medicaid payments would meet the definition of applicant for credit under the ECOA.

The exception for incidental consumer credit, however, may exclude medical service providers from certain specific ECOA provisions, including the record retention requirements which may be essential to prove discrimination.[54] State and federal laws, such as those which prohibit discrimination by nursing homes or which require provision of emergency medical service, may provide an alternative remedy.[55]

2.2.2.7 ECOA Coverage by Agreement of the Parties

A transaction may also be subject to the ECOA when it is so designated by the creditor, even if it would not otherwise fall within the statutory definition. A creditor may contract to subject itself to a consumer protection law.[56]

2.2.3 The ECOA Applies to All Stages of a Credit Transaction

Once a transaction involves credit, then all stages of that transaction are covered by the ECOA's general prohibition against discrimination, from the initial request for credit through the final payment or a collection action. The ECOA makes it unlawful for a creditor to discriminate in "any aspect of a credit transaction."[57] Regulation B defines credit transaction as including "[e]very aspect of an applicant's dealings with a creditor regarding an application for credit, or an existing extension of credit (including, but not limited to, information requirements; investigation procedures; standards of creditworthiness; terms of credit; furnishing of credit information; revocation, alteration, or termination of credit; and collection procedures.)"[58] Subsequent chapters detail the various stages of a credit transaction to which the ECOA applies.

2.2.4 The ECOA Prohibits Discrimination Against "Applicants"

2.2.4.1 Definition of Applicant

Only applicants are protected under most ECOA provisions.[59] Regulation B defines an applicant as including "any person who requests or who has received an extension of credit," including "any person who is or may become contractually liable regarding an extension of credit."[60]

Regulation B defines "contractually liable" as being expressly obligated to repay all debts on an account, pursuant to an agreement.[61] Regulation B defines "extension of credit" as the granting of credit in any form, including but not limited to credit granted in addition to existing credit, open-end credit, refinancings, renewals, and consolidations, or the continuation of existing credit.[62]

Thus, a cosigner is an applicant, but an authorized user on someone else's credit account may not be an applicant

49 *See* § 2.2.2.1, *supra* (definition of credit).
50 Official Staff Commentary, 12 C.F.R. § 202.3-1.
51 Official Staff Commentary, 12 C.F.R. § 202.2(z)-3.
52 Barney v. Holzer Clinic, Ltd., 110 F.3d 1207 (6th Cir. 1997).
53 *Id.* at 1210.
54 *See* § 2.2.6.3, *infra*.
55 *E.g.*, Conn. Gen. Stat. § 19a-533 (prohibiting nursing homes from discriminating on the basis of indigence).
56 Mack Fin. Corp. v. Crossley, 209 Conn. 163, 550 A.2d 303

(1988); Tim O'Neill Chevrolet v. Forristall, 551 N.W.2d 611 (Iowa 1996) (when promissory note provided "this loan is subject to the provisions of the Iowa Consumer Credit Code applying to consumer loans" and "this is a consumer credit transaction," transaction was subject to Iowa consumer credit code even though not subject to the code by force of statute alone); First Northwestern Nat'l Bank v. Crouch, 287 N.W.2d 151 (Iowa 1980); Farmers State Bank v. Haflich, 699 P.2d 553, 557 (Kan. 1985); *see* U.C.C. §§ 1-102(3), 1-105(2).
57 15 U.S.C. § 1691(a).
58 Reg. B, 12 C.F.R. § 202.2(m).
59 15 U.S.C. § 1691(a),(d),(e); Reg. B, 12 C.F.R. §§ 202.4, 202.5 (also applies to prospective applicants), 202.6, 202.7 (includes guarantors, sureties, endorsers and similar parties), 202.9.
60 Reg. B, 12 C.F.R. § 202.2(e).
61 Reg. B, 12 C.F.R. § 202.2(i).
62 Reg. B, 12 C.F.R. § 202.2(q).

unless the user is obligated to repay all debts on the account.[63] A spouse whose signature is improperly required is an applicant. Someone who does not sign the promissory note itself but who is required to sign a mortgage securing that note is contractually liable, because the note can be satisfied from that property.[64]

There are limits to who might be contractually liable and therefore a credit applicant under the Act. For example, individual members of a church were not considered applicants for a loan request made on behalf of the non-profit church corporation.[65] In addition, the sole shareholder and officer of a corporation was held not to be an applicant when a loan was sought on behalf of his corporation.[66]

2.2.4.2 Guarantors, Sureties and Similar Parties

One unclear area is whether guarantors, sureties and others who are secondarily liable on an obligation are applicants. Regulation B states that guarantors, sureties, endorsers and similar parties are applicants "for purposes of section 202.7(d) [dealing with spouses' signatures]."[67] One implication of this phrase is that guarantors and similar parties are *not* otherwise applicants. In fact, until 1985, Regulation B explicitly excluded guarantors, sureties, and

similar parties from the definition of applicant.[68]

On the other hand, guarantors, sureties and similar parties would seem to fall within the definition of those "who may become contractually liable" on the obligation. The pre-1985 version limited applicants to those who may *be* contractually liable, while the 1985 amendment changed that phrasing to those who may *become* contractually liable. The clear implication is that guarantors (who are not initially liable but who may become liable) are applicants.

Regulation B does specify that guarantors are applicants for purposes of section 202.7(d), but this should be viewed as an effort by the Federal Reserve Board to unambiguously overrule some earlier cases to the contrary, and not as an attempt to modify the ability of guarantors more generally to qualify as applicants.[69] Regulation B does not state that guarantors are applicants *only* for purposes of section 202.7(d).

Whatever the outcome as to the coverage of those secondarily liable, such as guarantors and sureties, cosigners are applicants. That is, if an individual is immediately liable on an obligation before another party defaults, that party should be considered an applicant.

63 Reg. B, 12 C.F.R. § 202.7(c); *see also* Official Staff Commentary, 12 C.F.R. §§ 202.7(c)(1)-1, 202.7(c)(2)-1; *cf.* Miller v. Am. Express Co., 688 F.2d 1235 (9th Cir. 1982) (in challenging American Express's policy of automatically canceling a supplementary cardholder's account upon the death of the principal cardholder, plaintiff was found to be more than a mere user of her husband's account; the ECOA applied because plaintiff was personally liable under the contract creating the supplementary account for all debts charged on her card by any person). Note that, under the ECOA, a creditor may require that a user become contractually liable on the account in order to be designated an authorized user, as long as the condition is not imposed on a discriminatory basis. Official Staff Commentary, 12 C.F.R. § 202.7(a)-1.
64 Ford v. Citizens & S. Nat'l Bank, 700 F. Supp. 1121 (N.D. Ga. 1988), *aff'd on other grounds*, 928 F.2d 1118 (11th Cir. Ga. 1991) (husband required to put up a mortgage to secure note signed by his wife was contractually liable and therefore was aggrieved party with standing to sue).
65 Hargraves v. City Mortgage Corp., 147 F.2d 1 (D.D.C. 2001) (claims of individual plaintiffs who did not receive or apply for credit as individuals, but rather were involved in obtaining the loan for their church, dismissed; the ECOA provides a cause of action for the church, but individuals cannot assert the church's legal interest; section 1981 claims also dismissed because the church, not the individual plaintiffs, was party to the loan contract); Church of Zion Christian Center, Inc. v. Southtrust Bank, 1997 U.S. Dist. LEXIS 12425 (S.D. Ala. July 30, 1997) (individual plaintiffs held not to have standing to bring an ECOA action when loan application was made on behalf of a corporation and plaintiffs never entered into any oral or written agreement with defendants).
66 Bentley v. Glickman, 234 B.R. 12 (N.D.N.Y. 1999).
67 *See* Reg. B, 12 C.F.R. § 202.2(e).
68 Section 202.2(e) (as amended in 1978 and 1979, but not as amended in 1985); *see also* Bank of Am. Nat'l Trust & Sav. Ass'n v. Hotel Rittenhouse Associates, 595 F. Supp. 800 (E.D. Pa. 1984); Morse v. Mut. Fed. Sav. & Loan Ass'n, 536 F. Supp. 1271 (D. Mass. 1982); Quigley v. Nash, 1981 U.S. Dist. LEXIS 18177 (D.D.C. Nov. 13, 1981); Delta Diversified, Inc. v. Citizens & S. Nat'l Bank, 171 Ga. App. 625, 320 S.E.2d 767 (1984).
The 1985 revision of § 202.2(e) is not retroactive. Comas v. Equibank, 1989 Bankr. LEXIS 905 (Bankr. W.D. Pa. June 9, 1989); Marine Am. State Bank v. Lincoln, 433 N.W.2d 709 (Iowa 1988); *see also* Mayes v. Chrysler Credit Corp., 37 F.3d 9 (1st Cir. 1994), *aff'd*, 167 F.3d 675 (rejecting loan guarantor's equitable argument that the policies embodied in the pre-amendment ECOA should allow her to assert an ECOA defense when, at the time she signed the guaranty, the then-operative version of 12 C.F.R. § 202.2(e) expressly provided that a guarantor was not an applicant). That guarantors are excluded from ECOA protections for transactions prior to 1985 does not resolve creditor's obligations on old accounts when creditors require new signatures after 1985. In *Boatmen's First Nat'l Bank v. Koger*, 784 F. Supp. 815 (D. Kan. 1992), the court erroneously ignored two post-1985 spousal signatures to deny the wife standing as an applicant, reasoning that the post-1985 signatures were merely continuances of pre-1985 guarantees. *Stern v. Espirito Santo Bank*, 791 F. Supp. 865 (S.D. Fla. 1992), on the other hand, reaches the correct conclusion that post-1985 signatures on old accounts are covered by the post-1985 definition of applicant.
69 *See* Silverman v. Eastrich Multiple Investor Fund, L.P., 857 F. Supp. 447 (E.D. Pa. 1994), *rev'd on other grounds*, 51 F.3d 28 (3d Cir. 1995); Gen. Elec. Capital Corp. v. Pulsifer, Clearinghouse No. 46,778 (D. Me. Oct. 28, 1991); Douglas County Nat'l Bank v. Pfeiff, 809 P.2d 1100 (Colo. Ct. App. 1991). *But see* Jordan v. Delon Olds Co., 887 F.2d 1089 (9th Cir. 1989) (unpublished) (text available on Westlaw) (guarantors or others requested as additional signatories found not to be applicants protected by ECOA); Bo Foods, Inc. v. Bojangles of Am., Inc., 1987 U.S. Dist. LEXIS 531 (N.D. Ill. Jan. 23, 1987).

2.2.4.3 Applicant Need Not Make an Application

To be an applicant, one need not submit a full application to a creditor.[70] An application is a defined term under the ECOA, and certain ECOA provisions apply only if there is an "application." But the definition of applicant does not require or even mention an application.

For example, in one case the plaintiff's telephone request for credit did not meet the creditor's usual standards for an application. Nevertheless, the court found that the plaintiff came within the definition of applicant.[71]

Prior to issuing the 1999 proposed revisions to Regulation B, the Federal Reserve Board (FRB) solicited comment on whether it should further clarify the distinction between an inquiry about credit and an application for credit.[72] The Board was motivated by the growth of new delivery channels for loan product information, such as the internet, and the growth in credit counseling and prequalification programs, which resulted in consumers asking for information about credit products and their creditworthiness before ever submitting an application.[73]

Regulation B currently defines an application as "an oral or written request for an extension of credit that is made in accordance with procedures established by the creditor for the type of credit request."[74] This definition gives creditors flexibility to establish the type of process they wish to use. The Commentary, however, encourages creditors to provide consumers with the information needed to shop for credit. Many industry commentators reported that they were unclear when inquiries about credit rose to the level of an "application," requiring a formal denial if credit was rejected.

Based on the various responses to the FRB, including the industry comments noted above, the Board has proposed that the definition of application be amended to include a request for preapproval under procedures in which a creditor will issue to creditworthy persons a written commitment, even if conditional, for credit up to a specified amount that is valid for a period of time.[75] The Official Commentary would be amended to reflect this change and to further explain when an inquiry or prequalification request becomes an application.[76] However, the Board declined to extend the

ECOA to cover prescreened credit solicitations.[77]

2.2.4.4 Applicant Need Not Be Seeking Credit

Applicants are not just persons attempting to open a new account. The statutory definition includes persons applying for an "extension, renewal or continuation of credit" and someone who "applies to a creditor indirectly by use of an existing credit plan for an amount exceeding a previously established credit limit."[78] The regulations clarify that the term also includes any person who has received an extension of credit.[79]

An applicant then could be a person who inquires about credit, a person who requests credit, a person who submits an actual application, a person whose application is approved and who opens an account, a person whose application is approved but who decides not to accept the credit offered, a person who requests an increase of an existing credit limit, or a person who just has existing credit with a creditor. The Commentary explicitly states that a home buyer is an applicant when that buyer seeks to assume the seller's mortgage loan unless the creditor's policy is not to permit assumptions.[80] The ECOA can apply even to *potential* applicants, so that creditors whose practices discourage applications on a prohibited basis will be liable.[81]

2.2.5 Creditors and Related Parties Subject to the ECOA

2.2.5.1 General

The ECOA and Regulation B identify three types of creditors who are subject to its requirements:

- Any person who regularly extends, renews, or continues credit;
- Any person who regularly arranges for the extension, renewal, or continuation of credit; or
- Any assignee of an original creditor who participates in the decision to extend, renew, or continue credit.[82]

70 *See, e.g.*, Cragin v. First Fed. Sav. & Loan Ass'n, 498 F. Supp. 379 (D. Nev. 1980) (although plaintiff held to be an applicant for credit, court found that plaintiff failed to prove a prima facie case of discrimination).
71 Cragin v. First Fed. Sav. & Loan Ass'n, 498 F. Supp. 379 (D. Nev. 1980).
72 63 Fed. Reg. 12,326 (Mar. 12, 1998).
73 64 Fed. Reg. 44,582, 44,589 (Aug. 16, 1999).
74 12 C.F.R. § 202.2(f).
75 64 Fed. Reg. 44,582, 44,594 (Aug. 16, 1999) (proposing to amend 12 C.F.R. § 202.2(f)). The proposed revisions to Regulation B are reproduced on the CD-Rom accompanying this volume.
76 64 Fed. Reg. 44,582, 44,619 (Aug. 16, 1999) (proposing to

amend Official Staff Commentary, 12 C.F.R. § 202.2(f)). The proposed revisions to the Official Staff Commentary for Regulation B are reproduced on the CD-Rom accompanying this volume.
77 64 Fed. Reg. 44,582, 44,584–44,585 (Aug. 16, 1999).
78 15 U.S.C. § 1691a(b).
79 Reg. B, 12 C.F.R. § 202.2(e).
80 Official Staff Commentary, 12 C.F.R. § 202.2(e)-1.
81 *See* § 5.3.2.1, *infra*.
82 15 U.S.C. § 1691a(e); Reg. B, 12 C.F.R. § 202.2(*l*). The Federal Reserve Board has proposed revisions to Regulation B that would clarify that the term creditor includes those who regularly participate in setting terms of credit, not just in the decision to extend or deny credit. 64 Fed. Reg. 44,582, 44,594 (Aug. 16, 1999) (proposing to amend 12 C.F.R. § 202.2(*l*)). The proposed

Understanding this definition is crucial to selecting appropriate defendants in an ECOA action. Often it is possible to select as defendants not only the creditor originally extending the loan, but also those who arranged the loan, assignees who participated in the credit determination, and even secondary market purchasers.[83]

2.2.5.2 "Regularly" Extends Credit

The ECOA applies to any person that "regularly" extends, renews, or continues credit.[84] Most creditors regularly extend credit and will admit as much in a request for admissions, which an ECOA plaintiff should send early in the litigation.[85]

Nevertheless, some ECOA cases will involve creditors who only infrequently extend credit.[86] Neither Regulation B and its Commentary nor ECOA case law define when a creditor regularly extends credit. The best precedent is that found under the old Truth in Lending Act and Regulation Z. Regulation Z's pre-Simplification (i.e. pre-1983) definition of creditor also required that such a person "regularly" extend credit in the ordinary course of business.[87] It seems clear that the Federal Reserve Board had this Regulation Z language in mind when it promulgated the Regulation B requirement that a creditor regularly extend credit. Under cases interpreting old Regulation Z, if a transaction represents more than an "isolated," "incidental" occurrence, then the creditor regularly extends credit.[88]

2.2.5.3 Arrangers of Credit

2.2.5.3.1 Definition of arranger

The ECOA's definition of creditor includes persons who regularly arrange for the extension, renewal, or continuation of credit.[89] Arrangers include certain real estate brokers, loan brokers, and car dealers, who may not provide credit but whose discrimination may prevent applicants from receiving credit.[90] Regulation B indicates that a creditor includes someone who refers applicants or prospective applicants to creditors, or who selects or offers to select creditors to whom requests for credit may be made.[91] The Commentary clarifies that this category may include certain persons such as real estate brokers who do not participate in credit decisions but who regularly refer applicants to creditors or who select or offer to select creditors to whom credit requests can be made.[92]

For example, some car dealers do not provide credit directly but may have arrangements with one or more creditors to provide car loans to their customers. The car dealer would violate the ECOA if it disproportionately directed purchasers from protected classes to high cost creditors.[93]

Other than the Regulation B standard, the best source of precedent defining when a person is an arranger of credit can be found in old Truth in Lending (TILA) cases on arrangers. After TILA was "simplified" in 1982, credit arrangers were no longer covered. But pre-Simplification, the Federal Reserve Board defined an arranger as a person who either received a fee or similar consideration for services, or had knowledge of the credit terms and participated in preparation of the contract documents.[94]

---

revisions to Regulation B are reproduced on the CD-Rom accompanying this volume.

83 Official Staff Commentary, 12 C.F.R. § 202.2(*l*); *see* §§ 2.2.5.3, 2.2.5.4, *infra.*

84 15 U.S.C. § 1691a(e).

85 The Federal Reserve Board has proposed amending the definition of creditor to make it clear that it also includes one who regularly participates in setting terms of credit, not just in the decision of whether to extend or deny credit. 64 Fed. Reg. 44,594 (Aug. 16, 1999). The proposed revisions to Regulation B are reproduced on the CD-Rom accompanying this volume.

86 *See, e.g.*, Riethman v. Berry, 113 F. Supp. 2d 765 (E.D. Pa. 2000) (attorneys not considered creditors under ECOA because they did not regularly extend credit to their clients).

87 Reg. Z, 12 C.F.R. § 226.2(s) (1973) (this section was deleted in the 1983 revisions).

88 *See, e.g.*, Eby v. Reb Realty, Inc., 495 F.2d 646 (9th Cir. 1974) (extension of credit in three out of seven land sales in a nineteen-month period made real estate broker a creditor); James v. Ragin, 432 F. Supp. 887 (W.D.N.C. 1977). Currently, Regulation Z defines regularly to mean twenty-five credit extensions per year, or five times per year for transactions secured by a dwelling. Reg. Z, 12 C.F.R. § 226.2(a)(17), n.3.

89 15 U.S.C. § 1691a(e).

90 The Federal Reserve Board has proposed amending the Official Staff Commentary to Regulation B to expressly provide that arrangers can include automobile dealers, home builders, home improvement contractors, and those who solely accept applications. Official Staff Commentary, 12 C.F.R. § 202.2-l; 64 Fed. Reg. 44,582, 44,620 (Aug. 16, 1999). The proposed revisions to the Official Staff Commentary are reproduced on the CD-Rom accompanying this volume.

91 Reg. B, 12 C.F.R. § 202.2(*l*); *see also* Official Staff Commentary, 12 C.F.R. § 202.2(*l*)-2.

92 Official Staff Commentary, 12 C.F.R. § 202.2(*l*)-2.

93 In a case brought not under the ECOA but under § 1981 of the Civil Rights Act, the Truth In Lending Act, and various other federal and state statutes, a car dealer misrepresented that it would find customers the best available credit. The dealer then referred customers to a lender who, unbeknownst to the customers, paid some of the interest it collected back to the dealer. Fairman v. Schaumberg Toyota, Inc., 1996 U.S. Dist. LEXIS 9669 (N.D. Ill. July 10, 1996). The defendants unsuccessfully argued that the ECOA should shield them from liability because the statute did not require them to disclose the pay-back scheme. *Id.; see also* Johnson v. Equicredit Corp. of Am., 2002 U.S. Dist. LEXIS 4817 (N.D. Ill. Mar. 21, 2002) (plaintiff presented sufficient evidence to state a claim against a mortgage origination company; company could be considered an arranger of credit).

94 Reg. Z, 12 C.F.R. § 226.2(h) (1973) (this section was deleted by the 1983 revisions); *see also* Price v. Franklin Inv. Co., 574 F.2d 594 (D.C. Cir. 1978); Hinkle v. Rock Springs Nat'l Bank, 538 F.2d 295 (10th Cir. 1976).

Regulation B slightly restricts the statutory definition of an arranger as creditor by requiring that the arranger be one who "in the ordinary course of business, regularly refers applicants."[95]

2.2.5.3.2 Limitations on arrangers' ECOA liability

Regulation B limits the liability of arrangers by indicating that arrangers need only comply with two ECOA provisions, the general rule against discrimination[96] and the prohibition against discouraging applications on a prohibited basis.[97] As a practical matter, these are the two provisions most applicable to arrangers of credit. However, the Regulation's limitation means that arrangers are not responsible for other ECOA violations even if they actively participate in, or are the actual cause of, the violation.

If an applicant wants to bring an ECOA violation against an arranger under one of these other ECOA provisions, the best approach is to try to establish that the arranger falls within the definition of creditor for other reasons than that it is an arranger. Generally, doing so will require that the consumer show that the arranger regularly participates in the decision whether to extend credit.[98]

Showing this participation may pose a problem because, although car dealers and brokers may receive a commission for referring the applicant to the lender, they may have little input into the actual credit approval process. However, participation might be shown by such actions as the dealer accessing the applicant's credit report before referring the customer to the lender, or the dealer making a judgment whether to refer that particular customer to the creditor.

2.2.5.4 Participants in the Credit Decision, Including Assignees

The term creditor includes any person who in the ordinary course of business regularly participates in the decision whether or not to extend credit.[99] The ECOA statute also specifically includes in the definition of creditor any *assignee* of an original creditor who participates in the decision to extend, renew or continue credit.[100] Regulation B further clarifies that this category includes persons such as a creditor's assignee, transferee, or subrogee who participates in the decision whether or not to extend credit.[101] The

Commentary elaborates that creditor includes all persons participating in the credit decision and may include an assignee or a potential purchaser of the obligation who influences the credit decision by indicating whether or not it will purchase the obligation if the transaction is consummated.[102]

Many assignees and other secondary creditors will fit into this definition because they participate in the credit decision in some way.[103] If the creditor is held not to have participated in the credit decision, the assignee can still be held liable, but the plaintiff will have to prove that the secondary creditor had knowledge or reasonable notice of the violation.[104]

There are limits to this broad standard. Most importantly, the person must participate in the decision whether to extend credit. FBI agents forwarding inaccurate credit information to a bank have not been considered "creditors."[105] A company was found not to be a creditor when it just received the mortgage application and acted as a conduit to the actual financier.[106]

A mortgage holder who forwarded a credit report to a second lender was, however, considered a creditor for purposes of ECOA liability.[107] A Department of Housing and Urban Development (HUD) mortgagee letter concluded that both HUD and mortgagee banks were creditors on applications for HUD-insured mortgage financing.[108] At least one court has held that the president and sole owner of a lending institution, who directed and controlled its actions, could be held liable as a creditor under the ECOA.[109]

---

95 Reg. B, 12 C.F.R. § 202.2(*l*).
96 As defined in Reg. B, 12 C.F.R. § 202.4.
97 *See* Reg. B, 12 C.F.R. § 202.2(l).
98 *See* § 2.2.5.4, *infra*.
99 Reg. B, 12 C.F.R. § 202.2(*l*).
100 15 U.S.C. § 1691a(e).
101 Reg. B, 12 C.F.R. § 202.2(*l*). The Federal Reserve Board has proposed amending the definition of creditor to make it clear that it also includes one who regularly participates in setting the terms credit will be available on, not just one who participates in the decision whether to extend or deny credit. 64 Fed. Reg.

44,582, 44,954 (Aug. 16, 1999). The proposed revisions to Regulation B are reproduced on the CD-Rom accompanying this volume.
102 Official Staff Commentary, 12 C.F.R. § 202.2(*l*)-1.
103 *See* § 2.2.5.5, *infra*.
104 Reg. B, 12 C.F.R. § 202.2(*l*); *see* § 2.2.5.5, *infra*.
105 Ricci v. Bancshares, 768 F.2d 456 (1st Cir. 1985).
106 Markham v. Colonial Mortgage Serv. Co., 605 F.2d 566 (D.C. Cir. 1979). *Contra* Kimberton Chase Realty Corp. v. Main Line Bank, 1997 U.S. Dist. LEXIS 17966 (E.D. Pa. Nov. 3, 1997) (individual who asked for clarification and updated financials, gave loan package to lenders, and provided guidance to credit applicant could be "creditor"; claim survives motion to dismiss).
107 Luby v. Fid. Bond & Mortgage Co., 662 F. Supp. 256 (E.D. Pa. 1985). The court reached this conclusion on the grounds that, although the mortgage holder was not the party who denied the plaintiff's mortgage application, it met the ECOA's definition of creditor and allegedly engaged in discriminatory acts that led to the denial of credit, including furnishing a credit report to the institution that denied the plaintiff's mortgage application.
108 Dep't of Hous. & Urban Dev., HUD Mortgagee Letter No. 77-17, Consumer Cred. Guide (CCH) ¶ 98,192 (Apr. 22, 1977).
109 Fed. Trade Comm'n v. Capital City Mortgage Corp., 1998 U.S. Dist. LEXIS 22115 (D.D.C. July 13, 1998); *see also* Kimberton Chase Realty Corp. v. Main Line Bank, 1997 U.S. Dist. LEXIS 17966 (E.D. Pa. Nov. 3, 1997) (CEO and 97% stockholder of lending institution could be creditor even if no actual participation).

2.2.5.5 Exclusions From Definition of Creditor

There are two exclusions from the definition of creditor. A person whose only participation in a credit transaction involves honoring a credit card is not a creditor.[110] In addition, the regulations state that a person is not a creditor regarding any violation of the act or regulation *committed by another creditor* unless the person knew or had reasonable notice of the violation before becoming involved in the credit transaction.[111] This requirement can make it much more difficult to pursue liability against assignees and other secondary creditors for ECOA violations.[112]

For example, a car dealer may make a preliminary credit determination and require the signature of a spouse before submitting the proposed transaction to a finance company. If this practice violates the ECOA, the finance company might then claim ignorance of the dealer's action and claim that it is not liable for the dealer's ECOA violations. This argument is only viable if the finance company is not directly liable as a creditor under the ECOA.

The first part of the definition of creditor in Regulation B defines creditors as those who in the ordinary course of business regularly participate in the decision whether or not to extend credit.[113] Immediately following this definition is an explanation that this category includes a creditor's assignee, transferee, or subrogee who regularly participates in the credit decision.[114] Therefore, assignees who regularly participate in the credit decision by setting terms regarding the loans they will buy, and other common secondary market practices, should be directly liable for ECOA violations even if the credit was actually extended by the dealer or another creditor.[115] Knowledge or reasonable notice of the violation is required only for assignees and other secondary creditors who do not participate in the credit decision in this way.

This distinction is critical as it allows plaintiffs to pursue claims against assignees, secondary market purchasers, and others who create financing policies and set the terms credit is offered on without having to prove that these creditors had specific knowledge or notice of the ECOA violations committed by dealers and other creditor partners. This issue has been a key point of contention in cases against General Motors Acceptance Corp. (GMAC) and Nissan Motor Acceptance Corp. (NMAC) alleging that their subjective mark-up pricing schemes result in significantly higher interest rates for African-American buyers than for white buyers with similar credit profiles.[116]

GMAC and NMAC, as assignees of the loans in question, argued that they did not fit into the ECOA definition of direct creditors. As a result, they argued that plaintiffs had to prove that they had knowledge of any discriminatory actions taken by the car dealers. The companies further alleged that they had no notice or knowledge of these violations, characterizing themselves as "mere paper buyers." In denying defendants' motions for summary judgment, the court agreed that the defendants could be held directly liable as participating creditors under the ECOA.[117]

2.2.5.6 The Government as Creditor

Transactions in which credit is extended *by* a government or a governmental subdivision, agency, or instrumentality are subject to the provisions of the ECOA and Regulation B, except that no action can be brought against governmental creditors for the recovery of punitive damages.[118] However, if a government agency is operating a special purpose credit program, it is exempted from some of the provisions of the ECOA and Regulation B.[119]

When a governmental agency, such as the Federal Deposit Insurance Corporation (FDIC) or the Resolution Trust Corporation (RTC), takes over a bank, the ECOA still applies.

---

110 Reg. B, 12 C.F.R. § 202.2(*l*).
111 Reg. B, 12 C.F.R. § 202.2(*l*).
112 The Federal Reserve Board (FRB) recently considered, but rejected, changes to this knowledge/reasonable notice requirement. 64 Fed. Reg. 44,582, 44,590 (Aug. 16, 1999). In its Advanced Notice of Proposed Rulemaking, the FRB solicited comments on whether it should modify the knowledge/reasonable notice standard. 63 Fed. Reg. 12,326 (Mar. 12, 1998). It chose to retain the present standard, however, stating "that it is not possible to specify with particularity the circumstances under which a creditor may or may not be liable for a violation committed by another creditor." 64 Fed. Reg. at 44,590. On the other hand, the FRB stated that under some circumstances the reasonable notice standard may carry with it the need for a creditor to exercise some degree of diligence with respect to third parties' involvement in credit decisions. 64 Fed. Reg. at 44,590 (Aug. 16, 1999).
113 Reg. B, 12 C.F.R. § 202.2(*l*).
114 Reg. B, 12 C.F.R. § 202.2(*l*); *see* § 2.2.5.4, *supra*.
115 For a government enforcement action alleging liability of a lender at least in part for the actions of its brokers, see U.S. v. Long Beach Mortgage Co., Clearinghouse No. 51, 944, No. CV 96-6159 (C.D. Cal. Sept. 5, 1996) (settlement agreement and order). *See also* § 12.4.3.9, *infra*.

116 Coleman v. Gen. Motors Acceptance Corp., Clearinghouse No. 53,036B, Civ. No. 3-98-0211 (M.D. Tenn. Aug. 9, 2000) (fourth amended complaint); Cason v. Nissan Motor Acceptance Corp., Clearinghouse No. 53,037A, Civ. No. 3-98-0223 (M.D. Tenn. June 9, 2000) (fourth amended complaint); *see* §§ 8.4, 12.4.3.9, *infra*.
117 Coleman v. Gen. Motors Acceptance Corp., 196 F.R.D. 315 (M.D. Tenn. 2000). The court in the *Cason* case issued an oral decision on August 24, 2000. *See also* Jones v. Ford Motor Credit Co., 2002 U.S. Dist. LEXIS 1098 (S.D.N.Y. Jan. 18, 2002) (in denying defendant's motion to dismiss, court held that defendant was a creditor under the ECOA because defendant participated in the credit decision-making process by arriving at an objective credit score for customers and then authorizing the dealers to subjectively mark it up).
118 15 U.S.C. § 1691e(b).
119 *See* § 3.9, *infra*.

Under the doctrine of *D'Oench Duhme & Co. v. FDIC*,[120] as partially codified in 12 U.S.C. § 1823(e), defenses based on unrecorded side agreements are not available. However, an ECOA violation is normally apparent on the face of the bank's records (for example, requirement of a spouse's signature when the credit application shows the applicant is creditworthy). Thus, courts agree that an ECOA violation may be raised against the RTC or the FDIC either as a special defense of illegality, or as a counterclaim for damages.[121]

In 1999, a consent decree was approved and entered against the U.S. Department of Agriculture (USDA) in a class action case alleging systemic discrimination against African-American farmers.[122] The class included approximately 20,000 members. Among other charges, the class alleged that the Farm Service Agency, an agency within the USDA, routinely discouraged applications from some farmers, delayed processing their applications, or denied applications for credit and benefits on a discriminatory basis.[123]

2.2.6 Transactions Partially Exempted From the ECOA

2.2.6.1 General

The Federal Reserve Board (FRB) has created *partial* exemptions from ECOA coverage for five classes of credit: public utility credit, incidental consumer credit, business credit, securities credit and credit extended to the government. It is important to realize that these are *partial* exemptions dealing with specific, itemized ECOA requirements, and that these partially exempt forms of credit must still comply with *all* other ECOA requirements. In every case, the general rule prohibiting discrimination against applicants on a prohibited basis applies to these five special forms of credit.[124]

2.2.6.2 Public Utility Credit

The FRB has enacted a very limited exemption for public utility credit. While public utilities must comply with most ECOA provisions, they need not comply with the following three Regulation B provisions:

- Section 202.5(d)(1), which forbids requests by creditors for information on marital status except in defined situations;
- Section 202.10, which concerns reporting of credit information in the names of both spouses; and
- Section 202.12(b), which requires creditors to retain records of credit applications for a prescribed period of time.[125]

In practice, this exemption means that public utilities may ask the marital status of applicants, that they are not required to report credit information in both spouses' names, and that they are not required to retain records of credit applications. All other provisions of Regulation B apply, including other provisions related to discrimination based on marital status.[126]

The three exemptions listed above apply *only* to the provision of service by a public utility, and thus do not apply to certain other utilities and other utility practices.

The exemption applies only to utilities whose charges are filed with or regulated by a governmental unit.[127] Thus the FRB exemption does not apply to rural electric cooperatives or other unregulated utilities.[128] Municipal utilities are gen-

---

120 315 U.S. 447, 62 S. Ct. 676, 86 L. Ed. 956 (1942).
121 CMF Va. Land, L.P. v. Brinson, 806 F. Supp. 90 (E.D. Va. 1992); Diamond v. Union Bank & Trust, 776 F. Supp. 542 (N.D. Okla. 1991); Fed. Deposit Ins. Corp. v. Allen, 1988 U.S. Dist. LEXIS 17565 (W.D. Okla. Nov. 3, 1988).
122 Pigford v. Glickman, 185 F.R.D. 82 (D.D.C. 1999) (consent decree), *aff'd*, 206 F.3d 1212 (D.C. Cir. 2000). This settlement was challenged by non-African-American farmers in Green v. Veneman, 159 F. Supp. 2d 360 (S.D. Miss. 2001). The court in *Green* upheld the *Pigford* settlement on the basis that the non-African-American farmers were not similarly situated to the *Pigford* class members.
123 *See generally* Stephen Carpenter, *Discrimination in Agricultural Lending*, 33 Clearinghouse Rev. 166 (1999).
124 Official Staff Commentary, 12 C.F.R. § 202.3-1.
125 Reg. B, 12 C.F.R. § 202.3(a); *see also* Official Staff Commentary, 12 C.F.R. § 202.3(a). The public utility exemption was republished for review without proposed change as a result of the 1988 Women's Business Ownership Act amendments. 54 Fed. Reg. 29,734 (July 14, 1989). It was subsequently re-adopted. 54 Fed. Reg. 50,482 (Dec. 7, 1989).
126 *See, e.g.*, McGee v. E. Ohio Gas Co., 111 F. Supp. 2d 979 (S.D. Ohio 2000) (defendant utility's summary judgment motion denied when plaintiff alleged marital status discrimination based on utility's conditioning of wife's account on payment of arrearages owed by her husband only on a previous account), 200 F.R.D. 382 (S.D. Ohio 2001) (granting class certification). Note that the Federal Reserve Board has proposed revisions to Regulation B that would amend the public utilities exemption to apply to record retention requirements only, requiring the utilities to comply with all other provisions of Regulation B. 64 Fed. Reg. 44,582, 44,595 (Aug. 16, 1999) (proposing to amend 12 C.F.R. § 202.3(a)(2)(ii)). The proposed revisions to Regulation B are reproduced on the CD-Rom accompanying this volume.
127 Reg. B, 12 C.F.R. § 202.3(a)(1); *see, e.g.*, Mays v. Buckeye Rural Elec. Coop., Inc., 227 F.3d 873 (6th Cir. 2002) (finding no public utilities credit when rural electric cooperative was not required to file rates with any government entity; however, transaction was considered incidental credit and therefore exempt from certain ECOA provisions).
128 As deregulation/restructuring of the electric industry unfolds around the country, it is likely that these exemptions will no longer apply to electric utilities. However, resolution of the exemption's application will depend largely on what, if anything, still has to be filed with or regulated by a government unit, or even what it means to be "filed." In any event, these are issues that vary from state to state and should be examined on

erally unregulated, and should be outside the FRB exclusion unless the government ownership of the utility is deemed sufficient to find that charges are filed with a government unit. The FRB exemption also does not apply to a telephone company which is not regulated by a government unit and which does not file its charges for service, delayed payment, or discount for prompt payment with a government unit.[129]

The utility exemption applies only to credit related to utility service. If even a regulated utility grants credit for purposes other than utility service, such as for financing the purchase of a gas dryer, telephone equipment, or other durable goods, or for insulation or other home improvements, then the ECOA is fully operative.[130] However, if the utility exemption does not apply, the transaction may still be exempt under the incidental consumer credit exemption.[131]

2.2.6.3 Incidental Consumer Credit

2.2.6.3.1 *Definition of incidental consumer credit*

Regulation B provides a limited exemption for "incidental consumer credit." Incidental consumer credit is defined as:[132]

- Primarily for personal, family, or household purposes;
- Not made pursuant to the terms of a credit card account;
- Not subject to any finance charge; and
- Not payable by agreement in more than four installments.[133]

In addition, the incidental credit category explicitly does not include public utilities or securities credit.[134] These types of credit are separately exempted from certain provisions of the ECOA.[135]

This definition in part mimics the scope of the federal Truth in Lending Act (TILA), which only applies to transactions involving a finance charge or more than four installments. While the ECOA is substantially broader in scope than the TILA, the Federal Reserve Board (FRB), through regulation, has in effect limited the scope of *certain* ECOA

provisions to the scope of the TILA.[136]

Typical examples of incidental consumer credit may include (depending on whether there is a finance charge or more than four installments) deferment of payment by doctors, home heating oil companies, lawyers, hospitals, and some small retailers.[137] However, the FRB's exclusion for incidental consumer credit (and TILA's similar exclusion) has led some not-so-incidental creditors to restructure their business so as to avoid many ECOA provisions (and TILA entirely).

For example, there is a growing use of "ninety-day same as cash" transactions in which the seller may hide the finance charge in a higher selling price. As this arrangement is incidental consumer credit, the creditor can avoid the ECOA prohibition of requiring a spouse to cosign such a purchase agreement. A great many such contracts are assigned to finance companies which then, at the end of ninety days, "flip" that contract (which has two signatures) into a loan with a finance charge, thereby ushering the spouse into a credit obligation through the back door.

2.2.6.3.2 *Exemption is limited to only certain Regulation B provisions*

In general, even if a particular transaction is found to be credit under the ECOA, the incidental credit exception allows the creditor to avoid compliance with key aspects of the law, including the notice provisions of section 202.9.[138]

In addition to the notice provisions, the following requirements of Regulation B do not apply to incidental consumer credit:[139]

---

a case-by-case basis. *See* National Consumer Law Center, Access to Utility Service § 3.7.2 (2d ed. 2001).

129 Official Staff Commentary, 12 C.F.R. § 202.3(a)-3.

130 Official Staff Commentary, 12 C.F.R. § 202.3(a)-1.

131 *See, e.g.,* Mays v. Buckeye Rural Elec. Coop., Inc., 227 F.3d 873 (6th Cir. 2002) (finding no public utilities credit when rural electric cooperative was not required to file rates with any government entity; however, transaction was considered incidental credit and therefore exempt from certain ECOA provisions); *see also* § 2.2.6.3, *infra*.

132 Reg. B, 12 C.F.R. § 202.3(c); *see also* Reg. B, 12 C.F.R. § 202.2(b); Official Staff Commentary, 12 C.F.R. § 202.3(c).

133 Reg. B, 12 C.F.R. § 202.3(c)(1).

134 Reg. B, 12 C.F.R. § 202.3(c)(1).

135 *See* § 2.2.6.2, *supra*; § 2.2.6.6, *infra*.

136 The numerous Truth in Lending cases that discuss finance charges and the four-installment rule are useful in ECOA cases involving this issue. *See* National Consumer Law Center, Truth in Lending § 2.3.4 (4th ed. 1999 and Supp.).

137 *See* Official Staff Commentary, 12 C.F.R. § 202.3(c)-1; *see also* Mays v. Buckeye Rural Elec. Coop., Inc., 227 F.3d 873 (6th Cir. 2002); Williams v. AT & T Wireless Services, Inc., 5 F. Supp. 2d 1142 (W.D. Wash. 1998) (application for cellular telephone service is a credit transaction, but qualifies for the incidental credit exception to the ECOA notice requirement).

138 Mays v. Buckeye Rural Electric Coop., Inc., 227 F.3d 873 (6th Cir. 2002); Williams v. AT & T Wireless Services, Inc., 5 F. Supp. 2d 1142 (W.D. Wash. 1998) (although plaintiff's cellular phone application was considered to be a credit transaction, creditor was exempt from notice requirement based on the incidental credit exception; court rejected plaintiff's argument that the exception did not apply because AT & T was a public utility).

139 Reg. B, 12 C.F.R. § 202.3(c)(a). The incidental consumer credit exemption was republished for review without proposed change as a result of the 1988 Women's Business Ownership Act amendments. 54 Fed. Reg. 29,734 (July 14, 1989). It was subsequently readopted. 54 Fed. Reg. 50,482 (Dec. 7, 1989). The Federal Reserve Board has proposed extending the definition of incidental credit to include incidental business credit as well. 64 Fed. Reg. 44,582, 44,595 (Aug. 16, 1999) (proposing to amend 12 C.F.R. § 202.3(c)(1)).

- Section 202.5(c), which limits inquiries about the applicant's spouse or former spouse;
- Section 202.5(d)(1), which forbids requests by creditors for information on marital status except in defined situations;
- Section 202.5(d)(2), which limits inquiries about income derived from alimony, child support, and separate maintenance payments;
- Section 202.5.(d)(3), which forbids inquiries about the applicant's sex;[140]
- Section 202.7(d), which restricts the circumstances in which creditors may request the signature of a cosigner;
- Section 202.9, which requires notification of adverse action, reasons for the action, and ECOA rights;
- Section 202.10, which concerns reporting of credit information in the names of both spouses; and
- Section 202.12(b), which requires creditors to retain records of credit applications for a prescribed period of time.

All other ECOA provisions apply to incidental consumer credit, including the general prohibition against discrimination.[141]

2.2.6.4 FRB's Authority to Exempt Public Utility and Incidental Consumer Credit from Certain ECOA Provisions

There was considerable controversy over whether the Federal Reserve Board had the authority to exempt certain transactions from the ECOA, particularly with respect to public utility and incidental credit. The Women's Business Ownership Act of 1988 (WBO) changed the standards as to when and how the Board could create exemptions.[142] The Board then reissued its regulations covering these exemptions under this new authority, essentially rendering moot the issue as to whether the FRB had the authority to issue the regulations *pre-1988*.[143]

There may still be some controversy as to whether the FRB had the authority to reissue the exemptions in 1988. This dispute will likely have limited practical significance to most litigants. The issue is likely to be relevant only when a consumer wishes to challenge a creditor's failure to comply with certain listed ECOA provisions, and the credit involves a public utility or incidental consumer credit.

In addition, even if the consumer prevails in arguing that the exemption the creditor is relying upon is in fact invalid, the consumer is unlikely to obtain any damages. The creditor presumably would not be liable for its past actions because they were complying in good faith with FRB rules.[144] As a result, any challenge to the FRB's authority to exempt certain forms of consumer and business credit may have prospective impact only.

2.2.6.5 Business Credit

The Federal Reserve Board had granted partial exemptions to credit extended primarily for business and commercial purposes,[145] but the Women's Business Ownership Act of 1988[146] amended the ECOA in ways which affected this exemption. The FRB, in response, deleted or altered each of those exemptions, to assure small business owners procedural rights more in line with consumer borrowers.[147]

---

140 This exemption applies only to the extent that the information is necessary for medical records or similar purposes. The Federal Reserve Board has proposed eliminating this exception in light of the proposed revision to allow creditors to seek information about an applicant's sex. 64 Fed. Reg. 44,582, 44,595 (Aug. 16, 1999); *see* § 4.4.8, *infra*.

141 Official Staff Commentary, 12 C.F.R. § 202.3-1.

142 Pub. L. No. 100-533, § 301, 102 Stat. 2689, 2692 (1988).

143 There were two reasons that the old exemptions were controversial. First, there was an issue as to whether the ECOA allowed the Federal Reserve Board (FRB) to make exemptions relating to consumer transactions, specifically its exemptions for incidental consumer credit and public utility credit. Read literally, the language of the statute precluded any regulatory authority to carve out exemptions in the consumer area. "[S]uch regulations may exempt from one or more provisions of [ECOA] any class of transactions *not primarily for personal, family, or household purposes.* . . ." 15 U.S.C. § 1691b(a)

(1976) (emphasis added). Transactions primarily for personal, family, or household purposes are consumer credit. *See* Reg. B, 12 C.F.R. § 202.3(g) (1975) (now 12 C.F.R. § 202.2(h)); *see also* Truth in Lending Act, 15 U.S.C. § 1602.

Secondly, it is also arguable that none of the exemptions were promulgated in a manner that complied with the statutory directives as to the proper procedure and standards to be used in creating them. In passing the Women's Business Ownership Act of 1988 (WBO), Congress severely criticized the FRB for failure to comply with the statute when it created the then existing business credit exemptions. The House Report accompanying the amendments notes that, contrary to the specific requirements of the Act, the FRB never made the required "'express finding' that application of the Act's provisions would not further the goals and purposes of the Act. No such findings have ever been made, nor evidence presented to support the special treatment accorded by Regulation 'B' to business credit transactions." H.R. Rep. No. 100-955, at 15–16, *reprinted in* 1988 U.S.C.C.A.N. 3535, 3544. As the same procedure and standards were used for all the original exemptions, then, by Congressional standards, none of them were created in compliance with the statute.

144 15 U.S.C. § 1691e(e).

145 Reg. B, 12 C.F.R. § 202.3(d) (1985) (this section was deleted in the 1989 revisions); Official Staff Commentary, 12 C.F.R. § 202.3(d) (this section was deleted in the 1990 revisions).

146 Pub. L. No. 100-533, § 301, 102 Stat. 2689, 2692 (1988).

147 *See* Supplementary Information, 54 Fed. Reg. 50,482 (Dec. 7, 1989). The Federal Reserve Board has proposed, however, extending the incidental credit exception to incidental business credit as well. 64 Fed. Reg. 44,582, 44,595 (Aug. 16, 1999) (proposing to amend 12 C.F.R. § 202.3(c)(1)). Incidental credit is discussed in § 2.2.6.3, *supra*. The proposed revisions are reproduced on the CD-Rom accompanying this volume.

As it now stands, business credit is subject to different procedural standards in a few areas,[148] and the requirement that the reporting of credit information be in the names of both spouses applies only to consumer and not business credit.[149] In deciding whether something is business or consumer credit, the primary purpose of the application controls.[150] For example, if a consumer purchases a pick-up truck primarily for consumer use but also for occasional business use, the transaction involves consumer credit.

2.2.6.6 Securities Credit

A partial exemption from Regulation B is provided for extensions of credit subject to regulation by the Securities Exchange Act of 1934 or offered by a broker or dealer under that Act.[151] The following specific provisions of Regulation B are not applicable to securities credit transactions:[152]

- Section 202.5(c), which limits inquiries about the applicant's spouse or former spouse;
- Section 202.5(d)(1), which forbids requests by creditors for information on marital status except in defined situations;
- Section 202.5(d)(3), which forbids inquiries about the applicant's sex;
- Section 202.7(b), which requires creditors to allow applicants to open or maintain accounts in various combinations of first names and surnames;[153]
- Section 202.7(c), which limits the circumstances under which creditors may require reapplication, change terms, or terminate an existing open-end credit account;[154]
- Section 202.7(d), which restricts the circumstances in which creditors may request the signature of a cosigner;
- Section 202.10, which concerns reporting of credit information in the names of both spouses; and
- Section 202.12(b), which requires creditors to retain records of credit applications for a prescribed period of time.

All other aspects of Regulation B apply.[155]

2.2.6.7 Credit Extended to the Government

The Federal Reserve Board has largely exempted from ECOA coverage transactions in which credit is extended *to* governments or governmental subdivisions, agencies, or instrumentalities. The only provision of Regulation B applicable to such a transaction is the general rule against discrimination, forbidding discrimination against credit applicants on a prohibited basis.[156]

It is important to note that this exemption is only for credit extended *to* a government agency, and not for credit extended *by* a housing agency or some other government agency to a consumer.[157] Remedies for government agencies violating the ECOA nevertheless are limited.[158]

2.3 Scope of the Fair Housing Act

2.3.1 Overview

The scope of the Fair Housing Act is complicated by the fact that three different provisions of the statute may apply to credit discrimination. The major Fair Housing Act provision covering credit discrimination (42 U.S.C. § 3605) applies to "residential real estate-related transactions." The second Fair Housing Act provision (42 U.S.C. § 3604) covering credit discrimination applies to the sale, rental, or advertising of dwellings. The third relevant provision (42 U.S.C. § 3617) provides that it is unlawful to coerce, intimidate, threaten, or interfere with the exercise or enjoyment of various rights granted or protected by the Fair Housing Act, including the rights set forth in sections 3604 and 3605. The discussion that follows analyzes the differing scope of each of these provisions.

---

148 *See* § 10.2.14, *infra* (notification of adverse action); § 10.3.2, *infra* (recordkeeping).

149 Official Staff Commentary, 12 C.F.R. § 202.10-1.

150 Official Staff Commentary, 12 C.F.R. § 202.2(g)-1. Truth in Lending also uses the primary purpose test, and cases interpreting that provision may provide useful guidance. *E.g.*, Gallegos v. Stokes, 593 F.2d 372 (10th Cir. 1979); Redhouse v. Quality Ford Sales, Inc., 523 F.2d 1 (10th Cir. 1975) (en banc) (per curiam) (superseding 511 F.2d 230 (10th Cir. 1975)); Smith v. Chapman, 436 F. Supp. 58 (W.D. Tex. 1977). *See generally* National Consumer Law Center, Truth in Lending § 2.4.2.1 (4th ed. 1999 and Supp.).

151 Reg. B, 12 C.F.R. § 202.3(b). The securities exemption was republished for review without proposed change as a result of the 1988 Women's Business Ownership Act amendments. 54 Fed. Reg. 29,734 (July 14, 1989). It was readopted. 54 Fed. Reg. 50,482 (Dec. 7, 1989). The Federal Reserve Board has proposed eliminating § 202.3(b)(2)(iii) from the list of inapplicable provisions in light of the proposed revision to allow creditors to seek information about an applicant's sex. 64 Fed. Reg. 44,582, 44,595 (Aug. 16, 1999). The proposed revisions to Regulation B are reproduced on the CD-Rom accompanying this volume.

152 Reg. B, 12 C.F.R. § 202.3(b)(2). The Federal Reserve Board has proposed revisions to § 202.3(b)(2) to reflect the proposed revision to allow creditors to seek information about an applicant's sex. 64 Fed. Reg. 44,582, 44,595 (Aug. 16, 1999). The proposed revisions to Regulation B are reproduced on the CD-Rom accompanying this volume.

153 This exemption is effective only to the extent necessary to prevent the violation of rules concerning accounts in which a broker or dealer has an interest, or necessitating the aggregation of spouse's accounts.

154 This exemption is effective only to the extent that such action is taken following a change in the account holder's name or marital status.

155 Official Staff Commentary, 12 C.F.R. § 202.3-1.

156 Reg. B, 12 C.F.R. § 202.3(d).

157 Official Staff Commentary, 12 C.F.R. § 202.3(d)-1.

158 *See* § 11.8.3.4, *infra*.

2.3.2 *Residential Real Estate-Related Transactions: Scope of Section 3605*

2.3.2.1 General

Section 3605 of the Fair Housing Act prohibits discrimination in "residential real estate-related transactions."[159] Residential real estate-related transactions are defined as the making or purchasing of loans or providing other financial assistance:

- For purchasing, constructing, improving, repairing or maintaining a dwelling[160], or
- Secured by residential real estate.[161]

Residential real estate-related transactions also include the selling, brokering, or appraising of residential real property.[162]

2.3.2.2 Transactions Covered by Section 3605

2.3.2.2.1 *Loans used to buy, improve, repair or maintain a dwelling*

Section 3605 of the federal Fair Housing Act applies to any loan used to purchase, build, improve, repair or maintain a dwelling.[163] The loan does not have to come from the entity doing the selling, building or improving. The loan does not have to be secured by the dwelling.

For example, the Fair Housing Act applies to mortgages to purchase a home, a loan to purchase building materials, a loan to finance a home improvement contract, or loans to pay for plumbers, roofers, carpenters, electricians, even carpet cleaners or window washers. The Act should apply if a homeowner obtains a $500 unsecured loan from a finance company to buy some paint, wood, and other items that the homeowner intends to use to spruce up his or her home. Arguably, the Act would apply even to loans to purchase refrigerators, sinks, stoves, or other appliances necessary to improve or maintain a dwelling.

The loan must be used to purchase, improve or maintain a "dwelling." The term dwelling is broadly construed. A dwelling is defined as any structure or portion of a structure that is occupied or intended to be occupied as a *residence* by one or more families, and any vacant land offered for sale or lease for the construction or location of such a structure.[164]

The term residence is not defined in the Act. Courts have generally found that residence means either a temporary or permanent dwelling place to which one intends to return.[165] Although this category generally does not include transient dwelling places, the line is not always clear. Places such as homeless shelters have been held to be "residences" for purposes of the Act.[166]

As the Act does not specify who must live or intend to live in a building for it to be considered a dwelling, a plaintiff does not have to live in a building in order to bring a claim under the Act.[167] Therefore, dwelling may include a residence the consumer has recently vacated or intends to move into, or even one the consumer does not plan to live in but intends to use as rental property, or even leave vacant, at a particular point in time.

2.3.2.2.2 *Home equity and other loans taking home as collateral*

Section 3605 of the Fair Housing Act also applies to other types of loans as long as the loan is secured by residential real estate.[168] The loan proceeds do not have to be used in any way related to the dwelling provided the residential real estate is taken as collateral for the loan.

This definition applies to home equity loans, in which the consumer establishes a credit line using residential real estate as collateral. In addition, homes and other real estate are frequently used as collateral on many finance company refinancings and even some car loans, credit card obligations, and other types of credit transactions. Because many subprime and predatory lenders take a security interest in a borrower's home to finance home improvements and other work, section 3605 can be a powerful tool to challenge the actions of predatory lenders.[169]

The Fair Housing Act applies to any loan that takes "residential real estate" as collateral. Unlike dwelling, this term is not defined. Residential real estate should include

---

159 42 U.S.C. § 3605.
160 42 U.S.C. § 3605(b)(1)(A).
161 42 U.S.C. § 3605(b)(1)(B).
162 42 U.S.C. § 3605(b)(2).
163 42 U.S.C. § 3605(b)(1); *see* 24 C.F.R. § 100.115(a).
164 42 U.S.C. § 3602(b); 24 C.F.R. § 100.20.

165 *See, e.g.*, United States v. Columbus Country Club, 915 F.2d 877, 881 (3d Cir. 1990) (seasonal bungalows used by annual members who returned each year for five months at a time fell within the meaning of the statute); The Tara Circle, Inc. v. Bifano, 1997 U.S. Dist. LEXIS 10153 (S.D.N.Y. July 15, 1997) (citing Hovsons, Inc. v. Township of Brick, 89 F.3d 1096, 1102 (3d. Cir. 1996)); Woods v. Foster, 884 F. Supp. 1169, 1173 (N.D. Ill. 1995) (homeless shelter determined to be a "residence"); United States v. Hughes Mem'l Home, 396 F. Supp. 544 (W.D. Va. 1975) (home for needy children, although not intended as a permanent home, was a residence within the meaning of the Act).
166 *See* Woods v. Foster, 884 F. Supp. 1169, 1173 (N.D. Ill. 1995).
167 *See, e.g.*, Hovsons, Inc. v. Township of Brick, 89 F.3d 1096 (3d Cir. 1996) (Act covered those living in a nursing facility as well as one plaintiff who did not); *see also* Brief of the United States as Amicus Curiae In Support of Plaintiffs' Opposition to Defendants' Motion for Judgment on the Pleadings or, In the Alternative, For Summary Judgment, Hargraves v. Capital City Mortgage Corp., 140 F. Supp. 2d 7 (D.D.C. 2000) [reproduced on the CD-Rom accompanying this volume].
168 42 U.S.C. § 3605(b)(1)(B).
169 *See* § 8.2, *infra*.

any piece of realty used for residential purposes, whether or not the owner is the resident. It should apply to any form of realty used for that purpose, but may not apply to personalty. Thus, there will be an issue whether a mobile home is residential real estate if the security is taken only in the structure and not in the land on which the home is situated. Land used as the site of a mobile home should certainly be considered residential real estate.

2.3.2.3 Credit Actors Covered by Section 3605

2.3.2.3.1 General

Residential real estate-related transactions do not include just creditors making loans. Such transactions also include those providing other financial assistance related to the making of the loans.[170] Thus the Fair Housing Act applies to loan brokers, financial consultants, or anyone else providing financial assistance related to a loan covered by the Fair Housing Act.

The only possible exclusion (when a residential real estate-related transaction is involved) would be if the person is not in the "business" of making such transactions but merely engages in one such isolated transaction. No court or agency interpretation has clarified this issue, however.

The various credit actors that may be covered under section 3605 are discussed in the following sections.

2.3.2.3.2 "Makers" of loans

Section 3605 applies to a wide range of actors involved in *making* loans. The regulations identify some of the prohibited practices in this category.[171]

Prohibited practices under this section include, but are not limited to, failing or refusing to provide to any person, in connection with a residential real estate-related transaction, information regarding the availability of loans or other financial assistance, application requirements, procedures or standards for the review and approval of loans or financial assistance, or providing information which is inaccurate or different from that provided others because of a prohibited basis.[172]

Those making loans or providing other financial assistance related to the purchase, construction, improvement, repair or maintenance of a dwelling, or secured by residential real estate, are also prohibited from discriminating in the *terms and conditions* for making those loans available.[173]

Prohibited conduct under this section includes, but is not limited to, using different policies, practices or procedures in evaluating or in determining the creditworthiness of any person in connection with the provision of any loan or other financial assistance for a dwelling or for any loan or other financial assistance which is secured by residential real estate because of a prohibited basis. This section also prohibits financial actors from determining the type of loan or other financial assistance to be provided, or fixing the amount, interest rate, duration or other terms for a loan because of a prohibited basis.

2.3.2.3.3 Purchasers of loans

The Fair Housing Act also applies to the activities of one who purchases loans[174]—that is, to the activities of those who buy mortgages and other loan paper from the originating lender, as long as the loans themselves are covered by the Fair Housing Act. This provision means that lenders who participate in the original loan decision are covered and also lenders who do not participate before the fact, but whose decision as to which loans to purchase involves discrimination on a prohibited basis are covered. The pooling and sale of not only loans but also loan servicing rights are included.

The regulations present a non-exhaustive list of unlawful practices, including the purchasing of loans or other debts or securities in certain communities but not in others on a discriminatory basis.[175] This regulation applies to traditional "redlining" practices.[176] It prohibits redlining practices not only in connection with the purchasing of loans, but also in connection with the pooling or packaging of loans or other debts.[177]

The FHA, therefore, may be used to extend liability to secondary market purchasers. The ECOA also may apply to secondary market actors. However, in some cases, the ECOA requires that these actors have knowledge or reasonable notice of the discriminatory actions of the primary lenders.[178] There is no similar requirement in the FHA. However, the regulation does specify that it is not meant to preclude loan purchasers from considering factors justified by business necessity.[179]

2.3.2.3.4 Sellers, brokers, and appraisers

The FHA also applies to persons or businesses engaging in the selling, brokering, or appraising of residential real

---

170 42 U.S.C. § 3605(a); 24 C.F.R. § 100.115(a).

171 24 C.F.R. § 100.120.

172 *See, e.g.*, Honorable v. The Easy Life Real Estate Sys., 100 F. Supp. 2d 885 (N.D. Ill. 2000) (plaintiffs alleged that defendant real estate company took advantage of a segregated housing market by, among other actions, falsely telling plaintiff borrowers that their company's financing program was the only program available to plaintiffs).

173 24 C.F.R. § 100.130.

174 24 C.F.R. § 100.115(a).

175 24 C.F.R. § 100.125.

176 *See generally* Ch. 7 (redlining), *infra*.

177 24 C.F.R. § 100.125(b)(2).

178 *See* § 2.2.5.5, *supra*.

179 24 C.F.R. § 100.125(c).

property.[180] The regulations define broker or agent as including any person authorized to act on behalf of another person regarding any matter related to the sale or rental of a dwelling.[181] Brokers should also be covered under the provisions prohibiting discrimination in the terms and conditions for making loans or other financial assistance available.[182]

Appraisal practices that are unlawful include, but are not limited to, using an appraisal of residential real property when the person knows or reasonably should know that the appraisal improperly takes into consideration race, color or other characteristics protected by the Act.[183]

2.3.3 Scope of Section 3604

2.3.3.1 Transactions Covered Under Section 3604

2.3.3.1.1 General

Section 3604 is titled "Discrimination in the Sale or Rental of Housing and Other Prohibited Practices." Of most relevance to consumer credit, the first two subsections make it unlawful:

> (a) To refuse to sell or rent after the making of a bona fide offer, or to refuse to negotiate for the sale or rental of, or otherwise make unavailable or deny, a dwelling to any person because of race, color, religion, sex, familial status, or national origin.
>
> (b) To discriminate against any person in the terms, conditions, or privileges of sale or rental of a dwelling, or in the provision of services or facilities in connection therewith, because of race, color, religion, sex, familial status, or national origin.[184]

The broad scope of the term dwelling is detailed above[185]—it includes homes, apartments, mobile homes, mobile home parks and trailer courts, house boats and about any other structure within which an individual could reside.

2.3.3.1.2 Does section 3604 apply to home equity loans?

Although most courts have agreed that sections 3604 and 3605 are not mutually exclusive,[186] they have been less clear about whether section 3604 can be applied to non-purchase money (or home equity) financing.

The Department of Justice (DOJ) made an extensive analysis of this issue in an amicus brief filed in 2000 in a predatory lending case.[187] The DOJ argued that both subsections (a) and (b) of § 3604 should apply to home equity financing.

The DOJ argued that § 3604(a) covers "discrimination that adversely affects the availability of housing."[188] Home equity financing, particularly predatory lending, can have this effect. According to the DOJ, under the broad language of the Act, a direct refusal to rent or sell housing is not required for either § 3604(a) or § 3604(b) to apply.

The DOJ also argued that § 3604(b), the provision addressing terms and conditions of the sale or rental of dwellings or of the provision of related services, applies to home equity financing. The DOJ argued that this provision should not be narrowly confined to purchase money loans.[189]

In many cases it will not matter whether a § 3604 claim is available because § 3605, discussed above, will clearly apply. However, some potentially discriminatory practices do not fit within the parameters of § 3605 but may fit within a broad reading of § 3604.

The provision of § 3604(a) prohibiting any practice that has the effect of making housing unavailable is probably the main advantage of adding a § 3604 claim in a home financing case, particularly in a predatory lending case.[190] A wide range of predatory loans and a wide range of predatory lending creditors may be covered by the Act because predatory lending is a practice, according to the DOJ, of making loans that are designed to fail.[191] Housing is made unavail-

---

180 42 U.S.C. § 3605(b)(2); 24 C.F.R. § 100.135.

181 24 C.F.R. § 100.20.

182 *See* § 2.3.2.3.2, *supra.* For a government enforcement case involving loan brokers, see U.S. v. Long Beach Mortgage Co., Clearinghouse No. 51, 944, No. CV-96-6159 (C.D. Cal. Sept. 5, 1996) (settlement agreement and order).

183 Cases involving appraisal practices include: Latimore v. Citibank, 979 F. Supp. 662 (N.D. Ill. 1997) (finding that plaintiff did not bring a prima facie case of discrimination; court registered displeasure with plaintiff's joining of the appraiser as a defendant—even though appraisers can be covered by the FHA and ECOA, court found no evidence of racial motives here), *aff'd,* 151 F.3d 712 (7th Cir. 1998); Steptoe v. Sav. of Am., 800 F. Supp. 1542 (N.D. Ohio 1992); Old W. End Ass'n v. Buckeye Fed. Sav. & Loan, 675 F. Supp. 1100 (N.D. Ohio 1987).

184 42 U.S.C. § 3604(a), (b).

185 *See* § 2.3.2.2, *supra.*

186 *See* Nationwide Mut. Ins. Co. v. Cisneros, 52 F.3d 1351 (6th Cir. 1995) (§§ 3604 and 3605 overlap and are not mutually exclusive); Eva v. Midwest Nat'l Mortgage Banc, Inc., 2001 U.S. Dist. LEXIS 2748, at *49 (N.D. Ohio Feb. 15, 2001) (although court found that section 3604 did not apply to refinancing loans, court agreed that sections 3604 and 3605 are not mutually exclusive).

187 *See* Brief of the United States as Amicus Curiae In Support of Plaintiffs' Opposition to Defendants' Motion for Judgment on the Pleadings or, In the Alternative, For Summary Judgment, Hargraves v. Capital City Mortgage Corp., 140 F. Supp. 2d 7 (D.D.C. 2000) [reproduced on the CD-Rom accompanying this volume].

188 *Id.* at 21 (citing Clifton Terrace Associates v. United Tech. Corp. 929 F.2d 714, 719 (D.C. Cir. 1991)).

189 *Id.* at 40–41.

190 *See* § 8.2, *supra.*

191 Brief of the United States as Amicus Curiae In Support of Plaintiffs' Opposition to Defendants' Motion for Judgment on the Pleadings or, In the Alternative, For Summary Judgment, at

able if borrowers lose their homes because they cannot repay predatory loans. In addition, the denial of reasonably priced financing to protected groups, often resulting in foreclosure, makes housing unavailable.[192]

The *Hargraves* court noted that it was a close issue whether § 3604, as well as § 3605, applies to home equity loans but dismissed the § 3604 claim with respect to the one defendant in the case sued over a home equity loan because the plaintiffs failed to pursue the argument.[193]

In other cases, plaintiffs have attempted to apply § 3604 to a broad range of practices, including home equity financing. Although most courts have agreed that a direct refusal to rent or sell housing is not required for § 3604 to apply, they differ on how much it covers.[194] This is a close issue without a settled result.

2.3.3.2 Credit Actors Covered by Section 3604

The Fair Housing Act provision prohibiting discrimination in the sale or rental of property[195] applies to any person selling or renting property, with the following two exemptions. The Fair Housing Act (except for the discriminatory advertising section) does not apply to the sale or rental of a single family house by an owner as long as the owner has an interest only in three or fewer homes and as long as the owner does not use an agent or broker or other person in the business of selling or renting dwellings.[196] The Act also does not apply to the rental of units in an owner-occupied four-family or smaller home.[197]

2.3.4 Interference, Coercion, Intimidation, or Threats: Scope of Section 3617

Section 3617 of the Fair Housing Act makes it unlawful to coerce, intimidate, threaten, or interfere with any person in the exercise or enjoyment of, or on account of his having exercised or enjoyed, or on account of his having aided or encouraged any other person in the exercise or enjoyment of, the rights granted or protected by sections 3603, 3604, 3605 or 3606 of the Fair Housing Act.[198] Thus, if defendants have violated one of the four enumerated sections, they have also violated section 3617.[199]

Plaintiffs have brought suit under section 3617 in cases involving mortgage redlining,[200] insurance redlining,[201] and other practices[202] on the theory that such discrimination "interferes" with the exercise and enjoyment of Fair Housing Act rights. Although many cases alleging violations of section 3617 involve violent conduct, violence or physical coercion is not a prerequisite to a section 3617 claim.[203]

21–23, Hargraves v. Capital City Mortgage Corp., 140 F. Supp. 2d 7 (D.D.C. 2000) [reproduced on the CD-Rom accompanying this volume].

192 *Id.* at 21–22.

193 Hargraves v. Capital City Mortgage Corp., 140 F. Supp. 2d 7, 22 (D.D.C. 2000).

194 *See, e.g.,* Nationwide Mut. Ins. Co. v. Cisneros, 52 F.3d 1351, 1357 (1995) (§ 3604 applies to property insurance); United States v. Yonkers Bd. of Educ., 837 F.2d 1181 (2d Cir. 1987) (applying § 3604 to exclusionary zoning); Hanson v. Veterans Admin., 800 F.2d 1381 (5th Cir. 1986) (applying § 3604 to discriminatory appraisals); Laufman v. Oakley Bldg. & Loan Co., 408 F. Supp. 489 (S.D. Ohio 1976) (court agreed with plaintiffs that § 3604(a) not only prohibits conduct constituting a refusal to sell or rent, but also conduct that otherwise makes dwellings unavailable; applied in this case to mortgage redlining); *see also* Brief of the United States as Amicus Curiae In Support of Plaintiffs' Opposition to Defendants' Motion for Judgment on the Pleadings or, In the Alternative, For Summary Judgment, Hargraves v. Capital City Mortgage Corp., 140 F. Supp. 2d 7 (D.D.C. 2000) [reproduced on the CD-Rom accompanying this volume]. *But see* Matthews v. New Century Mortgage Corp., 185 F. Supp. 2d 874 (S.D. Ohio 2002) (transactions involving financial assistance for improving, repairing, or maintaining a dwelling that the owner had previously acquired fall outside the scope of § 3604); Eva v. Midwest Nat'l Mortgage Banc Inc., 143 F. Supp. 2d 862 (N.D. Ohio 2001) (courts have generally stretched § 3604 to address insurance issues; although § 3604 applies beyond the literal sale or rental of housing, not applicable in case involving discrimination based on gender in refinancing loans; court granted creditors' motion to dismiss § 3604 claims, but denied motion to dismiss § 3605 claims); Thomas v. First Fed. Sav. Bank of Ind., 653 F. Supp. 1330 (N.D. Ind. 1987) (redlining practices which affect the availability of housing are actionable under § 3604, redlining practices which affect the availability of financing are more properly brought under § 3605).

195 42 U.S.C. § 3604.

196 24 C.F.R. § 100.10(c)(1); *see also* 24 C.F.R. § 100.20 (definitions of dwelling, broker or agent, and person in the business of selling or renting dwellings).

197 24 C.F.R. § 100.10(c)(2).

198 42 U.S.C. § 3617.

199 *See* Bryant v. Polston, 2000 U.S. Dist. LEXIS 16368 (S.D. Ind. Nov. 2, 2000) (plaintiffs stated a claim under § 3617 when Caucasian homeowners sued neighbors for intimidating and harassing them because of their association with African-Americans); Dunn v. Midwestern Indem. Mid-Am. Fire & Cas. Co., 472 F. Supp. 1106, 1111 (S.D. Ohio 1979). It is also possible to bring an action under § 3617 even if there is no claim of a violation of one of the enumerated sections. *See* Stackhouse v. DeSitter, 620 F. Supp. 208 (N.D. Ill. 1985) (firebombing case). As discussed above, however, credit discrimination suits brought under the Fair Housing Act generally involve violations of §§ 3604 or 3605. *See* §§ 2.3.2 (§ 3605), 2.3.3 (§ 3604), *supra.*

200 Laufman v. Oakley Bldg. & Loan Co., 408 F. Supp. 489, 498 (S.D. Ohio 1976).

201 Dunn v. Midwestern Indem. Mid-Am. Fire & Cas. Co., 472 F. Supp. 1106 (S.D. Ohio 1979).

202 *See, e.g.,* United States v. Am. Inst. of Real Estate Appraisers, 442 F. Supp. 1072 (N.D. Ill. 1977) (the promulgation of standards which cause real estate appraisers and lenders to treat race and national origin as negative factors in determining the value of dwellings and in evaluating the soundness of home loans violates § 3617).

203 *See, e.g.,* Mich. Prot. & Advocacy Serv., Inc. v. Babin, 18 F.3d 337, 347 (6th Cir. 1994); Fowler v. Borough of Westville, 97 F. Supp. 2d 602 (D.N.J. 2000); People Helpers, Inc. v. City of Richmond, 789 F. Supp. 725 (E.D. Va. 1992).

Credit Discrimination

2.3.5 *Only Aggrieved Persons May Bring Actions*

The Fair Housing Act prohibits certain types of discrimination, and specifies that these prohibitions protect "any person."[204] The only limit as to who can bring a Fair Housing Act case is that the individual be "aggrieved."[205] Aggrieved person is defined in the Fair Housing Act regulations as any person who claims to be injured by a discriminatory housing practice or believes he or she will be injured by a discriminatory housing practice that is about to occur.[206] This requirement that the plaintiff be aggrieved under the Fair Housing Act is to be generously construed to foster "truly integrated and balanced living patterns."[207]

The Supreme Court has held that Congress intended standing under the Fair Housing Act to "extend to the full limits of Article III," thereby eliminating the prudential barriers to standing.[208] There are limits to this broad standard. In particular, federal statutes may not abrogate the minimum requirement of Article III that a plaintiff demonstrate: 1) an injury in fact, 2) a causal connection between the injury and the conduct complained of, and 3) the likelihood, as opposed to mere speculation, that the injury will be redressed by a favorable decision.[209] Thus members of non-protected classes may bring claims as well if they are alleging discrimination based on their association with members of protected classes.[210]

Moreover, a series of Supreme Court cases makes clear that testers, nonprofit housing organizations, and municipalities have standing to bring Fair Housing Act claims. Municipalities can be affected by racial discrimination in housing patterns in various ways, including their tax base, and such injury is sufficient for a municipality to bring a Fair Housing Act claim concerning discrimination as to its residents.[211]

The definition of aggrieved person under the Fair Housing Act is broader than the analogous term under the ECOA, which requires that an individual be an "applicant." An individual not seeking credit can bring a Fair Housing Act action, such as those who would benefit if credit were granted. For example, tenants of a two-family house could bring a Fair Housing Act claim if their landlord was unfairly deprived of a home improvement loan to fix up the tenant's apartment.

2.4 Scope of Federal Civil Rights Acts

The federal Civil Rights Acts apply only to discrimination based on race, certain ethnic origins, and citizenship status.[212] Within these parameters, however, they are generally broad in scope.

Section 1981 provides to all persons within the United States the same rights to make contracts as is enjoyed by white citizens. This statute applies to all types of contracts, all types of borrowers or related individuals, and any type of creditor or other type of merchant. For example, noncitizens are persons within the scope of the statute, so that noncitizens may bring section 1981 actions.[213]

The Civil Rights Act of 1991 added an express provision to the statute making it applicable to all aspects of the contractual relationship including, "making, performance, modification, and termination [of the contract], and the enjoyment of all benefits, privileges, terms, and conditions of the contractual relationship."[214] The amendments also make it clear that section 1981 bars both public and private discrimination.[215]

Section § 1982 grants all citizens the same rights as are enjoyed by white citizens to inherit, purchase, lease, sell, hold, and convey real and personal property. This statute does not apply to discrimination against noncitizens. Nevertheless, it applies to any form of sale or rental practice by any individual or entity that discriminates against a citizen on the basis of race or ethnic origin.

Section 1982 applies to a loan in any way used to purchase or rent property.[216] However, it is not limited to real estate lending. Some courts have interpreted the section quite broadly, allowing claims that do not relate specifically to real estate transactions. For example, plaintiffs alleging

---

204 42 U.S.C. §§ 3604, 3605, 3617; *see* Jordan v. Khan, 969 F. Supp. 29 (N.D. Ill. 1997).
205 42 U.S.C. § 3613.
206 24 C.F.R. § 100.20.
207 Trafficante v. Metro. Life Ins. Co., 409 U.S. 205, 211, 93 S. Ct. 364, 34 L. Ed. 2d 415 (1972).
208 Havens Realty Corp. v. Coleman, 455 U.S. 363, 373–75, 102 S. Ct. 1114, 71 L. Ed. 2d 214 (1982); Gladstone Realtors v. Vill. of Bellwood, 441 U.S. 91, 103, 99 S. Ct. 1601, 60 L. Ed. 2d 66 (1979); Trafficante v. Metro. Life Ins. Co., 409 U.S. 205, 211, 93 S. Ct. 364, 34 L. Ed. 2d 415 (1972).
209 Lujan v. Defenders of Wildlife, 504 U.S. 555, 560–61, 112 S. Ct. 2130, 119 L. Ed. 2d 351 (1992).
210 *See, e.g.*, Bryant v. Polston, 2000 U.S. Dist. LEXIS 16368 (S.D. Ind. Nov. 2, 2000) (FHA claim brought by white homeowners against neighbors, alleging discrimination based on plaintiffs' association with African-Americans).
211 Gladstone Realtors v. Vill. of Bellwood, 441 U.S. 91, 99 S. Ct. 1601, 60 L. Ed. 2d 66 (1979); Vill. of Bellwood v. Dwivedi, 895 F.2d 1521 (7th Cir. 1990); *see* § 11.2.2, *infra*.
212 *See* § 3.6, *infra*.
213 *See* Graham v. Richardson, 403 U.S. 365, 91 S. Ct. 1848, 29 L. Ed. 2d 534 (1971).
214 42 U.S.C. § 1981(b).
215 42 U.S.C. § 1981(c). Since the 1991 amendments to section 1981, courts have clarified that section 1981 provides a claim against private discrimination on the basis of alienage. *See* Anderson v. Conboy, 156 F.3d 167 (2d Cir. 1998); Angela M. Ford, Comment, *Private Alienage Discrimination and the Reconstruction Amendments: The Constitutionality of 42 U.S.C. § 1981*, 49 U. Kan. L. Rev. 457 (2001); § 3.6.3, *infra*.
216 *See* Evans v. First Fed. Sav. Bank, 669 F. Supp. 915 (N.D. Ind. 1987) (§ 1982 count allowed to stand when borrower alleged redlining in the denial of a home equity loan to be used to purchase a car and pay college tuition).

harassment and intimidating conduct by their neighbors have been found to state a claim under the provision requiring equality in the right to hold real and personal property.[217] The statute bars discrimination by both state and private actors.[218]

2.5 Scope of State Credit Discrimination Statutes

By and large the scope of state credit discrimination statutes follows the scope of the federal statute they are modeled after. Nevertheless, sometimes the scope of a state statute will be broader than the scope of the analogous federal statute and it may prove particularly valuable in those situations.

Because of significant state variations, readers are referred to Appendix E, *infra*, for a summary of the scope of various state credit discrimination statutes. Particularly because states continue to make changes to bring their state statutes more in line with the current version of the federal Fair Housing Act and other federal statutes, it is important to examine the most recent version of the state statute.

2.6 Scope of State UDAP Statutes

Occasionally, a state statute generally prohibiting unfair or deceptive acts or practices (a UDAP statute) may be used to challenge credit discrimination not prohibited by any other statute or a UDAP claim may be useful if a discrimination statute does not provide a sufficient remedy. Nevertheless, various scope issues may limit the applicability of a state UDAP statute to credit discrimination.

State UDAP statutes vary significantly, and this variation is most pronounced concerning scope issues. A thorough analysis of UDAP scope issues is found in National Consumer Law Center, *Unfair and Deceptive Acts and Practices* (5th ed. 2001). This section will only briefly list some of the possible scope problems found in *some* state UDAP statutes.

Some UDAP statutes apply only to the sale of goods and services and there will be an issue as to whether credit (related or unrelated to a sale) involves the sale of goods and services.[219] In other states, the statute applies to trade or commerce, and credit should clearly fall within the statute's coverage.[220]

Certain state UDAP statutes do not apply to banks or other creditors regulated by state agencies.[221] There may also be an issue as to whether a UDAP statute applies to debt collection practices (which may be the subject of a credit discrimination action),[222] or offers protections to loan guarantors[223] or businesses.[224]

It is important to note that each of these issues applies only to certain UDAP statutes and not to most state UDAP laws. Nevertheless, it is always important before bringing any UDAP claim to review carefully the particular state statute's scope.

---

217 *See, e.g.*, Bryant v. Polston, 2000 U.S. Dist. LEXIS 16368 (S.D. Ind. Nov. 2, 2000); Egan v. Schmock, 93 F. Supp. 2d 1090 (N.D. Cal. 2000) (applying same analysis to § 1982 claim as to FHA claim and holding that both statutes prohibit discriminatory conduct intended to drive individual out of her home); Bryd v. Brandeburg, 922 F. Supp. 60 (N.D. Ohio 1996) (allegations of racially motivated firebombing stated claim under § 1982). *But see* Spahn v. Colonial Vill., Inc., 899 F.2d 24, 35 (D.C. Cir. 1990) (in finding that § 1982 did not prohibit real estate advertising that indicated discriminatory preferences, court stated that §§ 1981 and 1982 are not meant to be all-purpose anti-discrimination statutes nor comprehensive open housing laws).

218 Jones v. Alfred H. Mayer Co., 392 U.S. 409, 88 S. Ct. 2186, 20 L. Ed. 2d 1189 (1968).

219 *See* National Consumer Law Center, Unfair and Deceptive Acts and Practices § 2.2.1.2 (5th ed. 2001).

220 *See id.* at § 2.2.1.4.

221 *See id.* at § 2.2.1.3.

222 *See id.* at § 2.2.2.

223 *See id.* at § 2.4.3.

224 *See id.* at § 2.4.5.

Chapter 3   Prohibited Bases for Discrimination

3.1 Introduction

Federal and state credit discrimination laws do not prohibit all forms of discrimination. They do not prevent creditors from making reasonable distinctions between applicants, denying credit, or offering less advantageous terms to higher risk borrowers. The credit discrimination laws generally do not even require that creditors act reasonably in making a determination as to which applicants are high risk.

Instead, credit discrimination laws prohibit creditors from utilizing certain factors, such as race, national origin, or sex, as the *basis* for the credit determination. Whether or not a credit determination is reasonable, it is prohibited if the determination is based upon a prohibited distinction. This chapter lists the various types of prohibited bases for credit discrimination found in the ECOA, the federal Fair Housing Act, the federal Civil Rights Acts, the Americans with Disabilities Act, and state credit discrimination laws.

The chapter also details the one major ECOA exception to this prohibition: under a special-purpose credit program, creditors can act on a prohibited basis to grant credit.[1] That is, under specified conditions (usually when a group traditionally discriminated against is provided special purpose credit opportunities), creditors may restrict a credit program only to those who share one common characteristic, even if that characteristic is race, national origin, sex, or some other prohibited basis.

A final credit discrimination principle detailed in this chapter is that a credit applicant can challenge discrimination even when the applicant is not part of the group discriminated against on a prohibited basis.[2] The applicant need only be affected by the discrimination and have dealings with, or be related to, the group discriminated against on a prohibited basis. For example, white credit applicants have a claim if their mortgage application is denied because they live in a predominantly African-American neighborhood.

---

1 *See* § 3.9, *infra.*

2 *See* § 3.10, *infra.* The issue of associational discrimination is closely related to the issue of standing in a credit discrimination case. The topic of standing is discussed in § 11.2, *infra.*

3.2 When is Discrimination on a Prohibited Basis?

Creditors are in the business of distinguishing between good and bad credit risks; creditors discriminate against bad risks all the time. Credit discrimination laws do not generally prevent creditors from denying credit or providing less favorable terms to bad credit risks. In fact, such laws do not generally prevent creditors from making bad judgments and denying credit to good credit risks.[3] What credit discrimination laws do is to outlaw the practice of treating individuals differently *because* of their race, religion, national origin, sex, or some other prohibited basis.

The laws prohibit creditors from using these criteria even if such criteria have some positive correlation to credit risk. If a creditor believes minorities tend to have higher unemployment rates, for example, and thus are greater credit risks, the creditor must not discriminate because an applicant is a minority. Instead, the creditor must determine the individual applicant's employment status.

At the same time, credit discrimination statutes are not violated merely because an applicant is adversely treated and the applicant is a member of a protected group.[4] Dis-

---

3 *See* Palmiotto v. Bank of N.Y., Clearinghouse No. 44,850 (S.D.N.Y. Sept. 29, 1989) (although it might be arbitrary and unfair to deny credit based merely on an excessive number of inquiries on the applicant's credit report, such an action is not prohibited by the ECOA).

4 *See* O'Dowd v. S. Cent. Bell, 729 F.2d 347 (5th Cir. 1984) (court rejected white couple's claim that telephone company discriminated in requiring a deposit because of their exchange's racial composition when couple had history of late payments and deposits were required of all such customers); Gross v. United States Small Bus. Admin., 669 F. Supp. 50 (N.D.N.Y. 1987) (no ECOA violation based on sex or marital status discrimination because applicant was rejected due to past delinquent loan with same agency), *aff'd*, 867 F.2d 1423 (2d Cir. 1988); Thomas v. First Fed. Sav. Bank, 653 F. Supp. 1330 (N.D. Ind. 1987) (no evidence of differing treatment of African-American second mortgage applicants or of "impermissible adverse impact"); Sayers v. Gen. Motors Acceptance Corp., 522 F. Supp. 835 (W.D. Mo. 1981) (married African-American woman did not establish discrimination on the basis of race, sex, or marital status, as the creditor's disparate treatment in approving twenty-five male applicants with similar credit histories was due to "extenuating circumstances," that is, prior dealings with creditor or larger equity in property purchased); Cherry v. Amoco Oil

crimination is prohibited if there is a link between the discrimination and the prohibited basis, such that the creditor's decision-making process results in individuals being treated differently because of a prohibited basis. This is called "disparate treatment." Chapter 4 discusses the fundamentals of disparate treatment in credit discrimination cases.

Another important credit discrimination principle is that a practice can involve illegal discrimination even when the creditor does not intend to discriminate on a prohibited basis. A practice can be illegal if it has the *effect* of discriminating on a prohibited basis.[5] This "effects test" provides an alternative approach when it is impossible to prove that the creditor intended to treat applicants differently. The effects test is discussed fully in Chapter 4.

3.3 Prohibited Bases Under Both the ECOA and the FHA

3.3.1 Race and Color

Race and color are prohibited bases under both the ECOA[6] and the Fair Housing Act.[7] They are also prohibited bases under the federal Civil Rights Acts[8] and virtually all state credit discrimination legislation.[9] Native American

Indians are a protected race.[10] Discrimination against whites is also actionable under the ECOA.[11]

Racial discrimination may include discrimination not only against minorities but against those living in predominantly minority neighborhoods.[12] Such determinations can be disparate treatment if the creditor is taking an action because of the racial composition of a community.

Such actions may also constitute discrimination based on disparate impact if the creditor does not know the racial composition of a particular community and only discriminates against areas because of average income levels, payment histories, or similar characteristics. This geographic discrimination may still have a disproportionate impact on certain races. Redlining and reverse redlining are discussed in full in Chapters 7 and 8.

3.3.2 Religion, Creed, Political Affiliation

Religion is a prohibited basis for discrimination under the ECOA,[13] the Federal Fair Housing Act,[14] and most state credit discrimination statutes.[15] The only exception under the ECOA is that creditors may favor applicants of a particular religion when offering a special purpose credit program meeting the standards set out in Regulation B.[16]

Co., 490 F. Supp. 1026 (N.D. Ga. 1980).

5 *See* § 4.3, *infra*.

6 15 U.S.C. § 1691(a)(1); Reg. B, 12 C.F.R. § 202.2(z). The FRB has proposed a number of changes to conform with its proposal to lift the ban on inquiring about an applicant's race, color, religion, national origin, or sex, but also to emphasize that such provision of information is voluntary and neither the information itself nor a decision to decline to provide the information can be considered in any aspect of the credit transaction. *See* § 5.5.4, *infra*. First, the FRB has proposed adding § 202.6(b)(9) to emphasize that a creditor may not consider race, color, religion, national origin, or sex to determine an applicant's creditworthiness except as permitted by law, nor may a creditor consider an applicant's decision not to provide the information. 64 Fed. Reg. 44, 582, 44,597 (Aug. 16, 1999). Second, the FRB proposed adding § 202.5(a)(4), which would prohibit a creditor from requiring an applicant to supply information about race, color, religion, national origin, or sex unless otherwise permitted or allowed by law, and would require a creditor who seeks such information to disclose to the applicant that providing such information is voluntary and that neither the information nor the decision not to provide the information will be taken into account in any aspect of the credit transaction. In addition, the FRB has proposed a new § 202.4(d) that would require the latter disclosure, and some others required by Regulation B, to be in writing, to be made in a clear and conspicuous manner, and to be provided in a form the applicant can retain. 64 Fed. Reg. at 44,597. The proposed revisions to Regulation B can be found on the CD-Rom accompanying this volume.

7 42 U.S.C. §§ 3604, 3605; *see* 24 C.F.R. § 100.110(b).

8 42 U.S.C. §§ 1981, 1982; *see* § 3.6.1, *infra*.

9 *See* Appx. E, *infra* (summaries of state credit discrimination statutes).

10 United States v. First Nat'l Bank of Gordon, Neb., Clearinghouse Nos. 51,295 (complaint), 51,295B (consent order), Civ. No. 95C 3239 (D.S.D. 1996); United States v. Blackpipe State Bank, Clearinghouse Nos. 49,955A (complaint), 49,955B (consent decree), Civ. No. 93-5115 (D.S.D. 1994); Saunsoci v. Sonny Gerber Auto Sales, Clearinghouse No. 49,723A, No. 8CV94-00048 (D. Neb. filed Feb. 1994) (complaint); Stuart v. First Sec. Bank, 15 P.3d 1198 (Mont. 2000).

11 Moore v. U.S. Dep't of Agric., *ex rel.* Farmer's Home Admin., 993 F.2d 1222 (5th Cir. 1993) (district court incorrectly dismissed action for race discrimination under the ECOA for lack of standing by white plaintiffs who were denied the opportunity to participate in sale of inventory farmland held by FmHA solely because they were white).

12 Cherry v. Amoco Oil Co., 481 F. Supp. 727 (N.D. Ga. 1979); Official Staff Commentary, 12 C.F.R. § 202.2(z)-1; *see also* § 3.10, *infra*.

13 15 U.S.C. § 1691(a)(1); *see* Reg. B, 12 C.F.R. § 202.2(z). The FRB has proposed a number of changes to conform with its proposal to lift the ban on inquiring about an applicant's race, color, religion, national origin, or sex, but also to emphasize that provision of such information is voluntary and neither the information itself nor a decision to decline to provide the information can be considered in any aspect of the credit transaction. *See* § 5.5.4, *infra* (note on proposed changes to Regulation B).

14 42 U.S.C. §§ 3604, 3605; *see* 24 C.F.R. § 100.110(b); *cf.* Tien Tao v. Kingsbridge Park Cmty. Ass'n, 953 S.W.2d 525, 532 (Tex. App. 1997) (enforcement of residential deed restrictions by neighborhood association did not violate federal or state FHA even though enforcement may impact manner that homeowners observed their religion).

15 *See* Appx. E, *infra* (summaries of state credit discrimination statutes).

16 *See* § 3.9, *infra*.

Creed might be a broader standard than religion because a creed may comprise a set of fundamental belief that are not necessarily religious in nature. Although federal discrimination laws do not list creed as a prohibited basis, a number of state credit discrimination statutes do.[17] At least one state statute lists political affiliation as a prohibited basis.[18]

3.3.3 National Origin

3.3.3.1 General

National origin is a prohibited basis under the ECOA,[19] the federal Fair Housing Act,[20] and most state credit discrimination statutes.[21]

3.3.3.2 Country of Birth or Ancestry

National origin is not defined in Department of Housing and Urban Development regulations but has been the subject of some interpretation under the ECOA. It seems clear that national origin is included as a prohibited basis to prevent discrimination based on an individual's ancestry. Examples of such discrimination include discrimination against individuals with Hispanic or Asian surnames or against individuals of Italian origin because of stereotypes involving organized crime.[22] It also includes discrimination against Native Americans.[23]

It is equally clear that national origin is included as a prohibited basis to prevent discrimination based on an individual's country of birth.[24] Similarly, creditors should not discriminate against anyone simply because they were born outside of the United States.

Any discrimination based on an individual's inability to speak English should be considered a form of discrimination based on national origin. For example, regulations set out by the Office of Thrift Supervision indicate that requiring fluency in the English language as a prerequisite for obtaining a loan may be discrimination based on national origin.[25] The Department of Justice (DOJ) has sued one bank for alleged discrimination against applicants who submitted credit card applications in Spanish.[26]

3.3.3.3 Immigration Status

3.3.3.3.1 The ECOA standard

For purposes of the ECOA, a denial of credit to a non-citizen of the United States is not per se discrimination.[27] The ECOA allows some latitude for credit discrimi-

---

17 *See, e.g.,* Colo. Rev. Stat. § 5-1-109 (Colorado Consumer Credit Code); Colo. Rev. Stat. § 24-34-502 (housing financing); Del. Code Ann. tit. 6, § 4604 (fair housing); Iowa Code § 537.3311 (Iowa Consumer Credit Code); Iowa Code § 216.8A (housing financing); Iowa Code § 216.10 (civil rights); La. Rev. Stat. Ann. § 51:2254 (West) (real estate financing); La. Rev. Stat. Ann. § 51:2255 (West); Md. Code Ann., Com. Law § 12-113; Md. Code Ann., Com. Law § 12-305; Md. Ann. Code art. 49B, § 22 (housing financing); Minn. Stat. § 363.03(2)(3) (housing financing); Mont. Code Ann. § 49-2-305(7) (housing financing); Mont. Code Ann. § 49-2-306; N.J. Stat. Ann. § 10:5-12(i) (West); N.Y. Exec. Law § 296-a (McKinney); 43 Pa. Cons. Stat. § 955(h) (housing financing); S.D. Codified Laws § 20-13-21 (Michie) (housing financing); Tenn. Code Ann. § 4-21-606 (housing financing); Vt. Stat. Ann. tit. 9, § 4503(a)(6); Wash. Rev. Code §§ 49.60.030(1)(d), 49.60.175, 49.60.176; Wash. Rev. Code § 49.60.222(j) (housing financing).

18 *See, e.g.,* Iowa Code § 537.3311 (Iowa Consumer Credit Code); 1 P.R. Laws Ann. § 13(e) (housing financing).

19 15 U.S.C. § 1691(a)(1); *see* Reg. B, 12 C.F.R. § 202.2(z). The FRB has proposed a number of changes to conform with its proposal to lift the ban on inquiring about an applicant's race, color, religion, national origin, or sex, but also to emphasize that provision of such information is voluntary and neither the information itself nor a decision to decline to provide the information can be considered in any aspect of the credit transaction. *See* § 5.5.4, *infra* (note on proposed changes to Regulation B).

20 42 U.S.C. §§ 3604, 3605; *see* 24 C.F.R. § 100.110(b).

21 *See* Appx. E, *infra* (summaries of state credit discrimination statutes).

22 *See* Ricci v. Key Bancshares, 662 F. Supp. 1132 (D. Me. 1987).

23 *See* United States v. First Nat'l Bank of Gordon, Neb., Clearinghouse Nos. 51,295 (complaint), 51,295B (consent order), Civ. No. 95C 3239 (D.S.D. 1996); United States v. Blackpipe State Bank, Clearinghouse Nos. 49,955A (complaint), 49,955B (consent decree), Civ. No. 93-5115 (D.S.D. 1994); Saunsoci v. Sonny Gerber Auto Sales, Clearinghouse No. 49,723A, No. 8CV94-00048 (D. Neb. filed Feb. 1994) (complaint).

24 Official Staff Commentary, 12 C.F.R. § 202.2(z)-2.

25 12 C.F.R. § 571.24(c)(2). Note that the Equal Employment Opportunity Commission's guidelines also state that a blanket English-only workplace rule may constitute national origin discrimination. 29 C.F.R. § 1606.7. However, the EEOC guideline has provoked mixed reactions from the federal courts. *Compare* Equal Employment Opportunity Comm'n v. Premier Operator Services, 113 F. Supp. 2d 1066 (N.D. Tex. 2000) (upholding EEOC guideline) *with* Garcia v. Spun Steak Co., 998 F.2d 1480 (9th Cir. 1993) (rejecting EEOC guidelines and holding that an English-only rule does not create an adverse impact prohibited by Title VII).

26 United States v. Associates Nat'l Bank, Clearinghouse No. 53,524, Civ. No. 99-196 (D. Del. Jan. 8, 2001), *available at* http://www.usdoj.gov. This lawsuit was settled with Associates agreeing to establish a $1.5 million fund to compensate Hispanic applicants and cardholders affected by the allegedly discriminatory practices. *Id.*

27 Official Staff Commentary, 12 C.F.R. § 202.6(b)(7)-2; *see also* Bhandari v. First Nat'l Bank of Commerce, 808 F.2d 1082 (5th Cir. 1987) (denial of credit to all aliens not an ECOA violation), *rev'd in part on other grounds*, 829 F.2d 1343 (5th Cir. 1987) (en banc), *vacated and remanded*, 492 U.S. 901, *reinstated*, 887 F.2d 609 (5th Cir. 1989). On the other hand, the Comptroller of the Currency has stated that national bank creditors under its jurisdiction may no longer maintain a blanket policy of refusing to grant credit to non-citizens; instead, such applications must

nation based on immigration status. Creditors may inquire about and consider an applicant's permanent residence status and immigration status.[28] A creditor may consider this information and other information necessary to determine the creditor's rights and remedies in case of default.[29]

For example, a creditor may discriminate between a non-citizen who is a long-time resident with permanent residence status and a non-citizen who is temporarily in this country on a student visa.[30] Nevertheless, the creditor may not discriminate against non-citizens of a specific national origin, only against those with a temporary immigration status. Each application must be judged on its individual merits.

A creditor also may refuse to grant credit because a law, regulation, or executive order imposes limitations on dealings with citizens or governments of certain other countries.[31] A prime example would be a creditor's refusal to extend credit to an applicant who wishes to conduct business with an officially-embargoed nation.

An interesting issue is whether discrimination based on immigration status, even if not per se prohibited, may be seen as having the effect of discriminating based on national origin. For example, any policy that discriminates against non-citizens may have a disparate impact upon individuals whose national origins are in Latin America or Asia. It is best to establish statistical or other evidence of this disparate impact on such individuals and not to rely solely on the theoretical argument that discrimination based on alienage is effectively discrimination against persons whose origins lie outside the United States.[32]

3.3.3.3.2 The Fair Housing Act standard

The Fair Housing Act is not clear as to whether its prohibition on discrimination based on national origin would apply to discrimination based on immigration status.[33] Unlike the ECOA, there is no explicit exception allowing discrimination based on immigration status. Thus, an action against discrimination based on immigration status could conceivably be available under the FHA. At the very least, discrimination based on alienage would violate the Fair Housing Act if it had the effect of discriminating against individuals of a particular national origin.[34]

3.3.4 Sex or Gender

An applicant's sex is a prohibited basis for credit discrimination under the ECOA,[35] the federal Fair Housing Act,[36] and many state credit discrimination statutes.[37] Sex discrimination is often related to discrimination based on marital status.[38] It is thus important to consider both bases in any case involving one or the other.

In addition, the ECOA provides women with specific protections against creditor inquiries or credit decisions based on a woman's childbearing or childrearing intentions, including plans for maternity leave.[39] For example, a civil

---

be considered on their individual merits. Comptroller of the Currency, Interpretive Staff Letter, Fed. Banking L. Rep. (CCH) ¶ 85,026 (Office of the Comptroller of the Currency Sept. 9, 1977) (William B. Glidden) (also available at 1977 OCC Ltr. LEXIS 64).

28 National bank creditors are permitted to inquire about and to consider an applicant's permanent residence and immigration status and may maintain a policy of requiring foreign student credit applicants to possess an alien registration card. Comptroller of the Currency, Interpretive Staff Letter, Fed. Banking L. Rep. (CCH) ¶ 85,026 (Office of the Comptroller of the Currency Sept. 9, 1977) (William B. Glidden) (also available at 1977 OCC Ltr. LEXIS 64; Comptroller of the Currency, Interpretive Staff Letter, Fed. Banking L. Rep. (CCH) ¶ 85,023 (Office of the Comptroller of the Currency Sept. 6, 1977) (Thomas W. Taylor) (also available at 1977 OCC Ltr. LEXIS 68).

29 Reg. B, 12 C.F.R. § 202.6(b)(7); *see also* Bhandari v. First Nat'l Bank of Commerce, 808 F.2d 1082 (5th Cir. 1987), *rev'd in part on other grounds*, 829 F.2d 1343 (5th Cir. 1987) (en banc); Nguyen v. Montgomery Ward & Co., 513 F. Supp. 1039 (N.D. Tex. 1981) (credit refusal based on lack of United States citizenship does not constitute discrimination on the basis of national origin; no ECOA violation because no evidence that alien was denied credit given to other aliens); Hanna v. Sec. Pac. Bus. Credit, 281 Cal. Rptr. 857 (Ct. App. 1991) (credit refusal based on lack of citizenship is not national origin discrimination); Abuzant v. Shelter Ins. Co., 977 S.W.2d 259 (Ky. Ct. App. 1998) (applying Kentucky civil rights statute, court found denial of insurance policy on basis of non-citizenship did not necessarily constitute discrimination on basis of national origin).

30 Official Staff Commentary, 12 C.F.R. § 202.6(b)(7)-1.

31 Official Staff Commentary, 12 C.F.R. § 202.2(z)-2.

32 *See* Bhandari v. First Nat'l Bank of Commerce, 808 F.2d 1082 (5th Cir. 1987), *rev'd in part on other grounds*, 829 F.2d 1343 (5th Cir. 1987) (en banc); Abuzant v. Shelter Ins. Co., 977 S.W.2d 259 (Ky. Ct. App. 1998) (applying Kentucky civil rights statute, court found denial of insurance policy on basis of non-citizenship did not necessarily constitute discrimination on basis of national origin).

33 *See* Espinoza v. Farah Mfg. Co., 414 U.S. 86, 94 S. Ct. 334, 38 L. Ed. 2d 287 (1973) (Equal Employment Opportunity Act's prohibition of discrimination based on national origin does not prohibit discrimination on the basis of alienage).

34 Espinoza v. Hillwood Square Mut. Ass'n, 522 F. Supp. 559 (E.D. Va. 1981) (housing cooperative's policy of excluding aliens could violate the Fair Housing Act if it had the effect of discriminating on the basis of national origin).

35 15 U.S.C. § 1691(a)(1); *see* Reg. B, 12 C.F.R. §§ 202.4, 202.2(z). The FRB has proposed a number of changes to conform with its proposal to lift the ban on inquiring about an applicant's race, color, religion, national origin, or sex, but also to emphasize that provision of such information is voluntary and neither the information itself nor a decision to decline to provide the information can be considered in any aspect of the credit transaction. *See* § 5.5.4, *infra* (note on proposed changes to Regulation B).

36 42 U.S.C. §§ 3604, 3605.

37 *See* Appx. E, *infra* (summaries of state credit discrimination statutes).

38 *See* § 3.4.1, *infra*.

39 *See* § 5.5.5.2.3, *infra*.

penalty has been assessed against a credit union which denied loans to female members who anticipated taking maternity leave.[40] Similarly, the Fair Housing Act prohibits discrimination on the basis of familial status which includes discrimination against women who are pregnant.[41]

Sex discrimination may also be prohibited based on how creditors treat income sources traditionally associated with women. Regulation B sets out detailed standards as to whether creditors may discriminate against applicants whose incomes are based on part-time employment or that consist of alimony, child support, separate maintenance, or public assistance.[42]

Sex discrimination may also take the form of discrimination based on gender-defined occupations. For example, the Federal Trade Commission has successfully challenged a credit scoring system which evaluated applications by giving waitresses no points for their occupation while giving waiters a positive number of points.[43]

Sex discrimination may also take the form of discrimination against applicants who do not conform to gender-specific stereotypes or behave in gender-specific ways. For example, a sex discrimination claim under the ECOA was allowed to proceed against a bank that refused to allow a man who dressed in "feminine" clothing to apply for credit.[44] Thus, the prohibition against sex discrimination may also cover discrimination based on sexual orientation or transgender identity if the animus is based upon the applicant's failing to appear or act "like a man/woman."[45] Rhode Island prohibits discrimination based upon an applicant's gender identity or expression.[46]

The prohibitions against sex discrimination may also extend to discrimination based on gender-related characteristics. For example, the ECOA and the FHA should prohibit discrimination by automobile dealers who routinely mark up financing higher for female customers than male customers based on the belief that "women tend not to be as aggressive in negotiations as men."

Because of historical differences as to how husbands and wives have been treated, factors that appear neutral—such as an individual's marital status—can have a disparate impact on women and discrimination based on these may be prohibited. For example, credit accounts traditionally were kept in only the husband's name, with the consequence that many women today do not have independent credit histories. The ECOA sets out special rules by which to judge the credit history of women whose accounts have been subsumed under the name of their husbands.[47]

Similarly, because telephone listings traditionally were often listed in only the husband's name, the ECOA prohibits creditors from considering whether a telephone is listed in the applicant's name. Instead, creditors may only consider whether there is a telephone at the applicant's residence.[48]

3.4 Prohibited Bases Under the ECOA But Not the FHA

3.4.1 Marital Status

Marital status is a prohibited basis under the ECOA[49] and many state credit discrimination and fair housing statutes.[50] Generally, marital status as a prohibited basis includes any discrimination against an individual because that individual is single, divorced, separated, married, or widowed.

It is an ECOA violation to discriminate not only between married and unmarried applicants but also between single and divorced applicants. The Federal Trade Commission (FTC) has successfully challenged the practices of a major creditor who divided credit applicants into divorced and single categories by circling or otherwise emphasizing information contained in credit reports run on the applicants.[51]

The prohibition on marital status discrimination also prevents various forms of discrimination favoring married over unmarried couples or favoring joint accounts between a married couple versus between two unmarried individuals who wish to share a credit account.[52] The Federal Reserve

40 United States v. Ga. Telco Credit Union, Clearinghouse No. 31,075 (N.D. Ga. July 25, 1980).
41 *See* § 3.5.1, *infra*.
42 These requirements are analyzed in § 6.5.2, *infra*.
43 *In re* Alden's, Inc., 92 F.T.C. 901 (Fed. Trade Comm'n 1978).
44 Rosa v. Park W. Bank & Trust, 214 F.3d 213, 216 (1st Cir. 2000) (noting that stereotyped remarks about dressing in a more feminine or masculine manner can be evidence of gender bias).
45 *See* Centola v. Potter, 2002 U.S. Dist. LEXIS 1504 (D. Mass. Jan. 29, 2002); Enriquez v. W. Jersey Health Sys., 777 A.2d 365 (N.J. Super. Ct. App. Div. 2001). *See generally* Taylor Flynn, *Transforming the Debate: Why We Need to Include Transgender Rights in the Struggles for Sex and Sexual Orientation Equality*, 101 Colum. L. Rev. 392 (2001).
46 R.I. Gen. Laws §§ 34-37-4(b) (housing financing), § 34-37-4.3.
47 *See* § 6.5.3, *infra*.
48 *See* § 6.5.4, *infra*.
49 15 U.S.C. § 1691(a)(1); *see* Reg. B, 12 C.F.R. § 202.2(z).
50 *See* Appx. E, *infra* (summaries of state credit discrimination statutes).
51 *In re* Westinghouse Credit Corp., 94 F.T.C. 1280 (Fed. Trade Comm'n 1979); *see also* United States v. Fireside Thrift, Clearinghouse No. 43,051 (N.D. Cal. Sept. 2, 1986) (consent order in which creditors agreed not to use terms other than married and separated on applications); United States v. Capitol Thrift & Loan Ass'n, Clearinghouse No. 43,052 (N.D. Cal. Mar. 20, 1986) (same); Shuman v. Standard Oil, 453 F. Supp. 1150 (N.D. Cal. 1978) (divorced woman alleged that the creditor discriminated against her on the basis of her marital status, as revealed in a credit report).
52 Official Staff Commentary, 12 C.F.R. § 202.6(b)(1)-1; *see also* Official Staff Commentary, 12 C.F.R. § 202.7(a)-2; Diaz v. Va. Hous. Dev. Auth., 101 F. Supp. 2d 415, 419–20 (noting ECOA generally prohibits discrimination against unmarried couples), *subsequent proceeding at* 117 F. Supp. 2d 500 (E.D. Va. 2000). However, in the context of a special purpose credit program expressly authorized by federal or state law, a creditor can

Board has proposed a revision to Regulation B emphasizing this prohibition.[53]

A creditor who would not aggregate the incomes of an unmarried man and woman applying jointly for a mortgage has been found to have discriminated based on marital status.[54] The FTC has had two significant settlements resulting from complaints alleging, among other things, marital status discrimination based on creditors' failing to combine incomes for unmarried co-applicants.[55] However, it would not be a violation of the ECOA for a creditor to refuse to combine the incomes of two parties when one is a cosigner or guarantor and not a joint applicant.[56]

Marital status as a prohibited basis does not directly address sexual orientation. However, the prohibition against favoring married couples over unmarried joint applicants should protect same-sex joint applicants. While the ECOA does not prohibit discrimination based on familial status, some forms of familial status discrimination may be challenged under the ECOA as discrimination based on sex or marital status. For example, discrimination based on an applicant being pregnant should be challenged under the

ECOA as sex discrimination.[57] If there is discrimination based on whether a family has children, it is unclear if this consitutes marital status discrimination. Children are more likely to be correlated with married couples than with single individuals, particularly those who have never married.

On the other hand, this correlation is not particularly uniform or accurate. Many divorced, separated, and unmarried individuals have children and many married couples do not. Thus, one court has rejected a challenge to a credit scoring system which gave positive consideration to applicants with children because there was no evidence that the end result of the credit scoring system was to differentiate based on marital status.[58]

Regulation B includes a number of detailed rules concerning marital status discrimination, which are discussed in later chapters, including:

- A creditor's ability to require that spouses join in credit applications if joint property is involved;[59]
- A creditor's ability to consider an applicant's marital status if it implicates the creditor's rights and remedies upon default;[60]
- The right of a creditor such as a utility to refuse to grant credit to one spouse on the basis of a delinquency owed by the other spouse to the same creditor;[61] and
- The manner in which a creditor must treat income that is associated with divorced or separated applicants, such as alimony, child support, and separate maintenance payments.[62]

3.4.2 Age

The ECOA[63] and a number of state credit discrimination laws[64] list age as a prohibited basis. In practice, however, the ECOA mainly prohibits discrimination against the elderly. That is, the central purpose and chief effect of the ECOA provision is to protect elderly persons, who historically have been subjected to arbitrary denial or revocation of credit when they reached a certain age, regardless of their actual credit history or income level.[65]

Regulation B defines the term elderly to include all persons aged sixty-two or older.[66] As a result, the ECOA offers special protections to those age sixty-two or older but

---

discriminate against unmarried couples even if marital status does not directly relate to characteristics shared by the specific population being served by the program. *Id.; see* § 3.9, *infra* (discussion of special purpose credit programs).

Note that states which prohibit marital status discrimination are split as to whether such provisions prohibit discrimination against unmarried couples. Levin v. Yeshiva Univ., 754 N.E.2d 1099 (N.Y. 2001); Hoy v. Mercado, 266 A.D.2d 803 (N.Y. App. Div. 1999). *See generally* Jason C. Long, *Housing Discrimination and the Status of Unmarried Cohabitants—Living with McCready v. Hoffus,* 76 U. Det. Mercy L. Rev. 99 (1998). New Mexico's credit discrimination law has substituted "spousal affiliation" for "marital status" as a prohibited basis. N.M. Stat. Ann. § 28-1-1 (Michie).

53 64 Fed. Reg. 44,582, 44,597 (Aug. 16, 1999) (revising 12 C.F.R. § 202.6(b)(8)) (emphasizing that, unless otherwise permitted or required by law, a creditor must evaluate married and unmarried applicants by the same standards and must not treat applicants differently based on the existence, absence, or likelihood of a marital relationship between the parties).

54 Markham v. Colonial Mortgage Serv. Co., 605 F.2d 566 (D.C. Cir. 1979). However, on remand, the court decided that the applicants had been denied credit because their combined income was insufficient and not because of their marital status. Consumer Cred. Guide (CCH) ¶ 97,403 (D.D.C. 1980).

55 United States v. Franklin Acceptance Corp., Civ. No. 99-CV-2435 (E.D. Pa. 1999) (consent decree); United States v. Ford Motor Credit Co., Clearinghouse No. 53,016, No. 99-75887 (E.D. Mich. Dec. 14, 1999) (consent decree). Both of these consent decrees are also available at http://www.ftc.gov. In *Franklin Acceptance Corp.,* the FTC also alleged that Franklin discriminated on the basis of marital status by failing to consider child support payments as part of the applicant's income (also sex discrimination) and requiring a married applicant to have his/her spouse and not any other person cosign a loan when required.

56 *See* Official Staff Commentary, 12 C.F.R. § 202.6(b)(1)-1 (explained at 60 Fed. Reg. 29,965, 29,967 (June 7, 1995)).

57 *See* § 3.3.4, *supra.*

58 Carroll v. Exxon Co., 434 F. Supp. 557 (E.D. La. 1977).

59 *See* § 5.6, *infra.*

60 *See* § 6.6.4, *infra.*

61 *See* § 5.5.5.4, *infra.*

62 *See* § 6.5.2.6, *infra.*

63 15 U.S.C. § 1691(a)(1); *see* Reg. B, 12 C.F.R. §§ 202.4, 202.2(z).

64 *See* Appx. E, *infra* (summaries of state credit discrimination statutes).

65 *See* H.R. Rep. No. 94-210, at 3–4 (1975) (legislative history of the ECOA provisions addressing age discrimination).

66 Reg. B, 12 C.F.R. § 202.2(o).

offers significantly less protection against discrimination, for example, to a sixty-year old.[67] Similarly, less protection is offered to a twenty-two-year-old who is discriminated against because of a brief work or credit history.[68]

There are a number of special ECOA rules that permit certain types of age discrimination.[69] These include:

- A creditor may consider the applicant's age to determine if the applicant is too young under state law to enter into a binding contract;[70]
- A creditor may consider the age of an applicant sixty-two years old or older in order to provide favorable treatment or more favorable credit terms to that applicant;[71]
- A creditor may consider the age of an applicant sixty-two years old or older in order to evaluate a pertinent element of creditworthiness for a reverse mortgage;[72]
- Under certain circumstances, a creditor may also take age into account as a factor in a credit scoring system, as long as those aged sixty-two and over receive the highest possible score for that factor.[73]

There are also special ECOA rules concerning the treatment of income associated with the elderly. These essentially prevent creditors from automatically excluding or considering only a portion of income derived from part-time employment, annuities, pensions, or other retirement benefits.[74] These rules are discussed in full in Chapter 6.

3.4.3 Public Assistance Status

The ECOA lists as a prohibited basis that "all or part of the applicant's income derives from any public assistance program."[75] This is an important category of prohibited discrimination for low-income consumers. It is not found in the federal Fair Housing Act. It is sometimes found in state fair housing laws and infrequently found as a prohibited

basis in state credit discrimination laws.[76] During the late 1990s, the Federal Trade Commission brought two cases involving discrimination against public assistance recipients.[77]

Under Regulation B, a protected public assistance program is "[a]ny federal, state, or local governmental assistance program that provides a continuing, periodic income supplement, whether premised on entitlement or need."[78] According to the Commentary, examples of such programs include, but are not limited to: Temporary Assistance to Needy Families, food stamps, rent and mortgage supplement or assistance programs, Social Security and Supplemental Security Income, and unemployment compensation.[79] Other programs within this definition should include veterans' benefits, emergency relief programs, and federal fuel assistance.

Medicare and Medicaid payments are public assistance benefits only for the purposes of doctors, hospitals or others to whom such benefits are payable.[80] Many doctors and hospitals are creditors[81] who extend credit.[82] thus the ECOA could be used against medical providers who, for example, treat Medicare recipients less favorably than private insurance patients during any phase of the credit transaction.[83]

Although public assistance status is generally a prohibited basis for discrimination under the ECOA, there are some exceptions. Although the fact that income derives from

67 Government enforcement of the age discrimination prohibition has also focused on the elderly. United States v. Money Tree, Inc., Clearinghouse No. 52,053, Civ. No. 6:97-CV-7 (M.D. Ga. Feb. 4, 1997) (settlement between the DOJ and The Money Tree, Inc. over allegations of discrimination against elderly applicants and applicants who received public assistance), *available at* http://www.ftc.gov.
68 The only official attention to the problems of young credit applicants is contained in Official Staff Commentary, 12 C.F.R. § 202.6(b), under which a creditor may consider an applicant's age, for example, to assess the significance of the applicant's length of employment or residence.
69 These rules are discussed in detail in § 6.6.2, *infra*.
70 *See* § 6.6.2.2, *infra*.
71 *See* § 6.6.2.2, *infra*.
72 *See* § 6.6.2.2, *infra*.
73 *See* § 6.6.2.4, *infra*.
74 *See* § 6.5.2.5, *infra*.
75 15 U.S.C. § 1691(a)(2); *see* Reg. B, 12 C.F.R. § 202.2(z).

76 *See, e.g.,* Conn. Gen Stat. § 46a-64c (housing finance) (source of income); D.C. Code Ann. § 1-2515 (human rights) (source of income); 815 Ill. Comp. Stat. § 120/3 (Fairness in Lending Act); Iowa Code § 537-3311 (Iowa Consumer Credit Code); Mass. Gen. Laws ch. 151B, § 4(10); Minn. Stat. § 363.03(2)(3) (housing financing); N.D. Cent. Code § 14-02.4-13 (housing financing), § 14-02.4-17; Okla. Stat. tit. 25, § 1452(A)(7)–(9) (housing financing) (public assistance, as specified); Or. Rev. Stat. § 659.033 (source of income); Tex. Fin. Code Ann. § 341.401 (Vernon) (social security and SSI income only); Utah Code Ann. § 57-21-5 (housing financing) (source of income); Vt. Stat. Ann. tit. 9, § 4503(a)(6) (housing financing); Wis. Stat. § 106.04 (housing finance) (source of income), § 224.77 (certain housing finance) (source of income).
77 United States v. Franklin Acceptance Corp., Civ. No. 99-CV-2435 (E.D. Pa. 1999); United States v. Money Tree, Inc., Clearinghouse No. 52,053, Civ. No. 6:97-CV-7 (M.D. Ga. Feb. 4, 1997). Both of these consent decrees are available at http://www.ftc.gov. *United States v. Franklin Acceptance Corp.* resulted in an $800,000 settlement, the largest civil penalty settlement obtained up to that time for alleged violations of the ECOA.
78 Official Staff Commentary, 12 C.F.R. § 202.2(z)-3. The Federal Reserve Board has proposed revisions to Official Staff Commentary, 12 C.F.R. § 202.2(z)-3 that would reflect the change in name of the Aid to Families with Dependent Children program to Temporary Aid to Needy Families (TANF). The proposed revisions to the Official Staff Commentary to Regulation B can be found on the CD-Rom accompanying this volume.
79 Official Staff Commentary, 12 C.F.R. § 202.2(z)-3.
80 Official Staff Commentary, 12 C.F.R. § 202.2(z)-3.
81 *See* § 2.2.2.6, *supra*.
82 *See* § 2.2.2.6, *supra*.
83 *See* § 2.2.2.6, *supra*.

public assistance may not be used in a credit scoring system, creditors using other systems may consider the source of such income to the extent it has a demonstrable relationship to determining creditworthiness. The Commentary gives several examples of such relationships, including how long the applicant will remain eligible for such income or whether the income may be garnished. These exceptions to the general rule against discrimination based on public assistance status are described in Chapter 6.[84]

3.4.4 Good Faith Exercise of Consumer Credit Protection Act, Other Legal Rights

3.4.4.1 General

A prohibited basis unique to the ECOA is the applicant's good faith exercise of federal Consumer Credit Protection Act (CCPA) rights.[85] While this basis does not appear in state credit discrimination laws, a few state statutes list exercise of rights under state credit legislation as a prohibited basis.[86] Also, the Fair Housing Act prohibits retaliating against any person because that person has made a complaint, testified, assisted, or participated in any manner in a proceeding under the Fair Housing Act.[87]

Under the ECOA, a creditor may not discriminate against an applicant because that person has exercised, in good faith, any right under the CCPA[88] or any state statute substituted for it, in whole or in part, with the Federal Reserve Board's approval.[89] The intent of this provision is to prevent "retaliatory credit denials or terminations"[90] of credit accounts when applicants exercise their legal rights. Similarly, a creditor may not condition granting new credit on an applicant releasing existing CCPA claims.[91]

The protection of this section is contingent on showing three separate elements:

- Rights were exercised under the Federal Consumer Credit Protection Act or a substituted state statute;
- The rights were exercised in good faith; and
- The rights were exercised by the applicant.

A recent case discussing this section has characterized it as prohibiting "retaliation" and used a framework that has been used in retaliation-based Title VII employment discrimination cases. In order to make out a prima facie case, the court held that a consumer must allege facts sufficient to show that he or she engaged in a statutorily protected activity and suffered an adverse credit action, and that there is a causal connection between the two (a retaliatory motive).[92]

3.4.4.2 Exercise of Rights Under the Federal Consumer Credit Protection Act or a Substituted State Statute

The federal Consumer Credit Protection Act[93] is an umbrella act comprised of a number of separately enacted statutes focusing on various credit issues. Exercise of rights under any of the following statutes triggers the protection of the ECOA for credit applicants:

- Truth in Lending Act;[94]
- Fair Credit Billing Act;[95]
- Consumer Leasing Act;[96]
- Federal Garnishment Act;[97]
- Federal Credit Repair Organization Act;[98]
- Fair Credit Reporting Act;[99]
- Fair Debt Collection Practices Act;[100]
- Electronic Funds Transfer Act;[101] and
- Equal Credit Opportunity Act.[102]

When a state has obtained an exemption from one of these acts because it has enacted its own equivalent or more protective statute,[103] exercise of rights under the state statute would also invoke the protection of the ECOA.

The exercise of rights is not limited merely to litigation

---

84 *See* § 6.6.3.2, *infra.*

85 15 U.S.C. § 1691(a)(3); *see* Reg. B, 12 C.F.R. § 202.2(z).

86 *See, e.g.,* Iowa Code § 537.3311 (Iowa Consumer Credit Code); Mo. Rev. Stat. § 408.550.

87 42 U.S.C. § 3617; *see* 24 C.F.R. § 100.400(c)(5).

88 15 U.S.C. §§ 1601–1693r.

89 15 U.S.C. § 1691(a)(3); *see* Reg. B, 12 C.F.R. §§ 202.4, 202.2(z). This protection does not extend to rights exercised by persons other than the applicant. *See* Official Staff Commentary, 12 C.F.R. § 202.2(z)-1.

90 S. Rep. No. 94-589, at 5, *reprinted in* 1976 U.S.C.C.A.N. 403, 407.

91 Owens v. Magee Fin. Serv., 476 F. Supp. 758 (E.D. La. 1979).

92 Lewis v. ACB Bus. Services, Inc., 135 F.3d 389 (6th Cir. 1998) (plaintiff failed to show a causal connection between the creditor's collection action and the plaintiff's earlier lawsuit against the creditor and therefore failed to claim an adverse credit action, as the creditor was just collecting its debt).

93 15 U.S.C. §§ 1601–1693r.

94 15 U.S.C. §§ 1601–1667f.

95 15 U.S.C. §§ 1666–1666j.

96 15 U.S.C. §§ 1667–1667f.

97 15 U.S.C. §§ 1671–1677.

98 15 U.S.C. §§ 1679–1679j.

99 15 U.S.C. §§ 1681–1681u.

100 15 U.S.C. §§ 1692–1692o.

101 15 U.S.C. §§ 1693–1693r.

102 15 U.S.C. §§ 1691 to 1691f; *see* Emigrant Sav. Bank v. Elan Mgmt. Corp., 668 F.2d 671 (2d Cir. 1982) (removal from state court refused when apartment building management corporation claimed that foreclosure action was racially motivated and was brought in retaliation for its exercise of ECOA rights).

103 For example, several states have been granted an exemption from the federal Truth in Lending Act, pursuant to 15 U.S.C. § 1633. *See, e.g.,* Conn. Gen. Stat. §§ 36-393 to 36-417j.

under the CCPA or substituted state statutes. Exercise of rights also includes procedures such as use of the billing statement dispute mechanisms of the Fair Credit Billing Act[104] and exercise of rescission rights under the Truth in Lending Act.[105] Furthermore, if the creditor denies credit because the applicant does not wish to buy credit insurance, which is supposedly optional under the creditor's Truth in Lending disclosure form, the applicant may have an ECOA claim for discrimination on the basis of good faith exercise of rights under the CCPA.[106]

3.4.4.3 Good Faith Exercise of Rights

The applicant is protected only when an exercise of rights under the CCPA was done in "good faith."[107] The legislative history of the 1976 amendments to the ECOA explains: "The 'good faith' qualification recognizes that some applicants may engage in frivolous or nuisance disputes which do reflect on their willingness to honor their obligations."[108]

Case law under various acts comprising the CCPA generally does not focus on the consumer's good faith or lack of it but rather on the good or bad faith of the creditor.[109] One reported case dealing with discrimination based on an applicant's exercise of Consumer Credit Protection Act rights concluded as a matter of law that the applicant had previously exercised her Truth in Lending rights in good faith, in the absence of any creditor claim to the contrary.[110]

One possible source of precedent as to the good faith issue is the award of attorney fees to defendants when plaintiffs have brought actions in bad faith under the CCPA or similar statutes. For instance, the Federal Debt Collection Practices Act (FDCPA) provides that a court may award attorney fees to a defendant when a plaintiff brings an action under the Act "in bad faith and for the purposes of harassment."[111]

The FDCPA provides a somewhat more stringent standard for fee awards than does the federal common law rule, which generally permits the award of attorney fees to the prevailing party when the losing party had "acted in bad

faith, vexatiously, wantonly, or for oppressive reasons."[112] In denying an award of fees to a prevailing defendant under the Equal Employment Opportunity Act, the Supreme Court's standard in another case was that the suit had not been "frivolous, meritless, or vexatious."[113]

Under these standards, the creditor claiming that a CCPA suit was not brought in good faith bears a heavy burden of proof. The creditor must prove that the consumer acted out of malice or with an intent to harass in instituting the action. Good faith should be proven automatically if the consumer's action was successful.

After an unsuccessful CCPA action, the creditor trying to argue for the consumer's lack of good faith would have to show not only that the consumer had no basis for believing that the CCPA had been violated, but also that the consumer in fact did not believe that such violations had occurred. Furthermore, the creditor must show that the purpose of the suit was harassment. Of course, a creditor's proof problems are complicated when the consumer brought the CCPA action against a different creditor, because the creditor wishing to show bad faith did not participate in that original transaction.

3.4.4.4 Applicant Must Exercise the Rights

The applicant must have exercised the CCPA rights. Applicant is a defined term under Regulation B and includes both a credit applicant, one who has been extended credit, and a cosigner or other party who is contractually obligated on the loan.[114] If any of these individuals had previously exercised CCPA rights, the creditor may not use that as a basis for discrimination.

3.5 Prohibited Bases Under the FHA

3.5.1 Familial Status

The federal Fair Housing Act lists familial status as a prohibited basis for credit discrimination,[115] as do most state credit discrimination and housing financing statutes.[116] Generally, this prohibition forbids creditors from discriminating on the basis that applicants have children (or do not have children), are pregnant, or are legal custodians of children.

The Fair Housing Act regulations define familial status as a parent, legal custodian, or designee of such person having one or more children under the age of eighteen domiciled

---

104 15 U.S.C. § 1666(a).

105 15 U.S.C. § 1635; Reg. Z, 12 C.F.R. § 226.9.

106 Bryson v. Bank of N.Y., 584 F. Supp. 1306 (S.D.N.Y. 1984).

107 15 U.S.C. § 1691(a)(3); Reg. B, 12 C.F.R. § 202.2(z).

108 S. Rep. No. 94-589, at 5, *reprinted in* 1976 U.S.C.C.A.N. 403, 407. An example of such an action would be the initiation of a Fair Credit Billing Act inquiry solely to delay payment of an outstanding credit card balance. Compare the legislative history of the Fair Debt Collection Practices Act, a subtitle of the Consumer Credit Protection Act, which recognizes that "the number of persons who willfully refuse to pay just debts is minuscule [sic]." S. Rep. No. 95-382 (1977), *reprinted in* 1977 U.S.C.C.A.N. 1695, 1697.

109 *See, e.g.,* Franklin v. First Money, Inc., 599 F.2d 615 (5th Cir. 1979) (Truth in Lending case dealing with a creditor's "good faith conformity" with Federal Reserve Board releases concerning that act).

110 Owens v. Magee Fin. Serv., 476 F. Supp. 758 (E.D. La. 1979).

111 15 U.S.C. § 1692k(a)(3).

112 Alyeska Pipeline Serv. v. Wilderness Soc'y, 421 U.S. 240, 258–59, 95 S. Ct. 1612, 44 L. Ed. 2d 141 (1975).

113 Christiansburg Garment Co. v. Equal Employment Opportunity Comm'n, 434 U.S. 412, 98 S. Ct. 694, 54 L. Ed. 2d 648 (1978).

114 *See* § 2.2.4, *supra.*

115 42 U.S.C. §§ 3604, 3605; *see* 24 C.F.R. § 100.110(b).

116 *See* Appx. E, *infra* (summaries of state credit discrimination and housing financing statutes).

with them.[117] Thus there is discrimination on the basis of familial status when an apartment complex has a policy of refusing to rent apartments to families with more than a certain number of family members (that is, total of adults and children) when it would rent the same unit to the same number of individuals if all the tenants were adults.[118]

In one case, the court found a prima facie violation on the basis of familial status when the condominium association published rules prohibiting children under twelve and neither removed those restrictions prior to the tenancy nor communicated their unenforceability to the tenant, even though the association took no action to enforce the rules and the tenancy was terminated for failure to pay rent.[119]

Familial status also includes being pregnant or in the process of gaining legal custody of a child under eighteen years of age.[120] Thus, discrimination against a family that takes in foster children should be discrimination under the Fair Housing Act.[121]

A lender may consider the *costs* of caring for children in determining creditworthiness but can not have a policy of treating those with children less favorably than those without.[122] Creditors also should not be able to discriminate on the basis of the number of children.[123]

In addition, the prohibition on familial status discrimination does not apply to certain housing for the elderly,[124] allowing elderly housing developments to restrict children. This exclusion should have little application to credit discrimination.

3.5.2 Disability or Handicap

The Fair Housing Act and many state credit discrimination statutes[125] directly prohibit credit discrimination based on an applicant's status as handicapped or disabled.[126] While the ECOA does not include this basis, as discussed below, the Americans with Disabilities Act (ADA)[127] prohibits discrimination by many types of lenders on the basis of disability.

In addition to directly prohibiting discrimination on the basis of disability, both the ADA[128] and the FHA[129] also provide that a refusal to make a reasonable accommodation for a disabled person is a form of discrimination. Reasonable accommodation can involve either physical access modifications or accommodations in rules, policies, practices or services.[130] Thus, a lender could be required to make an exception to its rules or policies in order to reasonably accommodate a disabled applicant.[131]

Handicap is defined in HUD's Fair Housing regulations and in the ADA as a physical or mental impairment which substantially limits one or more major life activities, having a record of such impairment, or being considered as having such an impairment.[132]

It is not enough to have an impairment. The handicap also must substantially limit one or more major life activities, such as caring for one's self, performing manual tasks, walking, seeing, hearing, speaking, breathing, learning, or working.[133]

---

117 24 C.F.R. § 100.20.

118 Glover v. Crestwood Lake Section 1 Holding Corp., 746 F. Supp. 301 (S.D.N.Y. 1990). Note that the FHA contains an exemption which states that occupancy limits per se do not violate the Act. 42 U.S.C. § 3607(b)(1). However, this exemption is to be narrowly construed, and occupancy limits cannot be based upon the familial relationships (or lack thereof) of the occupants. City of Edmonds v. Oxford House, 514 U.S. 725, 115 S. Ct. 1776, 131 L. Ed. 2d 801 (1995).

119 Martin v. Palm Beach Atl. Ass'n, 696 So. 2d 919 (Fla. Dist. Ct. App. 1997).

120 24 C.F.R. § 100.20.

121 *See* Gorski v. Troy, 929 F.2d 1183 (7th Cir. 1991). However, familial status does not include a group home consisting solely of the caretakers of the children actually live with them in the home. Keys Youth Services v. City of Olathe, 248 F.3d 1267 (10th Cir. 2001).

122 H.R. Rep. No. 100-711 (1988), *reprinted in* 1988 U.S.C.C.A.N. 2173, 2191–2192.

123 For example, occupancy limits based upon the number of children are prohibited. Indiana Civil Rights Comm'n v. County Line Park, 738 N.E.2d 1044 (Ind. 2000); *see also* Kelly v. United States Dep't of Hous. & Urban Dev., 3 F.3d 951, 952 (6th Cir. 1993).

124 *See* 24 C.F.R. § 100.300; Covey v. Hollydale Mobilehome Estates, 116 F.3d 830 (9th Cir. 1997); Massaro v. Mainlands Section 1 & 2 Civic Ass'n, 3 F.3d 1472 (11th Cir. 1993).

125 42 U.S.C. §§ 3604, 3605; *see* Appx. E, *infra* (summaries of state credit discrimination statutes). Some state statutes use the term "disability" rather than "handicapped." *See, e.g.,* Me. Rev. Stat. Ann. tit. 5, § 4582 (West) (housing financing); N.D. Cent. Code § 14-02.4-13 (housing financing); N.D. Cent. Code § 14-02.4-17; Wis. Stat. § 106.04.

126 *See* Mich. Prot. & Advocacy Serv., Inc. v. Babin, 18 F.3d 337 (6th Cir. 1994); United States v. Bank United, Clearinghouse Nos. 53,018 (complaint), 53,019 (consent decree) (W.D.N.Y. 1999), *available at* http://www.usdoj.gov.

127 42 U.S.C. § 12101.

128 42 U.S.C. § 12182(b)(2)(A)(ii).

129 42 U.S.C. § 3604(f)(3).

130 42 U.S.C. § 3604(f)(3)(A), (B); 42 U.S.C. § 12182(b)(2)(A)(ii).

131 The FHA's requirement of reasonable accommodation for disabled persons is a more stringent burden than the "reasonable accommodation" standards for religious practices under Title VII (but appears to be the same standard as set forth in the Americans with Disabilities Act). Shapiro v. Cadman Towers, 51 F.3d 328, 334 (2d Cir. 1995).

132 42 U.S.C. § 12102(2)(A),(B),(C); 24 C.F.R. § 100.201. Handicap for purposes of the Fair Housing Act's credit discrimination provision is actually defined at 24 C.F.R. § 100.20, but this provision merely refers to the definition found at 24 C.F.R. § 100.201.

133 Toyota Mfg. v. Williams, 534 U.S. 184, 122 S. Ct. 681, 151 L. Ed. 2d 615 (2002) (in this employment discrimination case a unanimous Supreme Court ruled that "to be substantially limited in performing manual tasks, an individual must have an impairment that prevents or severely restricts the individual from doing activities that are of central importance to most

On the other hand, the individual need not actually *presently* have such a physical or mental impairment. It is enough if a *record* of such impairment exists, meaning having a history of, or having been classified (or even misclassified) as having, a mental or physical impairment. Also, it is enough if the individual is *considered* as having such an impairment, meaning that the impairment does not substantially limit a major life activity, but others view and treat the individual as having an impairment which constitutes such a limitation.[134]

It always makes sense to compare the definition of handicap or disability under the Fair Housing Act and the ADA with definitions found in any relevant state credit discrimination law to determine if one or the other is more applicable in a particular case. For example, several state credit discrimination and housing financing laws[135] consider persons with AIDS or HIV to be disabled or handicapped (as does the ADA).[136]

In addition to the FHA, the ADA provides another possible avenue to combat credit discrimination involving applicants with disabilities or handicaps, especially for non-housing financing cases.[137] Title III of the ADA prohibits discrimination on the basis of disability by places of public accommodation.[138] Public accommodation is defined to include banks, retailers, and other service establishments.[139] Thus, many creditors should be covered by the ADA because they are places of public accommodation and are prohibited from discriminating on the basis of a disability in the full enjoyment of "goods, services, facilities, or privileges" provided by the creditor.[140] The ADA's legislative history also provides support for the application of the ADA to credit transactions. The House Report explains that a store may not ask on a credit application if a person has epilepsy, has ever been hospitalized for mental illness, or has any other disability.[141] The ADA further requires places of public accommodation to ensure effective communication and provision of auxiliary devices and prohibits unecessary inquiries about disabilities.[142]

To date, there has been very little litigation in this area.[143] In the context of homeowner's insurance, a court has ruled that the ADA prohibits an insurer from refusing to provide insurance on the basis of the disability of the residents of that home.[144] The court noted that several courts have held that the ADA applies to more than just physical access to an insurance office and also covers insurance products (and thus presumably credit products).

Also, the Department of Justice (DOJ) has taken enforcement action under the ADA against a department store that allegedly discriminated against disabled customers by granting check payment privileges only to customers with driver's licenses (which certain disabled individuals cannot obtain).[145] The DOJ has also issued an informal opinion letter stating that, under the ADA, a bank must modify its signature policies to accommodate a quadriplegic who was unable to sign his name because of his disability. Such modifications were necessary to allow the consumer to transact business with the bank. Such modifications must be reasonable and not fundamentally alter the nature of the services provided at the public accommodation.[146]

One explanation for the sparse case law under the ADA with respect to credit discrimination is that remedies for private plaintiffs under the ADA are limited to injunctive relief and attorney fees. Congress did not provide for compensatory relief in private rights of actions for violations of Title III of the ADA.[147]

3.6 Prohibited Bases Under the Federal Civil Rights Acts

3.6.1 *Race and Color*

Race is the sole prohibited basis under the federal Civil Rights Acts. One important issue in the definition of race is whether racial discrimination may be against ethnic or

---

people's daily lives, and the impairment must be permanent or long-term").

134 *Id.*

135 *See* Fla. Stat. Ann. § 760.25 (West); Haw. Rev. Stat. § 515-5; N.J. Stat. Ann. § 10:5-12(i) (West).

136 *See* Bragdon v. Abbott, 524 U.S. 624, 118 S. Ct. 2196, 141 L. Ed. 2d 540 (1998).

137 *See* § 1.6, *supra* (brief description of the ADA).

138 42 U.S.C. § 12182(a) ("No individual shall be discriminated against on the basis of disability in the full and equal enjoyment of the goods, services, facilities, privileges, advantages, or accommodations of any place of public accommodation by any person who owns, leases (or leases to), or operates a place of public accommodation.").

139 42 U.S.C. § 12181(7)(F).

140 42 U.S.C. § 12182(a).

141 *See* H.R. Rep. No. 101-485II, at 105 (1990), *reprinted in* 1990 U.S.C.C.A.N. 267, 388.

142 *See* United States Dep't of Justice, ADA Title III Technical

Assistance Manual, *available at* http://www.usdoj.gov/crt/ada/taman3.html.

143 In a case in which a pro se plaintiff had invoked the ADA in a credit discrimination context, the court dismissed the public accommodations claim by rather oddly citing only the ADA section concerning discrimination in employment while ignoring Title III. Kloth v. Citibank, 33 F. Supp. 2d 115 (D. Conn. 1998).

144 Wai v. Allstate Ins. Co., 75 F. Supp. 2d 1, 8–11 (D.D.C. 1999).

145 United States Dep't of Justice, Disability Rights Sec., Enforcing the ADA: Looking Back on a Decade of Progress § C.1 (2000), *available at* http://www.usdoj.gov.

146 United States Dep't of Justice, Informal Opinion Letter (Dec. 29, 1994), *available at* http://www.usdoj.gov/crt/foia/cltr149.txt.

147 42 U.S.C. § 12188(a); AR v. Kogan, 964 F. Supp. 269, 271 (N.D. Ill. 1997). In contrast, U.S. Attorneys can seek monetary relief for the victims of discrimination, as well as injunctive relief and civil penalties. 42 U.S.C. § 12188(b)(2).

Caucasian groups—such as Arabs, Jews, and Hispanics—under these laws.

A unanimous Supreme Court in 1987 interpreted racial discrimination under the federal Civil Rights Acts to be based on the nineteenth century notions of race (when the Civil Rights Acts were first enacted). The Court concluded that the statutes protected "identifiable classes of persons who are subjected to intentional discrimination solely because of their ancestry or ethnic characteristics."[148]

Thus discrimination is based on race when it is based, for example, on an individual being Arab rather than the individual being born in a particular country or in a particular place.[149] Similarly, the Court has held that the federal Civil Rights Acts apply to discrimination against Jews because, in the nineteenth century, Jews were also considered a separate race.[150] Hispanics are also considered racial minorities for purposes of the federal Civil Rights Acts.[151] Members of other ethnic groups such as Italian-Americans have also successfully asserted claims.[152] In addition, while the federal Civil Rights Acts do not prohibit discrimination on the basis of religion, ethnic groups who might have a common religion, such as Jews, may be covered.[153]

3.6.2 National Origin

The federal Civil Rights Acts do not explicitly prohibit discrimination on the basis of national origin. As discussed above, the statutes have been interpreted by the U.S. Supreme Court as prohibiting discrimination against certain ethnic groups such as Arabs and Jews.[154] As described below, there is also a good case to be made that section 1981 prohibits discrimination against non-citizens on the basis of immigration status.

However, only citizens are given the right to utilize

section 1982. On the other hand, non-citizens can utilitze the protections of section 1981.[155] Thus, a non-citizen can bring actions under that statute for discrimination based on race, ethnic origin, or immigration status.

3.6.3 Immigration Status

Section 1981 of the federal Civil Rights Acts[156] should apply to discrimination on the basis of alienage, i.e., citizenship status. The Supreme Court has ruled that section 1981 applies not only to discrimination based on race but also to discrimination based on an individual not being a citizen of the United States.[157] Prior to the enactment of the 1991 amendments, courts were split as to whether section 1981 applied to private alienage discrimination.[158] The highest court to date to rule on this issue since the adoption of the 1991 amendments found that section 1981 clearly provides a claim against private discrimination on the basis of alienage.[159] The 1991 amendments clarified that the rights enumerated in section 1981 are protected from private as well as governmental discrimination.[160] Prior decisions that required state action for a finding of alienage discrimination have therefore been legislatively superseded.[161] Thus, a

148 Saint Francis College v. Al-Khazraji, 481 U.S. 604, 95 L. Ed. 582, 107 S. Ct. 2022 (1987).
149 *Id.*
150 Shaare Tefila Congregation v. Cobb, 481 U.S. 615, 107 S. Ct. 2019, 95 L. Ed. 2d 594 (1987).
151 Rodriguez v. Beechmont Bus Serv., 173 F. Supp. 2d 139 (S.D.N.Y. 2001) (Hispanic employee allowed to bring racial discrimination claim, but not national origin discrimination claim, under § 1981; Cantu v. Nocona Hills Owners Ass'n, 2001 U.S. Dist. LEXIS 11010 (N.D. Tex. July 30, 2001) (Mexican-American plaintiff permitted to bring § 1981 claim as a racial minority).
152 *See, e.g.*, Bisciglia v. Kenosha Unified Sch. Dist. No. 1, 45 F.3d 223 (7th Cir. 1995) (Italian-Americans may state § 1981 claim, as they may be considered members of a race protected against discrimination); Sonaire v. NME Hosp., Inc., 27 F.3d 507 (11th Cir. 1994) (Filipino-Americans considered a protected class under § 1981), *aff'd*, 182 F.3d 903 (3d Cir. 1999) (table), *cert. denied*, 528 U.S. 951 (1999).
153 *But see* King v. Township of E. Lampeter, 17 F. Supp. 2d 394 (E.D. Pa. 1998) (Amish are not a protected group under § 1981, as they are a religious and not an ethnic group).
154 *See* § 3.6.1, *supra*.

155 *See* Graham v. Richardson, 403 U.S. 365, 91 S. Ct. 1848, 29 L. Ed. 2d 534 (1971); Anderson v. Conboy, 156 F.3d 167 (2d Cir. 1998).
156 42 U.S.C. § 1981.
157 Takahashi v. Fish & Game Comm'n, 334 U.S. 410, 68 S. Ct. 1138, 92 L. Ed. 1478 (1948).
158 *Compare* Bhandari v. First Nat'l Bank of Commerce, 829 F.2d 1343 (5th Cir. 1987), *vacated and remanded*, 492 U.S. 901, *reinstated*, 887 F.2d 609 (5th Cir. 1989) (§ 1981 prohibits only state action discriminating against aliens, not private discrimination) *with* Duane v. Geico, 37 F.3d 1036 (4th Cir. 1994) (holding that the pre-1991 version of § 1981 prohibited private as well as state alienage discrimination), *cert. granted*, 513 U.S. 1189, *cert. dismissed*, 515 U.S. 1101 (1995).
159 *See* Anderson v. Conboy, 156 F.3d 167 (2d Cir. 1998) (citizen of Jamaica who immigrated to the United States in 1968 filed complaint claiming discrimination on the basis of alienage; the Second Circuit held that § 1981 as amended by the Civil Rights Act of 1991 provides a claim against private discrimination on the basis of alienage). To date, the Supreme Court has not ruled squarely on this issue.
160 42 U.S.C. § 1981(c), *as added by* Pub. L. No. 102-166, § 101, 105 Stat. 1071 (1991).
161 *See* Anderson v. Conboy, 156 F.3d 167 (2d Cir. 1998); Nagy v. Baltimore Life Ins. Co, 49 F. Supp. 2d 822 (D. Md. 1999), *vacated and remanded, in part, on other grounds*, 2000 U.S. App. LEXIS 12307 (4th Cir. June 5, 2000); Chacko v. Tex. A & M Univ., 960 F. Supp. 1180 (S.D. Tex. 1997) (following *Cheung*); Cheung v. Merrill, Lynch, Pierce, Fenner & Smith, Inc., 913 F. Supp. 248 (S.D.N.Y. 1996) (1991 amendments mooted previous arguments over whether Congress meant to prohibit private citizenship discrimination; in agreement with *Anderson* decision). *See generally* Angela M. Ford, Comment, *Private Alienage Discrimination and the Reconstruction Amendments: The Constitutionality of 42 U.S.C. § 1981*, 49 U. Kan. L. Rev. 457 (2001).

section 1981 claim should be available to challenge credit discrimination against non-citizens, even when such discrimination would not be actionable under other fair lending laws, such as the ECOA or the FHA.

3.7 Prohibited Bases Under State Credit Discrimination Laws: Sexual Orientation

None of the federal credit discrimination statutes mention sexual orientation as a prohibited basis. In some cases, discrimination based on sexual orientation may be challenged as discrimination based on marital or familial status.[162] Sexual orientation bias may also be challenged as sex discrimination if the creditor discriminates on the basis that an applicant does not conform to gender-specific stereotypes.[163] More importantly, several state credit discrimination and housing financing statutes specifically list sexual orientation as a prohibited basis.[164]

3.8 Other Prohibited Bases

3.8.1 General

As described earlier, not all credit discrimination is actionable. The discrimination must be on a prohibited basis. This chapter has detailed the bases found in the ECOA, the federal Fair Housing Act, the federal Civil Rights Acts, and most bases listed under state credit discrimination statutes.

If discrimination does not involve one of these listed

prohibited bases, the consumer has three other strategies to show such discrimination to be actionable. First, does the basis for credit discrimination have a disparate impact on a protected class? For example, if credit is based on the income level associated with an applicant's zip code, does this have a disparate impact on minorities, even though the income level associated with the zip code is not itself a prohibited basis?[165]

Second, there are other, usually specialized, state or federal statutes that may prohibit discrimination on the basis utilized. Advocates should always check not only their own state's credit discrimination and fair housing statutes but also any other anti-discrimination or civil rights statutes that might apply. For example, two states prohibit discrimination based on genetic information.[166] Illinois prohibits discrimination based on an applicant's unfavorable discharge from the military.[167] A New Jersey statute prohibiting geographic redlining in the granting of home mortgages is not preempted by the ECOA.[168] Several other state statutes also prohibit discrimination based on the geographic area of residence.[169]

The United States Office of Thrift Supervision issues regulations for the provision of mortgage loans by savings associations. One regulation prohibits discrimination based on the location or age of the dwelling.[170] Instead, the creditor should consider the dwelling's market value and any factors that can be documented that would directly result in a change in that market value.[171]

In addition, other federal and state statutes may address specialized forms of discrimination, such as discrimination by nursing homes, in the sale of insurance, or against certain classes of individuals. For example, the United States Bankruptcy Code places certain limitations on creditors' ability to seek reaffirmation of a debt as a precondition to a new loan and may limit government entities' right to deny loans based on an applicant's prior bankruptcy.[172]

To the extent that these miscellaneous state or federal statutes prohibit the challenged discrimination but do not provide adequate private remedies for violation of such statutes, there is a good argument that a violation of these

---

162 *See* §§ 3.4.1, 3.5.1, *supra. But see* Levin v. Yeshiva Univ., 754 N.E.2d 1099 (N.Y. 2001) (university's housing policy giving preferential treatment to married couples over unmarried couples, including same-sex partners, did not violate New York fair housing law prohibition against marital status discrimination.).

163 Rosa v. Park W. Bank & Trust, 214 F.3d 213 (1st Cir. 2000) (allowing sex discrimination claim to proceed against bank that refused to allow cross-dresser to apply for credit, on the basis that bank may have treated men dressed like women less favorably than women dressed like men).

164 *See, e.g.*, Cal. Gov't Code § 12955 (West); Conn. Gen. Stat. §§ 46a-81f, 46a-98; D.C. Code Ann. § 1-2515 (human rights); Md. Ann. Code art. 49B, §§ 22, 23 (housing financing) (subject to confirmation by Nov. 2002 referendum); Mass. Gen. Laws ch. 151B, §§ 4(3B), 4(14) (excluding persons whose sexual orientation involves minor children as sex object); Minn. Stat. § 363.03(2)(3) (housing financing); Minn. Stat. § 363.03(8); N.H. Rev. Stat. Ann. § 354-A:10; N.J. Stat. Ann. § 10:5-12(i) (West); R.I. Gen. Laws §§ 34-37-4(b), 34-37-4.3, 34-37-5.4; Vt. Stat. Ann. tit. 8, §§ 1211, 1302, 10403; Vt. Stat. Ann. tit. 9, §§ 2362, 2410, 4503(a)(6); Wis. Stat. §§ 106.04, 224.77(1)(o). There are also a number of municipalities that include sexual orientation in their credit discrimination ordinances. The Lambda Legal Defense and Education Fund has a list of these municipalities on its website at http://www.lambdalegal.org.

165 *See* 12 C.F.R. § 571.24(c)(6) (U.S. Office of Thrift Supervision guidelines relating to nondiscrimination in lending). The disparate impact approach is described in § 4.3, *infra*.

166 Mass. Gen. Laws ch. 151B, § 4(3B); N.J. Stat. Ann. §§ 10:5-1 to 10:5-42 (West).

167 775 Ill. Comp. Stat. §§ 5/3-101, 5/4-101; 815 Ill. Comp. Stat. § 140/1a.

168 Nat'l State Bank v. Long, 630 F.2d 981 (3d Cir. 1980).

169 815 Ill. Comp. Stat. §§ 120/1 to 120/6; Iowa Code §§ 535A.1 to 535A.9; Md. Code Ann., Com. Law § 12-603; Mich. Comp. Laws §§ 445.1601 to 445.1614; Minn. Stat. § 363.03(2)(3); N.Y. Banking Law § 9-f (McKinney); Wash. Rev. Code §§ 30.04.500 to 30.04.515; *see* Ch. 7 (general discussion of redlining).

170 12 C.F.R. § 528.2(a); *see* Ch. 7 (general discussion of redlining).

171 12 C.F.R. § 528.2(a).

172 *See* National Consumer Law Center, Consumer Bankruptcy Law and Practice Ch. 14 (6th ed. 2000 and Supp.).

statutes is also a state UDAP violation, that is, a violation of the state's general statute prohibiting deceptive and unfair marketplace behavior.[173] For example, if a creditor is violating a state statute specifically prohibiting a type of discrimination, there is a legislative determination that the conduct is unfair, and the aggrieved applicant should be able to point to that legislative determination as evidence that the practice also violates the state UDAP statute.

Even if no state or federal statute prohibits a form of credit discrimination, the discrimination may still be actionable under a state UDAP statute, particularly a statute that prohibits not just deceptive but unfair or unconscionable practices. Although there is little precedent in this area,[174] the argument is fairly straightforward.[175]

An unfair practice is defined as one that causes substantial consumer injury, which consumers cannot reasonably avoid and which is not outweighed by the countervailing benefits to competition.[176] Thus, credit discrimination on a particular basis can be unfair because it injures less-favored applicants. The remaining issues are whether consumers may avoid the discrimination and whether the benefits of the discrimination to competition outweigh the injury.[177] The UDAP approach is therefore strongest when the consumer has limited alternative sources of credit (a utility transaction would be a classic example) and the discrimination is not based on a sound business justification but instead is based on creditor prejudice or an overly broad classification.

3.8.2 Discrimination and the Digital Divide

A growing practice that is likely to have a disparate impact on protected classes is the offering of preferential or exclusive credit terms to consumers who apply on-line.[178] A 2002 report by the Department of Commerce indicates that the so-called digital divide—that is, the gap between individuals who have internet access and those who do not have internet access—is even greater among most racial and ethnic minorities, the elderly, the disabled, and low-income individuals than among the general population.[179] There-

fore, a creditor who offers "internet-only" deals, or special discounts for applying on-line, is likely disproportionately excluding racial and ethnic minorities, the elderly, the disabled, and public assistance recipients.[180]

Such practices may be challenged under Regulation B's prohibition against advertising that discourages prospective applicants on a prohibited basis.[181] In cases involving housing finance, such practices may also be challenged under the FHA.[182] In particular, given the FHA's requirement of reasonable accommodation for disabled individuals, the FHA may be used to challenge housing finance programs on the internet that exclude the disabled.[183] For example, an internet-only mortgage program might effectively exclude all prospective visually impaired applicants.[184]

A related issue is the possibility that internet-based business will engage in old-fashioned redlining based on zip code or other geographic boundaries.[185] These concerns are exacerbated by the ease with which information, including information on race, ethnicity, gender, religion, and age, can be collected about users of the internet.[186] Such demographic information can also be easily "mined" by compa-

---

report states that only about 40% of African-Americans and 32% of Hispanics use the internet (whether from home or another location, such as work or school), as compared to nearly 60% of whites. As for older Americans, about 37% of persons over the age of 50 use the internet, in comparison to 53.9% of the overall U.S. population. Persons with a disability are about half as likely as the non-disabled to use the internet. Although this study did not focus on public assistance recipients, it did report that only 25% of households with incomes of less than $15,000 use the internet.

180 A related issue in electronic transactions is whether a creditor has met the consumer consent requirements of the Electronic Signatures in Global and National Commerce Act. 15 U.S.C. §§ 7001–31; *see* National Consumer Law Center, The Cost of Credit: Regulation and Legal Challenges, § 9.2.10 (2001 Supp.) (a more detailed discussion of these requirements); *see also* § 10.2.6.2, *infra* (discussion of Regulation B's requirements when ECOA notices are provided electronically).

181 Reg. B, 12 C.F.R. § 202.5. *See generally* § 5.3.2, *infra* (discussing ways to challenge marketing discrimination in lending).

182 In one internet-related advertising case, plaintiffs were allowed to bring an FHA claim against Norwest Mortgage for using an internet website that steered potential homebuyers to areas in which the person's race predominates. Isaac v. Norwest Mortgage, 2001 U.S. Dist. LEXIS 4146 (N.D. Tex. Mar. 30, 2001).

183 42 U.S.C. § 3604(f)(3). Recall that the ECOA does not include a prohibition against discrimination on the basis of disability.

184 In the case of non-mortgage lending, such discrimination might violate the public accommodations section of the Americans with Disabilities Act. 42 U.S.C. § 12182(a).

185 For example, a lawsuit was filed against the now-defunct internet-based delivery company Kozmo.com for allegedly excluding predominantly African-American neighborhoods from its delivery areas. Clive Thompson, *Redlining Online: The Door-to-Door Digital Divide*, New York Newsday, Apr. 30, 2000, at B15; *see* Ch. 7, *infra* (general discussion on redlining).

186 Gary A. Hernandez et al., *Symposium on Insurance and Technology: Insurance Weblining and Unfair Discrimination in Cyberspace*, 54 SMU L. Rev. 1953, 1970–1971 (2001).

---

173 *See* National Consumer Law Center, Unfair and Deceptive Acts and Practices § 3.2.7 (5th ed. 2001).

174 *See* Colvard v. Francis, 106 N.C. App. 277, 416 S.E.2d 579 (1992) ("acts designed to unfairly deny credit are unlawful").

175 *See* National Consumer Law Center, Unfair and Deceptive Acts and Practices § 4.3 (5th ed. 2001).

176 *Id.* at § 4.3.2.

177 *Id.*

178 Gary A. Hernandez et al., *Symposium on Insurance and Technology: Insurance Weblining and Unfair Discrimination in Cyberspace*, 54 SMU L. Rev. 1953 (2001); Cheryl R. Lee, *Cyberbanking: A New Frontier for Discrimination?*, 26 Rutgers Computer & Tech. L.J. 277 (2000).

179 U.S. Dep't of Commerce, Econ. & Statistics Admin. and Nat'l Telecomm. & Info. Admin., A Nation Online: How Americans are Expanding Their Use of the Internet (Feb. 2002), *available at* http://www.ntia.doc.gov. The Department of Commerce's

nies other than the business to whom the consumer origi-nally provided the information.[187] The ease of information gathering in electronic transactions may also exacerbate issues around customer profiling and whether such practices result in discrimination against protected groups.[188]

3.9 ECOA Prohibited Bases Do Not Apply to Special Purpose Credit Programs

3.9.1 General

The ECOA and Regulation B set out a clearly delineated and limited exception to the general rule prohibiting dis-crimination on a prohibited basis called special purpose credit programs[189] These programs may require that pro-gram participants share a common characteristic, such as race, national origin, or sex.[190] For example, a special purpose credit program may be set up to assist minorities, women, or young applicants.[191] The Congressional intent for the special purpose credit exception is to increase access to the credit market by persons previously foreclosed from the market.[192] The Official Staff Commentary clarifies this purpose to mean that programs may be designed to benefit a class of persons who not only would otherwise be denied credit but who would also receive credit on less favorable terms.[193]

This is an exception to the ECOA rule that does not apply to a Fair Housing Act claim or a federal Civil Rights Act claim. There is no case law as to how such special purpose

credit programs would fare under these other laws.

State credit discrimination laws can not be utilized to challenge the practices of a special purpose credit program if the ECOA and Regulation B authorize such practices. Regulation B specifically preempts state statutes that pro-hibit inquiries necessary to establish or administer a special purpose credit program.[194] The Federal Reserve Board views such laws as inconsistent with Regulation B because they are less protective of credit applicants.[195]

3.9.2 Qualifying as a Special Purpose Credit Program

A creditor does not violate the ECOA by denying credit solely because the applicant fails to qualify under the re-quirements of a special purpose credit program, provided that the program was not established for the purpose of evading the ECOA and it fits into one of the following categories:[196]

- *Government-established*: A credit assistance program of-fered pursuant to federal, state, or local statute, regulation or ordinance, or by judicial or administrative order to benefit an economically disadvantaged class.[197] The fed-eral Small Business Administration (SBA) loan program, which makes a special effort to extend credit to minority and female applicants, is such a program. A remedial program set up by a consent order to benefit past victims of discrimination is another example.[198]

---

187 *Id.*
188 *Id.*
189 15 U.S.C. § 1691(c); Reg. B, 12 C.F.R. § 202.8.
190 Reg. B, 12 C.F.R. § 202.8. The Federal Reserve Board has proposed deleting the phrase "to meet special social needs" from the requirements of qualifying special purpose credit programs listed in § 202.8. 64 Fed. Reg. 44,582, 44,598 (Aug. 16, 1999). The proposed revisions to Regulation B can be found on the CD-Rom accompanying this volume.
191 *See, e.g.*, Moore v. United States Dep't of Agric., 55 F.3d 991 (5th Cir. 1995) (status of program to benefit socially disadvan-taged applicants—which consisted of "Women, Blacks, Ameri-can Indians, Alaskan Natives, Hispanics, Asians, and Pacific Islanders"—not resolved).
192 *See* S. Rep. No. 94-589, at 7, *reprinted in* 1976 U.S.C.C.A.N. 403, 409; H.R. Rep. No. 94-873, at 8, *reprinted in* 1976 U.S.C.C.A.N. 403, 428.
193 Official Staff Commentary, 12 C.F.R. § 202.8(a)-5 (published at 60 Fed. Reg. 29,965 (June 7, 1995)). The Federal Reserve Board has proposed revising Official Staff Commentary, 12 C.F.R. § 202.8(a)-5 to clarify how creditors can determine the need for a special purpose credit program by providing additional ex-amples of analyses that can be used to determine such need. 64 Fed. Reg. 44,582, 44,625 (Aug. 16, 1999). The proposed revi-sions to the Official Staff Commentary to Regulation B can be found on the CD-Rom accompanying this volume.

194 Regulation B, 12 C.F.R. § 202.11(b)(1)(v). Special purpose credit programs address the credit needs of economically dis-advantaged groups and may request and consider information on race, sex, and other protected categories in ways forbidden to other forms of credit. The Federal Reserve Board ruled that two New York statutes were preempted by the ECOA to the extent that they barred creditors from taking a prohibited basis into account (national origin) when establishing eligibility for cer-tain special purpose programs based on national origin, and barred them from requesting and considering information re-garding characteristics required for eligibility for such pro-grams. Official Staff Commentary, 12 C.F.R. § 202.11(a)-1; *see also* 54 Fed. Reg. 9416 (Mar. 7, 1989); 53 Fed. Reg. 45,756 (Nov. 11, 1988).
195 15 U.S.C. § 1691d(f); Reg. B, 12 C.F.R. § 202.11(a).
196 15 U.S.C. § 1691(c); Reg. B, 12 C.F.R. § 202.8(b)(2). The Federal Reserve Board has proposed revising Official Staff Commentary, 12 C.F.R. § 202.8(a)-5 to clarify how creditors can determine the need for a special purpose credit program by providing additional examples of analyses that can be used to determine such need. 64 Fed. Reg. 44,582, 44,625 (Aug. 16, 1999). The proposed revisions to the Official Staff Commentary to Regulation B can be found on the CD-Rom accompanying this volume. *See also* Official Staff Commentary, 12 C.F.R. § 202.8 (which gives numerous examples of allowable pro-grams and credit-granting procedures).
197 *See* Official Staff Commentary, 12 C.F.R. § 202.8(a)-3.
198 *E.g.*, Green v. Veneman, 159 F. Supp. 2d. 360 (S.D. Miss. 2001) (consent decree providing for special program for African-

- *Non-profit*: A credit assistance program administered by a not-for-profit organization (as defined by I.R.S. Code § 501(c)) for its members or for an economically disadvantaged class;[199] or
- *For-profit*: A special purpose credit program offered by a for-profit organization to meet "special social needs." The Federal Reserve Board (FRB) requires that this type of program be established and administered under a written plan which identifies the class or classes to be benefitted and which sets forth the procedures and standards for extending credit.[200] The failure to have a written plan should be enough to disqualify a for-profit organization's program.[201] The FRB also requires that the program extend credit to a class of persons who, under the organization's usual creditworthiness standards, probably would not receive such credit or would receive it on less favorable terms than are ordinarily available.

An example of such a program run by a for-profit organization is a bank home mortgage program that extends credit on homes in a defined economically depressed neighborhood and gives favored treatment to present neighborhood residents. The special purpose credit program need not give this class of applicants its most favorable terms, only terms more favorable than it would offer absent the existence of the special purpose program.[202] Recognizing that special purpose credit programs are designed to fulfill a particular need, the written plan must contain information that supports the designated need and must also state a specific duration for the program or set a date when the program will be reevaluated to determine if there is a continuing need for it.[203]

The FRB does not determine for an organization whether a program qualifies as a special purpose credit program. The organization must make its own determination at its own

risk.[204] If the organization is mistaken, it is subject to an ECOA action. But a creditor does not violate the ECOA when it complies in good faith with a regulation promulgated by a government agency implementing a special purpose credit program expressly authorized by federal or state law to benefit an economically disadvantaged class.[205]

3.9.3 Special Purpose Credit Program Must Still Comply With Most ECOA Requirements

A special purpose credit program is exempt only to the extent necessary to carry out the program.[206] For example, a program to promote minority business ownership would still have to comply with the ECOA regarding provision of notices of adverse action taken on an application.[207]

For special purpose credit programs that are not government-established, a creditor may only require applicants to share those factors inextricably tied to the need being addressed.[208] However, a government-established special purpose credit program has more flexibility to establish eligibility requirements.[209]

Perhaps the most important limitation for non-government-established programs is that, once the program is set up to benefit one particular group, it must not discriminate on a prohibited basis within that group.[210] For example, if a program is set up to assist young applicants, it may not then provide its most favorable terms to young white unmarried female applicants.[211] The Federal Reserve Board (FRB) gives another example: "A creditor might establish a credit program for impoverished American Indians. If the program met the requirements of § 202.8(a), the creditor could refuse credit to non-Indians, but could not discriminate among Indian applicants on the basis of sex or marital status."[212]

Note that this limitation does not apply to special purpose credit programs that are government-established. These special purpose credit programs may discriminate on a prohibited basis within the group of potential beneficiaries.[213] Also, there is no violation when a bank establishes a loan program available only to active members of the military

---

American farmers who filed credit discrimination lawsuit, Pigford v. Glickman, 185 F.R.D. 82 (D.D.C. 1999), did not violate the ECOA). Interestingly, the court in this case did not rely on the special purpose credit exception to the ECOA; instead, the court held that there was no discrimination because the plaintiff non-African-American farmers could not show discrimination, as they were not similarly situated to the African-American farmers.
199 Reg. B, 12 C.F.R. § 202.8(a)(2).
200 Reg. B, 12 C.F.R. § 202.8(a)(3). The FRB has proposed deleting the phrase "to meet special social needs" from the requirements of qualifying special purpose credit programs listed in § 202.8. 64 Fed. Reg. 44,582, 44,598 (Aug. 16, 1999). The proposed revisions to Regulation B can be found on the CD-Rom accompanying this volume.
201 United States v. Am. Future Sys., Inc., 743 F.2d 169 (3d Cir. 1984).
202 *Id.*
203 *See* Official Staff Commentary, 12 C.F.R. § 202.8(a)-6 (published at 60 Fed. Reg. 29,965 (June 7, 1995)).

204 Official Staff Commentary, 12 C.F.R. § 202.8(a)-1.
205 Official Staff Commentary, 12 C.F.R. § 202.8(a)-2.
206 Reg. B, 12 C.F.R. § 202.8(b)(1).
207 Official Staff Commentary, 12 C.F.R. § 202.8(b)-1; *see* Ch. 10 (ECOA's notice requirements).
208 United States v. Am. Future Sys., 743 F.2d 169 (3d Cir. 1984).
209 Diaz v. Va. Hous. Dev. Auth., 101 F. Supp. 2d 415, *subsequent proceeding at* 117 F. Supp. 2d 500 (E.D. Va. 2000).
210 *See* Reg. B, 12 C.F.R. § 202.8(b)(2); United States v. Am. Future Sys., 743 F.2d 169 (3d Cir. 1984).
211 United States v. Am. Future Sys., Inc., 743 F.2d 169 (3d Cir. 1984).
212 42 Fed. Reg. 1248 (1977).
213 Diaz v. Va. Hous. Dev. Auth., 101 F. Supp. 2d at 419–420.

and refuses credit to the male spouse of an active member of the military.[214]

3.10 Protected Characteristics May Apply to Those Associated With Applicant

3.10.1 The General Rule

Prohibited credit discrimination under the ECOA may be based not only on the characteristics of the applicant but may also be based on the characteristics of the applicant's business partners, its officers (in the case of a corporate applicant), and the individuals with whom the applicant affiliates or associates.[215] Thus, the ECOA prevents discrimination in the offering of credit based on the race, religion, sex or other characteristics of those with whom the applicant deals or of those who will benefit if the applicant obtains the credit.

For example, a creditor is prohibited under the ECOA from discriminating against an applicant because of the applicant's business dealings with members of a certain religion.[216] Similarly, a creditor may not deny financing for an apartment complex because of the national origin of the complex's tenants.[217] A loan applicant planning to build an apartment building for the elderly is afforded the statute's protection, as is an applicant seeking a mortgage on property located in a neighborhood chiefly populated by elderly persons. Nor can a mortgage be denied because of the race of other residents in the neighborhood.[218]

The same rule applies in Fair Housing Act and Civil Rights Act cases. The plaintiff need not be a member of a protected class as long as consideration of a prohibited basis injured the plaintiff.[219] Standing has been granted to a white house seller suing his potential African-American buyers'

lender,[220] whites married to African-Americans,[221] whites associated with African-Americans,[222] whites buying houses in African-American neighborhoods,[223] whites selling houses in minority neighborhoods,[224] a white landlord seeking financing to convert his building in a minority neighborhood into cooperative housing that would likely have been minority-owned,[225] and whites indirectly injured by discrimination against African-American applicants.[226] In fact, the Fair Housing Act's scope is broader than the ECOA's, and anyone in any way aggrieved by discriminatory credit practices can bring an action.[227] The plaintiff need not even be a credit applicant.

The ECOA's applicability to discrimination based on the characteristics of those affiliated with or related to the applicant, however, has certain limits. The ECOA does not provide a basis for a plaintiff associated with the applicant to challenge the discrimination suffered by the applicant but not by the plaintiff.[228] The ECOA generally only provides remedies to those who *apply* for credit, not those affiliated with those who apply. For example, the ECOA would only provide a remedy for the landlord and not for the African-American tenants when the landlord was denied a loan to fix up the apartment because of the tenants' race.

3.10.2 Does the ECOA's Associational Protection Rule Apply to Public Assistance and to the Exercise of Rights Under the CCPA?

The general ECOA rule that a creditor may not discriminate against an applicant because of individuals the applicant associates with is at least true when the discrimination is based on the race, color, religion, national origin, sex,

---

214 Williams v. Amity Bank, 703 F. Supp. 223 (D. Conn. 1988).

215 Official Staff Commentary, 12 C.F.R. § 202.2(z)-1. The issue of associational discrimination is related to the issue of standing in a credit discrimination case. The topic of standing is covered in § 11.2, *infra*.

216 *See* Official Staff Commentary, 12 C.F.R. § 202.2(z)-1.

217 Official Staff Commentary, 12 C.F.R. § 202.2(z)-1.

218 Official Staff Commentary, 12 C.F.R. § 202.2(z)-1; Cherry v. Amoco Oil Co., 481 F. Supp. 727 (N.D. Ga. 1979) (a white woman living in a predominantly African-American area of Atlanta had been directly affected by the creditor's alleged racial discrimination because the creditor's scoring system penalized all applicants residing within her zip code). Ms. Cherry's case ultimately failed on the merits because she did not produce sufficient evidence that the creditor's practice actually treated otherwise qualified African-American and white applicants in a significantly different manner. *See* 490 F. Supp. 1026 (N.D. Ga. 1980).

219 Harrison v. Otto G. Heinzeroth Mortgage Co., 430 F. Supp. 893 (N.D. Ohio 1977); *see also* § 11.2, *infra* (general discussion on standing in credit discrimination cases).

220 Doane v. Nat'l Westminster Bank, 938 F. Supp. 149 (E.D.N.Y. 1996).

221 Stewart v. Furton, 774 F.2d 706 (6th Cir. 1985).

222 Woods-Drake v. Lundy, 667 F.2d 1198 (5th Cir. 1982) (whites entertaining African-American guests); Lane v. Cole, 88 F. Supp. 2d 402 (E.D. Pa. 2000).

223 Harrison v. Otto G. Heinzeroth Mortgage Co., 414 F. Supp. 66 (N.D. Ohio 1976).

224 Doane v. Nat'l Westminster Bank, 938 F. Supp. 149 (E.D.N.Y. 1996); Old W. End Ass'n v. Buckeye Fed. Sav. & Loan, 675 F. Supp. 1100 (N.D. Ohio 1987).

225 Simms v. First Gibraltar Bank, 83 F.3d 1546 (5th Cir. 1996).

226 Sec'y, United States Dep't of Hous. & Urban Dev., *ex rel.* Herron v. Blackwell, 908 F.2d 864 (11th Cir. 1990).

227 *See* § 2.3.5, *supra*; Hargraves v. Capital City Mortgage Corp., 2001 U.S. Dist. LEXIS 7738 (D.D.C. Jan. 2, 2001) (church pastor and financial secretary did not have standing to bring ECOA redlining claims on behalf of church but could bring FHA and § 1982 claims).

228 *See* Evans v. First Fed. Sav. Bank, 669 F. Supp. 915 (N.D. Ind. 1987) (non-profit organization lacked standing to bring ECOA action on behalf of individuals challenging mortgage redlining); Marine Am. State Bank v. Lincoln, 433 N.W.2d 709 (Iowa 1988).

marital status, or age of those with whom the applicant deals.[229] It is unclear whether this "associational" protection extends to the remaining two protected ECOA categories—receipt of public assistance and good faith exercise of rights under the Consumer Credit Protection Act.

Prior to 1985, these two bases were specifically excluded from this broader protection by a footnote to Regulation B.[230] However, that exclusion disappeared from the Regulation in the 1985 revisions, and, unlike the contents of other pre-1985 Regulation B footnotes, this one did not explicitly reappear in the Official Staff Commentary.[231] Instead, the Commentary specifically provides for associational protection generally—discrimination should not be based on the characteristics of individuals the applicant associates with. In listing examples of such characteristics, the Commentary

---

229 Official Staff Commentary, 12 C.F.R. § 202.2(z)-1.

230 Under then-existing Reg. B, 12 C.F.R. § 202.2(z) n.3 (1985 version).

231 *See* 50 Fed. Reg. 10,890 (Mar. 18, 1985) (proposed revisions); 50 Fed. Reg. 48,018 (Nov. 20, 1985) (final revisions). The explanatory material to the revisions, without referring specifically to the contents of pre-1985 footnote 3, generally indicate that no substantive changes were intended. This comment would support the proposition that these two exceptions remain in force.

does not include receipt of public assistance and good faith exercise of rights, but that list is only explanatory and not definitional.[232]

In addition, it is difficult to think of a valid reason why the Federal Reserve Board would want to exclude these two characteristics from the general rule favoring associational protection. For example, it is clear that a lender may not discriminate against a builder wishing to build an apartment complex in a minority neighborhood. There is no rational distinction between this situation and that of a builder who wishes to build low-income housing units (many of whose tenants might be recipients of public assistance) or a nursing home (many of whose residents might receive Social Security, SSI, or Medicare and Medicaid benefits). Similarly, some consumer lawyers who bring Truth In Lending or other Consumer Credit Protection Act suits regularly may be *persona non grata* to local creditors, who should not be allowed to discriminate against such lawyers or their other clients because of the advocates' association with persons who exercise their rights under the Consumer Credit Protection Act.

---

232 Official Staff Commentary, 12 C.F.R. § 202.2(z)-1.

Chapter 4   Proving Credit Discrimination

4.1 Introduction

Creditors are generally free to use whatever factors they want in making credit decisions as long as certain itemized factors are not utilized and the factors that are used do not have a disparate impact on protected groups.[1] At the same time, credit discrimination statutes are not violated merely because an applicant is adversely treated and the applicant is a member of a protected group. This type of treatment is prohibited only if there is a linkage between the treatment and a prohibited basis. Disparate treatment on a prohibited basis is one method for proving credit discrimination discussed in this chapter.

In practice it is often difficult to prove that a decision was made on a prohibited basis and not based on some other permissible factor. The creditor will almost always present a legitimate business justification for its actions. The disparate treatment case will then center on whether the stated reason for the creditor's adverse action was the real basis, or whether it was a mere pretext for discrimination on a prohibited basis. The plaintiff is not required to prove that the creditor used a prohibited basis knowingly, only that the prohibited basis in fact was a factor in the creditor's conduct. Disparate treatment can be proven either through direct evidence or through indirect or circumstantial evidence.[2]

If a creditor does not engage in disparate treatment, the creditor's conduct can still be challenged under the ECOA and the Fair Housing Act for its disparate impact. If the stated business justification for a practice is, in fact, the real basis for the creditor's conduct, the creditor's conduct may still be illegal if the business justification has a disparate impact on protected groups. This disparate impact theory or "effects test" is a critical tool for plaintiffs. It is available in addition to or as an alternative to disparate treatment analysis.

This chapter covers both the disparate treatment and disparate impact methods of proving credit discrimination. The section on legal requirements is followed by a discus-sion of sources of information that can be useful in proving credit discrimination.

This chapter focuses on proving general discrimination as opposed to a specific ECOA procedural violation such as failure to provide an applicant with a notice of adverse action. These ECOA procedural violations are generally easier to prove. It is, for example, less difficult to prove that a notice was not mailed or did not contain certain informa-tion than it is to show that a creditor discriminated on a prohibited basis. Procedural violations are discussed in Chapter 10 of this manual.

4.2 Proving Disparate Treatment

4.2.1 Introduction

Discrimination is prohibited if there is a linkage between the discrimination and a prohibited basis, so that the credi-tor's decision-making process results in individuals being treated differently because of a prohibited basis.

It is relatively easy to show that a creditor treated an individual differently than other applicants. For example, the creditor may have refused to offer credit to that applicant, but extended credit to many other applicants. The difficult part of a disparate treatment case is to show that the creditor acted on a prohibited basis in treating applicants differently.

It is not enough to show that the applicant denied credit was African-American, a woman, or had some other char-acteristic protected by credit discrimination legislation.[3] The

---

1 The various prohibited bases are discussed in Chapter 3. Credi-tors may take prohibited bases into account in limited circum-stances when considering applicants for "special purpose credit programs." *See* § 3.9, *supra.*

2 *See* § 4.2, *infra.*

3 *See, e.g.,* Matthiesen v. Banc One Mortgage Corp., 173 F.3d 1242 (10th Cir. 1999) (court found no prima facie case of gender discrimination because plaintiff did not prove that she was qualified for the loan); O'Dowd v. S. Cent. Bell, 729 F.2d 347 (5th Cir. 1984) (court rejected white couple's claim that tele-phone company discriminated in requiring a deposit because of their exchange's racial composition, when couple had history of late payments and deposits were required of all such customers); Sallion v. Suntrust Bank, Atlanta, 87 F. Supp. 2d 1323 (N.D. Ga. 2000) (plaintiff failed to show prima facie case of race and marital status discrimination because she was not qualified for the loan); Gross v. Small Business Admin., 669 F. Supp. 50 (N.D.N.Y. 1987), *aff'd without op.,* 867 F.2d 1423 (2d Cir. 1988) (no ECOA violation based on sex or marital status discrimina-tion because applicant was rejected due to past delinquent loan with same agency); Thomas v. First Fed. Sav. Bank, 653 F.

plaintiff must show that the credit decision was at least in part based on this characteristic. The creditor will typically claim that the credit denial was not based on such a protected characteristic, but was based on objective standards of creditworthiness or other legitimate factors.[4]

As most applicants have some kind of blemish on their credit record, employment history, or income potential, it is relatively easy for a creditor to point to a specific legitimate reason to deny credit to an applicant. The plaintiff will have to show that this legitimate reason was not the real reason for the creditor's action, but that the real reason was the applicant's race, sex, or some other protected characteristic.

If the creditor's business justification is a mere pretext for the real reason which is a prohibited basis, then it is irrelevant how good a business justification the creditor has presented. Even if the justification is an absolute business necessity, if the real reason for its actions was a prohibited basis, then there is disparate treatment.

Conversely, if the business justification is the real reason, it is irrelevant that the justification is not a good one or that there are other ways of accomplishing the same business goal with a narrower impact on a prohibited basis.[5] Instead, such a case should be brought for its disparate impact, not because of disparate treatment.

It is important to look for disparate treatment not only in the granting of credit, but also earlier on in the application process. For example, there is disparate treatment if whites are encouraged to apply and African-Americans are discouraged, even if a creditor treats all those who do apply equally.[6] There is also disparate treatment if whites are coached more in filling out their applications, even if all written applications are then treated equally.[7]

4.2.2 Direct Evidence of Disparate Treatment

There are two ways to prove that the creditor used a prohibited basis is making a credit decision—either through direct evidence or through circumstantial evidence. Direct evidence of disparate treatment on a prohibited basis will clearly constitute a prima facie violation of a credit discrimination statute.[8] If the plaintiff can show through direct evidence that the credit decision was based upon an impermissible factor, the creditor must then respond by proving by a preponderance of the evidence that it would have made the same decision even if it had not taken the impermissible factor into account.[9]

Although courts generally agree that it is rare for plaintiffs to provide sufficient direct evidence of discrimination, there are cases in which this evidence might be available.[10] Sometimes a creditor will actually admit that its credit decision was based on public assistance status—we do not handle Medicare or Medicaid patients, or we do not rent to those on public assistance—or that it was based on familial or marital status, or age. It is less likely that a creditor will admit to acting on an individual's race, religion, or national origin. However, use of a racial slur by a lending agent may provide direct evidence of discrimination.[11] Courts will require that there be a sufficient nexus between the remarks in question and the adverse action taken.[12]

Direct evidence can sometimes be obtained from former

Supp. 1330 (N.D. Ind. 1987) (no evidence of differing treatment of black second mortgage applicants or of "impermissible adverse impact").

4 *See* Thompson v. Marine Midland Bank, 198 F.3d 235 (2d Cir. 1999) (unpublished) (text available at 1999 U.S. App. LEXIS 22960) (although a member of a protected class, plaintiff failed to prove discrimination because defendant presented a legitimate reason for denying application; defendant argued that the history of large financial losses at the auto dealer together with the incomplete nature of plaintiff's submissions made full review of plaintiff's application impossible); Cartwright v. Am. Sav. & Loan Ass'n, 880 F.2d 912, 923 (7th Cir. 1989); Sassower v. Field, 752 F. Supp. 1182, 1188 (S.D.N.Y. 1990), *aff'd in part, vacated in part*, 973 F.2d 75 (2d Cir. 1992).

5 *See* Texas Dep't of Cmty. Affairs v. Burdine, 450 U.S. 248, 101 S. Ct. 1089, 67 L. Ed. 2d 207 (1981) (employment case); McDonnell-Douglas Corp. v. Green, 411 U.S. 792, 93 S. Ct. 1817, 36 L. Ed. 2d 668 (1973) (employment discrimination case).

6 For more information on pre-application and marketing discrimination, see § 5.3, *infra*.

7 *See* § 5.3.3, *infra*.

8 *See* Pinchback v. Armistead Homes Corp., 907 F.2d 1447, 1452–53 (4th Cir. 1990) (in §§ 1981 and 1982 case, plaintiff produced sufficient evidence of direct discrimination and thus *McDonnell-Douglas* method of proof was not relevant).

9 *See* Saldana v. Citibank, 1996 U.S. Dist. LEXIS 8327 (N.D. Ill. Jun. 13, 1996) (defendant's account executive made remarks about plaintiff's neighborhood including that it was not the same as it had been when he grew up there; court found these remarks did not constitute direct evidence of discrimination).

10 *See, e.g.*, Rhodes v. Guiberson Oil Tools, 75 F.3d 989, 993 (5th Cir. 1996) (en banc).

11 For cases in the employment area see, e.g., Cordova v. State Farm Ins. Co., 124 F.3d 1145, 1149 (9th Cir. 1997) (employer's reference to a new hire as a "dumb Mexican" was sufficient evidence to create an inference of discrimination). *But see* Jones v. Bessemer Carraway Med. Ctr., 151 F.3d 1321, 1323 (11th Cir. 1998) (holding that racial statements made by supervisor did not constitute direct evidence, and that it could not be inferred that it was more likely than not that plaintiff's termination was based on racial criteria, in light of event preceding her discharge); McCarthy v. Kemper Life Ins. Co., 924 F.2d 683 (7th Cir. 1991) (racial slurs by fellow employees insufficient to provide direct evidence and prove prima facie case of discriminatory discharge).

12 *See, e.g.*, Faulkner v. Glickman, 172 F. Supp. 2d 732 (D. Md. 2001) (to constitute direct proof of discriminatory intent statements in question must be more than stray or isolated remarks) (citing O'Connor v. Consolidated Coin Caterers Corp., 56 F.3d 542, 549 (4th Cir. 1995), *rev'd on other grounds*, 517 U.S. 308 (1996)).

employees of the creditor, from those with whom the creditor communicated, or from notations in the creditor's records. Any statements that the creditor made to the applicant should be scrutinized to see if they constitute admissions as to the reason for the creditor's action.

Plaintiffs should carefully decide what specific disparate treatment to attempt to prove. For instance, it may be difficult to show that an applicant's race was the basis for a denial of credit, but not difficult to show that the application *process* was different for whites than for nonwhites.[13]

4.2.3 Circumstantial Evidence

4.2.3.1 The *McDonnell-Douglas* Burden Shifting Analysis

If the plaintiff does not have direct evidence of disparate treatment, a prima facie case may be established through circumstantial evidence. To prove disparate treatment using circumstantial evidence, most courts will require that a plaintiff first establish a prima facie case of discrimination by showing: 1) membership in a protected class; 2) application for credit for which the plaintiff was qualified; 3) rejection despite qualification; and 4) that defendant continued to approve credit for similarly qualified applicants.[14] In a typical predatory lending case, a prima facie case would require showing that the plaintiff: 1) is a member of a protected class; 2) applied for and was qualified for a loan; 3) was given grossly unfavorable terms; and 4) that the lender continues to provide loans to other applicants with similar qualifications, but on significantly more favorable terms.[15]

This analysis is derived from a Supreme Court employment discrimination case, *McDonnell-Douglas Corp. v. Green.*[16] With certain exceptions discussed below, most courts use this test for claims brought under the ECOA, the FHA, and the federal Civil Rights Acts.

If the plaintiff can establish a prima facie case, the burden then shifts to the creditor to articulate a legitimate non-discriminatory basis for the adverse action.[17] If the defendant does so, the plaintiff must show that the "legitimate" reasons were merely a pretext for discrimination.[18]

Proving a circumstantial case may be somewhat different when a creditor uses a credit scoring or other objective system to evaluate applications than when it uses a judgmental system. When a creditor uses a credit scoring or other objective system, the circumstantial evidence might merely indicate that the applicant is a member of a protected class, received a passing grade under the creditor's objective system, but was still denied credit. Disparate treatment can be shown even if the applicant failed to obtain a passing grade on the creditor's test. The issue is whether other applicants received the same failing grade but were still offered credit. Issues related to credit scoring are discussed in detail in Chapter 6.

4.2.3.2 When Is Use of the *McDonnell-Douglas* Test Appropriate?

There is a split in the lower courts as to whether the *McDonnell-Douglas* standard is appropriate for use in credit discrimination claims based on violations of the ECOA.[19] The Supreme Court has yet to grant certiorari to resolve the issue.[20]

This issue is a critical one for plaintiffs hoping to bring credit discrimination cases. A rejection of the *McDonnell-Douglas* test means that courts will not immediately shift the burden of proof to the defendant upon a prima facie showing of discrimination by the plaintiff.[21] This requires plaintiffs to put on more evidence of discrimination before proceeding to discovery. The problem for plaintiffs is that direct evidence is rarely available at this stage.

The courts rejecting the *McDonnell-Douglas* test purport to be increasing judicial efficiency by weeding out "frivo-

13 For a discussion of discrimination in the application process, see generally Ch. 5, *infra.*

14 *See, e.g.,* Simms v. First Gibralter Bank, 83 F.3d 1546 (5th Cir. 1996); Saldana v. Citibank, 1996 U.S. Dist. LEXIS 8327 (N.D. Ill. Jun. 13, 1996); Farris v. Jefferson Bank, 194 B.R. 931 (Bankr. E.D. Pa. 1996).

15 *See* Frank Lopez, *Using the Fair Housing Act to Combat Predatory Lending,* 6 Geo. J. on Poverty L. & Pol'y 73 (1999).

16 McDonnell-Douglas Corp. v. Green, 411 U.S. 792, 93 S. Ct. 1817, 36 L. Ed. 2d 668 (1973).

17 *See, e.g.,* Sallion v. Suntrust Bank, Atlanta, 87 F. Supp. 2d 1323 (N.D. Ga. 2000).

18 *See, e.g.,* Simms v. First Gibraltar Bank, 83 F.3d 1546 (5th Cir.

1996) (must show similar applicants were treated differently); Saldana v. Citibank, 1996 U.S. Dist. LEXIS 8327 (N.D. Ill. Jun. 13, 1996); Farris v. Jefferson Bank, 194 B.R. 931 (Bankr. E.D. Pa. 1996).

19 *Compare* Greer v. Bank One, 2002 U.S. App. LEXIS 2195 (7th Cir. Feb. 6, 2002) (unpublished) *and* Latimore v. Citibank, 151 F.3d 712 (7th Cir. 1998) (holding that the *McDonnell-Douglas* standard is inappropriate in the credit discrimination context; the plaintiff in *Latimore* did not pursue certiorari) *with* Simms v. First Gibraltar Bank, 83 F.3d 1545 (5th Cir. 1996) (allowing use of the *McDonnell-Douglas* standard in a credit discrimination context). *See generally* Erin Elisabeth Dancy, *Latimore v. Citibank Federal Savings Bank: A Journey Through the Labyrinth of Lending Discrimination,* 3 N.C. Banking Inst. 233 (Apr. 1999); Richard A. Hill, Note, *Credit Opportunities, Race, and Presumptions: Does the McDonnell Douglas Framework Apply in Fair Lending Cases? Latimore v. Citibank Savings Bank,* 64 Mo. L. Rev. 479 (1999).

20 The Supreme Court denied certiorari in both Ring v. First Interstate Mortgage, 984 F.2d 924 (8th Cir. 1993) *cert. denied,* 523 U.S. 1006 (1998) and Simms v. First Gibraltar Bank, 83 F.3d 1545 (5th Cir. 1996), *cert. denied,* 519 U.S. 1041 (1996).

21 The court of appeals in *Latimore,* for example, required the plaintiff to present evidence of actual discrimination on some prohibited ground, such as race, in order to state a claim. Latimore v. Citibank, 151 F.3d 712 (7th Cir. 1998).

lous" lawsuits. On the other hand, it may prevent plaintiffs with meritorious cases from ever reaching the discovery phase.[22]

In the Seventh Circuit, the *Latimore* court reasoned that the *McDonnell-Douglas* test is more appropriate in an employment situation because members of protected classes compete directly with others for jobs. The court found it important that in a credit situation, in contrast, a person applying for credit is not in direct competition with other credit applicants.[23] The court explained further that the rejection of an African-American job applicant in favor of a white applicant has been considered sufficiently suspicious to shift the burden of proof to the employer to present a nondiscriminatory reason for the rejection of the African-American applicant.[24] This suspicion, according to the *Latimore* court, does not automatically arise in the context of a rejected credit application.

The result is that the *Latimore* court and others that follow its reasoning require plaintiffs to present more than just the mere rejection of credit applications in order to state a prima facie case of discrimination. The fact that essential evidence to make this claim may not be in the plaintiff's possession has not persuaded these courts to reconsider their position.[25]

This confusion arises only with respect to disparate treatment claims in ECOA cases. In disparate effects cases, in contrast, Congress directly addressed the burden of proof issue, specifically adopting the standard of proof used in

employment cases.[26] The standard is also clearer under the FHA because the *McDonnell-Douglas* test generally has been adopted in disparate treatment cases.[27]

4.3 Proving Disparate Impact

4.3.1 Introduction

An alternative under the Fair Housing Act and the ECOA to proving disparate treatment is proving disparate impact. Under a disparate impact theory, the creditor may not be treating applicants differently on a prohibited basis, but there still may be illegal discrimination if the *effect* of the creditor's practices is to adversely impact a particular protected class.

It is widely accepted that proof of discriminatory impact or effect can show a violation of the credit discrimination provisions of the Fair Housing Act[28] and the ECOA.[29]

---

22 *See generally* Erin Elisabeth Dancy, *Latimore v. Citibank Federal Savings Bank: A Journey Through the Labyrinth of Lending Discrimination*, 3 N.C. Banking Inst. 233 (1999).

23 Latimore v. Citibank, 151 F.3d 712, 714 (7th Cir. 1998).

24 *Id.* Note that the *Simms* court (Simms v. First Gibraltar Bank, 83 F.3d 1546 (5th Cir. 1996)) was also concerned about this issue even though it permitted the burden-shifting methodology to proceed.

25 Latimore v. Citibank, 151 F.3d 712, 714 (7th Cir. 1998). Subsequent courts have interpreted *Latimore* as a rejection of the *McDonnell-Douglas* standard in favor of conventional proof methods. However, these courts have avoided reaching the question whether the *McDonnell-Douglas* test is ever appropriate in credit discrimination cases. Instead, they have found that the plaintiffs did not meet the threshold creditworthiness criteria required under either the *McDonnell-Douglas* test or conventional proof methods. *See* Crawford v. Signet Bank, 179 F.3d 926 (D.C. Cir. 2000) (plaintiff failed to meet *McDonnell-Douglas* burden and therefore no need to reach issue of whether the test is appropriate in credit discrimination cases); Matthiesen v. Banc One Mortgage Corp., 173 F.3d 1242 (10th Cir. 1999) (because plaintiff did not demonstrate that he was a qualified borrower, court found no need to reach the question of whether the *McDonnell-Douglas* standard should be applied); Estate of Hilgert v. Mark Twain/Mercantile Bank, 2000 U.S. Dist. LEXIS 5922 (D. Kan. Apr. 19, 2000) (defendant's motion for summary judgment granted), *aff'd*, 246 F.3d 681 (10th Cir. Feb. 5, 2001) (unpublished) (text available at 2001 U.S. App. LEXIS 1667). In addition, some courts have made a distinction between the tests used to evaluate discrimination claims at the summary judgment phase versus those claims brought to trial. *See, e.g.,* Stuart v. First Sec. Bank, 15 P.3d 1198 (Mont. 2000).

26 In disparate effects cases, Congress specifically referred to the tests used in the employment context in cases such as Griggs v. Duke Power Co., 401 U.S. 424 (1971) and Albemarle Paper Co. v. Moody, 422 U.S. 405 (1971). For a discussion of Congressional action in disparate effects cases, see generally Richard A. Hill, Note, *Credit Opportunities, Race, and Presumptions: Does the McDonnell Douglas Framework Apply in Fair Lending Cases? Latimore v. Citibank Savings Bank*, 64 Mo. L. Rev. 479 (1999). *See also* § 4.3, *infra*.

27 The reason for courts' usage of the test in FHA cases may be in deference to the Department of Housing and Urban Development's adoption of the test to evaluate claims of discrimination under the Act. *See* Gamble v. City of Escondido, 104 F.3d 300, 304–5 (9th Cir. 1997); Ring v. First Interstate Mortgage, 984 F.2d 924 (8th Cir. 1993), *cert. denied*, 523 U.S. 1006 (1998) (no doubt that *McDonnell-Douglas* test applies to FHA cases); United States v. Badgett, 976 F.2d 1176, 1178 (8th Cir. 1992); Texas v. Crest Asset Mgmt., Inc., 85 F. Supp. 2d 722 (S.D. Tex. 2000).

28 All of the federal circuit courts, except for the D.C. Circuit which has not considered the issue, have held that the FHA encompasses claims based upon the disparate impact theory. *See, e.g.,* Langlois v. Abington Hous. Auth., 207 F.3d 43 (1st Cir. 2000); Mountain Side Mobile Estates P'ship v. Sec'y of Hous. & Urban Dev., 56 F.3d 1243 (10th Cir. 1995); United States v. Badgett, 976 F.2d 1176, 1179 (8th Cir. 1992); Keith v. Volpe, 858 F.2d 467, 484 (9th Cir. 1988); Huntington Branch N.A.A.C.P. v. Town of Huntington, 844 F.2d 926 (2d Cir. 1988), *aff'd*, 488 U.S. 15 (1988); Arthur v. City of Toledo, 782 F.2d 565, 575 (6th Cir. 1986); Metro. Hous. Dev. Corp. v. Vill. of Arlington Heights (*Arlington Heights II*), 558 F.2d 1283, 1289 (7th Cir. 1977). Although the D.C. Circuit has not addressed the issue, at least two D.C. district court judges have recognized the disparate impact theory in FHA cases. *See* Samaritan Inns v. District of Columbia, 1995 U.S. Dist. LEXIS 9294 (D.D.C. June 30, 1995), *aff'd in part, rev'd in part*, 114 F.3d 1227 (D.C. Cir. 1997) (the D.C. government's suspension of plaintiff's permit to rehabilitate home for disabled violated the FHA under theories of intentional discrimination and disparate impact); Brown v. Artery Org., Inc., 654 F. Supp. 1106, 1115 (D.D.C. 1987).

29 *See* Coleman v. Gen. Motors Acceptance Corp., 196 F.R.D. 315, 325 (M.D. Tenn. 2000) (granting plaintiff's motion for class

Courts have found that it is not available for federal Civil Rights Act claims.[30]

The disparate impact approach gives the plaintiff another avenue to pursue whenever disparate treatment cannot be proven. Even though the business justification is the real reason for the creditor's actions, the creditor's actions may still be illegal if they have a disparate impact on a protected class and use of some other factor would satisfy the creditor's legitimate business needs with less of a disparate impact. The plaintiff does not need to show intent to discriminate, but instead must show that a facially neutral policy has a discriminatory effect.

For instance, a creditor might refuse to grant credit to applicants from all zip code areas in which its computer indicates that default losses in the past have been greater than a stated frequency. It might be impossible to prove that this system is a mere pretext for illegal discrimination, particularly if the creditor claims not to even know the racial composition of various zip code areas. But it might be possible to prove that the affected zip code areas were predominantly nonwhite, and that this credit factor could be replaced by some other factor, such as the applicant's own credit history, that would have less of a disparate impact.

The disparate impact test also significantly broadens the reach of the prohibited bases listed in the ECOA and the Fair Housing Act, and, in effect, creates many new prohibited bases. When the factors that creditors utilize in differentiating credit applications have a disparate impact on a prohibited basis, these other, seemingly nonprohibited factors, can become prohibited bases.

For example, a creditor's practice may have a disparate effect on a protected category if the creditor denies credit to anyone who relies on child support payments as income. As this practice would affect divorced and separated women almost exclusively, it would have a disproportionately negative impact on the basis of sex and marital status and thus, in effect, becomes a prohibited basis.[31]

4.3.2 Burdens of Proof

4.3.2.1 General

Both FHA and ECOA cases rely heavily on the much more developed body of law in the employment discrimination area. There is little case law on the disparate impact theory of liability in credit discrimination cases. Thus, it is critical for practitioners to keep track of judicial and regulatory trends in both credit discrimination and employment discrimination cases.

The test for a prima facie case of employment discrimination has been described as requiring three elements: *identification* of a specific policy, disparate *impact* of the policy on a protected group, and *causation* (a causal link between the policy and the disparate impact).[32] Each of these categories is discussed in detail below in the credit discrimination context.

Once the plaintiff makes a prima facie showing, the defendant bears the burden of rebutting the plaintiff's case by demonstrating a "business necessity" for the practice. Even if a defendant meets this burden, they will prevail only if the plaintiff fails to show the availability of [a] less discriminatory alternative practice or action that would provide a comparably effective means of meeting that goal.[33]

Most courts will follow the employment cases fairly closely for both ECOA and FHA claims. The continuing evolution of the disparate impact theory in the employment area, therefore, has a significant effect on credit discrimination cases. The most consistent conflict in disparate impact cases in general is the extent to which the disparate impact test is truly an "effects test" or whether some sort of intentional discrimination is required.[34]

---

certification and denying, in part, defendant's motion for summary judgment) ("[T]he legislative history of the ECOA indicates that the Congress intended an 'effects test' concept, as outlined in the employment field in the Supreme Court in the cases of Griggs v. Duke Power Co., 401 U.S. 424 (1971) and Albemarle Paper Co. v. Moody, 422 U.S. 405 (1975).") (citing 12 C.F.R. § 202.6(a) n.2; Official Staff Commentary 12 C.F.R. § 202.6(a); Haynes v. Bank of Wedowee, 634 F.2d 266 (5th Cir. 1981) (noting use of disparate impact standard in ECOA case)); A.B. & S Auto Serv., Inc. v. S. Shore Bank of Chicago, 962 F. Supp. 1056 (N.D. Ill. 1997); Sayers v. Gen. Motors Acceptance Corp., 522 F. Supp. 835, 839 (W.D. Mo. 1981).

30 *See, e.g.*, Gen. Bldg. Contractors Ass'n v. Pennsylvania, 458 U.S. 375 (1982).

31 The drafters of Regulation B, recognizing this potential problem, specifically prohibited such a practice. *See* Reg. B, 12 C.F.R. § 202.6(b)(5).

32 *See, e.g.*, Equal Employment Opportunity Comm'n v. Steamship Clerks Union Local 1066, 48 F.3d 594, 601 (1st Cir. 1995).

33 *See* Albemarle Paper Co. v. Moody, 422 U.S. 405, 425, 95 S. Ct. 2362, 45 L. Ed. 2d 280 (1975) (once the Defendant shows that an employment requirement has a "manifest relationship" to a legitimate employer goal, the burden shifts back to the plaintiff to show the existence of a less discriminatory alternative in order to prove that the defendant's showing of job-relatedness was a pretext for discrimination); Fitzpatrick v. City of Atlanta, 2 F.3d 1112, 1118 (11th Cir. 1993); *see also* § 4.3.2.6, *infra*.

34 *See generally* Peter E. Mahoney, *The End(s) of Disparate Impact: Doctrinal Reconstruction, Fair Housing and Lending Law, and the Antidiscrimination Principle*, 47 Emory L.J. 409 (1998) (describing the conflict between the precedent set by Griggs v. Duke Power Co., 401 U.S. 424, 91 S. Ct. 849, 28 L. Ed. 2d 158 (1971) in which liability was found in employment discrimination upon disparate impact alone, versus the line of cases flowing from Washington v. Davis, 426 U.S. 229, 96 S. Ct. 2040, 48 L. Ed. 2d 597 (1976), finding that in order to sustain a constitutional challenge under the Equal Protection Clause, the plaintiff must prove that the conduct in question was motivated by a discriminatory purpose). In addition, there is a judicial trend in other areas of the law disfavoring the effects test. Although these cases are distinguishable on a number of

4.3.2.2 ECOA Burden of Proof

The burden of proof in disparate impact cases is some-what clearer for ECOA claims than for FHA claims. Unlike the FHA, the legislative history of the ECOA expressly instructs the courts to use employment discrimination cases in construing the ECOA "effects test."[35]

In addition, the Official Staff Commentary to Regulation B states:

> The act and regulation may prohibit a creditor practice that is discriminatory in effect because it has a disproportionately negative impact on a prohibited basis, even though the creditor has no intent to discriminate and the practice appears neutral on its face, unless the creditor practice meets a legitimate business need that cannot reasonably be achieved as well by means that are less disparate in their impact.[36]

Four standards are implicit in this statement:

- A practice that does not appear to discriminate on a prohibited basis can still be prohibited if the practice has a disparate impact on a prohibited basis;
- To be actionable, the impact must be disproportionately negative (by using this term, the Commentary suggests some balancing of the negative impact with the business justification);
- If the practice has such an impact, it is prohibited unless the practice meets a legitimate business need that cannot be achieved by a practice that has a less disparate impact;

- The creditor's intent to discriminate is irrelevant.

The Commentary also indicates that the ECOA standard as to disparate impact is based on two Supreme Court employment discrimination decisions, *Griggs v. Duke Power Co.*,[37] and *Albermarle Paper Co. v. Moody*.[38]

4.3.2.3 FHA Burden of Proof

The legal standard for disparate impact claims under the FHA was first clearly described in a Seventh Circuit case.[39] The Court articulated a test that asks four questions: 1) How strong is the plaintiff's showing of discriminatory effect? 2) Is there some evidence of discriminatory intent, though not enough to satisfy the constitutional standard of *Washington v. Davis*? 3) What is the defendant's interest in taking the action complained of? 4) Does the plaintiff seek to compel the defendant affirmatively to provide housing for a protected class, or merely to remove obstacles to private provision of such housing?[40] The Second Circuit later refined these factors into a burden shifting framework under which a plaintiff establishes a prima facie case by showing that the "challenged practice of the defendant 'actually or predictably results in racial discrimination; in other words that is has a discriminatory effect.'"[41]

In general, in cases involving government defendants, courts have utilized some variant of the Seventh Circuit's *Arlington Heights II* test. However, in cases involving private defendants, results have been mixed. Some courts have applied the Seventh Circuit standard without reference to a distinction between government and private defendants.[42] Other courts have turned more to employment law precedent, either because the case also involved an ECOA claim[43]

---

grounds, they may have consequences in the credit discrimination area eventually. For example, a U.S. Supreme Court decision in 2001 eliminated an individual's ability to enforce the Title IV disparate impact regulations through an implied private right of action. Alexander v. Sandoval, 532 U.S. 275, 121 S. Ct. 1511, 149 L. Ed. 2d 517 (2001). *See generally* Jane Perkins & Sarah Jane Somers, *Sandoval's Retrenchment on Civil Rights Enforcement: The Ultimate Sorcerer's Magic*, 35 J. of Poverty L. & Pol'y 433 (2001). Further evidence of judicial reluctance to extend disparate impact theory too far beyond employment discrimination cases can be found in case law under the Age Discrimination in Employment Act (ADEA). In 2002, the Supreme Court reversed a previous decision to consider the question, stating that their decision to hear the case was "improvidently granted." *See* Adams v. Fla. Power Corp., 255 F.3d 1322 (11th Cir. 2001) (disparate impact theory not available under ADEA), *cert. granted*, 122 S. Ct. 643 (2001), *cert. dismissed*, 122 S. Ct. 1290 (2002).

35 *See* S. Rep. No. 94-589 (1976) ("Thus, judicial construction of antidiscrimiation legislation in the employment field, in cases such as Griggs v. Duke Power Co. 401 U.S. 424 [, 91 S. Ct. 849, 28 L. Ed. 2d 158] (1971) and Albemarle Paper Co. v. Moody [422 U.S. 405, 95 S. Ct. 2362, 45 L. Ed. 2d 280 (1975)] are intended to serve as guides in the application of this Act, especially with respect to the allocations of burden of proof.").

36 Official Staff Commentary, 12 C.F.R. § 202.6(a)-2.

37 401 U.S. 424, 91 S. Ct. 849, 28 L. Ed. 2d 158 (1971) (establishing that discriminatory impact violates Title VII which prohibits employment discrimination).

38 422 U.S. 405, 95 S. Ct. 2362, 45 L. Ed. 2d 280 (1975) (setting out disparate impact analysis for prima facie employment discrimination case by plaintiff, defendant's burden of proving business necessity, and plaintiff's opportunity to show less discriminatory means).

39 Metro. Hous. Dev. Co. v. Vill. of Arlington Heights, 558 F.2d 1283 (7th Cir. 1977) (*Arlington Heights II*).

40 *Id.*

41 Huntington Branch N.A.A.C.P. v. Town of Huntington, 844 F.2d 926, 934 (2d Cir. 1988), *aff'd*, 488 U.S. 15 (1988) (quoting United States v. City of Black Jack, 508 F.2d 1179, 1184–85 (8th Cir. 1974)).

42 *See, e.g.*, United States v. Badgett, 976 F.2d 1176 (8th Cir. 1992) (applying *Arlington Heights II* test to private defendant); Old W. End Ass'n v. Buckeye Fed. Sav. & Loan, 675 F. Supp. 1100, 1105 (N.D. Ohio 1987) (in dismissing motion for summary judgment, court applied the *Arlington Heights II* standard to a claim of redlining). *See generally* Peter E. Mahoney, *The End(s) of Disparate Impact: Doctrinal Reconstruction, Fair Housing and Lending Law, and the Antidiscrimination Principle*, 47 Emory L.J. 409 (1998).

43 *See, e.g.*, A.B. & S Auto Serv. Inc. v. S. Shore Bank, 962 F.

or because that circuit has specifically rejected the *Arlington Heights II* standard.[44]

4.3.2.4 Prima Facie Case for ECOA and FHA Claims

4.3.2.4.1 Introduction

Despite the confusion in FHA cases, most courts in credit discrimination cases will follow the employment law standards, asking whether a policy, procedure, or practice specifically identified by the plaintiff has a significantly greater discriminatory impact on members of a protected class.[45] As discussed above, the plaintiff's prima facie case consists of three elements: identification, impact, and causation. Each is discussed below.

4.3.2.4.2 Identification of a specific policy

The plaintiff first must show that a specific policy caused a significant disparate effect on a protected group. Although the policy being challenged is often not in question, there are instances when the defendant will challenge whether the plaintiff has in fact identified a specific policy.[46]

Defendants may also challenge whether the particularity requirement is met when the plaintiff is challenging subjective discriminatory practices as opposed to neutral policies. In at least one case defendants argued that a policy that permits subjective treatment is not a neutral policy for disparate impact purposes.[47] The policy in question was a mark-up pricing scheme in which dealers, based on creditor instructions, were given discretion to mark up interest rates above the creditor's minimum buy rate.[48] The court disagreed with defendants, finding no discernible reason not to use disparate impact analysis in these circumstances.[49]

Sometimes it is difficult to pinpoint exactly which business practice has a particular disparate impact, but it is clear that a combination of factors has a disparate effect.[50] While some Supreme Court employment discrimination cases indicated that the plaintiff must specify what particular business practice had what particular disparate impact,[51] with the passage of the Civil Rights Act of 1991, Congress declared unequivocally that the specific discriminatory practices need not be separately proven, but a combination of policies may be shown to have a disparate impact.[52]

4.3.2.4.3 Disparate impact on a protected group

Second, the plaintiff must identify or demonstrate the adverse impact of the policy on a specific class of persons protected by the discrimination law. This element is further broken down into two categories. First, the plaintiff must show the adverse impact on protected persons. The plaintiff must then show that the unfavorable consequences are felt disproportionately by the members of the protected class in comparison to non-members who are similarly situated.[53]

Care must be taken in determining exactly what numbers are to be compared. Courts are unlikely to find persuasive statistics which merely show that a higher percentage of African-Americans are turned down for credit than whites, but instead will look to see if a higher percentage of *qualified* African-Americans are turned down than whites.[54] For example, if a creditor denies credit to those with active delinquencies, a court may not find that this shows a disparate impact on African-Americans when the only evidence produced is that African-Americans are more likely to be delinquent than whites, not that otherwise creditworthy African-Americans are more likely to be delinquent than otherwise creditworthy whites. On the other hand, courts will likely find a disparate impact if a plaintiff can show that a creditor's insistence on a credit history from a bank, and not just a finance company, is more likely to impact creditworthy African-Americans than creditworthy whites.

Supp. 1056 (N.D. Ill. 1997); Thomas v. First Fed. Sav. Bank, 653 F. Supp. 1330 (N.D. Ind. 1987); Cherry v. Amoco Oil Co., 490 F. Supp. 1026, 1031 (N.D. Ga. 1980).

44 *See, e.g.,* Bronson v. Crestwood Lake Section 1 Holding Corp., 724 F. Supp. 148 (S.D.N.Y. 1989).

45 *See, e.g.,* Simms v. First Gibraltar Bank, 83 F.3d 1546 (5th Cir. 1996).

46 *See, e.g., id.* (plaintiff failed to specifically identify a policy, procedure or practice of the defendant that had a disparate impact).

47 Coleman v. Gen. Motors Acceptance Corp., 196 F.R.D. 315, 325 (M.D. Tenn. 2000).

48 *Id.*

49 *Id.* at 326; *see* Buycks-Roberson v. Citibank Fed. Sav. Bank, 162 F.R.D. 322, 331 (N.D. Ill. 1995) (the subjective application of neutral underwriting criteria is standardized conduct because the loan originators have the opportunity to use their discretion with respect to each loan application and the standardized conduct can be readily identified for purposes of assessing evidence of disparate impact); *see also* Watson v. Forth Worth Bank & Trust, 487 U.S. 977, 990, 108 S. Ct. 2777, 101 L. Ed. 2d 827 (1988) (in Title VII employment case, court held that

---

disparate impact analysis is no less applicable to subjective employment criteria than to objective or standardized tests).

50 *See* United States v. Incorporated Vill. of Island Park, 888 F. Supp. 419 (E.D.N.Y. 1995).

51 *See* Wards Cove Packing Co. v. Atonio, 490 U.S. 642, 109 S. Ct. 2115, 104 L. Ed. 2d 733 (1989) (employment discrimination case). The legislative history of the Civil Rights Act of 1991 specifically discusses overruling *Wards Cove.* 1991 U.S.C.C.A.N. 561.

52 42 U.S.C. § 2000e-2(k)(1)(B)(i).

53 Donnelly v. Rhode Island Bd. of Governors for Higher Educ., 929 F. Supp. 583, 590 (D.R.I. 1996), *aff'd,* 110 F.3d 2 (1st Cir. 1997) (citing Equal Employment Opportunity Comm'n v. Steamship Clerks Union Local 1066, 48 F.3d 594, 601 (1st Cir. 1995)).

54 *See* Albemarle Paper Co. v. Moody, 422 U.S. 405, 95 S. Ct. 2362, 45 L. Ed. 2d 280 (1975) (employment discrimination case); Saldana v. Citibank, 1996 U.S. Dist. LEXIS 8327 (N.D. Ill. Jun. 13, 1996) (mortgage redlining case).

It is often difficult for plaintiffs to show that they used a proper pool for comparison purposes. The Supreme Court's general guidance in the employment area is that "while a statistical showing of disproportionate impact [need not] always be based on an analysis of the characteristics of actual applicants,"[55] "statistics based on an applicant pool containing individuals lacking minimal qualifications for the job would be of little probative value,"[56] and "evidence showing that the figures for the general population might not accurately reflect the pool of qualified job applicants' undermines the significance of such figures."[57]

Many cases rely on the "applicant pool" method set out in *Wards Cove Packing Co. v. Atonio*.[58] In that case the Court held that, in using the applicant pool method, the proper comparison was between the racial composition of those holding the more desirable (non-cannery) jobs and the racial composition of the qualified population in the relevant labor market.[59]

The test is slightly different in a reverse redlining case.[60] In a typical reverse redlining case, a plaintiff using the applicant pool approach collects applicant data from all of the lenders' branches. The plaintiff would then show that under the lenders' lending criteria, the percentage of qualified white applicants receiving terms at the favorable rate significantly exceeds the percentage of qualified nonwhites receiving such rates.[61] This data can be supplemented with census data, for example, to show the racial composition of particular neighborhoods and to show that predatory lenders target those areas for the highest price credit products.[62]

A problem with this approach is that many nonwhites may be deterred from applying for loans at the pre-application stage.[63] This discrimination will not show up in an analysis based on applicants only. As an alternative, plaintiffs could use general population statistics and compare, for example, the percentage of nonwhites holding the more desirable jobs versus the percentage of nonwhites in the general population for the targeted area. However, such a comparison pool is vulnerable to challenge for over-inclusiveness. For example,

in a mortgage lending case, defendants will likely argue that comparisons with the general population fail to discern between those who are creditworthy and those who would not qualify for credit.

4.3.2.4.4 Causation

Finally, plaintiffs must show causation. Establishing a prima facie case requires more than a mere showing of statistical disparities. The suspect practices must be identified and causally linked with the statistically demonstrated adverse impact.[64] Again, credit discrimination cases borrow from the employment area in determining what is required to show this element.

In employment cases, the Supreme Court decisions have generally required plaintiffs to show that the particular practice or policy has a disparate impact upon the identified pool of protected persons that is significant or substantial enough to raise an inference of causation.[65] In employment cases, plaintiffs typically make this showing by using statistical analyses.[66] However, the Court has not adopted a particular statistical standard that could show "significance" in every case, relying instead on a case-by-case approach.[67]

In home mortgage lending cases, in particular, the causation element is critical to balance "mere" findings from HMDA data (or other sources) of statistical disparities in approval and rejection rates. This element requires that the plaintiff show that the specific policy in question caused the disparate effect.[68]

---

55 Dothard v. Rawlinson, 433 U.S. 321, 330, 97 S. Ct. 2720, 53 L. Ed. 2d 786 (1977).

56 Watson v. Fort Worth Bank & Trust, 487 U.S. 977, 997, 108 S. Ct. 2777, 101 L. Ed. 2d 827 (1988).

57 New York City Transit Auth. v. Beazer, 440 U.S. 568, 587 n.29, 99 S. Ct. 1355, 59 L. Ed. 2d 587 (1979) (quoting Int'l Brotherhood of Teamsters v. United States, 431 U.S. 324, 340 n.20, 97 S. Ct. 1843, 52 L. Ed. 2d 396 (1977)).

58 Wards Cove Packing Co. v. Atonio, 490 U.S. 642, 650, 109 S. Ct. 2115, 104 L. Ed. 2d 733 (1989).

59 *Id.*

60 *See generally* § 8.2, *infra.*

61 *See generally* Frank Lopez, *Using the Fair Housing Act to Combat Predatory Lending*, 6 Geo. J. on Poverty L. & Pol'y 73 (1999).

62 *See, e.g.,* Hargraves v. Capital City Mortgage Corp., 140 F.2d 7 (D.D.C. 2000).

63 *See generally* § 5.3, *infra* (discussion of pre-application discrimination).

64 *See* A.B. & S. Auto Serv., Inc. v. S. Shore Bank, 962 F. Supp. 1056 (N.D. Ill. 1997); Saldana v. Citibank, 1996 U.S. Dist. LEXIS 8327 (N.D. Ill. Jun. 13, 1996); United States v. Incorporated Vill. of Island Park, 888 F. Supp. 419, 446 (E.D.N.Y. 1995) (the fact that no African-Americans received any of the forty-four homes constructed under a government-subsidized housing plan was combined with evidence of a facially neutral process which did not allow for selection of applications from African-Americans.).

65 *See* Watson v. Fort Worth Bank & Trust, 487 U.S. 977, 995, 108 S. Ct. 2777, 101 L. Ed. 2d 827 (1988) (plaintiffs in Title VII cases must show that the "test in question select applicants for hire or promotion in a racial pattern significantly different from that of the pool of applicants"); *see also* Connecticut v. Teal, 457 U.S. 440, 446, (1982); New York City Transit Auth. v. Beazer, 440 U.S. 568, 584, 99 S. Ct. 1355, 59 L. Ed. 2d 587 (1979); Dothard v. Rawlinson, 433 U.S. 321, 329, 97 S. Ct. 2720, 53 L. Ed. 2d 786 (1977); Washington v. Davis, 426 U.S. 229, 246–47, 96 S. Ct. 2040, 48 L. Ed. 2d 597 (1976).

66 *See, e.g.,* Watson v. Fort Worth Bank & Trust, 487 U.S. 977, 994, 108 S. Ct. 2777, 101 L. Ed. 2d 827 (1988).

67 *Watson*, 487 U.S. at 996 n.3.

68 The question of whether statistics alone can be used to prove discriminatory bias is the subject of much academic debate. *See generally* Stephen M. Dane, *Eliminating the Labyrinth: A Proposal to Simplify Federal Mortgage Lending Discrimination Laws*, 26 U. Mich. J.L. Reform 527, 530 (1993); Peter E. Mahoney, *The End(s) of Disparate Impact: Doctrinal Recon-*

4.3.2.5 Business Justification

If the plaintiff meets the prima facie burden described above, then the burden of proof shifts to the creditor to show a legitimate and necessary business justification.[69] That the plaintiff need only initially show the discriminatory impact and that the burden of showing the business justification then shifts to the creditor is buttressed by Congressional action in the employment area. Supreme Court employment discrimination cases had been increasingly placing a greater burden on the plaintiff concerning the business justification.[70] In response, Congress entered the Civil Rights Act of 1991, which unequivocally declares that the defendant retains the burden of proving that a challenged practice constitutes a business necessity.[71] Congress' purpose in passing the 1991 Act was to return to the principles of *Griggs v. Duke Power Co.*[72] and *Albemarle Paper Co. v. Moody*,[73] which contained more generous standards for the plaintiff[74] and were the cases upon which the ECOA standard of disparate impact was based.[75]

Although the 1991 Act clarified the burden of proof, it did not establish a clear standard of what constitutes a "business necessity." As a result, courts have articulated a number of different tests and definitions, including "compelling need,"[76] "manifest relationship,"[77] "legitimate, nondiscriminatory rationale,"[78] and "demonstrably necessary."[79] The legitimate nondiscriminatory rationale and manifest relationship tests are the most commonly used.

In a disparate impact case, the creditor carries the burden of proving not only that its business justification is the reason it acted but that its business justification is a legitimate and necessary basis to evaluate credit risks.[80] If the business justification is the real reason for the creditor's actions, but the justification is not relevant to creditworthiness, then the plaintiff's prima facie case of disparate impact will be sufficient for the plaintiff to prevail.[81] However, there is no particular type of evidence the defendant must present in order to carry this burden.[82]

With respect to claims under the ECOA, no guidance is given in Regulation B as to what might constitute a legitimate business necessity in credit discrimination cases. However, the Commentary does give this example:

> For example, requiring that applicants have incomes in excess of a certain amount to qualify for an overdraft line of credit could mean that women and minority applicants will be rejected at a higher rate than men and nonminority applicants. If there is a demonstrable relationship between the income requirement and creditworthiness for the level of credit involved, however, use of the income standard *would likely* be permissible.[83]

4.3.2.6 Are There Alternative Factors With Less Disparate Impact?

Once the creditor carries its burden of establishing a

---

struction, Fair Housing and Lending Law, and the Antidiscrimination Principle, 47 Emory L.J. 409 (1998); Peter P. Swire, *The Persistent Problem of Lending Discrimination: A Law and Economics Analysis*, 73 Tex. L. Rev. 787 (1995).

69 *See, e.g.*, Huntington Branch N.A.A.C.P. v. Town of Huntington, 844 F.2d 926 (2d Cir. 1988), *aff'd*, 488 U.S. 15, 16 (1988) (not reaching the question of appropriateness of the pure effects test because the defendant had not challenged its application, but commenting that it was "satisfied on this record that disparate impact was shown, and that the sole justification proffered to rebut the prima facie case was inadequate"); Betsey v. Turtle Creek Associates, 736 F.2d 983 (4th Cir. 1984); United States v. Parma, 661 F.2d 562 (6th Cir. 1981); Resident Advisory Bd. v. Rizzo, 564 F.2d 126 (3d Cir. 1977); United States v. City of Black Jack, 508 F.2d 1179 (8th Cir. 1974); Williams v. 5300 Columbia Pike Corp., 891 F. Supp. 1169 (E.D. Va. 1995) (because plaintiffs presented a valid prima facie claim under Fair Housing Act, burden shifted to defendants to assert a legitimate business purpose or purposes for the challenged practice); Interagency Policy Statement on Discrimination in Lending, 59 Fed. Reg. 18,266 (Apr. 15, 1994) (discussed at § 12.2.4, *infra*).

70 See *Wards Cove Packing Co. v. Atonio*, 490 U.S. 642, 109 S. Ct. 2115, 104 L. Ed. 2d 733 (1989) (employment discrimination case), which the legislative history of the Civil Rights Act of 1991 specifically discusses overruling. 1991 U.S.C.C.A.N. 561.

71 42 U.S.C. § 2000e-2(k)(1)(A).

72 401 U.S. 424, 91 S. Ct. 849, 28 L. Ed. 2d 158 (1971) (establishing that discriminatory impact violates Title VII's prohibition of employment discrimination).

73 422 U.S. 405, 95 S. Ct. 2362, 45 L. Ed. 2d 280 (1975) (setting out disparate impact analysis for prima facie case by plaintiff, defendant's burden of proving business necessity, and plaintiff's opportunity to show less discriminatory means).

74 *See* 1991 U.S.C.C.A.N. 561.

75 *See* § 4.3.2.2, *supra*.

76 *See, e.g.*, Bradley v. Pizzaco of Neb., Inc., 7 F.3d 795, 797 (8th Cir. 1993).

77 *See, e.g.*, Smith v. City of Des Moines, 99 F.3d 1466, 1271 (8th Cir. 1996); Mountain Side Mobile Estates P'ship v. Sec'y of Hous. & Urban Dev., 56 F.3d 1243 (10th Cir. 1995).

78 *See, e.g.*, Equal Employment Opportunity Comm'n v. Steamship Clerks Union Local 1066, 48 F.3d 594, 602 (1st Cir. 1995).

79 Fitzpatrick v. City of Atlanta, 2 F.3d 1112, 1119 (11th Cir. 1993).

80 Congress in 1991 codified this standard for employment discrimination cases. *See* 42 U.S.C. § 2000e-2(e)(1)(A).

81 *See* Wards Cove Packing Co. v. Atonio, 490 U.S. 642, 109 S. Ct. 2115, 104 L. Ed. 2d 733 (1989) (employment discrimination case); Watson v. Fort Worth Bank & Trust, 487 U.S. 977, 108 S. Ct. 2777, 101 L. Ed. 2d 827 (1988) (employment discrimination case); *see also* Town of Huntington v. Huntington Branch N.A.A.C.P., 488 U.S. 15, 16, 109 S. Ct. 276, 102 L. Ed. 2d 180 (1988) (sole justification offered to rebut the prima facie housing discrimination case was inadequate); *Mountain Side*, 56 F.3d at 1254 (mere insubstantial justification of manifest relationship is insufficient, because such a low standard would permit discrimination to be practiced through the use of spurious, seemingly neutral practices).

82 Watson v. Forth Worth Bank & Trust, 487 U.S. 977, 998, 108 S. Ct. 2777, 101 L. Ed. 2d 827 (1988).

83 Official Staff Commentary, 12 C.F.R. § 202.6(a)-2 (emphasis added).

legitimate and significant business justification, then the remaining issue is whether the legitimate business concern can be met in some other fashion with less of a disparate impact. If the creditor demonstrates a significant business justification, the plaintiff can still prove discrimination if another practice meeting the creditor's legitimate concerns would have less of a discriminatory impact.[84]

Although it is now well established in employment law that the plaintiff has the burden of showing an alternative practice with less of a discriminatory impact exists, the standards for showing this alternative are not clear.[85] Some courts in employment law cases have required the plaintiff to show that the alternative practice can be statistically proven to be equally effective in achieving the business objectives underlying the challenged practice and to have a less disproportionate effect.[86]

In the credit discrimination realm, courts and regulatory agencies have sent mixed messages as to whether the plaintiff or defendant must carry the burden of showing a less discriminatory alternative exists. In 1995, both the Department of Justice and the Department of Housing and Urban Development endorsed the Title VII (employment discrimination law) burden of proof standards as the appropriate standards in FHA cases.[87] The Federal Reserve Board has also adopted regulatory language indicating that the burdens of proof under the ECOA are to follow the employment law standards codified in the Civil Rights Act of 1991.[88] Although there is still some confusion on this issue, there is strong support that the burden is placed on the plaintiff.[89]

As in employment law, there is little guidance regarding the showing required to meet the burden of proving a less discriminatory alternative exists. However, assuming that courts in credit discrimination cases will follow the employment standards, a plaintiff will need to show that a less discriminatory alternative would be "equally effective" in meeting the defendant's legitimate business objective.[90]

4.4 Sources of Evidence

4.4.1 The Consumer's Own Records

The plaintiff should possess certain information useful for a credit discrimination case. The first item to check for is whether the plaintiff received a notice of action taken by the creditor, and whether this notice is in the proper format.[91] The ECOA requires that creditors provide notice of an adverse action, generally in writing.[92] The notice must either state the reason for the action taken or give the applicant the right to request the reason. In the latter case, the applicant must request the reason within sixty days of the notice of adverse action.[93] If notice was not sent, there may be an ECOA violation triggering a cause of action for actual and punitive damages as well as attorney fees.[94]

While every effort should be made to request the reasons for the adverse action within the sixty-day deadline, if the sixty-day deadline has passed, the information should still be requested. If the creditor refuses, the information should be sought through a formal request for production of documents. The ECOA in most cases requires the creditor to retain such information for twenty-five months.[95]

The Fair Credit Reporting Act requires the creditor to advise the consumer if an adverse action was taken due to information contained in a credit report from a reporting agency.[96] The creditor must advise the consumer of the name and address of the agency making the report, and the consumer may then obtain a copy of the credit report from the agency at no charge, as long as the request is made within sixty days. Otherwise, there may be a charge for the report.[97]

Another useful piece of information that is often in an applicant's possession is an appraisal report on the appli-

---

84 Albemarle Paper Co. v. Moody, 422 U.S. 405, 95 S. Ct. 2362, 45 L. Ed. 2d 280 (1975); Resident Advisory Bd. v. Rizzo, 564 F.2d 126, 149 (3d Cir. 1977) (Fair Housing Act case); Official Staff Commentary, 12 C.F.R. § 202.6(a)-2.

85 *See generally* Peter E. Mahoney, *The End(s) of Disparate Impact: Doctrinal Reconstruction, Fair Housing and Lending Law, and the Antidiscrimination Principle*, 47 Emory L.J. 409 (1998).

86 *See, e.g.,* York v. AT & T, 95 F.3d 948 (10th Cir. 1996); MacPherson v. Univ. of Montevallo, 922 F.2d 766, 771 (11th Cir. 1991).

87 *See* Mountain Side Mobile Estates P'ship v. Sec'y of Hous. & Urban Dev. (HUD), 56 F.3d 1243 (10th Cir. 1995) (Dep't of Justice petition for en banc rehearing of the 10th Circuit's decision). HUD also has stated (in the preamble to 1995 regulations interpreting affordable housing and fair lending standards applicable to federally chartered housing enterprises) that "when taken together, the Fair Housing Act regulations and case law, the Civil Rights Act of 1991, and the Interagency Policy Statement provide sufficient guidance" concerning interpretation of fair lending standards. 60 Fed. Reg. 61,846, 61,868 (Dec. 1, 1995). Earlier, HUD had implied that it believed the burden of proof on less discriminatory alternatives should be placed on defendants. *See, e.g.,* Unified Agenda of Federal Regulations, Dep't of Hous. and Urban Dev., Proposed Rules, Disparate Impact Rule, 59 Fed. Reg. 57,087, 57,102 (Nov. 14, 1994). HUD later withdrew the rule from its list of regulatory priorities.

88 Official Staff Commentary, 12 C.F.R. § 202.6(a)-2.

89 *See generally* Peter E. Mahoney, *The End(s) of Disparate Impact: Doctrinal Reconstruction, Fair Housing and Lending*

Law, and the Antidiscrimination Principle, 47 Emory L.J. 409 (1998).

90 *See* Wilson v. Glenwood Intermountain Properties, 876 F. Supp. 1231, 1242 (D. Utah 1995) (FHA case).

91 *See* § 10.2, *infra.*

92 *See* § 10.2.4, *infra.*

93 *See* § 10.2.7.2, *infra.*

94 *See generally* Ch. 11, *infra* (private remedies for ECOA violations).

95 *See* § 10.3.1, *infra.*

96 15 U.S.C. § 1681m(a); *see also* National Consumer Law Center, Fair Credit Reporting Act (4th ed. 1998 and Supp.).

97 *See* § 4.4.3, *infra.*

cant's home, especially if the applicant is applying for a mortgage or home equity loan. The ECOA requires that creditors provide applicants with notice of their right to receive a copy of any appraisal, specifying the address to which the applicant should send their written request.[98] The applicant's request must be received by the creditor within ninety days of the creditor's action on the application, or the creditor need not provide a copy of the report.[99] The report may also be obtained later through discovery. In many cases, to avoid the extra step of sending applicants the notice of a right to an appraisal report, the creditor has sent the report to the applicant unsolicited.

4.4.2 The Creditor's Own Files

The creditor's files are critical in any credit discrimination case. The ECOA sets out specific records that creditors must retain for twenty-five months following the date the creditor notifies an applicant of the action taken on an application (that is, the records are supposed to be retained until the statute of limitations usually has expired on possible ECOA actions).[100]

The creditor must retain the following documents:

- Any application form that the creditor receives;
- Information obtained for monitoring purposes;
- Any other written or recorded information used in evaluating the application and not returned to the applicant upon request;
- Written notification to the applicant of the action taken on the application, or notes concerning oral notification;
- Written notification to the applicant of the specific reasons for adverse action, or notes concerning oral notification; and
- Any written statement submitted by the applicant alleging a violation of the ECOA or Regulation B.[101]

When adverse action has been taken on a credit transaction outside of the application process, such as when the creditor has terminated or changed terms on an existing account, the creditor also must preserve the following records for twenty-five months after notification to the applicant of the adverse action:[102]

- Any written or recorded information concerning the adverse action; and
- Any written statement submitted by the applicant alleging a violation of the ECOA or Regulation B.[103]

Written copies need not be retained by creditors using a computerized system, provided that the information can be regenerated in a timely manner.[104]

In transactions involving more than one creditor, even those creditors not required to comply with the notification provisions of Regulation B must retain all written or recorded information they possess concerning the applicant, for a period as long as that required of the notifying creditor.[105] This information must include any notations concerning adverse actions.

In addition, once a creditor receives actual notice that a civil action has been filed or that the creditor is under investigation or is subject to an enforcement proceeding for an ECOA violation, the creditor must retain all required records until there is a final disposition of the matter, unless an earlier time is allowed by the agency or court.[106]

Certain creditors, including public utilities, creditors dealing in securities credit, and incidental consumer creditors, are exempt from certain of the record retention requirements.[107]

Creditors must also retain certain information obtained for monitoring purposes. This information can be very helpful for credit discrimination claims, because it consists of information concerning the race, sex and other characteristics of mortgage applicants.[108]

4.4.3 Credit Reporting Agency Files

Information collected on an applicant by a credit reporting agency is useful for several reasons. If information from a credit reporting agency is given by the creditor as the grounds for denial of credit, it is useful to check to see if the creditor in fact contacted the agency before denying credit and what the applicant's record indicates. In any case, as it is likely that the creditor will bring up that record as a

---

98 *See* § 10.2.12, *infra*.

99 *See* § 10.2.12, *infra*.

100 *See* § 10.3.1, *infra*. In its 1999 proposed revisions to Regulation B, the Federal Reserve Board expanded the record retention requirements to include information on preapproved credit solicitations. If the revisions become final, creditors who solicit potential customers for credit will be required to retain any preapproved credit solicitation, the list of criteria the creditor used to select the recipients of the solicitation, any correspondence related to complaints about the solicitation, and any component of any marketing plan related to the solicitation. 64 Fed. Reg. 44,582, 44,601 (Aug. 16, 1999) (proposing to add 12 C.F.R. § 202.12(b)(7)). Creditors will be required to keep the information for twenty-five months, or twelve months for certain business credit. *See* 64 Fed. Reg. at 44,584.

101 Reg. B, 12 C.F.R. § 202.12(b)(1).

102 Reg. B, 12 C.F.R. § 202.12(b)(2).

103 Chapter 10 provides more details on ECOA record retention requirements, particularly concerning exemptions from these requirements and the inadvertent error defense. *See* § 10.3, *infra*.

104 Official Staff Commentary, 12 C.F.R. § 202.12(b)-1.

105 Reg. B, 12 C.F.R. § 202.12(b)(3); *see* § 10.3.1, *infra*.

106 12 C.F.R. § 202.12(b)(4); *see* § 10.3.4, *infra*.

107 *See* § 10.3.2, *infra*.

108 This information is described in more detail in § 4.4.5, *infra*.

defense, it will be important for the applicant to know what the record contains.

If information from a reporting agency is the grounds for denial of credit, the creditor must disclose this fact, along with the name of the reporting agency utilized. The applicant may obtain a copy of the record for no charge if a request is made to the reporting agency within sixty days.[109]

If the applicant does not receive a notice of credit denial or fails to request a copy of the report within sixty days, she can still order a report directly from the main credit reporting agencies. Reports can be ordered from the three main agencies, Equifax, Experian, and Trans Union, by mail or phone, or via the internet.[110] For other credit reporting agencies, the best approach is to look up credit reporting in the yellow pages and contact several reporting agencies.

Consumers are entitled to a free report if, as noted above, they were denied credit because of information in the file within the past sixty days. In addition, consumers can obtain free reports annually in any of the following circumstances:

- The consumer lives in a state that allows one free report each year;[111]
- The consumer is unemployed and planning to apply for a job within sixty days;[112]
- The consumer is receiving public welfare assistance;[113] or
- The consumer reasonably believes the credit file contains errors due to fraud.[114]

In other cases, fees are limited by federal law and in some cases by state law.[115]

4.4.4 Testers

Testers are an important source of information about a creditor's practices. Testers are most frequently used by fair housing organizations, by other non-profit organizations and, in some cases, by the government. Typically, paired testers are used who have been similarly trained and who are instructed to act in an identical manner and provide identical information. The only difference is the tester's race, sex or other characteristic that would suggest discrimination on a prohibited basis.

Courts have approved the use of testers in the context of fair housing litigation, agreeing that it would be difficult to prove discrimination in housing without this means of gathering evidence and that the evidence from testing is frequently valuable if not indispensable.[116] Testers can even bring actions in their own name for Fair Housing Act violations, although they must be a legitimate "applicant" to bring an ECOA action.[117]

Testers are perhaps the best approach to use to determine if potential applicants are being turned away *before* they can submit an application. This is because Home Mortgage Disclosure Act (HMDA) data and other statistics on the racial or other composition of loan denials do not measure pre-application discrimination. Testers can discover, for example, if the white tester's application is taken at the local branch office while the African-American tester is sent across town to a different office.[118] Evidence of discrimination prior to application should on its own be sufficient to show violation of the credit discrimination laws, even without specific evidence of subsequent discrimination in the application process.[119]

4.4.5 Home Mortgage Disclosure Act (HMDA) Data

4.4.5.1 General

The Home Mortgage Disclosure Act[120] and Federal Reserve Board (FRB) Regulation C[121] require that lenders collect certain data on loan applicants, and that the Federal Financial Institutions Examination Council prepare disclosure statements and produce various reports on the practices of these individual lenders. For each metropolitan statistical area, each lender's disclosure statement shows lending pat-

---

109   15 U.S.C. § 1681m(b).

110   The websites, as of April 2002, are: Equifax: http://www. Equifax.com; Experian: http://www.experian.com; Trans Union: http://www.tuc.com. *See generally* National Consumer Law Center, Fair Credit Reporting Act § 3.4 (4th ed. 1998 and Supp.).

111   For a list of these states and additional information, see National Consumer Law Center, Fair Credit Reporting Act § 3.4.5.2 (4th ed. 1998 and Supp.).

112   15 U.S.C. § 1681j(c).

113   15 U.S.C. § 1681j(c).

114   15 U.S.C. § 1681j(c).

115   *See generally* National Consumer Law Center, Fair Credit Reporting Act § 3.4.5.1 (4th ed. 1998 and Supp.).

116   *See, e.g.,* Havens Realty Corp. v. Coleman, 455 U.S. 363, 102 S. Ct. 1114, 71 L. Ed. 2d 214 (1982); Richardson v. Howard, 712 F.2d 319 (7th Cir. 1983); Hamilton v. Miller, 477 F.2d 908, 910 n.1 (10th Cir. 1973); Zuch v. Hussey, 394 F. Supp. 1028 (E.D. Mich. 1975).

117   *See* §§ 11.2.2, 11.2.3, *infra.*

118   *See* § 5.3, *infra.*

119   *See, e.g.,* United States v. Lorantffy Care Ctr., 999 F. Supp. 1037 (N.D. Ohio 1998) (government used testers to look for possible discrimination by assisted living facility in treatment of "walk-ins" requesting information about the facility; defendants argued that because the facility did not admit residents on the basis of a walk-in visit, it could not be violating the FHA; the court disagreed, recognizing that decision makers can discriminate against applicants long before they reach the point of deciding whether to accept an application, and finding that evidence of discrimination in treatment of walk-ins could on its own be a FHA violation, even without evidence of discrimination in subsequent admittances—however, court dismissed claims against individual defendants).

120   12 U.S.C. §§ 2801–2810.

121   12 C.F.R. § 203.

terns by location, age of housing stock, income level, sex, and racial characteristics.[122] In addition to disclosures for each lender, the Council also produces aggregate reports for all lenders within each metropolitan statistical area, broken down by census tract.[123] Plaintiffs can then compare a particular lender's experience with that of the aggregate lenders for the same geographic area.

The FRB, in summarizing the purposes of the HMDA, stated that the HMDA is designed: 1) to provide the public and government officials with data that will help show whether lenders are serving the housing needs of the neighborhoods and communities in which they are located; 2) to help public officials target public investment to promote private investment where it is needed, and 3) to provide data to assist in identifying possible discriminatory lending patterns and in enforcing antidiscrimination statutes.[124]

HMDA data has been the focus of a number of reports and government enforcement actions.[125] In addition, the Department of Justice has used HMDA data in suits against banks for alleged discriminatory lending practices. One case, for example, was based on an alleged disparity in rejection rates between African-American and white credit applicants.[126]

4.4.5.2 Access to HMDA Data

The HMDA disclosure statements, aggregate data, and other reports are available to the public at central data depositories in each metropolitan area. A listing of these depositories can be obtained from the Federal Financial Institutions Examination Council, Washington, DC 20006.[127] Depository institutions are to make every effort to have disclosure statements available before July 1 of the following year.[128] The aggregate data should be produced a few months later.[129]

The Federal Reserve Board releases HMDA data on CD-Rom annually, usually in August. It is also available on-line.[130] Data obtained in this way is designed to allow users to look up one lender at a time. To do more in-depth analysis, users will need to import the data into statistical software or a database manager.[131]

The disclosure statement is also available to the public at the lender's own home office (certain data will also be available at branch offices) for five years after it has been completed.[132] In addition, the public has access to the bank's complete loan application register (that is, the original data before it is aggregated for statistical purposes) after the bank makes certain modifications to protect the individual applicants' privacy.[133] Requests for the previous calendar year's register received March 1 or before must be fulfilled by March 31. After March 31, requests must be fulfilled within thirty days.[134] Unlike the disclosure statement, the loan application register need only be retained for three years.[135] The lender must make the disclosure statement and the register available for copying and inspection during normal business hours, and it may impose a reasonable photocopying charge.[136]

4.4.5.3 Scope of HMDA

4.4.5.3.1 Current regulations

The HMDA reporting requirements only apply to federally insured or regulated lenders, or to loans which are insured by a federal agency or which the lender intends to sell to Fannie Mae or Freddie Mac.[137] Even then the Act does not apply to smaller institutions or to those that do not do business in a metropolitan area.[138] Institutions not subject to the HMDA requirements must still keep information for monitoring purposes pursuant to the ECOA.[139]

---

122 12 C.F.R. § 203.1(d).
123 12 U.S.C. § 2809.
124 67 Fed. Reg. 7222 (Feb. 15, 2002).
125 *See, e.g.*, Ass'n of Community Organizations for Reform Now (ACORN), Separate and Unequal: Predatory Lending in America (Nov. 2001), *available at* http://www.acorn.org; Ass'n of Community Organizations for Reform Now, The Great Divide: An Analysis of Racial and Economic Disparities in Home Purchase Mortgage Lending Nationally and in Sixty Metropolitan Areas (Oct. 2001); Daniel Immergluck & Marti Wiles, Two Steps Back: The Dual Mortgage Market: Predatory Lending and the Undoing of Community Development (Woodstock Inst. 1999).
126 United States v. Decatur Fed. Sav. & Loan Ass'n, Clearinghouse No. 49,126 (N.D. Ga. 1992) (complaint) [reproduced on the CD-Rom accompanying this volume]. The complaint resulted in a far-reaching consent decree. *See id.* (consent decree) [reproduced on the CD-Rom accompanying this volume]; *see also* § 12.4.3.2, *infra*.
127 12 C.F.R. § 203.1(d). For more information, see http://www.ffiec.gov.
128 12 U.S.C. § 2803(*l*).
129 12 U.S.C. § 2803(*l*).

130 To obtain more information by phone, call 202-452-2016 (HMDA Assistance Line); on-line, visit http://www.ffiec.gov/hmda.
131 *See generally* Jo Craven McGinty, Home Mortgage Lending: How to detect disparities (Investigative Reporters & Editors, Inc. 2000). A number of websites have information about analyzing and obtaining access to HMDA data, including: The Center for Community Change (http://www.communitychange.org); Inner City Press (http://www.innercitypress.org); and National Fair Housing Advocate (http://www.fairhousing.com).
132 12 C.F.R. § 203.5(b),(d).
133 12 C.F.R. § 203.5(c).
134 12 C.F.R. § 203.5(c).
135 12 C.F.R. § 203.5(d).
136 12 C.F.R. § 203.5(d).
137 12 C.F.R. § 203.2(e).
138 12 C.F.R. § 203.3(a). A bank, savings association or credit union is exempt if its total assets are less than $28 million. Other for-profit mortgage lenders must have total assets (including those of a parent) under $10 million and have originated fewer than one-hundred home purchase loans in the preceding year.
139 *See* § 4.4.7, *infra*.

The HMDA, however, is broader in scope than the ECOA in that lenders not only have to obtain monitoring data for loans to purchase or refinance a principal residence, but also for home improvement loans.[140] Beginning in January 2004, as discussed below, certain lenders will also be required to report data on subprime loans.

Currently, the lender must keep the following data for each covered loan: the type and purpose of the loan, the amount of the loan, the action taken, the date the action was taken, the location of the property, the applicant's race or national origin, sex, and income, and the loan purchaser.[141] The exact form this data is to be retained in is set forth in Regulation C, Appendix A.[142] Lenders will still be required to keep this same data after December 2003, but certain lenders will have additional data collection requirements.

4.4.5.3.2 Changes to HMDA effective January 2004[143]

In January 2002, the Federal Reserve Board (FRB) announced changes in Regulation C intended to provide more consistent and comprehensive information about mortgage lending activity and to aid in fair lending enforcement. These changes are summarized below.

Two changes relate to the reporting of subprime loans. The first is a new requirement that lenders designate on their HMDA reports which of the loans they originate are high-cost loans, subject to the provisions of the Home Ownership Equity Protection Act (HOEPA).[144]

The second predatory lending-related change requires additional reporting on loan pricing. The Board rejected a proposal to require reporting of annual percentage rates (APRs), instead adopting a scheme based on the difference between the APR on the loan and the yield on a comparable security issued by the U.S. Treasury. The Board set out tentative thresholds for reporting these spreads.[145] For first lien loans, if that spread is more than three percentage points, lenders will have to report how big the spread is. For junior lien loans, lenders will have to report the spread if it

is more than five percentage points.[146] This regulation is limited to originations of home purchase loans, secured home improvement loans, and refinancings.[147] The following are excluded from the reporting requirements: 1) applications that are incomplete, withdrawn, denied, or approved but not accepted; 2) purchased loans; and 3) unsecured home improvement loans.[148]

The FRB also made changes intended to expand the scope of lenders that must maintain HMDA data. Currently, non-depository for-profit lenders must maintain and report HMDA data only if they have assets above $10 million, originated at least one hundred home purchase or refinance loans in the previous calendar year, and their mortgage lending activity constituted 10% or more of their total loan volume (measured in dollars).[149] The Board responded to concerns that a number of large consumer finance companies that are active mortgage lenders apparently were not required to report HMDA data because they did not reach the 10% volume level.[150] Rather than eliminating the 10% requirement, the Board added a requirement that nondepository lenders whose mortgage lending activity amounted to $25 million in the previous calendar year must report HMDA data, even if this lending constituted less than 10% of the institutions' total loan volume.[151]

Among other important changes the FRB made is a requirement that lenders indicate which applications are for manufactured homes.[152] The new rule also changes the definition of a refinancing loan that must be reported under the HMDA. The new definition covers loans that pay off and replace an existing loan, when both loans are secured by a lien on the dwelling.[153] Previously, lenders could choose from among four scenarios in deciding which refinancing loans to report, leading to inconsistent data.[154]

The Board also changed the definition of a home improvement loan to include any loan secured by a dwelling that is made in whole or in part for home improvement purposes.[155] Previously, lenders had discretion whether to classify a loan as a home improvement loan. This discretion will remain only for home improvement loans that are not secured by a dwelling.[156] The exception to this new reporting requirement is "home equity lines of credit" which

---

140 12 C.F.R. § 203.4(a).

141 12 C.F.R. § 203.4(a).

142 12 C.F.R. § 203 app. A.

143 On May 2, 2002, the Federal Reserve Board announced a delay in the effective date of these changes from January 1, 2003, to January 1, 2004. The Board did, however, adopt an interim amendment mandating the use of 2000 Census data in HMDA reporting.

144 67 Fed. Reg. 7222, 7230 (Feb. 15, 2002) (amending 12 C.F.R. § 203.4(a)(13)). *See generally* National Consumer Law Center, Truth In Lending Ch. 10 (4th ed. 1999 and Supp.) (HOEPA); Center for Community Change, Home Mortgage Disclosure Act: Fed Announces New Mortgage Disclosure Rules—More Info on Subprime Lending, *available at* http://www.communitychange.org (last visited April 2002).

145 In the February 2002 final rules, the Board solicited additional comment on the thresholds. Final thresholds should be available in mid-2002.

146 67 Fed. Reg. 7222, 7228 (Feb. 15, 2002) (amending 12 C.F.R. § 203.4(a)(12) and (13)).

147 67 Fed. Reg. 7222, 7228 (Feb. 15, 2002).

148 67 Fed. Reg. 7222, 7228 (Feb. 15, 2002).

149 12 C.F.R. § 203.3(a)(2), § 203.2(e).

150 67 Fed. Reg. 7222, 7224 (Feb. 15, 2002) (amending 12 C.F.R. § 203.2(e)).

151 67 Fed. Reg. 7222, 7224 (Feb. 15, 2002).

152 67 Fed. Reg. 7222, 7226 (Feb. 15, 2002) (amending 12 C.F.R. § 203.2(i)).

153 67 Fed. Reg. 7222, 7226 (Feb. 15, 2002) (amending 12 C.F.R. § 203.2(k)).

154 67 Fed. Reg. 7222, 7226 (Feb. 15, 2002).

155 67 Fed. Reg. 7222, 7225 (Feb. 15, 2002) (amending 12 C.F.R. § 203.2(g)).

156 67 Fed. Reg. 7222, 7225 (Feb. 15, 2002).

lenders currently have the option to report or not. This discretion will remain unchanged.[157]

Another significant change is that lenders will now be required to report denials under "covered" pre-approval programs for home purchase loans. These are defined as programs under which the lender issues a written commitment to lend creditworthy borrowers up to a specific amount for a specific amount of time, subject only to limited conditions, such as finding a suitable property. Lenders will also be required to designate which approved loans resulted from a covered pre-appproval program, and will have the option to report on pre-approval requests that were approved but not accepted by the applicant.[158]

The Board also changed the way that race and ethnicity are reported to allow borrowers to designate more than one race or ethnicity. This change is in conformance with other government standards.[159]

These changes take effect for data collected under the HMDA beginning January 1, 2004.

4.4.5.4 Limits to HMDA Data

Great care must be taken in using HMDA and other monitoring data. Data showing higher rejection rates for members of protected groups may not prove illegal discrimination. It may be that these applicants have lower incomes, have different housing collateral, have different credit histories, or some other variable. Further refinement of data is needed to present a persuasive case.

While raw HMDA data can be indicative of discrimination, it can be made more persuasive by further analysis. The Federal Reserve Bank of Boston did the first study that actually took into account the missing variables—information related to legitimate indicators of creditworthiness not contained in HMDA data.[160]

The results of the Boston study go a long way toward explaining the difficulties of proving credit discrimination. The study found that for over eighty percent of borrowers of whatever race, there is a legitimate creditworthiness reason to deny credit. The minority of people who are truly creditworthy, irrespective of race, almost always will be offered credit.

However, the Boston study found that for the remaining eighty percent of applicants, while nondiscriminatory fac-

tors account for a large portion of the discrepancy in denial rates, race remains a significant factor.[161] In Boston, the raw HMDA data showed that the African-American denial rate was 170% higher than the white denial rate. However, the researchers found that some of this difference was not based on race, but on the fact that African-Americans were more likely to have higher loan-to-value ratios, had weaker credit histories, and were more likely to seek loans on multi-family instead of single family homes.

This expanded HMDA study looked at thirty-eight additional variables, identified from extensive discussions with lenders as to what they consider in making a credit decision. While the raw HMDA data showed the African-American denial rate was 170% higher than the white denial rate, the expanded Boston HMDA study, after controlling for all of the relevant characteristics, showed that the rate was still 56% higher. In other words, much of the difference could be explained by legitimate factors that more heavily impact African-Americans, but a significant part of the difference could only be explained by race.[162]

A major problem with HMDA or related data is that it tends to miss subtle forms of discrimination that prevent individuals from even applying to a lender, thus keeping these individuals out of the HMDA data completely. One way to discover if this sort of discrimination is happening is to use paired testers.[163] In addition, the location of the lender's branches, racial composition of its staff, advertising practices and other conduct may indicate whether there is discrimination on a prohibited basis as to the way consumers are encouraged or discouraged to apply.[164]

A second problem with HMDA data is that the legacy of discrimination affects standards of creditworthiness such as accumulated wealth, income, and property values in non-white neighborhoods. There is a debate as to whether differences in, for example, the granting of credit to nonwhites today is primarily due to these factors of creditworthiness that vary by race or ethnicity or due to ongoing discrimination. In any case, the HMDA data does not illuminate this debate because the data set does not question the premises of what it means to be creditworthy or to what extent the traditional standards are inherently biased due to past discrimination.[165]

---

157 67 Fed. Reg. 7222, 7225 (Feb. 15, 2002) (amending 12 C.F.R. § 203.2(f)).

158 67 Fed. Reg. 7222, 7223 (Feb. 15, 2002) (amending 12 C.F.R. § 203.2(b)).

159 67 Fed. Reg. 7222, 7228 (Feb. 15, 2002) (amending 12 C.F.R. § 202.4(a)(10)).

160 Alicia Munnell et al., Mortgage Lending in Boston: Interpreting HMDA Data (Fed. Reserve Bank of Boston, Working Paper Series No. 92-7, 1992) (available from Federal Reserve Bank of Boston, Research Library-D, P.O. Box 2076, Boston, MA 02016-2076, 617-973-3397) (also available as Clearinghouse No. 47,967).

161 *Id.*

162 *Id.*

163 *See* § 4.4.4, *supra.*

164 *See* § 5.3, *infra; see also* The Urban Inst., Mortgage Lending Discrimination: A Review of Existing Evidence ch. 1 (Margery Austin Turner & Felicity Skidmore, eds., 1999) (a summary of possible discrimination in all phases of a credit transaction, including a summary of the evidence from advertising and outreach, pre-application inquiries, loan approval or denial, loan administration).

165 The Urban Inst., Mortgage Lending Discrimination: A Review of Existing Evidence ch. 1 (1999)

4.4.6 Other Sources of Mortgage Data

There are some supplementary data sources that can be useful in analyzing HMDA data. Census data, for example, provides detailed information for each census tract and can be obtained from the Bureau of the Census.[166] Information about the location of lenders' offices is available from the Federal Deposit Insurance Corporation.[167] The Federal Reserve also has some useful information available on its website.[168]

Community Reinvestment Act ratings may also be helpful. These are available only from lenders who are required to provide the information.[169] Advocates should also consider contacting government enforcement agencies for information about public investigations and complaints.

4.4.7 Monitoring Data Required by the ECOA

In addition to the HMDA requirements, the ECOA also requires creditors to retain certain information for monitoring purposes. This requirement is significant for two reasons. First, certain smaller institutions, institutions that do not do business within a metropolitan area, and lenders with no federal connection need not comply with the HMDA requirements, while the ECOA requirements apply to all creditors, thus including every mortgage lender.[170] However, the ECOA requirement only applies when a consumer seeks a loan to purchase or refinance a principal residence, and does not apply to home improvement loans.[171]

Second, the ECOA requirement includes a few pieces of information not required by the HMDA (although much of the HMDA data is not required by the ECOA). The ECOA requires the creditor to obtain certain information also required by the HMDA (the applicant's race or national origin, and sex) and also requires information on marital status (married, unmarried, or separated) and age.[172]

The ECOA data is not routinely compiled into reports like the HMDA data, and the data is not generally open for inspection. Nevertheless, the relevant enforcement agency may have requested the data, and may have compiled it in some fashion. The enforcement agency may also require the lender to provide additional or different information.[173]

The monitoring information required by the ECOA should also be available through discovery from the creditor itself, although the creditor need not have compiled the information. The raw records must be retained by the creditor for at least twenty-five months, and cannot be disposed of once an investigation or civil action is instituted.[174]

4.4.8 Non-Mortgage Data

Except for HMDA and ECOA mortgage data, a creditor legally should not have statistics as to the racial, sexual or other characteristics of those denied or approved for credit. However, there are other possible sources of data. For example, in cases challenging the mark-up policies of car financing creditors, plaintiffs based their statistical proof of discrimination on race-coded drivers licenses.[175]

If proposed revisions to Regulation B become final, the amount of non-mortgage data available to show discrimination should be greatly expanded. In these revisions, the Federal Reserve Board proposed removing the prohibition on seeking information about an applicant's race, color, religion, national origin and sex for non-mortgage credit products.[176] This proposal was made in response to comments from the Department of Justice and the federal financial enforcement agencies that the enhanced ability to obtain data on race and ethnicity would aid fair lending enforcement, particularly with respect to small business lending.[177] The proposal simply removes the prohibition on collecting such data but does not require creditors to gather this information.

In addressing the concern that removing the prohibition might actually increase instances of discrimination, the 1999 proposed revisions require creditors who request information on these characteristics to disclose at the time of the request that providing the information is optional and that

---

166 Census data is available on-line at http://www.census.gov.

167 This information is available online at http://www.fdic.gov, or by mail or phone from Federal Deposit Insurance Corp., Office of the Ombudsman, 550 17th St., NW, Washington, D.C. 20429-9990, 877-ASK-FDIC (275-3342).

168 *See* http://www.ffiec.gov/NIC/default.htm.

169 *See* § 1.9, *supra*.

170 *See* Reg. B, 12 C.F.R. § 202.13(a).

171 Reg. B, 12 C.F.R. § 202.13(a).

172 Reg. B, 12 C.F.R. § 202.13(a).

173 Reg. B, 12 C.F.R. § 202.13(d); Official Staff Commentary, 12 C.F.R. § 202.13(d)-1.

174 *See* § 10.3, *infra*.

175 Expert reports in these cases are reproduced on the CD-Rom accompanying this volume. The report of Professor Mark Cohen reviewed the data on auto finance customers provided by Nissan Motors Acceptance Corp. (NMAC) through discovery, which was race-coded based upon the automobile license information subpoenaed from the eleven states that include race data in their registry of motor vehicle records. Since the time of the report, three additional states produced race-coded drivers license information. Since the success of the plaintiffs in defending against motions for summary judgment in these cases against NMAC and General Motors Acceptance Corp., consumers have filed nationwide class cases against Ford, Chrysler, and Toyota in federal courts. For more information on these cases, see http://www.faircreditlaw.com. *See* Coleman v. Gen. Motors Acceptance Corp., 196 F.R.D. 315 (M.D. Tenn. 2000). The court in the NMAC case issued an oral decision on August 24, 2000. *See also* Jones v. Ford Motor Credit Co., 2002 U.S. Dist. LEXIS 1098 (S.D.N.Y. Jan. 18, 2002).

176 64 Fed. Reg. 44,582, 44,586 (Aug. 16, 1999) (amending 12 C.F.R. § 202.5).

177 64 Fed. Reg. 44,582, 44,586 (Aug. 16, 1999).

the creditor will not take the information, or the applicant's decision not to provide the information, into account in any aspect of the credit transaction.[178] In addition, the Board proposed adding a new section to Regulation B to emphasize that a creditor may not consider race, color, religion, national origin or sex to determine an applicant's creditwor-

thiness, except as permitted by law, nor may a creditor consider an applicant's decision not to provide the information.[179] Borrowers are not required to provide the information. A sample disclosure form is included with the proposed rules.[180]

---

178 64 Fed. Reg. 44,582, 44,596 (Aug. 16, 1999).

179 64 Fed. Reg. 44,582, 44,597 (Aug. 16, 1999).
180 64 Fed. Reg. 44,582, 44,616 app. C (Aug. 16, 1999).

Chapter 5   Discrimination in Pre-Application and Application Procedures

5.1 Introduction

5.1.1 The Special ECOA Requirements

As a fundamental principle, the ECOA, the FHA, and other credit discrimination statutes set forth a general rule against discrimination in every aspect of a credit transaction. The ECOA also has special requirements that creditors must follow in the various stages of a credit transaction. The Fair Housing Act and Civil Rights Acts do not have equivalent special requirements.

For purposes of the special ECOA requirements, there are five major stages in a credit transaction:

- the application for credit and other initial procedures;
- the creditor's evaluation of that application;
- the decision to grant credit and on what terms credit is granted;
- notification to the applicant of the creditor's decision; and
- the various procedures after credit is granted.

It is important to remember that the special ECOA requirements are in addition to, and do not in any way limit, the general rule against discrimination in the ECOA, the FHA, and the federal Civil Rights Acts.[1]

5.1.2 Discussion of the Stages of a Credit Transaction In This Manual

The next few chapters of this manual will follow the four major stages in a credit transaction. Each chapter will discuss both general discriminatory practices and the special ECOA requirements specific to that stage of the credit process.

This chapter focuses on discrimination in the pre-application and application stages of a credit transaction. It will discuss general discrimination at these stages, including discriminatory marketing of credit and disparities in the application process for protected groups. This chapter also discusses the relevant special ECOA requirements, including what information creditors can request in an application and who can be required to cosign a credit obligation.

Next, Chapter 6 analyzes general discrimination and special ECOA requirements concerning the evaluation of an application. Chapter 7 focuses on discrimination in the granting of credit, focusing on the issue of redlining. Chapter 8 discusses discrimination regarding the terms of credit, focusing on the critical issue of predatory lending as a form of such discrimination. Chapter 9 discusses discrimination following the granting of credit. Chapter 10 discusses the special ECOA requirements for notification of action taken on an application for credit.

5.2 General Rule Against Discrimination

5.2.1 Introduction

Before discussing discrimination specific to each stage of the credit transaction, it is helpful to understand some principles about the general rule against discrimination embodied in the ECOA, the FHA, the Civil Rights Acts, and other credit discrimination statutes.

5.2.2 What Is "Discrimination" Under the General Rule?

To "discriminate" is defined by Regulation B as treating an applicant less favorably than other applicants.[2] Consequently, the ECOA prohibits treating an applicant less favorably than other applicants on a prohibited basis at any stage of the credit transaction, ranging from application procedures to terms of the transaction to subsequent handling of defaults. This broad standard can be aggressively

---

1 *See* Official Staff Commentary, 12 C.F.R. § 202.4-1 ("Thus, whether or not specifically prohibited elsewhere in the regulation, a credit practice that treats applicants differently on a prohibited basis violates the law because it violates the general rule.").

2 Reg. B, 12 C.F.R. § 202.2(n).

and innovatively applied to many types of creditor conduct that treats one debtor less favorably than others.

The Fair Housing Act also uses the term "to discriminate" but, unlike the ECOA and its implementing regulation, does not define the term. Most likely, it will be considered as having the same meaning as found under the ECOA. Similarly, the federal Civil Rights Acts require that individuals be treated the "same" as white citizens, indicating a similar standard to that found under the ECOA.

Even though unfavorable treatment constitutes discrimination, it is not necessarily *illegal* discrimination. Discrimination in credit transactions is generally legal unless the discrimination is on a prohibited basis. Another chapter discusses when discrimination is on a prohibited basis and therefore illegal.[3]

5.2.3 The General Rule Applies to All Aspects of a Credit Transaction

The general rule against discrimination applies during every stage of the credit transaction. This is true for the ECOA, the FHA, and the federal Civil Rights Acts.

The ECOA prohibits any creditor from discriminating against any applicant on a prohibited basis with respect to *any* aspect of a credit transaction.[4] The Commentary elaborates that this rule "covers all dealings, without exception, between an applicant and a creditor, whether or not addressed by other provisions of the regulation."[5]

The Fair Housing Act also offers a broad standard as to prohibited conduct. The two different sections that provide the main avenues for relief in credit discrimination cases are both broadly worded. The provision dealing with housing-related financing prohibits discrimination "in making available such a transaction, or in the terms or conditions of such a transaction."[6] The other provision, dealing with the sale or lease of realty, generally prohibits discrimination: in any conduct that would make unavailable the sale or rental of dwellings; in the terms, conditions, or privileges of a sale or rental; or in statements or advertisements offering dwellings for sale or rent.[7] Thus the Fair Housing Act would seem to apply to virtually every stage of a transaction involving the sale or rental of a dwelling, or involving the financing related to a dwelling.

The Federal Civil Rights Acts apply even more clearly to all aspects of a transaction. Section 1981, which ensures the right to "make and enforce contracts," explicitly applies to any aspect of a contractual relationship.[8] Section 1982 refers

to the right of all citizens to "inherit, purchase, lease, sell, hold, and convey real and personal property" and would seem to apply to every aspect of a transaction relating to purchasing or holding real or personal property, including every aspect of a credit transaction.

5.3 Discrimination in the Pre-Application Stage of a Credit Transaction

5.3.1 Overview

The first stage of a credit transaction in which discrimination may occur is before the actual application—when the creditor takes various actions to encourage or discourage persons from seeking credit from that creditor. While most of the ECOA applies only to "applicants,"[9] Regulation B does include a pre-application prohibition forbidding creditors from discouraging prospective applicants on a prohibited basis.[10] The FHA contains a similar prohibition.[11]

Attacking pre-application discrimination is critical because creditors who want to discriminate illegally have a strong incentive to keep minorities, public assistance recipients, or others from applying. If an individual never applies, it will be difficult for that individual to complain about being denied credit. Similarly, the federal Home Mortgage Disclosure Act requires creditors to report racial and other characteristics of mortgage applicants.[12] If individuals never apply, the lender need not report the individual as being denied credit.

In addition, pre-application discrimination has become important because of the growth in predatory lending targeted at minority communities, known as reverse redlining, discussed in Chapter 8. One potential factor supporting this growth is discriminatory marketing by lenders, resulting in white applicants being steered to prime products while applicants of color are steered to subprime products.

5.3.2 Marketing Discrimination

5.3.2.1 The ECOA Standard

Regulation B specifically prohibits any oral or written statement to prospective applicants in advertising or otherwise that would discourage, on a prohibited basis, a reason-

---

3 *See* Chapter 3, *supra.*
4 15 U.S.C. § 1691(a); *see* Reg. B, 12 C.F.R. § 202.4.
5 Official Staff Commentary, 12 C.F.R. § 202.4-1.
6 42 U.S.C. § 3605(a); *see* 24 C.F.R. § 100.110(b).
7 42 U.S.C. § 3604(a), (b); 24 C.F.R. § 100.50.
8 [T]he term "make and enforce contracts" includes the making, performance, modification, and termination of contracts, and the

enjoyment of all benefits, privileges, terms, and conditions of the contractual relationship. 42 U.S.C. § 1981.
9 Official Staff Commentary, 12 C.F.R. § 202.5(a)-1.
10 Reg. B, 12 C.F.R. § 202.5(a); *see* § 5.3.2.1, *infra.*
11 42 U.S.C. § 3604(a), (b); *see* § 5.3.2.2, *infra.*
12 20 U.S.C. § 2801; *see* § 4.4.5, *supra,* § 5.5.6, *infra.*

able person from pursuing an application.[13] Similarly, the ECOA's general rule against discrimination prohibits advertising and other marketing that discriminates on a prohibited basis as to who is encouraged to apply.[14]

The Regulation B prohibition covers oral or written statements by the creditor in advertising or otherwise.[15] A reasonable person test is used to determine whether the applicant "should have been" discouraged by the creditor's actions.[16]

The Commentary gives examples of prohibited discouragement, which include:[17]

- A statement that the applicant should not bother to apply after the applicant states that he is retired;
- Use of words, symbols, models or other communication in advertising that even implies or suggests a discriminatory preference; and
- Use of interview scripts that discourage applicants on a prohibited basis.

However, prohibited discouragement is not limited to these examples.

Other creditor actions which discourage applications include creditor practices at its place of business, such as sending minorities to different locations to apply, encouraging potential applicants to apply at other banks, and indicating it would take a long time to have an application processed.[18] Another means of discouraging minority applicants is through the hiring of an all-white workforce by the creditor or using solely white actors in advertisements.[19] Unreasonably delaying the processing of applications from members of protected groups may also be discriminatory.[20] But one court has ruled that creditors need not provide prospective credit applicants with pamphlets or other informational literature explaining their rights under the ECOA, concluding that failure to provide such literature was irrel-

evant to whether the creditor was discouraging credit applications.[21]

Another means of discouraging applicants on a prohibited basis is a practice called "steering." Steering occurs when a loan officer refers potential applicants away from one type of product or market (e.g., a prime product) to another (e.g., a subprime product).[22] While steering may be legitimate, it can be discriminatory if mostly minority applicants are being steered from more favorable to less favorable products. Steering sometimes occurs when lenders offer government-backed mortgages as well as conventional mortgage or when they operate in both the prime and subprime markets.[23] A guidance document issued by several financial regulatory agencies suggests that steering on a prohibited basis violates Regulation B.[24]

Another means of discouraging applicants is through discriminatory marketing practices.[25] A self-assessment guide from the Federal Deposit Insurance Corp. (FDIC) on fair lending practices cautions lenders about the following marketing practices that may discourage applicants on a prohibited basis:

- Marketing strategies that fail to include contact with minority realtors and other realtors serving predominantly minority areas—the FDIC guide notes that, in those instances, there is almost always a low level of minority applicants;
- Failing to advertise in media directed to minority areas, or in media known to appeal to minorities, which can

---

13 Reg. B, 12 C.F.R. § 202.5(a).

14 *See* § 5.2.2, *supra*.

15 Reg. B, 12 C.F.R. § 202.5(a).

16 Reg. B, 12 C.F.R. § 202.5(a). No guidance is given as to what constitutes a reasonable person under this provision. Arguably, reference should be to a reasonable person belonging to the protected category. Clearly, the test should not be whether a reasonable middle-class white male applicant who has never encountered discrimination based on race or sex would have been discouraged by the creditor's actions.

17 Official Staff Commentary, 12 C.F.R. § 202.5(a)-1.

18 *See* § 5.3.3, *infra*.

19 *See, e.g.*, Ragin v. Harry Macklowe Real Estate, Co., 6 F.3d 898 (2d Cir. 1993); Saunders v. Gen. Services Corp., 659 F. Supp. 1042 (E.D. Va. 1987).

20 *See* Thompson v. Marine Midland Bank, 1999 U.S. App. LEXIS 22960 (2d Cir. Sept. 16, 1999) (although plaintiffs' allegations of delay in processing of applications may have constituted disparate treatment, the court found that defendant provided a legitimate, non-discriminatory reason for the delay; therefore, a prima facie case of discrimination was not established).

21 Vander Missen v. Kellogg-Citizens Nat'l Bank, 481 F. Supp. 742 (E.D. Wis. 1979).

22 Fed. Fin. Institutions Examination Council, Interagency Fair Lending Examination Procedures Guide 21, Clearinghouse No. 53,526 (1999), *available at* http://www.ffiec.gov/PDF/fairlend/pdf. The F.F.E.I.C. is a formal interagency body that prescribes uniform standards for the examination of financial institutions by the Federal Reserve Board (FRB), the Federal Deposit Insurance Corporation (FDIC), the National Credit Union Administration (NCUA), the Office of the Comptroller of the Currency (OCC), and the Office of Thrift Supervision (OTS). The F.F.E.I.C. is also responsible for reporting HMDA data. *See* § 4.4.5.2, *supra*, § 12.2.4, *infra*.

23 *Id.*; *see, e.g.*, Johnson v. Equicredit Corp., 2002 U.S. Dist. LEXIS 4817 (N.D. Ill. Mar. 22, 2002) (allegations of steering against Bank of America, a prime lender, which owns Equicredit, a subprime lender).

24 Fed. Fin. Institutions Examination Council, Interagency Fair Lending Examination Procedures Guide 21, Clearinghouse No. 53,526 (1999), *available at* http://www.ffiec.gov/PDF/fairlend/pdf.

25 Examples of discriminatory marketing practices are discussed at § 5.3.2.3, *infra*. Some commentators have argued that marketing discrimination is not actionable under the ECOA and the FHA because there is no individual applicant who has been discriminated against. *See* Michael B. Mierzewski & Richard L. Jacobs, *What Hath Justice Department Wrought*, Banking Pol'y Rep., Feb. 6, 1995, at 8; John Spina, *United States v. Albank, FSB: Is 'Justice' Served in the Enforcement of Fair Lending Laws*, 2 N.C. Banking Inst. 207 (1998). These commentators seemed to have ignored Regulation B, 12 C.F.R. § 202.5(a).

limit the ability of the institution to attract minority applicants.[26]

The prohibition against acts to discourage applicants in no way prevents creditors from encouraging applications from disadvantaged groups. The Commentary specifically states: "A creditor may affirmatively solicit or encourage members of traditionally disadvantaged groups to apply for credit, especially groups that might not normally seek credit from that creditor."[27]

For example, the Federal Reserve Board gave approval to a California statute that requires creditors to provide Spanish-speaking applicants with the opportunity to obtain an unexecuted Spanish language contract.[28] The Board reasoned that the statute made contract terms more understandable to applicants of one national origin without interfering with the interests of any other group and therefore did not frustrate the intent of the ECOA.[29]

5.3.2.2 The Fair Housing Act Standard

The Fair Housing Act regulations prohibit discrimination on a prohibited basis concerning the provision of information, including information concerning the availability of loans or other financial assistance, application requirements, procedures or standards for the review and approval of loans and financial assistance.[30] The Fair Housing Act explicitly applies to advertising and should also apply to any other type of marketing that discriminates on a prohibited basis as to its target audience.[31]

5.3.2.3 Marketing Discrimination as a Force in Predatory Lending

Recent studies have shown that subprime lenders com-

prise the greater share of lending in non-white neighborhoods.[32] This pattern appears to hold true even in middle-class and higher-income areas, indicating that the segmentation of the market into prime and subprime is correlated more strongly with race than with income.[33]

If the prime and subprime markets are segmented more by race than income, it means that many African-Americans and Hispanics who receive subprime loans were actually qualified for prime loans.[34] This phenomenon raises questions as to why the prime and subprime market are so strongly segmented by race and why such an inordinate number of applicants of color who potentially qualify for prime loans end up with subprime loans.

One reason for this troubling dual market is the use of disparate and even discriminatory marketing practices by lenders. On the one hand, prime lenders focus their marketing efforts almost exclusively in white neighborhoods. These lenders locate their branches in predominately white neighborhoods, making it convenient for white applicants to apply and obtain prime loans. They advertise only in mainstream media. Their loan officers, who are mostly white, market loans almost exclusively to realtors serving white neighborhoods. These lenders may even offer better deals on the internet, which has its own racial divide.[35]

On the other hand, subprime lenders focus their market-

---

26 Fed. Deposit Ins. Co., Side-by-Side, A Guide to Fair Lending 28 (June 1996), *available at* http://www.fdic.gov.

27 Official Staff Commentary, 12 C.F.R. § 202.5(a)-2.

28 Cal. Civ. Code § 1632 (West). The Federal Reserve Board has also recently issued an amendment to Regulation B that specifically permits creditors to provide ECOA notices in a language other than English as long as it is available in English upon request. Reg. B, 12 C.F.R. § 202.4(b). This provision was added as part of the Board's interim final rule issued March 30, 2001, concerning electronic disclosures. 66 Fed. Reg. 17,779–17,786 (Apr. 4, 2001); *see* § 10.2.6.2.1, *infra*.

29 Fed. Reserve Bd., Official Board Interpretation § 202.1102, 42 Fed. Reg. 22,861 (May 5, 1977). This interpretation was not included in the 1985 Official Commentary to Regulation B. However, the FRB chose not to include in the Official Commentary any interpretation which did not preempt state law and so, presumably, the California statute remains acceptable. Moreover, § 202.1102 is an official board interpretation, not a staff interpretation, and should therefore not be superseded by staff commentary.

30 24 C.F.R. § 100.120(b).

31 42 U.S.C. § 3604(a), (b).

32 *See, e.g.,* Daniel Immergluck & Marti Wiles, Two Steps Back: The Dual Mortgage Market, Predatory Lending, and the Undoing of Community Development (Woodstock Inst. Nov. 1999), *available at* http://www.woodstockinst.org; Ass'n of Community Organizations for Reform Now (ACORN), The Great Divide: An Analysis of Racial and Economic Disparities in Home Purchase Mortgage Lending Nationally and in Sixty Metropolitan Areas, (Oct. 2001); U.S. Dep't of Hous. & Urban Dev. (HUD), Unequal Burden: Income & Racial Disparities in Subprime Lending in America (Apr. 2000), *available at* http://www.hud.gov. *See generally* Frank Lopez, *Using the Fair Housing Act to Combat Predatory Lending*, 6 Geo. J. on Poverty L. & Pol'y 73 (1999).

33 Daniel Immergluck & Marti Wiles, Two Steps Back: The Dual Mortgage Market, Predatory Lending, and the Undoing of Community Development (Woodstock Inst. Nov. 1999), *available at* http://www.woodstockinst.org; Ass'n of Community Organizations for Reform Now (ACORN), The Great Divide: An Analysis of Racial and Economic Disparities in Home Purchase Mortgage Lending Nationally and in Sixty Metropolitan Areas, (Oct. 2001); U.S. Dep't of Hous. & Urban Dev. (HUD), Unequal Burden: Income & Racial Disparities in Subprime Lending in America (Apr. 2000), *available at* http://www.hud.gov. *See generally* Frank Lopez, *Using the Fair Housing Act to Combat Predatory Lending*, 6 Geo. J. on Poverty L. & Pol'y 73 (1999). For more information on this issue, see Chapter 8, *infra*.

34 *See* Freddie Mac, Automated Underwriting: Making Mortgage Lending Simpler and Fairer for America's Families, ch. 5 n.5 (1996) (based on 15,000 loans from four lenders, finding that 10% to 35% of borrowers who got subprime mortgages qualified for conventional mortgages), *available at* http://www.freddiemac.com/corporate/reports.

35 *See* § 3.8.2, *supra* (on credit discrimination and the digital divide).

ing efforts on communities of color. These lenders place their advertisements in traditional African-American or Hispanic media outlets. They solicit business from mortgage brokers who serve communities of color. They locate their offices in these communities and often represent the sole option for borrowers, given the lack of bank branches in these neighborhoods.

In some instances, the subprime lender is actually a subsidiary of or otherwise related to a prime lender. For example, Bank of America, a prime lender, owned Equicredit, a subprime lender. A credit discrimination lawsuit brought in Chicago alleged that Equicredit made loans almost exclusively in minority areas while Bank of America made loans in predominately white areas.[36] Another major financial institution with subprime subsidiaries is Citigroup, which acquired subprime lender Associates National Bank in November 2000. Community groups objected to the acquisition for a number of reasons, including the fact that Citigroup's prime lending unit primarily made loans in white neighborhoods, while Associates's subprime and often predatory loans were made in neighborhoods of color.[37]

5.3.2.4 How Discrimination in Marketing Happens

A good example of how the dual market for credit develops can be found by contrasting the cases of two lenders in the Washington, D.C. area: Chevy Chase Federal Savings Bank and Capital City Mortgage Corp. Chevy Chase, a metropolitan District of Columbia bank, and its subsidiary, B.F. Saul Mortgage, Co., were sued by the U.S. Department of Justice for engaging in a pattern of encouraging white and discouraging African-American mortgage applicants.[38] According to the DOJ, Chevy Chase located

nearly 95% of its bank branches and mortgage offices in white neighborhoods, excluding the vast majority of the D.C area's predominately African-American population. Nearly 98% of the loan officers/originators hired by the mortgage company were not African-American, despite the fact that over 65% of the city's population is African-American. These loan officers actively solicited real estate brokers serving white neighborhoods but rarely solicited brokers serving African-American neighborhoods. Chevy Chase also did not advertise in African-American media outlets.[39]

As a result of the bank's practices, in 1993, about 95% of its mortgage applicants came from white neighborhoods and only 5% came from African-American neighborhoods. Of the mortgages granted by the bank and its mortgage subsidiary, 95% were secured by properties located in majority white neighborhoods while only 5% were secured by property located in predominantly African-American neighborhoods.[40]

Contrast Chevy Chase's marketing practices with that of Capital City Mortgage Corp. Capital City is a subprime lender, also located in the metropolitan Washington, D.C., area, which was sued by both the Federal Trade Commission[41] and private parties for engaging in predatory lending.[42]

Unlike Chevy Chase Bank, Capital City made every effort to reach out to African-Americans in the District of Columbia. It located its offices in African-American neighborhoods.[43] It distributed flyers and advertisements to the African-American community.[44] Capital City courted and solicited brokers who worked predominately in the African-American community.[45] Capital City's office even promi-

---

36 Johnson v. Equicredit Corp., 2002 U.S. Dist. LEXIS 4817 (N.D. Ill. Mar. 22, 2002).

37 *See, e.g.,* Letter from Malcolm Bush, President, Woodstock Institute, to the Office of the Comptroller of Currency (Oct. 2, 2000) (re: Citigroup/Associates Merger), *available at* http://www.woodstockinst.org; *Hearing Before the New York Banking Comm'n, California Reinvestment Comm.* (Nov. 10, 2000) (testimony of Alan Fisher), *available at* http://www.calreinvest.org; *see also* Lew Sichelman, *Community Groups Claim CitiFinancial Still Predatory,* Am. Banker, Jan. 2002, at 25 (noting that prime loans are still only available through Citibank, while CitiFinancial subsidiary—formerly Associates—offers only subprime loans).

38 *See* United States v. Chevy Chase Fed. Sav. Bank, No. 94-1824-J6 (D.D.C. 1994) [consent decree reproduced on the CD-Rom accompanying this volume]. The *Chevy Chase* case is also discussed at § 12.4.3.3, *infra.*

Some commentators have been critical of the DOJ's actions against Chevy Chase and other banks allegedly engaged in marketing discrimination. In the view of these commentators, marketing discrimination is not actionable under ECOA and FHA because there is no individual applicant who has been discriminated against. *See* Michael B. Mierzewski & Richard L.

Jacobs, *What Hath Justice Department Wrought,* Banking Pol'y Rep., Feb. 6, 1995, at 8; John Spina, *United States v. Albank, FSB: Is 'Justice' Served in the Enforcement of Fair Lending Laws,* 2 N.C. Banking Inst. 207 (1998).

39 United States v. Chevy Chase Fed. Sav. Bank, No. 94-1824-J6 (D.D.C. 1994).

40 *Id.* A few years earlier, the Department of Justice had alleged that the Decatur Savings Federal Savings and Loan Association engaged in similar conduct that had the effect of discouraging applications from African-Americans in the Atlanta, Georgia area. *See* United States v. Decatur Fed. Sav. & Loan Ass'n, Clearinghouse No. 49,126 (N.D. Ga. 1992) (consent decree). The *Decatur* case is discussed at § 12.4.3.2, *infra.*

41 Fed. Trade Comm'n v. Capital City Mortgage Corp., 1998 U.S. Dist. LEXIS 22115 (D.D.C. July 13, 1998).

42 Hargraves v. Capital City Mortgage Corp., 140 F. Supp. 2d 7 (2000). The Department of Justice filed an amicus brief in this case supporting the private plaintiffs. Brief of the United States as Amicus Curiae in Support of Plaintiffs' Opposition to Defendants' Motion for Judgment on the Pleadings, or, In the Alternative, For Summary Judgment, Hargraves v. Capital City Mortgage Corp., 140 F. Supp. 2d 7 (D.D.C. 2000) (Civ. Action No. 98-1021) [reproduced on the CD-Rom accompanying this volume].

43 *Hargraves,* 140 F. Supp. 2d at 21.

44 *Id.*

45 *Id.*

nently displayed a portrait of its president standing next to the Reverend Jesse Jackson and former Washington, D.C., Mayor Marion Barry.[46]

As a result of Capital City's practices, about 95% of the mortgages it made in the District of Columbia were secured by properties located in African-American neighborhoods, as were 74% of its mortgages in Prince George's County.[47]

5.3.2.5 Market Segmentation and Pre-Screened Marketing

Another form of potential marketing discrimination occurs when lenders use direct marketing to send solicitations, including pre-approved credit offers, to potential applicants. Lenders, like many other businesses, will pre-screen potential applicants using sophisticated computer technology.[48] Often, the technology consists of enormous databases of computer information that is easily and cheaply analyzed and sorted, allowing lenders to "segment" their target population into ever smaller subsets of consumers.[49] Lenders have the added advantage of using the plethora of information available from credit reporting agencies to conduct this pre-screening.[50]

This pre-screening often segments the target audience by factors such as geography, demographics (including age and sex), and income—the very factors that are either prohibited bases or proxies for prohibited bases.[51] Despite these concerns, and the mounting evidence discussed above that lenders regularly engage in marketing discrimination, the Federal Reserve Board declined in its 1999 proposed revisions to Regulation B to extend the ECOA to cover pre-screened credit offers.[52]

5.3.3 Discrimination in Treatment of Potential Applicants

Even if an applicant from a protected group can get past the marketing discrimination and through the creditor's door, pre-application discrimination may still take place in the creditor's office. Sometimes, differential encouragement at this stage can be very subtle and may be discovered only through the use of paired testers. A number of studies involving paired testers have shown that loan officers often subtly encourage white applicants and not minority applicants by providing better treatment, giving more information, and spending more time with the white applicants.

A series of studies conducted by the National Fair Housing Alliance used paired testers to show significant differences in treatment at the pre-application stage.[53] These studies matched white and minority testers, giving them similar debt-to-income ratios.[54] The testers posed as potential mortgage applicants seeking information about the types and terms of mortgage loans for which they might qualify. The studies found that:

- Minority testers were more likely to be denied the opportunity to speak with a loan officer at the pre-application stage;
- Even when they were able to meet with a loan officer, minority testers were more likely to be denied basic information, such as what types of loans they would qualify for;
- Lenders spent longer amounts of time with white testers than with their minority counterparts;
- Lenders provided more information to white testers, including a greater number of quotes on loan products; and
- Minority testers were more likely to be quoted a higher interest rate than their white counterparts.

An earlier study by the same organization found that lender employees actively discouraged African-American testers who walked into their office.[55] Employees told African-American testers that the lender did not accept applications at that office and that they needed to go across town to the bank's mortgage lending division, while white applicants were told they were in the right place. African-American applicants were often told that the loan process was long and complicated and that all the paperwork must first be completed, while white borrowers were quickly told that they were likely to qualify even though a full application was not provided.

Another series of studies conducted by the Fort Worth Human Relations Commission uncovered evidence of pre-application discrimination with respect to pre-qualification

---

46 *Id.*

47 Brief of the United States as Amicus Curiae in Support of Plaintiffs' Opposition to Defendants' Motion for Judgment on the Pleadings, or, In the Alternative, For Summary Judgment, Hargraves v. Capital City Mortgage Corp., 140 F. Supp. 2d 7 (D.D.C. 2000) (Civ. Action No. 98-1021) [reproduced on the CD-Rom accompanying this volume].

48 *See generally* Timothy C. Lambert, *Fair Marketing: Challenging Pre-Application Lending Practices*, 87 Geo. L.J. 2181 (1999).

49 *Id.*

50 *See* National Consumer Law Center, Fair Credit Reporting Act § 4.3.7 (4th ed. 1998 and Supp.).

51 *See generally* Timothy C. Lambert, *Fair Marketing: Challenging Pre-Application Lending Practices*, 87 Geo. L.J. 2181 (1999).

52 64 Fed. Reg. 44,582, 44,584–44,585 (Aug. 16, 1999).

53 Robin Smith & Michelle DeLair, *New Evidence from Lender Testing: Discrimination at the Pre-Application Stage*, in Mortgage Lending Discrimination: A Review of Existing Evidence 23–41 (Urban Inst. 1999). The Urban Institute report constitutes a re-analysis of raw data provided by the National Fair Housing Alliance.

54 *Id.* at 24.

55 Cathy Cloud & George Galster, *What Do We Know About Racial Discrimination in Mortgage Markets*, 22 Rev. of Black Pol. Econ. 101 (1993) (available as Clearinghouse No. 47,964).

or pre-approval quotes given by lenders.[56] African-Americans and Hispanics who had similar financial profiles to their white counterparts received significantly lower quotes for pre-approval or pre-qualification. In one case, a white tester was qualified for a $70,000 loan on the same day that an African-American tester, who had more favorable finances, was qualified for only $55,000.[57] At another bank, a white tester was told he would qualify for a loan of $158,000, while an African-American tester was told that he would qualify for a loan of only $100,000, even though the latter had a slightly higher income, a higher down payment, more savings, and less debt.[58]

5.4 Application Procedures

5.4.1 General

The next stage of the credit transaction involves the procedures for application for credit. Discrimination may involve rules concerning requests for different types of information from or about the applicant. This section also focuses on issues concerning oral applications, whether spouses or others must act as cosigners to a loan, and under what name the consumer may request a credit account.

In general, under the ECOA, there can be no differences in the application procedures if those differences are on a prohibited basis.[59] The Fair Housing Act's general rule against discrimination also prohibits such discrimination in housing financing.

5.4.2 Oral Applications for Credit

5.4.2.1 General

A caveat exists with regard to the application process in that Regulation B permits creditors to take either oral or written applications for credit. However, applications must be in writing when credit is used to purchase or refinance the applicant's principal residence and when the residence is taken as security for the loan.[60] Thus, except for home mortgage applications, creditors may base their credit decisions on information taken orally from applicants and on notations of conversations.

This provision is both a help and a hindrance to applicants. On the one hand, it brings a great deal of creditor activity within the scope of the statute because the protective provisions can be triggered by a mere conversation between a prospective customer and a creditor's employee, if credit is extended or denied on the basis of that conversation. On the other hand, the lack of a written application requirement makes an ECOA plaintiff's burden of proof more difficult because the only written record of the transaction is often the employee's own memorandum of any conversation.

When a creditor conducts the application process orally, it must still maintain written records of the process and of its reasons for taking a particular action on the application.[61] Some enforcing agencies have formally recognized that evasions of the statute may possibly occur when a creditor uses oral applications. For instance, the Office of the Comptroller of the Currency requires banks within its jurisdiction to retain certain records, including loan officers' memoranda, when an application has been taken orally.[62] The lack of specific overall record retention requirements for oral applications increases the risk of both arbitrary and evasive action by creditors, and increases the ECOA plaintiff's difficulties in proving discrimination.

5.4.2.2 The Home Mortgage Exception

Applications must be in writing when credit is used to purchase or refinance the applicant's principal residence and

---

56 *See* Fort Worth Human Relations Commission Study Leads to $1.375 Billion Fair Lending Settlement, Nat'l Fair Housing Advocate, Apr. 1998, at 1; Michael Janofsky, *Texas Lenders Pledge $1.4 Billion in Housing Case*, The New York Times, Mar. 10, 1998; *HUD Settles With Texas Mortgage Lender Charged With Fair Housing Act Violations*, 70 Banking Rep. (BNA) 688 (Apr. 27, 1998). These studies prompted the Department of Housing and Urban Development to take action against five lenders, resulting in settlements providing $3.5 billion in loan commitments for minority borrowers. *See* § 12.3.1, *infra.*

57 Michael Janofsky, *Texas Lenders Pledge $1.4 Billion in Housing Case*, The New York Times, Mar. 10, 1998.

58 *HUD Settles With Texas Mortgage Lender Charged With Fair Housing Act Violations*, 70 Banking Rep. (BNA) 688 (Apr. 27, 1998).

59 Official Staff Commentary, 12 C.F.R. § 202.4-1. The Federal Reserve Board has proposed redesignating Official Staff Commentary § 202.4-1 as §§ 202.4(a)-1 and 202.4(a)-2 to clarify the Commentary and to provide additional examples of disparate treatment. 64 Fed. Reg. 44,582, 44,621 (Aug. 16, 1999). The proposed revisions to the Official Staff Commentary can be found on the CD-Rom accompanying this volume.

60 Reg. B, 12 C.F.R. § 202.5(e). Information entered directly into and retained by a computerized system qualifies as a written application. Official Staff Commentary, 12 C.F.R. § 202.5(e)-3 (as revised Sept. 30, 1996).

61 Reg. B, 12 C.F.R. § 202.12(b). The Federal Reserve Board has proposed extending the record retention requirement for applications pertaining to businesses with one million dollars or less in gross revenues from twelve to twenty-five months. Larger businesses would remain subject to the shorter sixty-day period allowed by 12 C.F.R. § 202.12(b)(5). 64 Fed. Reg. 44,582, 44,600–44,601 (Aug. 16, 1999). The proposed revisions to Regulation B can be found on the CD-Rom accompanying this volume.

62 Comptroller of Currency, Examining Circular No. 152, Consumer Cred. Guide (CCH) ¶ 98,239 (Mar. 7, 1977).

when the residence is taken as security for the loan.[63] This requirement assists federal supervisory agencies in their enforcement of the ECOA and the Fair Housing Act.[64]

The creditor need not use a pre-printed form, and it is sufficient for the creditor just to write down the information that it normally considers in making a credit decision. The creditor may complete the application for the applicant and need not ask for a signature from the applicant.[65] This process can even be done over the telephone.[66] The written application requirement is also satisfied if the information is entered directly into and retained by a computerized system.[67]

5.4.3 Providing Disparate Levels of Assistance in the Application Process

Most credit discrimination appears to occur among those marginally qualified. That is, those clearly qualified or clearly unqualified are treated in the same manner no matter what their race or other characteristics. But most applicants, perhaps as many as eighty percent, have some blemish on their application, and the question is whether creditors differentiate on the basis of race or some other prohibited characteristic among this group.[68] If an individual is denied credit, the creditor can point to the blemish as the basis for the denial.

Nevertheless, even if applicants have credit blemishes, illegal discrimination occurs if, for example, creditors work more with white applicants with credit blemishes to qualify them for a loan than they do with similarly situated African-American applicants. It is discriminatory to facilitate the application process for certain applicants but to place roadblocks before other applicants when the difference in treatment is based on the applicant's race or some other prohibited basis. For example, a marginal white applicant might be coached on how to make the grade, while a minority applicant—though being treated quite nicely—may not receive such coaching.

One study using paired testers found subtle distinctions between how marginally qualified white and African-American applicants were treated.[69] White applicants were more likely to be provided helpful hints and secrets that are often critical for the qualification of marginal applicants. African-Americans might be told the rules but not the exceptions. For example, both white and African-American applicants were told that a ten-percent down payment would require the applicant to keep six monthly payments in escrow. But only whites might be told that, if an eleven percent down payment were made, the escrow would be reduced to only two months' payments. Similarly, only white applicants might be told that they could improve their chances by obtaining gift letters from relatives or by applying on pay day, when they would have the most money in the bank. Related conduct has sometimes been described as the "fat file" phenomenon. White applicants are provided the opportunity to explain credit blemishes and document the applicant's suitability while loan officers do not provide African-American applicants with the same opportunity. Studies have found that many applicants fail to meet minimum loan underwriting standards—such as loan amount to income or total outstanding debt to income—and still obtain credit. The issue is not whether an applicant meets the creditor's stated minimum standards but what additional information is placed in the file that allows for an exception. It would be illegal not to assist African-Americans (or another protected class) to the same extent that the creditor assists white applicants in building the case for an exception from normal underwriting standards.

5.4.4 Requesting More Information About Applicants from Protected Groups

One type of discrimination in the application process involves how much and what types of information a creditor requires from an applicant. Requiring too much personal or hard- to-obtain information may discourage applicants from completing their applications. Regulation B specifically prohibits discrimination on a prohibited basis as to "information requirements."[70] Thus it would be discriminatory to require more information from public assistance recipients than from other applicants.[71]

Regulation B also prohibits engaging in different investigatory procedures on a prohibited basis. The Regulation specifically prohibits discrimination on a prohibited basis as

---

63　Reg. B, 12 C.F.R. § 202.5(e).

64　Official Staff Commentary, 12 C.F.R. § 202.5(e)-1.

65　Official Staff Commentary, 12 C.F.R. § 202.5(e)-1.

66　Official Staff Commentary, 12 C.F.R. § 202.5(e)-2.

67　Official Staff Commentary, 12 C.F.R. § 202.5(e)-3 (as revised Sept. 30, 1996).

68　Alicia Munnell et al., Mortgage Lending in Boston: Interpreting HMDA Data (Fed. Reserve Bank of Boston, Working Paper Series No. 92-7, 1992) (available from Federal Reserve Bank of Boston, Research Library-D, P.O. Box 2076, Boston, MA 02016-2076, 617-973-3397) (also available as Clearinghouse No. 47,967).

69　Cathy Cloud & George Galster, *What Do We Know About Racial Discrimination in Mortgage Markets*, 22 Rev. of Black Pol. Econ. 101 (1993) (available as Clearinghouse No. 47,964).

70　Reg. B, 12 C.F.R. § 202.2(m), defines information requirements as part of a credit transaction, and Reg. B, 12 C.F.R. § 202.4, prohibits discrimination concerning any aspect of a credit transaction.

71　*But see* Cartwright v. Am. Sav. & Loan Ass'n, 880 F.2d 912 (7th Cir. 1989) (mortgage lender did not violate the ECOA by placing an application on indefinite hold after requesting that the applicant herself provide information on comparable housing prices in a largely minority neighborhood—a burden generally borne by lenders).

to "investigation procedures."[72] Thus creditors may not order credit reports on the spouses of married women who apply for individual accounts but not on the spouses of married male applicants for individual accounts.[73]

Similarly, creditors may not discriminate as to the information they actually review. When a couple applies for a joint account, it would be discriminatory to solely or primarily consider the husband's credit report, without considering the wife's credit record.[74]

5.5 Prohibited Requests For Information

5.5.1 General

There are a number of special ECOA requirements and prohibitions concerning requests for information, especially information relevant to the prohibited bases. These requirements specify that various types of information may not be requested or may be requested only in certain situations.

Aside from the special ECOA requirements, the ECOA does not limit a creditor from requesting any information in connection with a credit application.[75] Even if a request for information is not specifically covered by the ECOA or Regulation B, advocates should analyze whether it discourages applicants on a prohibited basis (as detailed immediately above). Furthermore, such a request may be prohibited by some other federal or state law regarding privacy, privileged information, credit reporting limitations, or similar restrictions.[76]

5.5.2 ECOA Restricts Creditor from "Requesting" Information About an "Applicant"

An important aspect to the general rule about prohibited requests for information is the term applicant, because the prohibitions only cover information requests about applicants. Regulation B defines applicant to include "any person who requests or who has received an extension of credit"

and "any person who is or may become contractually liable regarding an extension of credit."[77] Regulation B defines "contractually liable" as being expressly obligated to repay all debts on an account, pursuant to an agreement.[78]

An issue that remains unclear is whether guarantors, sureties and others who are secondarily liable on an obligation are applicants. Regulation B includes guarantors, sureties, endorsers and similar parties as applicants "for purposes of section 202.7(d) [dealing with spouses' signatures]."[79] One implication of this phrase is that guarantors and similar parties are *not* otherwise applicants.[80] On the other hand, guarantors, sureties and similar parties would seem to fall within the definition of those "who may become contractually liable" on the obligation.[81] It seems equally repugnant to the purposes of the ECOA to request racial, ethnic, religious or similar information from a guarantor as from the applicant.

Regardless of the outcome as to the coverage of those who are secondarily liable, such as guarantors and sureties, it seems clear that cosigners are applicants. That is, if an individual is immediately liable on an obligation before another party defaults, that party should be an applicant.

To be an applicant, one need not submit a full application to a creditor. Only a request for credit needs to be made, even if the request does not constitute an "application"

---

72 Reg. B, 12 C.F.R. § 202.2(m), defines investigating procedures as part of a credit transaction, and Reg. B, 12 C.F.R. § 202.4, prohibits discrimination concerning any aspect of a credit transaction.

73 *In re* Alden's, Inc., 92 F.T.C. 901 (Fed. Trade Comm'n 1978); *see also* Shuman v. Standard Oil Co., 453 F. Supp. 1150 (N.D. Cal. 1978) (divorced woman's suit withstood a motion for partial summary judgment when she alleged that the creditor had discriminated on the basis of sex or marital status as revealed in a credit report).

74 United States v. John Wanamaker, Philadelphia, Clearinghouse No. 44,328 (E.D. Pa. Apr. 14, 1989) (consent order).

75 *See* Reg. B, 12 C.F.R. § 202.5(b)(1).

76 Reg. B, 12 C.F.R. § 202.5(b)(1) n.1.

77 Reg. B, 12 C.F.R. § 202.2(e); *see* § 2.2.4, *supra*.

78 Reg. B, 12 C.F.R. § 202.2(i).

79 *See* Reg. B, 12 C.F.R. § 202.2(e); Silverman v. Eastrich Multiple Investor Fund, L.P., 857 F. Supp. 447 (E.D. Pa. 1994), *rev'd on other grounds*, 51 F.3d 28 (3d Cir. 1995); Gen. Elec. Capital Corp. v. Pulsifer, Clearinghouse No. 46,778 (D. Me. Oct. 28, 1991); Douglas County Nat'l Bank v. Pfeiff, 809 P.2d 1100 (Colo. Ct. App. 1991). *But see* Jordan v. Delon Olds Co., 887 F.2d 1089 (9th Cir. 1989) (unpublished) (text available at 1989 U.S. App. LEXIS 15429) (guarantors or others requested as additional signatories found not to be applicants protected by the ECOA).

80 In fact, until 1985, Regulation B explicitly excluded guarantors, sureties, and similar parties from the definition of applicant. Thus, the 1985 change can be seen as expanding the scope of the term applicant in this area solely for the purposes of section 202.7(d). *See* Fed. Deposit Ins. Corp. v. Deglau, 1998 U.S. Dist. LEXIS 380 (E.D. Pa. Jan. 16, 1998) (defendant's ECOA claim was rejected because guarantors fell outside the statutory definition of applicant as it read before Dec. 16, 1985), *aff'd in part, rev'd in part on other grounds*, 207 F.3d 153 (3d Cir. 2000).

81 The pre-1985 version of Regulation B limited applicants to those who may be contractually liable, while the 1985 amendment changed the definition to read those who may *become* contractually liable. *See* Fed. Deposit Ins. Corp. v. Deglau, 1998 U.S. Dist. LEXIS 380 (E.D. Pa. Jan. 16, 1998), *aff'd in part, rev'd in part on other grounds*, 207 F.3d 153 (3d Cir. 2000). The clear implication is that guarantors (who are not initially liable but who may become liable) are applicants. *See* § 2.2.4.2, *supra*. The fact that the regulation spelled out with crystal clarity that they are definitely applicants under section 202.7(d) can be seen as an attempt to unambiguously overrule some earlier cases and not as an attempt to more generally modify the status of guarantors as applicants.

according to the creditor's usual standards.[82] An application is a defined term under the ECOA, and certain ECOA provisions apply only if there is an application. But the definition of applicant does not require or even mention an application.[83]

5.5.3 Information Legally Obtained Sometimes May Not Be Utilized By Creditor

Regulation B's specific prohibitions on seeking information are constrained to "requests" for information or "inquiries" about an applicant.[84] Thus, the Regulation only prohibits active steps by the creditor to obtain prohibited information about the applicant. The creditor may still *receive* information from the applicant, a reporting agency, or other source, as long as the creditor did not seek out the information.[85] If the creditor receives information concerning a prohibited basis, however, it still cannot use that information to discriminate against the applicant on a prohibited basis.[86] Thus, even if a creditor is permitted to obtain certain information, there may still be restrictions as to how that information may be used. Chapter 6 details such restrictions.

5.5.4 The Proposed 1999 Revisions to Regulation B

One of the most significant changes in the Federal Reserve Board's (FRB) proposed set of revisions to Regulation B issued in 1999 concerns prohibited requests for information. The FRB proposed removing the prohibition on seeking information about an applicant's race, color, religion, national origin and sex for non-mortgage credit products.[87] This change was made in response to comments from the Department of Justice and other federal financial enforce-ment agencies that the enhanced ability to obtain data on race and ethnicity would aid fair lending enforcement, particularly with respect to small business lending.[88] The Board recognized the obvious concern—that removing the prohibition would give loan officers access to information on applicant characteristics that would aid discrimination—but found in favor of allowing the collection of that information.[89] The lifting of this prohibition would not affect the substantive rules barring creditors from discriminating against applicants on a prohibited basis.[90]

As an additional safeguard, the 1999 proposed revision would require creditors who request information on these characteristics to disclose at the time of the request that providing the information is optional and that the creditor would not take the information, or the applicant's decision not to provide the information, into account in any aspect of the credit transaction.[91] Also, the FRB proposed adding a new section to Regulation B emphasizing that a creditor may not consider race, color, religion, national origin or sex in determining an applicant's creditworthiness, except as permitted by law, nor may a creditor consider an applicant's decision not to provide the information.[92]

The FRB's proposal to allow voluntary data collection was particularly controversial. According to the FRB, most banking organizations were against the change, arguing that it would increase their regulatory burden and would be an invasion of their customers' privacy. On the other side, most regulators, including the Departments of Justice and Housing and Urban Development, as well as consumer and small business advocates, supported the change. Many of these groups, however, argued that voluntary data collection should only be a temporary step and that, ultimately, this data collection must be mandatory in order to be effective.[93]

5.5.5 Types of Information That Creditors Cannot Seek

5.5.5.1 Race, Color, Religion, and National Origin

With certain special exceptions set out later in § 5.5.6, *infra*, the current Regulation B prohibits creditors from requesting the race, color, religion, or national origin of the applicant or any other person in connection with a credit

---

82 Cragin v. First Fed. Sav. & Loan Ass'n, 498 F. Supp. 379 (D. Nev. 1980).

83 The term applicant is analyzed in more detail in § 2.2.4, *supra*.

84 Reg. B, 12 C.F.R. §§ 202.5, 202.12(a).

85 Reg. B, 12 C.F.R. § 202.12(a).

86 Reg. B, 12 C.F.R. § 202.6(a); *see also* 15 U.S.C. § 1691(a)(1); Reg. B, 12 C.F.R. § 202.4. The Federal Reserve Board has proposed redesignating the material at 12 C.F.R. § 202.4 as § 202.4(a) without substantive change. 64 Fed. Reg. 44,582, 44,595 (Aug. 16, 1999). The Board has also proposed adding § 202.6(b)(9) to expressly prohibit a creditor from considering an applicant's race, color, religion, national origin, or sex, or to consider the applicant's decision not to provide such information, in any aspect of the credit transaction except as allowed by law. 64 Fed. Reg. 44,582, 44,597 (Aug. 16, 1999). The proposed revisions to Regulation B can be found on the CD-Rom accompanying this volume.

87 64 Fed. Reg. 44,582, 44,596 (Aug. 16, 1999) (amending 12 C.F.R. § 202.5). The proposed revisions to Regulation B can be found on the CD-Rom accompanying this volume.

88 64 Fed. Reg. 44,582, 44,586 (Aug. 16, 1999).

89 64 Fed. Reg. 44,582, 44,586 (Aug. 16, 1999).

90 *See* § 5.2, *supra* (discussing the general rule against discrimination).

91 64 Fed. Reg. 44,582, 44,596 (proposing 12 C.F.R. § 202.5(a)(4)). The proposed revisions to Regulation B can be found on the CD-Rom accompanying this volume.

92 64 Fed. Reg. 44,582, 44,597 (Aug. 16, 1999) (proposing 12 C.F.R. § 202.6(b)(9)). The proposed revisions to Regulation B can be found on the CD-Rom accompanying this volume.

93 Final rules were not available at the time this manual was written.

transaction.[94] For example, if the director of a day care center serving African-American families applies for a bank loan to defray some of the center's debts until payments are received, the bank may not ask the race of the center's director or students.

However, a creditor may inquire about an applicant's permanent residence and immigration status.[95] The Comptroller of the Currency has authorized national banks to maintain a policy of requiring foreign student credit applicants to possess an alien registration card.[96]

The general restriction on requests for information on an applicant's national origin should not prevent a creditor from determining the language spoken by the applicant so as to provide that applicant with information in the appropriate language. In fact, Regulation B specifically permits creditors to provide ECOA notices in a language other than English, as long as it is available in English upon request.[97] Also, the Federal Reserve Board (FRB) has given approval to a California statute which requires creditors to provide Spanish-speaking applicants with the opportunity to obtain an unexecuted Spanish-language contract.[98] The FRB reasoned that the statute made contract terms more understandable to applicants of one national origin without interfering with the interests of any other group and therefore did not frustrate the intent of the ECOA.[99]

5.5.5.2 Sex; Optional Use of Courtesy Titles

5.5.5.2.1 Inquiries about applicant's gender

A creditor generally may not request the sex of the applicant as required information.[100] There are five excep-

tions. A creditor may inquire into the applicant's gender: 1) when securities credit is involved;[101] 2) when incidental consumer credit is involved, but only to the extent necessary for medical records or similar purposes;[102] 3) to determine eligibility and premium rates for insurance;[103] 4) when a residential real estate-related loan is involved;[104] and 5) when a special purpose credit program is involved.[105] However, as discussed in the previous section, the Federal Reserve Board proposed in its 1999 proposed revisions to Regulation B to allow creditor to voluntarily seek information about an applicant's gender.[106]

Unless the creditor employs mail-in applications and the applicant uses only initials, or the creditor's employee who takes the application is not the person making the credit decision, the prohibition concerning requesting the applicant's sex is of limited practical effect.[107] The creditor will usually be able to determine for itself whether the applicant is a man or woman.

5.5.5.2.2 Courtesy titles

The applicant may be asked, but not required, to designate a courtesy title for the account (Ms., Miss, Mrs., or Mr.),[108] and the application form must "appropriately" indicate that selection of such a designation is optional.[109] All other terms used on the application must be gender-neutral.[110]

5.5.5.2.3 Birth control, childbearing or rearing

A creditor may not request any information about the applicant's birth control practices, intention or capacity to bear children, or intention to rear children.[111] A creditor, however, may request information about the applicant's present dependents (such as the number of dependents and their age) and related financial obligations for these present

---

94 Reg. B, 12 C.F.R. § 202.5(d)(5).

95 Reg. B, 12 C.F.R. § 202.5(d)(5); *see also* Comptroller of Currency, Interpretive Staff Letter, Fed. Banking L. Rep. (CCH) ¶ 85,026 (Office of the Comptroller of the Currency Sept. 9, 1977) (William B. Glidden) (also available at 1977 OCC Ltr. LEXIS 64) (similar rule for national banks).

96 Comptroller of Currency, Interpretive Staff Letter, Fed. Banking L. Rep. (CCH) ¶ 85,023 (Office of the Comptroller of the Currency Sept. 6, 1977) (Thomas W. Taylor) (also available at 1977 OCC Ltr. LEXIS 68).

97 Reg. B, 12 C.F.R. § 202.4(b). This provision was added as part of the Federal Reserve Board's interim final rule issued March 30, 2001, concerning electronic disclosures. 66 Fed. Reg. 17,779–17,786 (Apr. 4, 2001); *see* § 10.2.6.2.1, *infra*.

98 Cal. Civ. Code § 1632 (West).

99 Fed. Reserve Bd., Official Board Interpretation § 202.1102, 42 Fed. Reg. 22,861 (May 5, 1977). This interpretation was not included in the 1985 Official Commentary to Regulation B. However, the Board chose not to include in the Commentary any interpretation which did *not* preempt a state law, such as § 202.1102, and so, presumably, the California statute remains acceptable. Moreover, § 202.1102 is an Official Board Interpretation, not a staff interpretation, and thus should not be superseded by staff commentary.

100 Reg. B, 12 C.F.R. § 202.5(d)(3).

101 *See* § 2.2.6.6, *supra*.

102 Reg. B, 12 C.F.R. § 202.3(c)(2)(iv). The Federal Reserve Board has proposed eliminating 12 C.F.R. § 202.3(c)(2)(iv) to reflect the intended change to § 202.5(d)(3) that would allow creditors to request information about sex. 64 Fed. Reg. 44,582, 44,596 (Aug. 16, 1999). The proposed revisions to Regulation B can be found on the CD-Rom accompanying this volume. *See also* § 5.5.4, *supra*.

103 This information may not be sought for purposes of making the credit decision. *See* Official Staff Commentary, 12 C.F.R. § 202.7(e)-2.

104 *See* § 5.5.6.1, *infra*.

105 *See* § 5.5.6.4, *infra*.

106 *See* § 5.5.4, *supra*.

107 *See* United States v. Household Fin. Corp., Clearinghouse No. 38,903 (N.D. Ill. Oct. 31, 1984) (consent order based partially on allegations that creditor generally considered the sex of applicants in evaluating credit applications).

108 Reg. B, 12 C.F.R. § 202.5(d)(3).

109 Reg. B, 12 C.F.R. § 202.5(d)(3).

110 Reg. B, 12 C.F.R. § 202.5(d)(3).

111 Reg. B, 12 C.F.R. § 202.5(d)(4).

dependents, as long as this information is not solely requested from a group protected by the statute.[112] For example, a creditor would violate the ECOA if it requested information on child care expenses only from female applicants or only from recipients of public assistance.

5.5.5.3 Marital Status

5.5.5.3.1 *When marital status information may be requested*

Whether a creditor may ask about an applicant's marital status will depend on the type of credit account being sought. If an account is joint between husband and wife, or if the credit account is secured by property, the creditor may seek information about the applicant's marital status.[113]

But a creditor must allow a married applicant to apply for an individual account if the applicant so desires.[114] If the applicant seeks an individual, unsecured account, a creditor is severely restricted as to when it can seek marital status information. The creditor in that situation may *not* ask the applicant's marital status unless:

- The applicant resides in a community property state or is relying on any property located in such a state to establish creditworthiness;[115]
- The credit involves a regulated utility company, incidental consumer credit, or securities credit;[116]
- The creditor seeks the information solely to determine eligibility and premium rates for insurance;[117]

- A residential real estate-related loan is involved;[118] or
- The creditor seeks the information solely to determine eligibility for a special purpose credit program.[119]

Unless the transaction involves only incidental consumer credit,[120] the creditor also must make an "appropriate" disclosure to the applicant that income from alimony, child support, or separate maintenance payments need not be revealed unless the applicant wants it to be considered in evaluating the application.[121] Regulation B does not define the term appropriate, although a good standard to measure appropriateness may be found on the Federal Reserve Board's model credit application forms. These model forms indicate in bold letters that: "Alimony, child support, or separate maintenance income need not be revealed if you do not wish to have it considered as a basis for repaying this obligation."[122]

This disclosure must *precede* any general request for income information so that it can be seen before the applicant answers the question.[123] On the other hand, the disclosure need not be made at all if the creditor seeks only specific income information that would not include alimony, support payments or the like—for example, if the creditor asks for salary, wages, and investment income.[124]

If the applicant does not want alimony, child support, or separate maintenance income to be considered then the creditor is prohibited from making any inquiries about these sources of income.[125] The creditor must instead evaluate the application based on the applicant's other income sources.

At least one court has held that a creditor who asked a female applicant if she anticipated getting married did not violate the ECOA, as the question was posed in the context of a discussion of the applicant's financial troubles and her need for a guarantor.[126]

112　Reg. B, 12 C.F.R. § 202.5(d)(4).

113　Reg. B, 12 C.F.R. § 202.5(d)(1). The Federal Reserve Board had at one time given approval to state statutes which banned creditor inquiries concerning marital status altogether; however, it then reconsidered and suspended its official interpretation on this subject. *See* Fed. Reserve Bd., Official Board Interpretation § 202.1104 (effective Sept. 26, 1979; suspended Jan. 21, 1980).

114　15 U.S.C. § 1691d(c); Reg. B, 12 C.F.R. § 202.7(a). The statute explicitly overrides any state laws prohibiting the separate extension of consumer credit to spouses.

115　Reg. B, 12 C.F.R. § 202.5(d)(1); *see also* United States v. Allied Fin. Co., Clearinghouse No. 38,922 (N.D. Tex. 1985) (consent decree forbidding creditor from requesting information on the marital status of consumers applying for individual, unsecured credit); United States v. Household Fin. Corp., Clearinghouse No. 38,903 (N.D. Ill. Oct. 31, 1984) (consent order forbidding creditor from asking about marital status of individual applicants for unsecured credit when such credit information was unrelated to creditworthiness and the spouse would neither use the account nor be contractually liable on it); *In re* Alden's, Inc., 92 F.T.C. 901 (Fed. Trade Comm'n 1978) (creditor was ordered to stop asking about applicants' marital status when an individual, unsecured account was requested in a noncommunity property state).

116　*See* § 2.2.6.2, *supra.*

117　This information may not be sought for purposes of making the credit decision. *See* Official Staff Commentary, 12 C.F.R. § 202.7(e)-2.

118　*See* § 5.5.6.1, *infra.*

119　*See* § 5.5.6.4, *infra.*

120　*See* § 2.2.6.3, *supra.*

121　Reg. B, 12 C.F.R. § 202.5(d)(2); *see also* United States v. Household Fin. Corp., Clearinghouse No. 38,903 (N.D. Ill. Oct. 31, 1984) (consent order based partially on allegations that creditor failed to advise applicants that they did not have to disclose such sources of income if they did not want them to be considered in evaluating creditworthiness).

122　Fed. Reserve Bd., Model Form for Credit Application, *reprinted at* Appx. B, *infra.* The Federal Reserve Board has proposed revisions to the Model Form to reflect proposed changes to 12 C.F.R. § 202.5 and to add clarity. 64 Fed. Reg. 44,582, 44,617 (Aug. 16, 1999). The proposed revisions to Regulation B can be found on the CD-Rom accompanying this volume.

123　Official Staff Commentary, 12 C.F.R. § 202.5(d)(2)-2.

124　Official Staff Commentary, 12 C.F.R. § 202.5(d)(2)-3.

125　Reg. B, 12 C.F.R. § 202.5(d)(2).

126　Para v. United Carolina Bank, 1998 U.S. Dist. LEXIS 16843 (E.D.N.C. Aug. 25, 1998).

5.5.5.3.2 *Types of marital status information that may be requested*

In situations in which creditors may request an applicant's marital status, creditors may categorize the applicant only as unmarried (which includes single, divorced, and widowed persons), married, or separated.[127] These terms are to be defined by applicable state law.[128] The creditor may explain that the category "unmarried" includes single, divorced, and widowed persons but is not required to do so.[129]

5.5.5.3.3 *Creditors may also seek information which indirectly discloses marital status*

Creditors also may ask for certain information which indirectly discloses the applicant's marital status. Examples of such permissible indirect inquiries include:[130]

- Whether the applicant is responsible for paying alimony, child support, or separate maintenance payments;
- The source of income to be used as a basis for the repayment of the credit requested (which may disclose that it is a spouse's income);
- Whether any obligation disclosed by the applicant has a co-obligor (which may disclose that the co-obligor is a spouse or former spouse); or
- The form of ownership of assets relied on in extending credit (which may disclose the interest of a spouse).

A creditor may also ask the applicant to list any other account for which the applicant is liable and to provide the name and address in which the account is carried.[131] The creditor also may ask for the names under which the applicant has previously received credit.[132] This provision serves chiefly as a means of obtaining credit reports on women who have changed names through marriage or divorce and to track experience with prior business loans.

5.5.5.4 Information About Spouse or Former Spouse

With enumerated exceptions, a creditor may not make any inquiry about an applicant's spouse or former spouse.[133] This prohibition applies not only to inquiries directed to the applicant but also to inquiries directed to a credit reporting agency, other creditors, or other sources. For instance, one creditor signed a consent agreement with the Federal Trade Commission in which it agreed to stop obtaining credit

reports on the deceased spouses of applicants.[134] Another creditor was ordered to stop denying married persons' applications for separate accounts based on credit reports obtained on their spouses.[135]

The prohibition on inquiring about a spouse or former spouse does not prohibit a creditor from reviewing information about the spouse if it is already included in a credit report on the applicant. However, several cases have prohibited the denial of credit based on information that the creditor received on the applicant's spouse or former spouse.[136] In particular, these creditors violated the ECOA because they refused to grant individual credit to one spouse on the basis of a delinquency owed by the other spouse to the same creditor.

A creditor may request information about the applicant's spouse or former spouse *only* if:[137]

- The spouse will be permitted to use the account;[138]
- The spouse will be contractually liable on the account;[139]
- The applicant is relying on the spouse's income for repayment of the credit;[140]

---

127 Reg. B, 12 C.F.R. §§ 202.5(d)(1), 202.2(u).
128 Reg. B, 12 C.F.R. § 202.2(u).
129 Reg. B, 12 C.F.R. § 202.5(d)(1).
130 Official Staff Commentary, 12 C.F.R. § 202.5(d)(1)-1.
131 Official Staff Commentary, 12 C.F.R. § 202.5(c)(3).
132 Official Staff Commentary, 12 C.F.R. § 202.5(c)(3).
133 Reg. B, 12 C.F.R. § 202.5(c)(1).
134 *In re* Westinghouse Credit Corp., 94 F.T.C. 1280 (Fed. Trade Comm'n 1979).
135 *In re* Alden's, Inc., 92 F.T.C. 901 (Fed. Trade Comm'n 1978).
136 *See* McGee v. E. Ohio Gas Co., 111 F. Supp. 2d 979 (S.D. Ohio 2000) (ECOA prohibits utility from refusing credit to one spouse on the basis of a delinquency owed by the other spouse to the same utility), *class certification granted*, 200 F.R.D. 382 (S.D. Ohio 2001); *In re* Brazil, 21 B.R. 333 (Bankr. N.D. Ohio 1982) (a public utility company discriminated against a bankruptcy petitioner on the basis of marital status by refusing to accept her application for service while her husband was still residing in their home and there was an outstanding bill in his name); *see also* § 2.2.2.3, *supra* (a more extensive discussion on prohibited forms of credit discrimination by utilities). *But see* Haynes v. Bank of Wedowee, 634 F.2d 266 (5th Cir. 1981) (no discrimination on basis of marital status shown when bank accelerated wife's loan due to husband's bankruptcy filing and bank had relied on existence of a joint account in original credit extension); Haynsworth v. S.C. Elec. & Gas Co., 488 F. Supp. 565 (D.S.C. 1979) (no unlawful discrimination when a utility company refused to open an account in a woman's name because of an outstanding bill at the same residence in the name of her separated husband); Vander Missen v. Kellogg-Citizens Nat'l Bank, 481 F. Supp. 742 (E.D. Wis. 1979); Cherry v. Hughes Supply Co., 539 S.E.2d 536 (Ga. Ct. App. 2000) (holding that a creditor does not violate the ECOA by requiring applicant to pay spouse's delinquency to that same creditor before granting new credit when the creditor justifiably believes that the applicant is liable for the spouse's delinquency).
137 Reg. B, 12 C.F.R. § 202.5(c)(1), (2).
138 Reg. B, 12 C.F.R. § 202.5(c)(2)(i). The term "use" refers only to open-end credit accounts. *See* Reg. B, 12 C.F.R. § 202.2(a), (w).
139 Reg. B, 12 C.F.R. § 202.5(c)(2)(ii). A person is contractually liable when he or she is expressly obligated (for example, by written agreement) to repay all debts arising on an account. *See* Reg. B, 12 C.F.R. § 202.2(i).
140 Reg. B, 12 C.F.R. § 202.5(c)(2)(iii). A creditor may not presume that, because the spouse's income is listed, the applicant is

- The applicant resides in a community property state or is relying on property which is located in such a state for repayment;[141]
- The applicant is relying on alimony, child support, or separate maintenance payments from a spouse or former spouse for repayment of the credit;[142] or
- The transaction involves incidental consumer or securities credit.[143]

In the above situations, the creditor may request any information about the spouse or former spouse that may be requested about the applicant.[144] It may prove difficult for divorced applicants to comply with creditor requests for information about their ex-spouses, because the applicant may not have easy access to current financial information concerning an ex-spouse.

The Federal Trade Commission (FTC) has issued an interpretation of the Fair Credit Reporting Act concerning when a credit reporting agency is permitted to provide creditors with the credit history of the credit applicant's spouse. Under this interpretation, a creditor can seek a spouse's credit history whenever:

- The spouse will be permitted to use the account;
- The spouse will be contractually liable on the account;
- The applicant is relying on the spouse's income for repayment of the credit;
- The state law doctrine of necessaries applies to the transaction;[145]
- The applicant resides in a community property state or the property, upon which the applicant is relying to establish creditworthiness, is located in a community property state; or
- The applicant is acting as the agent of the nonapplicant spouse.[146]

Other than in these situations, the creditor does not have a permissible purpose to request a credit report on a non-applicant spouse, and the Fair Credit Reporting Act prohibits reporting agencies from furnishing such reports.[147] Note that the FTC's Staff Commentary allows creditors to access a spouse's credit history in two situations not provided for in Regulation B: when a state necessaries doctrine applies and when the applicant is acting as the spouse's agent. There could conceivably be some situations in which the FTC Staff Commentary could conflict with Regulation B. However, the FTC Staff Commentary also states that there is never a permissible purpose for seeking a credit report when Regulation B prohibits a creditor from seeking such information or when the nonapplicant spouse is divorced, separated, or has expressed an intent to legally disassociate from the marriage.[148]

5.5.5.5 Public Assistance Status

With the exceptions of home mortgages and special purpose credit programs,[149] a creditor is likely to be limited in the information it may seek about an applicant's public assistance status. Whether or not a creditor may ask about the applicant's public assistance status depends on what kind of credit evaluation system it uses. If the creditor utilizes a credit scoring system it may not consider, and therefore presumably may not ask about, public assistance status.[150]

If a creditor uses a judgmental system, it may ask whether an applicant's income derives from public assistance payments in order to determine the amount and probable continuance of the payments, the applicant's credit history, and other "pertinent elements of creditworthiness."[151] A creditor may be able to ask, for example, how long the applicant has been receiving public assistance, whether the applicant intends to remain in a state that provides income from a state-funded program not offered in adjoining states, or the age of the applicant's dependents, in order to ascertain how long present benefits will continue. If the creditor's inquiries

---

relying on that income to establish creditworthiness. "Whether an applicant is relying on the future earnings of a nonapplicant spouse is for the creditor to determine. Because section 202.5(c)(2)(iv) permits a creditor routinely to request information about a nonapplicant spouse, the mere fact that the nonapplicant spouse's income is listed on an application form is insufficient to show that the applicant is relying on the spouse's income." 50 Fed. Reg. 11,044, 11,045 (Apr. 5, 1988) (explanatory material for revision of Official Staff Commentary, 12 C.F.R. § 202.7(d)(5)-2).

141 Reg. B, 12 C.F.R. § 202.5(c)(2)(iv).
142 Reg. B, 12 C.F.R. § 202.5(c)(2)(v).
143 *See* § 2.2.6.3, *supra.*
144 Reg. B, 12 C.F.R. § 202.5(c)(2).
145 *See* § 9.3, *infra* (impact of the ECOA on necessaries doctrines and family expense statutes).
146 Fed. Trade Comm'n, Official Staff Commentary on the Fair Credit Reporting Act § 604(3)(A) item 5A (interpreting 15 U.S.C. § 1681(b)).

147 Fed. Trade Comm'n, Official Staff Commentary on the Fair Credit Reporting Act § 604(3)(A) item 5B.
148 Fed. Trade Comm'n, Official Staff Commentary on the Fair Credit Reporting Act § 604(3)(A) item 5B. In another interpretation of the Fair Credit Reporting Act, the Federal Trade Commission set out requirements for credit reporting agencies which allow the applicant to request that favorable reports be considered. The agencies were asked to adopt procedures to ensure that "undesignated information" in the file of married persons (that is, information reported in only one spouse's name, information on joint accounts, or information on individual accounts on which the other spouse was an authorized user of the account) could be "accessed" in the name of either spouse who wishes to rely on it. *See* Fed. Trade Comm'n, Official Staff Commentary on the Fair Credit Reporting Act § 607(3)(A).
149 *See* § 5.5.6, *infra.*
150 Reg. B, 12 C.F.R. § 202.6(b)(2); *see* § 6.3, *infra* (an explanation of the different types of credit evaluation systems).
151 Reg. B, 12 C.F.R. § 202.2(y). The use of public assistance status in credit evaluation is discussed in further detail at § 6.6.3, *infra.*

become demeaning, Regulation B can arguably be invoked to prohibit statements which would discourage a reasonable person from making or pursuing a credit application.[152]

5.5.6 Exceptions to Restrictions on Requested Information

5.5.6.1 The Home Mortgage Monitoring Requirements

The major exception to the ECOA's prohibitions on prohibited inquiries is in the area of home mortgages. Both Regulation B and the Home Mortgage Disclosure Act (HMDA)[153] require lenders to collect certain information regarding the residential real estate-related loans that they make. The HMDA requires lenders to collect information including the race, sex, and income of each applicant for a home mortgage, as well information about the location of the property securing the loan.[154] Regulation B requires lenders to collect information including race, national origin, sex, marital status, and age so that creditor compliance with the ECOA and other statutes can be monitored.[155]

Although the creditor is required to seek this information, the applicant is not required to provide it. Under Regulation B, if the applicant does not provide the required information or any part of it, the creditor must note that fact on its form(s) and, to the extent possible, also note the applicant's race or national origin and sex on the basis of visual observation or surname. This information may be used only for monitoring; it may not be used to discriminate against the applicant.[156]

The impact of the HMDA and the ECOA provisions requiring collection of information on race, gender, and income have been very positive for protected groups.

HMDA data has been used quite effectively to reveal startling racial disparities in the area of home mortgages, including disparities in approval rates and rates of subprime versus prime loans based on racial composition of neighborhoods.[157] HMDA data is also useful in litigation to prove credit discrimination.[158] These studies and lawsuits in turn have attracted more attention and activism to efforts to increase lending to protected groups.[159] In fact, the success of the HMDA may have provided an impetus to the proposed revisions to Regulation B allowing requests for information on prohibited bases in non-mortgage credit.

5.5.6.2 Coverage of the Home Mortgage Monitoring Requirements

Creditors are required to seek out information on race, national origin, and gender (and marital status and age if the Regulation B monitoring requirements apply) in the following situations:

- Under both Regulation B and the HDMA/Regulation C: Applications for credit[160] primarily for the purchase or refinancing of a dwelling;[161] Regulation B's requirements only apply to dwellings occupied by the applicant as a principal residence when the dwelling will be collateral for the loan;[162] dwelling means residential structure, whether or not the structure is attached to real property, including condominiums, cooperatives, and mobile homes;[163]

---

152 Reg. B, 12 C.F.R. § 202.5(a).

153 12 U.S.C. § 2801–2810. For more on the HDMA and its implementing regulation, Regulation C, see § 4.4.5, *supra.*

154 12 C.F.R. § 203.4(a). Beginning in January 2004, lenders will also be required to disclose whether the loan is a high cost loan subject to the Home Ownership Equity Protection Act, and information about loan pricing for certain loans. 67 Fed. Reg. 7222, 7230 (Feb. 15, 2002) (adding 12 C.F.R. § 203.4(a)(12), (13). See § 4.4.5.3.2, *supra.*

155 Reg. B, 12 C.F.R. § 202.13.

156 Reg. B, 12 C.F.R. §§ 202.13(c), 202.6(a). 12 C.F.R. § 202.13(c) provides that the creditor must inform the applicant that the information is being requested for the purpose of monitoring compliance with federal anti-discrimination statutes and that, if the applicant chooses not to provide the information, the creditor is required to note the race or national origin and sex on the basis of visual observation or surname. The Federal Reserve Board has proposed requiring that this information be clear and conspicuous and in a form the applicant can retain. 64 Fed. Reg. 44,582, 44,596 (Aug. 16, 1999) (proposing to add 12 C.F.R. § 204(d)). The proposed revisions to Regulation B can be found on the CD-Rom accompanying this volume.

157 Both the ACORN and HUD studies discussed in § 5.3.2.3, *supra*, used HDMA data. Ass'n of Community Organizations for Reform Now, The Great Divide: An Analysis of Racial and Economic Disparities in Home Purchase Mortgage Lending Nationally and in Sixty Metropolitan Areas (Oct. 2001); Dep't of Hous. & Urban Dev., Unequal Burden: Income & Racial Disparities in Subprime Lending in America (Apr. 2000), *available at* http://www.hud.gov.

158 *See* § 4.4.5, *supra* (using HDMA to prove credit discrimination).

159 Richard D. Marsico, *Shedding Some Light on Lending: The Effect of Expanded Disclosure Laws on Home Mortgage Marketing, Lending and Discrimination in the New York Metropolitan Area*, 27 Fordham Urb. L.J. 481 (1999).

160 Regulation B's requirements only apply to applications by natural persons. Official Staff Commentary, 12 C.F.R. § 202.13(a)-1.

161 Reg. C, 12 C.F.R. § 203.4(a); Reg. B, 12 C.F.R. § 202.13(a).

162 Reg. B, 12 C.F.R. § 202.13(a). A dwelling is a principal residence if the applicant intends to make the dwelling his or her principal residence within one year of completion of construction. Official Staff Commentary, 12 C.F.R. § 202.13(a)-2. Principal residence does not include a vacation home or a rental unit. Official Staff Commentary, 12 C.F.R. § 202.13(a)-2. An application for temporary financing to construct a dwelling is not covered, and neither are loans not obtained to purchase the residence but rather obtained for home improvements, debt consolidations, or home equity lines of credit. Official Staff Commentary, 12 C.F.R. §§ 202.13(a)-3, 202.13(a)-5.

163 Reg. C, 12 C.F.R. § 203.2(d); Reg. B, 12 C.F.R. § 202.13(a).

- Under the HDMA/Regulation C: Applications for certain home improvement loans and open-ended home equity loans;[164]
- Regulation B also provides that loan brokers do not violate the ECOA when they collect information otherwise prohibited for purposes of providing it to creditors that are required to collect that data under the HMDA or another statute or regulation requiring such data collection.[165]

5.5.6.3 Information Required By Any Other Federal or State Statute or By Court Order For Monitoring Purposes

In addition to the home mortgage exception, creditors may make requests for information otherwise prohibited by Regulation B if any other federal or state statute or regulation requires collection of the information.[166] Creditors may also make otherwise forbidden inquiries if required to by an order or agreement issued by, or entered into with, a court or an enforcement agency.[167] The most common example of such an order would be one issued in an ECOA or Fair Housing lawsuit in which a creditor's future performance is to be monitored by a government enforcement agency.

5.5.6.4 Special Purpose Credit Programs

Regulation B creates special rules for special purpose credit programs, which are programs that address the credit needs of economically disadvantaged groups[168] If participants in such a program are required to possess one or more

common characteristics (such as race, national origin or sex), a creditor may request information regarding those common characteristics.[169] For example, if an energy conservation program is created to assist the elderly, the creditor may ask the applicant's age. A creditor may also inquire about the applicant's minority status when offering credit under a Minority Enterprise Small Business Investment Corporation program.[170]

If financial need is one of the criteria for the special purpose credit program, the creditor may also request information about marital status, alimony, child support, separate maintenance income, and the spouse's or parents' financial resources.[171] Examples of such programs are subsidized housing programs for low to moderate income households and student loan programs based on the family's financial need.[172]

5.6 Cosignature of Spouse or Other Person

5.6.1 General

The general rule against discrimination prevents a creditor from seeking a spouse or other person to cosign or guaranty a loan on a prohibited basis.[173] Thus creditors may not ask husbands to cosign loans while not requiring wives to do so or require only applicants on public assistance to provide cosigners.

The ECOA also sets other limitations as to when a creditor may seek a guarantor or cosigner, which apply particularly to creditor requirements that spouses cosign loans. The rules vary depending on whether an applicant's creditworthiness depends on property that is jointly owned, whether a community property state is involved, and whether the application is for joint credit. The rest of this chapter details these differing rules.

Before addressing specific rules, certain rules that are generally applicable should be mentioned. Regulation B specifically indicates that, when a creditor violates the rules governing when cosigners and sureties can be required, not only the applicant but also guarantors, sureties, endorsers and similar parties have the right to bring ECOA actions for damages.[174] However, these rights are still limited to ag-

Regulation B's definition of dwelling includes multi-family structures of two to four units, if the applicant intends to occupy one of the units as a principal residence. Official Staff Commentary, 12 C.F.R. § 202.13(a)-2.

164 Reg. C, 12 C.F.R. 203.4(a); *see also* Official Staff Commentary, 12 C.F.R. § 202.5(b)(2)-2. The Federal Reserve Board's proposed revisions to the Official Staff Commentary would delete § 202.5(b)(2)-2 in accordance with proposed changes to 12 C.F.R. § 202.5 that would allow creditors to request information about an applicant's race, color, religion, national origin, or sex. 64 Fed. Reg. 44,582, 44,622 (Aug. 16, 1999); *see also* § 5.5.4, *supra*. The proposed revisions to the Official Staff Commentary can be found on the CD-Rom accompanying this volume.

165 Official Staff Commentary, 12 C.F.R. § 202.5(b)(2)-3. The Federal Reserve Board's proposed revisions to the Official Staff Commentary delete § 202.5(b)(2)-3 in accordance with proposed changes to 12 C.F.R. § 202.5 that would allow creditors to request information about an applicant's race, color, religion, national origin, or sex. 64 Fed. Reg. 44,582, 44,622 (Aug. 16, 1999); *see* § 5.5.4, *supra*. The proposed revisions to the Official Staff Commentary can be found on the CD-Rom accompanying this volume.

166 Reg. B, 12 C.F.R. § 202.5(b)(2).
167 Reg. B, 12 C.F.R. § 202.5(b)(2).
168 Reg. B, 12 C.F.R. § 202.8; *see* § 3.9, *supra* (a description of the requirements for a special purpose credit program).

169 Reg. B, 12 C.F.R. § 202.8(c).
170 Official Staff Commentary, 12 C.F.R. § 202.8(c)-2.
171 Reg. B, 12 C.F.R. § 202.8(d).
172 Official Staff Commentary, 12 C.F.R. § 202.8(d)-2.
173 *See* Fed. Deposit Ins. Corp. v. Medmark, Inc., 897 F. Supp. 511 (D. Kan. 1995) (court granted summary judgment in favor of wife-guarantor because lender failed to set forth any facts to controvert assertion that wife's guaranty violated ECOA because husband was independently creditworthy).
174 Reg. B, 12 C.F.R. § 202.2(e); *see* Silverman v. Eastrich Multiple Investor Fund, L.P., 857 F. Supp. 447 (E.D. Pa. 1994), *rev'd on*

grieved parties—persons for whom accommodation signers were required and the accommodation signers themselves. Mere involvement in a transaction in which the ECOA may have been violated does not give one standing to sue under the ECOA.[175]

In addition to bringing an affirmative ECOA action, an aggrieved party whose signature was obtained illegally may be able to challenge the ECOA violations defensively through recoupment.[176]

Even when the ECOA would otherwise limit a creditor's ability to seek an additional signatory, a creditor may require such an additional signature pursuant to a special purpose credit program.[177] For example, a creditor may obtain a parent's signature as guarantor on a guaranteed student loan when required to do so by federal or state law or agency regulations.[178] In addition, the rules concerning cosigners do not apply to securities credit or incidental consumer credit.[179] Courts are also reluctant to apply these rules in a business context—for example, when a businessperson is guaranteeing a corporation as opposed to a spouse being asked to cosign a consumer loan—as none of the ECOA's purposes appear to be relevant.[180]

State laws addressing credit discrimination are preempted to the extent that they are inconsistent with the ECOA and Regulation B.[181] Regulation B specifies that state laws prohibiting the individual extension of consumer credit to both parties to a marriage if each spouse individually and voluntarily applies for such credit are inconsistent with the ECOA and therefore are preempted by it.[182]

5.6.2 Individual Credit When No Joint Property Is Involved

A creditor may not require the signature of a spouse or any other additional person on a credit instrument if the applicant has requested an individual account, no jointly held or community property is involved, and the applicant individually meets the creditor's standards for creditworthiness for the amount and terms of credit requested.[183] For example, a creditor may not automatically require that applications by married women for individual credit be signed by their husbands or that unmarried female applicants obtain cosigners for loans, because many of these applicants have sufficient individual assets to qualify for credit.[184]

---

other grounds, 51 F.3d 28 (3d Cir. 1995); Gen. Elec. Capital Corp. v. Pulsifer, Clearinghouse No. 46,778 (D. Me. Oct. 28, 1991); Douglas County Nat'l Bank v. Pfeiff, 809 P.2d 1100 (Colo. Ct. App. 1991). This right did not always exist, at least with regard to guarantors and sureties. *See* Reg. B, 12 C.F.R. § 202.2(e) (as amended in 1978 and 1979 but not as amended in 1985); *see also* Bank of Am. Nat'l Trust & Sav. Ass'n v. Hotel Rittenhouse Associates, 595 F. Supp. 800 (E.D. Pa. 1984); Morse v. Mut. Fed. Sav. & Loan Ass'n, 536 F. Supp. 1271 (D. Mass. 1982); Quigley v. Nash, Consumer Cred. Guide (CCH) ¶ 97,051 (D.D.C. Nov. 13, 1981) (also available at 1981 U.S. Dist. LEXIS 18177); Delta Diversified, Inc. v. Citizens & S. Nat'l Bank, 171 Ga. App. 625, 320 S.E.2d 767 (1984).

175 Riggs Nat'l Bank v. Linch, 36 F.3d 370 (4th Cir. 1994) (party whose independent creditworthiness was established and whose spouse was not required to cosign guaranty has no standing to sue under the ECOA because the creditor required the signature of a co-guarantor's spouse); *see also* Integra Bank/Pittsburgh v. Freeman, 839 F. Supp. 326 (E.D. Pa. 1993) (guarantor of loans could not invoke lender's alleged ECOA violation in requiring another guarantor's wife to sign guaranty agreements either as defense to liability or by way of recoupment) (discussed at §§ 11.6.5.2, 11.7.2, *infra*).

176 Sections 11.6.5.2, 11.7.2, *infra*, discuss this issue in more detail.

177 Official Staff Commentary, 12 C.F.R. § 202.8(d)-1; *see* § 3.9, *supra* (a discussion as to when credit qualifies for the special credit program exception and the scope of this exception).

178 Official Staff Commentary, 12 C.F.R. § 202.8(d)-3.

179 *See* Reg. B, 12 C.F.R. §§ 202.3(b)(2)(vi), 202.3(c)(2)(v); §§ 2.2.6.3, 2.2.6.6, *supra*. The Federal Reserve Board's proposed revisions to Regulation B would redesignate 12 C.F.R. § 202.3(b)(2)(vi) as § 202.3(b)(2)(v) and § 202.3(b)(2)(v) as § 202.3(b)(2)(iv) in accordance with proposed changes to 12 C.F.R. § 202.5 that would allow creditors to request information about an applicant's race, color, religion, national origin, or sex. 64 Fed. Reg. 44,582, 44,595 (Aug. 16, 1999); *see* § 5.5.4, *supra*.

180 *See* First Fid. Bank v. Best Petroleum, Inc., 757 F. Supp. 293 (S.D.N.Y. 1991) (cosigner for corporation had no ECOA stand-

ing in absence of allegation that he was subjected to discrimination on improper basis).

181 15 U.S.C. § 1691d(f); Reg. B, 12 C.F.R. § 202.11(a); *see* § 11.5.1.3, *infra*.

182 Reg. B, 12 C.F.R. § 202.11(b)(1)(ii).

183 Reg. B, 12 C.F.R. § 202.7(d)(1). The Federal Reserve Board's proposed revisions to Regulation B would amend 12 C.F.R. § 202.7(d)(1) to expressly prohibit a creditor from deeming the submission of a joint financial statement or other evidence of jointly held assets as an application for joint credit. 64 Fed. Reg. 44,582, 44,598 (Aug. 16, 1999). The proposed revisions to Regulation B can be found on the CD-Rom accompanying this volume. *See also* Bolduc v. Beal Bank, 994 F. Supp. 82 (D.N.H. 1998), *vacating preliminary injunction*, 167 F.3d 667 (1st Cir. 1999) (ECOA violation when wife was required to cosign credit instrument despite husband being independently creditworthy); United States v. Capitol Thrift & Loan Ass'n, Clearinghouse No. 43,052 (N.D. Cal. 1986) (consent order based on allegations that married applicants for individual credit were required to have spouse cosign); United States v. Allied Fin. Co., Clearinghouse No. 38,922 (N.D. Tex. 1985) (same); United States v. Household Fin. Corp., Clearinghouse No. 38,903 (N.D. Ill. Oct. 31, 1984) (creditor allegedly required applicant's spouse to sign credit documents even when the application was for individual, unsecured credit); Marine Am. State Bank v. Lincoln, 433 N.W.2d 709 (Iowa 1988) (bank violated ECOA by requiring spouse's signature when applicant was qualified individually). *But see* First Fid. Bank v. Best Petroleum, Inc., 757 F. Supp. 293 (S.D.N.Y. 1991) (bank could ask owner to cosign for corporation even if corporation was creditworthy; owner did not claim to be member of protected class).

184 However, one court has held that a blanket policy of requiring spousal signatures regardless of creditworthiness of the applicant does not violate the ECOA if the applicant and spouse presented themselves as joint applicants. Southwestern Pa. Regional Council v. Gentile, 776 A.2d 276 (Pa. Super. Ct. 2001).

Creditors may determine that an individual does not meet its standards of creditworthiness and condition credit on the applicant obtaining a cosigner.[185] In making its determination of creditworthiness, a creditor is permitted to apply its own criteria, as long as they are valid, reasonable, and nondiscriminatory.[186] In order to prove a violation of the ECOA, the plaintiff must show that the credit denial constitutes marital status discrimination.[187]

If the creditor requires a cosignor, it may not require that the spouse be this person, nor may the creditor impose any requirements on the additional person that may not be imposed on the applicant.[188] If the applicant's income alone will not support the credit, creditors may not tell an applicant that their spouses will have to cosign. Instead, the creditor should, without specifying the spouse, state that a cosigner is necessary.[189]

The creditor may place certain restrictions on who the cosigner is. For example, the creditor could insist that the additional signatory live in the creditor's market area.[190] But the creditor may not discriminate on the basis of sex, marital status, or any other prohibited basis. For example, creditors may not discriminate on a prohibited basis by giving greater credibility to male as opposed to female cosigners.[191]

Similarly, if an applicant is relying on another's income in making the credit application, the creditor may require the signature of that person so that the income will be available

to pay the debt.[192] A creditor may likewise require the signature of the owner of a spouse's property used in an applicant's disclosure of net worth.[193] The same is true in a community property state if the applicant is relying on the spouse's separate income or future earnings that cannot be characterized as community property until earned.[194]

5.6.3 Reliance on Jointly Owned Property to Establish Creditworthiness

If an applicant requests individual unsecured credit and relies on jointly owned property to establish creditworthiness, the creditor may require the signature of a spouse or other person on an instrument necessary to make the property available to the creditor in case of death or default.[195] For example, if a house is held in tenancy by the entirety under state law and cannot be transferred by only one spouse, the creditor may request the wife's signature if the husband applies for credit and relies on the house to establish creditworthiness. In the context of loans for small businesses, the spouse is often listed as a partner or principal in the business, and the creditor may in those instances require the spouse's signature.[196]

This exception is a sweeping one. Many married applicants jointly own a house or car and rely upon them as assets in an application for credit, even if that property does not secure the loan. Therefore, creditors can frequently obtain a spouse's signature legitimately, even for unsecured credit accounts.

The first issue, however, is whether the individual is relying on the jointly owned property to establish creditworthiness. Simply because a creditor's application asks an applicant to list property should not be taken to indicate that the applicant is relying on such property to establish creditworthiness.[197] However, even if the applicant does not rely on jointly owned property to establish creditworthiness,

---

185 *See, e.g.,* Miller v. Elegant Junk, 616 F. Supp. 551 (S.D. W. Va. 1985) (cosignature requirement based on applicant's lack of creditworthiness); Paulson v. Centier Bank, 704 N.E.2d 482 (Ind. Ct. App. 1998) (requiring wife's signature did not violate the ECOA because bank could have reasonably concluded husband was not independently creditworthy); Spears v. Voss Chevrolet, Inc., 1986 Ohio App. LEXIS 9412 (Ohio Ct. App. Dec. 16, 1986) (no ECOA violation when woman wished to apply individually for a loan, but creditor took information on both her and her husband and approved financing contingent on his cosignature, in the absence of evidence that the woman was qualified individually); Roper Bros. Lumber Co. v. Westover Homes, Inc., 44 Va. Cir. 448 (1998) (no ECOA violation when wife's cosignature was required after creditor determined husband was not independently creditworthy).

186 Riggs Nat'l Bank v. Linch, 36 F.3d 370 (4th Cir. 1994).

187 Haynes v. Bank of Wedowee, 634 F.2d 266, 270 (5th Cir. 1981) (no discrimination under ECOA when bank considered bankruptcy of plaintiff's husband in deciding whether to accelerate plaintiff's loan); Cherry v. Hughes Supply Co., 539 S.E.2d 536 (Ga. Ct. App. 2000) (no evidence that denial was a pretext for marital status discrimination). A key issue is whether this claim may be raised as an affirmative defense or only as a counterclaim. *See* §§ 11.6.5.2, 11.7.2, *infra.*

188 Reg. B, 12 C.F.R. § 202.7(d)(5), (6); *see also* Thames v. City Nat'l Bank of Baton Rouge, 370 So. 2d 892 (La. Ct. App. 1978).

189 *See* Reg. B, 12 C.F.R. § 202.7(d)(5). When a spouse's income is being relied upon to support the ability to repay, the spouse may be required to sign to the extent necessary to make that income available to pay the debt. *See* Official Staff Commentary, 12 C.F.R. § 202.7(d)(5)-2.

190 Official Staff Commentary, 12 C.F.R. § 202.7(d)(5)-1.

191 United States v. Citizens Bank & Trust Co., Clearinghouse No. 31,077 (E.D. Ky. 1979).

192 Official Staff Commentary, 12 C.F.R. § 202.7(d)(5)-2; Riggs Nat'l Bank v. Webster, 832 F. Supp. 147, 151 (D. Md. 1993).

193 Riggs Nat'l Bank v. Webster, 832 F. Supp. 147, 151 (D. Md. 1993).

194 Official Staff Commentary, 12 C.F.R. § 202.7(d)(5)-2; *see also* Resolution Trust Corp. v. Forest Grove, Inc., 1993 U.S. Dist. LEXIS 12575 (E.D. Pa. Sept. 7, 1993), *reversed in part on other grounds,* 33 F.3d 284 (3d. Cir. 1994).

195 Reg. B, 12 C.F.R. § 202.7(d)(2); Official Staff Commentary, 12 C.F.R. §§ 202.7(d)(2)-1, 202.7(d)(4)-3.

196 Taylor v. Albina Cmty. Bank, 2001 U.S. Dist. LEXIS 21519 (D. Or. Nov. 23, 2001); Cherry v. Hughes Supply Co., 539 S.E.2d 536 (Ga. Ct. App. 2000).

197 *See* Reg. B, 12 C.F.R. § 202.7(d)(3) (dealing with community property states). *But see* Riggs Nat'l Bank v. Linch, 36 F.3d 370 (4th Cir. 1994) (lender did not violate ECOA by requiring wife to sign as co-guarantor in loan to husband's business after lender discovered that many of the assets listed on husband's personal financial statement were jointly owned by husband and wife and that husband was not independently creditworthy for loan amount requested).

merely listing the property may be seen to imply that the spouse voluntarily signed.[198]

Furthermore, if the applicant is relying on jointly held property to establish creditworthiness and can, under state law, individually transfer enough of that property to meet the creditor's creditworthiness standards, no additional signature may be required.[199] In determining the value of the applicant's interest in jointly owned property, a creditor may consider factors such as the form of ownership and the property's susceptibility to attachment, execution, severance, or partition, and the cost of such action.[200] However, the value of an applicant's interest prior to or at consummation (without factoring in the possibility of subsequent changes resulting from marriage or divorce, for example) is the relevant issue in making a credit decision.[201]

If the applicant's interest in the property is not sufficient to protect the creditor, the creditor may give the applicant another option of providing additional support for the extension of credit, such as finding another party (that is, not the spouse) to act as a cosigner, converting the application to one for secured credit, or asking for the signature of the co-owner of the property on an instrument that ensures access to the property but does not impose personal liability unless necessary under state law.[202]

Finally, if the creditor requires a signature from the co-owner of the property, the signature is required only on instruments necessary (or reasonably believed to be necessary) under state law to make the property available in the event of death or default.[203] That is, the co-owner may not have to sign the note evidencing the obligation to pay but only a document protecting the creditor's access to the property in the case of default.

The creditor will not be held liable if it can show it "reasonably believed" that the spouse's signature was necessary. Reasonable belief can be shown if the creditor came to this conclusion based on a "thorough review" of applicable statutes and case law.[204]

5.6.4 Reliance on Community Property to Establish Creditworthiness

If a married applicant requests individual unsecured credit in a community property state, or relies on property located in such a state, the creditor may request the spouse's signature on instruments necessary to make community property available in case of death or default.[205] Similarly, in a community property state, if an applicant for individual credit relies on the future earnings or income of another person, the creditor may require the signature of that individual[206] (the Commentary allows creditors to assume that

---

198 Southwestern Pa. Regional Council v. Gentile, 776 A.2d 276 (Pa. Super. Ct. 2001).

199 Reg. B, 12 C.F.R. § 202.7(d)(1). The Federal Reserve Board's proposed revisions to Regulation B would amend 12 C.F.R. § 202.7(d)(1) to expressly prohibit a creditor from deeming the submission of a joint financial statement or other evidence of jointly held assets as an application for joint credit. 64 Fed. Reg. 44,582, 44,598 (Aug. 16, 1999). The proposed revisions to Regulation B can be found on the CD-Rom accompanying this volume. The Board has also proposed to redesignate the portion of Official Staff Commentary, 12 C.F.R. § 202.6(b)(1)-1— related to a creditor's right to consider an applicant's or joint applicant's marital status for purposes of ascertaining rights and remedies applicable to the particular extension of credit, such as when state law gives the applicant's spouse an interest in the property offered as collateral—as new Official Staff Commentary, 12 C.F.R. § 202.6(b)(8)-1. 64 Fed. Reg. 44,582, 44,624 (Aug. 16, 1999); *see also* Comptroller of the Currency, Interpretive Staff Letter, Fed. Banking L. Rep. (CCH) ¶ 85,042 (Office of the Comptroller of the Currency Oct. 27, 1977) (Roberta W. Boylan) (also available at 1977 OCC Ltr. LEXIS 28); Comptroller of the Currency, Interpretive Staff Letter, Fed. Banking L. Rep. (CCH) ¶ 85,043 (Office of the Comptroller of the Currency Oct. 27, 1977) (Roberta W. Boylan) (also available at 1977 OCC Ltr. LEXIS 29).

200 Official Staff Commentary, 12 C.F.R. § 202.7(d)(2)-1a.

201 Official Staff Commentary, 12 C.F.R. § 202.7(d)(2)-1a.

202 Official Staff Commentary, 12 C.F.R. § 202.7(d)(2)-1b.

203 Reg. B, 12 C.F.R. § 202.7(d)(2); *In re* McMullan, 196 B.R. 818 (Bankr. W.D. Ark. 1996), *aff'd*, 162 F.3d 1164 (8th Cir. 1998)

(Arkansas and Louisiana state law required wife's signature on note to obtain valid lien on personal and real property); *see also* Anderson v. United Fin. Co., 666 F.2d 1274 (9th Cir. 1982) (discrimination shown when finance company insisted that loan applicant obtain her husband's signature on note, when applicant specifically desired to establish individual credit, husband was disabled and receiving public benefits, and creditor did not show that a valid lien on joint property could not be created without husband's signature on note); Comptroller of the Currency, Interpretive Staff Letter, Fed. Banking L. Rep. (CCH) ¶ 85,042 (Office of the Comptroller of the Currency Oct. 27, 1977) (Roberta W. Boylan) (also available at 1977 OCC Ltr. LEXIS 28); Comptroller of the Currency, Interpretive Staff Letter, Fed. Banking L. Rep. (CCH) ¶ 85,043 (Office of the Comptroller of the Currency Oct. 27, 1977) (Roberta W. Boylan) (also available at 1977 OCC Ltr. LEXIS 29); *cf.* Evans v. Centralfed Mortgage Co., 815 F.2d 348 (5th Cir. 1987) (husband's signature on deed could be seen as reasonably thought to be necessary).

204 Farris v. Jefferson Bank, 194 B.R. 931 (Bankr. E.D. Pa. 1996).

205 Reg. B, 12 C.F.R. § 202.7(d)(3); *see also* McKenzie v. U.S. Home Corp., 704 F.2d 778 (5th Cir. 1983) (no violation of ECOA when a mortgage company told an applicant she could not obtain a loan unless her divorce was finalized or her husband signed the deed of trust, because the company was acting lawfully to ensure a valid lien on the mortgaged property in a community property state); United States v. ITT Consumer Fin. Corp., Clearinghouse No. 38,924 (N.D. Cal. 1985), *aff'd*, 816 F.2d 487 (9th Cir. 1987) (no ECOA violation for requiring husbands to cosign loans on applications by creditworthy women in equal management community property states); Fed. Trade Comm'n, Informal Staff Opinion, Clearinghouse No. 37,097 (Jan. 7, 1985) (creditor in a community property state may obtain a nonapplicant spouse's signature on a security agreement, but not a promissory note, when the other spouse has applied for individual, secured credit and is qualified).

206 Official Staff Commentary, 12 C.F.R. § 202.7(d)(5)-2; *see also* United States v. ITT Consumer Fin. Corp., 816 F.2d 487 (9th Cir. 1987) (future earnings cannot be characterized prospec-

anyone applying for credit in a community property state is a resident of that state).[207] But the request for the spouse's signature may only be made if the applicant does not have enough separate property to be considered individually creditworthy and state law denies the applicant control over sufficient community property to be considered individually creditworthy.[208]

A creditor may not presume that, because income or assets are listed, the applicant is relying on them to establish creditworthiness.[209] Moreover, the creditor may request the spouse's signature only on the documents which would make the property available in case of default; there is no reason to make the spouse jointly liable on the note if a signature on some other document would suffice.[210]

5.6.5 Individual Credit When Jointly Owned Property Is Taken As Security

If an applicant requests individual *secured* credit, the creditor may require the signature of the spouse or other person jointly holding property offered as security but only on instruments necessary under state law to ensure its availability in case of default.[211] Examples of such docu-

ments include instruments to create a valid lien, pass clear title, waive inchoate rights, or assign earnings.[212]

Generally, a signature to make secured property available will be needed only on a security agreement.[213] According to the Commentary, before a creditor requests the other party's signature on the note itself, the creditor must thoroughly review statutory and decisional law or an opinion of the state attorney general.[214]

It is particularly important for advocates representing borrowers to scrutinize transactions in which the creditor uses integrated documents. These are documents in which the note, security agreement and, sometimes, the Truth in Lending disclosure statement are combined. If the nonapplicant spouse's signature is needed only on the security agreement, the creditor may not require the nonapplicant spouse to sign an integrated document unless the document makes clear that the signature is only for the purpose of granting a security interest and that no personal liability is imposed.[215]

5.6.6 When Do Applicants Voluntarily Enter into a Joint Account?

When a joint, rather than an individual, application for credit is made, the creditor clearly has the right to ask for the signature of both persons involved.[216] This is another

tively as community property, so it was not an ECOA violation to require the signature of an applicant's spouse when the applicant was relying on a spouse's future earnings to qualify for a loan).

207 Official Staff Commentary, 12 C.F.R. § 202.7(d)(3)-1.

208 Reg. B, 12 C.F.R. § 202.7(d)(3); *see also* Clark v. Avco Fin. Services of Maricopa, Inc., Clearinghouse No. 33,885 (D. Ariz. June 24, 1981) (creditor violated ECOA by requiring an applicant's spouse to sign an application for an unsecured loan when the applicant had authority under state law to bind enough community property to make her individually creditworthy).

209 "Whether an applicant is relying on the future earnings of a nonapplicant spouse is for the creditor to determine. Because section 202.5(c)(2)(iv) permits a creditor routinely to request information about a nonapplicant spouse, the mere fact that the nonapplicant spouse's income is listed on an application form is insufficient to show that the applicant is relying on the spouse's income." 50 Fed. Reg. 11,044, 11,045 (Apr. 5, 1988) (explanatory material for revision of Official Staff Commentary, 12 C.F.R. § 202.7(d)(5)-2)).

210 *See* Fed. Trade Comm'n, Informal Staff Opinion, Clearinghouse No. 37,097 (Jan. 7, 1985). *But cf.* Evans v. Centralfed Mortgage Co., 815 F.2d 348 (5th Cir. 1987) (husband's signature on deed could be seen as reasonably thought to be necessary).

211 12 C.F.R. § 202.7(d)(4); *see also* Evans v. Centralfed Mortgage Co., 815 F.2d 348 (5th Cir. 1987) (no ECOA violation when creditor required all married borrowers to obtain their spouse's signatures on the warranty deed and deed of trust for the property purchased but not on the note); Bolduc v. Beal Bank, 994 F. Supp. 82 (D.N.H. 1998), *vacating preliminary injunction*, 167 F.3d 667 (1st Cir. 1999) (creditor is permitted to require spouse's signature on documents necessary to create an undisputed interest in jointly held property offered as security); Tease v. First Union Home Equity Bank, 974 F. Supp. 1408 (D. Kan. 1997) (creditor may escape ECOA liability by showing it has policy of requiring all individuals with actual or potential

interest in pledged property to sign loan documents); Liberty Sav. Bank v. Sortman, 1998 Ohio App. LEXIS 1667 (Ohio Ct. App. Apr. 17, 1998) (no ECOA violation because spouse's signature was required to create a valid lien against jointly held property).

212 Reg. B, 12 C.F.R. § 202.7(d)(4).

213 United States v. Sec. Pac. Fin. Sys., Clearinghouse No. 37,095 (S.D. Cal. 1983) (creditor may not generally require nonapplicant spouse to assume liability on note or on integrated note and security agreement). *But see* Riggs Nat'l Bank v. Webster, 832 F. Supp. 147, 151 (D. Md. 1993) (when bank could have required applicant's spouse to sign lien documents on her solely owned property, it causes no injury to require her to sign the promissory note instead). The *Webster* court failed to consider the personal liability which attached upon signing the promissory note which does not attach upon signing lien documents alone. If the house burned down, she would be injured by having personal liability on the note when none should have attached.

214 Official Staff Commentary, 12 C.F.R. § 202.7(d)(4)-2; *cf.* Rooms with A View v. Private Nat'l Mortgage Ass'n, 7 S.W.3d 840 (Tex. App. 1999), *cert. denied*, 531 U.S. 826 (2000) (state constitutional amendment requiring both spouses' signature on a home improvement contract in order to create a valid mechanic's lien against the homestead does not violate the ECOA).

215 *See* Official Staff Commentary, 12 C.F.R. § 202.7(d)(4)-3.

216 Reg. B, 12 C.F.R. § 202.7(d)(1); *see also* Midlantic Nat'l Bank v. Hansen, 48 F.3d 693 (3d Cir. 1995); Bank of Am. Nat'l Trust & Sav. Ass'n v. Hotel Rittenhouse Associates., 595 F. Supp. 800 (E.D. Pa. 1984). However, the Federal Reserve Board's proposed revision to 12 C.F.R. § 202.7(d)(1) makes it clear that a creditor cannot deem the submission of a joint financial statement or other evidence of jointly held assets as an application for joint credit. 64 Fed. Reg. 44,582, 44,598 (Aug. 16, 1999).

sweeping exception and has even been used to justify lenders' policies that should otherwise be illegal under the ECOA.[217]

However, the fact that two people have signed an application for an account does not make it a joint account—otherwise, any illegally procured cosignature would become legal because the application would be transformed into one for a joint account. In order for an account to be truly joint, and thus avoid ECOA cosigner limitations, the cosigner must have voluntarily entered into the loan.[218] The issue is whether the individual actually wanted to make a joint application or was required or convinced to do so by the creditor. The Commentary states that joint applicant "refers to someone who applies contemporaneously with the applicant for shared or joint credit. It does not refer to someone whose signature is required by the creditor as a condition for granting the credit requested."[219]

The distinction hinges on the intent of the applicants. Typically, debtors do not know that spousal signatures are often not required, and the creditor is under no obligation to disclose the debtor's ECOA rights. Thus it is usually not difficult for a creditor to procure both spouses' signatures, especially if both are physically present when one spouse is applying for credit. But that does not make the signature voluntary.

Advocates should ascertain if the creditor encouraged both spouses to be physically present or indicated that both spouses' signatures were required on the promissory note for a secured debt (even though the second signature on the security agreement alone might be adequate under state law to protect the creditor's security interest in such collateral).[220]

An issue of interest is whether a creditor may require both signatures on the refinancing of an account originally signed by two parties. Consider a case in which one party wishes to take out a new loan individually to pay off the old joint loan and meets the creditor's standards for creditworthiness for that new loan even without relying on jointly owned property. That party should be able to obtain the new loan individually with no cosigner and pay off the old joint obligation. There seems no reason to require two signatures for a new loan simply because the loan proceeds will go to pay off a loan with two signatories.[221] In fact, for renewals, the Commentary specifies that, if a borrower's creditworthiness is reevaluated when credit is renewed, the creditor must determine whether an additional party is still warranted and, if not, release the additional party.[222]

5.6.7 Authorized Users

Credit card and other credit accounts often provide the individual borrower the opportunity to designate another individual as an authorized user. The latter may use the account but is not liable for payment of debts accrued to the account. Although creditors are permitted to decide whether or not to allow authorized users on an account, they may not decide on a prohibited basis which individuals are allowed to be authorized users.[223] Thus, if a creditor accepts spouses as authorized users, it may not refuse to accept others as authorized users.[224]

A creditor can restrict the number of authorized users on a card. However, the creditor may not restrict the number of authorized users on a prohibited basis. For example, a creditor may restrict all accounts to one authorized user but may not restrict only the accounts of married women to one authorized user.

Sometimes, the creditor may allow the designation of an authorized user by the account holder on the condition that the authorized user becomes contractually liable for the account. This requirement is permissible as long as the creditor does not differentiate on any prohibited basis in imposing this requirement.[225] Thus, creditors can require that all authorized users sign the credit agreement but may not require that only authorized users who are spouses sign the agreement. If a checking or NOW account includes an overdraft line of credit, the creditor may require that all

---

The proposed revisions to Regulation B can be found on the CD-Rom accompanying this volume.

217 *See* Southwestern Pa. Regional Council v. Gentile, 776 A.2d 276 (Pa. Super. Ct. 2001) (not a violation of ECOA for lender to require spouse's signature under a blanket policy of requiring spousal guarantees regardless of creditworthiness, if the applicant and spouse presented themselves as joint applicants).

218 *Cf.* United States v. Meadors, 753 F.2d 590 (7th Cir. 1985) (signature voluntary when creditor did not provide signature block for applicant's spouse and creditor was not present when applicant's spouse added signature).

219 Official Staff Commentary, 12 C.F.R. § 202.7(d)(1)-1. The Federal Reserve Board has proposed adding a new Official Staff Comment § 202.7(d)(1)-1 to clarify that a creditor may not require an applicant who is individually creditworthy to provide a cosigner even if the creditor applies the requirement without regard to sex, marital status, or any other prohibited basis. 64 Fed. Reg. 44,582, 44,624 (Aug. 16, 1999). The proposed revisions to the Official Staff Commentary can be found on the CD-Rom accompanying this volume.

   See Baybank v. Bornhofft, 694 N.E.2d 854 (Mass. 1998) (combination of contemporaneous application for credit and shared ownership interest in the collateral makes the defendant a joint applicant).

220 Farris v. Jefferson Bank, 194 B.R. 931 (Bankr. E.D. Pa. 1996) (wife not co-applicant when husband applied for the loan for a

business in which wife was not involved; only husband negotiated the loan; the application referred to his assets; and she first learned of the loan the evening before signing the papers).

221 *But see* Sutliff v. County Sav. & Loan Co., 533 F. Supp. 1307 (N.D. Ohio 1982) (no unlawful discrimination when husband and wife were obligors on 1967 demand note and creditor required both spouses to be obligors on 1980 refinancing).

222 Official Staff Commentary, 12 C.F.R. § 202.7(d)(5)-3.

223 Official Staff Commentary, 12 C.F.R. § 202.7(a)-1.

224 Official Staff Commentary, 12 C.F.R. § 202.7(a)-2.

225 Official Staff Commentary, 12 C.F.R. § 202.7(a)-1.

persons authorized to draw on the transaction account assume liability for the overdraft.[226]

5.6.8 Signature of Guarantor's Spouse

The rules limiting a creditor's ability to require the signature of an applicant's spouse apply as well to a creditor's attempt to obtain the signature not only of a guarantor but also a guarantor's spouse.[227] For example, if a creditor requires one parent's signature on a credit application in addition to the applicant's, it may not require that the father sign in addition to the mother.

Another example provided by the Commentary indicates that, when all the officers of a closely held corporation are required to personally guarantee a corporate loan, the creditor may not automatically require that spouses of married officers also sign. However, if an evaluation of an officer's financial circumstances indicates that an additional signature is required, under appropriate circumstances, this extra signatory can be the officer's spouse.[228] Similarly, the ECOA does not prohibit a spouse from signing in a capacity unrelated to marital status, for example, as a guarantor limited partner of a partnership for which the husband is the general partner.[229]

5.7 Designation of Name on Account

The creditor may not prohibit an applicant from opening (or maintaining) an account under any of the following names:[230]

- Birth-given first name (e.g., Jane Applicant, rather than Mrs. John Applicant);[231]
- Birth-given surname (e.g., Jane Birthname);[232]
- Spouse's surname (e.g., Jane Marriedname); or
- Combined surname (e.g., Jane Birthname-Marriedname).[233]

A creditor may require, however, that joint applicants on an account designate a single name for purposes of administering the account and that a single name be embossed on any credit cards issued on the account. The creditor may also require that all accounts opened or maintained at the same time be listed in the same way to prevent fraud and to simplify recordkeeping.[234] But the creditor may not require that the name designated on the account or accounts be the husband's name.[235]

There is an exception from these requirements for securities credit, but only to the extent necessary to prevent violation of rules regarding an account in which a broker or dealer has an interest or of rules dealing with the aggregation of accounts of spouses.[236]

5.8 Collateral, Security Deposits, Sureties, Other Forms of Creditor Protection

5.8.1 Discriminatory Practices

In addition to the ECOA's co-signature rules, a creditor

---

226 Official Staff Commentary, 12 C.F.R. § 202.7(a)-3.

227 Official Staff Commentary, 12 C.F.R. § 202.7(d)(6)-1.

228 Official Staff Commentary, 12 C.F.R. § 202.7(d)(6)-1.; Riggs Nat'l Bank v. Linch, 36 F.3d 370 (4th Cir. 1994) (lender did not violate ECOA by requiring wife to sign as co-guarantor in loan to husband's business after lender discovered that many of the assets listed on husband's personal financial statement were jointly owned by husband and wife and that husband was not independently creditworthy for loan amount requested); Resolution Trust Corp. v. Townsend Assocs. Ltd. P'ship, 840 F. Supp. 1127 (E.D. Mich. 1993) (creditor had legitimate business justification for requiring wife's, as well as husband's, personal guaranty on loans to husband's partnership when creditor determined that husband was not creditworthy because he did not separately own sufficient assets and because the assets listed were those jointly held with his wife; guarantors did not come forward with any evidence to show that this determination was purely a pretext to discriminate based upon marital status); *see also* Resolution Trust Corp. v. Forest Grove, Inc., 1993 U.S. Dist. LEXIS 12575 (E.D. Pa. Sept. 7, 1993), *reversed in part on other grounds*, 33 F.3d 284 (3d. Cir. 1994); United States v. Lowy, 703 F. Supp. 1040 (E.D.N.Y. 1989) (Small Business Administration's standards of creditworthiness require guarantors for loans to marginal small businesses; proper to require guarantor's wife to sign as well, when she had sole title to house which was collateral, and to prevent fraudulent transfers from her husband to her).

229 *See* Wilmington Trust Co. v. Bethany Group Ltd. P'ship, 1994 Del. Super. LEXIS 146 (Del. Super. Ct. Feb. 1, 1994).

230 Reg. B, 12 C.F.R. § 202.7(b).

231 For an interesting twist on this provision, see Harbaugh v. Cont'l Ill. Nat'l Bank & Trust, 615 F.2d 1169 (7th Cir. 1980) (creditor had no affirmative duty to issue a separate account when plaintiff wife applied for credit using her husband's full name preceded by "Mrs."; offer of credit had been extended to husband only and creditor issued two cards in husband's name which wife was also entitled to use).

232 *See* United States v. Household Fin. Corp., Clearinghouse No. 38,903 (N.D. Ill. Oct. 31, 1984) (consent order based partially on allegations that creditor refused to permit married women to open accounts in their maiden names); *In re* Alden's, Inc., 92 F.T.C. 901 (Fed. Trade Comm'n 1978) (creditor was ordered to stop refusing to extend joint accounts to married couples when the wife used her birth-given surname or a combined surname rather than her husband's surname).

233 Reg. B, 12 C.F.R. § 202.7(a), (b); *see also In re* Alden's, Inc., 92 F.T.C. 901 (Fed. Trade Comm'n 1978) (creditor was ordered to stop refusing to extend joint accounts to married couples when the wife used her birth-given surname or a combined surname rather than her husband's surname).

234 Official Staff Commentary, 12 C.F.R. § 202.7(b)-1.

235 Official Staff Commentary, 12 C.F.R. § 202.7(b)-1.

236 Reg. B, 12 C.F.R. § 202.3(b)(2)(iv).

may not discriminate on a prohibited basis as to the type of protection it demands on a loan, including collateral or security. For example, a creditor can not require that married women alone put up a home as collateral on a small loan when other applicants need not do so.

Lenders often offer both secured and unsecured loans and may offer lower interest rates for the secured loans. Nevertheless, if a creditor offers only secured loans to applicants of certain races, even if the interest is lower, this practice is discriminatory if other applicants are given the choice between higher-rate unsecured loans and lower-rate secured loans.

The general rule against discrimination applies not only to collateral but also to cosigners, security deposits and other forms of protection. For example, under the ECOA, a security deposit or cosigner may not be sought from public assistance recipients if it is not sought from others.[237]

If all a merchant requires as security is a credit card in the consumer's name or a telephone number listed under the consumer's own name, even this requirement may be discriminatory if the creditor does not accept a credit card or telephone number that is in the name of the consumer's spouse.[238] This practice may be viewed as having the effect of discriminating against married, separated, or divorced women who, for historical reasons, never obtained a separate listing under their own name.

---

237 *See, e.g.,* Reed v. Northwestern Bell Tel., Clearinghouse No. 27,524 (D. Minn. 1981).

238 *See* Reg. B, 12 C.F.R. § 202.6(b)(4) (can only require telephone listing at applicant's residence, not in applicant's name); Fed. Trade Comm'n, Informal Staff Opinion, Clearinghouse No. 37,084 (May 26, 1983) (ECOA violation when car rental agency required that a customer without a major credit card have a telephone listing in their own name).

The ECOA and Regulation B do not alter or annul any state banking regulations directed only toward ensuring the solvency of financial institutions.[239] These regulations would include those requiring banks to obtain adequate security for loans and adequate documentation of that security.

5.8.2 Injury Caused By Such Discrimination

Merely requiring extra security may not seem injurious to a consumer, but such discrimination can often cause the consumer financial damage *even* if the loan never goes into default, and these damages should be recoverable under the ECOA. If a consumer must put up personal property as collateral, the creditor may require the consumer to purchase property insurance on that collateral. Using a home as security may require various closing costs. These costs are further increased because they are often included in the amount financed, which in turn increases the finance charges and the cost of any credit insurance.

There may be additional damages if the loan goes into default. It might be possible in such a situation, when there is an ECOA violation, to seek not only actual and punitive damages but also the voiding of the cosigner's obligation under the note or other instrument.[240] It should be argued that, were it not for the illegal discrimination, the property would not have been offered as collateral or a cosignor would not have been required to sign the loan.

---

239 Reg. B, 12 C.F.R. § 202.11(d). Similar federal banking regulations are also unaffected.

240 *See* §§ 11.6.5.2, 11.7.2, *infra.*

Chapter 6

Discrimination in Credit Evaluation

6.1 Introduction

This chapter focuses on discrimination in the credit evaluation process. It discusses both examples of credit evaluation practices that violate the general rule against discrimination as well the special ECOA requirements with respect to credit evaluation.

Some of these special ECOA requirements prohibit certain types of credit discrimination even though the discrimination is not on a prohibited basis or is only indirectly linked to a prohibited basis. Examples are credit decisions based on the applicant's likelihood of childbearing, type of income, telephone listing, and certain aspects of credit history. As discussed in § 5.2, *supra*, these special ECOA rules provide protections for women and, to a lesser extent, for applicants aged sixty-two or over.

Other special ECOA requirements permit creditors in certain situations to take into consideration three of the prohibited bases—the applicant's age, public assistance status, and marital status. These exceptions are set out in §§ 6.6.2, 6.6.3, and 6.6.4, *infra*.

This chapter also devotes significant attention to the topic of credit scoring, one of the types of credit evaluation systems, because the use of credit scoring has grown dramatically in the past few years. The credit scoring section sets forth the arguments as to whether credit scoring has had a positive or a discriminatory effect on protected groups, especially with regard to race and ethnicity.

6.2 Credit Evaluation Practices That Violate the General Rule Against Discrimination

6.2.1 The ECOA and FHA Standards

The ECOA and Regulation B prohibit discrimination in credit evaluation on a prohibited basis. Regulation B specifically states that a creditor shall not take a prohibited basis into account "in any system of evaluating the creditworthiness of applicants."[1] Regulation B also prohibits a creditor from using any information it obtains on an applicant to

---

1   Reg. B, 12 C.F.R. § 202.6(b)(1).

discriminate on a prohibited basis.[2] These standards essentially apply the general rule against discrimination to credit evaluation.

The Fair Housing Act also generally prohibits any type of discrimination in the evaluation or denial of credit. Department of Housing and Urban Development regulations prohibit using different policies, practices, or procedures in evaluating or in determining creditworthiness because of the applicant's race, color, religion, sex, handicap, familial status, or national origin.[3] Furthermore, a lender may not rely on an appraisal which it knows or should have known uses impermissible bases of evaluation.[4]

Thus, both the ECOA and Fair Housing Act standards prohibit virtually any discrimination on a prohibited basis as to credit evaluation.

6.2.2 Examples of Credit Evaluation Practices That Violate the General Rule

6.2.2.1 Applying Different Standards on a Prohibited Basis

The general rule against discrimination prohibits creditors from applying different standards to applicants on a prohibited basis. For example, creditors may not use one set of underwriting standards for white applicants and another, more stringent, set of standards for protected groups.

Discrimination can also be present even if an applicant failed to obtain a passing grade on the creditor's test for

---

2   Reg. B, 12 C.F.R. § 202.6(a).

3   24 C.F.R. § 100.130(b)(1). It is critical that the plaintiff link the different treatment of credit applicants with an impermissible basis for such treatment. For example, in Simms v. First Gibraltar Bank, 83 F.3d 1546 (5th Cir. 1996), the plaintiff presented evidence discrediting the lender's articulated reasons for denying credit and showing that the bank's less-than-thorough handling of the plaintiff's mortgage application did not conform generally to customary industry practices. The court nonetheless ruled that this evidence did not support an inference of discrimination, because there was no evidence that the bank treated similar, "non-protected" applications differently. *Id.* at 1559.

4   24 C.F.R. § 100.135; 12 C.F.R. § 528.2a (Office of Thrift Supervision Nondiscrimination Requirements); *see also* Steptoe v. Sav. of Am., 800 F. Supp. 1542 (N.D. Ohio 1992). For more on discrimination in the appraisal process, see § 6.2.2.3, *infra*.

creditworthiness. The issue is whether other applicants received the same failing grade but were still offered credit. For example, one of the most common standards used in mortgage lending is that a loan must not exceed a certain percentage of the home's value. This loan-to-value ratio is a fairly objective standard; it would not be illegal discrimination to deny credit to all applicants whose ratios were over a certain level.[5] On the other hand, it would be illegal discrimination to almost always deny mortgages to minorities when a loan is above the stated ratio, while often making exceptions for white applicants.[6]

Sometimes the differences in credit evaluation are hard to spot and can only be uncovered by using paired testers. For example, one study found that when paired testers approached a lender their expense/income ratios were computed differently, with utility costs being included only for African-American applicants.[7] At other times, African-American testers with the same ratio were told they were just over the limit, but whites were told they qualified.

6.2.2.2 Using Different Investigation Procedures on a Prohibited Basis

The general rule against discrimination prohibits creditors from implementing different investigatory procedures on a prohibited basis. Regulation B specifically states that creditors may not discriminate on a prohibited basis as to "investigation procedures."[8] Thus creditors may not order credit reports on the spouses of married women who apply for individual accounts but not on the spouses of married men who apply for individual accounts.[9]

Similarly, creditors may not discriminate as to the information they actually review. When a couple applies for a joint account, it would be discriminatory to solely or primarily consider the husband's credit report without considering the wife's credit report.[10]

6.2.2.3 Appraisal Practices That Violate the General Rule Against Discrimination

In applying for home mortgage loans, the appraisal of the real estate can have a significant impact on whether an applicant qualifies. Differences in appraisal practices because of a prohibited basis are specifically prohibited by the Fair Housing Act[11] and should violate the ECOA and sections 1981 and 1982 of the Civil Rights Act as well.[12]

In addition, creditors who employ predominantly white appraisers can adversely impact the appraisal of African-American-owned property. In one disturbing example, an African-American editor for the *Wall Street Journal* reported that he received a surprisingly low appraisal on his home. He had the home reappraised after removing his family pictures from the home and replacing them with pictures of his white secretary and her family. The second appraisal came back significantly higher.[13]

6.2.2.4 Failure to Combine Joint Applicant Income on the Basis of Marital Status

Creditors may not use marital status as grounds for determining whether to grant credit.[14] A creditor that would not aggregate the incomes of an unmarried man and woman applying jointly for a mortgage violated the ECOA by discriminating on the basis of marital status.[15] The court noted that, had the couple been married, the creditor would have been required to consider both of their incomes.

---

5 Thomas v. First Fed. Sav. Bank of Ind., 653 F. Supp. 1330 (N.D. Ind. 1987).

6 *See* § 6.4.3.3.3, *infra* (cases involving a similar phenomenon, i.e., discriminatory "overrides" with respect to credit score thresholds).

7 Cathy Cloud & George Galster, *What Do We Know About Racial Discrimination in Mortgage Markets*, 22 Rev. of Black Pol. Econ. 101 (1993) (available as Clearinghouse No. 47,964).

8 Reg. B, 12 C.F.R. § 202.2(m), defines investigation procedures as part of a credit transaction, and Reg. B, 12 C.F.R. § 202.4, prohibits discrimination concerning any aspect of a credit transaction.

9 *In re* Alden's, Inc., 92 F.T.C. 901 (Fed. Trade Comm'n 1978).

10 United States v. John Wanamaker, Philadelphia, Clearinghouse No. 44,328 (E.D. Pa. Apr. 14, 1989) (consent order).

11 24 C.F.R. § 100.135; *see also* 12 C.F.R. § 528.2a (Office of Thrift Supervision Nondiscrimination Requirements).

12 For example, the plaintiffs in Steptoe v. Sav. of Am., 800 F. Supp. 1542 (N.D. Ohio 1992) sued under both the Fair Housing Act and sections 1981 and 1982. In this case, an African-American couple attempted to buy a home that their lender initially appraised at their offer price of $115,000. The bank's chief appraiser disagreed with the valuation, however, and ordered his staff appraiser to redo the numbers. The second appraisal came in at $94,500, and the bank refused to lend the Steptoes the entire sum which they needed to purchase the house. Less than a month later, another buyer bought the house for $115,000. In denying the bank's motion for summary judgment, the court ruled that the Steptoes had made a prima facie case of discrimination in violation of the Fair Housing Act and sections 1981 and 1982 of the Civil Rights Act.

13 Joseph Boyce, *L.A. Riots and the "Black Tax"*, Wall St. J., May 12, 1992, at A24.

14 Shuman v. Standard Oil Co., 453 F. Supp. 1150 (N.D. Cal. 1978) (divorced woman's suit withstood motion for partial summary judgment when she alleged that the creditor had discriminated on the basis of sex or marital status as revealed in a credit report).

15 Markham v. Colonial Mortgage Serv. Co., 605 F.2d 566 (D.C. Cir. 1979). However, on remand, the court decided that the applicants had been denied credit because their combined income was insufficient and not because of their marital status. Markham v. Colonial Mortgage Serv. Co., Consumer Cred. Guide (CCH) ¶ 97,403 (D.D.C. 1980). For more discussion of whether discrimination against unmarried couples constitutes marital status discrimination, see § 3.4.1, *supra*.

6.2.2.5 Requirements for Immediate Payment

One form of discrimination that is not obvious is the refusal to allow a customer to delay payment until some time after the goods or services have been delivered. For example, various tradespeople, doctors or merchants, while not formally offering credit, will allow certain customers to mail in their payments later while requiring immediate payment up-front from other customers.

Such informal arrangements to defer payment when there is no installment payment schedule or finance charge are generally considered incidental consumer credit under Regulation B.[16] While the ECOA generally applies to incidental consumer credit,[17] the Federal Reserve Board (FRB) exempts such credit from many specific ECOA provisions.[18] The FRB has proposed exempting incidental business credit from these provisions as well.[19] Nevertheless, the FRB does not exclude incidental consumer credit from the general rule against discrimination, so discrimination on a prohibited basis as to when a creditor will defer payment clearly violates the ECOA.[20]

For example, a doctor who does not ordinarily require patients to pay immediately may not demand cash from elderly patients to avoid a lengthy wait for Medicare payments. Similarly, a grocery store may not run a tab for most customers but refuse to do so for those who pay with food stamps.

6.2.2.6 Discrimination in Credit Limits

The amount of credit to be extended is also subject to the general rule against discrimination. Thus, an individual unmarried applicant should be evaluated for and receive the same credit limit as a similarly situated but married applicant.

State law sometimes treats married and unmarried applicants differently with regard to the amount of credit that may be extended. In many states, loan statutes provide for graduated interest rates such that loans up to a certain amount carry one interest rate while any balances above that amount carry a different interest rate. For example, the rate of interest may be 18% on the first $500 of a loan and 12% on the balance above $500. Often, these state statutes also impose ceilings on the loan amount and, prior to the enactment of the ECOA, many statutes contained provisions prohibiting separate extensions of credit to a husband and wife because higher interest rates would result, or the practice might be an attempt to circumvent the ceilings imposed on the amount that could be loaned.

The ECOA preempts those state laws which prohibit the separate extension of consumer credit to a husband and wife.[21] State statutes which aggregate or otherwise combine the separate accounts of spouses for the purpose of determining permissible finance charges or loan ceilings are also preempted.[22]

Statutes establishing permissible loan ceilings are to be construed as permitting each spouse to become individually liable to a creditor up to the amount of the loan ceiling, minus the amount for which each is jointly liable. For instance, if a state's permissible loan ceiling is $1,000, and a married couple are jointly liable to a creditor for an unpaid debt of $250, each could subsequently become individually liable for $750.[23]

There is potential for creditor abuse in these situations, as an applicant's spouse may be pressured to "voluntarily" apply for an individual account, which would result in higher interest rates for that applicant. When there are two such individual accounts the advocate should carefully interview the clients carefully to ensure that the creditor was not attempting to use the ECOA to circumvent usury laws.

6.2.2.7 Denial of Credit for Exercise of Rights Under the Consumer Credit Protection Act

One interesting potential use of the ECOA is when a creditor denies credit (or in any other way distinguishes the applicant) because the applicant does not wish to buy optional credit insurance. The applicant may have an ECOA claim for discrimination on the basis of the good faith exercise of rights under the Consumer Credit Protection Act.[24] Although the creditor's actions may also violate other federal and state laws, ECOA punitive damages may be a particularly attractive remedy.

---

16 *See* § 2.2.6.3, *supra.*
17 *See* § 2.2.6.3, *supra.*
18 Reg. B, 12 C.F.R. § 202.3(c).
19 64 Fed. Reg. 44,582, 44,595 (Aug. 16, 1999). The proposed revisions to Regulation B can be found on the CD-Rom accompanying this volume.
20 Official Staff Commentary, 12 C.F.R. § 202.3-1.

21 15 U.S.C. § 1691d(c); *see also* Reg. B, 12 C.F.R. § 202.7(a).
22 15 U.S.C. § 1691d(d); Reg. B, 12 C.F.R. § 202.11(c).
23 Reg. B, 12 C.F.R. § 202.11(c) n.16, which contained this example, was not included in the 1985 revised Regulation B or the Official Staff Commentary, but the requirements are unchanged.
24 Bryson v. Bank of N.Y., 584 F. Supp. 1306 (S.D.N.Y. 1984). For a discussion of credit insurance and its treatment under the Truth in Lending Act, see National Consumer Law Center, Truth in Lending § 3.9.4 (4th ed. 1999 and Supp.).

6.3 Understanding Credit Evaluation Systems

6.3.1 Introduction to the Three Types of Credit Evaluation Systems

In order to understand discrimination in the credit evaluation process, it is essential to understand the different systems used for credit evaluation and how these systems operate. There are basically three types of credit evaluation systems used by creditors: credit scoring systems; judgmental systems; or combined systems, which share aspects of both of the other two systems.

Each of these systems base their method of evaluating credit applications on the assumption that past credit history is the best predictor of how credit obligations will be handled in the future. Using these systems, some creditors will look only at the credit history and present financial situation of an individual applicant when deciding whether or not to extend credit to that person. Other creditors will look at both the applicant's history of making payments and at how the applicant compares to an "ideal" credit applicant. Applicants seeking credit from the latter type of creditor may be rejected despite their good credit histories merely because their characteristics as a credit applicant vary too much from those of the ideal applicant.[25]

Theoretically, credit evaluation systems should measure only those characteristics shown by experience to be predictors of a good or bad credit risk. Nevertheless, the legislative history of the ECOA is replete with examples of creditors that rejected whole classes of credit applicants, such as elderly persons, minorities, or single women, on the unfounded assumption that they were poor credit risks. Many of these assumptions are still built into credit evaluation systems. This type of residual or built-in discrimination is hard to identify because the inner workings of credit evaluation systems remain a closely guarded secret within the credit industry.

6.3.2 Credit Scoring Systems

6.3.2.1 Description of Credit Scoring

6.3.2.1.1 Overview

A credit scoring system is one that numerically weighs or "scores" some or all of the factors considered in the underwriting process. There has been an explosive growth in the use of credit scoring systems over the last decade, and this growth has been accompanied by some controversy. This controversy, as well as the relationship between credit scoring and credit discrimination, is discussed in § 6.4, *infra*.

Factors used in a credit scoring system may include payment history on past financial obligations, amounts owed, length of credit history, types of credit already held, length of employment, and income level.[26] The number of points received often determines whether the applicant is offered credit and how much credit is granted.

Exactly what is meant by a "credit score" varies depending on the score's creator and the specific industry involved. Basically, there are two types of credit scores: credit history scores and credit application scores.

6.3.2.1.2 Credit history or generic credit score

A credit bureau score, also known as a generic credit score, is a number that is calculated based on information obtained from a consumer's credit file at a credit bureau. This number purports to predict the risk that a consumer will default on credit in the future and is based on the historic performance of credit extended to consumers with similar characteristics. The number is calculated from an algorithm or mathematical model.

The leading creator of models is Fair, Isaac & Co. (Fair Isaac), also known as FICO; hence, a credit score is sometimes referred to as a "FICO score." Fair Isaac has developed credit scoring models for each of the three major credit bureaus (Trans Union, Experian, and Equifax). These models take data from a consumer's file and generate a number. Depending on the model used, a generic credit score will fall within a range, from a low of 300 to 400 to a high of 800 to 900. The higher the score, the better. A credit applicant with a score of 660 or greater is generally considered to be less of a risk for the lender, while a score of 620 or lower is considered a poor risk. FICO products return a score along with reason codes showing why the consumer's score deviated from the optimal score. Creditors sometimes use these reason codes to specify the reasons for their decision to deny credit.[27]

6.3.2.1.3 Credit application scores

Credit application scores combine credit history information with information derived from an application for a particular type of credit. This information may include employment history, income, loan collateral, debt-to-income ratio, and cash reserves. Custom or credit application scores are often used for automobile loan and mortgage applications.

---

25 *See, e.g.,* Cherry v. Amoco Oil Co., 490 F. Supp. 1026 (N.D. Ga. 1980) (applicant denied credit because creditor had experienced poor payments on accounts of customers in applicant's zip code area).

26 For a description of some of the factors used in some of the most popular credit scoring systems, see § 6.4.2.3, *infra*.

27 For a further description of FICO scores, see § 6.4.2.3, *infra*.

Credit application scores are increasingly being used in the form of "automated underwriting systems." These systems contain computerized decision-making programs that determine whether or not an applicant should receive a loan. The best-known automated underwriting systems are the ones developed by Freddie Mac and Fannie Mae for the purpose of deciding whether they will consider purchasing a loan on the secondary market.[28]

6.3.2.2 Regulation B Definition of Credit Scoring

Regulation B includes a definition of credit scoring system, which is described under the regulation as "an empirically derived, demonstrably and statistically sound, credit scoring system."[29] However, Regulation B makes limited use of this definition, referring to it only with respect to when creditors are permitted to consider information about age and public assistance status.[30]

Under Regulation B, an empirically derived, demonstrably and statistically sound, credit scoring system is one which compares, by assignment of points or by other methods, certain key attributes of the applicant or of the transaction[31] to the attributes of sample groups or the population of creditworthy and non-creditworthy applicants who have applied to the creditor within a "reasonably preceding" period of time.[32] The total score, taken alone or in conjunction with other information about the applicant, is used to determine whether credit should be granted or denied.[33]

Such a system must satisfy four criteria:[34]

- The data used to develop the system must constitute either the entire applicant file or an appropriate sample of it;[35]
- The system must have the purpose of predicting applicants' creditworthiness with respect to the "legitimate

business interests" of the creditor using it—legitimate interests include minimizing operating expenses and bad debts; although no examples of "illegitimate" interests are given in the regulation, one such interest might be the desire to maintain an all-white clientele in a mortgage market;[36]
- The system must be "developed and validated using accepted statistical principles and methodology";[37] and
- The system should be periodically reviewed and revalidated as to its predictive ability and adjusted accordingly.[38]

Despite the requirement for validating and revalidating a credit scoring system, there are no procedures or standards set forth for these requirements. Moreover, a creditor suffers few consequences if its system does not meet the Regulation B standards for credit scoring systems. Recall that Regulation B's definition of a credit scoring system is only relevant to the consideration of age and public assistance status in evaluating credit. Furthermore, if a credit scoring system fails to meet Regulation B's definition, then the creditor need merely comply with the requirements of a judgmental system.[39] Practically speaking, any impetus for validation will most likely come from regulatory agencies and from individuals suing creditors under the ECOA.

6.3.3 Judgmental Systems

A judgmental system is defined by Regulation B as any credit evaluation system other than a "demonstrably and statistically sound, empirically derived credit system," that is, a system other than a credit scoring system.[40] A judgmental system generally involves a subjective examination of the overall application—often, a general search of the application for characteristics that are "acceptable" to the creditor based on past experience.

At times, a judgmental system operates much like a credit scoring system because the judgmental creditor may favorably assign value to certain characteristics on a credit report, such as a positive payment history. However, unlike the credit scoring system, the judgmental system grants or denies credit based on a general overview of the application rather than on a list of specific factors. The decision to grant or deny credit can be based on a single factor which

---

28 Freddie Mac's automated underwriting system is known as "Loan Prospector." Fannie Mae's system is called "Desktop Underwriter." Freddie Mac's system is described in detail at § 6.4.2.3, *infra.*

29 Reg. B, 12 C.F.R. § 202.2(t).

30 *See* Official Staff Commentary, 12 C.F.R. § 202.2(p)-1 (which explains that the purpose of the definition of credit scoring system is to define when a system may use age as a predictive factor).

31 Reg. B, 12 C.F.R. § 202.2(p)(1); *see also* Official Staff Commentary, 12 C.F.R. § 202.2(p)-1.

32 Reg. B, 12 C.F.R. § 202.2(p)(1) The regulation provides no further guidance on what constitutes a valid "sample group," a "reasonably preceding" period of time, or an "empirical" comparison of applicants or sample groups. *See* Hsia, *Credit Scoring and the Equal Credit Opportunity Act*, 30 Hastings L.J. 371 (1978) (Federal Reserve Board employee's discussion of the intricacies of credit scoring systems).

33 Reg. B, 12 C.F.R. § 202.2(p)(1); *see also* Official Staff Commentary, 12 C.F.R. § 202.2(p).

34 Reg. B, 12 C.F.R. § 202.2(p)(1).

35 Reg. B, 12 C.F.R. § 202.2(p)(1)(i).

36 Reg. B, 12 C.F.R. § 202.2(p)(1)(ii).

37 Reg. B, 12 C.F.R.§ 202.2(p)(1)(iii). The services of an expert may be required to establish whether a system satisfies this criterion.

38 Reg. B, 12 C.F.R. § 202.2(p)(1)(iv). No definition of "periodically" is given in the regulation. See also Official Staff Commentary, 12 C.F.R. § 202.2(p)-2, which gives some guidance on revalidation procedures.

39 *See* § 6.6.2.5, *infra* (requirements with respect to age), § 6.6.3.2, *infra* (requirements with respect to public assistance status).

40 Reg. B, 12 C.F.R. § 202.2(t).

overshadows the rest of the application. Thus, the outcome is often less predictable under a judgmental system.

There is great potential for judgmental systems to produce discriminatory results because Regulation B does not provide adequate standards for their use. At worst, they involve a creditor's judgment, which is based solely on isolated experiences with supposedly similar applicants, that an applicant is a bad credit risk. In a judgmental system, standards for granting credit can and do vary from one applicant to the next. If the person who takes the application finds the applicant unimpressive, pushy, or difficult to communicate with, credit can be denied merely on that employee's recommendation. When judgmental systems are involved, the leeway given to creditors can also perpetuate past patterns of discrimination because employees are apt to approve applicants most similar to those found suitable in the past.

6.3.4 Combination Systems

Regulation B allows combination systems of credit evaluation, that is, systems that require applicants to pass both a credit scoring and judgmental evaluation. In this fashion, any credit scoring system may be transformed into a combination system whenever an applicant obtains a passing score but is still considered an undesirable applicant by the creditor. Such a combination system would violate the general rule against discrimination if the additional requirements were applied only to protected groups or if they were applied to all applicants but had a disparate impact on protected groups.[41]

6.3.5 Different Requirements for Credit Scoring and Judgmental Systems

Despite the fact that Regulation B goes to some length to define credit scoring systems, judgmental systems, and combination systems, the requirements for the two main types of systems are not significantly different. The only provisions of the regulation that differ depending on whether the creditor uses a credit scoring or a judgmental system are those concerning the consideration of age and public assistance in credit evaluation. These rules are discussed in §§ 6.6.2 and 6.6.3, *infra*.

6.4 Special Issues Concerning Credit Scoring Systems

6.4.1 Dramatic Increase in the Use of Credit Scores

The use of credit scores to determine whether to extend consumer credit, and on what terms to extend credit, has grown dramatically, particularly in the home mortgage business. According to industry leader Fair Isaac, credit scores are a determining factor in three-quarters of mortgage decisions.[42]

One reason for the growth in the use of credit scores is that Freddie Mac and Fannie Mae—which, together, dominate the secondary market for home mortgages—have recommended that mortgage lenders use credit scores in deciding whether to grant mortgage requests and whether to charge higher interest rates and fees. While Freddie Mac and Fannie Mae state that they caution their lenders not to exclude borrowers solely on the basis of their credit scores,[43] both have urged lenders to use their automated underwriting systems, which factor in credit history scores in determining creditworthiness.[44]

Credit scores are also increasingly being used for purposes that extend well beyond the initial question of whether to grant loans. For example, scoring systems are used to prescreen and preselect consumers for the purposes of direct marketing, to determine interest rates and credit limits, to collect on mortgage loans, and in the sale of loans to Wall Street and secondary market purchasers.[45] Some credit card issuers have begun periodically reviewing card holders' credit scores to reset rates for lower-scoring holders. Credit scores are even being used to determine eligibility and rates for automobile and homeowner's insurance.

---

41 For an example in which requirements were lowered for groups on a prohibited basis, see § 6.4.3.3.3, *infra*, regarding discriminatory use of credit score "overrides."

42 Brian Deagon, *Fair Isaac's New Scoring Service Attracts Banks*, Investor's Business Daily, July 25, 2001.

43 Henry Cassidy & Robert Englestad, Credit Scoring and the Secondary Market: Perceptions, Policies, Practices, Community Investments 5 (Fed. Reserve Bank of San Francisco 1998).

44 Loretta J. Mester, *What's the Point of Credit Scoring?*, Bus. Rev.-Fed. Reserve Bank of Philadelphia, Sept./Oct. 1997, at 6. Fannie Mae's automated underwriting system is known as "Desktop Underwriter" while Freddie Mac's is known as "Loan Prospector."

45 *See* Edward Kulkosky, *Credit Scoring Appeal Transcends Underwriting*, Am. Banker, May 15, 1996, at 8.

6.4.2 Lack of Information and Regulation of Credit Scores

6.4.2.1 Credit Scores Do Not Have to Be Disclosed Under the FCRA

One reason for the controversy over credit scores has been the fact that, until recently, consumers were not able to find out their credit scores. They still do not have a legal right to access it. The federal Fair Credit Reporting Act (FCRA), which in general requires consumer reporting agencies to disclose all information in a consumer's file, specifically exempts credit scores from disclosure.[46] Several states have laws requiring disclosure of credit scores, which are not preempted by the FCRA.[47]

6.4.2.2 Recent Availability of Credit Scores

For many years, Fair Isaac and the three major credit reporting agencies refused to provide consumers with their own credit scores. Recently, the industry has begun to provide access to credit scores for a fee. It is unclear how closely these credit scores resemble those actually provided to lenders.[48] If consumers wish to obtain their credit scores, they have the following options:

- Fair Isaac and Equifax currently make credit scores available for a fee of $12.95, which entitles the purchaser to a copy of their credit report. As part of their credit report, consumers receive charts, details and analysis of the main factors that determined their scores. In addition, Equifax/Fair Isaac now offers a service that provides consumers with a personalized analysis of ways to improve their credit scores.[49] Consumers can order their FICO score

from http://www.myfico.com, http://www.equifax.com, or http://www.scorepower.com.

- TransUnion has its own version of a credit score, which is included with any credit report ordered from the company for the regular credit report price mandated by the FCRA, currently $9.00. TransUnion credit reports and scores can be ordered from http://www.transunion.com, by calling 800-888-4213, or by writing Trans Union, Consumer Disclosure Center, P.O. Box 1000, Chester, PA 19022.

- Experian currently offers a product called Experian Scorecard for a fee of $12.95, which entitles the purchasor to both their credit report and credit score from Experian. Experian also provides a "score simulator" with its report, which allows consumers to see how their scores will be affected if certain factors in their credit report change. The Experian Scorecard is available at http://www.experian.com.

There may be significant variations in the credit scores provided by the three credit reporting agencies. One journalist who ordered her credit score from all three services found a 100 point spread between the credit scores she received from these credit score services.[50]

6.4.2.3 How a Credit Score Is Calculated: The Black Box

Another reason for the controversy over credit scores is that, even with their availability to consumers, the method by which they are calculated is not known to consumers, advocates, or even regulators. The process by which a credit score is calculated has been likened to a "black box."

Freddie Mac and Fair Isaac have disclosed a list of general factors they use to generate credit scores and the general level of importance they attach to each factor.[51] However, critical information is still lacking from the industry's new disclosures. For example, Fair Isaac failed to identify all the factors that go into scoring an applicant and has not identified which of these factors help and which hinder the borrower. Furthermore, they have not revealed the algorithms or mathematical models used to calculate the credit scores.

Fair Isaac has stated that the following factors are used to derive FICO scores (a weighting of each factor is given in parentheses):

- Payment History (35%);

---

46 15 U.S.C. § 1681g(a) (Fair Credit Reporting Act § 609(a)).

47 Cal. Civ. Code § 1785.20.2 (West) (includes disclosure and notice requirements); N.M. Stat. Ann. § 56.3-2(B) (Michie); Okla. Stat. tit. 24, § 84; Vt. Stat. Ann. tit. 9, § 2480b(a). *See generally* National Consumer Law Center, Fair Credit Reporting Act § 3.5.7.1 (4th ed. 1998 and Supp.). In addition, some state laws require disclosure of all information in a consumer's credit files upon the consumer's request, which would include the credit score. *See* National Consumer Law Center, Fair Credit Reporting Act Appx. B.3 (4th ed. 1998 and Supp.) (summaries of state fair credit reporting laws).

48 Neal Walters & Sharon Hermanson, Credit Scores and Mortgage Lending 3 (AARP Pub. Pol'y Inst., Aug. 2001); Michelle Singletary, *Ratings for the Credit Raters*, Wash. Post, Mar. 24, 2002, at H1 (noting that scores provided to consumers from Fair Isaac/Equifax contain a disclaimer that "it's unlikely that a lender would use this credit report or score in considering a credit application").

49 Ruth Simon, *Fair Isaac Plans Credit-Score Help*, Wall St. J., Mar. 19, 2002, at 1. Fair Isaac states that more than one million consumers have paid for a FICO/Equifax score since the company started providing them in 2001.

50 Michelle Singletary, *Ratings for the Credit Raters*, Wash. Post, Mar. 24, 2002, at H1.

51 *See* Press Release, Freddie Mac, *Freddie Mac Releases Automated Underwriting Factors Used by Loan Prospector* (June 7, 2000), *available at* http://www.freddiemac.com; Press Release, Fair, Isaac & Co., *Fair Isaac 'Demystifies' FICO Scores with List of Score Factors, Web-based Explanation Service* (June 8, 2000), *available at* http://www.fairisaac.com.

- Amounts Owed (30%);
- Length of Credit History (15%);
- New Credit (10%); and
- Types of Credit in Use (10%).[52]

On its website, Freddie Mac lists the factors used in its automated underwriting system, Loan Prospector. Freddie Mac has not revealed the relative weight or importance given to each factor:

- Collateral;
- Credit history and credit bureau score;
- Capacity (debt ratios, salaried versus self-employed borrower, and cash reserves); and
- Loan type and purpose.[53]

6.4.2.4 Discovery of How Creditor Utilizes Scoring System

Even with these revelations by the credit scoring industry, much of the "black box" characteristics of credit scoring systems still persist. Attorneys seeking detailed information on how a client's credit score was calculated or how it was used in underwriting probably will be told initially by the creditor that the actual process is a trade secret.

This trade secret objection to obtaining information on credit scoring systems can be overcome in discovery. Federal Rule of Civil Procedure 26(c) allows a creditor to seek a protective order barring or restricting discovery related to "a trade secret or other confidential research, development, or commercial information." However, if the information sought is relevant and necessary to the initial presentation of the plaintiff's credit discrimination claims, it must be produced.[54] The ECOA itself indicates that nothing in the statute shall be construed to prohibit discovery of a creditor's credit-granting standards under appropriate discovery procedures.[55]

It is thus possible to gain access to credit evaluation systems by showing, for example, that this information is necessary to prove the following:

- The creditor's discriminatory actions were the result of

---

52 Press Release, Fair, Isaac & Co., *Fair, Isaac 'Demystifies' FICO Scores with List of Score Factors, Web-based Explanation Service* (June 8, 2000), *available at* http://www.fairisaac.com.

53 Press Release, Freddie Mac, *Freddie Mac Releases Automated Underwriting Factors Used by Loan Prospector* (June 7, 2000), *available at* http://www.freddiemac.com.

54 *See, e.g.*, Fed. Open Market Comm. v. Merrill, 443 U.S. 340, 995 S. Ct. 2800, 61 L. Ed. 2d 587 (1979); Carter Products, Inc. v. Eversharp, Inc., 360 F.2d 868 (7th Cir. 1966); United States v. Aluminum Co. of Am., 193 F. Supp. 249 (N.D.N.Y. 1960); *see also* 6 James Wm. Moore et al., Moore's Federal Practice § 26.105[8][a] (3d ed. 2001) (discussion of trade secrets discovery).

55 15 U.S.C. § 1691e(j).

policy and practice rather than an excusable clerical error;[56]
- The creditor's actions were intentional, which is relevant to an award of punitive damages under the ECOA;[57] or
- The parent company of the branch creditor with whom the client dealt created the system and so shares liability for any violations.

Being able to show that these factors cannot be established by alternative means will strengthen the argument for discovery. If a court seems inclined to deny access through discovery, advocates might suggest restrictions on the use of the information discovered. Such restrictions could include use of the information only for the purposes of the present suit, use only by the attorney and assistants, use by a mutually acceptable expert, or use only in proceedings conducted in the judge's chambers.

6.4.3 Problems with Credit Scoring Systems

6.4.3.1 Lack of Flexibility

One concern with credit scoring systems has to do with the discomfiting concept that, with their use, a person's entire "credit persona" is reduced to a number. The rigidity of a credit scoring system and its mechanistic application leave no room for the exercise of human insight and discretion in evaluating applicants. An applicant who may pose a very questionable credit risk in some respects might qualify under a rigid credit scoring system, while another applicant who in every respect is dependable and conscientious may not qualify under the same system because a temporary financial setback in their past can not be justified numerically. A judgmental system allows a lender flexibility to consider mitigating factors that would turn an otherwise unacceptable credit risk into a successful loan. Human judgment is by no means infallible, but it provides insight that is not quantifiable.

On the other hand, some lenders exercise their judgment in a discriminatory way such that certain applicants benefit from "human judgment" while other similarly situated applicants do not. Often, people are not even aware of the discriminatory aspects in their judgment. Credit scoring proponents have consistently argued that removing human discretion from the credit evaluation process also removes the potential for discrimination in that process.[58]

The rigidity of credit scores may have particularly nega-

---

56 *See, e.g.*, Desselles v. J.C. Penney Co., [1974-1980 Decisions Transfer Binder] Consumer Cred. Guide (CCH) ¶ 97,536 (E.D. La. Nov. 26, 1979).

57 *See* § 11.6.4.3.7, *infra*.

58 This argument is set forth more fully in § 6.4.3.3.2, *infra*.

tive consequences for low-income consumers. Both Freddie Mac and Fannie Mae have issued guidelines for lenders on what they consider to be an acceptable credit bureau score.[59] This may cause lenders to err on the side of denying loans to applicants with scores below the recommended cut-off points. As a result, more low-income borrowers and those who do not have conventional credit backgrounds may be unnecessarily forced into the fringe or "subprime" market, in which interest rates are considerably higher and many lenders charge excessive points and fees.

Government officials have also articulated concerns about the inflexibility of credit scoring evaluation systems. A former assistant attorney general in the Department of Justice's Civil Rights Division has expressed a preference for lender exercise of discretion rather than "mechanistic" scoring systems, with the caveat that lenders must not exercise discretion in an unlawful way.[60] Moreover, the Department of Justice took an official position against a provision in a proposed amendment to the ECOA that would have deemed a creditor to be in compliance with the non-discrimination provisions of the Act if the creditor based its credit decisions solely on an "empirically derived, demonstrably and statistically sound" credit scoring system which does not utilize prohibited factors.[61]

6.4.3.2 Accuracy

6.4.3.2.1 Validation of the system

Under Regulation B, a credit scoring system is defined as a system that is "validated using accepted statistical principles and methodology."[62] Regulation B also requires the system to be periodically revalidated as to its predictive ability and for it to be adjusted accordingly.[63] Without revalidation, a credit scoring model can lose its accuracy. The Federal Reserve Board has warned that validity levels can deteriorate over time and must be rechecked periodi-

cally.[64] The Office of the Comptroller of the Currency (OCC) has reported that some banks have been unable to track the validity of their credit scoring model over time.[65]

Even a validated credit scoring model may produce wrong results if it is used for a purpose for which it was not intended. The OCC reports finding problems with the application of credit scoring models to products, customers, or neighborhoods for which they were not designed and that bank staff were often poorly trained in the use of these models.[66]

6.4.3.2.2 Garbage in, garbage out: the effect of credit report inaccuracies on credit scores

No matter how valid a model may be, however, it is no better than the data it is given. If a consumer's credit history contains inaccuracies, her credit score will be inaccurate. Maintaining an accurate consumer file has never been so important.

Yet the credit history files at the major credit reporting agencies are notorious for their lack of accuracy. Studies have found that between fifty to seventy percent of credit reports contain inaccurate information.[67] Even if the consumer discovers an error and is able to get the credit reporting agency to correct the error, it can take up to ninety days for the consumer's credit score to reflect the corrected information.

If a credit reporting agency or creditor refuses to delete negative information on a credit report, the Fair Credit Reporting Act (FCRA) allows consumers to include a written protest disputing the information.[68] This right is part of the FCRA's protective measures to ensure the accuracy of credit reports. Yet consumers' credit scores are unlikely to reflect the consumers' written protests.

Furthermore, there is evidence that certain subprime lenders deliberately fail to report positive information to credit reporting agencies that would help boost a consumer's credit scores. There are allegations that these creditors omit this information for the purpose of keeping their borrowers' credit scores artificially low so that these borrowers do not

---

59 Freddie Mac advises lenders that applicants with FICO scores below 620 indicate high risk, between 620 and 660 indicate an uncertain credit profile, and above 660 indicate that they are likely to have acceptable credit reputations. *See* Freddie Mac, Automated Underwriting: Making Mortgage Lending Simpler and Fairer for America's Families (Sept. 1996), *available at* http://www.freddiemac.com/corporate/reports/moseley/mosehome.htm.

60 Letter from Deval L. Patrick, Assistant Att'y Gen., Civil Rights Div., Dep't of Justice, to lender association representatives (Feb. 21, 1995) (concerning Department of Justice Fair Lending Enforcement Program) (available as Clearinghouse No. 52,064).

61 Letter from John R. Schmidt, Associate Att'y Gen., Dep't of Justice, to the Honorable Jim Leach, Chairman, Comm. on Banking & Fin. Services, U.S. House of Representatives (June 10, 1995) (commenting on H.R. 1362, The Financial Institutions Regulatory Relief Act of 1995).

62 Reg. B, 12 C.F.R. § 202.2(p)(1)(iii).

63 Reg. B, 12 C.F.R. § 202.2(p)(1)(iv). No definition of periodically is given in the regulation.

64 *See Credit Risk, Credit Scoring, and the Performance of Home Mortgages,* Fed. Reserve Bull., July 1996, at 621, 628; *see also* Press Release, Office of the Comptroller of the Currency, OCC Alerts Banks to Potential Benefits and Risks of Credit Scoring Models (No. 97-46, May 20, 1997), *available at* http://www.occ.treas.gov.

65 Office of the Comptroller of the Currency, Credit Scoring Models (OCC Bull. 97-24, May 20, 1997).

66 *Id.*

67 U.S. Pub. Interest Research Group, Mistakes Do Happen: Credit Report Errors Mean Consumers Lose (1998); *Credit Reports: How Do Potential Lenders See You?,* Consumer Reports, July 2000.

68 *See* National Consumer Law Center, Fair Credit Reporting Act § 9.7 (4th ed. 1998 and Supp.).

have better credit alternatives.[69] As a disproportionate number of subprime loan borrowers are African-American and Hispanic, such a practice of withholding good credit information has a disparate impact on protected groups.

6.4.3.2.3 Risk-based pricing

The current trend is to use credit scores to determine not only whether a consumer will be approved for credit but at what price the credit will be provided. Essentially, the higher the credit score, the lower the price for credit. The website for Fair Isaac even provides interest rates quotes for home mortgages based upon a consumer's credit score. However, there are questions as to the justifiability of risk-based pricing, that is, whether the additional prices charged by some lenders for so-called "risky" loans legitimately compensate them for additional risk or actually represent pure additional profit.[70]

6.4.3.3 Do Credit Scores Discriminate?

6.4.3.3.1 Concerns that minority and other protected groups are disadvantaged by credit scoring

As long as there have been credit scores, there have been concerns that scoring systems contain biases which disproportionately impact protected groups.[71] These concerns are heightened by data showing that, as a group, certain racial and ethnic groups have lower credit scores than whites. A 1996 Freddie Mac study found that African-Americans are three times as likely to have FICO scores below 620 as whites. The same study showed that Hispanics are twice as likely as whites to have FICO scores under 620.[72]

A later study conducted by researchers at the University of North Carolina showed that one-third of African-Americans had credit scores under 620, as compared to only fifteen percent of whites. Furthermore, the same study found that another one-third of African-Americans had credit scores between 621 and 660 (as compared to twenty percent of whites), which means that two-thirds of African-Americans have what is considered marginal or poor credit ratings.[73]

In addition to having lower credit scores, minority consumers are also more likely to lack the credit history necessary to even generate a credit score because they are less likely to have those forms of traditional credit that are reported to credit bureaus.[74] The University of North Carolina study discussed above found that twenty-two percent of Hispanics did not have a sufficient credit history to generate a credit score.[75]

6.4.3.3.2 Factors in a credit scoring system may disfavor minorities and other protected groups

If even a single factor in a credit scoring model correlates to race or other prohibited bases, the results of the model may be discriminatory.[76] A 1995 amendment to the Official Staff Commentary appears to concur, noting that an "empirically derived, demonstrably and statistically sound" credit scoring system may be flawed and thus subject to review and challenge under the ECOA.[77] These concerns are

---

69 Kenneth Harney, *Improve Credit Rating By Paying On Time? Don't Count On It*, Wash. Post, Jan. 29, 2000, at G1.

70 *See* National Consumer Law Center, The Cost of Credit: Regulation and Legal Challenges § 11.1.1.3 (2d ed. 2000 and Supp.) (a critique of risk-based pricing).

71 Fed. Reserve Bank of Boston, *Perspectives on Credit Scoring and Fair Lending: A Five-Part Article Series* (pt. 1), Communities & Banking, Spring 2000, at 2.

72 *See* Freddie Mac, Automated Underwriting: Making Mortgage Lending Simpler and Fairer for America's Families (Sept. 1996), *available at* http://www.freddiemac.com/corporate/reports/moseley/mosehome.htm.

73 Michael Stegman et al., Automated Underwriting: Getting to "Yes" for More Low-Income Applicants, Presentation to the Research

---

Institute for Housing America Conference (Apr. 2001), *available at* http://www.housingamerica.org/CHO2001-slideshow.html. The credit score cut-offs for what is considered poor, marginal and good credit are derived from Freddie Mac's categories used in its Loan Prospector system. Freddie Mac advises lenders that applicants with FICO scores below 620 indicate high risk, between 620 and 660 indicate an uncertain credit profile, and above 660 indicate that they are likely to have acceptable credit reputations. *See* Freddie Mac, Automated Underwriting: Making Mortgage Lending Simpler and Fairer for America's Families (Sept. 1996), *available at* http://www.freddiemac.com/corporate/reports/moseley/mosehome.htm.

74 For example, one survey from central Ohio found that African-Americans are twice as likely as whites not to have a credit card. Mark A. Fisher, *Minorities Score Lower in "Colorblind" Ratings*, Columbus Dispatch, Apr. 14, 1999, at 5A. The same survey found that African-Americans who do have credit cards miss their minimum payments more than twice as often as whites do.

75 Michael Stegman et al., Automated Underwriting: Getting to "Yes" for More Low-Income Applicants Presentation to the Research Institute for Housing America Conference (Apr. 2001), *available at* http://www.housingamerica.org/CH02001-slideshow.html.

76 *See* Office of the Comptroller of the Currency, Credit Scoring Models (OCC Bull. 97-24, May 20, 1997) (warning against the use of "models that may include characteristics that may have a disparate impact on a prohibited basis or raise other Equal Credit Opportunity Act (Regulation B) or Fair Housing Act concerns"); Press Release, Office of the Comptroller of the Currency, OCC Alerts Banks to Potential Benefits and Risks of Credit Scoring Models (No. 97-46, May 20, 1997), *available at* http://www.occ.treas.gov (advising national banks "to avoid illegal disparate treatment by insuring that adequate controls exist during the pre-scoring, scoring, and post-scoring states of the credit application process").

77 Official Staff Commentary, 12 C.F.R. § 202.2(p)-4 (published in 60 Fed. Reg. 29,965 (June 7, 1995)); *see, e.g.,* Stackhaus v. NationsBank Corp., Clearinghouse No. 52,065, Civ. No. 96-CV-1077 (NHJ) (D.D.C. 1996) (complaint) (class action

intensified by the "black box" nature of credit scoring systems.

Furthermore, if certain groups have been denied access to credit in the past as a result of discrimination, the use of credit scoring systems may perpetuate that lack of access.[78] African-Americans, Hispanics and women probably still lag behind other groups under credit scoring systems because in terms of credit access the proverbial playing field is far from level.[79] Indeed, the Federal Reserve Board has observed that the scores "may lack predictive power for the underrepresented segments of the overall population."[80]

One issue is that scoring models often fail to adequately weigh rent, utility, and other nonstandard payment histories that are more typical of lower-income populations. Thus, existing credit scoring models may unwittingly overrate the real risk of nonpayment by these groups.

Another issue is that groups who have historically been discriminated against may rely more heavily on credit obtained from non-traditional sources such as finance companies. Credit scoring models may assign a higher risk rating to such credit sources.[81] Fair Isaac claims that the latest generation of credit scoring models does not penalize consumers for having loans from finance companies. However, Fair Isaac admits that many lenders have not adopted these updated scoring models.[82]

A third issue is whether minorities and other protected groups are adequately represented in the samples used to calculate credit scores. Because of past discrimination, the pool of past credit recipients may contain a disproportionately low number of members of protected groups. If such is the case, a credit scoring model may underestimate the likelihood of repayment by applicants from these underrepresented groups. For example, Fair Isaac develops its models using a sample of files from credit reporting agencies that may be as small as 750,000.[83] This is a fraction of one percent of the roughly 190,000,000 files each credit report-

ing agency maintains.[84] Fair Isaac has admitted that the databases used to generate their models underrepresent communities of color but claims there is only a slight underrepresentation.[85]

In response to these concerns, the credit scoring industry and its proponents have consistently maintained that their systems are not discriminatory.[86] Moreover, they claim that credit scoring actually reduces discrimination against protected groups. Credit scoring proponents contend that the human, and potentially discriminatory, element in credit evaluation has been replaced by a system that is blind to race and other prohibited bases. In fact, they point to studies showing that credit scoring systems approve a higher number of minority borrowers than do traditional manual underwriting systems.[87]

6.4.3.3.3 *Discriminatory credit score thresholds or overrides*

One use of credit scores that clearly puts minority applicants at a disadvantage is the use of different credit score thresholds or "cut-offs" by creditors for white and minority applicants. For example, the Department of Justice (DOJ) filed a lawsuit in 1999 against Associates National Bank (ANB), alleging that ANB implemented different credit score cut-offs for English-language applicants than for Spanish-language applicants.[88] According to the DOJ, ANB segregated its Spanish-language applications into a separate file then lowered the credit score cut-off for English-language applicants but not for Spanish- language applicants. As a result, the denial rate of credit cards for Spanish-language applicants was higher.[89]

Another concern, raised by the Office of Comptroller of the Currency (OCC) in 1997, is that because the credit scores of a large percentage of applicants fall in a gray area, lenders will continue to use subjective or "human" under-

---

brought by Washington Lawyers' Committee for Civil Rights & Urban Affairs alleging, *inter alia*, that defendant's credit scoring system had a racially discriminatory adverse impact on African-American applicants for mortgage loans in the Washington, D.C., area).

78 Therefore, such systems may be vulnerable to challenge using a disparate impact theory. *See* § 4.3, *supra*.

79 A similar observation has been made by at least one Federal Reserve Board governor. *Governor Lindsey Points to Difficulties with Statistics as Loan-Eligibility Tool*, 63 Banking Rep. (BNA) 280 (Aug. 29, 1994).

80 *Credit Risk, Credit Scoring, and the Performance of Home Mortgages*, Fed. Reserve Bull., July 1996, at 621, 630.

81 Allen Fishbein, *Is Credit Scoring a Winner for Everyone?*, Stone Soup, Spring 1996, at 14.

82 Kenneth Harney, *Outdated Credit-Scoring System Can Penalize Borrowers*, Wash. Post, Feb. 23, 2002, at H1.

83 *See* Fed. Trade Comm'n, Credit Scoring (Aug. 1998); *see also Credit Risk, Credit Scoring, and the Performance of Home Mortgages*, Fed. Reserve Bull., July 1996, at 621, 628.

84 *See* National Consumer Law Center, Fair Credit Reporting Act § 3.2 (4th ed. 1998 and Supp.).

85 Fair, Isaac & Co., The Effectiveness of Scoring on Low-to-Moderate Income and High-Minority Area Populations 22 (Aug. 1997), *available at* http://www.fairisaac.com (database used to develop TransUnion's credit scoring system composed of 6.7% residents of minority neighborhoods, in comparison to 7.8% of the overall U.S. population of adults).

86 *Id.*

87 Peter Zorn et al., Automated Underwriting and Lending Outcomes: The Effect of Improved Mortgage Risk Assessment on Under-Served Populations (Inst. of Bus. & Econ. Research, Univ. of Cal.-Berkeley, Aug. 2001) (study showing that manual underwriting approved only 52% of a sample of minority applicants for affordable loans, but Freddie Mac's Loan Prospector system approved 79%).

88 United States v. Associates Nat'l Bank, Civ. No. 99-196 (D. Del. Mar. 29, 1999) [reproduced on the CD-Rom accompanying this volume]. For more about the DOJ's action against ANB, see § 12.4.3.5, *infra*.

89 *Id.*

writing to review these applications. The OCC expressed concern that decisions to override the credit scores in these situations may undermine the objectivity and/or integrity of credit scoring and lead to discriminatory results.[90]

One instance of discriminatory overrides was challenged by the DOJ in their lawsuit against Deposit Guaranty National Bank (DGNB) which focused on actions taken by DGNB's loan officers in a home improvement loan program. The DOJ alleged that DGNB allowed its loan officers broad discretion to override decisions pertaining to credit-scored loan applications. Many of these decisions were inconsistent with the credit scores of individual applicants.[91] The purpose and effect, according to the DOJ, was to grant credit less frequently to African-American loan applicants in violation of the FHA and ECOA.[92]

The potential for discrimination in the supposedly objective process of generating credit scores also arises when loan officers engage in selective "coaching" of applicants. If a loan officer provides more information and assistance to white applicants in filling out their applications, those applications may be more likely to generate higher credit application scores and to qualify under automated underwriting systems.[93]

6.4.3.4 Credit Scores and Insurance

A particularly controversial issue is the use of credit scores by automobile and home insurers to determine whether to insure a consumer and at what price. The credit scores used by insurers, or "insurance scores," are specially developed for insurers and not the same as generic credit scores, but they nonetheless are based solely on credit history. The practice has become widespread, with a recent survey showing that ninety-two percent of auto insurers surveyed use insurance scores.[94] As a result, a consumer with a poor credit history may be charged forty to seventy-five percent more in premiums for automobile insurance.[95]

The practice of using insurance scores has been criticized as being fundamentally unfair as well as being particularly burdensome to low-income consumers least able to afford

high insurance rates. In addition, the use of insurance scores probably disproportionately burdens racial minorities, given that they have lower credit scores as a group.[96] Several states have passed legislation regulating the practice,[97] and legislation has been proposed in many other states.[98] Insurance companies defend their actions by noting the high correlation between credit scores and loss experience.[99]

6.5 Special ECOA Rules Concerning Credit Evaluation

6.5.1 Introduction

The following section discusses the special ECOA prohibitions of certain types of credit discrimination that are indirectly linked to a prohibited basis. Examples are credit decisions based on the applicant's likelihood of childbearing, type of income, telephone listing, and certain aspects of credit history. These special ECOA rules provide protection for women and, to a lesser extent, for applicants aged sixty-two or over.

6.5.2 Income Sources

6.5.2.1 General

The ECOA protects applicants from a creditor's inappropriate consideration of certain sources of the applicant's income. These special rules apply to what is called "protected income." Protected income includes income derived from part-time employment, alimony, child support, separate maintenance, retirement benefits, or public assistance.[100] These sources of income are related to age, sex, marital status, and public assistance status, and the Federal Reserve Board therefore believes it is important to prevent discrimination based on these sources of income which could have a disparate impact on a protected group.

6.5.2.2 Appropriate Methods to Evaluate Protected Income

The ECOA protects applicants from inappropriate evaluation of sources of protected income, but does not guarantee that every applicant with such income be granted credit. A creditor need not consider income at all in evaluating cred-

---

90 *See* Office of the Comptroller of the Currency, *OCC Alerts Banks to Potential Benefits and Risks of Credit Scoring Models* (May 20, 1997), *available at* http://www.occ.treas.gov.

91 *See* United States v. Deposit Guar. Nat'l Bank, Civ. Action No. 3:99CV67OLN (S.D. Miss. 1999) [reproduced on the CD-Rom accompanying this volume]. For more about the DOJ's action against DGNB, see § 12.4.3.5, *infra*.

92 *Id.*

93 James Carr, *Risk-Based Pricing: Are There Fair Lending Implications?*, Hous. Facts & Findings (vol. 1, issue 2, Summer 1999), *available at* http://www.fanniemaefoundation.org.

94 Brian Grow & Pallavi Gogoi, *Insurance: A New Way to Squeeze the Weak?*, Business Week, Jan. 28, 2002, at 92 (citing study by Conning & Co.).

95 Pamela Yip, *One Number, Many Uses*, Dallas Morning News, Apr. 8, 2002, at 1D.

96 *See* § 6.4.3.3, *supra*.

97 2002 Idaho Sess. Laws 264; 2002 Utah Laws 110; 2002 Wash. Laws 360.

98 Pamela Yip, *One Number, Many Uses*, Dallas Morning News, Apr. 8, 2002, at 1D.

99 *Id.*

100 Official Staff Commentary, 12 C.F.R. § 202.6(b)(5)-1.

itworthiness.[101] If the creditor does consider income, there are several acceptable methods of evaluating income.

A creditor may consider the total amount of income stated by the applicant without taking any steps to evaluate the different sources or components of that income.[102] Alternatively, the creditor may review *every* component of income separately, placing every component in one of two categories—reliable income and unreliable income. The creditor can then disregard *all* the unreliable income or evaluate the applicant based on these two total numbers—reliable and unreliable income.[103] If the creditor does not evaluate each component for reliability (e.g., it evaluates some components for reliability, but not others), then it must automatically treat all protected income as reliable.[104]

6.5.2.3 Individual Evaluation of Protected Income

If the creditor is using the second approach and evaluating every component of the applicant's income for reliability, the creditor may not discount or exclude from consideration the income of an applicant or the spouse of an applicant because of a prohibited basis.[105] In addition, the creditor may not automatically discount or exclude from consideration *any* protected income. The discount or exclusion must be based on the applicant's actual circumstances.[106]

Creditors, therefore, may not use blanket rules which automatically deem a certain type of protected income to be unreliable.[107] The decision must be made on an individual basis, and not be based on aggregate statistical relationships such as those underlying credit scoring models.[108]

Creditors may not treat applicants negatively on the basis that their only earned income is derived from a part-time job,[109] or that their income is derived from an annuity, pension, or other retirement benefit.[110] The creditor instead may only consider in each individual case the amount and probable continuity of the income.[111] Similarly, alimony, child support, or separate maintenance payments must be considered as income as long as they will be consistently received in the individual applicant's case.[112]

For instance, a creditor may not count only half of the income of a married woman when it would consider all of the income of a married man, or only half of a married woman's income when it would consider the full amount of a single woman's income. Similarly, the creditor may not discount income derived from part-time jobs or from retirement benefits or alimony.

6.5.2.4 Income from Multiple Sources

The previous subsection discussed whether a creditor could treat certain types of protected income as unreliable, and thus discount or ignore that income. A separate but related issue is whether creditors may treat income differently if it comes from multiple sources rather than from a single source. This issue is particularly important because women and elderly applicants are more likely to have multiple sources of income.

The Commentary states that creditors may not take into account the *number* of sources for protected income (such as alimony, child support, and Social Security). Further, they may not treat negatively the fact that the sole source of *earned* income is from a part-time job.[113]

However, creditors may take into account the fact that the applicant has more than one source of *earned* income, even if one such source is the otherwise protected category of part-time employment. In other words, Regulation B allows consideration of the fact that income is derived from two part-time jobs or from one full-time and one part-time job.[114] The creditor may also treat income earned from an applicant's primary job differently than income from an applicant's second job.[115] These standards apply to both credit scoring and judgmental evaluation systems.[116]

6.5.2.5 Income Sources Associated With Older Applicants

A creditor may not automatically exclude income of an applicant or applicant's spouse derived from part-time employment, annuities, pensions, or other retirement benefits from consideration, or consider only a portion of such income.[117] Evaluation of protected income from sources

---

101 Official Staff Commentary, 12 C.F.R. § 202.6(b)(5)-3.

102 Official Staff Commentary, 12 C.F.R. § 202.6(b)(5)-3.

103 Official Staff Commentary, 12 C.F.R. § 202.6(b)(5)-3.

104 Official Staff Commentary, 12 C.F.R. § 202.6(b)(5)-3.

105 Reg. B, 12 C.F.R. § 202.6(b)(5).

106 Official Staff Commentary, 12 C.F.R. § 202.6(b)(5)-3.

107 Official Staff Commentary, 12 C.F.R. §§ 202.6(b)(5)-1, 202.6(b)(5)-3. The Federal Reserve Board has proposed minor, clarifying revisions to these sections of the Official Staff Commentary, and removal of the phrase "protected income." 64 Fed. Reg. 44,582, 44,623 (Aug. 16, 1999). The proposed revisions to the Official Staff Commentary can be found on the CD-Rom accompanying this volume.

108 Official Staff Commentary, 12 C.F.R. § 202.6(b)(5)-1.

109 Reg. B, 12 C.F.R. § 202.6(b)(5); Official Staff Commentary, 12 C.F.R. § 202.6(b)(5)-4.

110 Reg. B, 12 C.F.R. § 202.6(b)(5).

111 Reg. B, 12 C.F.R. § 202.6(b)(5).

112 Reg. B, 12 C.F.R. § 202.6(b)(5).

113 Official Staff Commentary, 12 C.F.R. § 202.6(b)(5)-4.

114 Official Staff Commentary, 12 C.F.R. § 202.6(b)(5)-4.

115 Official Staff Commentary, 12 C.F.R. § 202.6(b)(5)-4.

116 United States v. Aristar, Inc., Clearinghouse No. 37,083 (S.D. Fla. Apr. 7, 1983).

117 Reg. B, 12 C.F.R. § 202.6(b)(5); *see also* United States v. City Fin. Co., Clearinghouse No. 45,752 (N.D. Ga. 1990) (five finance companies agreed to stop refusing to consider income derived from public assistance programs, part-time employment and retirement benefits); United States v. Gen. Elec. Capital Corp., Clearinghouse No. 45,754 (D. Conn. 1989) (lender

such as Social Security or retirement benefits must be made on an individual basis, and not be based on aggregate statistical relationships such as those underlying credit scoring models. Creditors may not use blanket rules which automatically deem a certain type of protected income to be unreliable, and therefore predictive of a higher risk of nonpayment.[118]

However, although creditors may not take into account the number of sources of unearned protected income (such as retirement income or Social Security), Regulation B allows consideration of multiple earned income sources (e.g., two part-time jobs).[119] But creditors may not treat adversely the fact that an applicant's only source of earned income is from a single part-time job.[120]

6.5.2.6 Income Sources Associated With Women Applicants

Regulation B prohibits creditors from discounting income from certain sources historically associated with women, such as part-time employment.[121] Other sources of income traditionally available primarily to women, such as alimony, child support, and separate maintenance payments, also may not be discounted automatically when an applicant is relying on such income to support the application,[122] although they may be evaluated on an individual basis for reliability and probable continuity.[123]

The creditor must consider such payments as income "to the extent that they are likely to be consistently made."[124] Factors which may be used to measure the likelihood of consistent payments include:[125]

- Whether the payments are received pursuant to a written agreement or court decree;
- The length of time that the payments have been received;
- The regularity of receipt of payments;
- The availability of procedures to compel payment; and
- The creditworthiness of the person making the payments to the applicant.

The creditor also may consider the amount and probable continuity of such income.[126]

---

agreed not to require applicants to be employed full-time and not to exclude income from public assistance, part-time employment or retirement plans); United States v. Capitol Thrift & Loan Ass'n, Clearinghouse No. 43,052 (N.D. Cal. 1986) (consent order settling charges that creditor discriminated against elderly credit applicants based on their reliance on retirement income).

118 *See* United States v. Aristar, Inc., Clearinghouse No. 37,083 (S.D. Fla. 1983).

119 *See* § 6.5.2.4, *supra.*

120 Official Staff Commentary, 12 C.F.R. § 202.6(b)(5)-4.

121 Reg. B, 12 C.F.R. § 202.6(b)(5).

122 A person receiving such income may choose not to include it when submitting a credit application. *See* Reg. B, 12 C.F.R. § 202.5(d)(2); Official Staff Commentary, 12 C.F.R. § 202.5(d)(2).

123 Reg. B, 12 C.F.R. § 202.6(b)(5); Official Staff Commentary, 12 C.F.R. § 202.6(b)(5)-1 to -4. The Federal Reserve Board has proposed minor, clarifying revisions to Official Staff Commentary, 12 C.F.R. §§ 202.6(b)(5)-1, 202.6(b)(5)-3, and 202.6(b)(5)-4, and removal of the phrase "protected income." 64 Fed. Reg. 44,582, 44,623 (Aug. 16, 1999). The proposed revisions to the Official Staff Commentary can be found on the CD-Rom accompanying this volume. *See also* Sallion v. Suntrust Bank, 87 F. Supp. 2d 1323 (N.D. Ga. 2000) (no ECOA violation found when bank required verification of alimony income and plaintiff could not substantiate receipt of payments as required by bank's underwriting guidelines); United States v. Franklin Acceptance Corp., Civ. No. 99-CV-2435 (E.D. Pa. 1999) (consent decree in which creditor agreed not to discount or exclude income from child support or public assistance) [reproduced on the CD-Rom accompanying this volume];

United States v. City Fin. Co., Clearinghouse No. 45,752 (N.D. Ga. 1990) (five finance companies agreed to stop refusing to consider income derived from public assistance programs, part-time employment, retirement benefits, alimony and child support); United States v. Capitol Thrift & Loan Ass'n, Clearinghouse No. 43,052 (N.D. Cal. 1986) (consent order in which creditor agreed not to discount or exclude income from alimony, child support, or separate maintenance payments); United States v. Household Fin. Corp., Clearinghouse 38,903 (N.D. Ill. 1984) (consent order based partially on allegations that creditor failed to consider alimony, child support, or separate maintenance payments as income); United States v. Amoco Oil Co., Clearinghouse No. 33,836 (D.D.C. 1980) (creditor agreed not to use credit scoring system which allegedly discriminated against women, by giving income from full-time employment or other sources a greater value than "protected sources" commonly associated with women, such as part-time employment, alimony and child support payments).

124 Reg. B, 12 C.F.R. § 202.6(b)(5); Official Staff Commentary, 12 C.F.R. § 202.6(b)(5)-2. The Federal Reserve Board has proposed minor, clarifying revisions to Official Staff Commentary, 12 C.F.R. §§ 202.6(b)(5)-1, 202.6(b)(5)-3, and 202.6(b)(5)-4, and removal of the phrase "protected income." 64 Fed. Reg. 44,582, 44,623 (Aug. 16, 1999). The proposed revisions to the Official Staff Commentary can be found on the CD-Rom accompanying this volume.

125 Official Staff Commentary, 12 C.F.R. § 202.6(b)(5)-2

126 Reg. B, 12 C.F.R. § 202.6(b)(5). Official Staff Commentary, 12 C.F.R. § 202.6(b)(5) is equally applicable to the treatment of income from sources such as alimony, child support, and separate maintenance payments. *See also* United States v. Sec. Pac. Fin. Sys., Clearinghouse No. 37,095 (S.D. Cal. Dec. 21, 1983) (civil penalty based on allegations that creditors discounted or failed to consider payments from alimony, child support, or separate maintenance); United States v. Amoco Oil Co., Clearinghouse 33,836 (D.D.C. 1980) (creditor barred from using credit scoring system which gave income from "protected sources," such as part-time employment, alimony and child support payments, less value than full-time employment or other sources); Anchor Sav. & Loan Ass'n v. Equal Opportunities Comm'n, 116 Wis. 2d 672, 343 N.W.2d 122 (Ct. App. 1983), *rev'd on other grounds*, 120 Wis. 2d 391 (Wis. 1984) (creditor discriminated against borrower on the basis of marital status—in action brought under a city ordinance, *not* the ECOA—when it denied a loan to divorced borrower who had

6.5.2.7 Income Sources Associated With Public Assistance Recipients

Public assistance status as a prohibited basis and treatment of public assistance income as protected income are so closely related that a discussion of one effectively merges into the other. Therefore, discussion of income sources associated with public assistance is detailed in conjunction with the discussion later in this chapter of the ECOA rules concerning public assistance generally.[127]

6.5.3 Spousal Credit History

6.5.3.1 Background

Regulation B attempts to aid two groups of women who have had problems with credit histories.[128] First, the ECOA gives special rights to women (whether married, divorced, or widowed) who have not been able to reap the benefits of their good credit histories because their accounts were recorded in their husbands' names. Second, women with poor credit histories due to their accounts being recorded in their husbands' names or in both spouses' names may show that this history does not reflect their individual creditworthiness.

6.5.3.2 Supplementing a Minimal Credit History

Regulation B requires creditors who consider the credit history of applicants to consider the credit history, when "available," of accounts designated as accounts that both the applicant and applicant's spouse are permitted to use, or for which both are contractually liable.[129] What information is considered available is not defined in Regulation B, but the Federal Reserve Board (FRB) has stated that creditors are not required to conduct any investigation of whether a spousal account exists given the prohibition against asking about marital status.[130] Essentially, the FRB is requiring that information about a spousal account, including the fact that the primary or joint account holder is a spouse, must be apparent on the face of whatever document or source of information the creditor is evaluating. For example, if the source of information is a credit report, the credit report

must show not only that the applicant is an authorized user of a credit account but that the identity of the primary account holder is the applicant's spouse.[131] Thus, the safest course would be for applicants to provide information directly to new creditors about all spousal joint or authorized user accounts.[132]

A creditor who considers the credit history of applicants also must consider, on the applicant's request, the credit history, when available, of any account reported in the name of the applicant's spouse or former spouse which the applicant can demonstrate accurately reflects the applicant's own creditworthiness.[133] The burden is placed on the applicant to present information on these accounts, without any affirmative duty on the creditor to request the information. The applicant carries the further burden of demonstrating that these accounts "accurately reflect" the applicant's own creditworthiness.[134]

One method of meeting this burden is to produce checks written on a joint account as payments for accounts listed in the spouse's name. Another is to produce employment records or deposit slips indicating that the applicant actually provided the funds which paid accounts listed in the spouse's name.

A creditor may restrict the types of credit history and credit references that it will consider, provided that the restrictions are applied to all credit applicants without regard to sex, marital status, or any other prohibited basis.[135] The provisions concerning credit history apply only to the extent that the creditor considers credit history in evaluating the creditworthiness of "similarly qualified applicants for a similar type and amount of credit."[136] However, on the applicant's request, a creditor must consider credit information not reported through a credit reporting agency when the information relates to the same types of credit references and history that the creditor would consider if reported through a credit reporting agency.[137]

---

support obligations, but did not consider similar obligations of married borrowers).

127 *See* § 6.6.3, *infra*.

128 Reg. B, 12 C.F.R. § 202.6(b)(6).

129 Reg. B, 12 C.F.R. § 202.6(b)(6)(i). This requirement is in addition to the requirement in Reg. B, 12 C.F.R. § 202.10, that a creditor furnish information to credit reporting agencies regarding the participation of both spouses for any joint or authorized user accounts. *See* § 9.4.2, *infra*.

130 Letter from Shawn McNulty, Ass't Dir., Div. of Consumer & Cmty. Affairs, Fed. Reserve Bd., to officers and managers in charge of consumer affairs (No. CA 02-6, Mar. 28, 2002).

131 *Id.*

132 Also, the requirement to consider "available" credit history about spousal joint or authorized user accounts should be read in conjunction with Reg. B, 12 C.F.R. § 202.10, regarding creditors' obligations to report the participation of both spouses on an account when the creditors furnish information to credit reporting agencies. Thus, if the creditors with whom an applicant previously had an account complied with § 202.10, the new creditor should have that history "available" to it for purposes of § 202.6(b)(6). If the prior creditors failed to provide such history, consider sending both the prior creditor and the credit reporting agency a written dispute seeking to have such information added. This request will trigger responsibilities under both § 202.10, see § 9.4.2, *infra*, and the FCRA, see National Consumer Law Center, Fair Credit Reporting Act Ch. 9 (4th ed. 1998 and Supp.).

133 Reg. B, 12 C.F.R. § 202.6(b)(6)(iii).

134 Reg. B, 12 C.F.R. § 202.6(b)(6)(iii).

135 Official Staff Commentary, 12 C.F.R. § 202.6(b)(6)-1.

136 Reg. B, 12 C.F.R. § 202.6(b)(6).

137 Official Staff Commentary, 12 C.F.R. § 202.6(b)(6)-1.

Note that an inadvertent error by the creditor is not a violation of the above requirements.[138] Inadvertent errors include clerical mistakes, calculation errors, computer malfunctions, and printing errors. An error of legal judgment is not an inadvertent error.[139]

6.5.3.3 Avoiding a Spouse's Bad Credit History

On the applicant's request, the creditor must consider any information that the applicant presents "tending to indicate" that the credit history being considered by the creditor does not accurately reflect the applicant's creditworthiness.[140] The creditor has no affirmative duty to request this information; the burden is placed on the applicant to explain why the applicant should not be denied credit because of a poor credit rating attributable to an ex-spouse during the marriage. Also, even though the creditor has an obligation to consider expiating information presented by such an applicant, it is not required to ignore the bad history altogether.

In many cases, there is no legitimate reason under the ECOA for a creditor to obtain the credit history of a spouse or ex- spouse if the applicant is seeking an individual account and does not wish to rely on the credit history built up in that other person's name.[141] In that case, the applicant need not be judged on the bad history of the spouse or ex-spouse at all.[142]

However, sometimes bad history involving a spouse will show up on an applicant's credit history because the applicant was an authorized user of a spouse's account.[143] In that case, it is important for the applicant to affirmatively show why the spouse's negative actions on that account do not accurately reflect the applicant's creditworthiness.

Some creditors have been reporting bankruptcy information regarding a spouse if there is a joint or authorized user spousal account. As a result, the spouse's bankruptcy information appears in the consumer's credit history. Creditors have defended this practice by arguing that this reporting is required by Regulation B.[144] Whether this argument is correct remains to be resolved.

6.5.4 Telephone Listing

A creditor may not consider whether there is a telephone listing in the applicant's name as a factor relevant to creditworthiness; but it may consider the existence of a telephone at the applicant's residence as such a factor.[145] This provision is primarily designed to protect married women, who often do not have telephone listings in their own names.

6.5.5 Likelihood of Bearing or Rearing Children

In evaluating an applicant's creditworthiness, a creditor may not make assumptions or use aggregate statistics concerning the likelihood that the income of any group of persons will be interrupted or diminished at a future time because those persons will bear or rear children.[146] In addition, creditors are forbidden from denying loans to women who anticipate taking maternity leaves.[147] Read together with the provision of Regulation B[148] which bars creditors from requesting information about an applicant's birth control practices and childbearing or childrearing intentions and capability, this provision prevents creditors from arbitrarily denying credit merely because they assume that a young female applicant will marry, have children, quit her job, and then probably default on her credit obligations.

6.5.6 Availability of Credit Insurance

A creditor may not refuse to extend credit or terminate an account merely because the applicant's age makes him or her ineligible for credit life, health, accident, or disability insurance.[149]

---

138 Reg. B, 12 C.F.R. § 202.14(c); *see also* Sayers v. Gen. Motors Acceptance Corp., 522 F. Supp. 835 (W.D. Mo. 1981) (no ECOA violation when credit denial was based on an inadvertent misinterpretation of the credit history; however, creditor's subsequent willful refusal to comply with notification requirements after being informed of its error did constitute an ECOA violation).

139 Official Staff Commentary, 12 C.F.R. § 202.14(c)-1.

140 Reg. B, 12 C.F.R. § 202.6(b)(6)(ii). For instance, an applicant could show that she was unemployed at the time a joint account went into default and had no way to ensure that her then-spouse, who was employed, would make payments. *See* Fed. Trade Comm'n, Informal Staff Opinion, Clearinghouse No. 37,088 (Apr. 5, 1983) (when unmarried cohabitants share use of an account and the account holder's negative credit history is imputed to another cohabitant, the cohabitant may make countervailing information available, and the creditor must consider it).

141 *See, e.g.,* In re Westinghouse Credit Corp., 94 F.T.C. 1280 (Fed. Trade Comm'n 1979) (creditor agreed not to conduct prohibited credit checks on the deceased spouses of applicants); *In re* Alden's, Inc., 92 F.T.C. 901 (Fed. Trade Comm'n 1978) (creditor ordered to stop rejecting married persons' applications for individual accounts on the basis of credit reports obtained on their spouses).

142 *See* § 5.5.5.4, *supra.*

143 As required by 12 C.F.R. § 202.10. *See* § 9.4.2, *infra.*

144 *See* Reg. B, 12 C.F.R. § 202.10(a)(1).

145 Reg. B, 12 C.F.R. § 202.6(b)(4); *see also* Fed. Trade Comm'n, Informal Staff Opinion, Clearinghouse No. 37,084 (May 26, 1983) (a rental car company would violate the ECOA if it required that a customer without a major credit card have a telephone listing in her own name, if the customer was permitted to defer payment and hence would receive "incidental credit").

146 Reg. B, 12 C.F.R. § 202.6(b)(3).

147 United States v. Ga. Telco Credit Union, Clearinghouse No. 31,075 (N.D. Ga. 1980).

148 Reg. B, 12 C.F.R. § 202.5(d)(4).

149 Reg. B, 12 C.F.R. § 202.7(e); *see also* United States v. Money Tree, Inc., Clearinghouse No. 52,053, Civ. No. 6:97-CV-7

6.6 Allowable Discrimination on a Prohibited Basis

6.6.1 Introduction

In certain special situations, creditors may make credit decisions taking into consideration three of the prohibited bases: the applicant's age, public assistance status, and marital status. These three prohibited bases are not found in other federal discrimination laws, and thus the ECOA limitations on these bases may be determinative.

6.6.2 Age

6.6.2.1 Introduction

Although age is a prohibited basis for discrimination under the ECOA, age is a very different type of prohibited basis than, for example, race or religion. Many types of age discrimination are explicitly authorized under the ECOA, and the ECOA can be seen more as regulating age discrimination than as prohibiting it.

There are detailed rules as to how a creditor may take the age of an applicant into consideration, and some of these rules differ depending on whether a credit scoring or judgmental system is used while others do not. The general rule, which applies no matter what evaluation system is used, is that age may not be taken into consideration at all unless provided for by the regulation.[150] To use age at all in either a credit scoring or judgmental system, the creditor must show that one of the specific exceptions to the general rule applies.

6.6.2.2 General Exceptions to the Prohibition Against Age Discrimination

The first general exception to the rule against age discrimination—that is, one that applies to both credit scoring and judgmental systems—is that the creditor can consider the applicant's age to determine if the applicant has the legal capacity to enter into a binding contract.[151] Legal capacity refers primarily to the legal age of majority. That is, if under state law an applicant is too young to enter into a binding contract, the creditor may reject the application on that basis.

The second exception—which also applies whether the creditor is using a credit scoring system or a judgmental

system—is that a creditor may consider the age of an applicant sixty-two years old or older in order to give favorable treatment to that applicant[152] or to evaluate a pertinent element of creditworthiness for a reverse mortgage.[153] Thus, assigning the highest point value or bonus points in a credit scoring system to an applicant sixty-two years of age or older would not constitute age discrimination. Nor would it be improper, in a judgmental system, to grant credit to an applicant sixty-two years of age or older who owned no real property, even if younger applicants would not receive a loan without such security.

A creditor may also provide more favorable credit terms to applicants over the age of sixty-two, such as lower interest rates or higher credit limits. More favorable terms may not be offered to those under age sixty-two than those over aged sixty-two except in special purpose credit programs.[154]

6.6.2.3 Relationship to State Laws

State laws addressing credit discrimination are preempted to the extent that they are inconsistent with the ECOA and Regulation B.[155] As described below, Regulation B allows credit discrimination in favor of elderly applicants and Regulation B specifically preempts state laws that prohibit creditors from asking or considering an applicant's age in order to favor an elderly applicant.[156]

Somewhat more confusing is a related Regulation B preemption of state laws dealing with age discrimination. As discussed below, Regulation B allows creditors using a credit scoring system to utilize age as a predictive factor, but only allows other systems to use age as a "pertinent element of creditworthiness." Regulation B preempts state laws that prohibit *credit scoring systems* from using age as a pertinent element of creditworthiness.[157] In other words, a state statute can prohibit creditors using a judgmental system from considering age at all, except to favor those over the age of sixty-two. The state statute could only limit a credit scoring system's use of age as a pertinent element of creditworthiness.

The ECOA does not preempt state laws which establish an age of majority for various purposes, such as an age below which a person may not enter into an enforceable contract.[158] Nor does it preempt state laws which set a

(M.D. Ga. Feb. 4, 1997) (consent order settling allegations that creditor discriminated against elderly applicants who were not eligible for credit life or credit disability insurance because of age), *available at* http://www.ftc.gov.
150 Reg. B, 12 C.F.R. § 202.6(b)(1).
151 Reg. B, 12 C.F.R. § 202.6(b)(2).
152 15 U.S.C. § 1691(b)(4); Reg. B, 12 C.F.R. §§ 202.6(b)(2)(iv), 202.2(o).
153 Official Staff Commentary, 12 C.F.R. § 202.6(b)(2)-4.
154 Official Staff Commentary, 12 C.F.R. § 202.6(b)(2)-1.
155 15 U.S.C. § 1691d(f); Reg. B, 12 C.F.R. § 202.11(a).
156 Reg. B, 12 C.F.R. § 202.11(b)(1)(iv).
157 Reg. B, 12 C.F.R. § 202.11(b)(iv).
158 Fed. Reserve Bd., Official Board Interpretation § 202.1103, 42 Fed. Reg. 36,810 (July 18, 1977), *as modified by* 42 Fed. Reg. 39,368 (Aug. 4, 1977). Interpretation § 202.1103 was not included in the Official Staff Commentary, because the Federal

different age of majority for married and unmarried persons.[159]

6.6.2.4 Age Discrimination Rules Applying Only to Credit Scoring Systems

When a creditor uses a credit scoring system, it may use the age of applicants as a predictor of creditworthiness.[160] For example, a forty-year-old applicant may receive five points and a twenty-five-year-old applicant only two points, if the creditor's scoring system predicts that forty-year-olds are substantially better risks.

However, creditors may not attach a negative factor or value to applicants who are sixty-two years of age or older.[161] A "negative factor or value" is defined by Regulation B as a factor, value, or weight that:

- Is less favorable to elderly applicants than the creditor's experience warrants; or
- Is less favorable than that assigned to the non-elderly applicants most favored by the creditor in terms of age.[162]

For example, the creditor might assign the following point values to certain age categories:

- Under 25 = 1 point;
- 26–34 = 2 points;
- 36–50 = 3 points;
- 51–61 = 4 points.

Under this system, the creditor could not assign less than four points to an applicant sixty-two or older. Those aged sixty-two or older may receive a factor higher than any other age group, though,[163] so that in this example, they could receive five points. Similarly, it is arguably impermissible to weigh favorably the fact that an applicant has young children, because this factor would penalize elderly applicants.

6.6.2.5 Age Discrimination Rules Applying Only to Judgmental Systems

When a creditor uses a judgmental system,[164] it may consider age only to determine a "pertinent element of creditworthiness."[165] According to Regulation B, a pertinent element of creditworthiness is "any information about applicants that a creditor obtains and considers and that has a demonstrable relationship to a determination of creditworthiness."[166]

Several examples of information displaying this "demonstrable relationship" are listed in the Commentary.[167] A creditor may not reject an application or terminate an account because the applicant is sixty-two years old. But the creditor that uses a judgmental system may relate the applicant's age to other factors that the creditor considers in measuring creditworthiness. For example, a creditor may consider:[168]

- The applicant's occupation and time remaining before retirement, to ascertain whether the applicant's income (including retirement income) would support the extension of credit until its maturity;[169]
- The adequacy of security offered by the applicant, if the duration of the credit extension would exceed the applicant's life expectancy; "An elderly applicant might not qualify for a 5-percent down, 30-year mortgage loan but might qualify with a larger downpayment or a

---

Reserve Board did not include any interpretations which did not preempt state laws. The reasoning of this interpretation thus apparently is still valid. Moreover, § 202.1103 is an Official Board Interpretation, not a staff interpretation, and thus should not be superseded by a staff commentary.

159 *Id.*

160 Reg. B, 12 C.F.R. § 202.6(b)(2)(ii); *see, e.g.*, Saunders v. Citibank S.D., Clearinghouse No. 45,760, Civ. No. JH-87-2930 (E.D. Md. 1988) (memorandum and order of summary judgment) (creditor did not discriminate against fifty-four year old applicant on basis of age, as it had used age permissibly in its empirically derived credit scoring system), *aff'd*, 872 F.2d 419 (4th Cir. 1989) (unpublished).

161 Reg. B, 12 C.F.R. § 202.6(b)(2)(ii). Reg. B, 12 C.F.R. § 202.2(o) defines elderly as aged sixty-two or older.

162 Reg. B, 12 C.F.R. § 202.2(v). Thus elderly applicants must be given "the *higher* of (1) the score warranted on the basis of the creditors experience with elderly applicants or (2) the score assigned to the class of nonelderly applicants most favored on the basis of age." Hsia, *Credit Scoring and the Equal Credit Opportunity Act*, 30 Hastings L.J. 371, 411 (1978).

163 Reg. B, 12 C.F.R. § 202.6(b)(2)(iv); *see also* 15 U.S.C. § 1691(b)(4).

164 Reg. B, 12 C.F.R. § 202.6(b)(2)(iii).

165 Reg. B, 12 C.F.R. § 202.2(y).

166 Reg. B, 12 C.F.R. § 202.2(y).

167 Official Staff Commentary, 12 C.F.R. § 202.6(b)(2)-3; *cf.* United States v. Landmark Fin. Services, Inc., Clearinghouse No. 41,275 (D. Md. 1986) (consent order and prior order on summary judgment motion) (limiting a creditor from using age-based mortality statistics to justify shorter terms of repayment for elderly loan applicants, but allowing shorter terms based on the creditor's own experience with that age group, provided that a lower rate of default is not set for elderly applicants). *But see* Official Staff Commentary, 12 C.F.R. §§ 202.6(b)(2)-1, 202.6(b)(2)-3 (an apparent response to the *Landmark* litigation which rejects age-related aggregate statistical data as the basis for decisions in a judgmental system).

168 Official Staff Commentary, 12 C.F.R. § 202.6(b)(2). The Federal Reserve Board has proposed revisions to Official Staff Commentary, 12 C.F.R. § 202.6(b)(2) that would reflect the change in name of the Aid to Families with Dependent Children program. The proposed revisions to the Official Staff Commentary can be found on the CD-Rom accompanying this volume.

169 Official Staff Commentary, 12 C.F.R. § 202.6(b)(2)-3.

shorter loan maturity";[170] and

• An applicant's age to assess the significance of the applicant's length of employment or length of residence at current address, for example, a young applicant who has a short work history, or an elderly applicant who has retired recently and moved from a long-time residence.[171]

However, these factors must be evaluated from facts and circumstances relating to the applicant on an individual, case-by-case basis, and a creditor cannot "base its decision on age or information related exclusively to age."[172] "Information related exclusively to age" encompasses mortality or life expectancy data.[173] Thus, creditors have been restricted in using age-based mortality statistics to justify a practice of requiring shorter repayment terms for older applicants and prohibited from automatically requiring higher down payments from applicants over the age of sixty-five.[174] Creditors are also prohibited from discriminating against older applicants because their age makes them ineligible for credit life, health, accident, or disability insurance.[175]

If a judgmental system in effect uses the "intuition" of the creditor's employee as a factor weighing against an older applicant, an argument should be made that such consideration is not related to a "pertinent element" of creditworthiness.[176] The burden should then shift to the creditor to

prove the "demonstrable relationship" of age to a determination of creditworthiness in the applicant's situation.[177]

6.6.2.6 Combination Systems

The Commentary authorizes a credit evaluation process which combines a credit scoring system and a judgmental system.[178] The credit scoring component of the combination system must comply with the special requirements (concerning age and public assistance evaluations) of a credit scoring system. The judgmental component (that component that is not a credit scoring system) must comply with the requirements (concerning age and public assistance evaluations) of a judgmental system.[179] This rule allows the creditor to use age twice, once pursuant to the limitations which apply to credit scoring systems, and once pursuant to the different limitations which apply to judgmental systems.

6.6.3 Public Assistance Status

6.6.3.1 General Rule Against Evaluations Based on Public Assistance Status

A creditor may not consider whether an applicant's income is derived from any public assistance program, except as expressly permitted by Regulation B.[180] Credit scoring systems can not consider the fact that income derives from a public assistance program because Regulation B contains no provision allowing the creditor using a credit scoring system to consider the applicant's public assistance status.[181] Income derived from public assistance programs should not be assigned a negative score in comparison to other forms of income of the same dollar amount.[182]

170 Official Staff Commentary, 12 C.F.R. § 202.6(b)(2)-3. The creditor's statistics might show that, in this mobile society, a large percentage of mortgages are paid off within five to ten years, so that concern about a thirty-year mortgage is arguably a pretext for age discrimination.

171 Official Staff Commentary, 12 C.F.R. § 202.6(b)(2)-3.

172 Official Staff Commentary, 12 C.F.R. § 202.6(b)(2)-3.

173 *See* Fed. Trade Comm'n v. Green Tree Acceptance, Clearinghouse No. 44,437 (N.D. Tex. Dec. 16, 1988) (consent decree).

174 Fed. Trade Comm'n v. Green Tree Acceptance, Clearinghouse No. 44,327 (N.D. Tex. 1988) (consent decree) (amended complaint alleges creditor violated ECOA by offering or granting loans to elderly applicants on less favorable terms than equally qualified nonelderly applicants; creditor's policy allegedly was to require down payment higher by three percent of the amount financed than that required of nonelderly applicants for each year the applicant was over sixty-five).

175 Reg. B, 12 C.F.R. § 202.7(e); *see* § 5.6, *supra*; *see also* United States v. Money Tree, Inc., Clearinghouse No. 52,053, Civ. No. 6:97-CV-7 (M.D. Ga. Feb. 4, 1997) (consent order settling allegations that creditor discriminated against elderly applicants who were not eligible for credit life or credit disability insurance because of age), *available at* http://www.ftc.gov.

176 Enforcement actions by federal agencies have made it clear that neither age nor information relating exclusively to age—such as mortality or life expectancy data—are reasonably related to a pertinent element of creditworthiness. *See, e.g.*, Fed. Trade Comm'n v. Green Tree Acceptance, Inc., Clearinghouse No. 44,327 (N.D. Tex. 1988) (agreed motion for leave to amend complaint ¶¶ 9-12; consent order ¶ 5(a)); United States v. Landmark Fin. Services, Inc., Clearinghouse No. 41,275, Civ. No. N-84-3510 (D. Md. Dec. 9, 1986) (consent order; also prior

decision on summary judgment motion).

177 *See* Reg. B, 12 C.F.R. §§ 202.6(b)(2), 202.2(y); Official Staff Commentary, 12 C.F.R. § 202.6(b)(2)-3.

178 Official Staff Commentary, 12 C.F.R. § 202.6(b)(2)-5 (as renumbered Sept. 30, 1996).

179 Official Staff Commentary, 12 C.F.R. § 202.6(b)(2)-5 (as renumbered Sept. 30, 1996).

180 Reg. B, 12 C.F.R. § 202.6(b)(2)-5.

181 *See* United States v. Aristar, Inc., Clearinghouse No. 37,083 (S.D. Fla. Apr. 7, 1983); Reed v. Northwestern Bell Tel. Co., Clearinghouse No. 27,524 (D. Minn. 1981) (credit scoring system unlawfully discriminated against public assistance recipients).

182 *See* United States v. Franklin Acceptance Corp., Civ. No. 99-CV-2435 (E.D. Pa. 1999) (consent decree settling allegations that creditor excluded or discounted public assistance income) [reproduced on the CD-Rom accompanying this volume]; United States v. Household Fin. Corp., Clearinghouse No. 38,903 (N.D. Ill. 1984) (consent order based partially on allegations that creditor did not give equal weight to income from public assistance as it did to income from other sources).

6.6.3.2 Exception for Judgmental System

When the creditor uses a judgmental system, it may consider whether the applicant's income is derived from a public assistance program, but only to determine a "pertinent element of creditworthiness."[183] According to Regulation B, a pertinent element of creditworthiness is "any information about applicants that a creditor obtains and considers and that has a demonstrable relationship to a determination of creditworthiness."[184]

Several examples of information displaying this "demonstrable relationship" are listed in the Commentary:[185]

- The length of time an applicant will likely remain eligible to receive such income;
- Whether the applicant will continue to qualify for benefits based on the status of the applicant's dependents (for instance, the age of the applicant's children may affect future Temporary Assistance to Needy Families payments or Social Security payments to a minor);
- Whether the creditor can attach or garnish the income to assure payment of the debt in the event of default (this exception, if followed, would nullify the general rule—most public benefits are exempt from execution; the Commentary example would in effect nullify the statutory protections granted to recipients of public assistance, placing the validity of this Commentary provision in doubt).

The prohibition against discrimination based on public assistance status provides certain clear cut limitations on creditor behavior. A creditor absolutely may not maintain a blanket policy of refusing to extend credit to public assistance recipients. It also may not impose stricter loan terms or additional restrictions based upon applicants' receipt of public assistance.[186]

In addition, when the public assistance is based on entitlement, and will remain continuous (e.g., Social Security benefits), it should be considered comparable to any other form of income. When an applicant's assistance is based on need rather than entitlement (e.g., food stamps), any creditor which has denied credit should be required to present evidence that it attempted to determine the amount, the expected duration, and the continuity of assistance. Without such evidence the creditor cannot support the argument that it has considered applications in an individual, nondiscriminatory manner, particularly if termination of needs-based benefits may mean that a new, larger source of income has been established.

Further, a creditor should be required to show that its inquiries about the level of assistance and its continuance bear a relationship to the duration of the credit transaction; an applicant should not be forced to show that benefits will be received indefinitely in order to obtain a one-year loan. If the creditor's inquiries become demeaning, Regulation B arguably can be invoked to prohibit statements which would discourage a reasonable person from making or pursuing a credit application.[187]

6.6.4 Marital Status

A creditor may not consider an applicant's marital status to determine the applicant's creditworthiness, except to ascertain the creditor's rights and remedies upon default.[188] For example, in a secured transaction involving real estate, a creditor may take into account whether state law gives the applicant's spouse an interest in the property being offered as collateral.[189]

This provision must be read along with the provision which sets standards for determining when an applicant's spouse may be required to act as cosigner on a credit instrument,[190] and with the applicable state property law

---

183 Reg. B, 12 C.F.R. § 202.2(y).
184 Reg. B, 12 C.F.R. § 202.2(y).
185 Official Staff Commentary, 12 C.F.R. § 202.6(b)(2)-6. The Federal Reserve Board has proposed revisions to Official Staff Commentary, 12 C.F.R. § 202.6(b)(2)-6 that would reflect the change in name of the Aid to Families with Dependent Children program. The proposed revisions to the Official Staff Commentary can be found on the CD-Rom accompanying this volume.
186 United States v. Money Tree, Inc. Clearinghouse No. 52,053, Civ. No. 6:97-CV-7 (M.D. Ga. Feb. 4, 1997) (consent order settling allegations that creditor imposed stricter loan terms on public assistance recipients, required them to make payments earlier than the payments were due, and required them to directly deposit their benefits in repayment of loan).
187 Reg. B, 12 C.F.R. § 202.5(a).
188 Official Staff Commentary, 12 C.F.R. § 202.6(b)(1)-1. The Federal Reserve Board has proposed redistributing Official Staff Commentary, 12 C.F.R. § 202.6(b)(1)-1 among other sections of Regulation B and the Commentary. The portions of § 202.6(b)(1)-1 requiring creditors to evaluate married and unmarried applicants by the same standards, and not treating joint applicants differently based on the existence, absence or likelihood of a marital relationship between the parties would become 12 C.F.R. § 202.6(b)(8). 64 Fed. Reg. 44,582, 44,597 (Aug. 16, 1999). The portion relating to a creditor's right to consider an applicant's or joint applicant's marital status for purposes of ascertaining the rights and remedies applicable to the particular extension of credit, such as when state law gives the applicant's spouse an interest in the property offered as collateral, would become new Official Staff Commentary, 12 C.F.R. § 202.6(b)(8)-1. 64 Fed. Reg. 44,582, 44,624 (Aug. 16, 1999). The proposed revisions to Regulation B and the Official Staff Commentary can be found on the CD-Rom accompanying this volume.
189 Official Staff Commentary, 12 C.F.R. § 202.6(b)(1)-1.
190 Reg. B, 12 C.F.R. § 202.7(d). The Federal Reserve Board's proposed revisions to Regulation B would amend 12 C.F.R. § 202.7(d)(1) to expressly prohibit a creditor from deeming the submission of a joint financial statement or other evidence of jointly held assets as an application for joint credit. 64 Fed. Reg. 44,582, 44,598 (Aug. 16, 1999). The proposed revisions to

concerning spouses' interest in property and liability for their partners' debts.

In situations in which creditors may request an applicant's marital status, they may categorize the applicant only as unmarried (which includes single, divorced, and widowed persons), married, or separated.[191] The creditor may explain that the category unmarried includes single, divorced, and widowed persons, but it is not required to do so.[192]

Some creditors have been reluctant to comply with even this basic requirement. One major creditor was alleged to routinely divide credit applicants into divorced and single categories, by circling or otherwise emphasizing information contained in the credit reports obtained on applicants. It agreed to halt this practice after an action was initiated by the Federal Trade Commission.[193]

Soon after the ECOA was enacted, the Comptroller of the Currency decided that national bank creditors were not liable for an ECOA violation contained on forms for federally-insured loans distributed to them by the Department of Health, Education and Welfare (the former name for the Department of Education and the Department of Health and Human Services) and the Federal Housing Administration. The use of marital status categories other than married, unmarried, and separated on these application forms was considered "a mere technicality . . . beyond the power of the bank to correct."[194]

Regulation B can be found on the CD-Rom accompanying this volume. *See also* § 5.6, *supra*.

191 Reg. B, 12 C.F.R. §§ 202.5(d)(1), 202.2(u).

192 Reg. B, 12 C.F.R. § 202.5(d)(1).

193 *In re* Westinghouse Credit Corp., 94 F.T.C. 1280 (Fed. Trade Comm'n 1979); *see also* United States v. Fireside Thrift, Clear-

inghouse No. 43,051 (N.D. Cal. Sept. 2, 1986) (consent order in which creditor agreed not to use terms other than "married," and "separated" on applications); United States v. Capitol Thrift & Loan Ass'n, Clearinghouse No. 43,052 (N.D. Cal. Mar. 20, 1986) (same); Shuman v. Standard Oil, 453 F. Supp. 1150 (N.D. Cal. 1978) (divorced woman alleged that the creditor discriminated against her on the basis of her marital status as revealed in a credit report).

194 Comptroller of Currency, Interpretive Staff Letter, Fed. Banking L. Rep. (CCH) ¶ 85,041 (Office of the Comptroller of the Currency, Oct. 27, 1977) (Roberta W. Boylan).

Chapter 7   Redlining

7.1 Introduction and History of Redlining

Redlining refers to the practice of separating out certain neighborhoods for disparate treatment as to mortgage or other types of lending. Redlining began as a result of the policies of the Home Owners' Loan Corp. (HOLC) in the 1930s. The HOLC was created to help families prevent the loss of homes through foreclosure.[1]

The HOLC created a uniform appraisal system. HOLC-trained appraisers then divided cities into different zones and developed a rating system to assess the risks associated with loans made in certain neighborhoods. The rating system consisted of four color-coded categories. The (A) category was considered the least risky and was coded green. The next category, (B), was coded blue. Category (C) was coded yellow and defined as neighborhoods that were in decline. The fourth and lowest category, (D), was coded red.[2]

The HOLC explicitly incorporated ethnic and racial worth into these categories. For example, a 1935 Federal Housing Administration manual for agency underwriters stated that acceptable ratings would depend on neighborhoods being protected against "the occurrence or development of unfavorable influences" such as the "infiltration of inharmonious racial or nationality groups."[3] As a result, many predominantly African-American neighborhoods were rated in category (D) and therefore "redlined." Although evidence suggests that the HOLC made loans even to these red-coded neighborhoods, the system it developed was copied by other lenders, ultimately contributing to the spread of racial redlining.[4]

For example, the Federal Housing Administration, established in 1934, used the HOLC system as a model. The Administration developed an underwriting manual that at least partially attributed stability in neighborhoods to racial homogeneity.[5] It follows that various studies over the years have found patterns of racial redlining in Federal Housing Administration lending.[6]

The Fair Housing Act (FHA) was passed in the 1960s to address this long history of racial redlining in the housing market, expand housing opportunities for members of protected groups and to foster residential integration. Despite progress, studies continue to show the existence of redlining in the provision of home mortgage loans.[7] Government enforcement actions, particularly in the 1990s, provide further evidence of the continued existence of redlining.[8]

7.2 Legal Claims Available to Challenge Redlining

7.2.1 The ECOA, FHA, and Federal Civil Rights Acts

To the extent redlining is based on a desire to avoid making loans to certain ethnic or racial groups, or to avoid making loans in areas where such groups predominate, the practice involves disparate treatment on a prohibited basis in clear violation of credit discrimination statutes.[9] Precedent has developed over the years allowing plaintiffs to use the FHA to challenge such redlining practices.[10] The ECOA and

---

1   *See generally* Charles L. Nier, III, *Perpetuation of Segregation: Toward a New Historical And Legal Interpretation of Redlining Under the Fair Housing Act*, 32 J. Marshall L. Rev. 617 (1999).

2   *Id.*

3   *See* Ira Rheingold, Michael Fitzpatrick & Al Hofeld Jr., *From Redlining to Reverse Redlining: A History of Obstacles for Minority Homeownership in America*, 34 Clearinghouse Rev. 642 (2001) (quoting John O. Calmore, Spatial Equality and the Kerner Commission Report: A Back to the Future Essay, in Race, Poverty, and American Cities 324 (John Charles Boger & Judith Welch Wegner eds., 1998)).

4   Charles L. Nier, III, *Perpetuation of Segregation: Toward a New Historical And Legal Interpretation of Redlining Under the Fair Housing Act*, 32 J. Marshall L. Rev. 617 (1999) (citing Douglas

A. Massey & Nancy A. Denton, American Apartheid: Segregation and the Making of the Underclass 51–52 (1993)).

5   *Id.* (citing Kenneth T. Jackson, Crabgrass Frontier: The Suburbanization of the United States (1985)).

6   *Id.* (citing Melvin L. Oliver & Thomas M. Shapiro, Black Wealth/White Wealth: A New Perspective on Racial Inequality (1995)).

7   *See, e.g.,* Jonathan Brown, Racial Redlining: A Study of Racial Discrimination by Bankers and Mortgage Companies in the United States (1993).

8   *See* § 12.4.3.3, *infra.*

9   *See, e.g.,* Harrison v. Otto G. Heinzeroth Mortgage Co., 430 F. Supp. 893 (N.D. Ohio 1977); Laufman v. Oakley Bldg. & Loan Co., 408 F. Supp. 489 (S.D. Ohio 1976).

10   In general, courts have allowed claims to be brought under both sections 3604 and 3605 of the FHA. *See, e.g.,* Thomas v. First

civil rights statutes may also be used to challenge redlining.[11]

Proving a redlining violation using these statutes becomes more complicated when the creditor is not motivated by the racial or ethnic composition of a neighborhood but by various legitimate factors relating to creditworthiness that are also correlated to geographic location. Such factors include the average income, default rates, age of housing stock, or housing value in a particular area. The creditor is then using geographic location as a proxy for these other factors.[12]

Because using geographic location to determine creditworthiness often has a disproportionate impact on various racial or ethnic groups, the issue becomes whether alternative credit factors would meet the creditor's needs without causing as much of a disparate impact.[13] For example, could the creditor more directly consider the individual applicant's income and credit history and the age and value of the applicant's residence instead of using geographic area as a proxy for these factors?

Some courts have imposed additional burdens of proof in redlining cases, departing in some cases from standards commonly used to determine whether a plaintiff has shown a prima facie case of discrimination.[14] These courts are often

sympathetic to lenders' arguments that their decisions not to lend in particular areas are based on sound business principles, not discrimination.[15]

At least partially in response to this judicial trend, plaintiffs have developed additional theories of relief for lender practices associated with a segregated market. For example, plaintiffs have argued that intentional exploitation of the dual market created by segregation violates the FHA.[16] The elements required to prove such an exploitation theory, as set out by the Seventh Circuit, are: 1) dual housing markets existed as a result of racial segregation, and 2) sellers took advantage of this situation by demanding prices and terms from members of protected groups unreasonably in excess of the prices and terms available to whites for comparable housing.[17]

7.2.2 Government Enforcement Actions

A number of government enforcement actions have focused on alleged illegal redlining practices. Most of the government enforcement actions are filed with simultaneous settlement agreements or consent decrees. Although these cases have no direct precedential value, they are important models for future public and private fair lending cases.[18]

For example, in a case against Chevy Chase Federal Savings Bank, the Department of Justice (DOJ) alleged that Chevy Chase and its subsidiary, B.F. Saul Mortgage Co., intentionally excluded majority African-American census tracts in their metropolitan District of Columbia service area from access to many of the institution's credit-related services.[19] The complaint also alleged that Chevy Chase engaged in other practices that effectively denied African-Americans access to banking services.[20] While Chevy Chase and its subsidiary admitted to no wrongdoing, they agreed to take reasonable actions to obtain a market share of mortgage

---

Fed. Sav. Bank of Ind., 653 F. Supp. 1330 (N.D. Ind. 1987) (defining redlining as mortgage credit decisions based on the characteristics of the neighborhood surrounding the would-be borrower's dwelling); Laufman v. Oakley Bldg. & Loan Co., 408 F. Supp. 489 (S.D. Ohio 1976) (plaintiffs also alleged violations of § 3617 of the FHA).

11 Some plaintiffs have coupled substantive FHA claims with ECOA procedural claims for lack of proper notice of credit decisions. *See, e.g.,* Cartwright v. Am. Sav. & Loan Ass'n, 880 F.2d 912 (7th Cir. 1989) (court rejected ECOA substantive and procedural claims because plaintiff's application was properly placed on hold and thus no adverse action taken); Saldana v. Citibank, 1996 U.S. Dist. LEXIS 8327 (N.D. Ill. June 13, 1996) (court found plaintiff did not submit a completed application and therefore rejected ECOA procedural claims). Note, however, that recovery cannot be had for the same transactions and same violations under both the ECOA and FHA. *See* § 11.5.2, *infra.*

12 Note, however, that as far as the Justice Department is concerned avoidance of tribal court jurisdiction is not a legitimate business justification for refusing to make secured loans when the collateral is located on a Native American reservation. United States v. Blackpipe State Bank, Civ. No. 93-5115 (D.S.D. 1994), Clearinghouse Nos. 49,955A (complaint), 49,955B (consent decree); *see also* § 12.4.3.3 (further discussion of *Blackpipe*, *infra.*

13 *See* Old W. End Ass'n v. Buckeye Fed. Sav. & Loan, 675 F. Supp. 1100 (N.D. Ohio 1987); Harrison v. Otto G. Heinzeroth Mortgage Co., 430 F. Supp. 893 (N.D. Ohio 1977); Laufman v. Oakley Bldg. & Loan Co., 408 F. Supp. 489 (S.D. Ohio 1976).

14 *See, e.g.,* Cartwright v. Am. Sav. & Loan Ass'n, 880 F.2d 912 (7th Cir. 1989) (plaintiffs' claims did not fall within § 3604 of the FHA and defendant did not engage in redlining within the definition of § 3605; court also denied relief under 42 U.S.C. §§ 1981 and 1982 because plaintiff failed to show intentional discrimination); Saldana v. Citibank, 1996 U.S. Dist. LEXIS

8327 (N.D. Ill. June 13, 1996) (plaintiff failed to show prima facie case of disparate treatment or disparate impact).

15 Cartwright v. Am. Sav. & Loan Ass'n, 880 F.2d 912 (7th Cir. 1989) (FHA prohibition against denying a loan based on location of the dwelling does not require that a lender disregard its legitimate business interests or make an investment that is not economically sound).

16 *See, e.g., Honorable v. The Easy Life Real Estate Sys., Inc.,* 100 F. Supp. 2d 885 (N.D. Ill. 2000); *see also* Hobson v. Lincoln Ins. Agency, Inc., 2001 U.S. Dist. LEXIS 476 (N.D. Ill. 2001) (denying defendant's motion to dismiss §§ 1981 and 1982 claims in insurance redlining case; court noted that dual market theory not limited to the real estate market).

17 Clark v. Universal Builders, Inc., 706 F.2d 204 (7th Cir. 1983) (*Clark II*); Clark v. Universal Builders, Inc., 501 F.2d 423 (7th Cir. 1974) (*Clark I*).

18 *See generally* Ch. 12, *infra* (further discussion of government enforcement actions).

19 United States v. Chevy Chase Fed. Sav. Bank, No. 94-1824-J6 (D.D.C. 1994) (consent decree) [reproduced on the CD-Rom accompanying this volume].

20 *Id.*

loans in African-American neighborhoods comparable to their market share in white neighborhoods.

In another redlining case, *United States v. Blackpipe State Bank*,[21] the DOJ alleged that the bank discriminated against Native Americans by refusing to make secured loans when the collateral was located on a reservation, by placing credit requirements on Native Americans that it did not require of whites, and by charging Native Americans greater interest rates and finance charges than those it charged to whites. Among other things, the bank allegedly had a policy of refusing to make loans secured by collateral subject to tribal court jurisdiction, even though all other lending criteria were met and even though the tribal courts have repossession and collection remedies available.

In *United States v. Albank*[22] the DOJ alleged that Albank refused to fund mortgage loans secured by residential properties located in certain areas in Connecticut and in Westchester County, New York, where significant populations of African-Americans and Hispanics lived. Although Albank made exceptions to its policies, the exceptions were made predominately for white borrowers.[23]

7.2.3 Other Federal and State Statutes

The federal credit discrimination statutes and civil rights laws are not the only possible bases for claims in redlining cases. For example, the federal Office of Thrift Supervision promulgates regulations for savings associations' provision of mortgage loans. One regulation prohibits discrimination based on the location and age of the dwelling.[24] Instead, the creditor should consider the dwelling's market value and any factors that can be documented that would directly result in a change in that market value.[25] Consideration of age and location may appear to be neutral, but past forms of discrimination may color the use of such a factor so that use of the factor would perpetuate old sources of discrimination. For example, use of criteria such as prior history with the same lender, home ownership, or education may foster past

practices that prevented individuals in protected groups from receiving home mortgages, owning homes, or attending higher educational institutions.[26]

State statutes and regulations may also specifically prohibit redlining. For example, a New Jersey statute prohibiting geographic redlining in the granting of home mortgages was not preempted by the ECOA.[27] Several other state statutes prohibit discrimination based on the geographic area of residence.[28]

7.3 Insurance Redlining

7.3.1 General

Insurance redlining is the practice of "charging higher rates or declining to write insurance for people who live in particular areas (figuratively, sometimes literally enclosed with a red line on a map)."[29] The definition is usually expanded to include discrimination against individuals on the basis of a factor unrelated to risk in providing residential property and casualty insurance.

Insurance redlining occurs in several forms. Common insurer practices include imposing unnecessary application eligibility criteria, failing to place agents in particular communities, making limited marketing efforts, offering a limited portfolio of insurance products, and offering uncompetitive premiums for homes in certain neighborhoods.[30] The following examples demonstrate how insurance industry activities may discriminate:

Application Eligibility: An agent who claims only to write insurance for dwellings above a certain value or under a certain age is effectively shutting out the poor and minorities in urban areas who proportionally purchase a greater number of older, less expensive homes.

Placement of Agents: Homeowners insurance policies are generally sold through insurance agents. Companies without a sufficient number of agents in a given area may be inadvertently discriminating by limiting access to their products and services in that area. Lower-income homeowners are disproportionately affected because they do not always

---

21   Civ. No. 93-5115 (D.S.D. 1994), Clearinghouse Nos. 49,955A (complaint), 49,955B (consent decree).

22   United States v. Albank, Clearinghouse No. 52,054, Civ. No. 97-1296 (N.D.N.Y. Aug. 13, 1997) (complaint and consent decree) [reproduced on the CD-Rom accompanying this volume].

23   Some commentators have been critical of the DOJ's actions against Chevy Chase and other banks allegedly engaged in discrimination in their marketing. In the view of these commentators, discrimination in marketing is not actionable under the ECOA and the FHA because there is no individual applicant who has been discriminated against. *See* John Spina, *United States v. Albank, FSB: Is 'Justice' Served in the Enforcement of Fair Lending Laws*, 2 N.C. Banking Inst. 207 (1998); Michael B. Mierzewski & Richard L. Jacobs, *What Hath the Justice Department Wrought*, Banking Pol'y Rep., Feb. 6, 1995, at 8.

24   12 C.F.R. § 528.2(a).

25   12 C.F.R. § 528.2(a).

26   *See* 12 C.F.R. §§ 528.1–528.9 (Office of Thrift Supervision guidelines relating to nondiscrimination in lending).

27   Nat'l State Bank v. Long, 630 F.2d 981 (3d Cir. 1980).

28   *See, e.g.*, 815 Ill. Comp. Stat. §§ 120/1 to 120/6; Iowa Code §§ 535A.1 to 535A.9; Md. Code Ann., Com. Law § 12-603; Mich. Comp. Laws §§ 445.1601 to 445.1614; Minn. Stat. § 363.03(2)(3); N.Y. Banking Law § 9-f (McKinney); Wash. Rev. Code §§ 30.04.500 to 30.04.515; *see* Appx. E (detailed summary of state credit discrimination laws).

29   *See* N.A.A.C.P. v. Am. Family Mut. Ins. Co., 978 F.2d 287, 290 (7th Cir. 1992) (consent decree available as Clearinghouse No. 52,059).

30   Another insurance issue that may disproportionately affect protected groups is the use of credit scores in insurance underwriting and pricing. *See* § 6.4.3.4, *supra*.

have the resources to get to an agency outside their neighborhood.

Marketing: Access to insurance companies can also be limited if the insurer chooses not to list its telephone number in certain telephone books, does not advertise on certain radio stations, omits specific zip codes from its mailing lists, and sends different mail offers to different neighborhoods.

Limited Portfolio of Insurance Offerings: Another practice used by insurers to avoid adequately serving certain areas is offering a subset of their normal product line—e.g., limiting the products offered in lower-income areas to either high-priced or low-risk coverage.

Uncompetitive Premiums for Homes: Many insurers charge higher premiums in low-income predominantly minority urban neighborhoods, pricing these consumers out of the marketplace.

Weblining: The widespread use of the internet to sell products and services has produced a new set of questions and concerns regarding insurance redlining.[31] "Weblining" is the use of the World Wide Web to practice any form of redlining. With respect to insurance, weblining generally occurs either because of unequal access to the internet or through profiling of potential customers.[32] For example, the practice of offering discounts to consumers who purchase policies on-line may have a disproportionate impact on protected groups to the extent that those groups are less likely to have access to the internet.[33]

"Digital divide" is the term given to the disparity between high-income and low-income households with respect to access to the internet. It also refers to the lower numbers of minority internet users. Some studies show this gap is closing while others show a persistent problem.[34] Even if the divide is closing, there is still a huge gap between those with access to broadband services and those without.[35]

Some commentators believe the internet has the potential to reduce the incidence of discrimination in the insurance industry because on-line shopping allows consumers to avoid face-to-face encounters, during which discrimination often occurs. The internet may also help improve access to insurance for consumers in neighborhoods where there are no insurance agents. However, these potential benefits can be easily overridden by discriminatory customer profiling. This type of profiling occurs when, for example, internet users inquiring about special offers are required to provide seemingly innocuous information such as their zip code. Violations may arise if this information is used to deny applications on a discriminatory basis.[36]

7.3.2 The Impact of Insurance Redlining

Insurance redlining seriously undermines the ability of affected individuals to purchase and safeguard their homes. According to one court: "[T]he availability of housing is . . . dependent on the availability of insurance. It is elementary that without insurance, mortgage financing will be unavailable, because a mortgage lender simply will not lend money on the [uninsured] property. Without mortgage financing, homes cannot be purchased."[37] In addition to discouraging the purchase of new homes, redlining puts existing homeowners in jeopardy of losing their homes.[38] The Seventh Circuit Court of Appeals provided a concise summary of the problem, stating, "no insurance, no loan; no loan, no house."[39]

Without insurance alternatives, many homeowners are forced or coaxed into purchasing insurance from an industry-financed high-risk pool. There are numerous problems with this type of insurance. Although the premiums are generally less expensive:

- Deductibles are higher;
- Options are few;
- Personal property coverage is normally not available;
- Overall coverage is usually lower;
- Home inspection and maintenance requirements can be overly rigorous (and too expensive for low-income homeowners); and
- This type of insurance gives insurers who do not want to conduct business in a particular neighborhood an excuse not to sell insurance there.

7.3.3 Detecting Insurance Redlining

Insurance redlining, like other forms of discrimination, occurs in overt as well as in subtle ways. Listed below are

---

31 *See generally* Gary A. Hernandez, Katherine J. Eddy & Joel Muchmore, *Insurance Weblining and Unfair Discrimination in Cyberspace*, 54 SMU L. Rev. 1953 (2001).

32 *See* § 5.3.2.5, *supra*.

33 Offering such discounts may violate insurance ratings laws in some states, as well as credit discrimination laws. *See generally* Gary A. Hernandez, Katherine J. Eddy & Joel Muchmore, *Insurance Weblining and Unfair Discrimination in Cyberspace*, 54 SMU L. Rev. 1953 (2001).

34 *See generally id.*; Dep't of Commerce, Nat'l Telecommunications & Info. Admin., A Nation Online: How Americans Are Expanding Their Use of the Internet (Feb. 2002), *available at* http://www.ntia.doc.gov; *see also* § 3.8.2, *supra*.

35 Dep't of Commerce, Nat'l Telecommunications & Info. Admin., A Nation Online: How Americans Are Expanding Their Use of the Internet (Feb. 2000), *available at* http://www.ntia.doc.gov.

36 *See* Gary A. Hernandez, Katherine J. Eddy & Joel Muchmore, *Insurance Weblining and Unfair Discrimination in Cyberspace*, 54 SMU L. Rev. 1953 (2001).

37 McDiarmid v. Economy Fire & Cas. Co., 604 F. Supp. 105, 107 (S.D. Ohio 1984).

38 A *Boston Globe* article highlighted a situation in which individuals who owned their homes outright were denied disaster insurance. Stephen Kurkjian, *Boston's Uninsured Homes*, The Boston Globe, Apr. 25, 1995, at 1, 24.

39 N.A.A.C.P. v. Am. Family Mut. Ins. Co., 978 F.2d 287, 297 (7th Cir. 1992).

a few ways to detect unlawful insurance discrimination practices:

Application Criteria: Suspicious signs include applications that require, for example, information on the age or value of a dwelling, prior insurance history (some insurers will not accept customers who have been turned down by other insurance companies), credit rating, or property inspections only in certain neighborhoods.

Insurance Company Training Manuals: Sales and underwriting training, policy, or procedural texts and memos can be very revealing. These documents, in which management communicates their sales and underwriting philosophy, should be checked for overt or subtle bias.

Accessibility of Insurance Company in Certain Areas: The scope of the insurer's marketing efforts, the number of agents, the number of minority and/or bilingual agents, limitations on product offerings, and above-market pricing are all indications that an insurer may be engaged in redlining.

Disclosure Legislation: The insurance industry generally contends that urban pricing patterns are based solely on risk and that pricing disparities between urban and suburban areas and between minority and non-minority neighborhoods are a result of higher incidences and greater severity of losses in urban areas.[40] In the absence of public data on insurance pricing and underwriting, it is difficult to ascertain the accuracy of that pronouncement, and insurance companies are not presently required to share that information. In at least a few states, advocates have succeeded in their push for expanded disclosure requirements for insurance data.[41]

Testing and Investigation of Insurers: Because information about insurance underwriting and pricing is so difficult to obtain, insurer policies, practices, and pricing that may be discriminatory in intent or effect are not easily uncovered. However, fair housing organizations have successfully used matched-pair testing to determine whether an insurer is unfairly discriminating.[42]

---

40 *See, e.g.*, Mass. Affordable Hous. Alliance, Opening the Books: The Case for Public Disclosure of Homeowners Insurance Data 4 (1995).

41 In California, for example, regulations require specified insurers to file a "community service statement" annually with the Department of Insurance reporting certain information for each zip code in which the insurer sells insurance or maintains agents. Cal. Code Regs. tit. 10, § 2646.6(a). The regulation makes those statements available for public inspection. *See* Cal. Code Regs. tit. 10, § 2646.6(c); Cal. Ins. Code § 1861.07 (West). As of 2001, proposed legislation to enact these regulations into statute had failed to pass the California legislature. Congress has also considered, but to date has not passed, federal insurance disclosure legislation.

42 Shanna L. Smith & Cathy Cloud, *Documenting Discrimination by Homeowners Insurance Companies Through Testing*, in Insurance Redlining 97 (Gregory D. Squires, ed., 1997); *see* § 4.4.4, *supra*.

7.3.4 *Legal Claims Available to Challenge Insurance Redlining*

7.3.4.1 The Equal Credit Opportunity Act

The Commentary explicitly states that Regulation B under the ECOA is applicable only to discrimination in the issuance of credit. It is *not* a violation of Regulation B for a creditor to obtain and use information about an applicant's age, sex, or marital status for the purpose of discriminating in the issuance of insurance.[43]

Still, the ECOA may be applicable when credit has been denied or some other adverse action taken because the applicant refused to purchase insurance. If credit is denied because the applicant refuses to buy optional credit insurance, the applicant may have an ECOA claim for discrimination on the basis of a good faith exercise of rights under the Consumer Credit Protection Act.[44] Borrowers cannot be denied access to credit for merely exercising, in good faith, their right not to insure. In addition, if a lender required *only* members of a protected group to purchase credit insurance, these applicants may have an ECOA claim.

7.3.4.2 The Fair Housing Act

The federal Fair Housing Act (FHA) is another important option, particularly with respect to the sale of insurance related to a dwelling, such as homeowners insurance.[45] However, there is no definitive statutory provision or judicial decision holding that the FHA applies to insurance. Throughout the 1980s, there was a split among the circuit courts on this issue.[46] The tide began to turn in 1989 when the Department of Housing and Urban Development (HUD) enacted a regulation prohibiting discriminatory refusals to provide "property or hazard insurance for dwellings" or providing insurance services on a discriminatory basis.[47] In January 1994, President Clinton issued an executive order mandating that HUD promulgate a regulation to clarify the application of the FHA to property insurance.[48] In 1995, HUD temporarily suspended rulemaking on this issue and,

---

43 Official Staff Commentary, 12 C.F.R. § 202.7(e).

44 *See, e.g.*, Bryson v. Bank of N.Y., 584 F. Supp. 1306 (S.D.N.Y. 1984).

45 Note, however, that the sale of credit-related insurance, such as mortgage disability insurance, is not a form of "financial assistance" for purchasing or maintaining a dwelling and therefore is not covered by the Fair Housing Act. *See* Doukas v. Metro. Life Ins. Co., 882 F. Supp. 1197, 1202 (D.N.H. 1995).

46 *See generally* William E. Murray, *Homeowners Insurance Redlining: The Inadequacy of Federal Remedies and the Future of the Property Insurance War*, 4 Conn. Ins. L.J. 735, 747 (1997–98).

47 24 C.F.R. § 100.70(d)(4).

48 Exec. Order No. 12,892, 59 Fed. Reg. 2939 (Jan. 20, 1994).

to date, has not returend to it.[49]

However, at least partially in response to the 1989 regulation, courts began to allow FHA claims for insurance redlining. The Seventh Circuit Court of Appeals, in *NAACP v. American Family Mutual Insurance Co.*, established the current standard, subsequently followed by many courts, that the provision of property insurance can be reasonably interpreted as the "provision of services or facilities in connection" with the sale or rental of a dwelling and therefore is covered by the FHA.[50]

The rationale for applying the FHA to insurance is that refusing to sell insurance prevents the potential insured from obtaining a mortgage, thereby preventing the individual from purchasing the home.[51] The FHA applies not only when redlining involves higher insurance premiums but also applies to decisions involving renewal of property insurance policies.[52] Government enforcement actions have also challenged insurance redlining practices.[53]

Assuming the court agrees with the majority view that the FHA applies, the court must still determine whether the McCarran-Ferguson Act[54] prevents the FHA from applying to the sale of insurance.[55] The McCarran-Ferguson Act prohibits federal statutes from invalidating, superseding, or impairing a state law regulating the business of insurance unless the federal statute refers specifically to insurance.

The Seventh Circuit in *NAACP v. American Family Mutual Insurance Co.* avoided the McCarran-Ferguson issue by finding no conflict between the federal Fair Housing Act and Wisconsin's insurance statutes.[56] It upheld the application of the Fair Housing Act to insurance because both federal and state law prohibited racial discrimination in the sale of insurance. According to the court, a federal remedy under the FHA would not frustrate any state policy.[57] Although the FHA provided an effective private remedy and state law did not, the court found this distinction did not create a conflict between the two statutes.[58]

An earlier case used a different approach to avoid the McCarran-Ferguson Act issue, holding that the Act does not apply to federal civil rights statutes enacted after the date the McCarran-Ferguson Act was adopted.[59] The Seventh Circuit, while reaching the same result (that the McCarran-Ferguson Act does not preempt a Fair Housing Act claim), harshly criticized the Second Circuit's reasoning.[60] Yet another approach argues that illegal discrimination in the sale of insurance does not involve the "business of insurance."[61]

In 1998, the first jury verdict in an insurance redlining case was awarded. The plaintiff was awarded $500,000 in compensatory damages and $100 million in punitive damages.[62] The plaintiff in this case alleged that urban African-

49 *See* Gregory D. Squires, *Why an Insurance Regulation to Prohibit Redlining?*, 31 J. Marshall L. Rev. 489, 503 (1998) (arguing that HUD should proceed with rulemaking on property insurance issues under the Fair Housing Act).

50 N.A.A.C.P. v. Am. Family Mut. Ins. Co., 978 F.2d 287 (7th Cir. 1992); *see also* Nationwide Mut. Ins. Co. v. Cisneros, 52 F.3d 1351 (6th Cir. 1995) (HUD regulations interpreting FHA and prohibiting redlining in property insurance underwriting were upheld; no McCarran-Ferguson Act preclusion of HUD regulations by Ohio insurance law); United Farm Bureau Mut. Ins. Co. v. Metro. Human Relations Comm'n, 24 F.3d 1008 (7th Cir. 1994) (reaffirms *American Family* holding); Lindsey v. Allstate Ins. Co., 34 F. Supp. 2d 636 (W.D. Tenn. 1999) (defendant's motion to dismiss FHA-based insurance redlining case denied; plaintiffs alleged discrimination on the basis of race in premiums, claims handling procedures, and policy renewal); Strange v. Nationwide Mut. Ins. Co., 867 F. Supp. 1209 (E.D. Pa. 1994) (FHA bars discrimination in provision of property and hazard insurance).

51 N.A.A.C.P. v. Am. Family Mut. Ins. Co., 978 F.2d 287 (7th Cir. 1992) (consent decree available as Clearinghouse No. 52,059); United States v. Nationwide Mut. Ins. Co., Clearinghouse Nos. 52,026A (complaint), 52,026B (consent decree) (S.D. Ohio 1997) [reproduced on the CD-Rom accompanying this volume].

52 Lindsey v. Allstate Ins. Co., 34 F. Supp. 2d 636 (W.D. Tenn. 1999).

53 N.A.A.C.P. v. Am. Family Mut. Ins. Co., 978 F.2d 287 (7th Cir. 1992); United States v. Nationwide Mut. Ins. Co., Clearinghouse Nos. 52,026A (complaint), 52,026B (consent decree) (S.D. Ohio 1997) [reproduced on the CD-Rom accompanying this volume]. *N.A.A.C.P. v. American Family Mutual Ins. Co.* was the first case the Department of Justice (DOJ) brought under the Fair Housing Act to challenge the use of race as a factor in issuing homeowner insurance. The complaint alleged that, since at least 1968, American Family Mutual denied homeowner's insurance to or provided inferior insurance for homes in the predominantly African-American areas of metropolitan Milwaukee. In addition to locating its sales offices in white communities, the DOJ's complaint alleged that American Family also closed sales offices once the racial composition of the community changed from white to black. In the consent decree settling the case, American Family agreed to pay $14.5 million to compensate the victims. The consent decree also required the

company to conduct random testing, to recruit qualified prospective customers, and to refrain from excluding homes solely on the basis of sale price of the home or age of the home. *See also* N.A.A.C.P. v. Am. Family Mut. Ins. Co., Clearinghouse No. 52,059, No. 90-C-0759 (N.D. Ill. 1995) (consent decree).

54 15 U.S.C. § 1012(b).

55 *See* Dep't of the Treasury v. Fabe, 508 U.S. 491, 113 S. Ct. 2202, 124 L. Ed. 23 449 (1993).

56 N.A.A.C.P. v. Am. Family Mut. Ins. Co., 978 F.2d 287 (7th Cir. 1992).

57 *Id.* at 297 (court noted that, if the state wanted to authorize redlining, it need only say so and then a FHA challenge to the practice would be untenable; however, in this case, federal and state policies determined not to conflict).

58 *Id.*

59 Spirit v. Teachers Ins. & Annuities Ass'n, 691 F.2d 1054 (2d Cir. 1982), *vacated on other grounds*, 463 U.S. 1223, 103 S. Ct. 3565, 77 L. Ed. 2d 1406 (1983); *accord* Stephens v. Nat'l Distillers & Chem. Corp., 69 F.3d 1226 (2d Cir. 1995).

60 N.A.A.C.P. v. Am. Family Mut. Ins. Co., 978 F.2d 287 (7th Cir. 1992) (consent decree available as Clearinghouse No. 52,059).

61 Duane v. Gov't Employees Ins. Co., 784 F. Supp. 1209 (D. Md. 1992), *aff'd*, 37 F.3d 1036 (4th Cir. 1994).

62 Hous. Opportunities Made Equal, Inc. v. Nationwide Mut. Ins. Co., No. LB-2704 (Circuit Court for the City of Richmond) (jury verdict Oct. 26, 1998). The Supreme Court of Virginia initially reversed the verdict, finding that the plaintiff lacked

Americans were specifically excluded from Nationwide Mutual Insurance Co.'s insurance market through discrimination in the underwriting, marketing, advertising, sales and actuarial practices of the company.

7.3.4.3 The Federal Civil Rights Acts

The federal Civil Rights Acts should apply to discrimination in the sale of any form of insurance, because insurance is a contract.[63] While the McCarran-Ferguson Act prevents federal statutes from invalidating state laws that regulate insurance unless the federal statute refers specifically to insurance, preemption of the federal regulation of insurance here is unlikely.[64] Similar to their analysis under the FHA, the courts have almost unanimously found that the Civil Rights Acts are applicable to insurance discrimination and do not violate the McCarran-Ferguson Act.[65]

7.3.4.4 State Laws

In addition to federal laws and regulations, the majority of states have some form of general discrimination laws or unfair insurance practices (UNIP) statute (also known as unfair trade practices acts or UTPA), under which insurance discrimination claims may be brought.

State credit discrimination laws generally provide an excellent vehicle to challenge insurance-related discrimination. For example, New York's highest court allowed a case to proceed in which the plaintiff used the state credit discrimination statute to challenge a credit insurer's exclusion of pregnancy as a covered disability.[66] The court specifically found that the practice involved gender discrimination and that credit insurance terms were terms of the credit offered.[67] The only remaining issue was whether the state insurance code, which also prohibits discrimination, displaces the state credit discrimination statute.[68] The court found that the state credit discrimination statute still applied.[69]

Another approach is to utilize the state UNIP or UTPA statute to challenge insurance discrimination.[70] With wide variations, state UNIP laws prohibit unfair discrimination in the issuance, renewal or extent of coverage, rates charged, or other terms or conditions of certain types of insurance. Selected UNIP statutes prohibit property and casualty insurers from discriminating based on the geographic location of the property to be insured[71] or on the age of the residential property.[72] At least three UNIP statutes also prohibit prop-

---

standing to file suit. Nationwide Mut. Ins. Co. v. Hous. Opportunities Made Equal, Inc., 523 S.E.2d 217 (Va. 2000). The same court later vacated that ruling. Nationwide Mut. Ins. Co. v. Hous. Opportunities Made Equal, Inc., 2000 Va. LEXIS 56 (Va. Mar. 3, 2000). The case settled in April 2000.

63 *See* 42 U.S.C. § 1981.

64 *See* Duane v. Gov't Employees Ins. Co., 784 F. Supp. 1209 (D. Md. 1992), *aff'd*, 37 F.3d 1036 (4th Cir. 1994).

65 Moore v. Liberty Nat'l Life Ins. Co., 267 F.3d 1209, 1221 (11th Cir. 2001) (§§ 1981 and 1982 do not invalidate, impair or supersede Alabama's scheme of insurance regulation); Nationwide Mut. Ins. Co. v. Cisneros, 52 F.3d 1351, 1360 (6th Cir. 1995) (the FHA does not specifically mention insurance and thus cannot be construed in such a way as to invalidate, impair, or supersede any state law enacted to regulate the business of insurance); N.A.A.C.P. v. Am. Family Mut. Ins. Co., 978 F.2d 287, 295 (7th Cir. 1992) (consent decree available as Clearinghouse No. 52,059) (the FHA is an "Act of Congress" that does not specifically relate to the business of insurance and, therefore, does not invalidate, impair, or supersede any law enacted by any state for the purpose of regulating the business of insurance); Mackey v. Nationwide Ins. Companies, 724 F.2d 419 (4th Cir. 1984) (court disagreed with conclusion of lower court that the McCarran-Ferguson Act bars the plaintiff's claims under the Fair Housing and the Civil Rights Acts); Spirt v. Teachers Ins. & Annuities Ass'n, 691 F.2d 1054 (2d Cir. 1982) (Congress, in enacting a statute primarily intended to deal with the conflict between state regulation of insurers and federal antitrust laws, had no intention of declaring that subsequently enacted civil rights legislation would be inapplicable to any and all of the activities of an insurance company that can be classified as the business of insurance); Hobson v. Lincoln Ins. Agency, Inc., 2001 U.S. Dist. LEXIS 476 (N.D. Ill. Jan. 18, 2001).

66 Binghamton GHS Employees Fed. Credit Union v. New York State Div. of Human Rights, 77 N.Y.2d 12, 564 N.E.2d 1051 (1990).

67 *Id.*

68 *See* N.Y. Exec. Law § 296-a(1) (McKinney).

69 Binghamton GHS Employees Fed. Credit Union v. New York State Div. of Human Rights, 77 N.Y.2d 12, 564 N.E.2d 1051 (1990); *cf.* N.A.A.C.P. v. Am. Family Mut. Ins. Co., 978 F.2d 287 (7th Cir. 1992) (consent decree available as Clearinghouse No. 52,059) (all parties appear to agree that state's general credit discrimination statute applies to sale of property insurance).

70 The source of most state UNIP statutes is the National Association of Insurance Commissioners' model Unfair Trade Practices Act (UTPA), which attempts to establish minimum standards of insurance practices for consumer protection. *See* Nat'l Ass'n of Ins. Commissioners, Model Laws, Regulations and Guidelines, 900-1 (NIARS Corp. 1984), *as amended*, 880-1 (Jan. 1993).

71 Alaska Stat. § 21.36.120 (Michie); Ark. Code Ann. § 23-66-206(7)(C) (Michie); Colo. Rev. Stat. § 10-3-1104(1)(f); Conn. Gen. Stat. § 38a-824 (see also Conn. Agencies Regs. § 38a-824-3(a)(1)); Ga. Code Ann. § 33-6-4(b)(8)(A)(iii); Haw. Rev. Stat. § 431:13-103(7)(C); 215 Ill. Comp. Stat. § 5/155.22; Ind. Code § 27-2-17-5(b)(2); Ky. Rev. Stat. Ann. § 304.20-340(3) (West); La. Rev. Stat. Ann. § 22:652.4 (West); Mich. Comp. Laws § 500.2027(a)(iii); Minn. Stat. § 72A.20(13)(a); Mo. Rev. Stat. § 375.936(11)(c); Mont. Code Ann. § 33-18-210(5); Neb. Rev. Stat. § 44-1525(7)(c); N.C. Gen. Stat. § 58-63-15(7)(c); N.D. Cent. Code § 26.1-39-17(3); Or. Rev. Stat. § 746.018(2); R.I. Gen. Laws § 27-29-4(7)(iii); Va. Code Ann. § 38.2-508(4) (Michie).

72 Ark. Code Ann. § 23-66-206(7)(D) (Michie); Conn. Gen. Stat. § 38a-824 (see also Conn. Agencies Regs. § 38a-824-3(a)(5)); Ga. Code Ann. § 33-6-4(b)(8)(A)(iii); Haw. Rev. Stat. § 431:13-103(7)(D); Ky. Rev. Stat. Ann. § 304.20-340(3) (Michie); La. Rev. Stat. Ann. § 22:652.4A (West); Minn. Stat. § 72A.20 (13)(b); Mo. Rev. Stat. § 375.936(11)(d); Mont. Code Ann. § 33-18-210(6); Neb. Rev. Stat. § 44-1525(7)(d); N.C. Gen. Stat. § 58-63-15(7)(d); N.D. Cent. Code § 26.1-39-17(3); R.I.

erty and casualty insurers from canceling or refusing to issue or renew coverage because of the physical or mental disability of the insured.[73]

The majority of UNIP statutes and regulations specifically prohibit discrimination in all types of insurance, based on certain of the following grounds: race, creed, color, gender, marital status, mental or physical impairments, age, occupation, religion, national origin, domestic abuse, or prenatal or genetic testing.[74] Several other state statutes generally prohibit discrimination without making reference to specific types of discriminatory grounds.[75]

The UNIP statutes vary as to the prohibited practices—for example, whether discrimination is prohibited in the issuance, amount of coverage, renewal, modification or termination, rates, or other terms and conditions—and the types of insurance covered.[76] In addition, the prohibition on discrimination may be limited both as to the type of insurance and the protected class.[77]

Gen. Laws § 27-29-4(7)(iv); Va. Code Ann. § 38.2-508(5) (Michie).

73 Ga. Code Ann. § 33-6-5(8); Haw. Rev. Stat. § 431:13-103(a)(7)(F); Mont. Code Ann. § 33-18-210(8).

74 Ark. Code Ann. § 23-66-206(7) (Michie) (marital status, mental or physical impairment, race, color, creed or gender); Ariz. Rev. Stat. § 20-448 (genetic condition, developmental delay, developmental disability, or domestic abuse); Colo. Rev. Stat. § 10-3-1104 (marital status, sex, blindness, partial blindness, disability, or sexual orientation); Conn. Gen. Stat. §§ 38a-816(12), (13) (physical disability, mental retardation, blindness or partial blindness); Del. Code Ann. tit. 18, § 2304(22) (race, color, religion, national origin, residence, lawful occupation, age, or domestic abuse); Fla. Stat. Ann. § 626.9441(x) (West) (race, color, creed, marital status, sex, national origin, residence, age, or lawful occupation); Haw. Rev. Stat. § 431:13-103(7)(E) to (H) (sex, marital status, or mental or physical impairment); 215 Ill. Comp. Stat. § 5/424(3), (4) (race, color, religion, national origin, or physical handicap); Ind. Code § 27-4-1-4(15) (blindness or partial blindness); Iowa Code § 507B.4(7)(C) (domestic abuse); Kan. Stat. Ann. § 40-2404(7) (blindness or partial blindness, physical or mental condition, or domestic abuse); Ky. Rev. Stat. Ann. § 304.12-085 (Michie) (race, color, religion, national origin or sex); La. Rev. Stat. Ann. §§ 22:652.1 (severe disability or sickle cell trait), 22:652.4(A) (race), 22:1214(7)(f), (g) (sex, marital status, race, religion, national origin, or mental or physical impairment), 22:1214(22), (23) (prenatal or genetic testing) (West); Me. Rev. Stat. Ann. tit. 24A, §§ 2159-A to 2159-C (West) (blindness or partial blindness, physical or mental handicap, or genetic testing); Md. Code Ann., Ins. § 27-501 (race, creed, color, sex, religion, national origin, residence, blindness, or physical or mental disability); Mich. Comp. Laws § 500.2027(a), (c) (race, color, creed, marital status, sex, national origin, residence, age, handicap or lawful occupation); Minn. Stat. §§ 72A.20(8), (9) (disability or domestic abuse); Mo. Rev. Stat. § 375.936(11)(e), (g), (h) (race, gender, marital status, color, creed, national origin, ancestry, or physical or mental impairment); Mont. Code Ann. §§ 33-18-206(3) (genetic condition, developmental delay, or developmental disability), 33-18-210(7), (8) (sex, marital status, race, color, creed, religion, or national origin), 33-18-216(1) (domestic abuse); Neb. Rev. Stat. § 44-1525(7) (sex, marital status, or physical or mental impairment); N.H. Rev. Stat. Ann. § 417:4(VIII) (age, residence, race, color, creed, national origin, ancestry, marital status, lawful occupation or domestic abuse); N.J. Stat. Ann. § 17B:30-12 (West) (race, creed, color, national origin or ancestry); N.M. Stat. Ann. §§ 59A-16-12, 59A-16-13 (Michie) (sex, race, color, religion, national origin, blindness or partial blindness); N.Y. Ins. Law §§ 2606–2608 (race, color, creed, national origin, disability, sex, marital status or mental disability), 2612 (domestic violence) (McKinney); N.D. Cent. Code. § 26.1-04-03 (blindness or partial blindness); Ohio Rev. Code Ann. § 3901.21(L), (Q) (West) (sex, marital status, blindness or partial blindness); Or. Rev. Stat. § 746.015(2), (3) (age, physical

handicap); 40 Pa. Cons. Stat. § 1171.5(7) (race, religion, nationality, ethnic group, age, sex, family size, occupation, residence or marital status); R.I. Gen. Laws § 27-29-4(7) (sex, marital status, or mental or physical impairment); S.D. Codified Laws §§ 58-33-12.1 (blindness or partial blindness), 58-33-13.2(1) (sex or marital status) (Michie); Tenn. Code Ann. §§ 56-8-104(6), 56-8-303 (domestic abuse); Vt. Stat. Ann. tit. 8, § 4724(7) (sex, sexual orientation, or marital status); Va. Code Ann. § 38.2-508 (Michie) (blindness, partial blindness, or physical or mental impairment); Wash. Rev. Code §§ 48.18.480, 48.30.300 (sex, marital status, or sensory, mental or physical handicap); Wis. Stat. § 628.34(3)(b) (mental or physical disability).

75 Ala. Code § 27-12-11; Alaska Stat. § 21.36.090 (Michie); Cal. Ins. Code § 790.03 (West); Ga. Code Ann. § 33-6-4(b)(8); Idaho Code § 41-1313 (Michie); Mass. Gen. Laws. ch. 176D, § 3(7); Miss. Code Ann. § 83-5-35; Nev. Rev. Stat. § 686A.130(4); N.C. Gen. Stat. § 58-63-15(7); Okla. Stat. tit. 36, § 1204(7); S.C. Code Ann. § 38-55-50 (Law. Co-op.); Tex. Ins. Code Ann. § 21.21(4)(7)(a) (Vernon); Utah Code Ann. § 31A-23-302(3)(a); W. Va. Code § 33-11-4(7); Wyo. Stat. Ann. § 26-13-112(c) (Michie).

76 *See* Ariz. Rev. Stat. § 20-448 (life and disability); Cal. Ins. Code § 790.03 (West) (life insurance or annuity); Del. Code Ann. tit. 18, § 2304; Idaho Code § 41-1313 (Michie) (life insurance, annuities, disability insurance); Minn. Stat. § 72A.20(8)(a) (life insurance or annuity); Miss. Code Ann. § 83-5-35 (life insurance and annuities, accident or health insurance); Nev. Rev. Stat. § 86A.130(4) (property, casualty, surety or title insurance); N.D. Cent. Code § 26.1-04-03(7)(c) (life, accident, or health); Okla. Stat. tit. 36, § 1204(7) (life, accident or health); Tex. Ins. Code Ann. § 21.21 (Vernon) (life insurance or annuity).

77 *See, e.g.,* Ariz. Rev. Stat. § 20-448(D), (G) (discrimination in life or disability insurance on the basis of genetic condition, developmental disability, or status as victim of domestic abuse); 215 Ill. Comp. Stat. § 5/424 (3), (4) (discrimination in casualty, fidelity and surety insurance, and in fire and marine insurance, on the basis of race, color, religion, national origin, and physical handicap (if motor vehicle insurance)); La. Rev. Stat. Ann. § 22:1214(7)(g) (West) (discrimination in property or casualty insurance on the basis of mental or physical impairment); Mont. Code Ann. § 33-18-206(3) (discrimination in life or disability insurance on the basis of genetic condition, developmental delay, or developmental disability); Neb. Rev. Stat. § 44-1525(7)(f) (discrimination in property or casualty insurance on the basis of mental or physical impairment); N.H. Rev. Stat. Ann. § 417:4(VIII)(e) (discrimination on the basis of age, race, color, creed, national origin, ancestry, marital status, lawful occupation except for life, accident or health insurance); N.J. Stat. Ann. § 17B:30 (West) (discrimination in life or health insurance annuity on the basis of race, creed, color, national origin or ancestry); N.D. Cent. Code § 26.1-04-03(7)(c) (discrimination in life, accident and health insurance on the basis of blindness or partial blindness); Ohio Rev. Code Ann.

UNIP statutes, however, do not generally provide an explicit private right of action. Courts are split on whether such a right should be implied, with a majority refusing to imply a private UNIP right of action.[78] Even if a private

action is available, the remedy may be limited to actual damages, and attorney fees may not be available.[79] Moreover, the court decisions finding an implied right of action generally involve unfair claims settlement practices rather than insurance discrimination.[80]

---

§§ 3901.21(L), (Q) (West) (discrimination in life, accident and health insurance on the basis of blindness or partial blindness); S.D. Codified Laws § 58-33-12.1 (Michie) (discrimination in life insurance on the basis of blindness or partial blindness).

78 *States in which there is no private cause of action under the UNIP statute are*:
ALABAMA: Farlow v. Union Cent. Life Ins. Co. 874 F.2d 791 (11th Cir. 1989); Allen v. State Farm Fire & Cas. Co., 59 F. Supp. 2d 1217 (S.D. Ala. 1999).
ALASKA: O.K. Lumber Co. v. Providence Wash. Ins. Co., 759 P. 2d 523 (Alaska 1988).
CALIFORNIA: Moradi-Shalal v. Fireman's Fund Ins. Co., 250 Cal. Rptr. 116, 46 Cal. 3d 287, 758 P.2d 58 (1988). However, California has found a private cause of action for violations of the UNIP provision dealing with twisting. Ky. Cent. Life Ins. Co. v. LeDuc, 814 F. Supp. 832 (N.D. Cal. 1992).
COLORADO: Schnacker v. State Farm Mut. Auto. Ins. Co., 843 P.2d 102 (Colo. Ct. App. 1992).
DELAWARE: Brown v. Liberty Mut. Ins., Co., 1999 Del. Super. LEXIS 525 (Del. Super. Ct. Aug. 20, 1999).
FLORIDA: Keehn v. Carolina Casualty Ins. Co., 758 F.2d 1522 (11th Cir. 1985) (Fla. law).
HAWAII: Genovia v. Jackson Nat'l Life Ins. Co., 795 F. Supp. 1036 (D. Haw. 1992).
IDAHO: State v. Bunker Hill Co., 647 F. Supp. 1064 (D. Idaho 1986); Greene v. Truck Ins. Exch., 753 P.2d 274 (Idaho Ct. App. 1988).
ILLINOIS: Scroggins v. Allstate Ins. Co., 74 Ill. App. 3d 1027, 393 N.E.2d 718 (1979).
IOWA: Bates v. Allied Mut. Ins. Co., 467 N.W.2d 255 (Iowa 1991).
KANSAS: Earth Scientists Ltd. v. U.S. Fid. & Guar. Co., 619 F. Supp. 1465 (D. Kan. 1985).
LOUISIANA: *Compare* Clausen v. Fid. & Deposit Co., 660 So. 2d 83 (La. Ct. App. 1995) *with* La. Rev. Stat. Ann. § 22:652.4(D) (private action for discrimination based upon race).
MARYLAND: Magan v. Med. Mut. Liab. Ins. Soc'y, 81 Md. App. 301, 567 A.2d 503 (1989).
MASSACHUSETTS: Thorpe v. Mut. of Omaha Ins. Co., 984 F.2d 541 (1st Cir. 1993).
MICHIGAN: Bd. of Trustees of Mich. State Univ. v. Cont'l Cas. Co., 730 F. Supp. 1408 (W.D. Mich. 1990).
MINNESOTA: Morris v. Am. Family Mut. Ins. Co., 386 N.W.2d 233 (Minn. 1986).
MISSISSIPPI: Davenport v. St. Paul Fire & Marine Ins. Co., 978 F.2d 927 (5th Cir. 1992).
MISSOURI: Wenthe v. Willis Corroon Corp., 932 S.W.2d 791 (Mo. Ct. App. 1996).
NEW HAMPSHIRE: Shaleen v. Preferred Mut. Ins. Co., 668 F. Supp. 716 (D.N.H. 1987).
NEW JERSEY: Pierzga v. Ohio Cas. Group of Ins. Cos., 208 N.J. Super. 40, 504 A.2d 1200 (Super. Ct. App. Div. 1986).
NEW MEXICO: Patterson v. Globe Am. Casualty Co., 101 N.M. 541, 685 P.2d 396 (Ct. App. 1984).
NEW YORK: N.Y. Univ. v. Cont'l Ins. Co., 87 N.Y.2d 308, 662 N.E.2d 763 (1995).
NORTH CAROLINA: First Fin. Sav. Bank v. Am. Bankers Ins. Co., 783 F. Supp. 963 (E.D.N.C. 1991).
OHIO: Strack v. Westfield Cos., 33 Ohio App. 3d 336, 515

N.E.2d 1005 (1986).
OKLAHOMA: Lewis v. Aetna U.S. Healthcare, Inc., 78 F. Supp. 2d 1202 (N.D. Okla. 1999).
PENNSYLVANIA: Smith v. Nationwide Mut. Ins. Co., 935 F. Supp. 616 (W.D. Pa. 1996).
RHODE ISLAND: Cowdell v. Cambridge Mut. Ins. Co., 808 F.2d 160 (1st Cir. 1986).
TENNESSEE: Lindsey v. Allstate Ins. Co., 34 F. Supp. 2d 636 (W.D. Tenn. 1999).
VERMONT: Wilder v. Aetna Life & Cas. Ins. Co., 140 Vt. 16, 433 A.2d 309 (1981).
VIRGINIA: A & E Supply Co. v. Nationwide Mut. Fire Ins. Co., 798 F.2d 669 (4th Cir. 1986).
WISCONSIN: Kranzush v. Badger State Mut. Cas. Co., 103 Wis. 2d 56, 307 N.W.2d 256 (Wis. 1981).
WYOMING: Wilson v. State Farm Mut. Auto Ins. Co., 795 F. Supp. 1077 (D. Wyo. 1992).
   States that imply a private cause of action under the UNIP statute are:
ARIZONA: Sparks v. Republic Nat'l Life Ins. Co., 132 Ariz. 529, 647 P.2d 1127 (Ariz. 1982) (misrepresentation and false advertising of policies).
KENTUCKY: State Farm Mut. Auto Ins. Co. v. Reeder, 763 S.W.2d 116 (Ky. 1988).
MONTANA: Fode v. Farmers Ins. Exch., 719 P.2d 414 (Mont. 1986); Klaudt v. Fink, 658 P.2d 1065 (Mont. 1983). *But see* Shupak v. N.Y. Life Ins. Co., 780 F. Supp. 1328 (D. Mont. 1991).
NEVADA: Albert H. Wohlers & Co. v. Bartgis, 969 P.2d 949 (Nev. 1998).
WEST VIRGINIA: Maher v. Cont'l Cas. Co. 76 F.3d 535 (4th Cir. 1996) (unfair claims settlement practices).
   States that have mixed case law include:
CONNECTICUT: Baroni v. W. Reserve Life Assurance Co., 1999 Conn. Super. LEXIS 2641 (Conn. Super. Ct. Sept. 29, 1999) (concluding that Connecticut superior courts are currently split regarding the availability of a private right of action). *But see* Peck v. Pub. Serv. Mut. Ins. Co., 114 F. Supp. 2d 51 (D. Conn. 2000) (interpreting Connecticut's direct action statute to allow third party to assert UDAP and UNIP claims against tortfeasor's insurance company after winning judgment against tortfeasor).
INDIANA: Dietrick v. Liberty Mut. Ins. Co., 759 F. Supp. 467 (N.D. Ind. 1991) (no private right of action); Dryden v. SunLife Assurance Co. of Canada, 737 F. Supp. 1058 (S.D. Ind. 1989) (private right of action).
NORTH DAKOTA: Farmer's Union Cent. Exch., Inc. v. Reliance Ins. Co., 675 F. Supp. 1534 (D.N.D. 1987) (no private right of action).
79 *See* National Consumer Law Center, Unfair and Deceptive Acts and Practices § 5.3.2.3.2 (5th ed. 2001); *see also* N.A.A.C.P. v. Am. Family Mut. Ins. Co., 978 F.2d 287 (7th Cir. 1992) (consent decree available as Clearinghouse No. 52,059) (no implied private right of action particularly when the standard is so broad as unfair discrimination, thus requiring administrative guidance).
80 *See, e.g.*, Maher v. Cont'l Cas. Co., 76 F.3d 535 (4th Cir. 1996) (W. Va. law); State Farm Fire & Cas. Co. v. Nicholson, 777 P.2d 1152 (Alaska 1989) (insured may have tort claim for bad faith

Therefore, a better approach is to challenge the violation of the UNIP statute as a violation of the state general unfair and deceptive acts and practices (UDAP) statute, which usually provides for attorney fees and other significant remedies.[81]

---

handling of claim); Heyman Associates No. 1 v. Ins. Co., 231 Conn. 756, 653 A.2d 122 (1995); Klaudt v. Fink, 658 P.2d 1065 (Mont. 1983); Pickett v. Lloyd's, 131 N.J. 457, 621 A.2d 445 (1993) (recognizing common law cause of action for bad faith refusal to settle first party claims).

81　*See* National Consumer Law Center, Unfair and Deceptive Acts and Practices § 5.3.2.2.1 (5th ed. 2001).

Chapter 8

Reverse Redlining to Price Gouging: Discrimination in Credit Terms and Pricing

8.1 Introduction

Redlining is the practice of *denying* credit to particular communities on a discriminatory basis.[1] The flip side is reverse redlining, the practice of targeting these same communities for the most expensive types of credit. The creditor may or may not offer better terms to others, but the key element of reverse redlining is the singling out of protected racial groups, elders, and others for unusually bad credit terms. In addition, reverse redlining includes the practice of some creditors of making loans at one rate in white communities through a creditor's banking arm, while making loans at higher rates in communities of color or to elders through separate finance company subsidiaries.

There are many legal tools available to challenge predatory lending practices. This chapter focuses only on credit discrimination remedies. Other National Consumer Law Center publications cover additional claims, including those made under the Truth in Lending Act, Racketeering Influenced and Corrupt Organizations Act (RICO), and UDAP statutes.[2]

In addition to discriminatory predatory lending practices, this chapter covers other types of discrimination in credit terms and pricing, including tier-based pricing (or overages) and discrimination in the pricing of related goods and services.

8.2 Subprime and Predatory Lending

8.2.1 General

Lenders divide prospective borrowers into different categories, based allegedly on risk of default. In general, lending is divided into prime and subprime loans. Subprime lenders loan at higher cost to those borrowers with past credit problems or low incomes. Subprime loans are divided into grades: A, B, C, or D. The minimum costs of the loan go up with each credit downgrade.[3]

The subprime market is also known as the "alternative financial services" or "fringe banking" sector. It has become a major source of traditional banking services for low-income and working poor consumers, residents of minority neighborhoods, and people with blemished credit histories.

The growth in subprime lending followed the overall growth in home equity lending during the mid-to-late 1980s. Its growth was also connected to earlier redlining practices which left many communities of color and other low-income communities without access to mainstream financial institutions in their neighborhoods.[4]

In 1983, subprime lending constituted only 1.4% of all loans. By 1998, these loans constituted 10.2% of all loans.[5] The earnings of small-volume subprime mortgage lenders are matching or surpassing the earnings of conventional mortgage lenders who have significantly greater loan volume.[6]

A part of the subprime market includes the predatory lenders. Although definitions of predatory loans vary, generally the term refers to high-rate loans that are aggressively marketed by lenders using fraudulent, high-pressure, or misleading sales tactics.[7]

---

1 *See* Ch. 7, *supra*.

2 *See* National Consumer Law Center, Truth in Lending (4th ed. 1999 and Supp.); National Consumer Law Center, The Cost of Credit: Regulation and Legal Challenges (2d ed. 2000 and Supp.); National Consumer Law Center, Unfair and Deceptive Acts and Practices (5th ed. 2001); National Consumer Law Center, STOP Predatory Lending (2002).

3 For an excellent history of subprime lending, see Cathy Lesser Mansfield, *The Road to Subprime "HEL" Was Paved With Good Congressional Intentions: Usury Deregulation and the Subprime Home Equity Market*, 51 S.C. L. Rev. 473 (2000).

4 *See* Ch. 7, *supra*; Ira Rheingold, Michael Fitzpatrick & Al Hofeld, Jr., *Redlining to Reverse Redlining: A History of Obstacles for Minority Homeownership in America*, 34 Clearinghouse Rev. 642 (2001).

5 Cathy Lesser Mansfield, *The Road to Subprime "HEL" Was Paved With Good Congressional Intentions: Usury Deregulation and the Subprime Home Equity Market*, 51 S.C. L. Rev. 473, 527 (2000).

6 Glenn B. Canner, Thomas A. Durkin & Charles A. Luckett, *Recent Developments in Home Equity Lending*, 84 Fed. Res. Bull. 241, 250 (1998).

7 At least one court disagreed with defendant lenders' argument that predatory lending is too amorphous a concept to support a legal claim. *See* Hargraves v. Capital City Mortgage Corp., 140 F. Supp. 2d 7 (D.D.C. 2000). The court found predatory lending

The court in *Hargraves v. Capital City Mortgage Corp.* identified some of the characteristics of predatory loans, including exorbitant interest rates, lending based on the value of the asset securing the loan rather than on a borrower's ability to repay (equity stripping or, in other words, issuing a loan designed to fail and profiting by acquiring the property through default rather than by receiving loan payments), repeated foreclosures, and loan servicing procedures in which excessive fees are charged.[8] Most of these loans are "packed" with unnecessary and often illegal fees.[9]

8.2.2 Discriminatory Impact of Subprime and Predatory Lending

Recent studies have shown that subprime lenders comprise the greater share of lending in nonwhite neighborhoods.[10] This pattern appears to hold true even in middle class and higher- income areas, indicating that the segmentation of the market into prime and subprime is considerably stronger by race than by income.[11]

For example, a 1999 Woodstock Institute study examined Home Mortgage Disclosure Act (HMDA) data for 1993 to 1998 in a six county Chicago metropolitan area. It found that

58% of conventional refinance loans in predominantly African-American neighborhoods were made by subprime lenders, compared to less than 10% in predominantly white neighborhoods. The difference in the proportion of refinance loans made by subprime lenders remained high in African-American middle-income neighborhoods.[12] The Department of Housing and Urban Development has found that in predominantly African-American neighborhoods subprime lending accounted for 51% of home loans in 1998, compared with only 9% in predominantly white areas.[13]

8.2.3 The Rationale for Subprime Lending: Are the Higher Prices Charged Connected to Higher Risk?

This manual does not address challenges to risk-based pricing in general. However, it is important to note that the accuracy of the assumption that lending to people with poor credit histories justifies higher prices is by no means clearly established.

First, many borrowers who end up with subprime loans have credit histories that should qualify them for lower-cost conventional financing.[14] Thus, they are misplaced into the subprime market and are not higher lending risks.

Second, claims of increased losses due to poor credit histories are overstated given the lenders' underwriting guidelines and how loans are structured. The typical structure of subprime loans creates minimal risk of loss due to either a default or a foreclosure. When credit is secured by a home, and the loan-to-value ratio is more than sufficient to protect against foreclosure losses (70% or less), there is no basis for significantly increased rates and fees. In reality, the higher pricing itself arguably creates more risk, and the excessive fees charged up front cause the most damage to the homeowner by stripping equity from the home.[15]

In general, it would seem that if higher prices were compensating for higher transaction costs and higher risk, subprime lenders' profits would be comparable to the profits earned by creditors lending to "lower risk" populations. In fact profits for subprime lenders are often higher, indicating

definable because Congress has studied the issue and found certain characteristics, such as exorbitant interest rates and excessive fees, to be typical of most predatory loans. In coming to this conclusion, the court relied on the enactment of the Home Ownership and Equity Protection Act, 15 U.S.C. § 1639, and noted plaintiffs' specific allegations of unfair lending practices, including exorbitant interest rates, equity stripping, repeated foreclosures, and excessive loan servicing charges. 140 F. Supp. 2d at 20–21.

8 Hargraves v. Capital City Mortgage Corp., 140 F. Supp. 2d 7, 20–21 (D.D.C. 2000).

9 The Home Ownership and Equity Protection Act defines high rate mortgages as those bearing annual percentage rates more than ten percentage points above the yield on Treasury securities or those including total fees and points exceeding 8% of the loan or $400, whichever is greater. *See* National Consumer Law Center, Truth in Lending Ch. 10 (4th ed. 1999 and Supp.).

10 *See, e.g.,* Daniel Immergluck & Marti Wiles, Two Steps Back: The Dual Mortgage Market, Predatory Lending, and the Undoing of Community Development (Woodstock Inst. 1999), *available at* http://www.woodstockinst.org; Ass'n of Community Organizations for Reform Now (ACORN), The Great Divide: An Analysis of Racial and Economic Disparities in Home Purchase Mortgage Lending Nationally and in Sixty Metropolitan Areas (2001); Dep't of Hous. & Urban Dev. (HUD), Unequal Burden: Income and Racial Disparities in Subprime Lending in America (2000), *available at* http://www.hud.gov. *See generally* Frank Lopez, *Using the Fair Housing Act to Combat Predatory Lending,* 6 Geo. J. on Poverty L. & Pol'y 73 (1999).

11 *See* Daniel Immergluck & Marti Wiles, Two Steps Back: The Dual Mortgage Market, Predatory Lending, and the Undoing of Community Development (Woodstock Inst. 1999), *available at* http://www.woodstockinst.org; Dep't of Hous. & Urban Dev. (HUD), Unequal Burden: Income and Racial Disparities in Subprime Lending in America (2000), *available at* http://www.hud.gov.

12 *See* Daniel Immergluck & Marti Wiles, Two Steps Back: The Dual Mortgage Market, Predatory Lending, and the Undoing of Community Development (Woodstock Inst. 1999), *available at* http://www.woodstockinst.org.

13 Dep't of Hous. & Urban Dev., Unequal Burden: Income and Racial Disparities in Subprime Lending in America (2000), *available at* http://www.hud.gov.

14 *See generally* Cathy Lesser Mansfield, *The Road to Subprime "HEL" Was Paved With Good Congressional Intentions: Usury Deregulation and the Subprime Home Equity Market,* 51 S.C. L. Rev. 473, 560 (2000) (summarizing studies that show that credit history does not appear to be the determining factor in whether borrowers are offered conventional or subprime loans).

15 *See* National Consumer Law Center, STOP Predatory Lending § 2.3.3 (2002) (in-depth analysis of various creditor arguments regarding risk).

that the standard justifications for allowing high-priced fringe market loans are not as solid as they seem.[16]

8.3 Challenging Reverse Redlining Using Credit Discrimination Statutes

It may appear contradictory to find that a creditor discriminates by offering racial minorities and other protected groups credit. However, a creditor which targets protected groups for the most expensive products is discriminating within the language of the various credit discrimination statutes by treating potential applicants less favorably. Nothing in the ECOA, the Fair Housing Act (FHA), or the Civil Rights Acts require that a challenged practice involve the denial of credit. Not only the originating lender but arrangers and participating assignees may be liable for the discrimination.[17]

Creditors often defend their practices by claiming that they cannot be discriminating if they make more loans to minority and other protected communities than they make to others. For example, a lender in one case argued that it could not be found to have made housing unavailable because of race when in fact it had made loans to African-Americans. The lender also claimed that its practices did not violate the ECOA or the FHA because it made loans to African-Americans on the same terms it made loans to whites and it did not target African-Americans in its marketing practices.[18]

In an amicus brief filed in that case, the Department of Justice argued that the fact that a lender does business only in minority neighborhoods should not shield it from the mandates of the ECOA or the FHA, further pointing out that redlining and reverse redlining work hand-in-hand to create racial ghettos.[19] The court agreed, stating that it was not necessary for plaintiffs to show that the defendants make loans on more favorable terms to anyone other than the targeted class.[20] The court also rejected the defendants' argument that permitting a cause of action based on predatory lending would discourage lenders from making loans to minorities.[21]

Legal theories challenging reverse redlining under the FHA, the ECOA and the federal civil rights statutes have begun to gain credibility in the courts.[22] Government enforcement actions have also alleged that reverse redlining practices violate both the FHA and the ECOA.[23]

The FHA should apply whenever predatory lending is discriminatory and involves lending secured by a borrower's home or used to finance a home. There is some question whether reverse redlining claims can be brought under both sections 3604 and 3605 of the FHA, or whether only claims under section 3605 will be allowed. Section 3605, covering residential real estate-related transactions, is generally the key statute with respect to housing lending and financing. However, plaintiffs are increasingly attempting to bring section 3604 claims as well. Section 3604 applies to the sale, rental or advertising of dwellings.[24]

Although most courts agree that these two sections of the FHA are not mutually exclusive,[25] they have been less clear as to whether section 3604 can be used to challenge predatory lending practices.[26]

16 *See* Lynn Drysdale & Kathleen E. Keest, *The Two-Tiered Consumer Financial Services Marketplace: The Fringe Banking System and its Challenge to Current Thinking About the Role of Usury Laws in Today's Society*, 51 S.C. L. Rev. 589 (2000) (noting the need for additional study of this issue); *see also* Cathy Lesser Mansfield, *The Road to Subprime "HEL" Was Paved with Good Congressional Intentions: Usury Deregulation and the Subprime Home Equity Market*, 51 S. Car. L. Rev. 473 (2000) (discussion of the justifications for the subprime mortgage market).

17 *See* §§ 2.2.5, 2.3.2.3, 2.3.3.2, *supra*.

18 *See* Hargraves v. Capital City Mortgage Corp., 140 F. Supp. 2d 7 (D.D.C. 2000).

19 *See* Brief of the United States as Amicus Curiae in Support of Plaintiffs' Opposition to Defendants' Motion for Judgment on the Pleadings, or, In the Alternative, For Summary Judgment at 15, Hargraves v. Capital City Mortgage Corp., 140 F. Supp. 2d 7 (D.D.C. 2000) (Civ. Action No. 98-1021) [reproduced on the CD-Rom accompanying this volume].

20 Hargraves v. Capital City Mortgage Corp., 140 F. Supp. 2d 7, 20 (D.D.C. 2000).

21 *Id.* at 20–21.

22 *See, e.g.*, Matthews v. New Century Mortgage Corp., 185 F. Supp. 2d 874 (S.D. Ohio 2002); Hargraves v. Capital City Mortgage, 140 F. Supp. 2d 7 (D.D.C. 2000); Honorable v. The Easy Life Real Estate Sys., 100 F. Supp. 2d 885 (N.D. Ill. 2000) (reverse redlining claim survived summary judgment but court relied on fact that the defendant failed to contest this issue); Associates Home Equity Services, Inc. v. Troup, 778 A.2d 529, 537 (N.J. Super. Ct. App. Div. 2001) (citing *Hargraves* for the proposition that a plaintiff may establish a colorable claim of reverse redlining by demonstrating that defendants' lending practices and loan terms were "unfair" and "predatory" and that the defendants either intentionally targeted on the basis of race or that there is a disparate impact on the basis of race).

23 *See, e.g.*, United States v. Delta Funding Corp., Civ. No. CV 00 1872 (E.D.N.Y. Mar. 30, 2000) [reproduced on the CD-Rom accompanying this volume]; Fed. Trade Comm'n v. Capital City Mortgage Corp., Clearinghouse No. 53,523, Civ. No. 98-237 (D.D.C. Jan. 29, 1998), *available at* http://www.ftc.gov; U.S. v. Long Beach Mortgage Co., Clearinghouse No. 51,944, No. CV 96-6159 (C.D. Cal. Sept. 5, 1996) (settlement agreement and order) [reproduced on the CD-Rom accompanying this volume]; *see also* § 12.4.3.8, *infra*.

24 *See* § 2.3.3, *supra*.

25 *See* Nationwide Mut. Ins. Co. v. Cisneros, 52 F.3d 1351 (6th Cir. 1995) (§§ 3604 and 3605 overlap and are not mutually exclusive); Eva v. Midwest Nat'l Mortgage Banc, Inc., 143 F. Supp. 2d 862 (N.D. Ohio 2001) (although finding that § 3604 did not apply to refinancing loans, court agreed that §§ 3604 and 3605 are not mutually exclusive).

26 The U.S. Department of Justice filed a brief in *Hargraves v. Capital City Mortgage* arguing that § 3604 should apply to predatory lending generally and specifically to predatory home equity lending. *See* Brief of the United States as Amicus Curiae

The ECOA may be used even more broadly to challenge predatory lending because it is not confined to housing financing and applies to every aspect of a credit transaction.[27] The court in *Hargraves v. Capital City Mortgage Corp.* noted that the plain language of the ECOA prohibits discrimination in any aspect of a credit transaction and is therefore not limited to the denial of credit.[28] The court also found support for ECOA's application to reverse redlining in its implementing regulations, which define credit transaction to include investigation procedures, terms of credit, collections procedures, and other matters.[29]

8.4 Discriminatory Credit Markup Policies

Some lenders offer "tiered-pricing," whereby they rank the credit risk of their applicants and vary the price of the credit granted depending, in theory, upon that ranking. This system of overages produces high profits for the lender and corresponding high costs to the borrower that may give rise to unconscionability or UDAP claims. In addition, failing to disclose the fact that the loan could be obtained more cheaply may itself be actionable.[30] When applicable, as in the case of yield-spread premiums, a broker should have a fiduciary duty to disclose that lower rates are available to the applicant.[31]

Most critically, this kind of price gouging is targeted at vulnerable consumers who are often members of protected groups. Only those who do not know what the typical rate range is, or that they could get typical rates, or do not know that the rate is negotiable, will be charged the higher price. If the result is that the creditor, acting through the broker, writes higher-priced loans for the elderly, women, or minorities, then fair lending laws are violated, either because of the disparate impact on protected classes or because it results in disparate treatment.[32] Regulators have noted the potential for discriminatory pricing inherent in this practice and have warned creditors about it.[33]

A number of cases have challenged the discriminatory aspects of overage policies in the auto lending industry. For example, two cases filed against major auto financing creditors in 2000 in federal court in Tennessee focus on the ways in which subjective markups disproportionately impact African-American consumers.[34]

Both of the lenders sued in these cases admitted to using a pricing scheme in which they set a minimum buy rate for loans to consumers falling in different credit risk categories. The dealer is then allowed to mark up the rate. The amount of the markup is not tied to risk; rather, it depends upon the dealer's ability to sell the higher rate to an unsuspecting consumer. The lenders then determine how to split the markup between themselves and the dealer, collect the markup, and pay a share to the dealer. The dealer never discloses to the consumer the particular minimum "buy rate" that the dealer's credit partner has set for the purchase

---

in Support of Plaintiffs' Opposition to Defendants' Motion for Judgment on the Pleadings, or, In the Alternative, For Summary Judgment, Hargraves v. Capital City Mortgage Corp., 140 F. Supp. 2d 7 (D.D.C. 2000) (Civ. Action No. 98-1021) [reproduced on the CD-Rom accompanying this volume]. Only one of the loans at issue in this case was a home equity loan. The court noted that it was a close issue whether § 3604, as well as § 3605, applies to home equity loans but dismissed the claim with respect to the home equity loan because plaintiffs failed to pursue the argument. The § 3604 claims against the other defendants survived the motion for summary judgment. Hargraves v. Capital City Mortgage Corp., 140 F. Supp. 2d 7 (D.D.C. 2000). *But see* Matthews v. New Century Mortgage Corp., 185 F. Supp. 2d 874 (S.D. Ohio 2002) (§ 3604 did not apply to financial transactions related to acquiring a home, but § 3605 reverse redlining claim survived motion to dismiss); Eva v. Midwest Nat'l Mortgage Banc, Inc., 143 F. Supp. 2d 862 (N.D. Ohio 2001) (in gender discrimination case involving refinancing loans, court granted creditors' motion to dismiss § 3604 claims, but denied motion to dismiss § 3605 claims).

27 Hargraves v. Capital City Mortgage Corp., 140 F. Supp. 2d 7, 22–23 (D.D.C. 2000) (some individual ECOA and § 1981 claims dismissed for lack of standing). Note that a person aggrieved by an ECOA violation and by a violation of section 3605 of the Fair Housing Act in the same transaction cannot recover under both statutes. 15 U.S.C. § 1691e(i); *see* § 11.5.2, *infra*.

28 140 F. Supp. 2d at 22–23 (citing 15 U.S.C. § 1691(a)).

29 140 F. Supp. 2d at 22–23 (citing Reg. B, 12 C.F.R. § 202.2(m)); *see also* Matthews v. New Century Mortgage Corp., 185 F. Supp. 2d 874 (S.D. Ohio 2002).

30 *See* National Consumer Law Center, Unfair and Deceptive Acts and Practices § 5.1.11.3 (5th ed. 2001).

31 *See, e.g.*, Besta v. Beneficial Loan Co., 855 F.2d 532 (8th Cir. 1988); *In re* Milbourne, 108 B.R. 522 (Bankr. E.D. Pa. 1989); National Consumer Law Center, The Cost of Credit: Regulation and Legal Challenges Ch. 11 (2d ed. 2000 and Supp.); *see also* Dwight Golann, *Beyond Truth in Lending: The Duty of Affirmative Disclosure*, 46 Bus. Law. 1307 (1991).

32 *See* § 4.2, *supra* (disparate treatment), § 4.3, *supra* (disparate impact).

33 Letter from E. Philip A. Simpson, Jr., Vice President, Fed. Reserve Bank of Boston, to the Chief Executive Officer of Each State Member Bank and Holding Company in the First Federal Reserve District (May 26, 1994), Clearinghouse No. 49,964; Letter from Deval L. Patrick, Assistant Att'y Gen., Civil Rights Div., Dep't of Justice, to Lender Association Representatives Concerning Department of Justice Fair Lending Enforcement Program (Feb. 21, 1995), Clearinghouse No. 52,064 (overages in and of themselves are not unlawful unless a correlation between higher rates and race comes about as a result of unlawful discrimination). Assistant Attorney General Patrick's letter is discussed at § 12.2.4, *infra*.

34 Coleman v. Gen. Motors Acceptance Corp., Clearinghouse No. 53,036B, Civ. No. 3-98-0211 (M.D. Tenn. Aug. 9, 2000) (fourth amended complaint); Cason v. Nissan Motor Acceptance Corp., Clearinghouse No. 53,037A, Civ. No. 3-98-0223 (M.D. Tenn. June 9, 2000) (fourth amended complaint). The sixth amended complaint in *Cason* is reproduced on the CD-Rom accompanying this volume. Note that NCLC is co-counsel in both cases.

of the loan. Furthermore, the consumer is not informed that the dealer has discretion to increase the buy rate, which may result in the consumer paying a higher rate than someone else in the same risk category.

The Tennessee litigation does not challenge the markup practice itself but, rather, its discriminatory impact. In both cases, the private plaintiffs alleged that African-Americans were over two-hundred percent more likely to be charged a marked-up interest rate than similarly situated whites. Furthermore, the complaints alleged that the markups charged African-Americans were larger than the markups charged similarly situated white borrowers.[35]

Plaintiff's experts found that 71.8% of African-American borrowers were charged a markup, compared to only 46.7% of white borrowers. On average, African-American borrowers paid more than twice the amount of discretionary markup charged to whites.[36] Judges in both cases granted conditional class certification and denied virtually all of defendants' motions for summary judgment.[37]

Government enforcement actions have also challenged discriminatory overages. For example, in 1996, the Department of Justice (DOJ) settled a suit alleging a discriminatory impact of California-based mortgage lender Long Beach Mortgage Co.'s markup policies.[38] The complaint did not explicitly challenge risk-based pricing itself even though Long Beach's arrangement with its own originators and "wholesale" brokers allowed them to add up to twelve points to a loan. Instead, the complaint focused on who was paying the greatest surcharge.

According to the complaint, those who paid the most were members of protected classes under the FHA and the ECOA. Those who were members of more than one protected class were at a higher risk of the greatest pricing abuse. On the broker-originated or wholesale loans, for example, the complaint alleged that older African-American women were nearly four times as likely to pay more than six percent of the loan in fees and points as compared to white men.[39] Long Beach denied any wrongdoing and disputed the validity of these statistics.

In another case, the DOJ filed suit against Delta Funding Corp., a subprime mortgage lender, claiming that it violated the ECOA and the FHA as well as the Home Ownership Equity Protection Act (HOEPA) and the Real Estate Settlement Procedures Act (RESPA).[40] The suit alleged that Delta engaged in the business of making subprime refinance home mortgage loans and that it concentrated its business primarily in African-American and Hispanic residential areas. The DOJ alleged that Delta approved and funded loans that included higher broker fees for African-American women than for similarly situated white borrowers. The complaint also brought other claims based on illegal kickbacks to brokers and approval of loans without regard to borrowers' ability to repay.

8.5 Discrimination In Pricing of Related Goods, Services

8.5.1 Introduction

Although this manual focuses on credit discrimination, discrimination in the price of goods and services is a closely related practice that may be challenged under the ECOA, the Fair Housing Act, and the federal Civil Rights Acts.

It has been argued that minority and low-income consumers pay higher prices for inferior products and have little or no access to refunds, exchanges, or warranties when problems arise.[41] It is no surprise that many of these consumers have lower expectations about credit terms, counter service, and treatment by service providers. According to one commentator, "[f]airness for many is often counterposed not only with the possibility of getting a bad deal, but with being the victim of discrimination."[42]

8.5.2 Types of Price Discrimination

There are different types of price discrimination, including discrimination in the pricing of credit. Another example of illegal price discrimination is when identical goods are sold at different stores owned by the same merchant at different prices, and the clientele of those stores are differentiated on a prohibited basis.

---

35   Coleman v. Gen. Motors Acceptance Corp., Clearinghouse No. 53,036B, Civ. No. 3-98-0211 (M.D. Tenn. Aug. 9, 2000) (fourth amended complaint); Cason v. Nissan Motor Acceptance Corp., Clearinghouse No. 53,037A, Civ. No. 3-98-0223 (M.D. Tenn. June 9, 2000) (fourth amended complaint).

36   Report of Professor Mark Cohen, Assoc. Professor of Mgmt., Owen Graduate Sch. of Mgmt., Vanderbilt Univ. & Chair, Comm. on L. & Justice, Am. Statistical Ass'n, Cason v. Nissan Motor Acceptance Corp., Civ. No. 3-98-0223 (M.D. Tenn. May 17, 2001) [reproduced on the CD-Rom accompanying this volume].

37   Coleman v. Gen. Motors Acceptance Corp., 196 F.R.D. 315 (M.D. Tenn. 2000). The court in the *Cason* case issued an oral decision on August 24, 2000. A key issue in both cases was whether the creditors could be held liable under the ECOA. The *Coleman* court allowed plaintiffs to proceed on the theory that creditor could be liable. *Coleman*, 196 F.R.D. at 324–325; *see also* Jones v. Ford Motor Credit Co., 2002 U.S. Dist. LEXIS 1098 (S.D.N.Y. Jan. 18, 2002).

38   United States v. Long Beach Mortgage Co., Clearinghouse No. 51,944, No. CV 96-6159 (C.D. Cal. Sept. 5, 1996) (settlement agreement and order).

39   *Id.*

40   United States v. Delta Funding Corp., No. CV 00 1872 (E.D.N.Y. Mar. 30, 2000), *available at* http://www.usdoj.gov [reproduced on the CD-Rom accompanying this volume]; *see* § 12.4.3.9, *infra.*

41   *See generally* David Dante Trott, *Ghettoes Revisited: Antimarkets, Consumption, and Empowerment*, 66 Brook. L. Rev. 1 (2000).

42   *Id.*

Another form of price discrimination occurs when a merchant sets a uniform price but discounts that price only to certain customers. Perhaps even more common is for the price of a good or service to be open to negotiation, and the merchant negotiates different prices for each customer. Such a practice would be illegal discrimination if the basis of the differing prices was a prohibited basis. A dramatic example of this practice was found in a study of ninety car dealers in Chicago.[43]

The study used paired testers—white men, white women, African-American men, and African-American women—whose given identities fit a middle-class profile. They also used a uniform bargaining strategy, to control for negotiating skills.

Using as a benchmark the amount of markup over dealer cost charged to white men, white women paid forty percent higher markups, African-American males paid twice the markup, and African-American females paid three times the markup. Those figures represent the "final" offer. The study also found a dramatic discrepancy in the initial offers made to the different test shoppers.

A later study, with a larger data set, confirmed the finding that dealers systematically offer lower prices to white males than to other tester types. However, while the more comprehensive data also showed that dealers offered all African-American testers significantly higher prices than those offered to white males, unlike the original study, the comprehensive data showed that African-American males were charged higher prices than African-American females.[44]

Price discrimination may involve more than just different selling prices of the goods or services. It may involve differing valuation of trade-ins and differing charges for various options and fees. For example, in a case brought as a class action for price discrimination based on race, the defendant automobile dealership chain was alleged, on average, to have made double the profit on its African-American customers as it made on its white customers for vehicle purchases, leases, and related services.[45]

8.5.3 Why Members of Protected Groups Often Pay More

The Chicago study discussed in the previous subsection provides insight into why minorities pay more for goods and services as well as credit. The author of the study speculated that, while actual bias may have played a role, the more likely explanation was that dealers were looking for "sucker sales." As profits are not uniformly spread across all sales but rather are concentrated in a few high markup sales, salespeople will look for those who are more likely to pay that high markup.

In turn, the salespeople may have stereotypes about who is more likely to pay high prices, and "[e]ven a small difference in the percentage of high mark-up buyers represented by consumers of any one race or gender class may lead to large differences in the way dealers treat the entire class."[46]

The explanations for why certain groups pay more are complex, involving a mix of psychological, political, and sociological factors. Some believe that those who have historically received worse deals ultimately see themselves as less worthy of better deals. Others argue that low-income consumers are aware that they are getting bad deals but simply do not have more affordable alternatives in their communities.[47] Many mainstream banks simply do not open branches in low-income minority neighborhoods. Segregation, both subtle and overt, keeps many residents of these communities from crossing the line into neighborhoods where they know they can get better deals.

Holding creditors liable for discriminatory pricing can be difficult because many courts, relying on traditional models of economic decision-making, are less likely to understand market realities and more likely to blame the victims for making "bad choices." The problem with rational economic theory is that it does not account for why consumers sometimes choose to buy high-cost products that they theoretically can obtain more cheaply elsewhere.

At least a few courts have begun to consider alternative economic theories to explain consumer decision-making in discrimination cases.[48] In denying the defendant's motion for summary judgment in one case, the court directly challenged the use of economic theories that "imply that market prices are efficient, thus beneficial for consumers, presuppose that consumers are informed, markets are competitive and the costs of making transactions are not excessively burdensome."[49] The court reasoned that these assumptions might need to be relaxed and even possibly replaced if

---

43 Ian Ayres, *Fair Driving: Gender and Race Discrimination in Retail Car Negotiations*, 104 Harv. L. Rev. 817 (1991).

44 Ian Ayres, *Further Evidence of Discrimination in New Car Negotiations and Estimates of Its Cause*, 94 Mich. L. Rev. 109 (1995).

45 Williams v. Sutherlin, Clearinghouse No. 52,062, Civ. No. 1-96-CV-1215-RCF (N.D. Ga. 1997) (third amended complaint).

46 Ian Ayres, *Fair Driving: Gender and Race Discrimination in Retail Car Negotiations*, 104 Harv. L. Rev. 817 (1991).

47 *See generally* David Dante Trott, *Ghettoes Revisited: Antimarkets, Consumption, and Empowerment*, 66 Brook. L. Rev. 1 (2000).

48 *See, e.g.*, Honorable v. The Easy Life Real Estate Sys., 100 F. Supp. 2d 885 (N.D. Ill. 2000) (denying defendant's motion for summary judgment). The judge in this case noted his wariness of arguments that low-income consumers are, per se, too ignorant to fend for themselves but found the facts in this case persuasive because the plaintiffs characterized themselves in this way. *Id.* at 888.

49 *Id.* at 888.

economic theory is to have any application to what happens in actual markets.[50]

8.5.4 Legal Theories to Challenge Price Discrimination

The Fair Housing Act has two major provisions, one dealing with discrimination in financing and the other with discrimination in the sale or rental of a dwelling.[51] Consequently, as long as a transaction is within the scope of the Fair Housing Act, any form of discrimination concerning purchase price, availability, or lease terms of a dwelling should be covered under at least one of the two major Fair Housing Act provisions.[52]

Discrimination as to purchase price and other aspects of any sales or lease transaction, whether realty or personalty, is also covered by the federal Civil Rights Acts—as long as the prohibited basis of the discrimination is race or ethnic origin.[53] The Civil Rights Acts' prohibition on price discrimination will apply whether or not credit is involved.[54]

Price discrimination should also violate the ECOA if the discrimination involves both credit and a creditor. The statute applies to every aspect of the applicant's dealings with a creditor regarding an extension of credit.[55]

---

50 *Id.*

51 42 U.S.C. §§ 3604, 3605; *see also* 24 C.F.R. pt. 100, Subpart B—Discriminatory Housing Practices.

52 *See* § 2.3, *supra.*

53 42 U.S.C. §§ 1981, 1982; *see* § 2.4, *supra.*

54 *See* Williams v. Sutherlin, Clearinghouse No. 52,062, Civ. No. 1-96-CV-1215-RCF (N.D. Ga. 1997) (third amended complaint).

55 Reg. B, 12 C.F.R. § 202.2(m); *see* § 2.2, *supra.*

Chapter 9 — Discrimination Subsequent to the Granting of Credit

9.1 Introduction

Federal and state credit discrimination statutes cover a wide range of credit activity. Most of the litigation in this area focuses on the application process and other transactions in which consumers are denied credit on a discriminatory basis. This chapter discusses often overlooked claims that might arise *after* credit is granted.

9.2 Types of Discrimination Subsequent to the Granting of Credit

9.2.1 Loan Servicing

The Official Staff Commentary to Regulation B gives "administration of accounts" as an example of the types of dealings between creditor and applicant that are covered by the ECOA's general prohibition against discrimination.[1] Thus, a creditor cannot discriminate on a prohibited basis concerning ease of payment, willingness to restructure or postpone payments, or providing information about account balances. Under the Fair Housing Act, such discrimination is likely to violate the prohibition on discrimination concerning the terms and conditions of a loan.[2]

9.2.2 Compliance With Warranties, Other Post-Sale Service

To the extent that a credit discrimination statute covers discrimination concerning the sale price of property or a service, it should also cover discrimination concerning compliance with warranties and other post-sale performance. For example, one court found that a car dealer violated the ECOA when it refused to honor a money-back guarantee because the consumer was Hispanic.[3]

In addition, discrimination related to sales transactions should be covered by the federal Civil Rights Acts—as long as the prohibited basis is race or ethnic origin. Section 1982 of the federal Civil Rights Acts provides that all citizens shall have the same right to purchase and hold real and personal property. Differences in performance under a warranty certainly relate to an individual's right to purchase and hold the property.[4]

9.2.3 Changes in Account Status

The ECOA's general rule against discrimination applies not only to the initial granting of credit, but to any changes in an account, such as raising the credit limit, changing credit terms, renewing the account, or terminating credit. Regulation B states that the general prohibition applies to "revocation, alteration, or termination of credit."[5]

Changes in the terms or conditions of a residential real estate-related transaction also fall under the scope of the Fair Housing Act.[6] Thus, the FHA should apply as well to changes in credit limits or terms or termination of accounts.

9.2.4 Treatment Upon Default

When a consumer is delinquent on an account, a creditor can take various steps to collect the amount due or to enforce the credit agreement. Such actions are related to the credit transaction and, under the ECOA, creditors may not treat debtors differently post-default based on a prohibited basis. Regulation B specifically mentions collection procedures and termination of credit as covered by the ECOA.[7] The Official Staff Commentary states that the general rule

---

1 Official Staff Commentary, 12 C.F.R. § 202.4-1.

2 42 U.S.C. § 3604(b); *see* 24 C.F.R. §§ 100.110(b), 100.130(a).

3 Luera v. Hilton, Clearinghouse No. 48,549 (Ill. Cir. Ct. Jackson County 1992).

4 42 U.S.C. § 1982; *see* § 2.4, *supra* (scope of federal Civil Rights Acts).

5 Reg. B, 12 C.F.R. § 202.2(m) defines revocation, alteration, or termination of credit as part of a credit transaction, and Reg. B, 12 C.F.R. § 202.4 prohibits discrimination concerning any aspect of a credit transaction.

6 42 U.S.C. § 3604(b); *see* 24 C.F.R. § 100.110(b).

7 Reg. B, 12 C.F.R. § 202.2(m).

against discrimination covers the "treatment of delinquent or slow accounts."[8]

The Fair Housing Act also prohibits discrimination concerning treatment of defaults. The statute has been interpreted to bar discrimination in mortgage foreclosures on the basis that this constitutes one of the terms or conditions of a loan.[9]

The Civil Rights Acts could also provide a framework for contesting mortgage foreclosures. One case brought pursuant to section 1982 failed, however, because the plaintiffs did not show that the defendant had foreclosed disproportionately against African-American mortgagors who were in default as compared with white mortgagors in default.[10] Although the bank had brought a high number of foreclosure actions against African-Americans, the evidence did not show that it attempted to foreclose "solely, primarily, or in a disproportionate way against African-American mortgagors."[11]

Other examples of post-default practices covered by both the ECOA and Fair Housing Act include how soon a creditor turns an account over for collection or cancels a consumer's line of credit, how soon collateral is seized, how willing a creditor is to reinstate the contract, and how soon a creditor institutes a collection lawsuit. Thus it should be a violation if collection procedures begin earlier when the consumer in default is a member of a protected group or if, for example, repossessions are more readily instituted in African-American neighborhoods.[12] The use of racial or gender-based epithets in collection efforts is another example of discriminatory behavior which violates credit discrimination statutes.[13]

Also actionable is any discrimination as to the method of charging default penalties. For example, it is discriminatory if one group of borrowers loses all down payments and the product purchased while another group pays a smaller penalty for default.[14]

9.3 Collection Against Non-Obligated Spouse Under Necessaries, Family Expense Laws

Many states still have laws on the books dating from the early nineteenth century, when it was widely held that a married woman could not contract in her own name.[15] The courts developed a fiction that the wife was acting as her husband's agent. The husband was presumed to have authorized his wife's purchases, unless the creditor was otherwise notified. Essentially, common law placed a unilateral obligation on the husband to support his wife financially. Although courts generally did not choose to set a minimum level of support, they did hold husbands liable to pay for necessaries under the doctrine of necessaries.[16]

These laws may be preempted by the provision of the ECOA which states that laws prohibiting the separate extension of consumer credit to each party in a marriage shall not apply when each party to the marriage voluntarily applies for separate credit from the same creditor.[17] Thus, when a creditor pursues a non-contractually liable spouse utilizing the necessaries statute, the creditor may be violating the ECOA by discriminating in the collection of debts on the basis of marital status.[18]

---

8 Official Staff Commentary, 12 C.F.R. § 202.4-1. Conversely, exercising rights upon default, standing alone, does not violate the ECOA. *See, e.g.,* Marine Midland Bank v. Yoruk, 662 N.Y.S.2d 957, 958 (App. Div. 1997) (denial of extension of credit to defaulted mortgagor insufficient to sustain counterclaim for violation of ECOA in action to foreclose).

9 Harper v. Union Sav. Ass'n, 429 F. Supp. 1254 (N.D. Ohio 1977); Lindsey v. Modern Am. Mortgage Corp., 383 F. Supp. 293 (N.D. Tex. 1974); *cf.* Little Earth of United Tribes v. Dep't of Hous. & Urban Dev., 675 F. Supp. 497 (D. Minn. 1987), *aff'd,* 878 F.2d 236 (8th Cir. 1989) (foreclosure decisions by HUD fully justified and no violation of Fair Housing Act).

10 Shipley v. First Fed. Sav. & Loan Ass'n, 703 F. Supp. 1122 (D. Del. 1988), *aff'd,* 877 F.2d 57 (3d Cir. 1989) (table).

11 703 F. Supp. at 1138.

12 For example, preliminary survey results of replevin court filings in Minnesota by the nation's largest rent-to-own company showed, among other things, that African-American customers were subject to repossession at a higher rate than white customers and that they were in default prior to repossession for a shorter period on average than white customers, even though both groups had similar income levels. *See* § 2.2.2.5, *supra.*

13 *See* Sharp v. Chartwell Fin. Services Ltd., 2000 U.S. Dist. LEXIS 3143 (N.D. Ill. Feb. 28, 2000) (a debt collector's invoking of racial and gender-based epithets during collection phone calls held actionable).

14 United States v. Am. Future Sys., Inc., 743 F.2d 169 (3d Cir. 1984).

15 *See also* National Consumer Law Center, Fair Debt Collection § 14.6 (4th ed. 2000 and Supp.). *See generally* Mechele Dickerson, *To Love, Honor & (Oh!) Pay: Should Spouses Be Forced to Pay Each Other's Debts?,* 78 B.U. L. Rev. 961 (1998).

16 *See* Mechele Dickerson, *To Love, Honor & (Oh!) Pay: Should Spouses Be Forced to Pay Each Other's Debts?,* 78 B.U. L. Rev. 961 (1998). Some states have addressed constitutional equal protection challenges to these statutes by either abolishing them or by extending them to women. *See, e.g.,* Account Specialists & Credit Collections, Inc. v. Jackman, 970 P. 2d 202 (Okla. Civ. App. 1998); Med. Ctr. Hosp. of Vt. v. Lorrain, 675 A.2d 1326 (Vt. 1996).

17 15 U.S.C. § 1691d(c); *see also* Reg. B, 12 C.F.R. § 202.11(b). No court has held that the ECOA preempts the doctrine of necessaries. However, one court stated in dicta that it believes the doctrine may be preempted. Edwards v. McCormick, 136 F. Supp. 2d 795, 803 n.9, *class certification denied,* 196 F.R.D. 487 (S.D. Ohio 2001). A few other state courts have considered the ECOA in the context of the doctrine of necessaries but have not directly confronted the issue because these cases did not involve credit. *See, e.g.,* Bartrom v. Adjustment Bureau, 618 N.E.2d 1, 7 (Ind. 1993); Med. Ctr. Hosp. of Vt. v. Lorrain, 675 A.2d 1326 (Vt. 1996). These courts cited the ECOA for its policy bases and for the congressional studies leading to its enactment.

18 15 U.S.C. § 1691d(c) specifically provides that "where such a State law is so preempted, each party to the marriage shall be

However, the ECOA and Regulation B allow a creditor to consider state property laws "directly or indirectly affecting creditworthiness."[19] The issue then becomes whether a family expense or necessaries statute affects an individual spouse's creditworthiness.[20] It might be argued that the amount of outstanding inchoate liability for a spouse's debts under a family necessaries statute affects creditworthiness. However, if such debts cannot be collected without violating the ECOA, they arguably should not even be considered in an evaluation of creditworthiness.[21]

In addition to possible violations of a credit discrimination statute, attempting to collect a debt based solely on a family expense statute may violate the Fair Debt Collection Practices Act. Courts have found that, because the ECOA prohibits spousal co-signatures in certain circumstances during the application stage of a transaction, debt collectors cannot later try to go after the non-signing spouse as though she had signed as a financially responsible party.[22]

9.4 Credit Reporting

9.4.1 General; Scope of Requirement

Regulation B establishes procedures that creditors must follow when they furnish information about certain accounts to credit reporting agencies.[23] These procedures are designed to ensure that each spouse may build a credit history on the basis of accounts which they both use or for which both are contractually liable even if only one spouse is listed as the primary obligor.

As there is no requirement that a creditor furnish credit information on its accounts, these requirements apply only to creditors that choose to furnish credit information to credit bureaus or to other creditors.[24] The requirements do not apply to public utility credit,[25] incidental consumer credit,[26] business credit,[27] or securities credit.[28]

9.4.2 Requirements Concerning Reporting Information to Reporting Agencies

9.4.2.1 Designation of Separate Accounts for Spouses

A creditor that furnishes credit information to a reporting agency must designate any new account to reflect the participation of both spouses, if the applicant's spouse is permitted to use the account or if the applicant's spouse is contractually liable on the account.[29] The creditor need not distinguish between accounts on which the spouse is an authorized user or is a contractually liable party.[30] The creditor is not required to designate a new account to reflect that the spouse is a guarantor, surety, endorser, or similar party.[31]

When new parties who are spouses assume a loan, the creditor should change the designation of the account to reflect the new obligors and should subsequently report

---

solely responsible for the debt so contracted." An early interpretation of 15 U.S.C. § 1691d(c), which appears in the explanatory material accompanying the original publication of Regulation B states: "[I]n states that have laws prohibiting separate extensions of credit for married persons, this section [then Reg. B, 12 C.F.R. § 202.8(a)] . . . will not only pre-empt such laws but also any other provision which would hold one spouse responsible for the debts contracted by the other, for example, a family expense statute." 40 Fed. Reg. 49,298, 49,304 (Oct. 22, 1975) (former Reg. B, 12 C.F.R. § 202.8(a), is now 12 C.F.R. § 202.11(b)(ii)).

19 15 U.S.C. § 1691d(b); Reg. B, 12 C.F.R. § 202.6(c).
20 "Among the state laws that may be considered by a creditor under this section are laws relating to the doctrines of agency between the spouses' 'necessaries'; and 'family expense statutes.' Also included are principles of community property management, as those principles affect an applicant's creditworthiness." 40 Fed. Reg. 49,298, 49,304 (Oct. 22, 1975).
21 In addition, Reg. B, 12 C.F.R. § 202.5(c)(1) and (2) seem to preclude such an inquiry, although subsection (3) arguably would permit it.
22 *See, e.g.*, Edwards v. McCormick, 136 F. Supp. 2d 795, *class certification denied*, 196 F.R.D. 487 (S.D. Ohio 2001); *see also* § 5.6, *supra* (discussion of when the ECOA prohibits requiring spousal cosignatures).
23 *See generally* National Consumer Law Center, Fair Credit Reporting Act (4th ed. 1998 and Supp.).

24 Official Staff Commentary, 12 C.F.R. § 202.10-1.
25 Reg. B, 12 C.F.R. § 202.3(a)(2)(ii). The Federal Reserve Board has proposed revisions that would apply the requirements to public utility credit. 64 Fed. Reg. 44,582, 44,595 (Aug. 16, 1999) (proposing to amend 12 C.F.R. § 202.3(a)(2)(ii)). The Board noted that creditors are considering public utility payments more frequently and that it would be helpful to consumers if public utility companies that furnish credit payment information were subject to the same reporting requirements as other creditors subject to the ECOA. 64 Fed. Reg. at 44,583.
26 Reg. B, 12 C.F.R. § 202.3(c)(2)(vii); *see also* § 2.2.6.3, *supra*.
27 Official Staff Commentary, 12 C.F.R. § 202.10-1. This business credit exemption was initially found in Regulation B. Although that exemption was rescinded because of the Women's Business Ownership Act of 1988, the exemption still lives on in the Commentary. The Supplementary Information accompanying the Commentary explains that no specific regulatory exemption is necessary as a basis for this exclusion because the reporting rule was designed to protect married women who become divorced or widowed from being left without a credit history of their own. Consequently, it "is not relevant to business applicants such as corporations or partnerships, nor is it intended to apply to individual business applicants such as sole proprietors." 54 Fed. Reg. at 50,482, 50,484 (Dec. 7, 1989). The complete exclusion of business credit ignores the possibility that the same problem of a woman's credit invisibility might occur when the "Pop" in a Mom-and-Pop small business dies or the marriage dissolves.
28 Reg. B, 12 C.F.R. § 202.3(b)(2)(vii); *see also* § 2.2.6.6, *supra*.
29 Reg. B, 12 C.F.R. § 202.10(a)(1).
30 Official Staff Commentary, 12 C.F.R. § 202.10-3.
31 Reg. B, 12 C.F.R. § 202.10(a)(1).

credit information on the account in the new names.[32] A request to change the manner in which information concerning the account is furnished does not alter the legal liability of either spouse and does not require the creditor to change the name under which the account is maintained.[33]

Regulation B does not require any special system of indexing or recordkeeping, but the creditor must be able to report information in the name of each spouse. If a creditor receives a credit inquiry about the wife, the creditor should be able to locate her credit file without asking for the husband's name.[34] In addition, if the creditor furnishes information about the account to a credit reporting agency, the information should be provided so that the reporting agency can gain access to the information in the name of each spouse.[35]

When reporting credit information in response to an inquiry about one spouse, the creditor must furnish the information only in the name of the spouse mentioned in the inquiry.[36] In response to any other request for credit information, the creditor is required to furnish the information in such a way that the credit reporting agency has access to the information in the name of each spouse.[37]

The requirements apply only to accounts held or used by spouses. Nevertheless, a creditor has the option to designate all joint accounts to reflect the participation of both parties even if the parties are not married to each other.[38]

A failure to comply with these credit reporting requirements is not considered a violation when caused by an inadvertent error, but the creditor must correct the error as soon as possible after discovering it.[39] Inadvertent errors include clerical mistakes, calculation errors, computer malfunctions, and printing errors. An error of legal judgment is not an inadvertent error.[40]

9.4.2.2 Other Credit Reporting Violations

When a consumer in good faith exercised rights under the Consumer Protection Act, creditors may not discriminate in reporting that consumer's credit information to other creditors or to reporting agencies.[41] For example, a creditor may not report a debt as "charged-off,"[42] or give it a similar adverse characterization, when in fact the account was paid or canceled as part of a settlement or judgment in a suit

brought by the consumer under the Consumer Credit Protection Act (CCPA).

The consumer in such a situation might have a cause of action against the creditor under a federal or state fair credit reporting law.[43] In addition, the consumer should have a cause of action under the ECOA for discrimination in the furnishing of credit information, on the basis of good faith exercise of Consumer Protection Act rights.[44] The prohibition concerning discrimination in reporting information should apply even after a creditor has closed an account. Nothing in the ECOA or Fair Housing Act indicates that a credit transaction ceases to be covered once the creditor closes the account.

9.5 Creditor Actions Triggered By Borrower's Increased Age or Change in Name or Marital Status

9.5.1 Rules Limiting Creditor Actions

A creditor may not require reapplication for an open-end account, change the terms of an open-end account, or terminate an open-end account merely because account holders reach a certain age, retire, or change their name or marital status.[45] The creditor may take such actions only if there is evidence of the account holder's inability or unwillingness to repay.

For example, a creditor violates this provision if it has a policy of automatically canceling a wife's supplementary credit card when her husband dies and then automatically renewing her credit after receiving her written consent to become liable for all charges on the new account.[46] Simi-

---

32 Official Staff Commentary, 12 C.F.R. § 202.10(a)-1.
33 Official Staff Commentary, 12 C.F.R. § 202.10(a)-2.
34 Official Staff Commentary, 12 C.F.R. § 202.10-4.
35 Reg. B, 12 C.F.R. § 202.10(b).
36 Reg. B, 12 C.F.R. § 202.10(b).
37 Reg. B, 12 C.F.R. § 202.10(b).
38 Official Staff Commentary, 12 C.F.R. § 202.10-2.
39 Reg. B, 12 C.F.R. § 202.14(c).
40 Official Staff Commentary, 12 C.F.R. § 202.14(c)-1.
41 *See* § 3.4.4, *supra* (prohibitions on discrimination based on exercise of rights under the Consumer Credit Protection Act).
42 A term indicating the debt was written off as a bad debt.

43 However, creditors reporting their own experience with a consumer are not subject to liability under the federal Fair Credit Reporting Act (FCRA). 15 U.S.C. § 1681a(d)(2)(A)(i); *see* National Consumer Law Center, Fair Credit Reporting Act §§ 2.4.1, 2.5.4, 2.5.5 (4th ed. 1998 and Supp.). If the credit information is incorrect, however, a creditor may be liable under a state provision or based on a deceit or negligent misrepresentation theory. In addition, the creditor can sometimes be held liable under the FCRA if the consumer challenges incorrect information with a credit reporting agency, and the creditor fails to fulfill its obligation to investigate the accuracy of the information. *See* National Consumer Law Center, Fair Credit Reporting § 2a.14.3 (2001 Supp.).
44 In settlement of many types of disputes, a consumer's attorney should consider requiring, as part of the settlement, that the creditor send a letter to credit reporting agencies correcting any errors in the consumer's credit report. For a more complete discussion of this issue and sample settlement provisions, see National Consumer Law Center, Fair Credit Reporting Act Ch. 7 (4th ed. 1998 and Supp.).
45 Reg. B, 12 C.F.R. § 202.7(c)(1), (2); Official Staff Commentary, 12 C.F.R. § 202.7(c).
46 Miller v. Am. Express Co., 688 F.2d 1235 (9th Cir. 1982) (in challenging American Express' policy of automatically cancel-

larly, a creditor may not terminate an account because credit life, health, accident, or disability insurance is unavailable or is no longer available due to the account holder's age.[47]

There are two exceptions to this rule. The creditor may require reapplication from a borrower who is contractually liable on an account on the basis of a change of marital status if 1) the credit was originally granted based on income earned by the borrower's spouse, and 2) the creditor has information available indicating that the borrower's income alone may not support the amount of credit currently available.[48] A creditor also may terminate an account when the spouses are jointly liable (even if the action coincides with a change in marital status), when one or both spouses repudiates responsibility for future charges, requests a separate account in his or her own name, or requests that the joint account be closed.[49]

9.5.2 Scope of the Rules Limiting Creditor Actions

9.5.2.1 Rules Apply Only to Open-End Accounts

The rules limiting creditor actions in closing or altering existing accounts apply only to open-end accounts. Open-end credit is defined in Regulation B as "credit extended under a plan under which a creditor may permit an applicant to make purchases or obtain loans from time to time,"[50] as opposed to one-time transactions such as auto loans. The classic example of open-end credit is the bank or retail store credit card with which the consumer can make as many or as few purchases or cash advances as desired, usually subject to a dollar limit. The credit may be obtained directly from the creditor or indirectly by use of a credit card, check, or other device.[51]

9.5.2.2 Rules Protect Only Applicants Who Are Contractually Liable

The rules limiting creditor actions in closing or altering existing accounts protect "applicants" who are "contractually liable."[52] Under Regulation B, a person who is contractually liable for a debt is expressly obligated to repay all debts on an account, pursuant to an agreement.[53] Thus, a man who had signed an agreement jointly with his wife may have protections against a reapplication requirement upon divorce or the death of his wife, while a man who was merely an authorized user on his wife's account may not.[54]

9.5.3 Status of Account During Reapplication

If a creditor requires a customer to reapply for an existing account, the applicant must be allowed full access to the account under existing terms while the reapplication is pending. The creditor may, however, specify a reasonable time period within which the account holder must submit the required information.[55]

9.5.4 When Creditor Can Request Updated Information From Account Holders

Creditors are not prohibited from periodically reevaluating the financial status of account holders to determine their ability to repay. For instance, creditors may ask account holders for regular income reports. They may also obtain credit reports on account holders for the purpose of reviewing the account.[56] If such a report indicates that an account holder has retired and as a result has a reduced income, the creditor could use this report as evidence of inability to repay and terminate the account. However, events related to a prohibited basis, such as retirement, reaching a particular age, or change in name or marital status, may not be used to trigger a request for updated information.[57] Similarly, it should violate the ECOA to target only members of protected categories, such as married women, for such updates.

9.6 Continuing Requirement of Cosigner on Credit Renewal

An earlier chapter details when a creditor may seek a spouse or other party's signature on a loan obligation as a

---

ing a supplementary cardholder's account upon the death of the principal cardholder, plaintiff was found to be more than a mere "user" of her husband's account; the ECOA applied because plaintiff was personally liable under the contract creating the supplementary account for all debts charged on her card by any person).

47 Reg. B, 12 C.F.R. § 202.7(e).

48 Reg. B, 12 C.F.R. § 202.7(c)(2).

49 Official Staff Commentary, 12 C.F.R. § 202.7(c)(1)-1.

50 Reg. B, 12 C.F.R. § 202.2(w).

51 Reg. B, 12 C.F.R. § 202.2(w).

52 Reg. B, 12 C.F.R. § 202.7(c).

53 Reg. B, 12 C.F.R. § 202.2(i).

54 Reg. B, 12 C.F.R. § 202.7(c); *see also* Official Staff Commentary, 12 C.F.R. §§ 202.7(c)(1)-1, 202.7(c)(2)-1; *cf.* Miller v. Am. Express Co., 688 F.2d 1235 (9th Cir. 1982) (though the creditor termed it a "supplementary" account, the court found that wife's account was in fact a separate account on which she was personally liable). Note that the ECOA permits an open-end creditor to condition the designation of an authorized user by the account holder on the authorized user's becoming contractually liable for the account, as long as the condition is not imposed on a discriminatory basis. Official Staff Commentary, 12 C.F.R. § 202.7(a)-1.

55 Official Staff Commentary, 12 C.F.R. § 202.7(c)(2)-1.

56 Fair Credit Reporting Act, 15 U.S.C. § 1681b(a)(3)(A).

57 Official Staff Commentary, 12 C.F.R. § 202.7(c)(1)-2.

cosigner or other surety.[58] Even when a creditor may obtain this extra signature, the creditor may not automatically seek the second signature on a renewal of the obligation.

Instead, if the borrower's creditworthiness is reevaluated when a credit obligation is renewed, the creditor must determine whether an additional party is still warranted—if not, the creditor must release the additional party.[59] The decision to require an additional party on renewal also may not be made on a prohibited basis.[60]

---

58 *See* Ch. 5, *supra.*

59 Official Staff Commentary, 12 C.F.R. § 202.7(d)(5)-3; Stern v. Espirito Santo Bank, 791 F. Supp. 865 (S.D. Fla. 1992).

60 Stern v. Espirito Santo Bank, 791 F. Supp. 865 (S.D. Fla. 1992).

Chapter 10   ECOA Procedural Requirements

10.1 Introduction

Previous chapters have focused on the ways in which the ECOA and other federal credit discrimination statutes may be used to challenge discriminatory creditor behavior. The ECOA, in particular, applies even more broadly. Creditors may violate the ECOA not only by engaging in discriminatory actions but also by violating any of a number of ECOA notice and record retention provisions.

The ECOA procedural provisions can be powerful tools even in situations in which discrimination is not at issue.[1] Despite the lack of "substantive" discrimination claims, borrowers who prevail on procedural claims may collect punitive damages plus actual damages and attorney fees against creditors who fail to strictly comply with the required procedures.[2]

Although procedural claims may be brought even without discrimination, there is a strong connection between the procedural and substantive aspects of the ECOA. The ECOA notice provisions require that creditors provide credit applicants with notices stating the reasons for denial or for taking other actions on an application. These notices may provide clues to help uncover whether the creditor's decision was discriminatory. The ECOA legislative history indicates, "only if creditors know they must explain their decisions will they effectively be discouraged from discriminatory practices."[3] Similarly, record retention requirements were enacted to help ensure that consumers would have access to records needed to help prove discrimination claims.

10.2 ECOA Notice Requirements

10.2.1 Introduction

Creditor notification requirements vary depending on the situation, and this chapter treats each of these six different situations separately: 1) applications approved by the creditor; 2) applications in which the creditor makes a counter-offer as to the terms or amount of credit; 3) applications involving credit denials, terminations or other adverse actions by the creditor; 4) incomplete applications; 5) withdrawn applications; and 6) applications in which a dwelling will secure the loan. This section also covers issues related to the timing, content and format of notices, including rules allowing electronic disclosures in certain circumstances.

Other federal and state statutes may have notice provisions similar to those found in the ECOA. For example, the Fair Credit Reporting Act requires notice when a credit report forms the basis of a credit denial.[4] Similarly, HUD or other government programs may require notice of action taken on an application. These requirements are in addition to, and do not absolve the creditor from complying with, the ECOA notice requirements.[5]

10.2.2 Notification Requirement for Approved Applications

A creditor must notify an applicant of its decision to approve an application within thirty days after receiving the completed application.[6] This notification may be either express or implicit. Implicit notification is given when the applicant receives, for example, a credit card, money, property, or other requested services.[7]

Notification need not be given each time a consumer uses a line of credit, credit card or other open-end account.

---

1 *See* Jochum v. Pico Credit Corp., 730 F.2d 1041 (5th Cir. 1984); Rayburn v. Car Credit Ctr. Corp., 2000 U.S. Dist. LEXIS 14944 (N.D. Ill. Oct. 6, 2000) (discrimination is not a prerequisite to an actionable ECOA claim); Williams v. Thomas Pontiac-GMC-Nissan-Hyundai, 1999 U.S. Dist. LEXIS 15045 (N.D. Ill. Sept. 22, 1999); Pinkett v. Payday Today Loans, L.L.C., 1999 U.S. Dist. LEXIS 12098 (N.D. Ill. July 22, 1999) (failure to provide ECOA rejection notice may be actionable without allegations of discrimination).

2 *See generally* Ch. 11, *infra*.

3 S. Rep. No. 94-589 (1976), *reprinted in* 1976 U.S.C.C.A.N. 403, 406.

4 15 U.S.C. § 1681m(a); *see also* National Consumer Law Center, Fair Credit Reporting Act § 5.4 (4th ed. 1998 and Supp.).

5 Official Staff Commentary, 12 C.F.R. § 202.9(b)(2)-9; Dep't of Hous. & Urban Dev., Mortgagee Letter 77-17, Consumer Cred. Guide (CCH) ¶ 98,192 (Apr. 22, 1977) (must comply with ECOA and with HUD notification requirement).

6 Reg. B, 12 C.F.R. § 202.9(a)(1)(i); *see also* §§ 10.2.4.1, 10.2.8, *infra* (discussion of what constitutes a completed application).

7 Official Staff Commentary, 12 C.F.R. § 202.9(a)(1)-2.

Regulation B indicates that such action—that is, the use of an account[8] or line of credit that does not exceed a previously established credit limit—should not be treated as an application.[9]

10.2.3 Notification Requirement If Creditor Makes a Counteroffer

10.2.3.1 The General Rule

Sometimes the creditor's response to a completed application will be to offer to extend credit, but on substantially different terms or in substantially different amounts than those requested by the applicant. Regulation B requires that a creditor notify an applicant of any counteroffer to the credit requested within thirty days after receiving an application.[10]

If the applicant does not expressly accept or use the counteroffered credit, the creditor then must make a determination whether to accept or reject the applicant's original credit request. In that case, the creditor, within ninety days of its counteroffer, must notify the applicant of the action it has decided to take on the original application.[11] This does not, however, require creditors to hold counteroffers open for ninety days or any other particular length of time.[12]

The creditor may also combine a counteroffer with a notice of adverse action.[13] In this instance, the creditor does not need to send a second notice of the action it has taken if the applicant does not accept the counteroffer.[14] A sample of such a combined notice is provided in the Federal Reserve Board's forms appended to Regulation B.[15]

The counteroffer notice provision is critical in alerting a borrower to differences between the loan presented to her at closing and the loan she had applied for. For example, borrowers often come to a lender with a specific loan amount in mind to pay for home improvements or other uses. The lender may try to inflate that amount, proposing a loan that is significantly different in amount, in terms or in both amount and terms, than what the borrower initially requested. The ECOA notice of counteroffer can raise a red flag and possibly help convince the borrower to reconsider signing a bad loan.[16]

Unfortunately, most borrowers seek legal help long after closing and only after they are having trouble paying back the loan. ECOA counteroffer notice violation claims are still important at this point though, as they can afford additional remedies to borrowers, including actual and punitive damages.[17]

10.2.3.2 Is Notice Required When the Borrower Accepts the Counteroffer?

The notice requirement is generally clear if the borrower rejects the counteroffer. In that case, the creditor, within ninety days of its counteroffer, must notify the applicant of the action it has decided to take on the original application.[18]

The situation is less clear when a borrower appears to have accepted the counteroffer by, for example, signing the counteroffered loan at closing. Borrowers may not know that they have signed the counteroffered loan, believing instead that they received the loan they had originally applied for. The counteroffer notice can be critical in these circumstances to help alert the borrower that the loan she is about to sign is different than what she had applied for. The key issue in these cases is whether the borrower must be given notice of the counteroffer and, if so, whether the notice must be in writing.

The few courts that have addressed this issue have come to different conclusions. One court concluded that creditors are required to give borrowers written notice of the counteroffer regardless of whether the borrower accepts or rejects the counteroffer.[19] In a more recent case, another court concluded that the notice does not have to be in writing.[20] The first case included challenges to a wide range of abusive practices. In the second case, in contrast, the ECOA procedural notice violation was the only issue remaining on appeal.[21]

---

8   Use of an account is a term of art in Regulation B referring only to open-end credit. *See* Reg. B, 12 C.F.R. § 202.2(a).

9   Reg. B, 12 C.F.R. § 202.2(f).

10   Reg. B, 12 C.F.R. § 202.9(a)(1)(i).

11   Reg. B, 12 C.F.R. § 202.9(a)(1)(i).

12   Official Staff Commentary, 12 C.F.R. § 202.9(a)(1)-5.

13   *See* § 10.2.4, *infra* (adverse action).

14   Official Staff Commentary, 12 C.F.R. § 202.9(a)(1)-6.

15   *See* Form C-4, Reg. B, 12 C.F.R. § 202 app. C. The Federal Reserve Board has proposed some technical, non-substantive revisions to Form C-4 to reflect that age cannot be considered, provided that the applicant has the capacity to contract. 64 Fed. Reg. 44,582, 44,617 (Aug. 16, 1999). The proposed revisions to Regulation B are reproduced on the CD-Rom accompanying this volume.

16   The Federal Reserve Board has proposed amending the Official Staff Commentary to clarify that when a consumer receives a solicitation for a specific amount and the creditor subsequently offers a different amount, the creditor's action constitutes a counteroffer. 64 Fed. Reg. 44,582, 44,588–89 (Aug. 16, 1999).

17   *See generally* Ch. 11, *infra*.

18   Reg. B, 12 C.F.R. § 202.9(a)(1)(i).

19   Newton v. United Companies Fin. Corp., 24 F. Supp. 2d 444 (E.D. Pa. 1998).

20   Diaz v. Va. Hous. Dev. Auth., 117 F. Supp. 2d 500 (E.D. Va. 2000).

21   The substantive claims were dismissed in an earlier decision. Diaz v. Va. Hous. Dev. Auth., 101 F. Supp. 2d 415 (E.D. Va. 2000). Plaintiffs had alleged that the housing authority's decision to deny their loan applications because they were not married violated the ECOA. The court found that the creditors' refusal to extend credit was permissible under the exception in the ECOA for credit programs designed to help economically disadvantaged borrowers. 15 U.S.C. § 1691(c)(1); *see* § 3.9, *supra* (special purpose credit programs).

The *Diaz* court cited the lack of specificity on this issue in both the statute and the regulations. The statute requires that creditors notify applicants of actions on completed applications within thirty days.[22] It does not specify whether this notice must be in writing. A later paragraph clarifies that only applicants against whom adverse actions are taken must receive a written statement of reasons.[23]

It is clear therefore that written notice must be given if there is an adverse action. Not all counteroffers, however, fit into the definition of adverse action. The statute defines adverse action as "a denial or revocation of credit, a change in the terms of an existing credit arrangement, or a refusal to grant credit in substantially the amount or on substantially the terms requested."[24] The last element in the definition includes situations in which the loan signed by the applicant is significantly different than what she had applied for. However, Regulation B refines this statutory definition, explicitly exempting from the definition of adverse action denials of credit coupled with a counteroffer that is accepted or used by the borrower.[25]

This exception is significant because most borrowers who are presented with different loan terms or amounts at closing are not aware of the changes or are otherwise coerced into accepting the "new" loan. The key question is whether under these circumstances notice of counteroffer is still required, and if so, whether this notice must be in writing. The *Newton* court concluded that written notice must be given as long as the lender has received a completed application.[26] The *Diaz* court found that oral notice was sufficient.[27]

This issue of whether written or oral notice is required can be crucial. Without a written requirement, lenders can later claim that they verbally informed the borrower of a counteroffer. The only evidence that a counteroffer notice was not given may be the borrower's testimony. Judges and juries are often sympathetic to predatory lending victims and thus these cases still may be resolved in the borrower's favor. However, when presented in conjunction with other claims, such as Truth in Lending violations, that can be proven with written documentation, the court may be more likely to dismiss the ECOA claims when no written documentation is available.

10.2.3.3 Special Notice Issues Related to Automobile Fraud

Car dealers, particularly used car dealers, routinely engage in deceptive tactics aimed at confusing prospective buyers and hiding the true cost of the credit being offered. A wide range of state and federal laws can be used to challenge these practices, including state unfair and deceptive acts and practices (UDAP) statutes, odometer statutes, and the federal Truth-in-Lending Act.[28] The ECOA's procedural and substantive requirements are an often overlooked, yet powerful, addition to this array of consumer protections.

As discussed throughout this chapter, ECOA notice requirements are triggered whenever a creditor denies an application or makes a counteroffer.[29] Many car dealers violate these notice requirements because they do not want to call attention to changes in credit terms or to changes from sales to leases.

For example, dealers who engage in the deceptive practice of spot delivery (also known as "yo-yo," "take-back" or "gimme-back" sales) frequently do not comply with the ECOA. Spot delivery occurs when a dealer supposedly finalizes an installment sale of a car, gives the consumer possession of the car "on the spot," even transfers title to the consumer, and then later tells the consumer to return the car because the financing has fallen through.[30] This practice leads to either the consumer agreeing to rewrite the loan at higher payments, to repossession, or both.

Dealers often fail to provide the ECOA notice of credit denial in these situations. The mere failure to provide these written notices should be a violation of the ECOA even in the absence of actual damages and may be enough to meet the standard for punitive damages.[31]

Dealers may argue that a denial notice was not required because they did not actually deny credit but rather made a counteroffer. This argument should not get the creditor off the hook. There are a number of different scenarios that may arise, but in each case, the dealer should be required under the ECOA to provide the consumer with some type of notice.

First, it is important to determine whether a counteroffer was in fact made. For example, in many spot delivery cases, the consumer will accept a particular deal and then the dealer will call her back hours or days later to sign a different contract. The second deal in this situation would

---

22 15 U.S.C. § 1691(d)(1).

23 15 U.S.C. § 1691(d)(2).

24 15 U.S.C. § 1691(d)(6); *see* § 10.2.4.2, *infra* (adverse action).

25 Reg. B, 12 C.F.R. § 202.2(c)(1)(i).

26 Newton v. United Companies Fin. Corp., 24 F. Supp. 2d. 444, 459 (E.D. Pa. 1998).

27 Diaz v. Va. Hous. Dev. Auth., 117 F. Supp. 2d 500, 503 (E.D. Va. 2000) (oral notice sufficient when loan officer called plaintiffs to inform them that their original application had been denied but that they qualified instead for a different loan).

28 *See generally* National Consumer Law Center, Automobile Fraud (1998 and Supp.).

29 *See* § 10.2.3.1, *supra* (counteroffer), § 10.2.4, *infra* (adverse action).

30 *See* National Consumer Law Center, Unfair and Deceptive Acts and Practices § 5.4.5 (5th ed. 2001 and Supp.).

31 *See* Rayburn v. Car Credit Ctr. Corp., 2000 U.S. Dist. LEXIS 14944 (N.D. Ill. Oct. 6, 2000); Williams v. Thomas Pontiac-GMC-Nissan-Hyundai, 1999 U.S. Dist. LEXIS 15045 (N.D. Ill. Sept. 22, 1999) (denial of motion to dismiss).

not be a counteroffer, but instead a rejection of the first application requiring notice of a credit denial. Any rider that gives the dealer the right to back out of an offer if financing does not come through is not a true counteroffer.

If the dealer made a counteroffer, it must have provided the required ECOA notice of a counteroffer within thirty days after receiving the application.[32] A counteroffer occurs if the dealer/creditor offers credit on substantially different terms or in substantially different amounts than those requested by the applicant.[33] At that point, the consumer may accept the counteroffered credit. Even if the consumer accepted the "new deal," she should still have received notice of the counteroffer. The failure to provide this notice may arguably be an ECOA violation. Advocates should also confirm in these cases that the consumer truly accepted the counteroffer.

If instead the consumer rejected the counteroffer, the creditor must then have made a determination whether to accept or reject the applicant's original credit request. In that situation, within ninety days of the counteroffer, the creditor must notify the applicant of the action it has taken on the original application.[34]

It is common practice for dealers to deny an application to buy a car and then offer to lease the car to the consumer. An immediate offer of lease terms may also be considered a counteroffer, triggering ECOA notice requirements. Even if the same credit application is used, there are two separate transactions in these circumstances. The first action by the dealer, denying credit for a sale, should trigger ECOA notice requirements.

In any of these scenarios, it is very likely that ECOA notice violations will be found. Dealers have various arguments they use to try to avoid these requirements. For example, in some cases, dealers may argue that notice was not required because the consumer withdrew her application.[35] However, if the application was not withdrawn but merely incomplete, the creditor is still obligated to notify the applicant of action taken on the application or that additional information is needed.[36]

Dealers may also attempt to avoid ECOA requirements by arguing that they do not fit within the ECOA definition of creditor. Dealers should fit the definition either as persons that regularly extend, renew or continue credit, or as persons who regularly arrange for credit.[37] It is preferable to argue that dealers regularly extend credit rather than arrange for credit because the ECOA limits the liability of arrangers.[38]

The dealer may also argue that because they assigned the financing immediately after purchase, it is the assignee and not the dealer who is responsible for sending the ECOA notices. The borrower's response should be that the dealer is the original creditor and therefore is required to give ECOA notices.[39] In the spot delivery context, the dealer may have agreed to finance the purchase thereby creating an account. An assignee's subsequent denial of the credit terms should be considered an adverse action on an existing account, also requiring notice.[40] On the other hand, the ECOA only requires one party to provide notice of adverse action. If the assignee has already provided that notice to the consumer, there is no requirement that the dealer do so as well.[41]

---

32 Reg. B, 12 C.F.R. § 202.9(a)(1)(i). At least one court has found that the notice of counteroffer does not have to be in writing. *See* Diaz v. Va. Hous. Dev. Auth., 117 F. Supp. 2d 500 (E.D. Va. 2000); § 10.2.3.2, *supra*.

33 Reg. B, 12 C.F.R. § 202.2(c)(1)(i).

34 Reg. B, 12 C.F.R. § 202.9(a)(1)(iv); *see* § 10.2.3.1, *supra* (notice of counteroffer).

35 *See* Thompson v. Galles Chevrolet Co., 807 F.2d 163 (10th Cir. 1986) (court acknowledged the lack of a withdrawal exception to notice requirements, but found that strict adherence to the letter of Regulation B in this case would not advance the basic purposes of the ECOA; notice of adverse action not required when plaintiffs asked for rescission of purchase order and arguably withdrew their application); Freeman v. Koerner Ford, 536 A.2d 340 (Pa. Super. Ct. 1987); § 10.2.9, *infra* (withdrawn applications).

36 Reg. B., 12 C.F.R. § 202.9(c); *see* § 10.2.8, *infra* (incomplete applications).

37 Reg. B, 12 C.F.R. § 202.2(l); *see* Burns v. Elmhurst Auto Mall, Inc., 2001 U.S. Dist. LEXIS 6385 (N.D. Ill. May 16, 2001) (dealer who regularly refers applicants to creditors and selects creditors to whom applications can be made is a creditor within meaning of the ECOA); Hudson v. Richfield Mitsubishi, 1997 U.S. Dist. LEXIS 23674 (D. Minn. July 11, 1997) (denial of defendant's argument in summary judgment motion that it was not covered by the ECOA); § 2.2.5, *supra*; *see also* Patterson v. Bob Ryan Oldsmobile, Inc., 1997 U.S. Dist. LEXIS 23692 (D. Minn. Oct. 31, 1997) (car dealer did not function as a creditor in first transaction with plaintiff because dealer only forwarded credit applications to creditors, who then sent required ECOA notices of denial; dealer did function as a creditor during subsequent transaction that occurred after initial denial by other creditors even though dealer applied credit guidelines developed by a secondary creditor and intended to extend credit for only a short period of time; ECOA claim failed, however, because there was no adverse action), *aff'd*, 162 F.3d 1164 (8th Cir. 1998) (unpublished) (text available at 1998 U.S. App. LEXIS 14771); *cf.* Sharlow v. Wally McCarthy's Pontiac-GMC Trucks-Hyundai, 1998 U.S. Dist. LEXIS 22746 (D. Minn. Feb. 4, 1998) (summary judgment granted because dealer not considered a creditor for ECOA purposes when it merely received the credit application and forwarded it to several potential lenders), *aff'd*, 221 F.3d 1343 (8th Cir. 2000) (unpublished) (text available at 2000 U.S. App. LEXIS 15627).

38 *See* § 2.2.5.3, *supra*. The Federal Reserve Board (FRB) has proposed amending the ECOA definition of creditor to clarify that it also includes one who regularly participates in setting terms of credit, not just in the decision of whether to extend or deny credit. 64 Fed. Reg. 44,582, 44,594 (Aug. 16, 1999). The FRB has also proposed amending the Official Staff Commentary to expressly provide that arrangers can include automobile dealers, home builders and home improvement contractors, and those who solely accept applications. Official Staff Commentary, 12 C.F.R. § 202.2-1, 64 Fed. Reg. at 44,620.

39 *See* §§ 2.2.5.4, 2.2.5.5, *supra*.

40 Reg. B, 12 C.F.R. § 202.2(c)(1)(ii); *see* § 10.2.4.2.2, *infra*.

41 *See* Burns v. Elmhurst Auto Mall, Inc., 2001 U.S. Dist. LEXIS 6385 (N.D. Ill. May 16, 2001) (Reg. B foresees that multiple entities may be involved, but only requires one notice to appli-

10.2.4 *Notification Requirement for Adverse Actions*

10.2.4.1 Notification Required Only If There Is an Application

The creditor must notify applicants when an adverse action is taken after the creditor receives an "application."[42] This is not a requirement that the creditor receive a *completed* application, only an application.[43]

Application is defined in Regulation B as "an oral or written request for an extension of credit that is made in accordance with procedures established by a creditor for the type of credit requested."[44] A creditor has latitude to establish its own application process and to decide the type and amount of information it will require from applicants.[45] If the application is in general accordance with the creditor's procedures, but not all required information has been provided, this should be treated as an incomplete application, but an application nevertheless.[46] If the application is incomplete, the creditor must notify the applicant within thirty days of any action taken on the application or notify the applicant that more information is needed.[47]

"Procedures established by a creditor" includes not only the creditor's stated procedures, but also the actual practices that the creditor follows in making credit decisions.[48] Thus, even if the creditor's stated policy is to require a written application, an oral application is sufficient if the creditor routinely decides to grant or deny credit based on an oral request for credit.[49]

An application, for instance, can consist of a telephone inquiry to a lender, if the lender has a policy or practice of making credit decisions solely on the basis of information received by telephone. When a creditor treats a telephone call as sufficient to take an adverse action, the creditor must request the applicant's name and address in order to provide written notification. If the applicant declines to provide that information, then the creditor has no further notification responsibility.[50]

Even if a creditor does not have a general practice of treating an oral inquiry as an application, if it does so in a particular case, then the inquiry is an application even if it does not meet the creditor's normal standards for an application.[51] Similarly, prequalification and preapproval programs could trigger the right to notice under certain circumstances.[52] Thus, if a creditor, in giving information about loan terms to a potential applicant, evaluates information about the applicant and decides to decline the request, and communicates this decision to the applicant, then the inquiry must be treated as an application and the creditor must notify the potential applicant of the adverse decision.[53]

Despite this broad definition, not every inquiry constitutes an application requiring notice of the creditor's action on that inquiry. The following, according to the Official Staff Commentary, are *not* applications:

- When a consumer calls to ask about loan terms and the employee explains the creditor's basic loan terms, such as interest rates, loan-to-value ratio, and debt-to-income ratio;
- When a consumer calls to ask about interest rates for car loans and, in order to quote the appropriate rate, the loan officer asks for the make and sales price of the car and the amount of down payment, then gives the consumer the rate;
- When a consumer asks about terms for a loan to purchase a home, and tells the loan officer her income and intended down payment, but the loan officer only explains the creditor's loan-to-value ratio policy and other basic lending policies, without telling the consumer whether she qualifies for the loan; and
- When a consumer calls to ask about terms for a loan to purchase vacant land, states his income and the sales price of the property to be financed, and asks whether he qualifies for a loan, and the employee responds by describing the general lending policies, explaining that she would need to look at all of the applicant's qualifications before making a decision, and offering to send

cant); Leguillou v. Lynch Ford, Inc., 2000 U.S. Dist. LEXIS 1668 (N.D. Ill. Feb. 10, 2000) (granting motion to dismiss). Even though the assignee is not the original creditor, it may still be directly liable for ECOA violations. *See* §§ 2.2.5.4, 2.2.5.5, *supra,* § 10.2.11, *infra* (multiple creditors).

42 Reg. B, 12 C.F.R. § 202.9(a).
43 Procedures required when the application is not completed are set out in § 10.2.8.2, *infra.*
44 Reg. B, 12 C.F.R. § 202.2(f). Application is not defined in the statute. *See also* Official Staff Commentary, 12 C.F.R. § 202.2(f).
45 Official Staff Commentary, 12 C.F.R. § 202.2(f)-1.
46 *See* Reg. B, 12 C.F.R. § 202.2(f); Riggs Nat'l Bank v. Webster, 832 F. Supp. 147, 151 (D. Md. 1993) (application for extension of maturity date of promissory note not complete without receipt of required appraisals of collateral).
47 Reg. B, 12 C.F.R. § 202.9(c); *see* § 10.2.8 (incomplete applications).
48 Official Staff Commentary, 12 C.F.R. § 202.2(f)-2; *see* Newton v. United Companies Fin. Corp., 24 F. Supp. 2d 444 (E.D. Pa. 1998) (communication with lender found to be de facto application because all information the lender regularly obtained was provided and the lender regularly treated such communications as applications for credit and made decisions based upon them).
49 Official Staff Commentary, 12 C.F.R. § 202.2(f)-2.

50 Official Staff Commentary, 12 C.F.R. § 202.9(a)(1)-7.
51 Official Staff Commentary, 12 C.F.R. § 202.2(f)-2.
52 Official Staff Commentary, 12 C.F.R. § 202.9-5.
53 Official Staff Commentary, 12 C.F.R. § 202.2(f)-3. The Federal Reserve Board has proposed revising Official Staff Commentary, 12 C.F.R. § 202.2(f)-3 to clarify that prequalifications are subject to the test currently applicable to inquiries. 64 Fed. Reg. 44,582, 44,619 (Aug. 16, 1999). The proposed revisions to the Official Staff Commentary to Regulation B are reproduced on the CD-Rom accompanying this volume.

an application form to the consumer.[54]

The clear implication from these Commentary examples is that even if a consumer does not follow the creditor's application procedures, if a creditor discourages a particular applicant or indicates that the particular applicant may not obtain credit, then an application *has* been made, and the creditor must notify the consumer of the adverse action.

The same general principles apply when evaluating whether an on-line communication with a lender amounts to an application. In fact, it may be that on-line communications are more likely than off-line communications to be considered applications, especially if consumers are able to provide credit-related information about themselves, allowing the system to perform a credit analysis.

To address issues related to on-line lending, the Federal Reserve Board (FRB) solicited comment on whether it should further clarify the distinction between an inquiry about credit and an application for credit.[55] The Board was motivated in large part by the growth of new delivery channels for information about loan products, such as the internet, but also by the growth in credit counseling and prequalification programs, which have resulted in consumers asking for information about credit products and their creditworthiness before ever submitting an application.[56] Many industry comments to the FRB reported that they were unclear about when inquiries about credit rose to the level of an application requiring a formal denial if credit was rejected.

Based on the various responses received, including the industry comments noted above, the FRB has proposed adding to the definition of application. Under the enhanced definition, an application would include a request for pre-approval following procedures whereby a creditor will issue a written commitment, even if conditional, to creditworthy persons for credit up to a specified amount that is valid for a period of time.[57] The Official Staff Commentary would be amended to reflect this change and to further explain when an inquiry or prequalification request becomes an applica-

tion.[58] However, the Board declined to extend the ECOA to cover prescreened credit solicitations.[59]

10.2.4.2 Notification Required Only If There Is an Adverse Action

10.2.4.2.1 Adverse actions involving new credit accounts

The creditor must notify an applicant of an adverse action.[60] Conversely, if Regulation B does not treat an action as adverse, Regulation B does not require the creditor to notify the applicant of the action (although the failure to disclose the action taken may be a deceptive trade practice).

An adverse action is defined as any refusal to grant credit "in substantially the amount or on substantially the terms requested in an application, unless the creditor makes a counteroffer (to grant credit in a different amount or on other terms) and the applicant uses or expressly accepts the credit offered."[61]

An adverse action is not involved when applicable law prohibits the creditor from extending the credit requested.[62] It is not adverse action, for instance, for an automobile dealer to refuse to extend a small loan for a purpose unrelated to the purchase of an automobile, if such loans must be made by a licensed lender under state law.

The refusal to extend credit also is not an adverse action when the creditor does not offer the type of credit or credit plan requested.[63] For example, a creditor does not take adverse action when it rejects an application for a used car loan because its policy is to offer loans only on new cars.[64] Nevertheless, when a creditor does not offer the credit *terms* (such as interest rate or security) requested by the applicant

---

54 Official Staff Commentary, 12 C.F.R. § 202.2(f)-4. The Federal Reserve Board has proposed revisions to Official Staff Commentary, 12 C.F.R. § 202.2(f)-4 to provide additional examples of inquiries that would not be considered applications. 64 Fed. Reg. 44,582, 44,620 (Aug. 16, 1999). The proposed revisions to the Official Staff Commentary to Regulation B are reproduced on the CD-Rom accompanying this volume.

55 63 Fed. Reg. 12,326 (Mar. 12, 1998).

56 *See* 64 Fed. Reg. 44,582, 44,589 (Aug. 16, 1999).

57 64 Fed. Reg. 44,582, 44,594 (Aug. 16, 1999) (proposing to amend 12 C.F.R. § 202.2(f)). The proposed revisions to Regulation B are reproduced on the CD-Rom accompanying this volume.

58 64 Fed. Reg. 44,582, 44,619 (Aug. 16, 1999) (proposing to amend Official Staff Commentary, 12 C.F.R. § 202.2(f)). The proposed revisions to the Official Staff Commentary to Regulation B are reproduced on the CD-Rom accompanying this volume.

59 64 Fed. Reg. 44,582, 44,584–44,585 (Aug. 16, 1999); *see also* § 5.3.2.5, *supra* (prescreened solicitations).

60 Reg. B, 12 C.F.R. § 202.9(a).

61 Reg. B, 12 C.F.R. § 202.2(c)(1)(i); *see also* Dorsey v. Citizens & S. Fin. Corp., 678 F.2d 137 (11th Cir. 1983) (when consumer applied for 95% mortgage, but accepted a mortgage of only 90%, there was no adverse action requiring notice to the consumer), *aff'd*, 706 F.2d 1203 (1983); United States v. Am. Future Sys., Inc., 571 F. Supp. 551 (E.D. Pa. 1983) (creditor violated the ECOA by failing to give customers notice of adverse action when they were accepted on less favorable terms than the terms extended to persons who were identically situated, except for their race, sex, and marital status), *aff'd on other grounds*, 743 F.2d 169 (3d Cir. 1984) ; § 10.2.3.2, *supra* (discussing whether an "accepted" counteroffer is an adverse action).

62 Reg. B, 12 C.F.R. § 202.2(c)(2)(iv).

63 Reg. B, 12 C.F.R. § 202.2(c)(2)(v).

64 The acceptance of telephone service conditioned upon payment of a $50 security deposit has also been held not to constitute an adverse credit action. Edwards v. Sprint, Inc., 1998 U.S. App. LEXIS 21040 (9th Cir. Aug. 17, 1998).

(as opposed to the type of credit), a denial of the application is an adverse action unless the creditor makes a counteroffer that is accepted by the applicant.[65]

10.2.4.2.2 Adverse actions involving existing accounts

The issue of when a creditor has taken an adverse action concerning an existing account is somewhat more complex. Termination of an account or an unfavorable change in the terms of an account that does not affect all or a substantial portion of a class of the creditor's accounts is an adverse action.[66] An example of this type of adverse action is the automatic termination of the paid-up account of a recently divorced woman, when no other paid-up accounts are terminated.

Similarly, a telephone company's requirement that only certain existing customers pay a $100 deposit would constitute adverse action and entitle the consumers to a statement of specific reasons.[67] In contrast, an increase in the interest rate on all credit cards issued by the creditor would not be an adverse action.[68]

Refusal to increase the amount of credit available to an applicant who has made an application for an increase is an adverse action.[69] For example, it is an adverse action to reject a consumer's application for an increase of an existing $500 credit limit when the creditor's maximum limit is $1000 and the requirements for requesting an increase were met. It is also an adverse action to lower a previously established credit limit unless the limit was lowered due to account inactivity, default, or delinquency.[70] A refusal to automatically increase a credit line would not be an adverse action if the consumer had overrun the established credit line on a specific credit card purchase without prior authorization.[71]

Termination because the customer moved from the card issuer's service area is still an adverse action unless termination on this ground is explicitly provided for in the credit agreement between the parties.[72] If a creditor decides to terminate all credit accounts with low credit limits (e.g., under $400) but keeps other credit accounts, this decision is also an adverse action.[73]

On the other hand, the following would not be adverse actions concerning existing accounts:

- *A change in the terms of an account expressly agreed to by the borrower.*[74]
- *Any action or forbearance relating to an account taken in connection with inactivity, default, or delinquency on that account.*[75] It is not an adverse action, for example, to repossess collateral, accelerate a defaulted loan, or to request the return of a credit card when the consumer has overrun the credit line.[76] Similarly, if the applicable contract defined the death of the primary cardholder as a default on the account, then termination on this ground would not be an adverse action.[77] Termination of an account based on a *current* default or delinquency is not an adverse action, but termination based upon a *past* default or delinquency is an adverse action.[78]
- *A refusal to extend additional credit under an existing credit arrangement when the additional credit would exceed a previously established credit limit.*[79] This provision has been held to include an application for an extension of a promissory note's maturity date.[80]
- *A refusal or failure to authorize an account transaction*

---

65 Official Staff Commentary, 12 C.F.R. § 202.2(c)(2)(v)-1; *see* § 10.2.3.2, *supra.*

66 Reg. B, 12 C.F.R. § 202.2(c)(1)(ii); *see, e.g.,* Pierce v. Citibank (S.D.), 843 F. Supp. 646 (D. Or. 1994) (termination of wife's account occurred automatically when husband's delinquent accounts were terminated, even though accounts were unrelated and each was obtained based on establishment of independent creditworthiness). The court later granted the defendant's motion for summary judgment because, among other reasons, the statute of limitations for bringing the ECOA claims had expired. Pierce v. Citibank (S.D.), 856 F. Supp. 1451 (D. Or. 1994), *aff'd,* 92 F.3d 1193 (9th Cir. Or. 1996) (unpublished) (text available at 1996 U.S. App. LEXIS 18496). The Federal Reserve Board has proposed replacing the phrase "substantial portion" with "substantially all" to emphasize that a creditor's action must affect the overwhelming majority of accounts in a designated class to be excluded from the definition of adverse action. 64 Fed. Reg. 44,582, 44,583, 44,593–44,594 (Aug. 16, 1999).

67 *See* O'Dowd v. S. Cent. Bell, 729 F.2d 347 (5th Cir. 1984).

68 *See* Sutliff v. County Sav. & Loan Co., 533 F. Supp. 1307 (N.D. Ohio 1982) (increase in the interest rate on all demand mortgage notes in the same classification as the plaintiffs' note was not adverse action requiring notice to the plaintiffs).

69 Reg. B, 12 C.F.R. § 202.2(c)(1)(iii).

70 Fed. Trade Comm'n, Unofficial Staff Letter, Clearinghouse No. 37,089 (Mar. 1983).

71 Official Staff Commentary, 12 C.F.R. § 202.2(c)(2)(iii).

72 Official Staff Commentary, 12 C.F.R. § 202.2(c)(1)(ii)-1.

73 Official Staff Commentary, 12 C.F.R. § 202.2(c)(1)(ii)-2.

74 Reg. B, 12 C.F.R. § 202.2(c)(2)(i).

75 Reg. B, 12 C.F.R. § 202.2(c)(2)(ii).

76 *See* Haynes v. Bank of Wedowee, 634 F.2d 266 (5th Cir. 1981) (consumer was in default when the creditor accelerated the loan, and therefore the acceleration did not constitute adverse action under the exception contained in Reg. B, 12 C.F.R. § 202.2(c)(ii)).

77 15 U.S.C. § 1691(d)(6); Reg. B, 12 C.F.R. § 202.2(c)(2)(ii).

78 Official Staff Commentary, 12 C.F.R. § 202.2(c)(2)(ii). The Federal Reserve Board has proposed revising Official Staff Commentary, 12 C.F.R. § 202.2(c)(2)(ii) to clarify that an adverse action does not include another action or a termination of an account due to a current delinquency or default on that account. 64 Fed. Reg. 44,582, 44,619 (Aug. 16, 1999). The proposed revisions to the Official Staff Commentary to Regulation B are reproduced the CD-Rom accompanying this volume.

79 15 U.S.C. § 1691(d)(6).

80 Riggs Nat'l Bank v. Webster, 832 F. Supp. 147, 150 (D. Md. 1993) (application for an extension is an application for additional credit beyond a previously established credit limit; denial of said application is not an adverse action).

at a point of sale or loan,[81] except when the refusal is a termination or an unfavorable change in the terms of an account that does not affect "all or a substantial portion" of a class of the creditor's accounts, or when the refusal is a denial of an application to increase the amount of credit available.[82] The Official Staff Commentary gives several examples of point-of-sale activity that is not considered adverse action. There is no adverse action when credit is refused because a cardholder attempts to use an expired card or a card that has been reported as stolen or lost or the transaction is over the card's credit limit. Similarly, there is no adverse action when credit is refused because it appears fraud is involved, the card authorization process is not working, or billing statements have been returned for lack of a forwarding address.[83]

- *A mortgagee's acceleration of the mortgage loan following the mortgagor's unauthorized sale of the property.[84]* Notice need not be sent to the mortgagor or to the property purchaser.[85] If a mortgagor sells property and the buyer makes an application to the creditor to assume the mortgage loan, then the creditor must notify the buyer of the action taken unless the creditor's policy is not to permit assumptions.[86]

These creditor actions, such as those taken in connection with delinquent accounts, may not constitute adverse actions, and thus may not trigger a requirement that creditors notify consumers of the actions taken. Nevertheless, creditors may not discriminate on a prohibited basis in taking such actions, because the ECOA's general prohibition on discrimination applies to all aspects of a credit transaction, including revocation, alteration, or termination of credit and collection procedures.[87] Thus, for example, it would violate the ECOA to accelerate loans of Temporary Aid to Needy Families recipients when one payment is in arrears if all other account holders are not treated similarly.

10.2.4.2.3　Are authorized users entitled to notification?

It is unclear whether authorized users should receive notice of adverse actions on an existing account, or whether the notice need only be sent to those contractually obligated on the account. Regulation B requires that the creditor notify an applicant (defined as one who has received an extension of credit from a creditor) when adverse action is taken on an existing account.[88] Applicant describes a broader category than contractually liable. The regulation recognizes this distinction, stating that an applicant is "any person who requests or who has received an extension of credit . . . and *includes* any person who is or may become contractually liable regarding an extension of credit."[89] The use of the word includes implies that contractual liability is not the sole criteria for the category.

Authorized users are clearly entitled to notification if they are contractually obligated. This will be decisive in most cases because, typically, language on a charge slip or elsewhere will contractually obligate an authorized user for charges for which that user signs.[90]

10.2.5　Timing of Notices

A creditor must notify an applicant of any adverse action taken on an application or an existing account within prescribed time periods, as follows:

- The creditor must send notification of adverse action taken on a completed application for credit within thirty days after receiving the application.[91] The application is considered complete once a creditor has obtained all the information it normally considers in making a credit decision;[92]
- The creditor must send notification of adverse action taken on an incomplete application for credit within thirty days after taking the adverse action;[93]
- The creditor must send notification of adverse action taken regarding an existing account within thirty days after taking the adverse action; and
- The creditor must send notification of adverse action taken within ninety days after notifying the applicant of a counteroffer, if the applicant has not expressly accepted or used the proffered credit.[94]

81　Reg. B, 12 C.F.R. § 202.2(c)(2)(iii). For example, a store's refusal to approve a credit card sale over $50 on a weekend, when no credit check can be made by phone, is not an adverse action.

82　Reg. B, 12 C.F.R. § 202.2(c)(2)(iii).

83　Official Staff Commentary, 12 C.F.R. § 202.2(c)(2)(iii).

84　Official Staff Commentary, 12 C.F.R. § 202.2(c)(2)(ii)-1.

85　Official Staff Commentary, 12 C.F.R. § 202.2(c)(2)(ii)-1.

86　Official Staff Commentary, 12 C.F.R. § 202.2(c)(2)(ii)-1.

87　Reg. B, 12 C.F.R. §§ 202.4, 202.2(m).

88　Reg. B, 12 C.F.R. § 202.9(a)(1)(iii).

89　Reg. B, 12 C.F.R. § 202.2(e) (emphasis added).

90　*See* § 2.2.4.1, *supra* (ECOA coverage of authorized users).

91　Reg. B, 12 C.F.R. § 202.9(a)(1)(i). The creditor thus must both evaluate the application and notify the applicant of the results within this thirty-day period.

92　Official Staff Commentary, 12 C.F.R. § 202.9(a)(1)-1. There may be a factual question as to when the application was completed, or as to whether the creditor acted with reasonable diligence in processing the loan. When the property appraisal is challenged, the creditor's reevaluation starts the thirty-day period again. Dufay v. Bank of Am., 94 F.3d 561 (9th Cir. 1996).

93　Reg. B, 12 C.F.R. § 202.9(a)(1)(ii). The creditor dealing with an incomplete application thus need not conform to the thirty-day evaluation timetable required for completed applications. The regulation does require that a creditor exercise "reasonable diligence" in obtaining all required information. *See* Reg. B, 12 C.F.R. § 202.2(f); § 10.2.8.2, *infra* (incomplete applications).

94　Reg. B, 12 C.F.R. § 202.9(a)(1)(iv); *see* § 10.2.3.2, *supra* (discussion of counteroffer notices).

These timing requirements can take on special significance when the creditor makes an oral or written promise to supply credit, but then goes back on that promise months later. For example, a home improvement contractor violates the ECOA by taking a credit application but only denying the loan (or changing the terms or creditor) months later after the work has been completed.[95]

10.2.6 Form of the Notification

10.2.6.1 General

The creditor must give the applicant written notification of an adverse action.[96] The written notice may be delivered or mailed to the applicant's last known address.[97] Creditors that have acted on one-hundred-fifty or fewer applications during the preceding calendar year may notify the applicant orally.[98] An oral notification is considered complete when the creditor "communicates" with the applicant.[99]

The ECOA notification may appear on the front or back or on both sides of a form or letter.[100] The notification can be made in a language other than English, so long as it is available in English upon request.[101] The Federal Reserve Board (FRB) has proposed adding a requirement that the notice be both clear and conspicuous and in a form the applicant can retain.[102]

The FRB provides a series of sample notices of action taken and statement of reasons.[103] The forms are illustrative and may not be appropriate for all creditors. The forms may require modification for particular applications, but proper use of the forms will satisfy the ECOA's notice requirement.[104]

10.2.6.2 Electronic Notifications

10.2.6.2.1 *The interim rule*

In April 2001, the Federal Reserve Board (FRB) published an interim final rule amending Regulation B to provide for electronic delivery of ECOA notifications.[105] The interim final rule was issued in response to passage of the Electronic Signatures in Global and National Commerce Act (E-Sign Act).[106] In August 2001, the FRB rescinded the October 1, 2001 deadline for compliance with the interim final rule.[107]

The interim rule makes some significant interpretations of the requirements of the E-Sign Act for the purposes of the ECOA, as well as addressing issues not covered by the E-Sign Act, such as the format of electronic notifications. Accompanying the interim rule, the FRB also issued a Supplement to the Official Staff Commentary with .[108]

In general, the E-Sign Act allows creditors to replace written disclosures with electronic documents if: a) certain disclosures are made to the consumer,[109] b) the consumer consents electronically, or confirms her consent electronically, in a manner that reasonably indicates that she can access information electronically in the format used by the provider of the information,[110] and c) the electronic document is in a form that is capable of being retained and accurately reproduced for later reference by all parties or

---

95 *See* Jochum v. Pico Credit Corp., 730 F.2d 1041 (5th Cir. 1984) (a creditor that failed to notify applicants for a second mortgage home improvement loan that they had been rejected for the loan until after the home improvements had been completed, and then only via the contractor, had no justifiable defense for failing to provide notice of the rejection).

96 Reg. B, 12 C.F.R. § 202.9(a)(2); *see also* Pierce v. Citibank (S.D.), 843 F. Supp. 646 (D. Or. 1994) (notice of termination of wife's account included in notice to husband of termination of his accounts, when accounts were unrelated, is insufficient notice to wife). The court later granted the defendant's motion for summary judgment based on, among other grounds, the expiration of the ECOA statute of limitations to bring claims. Pierce v. Citibank (S.D.), 856 F. Supp. 1451 (D. Or. 1994), *aff'd*, 92 F.3d 1193 (9th Cir. 1996) (unpublished) (text available at 1996 U.S. App. LEXIS 18496).

97 Official Staff Commentary, 12 C.F.R. § 202.9-3.

98 Reg. B, 12 C.F.R. § 202.9(d). *But see* Palmiotto v. Bank of N.Y., 1989 U.S. Dist. LEXIS 11546 (S.D.N.Y. Sept. 29, 1989) (creditor who did not show that it was eligible to give only oral notice could not prevail on its argument that consumer's ECOA claim was time-barred based on date of oral notice).

99 Official Staff Commentary, 12 C.F.R. § 202.9-3; *cf.* Birkett Williams Ford, Inc. v. E. Woodworking Co., 456 N.E.2d 1304 (Ohio Ct. App. 1982) (oral notice at the time of purchase was sufficient).

100 Official Staff Commentary, 12 C.F.R. § 202.9-4; *cf.* Barber v. Rancho Mortgage & Inv. Corp., 26 Cal. App. 4th 1819, 32 Cal. Rptr. 2d 906 (1994).

101 Reg. B, 12 C.F.R. § 202.4(b). This section was added as part of the Federal Reserve Board's interim final rule concerning electronic disclosures. 66 Fed. Reg. 17,779 (Apr. 4, 2001).

102 64 Fed. Reg. 44,582, 44,596 (Aug. 16, 1999) (proposing to add 12 C.F.R. § 204(d)).

103 *See* Reg. B, 12 C.F.R. § 202 app. C. The Federal Reserve Board has proposed changes to appendix C to reflect proposed changes to Regulation B and its Official Staff Commentary. 64 Fed. Reg. 44,582, 44,617–44,618 (Aug. 16, 1999). The proposed revisions to Regulation B's appendix C can be found on the CD-Rom accompanying this volume.

104 Reg. B, 12 C.F.R. § 202 app. C.

105 66 Fed. Reg. 17,779 (Apr. 4, 2001). The interim final rules are reproduced on the CD-Rom accompanying this volume.

106 Pub. L. No. 106-229, 114 Stat. 464 (June 30, 2000) (codified at 15 U.S.C. §§ 7001–7031).

107 66 Fed. Reg. 41,439 (Aug. 8, 2001). As of the printing of this volume, the Federal Reserve Board has not issued a revised final or interim rule.

108 66 Fed. Reg. at 17,786.

109 15 U.S.C. §§ 7001(c)(1)(B), 7001(c)(1)(C)(i).

110 15 U.S.C. § 7001(c)(1)(C)(ii).

persons who are entitled to retain it.[111]

The interim rule permits ECOA notifications to be delivered electronically so long as the creditor complies with the consumer consent provisions of the E-Sign Act.[112] These requirements apply when a lender wants to electronically deliver a document that the ECOA requires to be in writing, including the notice of adverse action and the notice of right to the statement of reasons (or the statement itself).[113] However, the E-Sign Act's requirements do not apply to the notice of the right to a copy of the appraisal[114] and requests for monitoring information.[115]

The interim rule imposes a new clear and conspicuous standard for electronic notices.[116] This standard only applies to electronic notices, because there is no similar standard for paper ECOA notifications.[117] The creditor is permitted to place other text, including advertisements, on the same screen as the ECOA notices, so long as the clear and conspicuous standard is met.[118]

The interim rule permits creditors to provide ECOA notifications electronically either by sending them via e-mail,[119] or by posting them on the creditor's website.[120] If a creditor provides notifications by posting them on its website, the creditor must also send a notice to consumers informing them of the availability of the notifications (an alert notice). The creditor has the option of sending this alert notice by e-mail *or* by postal mail.[121] This last option may prove troubling because it creates substantial barriers for consumers to actually access the disclosure on the internet. These barriers include physically getting to a computer and logging on to the internet once at the computer. Furthermore, consumers who have the most limited access to the internet (such as those who use public access computers or equipment controlled by the creditor) are the ones most likely to receive the alert notice by postal mail.

If an ECOA notification is posted to the creditor's website, the interim rule requires that the notice be retained on the website for ninety days.[122] This ninety-day retention requirement may contradict the E-Sign Act's requirement that an electronic document be "capable of being retained and accurately reproduced for later reference *by all parties.*"[123] A document posted to a website for only ninety days is not capable of being retained by the consumer unless the consumer has the ability to store or print the information, which may not be the case for a consumer who does not own a personal computer (most likely for consumers accessing the internet from the creditor's equipment or from a public access computer). The interim rule does not affect ECOA's requirement that the creditor itself retain records of a consumer credit transaction for twenty-five months.[124]

The interim rule does not require the creditor to verify that a consumer has actually received an electronic ECOA notification.[125] The rule does require that a creditor attempt redelivery of an electronic notification, based upon address information in the creditor's files, if the creditor receives actual notice that the electronic disclosure was not delivered.[126]

Finally, the interim rule exempts certain notices required by the ECOA and Regulation B from the E-Sign Act's consumer consent requirements, permitting them to be provided solely in electronic form if they are included on or with an application.[127] These notices include the notice of the right to a copy of the appraisal,[128] the notice of the right to a statement of reasons for adverse actions for small business applicants,[129] and the request for monitoring information.[130]

10.2.6.2.2 Potential pitfalls of electronic notifications for consumers

One potential pitfall of electronic disclosure may be

111 15 U.S.C. § 7001(e).
112 12 C.F.R. § 202.17(b). The interim rule also allows third parties who provide ECOA notifications on behalf of creditors to do so electronically. 12 C.F.R. § 202.9(h).
113 *See* 15 U.S.C. § 1691(d); Reg. B, 12 C.F.R. § 202.9(a), (b).
114 *See* 15 U.S.C. § 1691(e); Reg. B, 12 C.F.R. § 202.5a; § 10.2.12, *infra.*
115 *See* Reg. B, 12 C.F.R. § 202.13(a).
116 12 C.F.R. § 202.17(b).
117 However, the 1999 proposed revisions to Regulation B would impose the clear and conspicuous standard on all notices required by ECOA. 64 Fed. Reg. 44,582, 44,596 (Aug. 16, 1999); *see* § 10.2.6.1, *supra.*
118 66 Fed. Reg. 17,779, 17,781 (Apr. 4, 2001).
119 12 C.F.R. § 202.17(d)(1). The Official Staff Commentary prohibits creditors from sending electronic notifications to an e-mail address whose purpose is limited solely to receiving communications from the creditor. Official Staff Commentary, 12 C.F.R. § 202.17(d)(1)-1.
120 12 C.F.R. § 202.17(d)(2).
121 12 C.F.R. § 202.17(d)(2)(i).
122 12 C.F.R. § 202.17(d)(2)(ii).
123 15 U.S.C. § 7001(e) (emphasis added). The interim rule also has its own requirement that electronic notifications be "in a form that the applicant may retain." 12 C.F.R. § 202.17(b).
124 12 C.F.R. 202.12(b); *see* § 10.3.1, *infra.*
125 The Federal Reserve Board discusses its reasons for not including a verification requirement in the preamble to the interim rule. 66 Fed. Reg. 17,779, 17,783–17,784 (Apr. 4, 2001).
126 12 C.F.R. § 202.17(e).
127 12 C.F.R. § 202.17(c).
128 12 C.F.R. § 202.5a(a)(2)(i); *see* § 10.2.12, *infra.*
129 12 C.F.R. § 202.9(a)(3)(i)(B); *see* § 10.2.14.2, *infra.*
130 12 C.F.R. § 202.13(a). With respect to the request for monitoring information, note that the Official Staff Commentary states that a creditor may treat an application taken through an electronic medium without video capability (which would include the internet) as a telephone application. Official Staff Commentary, 12 C.F.R. § 202.13(b)-4. Creditors are not required to request monitoring information for telephone applications. Official Staff Commentary, 12 C.F.R. § 202.13(b)-3. However, the Federal Reserve Board has proposed in its 1999 proposed revisions to Regulation B to treat electronic applications taken without video capability as a postal application. 64 Fed. Reg. 44,582, 44,629 (Aug. 16, 1999).

attempts by overbearing creditors to entice or coerce consumers into consenting to electronic notifications when the consumers do not actually have internet access. Creditors might do this by penalizing consumers who decline to accept electronic notifications, even if these consumers do not have the ability to access them. Not only would such penalties raise the issue of coerced consent, they might constitute discrimination against the computerless, which is likely to have a disparate impact on protected classes under the ECOA.[131]

Another potential pitfall is notifications given on equipment provided by the creditor. The Supplement to the Official Staff Commentary authorizes this practice so long as the notifications are also automatically printed from the creditor's equipment, sent to the consumer's e-mail address, *or posted on the creditor's website.*[132] This last option is troubling because it could apply to consumers who cannot access the internet, i.e., it allows a creditor to show the consumer the ECOA notification on the creditor's equipment and then post the document to its website without ensuring the consumer has future access to the notification on the internet. However, such conduct would still be a violation of the E-Sign Act's basic consumer consent requirements, because the creditor has not "reasonably demonstrated that the consumer can access information in electronic form."[133]

10.2.7 Content of Notice

10.2.7.1 General

The notification of adverse action must contain the following elements:[134]

- A statement of the action taken (the notice does not have to use the term "adverse action"—the creditor may use any phrase or words that describe the action taken);[135]
- The creditor's name and address;
- The name and address of the federal agency with enforcement authority concerning the transaction;[136] and
- A statement of specific reasons for the action taken; or a disclosure of the applicant's right to request a statement of such reasons, with the name, address, and

telephone number of the person or office from which the statement of reasons can be obtained.[137]

The notification must also include the following language (or substantially similar language) detailing the applicant's ECOA rights as set out in Regulation B:

> The Federal Equal Credit Opportunity Act prohibits creditors from discriminating against credit applicants on the basis of race, color, religion, national origin, sex, marital status, age (provided the applicant has the capacity to enter into a binding contract); because all or part of the applicant's income derives from any public assistance program; or because the applicant has in good faith exercised any right under the Consumer Credit Protection Act. The federal agency that administers compliance with this law concerning this creditor is (name and address as specified by the appropriate agency listed in appendix A of this regulation).[138]

The exact language used need not be identical to the above quoted language, but it must be substantially similar.[139] For example, a creditor may add a reference to the fact that the ECOA permits age to be considered in certain credit scoring systems, add a reference to a similar state statute or regulation and to a state enforcement agency, or add certain disclosures required under the Fair Credit Reporting Act.[140]

10.2.7.2 The Reasons for Adverse Action

10.2.7.2.1 *Reasons must be specific*

The Federal Reserve Board (FRB) has drafted sample forms listing "specific reasons for adverse action."[141] Several of the sample forms contain lists of reasons, and the creditor is required to check off the appropriate boxes. Examples of the listed reasons include: credit application incomplete, insufficient number of references, unacceptable type of references provided, unable to verify credit references, temporary or irregular employment, unable to verify employment, income insufficient for amount of credit requested, excessive obligations in relation to income, length of residence, limited credit experience, delinquent credit obligations, garnishment, attachment, foreclosure, repossession, or value of collateral not sufficient.

If the creditor uses the FRB sample form, it may not rely solely on the listing of reasons on the sample, and it may not

131 *See* § 3.8.2, *supra.*
132 Official Staff Commentary, 12 C.F.R. § 202.17(b)-5; *see* National Consumer Law Center, The Cost of Credit: Regulation and Legal Challenges § 9.2.10.3 (2001 Supp.) (further discussion of the risks posed by providing consumer consent or electronic notifications on equipment controlled by creditors).
133 15 U.S.C. § 7001(c)(1)(C)(ii).
134 Reg. B, 12 C.F.R. § 202.9(a)(2).
135 Official Staff Commentary, 12 C.F.R. § 202.9-1.
136 *See* Reg. B, 12 C.F.R. § 202 app. A (list of agencies with enforcement authority).
137 Reg. B, 12 C.F.R. § 202.9(a)(2)(i), (ii).
138 *See* Reg. B, 12 C.F.R. § 202.9(b)(1).
139 Reg. B, 12 C.F.R. § 202.9(b)(1); Official Staff Commentary, 12 C.F.R. § 202.9(b)(1)-1.
140 Official Staff Commentary, 12 C.F.R. §§ 202.9(b)(1)-1, 202.9(b)(2)-9; *see* Reg. B, 12 C.F.R. § 202 app. C (forms C-1 through C-5; a combination of the ECOA and FCRA disclosures).
141 *See* Reg. B, 12 C.F.R. § 202 app. C.

just check the listed reason closest to the creditor's actual reason. The creditor must adapt the form to state the exact reason for the adverse action.[142]

A creditor may choose to use some other form, but the form must be specific and indicate the principal reason or reasons for the action taken.[143] A creditor may not merely state that the adverse action was based on "internal standards or policies," or that the applicant failed to achieve the qualifying score on a credit scoring system, without indicating specific shortcomings.[144] Moreover, a creditor cannot merely reinstate a terminated account without also specifying why the adverse action was taken.[145]

The creditor must disclose these reasons even if the relationship of a reason to predicting creditworthiness may not be clear to the applicant.[146] In providing reasons for adverse action, creditors are not required to describe how or why a factor adversely affected an applicant. For example, the notice may say "length of residence" rather than "too short a period of residence".[147]

Regulation B includes instructions for use of the sample notification forms, and gives an example that indicates how specific the creditor must be in providing its reasons for adverse action. For example, it is inadequate to state "insufficient credit references" when the applicant had finance company references, but the creditor accepts only bank references. Instead, the notice should indicate "insufficient bank references."[148]

The Fair Credit Reporting Act (FCRA) requires a creditor to disclose when it has based its decision in whole or in part on information from a source other than the applicant or from its own files.[149] Such a disclosure is not sufficient under the ECOA to disclose the reason for a denial.[150] For example, if the applicant's credit history indicates a delinquent debt and the creditor denies the application on that basis, the ECOA requires that the creditor notify the applicant that the reason for the denial is a delinquent account. The FCRA requires only that the creditor disclose that a credit report was obtained and used to deny credit.

10.2.7.2.2 Reasons must be the real ones

The reasons disclosed must relate to and accurately describe those factors actually reviewed, considered, or scored.[151] If the creditor uses a credit scoring system, the reasons disclosed must relate only to those factors actually scored in the system. Moreover, no factor that was a principal reason for the adverse decision may be excluded, even if the relationship of that factor to creditworthiness may not be clear to the applicant.[152]

A creditor may not disclose only "safe" reasons for denying credit, such as the lack of collateral, if the actual reason for denial of credit was a suspicious attribute such as residential zip code or age.[153] A creditor may not give one or two vague reasons for denial of credit when its actual

142 Reg. B, 12 C.F.R. § 202 app. C; *see also* Fischl v. Gen. Motors Acceptance Corp., 708 F.2d 143 (5th Cir. 1983) (creditor's "perfunctory reliance" on the sample form was considered "manifestly inappropriate," because the creditor had indicated that credit had been denied due to insufficient credit references, when the actual reasons were brevity of credit history and excessiveness of the amount to be financed).

143 Official Staff Commentary, 12 C.F.R. § 202.9(b)(2)-1.

144 Reg. B, 12 C.F.R. § 202.9(b)(2); *see also* United States v. Moore & Mothershead, Clearinghouse No. 45,755 (N.D. Tex. Oct. 20, 1989) (consent decree based on allegations that creditor failed to disclose that a consumer report or other third-party information was used in deciding to deny credit); Fed. Trade Comm'n v. Green Tree Acceptance, Inc., Clearinghouse No. 44,327 (N.D. Tex. 1988) (consent decree requiring $115,000 penalty and injunctive relief for, among other things, failing to give reasons for adverse action by merely stating that applicants failed to meet the creditor's internal credit underwriting standards); United States v. Winkleman Stores, Clearinghouse No. 40,626 (N.D. Ohio 1985) (consent order based on alleged failure to disclose actual negative factors in credit scoring system); O'Quinn v. Diners Club, Inc., 1978 U.S. Dist. LEXIS 15733 (N.D. Ill. Sept. 1, 1978).

145 Pierce v. Citibank (S.D.), 843 F. Supp. 646 (D. Or. 1994). The court later granted the defendant's motion for summary judgment based on, among other grounds, the expiration of the ECOA statute of limitations. Pierce v. Citibank (S.D.), 856 F. Supp. 1451 (D. Or. 1994), *aff'd*, 92 F.3d 1193 (9th Cir. 1996) (unpublished) (text available at 1996 U.S. App. LEXIS 18496).

146 Official Staff Commentary, 12 C.F.R. § 202.9(b)(2)-4.

147 Official Staff Commentary, 12 C.F.R. § 202.9(b)(2)-3.

148 Reg. B, 12 C.F.R. § 202 app. C.

149 15 U.S.C. § 1681m(a); *see* National Consumer Law Center, Fair Credit Reporting Act § 5.4 (4th ed. 1998 and Supp.).

150 Official Staff Commentary, 12 C.F.R. § 202.9(b)(2)-9.

151 Official Staff Commentary, 12 C.F.R. § 202.9(b)(2)-2; *see* Fischl v. Gen. Motors Acceptance Corp., 708 F.2d 143 (5th Cir. 1983) (creditor's "perfunctory reliance" on the sample form was considered "manifestly inappropriate," because the creditor had indicated that credit had been denied due to insufficient credit references, when the actual reasons were brevity of credit history and excessiveness of the amount to be financed); Carroll v. Exxon Co., 434 F. Supp. 557 (E.D. La. 1977). *But see* Para v. United Carolina Bank, 1998 U.S. Dist. LEXIS 16843 (E.D.N.C. Aug. 25, 1998) (discriminatory animus is clearly not a specific reason a lender might be expected to include in an ECOA notice; notice stating that application was denied because of lack of established earnings record and inadequate capital or assets was considered sufficient even if not the true reasons for denial); Higgins v. J.C. Penney, Inc., 630 F. Supp. 722 (E.D. Mo. 1986) (adverse action notice was adequate which gave "credit bureau report/delinquent history," "type of bank accounts" and "type of credit references" as reasons for denial of credit).

152 Official Staff Commentary, 12 C.F.R. § 202.9(b)(2)-4.

153 *See* United States v. Fidelity Acceptance Corp., Clearinghouse No. 38,923 (D. Minn. 1985) (consent order based on alleged failure to disclose to elderly applicants the actual, illegal reasons for denial of credit); United States v. Gen. Motors Acceptance Corp., Clearinghouse No. 38,902 (D.N.M. 1984) (creditor failed to disclose to applicants that rejection or less favorable credit terms were based on their being Native Americans); United States v. Household Fin. Corp., Clearinghouse No. 38,903 (N.D. Ill. 1984) (consent order partially based on allegations that creditor failed to provide rejected applicants with accurate and

reasons were the applicant's age, type of employment, or residential zip code.[154]

Courts may be more likely to find notices inadequate because a creditor used safe reasons rather than the real reasons if the creditor might actually have listed the real reasons for a denial.[155] Evidence that the creditor's real reason for denying an application was due to discrimination may help prove an ECOA substantive claim, but at least in one court's view, does not violate the provision requiring specific notice of the actual reasons for denial.[156]

It is inadequate to state that no reasons could be provided if the creditor simply failed to locate information on an applicant.[157] It is also inadequate for the creditor's reasons to be based on a credit report the creditor obtained *after* the applicant requested reasons for the denial. On the other hand, if the reasons are based on a credit report or other third party source, the creditor may not hide this fact.[158]

Listing only one of several reasons is not sufficient. The creditor must disclose the principal reasons, but a specific number of reasons is not mandated, and the Official Staff Commentary states that disclosure of more than four reasons is not likely to be helpful to the applicant.[159]

Sometimes a denial is based on an "automatic-denial factor," that is, a negative factor that always results in a

denial of credit no matter what other factors are present in the application. Examples might be that the applicant is a minor or is still in default with that creditor. In such situations, the applicable automatic-denial factors must always be disclosed as a reason for denial.[160]

If an application is incomplete and the creditor lacks sufficient data to make a decision, the creditor may either deny the application on that basis or provide a notice of incompleteness.[161] If the creditor denies the application for reasons other than incompleteness, the creditor must provide those reasons.[162]

The reasons given have to be the ones utilized by the creditor, but the reasons do not have to be good ones. For example, if the creditor's reason is based on a credit report containing outdated or unreliable information, there is no ECOA violation. Although the consumer should certainly bring these matters to the creditor's attention and the consumer has important rights under the Fair Credit Reporting Act,[163] there is no *ECOA* violation for a creditor making a bad credit decision. Under the ECOA, the creditor need not reconsider its denial when the consumer shows that the credit report was wrong.[164]

10.2.7.2.3 Reasons that must be disclosed when a credit scoring system is used

It is not always obvious what the actual reason for denial of credit is when a creditor uses a credit scoring system, as the system combines the applicant's score on many different variables.[165] Although the credit score is a single number, numerous factors are used to derive that number. The problem is how to isolate the variables that adversely affected an applicant's credit score, causing the denial of the credit application. Analysis is difficult because, to date, credit scoring companies and creditors that use the scores have not been required, for the most part, to disclose information about how these numbers are derived.[166]

The Official Staff Commentary indicates that there is no one right system for determining the reasons for a denial based on a credit scoring system, but does offer suggestions.

specific reasons, when actual reasons for rejection were based on discriminatory factors).

154 United States v. Montgomery Ward & Co., [1974-1980 Decisions Transfer Binder] Consumer Cred. Guide (CCH) ¶ 97,732 (D.D.C. 1979); United States v. Federated Dep't Stores, Inc., Clearinghouse No. 31,076 (S.D. Ohio 1978).

155 For example, in one case, the creditor's statement that "credit references are insufficient" was inadequate when the real reasons were brevity of credit history and excessive loan amount. These real reasons were ones that creditors should not be hesitant to give. Para v. United Carolina Bank, 1998 U.S. Dist. LEXIS 16843 (E.D.N.C. Aug. 25, 1998), *citing* Fischl v. Gen. Motors Acceptance Corp., 708 F.2d 143 (5th Cir. 1983).

156 *See* Para v. United Carolina Bank, 1998 U.S. Dist. LEXIS 16843 (E.D.N.C. Aug. 25, 1998) (discriminatory animus is clearly not a specific reason a lender might be expected to include in an ECOA notice).

157 *In re* Alden's, Inc., 92 F.T.C. 901 (Fed. Trade Comm'n 1978); *see also* Carroll v. Exxon Co., 434 F. Supp. 557 (E.D. La. 1977) (ECOA violation when only reason given for adverse action was that credit bureau contacted concerning applicant had been unable to furnish sufficient information about her, when, in fact, creditor had denied her credit for four other reasons).

158 United States v. Moore & Mothershead, Clearinghouse No. 45,755 (N.D. Tex. Oct. 20, 1989) (consent decree based on allegations that creditor failed to disclose that a consumer report or other third-party information was used in deciding to deny credit); United States v. Strawbridge & Clothier, Clearinghouse No. 38,925 (E.D. Pa. 1985) (alleged failure to disclose that credit was denied based on information received in credit reports).

The failure to disclose that a credit report was the reason for denial of credit also violates the Fair Credit Reporting Act. *See* 15 U.S.C. § 1681m(a); National Consumer Law Center, Fair Credit Reporting Act § 5.4 (4th ed. 1998 and Supp.).

159 Official Staff Commentary, 12 C.F.R. § 202.9(b)(2)-1.

160 Official Staff Commentary, 12 C.F.R. § 202.9(b)(2)-8.

161 Official Staff Commentary, 12 C.F.R. § 202.9(a)(1); Reg. B, 12 C.F.R. § 202.9(c) (notice requirement); *see* § 10.2.8.2, *infra*.

162 Official Staff Commentary, 12 C.F.R. § 202.9(a)(1)-3.

163 *See* National Consumer Law Center, Fair Credit Reporting Act (4th ed. 1998 and Supp.).

164 Grant v. World Class Mortgage Corp., 1990 U.S. Dist. LEXIS 2207 (N.D. Ill. Feb. 20, 1990) ("the statute and regulations do not . . . require that adverse action be based on reliable information, and do not require reconsideration of an application when it turns out that adverse action had been taken upon unreliable information").

165 *See* § 6.3.2, *supra* (discussion of credit scoring systems), § 6.3.2.2, *supra* (rules to determine whether a system qualifies as a credit scoring system).

166 *See* § 6.4.2.3, *supra*.

The creditor could identify the factors on which the applicant's score fell furthest behind the average score for those who were granted credit, or behind the average score for all applicants. Any other method that produces substantially similar results would also be acceptable.[167]

In a judgmental system, the reasons for the denial must relate to those factors in the applicant's record actually reviewed by the person making the decision.[168] If the creditor uses a combined system of credit scoring and judgment, the reasons must relate to the part of the combined system that the applicant failed, that is, either the credit scoring system or the judgmental system.[169]

10.2.7.2.4 When creditor discloses only the applicant's right to a statement of reasons

The creditor's notice of adverse action may either state the specific reasons for the action taken, or disclose the applicant's right to request a statement of the reasons for the action taken and how that request should be made.[170] When the creditor discloses the right to request a statement of the reasons, the creditor also must disclose the applicant's right to have a creditor's subsequent oral statement of the reasons confirmed in writing.[171]

The applicant has sixty days from being notified of the adverse action to request such reasons.[172] The creditor then must provide the applicant with the reasons for the adverse action taken within thirty days after receiving the request. At this point, the creditor may provide the reasons orally. After receiving the reasons orally, the applicant has the right to request a written confirmation. The creditor must provide the written confirmation within thirty days after receiving such a request.[173]

10.2.8 Incomplete Applications for Credit

10.2.8.1 When Is an Application Incomplete?

Application is defined in Regulation B as "an oral or

written request for an extension of credit that is made in accordance with procedures established by a creditor for the type of credit requested."[174] A creditor has latitude to establish its own application process and to decide the type and amount of information it will require from applicants.[175] If the application is in general accordance with the creditor's procedures, but not all required information has been provided, it should be treated as an incomplete application, but an application nevertheless.[176] If the application is incomplete, as discussed in the next subsection, the creditor must notify the applicant within thirty days of any action taken on the application or notify the applicant that more information is needed.[177]

"Procedures established by a creditor" includes not only the creditor's stated procedures, but also the actual practices that the creditor follows in making credit decisions.[178] Thus, even if the creditor's stated policy is to require a written application, an oral application is sufficient if the creditor routinely bases its decision to grant or deny credit on an oral request for credit.[179]

For instance, an application can consist of a telephone inquiry to a lender, if the lender has a policy or practice of making credit decisions solely on the basis of information received by telephone. When a creditor treats a telephone call as sufficient to take an adverse action, the creditor must request the applicant's name and address in order to provide written notification. If the applicant declines to provide that information, then the creditor has no further notification responsibility.[180]

If an application is incomplete, the creditor, nevertheless, must act with reasonable diligence to collect information needed to complete the application.[181] For example, the creditor should request information from third parties, such as credit reports, promptly after receiving the application. If an applicant has not submitted necessary and available information, the creditor must make a reasonable effort to

---

167 Official Staff Commentary, 12 C.F.R. § 202.9(b)(2)-5.
168 Official Staff Commentary, 12 C.F.R. § 202.9(b)(2)-6.
169 Official Staff Commentary, 12 C.F.R. § 202.9(b)(2)-7. The Federal Reserve Board has proposed revising the Official Staff Commentary to clarify that, if an application is not approved or denied as a result of the credit scoring and the creditor performs a judgmental assessment and then denies the credit after that assessment, the reasons disclosed must come from both components of the system. 64 Fed. Reg. 44,582, 44,627 (Aug. 16, 1999) (proposing to revise Official Staff Commentary, 12 C.F.R. § 202.9(b)(2)-7).
170 Reg. B, 12 C.F.R. § 202.9(a)(2)(ii).
171 Reg. B, 12 C.F.R. § 202.9(a)(2)(ii).
172 Reg. B, 12 C.F.R. § 202.9(a)(2)(ii). The regulation does not indicate whether this sixty-day period begins running when the notification is sent, or when the applicant receives it.
173 Reg. B, 12 C.F.R. § 202.9(a)(2)(ii).

174 Reg. B, 12 C.F.R. § 202.2(f). This term is not defined in the statute. *See also* Official Staff Commentary, 12 C.F.R. § 202.2(f); § 10.2.4.1, *supra* (definition of application).
175 Official Staff Commentary, 12 C.F.R. § 202.2(f)-1.
176 *See* Reg. B, 12 C.F.R. § 202.2(f); Riggs Nat'l Bank v. Webster, 832 F. Supp. 147, 151 (D. Md. 1993) (application for extension of maturity date of promissory note not complete without receipt of required appraisals of collateral).
177 Reg. B, 12 C.F.R. § 202.9(c); *see* § 10.2.8.2, *infra* (incomplete applications).
178 Official Staff Commentary, 12 C.F.R. § 202.2(f)-2; *see* Newton v. United Companies Fin. Corp., 24 F. Supp. 2d 444 (E.D. Pa. 1998) (communication with lender found to be de facto application because all information the lender regularly obtained was provided and the lender regularly treated such communications as applications for credit and made decisions based on them).
179 Official Staff Commentary, 12 C.F.R. § 202.2(f)-2.
180 Official Staff Commentary, 12 C.F.R. § 202.9(a)(1)-7.
181 Reg. B, 12 C.F.R. § 202.2(f). Proposed changes to Regulation B's definition of application, found at 12 C.F.R. § 202.9(f), are discussed at § 10.2.4.1, *supra*.

notify the applicant and provide the applicant a reasonable opportunity to complete the application.[182] The creditor may violate the ECOA if it deliberately delays obtaining the information necessary to complete an application.[183]

The implication of these standards is that the creditor may not avail itself of the special notification standards for incomplete applications if it has not acted reasonably in collecting the necessary information. Instead, the creditor must either offer the credit or comply with the time deadlines and other requirements for issuing an adverse action notice.[184]

10.2.8.2 Creditor Notification Options When Application Is Incomplete

The creditor must take one of two actions within thirty days after receiving an incomplete application: 1) notify the applicant of action taken on the application, or 2) notify the applicant that further information is needed.[185] Creditors that have acted on one-hundred-fifty or fewer applications during the preceding calendar year may notify the applicant orally of these facts.[186]

In considering the first option, the creditor must first ascertain that the incompleteness is based on information that the applicant must provide and that the creditor lacks sufficient data for a credit decision. The creditor may then deny the application, giving as the reason for the denial that the application is incomplete.[187] If the incompleteness does not prevent a credit decision from being made, the creditor may evaluate the application and make a decision. In that situation, the incompleteness is not the reason for the adverse action.[188]

When choosing the second option, the creditor must send an oral or written notice to the applicant specifying the information needed, designating a reasonable period of time to provide the information, and informing the applicant that failure to provide the information requested will result in no further consideration being given to the application.[189] If the applicant does not respond to an oral notice, the creditor must then within thirty days send a written notice with a new time period to respond.[190]

If the applicant does not respond within the designated reasonable period of time to a written notice, the creditor does not need to take further action.[191] If information requested by the creditor is submitted after the time period designated by the creditor, the creditor may require the applicant to make a new application.[192] If the applicant supplies the requested information within the time period specified in either the oral or written notice, the creditor must then take action and notify the applicant of the action taken as if the application was first submitted on that date.[193]

10.2.9 Withdrawn Applications for Credit

When an applicant expressly withdraws an application for credit, the creditor need not comply with the notification requirements.[194] The creditor must still comply, however, with the record retention provisions required by the ECOA.[195]

Regulation B makes special provision for situations in which it is contemplated that the applicant will inquire about the application's status.[196] If such an application is denied, the usual requirements for adverse action notification must be met.[197] If such an application for credit is approved, but

182 Official Staff Commentary, 12 C.F.R. § 202.2(f)-5.
183 *See, e.g.,* Saldana v. Citibank, 1996 U.S. Dist. LEXIS 8327 (N.D. Ill. June 13, 1996) (because Citibank regularly obtains and considers appraisals to complete an application, plaintiff's application was not complete until creditor received appraisal; although not the case here, court stated that there may be an impermissible motive if creditor deliberately delays obtaining the information necessary to complete an application).
184 *But see* Howard Oaks, Inc. v. Md. Nat'l Bank, 810 F. Supp. 674, 678 (D. Md. 1993) (when plaintiff, a defaulting commercial borrower, conceded that it never submitted a formal application for additional credit but instead supplied letters and documents, no ECOA liability found; "ECOA liability [for violation of 15 U.S.C. § 1691(d)(1)] cannot rest upon anything but a 'completed application'").
185 Reg. B, 12 C.F.R. § 202.9(c); *see also* Official Staff Commentary, 12 C.F.R. § 202.9(c).
186 Reg. B, 12 C.F.R. § 202.9(d); *cf.* Palmiotto v. Bank of N.Y., 1989 U.S. Dist. LEXIS 11546 (S.D.N.Y. Sept. 29, 1989) (creditor who did not show that it was eligible to give only oral notice could not prevail on its argument that consumer's ECOA claim was time-barred based on date of oral notice).
187 Official Staff Commentary, 12 C.F.R. § 202.9(a)(1)-3.
188 Official Staff Commentary, 12 C.F.R. § 202.9(a)(1)-4.
189 Reg. B, 12 C.F.R. § 202.9(c)(2).
190 Reg. B, 12 C.F.R. § 202.9(c)(3); Official Staff Commentary, 12 C.F.R. § 202.9(c)(3)-1.
191 *See* Reg. B, 12 C.F.R. §§ 202.9(c), 202.2(f); *see also* Cartwright v. Am. Sav. & Loan Ass'n, 880 F.2d 912 (7th Cir. 1989) (mortgage lender did not violate ECOA when it placed application on indefinite hold after requesting that applicant herself provide information on comparable housing prices in a largely minority neighborhood; nor was lender required to provide notice of adverse action, because none had occurred).
192 Official Staff Commentary, 12 C.F.R. § 202.9(c)(2)-1.
193 Reg. B, 12 C.F.R. § 202.9(c)(2); Official Staff Commentary, 12 C.F.R. § 202.9(c)(3)-1.
194 Official Staff Commentary, 12 C.F.R. § 202.9-2; *see also* Thompson v. Galles Chevrolet Co., 807 F.2d 163 (10th Cir. 1986) (when truck purchasers submitted two credit applications to the same finance company through two different dealers and credit was approved on the second application, there was no need for written notification that the creditor had stopped considering the first application, which was incomplete and arguably withdrawn); Freeman v. Koerner Ford of Scranton, 536 A.2d 340 (Pa. Super. Ct. 1987) (creditor need not give notice of adverse action when plaintiff purchased same vehicle elsewhere three days after application, effectively withdrawing the application).
195 Official Staff Commentary, 12 C.F.R. § 202.9-2; *see* § 10.3, *infra* (record retention requirements).
196 Reg. B, 12 C.F.R. § 202.9(e).
197 *See* Reg. B, 12 C.F.R. § 202.9(a)(1)(ii).

the applicant does not inquire about its status within thirty days after submission of the application, the creditor may consider the application withdrawn and need not comply with Regulation B's notification requirements.[198]

10.2.10 Notice to Multiple Applicants

When there is more than one applicant for credit, the required notification need be given to only one applicant—the primary applicant, if one is apparent.[199] There is a possibility of unlawful discrimination in the identification of the primary applicant. A creditor might assume, for instance, that the husband in a married couple is the primary applicant.

10.2.11 Notice By Multiple Creditors

Often, a credit applicant simultaneously submits applications to several creditors to ensure that credit will be obtained from one of them. This frequently occurs in real estate transactions and auto purchases, in which a broker or dealer might send information about an applicant to several lending sources.

If the applicant expressly accepts or uses the credit offered by any one creditor in connection with an application to multiple creditors submitted through a third party, no notice of adverse action need be provided by any other creditor that may have rejected the application.[200] If, on the other hand, no credit is offered by any creditor, or the applicant does not expressly accept or use any credit offered, each creditor that took adverse action must comply with Regulation B's adverse action notification requirements.[201]

Although multiple entities may be involved, only one notice to the applicant is required.[202] A third party, such as a broker or dealer, or one of the creditors may provide this notification on behalf of all of the creditors, identifying each creditor that took adverse action.[203] A creditor is not liable if the third party violates the notice requirements if the creditor accurately and in a timely manner provided the third party with the information necessary for the notification *and* maintained reasonable procedures adapted to prevent such violations by the third party.[204] Reasonable procedures might include a contract imposing on the third party both an obligation to notify the applicant and a procedure for verifying to the creditor that the notification was given.

10.2.12 Notification Requirement for Loans to Be Secured By a Dwelling

A 1991 amendment to the ECOA[205] requires that creditors provide applicants with notice of their right to receive a copy of any appraisal report on a dwelling which would secure the loan obligation being sought.[206] The statute gives this right concerning any loan that will be secured by a lien on residential real property,[207] whether or not the credit is for a consumer or business purpose.[208] The statute also specifies that the creditor may require reimbursement from the applicant for the cost of the appraisal.[209]

---

198 Reg. B, 12 C.F.R. § 202.9(a)(1).

199 Reg. B, 12 C.F.R. § 202.9(f).

200 Reg. B, 12 C.F.R. § 202.9(g); *see also* Thompson v. Galles Chevrolet Co., 807 F.2d 163 (10th Cir. 1986) (when truck purchasers submitted two credit applications to the same finance company through two different dealers and credit was approved on the second application, there was no need for written notification that the creditor had stopped considering the first application, which was incomplete and arguably withdrawn).

201 Reg. B, 12 C.F.R. § 202.9(g); *see also* High v. McLean Fin. Corp., 659 F. Supp. 1561 (D.D.C. 1987). In this case, the plaintiffs submitted a mortgage application to McLean Financial Corporation. But it was AmeriWest Mortgage Corporation, an entity unknown to the plaintiffs at the time they made the application, who notified them that their mortgage application had been denied. McLean did not provide a notice of adverse action.

The question of McLean's liability for failing to provide a notice of adverse action hinged upon whether AmeriWest was merely McLean's "assignee, transferee, or subrogee" and therefore within Regulation B's definition of creditor, or whether the two entities were separate creditors. The court noted that "[w]hile neither the law nor the regulations provides that a primary lender must inform an applicant that another financial institution is involved in the decision to extend credit, the

regulations clearly provide that each 'creditor' taking adverse action against the applicant must notify the applicant of that decision." *Id.* at 1564 (citation omitted).

202 *See, e.g.*, Burns v. Elmhurst Auto Mall Inc., 2001 U.S. Dist. LEXIS 6385 (N.D. Ill. May 16, 2001).

203 Reg. B, 12 C.F.R. § 202.9(g); Official Staff Commentary, 12 C.F.R. § 202.9(g)-1. If the creditors are under the jurisdiction of different federal enforcement agencies, the notice need not name each agency; disclosure of just one will suffice. Official Staff Commentary, 12 C.F.R. § 202.9(g)-2.

204 Official Staff Commentary, 12 C.F.R. § 202.9(g)-3.

205 The Federal Deposit Insurance Corporation Improvement Act of 1991, Pub. L. No. 102-242, 105 Stat. 2300, 2306 (1991) (adding 15 U.S.C. § 1691(e)).

206 The Federal Reserve Board has proposed requiring this notice to be clear and conspicuous and in a form the applicant can retain. 64 Fed. Reg. 44,582, 44,596 (Aug. 16, 1999).

207 15 U.S.C. § 1691(e).

208 Official Staff Commentary, 12 C.F.R. § 202.5a(a)-1. This applies to applications for renewal of existing credit secured by a dwelling as well, if the creditor obtains and uses a new appraisal report in evaluating the request. Official Staff Commentary, 12 C.F.R. § 202.5a(a)-2. In April 2001, the Federal Reserve Board published an interim final rule amending Regulation B to provide for electronic disclosures. The rule would permit ECOA disclosures to be made using electronic means of communication as long as the creditor complies with the consumer consent provisions of the E-Sign Act. The rule would exempt a few ECOA notices from the E-Sign Act protections, including the notice of appraisal. This notice may be provided solely in electronic form, even if the application is submitted on paper. *See* 66 Fed. Reg. 17,779 (Apr. 4, 2001); § 10.2.6.2.1, *supra*.

209 15 U.S.C. § 1691(e).

Appraisal reports include any report prepared by an appraiser, any document prepared by the creditor's staff that assigns value to the property when no third-party report was used, and internal review documents reflecting that the creditor's valuation is different from that in a third party's report or different from valuations that are publicly available.[210] However, the term does not include other reports such as internal documents when a third-party appraisal report was used to establish property value, government agency statements of appraised value, valuation lists that are publicly available (such as published sales prices or mortgage amounts, tax assessments, and retail price ranges), or valuations such as manufacturer's invoices for mobile homes.[211]

Creditors must disclose to applicants their right to receive a copy of the appraisal report, unless the creditor automatically provides appraisal reports to all applicants without being requested to do so.[212] The regulation requires that notice of this right to an appraisal report be made in writing, and must state that the request for the report must made be in writing, give the time for making a request, and include the creditor's address.[213] This notice may be delivered at any time during the application process, but no later than when the creditor provides the requisite notice of action taken.[214] When a transaction involves more than one applicant, notice need only be given to one applicant, but it must given to the primary applicant—if readily apparent who that is.[215]

The statute requires that the applicant make the request for the appraisal report within a reasonable period of time of the application.[216] Regulation B states that the written request must be received by the creditor within ninety days of the creditor's notice of action taken or the applicant's withdrawal of the application.[217]

The statute also requires that the creditor "promptly" furnish the appraisal report to the applicant.[218] The regulation states that if the applicant timely sends a written request for an appraisal report, the creditor should provide the applicant with the report within thirty days of receiving the request, the report, or reimbursement of the cost of the appraisal, whichever occurs last.[219]

10.2.13 Exceptions to Notice Requirements

10.2.13.1 Incidental Consumer Credit

The ECOA notice requirements do not apply to incidental consumer credit.[220] Incidental consumer credit is defined as:

- Primarily for personal, family, or household purposes;
- Not made pursuant to the terms of a credit card account;
- Not subject to any finance charge or interest; and
- Not payable by agreement in more than four installments.[221]

Examples of incidental consumer credit may include (as long as there is no finance charge and no more than four installments) deferment of payment by doctors, home oil companies, hospitals, and some small retailers.[222]

Even though courts have found these types of transactions to be "credit" transactions under the ECOA, the incidental credit exception allows the creditors to avoid complying with important ECOA requirements, including the notice requirements.[223] However, incidental creditors are required to comply with the general prohibition against discrimination, among other ECOA provisions.[224]

10.2.13.2 Potential Legal Challenges to Failure to Notify Consumer of Denial of Incidental Consumer Credit

There are two main legal theories why a consumer is entitled to some notification of the denial of incidental consumer credit. One possible, but not very practical, approach is to challenge the Federal Reserve Board's authority to make this exception.[225]

However, even if a challenge to the regulatory exclusion were successful, the consumer would obtain only prospective relief and perhaps attorney fees. The creditor would not be liable for money damages for the failure to notify the consumer because the creditor will assert the ECOA defense of good faith compliance with Federal Reserve Board regulations.[226]

A state UDAP claim is a more direct way to challenge the failure to notify the consumer of denial of incidental con-

210 Official Staff Commentary, 12 C.F.R. § 202.5a(c)(1).
211 Official Staff Commentary, 12 C.F.R. § 202.5a(c)(2).
212 Official Staff Commentary, 12 C.F.R. § 202.5a(a)(2).
213 Official Staff Commentary, 12 C.F.R. § 202.5a(a)(2)(i).
214 Official Staff Commentary, 12 C.F.R. § 202.5a(a)(2)(i).
215 Official Staff Commentary, 12 C.F.R. § 202.5a(a)(2)(i)-1.
216 15 U.S.C. § 1691(e).
217 Reg. B, 12 C.F.R. § 202.5a(a)(2)(ii).
218 15 U.S.C. § 1691(e).
219 Reg. B, 12 C.F.R. § 202.5a(a)(2)(ii).

220 Reg. B, 12 C.F.R. § 202.3(c)(2)(vi).
221 Reg. B, 12 C.F.R. § 202.3(c); *see also* Official Staff Commentary, 12 C.F.R. § 202.3(c); § 2.2.6.3, *supra*.
222 *See* § 2.2.6.3, *supra*.
223 *See, e.g.*, Mays v. Buckeye Rural Coop. Inc., 277 F.3d 873 (6th Cir. 2002); Williams v. AT & T Wireless Services, Inc., 5 F. Supp. 2d 1142 (W. D. Wash. 1998) (application for cellular phone service held to be incidental credit and creditor exempted from notice requirements.).
224 Official Staff Commentary, 12 C.F.R. § 202.3-1.
225 *See* § 2.2.6.4, *supra*.
226 15 U.S.C. § 1691e(e); *see also* § 11.8.3.1, *infra*.

sumer credit.[227] The creditor's failure to disclose the action taken is an unfair and deceptive act because it is deceptive to fail to disclose an important part of a sales transaction, in this case that the creditor will not defer payment.[228] Nevertheless, it is more difficult to prove a UDAP violation when the creditor has notified the consumer of the denial of credit, but has not disclosed the reason for the denial. The reason for the denial of credit may not be a material factor in the purchase of the goods or services.

10.2.14 Business Credit

10.2.14.1 General

The notification rules are looser for business credit, with one set of rules for relatively small business applicants and another set for larger business applicants. Creditors may, if they choose, comply with the consumer notification requirements for business credit or they may comply with the small business requirements for all businesses.[229]

In deciding whether business or consumer credit is involved, the primary purpose of the application controls.[230] Thus if a consumer purchases a pick-up truck primarily for consumer use, but also for occasional business use, the transaction involves consumer credit. The Truth in Lending Act also uses the primary purpose test, and cases interpreting that provision may provide useful guidance in this area.[231] Under Truth in Lending, there is little doubt that primary is not synonymous with exclusive. At the very least, though, primary must refer to the use of more than half the proceeds of the transaction.[232]

10.2.14.2 Rules for Small Business Applicants

The Federal Reserve Board has set out special notification rules for certain small businesses. These rules apply to businesses with gross revenues of one million dollars or less (except for trade or factoring credit[233]), to applications to start a business, and to most applications by an individual for business purpose credit (except that when an applicant applies for credit as a sole proprietor, the revenues of the sole proprietorship govern.)[234]

For these small business applicants, the creditor has to comply with the normal notification requirements with the following three exceptions. First, the creditor's notice of any adverse action taken may be made either orally or in writing[235] (for non-business credit, only very small creditors may utilize oral notification).

Second, for most credit applicants, if a creditor opts not to disclose the reasons for taking an adverse action, the creditor must disclose to the applicant *after the adverse action is taken* that the applicant has a right to a statement of the reasons for the adverse action. For business applicants, the creditor has the option to disclose the applicant's right to a statement of reasons in writing *at the time of the application*.[236]

The third exception for small business applicants is that, for telephone applications, a creditor may simply give notice of the action taken or of the right to a statement of reasons over the telephone.[237]

10.2.14.3 Rules for Other Business Applicants

Creditors may comply, if they like, with an even looser set of notification rules for other business applicants. These different rules apply for businesses with revenues over one million dollars and with respect to applications for trade credit and credit incident to a factoring agreement. The creditor may rely on the applicant's assertion as to the size of the business's revenue.[238]

The creditor may notify the applicant either orally or in writing of action taken within a reasonable time, without any notice of the reasons for the action taken or notice of the right to obtain those reasons.[239] The creditor only needs to provide a written statement of the reasons for the action taken if the applicant makes a written request within sixty days after being notified of the adverse action.[240]

227 *See* § 1.8, *supra* (discussion of state UDAP statutes).

228 *See* National Consumer Law Center, Unfair and Deceptive Acts and Practices § 4.2.14 (5th ed. 2001).

229 Official Staff Commentary, 12 C.F.R. § 202.9(a)(3)-4.

230 Official Staff Commentary, 12 C.F.R. § 202.2(g)-1, *as amended by* 54 Fed. Reg. 12,471 (Apr. 4, 1990) (formerly § 202.3(d)(1)-1).

231 *E.g.*, Gallegos v. Stokes, 593 F.2d 372 (10th Cir. 1979); Redhouse v. Quality Ford Sales, Inc., 523 F.2d 1 (10th Cir. 1975) (en banc) (per curiam) (superseding 511 F.2d 230 (10th Cir. 1975)); Smith v. Chapman, 436 F. Supp. 58 (W.D. Tex. 1977). *See generally* National Consumer Law Center, Truth in Lending § 2.4.2.1 (4th ed. 1999 and Supp.).

232 *See, e.g.*, Palmer v. Statewide Group, 134 F.3d 378 (9th Cir. 1998) (consumers' use of their home for child care business did not make loan a business loan); Semar v. Platte Valley Fed. Sav. & Loan Ass'n, 791 F.2d 699 (9th Cir. 1986) (loan primarily for personal use if only ten percent of proceeds used for business purposes and primary purpose of loan was to pay off a second trust deed loan on the consumer's house); Gombosi v. Carteret Mortgage Corp., 894 F. Supp. 176 (E.D. Pa. 1995) (majority of loan proceeds used for business purpose). *See generally* National Consumer Law Center, Truth in Lending § 2.4.2.1 (4th ed. 1999 and Supp.).

233 *See* Official Staff Commentary, §§ 12 C.F.R. § 202.9(a)(3)-2, 202.9(a)(3)-3 (definitions of trade and factoring credit).

234 Official Staff Commentary, 12 C.F.R. § 202.9(a)(3)-1.

235 Reg. B, 12 C.F.R. § 202.9(a)(3)(i)(A).

236 Reg. B, 12 C.F.R. § 202.9(a)(3)(i)(B).

237 Reg. B, 12 C.F.R. § 202.9(a)(3)(i)(C).

238 Official Staff Commentary, 12 C.F.R. § 202.9(a)(3).

239 If the notification occurs within the general time frames prescribed in 12 C.F.R. § 202.9(a)(1), that is deemed reasonable. Official Staff Commentary, 12 C.F.R. § 202.9(a)(3)- 5.

240 Reg. B, 12 C.F.R. § 202.9(a)(3)(ii). The Federal Reserve Board

10.2.15 Creditor's Inadvertent Error May Excuse Notice Violations

An inadvertent error by the creditor is not a violation of the notification requirements, provided that the creditor corrects the error as soon as possible after discovering it.[241] Inadvertent errors include clerical mistakes, calculation errors, computer malfunctions, and printing errors. An error of legal judgment is not an inadvertent error.[242] One case discussing the thirty-day period for responding to requests for specific reasons for adverse action taken has held that a creditor that failed to respond to these requests within the prescribed period could not avail itself of an inadvertent error defense based on the allegation that it employed insufficient staff to respond in a timely fashion.[243]

10.3 ECOA Record Retention Requirements

10.3.1 Preservation of Records

Creditors generally must retain records of credit transactions for approximately as long as the ECOA statute of limitations. A creditor must retain the original or a copy of each of the following documents for twenty-five months following the date it notifies an applicant of the action taken on an application (or of an incomplete application):[244]

- Any application form that the creditor receives;
- Information obtained for monitoring purposes;[245]
- Any other written or recorded information used in evaluating the application and not returned to the applicant upon request;
- Written notification to the applicant of the action taken on the application, or notes concerning oral notification;
- Written notification to the applicant of the specific reasons for adverse action taken, or notes concerning oral notification; and
- Any written statement submitted by the applicant alleging a violation of the ECOA or Regulation B.

Written copies need not be retained by creditors using a computerized system providing that the information can be regenerated in a timely fashion.[246]

When adverse action has been taken on a credit transaction outside of the application process, such as when the creditor has terminated or changed the terms of an existing account, the creditor also must preserve the following records for twenty-five months after notifying the applicant of the adverse action taken:[247]

- Any written or recorded information concerning the adverse action taken; and
- Any written statement submitted by the applicant alleging a violation of the ECOA or Regulation B.

The Federal Reserve Board has also proposed that creditors who solicit potential customers for credit be required to retain any preapproved credit solicitation, the list of criteria the creditor used to select the recipients of the solicitation, any correspondence related to complaints about the solicitation, and any component of any marketing plan related to the solicitation.[248] The creditor would be required to keep the information for twenty-five months, or for twelve months for certain types of business credit.[249] The Board

---

has proposed requiring creditors to disclose to such other business applicants their right to a written statement of reasons for adverse action taken. 64 Fed. Reg. 44,582, 44,599 (Aug. 16, 1999).

241 Reg. B, 12 C.F.R. § 202.14(c); *see also* Sayers v. Gen. Motors Acceptance Corp., 522 F. Supp. 835 (W.D. Mo. 1981) (no ECOA violation when credit denial was based on an inadvertent misinterpretation of the credit history; however, creditor's subsequent willful refusal to comply with notification requirements after being informed of its error did constitute an ECOA violation).

242 Official Staff Commentary, 12 C.F.R. § 202.14(c)-1.

243 *See* Desselles v. J.C. Penney Co., [1974-1980 Decisions Transfer Binder] Consumer Cred. Guide (CCH) ¶ 97,536 (E.D. La. 1979).

244 Reg. B, 12 C.F.R. § 202.12(b). The Federal Reserve Board has proposed extending the record retention requirement for credit applications of businesses with one million dollars or less in gross revenues from twelve to twenty-five months. Larger businesses would remain subject to the shorter sixty-day period allowed by 12 C.F.R. § 202.12(b)(5). 64 Fed. Reg. 44,582, 44,600–44,601 (Aug. 16, 1999) (proposing revisions to 12 C.F.R. § 202.12(b)); *see also* Maunsell v. Greenspan, 1998 U.S. App. LEXIS 10306 (2d Cir. May 11, 1998) (Federal Reserve Board acted within the scope of its authority in establishing the record retention requirement); United States v. City Fin. Co., Clearinghouse No. 45,752 (N.D. Ga. 1990) (consent decree partially based on allegations that creditor did not retain written records of applications or statements of adverse action for the required time period); United States v. Fidelity Acceptance

Corp., Clearinghouse No. 38,923 (D. Minn. 1985) (consent order partially based on creditor's alleged failure to retain records of rejected applications); United States v. Sec. Pac. Fin. Sys., Clearinghouse No. 37,095 (S.D. Cal. 1983) ($140,000 civil penalty partially based on allegations that creditor failed to retain credit applications and related information for twenty-five months following notice of adverse action); United States v. Lender Serv., Inc., Clearinghouse No. 33,788 (N.D. Okla. 1982) (creditor agreed to pay a $10,000 civil penalty partially based on its alleged repeated failure to keep rejected credit applications on file for the required twenty-five months).

245 *See* § 4.4.7, *supra.*

246 Official Staff Commentary, 12 C.F.R. § 202.12(b)-1.

247 Reg. B, 12 C.F.R. § 202.12(b)(2). The Federal Reserve Board has proposed revising 12 C.F.R. § 202.12(b)(2) to reflect the proposed extension of the record retention period for small businesses. 64 Fed. Reg. 44,582, 44,600 (Aug. 16, 1999).

248 64 Fed. Reg. at 44,601 (proposing to add 12 C.F.R. § 202.12(b)(7)).

249 64 Fed. Reg. at 44,601.

opted for this requirement, believing the information would allow review and analysis of creditors' possible use of prohibited bases in their preapproved credit solicitations, rather than extending the ECOA to govern prescreened credit solicitations.[250]

10.3.2 Transactions Exempt From Record Retention Requirements

Certain creditors are exempt from some of Regulation B's record retention requirements. Among those creditors who are exempt are public utilities,[251] creditors dealing in securities credit,[252] incidental consumer creditors,[253] and creditors extending credit to governments or governmental subunits and agencies.[254]

Creditors providing business credit have different record retention requirements.[255] In the case of relatively small business applicants, the same rules apply as for consumer applicants, except that the twenty-five-month retention period is shortened to twelve months. However, the Federal Reserve Board has proposed extending the record retention period for small business applications to twenty-five months,[256] believing that technical advances have alleviated concerns that such storage would be too costly and space consuming.[257]

In the case of larger business applicants, or with respect to certain specified types of business credit,[258] records need be retained only for sixty days unless, within that time, the applicant makes a written request *either* for a statement of the reasons for an adverse action taken or that the records be retained. In that case, the records are to be retained for twelve months.[259]

In deciding whether an application is for business or consumer credit, the primary purpose of the application controls.[260] Thus, if a consumer purchases a pick-up truck primarily for consumer use but also for occasional business use, the transaction involves consumer credit.

10.3.3 Retention of Prohibited Information

The ECOA and Regulation B prohibit creditors from requesting certain types of information.[261] However, creditors may retain any information in their files, even if use of it would violate the ECOA or Regulation B, provided that the information was obtained:

- From any source prior to March 23, 1977;
- At any time, from consumer reporting agencies or others without the specific request of the creditor;
- At any time, from the applicant if the creditor did not specifically request the information; or
- At any time, if required for federal or state monitoring.[262]

Thus, creditors may retain in their files the type of information which was the basis of much past credit discrimination. For example, they may retain information on birth control and childbearing; information about marital status even when it is irrelevant to creditworthiness; or references to the race of the applicant or the ethnic makeup of the applicant's neighborhood, provided the information was obtained either voluntarily from the applicant or from a third party such as a neighbor or a credit reporting agency. However, creditors may not use prohibited information in evaluating credit applications unless expressly permitted to do so.[263]

10.3.4 Preservation of Records in Case of an Investigation, Enforcement Proceeding, or Civil Action

Any creditor which has actual notice that it is under investigation or is subject to an enforcement proceeding for a violation of the ECOA or Regulation B, or which has been

250 64 Fed. Reg. at 44,584–44,585; *see* § 5.3.2.5, *supra*.
251 Reg. B, 12 C.F.R. § 202.3(a)(2)(iii); *see also* § 2.2.6.2, *supra*.
252 Reg. B, 12 C.F.R. § 202.3(b)(2)(viii); *see* § 2.2.6.6, *supra*.
253 Reg. B, 12 C.F.R. § 202.3(c)(2)(viii); *see* § 2.2.6.3, *supra*.
254 Reg. B, 12 C.F.R. § 202.3(d)(2); *see also* § 2.2.6.7, *supra*.
255 Reg. B, 12 C.F.R. § 202.12(b).
256 64 Fed. Reg. 44,582, 44,601 (Aug. 16, 1999) (proposing revisions to 12 C.F.R. § 202.12(b)). The proposed revisions to Regulation B are reproduced on the CD-Rom accompanying this volume.
257 64 Fed. Reg. 44,582, 44,601 (Aug. 16, 1999).
258 Reg. B, 12 C.F.R. § 202.9(a)(3). "Trade credit, credit incident to a factoring agreement, or other similar types of business credit," defined at Official Staff Commentary, 12 C.F.R. § 202.9(a)(3)-2, -3.
259 Reg. B, 12 C.F.R. § 202.12(b)(5). The Supplementary Information published when this regulation was enacted makes it clear that either request from the applicant will trigger the twelve-month retention requirement, thus eliminating the need for the applicant to make two separate requests. 54 Fed. Reg. 50,485 (Dec. 7, 1989).
260 Official Staff Commentary, 12 C.F.R. § 202.2(g)-1, *as amended*

by 54 Fed. Reg. 12471 (Apr. 4, 1990) (formerly § 202.3(d)(1)-1). The Truth in Lending Act also uses the primary purpose test, and cases interpreting that provision may provide useful guidance. *E.g.*, Gallegos v. Stokes, 593 F.2d 372 (10th Cir. 1979); Redhouse v. Quality Ford Sales, Inc., 523 F.2d 1 (10th Cir. 1975), (en banc) (per curiam) (superseding 511 F.2d 230 (10th Cir. 1975); Smith v. Chapman, 436 F. Supp. 58 (W.D. Tex. 1977). *See generally* National Consumer Law Center, Truth in Lending § 2.4.2.1 (4th ed. 1999 and Supp.).
261 *See* § 4.4.8, *supra* (prohibit requests for information). Note that the Federal Reserve Board proposed revisions to Regulation B that would allow creditors to make requests for this information with certain safeguards. 64 Fed. Reg. 44,582, 44,594 (Aug. 16, 1999).
262 Reg. B, 12 C.F.R. § 202.12(a).
263 Official Staff Commentary, 12 C.F.R. § 202.12(a)-2.

served with notice that a civil action has been filed, must retain all required records concerning applications in general and those concerning other transactions in which adverse action has been taken. These records must be retained until final disposition of the enforcement proceeding or civil action, unless an earlier time is allowed by order of the agency or court involved.[264]

10.3.5 Multiple Creditors

In transactions involving more than one creditor, even those creditors not required to comply with the notification provisions of Regulation B[265] must retain all written or recorded information they possess concerning the applicant, for a period as long as that required of the creditor who is required to notify.[266] This information must include any notations concerning adverse actions taken.

---

264 Reg. B, 12 C.F.R. § 202.12(b)(4).

265 *See* § 10.2.11, *supra.*

266 Reg. B, 12 C.F.R. § 202.12(b)(3). The Federal Reserve Board has proposed revising 12 C.F.R. § 202.12(b)(3) to reflect the proposed extension of the retention period for small business applications. 64 Fed. Reg. 44,582, 44,600 (Aug. 16, 1999). The proposed revisions to Regulation B are reproduced on the CD-Rom accompanying this volume.

10.3.6 Inadvertent Error

Failure to comply with the ECOA record retention requirements does not constitute a violation when caused by an inadvertent error.[267] Inadvertent errors include clerical mistakes, calculation errors, computer malfunctions, and printing errors. An error of legal judgment is not an inadvertent error.[268] One case discussing the thirty-day period for responding to requests for specific reasons for adverse action taken has held that a creditor which failed to respond to these requests within the prescribed period could not avail itself of an inadvertent error defense based on the allegation that it employed insufficient staff to respond in a timely fashion.[269]

When a creditor engages in an inadvertent error concerning recordkeeping, the creditor need not correct the past error. The creditor need only correct the error prospectively.[270]

---

267 Reg. B, 12 C.F.R. § 202.14(c).

268 Official Staff Commentary, 12 C.F.R. § 202.14(c)-1.

269 *See* Desselles v. J.C. Penney Co., [1974-1980 Decisions Transfer Binder] Consumer Cred. Guide (CCH) ¶ 97,536 (E.D. La. 1979).

270 Official Staff Commentary, 12 C.F.R. § 202.14(c)-2.

Chapter 11   Litigating a Credit Discrimination Case

11.1 Introduction

This chapter reviews key issues to consider in bringing private credit discrimination litigation. The next chapter focuses on government enforcement actions.

Plaintiffs may have difficulty establishing standing in credit discrimination cases. These issues are covered in section 11.2, including a separate section focusing on standing for testers and non-profit organizations. The next section (§ 11.3) discusses possible defendants to sue in credit discrimination litigation.

Section 11.4 covers forum selection issues, particularly choices regarding federal versus state court, administrative procedures for FHA claims, and issues related to mandatory arbitration clauses. Section 11.5 provides a guide for advocates in selecting causes of action in credit discrimination cases. This section is followed by an extensive discussion of private remedies in section 11.6. A key issue is whether plaintiffs may be awarded punitive damages in credit discrimination cases.

The final sections review creditor defenses, including statute of limitations issues (§ 11.7) and other creditor defenses unique to credit discrimination cases (§ 11.8).

11.2 Does the Plaintiff Have Standing?

11.2.1 General

Under any of the credit discrimination statutes, it is important that the plaintiff be "aggrieved" by the statutory violation. Otherwise, the plaintiff may not have standing under Article III of the U.S. Constitution. Moreover, both the ECOA and the Fair Housing Act provide private remedies only for "aggrieved" persons.[1]

Aggrieved person is defined in Fair Housing regulations as any person who claims to be injured by a discriminatory housing practice or believes he or she will be injured by a discriminatory housing practice that is about to occur.[2] This requirement that the plaintiff be aggrieved under the Fair Housing Act is to be generously construed to foster "truly integrated and balanced living patterns."[3]

The Supreme Court has held that Congress intended standing under the Fair Housing Act to "extend to the full limits of Article III," thereby eliminating the prudential barriers to standing.[4] There are limits to this broad standard. In particular, federal statutes may not abrogate the minimum requirement of Article III that a plaintiff demonstrate: 1) an injury in fact, 2) a causal connection between the injury and the conduct complained of, and 3) the likelihood, as opposed to mere speculation, that the injury will be redressed by a favorable decision.[5]

The broad FHA standing provisions, for the most part, also apply to Civil Rights Act claims. However, there are a few limits to consider when seeking standing for plaintiffs under the federal Civil Rights Acts. If an action is brought under section 1982, the plaintiff must be a United States citizen.[6] The same requirement does not apply for section 1981, the ECOA, or the Fair Housing Act.

Section 1981 protects the right to make and enforce contracts.[7] Thus only parties to the contract at issue will generally have standing.[8] However, those who are not parties to contracts may have standing under section 1982, which protects the right to "inherit, purchase, lease, sell, hold and convey real and personal property."

The ECOA has an important standing limitation. Only "applicants" can bring actions. The definition of applicant is broader than the term implies, including not only those who seek credit but those who have been extended credit. The term also applies not just to the primary obligor but also to

---

1   15 U.S.C. § 1691e; 42 U.S.C. § 3613; *see, e.g.,* Lee v. Fed. Deposit Ins. Corp., 1997 U.S. Dist. LEXIS 13885 (S.D.N.Y. Sept. 12, 1997); *cf.* Assisted Living Group, Inc. v. Upper Dublin Township, 1997 U.S. Dist. LEXIS 19554 (E.D. Pa. Dec. 2, 1997) (intervention denied in FHA case).

2   24 C.F.R. § 100.20.

3   Trafficante v. Metro. Life Ins. Co., 409 U.S. 205, 211, 93 S. Ct. 364, 34 L. Ed. 2d 415 (1972).

4   Havens Realty Corp. v. Coleman, 455 U.S. 363, 373–75, 102 S. Ct. 1114, 71 L. Ed. 2d 214 (1982); Gladstone Realtors v. Vill. of Bellwood, 441 U.S. 91, 103, 99 S. Ct. 1601, 60 L. Ed. 2d 66 (1979); Trafficante v. Metro. Life Ins. Co., 409 U.S. 205, 93 S. Ct. 364, 34 L. Ed. 2d 415 (1972).

5   Lujan v. Defenders of Wildlife, 504 U.S. 555, 560–61, 112 S. Ct. 2130, 119 L. Ed. 2d 351 (1992).

6   *See* § 2.4, *supra.*

7   *See* §§ 1.5, 2.4, *supra.*

8   *See, e.g.,* Hargraves v. Capital City Mortgage Corp., 147 F. Supp. 2d 1, 3 (D.D.C. 2001).

others obligated on the debt.[9] For example, a husband required to put up a mortgage to secure a note signed by his wife is an applicant.[10] A major practical implication of the applicant standing requirement under the ECOA is that it will be more difficult for an organization representing applicants to bring an ECOA action than a Fair Housing Act case.[11]

11.2.2 Do Testers and Non-Profit Organizations Have Standing?

11.2.2.1 General

As noted in the previous section, the ECOA's limiting of actions to applicants poses a major barrier for testers and non-profit organizations hoping to bring ECOA claims. Although the definition of applicant may be interpreted broadly, it generally will not apply to organizations acting on behalf of persons alleging discrimination.[12]

Standing for organizations and testers is much more likely to be obtained in FHA cases. The Department of Housing and Urban Development (HUD) has consistently interpreted the provisions of the fair housing laws to permit the filing of a complaint by any person or organization if an action that occurred or is about to occur would result in an injury to that person or organization.[13] Moreover, a series of United States Supreme Court cases, mainly from the 1970s and early 1980s, found that testers, nonprofit housing organizations, and municipalities had standing to bring Fair Housing Act claims. These cases made clear that municipalities can be affected by racial discrimination in housing patterns in various ways, including their tax base, and such injury is sufficient for a municipality to bring a Fair Housing Act case concerning discrimination as to its residents.[14] Similarly, the individual residents of an affected community have standing

by virtue of the loss of the benefits of an integrated community.[15]

The Supreme Court last ruled on this issue in 1982.[16] During this period of Supreme Court silence, the lower courts have split, in many cases eroding the previously generous standing requirements for testers and organizations.[17]

11.2.2.2 FHA Standing for Testers

Fair housing organizations often employ testers to uncover unlawful housing discrimination. Both the testers and the organizations that employ them may attempt to bring claims of unlawful discrimination. There are distinct issues when considering standing for testers as opposed to standing for organizations.

With respect to testers, courts have come to different conclusions depending on whether the testers can show that they were directly injured by the alleged discriminatory practices. The Supreme Court ruled in *Havens Realty Corp. v. Coleman* that section 3604(d) of the FHA, which entitles any person to truthful information concerning the availability of housing, is a statutorily created right sufficient to confer Article III standing.[18] However, the Court concluded that the white tester in this case did not have standing because he was not provided false information about the availability of housing and therefore was not injured.[19] The African-American tester, even though expecting to receive false information and even though not intending to rent an apartment, did suffer an injury according to the Court and therefore had standing under the FHA.[20] Since the *Havens* ruling, courts have split as to whether tester standing under § 3604(d) is applicable to other provisions of the FHA.[21]

Testers may also show standing through indirect injury.

9 *See* Reg. B, 12 C.F.R. § 202.2(e); §§ 2.2.4.1, 2.2.4.4, *supra*.
10 *See* Ford v. Citizens & S. Nat'l Bank, 700 F. Supp. 1121 (N.D. Ga. 1988).
11 *See* § 11.2.2, *infra*.
12 *See, e.g.*, Evans v. First Fed. Sav. Bank, 669 F. Supp. 915 (N.D. Ind. 1987) (nonprofit organization was not an applicant under the ECOA and so lacked standing to bring an ECOA action).
13 Preamble to Final Rule Implementing Fair Housing Act of 1988 § 100.20, 54 Fed. Reg. 3234 (Jan. 23, 1989). Note that the Preamble was withdrawn from 24 C.F.R. pt. 100, 61 Fed. Reg. 41,282 (Aug. 7, 1996), as part of the streamlining of regulations. "[T]his rule removes from title 24 the unnecessarily codified preamble to the final rule implementing the Fair Housing Amendments Act of 1988."
14 Havens Realty Corp. v. Coleman, 455 U.S. 363, 102 S. Ct. 1114, 71 L. Ed. 2d 214 (1982); Gladstone Realtors v. Vill. of Bellwood, 441 U.S. 91, 99 S. Ct. 1601, 60 L. Ed. 2d 66 (1979); Vill. of Bellwood v. Dwivedi, 895 F.2d 1521 (7th Cir. 1990).

15 Gladstone Realtors v. Vill. of Bellwood, 441 U.S. 91, 99 S. Ct. 1601, 60 L. Ed. 2d 66 (1979).
16 Havens Realty Corp. v. Coleman, 455 U.S. 363, 102 S. Ct. 1114, 71 L. Ed. 2d 214 (1982).
17 *See generally* Dash T. Douglas, *Standing on Shaky Ground: Standing Under the Fair Housing Act*, 34 Akron L. Rev. 613 (2001).
18 Havens Realty Corp. v. Coleman, 455 U.S. 363, 102 S. Ct. 1114, 71 L. Ed. 2d 214 (1982).
19 *Id*. at 375.
20 *Id*. at 374.
21 *Compare* Ragin v. Harry Macklowe Real Estate Co., 6 F.3d 898 (2d Cir. 1993) (testers who read allegedly discriminatory housing advertisements but were not necessarily in the market for housing had standing) *with* Wilson v. Glenwood Intermountain Properties, Inc. 98 F.3d 590 (10th Cir. 1996) (reading of a discriminatory advertisement by one who is not in the market for housing is insufficient to confer standing) *and* Ricks v. Beta Dev. Co., 92 F.3d 1193 (9th Cir. 1996) (unpublished) (text available at 1996 U.S. App. LEXIS 19743) (in denying standing, court limited the *Havens* result to provisions of the act explicitly providing protection to "any person."). *See generally* Dash T. Douglas, *Standing on Shaky Ground: Standing Under the Fair Housing Act*, 34 Akron L. Rev. 613 (2001).

This is most common in cases of racial steering when white residents of a neighborhood, for example, may suffer injury due to the loss of a diverse and integrated neighborhood. In *Havens*, the Court found that the white tester, as noted above, did not suffer a direct injury. In determining whether he had suffered an indirect injury, the key question considered was how wide of a geographic impact racial steering practices could have.

In *Havens*, the Court found that it was implausible that the discrimination could affect the entire city of Richmond.[22] The Court noted that it had upheld standing in other cases but only within a relatively compact neighborhood. However, the Court found that an injury could still be proven, leaving open the question of how broad an area fits within the definition of a "relatively compact neighborhood."[23]

11.2.2.3 FHA Standing for Organizational Plaintiffs

An organization, such as a non-profit fair housing organization, may have standing to assert its own interests in an FHA case. A fair housing organization may recover even if unlawful discrimination is found only involving its testers and not involving others.[24]

Although courts agree that organizations may attain standing on behalf of their members or on their own behalf, the key issue is what is required to show that the organization has suffered an injury. In general, the organization must have suffered a concrete and demonstrable injury to its activities, not merely a setback to the organization's abstract social interests.[25]

To date, the Second, Sixth, and Seventh Circuits have found that organizations may be injured if they can show that the time and resources spent investigating and pursuing the discrimination claims kept them from accomplishing other services, such as counseling individual clients. In essence, a drain on the organizations' resource can constitute the requisite injury in these circuits.[26] The D.C., Third, and Fifth Circuits reject this broad interpretation, holding that in order for an organization to demonstrate the requisite injury it must show an expenditure of resources on organizational activities independent of the lawsuit.[27] Other courts have

found a middle ground, holding that while resources expended on legal efforts do not in and of themselves result in the requisite injury, they should be considered when analyzing whether the organization has been injured.[28]

11.2.3 Associational Standing

The aggrieved individual bringing an ECOA, Fair Housing or Civil Rights Act suit need not be a member of the protected group being discriminated against, as long as the individual is injured by the discrimination.[29] For example, a white person can bring an action under any of the credit discrimination laws if denied credit because she lives in a predominantly African-American neighborhood or associates with African-Americans.[30]

The aggrieved individual under the Fair Housing Act and Civil Rights Acts need not even be the individual turned down for credit, but just someone aggrieved by that action. An individual not seeking credit can bring an action, such as those who would benefit if credit were granted to some other party. For example, consider an owner who rents a two-family home to one white family and one African-American family. If the owner is turned down for a loan to repair the home because an African-American family lives in the house, both the white tenants and the African-American tenants could bring a Fair Housing Act claim.

The ECOA, however, does not provide a right for a plaintiff associated with the applicant to challenge the discrimination suffered by the applicant, but not by the plaintiff.[31] The ECOA generally only provides remedies to those

22 *Havens Realty Corp. v. Coleman*, 455 U.S. at 377.
23 *Id.*
24 *See, e.g.*, Cent. Ala. Fair Hous. Ctr., Inc. v. Lowder Realty Co., 236 F.3d 629 (11th Cir. 2000) (even if none of the individual plaintiffs prevail, organization is still entitled to seek damages proximately caused by defendant's unlawful discrimination toward the testers; trial court erred by instructing jury that it could find for the organization only if it first found for one of the individual plaintiffs).
25 *Havens Realty Corp. v. Coleman*, 455 U.S. at 379.
26 *See* Ragin v. Harry Macklowe Real Estate Co., 6 F.3d 898 (2d Cir. 1993); Hooker v. Weathers, 990 F.2d 913 (6th Cir. 1993); Vill. of Bellwood v. Dwivedi, 895 F.2d 1521 (7th Cir. 1990).
27 Fair Hous. Council v. Montgomery Newspapers, 141 F.3d 71,

79 (3d Cir. 1998); Fair Employment Council v. BMC Mktg. Corp., 28 F.3d 1268 (D.C. Cir. 1994); Ass'n for Retarded Citizens v. Dallas County Mental Health & Mental Retardation Ctr. Bd.of Trustees, 19 F.3d 241 (5th Cir. 1994); Spann v. Colonial Vill. Inc., 899 F.2d 24 (D.C. Cir. 1990).
28 *See* Williams v. Poretsky Mgmt., Inc., 955 F. Supp. 490 (D. Md. 1996).
29 *See* § 3.10, *supra*.
30 *See, e.g.*, Simms v. First Gibraltar Bank, 83 F.3d 1546 (5th Cir. 1996) (white owner of apartment complex in predominantly minority area); Woods-Drake v. Lundy, 667 F.2d 1198 (5th Cir. 1982) (in an eviction case, white plaintiff had minority guests); Cherry v. Amoco Oil Co., 481 F. Supp. 727 (N.D. Ga. 1979); Harrison v. Otto G. Heinzeroth Mortgage Co., 430 F. Supp. 893 (N.D. Ohio 1977) (African-American neighborhood); Official Staff Commentary, 12 C.F.R. § 202.2(z)-1; *see also* § 3.10, *supra*.
31 *See, e.g.*, Hargraves v. Capital City Mortgage Corp., 147 F. Supp. 2d 1 (D.D.C. 2001) (claims of individual plaintiffs who did not receive or apply for credit as individuals, but rather were involved in obtaining a loan for their church, dismissed; the ECOA provides a cause of action for the church, but individuals cannot assert the church's legal interest; section 1981 claims also dismissed because the church, not the individual plaintiffs, was party to the loan contract); Church of Zion Christian Ctr., Inc. v. Southtrust Bank, 1997 U.S. Dist. LEXIS 12425 (S.D. Ala. July 30, 1997) (individual plaintiffs held not to have standing to bring an ECOA action when loan application was

who apply for credit, not those affiliated with those who apply. For example, the ECOA would only provide a remedy for the landlord and not the African-American tenants if the landlord were denied a loan to fix up the apartment because of the tenants' race.

11.2.4 Class Actions

Class actions are available under all the credit discrimination statutes, and the same issues arise in such class actions as with any other type of consumer class action.[32] Several unique issues also arise in deciding whether to bring a discrimination suit as an individual or class action.[33]

Under the ECOA, punitive damages in class actions are limited to the lesser of $500,000 or one percent of the creditor's net worth.[34] As there are no limits to the size of punitive damages under the Fair Housing Act and Civil Rights Acts, there may be no need to bring a class action if punitive damages are the major relief sought, as an individual action may produce a large punitive damages award that would deter future misconduct.

In addition, there may be significant differences in damages among class members. For example, in a redlining case, potential class members may all live in the designated geographic area or be members of a protected group but will differ as to individual qualifications for credit. In this case, courts may certify the class for injunctive relief only and require individual claims for damages to proceed separately.[35]

11.3 The Defendant—Who Is Liable?

11.3.1 Direct Creditor Liability

Creditors that directly extend or refuse to extend credit are almost always covered by the credit discrimination laws. There are only a few exceptions. For example, ECOA

remedies are limited when a government entity is the creditor.[36] In addition, suits against public agencies charged with supervisory or enforcement duties are unlikely to succeed for lack of standing or because the statute does not grant a private right of action.[37]

The ECOA and Fair Housing Act also do not apply to an individual creditor who only makes one or two isolated loans.[38] The Fair Housing Act is further limited to credit discrimination related to a dwelling. Either the credit must be used in relation to purchasing, fixing, or maintaining a dwelling, or a security interest must be taken on residential real estate.[39] The federal Civil Rights Acts apply only to discrimination based on race, certain ethnic origins, and citizenship status.[40] Within these parameters, the Civil Rights Acts are generally broad in scope.

11.3.2 Finding Deep Pockets: Extending Liability Beyond Direct Creditors

Liability under both the ECOA and the FHA may stretch well beyond the direct creditors who extend or deny credit. This liability is critical because financial players other than the direct creditors often have the deepest pockets.

The ECOA covers those who regularly participate in the decision of whether or not to extend credit. These creditors or assignees or loan purchasers are directly liable for ECOA violations even if the credit was actually extended by a dealer or another creditor.[41] This category includes assignees, transferees, and subrogees of the original creditor.[42] Arrangers of credit, including brokers and dealers, may also be liable under the ECOA for general discrimination violations and for violations of the prohibition against discouraging applicants on a prohibited basis.[43]

The FHA also explicitly extends liability to arrangers and brokers and others providing financial assistance related to a loan covered by the FHA.[44] In general, section 3605 of the FHA (related to residential real estate transactions) covers a wide range of actors including makers of loans, purchasers, and those selling, brokering, and appraising real estate.[45] Section 3604, with a few limited exceptions, applies to any seller or renter of property.[46]

made on behalf of a corporation and plaintiffs never entered into any oral or written agreement with defendants).

32 *See generally* National Consumer Law Center, Consumer Class Actions: A Practical Litigation Guide (4th ed. 1999).

33 *See, e.g.,* Coleman v. Gen. Motor Acceptance Corp., 196 F.R.D. 315 (M.D. Tenn. 2000) (granting class certification under Rule 23(b)(2) and denying certification under Rule 23(b)(3)); Buycks-Roberson v. Citibank Fed. Sav. Bank, 162 F.R.D. 322 (N.D. Ill. 1995) (disparate impact case in which court certified class only for purposes of determining defendant's liability, if any, and fashioning injunctive relief, at the same time acknowledging that later it will be necessary for individual damage claims to proceed separately).

34 15 U.S.C. § 1691e(b). Punitive damages are also limited in individual ECOA actions. *See* § 11.6.4.3.2, *infra.*

35 *See* Buycks-Roberson v. Citibank Fed. Sav. Bank, 162 F.R.D. 322 (N.D. Ill. 1995); Fischer v. Dallas Fed. Sav. & Loan Ass'n, 106 F.R.D. 465 (N.D. Tex. 1985), *aff'd*, 835 F.2d 567 (5th Cir. 1988).

36 *See* § 11.8.3.4, *infra.*

37 Lee v. Board of Governors, 118 F.3d 905 (2d Cir. 1997); Jones v. Comptroller of the Currency, 983 F. Supp. 197 (D.D.C. 1997).

38 *See* §§ 2.2.5.2, 2.3.2.3.1, 2.3.3.2, *supra.*

39 *See* § 2.3, *supra.*

40 *See* § 2.4, *supra.*

41 15 U.S.C. § 1691a(3); Reg. B, 12 C.F.R. § 202.2(l). Knowledge or reasonable notice of the violation is required only for assignees and secondary creditors who did not participate in the credit decision. *See* §§ 2.2.5.4, 2.2.5.5, *supra.*

42 Reg. B, 12 C.F.R. § 202.2(l).

43 Reg. B, 12 C.F.R. § 202.2(l); *see* § 2.2.5.3, *supra.*

44 *See* § 2.3, *supra.*

45 *See* § 2.3.2.3, *supra.*

46 *See* § 2.3.3.2, *supra.*

Others with deep pockets should also be considered. For example, corporate principals may be individually responsible for the acts of the corporation's agent.[47] Holding the principals responsible for the acts of the corporation and its agents can be critical in collecting on a judgment.[48] Corporations and other entities that are wholly owned by one or a few individuals may be merely a shell to protect the individuals from liability. The individuals may, in reality, have the deep pockets. Informal investigation before the filing of a case can clarify the corporate and/or familial relationships and agency ties that bind the various players in a fraudulent scheme together.

Even if they do not have deep pockets, adding additional parties may result in a higher total punitive damages award or in a higher settlement. This possibility will be particularly important in an ECOA class action, because punitive damages will be capped.[49] The credit arrangers or assignees may also be the most culpable parties, again leading to higher punitive damage awards and also helping the lawsuit to have the most appropriate deterrent effect.

11.4 Selecting the Forum

11.4.1 Federal or State Court

11.4.1.1 Reasons to Choose One Forum or the Other

Credit discrimination cases can be brought in either federal or state court.[50] Courts have found that the federal discrimination laws should be laws "providing for the equal civil rights of citizens" but it will rarely be the case that such laws cannot be enforced in state court.[51]

The choice of forum should be carefully considered. Relevant factors include:

- Whether a forum's judges are sympathetic to debtors and to civil rights claims;
- Whether state court judges are familiar with the statutes' provisions;
- Whether the client desires or needs a quick determination, and the speed of proceedings in each forum;
- Whether there are pendent state law claims, such as deceptive practices, which would be better heard in state court;
- Which court is willing to award truly reasonable fees to attorneys representing low-income consumers;
- The amount of the filing fee, the ability to obtain *in forma pauperis* status, and any plaintiff's bond requirements;
- Differences in discovery rules; and
- Desirability of available remedies under similar state laws, such as minimum/maximum damages, or restriction to mandatory administrative proceedings.

11.4.1.2 Obtaining the Desired Forum

If federal court is the preferred forum, then at least one claim must be made under the federal credit discrimination laws—the ECOA, the Fair Housing Act, or the federal Civil Rights Acts. If the plaintiff prefers a state forum, the plaintiff must anticipate that the defendant will prefer a federal forum.

If the plaintiff's complaint includes a claim under a federal discrimination law, the defendant may be able to remove the case to federal court pursuant to 28 U.S.C.

---

47 *See* Hargraves v. Capital City Mortgage Corp., 140 F. Supp. 2d 7, 27–28 (D.D.C. 2000) (plaintiffs sued corporate principal Thomas Nash individually for fraud based upon misrepresentations allegedly made by defendant's agent in the course of arranging loans; court denied Nash's motion for summary judgment due to Nash's ownership and control over Capital City as well as allegations that he signed the contract to sell the property to the homeowners, hired the agent to list the property, received information from the agent regarding the homeowner's financial status, and made the decision to make the loan in the form it was offered). ECOA claims by two plaintiffs who did not receive or apply for credit were ultimately denied in defendant's summary judgment motion. Hargraves v. Capital City Mortgage Corp., 147 F. Supp. 2d 1 (D.D.C. 2001). In addition to the private plaintiffs' case, the Federal Trade Commission (FTC) filed a case against Capital City, in which the court also denied a summary judgment motion by Nash on the issue of individual liability. In addition to ECOA claims, the FTC's complaint alleged violations of the FTC Act, the Truth in Lending Act, and the Fair Debt Collection Practices Act. Fed. Trade Comm'n v. Capital City Mortgage Corp., Clearinghouse No. 53,523, Civ. No. 98-237 (D.D.C. Jan. 29, 1998), *available at* http://www.ftc.gov. The court denied summary judgment on the issue of individual liability with respect to all of these claims. Fed. Trade Comm'n v. Capital City Mortgage Corp., 1998 U.S. Dist. LEXIS 22115 (D.D.C. July 13, 1998).

48 *See generally* National Consumer Law Center, The Cost of Credit: Regulations and Legal Challenges § 11.13 (2d ed. 2000 and Supp.).

49 *See* § 11.6.4.3.2, *infra*.

50 15 U.S.C. § 1691e(f); 42 U.S.C. § 3613(a)(1)(A).

51 *See* Emigrant Sav. Bank v. Elan Mgmt. Corp., 688 F.2d 671 (2d Cir. 1982) (removal from state court refused when apartment building management corporation claimed that foreclosure action was racially motivated and was brought in retaliation for its exercise of ECOA rights); Bledsoe v. Fulton Bank, 940 F. Supp. 804 (E.D. Pa. 1996) (plaintiff could not seek declaratory or injunctive relief under ECOA in federal court when she had raised issue defensively in state court).

§ 1441. Federal law provides for removal of an action to federal court "[a]gainst any person who is denied or cannot enforce in the courts of such State a right under any law providing for the equal civil rights of citizens of the United States or of all persons with the jurisdiction thereof."[52]

If the case is removed, the plaintiff can try to remand the case to state court.[53] When appropriate, the plaintiff should challenge the defendant's claim of original jurisdiction. Alternatively, in cases in which federal claims are asserted along with other claims based on state law, the plaintiff should request that the federal court exercise its discretion to remand "all matters in which State law predominates."[54] This principle has generally been construed to authorize remand back to state court of either the entire case or individual state law claims when the state law claims predominate over the federal question claims. The plaintiff may also challenge the removal if it was not timely made.[55]

If the plaintiff wants to stay in state court, the safest course will be to plead an action solely under a state credit discrimination statute or other state law. This alternative is a viable option only when the state claim provides an adequate remedy and covers the challenged practice. A matter removed to federal court on the basis that the plaintiff could have raised federal claims instead of, or in addition to, state law claims should be remanded by the federal court. One exception to this rule is when the state law claims are completely preempted by federal law. In that case, the defendants may object to the remand, but such blanket preemption is generally found only in extraordinary circumstances.[56]

A consumer may wish to bring a federal credit discrimination law claim as a counterclaim in a creditor's state court collection action. The counterclaim will generally not provide a basis to remove an action to federal court, because the federal question must appear in the complaint.[57]

When precedent requires that a consumer assert ECOA, FHA or other federal claims in the state collection action to avoid a res judicata bar, and the consumer would prefer to be in federal court, the consumer may consider affirmatively filing a parallel action in the federal court. While the creditor will likely argue that the federal court action should be stayed, strong arguments can be made that the court should exercise federal jurisdiction and retain the case.[58] Abstention is particularly disfavored when the applicable substantive law is federal.[59] Nevertheless, the district court will have some discretion in the matter.[60] To minimize problems, the consumer should move the federal case along expeditiously and consider filing an early motion for summary judgment in federal court.[61]

11.4.2 Deciding Whether to Select an Administrative Determination in FHA Cases

11.4.2.1 Administrative Option May Be Pursued Simultaneously With Court Action

There are two ways to make a claim under the Fair Housing Act. The aggrieved party may file an administrative complaint with the Department of Housing and Urban Development (HUD) or commence a private civil action.[62] These two procedures are not mutually exclusive and may be pursued contemporaneously or sequentially. There is no requirement that the administrative remedies be exhausted prior to instituting a private action.[63] The only restriction is that trial of the private action may not be commenced once the actual administrative hearing has begun[64] and an administrative hearing may not go forward if a civil trial has begun.[65]

---

52 28 U.S.C. § 1443(*l*).

53 *See* 28 U.S.C. § 1441(c). A motion to remand on grounds other than lack of subject matter jurisdiction must be filed within thirty days after the filing of the notice of removal. 28 U.S.C. § 1447(c).

54 *See* 28 U.S.C. § 1441(c). If the plaintiff is successful in having a removed case remanded to state court based on a lack of subject matter jurisdiction, the plaintiff may be awarded costs and expenses, including reasonable attorney fees. 28 U.S.C. § 1447(c).

55 The notice of removal generally must be filed within thirty days of receipt of the initial pleading that makes the case removable. *See* 28 U.S.C. § 1446(b).

56 *See generally* National Consumer Law Center, The Cost of Credit: Regulation and Legal Challenges § 3.9 (2d ed. 2000 and Supp.).

57 *See* Gen. Elec. Capital Auto Lease, Inc. v. Mires, 788 F. Supp. 948 (E.D. Mich. 1992) (TILA counterclaim).

58 *See generally* National Consumer Law Center, Truth in Lending § 7.5.4 (4th ed. 1999 and Supp.). The Supreme Court has enunciated an "exceptional circumstances test" for surrender of a federal court's obligation to exercise federal jurisdiction. This test applies to cases that do not fall within a specific abstention doctrine. Moses H. Cone Mem'l Hosp. v. Mercury Constr. Corp., 460 U.S. 1, 15, 19, 103 S. Ct. 927, 74 L. Ed. 2d 765 (1983).

59 Vill. of Westfield v. Welch's, 170 F.3d 116 (2d Cir. 1999).

60 Moses H. Cone Mem'l Hosp. v. Mercury Constr. Corp., 460 U.S. 1, 103 S. Ct. 927, 74 L. Ed. 2d 765 (1983); Kent v. Celozzi-Ettleson Chevrolet, Inc., 1999 U.S. Dist. LEXIS 17282 (N.D. Ill. Nov. 1, 1999) (granting stay in favor of state court case raising similar claims).

61 *See* National Consumer Law Center, Truth in Lending §§ 7.5.4, 8.12 (4th ed. 1999 and Supp.). This tactic not only may help prevent a stay, but may also help avoid the preclusive effect in federal court of a prior state court adjudication. For information on litigating in bankruptcy court, see National Consumer Law Center, Consumer Bankruptcy Law and Practice Ch. 13 (6th ed. 2000 and Supp.).

62 42 U.S.C. §§ 3610–3613.

63 42 U.S.C. § 3613(a)(2); *see* Bryant Woods Inn, Inc. v. Howard County, 124 F.3d 597 (4th Cir. 1997); Murphy v. Zoning Comm'n, 148 F. Supp. 2d 173 (D. Conn. 2001).

64 42 U.S.C. § 3613(a)(3).

65 42 U.S.C. § 3612(f).

11.4.2.2 Reasons to Choose Administrative or Judicial Option

The administrative complaint procedure will, in many cases, offer a satisfactory method of redress at a substantially lower cost than a private action. The greatest advantage of the administrative route is this low cost to the complainant as the government bears the burden of investigating and proving the case even after it is removed to federal court. The complainant need not have an attorney or pay any filing fees. The complainant, nevertheless, has the right to intervene in the administrative proceeding and conduct an independent investigation.

There are other advantages to the administrative process. In theory it may be faster than a judicial proceeding, although in practice it is not usually any faster. The HUD conciliation process, discussed below, may help facilitate satisfactory settlements.

On the other hand, there are drawbacks to the administrative option.[66] The greatest disadvantage is loss of control over the case. Moreover, the administrative complaint may still end up in federal court, but will have been delayed getting there during several layers of administrative review.

Remedies are also not as robust in an administrative proceeding. The administrative law judge can award injunctive and equitable relief, actual damages and attorney fees,[67] but may not award punitive damages (although the administrative law judge can assess civil fines that are to be paid to the government, not the complainant). A federal judge, in contrast, is authorized to order all this relief plus unlimited punitive damages.[68]

There are also possible conflict of interest issues. If the administrative judge does not rule in the victim's favor or does not grant all of the relief sought, HUD is not required to seek reconsideration on behalf of the complainant or pursue an appeal. In addition, precedent in the employment discrimination area suggests that once findings of fact and conclusions of law have been issued in the administrative proceeding, the plaintiff may be collaterally estopped from proceeding on the same claims and facts in federal court.[69]

11.4.2.3 How the Administrative Procedure Works

An individual begins the administrative process by filing a complaint with the Department of Housing and Urban Development (HUD). Although HUD has developed a form to use for housing discrimination complaints, the agency will accept any written statement that contains the allegations of a discriminatory housing practice, provided that the following information is included in the complaint:

- 1) Complainant's name and address;
- 2) Respondent's name and address;
- 3) A description and address of the dwelling which is at issue; and
- 4) A concise statement of the violation including the relevant facts and dates.[70]

HUD is required to refer the complaint to the state or local agency in whose jurisdiction the alleged discrimination occurred, if that agency is "certified" as having a law comparable to the federal Fair Housing Act.[71] The list of certified agencies is updated annually.[72]

The state or local agency is given thirty days to commence a proceeding.[73] If the agency fails to do so, the complaint reverts back to HUD.[74] It is important to keep track of these dates and push HUD to begin its investigation if necessary.

After the complaint is filed, or reverts back to HUD due to the inaction of a state or local agency, HUD has one hundred days to conduct an investigation.[75] During the investigatory period, HUD is required to attempt to conciliate the case by negotiating with the aggrieved party and the respondent.[76] If conciliation is successful, both parties must execute an agreement describing the resolution of the complaint or providing for binding arbitration.[77]

If conciliation is not successful and the investigation leads to a finding of reasonable cause, the government must issue

---

66 For a discussion of advantages and disadvantages of the administrative process and litigation, see John P. Relman, Housing Discrimination Practice Manual § 3.2(2)(a), (b) (2000 Supp.).

67 While the Fair Housing Act previously required a showing of need to recover attorney fees, the 1988 Amendments eliminated that requirement. 42 U.S.C. § 3612(p).

68 42 U.S.C. § 3613(c). A federal judge is also expressly authorized to order affirmative action relief, 42 U.S.C. § 3613(c), while the administrative law judge's mandate is the more vague "equitable relief." 42 U.S.C. § 3612(g)(3).

69 *See, e.g.*, Univ. of Tenn. v. Elliot, 478 U.S. 788, 106 S. Ct. 3220, 92 L. Ed. 2d 635 (1986) (collateral estoppel barred § 1981 claim in federal court when state agency made findings of fact after parties had adequate opportunity to litigate). *See generally* The Chicago Lawyers' Committee for Civil Rights Under the Law, The Law of Mortgage Lending and Insurance Discrimination,

available at http://www.clccrul.org; John P. Relman, Housing Discrimination Practice Manual § 3.2(2) (2000 Supp.); Robert G. Schwemm, Housing Discrimination: Law and Litigation (7th ed. 1997).

70 24 C.F.R. § 103.30(b).

71 42 U.S.C. § 3610(f); 24 C.F.R. § 103.100-110.

72 For interim updates check the Federal Register or the Housing Development Reporter.

73 42 U.S.C. § 3610(f)(2)(a).

74 24 C.F.R. § 103.110.

75 24 C.F.R. § 103.225.

76 24 C.F.R. § 103.300.

77 24 C.F.R. § 103.310; *see* § 11.4.3, *infra* (discussion of problems with binding arbitration).

a charge on behalf of the aggrieved person.[78] If the government determines that no reasonable cause exists, the complaint will be dismissed.[79]

If the government files a charge, the respondent or the complainant has the right at this stage to elect that the case be removed to federal district court.[80] The purpose of this provision is to assure that the statute does not violate the respondent's constitutional right to a jury trial. If neither party elects to remove the case, the case is heard by an administrative law judge. The aggrieved party may intervene in the administrative action, and is entitled to monetary relief even if she does not intervene.[81] The hearing must be held within 120 days after the charge is filed.[82]

11.4.3 Mandatory Arbitration

11.4.3.1 Introduction

Another NCLC manual, *Consumer Arbitration Agreements* (2d ed. 2002), examines the enforceability of arbitration agreements in detail. This section introduces the topic and considers issues of special relevance to ECOA and FHA claims.

It is not surprising that binding arbitration clauses are becoming standard in credit agreements. Forcing consumers to arbitrate their claims allows creditors to avoid exposure to class action liability, because joinder of individual claims is generally unavailable in arbitration. In addition, punitive damage awards are largely precluded, either by the express terms of the arbitration clause, or because arbitrators as a rule are less inclined than juries to award punitive damages.

Discovery is limited in arbitration proceedings, which benefits creditors who, of course, have automatic access to the extensive information contained in their own files, and who want to avoid discovery of their illegal practices. Moreover, individual actions for actual damages in arbitration are often impractical because hearing fees are high in comparison to the amount of damages suffered. By way of contrast, the consumer need not pay for the judge and jury's time in a court case. In arbitration, erroneous interpretations of the law can not be appealed and arbitrators tend to be more sympathetic to defendant companies who are repeat users of the arbitration forum than to unfamiliar, one-time user plaintiffs.

Consequently, an initial issue in much consumer litigation today is whether the consumer can press claims in court, or whether the creditor can insist that the consumer take those claims to arbitration instead. This section examines several theories why an arbitration clause should not be enforced against an ECOA or FHA claim, but a more comprehensive discussion of such theories is found in NCLC's *Consumer Arbitration Agreements* (2d ed. 2002).

11.4.3.2 Has a Binding Arbitration Agreement Been Formed?

It is axiomatic that an arbitration agreement is not binding if there is no agreement with the consumer to submit disputes to arbitration.[83] For example, if a creditor's standard form contract includes an arbitration clause, that clause should not apply to an applicant who was denied credit and who thus never entered into the credit agreement. Even if a credit application states that the applicant agrees to abide by certain provisions if credit is granted, this should not be binding if credit is not granted. The terms have, in effect, been agreed to by the borrower, but rejected by the creditor. Because only one side has agreed, there is no binding agreement.

Similarly, an arbitration agreement on an application is not binding if the creditor provides a counteroffer of credit on different terms, and that counteroffer does not include an arbitration clause. The binding agreement is based on the counteroffer, not the original offer.

Another common practice is for the creditor, after the credit agreement has been consummated, to send a change of terms that includes an arbitration clause and which indicates that the consumer's continued use of the credit is deemed acceptance of the change in terms. Whether this change in terms is binding on a consumer who continues to use the credit after receiving such a notice is an unresolved issue, which is discussed in another NCLC manual.[84] But the change in terms should certainly not apply to a consumer who does not borrow additional funds after the change in terms is announced.

A consumer's claim under a credit discrimination statute may be brought against a credit arranger, the originating creditor, or a subsequent assignee. The consumer attorney should determine what parties are explicitly covered by the arbitration agreement, and what legal basis a defendant has to claim that it can enforce an arbitration agreement that does not explicitly apply to it.[85]

Also note whether the arbitration agreement is found in a document other than the credit agreement, such as the purchase agreement between the dealer and the consumer. Even if an assignee has grounds to enforce an arbitration agreement found in the loan assigned to it, can it enforce a clause found in a purchase agreement which has not been assigned to it and in which it has no interest?

---

78 42 U.S.C. § 3610(g); 24 C.F.R. § 103.405.

79 24 C.F.R. § 103.400(a)(1).

80 42 U.S.C. § 3612(a).

81 42 U.S.C. § 3612(c).

82 42 U.S.C. § 3612(g)(1).

83 *See* Equal Employment Opportunity Comm'n v. Waffle House, Inc., 122 S. Ct. 754, 151 L. Ed. 2d 755 (2002); First Options of Chicago, Inc. v. Kaplan, 514 U.S. 938, 943, 115 S. Ct. 1920, 1924, 131 L. Ed. 2d 985 (1995).

84 *See* National Consumer Law Center, Consumer Arbitration Agreements § 3.7 (2d ed. 2002).

85 *Id.* § 6.3.

If the arbitration agreement is found in a document signed by the principal consumer obligor, but not in the agreement signed by the cosigner, the arbitration agreement should not be binding on the cosigner, particularly if the cosigner does not benefit from the agreement containing the arbitration clause.[86]

11.4.3.3 Was the Arbitration Agreement Made Knowingly and Willingly?

Some courts find that a voluntary, knowing and intelligent waiver is required when an arbitration clause requires individuals to give up the constitutional right to a jury, arbitrate claims arising under civil rights-type statutes or under other statutes that provide a judicial remedy. In *Prudential Insurance Co. v. Lai*, for example, the Ninth Circuit held that "Congress intended there to be at least a knowing agreement to arbitrate employment disputes before an employee may be deemed to have waived the comprehensive statutory rights, remedies and procedural protections prescribed in Title VII and related state statutes."[87] The Ninth Circuit's adoption of a voluntary, knowing standard for civil rights claims has been rejected by some other courts, however, and the law appears to differ from one jurisdiction to the next.[88]

11.4.3.4 When Arbitration Conflicts with Statute's Remedial Scheme

11.4.3.4.1 General

An arbitration agreement that prevents a consumer from obtaining relief under a federal statutory claim is unenforceable because it conflicts with the legislature's purpose in enacting the statute. The Supreme Court, in *Mitsubishi Motors Corp. v. Soler Chrysler-Plymouth, Inc.*, stated that if an arbitration clause waives the plaintiff's "right to pursue statutory remedies for antitrust violations, we would have little hesitation in condemning the agreement as against

public policy.... [S]o long as the prospective litigant effectively may vindicate [her] statutory cause of action in the arbitral forum, the statute will continue to serve both its remedial and deterrent function."[89] The clear implication is that if the consumer cannot effectively vindicate a statutory cause of action in arbitration, the arbitration clause is unenforceable.

The California Supreme Court recently summarized the extent of the consensus on this point as follows: "The principle that an arbitration agreement may not limit statutorily imposed remedies such as punitive damages and attorney fees appears to be undisputed."[90] The Southern District of New York has held that "contractual clauses purporting to mandate arbitration of statutory claims as a condition of employment are enforceable only if the arbitration preserves the substantive protections and remedies afforded by the statute."[91] The Eleventh Circuit, in *Paladino v. Avnet Computer Technologies, Inc.*,[92] has found similarly that a binding arbitration agreement that nominally applied to all of an employee's claims should be interpreted as not applying to a claim under an employment discrimination statute because the arbitration clause only allowed the arbitrator to award damages for breach of contract, and not damages for statutory claims. The rule is that if the arbitrator cannot provide relief under the legal claim relied upon by an individual employee or consumer, the arbitration clause cannot be enforced against such a claim.

11.4.3.4.2 Limits on punitive damages

The ECOA and the FHA both explicitly provide a statutory right to punitive damages.[93] Consequently, an arbitration agreement that either explicitly restricts punitive damages or has that practical effect should not be enforced as to a consumer's ECOA or FHA claims.[94] In a civil rights context, this result is particularly appropriate because the courts have recognized that the threat of punitive damages is crucial to the enforcement of anti-discrimination statutes

---

86 *Id.* § 6.4.

87 42 F.3d 1299, 1304 (9th Cir. 1994); *see also* Renteria v. Prudential Ins. Co., 113 F.3d 1104 (9th Cir. 1997).

88 *Compare* Rosenberg v. Merrill Lynch, Pierce, Fenner & Smith, Inc., 170 F.3d 1 (1st Cir. 1999) (not adopting the Ninth Circuit's knowing and voluntary standard, but nonetheless holding that it was "inappropriate to enforce" an arbitration clause with which the employee was not "familiar" in light of the New York Stock Exchange Rules and other matters) *with* Haskins v. Prudential Ins. Co., 230 F.3d 231, 239 (6th Cir. 2000) (holding that "absent a showing of fraud, duress, mistake, or some other ground upon which a contract may be voided, a court must enforce a contractual agreement to arbitrate," and finding that this rule "is superior to the standards set forth in *Rosenberg* and *Lai* because it does not plainly ignore long-standing rules of contract law"), *cert. denied*, 531 U.S. 1113 (2001). *See generally* National Consumer Law Center, Consumer Arbitration Agreements § 3.5 (2d ed. 2002).

89 473 U.S. 614, 105 S. Ct. 3346, 87 L. Ed. 2d 444 (1985).

90 Armendariz v. Found. Health Psychcare Services, Inc., 24 Cal. 4th 83, 99 Cal. Rptr. 2d 745, 6 P.3d 669 (2000).

91 DeGaetano v. Smith Barney, Inc., 983 F. Supp. 459, 469 (S.D.N.Y. 1997).

92 134 F.3d 1054 (11th Cir. 1998).

93 *See* § 11.6, *infra*.

94 *See* Graham Oil Co. v. ARCO Products Co., 43 F.3d 1244 (9th Cir. 1994); *see also In re* Managed Care Litig., 2000 U.S. Dist. LEXIS 19247, at *32–*33 (S.D. Fla. Dec. 11, 2000); *Ex Parte* Thicklin, 2002 Ala. LEXIS 11 (Ala. Jan. 11, 2002); Cavalier Mfg., Inc. v. Jackson, 2001 Ala. LEXIS 373 (Ala. Oct. 5, 2001); Armendariz v. Found. Health Psychcare Services, Inc., 24 Cal. 4th 83, 99 Cal. Rptr. 2d 745, 6 P.3d 669 (2000); Kinney v. United HealthCare Services, Inc., 70 Cal. App. 4th 1322, 83 Cal. Rptr. 2d 348 (1999); Stirlen v. Supercuts, Inc., 51 Cal. App. 4th 1519, 60 Cal. Rptr. 2d 138 (1997); Powertel, Inc. v. Bexley, 743 So. 2d 570 (Fla. Dist. Ct. App. 1999); Richard A. Lord, Williston on Contracts § 18.13 (4th ed. 1998).

and that arbitration clauses which bar punitive damages conflict with those statutes.[95]

11.4.3.4.3 Limits on class actions

Businesses often draft arbitration clauses, either by their express terms or through their silence on the subject, in order to prohibit consumers from bringing ECOA, FHA, or other claims as class actions, either in court or in arbitration.[96] Most cases considering whether this restriction conflicts with a federal statutory scheme relate to the Truth in Lending Act (TILA), and find that the TILA does not provide a substantive statutory right to bring a claim as a class, but rather only caps the amount of the consumer's recovery in a class action under the TILA.[97]

On the other hand, the ECOA's provisions as to class actions are different than the TILA's. Limits on class action punitive damages found in the ECOA at 15 U.S.C. § 1691e(b) are similar to those found in the TILA, but 15 U.S.C. § 1691e(a) contains an explicit and substantive provision for class action relief under the ECOA, a provision not found in the TILA: "Any creditor who fails to comply . . . shall be liable . . . for any actual damages sustained by such applicant acting either in an individual capacity or as a member of a class." There is thus a strong argument that a class action under the ECOA cannot be forced into arbitration unless the arbitration agreement explicitly authorizes class-wide arbitration.[98]

11.4.3.4.4 Injunctive relief

When a federal statute explicitly provides for injunctive relief (as the ECOA and the FHA do), and the consumer seeks this relief, can that claim be forced into arbitration? It is clear that when an arbitration clause or the rules of an arbitration mechanism prevent a consumer from obtaining injunctive relief, then the consumer's action seeking injunctive relief cannot be forced into arbitration.[99]

The closer question is whether an arbitration clause and arbitration mechanism that allow the consumer to seek injunctive relief through the arbitrator really provide a viable remedy. Are arbitrators capable of ordering injunctive relief and is this injunctive relief the same as that ordered by a court?

Perhaps the most detailed discussion of an arbitration mechanism's ability to provide injunctive relief is the California Supreme Court's decision in *Broughton*.[100] The court discussed the difficulty an arbitrator would encounter monitoring an injunction and issuing subsequent orders. The court especially found that private arbitration could not provide the type of equitable relief that the legislature had intended in passing the Consumer Legal Remedies Act.

The result in *Broughton* can be distinguished from that in *Gilmer*, in which an employee argued before the Supreme Court that Age Discrimination in Employment Act (ADEA) claims need not be submitted to arbitration.[101] The Supreme Court responded that in the arbitration at issue, the arbitrator had the power to fashion equitable relief and such relief was not restricted by the rules of the arbitration mechanism. In addition, the Court pointed out that the Equal Employment Opportunity Commission can intervene at any time and stop the individual action and instead bring its own action in court seeking equitable relief.

---

95 *See* Derrickson v. Circuit City Stores, Inc., 1999 U.S. Dist. LEXIS 21100, 81 Fair Empl. Prac. Cas. (BNA) 1533, 1538 (D. Md. Mar. 19, 1999) ("Punitive damages and back pay are powerful deterrents to employers who might otherwise discriminate on the basis of race. The failure of the Circuit City arbitration provision to provide those remedies shields Circuit City from the full force of Section 1981 and prevents Plaintiff from effectively vindicating her rights."), *aff'd sub nom.* Johnson v. Circuit City Stores, Inc., 203 F.3d 821 (4th Cir.), *cert. denied*, 120 S. Ct. 2744 (2000).

96 For discussion of federal and state law governing *whether* an arbitration clause allows for class action proceedings, see National Consumer Law Center, Consumer Arbitration Agreements § 9.3 (2d ed. 2002). The instant subsection focuses solely on the legal effect of arbitration clauses that limit class-based claims.

97 *See* Green Tree Fin. Corp. v. Randolph, 244 F.3d 814 (11th Cir. 2001); Johnson v. W. Suburban Bank, 225 F.3d 366 (3d Cir. 2000), *cert. denied*, 531 U.S. 1145 (2001); *see also* Bowen v. First Family Fin. Servs., Inc., 233 F.3d 1331, 1338 (11th Cir. 2000).

98 *See* National Consumer Law Center, Consumer Arbitration Agreements § 5.3.2.5 (2d ed. 2002); *see also* Bailey v. Ameriquest Mortgage Co., 2002 U.S. Dist. LEXIS 1343 (D. Minn. Jan. 23, 2002); Ting v. AT & T, 182 F. Supp. 2d 902, 930–31 (N.D. Cal. 2002). *But see* Adkins v. Labor Ready, Inc., 185 F. Supp. 2d 628 (S.D. W. Va. 2001) (finding that arbitration clause waives right of individual workers to proceed as class under federal Fair Labor Standards Act); Gras v. Associates First Capital Corp., 786 A.2d 886 (N.J. Super. Ct. App. Div. 2001) (finding arbitration clause prohibiting class actions enforceable

in case involving consumer claims under New Jersey's Consumer Fraud Act).

99 Lozada v. Dale Baker Oldsmobile, Inc., 91 F. Supp. 2d 1087 (W.D. Mich. 2000); Broughton v. CIGNA Healthplans, 21 Cal. 4th 1066, 90 Cal. Rptr. 2d 334, 988 P.2d 67 (1999); Stirlen v. Supercuts, Inc., 51 Cal. App. 4th 1519, 60 Cal. Rptr. 2d 138 (1997); *see also* Simitar Entm't, Inc. v. Silva Entm't, Inc., 44 F. Supp. 2d 986 (D. Minn. 1999).

100 Broughton v. CIGNA Healthplans, 21 Cal. 4th 1066, 90 Cal. Rptr. 2d 334, 988 P.2d 67 (1999). One federal court has pronounced *Broughton*'s reasoning "persuasive" and adopted it. Gray v. Conseco, Inc., 2000 U.S. Dist. LEXIS 14821 (C.D. Cal. Sept. 29, 2000). Another federal court has concluded that the California Supreme Court erred in the *Broughton* case, however, and that federal law preempts any California law that would ban arbitration of certain statutory claims. Arriaga v. Cross County Bank, 163 F. Supp. 2d 1189 (S.D. Cal. 2001).

101 Gilmer v. Interstate/Johnson Lane Corp., 500 U.S. 20, 111 S. Ct. 1647, 114 L. Ed. 2d 26 (1991).

11.4.3.4.5 Limits on recovery of attorney fees and costs; high arbitration fees

Essential to the ECOA and FHA regulatory scheme is the authority for courts to award attorney fees to a prevailing consumer, but not to a prevailing creditor. This statutory provision, more than any other, makes enforcement of the statute practical. It also deters creditors from improperly contesting meritorious claims. Otherwise, creditors with deep legal pockets could overwhelm any attempt by a consumer to press an action.[102]

Consequently, arbitration agreements that require each party to bear its own attorney fees and costs, regardless of which party prevails, are fundamentally in conflict with the congressional intent underlying the ECOA and the FHA. Such an arbitration provision is unenforceable.[103] This result is particularly appropriate in an FHA claim because the statute reveals its congressional purpose with an unusual provision that upon application the court may appoint an attorney for the consumer or authorize an action without the payment of fees, costs, or security.[104]

Contrast this congressional purpose with an arbitration proceeding in which arbitration charges can easily exceed $10,000, and in which the consumer may have to front a portion of these fees or even be liable for all of these fees if the consumer does not prevail. While the Supreme Court places the burden on the consumer to prove that high arbitration fees make pursuing a statutory claim in arbitration impractical,[105] implicit to this holding is the principle that high fees in relation to the consumer's claim can render an arbitration agreement unenforceable. A significant number of courts have in fact examined the consumer's resources and the cost of the arbitration proceeding and determined that the arbitration requirement either conflicts with a statutory purpose or is unconscionable, and thus unenforceable.[106]

Consequently, as a matter of practice, consumers should seek clarification as to their potential liability for arbitration filing fees and the cost of the arbitrator(s). Will the fees be waived because of the consumer's indigency? If so, will just the filing fee be waived, or will the much larger hourly fees for the arbitrator also be waived? Will fees be assessed to the losing party only? What retainer must the consumer pay up front? The key to any arbitration fee challenge is a thorough presentation to the court of admissible evidence establishing the actual fees and charges the arbitration is likely to involve and whether the consumer will in fact be liable for those charges. A detailed analysis of how to challenge excessive arbitration costs as inconsistent with an arbitration requirement is found in National Consumer Law Center, *Consumer Arbitration Agreements* § 4.5 (2d ed. 2002).

11.4.3.5 Does the ECOA Prohibit Arbitration of Claims Brought Under the Consumer Credit Protection Act?

Consumers have argued that the ECOA prohibits credit agreements which require that consumers arbitrate Truth in Lending, Fair Credit Reporting, Equal Credit, Fair Debt Collection Practices, and other claims brought under the umbrella federal Consumer Credit Protection Act. This argument rests upon the ECOA provision which prohibits discrimination in any aspect of a credit transaction because the applicant has in good faith exercised any right under the federal Consumer Credit Protection Act.[107]

The Eleventh Circuit in *Bowen* found no merit to a claim that a creditor violates this ECOA provision by forcing a consumer, as a precondition for obtaining credit, to enter into an arbitration agreement—even if the effect of this agreement is to prevent the consumer from bringing a class action under the Truth in Lending Act (TILA).[108] The

---

102 *See* Graham Oil Co. v. ARCO Products Co., 43 F.3d 1244 (9th Cir. 1994).

103 Perez v. Globe Airport Sec. Services, Inc., 253 F.3d 1280 (11th Cir. 2001); Baron v. Best Buy Co., 75 F. Supp. 2d 1368 (S.D. Fla. 1999); *see also* Graham Oil Co. v. ARCO Products Co., 43 F.3d 1244 (9th Cir. 1994) (Petroleum Marketing Practices Act); Gourley v. Yellow Transp., L.L.C., 178 F. Supp. 2d 1196 (D. Colo. 2001) (agreement denying attorney fees violates public policy); Horenstein v. Mortgage Mkt., Inc., Clearinghouse No. 52,506, Civ. No. 98-1104-AA (D. Or. Jan. 11, 1999) (employment case); DeGaetano v. Smith Barney, Inc., 983 F. Supp. 459 (S.D.N.Y. 1997); Broughton v. CIGNA Healthplans, 21 Cal. 4th 1066, 90 Cal. Rptr. 2d 334, 988 P.2d 67 (1999) (indicating that restriction of UDAP attorney fees and costs was inconsistent with statutory intent, and agreement construed so such fees could be recovered); Maciejewski v. Alpha Sys. Lab, Inc., 73 Cal. App. 4th 1372, 87 Cal. Rptr. 2d 390 (1999) (limitation on attorney fees was unconscionable), *review granted, opinion superseded,* 89 Cal. Rptr. 2d 834, 986 P.2d 170 (Cal. 1999), *vacated and transferred,* 101 Cal. Rptr. 2d, 11 P.3d 954 (Cal. 2000); Stirlen v. Supercuts, Inc., 51 Cal. App. 4th 1519, 60 Cal. Rptr. 2d 138 (1997) (same).

104 42 U.S.C. § 3613(b).

105 Green Tree Fin. Corp. v. Randolph, 531 U.S. 79, 121 S. Ct. 513, 521, 148 L. Ed. 2d 373 (2000).

106 Circuit City Stores, Inc. v. Adams, 279 F.3d 889 (9th Cir. 2002); Cole v. Burns Int'l Sec. Services, 105 F.3d 1465 (D.C. Cir. 1997); Bailey v. Ameriquest Mortgage Co., 2002 U.S. Dist. LEXIS 1343 (D. Minn. Jan. 23, 2002); Popovich v. McDonald's Corp., 2002 U.S. Dist. LEXIS 406 (N.D. Ill. Jan. 14, 2002); Phillips v. Associates Home Equity Services, Inc., 179 F. Supp. 2d 840 (N.D. Ill 2001); Gourley v. Yellow Transp., L.L.C., 178 F. Supp. 2d 1196 (D. Colo. 2001); Camacho v. Holiday Homes, Inc., 167 F. Supp. 2d 892 (W.D. Va. 2001); Lelouis v. W. Directory Co., 2001 U.S. Dist. LEXIS 12517 (D. Or. Aug. 10, 2001); Ball v. SFX Broadcasting, Inc., 165 F. Supp. 2d 230 (N.D.N.Y. 2001); Wood v. Cooper Chevrolet, Inc., 102 F. Supp. 2d 1345 (N.D. Ala. 2000); Mercuro v. Superior Court, 96 Cal. App. 4th 167, 116 Cal. Rptr. 2d 671 (2002); Licitra v. Gateway, Inc., 189 Misc. 2d 721, 734 N.Y.S.2d 389 (Civ. Ct. 2001).

107 *See* § 3.4.4.3, *supra.*

108 Bowen v. First Family Fin. Services, Inc., 233 F.3d 1331 (11th Cir. 2000).

primary reason for this holding is that the court found no statutory right under the TILA to bring a TILA action in court as opposed to in an arbitration proceeding. Consequently, no TILA right is at issue.

The *Bowen* court also questioned whether the consumer was discriminated against because the consumer had, in fact, received credit. The court also noted that there was no evidence that the consumer attempted to reject the arbitration clause.

Nevertheless, consider this situation. The creditor requires, as a precondition of obtaining credit, that the consumer arbitrate all disputes, without a right to obtain punitive damages or bring the arbitration on a class-wide basis. The consumer refuses to sign the arbitration agreement because the consumer in good faith believes this will restrict the consumer's Consumer Credit Protection Act rights. The creditor refuses to grant credit on this basis. Is this an ECOA violation?

11.5 Selecting Causes of Action

11.5.1 Advantages of Various Claims

11.5.1.1 General

Plaintiffs in credit discrimination cases can choose from claims under the ECOA, the Fair Housing Act, 42 U.S.C. § 1981, 42 U.S.C. § 1982, state credit discrimination statutes, and state statutes that prohibit unfair or deceptive practices (UDAP statutes). With certain exceptions detailed below, the best strategy is often to plead as many causes of action as are viable.

Each statute has special characteristics that make it appropriate for only certain types of cases. Although these differences are detailed throughout this manual, this subsection will provide a brief overview.

The first question to ask is whether the challenged practice generally involves discrimination on a prohibited basis, or whether it only involves a violation of one of the ECOA procedural requirements.[109] For example, a creditor who requires applicants to state their marital status violates a specific ECOA procedural prohibition.

The ECOA procedural provisions are powerful tools even in situations in which discrimination is not at issue. Courts have agreed that violations of the ECOA notice requirements, in particular, may arise with or without additional discrimination claims.[110] There is also a possibility that a

state equal credit opportunity statute will prohibit the same practice.[111] In these circumstances, the state claim might be considered as an alternative to the federal one.[112]

If a challenged practice involves general discrimination, the next step is to determine the illegal basis for the discrimination. Credit discrimination statutes do not prohibit discrimination generally, but only prohibit discrimination based on certain itemized bases.[113]

If the basis for discrimination is not included in one of the credit discrimination statutes, the plaintiff should look for another state statute that prohibits this type of discrimination or rely on a state's general prohibition of unfair or deceptive acts or practices under its UDAP statute. Finally, even if a practice is discriminatory, but only on a nonprohibited basis, it may violate the ECOA, the FHA and state laws if it also has the effect of discriminating on a prohibited basis.[114]

Sample pleadings and discovery can be found in Appendices F and G, *infra*, and on the CD-Rom accompanying this volume.

11.5.1.2 Remedy, Forum, and Defenses

The federal discrimination laws all have similar remedies, in that they provide for actual and punitive damages, attorney fees and equitable relief.[115] Remedies issues are discussed in detail in section 11.6, *infra*.

Federal jurisdiction is available under any of the federal statutes, and state claims could then be brought as well based on pendent jurisdiction. If a state court forum is deemed important, it is wiser to bring only state claims, because federal claims may be removed to federal court. If an administrative remedy is desired, the action must be brought under the federal Fair Housing Act or a state statute with a similar remedial scheme. Forum issues are covered in section 11.4, *infra*.

As a general rule, the limitations period for both the ECOA and the Fair Housing Act is two years. A controversial issue is whether claims may also be brought defensively beyond the two-year period. If claims under the federal statutes are problematic, the applicable state limitations period should be examined. A state credit discrimination statute may, but is not likely to, have a longer limitations period. In addition, the federal Civil Rights Acts utilize the analogous state limitations period. Section 11.7, *infra*, covers statute of limitations issues in detail.

---

109 *See generally* Ch. 10, *supra*.
110 *See* Jochum v. Pico Credit Corp., 730 F.2d 1041 (5th Cir. 1984); Rayburn v. Car Credit Ctr. Corp., 2000 U.S. Dist. LEXIS 14944 (N.D. Ill. Oct. 6, 2000) (discrimination is not a prerequisite to an actionable ECOA claim); Williams v. Thomas Pontiac-GMC-Nissan-Hyundai, 1999 U.S. Dist. LEXIS 15045 (N.D. Ill. Sept.

22, 1999) (denial of motion to dismiss); Pinkett v. Payday Today Loans, L.L.C., 1999 U.S. Dist. LEXIS 12098 (N.D. Ill. July 22, 1999) (failure to provide ECOA rejection notice without allegations of discrimination may be actionable); § 10.1, *supra*.
111 *See* Appx. E, *infra*.
112 *See* § 2.5, *supra*.
113 *See generally* Ch. 3, *supra*.
114 *See* § 4.3, *supra*.
115 *See* § 11.6, *infra*.

11.5.1.3 State Laws Not Preempted

The ECOA preempts only those state laws that are inconsistent with the Act and with Regulation B, and then only to the extent of the inconsistency.[116] A state law which is more protective of a credit applicant is not considered inconsistent with the ECOA and Regulation B and is therefore unaffected by them.[117]

Inconsistency may be determined by the Federal Reserve Board (FRB) in response to a request from a "creditor, state or other interested party" for a formal Board determination.[118] It may therefore be difficult to argue that a state law is inconsistent with the ECOA without the support of a previous FRB finding, although in clear cases the lack of an FRB ruling should not be fatal.

Regulation B lists several types of state laws that are inconsistent with the ECOA and therefore are preempted by it. These laws include:

- Those requiring or permitting a practice or act prohibited by the ECOA and Regulation B;[119]
- Those prohibiting the individual extension of consumer credit to both parties to a marriage if each spouse individually and voluntarily applies for such credit;[120]
- Those prohibiting inquiries or collection of data required to comply with the ECOA or Regulation B;[121]
- Those prohibiting asking or considering age in an empirically derived, demonstrably and statistically sound credit scoring system to determine a pertinent element of creditworthiness, or to favor an elderly applicant;[122] or
- Those prohibiting inquiries necessary to establish or administer a special purpose credit program.[123]

Just like the ECOA, the Fair Housing Act and federal Civil Rights Acts should not preempt state laws which afford similar or greater rights to consumers.

11.5.2 What Causes of Action May Be Brought in the Same Lawsuit?

Not all causes of action may be brought in the same lawsuit. The ECOA states that when a particular act or omission by a creditor would constitute a violation of both state law and the ECOA, an action may be brought to recover money damages under only one of them, either the ECOA or state law.[124] No such election of claims is necessary in a court action for relief other than money damages (e.g., injunctive or declaratory relief), or in an administrative action.[125]

In addition, the ECOA provides that no person aggrieved by an ECOA violation and, in the same transaction, by a violation of the Fair Housing Act's prohibitions concerning residential real estate-related discrimination can recover under both the ECOA and the Fair Housing Act.[126] This language seems to clearly indicate that the litigant may bring an action under both statutes, and must elect one remedy or the other before a final order is issued.

The election between the ECOA and state law, on the other hand, indicates that an "action may be brought" under either the ECOA or state law, but not both. It is thus safest to elect one theory or the other before bringing a complaint. Nevertheless, federal courts have ruled that cases should not be dismissed if plaintiffs fail to elect between federal and state remedies before bringing the complaint; rather, the plaintiff should be restricted to recovery under the federal statute if the action was primarily pursued under that theory.[127]

The ECOA rules do not require an election of remedies between an ECOA action and a federal Civil Rights Act claim or between an ECOA action and a Fair Housing Act

---

116 15 U.S.C. § 1691d(f); Reg. B, 12 C.F.R. § 202.11(a). Regulation B, 12 C.F.R. § 202.2(aa) defines "state" as all states, the District of Columbia, the Commonwealth of Puerto Rico, or any territory or possession of the United States.

117 15 U.S.C. § 1691d(f); Reg. B, 12 C.F.R. § 202.11(a); *see also* Nat'l State Bank v. Long, 630 F.2d 981 (3d Cir. 1980) (the ECOA does not preempt a New Jersey statute prohibiting geographic redlining in the granting of home mortgages, as applied to national banks). An equally or more protective state law dealing explicitly with credit discrimination also may be granted an exemption from the requirements of the ECOA by the Federal Reserve Board. *See* 15 U.S.C. § 1691d(g); Reg. B, 12 C.F.R. § 202.11(e). A state might seek such an exemption to strengthen state enforcement of anti-discrimination statutes.

118 Reg. B, 12 C.F.R. § 202.11(b)(2). Regulation B also sets out the procedural steps required of states when seeking a Board determination. Reg. B, 12 C.F.R. § 202.11(e).

119 Reg. B, 12 C.F.R. § 202.11(b)(1)(i).

120 Reg. B, 12 C.F.R. § 202.11(b)(1)(ii); *see* § 5.6.1, *supra.*

121 Reg. B, 12 C.F.R. § 202.11(b)(1)(iii). The data collection requirement referred to in the regulation is the monitoring information provision. Reg. B, 12 C.F.R. § 202.13.

122 Reg. B, 12 C.F.R. § 202.11(b)(1)(iv); *see* § 6.6.2.3, *supra.*

123 Reg. B, 12 C.F.R. § 202.11(b)(1)(v). Special purpose credit programs address the credit needs of economically disadvan-

taged groups, and may request and consider information on race, sex, and other protected categories in ways forbidden to other forms of credit. *See* § 3.9, *supra.*

124 15 U.S.C. § 1691d(e).

125 15 U.S.C. § 1691d(e).

126 15 U.S.C. § 1691e(i). The literal language in the statute is confusing. It provides that there cannot be recovery under both the ECOA and 42 U.S.C. § 3612 of the Fair Housing Act. Section 3612 previously authorized a private right of action for damages and injunctive relief. The private relief section has been moved to § 3613, however, and § 3612 now deals with administrative enforcement of the Fair Housing Act. The notes to § 1691e clarify this change, referring to 42 U.S.C. § 3613 as the relevant statute.

127 Saldana v. Citibank, 1996 U.S. Dist. LEXIS 8327 (N.D. Ill. Jun. 13, 1996); Milton v. Bancplus Mortgage Corp., 1996 U.S. Dist. LEXIS 5166 (N.D. Ill. Apr. 19, 1996) (federal claim adequately pleaded; state claim, based on "election of remedy" statute, dismissed; Fernandez v. Hull Coop. Bank, 1979 U.S. Dist. LEXIS 8657 (D. Mass. Nov. 8, 1979).

claim not based on a residential real estate-related transaction, but on discrimination in the sale, rental, or advertising of a dwelling (§ 3604) or another FHA provision. Moreover, nothing prevents simultaneous recovery on a Fair Housing Act claim, a federal Civil Rights Act claim, and a state credit discrimination or UDAP claim. However, only one actual damage recovery can be had for the same injury.

11.6 Private Remedies

11.6.1 Overview

The various federal statutes that prohibit credit discrimination provide similar remedial schemes. They all provide for actual and punitive damages, equitable relief, and attorney fees for successful claims. None of the federal statutes provide minimum or multiple damages, although such remedies may be available under state law.[128] In some states, a state statute may provide better or different remedies than those available under the federal statutes. Several state credit discrimination statutes provide for minimum statutory damages that are not available under the federal statutes. In addition, some state UDAP statutes provide for treble or statutory minimum damages.[129]

The remedies under federal credit discrimination statutes are somewhat similar to other titles found within the Consumer Credit Protection Act.[130] For example, ECOA's private remedies are similar to those provided in the Truth in Lending Act (TILA),[131] the Fair Debt Collection Practices Act (FDCPA),[132] and the Fair Credit Reporting Act (FCRA).[133] In many situations, it is possible to use case law under these statutes to support an ECOA claim, particularly if case law under the ECOA is limited.[134] All of these statutes have the same purpose of providing remedies for consumers treated unlawfully in credit transactions, all were drafted within a several-year time span and all use similar language. Nevertheless, there are some important differences between the ECOA's remedial scheme and that found in the other consumer protection statutes. For example, the ECOA provides for punitive damages[135] while TILA provides for minimum statutory damages.[136]

As discussed in the previous section, because a discrimi-

nation case may be brought under more than one discrimination statute it is important to know when remedies are cumulative and when a plaintiff must elect one remedy or another.[137]

11.6.2 Actual Damages

11.6.2.1 General

It should not be necessary for a plaintiff to establish actual damages in order to take advantage of other possible statutory remedies, such as punitive damages, equitable and declaratory relief, and attorney fees. There are, however, other sound reasons for establishing the existence of actual damages and aggressively pursuing such damages.

Some courts faced with claims for punitive damages may be reluctant to penalize a creditor when no "real," measurable damage has been done to the client. This requirement is becoming a trend in some circuits, particularly in FHA cases in which courts are requiring a showing of compensable harm in order to allow punitive damages.[138] It is important, therefore, to demonstrate whenever possible that actual harm is the basis for the punitive damages claim. Moreover, it would be a tactical mistake not to submit evidence of actual damages because the ECOA, for example, explicitly provides that an award of actual damages is one factor to be considered in measuring any award of punitive damages.[139] Also, although the ECOA places a strict limit on the amount of punitive damages which may be awarded, no such limit is placed on actual damages.

Despite the value of pleading actual damages in these cases, it is also important to recognize that compensable damages are often difficult to prove and are often under compensated. For this reason, plaintiffs should always consider seeking punitive damages as well.[140]

11.6.2.2 Tangible Injury

Actual, out-of-pocket expenses and other tangible injuries are recoverable as actual damages under the ECOA, the federal Fair Housing Act, the federal Civil Rights Acts, and state credit discrimination statutes. These damages can arise in a number of ways. The following should be explored with the consumer:

- Did the consumer, after being denied credit, obtain a loan from another creditor at a higher interest rate, or purchase an item at a higher price than that charged by the creditor who originally denied the consumer's application?

---

128 *See* § 2.5, *supra.*
129 *See* § 2.6, *supra. See generally* National Consumer Law Center, Unfair and Deceptive Acts and Practices Ch. 8 (5th ed. 2001).
130 15 U.S.C. §§ 1601–1693r.
131 15 U.S.C. § 1640(a).
132 15 U.S.C. § 1692k(a), (b).
133 15 U.S.C. § 1681n.
134 *See* Brothers v. First Leasing, 724 F.2d 789 (9th Cir. 1984) (considering truth in lending title of Consumer Credit Protection Act in interpreting equal credit title).
135 15 U.S.C. § 1691e(b).
136 15 U.S.C. § 1640(a); *see* National Consumer Law Center, Truth in Lending § 8.6.2 (4th ed. 1999 and Supp.).

137 *See* § 11.5.2, *supra.*
138 *See* § 11.6.4.2, *infra.*
139 15 U.S.C. § 1691e(b); *see* § 11.6.4.3.3, *infra.*
140 *See* § 11.6.4, *infra.*

- Did the denial of credit prevent the consumer from purchasing property below its market value, and thus deprive the consumer of the benefit of her bargain? Did the consumer's inability to purchase an item or services, because of the denial of credit, result in additional costs such as alternative lodging or transportation?
- Were any transportation or communication costs incurred by the consumer as a result of the denial of credit, such as extra trips to the creditor's office or store to discuss the denial, or long-distance phone calls to a central office?
- Was the consumer compelled to take time from work to travel to the creditor's office or store to discuss the denial of credit and, if so, was there a resulting loss of pay?
- Was the consumer, whose spouse was the actual credit applicant, required to cosign the credit contract even though she had no separate property or income? If so, it can be argued that the consumer suffered actual damages amounting to the total liability on the contract as a result of the creditor's unlawful requirement.
- Did the consumer incur expense in getting a copy of her credit report to investigate whether the reasons for credit denial were legitimate or discriminatory, or to add or delete a spouse's accounts to improve the credit record?

11.6.2.3 Intangible Damages

Courts under all of the federal discrimination statutes have allowed actual damages for intangible losses, such as pain and suffering, humiliation, or damage to credit rating. One reason for allowing such damages is the strong public policy against discrimination, a public policy opposed not only to the economic injury caused by discrimination, but to the damage that discrimination causes to individuals' sense of worth and civil rights and to the very fabric of our society.[141] In addition, the explicit provision for punitive damages in both the ECOA and the Fair Housing Act indicates a congressional intent that recovery not be limited to out-of-pocket expenses.

Courts award as actual damages injury caused by loss of a credit card's convenience, increased purchasing power, and protection in case of emergency;[142] injury from embarrassment, humiliation, and mental distress;[143] injury caused by inconvenience;[144] injury from the deprivation of constitutional rights;[145] and harm to the applicant's reputation for or actual creditworthiness.[146]

Actual damages for intangible injury are not in lieu of, or a form of, punitive damages but are to be awarded in *addition* to punitive damages. Thus, the Fifth Circuit affirmed an $1000 award for the "private, momentary and personal affront" caused by a flawed denial of credit even though it held that punitive damages were not available under the facts of the case.[147] In a case brought pursuant to California civil rights law, the jury assessed $150,000 in damages against a mortgage broker who discriminated against African-American loan applicants. The court that upheld the verdict noted that "damages for emotional distress may easily support the entire amount of the verdict."[148]

However, as noted earlier, intangible damages may be difficult to prove. Awards for emotional distress often understate the actual harm. Among other reasons, this low valuation can be due to judges or juries underestimating the emotional harm discrimination causes to those who experience it.[149] It may also be difficult to prove the intangible

---

141 *See generally* Larry Heinrich, *The Mental Anguish and Humiliation Suffered by Victims of Housing Discrimination*, 26 J. Marshall L. Rev. 39 (1992); Timothy J. Moran, *Punitive Damages in Fair Housing Litigation: Ending Unwise Restrictions on a Necessary Remedy*, 36 Harv. C.R.-C.L. L. Rev. 279 (2001). According to one court, there is little in-depth research on the personal costs of discrimination and racial exclusion. *See* Broome v. Biondi, 17 F. Supp. 2d 211, 225 n.9 (S.D.N.Y. 1997). The court cited some of the research that is available including Joe R. Feagin & Melvin P. Sikes, Living With Racism: The Black Middle Class Experience 23 (1994) and Ellis Cose, The Rage of a Privileged Class: Why are Middle Class Blacks Angry? Why Should America Care? (1993).

142 Shuman v. Standard Oil Co., 453 F. Supp. 1150 (N.D. Cal. 1978).

143 *See* Fischl v. Gen. Motors Acceptance Corp., 708 F.2d 143 (5th Cir. 1983) (ECOA actual damages may include mental anguish, humiliation or embarrassment); Anderson v. United Fin. Co., 666 F.2d 1274 (9th Cir. 1982) (same); Woods-Drake v. Lundy, 667 F.2d 1198 (5th Cir. 1982) (Fair Housing and Civil Rights Act claims); Smith v. Anchor Bldg. Corp., 536 F.2d 231 (8th Cir. 1976) (Fair Housing Act claim); Williams v. Matthews Co., 499 F.2d 819 (8th Cir. 1974) (same); Jeanty v. McKey & Poague, Inc., 496 F.2d 1119 (7th Cir. 1974) (same); Steele v. Title Realty Co., 478 F.2d 380 (10th Cir. 1973) (same); Sayers v. Gen. Motors Acceptance Corp., 522 F. Supp. 835 (W.D. Mo. 1981) (ECOA claim); Owens v. Magee Fin. Serv., 476 F. Supp. 758 (E.D. La. 1979) (ECOA claim); Shuman v. Standard Oil Co., 453 F. Supp. 1150 (N.D. Cal. 1978) (ECOA claim); Morehead v. Lewis, 432 F. Supp. 674 (N.D. Ill. 1977), aff'd, 594 F.2d 867 (7th Cir. 1979) (Fair Housing Act claim).

144 Morehead v. Lewis, 432 F. Supp. 674 (N.D. Ill. 1977).

145 *Id.*

146 *See* Fischl v. Gen. Motors Acceptance Corp., 708 F.2d 143 (5th Cir. 1983) (actual damages under ECOA may include injury to credit reputation); Anderson v. United Fin. Co., 666 F.2d 1274 (9th Cir. 1982) (same); Ford v. Citizens & S. Nat'l Bank, 700 F. Supp. 1121 (N.D. Ga. 1988) (ECOA damages from being required to sign a mortgage could be difficulty in obtaining credit due to that encumbrance); Shuman v. Standard Oil Co., 453 F. Supp. 1150 (N.D. Cal. 1978) (ECOA case).

147 Bhandari v. First Nat'l Bank of Commerce, 808 F.2d 1082 (5th Cir. 1987), *rev'd in part on other grounds*, 829 F.2d 1343 (5th Cir. 1987) (en banc), *vacated and remanded*, 492 U.S. 901, *reinstated* 887 F.2d 609 (5th Cir. 1989).

148 Green v. Rancho Santa Margarita Mortgage Co., 28 Cal. App. 4th 686, 699, 33 Cal. Rptr. 2d 706 (1994).

149 *See* Timothy J. Moran, *Punitive Damages in Fair Housing Litigation: Ending Unwise Restrictions on a Necessary Remedy*,

harm of living in a less desirable neighborhood. Thus, actual damages are critical, but most effective when pursued in conjunction with punitive damages.

11.6.3 Multiple and Minimum Statutory Damages

None of the federal discrimination statutes provide either multiple or minimum statutory damages. Nevertheless, some relevant state statutes do provide multiple or minimum statutory damages.

There are two types of such statutes. A number of states' general discrimination statutes provide for minimum statutory damages in the $50 to $1000 range, with $100 or $200 being the most common amount.[150] In addition, many state statutes of general application prohibiting unfair or deceptive acts or practices (UDAP statutes) provide treble damages or minimum damages.[151] It may be that a violation of a federal or state credit discrimination statute is a per se state UDAP violation, thus triggering UDAP remedies for violation of credit discrimination statutes.[152]

Minimum statutory damages are useful when actual damages are small or nonexistent and it is unlikely that a court will award any punitive damages. The court will have to award the amount specified by statute (e.g., $100 or $200) if the court finds a statutory violation, no matter the amount of actual damages suffered. Minimum damages are particularly attractive in class actions if the court will award the minimum amount to each class member.

Multiple damage awards (typically treble damages) are useful when actual damages are significant and when a court is unlikely to award punitive damages. In a few states, any UDAP violation mandates a treble damages award.

In considering these state law remedies, it is important to remember that a plaintiff may have to elect *before* filing a complaint whether to pursue a federal ECOA claim or a state law claim.[153]

11.6.4 Punitive Damages

11.6.4.1 General

Punitive damages are available under the ECOA, the Fair Housing Act and the Civil Rights Acts. While some courts are reluctant to award such damages, others are more aggressive in awarding significant punitive damages. The threat of punitive damages is effective not only in cases that go to trial, but also in any settlement negotiation. The creditor may be averse to even a relatively small chance of having to pay large punitive damages, and may settle the case far more generously than if actual damages alone were sought.

Despite the availability and importance of punitive damages, there are a number of potential barriers plaintiffs seeking these awards face. First, punitive damages under the Fair Housing Act and the federal Civil Rights Acts are at the court's discretion. On the other hand, the ECOA contains language that appears to mandate an award of punitive damages. A non-complying creditor "shall be liable . . . for punitive damages . . . in addition to any actual damages" awarded.[154]

There are also limits to the amount of punitive damages that may be awarded. This limit is explicit in the ECOA.[155] Although there is no similar statutory limit in the FHA or the federal Civil Rights Acts, judicial decisions in recent years have limited the availability and amount of punitive damages, as discussed in the following sections.

11.6.4.2 Punitive Damages in FHA and Federal Civil Rights Cases

Although discretionary, punitive damages are widely available under the FHA. However, if a consumer opts for an administrative hearing under the Fair Housing Act, the administrative law judge is *not* empowered to award punitive damages. Punitive damages under the Fair Housing Act are only available if an action is brought before a court.[156]

There are no limits to the size of punitive damage awards under the federal Civil Rights Acts or under the Fair Housing Act. The Fair Housing Act had a $1000 limit on punitive damages but Congress repealed this limit in 1988.[157] As a result, whether one individual, several individuals, or a class brings an action there are no limits to the size of punitive damages that may be awarded under these statutes.[158] Since the removal of the cap punitive damage awards in FHA cases have increased substantially with frequent awards of $100,000 and more.[159]

---

36 Harv. C.R.-C.L. L. Rev. 279, 290 (2001) (commenting that predominantly white juries, for example, may not understand the effect of discrimination on a nonwhite plaintiff).

150 *See* Appx. E, *infra*.

151 National Consumer Law Center, Unfair and Deceptive Acts and Practices (5th ed. 2001).

152 *Id.* at §§ 3.2.7, 5.1.9.5.

153 *See* §§ 11.5.1.3, 11.5.2, *supra*.

154 15 U.S.C. § 1691e(b); *see* Barber v. Rancho Mortgage & Inv. Corp., 26 Cal. App. 4th 1819, 32 Cal. Rptr. 2d 906 (1994).

155 15 U.S.C. § 1691e(b); *see* § 11.6.4.3.2, *infra*.

156 *See* § 11.4.2, *supra* (discussion of the administrative alternative to pursue a Fair Housing Act claim).

157 Pub. L. No. 100-430, 102 Stat. 1633 (1988) (adding 42 U.S.C. § 3613(c)). The House Judiciary Committee specifically identified "disadvantageous limitations on punitive damages" as one of the weaknesses in the existing fair housing law. H.R. Rep. No. 100-711, at 16 (1988).

158 *See* Stokes v. Cetner, 2000 U.S. Dist. LEXIS 2162 (E.D. Mich. Jan. 28, 2000); Broome v. Biondi, 17 F. Supp. 2d 211 (S.D.N.Y. 1997).

159 *See, e.g.,* United States v. Big D Enterprises, Inc., 184 F.3d 924, 932 (8th Cir. 1999) (upholding punitive damages awards total-

Generally, the standard for punitive damages is conduct that is motivated by evil motive or intent, or involves reckless or callous indifference to the federally protected rights of others.[160] This standard requires evidence of the defendant's state of mind and does not require objective proof that the defendant's behavior was outrageous or egregious.[161]

More recently, lower courts have begun to limit the awarding of punitive damages in FHA cases. Some courts have refused to allow juries to consider the issue of punitive damages, even in cases in which there is sufficient evidence of intentional discrimination.[162] Although these cases are often appealed and reversed, they have had a strong chilling effect because many plaintiffs can not or will not appeal these cases.[163]

A second restriction stems from the standard for awarding punitive damages, discussed above, that focuses on the defendant's state of mind rather than objective evidence of egregious conduct. Some courts have interpreted this standard to allow defendants to present a "good faith defense" to plaintiff's claims of punitive damages. Defendants may assert that they did not know their conduct violated the law or that they did not even know that there was a law prohibiting their conduct. The "good faith defense" to punitive damages theory was most recently set forth by the Supreme Court in a Title VII employment discrimination case.[164]

There is some question whether this standard should also apply to FHA cases when the FHA specifically permits the award of punitive damages in all cases in which liability is found.[165] The major problem with the *Kolstad* good faith concept is that it may allow defendants to escape punitive damages if they can successfully argue ignorance of the law. The deterrent effect of punitive damages will be seriously undermined if punitive damages are barred simply because the statute is ambiguous and defendants can make an argument to excuse their conduct.[166]

Another critical issue is whether punitive damages can be awarded if the plaintiff fails to prove any compensable harm. There is a split in the circuits on this issue in FHA cases. In contrast, when the plaintiff has experienced a constitutional violation under the federal Civil Rights Acts, courts have consistently upheld awards of punitive damages even in the absence of compensable damages.[167]

Courts that have addressed this issue under the FHA have come to different conclusions. For example, the Third Circuit has held that compensatory damages are not a prerequisite to punitive damages[168] while the Fourth and Fifth

---

ing $100,000 to three victims), *cert. denied*, 529 U.S. 1018 (2000); Little Field v. McGuffey, 954 F.2d 1337, 1348–50 (7th Cir. 1992) (upholding punitive damage award of $100,000 to single plaintiff); Edwards v. Flagstar Bank, 109 F. Supp. 2d 691, 698 (E.D. Mich. 2000) (awarding $325,000 in punitive damages to single victim of mortgage lending discrimination); Broome v. Biondi, 17 F. Supp. 2d 211 (S.D.N.Y. 1997) (affirming award of $410,000 to couple and $47,000 to single individual); Nationwide Mut. Ins. Co. v. Housing Opportunities Made Equal, Inc. 523 S.E.2d 217 (Va. 2000) (discussing jury's $100 million punitive damage award for fair housing organization in insurance discrimination case). The same court later vacated that ruling. 2000 Va. LEXIS 56 (Va. Mar. 3, 2000). The case was settled in April 2000.

160 Smith v. Wade, 461 U.S. 30, 56, 103 S. Ct. 1625, 75 L. Ed. 2d 632 (1983) (§ 1983 action).

161 Kolstad v. Am. Dental Ass'n, 527 U.S. 526, 119 S. Ct. 2118, 144 L. Ed. 2d 494 (1999) (in Title VII employment case, Court expressly rejected the need to show egregious conduct); Preferred Properties v. Indian River Estates, Inc., 276 F.3d 790, 799 (6th Cir. 2002) (citing Smith v. Wade, 461 U.S. 30, 56 (1983)); Alexander v. Riga, 208 F.3d 419 (3d Cir. 2000), *cert. denied*, 531 U.S. 1069 (2001).

162 *See, e.g.*, Badami v. Flood, 214 F.3d 994, 997 (8th Cir. 2000) (reversing district court determination that evidence of landlord's refusal to rent home to a family with eight children because of family size did not warrant punitive damage instruction); United States v. Ballistrieri, 981 F.2d 916, 936 (7th Cir. 1992) (reversing district court's decision to enter a directed verdict on punitive damages despite evidence that landlord systematically misrepresented availability of apartments to African-American home seekers).

163 *See* Badami v. Flood, 214 F.3d 994, 997 (8th Cir. 2000); United States v. Ballistrieri, 981 F.2d 916, 936 (7th Cir. 1992). *See generally* Timothy J. Moran, *Punitive Damages in Fair Housing Litigation: Ending Unwise Restrictions On A Necessary Remedy*, 36 Harv. C.R.-C.L. L. Rev. 279 (2001).

164 Kolstad v. Am. Dental Ass'n, 527 U.S. 526, 119 S. Ct. 2118, 144 L. Ed. 2d 494 (1999).

165 42 U.S.C. § 3613. To date, three circuits have concluded that the *Kolstad* reasoning does apply in FHA cases. *See* Preferred Properties Inc. v. Indian River Estates, Inc., 276 F.3d 790 (6th Cir. 2002) (court allowed good faith defense, but found that defendant did not meet the standard; court upheld punitive damages award because jury could reasonably have inferred that defendant knew or perceived the risk that his actions violated federal law); Badami v. Flood, 214 F.3d 994, 997 (8th Cir. 2000); Alexander v. Riga, 208 F.3d 419, 430–32 (3d Cir. 2000), *cert. denied*, 531 U.S. 1069 (2001).

166 *See generally* Timothy J. Moran, *Punitive Damages in Fair Housing Litigation: Ending Unwise Restrictions on A Necessary Remedy*, 36 Harv. C.R.-C.L. L. Rev. 279 (2001).

167 *See, e.g.*, La. ACORN Fair Hous. v. LeBlanc, 211 F.3d 298, 303 (5th Cir. 2000) (punitive damages may be awarded in the absence of compensatory damages for § 1982 claims where there is a constitutional violation, but not in FHA cases), *cert. denied*, 532 U.S. 904 (2001); Campos-Orrego v. Rivera, 175 F.3d 89, 98 (1st Cir. 1999) (noting that when the court finds a constitutional violation, an award of actual damages is not required to uphold an award of punitive damages); King v. Macri, 993 F.2d 294, 298 (2d Cir. 1993); Basista v. Weir, 340 F.2d 74, 85–88 (3d Cir. 1965) (holding that no actual damages were required to uphold an award of punitive damages in a § 1983 action).

168 Alexander v. Riga, 208 F.3d 419, 430 (3d Cir. 2000), *cert. denied*, 531 U.S. 1069 (2001). The Seventh and Ninth Circuits have also found that punitive damages may be awarded in housing discrimination cases in the absence of compensatory damages but their statements are arguably dicta. *See* Fountila v. Carter, 571 F.2d 487, 492 (1978); Rogers v. Loether, 467 F.2d 1110, 1112–13 (7th Cir. 1972), *aff'd sub nom.* Curtis v. Loether, 415 U.S. 189 (1974).

Circuits have held that they are.[169] Compounding this troubling trend for plaintiffs are appellate courts that reduce punitive damage awards from lower courts.[170]

11.6.4.3 ECOA and Punitive Damages

11.6.4.3.1 Punitive damages are mandatory under the ECOA

The ECOA contains language that appears to mandate an award of punitive damages. A non-complying creditor "shall be liable . . . for punitive damages . . . in addition to any actual damages" awarded.[171] The one statutory exception is that no punitive damages are available in actions brought against a creditor that is a government or a governmental subdivision, agency, or instrumentality.[172]

However, some courts have ignored the seemingly mandatory nature of ECOA punitive damages awards and have found such damages not appropriate under certain facts, even though an ECOA violation has been proven.[173] Because even unintentional discrimination can provide the basis of an ECOA action, some courts are troubled by the award of punitive damages in every case.

Plaintiffs may attempt to counter such reluctance by pointing out that ECOA punitive damages can not exceed $10,000 and can be as low as appropriate based on the standards set out in the statute.[174] In addition, the ECOA requirement that punitive damages "shall" be awarded should be strictly construed.[175]

When a court refuses to make an award of punitive damages mandatory, it will still award such damages either when the creditor's action is wanton, malicious, or oppressive or when the creditor recklessly disregarded applicable law.[176] In addition, proof of actual damage is not a prerequisite to a finding of punitive damages under the ECOA.[177] Instead, the size of actual damages is one factor among several in determining the size of the award. If there are no actual damages other factors may still argue for a large punitive damages award.[178]

Moreover, many of the same courts that refuse to make an award of punitive damages mandatory have been generous in awarding plaintiffs damages for such intangible injuries as humiliation, affront, and damage to credit reputation.[179] The clear implication is that the plaintiff should attempt to show both the creditor's wantonness or recklessness (to establish punitive damages) and also the impact of the practice on the applicant (to establish actual damages for intangible injury).

---

169   La. ACORN Fair Hous. v. LeBlanc, 211 F.3d 298, 303 (5th Cir. 2000) (vacating $10,000 punitive damages award to victims of racial discrimination when jury did not award compensatory damages), *cert. denied*, 532 U.S. 904 (2001); People Helpers Found., Inc. v. City of Richmond, 12 F.3d 1321, 1327 (4th Cir. 1993) (court acknowledged that the language of the FHA did not require an award of actual damages in order to award punitive damages but still found that when plaintiff had not demonstrated actual harm, punitive damages should also be barred). For a discussion of the ramifications of the *Louisiana ACORN* decision and flaws in the court's reasoning, see Johanna M. Lundgren, *A Weakened Enforcement Power: The Fifth Circuit Limits Punitive Damages Under the Fair Housing Act in Louisiana ACORN Fair Housing v. LeBlanc*, 46 Loy. L. Rev. 1325 (2000).

170   *See, e.g.*, Allahar v. Zahora, 59 F.3d 693 (7th Cir. 1995) (when white seller initially refused to sell his home to an Indian man, jury awarded $10,000 in compensatory damages and $7,500 in punitive damages; the district court set aside the punitive damage award entirely and the Seventh Circuit affirmed, noting that the $20,000 in attorney fees awarded together with the compensatory damages would provide adequate compensation); Szwast v. Carlton Apartments, 102 F. Supp. 2d 777 (E.D. Mich. 2000) (court reduced a punitive damages award of $400,000 to $30,000 in a case of intentional familial status discrimination when jury awarded only $3,000 in compensatory damages); Darby v. Heather Ridge, 827 F. Supp. 1296, 1300–01 (E.D. Mich. 1993) (reducing jury's punitive damages award of $250,000 to $50,000 to match compensatory damages award). *But see* United States v. Big D Enterprises, Inc., 184 F.3d 924 (8th Cir. 1999), *cert. denied*, 529 U.S. 1018 (2000) (court affirmed a punitive damages award of $100,000 to three victims even though the jury awarded only $1,000 in compensatory damages).

171   15 U.S.C. § 1691e(b); *see* Barber v. Rancho Mortgage & Inv. Corp., 26 Cal. App. 4th 1819, 32 Cal. Rptr. 2d 906 (1994).

172   15 U.S.C. § 1691e(b).

173   *See, e.g.*, Newton v. United Companies Fin. Corp., 24 F. Supp. 2d 444 (E.D. Pa. 1998) (punitive damages not awarded because the case was one of first impression).

174   *See* § 11.6.4.3.2, *infra*.

175   *See* Bhandari v. First Nat'l Bank of Commerce, 808 F.2d 1082 (5th Cir. 1987), *rev'd in part on other grounds*, 829 F.2d 1343 (5th Cir. 1987) (en banc), *vacated and remanded*, 492 U.S. 901, *reinstated*, 887 F.2d 609 (5th Cir. 1989) (while following earlier Fifth Circuit precedent that punitive damages were not mandatory, questioning this result).

176   *See* Fischl v. Gen. Motors Acceptance Corp., 708 F.2d 143 (5th Cir. 1983); Anderson v. United Fin. Co., 666 F.2d 1274 (9th Cir. 1982); Ricci v. Key Bancshares, 662 F. Supp. 1132 (D. Me. 1987); Sayers v. Gen. Motors Acceptance Corp., 522 F. Supp. 835 (W.D. Mo. 1981); Vander Missen v. Kellogg-Citizens Nat'l Bank, 481 F. Supp. 742 (E.D. Wis. 1979); Shuman v. Standard Oil Co., 453 F. Supp. 1150 (N.D. Cal. 1978); *see also* Fernandez v. Hull Coop. Bank, 1979 U.S. Dist. LEXIS 8657 (D. Mass. Nov. 8, 1979) (following *Shuman*).

177   Fischl v. Gen. Motors Acceptance Corp., 708 F.2d 143 (5th Cir. 1983); Anderson v. United Fin. Co., 666 F.2d 1274 (9th Cir. 1982); Ricci v. Key Bancshares, 662 F. Supp. 1132 (D. Me. 1987); Cherry v. Amoco Oil Co., 490 F. Supp. 1026 (N.D. Ga. 1980); Smith v. Lakeside Foods Inc., 449 F. Supp. 171 (N.D. Ill. 1978).

178   *See* § 11.6.4.3.3, *infra*.

179   *See* Bhandari v. First Nat'l Bank of Commerce, 808 F.2d 1082 (5th Cir. 1987), *rev'd in part on other grounds*, 829 F.2d 1343 (5th Cir. 1987) (en banc); Fischl v. Gen. Motors Acceptance Corp., 708 F.2d 143 (5th Cir. 1983); Shuman v. Standard Oil Co., 453 F. Supp. 1150 (N.D. Cal. 1978).

11.6.4.3.2 Limits on the size of ECOA punitive damage awards

The ECOA limits the size of a punitive damages award. For an individual action, the maximum punitive damages award is $10,000 in addition to any actual damages that are awarded.[180] For a class action, the limit on punitive damages is the lesser of $500,000 or one percent of the creditor's net worth[181] (when a creditor's net worth is less than one million dollars, higher total punitive damages are actually available in an individual action).

This limit only applies to punitive damages and there is no limit to the size of actual damages that may be recoverable in a class action. Thus, when the maximum punitive damages in a class action is relatively small, proof of actual damages becomes critical.

It appears that the $10,000 limit applies to each creditor, applicant, and violation involved in a case, so that the total punitive damages in an ECOA case can be significantly more than $10,000.[182] The statute says that "any" creditor is liable for $10,000 for failing to comply with "any" requirement relating to the aggrieved "applicant." Thus, if there is more than one creditor, more than one ECOA requirement that is violated, or more than one aggrieved applicant, there can be multiple punitive damage awards. For example, in one case, $10,000 in punitive damages was awarded against one creditor for discrimination based on national origin and another $10,000 in punitive damages was awarded against a different but related creditor for failure to notify the applicant of an adverse action.[183]

The ECOA also provides a list of relevant factors to be considered by a court when determining the amount of punitive damages to be awarded. These factors are:

- The amount of actual damages awarded;
- The frequency and persistence of noncompliance;
- The creditor's resources;
- The number of persons adversely affected;
- The extent to which noncompliance was intentional; and
- Other relevant factors.[184]

These factors are detailed in the following subsections.

11.6.4.3.3 Amount of actual damages awarded as factor in determining size of punitive damages award

The award of actual damages is not a prerequisite to the award of punitive damages under the ECOA, but a large actual damages award is one factor favoring a large punitive damages award. The statute provides that, to determine the amount of punitive damages to award, "the court shall consider, among other relevant factors, the amount of any actual damages awarded."[185]

The ECOA cases that have grappled with this issue have held consistently that an ECOA plaintiff may be entitled to recover punitive damages whether or not actual damages have been established.[186] Further, cases arising under statutes analogous to the ECOA, such as the Fair Credit Reporting Act and Title VIII of the Civil Rights Act of 1968, have also allowed recovery of punitive damages regardless of the award of actual damages.[187]

11.6.4.3.4 Frequency and persistence of creditor's noncompliance as factor in determining size of punitive damages award

Another factor used to determine the amount of punitive damages is the frequency and persistence of the creditor's failure to comply.[188] This factor can be interpreted in two different ways.

First, it can refer to repeated discriminatory acts committed against the consumer within the same or successive transactions. For example, a creditor might deny credit because of the consumer's race and also give an inaccurate statement of the reasons for the denial. Or the creditor, confronted with evidence of its unlawful actions, may repeatedly refuse to correct them for that applicant.

A second interpretation of this provision could be that "frequency and persistence of failures of compliance" by the creditor refers to violations committed against persons other than that particular claimant. To establish these other failures of compliance the following sources should be investigated:

- State and federal agency compliance reports;

---

180 15 U.S.C. § 1691e(b).
181 15 U.S.C. § 1691e(b).
182 *See* Ricci v. Key Bancshares, 662 F. Supp. 1132 (D. Me. 1987).
183 *Id.*
184 15 U.S.C. § 1691e(b).
185 15 U.S.C. § 1691e(b).
186 *See* Fischl v. Gen. Motors Acceptance Corp., 708 F.2d 143 (5th Cir. 1983) (punitive damages may be awarded, regardless of proof of actual damages, if the creditor's conduct is adjudged wanton, malicious, or oppressive, or if the creditor is deemed to have acted in reckless disregard of applicable law); Anderson v. United Fin. Co., 666 F.2d 1274 (9th Cir. 1982) (punitive damages may be awarded absent a showing of actual damages, although an award is not required for every violation); Cherry v. Amoco Oil Co., 490 F. Supp. 1026 (N.D. Ga. 1980); Smith v. Lakeside Foods, Inc., 449 F. Supp. 171 (N.D. Ill. 1978).
187 *See* Rogers v. Loether, 467 F.2d 1110, 1112 n.4 (7th Cir. 1972), *aff'd sub nom.* Curtis v. Loether, 415 U.S. 189 (1974) (Fair Housing Act); Ackerly v. Credit Bureau of Sheridan, Inc., 385 F. Supp. 658 (D. Wyo. 1974) (FCRA). However, some courts, particularly in FHA cases, have begun to require compensatory damages as a prerequisite to awarding punitive damages. *See* § 11.6.4.2, *supra.*
188 15 U.S.C. § 1691e(b).

- Court records, which may reveal other suits brought against the creditor;
- Complaints and enforcement proceedings brought against the creditor before state commissions enforcing state equal credit or other civil rights laws;
- The creditor's forms, which may contain facial violations of ECOA prohibitions, such as prohibited inquiries, or may provide no space for a cosigner to sign a security agreement without also becoming liable for the debt;
- The creditor's internal operations guidelines or training manuals as to credit-granting procedures or collection procedures; and
- The creditor's other contracts, which may suggest discriminatory practices; for example, a review may reveal a significant percentage of spousal signatures or a geographic analysis may suggest redlining.

11.6.4.3.5 Creditor's resources as factor in determining size of punitive damages award

Another factor in determining the amount of punitive damages is the resources of the creditor.[189] The statute does not define resources, which could refer to the creditor's net worth, assets, profits, or some other measure of resources. Most likely, Congress intended resources to mean the net worth of the creditor, as this standard is used in the statute to set the upper limit on awards of punitive damages in class actions.[190]

The Truth in Lending Act, which contains the same limitation on damages in class actions[191] as the ECOA does, has given rise to case law which may be helpful in determining a creditor's net worth. To date, only one reported TILA case has dealt extensively with the rights of the class in discovery to investigate the creditor's net worth. The court held that the plaintiff was entitled to discover information about the creditor's assets, liabilities, balance sheets, and audits but could not discover information about gross income, income tax returns, or the persons who prepared the defendant's income tax returns.[192] When the original creditor partnership was dissolved and the partners became the shareholders of a new corporation that allegedly acquired the accounts, assets, and liabilities of the partnership, discovery of the assets and liabilities of the corporation was permitted as possibly relevant to the partnership's net worth.[193] The class was also entitled to discover financial

information, including tax returns, from each partner of the partnership extending credit.[194]

In order to maximize the value and extent of the creditor's resources, the term creditor should be defined as broadly as possible. Plaintiffs should plead that the creditor is the parent of the finance company that denied credit to the client, as well as the local finance company. Plaintiffs should also bring assignees and any others who participated in the credit decision into the case as defendants.[195] For example, the creditor could be General Motors Acceptance Corporation as well as Honest Abe's Chevy Lot; the creditor could also be General Electric Credit Corporation, to whom Ace Furniture assigns its credit contracts.[196] Another issue involves defining the point in time to measure the creditor's worth. Because there are no ECOA cases on point, the best approach is to refer to analogous TILA cases.[197]

11.6.4.3.6 Number of persons adversely affected as factor in determining size of punitive damages award

In calculating punitive damages, another factor to consider is the number of persons adversely affected.[198] The meaning of this provision is relatively clear when applied to an ECOA class action. In a class action, in which there is a limit on punitive damages, a court would most likely award less than the maximum amount when the class affected is small.[199] Accordingly, there is an advantage to defining the class of ECOA plaintiffs as broadly as possible.

In an individual ECOA action, establishing the "number of persons adversely affected" is more problematic. It is important to show, if possible, that the creditor has discriminated against persons other than the individual claimant.

---

189 15 U.S.C. § 1691e(b).

190 15 U.S.C. § 1691e(b). Punitive damages in class actions may not exceed "the lesser of $500,000 or 1 per centum of the net worth of the creditor."

191 15 U.S.C. § 1640(a)(2)(B).

192 Hunter v. Miller, Clearinghouse No. 22,266 (W.D. Mo. 1977). *See generally* National Consumer Law Center, Truth in Lending § 8.8.3.3 (4th ed. 1999 and Supp.).

193 Hunter v. Miller, Clearinghouse No. 22,266 (W.D. Mo. 1977).

194 *Id.*

195 *See* § 11.3.2, *supra.*

196 Cases brought under the Truth in Lending Act dealing with a creditor's net worth, assignee liability, and reaching the parent company also may be helpful in this area of ECOA law. *See, e.g.*, Ransom v. S & S Food Ctr., Inc., 700 F.2d 670 (11th Cir. 1983) (combined net worth of both defendants considered); Barber v. Kimbrell's, Inc., 577 F.2d 216 (4th Cir. 1978) (limiting the parent company's liability to resources allocable to its one store which committed Truth in Lending violations); *see also* Edmondson v. Allen-Russell Ford, Inc., 577 F.2d 291 (5th Cir. 1978); Price v. Franklin Inv. Co., 574 F.2d 594 (D.C. Cir. 1978); Jones v. Goodyear Tire & Rubber Co., 442 F. Supp. 1157 (E.D. La. 1977); Clausen v. Beneficial Fin. Co., 423 F. Supp. 985 (N.D. Cal. 1976).

197 *See* National Consumer Law Center, Truth in Lending § 8.8.3.3 (4th ed. 1999 and Supp.).

198 15 U.S.C. § 1691e(b).

199 15 U.S.C. § 1691e(b).

11.6.4.3.7 *Extent to which creditor's noncompliance was intentional as factor in determining size of punitive damages award*

Another relevant factor in determining the amount of punitive damages is "the extent to which the creditor's failure of compliance was intentional."[200] This factor somewhat overlaps the "frequency and persistence of noncompliance" factor.[201]

In enacting the ECOA, Congress specifically refused to require that a creditor's violation of the ECOA be "willful" in order to warrant a punitive damages award,[202] despite intensive lobbying for such a clause by credit industry representatives.[203] Instead, Congress adopted the present punitive damages provision, in which the creditor's intent is merely one of several factors to be weighed by the court.

A related issue, discussed in a previous subsection, is whether an award of punitive damages is mandatory or whether they will only be awarded for certain types of violations, such as when the creditor acts recklessly.[204] However, even courts that refuse to make punitive damages mandatory do not require proof of intentional discrimination. Instead, punitive damages are triggered by wanton or reckless conduct, and intentional discrimination is one of the factors that will increase the size of a punitive damages award.

11.6.4.3.8 *Other relevant factors in determining size of punitive damages award*

The ECOA provides that a court shall also consider "other relevant factors," in determining the amount of punitive damages,[205] along with the specific factors discussed above.[206] Nothing in the statute, the legislative history, or case law under the ECOA indicates what might constitute other relevant factors. A case[207] brought under the federal Fair Debt Collection Practices Act, however, held that that statute's language[208] allowed "other relevant factors" to be considered in measuring the amount of "additional damages" under the statute.[209] The court weighed the following factors not specified in the statute to arrive at an award of additional damages:

- The violation occurred within one year of the effective date of the Act;
- The defendant had no specific intent to injure the plaintiff;
- The contact between the defendant debt collector and the plaintiff was limited; and
- The defendant was an interstate organization, with access to legal advice.

Factors such as these also would be relevant to establishing the amount of punitive damages under the ECOA. Additional factors which could be developed for particular situations might include the relative bargaining power and sophistication of the parties, particularly if the client's primary language is not English, the unavailability of other sources of credit, and the urgency of the client's need for credit.

11.6.5 Equitable and Declaratory Relief

11.6.5.1 Prospective Relief

Equitable and declaratory relief is available under all of the federal credit discrimination statutes. Not only is it clear that such relief is available for a violation of the federal Civil Rights Acts, but the Fair Housing Act specifically states that the court "may grant as relief, as the court deems appropriate, any permanent or temporary injunction, temporary restraining order, or other order."[210] Similarly, the ECOA states that an aggrieved credit applicant may obtain "such equitable and declaratory relief as is necessary to enforce the requirements" of the ECOA.[211]

Equitable relief is particularly important when the creditor involved is a government agency. The ECOA explicitly exempts governmental bodies, subdivisions, and agencies from liability for punitive damages under the ECOA.[212] Equitable relief can also be an effective way to quickly stop a creditor's practice not just on an individual basis but also on behalf of all other potential applicants.

---

200 15 U.S.C. § 1691e(b).

201 *See* § 11.6.4.3.4, *supra.*

202 The "willfulness" amendment was proposed in the House, H.R. 210, 94th Cong., at 9 (1975), but was later dropped by the House-Senate Conference Committee. Congresswoman Leonor Sullivan explained, in her separate comments appended to the original House bill, that the "willfulness" language should be omitted because it connoted a standard used in criminal rather than civil statutes. H.R. 210, 94th Cong., at 9, 18 (1975).

203 *See Proposed Amendments to the Equal Credit Opportunity Act: Hearings on H.R. 14856 and H.R. 14908 before the Subcomm. on Consumer Affairs of the House Comm. on Banking and Currency,* 93d Cong., 430 (1974) (statement of National Retail Merchants Ass'n representative Kerr); *id.* at 483 (statement of Interbank Card Ass'n counsel Morgan).

204 *See* § 11.6.4.3.1, *supra.*

205 15 U.S.C. § 1691e(b).

206 *See* §§ 11.6.4.3.3 to 11.6.4.3.7, *supra.*

207 Carrigan v. Cent. Adjustment Bureau, Inc., 502 F. Supp. 468 (N.D. Ga. 1980).

208 15 U.S.C. § 1692k(b).

209 The Fair Debt Collection Practices Act's "additional damages" provision corresponds to the ECOA's "punitive damages" provision in many respects. Relevant factors in awarding FDCPA damages include: the frequency and persistence of the noncompliance; the nature of the noncompliance; the extent to which the noncompliance was intentional; and "other relevant factors."

210 42 U.S.C. § 3613(c).

211 15 U.S.C. § 1691e(c).

212 15 U.S.C. § 1691e(b).

When seeking an injunction to stop a creditor's practice the issue may arise whether the individual plaintiff is likely to be injured in the future and thus has a stake in the injunctive relief. For example, when an individual is no longer doing business with a creditor and there is no evidence the individual intends to deal with that creditor in the future, a court has refused to grant injunctive relief because the plaintiff did not have standing to seek such relief.[213]

There will not be a standing issue when debtors continue to have a relationship with a creditor and wish to change the creditor's practices. For example, injunctive relief would be appropriate to prevent a creditor from improperly requiring a spouse's signature when credit is renewed.[214]

11.6.5.2 Voiding an Individual's Obligation Under a Note or Security Agreement

When creditors require cosigners or guarantors to sign a note or security agreement in violation of the ECOA it is often desirable to seek to void the cosigner or guarantor's liability under the note or security agreement. The most common instance in which the situation arises is when a creditor, in violation of the ECOA, requires a husband to obtain his wife's signature for a loan even though the husband was creditworthy on his own.[215]

Borrowers in such cases seek to have this claim treated as an affirmative defense because presence of this factual issue will likely prevent the entry of summary judgment. The ECOA claim will then be a factual issue to be addressed at trial. Lenders, in contrast, seek to have the ECOA claim treated as a compulsory counterclaim, which allows the lender to pursue a motion for summary judgment separately from the ECOA claim. Also, if the lenders' view prevails, ECOA claims cannot be used to void the underlying obligation.[216]

There is a split among federal courts on whether the ECOA claim should be treated as a defense or a counterclaim, although the current trend is for courts to allow the ECOA violation to be raised as an affirmative defense.[217] State courts are also divided.[218]

Most courts that allow the obligation to be voided will do so only with respect to the impermissibly obligated party (the wife in the above scenario). This party, in these courts' view, should be relieved of her obligation because, but for the ECOA violation, she would not otherwise have incurred the obligation.[219] The wife is relieved from her obligation but the underlying debt is not necessarily void. The husband remains liable. The husband can still make a claim for

---

213 Bhandari v. First Nat'l Bank of Commerce, 808 F.2d 1082 (5th Cir. 1987), *rev'd on other grounds*, 829 F.2d 1343 (5th Cir. 1987) (en banc), *vacated and remanded*, 492 U.S. 901, *reinstated*, 887 F.2d 609 (5th Cir. 1989).

214 Chestnut Hill Gulf, Inc. v. Cumberland Farms, Inc., 788 F. Supp. 616 (D. Mass. 1992) (franchisees were granted preliminary injunction stopping Cumberland's practice of requiring spouses to sign a guarantee as a condition to renewing franchises).

215 The general rule against discrimination prevents a creditor from requiring a spouse or other person to cosign or guaranty a loan on a prohibited basis. The ECOA also sets out other limitations as to when a creditor may require a guarantor or cosigner. Reg. B, 12 C.F.R. § 202.7(d)(1); *see* § 5.6, *supra*. Some commentators and courts question whether there is an ECOA violation in these circumstances because the husband was arguably the party discriminated against and the ECOA was intended to protect women from discrimination. *See, e.g.,* CMF Va. Land, L.P. v. Brinson, 806 F. Supp. 90, 96 (E.D. Va. 1992).

216 *See generally* Ami diLorenzo, *Regulation B: How Lenders Can Fight Back Against the Affirmative Use of Regulation B*, 8 U. Miami Bus. L. Rev. 215 (2000); Andrea Michele Farley, Note, *The Spousal Defense—A Ploy to Escape Payment or Simple*

Application of the Equal Credit Opportunity Act?, 49 Vand. L. Rev. 1287 (1996).

217 Cases allowing the affirmative defense: *See, e.g.,* Bolduc v. Beal Bank, 994 F. Supp. 82 (D.N.H. 1998), *vacating preliminary injunction*, 167 F.3d 667 (1st Cir. 1999) (bank's illegal requirement of wife's cosignature invalidates wife's obligation); Silverman v. Eastrich Multiple Investor Fund, L.P., 51 F.3d 28 (3d Cir. 1995)., *rev'g*, 857 F. Supp. 447 (E.D. Pa. 1994); Fed. Deposit Ins. Corp. v. Medmark, 897 F. Supp. 511 (D. Kan. 1995); Sharp Electronic Corp. v. Yoggev, 1995 U.S. Dist. LEXIS 5751 (E.D. Pa. Apr. 28, 1995); Integra Bank/Pittsburgh v. Freeman, 839 F. Supp. 326 (E.D. Pa. 1993); Am. Sec. Bank v. York, 1992 U.S. Dist. LEXIS 14309 (D.D.C. Sept. 1, 1992). Cases refusing to allow the affirmative defense: Fed. Deposit Ins. Corp. v. 32 Edwardsville, Inc., 873 F. Supp. 1474 (D. Kan. 1995) (wife could not assert ECOA violation as an affirmative defense that would invalidate the guaranty); CMF Va. Land, L.P. v. Brinson, 806 F. Supp. 90 (E.D. Va. 1992); Diamond v. Union Bank & Trust, 776 F. Supp. 542 (N.D. Okla. 1991). These cases refusing to allow the affirmative defense, however, fail to discern the difference between releasing only the liability of the illegally obtained cosignor versus voiding the underlying obligation entirely. *See* Andrea Michele Farley, Note, *The Spousal Defense—A Ploy to Escape Payment or Simple Application of the Equal Credit Opportunity Act?*, 49 Vand. L. Rev. 1287 (1996).

218 Cases allowing the affirmative defense: *See, e.g.,* Douglas County Nat. Bank v. Pfeiff, 809 P.2d 1100 (Colo. Ct. App. 1991); Nat'l Collectors & Liquidators, L.P. v. Millco of Danbury, Inc., 2001 Conn. Super. LEXIS 2254 (Conn. Super. Ct. July 31, 2001); Eure v. Jefferson Nat'l Bank, 448 S.E.2d 417 (Va. 1994); Transamerica Comm. Fin. Corp. v. Naef, 842 P.2d 539 (Wyo. 1992). Cases refusing to allow the affirmative defense: St. Paul Fire & Marine Ins. Co. v. Barge, 483 S.E.2d 883 (Ga. Ct. App. 1997); Spottiswoode v. Levine, 730 A.2d 166 (Me. 1999), *vacated and remanded on other grounds*, 769 A.2d 849 (Me. 2001); Stewart Title Guar. Co. v. WKC Restaurants Venture Co., 961 S.W.2d 874 (Mo. Ct. App. 1998).

219 *See* Silverman v. Eastrich Multiple Investor Fund, L.P., 51 F.3d 28 (3d Cir. 1995); Integra Bank/Pittsburgh v. Freeman, 839 F. Supp. 326, 329 (E.D. Pa. 1993) (while an ECOA violation should not void the underlying credit transaction, an offending creditor should not be permitted to look for payment to parties who, but for the ECOA violation, would not have incurred personal liability on the underlying debt in the first instance—the creditor is in no worse position than if it had followed the law when the credit transaction occurred; but the purpose of the ECOA is not furthered by allowing the permissibly obligated guarantor to assert an ECOA violation as a defense to liability).

damages which can be raised affirmatively within the two-year statute of limitations or by way of recoupment in jurisdictions which allow it.[220]

11.6.6 Attorney Fees and Costs

11.6.6.1 General Standards

All of the federal discrimination laws provide for attorney fees for prevailing plaintiffs, but the language of the various statutes' attorney fee provisions differ somewhat. The ECOA states that the costs of the action together with a reasonable attorney fee, as determined by the court, *shall* be awarded in the case of any successful action.[221] The Fair Housing Act and the federal Civil Rights Acts state that the court, in its discretion, may allow the prevailing party a reasonable attorney fee and costs.[222]

These two standards are not so dissimilar as a first reading might indicate. The ECOA standard requires a successful *applicant* to be awarded fees, but makes no provision for an award of fees to a prevailing creditor. Nevertheless, Federal Rule of Civil Procedure 11 provides a creditor with fees if the applicant's ECOA claim is not well grounded in fact, not warranted by existing law, not a good faith argument for the extension, modification or reversal of existing law, or is interposed for an improper purpose, such as to harass, cause unnecessary delay or needlessly increase the cost of litigation.

A unanimous U.S. Supreme Court in *Christiansburg Garment Co. v. Equal Employment Opportunity Commission*,[223] has interpreted the Civil Rights Act attorney fee standard[224] much in the same fashion as the ECOA standard is applied in practice. The Court found in this case that prevailing plaintiffs should recover "in all but special circumstances."[225] At the same time, according to the Court, prevailing defendants should not routinely recover fees, and should only do so when the plaintiff's claim was frivolous, unreasonable, or without foundation.[226]

The Supreme Court has also indicated that its rulings concerning Civil Rights Act attorney fee awards are equally applicable to other federal laws (such as the ECOA) providing attorney fees for prevailing plaintiffs.[227] As a result, for all practical purposes, the various attorney fee provisions found in discrimination laws can be treated as interchangeable, and the substantial case law in each circuit on federal fee-shifting statutes should apply to the ECOA, Fair Housing Act, and the federal Civil Rights Acts.

Because of the extensive treatment of federal fee-shifting statutes in other treatises, this section will only provide a brief overview, relying on case law interpreting various federal fee-shifting statutes. Practitioners are urged to supplement this description by consulting other treatises.[228]

11.6.6.2 When Is an Action Successful?

The ECOA awards fees in a "successful action" and the Civil Rights Act standard is that fees are awarded when the aggrieved party "prevails." One question raised by these standards is whether a consumer prevails when successful on one claim but not on a number of related credit discrimination claims. As a general rule, prevailing on only one claim is sufficient as long as the result is a good one for the plaintiff.[229] But attorney fees sometimes will not be awarded when the plaintiff prevails only in the technical sense of receiving nominal damages and fails to obtain any of the other relief sought.[230] On the other hand, even a default judgment can be a successful action.[231] Fees should also be

---

220 *Integra Bank/Pittsburgh*, 839 F. Supp. at 329–330 (injury may occur when, for example, an objectively qualified loan applicant or guarantor is nonetheless impermissibly required to secure a spouse's or other party's signature); *see* § 11.7.2, *infra*.

221 15 U.S.C. § 1691e(d). The ECOA standard for attorney fees is virtually identical to that found in the Truth in Lending Act. *See* National Consumer Law Center, Truth in Lending § 8.9 (4th ed. 1999 and Supp.).

222 42 U.S.C. §§ 1988(b), 3613(c)(2); *see* Hunter v. Trenton Hous. Auth., 698 A.2d 25, 27 n.4 (N.J. Super. Ct. App. Div. 1997) (common law under federal civil rights litigation that prevailing party should ordinarily recover attorney fees absent special circumstances is equally applicable to FHA).

223 434 U.S. 412, 98 S. Ct. 694, 54 L. Ed. 2d 648 (1978).

224 The Court was interpreting Title VII of the Civil Rights Act, 42 U.S.C. § 2000e-5(k), but the result should be the same under the Fair Housing Act and 42 U.S.C. § 1988.

225 434 U.S. at 417.

226 *Id.* at 421; *see* Bryant Woods Inn, Inc. v. Howard County, 124 F.3d 597 (4th Cir. 1997); *see also* Deadwyler v. Volkswagen of Am., Inc., 748 F. Supp. 1146 (W.D.N.C. 1990), *aff'd*, 1992 U.S. App. LEXIS 14891 (4th Cir. June 25, 1992) (per curiam) ("may" award defendant attorney fees interpreted as requiring fees only when action frivolous).

227 Hensley v. Eckerhart, 461 U.S. 424, 103 S. Ct. 1933, 76 L. Ed. 2d 40 (1983) (Civil Rights Acts case); *see also* DeJesus v. Banco Popular de Puerto Rico, 918 F.2d 232 (1st Cir. 1990) (jurisprudence concerning attorney fees under Civil Rights Acts and other fee-shifting statutes applicable to TILA).

228 In particular see National Consumer Law Center, Truth in Lending § 8.9 (4th ed. 1999 and Supp.), dealing with attorney fees under the Truth in Lending Act.

229 *See* Hensley v. Eckerhart, 461 U.S. 424, 103 S. Ct. 1933, 76 L. Ed. 2d 40 (1983); Postow v. OBA Fed. Sav. & Loan Ass'n, 627 F.2d 1370 (D.C. Cir. 1980) (Truth in Lending case); *cf.* Smith v. Norwest Fin. Acceptance, Inc., 129 F.3d 1408, 1418–19 (10th Cir. 1997); Johnson v. Liberty Mortgage Corp. Northwest, 1997 U.S. Dist. LEXIS 15985 (N.D. Ill. Sept. 30, 1997) (no requirement that fees be proportional to damages), *aff'd*, 192 F.3d 656 (7th Cir. 1999).

230 *See* Farrar v. Hobby, 506 U.S. 103, 113 S. Ct. 566, 121 L. Ed. 2d 494 (1992) (one dollar nominal recovery when twelve million dollars sought).

231 City Fin. Co. v. Boykin, 358 S.E.2d 83 (N.C. Ct. App. 1987) (state deceptive practices act claim); Rodriguez v. Holmstrom, 627 S.W.2d 198 (Tex. Civ. App. 1981) (same).

awarded if the consumer prevails on appeal.[232]

If the consumer raises an ECOA counterclaim to a creditor's collection action, the action is successful even if the action results in a net recovery for the creditor.[233] If an action is by way of recoupment (after the statute of limitations has run on the discrimination claim), so that the discrimination claim can at most offset the creditor's collection action, an attorney fee award is not therefore limited to the amount at issue in the collection action. A successful defense is a successful action meriting an attorney fee award even if this exceeds the amount sought by the creditor.[234]

An award of fees need not be predicated on litigating a claim to a final verdict. A default judgment is a successful action and, therefore, attorney fees should be awarded even if the creditor never responds to the complaint.[235] A consent decree,[236] injunctive relief,[237] or a settlement[238] also may be considered successful actions warranting fee awards.

However, a U.S. Supreme Court decision handed down in 2001 casts some doubt on whether a settlement that is not incorporated into a court order can be the basis for an award of attorney fees.[239] Prior to this decision, it was widely accepted that a voluntary change in practices or policies in response to a suit could qualify as a successful action. This "catalyst theory" held that a plaintiff prevails and is therefore entitled to a recovery under a federal statutory fee provision when the lawsuit is the cause of the defendant's change of conduct that results in the termination of the litigation.

In *Buckhannon*, the U.S. Supreme Court rejected the awarding of fees to plaintiffs as the prevailing parties under the catalyst theory.[240] Because the plaintiffs in that case had not obtained an enforceable judgment on the merits or a court-ordered consent decree, they were not entitled to an award of fees. The case construed the fee-shifting provisions of fair housing laws and the Americans with Disabilities Act, but the Supreme Court made it clear that it was announcing a general rule that applied to most, if not all, federal fee-shifting statutes.[241] Courts have since applied the ruling to the civil rights fee-shifting statute,[242] the Equal Access to Justice Act,[243] and the Individuals with Disabilities Education Act,[244] all of which, like the statute construed in *Buckhannon*, use the term "prevailing party."

The full effects of *Buckhannon* are not yet clear. On one hand, the case only controls as to federal claims, and not UDAP or other state law claims. Courts interpreting state fee-shifting statutes may find *Buckhannon* persuasive, but are still free to adopt their own views about the catalyst theory and the formal requirements of settlements.[245] Note that because the court must approve the settlement of class actions,[246] the *Buckhannon* ruling should not pose any additional complications in class actions.

11.6.6.3 Fees for Legal Services, Pro Bono, and Pro Se Attorneys

Attorney fees should be awarded to legal services attorneys or other pro bono attorneys, even though the client is not obligated to pay the attorney or even though a fee is not

232 Martinez v. Idaho First Nat'l Bank, 755 F.2d 1376 (9th Cir. 1985) (TILA case); Varner v. Century Fin. Co., 738 F.2d 1143 (11th Cir. 1984) (same); Dias v. Bank of Haw., 732 F.2d 1401 (9th Cir. 1984) (same); *In re* Pine, 705 F.2d 936 (7th Cir. 1983) (same).

233 *See* Hayer v. Nat'l Bank of Alaska, 619 P.2d 474 (Alaska 1980) (TILA case).

234 Carr v. Blazer Fin. Services, Inc., 598 F.2d 1368 (5th Cir. 1979) (TILA case); Plant v. Blazer Fin. Services, Inc., 598 F.2d 1357 (5th Cir. 1979) (same); Bostic v. Am. Gen. Fin., Inc., 87 F. Supp. 2d 611 (S.D. W. Va. 2000); Burley v. Bastrop Loan Co., 407 F. Supp. 773 (W.D. La. 1975) (same), *rev'd on other grounds*, 590 F.2d 160 (5th Cir. 1979); *In re* McCausland, 63 B.R. 665 (Bankr. E.D. Pa. 1986) (same); *In re* DiCianno, 58 B.R. 810 (Bankr. E.D. Pa. 1986) (same); *In re* Smith, No. 83-01921 (Bankr. D.S.C. Jan. 29, 1985) (same).

235 *See* City Fin. Co. v. Boykin, 358 S.E.2d 83 (N.C. Ct. App. 1987) (state deceptive practices act claim); Rodriguez v. Holmstrom, 627 S.W.2d 198 (Tex. Civ. App. 1981) (same).

236 Balark v. City of Chicago, 81 F.3d 658 (7th Cir. 1996) (§ 1988 case); LaRouche v. Keezer, 20 F.3d 68 (2d Cir. 1994) (§ 1988 case).

237 LeBlanc-Sternberg v. Vill. of Airmont, 143 F.3d 765 (2d Cir. 1998) (§ 1988 case); Riley v. City of Jackson, 99 F.3d 757 (5th Cir. 1996) (§ 1988 case); *cf.* Bisciglia v. Kenosha Uniform Sch. Dist. No. 1, 45 F.3d 223 (7th Cir. 1995) (§ 1988 case) (temporary restraining order which merely preserves status quo and does not result in relief on the merits is insufficient).

238 Sablan v. Dep't of Fin., 856 F.2d 1317 (9th Cir. 1988) (§ 1988 case); Gram v. Bank of La., 691 F.2d 728 (5th Cir. 1982) (TILA case); Folsom v. Heartland Bank, 2000 U.S. Dist. LEXIS 7890 (D. Kan. May 18, 2000) (TILA case). *See generally* National Consumer Law Center, Truth in Lending § 8.9.2.1 (4th ed. 1999 and Supp.).

239 Buckhannon Board & Care Home v. West Virginia Dep't of Health & Human Resources, 532 U.S. 598, 121 S. Ct. 1835, 149 L. Ed. 2d 855 (2001).

240 *Id.*

241 *Id.* at 1838.

242 42 U.S.C. § 1988; *see* Chambers v. Ohio Dep't of Human Services, 273 F.3d 690 (6th Cir. 2001); Nat'l Coalition for Students with Disabilities v. Bush, 173 F. Supp. 2d 1272 (N.D. Fla. 2001).

243 28 U.S.C. § 2412(d)(1); *see* Former Employees of Motorola Ceramic Prods. v. U.S., 176 F. Supp. 2d 1370 (Ct. Int'l Trade 2001); Sileikis v. Perryman, 2001 U.S. Dist. LEXIS 12737 (N.D. Ill. Aug. 20, 2001). *But see* Brickwood Contractors, Inc. v. U.S., 49 Fed. Cl. 738, 2001 U.S. Claims LEXIS 133 (Fed. Cl. 2001).

244 20 U.S.C. § 1451(I)(3); *see* Brandon K. v. New Lenox Sch. Dist., 2001 U.S. Dist. LEXIS 20006 (N.D. Ill. Nov. 30, 2001); John T. v. Delaware County Intermediate Unit, 2001 U.S. Dist. LEXIS 18254 (E.D. Pa. Nov. 7, 2001); Jose Luis R. v. Joliet Township High Sch. Dist. 204, 2001 U.S. Dist. LEXIS 13951 (N.D. Ill. Aug. 27, 2001).

245 *See, e.g.,* Wallerstein v. Stew Leonard's Dairy, 258 Conn. 299, 780 A.2d 916 (2001) (judgment entered under Connecticut equivalent of Rule 68 made plaintiff the prevailing party).

246 Fed. R. Civ. P. 23(e).

actually charged.[247] Most circuits though refuse to provide attorney fees to *pro se* litigants, irrespective of whether that litigant is an attorney.[248]

11.6.6.4 Calculating the Award

The different circuit courts have adopted somewhat different approaches to calculating attorney fee awards, and some Supreme Court decisions have further complicated the issue. This subsection will only briefly sketch the general approach used by the federal courts, known as the "lodestar" approach. The lodestar is the number of allowable hours times an hourly rate. Allowable hours must be actually documented and reasonably expended.[249] Duplicative or excessive time will not be compensated.

The exact amount of a fee award is in the court's discretion, and an appellate court will only review the amount for an abuse of discretion.[250] But the circuit courts have adopted standards for calculating these awards and failure to follow these standards, or even failure to show clearly that these standards were followed, may be an abuse of discretion.[251]

The allowable hours are those hours claimed and documented by the attorneys that were reasonably expended in reaching a favorable result.[252] If there is a common core of facts or if the legal theories are related, the attorney should be compensated not only for claims that succeeded but for all reasonable work on the case, even on counts that failed and even for claims that do not provide for attorney fees.[253] Attorney fees should compensate not only attorney time spent, but also time spent by paralegals and law clerks who work on a case.[254]

The number of hours reasonably spent is then multiplied by a reasonable hourly rate for the attorney (or paralegal or law clerk). The hourly rate is not based on the attorney's customary rate, the amount billed the client, or the cost of that attorney's time. Rather it is based on the prevailing rate in the community for an individual with that level of legal skill and experience.[255] Evidence of the prevailing market rate includes affidavits from similarly qualified attorneys, information about fees awarded in analogous cases, and evidence of the fee applicant's rates during the relevant time.[256] Legal aid attorneys and other pro bono attorneys should receive the same hourly rate as comparable attorneys in private practice.[257] While the attorney's customary hourly rate, the rate billed to the consumer, the cost of the attorney's time, or a contingent fee agreement may all be considered as evidence, none of these is dispositive.[258]

The product of the number of allowable hours times the

---

247 Blanchard v. Bergeron, 489 U.S. 87, 109 S. Ct. 939, 103 L. Ed. 2d 67 (1989) (lawyer taking case without compensation does not bar attorney fee award); Blum v. Stenson, 465 U.S. 886, 104 S. Ct. 1541, 79 L. Ed. 2d 891 (1984) (legal services attorneys entitled to market rates in Civil Rights Acts cases); Johnson v. Lafayette Fire Fighters Ass'n Local 472, 51 F.3d 726 (7th Cir. 1995) (§ 1988 case); Bostic v. Am. Gen. Fin., Inc. 87 F. Supp. 2d 611 (S.D. W. Va. 2000); *cf.* Alexander S. v. Boyd, 113 F.3d 1373 (4th Cir. 1997) (law firm acting pro bono entitled to reasonable attorney fees). *See generally* National Consumer Law Center, Truth in Lending § 8.9.3.2 (4th ed. 1999 and Supp.).

248 Kay v. Ehrler, 499 U.S. 432, 111 S. Ct. 1435, 113 L. Ed. 2d 486 (1991) (civil rights claim); Freeman v. Gunter, 1998 U.S. App. LEXIS 230 (10th Cir. Jan. 8, 1998) (§ 1988 case); Belmont v. Associates Nat'l Bank, 199 F. Supp. 2d 149 (E.D.N.Y. 2000); Alexy v. O'Neil Nissan, 1999 U.S. Dist. LEXIS 3271 (E.D. Pa. Mar. 19, 1999). *See generally* National Consumer Law Center, Truth in Lending § 8.9.3.3 (4th ed. 1999 and Supp.).

249 Hensley v. Eckerhart, 461 U.S. 424, 103 S. Ct. 1933, 76 L. Ed. 2d 40 (1983).

250 *See, e.g., id.;* Jaffee v. Redmond, 142 F.3d 409 (7th Cir. 1998); Coutin v. Young & Rubicam Puerto Rico, Inc., 124 F.3d 331 (1st Cir. 1997); Martinez v. Idaho First Nat'l Bank, 755 F.2d 1376 (9th Cir. 1985) (TILA case).

251 *See, e.g.,* Hensley v. Eckerhart, 461 U.S. 424, 103 S. Ct. 1933, 76 L. Ed. 2d. 40 (1983); Coutin v. Young & Rubicam Puerto Rico, 124 F.3d 331 (1st Cir. 1997); GMAC Mortgage Corp. v. Larson, 597 N.E.2d 1245 (Ill. App. Ct. 1992). *See generally* National Consumer Law Center, Truth in Lending § 8.9.4.1 (4th ed. 1999 and Supp.).

252 Hensley v. Eckerhart, 461 U.S. 424, 103 S. Ct. 1933, 76 L. Ed. 2d 40 (1983).

253 Hensley v. Eckerhart, 461 U.S. 424, 103 S. Ct. 1933, 76 L. Ed. 2d. 40 (1983); LeBlanc-Sternberg v. Vill. of Airmont, 143 F.3d 765 (2d Cir. 1998); Jaffee v. Redmond, 142 F.3d 409 (7th Cir. 1988). *But see* Laubach v. Fid. Consumer Discount Co., 686 F. Supp. 504 (E.D. Pa. 1988) (TILA case); Morris v. Resolution Trust Corp., 622 A.2d 708 (Me. 1993) (as central actions were breach of contact and breach of fiduciary duty and work on those claims only "fortuitously" established TILA claims, low fee award justified).

254 Postow v. Oriental Bldg. Ass'n, 455 F. Supp. 781 (D.D.C. 1978), *aff'd in part, rev'd in part, sub nom.* Postow v. OBA Fed. Sav. & Loan Ass'n, 627 F.2d 1370 (D.C. Cir. 1980); Frazier v. Franklin Inv. Co., 468 A.2d 1338 (D.C. 1983); Merchandise Nat'l Bank v. Scanlon, 86 Ill. App. 3d 719, 408 N.E.2d 248 (1980); *see also* City Consumer Services, Inc. v. Horne, 631 F. Supp. 1050 (D. Utah 1986); *cf.* Blanchard v. Bergeron, 489 U.S. 87, 109 S. Ct. 939, 103 L. Ed. 2d 67 (1989) (reserving for another day the issue of fees for legal assistants).

255 Blum v. Stenson, 465 U.S. 886, 104 S. Ct. 1541, 79 L. Ed. 2d 891 (1984); Copeland v. Marshall, 641 F.2d 880 (D.C. Cir. 1980); Rodriguez v. Taylor, 569 F.2d 1231 (3d Cir. 1977); Johnson v. Ga. Highway Express, 488 F.2d 714 (5th Cir. 1974); City Consumer Services, Inc. v. Horne, 631 F. Supp. 1050 (D. Utah 1986) (attorney fees not limited by fee agreement between attorney and consumers).

256 *See* Broome v. Biondi, 17 F. Supp. 2d 211, 230 (S.D.N.Y. 1997).

257 Blum v. Stenson, 465 U.S. 886, 104 S. Ct. 1541, 79 L. Ed. 2d 891 (1984); *see* § 11.6.6.3, *supra.*

258 Blanchard v. Bergeron, 489 U.S. 87, 97, 109 S. Ct. 939, 103 L. Ed. 2d 67 (1989); Keenan v. City of Philadelphia, 983 F.2d 459, 475 (3d Cir. 1992); Covington v. District of Columbia, 839 F. Supp. 894 (D.D.C. 1993); *cf.* People Who Care v. Rockford Bd. of Educ., 90 F.3d 1307 (7th Cir. 1996) (§ 1988 case) (attorney's actual billing rate for comparable work is presumptively appropriate to use as the market rate). *But see* Robins v. Scholastic Book Fairs, 928 F. Supp. 1027 (D. Or. 1996) (§ 1988 case) (whether the attorney charges a fixed or contingent fee cannot be a factor in determining a reasonable rate).

Credit Discrimination

allowable hourly rate is called the lodestar figure. Once this number is calculated, courts may increase or decrease that number based on various factors.[259]

11.6.6.5 Fee Applications

The Federal Rules of Civil Procedure require motions for attorney fees and expenses to be filed and served no later than fourteen days after judgment.[260] However, all that is required in this time period is notice to the court and to the opposite side that fees will be sought and a fair estimate of the total fees and expenses claimed. A detailed record of hours and rates, affidavits, time records, fee surveys and other supporting evidence and briefs may be submitted "in due course" following the motion for fees.[261]

The burden of justifying the amount of an attorney fee award falls on the consumer's attorney, who should justify in detail the number of hours claimed, the hourly rates, and any factors claimed to adjust the lodestar upward.[262] Insufficient documentation insufficiencies will be used to reduce the award.[263]

Once the consumer's attorney has adequately delineated and documented the request for fees and expenses, the other party must submit evidence, not merely argument, to overcome the lodestar presumption.[264] Courts have different

procedures as to whether a hearing on the fee application is required.[265]

The first step in a successful fee application is keeping detailed accounting of the time spent and the work performed on the case.[266] While the Supreme Court has not described the standards for record keeping in detail, contemporaneous time records are the preferred practice.[267] The petition should include some fairly definite information as to the following:

- The hours devoted to various classes of activities (for example, pretrial discovery or settlement negotiations), identifying the task, and the general subject matter of the task;
- The hours spent by various classes of attorneys—partners, associates—and paralegals;[268]
- If the case involves unrelated claims, the time should be broken down by each claim as well, records should indicate, when possible, the claim for which the work was done and, if the work relates to several claims or if the work cannot be effectively separated, the records should indicate these facts as well;[269] the Supreme Court has advised that counsel "should maintain time records in a manner which will enable a reviewing court to identify distinct claims."[270]

The fee claimant's burden is to provide the court with sufficient documentary evidence justifying the rates claimed[271]

259 Hensley v. Eckerhart, 461 U.S. 424, 103 S. Ct. 1933, 76 L. Ed. 2d 240 (1983). The seminal case setting out factors to consider in awarding fees was Johnson v. Georgia Highway Express, 488 F.2d 714 (5th Cir. 1974). Courts found it too indefinite to apply the *Johnson* test, however, and in Lindy Brothers Builders, Inc. v. American Radiator & Standard Sanitary Corp., 487 F.2d 161 (3d Cir. 1973) and 540 F.2d 102 (3d Cir. 1976), the Third Circuit set out the lodestar approach. Courts now adopt the lodestar approach, some adjusting the lodestar by the factors set out in *Lindy*, others by the factors set out in *Johnson*.

260 Fed. R. Civ. P. 54(d)(2)(B); *see* Mills v. Freeman, 118 F.3d 727 (11th Cir. 1997) (§ 1988 case) (fee application barred as untimely).

261 *See also* 1993 Advisory Committee's note; Diller, *The Impact of the 1993 Amendments to the Federal Rules of Civil Procedure on Legal Services Practice in the Federal Courts*, 28 Clearinghouse Rev. 134, 140 (June 1994).

262 Hensley v. Eckerhart, 461 U.S. 424, 103 S. Ct. 1933, 76 L. Ed. 2d 40 (1983); Duckworth v. Whisenant, 97 F.3d 1393 (11th Cir. 1996); Mares v. Credit Bureau of Raton, 801 F.2d 1197 (10th Cir. 1986); Varner v. Century Fin. Co., 738 F.2d 1143 (11th Cir. 1984); Carr v. Blazer Fin. Services, Inc., 598 F.2d 1368 (5th Cir. 1979); Folsom v. Heartland Bank, 2000 U.S. Dist. LEXIS 7890 (D. Kan. May 18, 2000) (time records must be meticulous or percentage reduction will be appropriate).

263 Hensley v. Eckerhart, 461 U.S. 424, 103 S. Ct. 1933, 76 L. Ed. 2d 40 (1983); Cohen v. Brown Univ., 2001 U.S. Dist. LEXIS 22438 (D.R.I. Aug. 10, 2001); In re Mattera, 128 B.R. 107 (Bankr. E.D. Pa. 1991).

264 People Who Care v. Rockford Bd. of Educ., 90 F.3d 1307 (7th Cir. 1996); Gates v. Deukmejian, 987 F.2d 1392 (9th Cir. 1992); United Steelworkers v. Phelps Dodge, 896 F.2d 403 (9th Cir. 1990); Northeast Women's Center v. McMonagle, 889 F.2d 466

(3d Cir. 1989); Varner v. Century Fin. Co., 738 F.2d 1143 (11th Cir. 1984).

265 *Compare* Henson v. Columbus Bank & Trust Co., 651 F.2d 320 (5th Cir. 1981) (hearing required) *with* Watkins v. Fordice, 7 F.3d 453 (5th Cir. 1993) (hearing not required); DeJesus v. Banco Popular de Puerto Rico, 951 F.2d 3, 14 (1st Cir. 1991) (hearing not required); Sablan v. Dep't of Fin., 856 F.2d 1317 (9th Cir. 1988) (hearing not required); Mirabal v. Gen. Motors Acceptance Corp., 576 F.2d 729 (7th Cir. 1978) (hearing not required) *and* Love v. Deal, 5 F.3d 1406, 1409 (11th Cir. 1993) (hearing required only when there is some dispute of material historical fact).

266 A sample schedule of attorney hours with the judge's marginal comments is appended to In re Mattera, 128 B.R. 107 (Bankr. E.D. Pa. 1991).

267 Keenan v. City of Philadelphia, 983 F.2d 459, 472 (3d Cir. 1992) (citing Webb v. Board of Educ., 471 U.S. 234, 238 n.6 (1985)).

268 Washington v. Philadelphia County Ct. of Common Pleas, 89 F.3d 1031 (3d Cir. 1996); Keenan v. City of Philadelphia, 983 F.2d 459, 473 (3d Cir. 1992); *cf.* Gill v. Mid-Penn Consumer Discount Co., 1988 U.S. Dist. LEXIS 11457 (E.D. Pa. Oct. 14, 1988) (no fees for time spent by substitute attorney when failed to specify hourly rate of that particular attorney).

269 *See also* Cruz v. Local No. 3, 150 F.R.D. 29, 35 (E.D.N.Y. 1993), *aff'd in part, rev'd in part*, 34 F.3d 1148 (2d Cir. 1994); Gary Smith, *Federal Statutory Attorney Fees: Common Issues and Recent Cases*, 28 Clearinghouse Rev. 744 (1994).

270 Hensley v. Eckerhart, 461 U.S. 424, 437, 103 S. Ct. 1933, 76 L. Ed. 2d 40 (1983).

271 *See* Davis v. City & County of San Francisco, 976 F.2d 1536 (9th Cir. 1992), *vacated in part on other grounds*, 984 F.2d 345

and the efficacy of the hours expended.[272] While contemporaneous time records are the standard, courts in some circuits may accept reconstructed records.[273] At a minimum, this evidence should include:

- An explanation of the fee arrangement with the client;
- The attorney's relevant experience and expertise in the type of litigation involved;
- Documentation of customary fees in the area for attorneys with the level of experience and skill possessed by the attorney claiming the fees, such as affidavits from other attorneys in the area or a fee survey;
- The attorney's customary fee for the type of litigation involved, if any; and
- Calculation of the amount of fees requested, using the appropriate factors, including any justification for and calculation of an upward adjustment to the lodestar.

Courts often reduce or discount hours which are deemed duplicative of other compensated work,[274] unnecessary or inefficient.[275] Courts may also devalue work which is perceived as not requiring a lawyer of the expertise, experience and reputation of the lawyer who claims the time,[276] although most courts will not require an attorney to so carefully parse time expenditures.[277]

Courts may disallow fees for purely clerical tasks undertaken by attorneys, even if billed at the rate for paralegals or interns.[278] As courts often further penalize fee applicants who submit such claims by a punitive denial or reduction in fees,[279] many attorneys excise questionable, borderline, or insufficiently documented time entries, and further volunteer a small reduction in overall claims to compensate for duplication of efforts, inefficiency and billing errors which are inevitable—at least in any large scale litigation.[280]

11.6.6.6 Costs and Witness Fees

A successful plaintiff should recover costs under an ECOA, Fair Housing Act, or Civil Rights Act claim.[281] Costs include filing fees, transcripts, deposition costs, and other court and litigation expenses not otherwise claimed as attorney fees.[282] There is some case law that restricts a plaintiff's ability to recover costs associated with an expert witness's appearance at a trial, but this precedent may not limit recovery for costs associated with an expert assisting the attorney for the trial.[283] In addition, for actions under 42 U.S.C. § 1981, Congress has explicitly authorized expert witness fees.[284]

(9th Cir. 1993) (admitting declarations of prevailing market rates in relevant legal community, affidavits of counsel with similar credentials, and informal fee surveys).

272 *In re* Mattera, 128 B.R. 107, 120 (Bankr. E.D. Pa. 1991).

273 Yohay v. Alexandria Employees Credit Union, 827 F.2d 967 (4th Cir. 1987); *see* Davis v. City & County of San Francisco, 976 F.2d 1536 (9th Cir. 1992); Jean v. Nelson, 863 F.2d 759 (11th Cir. 1988), *aff'd other grounds*, 496 U.S. 154 (1990); MacDissi v. Valmont Indus., 856 F.2d 1054 (8th Cir. 1988); Harris v. Marsh, 679 F. Supp. 1204 (E.D.N.C. 1987), *rev'd in part on other grounds sub nom.* Blue v. Dep't of the Army, 914 F.2d 525 (4th Cir. 1990). *But see* Phetosomphone v. Allison Reed Group, 984 F.2d 4, 8 (1st Cir. 1993) (absence of contemporaneous time records calls for disallowance of the fee award).

274 Fair Hous. Council v. Landlow, 999 F.2d 92 (4th Cir. 1993); Davis v. City & County of San Francisco, 976 F.2d 1536, 1544 (9th Cir. 1992) (hours claimed must reflect the distinct contribution of each lawyer).

275 Envtl. Defense Fund v. Reilly, 1 F.3d 1254, 1258 (D.C. Cir. 1993); Fair Hous. Council v. Landlow, 999 F.2d 92 (4th Cir. 1993); Keenan v. City of Philadelphia, 983 F.2d 459 (3d Cir. 1992); Varner v. Century Fin. Co., 738 F.2d 1143 (11th Cir. 1984) (TILA case); Mares v. Credit Bureau of Raton, 801 F.2d 1197, 1205 (5th Cir. 1986) (TILA case).

276 Envtl. Defense Fund v. Reilly, 1 F.3d 1254 (D.C. Cir. 1994); Fair Hous. Council v. Landlow, 999 F.2d 92 (4th Cir. 1993); Varner v. Century Fin. Co., 738 F.2d 1143 (11th Cir. 1984).

277 Davis v. City & County of San Francisco, 976 F.2d 1536, 1548 (9th Cir. 1992).

278 Envtl. Defense Fund v. Reilly, 1 F.3d 1254, 1258 (D.C. Cir. 1993); Davis v. City & County of San Francisco, 976 F.2d 1536,

1543 (9th Cir. 1992); Bailey v. District of Columbia, 839 F. Supp. 888, 891 (D.D.C. 1993) ("Yet attorneys like plaintiffs' counsel, operating either as solo practitioners or in small firms, often lack the resources to retain a large staff of junior lawyers who could handle such tasks more economically. Denying plaintiffs compensation for these tasks would unfairly punish plaintiffs and their counsel for not staffing this case as if they had the manpower of a major law firm."); *cf.* Walker v. Dep't of Hous. & Urban Dev., 99 F.3d 761 (5th Cir. 1996), *sanctions disallowed*, 129 F.3d 831 (1997), *cert. denied*, 528 U.S. 1131 (2000) (§ 1988 case) (clerical work done by attorneys should be compensated at a different rate from legal work).

279 DeJesus v. Banco Popular de Puerto Rico, 951 F.2d 3, 5 (1st Cir. 1991); S. Florida I Ltd. v. Perez, Clearinghouse No. 48,711 (Fla. Dade County Ct. 1993); *see also* Oviedo v. Oziercy, 304 N.W.2d 596 (Mich. Ct. App. 1981) (state law); Stern v. Stern, 415 N.Y.S.2d 225 (App. Div. 1979) (state law). Attorneys may also want to refer to standardized publications regarding approximate hours appropriately billed for routine services. *See* Relative Values: Determining Attorneys' Fees (Shepards, 1990).

280 Louisville Black Police Officers v. City of Louisville, 700 F.2d 268, 278 (6th Cir. 1983); Carver v. McWherter, Clearinghouse No. 49,797A (E.D. Tenn. Mar. 30, 1994).

281 15 U.S.C. § 1691e(d); 42 U.S.C. § 3613(c)(2); 42 U.S.C. § 1988(b).

282 Bhandari v. First Nat'l Bank of Commerce, 808 F.2d 1082 (5th Cir. 1987), *rev'd on other grounds*, 829 F.2d 1343 (5th Cir. 1987) (en banc), *vacated and remanded*, 492 U.S. 901, *reinstated*, 887 F.2d 609 (5th Cir. 1989).

283 *See* Denny v. Westfield State College, 880 F.2d 1465 (1st Cir. 1989) (finding appearance at trial not recoverable but reserving question of expert preparing attorney for trial); *see also* W. Va. Univ. Hospitals, Inc. v. Casey, 499 U.S. 83, 111 S. Ct. 1138, 113 L. Ed. 2d 68 (1991) (expert witness fee may not be recovered as part of "reasonable attorney fee" award under 42 U.S.C. § 1988. *But cf. In re* Mattera, 128 B.R. 107 (Bankr. E.D. Pa. 1991) (an appraisal fee, the appraiser's expert witness fee, and $365 in photocopying costs were allowed).

284 42 U.S.C. § 1988(c).

11.6.6.7 Appeals of Attorney Fee Awards

If the action is successful but the attorney fee award is inadequate, this issue alone may be appealed.[285] Even if the consumer does not wish to pursue the appeal the attorney has standing to pursue the appeal.[286] Time spent on such a successful appeal, time spent before the trial court justifying fees, and fees for separate counsel to litigate the fee issues should all be included in the attorney fee request.[287] If the appeal is unsuccessful but the consumer ultimately prevails on remand or thereafter hours spent on the unsuccessful appeal may be compensable.[288]

11.6.6.8 Interim Fees

In protracted litigation creditors may slowly deplete the resources of the consumer's attorney by requiring the expenditure of numerous hours which may not be compensated, if at all, until after the termination of the litigation. In some cases interim fees may be awarded, which may support the litigation or place additional pressure upon the lender to settle.[289] In order to qualify for an interim award of fees the applicant must have prevailed in seeking some relief on the merits of his or her claim, whether by way of preliminary injunction[290] or by judgment pending appeal.[291]

11.6.6.9 Apportionment of Award Among Defendants

Courts may apportion the fee award among several defendants to ensure that a single defendant is not liable for fees greater than those incurred to litigate the case against that defendant.[292] If not all the defendants settle, the total award may be reduced by the amount allocated to attorney fees by any settlement.[293]

11.6.7 Election of Remedies

The ECOA, federal Fair Housing Act, federal Civil Rights Acts, and state anti-discrimination laws all provide remedies for illegal discrimination. Aggrieved individuals can recover their actual damages only once, but issues do arise as to whether an individual can seek punitive damages under different statutes, or minimum or multiple damages under a state statute and punitive damages under a federal one.

The ECOA establishes rules about potential multiple recoveries. When a particular act or omission by a creditor would constitute a violation of both state law and the ECOA, an action may be brought to recover money damages under only one of them, either the ECOA or state law.[294] No such election of remedies is required when the court action is for relief other than money damages (e.g., injunctive or declaratory relief), or in an administrative action.[295]

In addition, no person aggrieved by an ECOA violation and, in the same transaction, by a violation of the Fair Housing Act's prohibitions concerning discrimination concerning residential real estate-related transactions shall recover under both the ECOA and the Fair Housing Act.[296] This language seems to indicate clearly that the litigant can bring an action under both statutes, and must only elect one remedy or the other before a final order is issued.[297]

The election between an ECOA action and a state law action, on the other hand, indicates that an "action may be

---

285 Price v. Franklin Inv. Co., 574 F.2d 594 (D.C. Cir. 1978). The judgment on the merits and the attorney fee award are separate appealable orders. Budinich v. Becton Dickinson & Co., 486 U.S. 196, 108 S. Ct. 1717, 100 L. Ed. 2d 178 (1988).

286 *See* National Consumer Law Center, Truth in Lending § 8.9.2.3 (4th ed. 1999 and Supp.).

287 Comm'r, Immigration & Naturalization Serv. v. Jean, 496 U.S. 154, 110 S. Ct. 2316, 110, L. Ed. 2d 134 (1990); DeJesus v. Banco Popular de Puerto Rico, 918 F.2d 232 (1st Cir. 1990); Rosenfeld v. S. Pac. Co., 519 F.2d 527 (9th Cir. 1975) (Civil Rights Act case); Jones v. Mid-Penn Consumer Discount Co., 93 B.R. 66 (E.D. Pa. 1988) (attorney fees for work appealing size of fee award). *See generally* National Consumer Law Center, Truth In Lending §§ 8.9.2.3, 8.9.6 (4th ed. 1999 and Supp.).

288 Corder v. Brown, 25 F.3d 833, 841 (9th Cir. 1994); Envtl. Defense Fund v. Reilly, 1 F.3d 1254, 1258 (D.C. Cir. 1993); Dague v. City of Burlington, 935 F.2d 1343, 1358–59 (2d Cir. 1991), *reversed on other grounds*, 505 U.S. 557 (1992) (district court did not abuse its discretion in awarding full fee requested on all aspects of the case, although plaintiffs were unsuccessful on preliminary injunction and interlocutory appeal, some arguments failed, and some were not fee-generating).

289 Tex. State Teachers Ass'n v. Garland Indep. Sch. Dist., 489 U.S. 782, 790–91, 109 S. Ct. 1486, 103 L. Ed. 2d 866 (1989) (citing to legislative history of 42 U.S.C. § 1988); Hanrahan v. Hampton, 446 U.S. 754, 757, 100 S. Ct. 1987, 64 L. Ed. 2d 670 (1980); Larouche v. Keezer, 20 F.3d 68 (2d Cir. 1994).

290 *See* Topanga Press, Inc. v. City of Los Angeles, 989 F.2d 1524, 1534 (9th Cir. 1993).

291 Hanrahan v. Hampton, 446 U.S. 754, 757, 100 S. Ct. 1987, 64 L. Ed. 2d 670 (1980); Gates v. Deukmejian, 987 F.2d 1392, 1396 (9th Cir. 1992); Rosenfeld v. United States, 859 F.2d 717 (9th Cir. 1988).

292 Jones v. Espy, 10 F.3d 690 (9th Cir. 1993); Baughman v. Wilson Freight Forwarding Co., 583 F.2d 1208 (3d Cir. 1978); *In re* Mattera, 128 B.R. 107, 113 (Bankr. E.D. Pa. 1991).

293 Corder v. Brown, 25 F.3d 833 (9th Cir. 1994).

294 15 U.S.C. § 1691d(e); *see also* Fernandez v. Hull Coop. Bank, 1979 U.S. Dist. LEXIS 8657 (D. Mass. Nov. 8, 1979).

295 15 U.S.C. § 1691d(e).

296 15 U.S.C. § 1691e(i). The literal language of the statute is confusing. It provides that there cannot be recovery under both the ECOA and 42 U.S.C. § 3612 of the Fair Housing Act. Section 3612 previously authorized a private right of action for damages and injunctive relief. The private relief section, however, has been moved to § 3613 and § 3612 now deals with administrative enforcement of the Fair Housing Act. The notes to § 1691e now clarify this change, referring to 42 U.S.C. § 3613 as the relevant statute.

297 Walton v. Centrust Mortgage Corp., Fair Hous.-Fair Lending Rep.(P-H) ¶ 15,719, No. 39:91 CV7317 (N.D. Ohio Sept. 25, 1991).

brought" under either the ECOA or state law, but not both. It is thus safest to elect one theory or the other *before* bringing a complaint. Nevertheless, a federal court has ruled that the case should not be dismissed if the plaintiff fails to elect between federal and state remedies before bringing the complaint; rather, the plaintiff should be restricted to recovery under the federal statute because it appeared that the action was primarily pursued under that theory.[298]

The ECOA does not require an election of remedies between an ECOA claim and a federal Civil Rights Act claim or between an ECOA claim and a Fair Housing Act claim not based on residential real estate-related transactions, in other words, one based on discrimination in the sale, rental, or advertising of a dwelling. Moreover, nothing prevents simultaneous recovery on a Fair Housing Act claim, a federal Civil Rights Act claim, and a state credit discrimination or UDAP claim. Of course, only one actual damage recovery can be had for the same injury.

11.7 Statute of Limitations

11.7.1 Affirmative Actions

11.7.1.1 ECOA Claims

11.7.1.1.1 General rule: two year statute of limitations

The ECOA statute of limitations for affirmative claims is two years from the date of the occurrence of the violation.[299] In general, the statute of limitations runs from the date the violation occurs and not the date credit is applied for or the date credit is granted. However, the date on which the claim accrues may be extended if the plaintiff did not discover the violation until later and the court follows the federal discovery rule.

In most cases courts will find that the plaintiff discovered the injury on the same date as the violation but sometimes the discovery will be later. In these circumstances, some courts will follow the federal discovery rule and find that the statute begins to run at the time the plaintiff discovered, or in the exercise of reasonable diligence should have discovered, the injury.[300]

Courts that use the discovery rule will generally apply it only to violations that are either not immediately evident or not readily discernible.[301] Some courts treat the discovery rule as tolling a statute of limitations that already began to run at the time of the violation.[302] Other courts find that the discovery rule actually determines when a claim accrues and is not a tolling doctrine.[303] Courts applying the discovery rule generally agree that what matters is a plaintiff's discovery of certain facts, not an understanding of the legal significance of these facts or a conclusion that a valid claim exists.[304]

For example, in a credit discrimination claim brought under the ECOA, the creditor argued that the alleged violation, if any, occurred on the date the plaintiff entered into the contract. The plaintiff argued, and the court agreed, that the statute did not begin to run until the plaintiff knew or should have known that she was being discriminated against, in this case when she met with attorneys to discuss the case.[305]

If the statute begins to run at the time of violation (or if a court applying the discovery rule determines that the plaintiff discovered or should have discovered the injury at the time of the violation), there is still some question as to the actual violation date. The date will vary depending on what the violation involves—application procedures, notice of adverse action, post-default collection procedures, etc. The violation date may be before or significantly after the application and loan dates. For example, if the violation occurs when a loan is renewed, the two-year period starts from that renewal date, not the date of the original loan.[306]

---

298 Milton v. Bancplus Mortgage Corp., 1996 U.S. Dist. LEXIS 5166 (N.D. Ill. Apr. 19, 1996) (federal claims adequately pleaded; state claims, based on "election of remedy" statute, dismissed); *see also* Saldana v. Citibank, 1996 U.S. Dist. LEXIS 8327 (N.D. Ill. Jun. 13, 1996); Fernandez v. Hull Coop. Bank, 1979 U.S. Dist. LEXIS 8657 (D. Mass. Nov. 8, 1979).

299 15 U.S.C. § 1691e(f).

300 *See, e.g.*, Jones v. Ford Motor Credit Co., 2002 U.S. Dist. LEXIS 1098 (S.D.N.Y. Jan. 18, 2002); Jones v. Citibank, 844 F. Supp. 437, 440–41 (N.D. Ill. 1994) (the statute in this case began to run on the date on which Citibank notified plaintiffs of its decision to deny their loan application because it is the date

on which the plaintiffs alleged they discovered that they suffered an injury). *But see* Mays v. Buckeye Rural Elec. Coop., Inc., 277 F.3d 873 (6th Cir. 2002); Lewis v. Glickman, 104 F. Supp. 2d 1311, 1319–20 (D. Kan. 2000) (following the "general rule in the discrimination context" that the cause of action accrues when the individual first receives notice of the adverse action against him, and not when the effects of that action are felt); Stern v. Espirito Santo Bank, 791 F. Supp. 865 (S.D. Fla. 1992).

301 *See, e.g.*, Cambridge Plating Co. v. NAPCO, Inc., 991 F.2d 21, 26–28 n.6 (1st Cir. 1993); Armstrong v. Trico Marine, Inc., 923 F.2d 55, 58 (5th Cir. 1991); Wilson v. Johns-Manville Sales Corp., 684 F.2d 111, 116 (D.C. Cir. 1982); Stoleson v. United States, 629 F.2d 1265, 1269 (7th Cir. 1980).

302 *See generally* James R. MacAyeal, *The Discovery Rule and the Continuing Violation Doctrine as Exceptions to the Statute of Limitations for Civil Environmental Penalty Claims*, 15 Va. Envtl. L.J. 589 (1996).

303 *See, e.g.*, Oshiver v. Levin, Fishbein, Sedran & Berman, 38 F.3d 1380, 1386 n.5 (3d Cir. 1994); Alexander v. Beech Aircraft Corp., 952 F.2d 1215, 1226 n.13 (10th Cir. 1991); Resolution Trust Corp. v. Farmer, 865 F. Supp. 1143, 1154 (E.D. Pa. 1994) (stating that the rule "delays" the accrual of a claim).

304 In the non-discrimination context, see United States v. Kubrick, 444 U.S. 111, 120, 100 S. Ct. 352, 62 L. Ed. 2d 259 (1979).

305 Jones v. Ford Motor Credit Co., 2002 U.S. Dist. LEXIS 1098 (S.D.N.Y. Jan. 18, 2002).

306 *See* Silverman v. Eastrich Multiple Investor Fund, L.P., 51 F.3d 28 (3d Cir. 1995) (because claims by way of recoupment are never barred by statutes of limitations so long as the main action

Another issue arises for violations related to collection procedures. The question is, in a transaction in which an alleged ECOA violation occurred in the initial contract, whether collection procedures initiated over the life of the loan represent a new ECOA violation for the purpose of measuring whether the statute has run on bringing an affirmative damage claim. At least one court ruled that the use of collection procedures did not represent a new violation.[307] The same court affirmed this ruling in another case, finding that the institution of a collection action by a lender's successor in interest without ensuring that the original transaction complied with the ECOA did not constitute a new ECOA violation for purposes of the running of the statute of limitations.[308]

The court in these cases limited its rulings to affirmative ECOA claims, agreeing that ECOA violations may still be raised defensively after the two-year statute has run.[309] In addition, in one of the cases, the court noted that this conclusion might not apply when the collection action itself is the first discriminatory action.[310] The court distinguished these situations from the case before the court, in which the alleged ECOA violation related to the initial contract and not necessarily to the collection process per se.[311]

These decisions appear to be wrong, based on the plain language of the ECOA (prohibiting discrimination "with respect to any aspect of a credit transaction"), and the plain language of Regulation B ("credit transaction" includes collection procedures). They also contradict the rulings of courts in non-ECOA cases finding that the statute begins to run upon filing of a collection complaint and that the statute begins again after each violation.[312]

Another area that has been the subject of some litigation is whether an illegal requirement that an individual cosign a note occurs when the individual signs the note or when the creditor first requests that the note be cosigned.[313] There is also uncertainty as to the violation date when a notice of adverse action is not properly made. One court has ruled that the violation date is not the date of oral notification, because the notice must be in writing.[314] On the other hand, if proper written notice is never received, is the date of violation when the consumer receives some notice of the adverse action or is it the latest date the creditor should have mailed a proper written notice? At least one court has stated that the date of the violation is the date by which the creditor was required to provide notice of its adverse action.[315]

11.7.1.1.2 *Extending the time period*

As discussed in the previous subsection, some courts will apply the discovery rule to extend the statute beyond the date when the violation actually occurred. In addition, when a violation clearly occurred more than two years before the claim is brought, the limitations period should be extended when the plaintiff can show that the defendant fraudulently concealed the violation. Fraudulent concealment is a more difficult standard to meet than the discovery rule as it requires that the creditor actively concealed the violation.[316]

To date, courts have not articulated a clear definition of the level of improper conduct necessary for the equitable tolling of the ECOA's statute of limitations, often borrowing

---

is timely, court did not address creditor's assertion that time in which wife-guarantor could raise a claim under ECOA for impermissibly being required to sign husband's guaranty expired two years after date she signed guaranty, nor whether approval of creditor's bankruptcy reorganization plan which provided for deferral of payment on debt constituted "renewal" of debt permitting resurrection of claim beyond initial statute of limitations), *rev'g*, 857 F. Supp. 447 (E.D. Pa. 1994); Stern v. Espirito Santo Bank, 791 F. Supp. 865 (S.D. Fla. 1992).

307   Roseman v. Premier Fin. Services-E., L.P., 1997 U.S. Dist. LEXIS 13836 (E.D. Pa. Sept. 3, 1997), *further proceeding at* 1998 U.S. Dist. LEXIS 15679 (E.D. Pa. Sept. 29, 1998) (denying motion for summary judgment).

308   Stornawaye Properties, Inc. v. Moses, 76 F. Supp. 2d 607 (E.D. Pa. 1999).

309   *Id.*; Roseman v. Premier Fin. Services-E., L.P., 1997 U.S. Dist. LEXIS 13836 (E.D. Pa. Sept. 3, 1997); *see* § 11.7.2, *infra*.

310   Roseman v. Premier Fin. Services-E., L.P., 1997 U.S. Dist. LEXIS 13836 (E.D. Pa. Sept. 3, 1997).

311   *Id.*

312   *See, e.g.*, Naas v. Stolman, 130 F.3d 892 (9th Cir. 1997) (Fair Debt Collection Practices (FDCPA) statute began to run upon filing of collection complaint: "Filing a complaint is the debt collector's last opportunity to comply with the Act"). Ordinarily, the date on which each violation occurs begins the running of the statute of limitations. Fox v. Citicorp Credit Services, Inc., 15 F.3d 1507 n.3 (9th Cir. 1994) (FDCPA); Hyde

v. Hibernia Nat'l Bank, 861 F.2d 446, 449–50 (5th Cir. 1988) (each transmission of an erroneous consumer report is a separate and distinct tort); Blakemore v. Pekay, 895 F. Supp. 972, 983 (N.D. Ill. 1995) (FDCPA); Schmidt v. Citibank (S.D.), 645 F. Supp. 214, 216 (D. Conn. 1986) (each monthly statement is a separately actionable truth in lending violation); *see also* Hargraves v. Capital City Mortgage Corp., 140 F. Supp. 2d 7 (D.D.C. 2000).

313   *Compare* Farrell v. Bank of N.H., 929 F.2d 871 (1st Cir. 1991) (violation occurred on date bank sent commitment letter requiring spouse to cosign, not on later date of actual signature) *and* Fed. Deposit Ins. Corp. v. Skotzke, 881 F. Supp. 364 (S.D. Ind. 1994) *with* Riggs Nat'l Bank v. Webster, 832 F. Supp. 147, 150 (D. Md. 1993) (statute of limitations runs from date that spouse signed the note).

314   Palmiotto v. Bank of N.Y., 1989 U.S. Dist. LEXIS 11546 (N.D.N.Y. Sept. 29, 1989).

315   Para v. United Carolina Bank, 1998 U.S. Dist. LEXIS 16843 (E.D.N.C. Aug. 25, 1998).

316   *See* Matthews v. New Century Mortgage Corp., 185 F. Supp. 2d 874 (S.D. Ohio 2002) (finding fraudulent concealment and therefore tolling statute under the FHA and the ECOA). Case law under other consumer statutes has effectively argued for the existence of fraudulent concealment. See cases discussed in National Consumer Law Center, Truth in Lending § 7.2.2 (4th ed. 1999 and Supp.) and National Consumer Law Center, Automobile Fraud § 4.4 (1998 and Supp.). *See also* National Consumer Law Center, Fair Debt Collection § 6.10 (4th ed. 2000 and Supp.).

from case law under other federal or state statutes.[317] The courts generally hold that the statute of limitations can be tolled for fraudulent concealment when the plaintiff demonstrates that: 1) the defendant took affirmative steps to conceal the plaintiff's cause of action; and 2) the plaintiff could not have discovered the cause of action despite exercising due diligence.[318]

It may also be possible to argue for a "continuing violation" in ECOA cases. This doctrine is established in FHA cases, as discussed in section 11.7.1.2, *infra*, but may also apply under the ECOA. The continuing violation doctrine allows plaintiffs to recover for incidents outside of the statutory time limit if at least one instance of the alleged practice occurred within the period and the earlier acts are part of a continuing pattern of discrimination.[319]

11.7.1.1.3 Exceptions to the ECOA two year statute of limitations

There are two situations in which the ECOA's two-year statute of limitations does not apply:

- When a federal administrative agency with ECOA enforcement powers[320] has commenced its own ECOA proceeding against the creditor within two years from the date of the occurrence of the violation;[321] or
- When the United States Attorney General has commenced a civil action under the ECOA against a creditor within two years from the date of the occurrence of the violation.[322]

In these situations, a victim of the discrimination at issue in the agency proceeding or Attorney General civil action may bring a private action up to one year after the commencement of that proceeding or civil action.[323]

11.7.1.2 Fair Housing Act Claims

The statute of limitations for a private cause of action arising under the Fair Housing Act is two years after the occurrence or termination of the discriminatory practice.[324]

An administrative complaint may be filed within one year of the occurrence.[325] The two-year period is tolled while any administrative action is proceeding.[326]

Courts will frequently follow the discovery rule in FHA cases.[327] Unlike under the ECOA, the continuing violation theory is well established in FHA cases. The continuing violation doctrine allows plaintiffs to recover for incidents outside of the statutory time limit if at least one instance of the alleged practice occurred within the period and the earlier acts are part of a continuing pattern of discrimination.[328] The theory is applied when the type of violation is one that could not reasonably have been expected to be made the subject of a lawsuit when it first occurred because its character as a violation did not become clear until it was repeated during the limitations period.[329]

The continuing violation theory allows a plaintiff to base a claim on a series of related wrongful acts even if some occurred before the limitations period. The original violation, however, must be closely related to the other violations that are not time-barred. Lingering effects of the past discrimination are not sufficient. Instead, plaintiffs must show that defendants continued to commit violations during the statutory period.[330] In reverse redlining cases, for example,

---

317 *See* Foster v. Equicredit Corp., 2001 U.S. Dist. LEXIS 1881 (E.D. Pa. Jan. 25, 2001).

318 *See* Matthews v. New Century Mortgage Corp., 185 F. Supp. 2d 874 (S.D. Ohio 2002) (finding that equitable tolling prevented the FHA and ECOA statutes of limitations from running until the date the borrowers learned of the terms of the loans and the fraud committed upon them).

319 Although there are no cases to date adopting this theory for ECOA claims, at least one court applied the test in an ECOA claim but found that plaintiffs failed to show that at least one instance of the practice occurred within the relevant time frame and that the claim was therefore time-barred. *See* Lewis v. Glickman, 104 F. Supp. 2d 1311 (D. Kan 2000).

320 *See* 15 U.S.C. § 1691c(a); Reg. B, 12 C.F.R. § 202 app. A (complete list of federal agencies with ECOA enforcement powers and the creditors subject to each agency's jurisdiction); § 12.2, *infra*.

321 15 U.S.C. § 1691e(f)(1). As there is no statute of limitations in 15 U.S.C. § 1691c, dealing with administrative enforcement, an enforcing agency may use the general five-year statute of limitations, 28 U.S.C. § 2462. United States v. Blake, 751 F. Supp. 951 (W.D. Okla. 1990); Fed. Trade Comm'n v. Green Tree Acceptance, Inc., 1987 U.S. Dist. LEXIS 16750, Consumer Cred. Guide (CCH) ¶ 95,905 (N.D. Tex. Sept. 30, 1987).

322 15 U.S.C. § 1691e(f)(2).

323 15 U.S.C. § 1691e(f).

324 42 U.S.C. § 3613(a)(1)(A).

325 42 U.S.C. § 3610.

326 42 U.S.C. § 3613(a)(1)(B); *see* § 11.4.2, *supra* (administrative proceedings).

327 *See, e.g.*, Jones v. Citibank, 844 F. Supp. 437, 440–41 (N.D. Ill. 1994) (the statute in this case began to run on the date on which Citibank notified plaintiffs of its decision to deny their loan application because it is the date on which the plaintiffs alleged they discovered that they suffered an injury). For a discussion generally of the discovery rule, see §§ 11.7.1.1.1, 11.7.1.1.2, *supra*.

328 *See* Havens Realty Corp. v. Coleman, 455 U.S. 363, 102 S. Ct. 1114, 1125, 71 L. Ed. 2d 214 (1982) (when a plaintiff, pursuant to the FHA, challenges not just one incident of conduct violative of the Act, but an unlawful practice that continues into the limitation period, the complaint is timely when it is filed within the statute of limitations for the last asserted occurrence of that practice); Spann v. Colonial Vill., Inc., 899 F.2d 24, 34–35 (D.C. Cir. 1990) (affirming finding of continuing violation when last of "long stream" of advertisements with white models occurred within statutory period); Hargraves v. Capital City Mortgage Corp., 140 F. Supp. 2d 7 (D.D.C. 2000).

329 *See* Hargraves v. Capital City Mortgage Corp., 140 F. Supp. 2d 7 (D.D.C. 2000) (citing Taylor v. Fed. Deposit Ins. Corp., 132 F.3d 753, 765 (D.C. Cir. 1997)).

330 *See id.* (allowing plaintiffs to proceed on the theory that con-

plaintiffs may argue that the violation occurs throughout the life of the loan, not merely at closing, especially when there are specific allegations of predatory acts in the creditor's servicing and foreclosure practices.[331] The statute of limitations should also be tolled for fraudulent concealment.[332]

11.7.1.3 Federal Civil Rights Act Claims

Neither 42 U.S.C. § 1981 nor § 1982 contains a specific statute of limitations. Courts hearing such claims must look to analogous state limitations periods.[333] The state analogy for these two general civil rights statutes need not be the state's *credit* discrimination statute so, depending on the state, the applicable period could be longer or shorter than that allowed under the Fair Housing Act or the ECOA.[334] The continuing violation theory, discussed above, should also apply to federal Civil Rights Acts claims.[335]

11.7.1.4 State Law Claims

State credit discrimination acts often have short limitations periods, typically one year but sometimes two or three years.[336] Just as commonly, the statute will not specify a limitations period. In these circumstances, states take varying approaches toward selecting an appropriate limitations period, some using those for statutory actions, some those for tort actions, or some those for specialty actions. These other limitations periods may be as short as one year but may be as long as four years or more.

Many state credit discrimination statutes provide an administrative procedure. Typically, complaints under this administrative procedure must be brought within six months, or even sooner.[337]

Another approach is to use a state unfair or deceptive acts or practices (UDAP) statute to challenge discrimination. If a UDAP statute has a longer limitations period (UDAP limitations periods vary significantly from one year to four or more years[338]), this advantage may be a reason to bring a discrimination case as a UDAP claim, even though another discrimination statute also applies.

11.7.2 Defensive Claims

In many situations a client does not seek legal assistance until the client is sued on a debt, and frequently the statute of limitations for various credit discrimination claims has run by that time. For example, a client who was coerced years ago to cosign a loan with a spouse prior to their divorce may be sued now because the ex-spouse cannot be located. Even though the statute of limitations may have run for bringing an affirmative credit discrimination claim against the creditor, such claims usually can be brought by way of setoff or recoupment (in other words, as a defense) to the creditor's collection action.

Numerous cases brought under the pre-Simplification Truth in Lending Act (TILA) also wrestled with whether recoupment claims were available after the TILA limitations period had run. (Truth in Lending Simplification makes it explicit that recoupment claims are available after the limitations period has run.) A majority of these cases concluded that a consumer may recover damages for TILA violations by way of counterclaim or recoupment, even though the statute of limitations for affirmative actions has expired, if the creditor has filed an action based on the same credit transaction.[339] This reasoning is equally applicable to ECOA cases.

Although the consumer cannot recover an amount in actual and punitive damages in excess of the debt upon which the creditor is seeking collection, the limitations period will not apply to a recoupment claim.[340] This defense is available even when asserted in a nominally separate action filed in federal court, for example for declaratory relief.[341] However, failure to raise a defensive counterclaim

tinuing violations might include continued charging of exorbitant interest rates for loans plaintiff took out before statutory period and continued collecting of other predatory fees, and any discriminatory actions used to enforce the loans).

331 *Id.*

332 *See, e.g.,* Matthews v. New Century Mortgage Corp., 185 F. Supp. 2d 874 (S.D. Ohio 2002); *see* § 11.7.1.1.2, *supra.*

333 *See, e.g.,* Slack v. Carpenter, 7 F.3d 418 (5th Cir. 1993); Jones v. Orleans Parish Sch. Bd., 679 F.2d 32, 35 (5th Cir.), *modified,* 688 F.2d 342 (5th Cir. 1982).

334 *See* §§ 11.7.1.1, 11.7.1.2, *supra.*

335 This doctrine has been applied in employment discrimination cases under § 1981. *See* Perez v. Laredo Junior College, 706 F.2d 731, 733 (5th Cir. 1983) (assuming that continuation theory is available under § 1981); Chung v. Pomona Valley Cmty. Hosp., 667 F.2d 788, 790 (9th Cir. 1982) (holding federal continuing violation rule applicable to claims under § 1981). However, the theory might not be available if it appears to conflict with state law as statute of limitations periods for federal Civil Rights Acts claims are borrowed from state law. *See, e.g.,* Thomas v. Denny's Inc., 111 F.3d 1506, 1513 (10th Cir. 1997).

336 *See* Appx. E, *infra.*

337 *See* Appx. E, *infra.*

338 *See* National Consumer Law Center, Unfair and Deceptive Acts and Practices § 7.3, Appx. A. (5th ed. 2001).

339 National Consumer Law Center, Truth in Lending § 7.2.4 (4th ed. 1999 and Supp.). In the past, Truth in Lending rescission claims were also permitted after the three-year period had run, when raised by recoupment. The Supreme Court foreclosed this possibility as a matter of federal law in Beach v. Ocwen Fed. Bank, 523 U.S. 410, 118 S. Ct. 1408, 140 L. Ed. 2d 566 (1998). However, there may be arguments permitting rescission by way of recoupment under state law. *See* National Consumer Law Center, Truth in Lending § 6.6.3 (4th ed. 1999 and Supp.).

340 *See* Stewart Title Guar. Co. v. WKC Restaurants Venture Co., 961 S.W.2d 874 (Mo. Ct. App. 1998) (a recoupment action can mitigate or extinguish the debtor's damages, but cannot result in an affirmative judgment for the debtor).

341 Roseman v. Premier Financial Services-E., L.P., 1997 U.S. Dist.

may bar a party from doing so in a subsequent action on the grounds of res judicata.[342]

The majority of reported ECOA cases that have addressed the issue have permitted recoupment claims after the limitations period has run.[343] Courts have also allowed recoupment claims in FHA cases.[344] While most courts agree that the ECOA may be employed to defend against nonpayment of a promissory note, courts disagree as to whether the setoff

or recoupment claim should be asserted as a counterclaim for damages or as a special defense of illegality.[345]

When a court finds a recoupment claim unavailable, another possibility in some cases is to argue that the credit discrimination violation makes the debt illegal. Another section of this manual discusses the split case law as to whether an ECOA violation renders a note or security interest void.[346]

11.8 Creditor Defenses

11.8.1 General

The most common creditor defense, expiration of the statute of limitations, is discussed in section 11.7, *supra*. This section focuses on additional defenses unique to FHA and ECOA claims. Although not discussed here, creditors may also raise common law defenses in credit discrimination cases.

11.8.2 Business Justification Defense

In most credit discrimination cases, the creditor will offer a legitimate business justification for its actions. The effectiveness of this business justification defense will depend on the type of action being brought. There will be no business justification defense when the creditor violates a specific ECOA requirement, such as failing to send notice of an adverse action or seeking information not permitted to be inquired about.

The business justification defense is only relevant when the plaintiff alleges a violation of the general rule against discrimination, based either on disparate treatment or disparate impact. The nature of the business justification defense varies depending on whether a case involves disparate treatment or impact.

In a disparate treatment case, the business justification for the discrimination cannot justify disparate treatment on a prohibited basis. Instead, the creditor will have to argue that it did not treat individuals differently on a prohibited basis and that the *sole* basis for its action was a legitimate business need.[347] The creditor must show that the prohibited basis did not affect its actions. The issue at trial will be what was the real basis of the creditor's actions, the prohibited basis or the business justification. This issue is covered in Chapter 4.

In a disparate impact case, the plaintiff might not even challenge the existence of a business justification or that this

---

LEXIS 13836 (E.D. Pa. Sept. 3, 1997).

342 *See* Olague v. Vill. of Bensenville, 1997 U.S. Dist. LEXIS 8539 (N.D. Ill. June 11, 1997); *see also* United States Fid. & Guaranty Co. v. Feibus, 1998 U.S. Dist. LEXIS 20837 (M.D. Pa. Apr. 2, 1998) (defendant denied leave to amend answer to include ECOA counterclaim because excessive time had passed since close of discovery, defendant offered no explanation for the delay, and new discovery would have been required).

343 Mayes v. Chrysler Credit Corp., 167 F.3d 675 (1st Cir. 1999); Bolduc v. Beal Bank, 167 F.3d 667 (1st Cir. 1999); Silverman v. Eastrich Multiple Investor Fund, L.P., 51 F.3d 28 (3d Cir. 1995) (because claims by way of recoupment are never barred by statute of limitations so long as main action is timely, court did not address creditor's assertion that time in which wife-guarantor could raise a claim under ECOA for impermissibly being required to sign husband's guaranty expired two years after date she signed guaranty, nor whether approval of creditor's bankruptcy reorganization plan which provided for deferral of payment on debt constituted "renewal" of debt permitting resurrection of claim beyond initial statute of limitations), *rev'g*, 857 F. Supp. 447 (E.D. Pa. 1994); Nowicki v. Green, 1999 U.S. Dist. LEXIS 7058 (E.D. Pa. May 12, 1999); Sharp Electronics Corp. v. Yoggev, 1995 U.S. Dist. LEXIS 5751 (E.D. Pa. May 1, 1995); Fed. Deposit Ins. Corp. v. Medmark, Inc., 897 F. Supp. 511 (D. Kan. 1995); Integra Bank/Pittsburgh v. Freeman, 839 F. Supp. 326 (E.D. Pa. 1993); Machias Sav. Bank v. Ramsdell, 689 A.2d 595 (Me. 1997); Mundaca Inv. Corp. v. Emery, 674 A.2d 923 (Me. 1996); Fed. Deposit Ins. Corp. v. Notis, 602 A.2d 1164 (Me. 1992); Norwest Bank Minn. v. Midwestern Mach. Co., 481 N.W.2d 875 (Minn. Ct. App. 1992); Boone Nat'l Sav. & Loan Ass'n v. Crouch, 47 S.W.3d 371 (Mo. 2001) (en banc); *see also* Roseman v. Premier Fin. Services-E.,L.P., 1997 U.S. Dist. LEXIS 13836 (E.D. Pa. Sept. 3, 1997), *further proceedings at* 1998 U.S. Dist. LEXIS 15679 (E.D. Pa. Sept. 29, 1998) (claim for monetary relief barred but defensive claim seeking declaration that obligation is void is not barred by statute of limitations); Marine Am. State Bank v. Lincoln, 433 N.W.2d 709 (Iowa 1988) ($5,000 attorney fees and $5,000 punitive damages on ECOA recoupment claim). *But see* Riggs Nat'l Bank v. Linch, 36 F.3d 370 (4th Cir. 1994); Household Bank v. Carlton, 7 F.3d 223 (4th Cir. 1993) (unpublished) (text available at 1993 U.S. App. LEXIS 25139); Fed. Deposit Ins. Corp. v. 32 Edwardsville, Inc., 873 F. Supp. 1474 (D. Kan. 1995); CMF Va. Land, L.P. v. Brinson, 806 F. Supp. 90 (E.D. Va. 1992); Am. Sec. Bank v. York, 1992 U.S. Dist. LEXIS 14309 (D.D.C. Sept. 1, 1992); Diamond v. Union Bank & Trust, 776 F. Supp. 542 (N.D. Okla. 1991); *In re* Fox, 162 B.R. 729, 732 (Bankr. E.D. Va. 1993) (common law recoupment is not available on a sealed instrument in Virginia); Ford City Bank v. Goldman, 98 Ill. App. 3d 522, 424 N.E.2d 761 (1981).

344 *See, e.g.,* Associates Home Equity Services, Inc. v. Troup, 778 A.2d 529, 539 (N.J. Super. Ct. App. Div. 2001) (in allowing recoupment in FHA case, court disagreed with defendants argument that recoupment was inappropriate because the defendant's complaint was in foreclosure, not in a collection action).

345 *See* § 11.6.5.2, *supra*.

346 *See* § 11.6.5.2, *supra*.

347 Nia Home Health Care, Inc. v. Whitney Nat'l Bank, 1998 U.S. Dist. LEXIS 5200 (E.D. La. Apr. 9, 1998) (summary judgment granted for the defendant because the defendant had legitimate, non-discriminatory reasons for denying credit and the plaintiff offered no evidence that those reasons were pretextual).

justification was in fact the basis for the creditor's actions. Instead, the plaintiff will allege that use of this business justification has a disparate impact on a prohibited basis, that the effect of using this legitimate business factor is to disproportionately deny credit to minorities or other protected groups. The issue then becomes whether the disparate impact is so great as to outweigh the business justification.

The issue in disparate impact cases is not whether there is a business justification or whether this justification was the real reason for the creditor's action. Instead, the issue will be how significant the business justification is and whether the same need may be met with less disparate impact. This topic is discussed in detail in Chapter 4.

11.8.3 Special ECOA Defenses

11.8.3.1 Good Faith Compliance

The ECOA states that a creditor is not liable for any act done or omitted in good faith in conformity with Regulation B or with the Official Staff Commentary, even if the regulation or commentary is amended or determined to be invalid.[348] The conduct must not only conform to the regulation but must have been in good faith conformity. Regulation B defines good faith as actions based on "honesty in fact" in the conduct or transaction.[349]

The most important application of this defense is when a consumer wishes to challenge the regulation or commentary as being an unreasonable interpretation of the statute. Even if the consumer prevails in that challenge, the creditor is still protected as to its *past* conduct that conformed with the regulation or commentary subsequently found to be in error. Similarly, a regulation or commentary amendment cannot be applied retroactively to a creditor that complied in good faith with the prior version.

11.8.3.2 The Inadvertent Error Defense

Regulation B establishes an inadvertent error defense in ECOA actions.[350] This defense is limited in scope. First, the inadvertent error defense excuses the creditor only from liability for violations of five specified provisions of Regulation B—those dealing with review of credit history of a spouse's account, notification of action taken on an application, furnishing of credit information to reporting agencies on joint accounts, record retention requirements, and information requested for monitoring purposes.[351] The defense does not apply to actions based on the general rule against discrimination, cosigner requirements, application procedures, credit evaluation systems, or many other specific ECOA provisions.

Even when the five specified provisions are at issue, the creditor must show its actions fall within the Regulation's definition of inadvertent error. An inadvertent error is defined by Regulation B as a mechanical, electronic, or clerical error that a creditor demonstrates was not intentional and occurred notwithstanding the maintenance of procedures reasonably adapted to avoid such errors.[352]

To make use of this defense the creditor thus has to overcome a number of burdens. It must show that an error was mechanical, electronic or clerical.[353] An error of law, such as failing altogether to provide appropriate adverse action notices to rejected applicants, should not fall in this category.[354]

The creditor also has the burden of demonstrating that the error was not intentional and that it occurred despite the maintenance of procedures "reasonably adapted" to avoid such errors.[355] For instance, if a creditor routinely fails to furnish information to credit reporting agencies as to both participating spouses when it reports its account experience, the inadvertent error defense is not available against a claim of sex discrimination, because this practice could be shown to be either intentional or preventable under a system with reasonable procedures for checking validity. At a minimum, there should be a showing of some standard verification procedure which is used for all applications. The inadvertent error defense closely corresponds to the "bona fide error" defense under the Truth in Lending Act and cases discussing that defense should be of use by analogy.[356]

---

vertent error defense. A creditor who can establish this defense is not liable for violations of §§ 202.6(b)(6) (consideration of credit history), 202.9 (notification requirements), 202.10 (credit history reporting on joint accounts), 202.12 (record retention requirements), or 202.13 (federal monitoring requirements). *See also* Official Staff Commentary, 12 C.F.R. § 202.14(c).

348 15 U.S.C. § 1691e(e); *see also* Official Staff Commentary, Introduction-1.

349 Reg. B, 12 C.F.R. § 202.2(r); *see also* Uniform Commercial Code § 1-201(19) (good faith).

350 Reg. B, 12 C.F.R. § 202.14(c).

351 The 1985 revisions to Regulation B created a new section, 12 C.F.R. § 202.14(c), which consolidated references to the inad-

352 Reg. B, 12 C.F.R. § 202.2(s).

353 *See* Harbaugh v. Cont'l Ill. Nat'l Bank & Trust Co., 615 F.2d 1169, 1174 (7th Cir. 1980) (apparently condoning "good faith computer programming deficiencies").

354 For a discussion in the Truth in Lending context, see National Consumer Law Center, Truth in Lending § 7.3.3 (4th ed. 1999 and Supp.).

355 *See* Sayers v. Gen. Motors Acceptance Corp., 522 F. Supp. 835 (W.D. Mo. 1981) (an adverse action notice, stating that the denial of credit was based on unfavorable information in the consumer's credit history, did not give rise to an ECOA violation when it was based on an inadvertent misinterpretation of the credit history; however, the creditor's willful refusal to comply with the notification requirements after being informed of its error did constitute an ECOA violation); *see also* Gallegos v. Stokes, 593 F.2d 372 (10th Cir. 1979) (TILA case); Hinkle v. Rock Springs Nat'l Bank, 538 F.2d 295 (10th Cir. 1976) (TILA case); National Consumer Law Center, Truth in Lending § 7.3.3 (4th ed. 1999 and Supp.).

356 15 U.S.C. § 1640(c); *see* National Consumer Law Center, Truth in Lending § 7.3.5 (4th ed. 1999 and Supp.).

Moreover, upon discovery of an error dealing with the furnishing of credit information to reporting agencies or notification of an action taken on an application, the creditor must correct the error as soon as possible.[357] Thus, the defense should not be available if the creditor knows of the inadvertent error before the applicant brings the ECOA claim.

It should be noted that Regulation B's inadvertent error defense has no counterpart in the ECOA itself. In contrast, as noted, the Truth in Lending Act does statutorily provide for a similar creditor defense,[358] as does the Fair Debt Collection Practices Act,[359] suggesting that the omission in the ECOA was purposeful. Thus it might be argued that the Equal Credit Opportunity Act is a "strict liability" statute,[360] and that the inadvertent error defense should be available only in administrative proceedings, and not in private litigation.

11.8.3.3 Creditor's Reasonable Notice of Violation

When a transaction involves more than one creditor, and one creditor violates the ECOA, the other creditors in a transaction are not liable for the violation to the extent that they lacked "reasonable notice" of the violation *before* becoming involved in the transaction.[361]

For example, a car dealer may make a preliminary credit determination and require the signature of a spouse, before submitting the proposed transaction to a finance company. If this practice violates the ECOA, the finance company might then claim ignorance of the dealer's action and that it is not liable for the dealer's ECOA violations. This argument is only viable if the finance company is not directly liable as a creditor under the ECOA.[362]

11.8.3.4 Special Defenses by FDIC and RTC

When a governmental agency, such as the Federal Deposit Insurance Corporation (FDIC) or the Resolution Trust Corporation (RTC) takes over a bank, the ECOA still applies. Under the doctrine of *D'Oench Duhme & Co. v. FDIC*,[363] as partially codified in 12 U.S.C. § 1823(e), defenses based on unrecorded side agreements are not available. However, an ECOA violation is normally apparent on the face of the bank's records (for example, requirement of a spouse's signature when the credit application shows the applicant is creditworthy). Thus, courts agree that an ECOA violation may be raised against the RTC or the FDIC either as a special defense of illegality, or as a counterclaim for damages.[364] However, when prescribed administrative claims procedures have not been followed, courts lack jurisdiction to entertain affirmative defenses and counterclaims to suits brought by the government receiver.[365]

In addition, a debtor who has broadly released the RTC from any claims and defenses, may not use the ECOA against a coguarantor in a suit for contribution.[366]

11.8.4 Defenses to Fair Housing Act and Civil Rights Acts Claims

The Fair Housing Act and the Civil Rights Acts do not provide for any special defenses. The Fair Housing regulations provide a defense when an entity purchases loans. Such an entity may consider factors justified by business necessity, such as considerations employed in normal and prudent transactions.[367] Business justification is an issue in any disparate treatment or impact case, as well.[368]

---

357 The 1985 revisions to Regulation B created a new section, 12 C.F.R. § 202.14(c), which consolidated references to the inadvertent error defense. A creditor who can establish this defense is not liable for violations of §§ 202.6(b)(6) (consideration of credit history), 202.9 (notification requirements), 202.10 (credit history reporting on joint accounts), 202.12 (record retention requirements), or 202.13 (federal monitoring requirements). *See also* Official Staff Commentary, 12 C.F.R. § 202.14(c).

358 15 U.S.C. § 1640(c); *see* National Consumer Law Center, Truth in Lending § 7.3.3.1 (4th ed. 1999 and Supp.).

359 15 U.S.C. § 1692k(c); *see* National Consumer Law Center, Fair Debt Collection § 7.4 (4th ed. 2000 and Supp.).

360 A rationale for such a distinction between this and the other titles of the Consumer Credit Protection Act is that the ECOA was intended to be a civil rights statute, rather than simply a consumer protection statute. *See, e.g.,* 50 Fed. Reg. 48,019 (Nov. 20, 1985).

361 Reg. B, 12 C.F.R. § 202.2(*l*); *see* § 2.2.5.5, *supra*.

362 *See* §§ 2.2.5.4, 2.2.5.5, *supra*.

363 315 U.S. 447, 62 S. Ct. 676, 86 L. Ed. 956 (1942).

364 CMF Va. Land, L.P. v. Brinson, 806 F. Supp. 90 (E.D. Va. 1992); Diamond v. Union Bank & Trust, 776 F. Supp. 542 (N.D. Okla. 1991); Fed. Deposit Ins. Corp. v. Notis, 602 A.2d 1164 (Me. 1992). *See generally* National Consumer Law Center, The Cost of Credit: Regulation and Legal Challenges § 10.7.2 (2d ed. 2000 and Supp.).

365 Fed. Deposit Ins. Corp. v. Parkway Executive Office Ctr., 1997 U.S. Dist. LEXIS 12318 (E.D. Pa. Aug. 15, 1997) (defendants did not raise their claims in an administrative proceeding within sixty days under 12 U.S.C. § 1821(d)(6)); Resolution Trust Corp. v. A.W. Assocs., Inc., 869 F. Supp. 1503 (D. Kan. 1994); Resolution Trust Corp. v. Laskin, 843 F. Supp. 1008 (D. Md. 1994) (defendants failed to file a claim with the receiver prior to the published claim bar date).

366 Wetzler v. Cantor, 202 B.R. 573 (D. Md. 1996).

367 24 C.F.R. § 100.125(c).

368 *See* § 4.3.2.5, *supra*.

Chapter 12   Government Enforcement

12.1 Introduction

Several federal and state agencies are responsible for ensuring compliance with the various laws prohibiting credit discrimination. This chapter identifies those agencies and their respective enforcement roles and responsibilities under each of the applicable statutes. It also describes some important cases brought by these agencies.

12.2 Agencies Responsible For ECOA Enforcement

12.2.1 The U.S. Attorney General

The United States Attorney General may bring a civil action against a creditor for violations of the ECOA when a) a federal agency with ECOA enforcement authority refers a case to the Attorney General for prosecution or b) the Attorney General has reason to believe that a creditor is engaging in a pattern or practice of ECOA violations.[1] Relief available in such actions includes actual and punitive damages and injunctive relief.[2]

During the last decade, the Attorney General brought a number of enforcement actions under both the ECOA and the FHA.[3] The Attorney General's enforcement efforts included, among other things, actions directed at marketing practices, underwriting policies and pricing practices.[4] Since 1992, the Attorney General has filed sixteen fair lending lawsuits. Ten of these were referred to the Attorney General by federal bank regulatory agencies, and six were the result of the Attorney General's own investigations.[5]

---

1   15 U.S.C. § 1691e(h); *see* § 12.4.3, *infra* (specific enforcement actions by the Attorney General).

2   15 U.S.C. § 1691e(h). A 1991 statute clarified that the Attorney General can seek not only injunctive but also monetary relief. Federal Deposit Insurance Corporation Improvement Act of 1991, Pub. L. No. 102-242, § 223(a)–(c), 105 Stat. 2306 (Dec. 19, 1991). Thus any contrary holding, such as United States v. Beneficial Corp., 492 F. Supp. 682 (D.N.J. 1980), *aff'd without opinion*, 673 F.2d 1302 (3d Cir. 1981), is no longer good law.

3   *See* Dep't of Justice, Fair Lending Enforcement Program (Jan. 2001), *available at* http://www.usdoj.gov.

4   *Id.*

5   *Id.*

12.2.2 Federal Trade Commission

Except to the extent that another federal agency has specific enforcement authority concerning a particular type of creditor,[6] the Federal Trade Commission (FTC) has overall enforcement authority under the ECOA.[7] The one major exception is that the Federal Reserve Board (FRB) has been delegated the authority to issue regulations under the ECOA.[8] Thus, the FTC has overall enforcement responsibility for the FRB's Regulation B, and the FRB's enforcement authority of its own regulation is limited to violations by certain banks.[9]

Any violation of the ECOA or Regulation B is deemed a violation of the FTC Act and is remedied by the FTC's normal enforcement powers. These powers include administrative proceedings that may lead to a cease and desist order, and federal court actions for civil penalties, restitution, and injunctive relief. As a practical matter, most FTC actions end in consent agreements.

12.2.3 Other Federal Agencies

The ECOA delegates specific enforcement authority to ten different federal agencies, each having jurisdiction over a particular type of credit institution.[10] Any transaction at an institution not covered by one of these ten agencies is covered by the Federal Trade Commission.[11] These ten agencies and their areas of responsibility are:

- The Comptroller of the Currency for national banks and federal branches of foreign banks;
- The Federal Reserve Board (FRB) for member banks of the Federal Reserve System (other than national banks) and foreign bank branches (other than foreign bank federal and insured state branches);
- The Federal Deposit Insurance Corp. (FDIC) for banks insured by the FDIC (other than member banks of the

---

6   *See* § 12.2.3, *infra*.

7   15 U.S.C. § 1691c(c).

8   15 U.S.C. § 1691b(a)(1).

9   *See* § 12.2.3, *infra*.

10   *See* 15 U.S.C. § 1691c; Reg. B, 12 C.F.R. § 202.14(a), app. A.

11   *See* § 12.2.2, *supra*.

Federal Reserve System) and insured state branches of foreign banks;

- The Office of Thrift Supervision for savings associations insured by the FDIC;
- The National Credit Union Administration for federal credit unions;
- The Secretary of Transportation for carriers regulated by the Surface Transportation Board, and for regulated air carriers;
- The Secretary of Agriculture for activities related to the Packers and Stockyards Act;
- The Farm Credit Administration for federal land banks and associations, federal intermediate credit banks and production credit associations;
- The Securities and Exchange Commission for brokers and dealers; and
- The Small Business Administration for small business investment companies.[12]

In general, ECOA violations may be enforced with the same remedies and powers that these agencies possess for other matters.[13] If the agency cannot obtain the violator's compliance, the agency may refer the matter to the Department of Justice for appropriate civil action.[14]

In addition, the Comptroller of the Currency, the FRB, the FDIC, the Office of Thrift Supervision, and the National Credit Union Administration are *mandated* to refer a matter to the Attorney General whenever the agency has reason to believe that one or more creditor(s) has engaged in a pattern or practice of denying credit applications on a prohibited basis. They are permitted to make such a referral even in the absence of a pattern or practice.[15]

When a creditor's ECOA violation may also constitute a violation of the Fair Housing Act,[16] the appropriate enforcing agency must notify the Secretary of the Department of Housing and Urban Development (HUD) if it does not notify the U.S. Attorney General; the enforcing agency must also notify the applicant or alleged victim of discrimination that the complaint was referred to HUD and that the Fair Housing Act may provide a remedy for the discriminatory conduct.[17]

12.2.4 Agency Enforcement Policies and Statements

The Federal Reserve Board (FRB) plays the most important role in setting ECOA standards, in that it has the responsibility for promulgating general regulations to carry out the purposes of the ECOA,[18] which it has done by issuing Regulation B.[19] The FRB also has issued an Official Staff Commentary which provides many examples applying Regulation B to specific situations.[20]

The FRB's authority to issue regulations under the ECOA does not impair the Federal Trade Commission (FTC) or the other enforcing agencies' authority to make rules respecting their own procedures in enforcing compliance with ECOA requirements.[21] That is, the FRB makes the regulations as to when a practice does or does not violate the ECOA, but the various enforcement agencies can make their own enforcement policies.

For example, in 1981, the Federal Financial Institutions Examination Council, a formal interagency group that prescribes examination standards for financial institutions, proposed a policy statement calling for vigorous ECOA enforcement by the federal agencies which make up the Council.[22] The policy statement was subsequently adopted by the Federal Reserve Board, the Office of the Comptroller of the Currency, the Federal Deposit Insurance Corp., and the National Credit Union Administration.[23]

The policy statement focuses on several "serious" ECOA violations which, if discovered by agency examiners, re-

12 *See* 15 U.S.C. § 1691c (as amended by Pub. L. No. 102-242, 105 Stat. 2236 (1991)); Reg. B, 12 C.F.R. § 202.14(a), app. A.
13 15 U.S.C. § 1691c(b).
14 15 U.S.C. § 1691e(g).
15 15 U.S.C. § 1691e(g) (as amended by Pub. L. No. 102-242, § 223, 105 Stat. 2236 (1991)).
16 42 U.S.C. § 3605.
17 15 U.S.C. § 1691e(k) (as added by Pub. L. No. 102-242, § 223, 105 Stat. 2236 (1991)); *see also* Memorandum of Understanding Between Department of Housing and Urban Development and the Federal Financial Institutions Examination Council (FFIEC) Member Agencies, Clearinghouse No. 49,127 (Nov. 1991).

18 15 U.S.C. § 1691b.
19 Reg. B, 12 C.F.R. § 202. The Federal Reserve Board has proposed a comprehensive set of revisions to Regulation B, the substance of which are discussed throughout this manual. 64 Fed. Reg. 44,593–44,603 (Aug. 16, 1999). The proposed revisions to Regulation B can be found on the CD-Rom accompanying this volume.
20 Prior to issuing the Official Staff Commentary, ECO-1 (effective Dec. 16, 1985), the Federal Reserve Board (FRB) issued numerous Official Board and Staff Interpretation and unofficial staff letters, all of which have been superseded by the Official Staff Commentary. The FRB now issues Commentary revisions from time to time rather than continuing the somewhat disorganized former procedure.
21 15 U.S.C. § 1691c(d).
22 Fed. Fin. Institutions Examination Council, Interagency Policy Statement Regarding Enforcement of the Equal Credit Opportunity and Fair Housing Acts, Clearinghouse No. 49,137 (1981). The Council consists of the Board of Governors of the Federal Reserve System, the Federal Deposit Insurance Corp., the Office of Thrift Supervision (formerly the Federal Home Loan Bank Board), the Office of the Comptroller of the Currency, and the National Credit Union Administration.
23 *See* 46 Fed. Reg. 56,500 (Nov. 17, 1981). The Federal Home Loan Bank Board decided not to approve the policy statement or the subsequent enforcement guidelines because the Board already had in place an anti-discrimination enforcement policy which it felt was working well. The Office of Thrift Supervision has now replaced the Federal Home Loan Bank Board.

quire the creditor involved to take action to prevent future violations and to correct the effects of the violations discovered. The policy statement included descriptions of violations considered serious which would possibly warrant retrospective corrective action.

The Council also proposed a Supervisory Enforcement Policy to implement the policy statement.[24] This enforcement policy was subsequently adopted by three of the five council members: the National Credit Union Administration, the Office of the Comptroller of the Currency, and the Federal Reserve Board. It sets out specific guidelines designed to correct serious violations of ECOA.

In 1993, the Comptroller of the Currency issued new procedures for all national bank examiners to use to identify discrimination in home mortgage loans made by national banks.[25] Yet another enforcement policy was issued in 1994, following the heightened scrutiny of credit availability which inspired a new, more informed look at racial patterns in lending, and which startled both the industry and government regulators out of their complacency about fair lending compliance.[26] As a result of the regulatory agencies' reevaluation of their fair lending examination and enforcement efforts, a Joint Policy Statement on Discrimination in Lending[27] was adopted by ten agencies.[28] This statement was issued partly in response to industry complaints regarding the compliance burdens imposed upon banks by the application of different examination standards by each agency, but also in recognition of the regulatory efficiency of applying uniform standards.

The statement informs lenders about what the agencies consider in determining whether lending discrimination exists, how the agencies will respond to lending discrimination, and what steps lenders can take to prevent discriminatory lending practices. In addition, the statement answers thirteen questions often asked by financial institutions and the public. While it specifically states that it does not create any enforceable rights, it provides concrete examples of the three categories of evidence of discrimination[29] that are useful to borrowers, as well as lenders, in understanding the contours of the rights conferred by the ECOA and the FHA.[30]

Lenders responded to the joint policy statement with questions and concerns about particular aspects of the statement, including self-testing, minority-only second review programs, employee compensation systems and overages,[31] and disparate impact analysis.[32] To clarify the Justice Department's position with regard to the Joint Policy Statement, on February 21, 1995, the assistant attorney general for civil rights wrote a letter to various lender association representatives.[33] The letter restates the Department's commitment to enforcing fair lending laws, and offers guidance to lenders on how certain practices will be treated during an investigation and eventual prosecution.

In 1999, the Federal Financial Institutions Examination Council issued Interagency Procedures on Fair Lending Examination. These Procedures established a uniform set of procedures for its member agencies to use in their examinations to determine compliance with the ECOA and the FHA.[34] Among other things, the Procedures include steps for identifying program discrimination risk factors, for identifying lending discrimination risk factors, and for compliance review and examination recommendations to evaluate compliance with the ECOA and FHA[35]

24 *See* ECOA Supervisory Enforcement Policy, Clearinghouse No. 49,138 (adopted by Fed. Reserve Bd. in 1981).

25 *See* Comptroller of the Currency, Examining Bulletin on Examining for Residential Lending Discrimination, Clearinghouse No. 49,130 (Apr. 30, 1993).

26 In 1992, after increased public scrutiny of credit availability in Boston and Atlanta, the Federal Reserve Bank of Boston issued a landmark study showing that race played a role in mortgage credit denials. The findings surprised the industry, which had assumed "everybody's money was green," and the regulatory agencies, which had not uncovered it before, as their examination techniques were not designed to catch the type of discrimination that was occurring. Alicia Munnell et al., Mortgage Lending in Boston: Interpreting HMDA Data (Fed. Reserve Bank of Boston, Working Paper Series No. 92-7, Oct. 1992) (available from Federal Reserve Bank of Boston, Research Library-D, P.O. Box 2076, Boston, MA 02016-2076, 617-973-3397) (also available as Clearinghouse No. 47,967); *see* § 4.4.5.4, *supra*; § 12.5, *infra* (discussing the study).

27 59 Fed. Reg. 18,266 (Apr. 15, 1994).

28 The agencies are the Department of Housing and Urban Development, Office of Federal Housing Enterprise Oversight, Department of Justice, Office of the Comptroller of the Currency, Office of Thrift Supervision, Federal Reserve Board, Federal Deposit Insurance Corp., Federal Housing Finance Board, Federal Trade Commission, and National Credit Union Administration.

29 Overt evidence, evidence of disparate treatment, and evidence of disparate impact. It notes that the "precise contours" of the latter are evolving but that disparate impact must be established (not assumed), often by quantitative or statistical methods, then it must be determined whether there is a business necessity for the practice and, if so, whether there is an alternative practice which has less discriminatory impact. 59 Fed. Reg. 18,266, 18,269 (Apr. 15, 1994); *see* § 4.3, *supra*.

30 *But see Lenders Nationwide Urge Agencies to Alter Policy on Fair Lending*, 62 Banking Rep. (BNA) 1096 (June 27, 1994).

31 *See* § 8.4, *supra*, § 12.4.3.9, *infra*.

32 *See* § 4.3, *supra*.

33 Letter from Deval L. Patrick, Assistant Att'y Gen., Civil Rights Div., United States Dep't of Justice, to lender association representatives (Feb. 21, 1995) (concerning Dep't of Justice Fair Lending Enforcement Program) (available as Clearinghouse No. 52,064).

34 Fed. Fin. Institutions Examination Council, Interagency Fair Lending Examination Procedures, Clearinghouse No. 53,526 (Feb. 12, 1999), *available at* http://www.ffiec.gov/PDF/fairlend/pdf.

35 *Id.*

12.3 Fair Housing Act Enforcement

12.3.1 HUD Administrative Enforcement

On its own initiative, and without receiving a consumer complaint, the United States Department of Housing and Urban Development (HUD) can investigate discriminatory practices[36] and initiate an administrative proceeding against a creditor alleging credit discrimination.[37] At all times, the Secretary must attempt to resolve the matter through conciliation.[38]

Conciliation may result in a settlement providing monetary and other affirmative relief. For example, in April 1998, HUD reached conciliation agreements[39] with five Texas lenders as a result of testing conducted by the Fort Worth Human Relations Commission which showed disparities in the way minority and white testers were being treated by these lenders.[40] The five conciliation agreements provide for a total of approximately $3.5 billion in loan commitments to minorities and low-income borrowers. In addition to conciliation, the Secretary can seek preliminary relief in federal court while an administrative proceeding is pending.[41]

If conciliation fails to resolve a matter, the case is referred to a state or local agency certified by HUD for this purpose.[42] If the certified agency does not act, or if there is no appropriate certified agency, then, after HUD determines there is reasonable cause to believe that discrimination exists, the case is referred to a HUD Administrative Law Judge.[43] The Administrative Law Judge may order actual damages, equitable relief, and civil penalties of $10,000 (increasing to $25,000 and $50,000 for repeat violators).[44] Decisions of the Administrative Law Judge are reviewable by the Secretary and by the federal courts.[45]

Either the respondent or the Secretary may avoid the administrative process, and instead have the complaint adjudicated immediately in federal court in an action brought by the Attorney General.[46] The aggrieved party can receive the same relief as if a private action were instituted in court. This election must be made in a timely manner.[47]

HUD also has authority, pursuant to the Federal Housing Enterprises Financial Safety and Soundness Act of 1992 (FHEFSSA),[48] to regulate and enforce fair lending laws against the two government-sponsored enterprises (GSEs)—the Federal National Mortgage Association (a.k.a. Fannie Mae) and the Federal Home Loan Mortgage Corp. (a.k.a. Freddie Mac). Under the FHEFSSA, the Secretary must, by regulation, prohibit the GSEs from discriminating in their mortgage purchases on the basis of race, color, religion, sex, handicap, familial status, age, or national origin. The GSEs also may not discriminate based on the location or age of the dwelling, or the neighborhood or census tract where the dwelling is located. In addition, the FHEFSSA authorizes the Secretary to require Fannie Mae and Freddie Mac—leaders in the secondary mortgage industry—to submit data to assist HUD in investigating whether a mortgage lender has failed to comply with either the FHA or the ECOA, and to take remedial action against lenders found to have violated the FHA or ECOA. HUD must periodically review and comment on the GSEs' underwriting and appraisal guidelines to ensure that they are consistent with fair lending laws, and obtain and make available to the GSEs information from other regulatory and enforcement agencies of violations by lenders of the FHA and ECOA. HUD has issued final rules implementing, among other things, the above requirements mandated by the FHEFSSA.[49]

---

36 *See* United States v. Sea Winds of Marco, Inc., 893 F. Supp. 1051, 1054 (M.D. Fla. 1995) (HUD's alleged failure to complete its investigation within 100 days of receiving complaints against defendants or to notify defendants of its inability to complete the investigation within that period, as prescribed under 42 U.S.C. § 3610(g)(1), is neither a jurisdictional bar nor a statute of limitations).

37 42 U.S.C. § 3610(a)(1)(A).

38 42 U.S.C. § 3610(b); *see* United States v. Sea Winds of Marco, Inc., 893 F. Supp. 1051, 1054–55 (M.D. Fla. 1995) (HUD's alleged failure to engage in good faith conciliation is not a jurisdictional issue).

39 Joint Agreements between the United States Dep't of Hous. & Urban Dev., the Ft. Worth Human Relations Comm'n and 1) Overton Bank & Trust; 2) Temple-Inland Mortgage Corp.; 3) Banc One Mortgage Corp.; 4) Accubanc Mortgage Corp. and 5) SFM Mortgage Corp., Clearinghouse Nos. 53,527 to 53,531 (dated between Mar. 11 and Apr. 9, 1998).

40 *See* § 5.3.3, *supra* (further description of the testing program conducted by the Forth Worth Human Relations Commission).

41 42 U.S.C. § 3610(e).

42 42 U.S.C. § 3610(f).

43 42 U.S.C. §§ 3612(a), (b); *see, e.g.,* Dep't of Hous. & Urban Dev. v. Mercantile-Safe Deposit & Trust Co., Clearinghouse No. 53,535, HUDALJ 03-91-0235-1 (June 10, 1993) (initial decision), *available at* http://www.hud.gov.

44 42 U.S.C. § 3612(g)(3).

45 42 U.S.C. § 3612(i).

46 42 U.S.C. § 3612(o); *see* United States v. Tierra Apartments Ltd. P'ship, 865 F. Supp. 624 (D. Neb. 1994) (time limit is not jurisdictional and mandatory, therefore, United State's failure to file action within thirty days did not divest court of jurisdiction or require dismissal); *see also* United States v. Weber, 1993 U.S. Dist. LEXIS 20732 (D. Neb. Oct. 19, 1993); United States v. Bank United, Clearinghouse Nos. 53,018 (complaint), 53,019 (consent decree) (W.D.N.Y. 1999).

47 42 U.S.C. § 3612(a); *cf.* Ramos v. Dep't of Hous. & Urban Dev., 1997 U.S. Dist. LEXIS 13894, at *8 (S.D.N.Y. Sept. 11, 1997) (plaintiff may bring FHA action in federal court regardless of status of HUD administrative proceeding); Green v. Konover Residential Corp., 1997 U.S. Dist. LEXIS 18893 (D. Conn. Nov. 24, 1997) (Fair Housing Act does not require exhaustion of administrative remedies).

48 *See* Federal Housing Enterprises Financial Safety and Soundness Act of 1992, Pub. L. No. 102-550, §§ 1301–1395, 106 Stat. 3672 (codified at 12 U.S.C. §§ 4501–4641).

49 24 C.F.R. pt. 81.

12.3.2 Civil Enforcement of the FHA by the United States Attorney General

The United States Attorney General can on her own initiative bring an action in federal court for credit discrimination under the FHA.[50] The case must involve a pattern or practice of discrimination or the discrimination must raise an issue of general public importance.[51]

The Secretary of HUD may also elect not to follow the administrative procedure in a given case and may request instead that the Attorney General bring an action directly in federal court.[52] Thus the Attorney General may bring a discrimination case in federal court either because the Attorney General determines that there is a pattern or practice of discrimination or because HUD requests that the Attorney General bring a case. In either case, the court may award equitable relief, monetary damages to aggrieved parties, and a civil penalty not to exceed $50,000 for a first violation (or $100,000 for subsequent violations).[53]

12.4 Agency Referrals of ECOA Cases to Department of Justice or HUD

12.4.1 General

The ECOA and Regulation B authorize any agency responsible for enforcing the ECOA[54] to refer to the Attorney General any matter for which it is unable to obtain compliance under the Act or Regulation, or which it has reason to believe is a violation of § 701(a) of the Act by one or more creditors.[55] In addition, whenever the Federal Reserve Board, Comptroller of the Currency, Federal Deposit Insurance Corp., Office of Thrift Supervision, or National Credit Union Administration has reason to believe that one or more creditors has engaged in a pattern or practice of discouraging or denying applications in violation of the Act or Regulation, it is required to refer such matter to the Attorney General.[56] The Attorney General, on referral or whenever it has reason to believe that one or more creditors has engaged in a pattern or practice in violation of the Act or Regulation, may bring a civil action for damages or injunctive relief.[57]

The Act and Regulation also require the above five agencies to notify the Department of Housing and Urban Development (HUD) whenever there is reason to believe that a violation of the ECOA also violates the Fair Housing Act, and the agencies have not referred the matter to the Attorney General.[58] These agencies must also notify the applicant or alleged victim of discrimination that the complaint was referred to HUD, and that remedies for the discriminatory conduct may be available under the Fair Housing Act.[59]

12.4.2 Selected Agency Enforcement Actions Under the ECOA

12.4.2.1 Office of the Comptroller of the Currency

Since April 1993, the Office of the Comptroller of the Currency (OCC) has made thirty-seven referrals to the Department of Justice or to HUD for fair lending violations by national banks. Of the thirty-seven cases, two involved allegations of discrimination on the basis of race/national origin, twelve concerned discrimination on the basis of age, and ten involved marital status discrimination. The OCC indicated that twenty-four of the referrals involved consumer loan transactions, ten involved residential real estate loan transactions and three involved both types of loans. The OCC also had success settling an ECOA and FHA discrimination case in 1999, when it alleged that First Central Bank discriminated against non-Asian mortgage loan applicants in violation of the ECOA and the FHA. The bank consented to pay $25,000 in civil penalties and establish a $400,000 settlement fund to compensate applicants for the alleged fair lending violations.[60]

12.4.2.2 Federal Trade Commission

In the 1990s, the Federal Trade Commission successfully

---

50 42 U.S.C. § 3614(a).

51 42 U.S.C. § 3614(a); *see* United States v. Incorporated Vill. of Island Park, 888 F. Supp. 419, 449 (E.D.N.Y. 1995).

52 *See* § 12.3.1, *supra.*

53 42 U.S.C. § 3614(d).

54 *See* § 12.2.3, *supra.*

55 Reg. B, 12 C.F.R. § 202.14(b)(3).

56 Reg. B, 12 C.F.R. § 202.14(b)(3). Statistics on FFB referrals to the Attorney General may be available in the FRB's Annual Report to Congress. *See, e.g.,* Fed. Reserve Bd., 86th Annual Report to Congress 1999 (May 2000), *available at* http://www.federalreserve.gov.

57 Reg. B, 12 C.F.R. § 202.14(b)(4). In 1996, as part of the

Omnibus Consolidated Appropriations Act, 1997, Pub. L. No. 104-208, 110 Stat. 3009 (1996), both the ECOA and FHA were amended, limiting the ability of regulatory agencies to refer a matter to the Attorney General or to notify the Secretary of HUD if the creditor has already identified the matter as a possible violation of the ECOA or the FHA as a result of self-testing or internal reviews for compliance under the Acts. *See* §§ 1.3.2.6, 1.4.2, *supra.*

58 15 U.S.C. § 1691e(k); Reg. B, 12 C.F.R. § 202.14(b)(5); *see also* Memorandum of Understanding Between Dep't of Housing and Urban Development and the Federal Financial Institutions Examination Council (FFIEC) Member Agencies, Clearinghouse No. 49,127 (Nov. 1991).

59 12 C.F.R. § 202.14(b)(5)(ii).

60 *See In re* First Cent. Bank, Clearinghouse No. 53,020 (Office of the Comptroller of the Currency) (Jan. 1999) (stipulation and consent order). *See generally* http://www.occ.treas.gov/cdd/fair.htm.

negotiated several credit discrimination settlements under the ECOA. Each of the following cases resulted in substantial monetary payments by the creditors and injunctive relief prohibiting future discrimination.

- *United States v. Franklin Acceptance Corp.,*[61] (alleging that Franklin violated the ECOA by refusing to consider income from public assistance or child support, by refusing to consider the income of unmarried co-applicants, while combining the incomes of married co-applicants, and, when cosigners were required, by allowing only a married applicant to have their spouse and not any other person cosign a loan).
- *United States v. Ford Motor Credit Co.,*[62] (alleging that from May 1994 to August 1995, Ford violated the ECOA by combining incomes for married applicants but not for unmarried joint applicants resulting in unmarried applicants obtaining credit on less favorable terms compared to their married counterparts).
- *United States v. Money Tree, Inc.,*[63] (alleging that the Money Tree discriminated against applicants who received public assistance and against elderly applicants by imposing stricter loan terms on applicants who received income from public assistance than on employed applicants, by collecting or attempting to collect payments from borrowers receiving public assistance before they were due, and by discouraging elderly applicants from applying for credit, by denying them credit, or by offering them credit on less favorable terms than younger applicants).
- *United States v. Bonlar Loan Co.,*[64] (alleging that Bonlar violated the ECOA by asking applicants for their marital status when such information was not necessary for evaluating the loan application, by failing to provide adverse action notices, and by failing to provide specific reasons for adverse action or to inform the applicant of their right to request such reasons).

12.4.3 Enforcement by Justice Department

12.4.3.1 Actions and Settlements in Discriminatory Lending and Insurance Practices

During the 1990s, the U.S. Department of Justice filed complaints against more than a dozen separate financial institutions for alleged discriminatory lending practices and against insurance companies for alleged insurance redlining. These cases allege numerous illegal practices, ranging from the level of availability of credit services for different customers or communities, to discriminatory marketing and differential pricing issues. Most of these cases were filed simultaneously with settlement agreements or consent decrees which attempt to provide redress to the individuals and communities that were affected by the alleged misconduct.

Although the settled cases have no direct precedential value, they were important models for private actions alleging lending discrimination. They also helped establish new theories for what constitutes credit discrimination. Part of their value also lies in their use of Home Mortgage Disclosure Act data and other statistics to support allegations of discrimination, especially in the absence of overt acts.[65] The fact that lenders of all sizes and reputations were the subject of these actions underscores the Justice Department's designation of fair lending enforcement as a high priority at the time.

Remedies in each of the settled cases included compensatory as well as remedial components. While these lenders and insurers all denied the respective allegations against them, they agreed to pay money damages (including civil penalties), and to establish new policies and guidelines that would correct the practices in question. Perhaps the greatest value to consumers, however, was the message sent to regulated institutions at all levels that regulators recognized that discrimination is a serious problem and intended to pursue the remedial measures at their disposal.

12.4.3.2 Discriminatory Marketing

The first seminal government lawsuit in the 1990s alleging a pattern or practice of race discrimination under the ECOA and the FHA against a mortgage lender was *United States v. Decatur Federal Savings & Loan Ass'n.*[66] The Department of Justice (DOJ) alleged Decatur engaged in numerous racially discriminatory practices which denied African-Americans in the Atlanta area the same credit opportunities that were given whites.[67] Specifically, Decatur allegedly defined its customer service area under the Com-

---

61 United States v. Franklin Acceptance Corp., Civ. No. 99-CV-2435 (E.D. Pa. 1999) (consent decree) [reproduced on the CD-Rom accompanying this volume].

62 United States v. Ford Motor Credit Corp., Clearinghouse No. 53,016, No. 99-75887 (E.D. Mich. Dec. 14, 1999) (consent decree), *available at* http://www.ftc.gov.

63 United States v. Money Tree, Inc., Clearinghouse No. 52,053, Civ. No. 6:97-CV-7 (M.D. Ga. Feb. 4, 1997), *available at* http://www.ftc.gov.

64 United States v. Bonlar Loan Co., Clearinghouse No. 53,017, Civ. No. 97-C-7274 (N.D. Ill. Oct. 17, 1997) (consent decree), *available at* http://www.ftc.gov.

65 *See* § 4.4.5, *supra.*

66 Civ. No. 1:92-CV-2198 (N.D. Ga. 1992), Clearinghouse No. 49,126 (complaint and consent decree) [reproduced on the CD-Rom accompanying this volume].

67 *Id.*

munity Reinvestment Act so as to exclude most black residents in South Fulton County; opened virtually all of its branch offices in neighborhoods that were predominantly white, while closing branches in neighborhoods that were or became predominantly black; advertised primarily to white consumers; focused solicitation efforts in white neighborhoods; avoided origination of loan products with appeal to black borrowers, such as Federal Housing Administration and Veterans Administration loans; and employed few blacks in key mortgage loan origination positions. Decatur also allegedly counseled white applicants during the loan origination process about their credit deficiencies and reworked their applications in order to help them qualify in accordance with the underwriting guidelines, but did not consistently supply comparable assistance to black applicants.[68] The case resulted in a consent decree with broad affirmative relief which included opening more branches in black neighborhoods, establishing greater safeguards on the treatment of applications by African-Americans, and close monitoring of compliance with the plan. Decatur also agreed to place $1,000,000 in a fund for those aggrieved by its prior actions.[69]

In another ECOA discrimination case based on race, the Justice Department obtained a consent decree barring the creditor from refusing loans to Native Americans and to residents of reservations.[70] The injunctive relief obtained by the DOJ required the bank to: notify officials of eight tribes that the creditor is an equal opportunity lender; explain its real estate lending policy; notify applicants for non-housing loans during the prior three years of the creditor's reasons for loan rejections; and furnish the DOJ with copies of accepted and rejected loan applications for the next three years.

12.4.3.3 Redlining

The Department of Justice's efforts to curtail banks' failure to provide access to credit and services to *all* segments of their service area was illustrated in its case against the Chevy Chase Federal Savings Bank of Chevy Chase, Maryland.[71] The complaint alleged that Chevy Chase and its subsidiary, B.F. Saul Mortgage Co., intentionally excluded majority African-American census tracts in their metropolitan District of Columbia service area from access to many of the institution's credit-related services. According to the evidence, seventy out of seventy-four bank branches and seventeen out of eighteen mortgage offices were located in predominately white census tracts, while the vast majority

of DC's 65.1% African-American population (according to the 1990 census) resided in predominately African-American neighborhoods.[72]

The Department of Justice (DOJ) further alleged that Chevy Chase effectively denied African-Americans access to bank services, by: compensating loan officers on a commission structure which rewarded mortgage loans on higher-priced homes which tended to be located in white residential areas; employing only 2.1% African-Americans in loan officer/originator positions; failing to utilize advertising media that were oriented to the African-American community; and failing to solicit the services of real-estate professionals and builders serving African-American residential areas. These acts and omissions were all asserted to have been based on racial considerations.

Of the 3,515 mortgage loan applications received by Chevy Chase during 1991, 97.6% (3,432) were from residents of white census tracts, while 2.4% were from residents of African-American census tracts. In 1993, of the 7,311 applications that the defendants received, 95.0% were from white census tracts while 5.0% were from African-American census tract residents.

The consent decree contained several remedial measures. The bank and mortgage company agreed to open branches and mortgage offices in underserved areas, to significantly expand outreach efforts to market loan products in African-American residential areas, and to invest eleven million dollars for special mortgage loans directed to the affected communities.[73]

In another redlining case, *United States v. Blackpipe State Bank*,[74] the DOJ alleged that the bank discriminated against Native Americans by refusing to make secured loans when the collateral was located on a reservation, by placing credit requirements on Native Americans that it did not require of whites, and by charging greater interest rates and finance charges to Native Americans than it charged to whites.

Blackpipe entered into a consent order setting up a $125,000 fund for compensatory damages, reducing interest rates on the discriminatorily-priced loans to Native Americans, expanding its services to bordering reservations, and marketing its products to Native Americans.

In *United States v. Albank*[75] the DOJ alleged that Albank refused to fund mortgage loans secured by residential properties located in certain areas in Connecticut and in Westchester County, New York, where significant popula-

---

68 Clearinghouse No. 49,126 (N.D. Ga. 1992) (consent decree).
69 Clearinghouse No. 49,126 (N.D. Ga. 1992) (consent decree).
70 United States v. Great W. Bank & Trust, Clearinghouse No. 33,837 (D. Ariz. 1982).
71 United States v. Chevy Chase Fed. Sav. Bank, No. 94-1824-J6 (D.D.C. 1994) (complaint and consent decree) [reproduced on the CD-Rom accompanying this volume].

72 *Id.*
73 United States v. Chevy Chase Fed. Sav. Bank, No. 94-1824-J6 (D.D.C. 1994) (complaint and consent decree); *see* § 5.3.2.4, *supra* (a discussion of *Chevy Chase* in the context of marketing discrimination).
74 Clearinghouse Nos. 49,955A (complaint), 49,955B (consent decree), Civ. No. 93-5115 (D.S.D. 1994).
75 United States v. Albank, Clearinghouse No. 52,054, Civ. No. 97-1296 (N.D.N.Y. Aug. 13, 1997) (complaint and consent decree) [reproduced on the CD-Rom accompanying this volume].

tions of African-Americans and Hispanics lived. Although Albank made exceptions to its policies, the exceptions were made predominately for white borrowers. Albank entered into a consent decree which required the bank to implement a remedial special mortgage lending program which provides homebuyer counseling and marketing tailored to the communities it previously refused to serve and to provide $55 million in loans at below-market rates to those areas.[76]

Redlining occurs not just in the context of the availability of consumer loans, especially for financing home purchases, but also in the context of the availability of homeowner's insurance. The inability to obtain homeowner insurance for many people impairs their ability to purchase a home because lenders routinely require proof of the placement of property insurance prior to closing. Thus, it is decided law that the Fair Housing Act applies to the sale of insurance for dwellings.[77] To date, the Department of Justice has been involved in two enforcement actions against insurance companies for alleged insurance redlining.[78] Both cases reached settlements which attempt to redress the harm suffered by the individuals and the communities affected by the companies' redlining policies and practices.

In *N.A.A.C.P. v. American Family Mutual Insurance Co.*, the DOJ brought its first case under the FHA to challenge the use of race as a factor in issuing homeowner insurance. The complaint alleged that, since at least 1968, American Family Mutual denied homeowner's insurance to, or provided inferior insurance for, homes in the predominantly African-American areas of metropolitan Milwaukee. The DOJ's complaint also alleged that American Family located its sales offices in white communities and closed sales offices once the racial composition of the community changed from white to black. In the consent decree settling the case, American Family agreed to pay $14.5 million to compensate the victims. The consent decree also required the company to conduct random testing, to recruit qualified prospective customers, and to refrain from excluding homes solely on the basis of sale price of the home or age of the home.[79]

12.4.3.4 Differential Denial Rates

In 1993, the Justice Department brought an action for alleged discriminatory mortgage lending practices against New England's then largest originator of home-purchase mortgages.[80] The complaint against Shawmut Mortgage Co. alleged that the company implemented policies and practices which had a disproportionate impact on African-American and Hispanic mortgage loan applicants in violation of the ECOA and the FHA.[81] Specifically, Shawmut's Home Mortgage Disclosure Act data showed that its mortgage denial rates in 1990 were 38.8% for African-Americans, 33.17% for Hispanics and 17.31% for whites; in 1991 the same rates were 33.98%, 30.63%, and 14.7%; and in 1992 they were 21.26%, 24.44% and 10.63% respectively.

The complaint further alleged that the discrepancies in denial rates were because of Shawmut's policy of allowing its employees broad discretion without an adequate mechanism by which to evaluate their loan origination performance, the result being that black and Hispanic loan applicants were treated differently than similarly qualified white applicants.

Shawmut's consent decree included measures requiring various programs targeted at increased investment, marketing, and outreach in African-American neighborhoods, and an increase in below-market loans to moderate-income homebuyers. The bank also committed, among other things, to opening a full-service branch in the predominately minority community of Roxbury, Massachusetts; to training its loan personnel in principles of fair lending;[82] and to implementing a "mystery shopper" program whereby the bank could test its own employees' adherence to fair lending principles. The decree further provided for a $960,000[83] fund to compensate applicants who were unfairly denied loans.

A second case challenging the disparity in denial rates for African-American and Hispanic loan applicants was brought against an Illinois lender in 1995.[84] The complaint alleged that the Northern Trust Co. and three of its subsid-

---

76 Some commentators have been critical of the DOJ's actions in the *Chevy Chase* and *Albank* cases. In the view of these commentators, marketing discrimination is not actionable under the ECOA and the FHA because there is no individual applicant who has been discriminated against. *See* Michael B. Mierzewski & Richard L. Jacobs, *What Hath Justice Department Wrought*, Banking Pol'y Rep., Feb. 6, 1995, at 8; John Spina, *United States v. Albank, FSB: Is 'Justice' Served in the Enforcement of Fair Lending Laws*, 2 N.C. Banking Inst. 207 (1998). These commentators seem to have ignored Reg. B, 12 C.F.R. § 202.5(a). *See* § 5.3.2, *supra* (discussion of when marketing discrimination constitutes a violation of the ECOA and the FHA).

77 *See* § 7.3.4.2, *supra*.

78 N.A.A.C.P. v. Am. Family Mut. Ins. Co., 978 F.2d 287 (7th Cir. 1992); United States v. Nationwide Mut. Ins. Co., Clearinghouse No. 52,026A (complaint and consent decree) (S.D. Ohio 1997) [reproduced on the CD-Rom accompanying this volume]; *see also* N.A.A.C.P. v. Am. Family Mut. Ins. Co., Clearinghouse No. 52,059, No. 90-C-0759 (N.D. Ill. 1995) (consent decree) [reproduced on the CD-Rom accompanying this volume].

79 N.A.A.C.P. v. Am. Family Mut. Ins. Co., Clearinghouse No. 52,059, No. 90-C-0759 (N.D. Ill. 1995) (consent decree).

80 United States v. Shawmut Mortgage Co., Clearinghouse NoS. 49,953A (complaint), 49,953B (consent decree), Civ. No. 3:93-CV-2453 (avc) (D. Conn. 1993).

81 *Id.*

82 *Id.*

83 The parties agreed that $160,000 of this total represents payment in lieu of civil money penalties that would have been payable, if assessed, to the United States Treasury. *Id.* at 10 (consent decree). In addition, should this amount be insufficient to compensate all eligible payees, Shawmut agreed to supplement the fund accordingly. *Id.* at 12 (consent decree).

84 United States v. N. Trust Co., Clearinghouse Nos. 51,292A

iaries had a higher denial rate for African-American and Hispanic loan applicants than for similarly qualified white applicants because white applicants received more assistance and were given more flexibility in meeting the bank's underwriting standards. The DOJ's investigation showed that the bank required a higher level of documentation from minorities; failed to make comparable efforts to obtain qualifying information and documentation for minorities; failed to provide comparable counseling (for example, about reducing monthly debt) to minorities; and applied underwriting standards more stringently to minorities.

Northern Trust entered into a consent decree agreeing to injunctive relief and agreeing to establish a fund of $700,000 to compensate over sixty eligible applicants.[85] In addition, the bank agreed to continue a voluntarily-initiated program to ensure that all applicants are treated in a non-discriminatory manner and have a chance to fully present their qualifications, and to submit to the Department reports on its mortgage lending activities for three years.

In 1997, the DOJ charged a New Mexico lender with discrimination against Hispanic mortgage loan applicants who sought financing for the purchase of mobile homes.[86] The complaint alleged that the First National Bank of Dona Ana County, the largest bank in Las Cruces,[87] applied more stringent underwriting standards to Hispanic loan applicants than it applied to similarly situated Anglo applicants. The complaint also alleged that the bank made greater efforts to obtain information from Anglo mobile home applicants that would demonstrate their eligibility for financing, but did not expend the same efforts for Hispanic applicants for the same type of loan. Like Shawmut Mortgage Co., the First National Bank of Dona Ana allegedly failed to provide its loan personnel with adequate underwriting and loan evaluation guidelines, leaving loan officers with de facto authority to establish application processing procedures and lending standards.

The consent order agreed to by First National Bank of Dona Ana County provided for the creation of two funds totalling $1.2 million as compensation. The agreement further required additional outreach and advertising to the Hispanic community and the development of uniform underwriting policies and guidelines.

12.4.3.5 Credit Scoring—Overrides

Another form of discrimination occurs when lenders allow "overrides" of low credit scores more frequently for non-minority applicants.[88] For example, the Office of the Comptroller of the Currency (OCC) discovered what it believed to be a pattern or practice of discriminating on the basis of race in the Deposit Guaranty National Bank's (DGNB) home improvement lending activities in Mississippi, Arkansas, and Louisiana. The OCC focused on DGNB's credit scoring override system, finding that DGNB loan officers had broad discretion to deny credit to applicants who scored at or above the cutoff level or approve credit to applicants who scored below the credit score cutoff level.[89]

In another example, the OCC evaluated the ECOA compliance of Associates National Bank (ANB), a credit card bank, and found what it believed to be a pattern of discrimination based on national origin. The OCC determined that ANB subjected applicants and cardholders that had submitted Spanish-language applications for credit cards to stricter underwriting standards and less favorable terms than those submitting English-language applications.[90] The DOJ settled with ANB in January 2001. The settlement agreement provided for a $1.5 million fund to compensate Hispanic applicants and cardholders.[91]

12.4.3.6 Differential Pricing

Several other Justice Department (DOJ) actions are particularly important for legal services clients, who often obtain credit that is too costly, rather than getting none at all. Currently, at least with respect to disparate treatment, the DOJ has implicitly adopted the position that charging too much based on a protected status is as much a violation of fair lending laws as denying credit is a violation.[92]

12.4.3.7 Interest Rates and Costs

Acting with the Office of the Comptroller of the Currency, the DOJ alleged that the First National Bank of Vicksburg, by providing different loan products, charged most of its African-American unsecured home improvement loan bor-

---

(complaint), 51,292B (consent decree), Civ. No. 95C3239 (N.D. Ill. 1995).

85 Press Release, Dep't of Justice, Chicago Area Lender Agrees With Justice Department To Settle Lending Discrimination Claims (June 1, 1995).

86 United States v. First Nat'l Bank of Dona Ana County, Clearinghouse Nos. 52,025A (complaint), 52,025B (settlement agreement), Civ. No. CIV97-0096 (D.N.M. 1997).

87 According to 1990 census data, more than 25% of all housing units in Las Cruces were mobile homes, 56% of those units were occupied by Hispanics, and 36% of Hispanic homeowners in Las Cruces resided in mobile homes.

88 For more on credit scoring, see §§ 6.3.2, 6.4, *supra.*

89 The OCC's examination resulted in DNGB entering into a settlement agreement with the DOJ.

90 United States v. Associates Nat'l Bank, Civ. No. 99-196 (D. Del. Mar. 29, 1999) (complaint) [reproduced on the CD-Rom accompanying this volume]; *see* § 6.4.3.3.3, *supra.*

91 United States. v. Associates Nat'l Bank, Clearinghouse No. 53,524, Civ. No. 99-196 (D. Del. Jan. 8, 2001) (settlement agreement) [reproduced on the CD-Rom accompanying this volume].

92 See Ch. 8, *supra*, regarding the practice of targeting minorities for high cost credit sometimes known as reverse redlining.

rowers interest rates of between fourteen and twenty-one percent while most of its white borrowers of such loans were charged about ten percent.[93] Factual investigations did not support the non-discriminatory justifications offered by the bank for the difference but all charges were denied. In its consent decree, Vicksburg agreed to provide compensatory damages for the affected African-American borrowers; to establish procedures to ensure fair treatment, including employee training, random testing, and loan review systems; and to establish customer assistance programs and a goal of a $1,000,000 lending program for low and moderate income borrowers.[94]

As in the case against the Blackpipe State Bank,[95] Native Americans were the victims of alleged discrimination in a case brought by the Justice Department against a Nebraska bank.[96] The First National Bank of Gordon had a service area that extended over the border into a South Dakota community where an American Indian reservation was located. The complaint alleged that Gordon discriminated against Native American applicants on the basis of national origin by charging them higher interest rates for consumer loans than similarly qualified white applicants. The complaint further alleged that the bank's lack of formal standards or written criteria for setting interest rates on its consumer loans and its failure to review interest rate or pricing decisions by loan officers contributed to the disparity, for which the bank failed to provide investigators with a non-discriminatory explanation. The consent order provided for $275,000 in compensatory relief and fee discounts, a money management education program for reservation residents, and recruitment and hiring of qualified Native American persons for employment at the bank.[97]

The practice of charging minority groups higher prices for credit manifests itself in different ways, of which a higher base interest rate is one. Another way is through the pricing of services. In 1995, the DOJ alleged that the Security State Bank of Pecos, Texas, engaged in a practice of charging higher annual percentage rates (APRs) on non-mortgage related installment and single-payment loans to its Hispanic borrowers than to its similarly qualified non-Hispanic borrowers.[98] As the APR includes not just interest, but also all fees that are imposed by the lender to compensate for its services,[99] it is an indicator of potential non-interest pricing differentials which are harder to classify as risk-based.

Security's stipulated judgment acknowledged that the established differential rates were the result of the actions of one employee, who at the time was no longer employed by the bank. To compensate eligible borrowers Security agreed to set up a $500,000 fund. In addition, the bank agreed to pay a $10,000 civil penalty and to establish a bilingual customer assistance program to provide information about the bank's consumer loans.

12.4.3.8 Reverse Redlining

In 1998, the Department of Justice (DOJ) filed an amicus brief in a reverse redlining case, *Hargraves v. Capital City Mortgage Corp.*[100] The private plaintiffs who brought suit alleged that Capital City targeted African-Americans in the Washington D.C. metropolitan area for loans that were destined to fail due to the high interest rates of the loans and the income levels of the borrowers.[101]

Capital City's motion for summary judgment asserted that reverse redlining does not violate the law because they provided credit to African-Americans, and on the same terms as provided to whites. The DOJ's amicus brief was filed in support of the private plaintiffs' opposition to Capital City's motion. The DOJ argued, among other things, that lending practices designed to induce minorities into loans destined to fail could violate the fair lending laws.[102]

In September, 2000, a district court agreed with the plaintiffs' and DOJ's analysis of the FHA and the ECOA, holding that both statutes could be applied to the practice of reverse redlining.[103]

With respect to the ECOA's application to reverse redlining, the court noted that the plain language of the ECOA at 15 U.S.C. § 1691(a) prohibits discrimination in "any aspect of a credit transaction," and thus is not limited to the denial of credit. The court also found support for ECOA's appli-

---

93 United States v. First Nat'l Bank of Vicksburg, Clearinghouse Nos. 49,954A (complaint), 49,954B (consent decree), Civ. No. 5:94-CV-6(b)(n) (S.D. Miss. 1994).

94 *Id.* (consent decree).

95 United States v. Blackpipe State Bank, Clearinghouse Nos. 49,955A (complaint), 49,955B (consent decree), Civ. No. 93-5115 (D.S.D. 1994); *see* § 12.4.3.3, *supra*.

96 United States v. First Nat'l Bank of Gordon, Neb., Clearinghouse Nos. 51,295 (complaint), 51,295B (consent order), Civ. No. 96-5035 (D.S.D. 1996).

97 *See id.*

98 United States v. Sec. State Bank of Pecos, Clearinghouse Nos. 51,293A (complaint), 51,293B (stipulated judgment), Civ. No. SA 95CA099 (W.D. Tex. 1995).

99 *See* National Consumer Law Center, Truth in Lending § 3.2.3 (4th ed. 1999 and Supp.).

100 Hargraves v. Capital City Mortgage Corp., Civ. Action No. 98-1021 (D.D.C. Apr. 24, 1998) (complaint). The DOJ brief was filed March 10, 2000 [reproduced on the CD-Rom accompanying this volume].

101 For more on this case, see §§ 5.3.2.4, 8.2.1, *supra*.

102 Brief of the United States as Amicus Curiae in Support of Plaintiffs' Opposition to Defendants' Motion for Judgment on the Pleadings, or, In the Alternative, For Summary Judgment 35, Hargraves v. Capital City Mortgage Corp., 140 F. Supp. 2d 7 (D.D.C. 2000) (Civ. Action No. 98-1021) (citing Anderson v. United Fin. Co., 666 F.2d 1274, 1276–77 (9th Cir. 1982) and Newton v. United Companies Fin. Corp., 24 F. Supp. 2d 444, 461–62 (E.D. Pa. 1998)) [reproduced on the CD-Rom accompanying this volume]. The brief also addresses defendant's arguments that the term "predatory lending" is overly vague and undefinable. *See id.* at 27.

103 Hargraves v. Capital City Mortgage Corp., 140 F. Supp. 2d 7, 19–21 (D.D.C. 2000).

cation to reverse redlining on the basis of Regulation B, 12 C.F.R § 202.2(m), which defines credit transaction to include investigation procedures, terms of credit, collection procedures, and other matters.[104] The private plaintiffs settled with Capital City. The Federal Trade Commission case remains active.[105]

12.4.3.9 Overages

The use of overages, another pricing scheme some lenders engage in,[106] has been challenged in two fair lending enforcement actions to date. The first case ever to apply credit discrimination laws to this practice was brought against the Huntington Mortgage Co. in Ohio.[107] The complaint alleged that Huntington allowed loan personnel at one of its branches to charge minority customers a greater overage than they charged non-minority customers. The amount that exceeded the company's base price for each loan was then shared equally between the loan originator and Huntington.

Huntington entered into a settlement agreement which provided for the creation of a $420,000 fund to compensate affected African-American customers, the implementation of new monitoring and oversight systems, and a change in company policies to ensure uniform pricing without regard to race.[108]

The second case to challenge the use of overages was brought against Fleet Mortgage Corp. for allegedly using discriminatory policies and practices at its branches in Westbury, New York and Woodbridge, New Jersey.[109] The complaint alleged that African-American and Hispanic loan applicants at these branches were charged interest rates above Fleet's minimum price more frequently than similarly qualified white applicants.

The complaint against Fleet also challenged the use of underages (below-minimum interest rates) for the first time.[110] The Fleet branches in question allegedly granted underages to African-American and Hispanic loan applicants less frequently than to similarly qualified white applicants. Thus, under both practices, African-Americans and Hispanics frequently paid more for their mortgage loans than did their white counterparts.

Fleet's settlement agreement with the Department of Justice provided for the creation of a four million dollar fund to compensate approximately 600 victims, conduct community outreach and education programs, and for the implementation of new monitoring and oversight systems and policies.

In 1996, the Department of Justice (DOJ) settled another key predatory pricing case with the California-based Long Beach Mortgage Co.[111] This case also exposed the conflict of interest problems inherent when loan originators, particularly loan brokers, are permitted to price credit with their own financial reward as a major focus.

The Department of Justice's complaint explicitly did not challenge Long Beach's risk-based pricing practices even though Long Beach's arrangement with its own originators and "wholesale" brokers allowed them to add up to twelve points to a loan. Instead, the complaint focused on who was paying the greatest surcharge. Not surprisingly, those who paid the most were members of the protected classes under the FHA and the ECOA. Those who were part of more than one protected class were at a higher risk of being subjected to the greatest pricing abuse. On the broker-originated or "wholesale" loans, for example, older African-American women were nearly four times as likely as comparable younger white men to pay more than six percent of the loan in fees and points.[112]

Under the terms of the settlement, Long Beach was required to pay three million dollars to 1,200 victims of its practices, and to spend one million dollars on consumer education programs. It was also required to improve its procedures to guard against further discrimination.

In the first combined action by the DOJ, the Department of Housing and Urban Development (HUD) and the Federal Trade Commission, the DOJ filed suit against Delta Funding Corp., a subprime mortgage lender, claiming that it violated

---

104 *Id.* at 23. However, in deciding a motion for reconsideration brought by the defendants, the court dismissed the individual plaintiffs' ECOA and Section 1981 claims. Hargraves v. Capital City Mortgage Corp., 2001 U.S. Dist. LEXIS 7738 (D.D.C. Jan. 2, 2001). The court dismissed these claims on the grounds that only the party who received credit, which in this case was the church to whom the individual plaintiffs belonged, had standing to bring the ECOA and Section 1981 claims. *Id.* at *4–*5. The court allowed the individual plaintiffs to proceed with their claims under the FHA and Section 1982. *Id.* at *6–*7; *see* § 11.2, *supra*.

105 On February 2, 2002, the FTC's motion for an injunction to temporarily freeze the assets of the defendants, in order to prevent performance of the final settlement reached between the private plaintffs and the defendants, was denied. Federal Trade Comm'n v. Chevy Chase Bank, 2002 U.S. Dist. LEXIS 2199 (D.D.C. Feb. 7, 2002).

106 "Overage" or "yield spread" refer to the practice of allowing loan personnel to charge customers a higher interest rate than the lender's base or minimum rate. As an incentive for bringing in loans at a higher rate, lenders frequently share the overage with the loan originator. *See* § 8.4, *supra*.

107 United States v. Huntington Mortgage Co., Clearinghouse Nos. 51,294A (complaint), 51,294B (settlement agreement), Civ. No. 1:95CV2211 (N.D. Ohio 1995).

108 *Id.* (settlement agreement).

109 United States v. Fleet Mortgage Corp., Clearinghouse Nos.

51,296A (complaint), 51,296B (settlement agreement), Civ. No. CV962279 (E.D.N.Y. 1996).

110 *Id.* at 3 (complaint).

111 U.S. v. Long Beach Mortgage Co., Clearinghouse No. 51,944, No. CV 96-6159 (C.D. Cal., settlement agreement and order filed Sept. 5, 1996) [reproduced on the CD-Rom accompanying this volume]. For an in-depth discussion of risk-based pricing, see National Consumer Law Center, The Cost of Credit: Regulation and Legal Challenges § 11.1.1.3 (2d ed. 2000 and Supp.).

112 These allegations are contained in the DOJ's complaint, which charges violations of the Fair Housing Act and the ECOA.

the ECOA and FHA as well as the Home Ownership Equity Protection Act (HOEPA) and the Real Estate Settlement Procedures Act (RESPA).[113] The suit alleged that Delta engaged in the business of making subprime refinance home mortgage loans and that it concentrated its business primarily in African-American and Hispanic residential areas. The DOJ alleged that Delta approved and funded loans that included higher broker fees for African-American women than for similarly situated white borrowers. The enforcement agencies also included other claims based on illegal kickbacks to brokers and approval of loans without regard to borrowers' ability to repay.

A consent decree was filed at the same time as the complaint. In addition to a monetary settlement of up to twelve million dollars to compensate victims, Delta agreed to refuse to fund loans with discriminatory or unearned broker fees and to reject loans proposed by brokers when the borrower has insufficient funds to afford the payments.[114]

The DOJ has also taken important actions in non-housing ECOA cases. In 2000, the DOJ filed an amicus brief in *Cason v. Nissan Motors Acceptance Corp.*(NMAC), one of two class action cases brought against major automobile financing creditors for discriminatory charging of subjective overages or "markups."[115] The markups occurred when auto dealers, with the approval of NMAC or General Motors Acceptance Corp.(GMAC), charged a higher interest rate than the minimum buy rate set by the auto finance company for different credit risk categories.[116]

12.5 Enforcement Activities at the State and Local Levels

At the state and local levels, government agencies responsible for enforcement of their respective anti-discrimination laws have also been active. In the wake of the landmark study by the Federal Reserve Bank of Boston which showed that African-Americans and Hispanics had increased chances of denial on a mortgage loan application in the Boston area after controlling for all legitimate indicators of creditworthiness,[117] the Massachusetts Attorney General reached a settlement with ten banks and with the Bankers' Association, which established an independent committee to review minority applications which were denied during 1990. The banks and Bankers' Association also established several initiatives to assure that minority borrowers and minority neighborhoods have equal access to credit.

In Georgia, the Atlanta-based mortgage subsidiary of Fleet Financial Group, Inc., agreed to pay $100 million to settle an investigation by the state attorney general into possible loan bias. The state's investigation centered around allegations that Fleet "preyed on minority borrowers by charging high fees and interest rates"[118] in violation of the state's Fair Business Practices Act. Some had accused the company of sending agents, (i.e., brokers and home improvement contractors) roaming through poor, mostly black neighborhoods to make these high-rate loans.[119]

Fleet agreed to refund some of the high fees, to prospectively reduce high interest rates on 1150 loans, to give a fresh start and waiver of past-due interest to delinquent borrowers, to make a small cash payment to all borrowers who had a loan on January 1, 1991, and to complete, correct, or reimburse victims of shoddy contracting financed by Fleet loans. It also offered unspecified relief to those who lost their homes to foreclosure. Additionally, Fleet agreed to make seventy million dollars available for affordable loans to qualified low-income borrowers in Georgia.

In Arizona, Banc One Mortgage Corp. agreed to provide five million dollars in loans to low and moderate income home buyers to end a lending discrimination investigation by the Arizona Attorney General. The investigation stemmed from complaints by Hispanic applicants in Yuma County, Arizona, that they were denied home loans on the basis of their ethnicity. Banc One also agreed to employ a Spanish-speaking loan officer in Yuma County.[120]

An example from the local level involves the Philadelphia

---

113 United States v. Delta Funding Corp., Civ. No. CV 00 1872 (E.D.N.Y. Mar. 30, 2000), *available at* http://www.usdoj.gov [reproduced on the CD-Rom accompanying this volume]. Delta was also the subject of actions brought by the New York Attorney General's Office and New York Banking Department. These actions resulted in a 1999 settlement in which Delta agreed to establish a $7.5 million remediation fund and to develop a new monitoring system and training program. People v. Delta Funding Corp., Clearinghouse No. 53,522, 99-Civ-4951 (E.D.N.Y. Sept. 17, 1999) (consent judgment); *In re* Delta Funding Corp., Clearinghouse No. 53,521 (New York Banking Dep't Aug. 20, 1999) (settlement agreement).

114 United States v. Delta Funding Corp., Civ. No. CV 00 1872 (E.D.N.Y. Mar. 30, 2000), *available at* http://www.usdoj.gov [reproduced on the CD-Rom accompanying this volume].

115 Cason v. Nissan Motor Acceptance Corp., Clearinghouse No. 53,037A, Civ. No. 3-98-0223 (M.D. Tenn. June 9, 2000) (fourth amended complaint). The sixth amended complaint is reproduced on the CD-Rom accompanying this volume. The other case is Coleman v. Gen. Motors Acceptance Corp., Clearinghouse No. 53,036B, Civ. No. 3-98-0211 (M.D. Tenn. Aug. 9, 2000) (fourth amended complaint). The DOJ filed its amicus brief in July 2000. Cason v. Nissan Motors Acceptance Corp., Clearinghouse No. 53,037B, Civ. No. 3-98-0223 (July 31, 2000), *available at* http://www.usdoj.gov (DOJ brief) [reproduced on the CD-Rom accompanying this volume]; *see also* Coleman v. Gen. Motors Acceptance Corp., 196 F.R.D. 315 (M.D. Tenn. 2000). NCLC is co-counsel in both cases.

116 See § 8.4, *supra*, for more about the NMAC and GMAC cases.

117 *See* Alicia Munnell et al., Mortgage Lending in Boston: Interpreting HMDA Data (Fed. Reserve Bank of Boston, Working Paper Series No. 92-7, 1992); *see also* §§ 4.4.5.4, 12.2.4, *supra*.

118 Mitchell Zuckoff & Kimberly Blanton, *Fleet to Pay $100m Loan Bias Settlement*, Boston Globe, Dec. 16, 1993, at 1.

119 Mitchell Zuckoff, *Georgia Probe Slams Fleet Loan Practices*, Boston Globe, Dec. 17, 1993, at 85.

120 Memorandum of Understanding (and Addendum) between Banc One Mortgage Corp. and the Arizona Attorney General,

Commission on Human Relations, which filed actions against four lending institutions for alleged violations of anti-discrimination provisions of the Philadelphia Code.[121]

As a result, each institution entered into a consent decree agreeing to comply with the Code's "fair practices" provisions on lending, to cease giving false or misleading information regarding lending to potential borrowers based upon the potential borrower's race or color, and to require that its employees receive training on fair lending laws from the Human Relations Commission. In addressing practices which were having a disparate impact, the four institutions agreed not to establish or maintain minimum loan amounts, and to advertise their mortgage products on an equal opportunity basis.

Clearinghouse No. 53,525 (memorandum) (Dec. 7, 1997), (addendum) (Jan. 10, 2000).

121 Philadelphia Comm'n on Human Relations v. Boulevard Mortgage Co., Clearinghouse No. 49,139A, Docket No. 92110885 (Philadelphia Comm'n on Human Relations, June 29, 1993) (consent order and decree); Philadelphia Comm'n on Human Relations v. St. Edmonds Savings & Loan, Clearinghouse No. 49,140A, Docket No. 92120892 (Philadelphia Comm'n on Human Relations, May 4, 1993) (consent order and decree); Philadelphia Comm'n on Human Relations v. Bank & Trust Co. of Old York Rd., Clearinghouse No. 49,141A, Docket No. 92110887 (Philadelphia Comm'n on Human Relations, Apr. 7, 1993) (consent order and decree); Philadelphia Comm'n on

Human Relations v. People's Mortgage Co., Clearinghouse No. 49,142A, Docket No. 92110886 (Philadelphia Comm'n on Human Relations, Feb. 3, 1993) (consent order and decree).

Appendix A   Federal Credit Discrimination Statutes

A.1 Equal Credit Opportunity Act, 15 U.S.C. §§ 1691–1691f

(Pub. L. No. 90-321, §§ 701–707, as added Pub. L. No. 93-495, § 503, 88 Stat. 1521–1524 (1974), and amended by Pub. L. No. 94-239, §§ 2–7, 90 Stat. 251, 252, 253, 255 (1976); Pub. L. No. 95-473, § 3(b), 92 Stat. 1466 (1978); Pub. L. No. 96-221, § 610(c), 94 Stat. 174 (1980); Pub. L. No. 98-443, § 9(n), 98 Stat. 1708 (1984); Pub. L. No. 100-533, § 301, 102 Stat. 2692 (1988); Pub. L. No. 101-73, § 744(m), 103 Stat. 439 (1989); Pub. L. No. 102-242, 105 Stat. 2300, 2306 (1991); Pub. L. No. 102-550, § 1604(a)(7), 106 Stat. 4082 (1992); Pub. L. No. 104-88, § 315, 109 Stat. 949 (1995); and Pub. L. No. 104-208, § 2302(a), 110 Stat. 3009-420 (1996))

Congressional Findings and Statement of Purpose

The Congress finds that there is a need to insure that the various financial institutions and other firms engaged in the extensions of credit exercise their responsibility to make credit available with fairness, impartiality, and without discrimination on the basis of sex or marital status. Economic stabilization would be enhanced and competition among the various financial institutions and other firms engaged in the extension of credit would be strengthened by an absence of discrimination on the basis of sex or marital status, as well as by the informed use of credit which Congress has heretofore sought to promote. It is the purpose of this Act to require that financial institutions and other firms engaged in the extension of credit make that credit equally available to all creditworthy customers without regard to sex or marital status.

(Pub. L. No. 93-495, § 502, 88 Stat. 1525 (1974))

§ 1691. Scope of prohibition

(a) Activities constituting discrimination

It shall be unlawful for any creditor to discriminate against any applicant, with respect to any aspect of a credit transaction—

(1) on the basis of race, color, religion, national origin, sex or marital status, or age (provided the applicant has the capacity to contract);

(2) because all or part of the applicant's income derives from any public assistance program; or

(3) because the applicant has in good faith exercised any right under this chapter.

(b) Activities not constituting discrimination

It shall not constitute discrimination for purposes of this subchapter for a creditor—

(1) to make an inquiry of marital status if such inquiry is for the purpose of ascertaining the creditor's rights and remedies applicable to the particular extension of credit and not to discriminate in a determination of credit-worthiness;

(2) to make an inquiry of the applicant's age or of whether the applicant's income derives from any public assistance program if such inquiry is for the purpose of determining the amount and probable continuance of income levels, credit history, or other pertinent element of credit-worthiness as provided in regulations of the Board;

(3) to use any empirically derived credit system which considers age if such system is demonstrably and statistically sound in accordance with regulations of the Board, except that in the operation of such system the age of an elderly applicant may not be assigned a negative factor or value; or

(4) to make an inquiry or to consider the age of an elderly applicant when the age of such applicant is to be used by the creditor in the extension of credit in favor of such applicant.

(c) Additional activities not constituting discrimination

It is not a violation of this section for a creditor to refuse to extend credit offered pursuant to—

(1) any credit assistance program expressly authorized by law for an economically disadvantaged class of persons;

(2) any credit assistance program administered by a nonprofit organization for its members or an economically disadvantaged class of persons; or

(3) any special purpose credit program offered by a profit-making organization to meet special social needs which meets standards prescribed in regulations by the Board; if such refusal is required by or made pursuant to such program.

(d) Reason for adverse action; procedure applicable; "adverse action" defined

(1) Within thirty days (or such longer reasonable time as specified in regulations of the Board for any class of credit transaction) after receipt of a completed application for

credit, a creditor shall notify the applicant of its action on the application.

(2) Each applicant against whom adverse action is taken shall be entitled to a statement of reasons for such action from the creditor. A creditor satisfies this obligation by—

(A) providing statements of reasons in writing as a matter of course to applicants against whom adverse action is taken; or

(B) giving written notification of adverse action which discloses (i) the applicant's right to a statement of reasons within thirty days after receipt by the creditor of a request made within sixty days after such notification, and (ii) the identity of the person or office from which such statement may be obtained. Such statement may be given orally if the written notification advises the applicant of his right to have the statement of reasons confirmed in writing on written request.

(3) A statement of reasons meets the requirements of this section only if it contains the specific reasons for the adverse action taken.

(4) Where a creditor has been requested by a third party to make a specific extension of credit directly or indirectly to an applicant, the notification and statement of reasons required by this subsection may be made directly by such creditor, or indirectly through the third party, provided in either case that the identity of the creditor is disclosed.

(5) The requirements of paragraph (2), (3), or (4) may be satisfied by verbal statements or notifications in the case of any creditor who did not act on more than one hundred and fifty applications during the calendar year preceding the calendar year in which the adverse action is taken, as determined under regulations of the Board.

(6) For purposes of this subsection, the term "adverse action" means a denial or revocation of credit, a change in the terms of an existing credit arrangement, or a refusal to grant credit in substantially the amount or on substantially the terms requested. Such term does not include a refusal to extend additional credit under an existing credit arrangement where the applicant is delinquent or otherwise in default, or where such additional credit would exceed a previously established credit limit.

(e) Appraisals; copies of reports to applicants; costs

Each creditor shall promptly furnish an applicant, upon written request by the applicant made within a reasonable period of time of the application, a copy of the appraisal report used in connection with the applicant's application for a loan that is or would have been secured by a lien on residential real property. The creditor may require the applicant to reimburse the creditor for the cost of the appraisal.

(Pub. L. No. 90-321, Title VII, § 701, as added Pub. L. No. 93-495, Title V, § 503, 88 Stat. 1521 (1974), and amended by Pub. L. No. 94-239, § 2, 90 Stat. 251 (1976); Pub. L. No. 102-242, Title II, §223(d), 105 Stat. 2306 (1991))

§ 1691a. Definitions; rules of construction

(a) The definitions and rules of construction set forth in this section are applicable for the purpose of this subchapter.

(b) The term "applicant" means any person who applies to a creditor directly for an extension, renewal, or continuation of credit, or applies to a creditor indirectly by use of an existing credit plan for an amount exceeding a previously established credit limit.

(c) The term "Board" refers to the Board of Governors of the Federal Reserve System.

(d) The term "credit" means the right granted by a creditor to a debtor to defer payment of debt or to incur debts and defer its payment or to purchase property or services and defer payment therefor.

(e) The term "creditor" means any person who regularly extends, renews, or continues credit; any person who regularly arranges for the extension, renewal, or continuation of credit; or any assignee of an original creditor who participates in the decision to extend, renew, or continue credit.

(f) The term "person" means a natural person, a corporation, government or governmental subdivision or agency, trust, estate, partnership, cooperative, or association.

(g) Any reference to any requirement imposed under this subchapter or any provision thereof includes reference to the regulations of the Board under this subchapter or the provision thereof in question.

(Pub. L. No. 90-321, Title VII, § 702, as added Pub. L. No. 93-495, Title V, § 503, 88 Stat. 1522 (1974))

§ 1691b. Promulgation of regulations by Board; establishment of Consumer Advisory Council by Board; duties, membership, etc., of Council

(a) Regulations

(1) The Board shall prescribe regulations to carry out the purposes of this subchapter. These regulations may contain but are not limited to such classifications, differentiation, or other provision, and may provide for such adjustments and exceptions for any class of transactions, as in the judgment of the Board are necessary or proper to effectuate the purposes of this subchapter, to prevent circumvention or evasion thereof, or to facilitate or substantiate compliance therewith.

(2) Such regulations may exempt from the provisions of this subchapter any class of transactions that are not primarily for personal, family, or household purposes, or business or commercial loans made available by a financial institution, except that a particular type within a class of such transactions may be exempted if the Board determines, after making an express finding that the application of this subchapter or of any provision of this subchapter of such transaction would not contribute substantially to effecting the purposes of this subchapter.

(3) An exemption granted pursuant to paragraph (2) shall be for no longer than five years and shall be extended only if the Board makes a subsequent determination, in the manner described by such paragraph, that such exemption remains appropriate.

(4) Pursuant to Board regulations, entities making business or commercial loans shall maintain such records or other data relating to such loans as may be necessary to evidence compliance with this subsection or enforce any action pursuant to the authority of this chapter. In no event shall such records or data be maintained for a period of less than one year. The Board shall promulgate regulations to implement this paragraph in the manner prescribed by chapter 5 of Title 5.

(5) The Board shall provide in regulations that an applicant for a business or commercial loan shall be provided a written notice of such applicant's right to receive a written statement of the reasons for the denial of such loan.

(b) Consumer Advisory Council

The Board shall establish a Consumer Advisory Council to advise and consult with it in the exercise of its functions under this chapter and to advise and consult with it concerning other consumer related matters it may place before the Council. In appointing the members of the Council, the Board shall seek to achieve a fair representation of the interests of creditors and consumers. The Council shall meet from time to time at the call of the Board. Members of the Council who are not regular full-time employees of the United States shall, while attending meetings of such Council, be entitled to receive compensation at a rate fixed by the Board, but not exceeding $100 per day, including travel time. Such members may be allowed travel expenses, including transportation and subsistence, while away from their homes or regular place of business.

(Pub. L. No. 90-321, Title VII, § 703, as added Pub. L. No. 93-495, Title V, § 503, 88 Stat. 1522 (1974), and amended by Pub. L. No. 94-239, § 3(a), 90 Stat. 252 (1976); Pub. L. No. 100-533, Title III, § 301, 102 Stat. 2692 (1988))

§ 1691c. Administrative enforcement

(a) Enforcing agencies

Compliance with the requirements imposed under this subchapter shall be enforced under:

(1) section 8 of the Federal Deposit Insurance Act [12 U.S.C. § 1818], in the case of—

  (A) national banks, and Federal branches and Federal agencies of foreign banks, by the Office of the Comptroller of the Currency;

  (B) member banks of the Federal Reserve System (other than national banks), branches and agencies of foreign banks (other than Federal branches, Federal agencies, and insured State branches of foreign banks), commercial lending companies owned or controlled by foreign banks, and organizations operating under section 25 or 25(a) of the Federal Reserve Act [12 U.S.C. §§ 601 et seq., 611 et seq.], by the Board; and

  (C) banks insured by the Federal Deposit Insurance Corporation (other than members of the Federal Reserve System) and insured State branches of foreign banks, by the Board of Directors of the Federal Deposit Insurance Corporation;

(2) Section 8 of the Federal Deposit Insurance Act [12 U.S.C. § 1818], by the Director of the Office of Thrift Supervision, in the case of a savings association the deposits of which are insured by the Federal Deposit Insurance Corporation.

(3) The Federal Credit Union Act [12 U.S.C. § 1751 et seq.], by the Administrator of the National Credit Union Administration with respect to any Federal Credit Union.

(4) Subtitle IV of Title 49, by the Secretary of Transportation, with respect to all carriers subject to the jurisdiction of the Surface Transportation Board.

(5) Part A of subtitle VII of title 49, by the Secretary of Transportation with respect to any air carrier or foreign air carrier subject to that part.

(6) The Packers and Stockyards Act, 1921 [7 U.S.C. § 181 et seq.](except as provided in section 406 of that Act [7 U.S.C. §§ 226, 227]), by the Secretary of Agriculture with respect to any activities subject to that Act.

(7) The Farm Credit Act of 1971 [12 U.S.C. § 2001 et seq.], by the Farm Credit Administration with respect to any Federal land bank, Federal land bank association, Federal intermediate credit bank, and production credit association;

(8) The Securities Exchange Act of 1934 [15 U.S.C. § 78a et seq.], by the Securities and Exchange Commission with respect to brokers and dealers; and

(9) The Small Business Investment Act of 1958 [15 U.S.C. § 661 et seq.], by the Small Business Administration, with respect to small business investment companies.

The terms used in paragraph (1) that are not defined in this subchapter or otherwise defined in section 3(s) of the Federal Deposit Insurance Act (12 U.S.C. 1813(s)) shall have the meaning given to them in section 1(b) of the International Banking Act of 1978 (12 U.S.C. 3101).

(b) Violations of subchapter deemed violations of preexisting statutory requirements; additional agency powers

For the purpose of the exercise by any agency referred to in subsection (a) of this section of its powers under any Act referred to in that subsection, a violation of any requirement imposed under this subchapter shall be deemed to be a violation of a requirement imposed under that Act. In addition to its powers under any provision of law specifically referred to in subsection (a) of this section, each of the agencies referred to in that subsection may exercise for the purpose of enforcing compliance with any requirement imposed under this subchapter, any other authority conferred on it by law. The exercise of the authorities of any of the agencies referred to in subsection (a) of this section for the purpose of enforcing compliance with any requirement imposed under this subchapter shall in no way preclude the exercise of such authorities for the purpose of enforcing compliance with any other provision of law not relating to the prohibition of discrimination on the basis of sex or marital status with respect to any aspect of a credit transaction.

(c) Overall enforcement authority of Federal Trade Commission

Except to the extent that enforcement of the requirements imposed under this subchapter is specifically committed to some other Government agency under subsection (a) of this section, the Federal Trade Commission shall enforce such requirements. For the purpose of the exercise by the Federal Trade Commission of its functions and powers under the Federal Trade Commission Act [15 U.S.C. § 11 et seq.], a violation of any requirement imposed under this subchapter shall be deemed a violation of a requirement imposed under that Act. All of the functions and powers of the

Federal Trade Commission under the Federal Trade Commission Act are available to the Commission to enforce compliance by any person with the requirements imposed under this subchapter, irrespective of whether that person is engaged in commerce or meets any other jurisdictional tests in the Federal Trade Commission Act, including the power to enforce any Federal Reserve Board regulation promulgated under this subchapter in the same manner as if the violation had been a violation of a Federal Trade Commission trade regulation rule.

(d) Rules and regulations by enforcing agencies

The authority of the Board to issue regulations under this subchapter does not impair the authority of any other agency designated in this section to make rules respecting its own procedures in enforcing compliance with requirements imposed under this subchapter.

(Pub. L. No. 90-321, Title VII, § 704, as added Pub. L. No. 93-495, Title V, § 503, 88 Stat. 1522 (1974), and amended by Pub. L. No. 94-239, § 4, 90 Stat. 253 (1976); Pub. L. No. 98-443, § 9(n), 98 Stat. 1708 (1984); Pub. L. No. 101-73, Title VI, § 744(m), 103 Stat. 439 (1989); Pub. L. No. 102-242, Title II, § 212(d), 105 Stat. 2300 (1991); Pub. L. No. 102-550, Title XVI, § 1604(a)(7), 106 Stat. 4082 (1992); Pub. L. No. 104-88, Title III, § 315, 109 Stat. 948 (1995))

§ 1691c-1. Incentives for self-testing and self-correction[1]

(a) Privileged information
(1) Conditions for privilege

A report or result of a self-test (as that term is defined by regulations of the Board) shall be considered to be privileged under paragraph (2) if a creditor—

(A) conducts, or authorizes an independent third party to conduct, a self-test of any aspect of a credit transaction by a creditor, in order to determine the level or effectiveness of compliance with this subchapter by the creditor; and

(B) has identified any possible violation of this subchapter by the creditor and has taken, or is taking, appropriate corrective action to address any such possible violation.

(2) Privileged self-test
If a creditor meets the conditions specified in subparagraphs (A) and (B) of paragraph (1) with respect to a self-test described in that paragraph, any report or results of that self-test—

(A) shall be privileged; and

(B) may not be obtained or used by any applicant, department, or agency in any—

　(i) proceeding or civil action in which one or more violations of this subchapter are alleged; or

　(ii) examination or investigation relating to compliance with this subchapter.

　(ii) the subject of an ongoing administrative law proceeding;

　(B) in the case of section 704A of the Equal Credit Opportunity Act [this section], the creditor has waived the privilege pursuant to subsection (b)(1)(A)(i) of that section; or

　(C) in the case of section 814A of the Fair Housing Act [42 U.S.C. § 3614-1], the person engaged in residential real estate related lending activities has waived the privilege pursuant to subsection (b)(1)(A)(i) of that section.

Issuance of regulations

Section 2302(a)(2) of Pub. L. 104-208 provided that:

　(A) In general.—Not later than 6 months after the date of enactment of this Act [Sept. 30, 1996], in consultation with the Secretary of Housing and Urban Development and the agencies referred to in section 704 of the Equal Credit Opportunity Act [15 U.S.C. § 1691c], and after providing notice and an opportunity for public comment, the Board shall prescribe final regulations to implement section 704A of the Equal Credit Opportunity Act, as added by this section [this section].

　(B) Self-test.—

　(i) Definition.—The regulations prescribed under subparagraph (A) shall include a definition of the term "self-test" for purposes of section 704A of the Equal Credit Opportunity Act, as added by this section [this section].

　(ii) Requirement for self-test.—The regulations prescribed under subparagraph (A) shall specify that a self-test shall be sufficiently extensive to constitute a determination of the level and effectiveness of compliance by a creditor with the Equal Credit Opportunity Act [this chapter].

　(iii) Substantial similarity to certain Fair Housing Act Regulations.—The regulations prescribed under subparagraph (A) shall be substantially similar to the regulations prescribed by the Secretary of Housing and Urban Development to carry out section 814A(d) of the Fair Housing Act, as added by this section [42 U.S.C. § 3614-1(d)].]

---

1 [*Editor's Note:* The Historical and Statutory Notes to § 1691c-1 provide:

Effective Dates

1996 Acts. Section 2302(c) of Pub. L. 104-208 provided that:

(1) In general.—Except as provided in paragraph (2), the privilege provided for in section 704A of the Equal Credit Opportunity Act [this section] or section 814A of the Fair Housing Act [42 U.S.C. § 3614-1] (as those sections are added by this section) shall apply to a self-test (as that term is defined pursuant to the regulations prescribed under subsection (a)(2) or (b)(2) of this section, as appropriate [section 2302(a)(2) of Pub. L. 104-208, set out as a note under this section or section 2302(b)(2) of Pub. L. 104-208, set out as a note under section 3614-1 of Title 42, The Public Health and Welfare]) conducted before, on, or after the effective date of the regulations prescribed under subsection (a)(2) or (b)(2), as appropriate.

(2) Exception.—The privilege referred to in paragraph (1) does not apply to such a self-test conducted before the effective date of the regulations prescribed under subsection (a) or (b), as appropriate, if—

(A) before that effective date, a complaint against the creditor or person engaged in residential real estate related lending activities (as the case may be) was—

(i) formally filed in any court of competent jurisdiction; or

(b) Results of self-testing

(1) In general

No provision of this section may be construed to prevent an applicant, department, or agency from obtaining or using a report or results of any self-test in any proceeding or civil action in which a violation of this subchapter is alleged, or in any examination or investigation of compliance with this subchapter if—

> **(A)** the creditor or any person with lawful access to the report or results—
>> **(i)** voluntarily releases or discloses all, or any part of, the report or results to the applicant, department, or agency, or to the general public; or
>> **(ii)** refers to or describes the report or results as a defense to charges of violations of this subchapter against the creditor to whom the self-test relates; or
> **(B)** the report or results are sought in conjunction with an adjudication or admission of a violation of this subchapter for the sole purpose of determining an appropriate penalty or remedy.

(2) Disclosure for determination of penalty or remedy

Any report or results of a self-test that are disclosed for the purpose specified in paragraph (1)(B)—

> **(A)** shall be used only for the particular proceeding in which the adjudication or admission referred to in paragraph (1)(B) is made; and
> **(B)** may not be used in any other action or proceeding.

(c) Adjudication

An applicant, department, or agency that challenges a privilege asserted under this section may seek a determination of the existence and application of that privilege in—

> **(1)** a court of competent jurisdiction; or
> **(2)** an administrative law proceeding with appropriate jurisdiction.

(Pub. L. No. 90-321, Title VII, § 704A, as added Pub. L. No. 104-208, Div. A, Title II, § 2302(a)(1), 110 Stat. 3009-420 (1996))

§ 1691d. Applicability of other laws

(a) Requests for signature of husband and wife for creation of valid lien, etc.

A request for the signature of both parties to a marriage for the purpose of creating a valid lien, passing clear title, waiving inchoate rights to property, or assigning earnings, shall not constitute discrimination under this subchapter: *Provided, however,* That this provision shall not be construed to permit a creditor to take sex or marital status into account in connection with the evaluation of creditworthiness of any applicant.

(b) State property laws affecting creditworthiness

Consideration or application of State property laws directly or indirectly affecting creditworthiness shall not constitute discrimination for purposes of this subchapter.

(c) State laws prohibiting separate extension of consumer credit to husband and wife

Any provision of State law which prohibits the separate extension of consumer credit to each party to a marriage shall not apply in any case where each party to a marriage voluntarily applies for separate credit from the same creditor: *Provided,* That in any case where such a State law is so preempted, each party to the marriage shall be solely responsible for the debt so contracted.

(d) Combining credit accounts of husband and wife with same creditor to determine permissible finance charges or loan ceilings under Federal or State laws

When each party to a marriage separately and voluntarily applies for and obtains separate credit accounts with the same creditor, those accounts shall not be aggregated or otherwise combined for purposes of determining permissible finance charges or permissible loan ceilings under the laws of any State or of the United States.

(e) Election of remedies under subchapter or State law; nature of relief determining applicability

Where the same act or omission constitutes a violation of this subchapter and of applicable State law, a person aggrieved by such conduct may bring a legal action to recover monetary damages either under this subchapter or under such State law, but not both. This election of remedies shall not apply to court actions in which the relief sought does not include monetary damages or to administrative actions.

(f) Compliance with inconsistent State laws; determination of inconsistency

This subchapter does not annul, alter, or affect, or exempt any person subject to the provisions of this subchapter from complying with, the laws of any State with respect to credit discrimination, except to the extent that those laws are inconsistent with any provision of this subchapter, and then only to the extent of the inconsistency. The Board is authorized to determine whether such inconsistencies exist. The Board may not determine that any State law is inconsistent with any provision of this subchapter if the Board determines that such law gives greater protection to the applicant.

(g) Exemption by regulation of credit transactions covered by State law; failure to comply with State law

The Board shall by regulation exempt from the requirements of sections 1691 and 1691a of this title any class of credit transactions within any State if it determines that under the law of that State that class of transactions is subject to requirements substantially similar to those imposed under this subchapter or that such law gives greater protection to the applicant, and that there is adequate provision for enforcement. Failure to comply with any requirement of such State law in any transaction so exempted shall constitute a violation of this subchapter for the purposes of section 1691e of this title.

(Pub. L. No. 90-321, Title VII, § 705, as added Pub. L. No. 93-495, Title V, § 503, 88 Stat. 1523 (1974), and amended by Pub. L. No. 94-239, § 5, 90 Stat. 253 (1976))

§ 1691e. Civil liability

(a) Individual or class action for actual damages

Any creditor who fails to comply with any requirement imposed under this subchapter shall be liable to the aggrieved applicant for any actual damages sustained by such applicant acting either in an individual capacity or as a member of a class.

(b) Recovery of punitive damages in individual and class actions for actual damages; exemptions; maximum amount of punitive damages in individual actions; limitation on total recovery in class actions; factors determining amount of award

Any creditor, other than a government or governmental subdivision or agency, who fails to comply with any requirement imposed under this subchapter shall be liable to the aggrieved applicant for punitive damages in an amount not greater than $10,000, in addition to any actual damages provided in subsection (a) of this section, except that in the case of a class action the total recovery under this subsection shall not exceed the lesser of $500,000 or 1 per centum of the net worth of the creditor. In determining the amount of such damages in any action, the court shall consider, among other relevant factors, the amount of any actual damages awarded, the frequency and persistence of failures of compliance by the creditor, the resources of the creditor, the number of persons adversely affected, and the extent to which the creditor's failure of compliance was intentional.

(c) Action for equitable and declaratory relief

Upon application by an aggrieved applicant, the appropriate United States district court or any other court of competent jurisdiction may grant such equitable and declaratory relief as is necessary to enforce the requirements imposed under this subchapter.

(d) Recovery of costs and attorney fees

In the case of any successful action under subsection (a), (b), or (c) of this section, the costs of the action, together with a reasonable attorney's fee as determined by the court, shall be added to any damages awarded by the court under such subsection.

(e) Good faith compliance with rule, regulation, or interpretation of Board or interpretation or approval by an official or employee of Federal Reserve system duly authorized by Board

No provision of this subchapter imposing liability shall apply to any act done or omitted in good faith in conformity with any official rule, regulation, or interpretation thereof by the Board or in conformity with any interpretation or approval by an official or employee of the Federal Reserve System duly authorized by the Board to issue such interpretations or approvals under such procedures as the Board may prescribe therefor, notwithstanding that after such act or omission has occurred, such rule, regulation, interpretation, or approval is amended, rescinded, or determined by judicial or other authority to be invalid for any reason.

(f) Jurisdiction of courts; time for maintenance of action; exceptions

Any action under this section may be brought in the appropriate United States district court without regard to the amount in controversy, or in any other court of competent jurisdiction. No such action shall be brought later than two years from the date of the occurrence of the violation, except that—

(1) whenever any agency having responsibility for administrative enforcement under section 1691c of this title commences an enforcement proceeding within two years from the date of the occurrence of the violation,

(2) whenever the Attorney General commences a civil action under this section within two years from the date of the occurrence of the violation,

then any applicant who has been a victim of the discrimination which is the subject of such proceeding or civil action may bring an action under this section not later than one year after the commencement of that proceeding or action.

(g) Request by responsible enforcement agency to Attorney General for civil action

The agencies having responsibility for administrative enforcement under section 1961c of this title, if unable to obtain compliance with section 1691 of this title, are authorized to refer the matter to the Attorney General with a recommendation that an appropriate civil action be instituted. Each agency referred to in paragraphs (1), (2), and (3) of section 1691c(a) of this title shall refer the matter to the Attorney General whenever the agency has reason to believe that 1 or more creditors has engaged in a pattern or practice of discouraging or denying applications for credit in violation of section 1691(a) of this title. Each such agency may refer the matter to the Attorney General whenever the agency has reason to believe that 1 or more creditors has violated section 1691(a) of this title.

(h) Authority for Attorney General to bring civil action; jurisdiction

When a matter is referred to the Attorney General pursuant to subsection (g) of this section, or whenever he has reason to believe that one or more creditors are engaged in a pattern or practice in violation of this subchapter, the Attorney General may bring a civil action in any appropriate United States district court for such relief as may be appropriate, including actual and punitive damages and injunctive relief.

(i) Recovery under both subchapter and fair housing enforcement provisions prohibited for violation based on same transaction

No person aggrieved by a violation of this subchapter and by a violation of section 3605 of Title 42 shall recover under this subchapter and section 3612 of Title 42, if such violation is based on the same transaction.[2]

(j) Discovery of creditor's granting standards

Nothing in this subchapter shall be construed to prohibit the discovery of a creditor's credit granting standards under appropriate discovery procedures in the court or agency in which an action or proceeding is brought.

(k) Notice to HUD of violations

Whenever an agency referred to in paragraph (1), (2), or (3) of section 1691c(a) of this title—

(1) has reason to believe, as a result of receiving a consumer complaint, conducting a consumer compliance examination, or otherwise, that a violation of this subchapter has occurred;

(2) has reason to believe that the alleged violation would be a

---

2 [*Editor's Note:* At the moment, the literal language of the statute is a bit confusing. It provides that there cannot be recovery under both the ECOA and 42 U.S.C. § 3612. Prior to the Fair Housing Amendments Act of 1988 (Pub. L. No. 100-430), 42 U.S.C. § 3612 authorized a private right of action for damages and injunctive relief. The private relief provision has been moved to 42 U.S.C. § 3613, however, and § 3612 now deals with administrative enforcement of the Fair Housing Act. Presumably, a technical correction to the ECOA will be passed at some point to correct the cross-reference.]

violation of the Fair Housing Act [42 U.S.C. § 3601 et seq.]; and

(3) does not refer the matter to the Attorney General pursuant to subsection (g) of this section,

the agency shall notify the Secretary of Housing and Urban Development of the violation, and shall notify the applicant that the Secretary of Housing and Urban Development has been notified of the alleged violation and that remedies for the violation may be available under the Fair Housing Act.

(Pub. L. No. 90-321, Title VII, § 706, as added Pub. L. No. 93-495, Title V, § 503, 88 Stat. 1524 (1974), and amended by Pub. L. No. 94-239, § 6, 90 Stat. 253 (1976); Pub. L. No. 102-242, § 223(a) to (c), 105 Stat. 2306 (1991))

§ 1691f. Annual reports to Congress; contents

Each year, the Board and the Attorney General shall, respectively, make reports to the Congress concerning the administration of their functions under this subchapter, including such recommendations as the Board and the Attorney General, respectively, deem necessary or appropriate. In addition, each report of the Board shall include its assessment of the extent to which compliance with the requirements of this subchapter is being achieved, and a summary of the enforcement actions taken by each of the agencies assigned administrative enforcement responsibilities under section 1691c of this title.

(Pub. L. No. 90-321, Title VII, § 707, as added Pub. L. No. 94-239, § 7, 90 Stat. 255 (1976), and amended by Pub. L. No. 96-221, Title VI, § 610(c), 94 Stat. 174 (1980))

A.2 Fair Housing Act, 42 U.S.C. §§ 3601–3631

(Pub. L. No. 90-284, Title VIII, §§ 801–819, Title IX, § 901, 82 Stat. 81–89 (1968); Pub. L. No. 93-383, Title VIII, § 808(b), 88 Stat. 729 (1974); Pub. L. No. 95-251, § 3, 92 Stat. 184 (1978); Pub. L. No. 95-454, Title VIII, § 801, 92 Stat. 1222 (1978); Pub. L. No. 95-598, Title III, § 331, 92 Stat. 2679 (1978); Pub. L. No. 100-242, Title V, §§ 561–562, 101 Stat. 1942–1944 (1988); Pub. L. No. 100-430, §§ 5–10, 102 Stat. 1619–1636 (1988); Pub. L. No. 101-625, Title IX, § 953, 104 Stat. 4419 (1990); Pub. L. No. 102-550, Title IX, § 905(b), 106 Stat. 3869 (1992); Pub. L. No. 103-322, § 320103(e), 108 Stat. 2110 (1994); Pub. L. No. 104-66, Title I, § 1071(e), 109 Stat. 720 (1995); Pub. L. No. 104-76, §§ 2–3, 109 Stat. 787 (1995); Pub. L. No. 104-208, Div. A, Title II, § 2302(b)(1), 110 Stat. 3009-421 (1996); Pub. L. No. 104-294, Title VI, § 604(b)(15),(27), 110 Stat. 3507, 3508 (1996))

Subchapter I—Generally

§ 3601. Declaration of policy

It is the policy of the United States to provide, within constitutional limitations, for fair housing throughout the United States.

(Pub. L. No. 90-284, Title VIII, § 801, 82 Stat. 81 (1968))

§ 3602. Definitions

As used in this subchapter—

(a) "Secretary" means the Secretary of Housing and Urban Development.

(b) "Dwelling" means any building, structure, or portion thereof which is occupied as, or designed or intended for occupancy as, a residence by one or more families, and any vacant land which is offered for sale or lease for the construction or location thereon of any such building, structure, or portion thereof.

(c) "Family" includes a single individual.

(d) "Person" includes one or more individuals, corporations, partnerships, associations, labor organizations, legal representatives, mutual companies, joint-stock companies, trusts, unincorporated organizations, trustees, trustees in cases under Title 11, receivers, and fiduciaries.

(e) "To rent" includes to lease, to sublease, to let and otherwise to grant for a consideration the right to occupy premises not owned by the occupant.

(f) "Discriminatory housing practice" means an act that is unlawful under section 3604, 3605, 3606, or 3617 of this title.

(g) "State" means any of the several States, the District of Columbia, the Commonwealth of Puerto Rico, or any of the territories and possessions of the United States.

(h) "Handicap" means, with respect to a person—
   (1) a physical or mental impairment which substantially limits one or more of such person's major life activities,
   (2) a record of having such an impairment, or
   (3) being regarded as having such an impairment,
but such term does not include current, illegal use of or addiction to a controlled substance (as defined in section 802 of Title 21).

(i) "Aggrieved person" includes any person who—
   (1) claims to have been injured by a discriminatory housing practice; or
   (2) believes that such person will be injured by a discriminatory housing practice that is about to occur.

(j) "Complainant" means the person (including the Secretary) who files a complaint under section 3610 of this title.

(k) "Familial status" means one or more individuals (who have not attained the age of 18 years) being domiciled with—
   (1) a parent or another person having legal custody of such individual or individuals; or
   (2) the designee of such parent or other person having such custody, with the written permission of such parent or other person.
The protections afforded against discrimination on the basis of familial status shall apply to any person who is pregnant or is in the process of securing legal custody of any individual who has not attained the age of 18 years.

(l) "Conciliation" means the attempted resolution of issues raised by a complaint, or by the investigation of such complaint, through informal negotiations involving the aggrieved person, the respondent, and the Secretary.

(m) "Conciliation agreement" means a written agreement setting forth the resolution of the issues in conciliation.

(n) "Respondent" means—
   (1) the person or other entity accused in a complaint of an unfair housing practice; and
   (2) any other person or entity identified in the course of investigation and notified as required with respect to respondents so identified under section 3610(a) of this title.

(o) "Prevailing party" has the same meaning as such term has in section 1988 of this title.

(Pub. L. No. 90-284, Title VIII, § 802, 82 Stat. 81 (1968); Pub. L. No. 95-598, Title III, § 331, 92 Stat. 2679 (1978); Pub. L. No. 100-430, § 5, 102 Stat. 1619 (1988))

§ 3603. Effective dates of certain prohibitions

(a) Application to certain described dwellings

Subject to the provisions of subsection (b) of this section and section 3607 of this title, the prohibitions against discrimination in the sale or rental of housing set forth in section 3604 of this title shall apply:
   (1) Upon enactment of this subchapter, to—

   (A) dwellings owned or operated by the Federal Government;
   (B) dwellings provided in whole or in part with the aid of loans, advances, grants, or contributions made by the Federal Government, under agreements entered into after November 20, 1962, unless payment due thereon has been made in full prior to April 11, 1968;
   (C) dwellings provided in whole or in part by loans insured, guaranteed, or otherwise secured by the credit of the Federal Government, under agreements entered into after November 20, 1962, unless payment thereon has been made in full prior to April 11, 1968: *Provided,* That nothing contained in subparagraphs (B) and (C) of this subsection shall be applicable to dwellings solely by virtue of the fact that they are subject to mortgages held by an FDIC or FSLIC institution; and
   (D) dwellings provided by the development or the redevelopment of real property purchased, rented, or otherwise obtained from a State or local public agency receiving Federal financial assistance for slum clearance or urban renewal with respect to such real property under loan or grant contracts entered into after November 20, 1962.
   (2) After December 31, 1968, to all dwellings covered by paragraph (1) and to all other dwellings except as exempted by subsection (b) of this section.

(b) Exemptions

Nothing in section 3604 of this title (other than subsection (c)) shall apply to—
   (1) any single-family house sold or rented by an owner: *Provided,* That such private individual owner does not own more than three such single-family houses at any one time: *Provided further,* That in the case of the sale of any such single-family house by a private individual owner not residing in such house at the time of such sale or who was not the most recent resident of such house prior to such sale, the exemption granted by this subsection shall apply only with respect to one such sale within any twenty-four month period: *Provided further,* That such bona fide private individual owner does not own any interest in, nor is there owned or reserved on his behalf, under any express or voluntary agreement, title to or any right to all or a portion of the proceeds from the sale or rental of, more than three such single-family houses at any one time: *Provided further,* That after December 31, 1969, the sale or rental of any such single-family house shall be excepted from the application of this title only if such house is sold or rented (A) without the use in any manner of the sales or rental facilities or the sales or rental services of any real estate broker, agent, or salesman, or of such facilities or services of any person in the business of selling or renting dwellings, or of any employee or agent of any such broker, agent, salesman, or person and (B) without the publication, posting or mailing, after notice, of any advertisement or written notice in violation of section 3604(c) of this title; but nothing in this proviso shall prohibit the use of attorneys, escrow agents, abstractors, title companies, and other such professional assistance as necessary to perfect or transfer the title, or
   (2) rooms or units in dwellings containing living quarters occupied or intended to be occupied by no more than four

families living independently of each other, if the owner actually maintains and occupies one of such living quarters as his residence.

(c) Business of selling or renting dwellings defined

For the purposes of subsection (b) of this section, a person shall be deemed to be in the business of selling or renting dwellings if—

(1) he has, within the preceding twelve months, participated as principal in three or more transactions involving the sale or rental of any dwelling or any interest therein, or

(2) he has, within the preceding twelve months, participated as agent, other than in the sale of his own personal residence in providing sales or rental facilities or sales or rental services in two or more transactions involving the sale or rental of any dwelling or any interest therein, or

(3) he is the owner of any dwelling designed or intended for occupancy by, or occupied by, five or more families.

(Pub. L. No. 90-284, Title VIII, § 803, 82 Stat. 82 (1968))

§ 3604. Discrimination in the sale or rental of housing and other prohibited practices

As made applicable by section 3603 of this title and except as exempted by sections 3603(b) and 3607 of this title, it shall be unlawful—

(a) To refuse to sell or rent after the making of a bona fide offer, or to refuse to negotiate for the sale or rental of, or otherwise make unavailable or deny, a dwelling to any person because of race, color, religion, sex, familial status, or national origin.

(b) To discriminate against any person in the terms, conditions, or privileges of sale or rental of a dwelling, or in the provision of services or facilities in connection therewith, because of race, color, religion, sex, familial status, or national origin.

(c) To make, print, or publish, or cause to be made, printed, or published any notice, statement, or advertisement, with respect to the sale or rental of a dwelling that indicates any preference, limitation, or discrimination based on race, color, religion, sex, handicap, familial status, or national origin, or an intention to make any such preference, limitation, or discrimination.

(d) To represent to any person because of race, color, religion, sex, handicap, familial status, or national origin that any dwelling is not available for inspection, sale, or rental when such dwelling is in fact so available.

(e) For profit, to induce or attempt to induce any person to sell or rent any dwelling by representations regarding the entry or prospective entry into the neighborhood of a person or persons of a particular race, color, religion, sex, handicap, familial status, or national origin.

(f)(1) To discriminate in the sale or rental, or to otherwise make unavailable or deny, a dwelling to any buyer or renter because of a handicap of—

(A) that buyer or renter;

(B) a person residing in or intending to reside in that dwelling after it is so sold, rented, or made available; or

(C) any person associated with that buyer or renter.

(2) To discriminate against any person in the terms, conditions,

or privileges of sale or rental of a dwelling, or in the provision of services or facilities in connection with such dwelling, because of a handicap of—

(A) that person; or

(B) a person residing in or intending to reside in that dwelling after it is so sold, rented, or made available; or

(C) any person associated with that person.

(3) For purposes of this subsection, discrimination includes—

(A) a refusal to permit, at the expense of the handicapped person, reasonable modifications of existing premises occupied or to be occupied by such person if such modifications may be necessary to afford such person full enjoyment of the premises except that, in the case of a rental, the landlord may where it is reasonable to do so condition permission for a modification on the renter agreeing to restore the interior of the premises to the condition that existed before the modification, reasonable wear and tear excepted;

(B) a refusal to make reasonable accommodations in rules, policies, practices, or services, when such accommodations may be necessary to afford such person equal opportunity to use and enjoy a dwelling; or

(C) in connection with the design and construction of covered multifamily dwellings for first occupancy after the date that is 30 months after September 13, 1988, a failure to design and construct those dwellings in such a manner that—

(i) the public use and common use portions of such dwellings are readily accessible to and usable by handicapped persons;

(ii) all the doors designed to allow passage into and within all premises within such dwellings are sufficiently wide to allow passage by handicapped persons in wheelchairs; and

(iii) all premises within such dwellings contain the following features of adaptive design:

(I) an accessible route into and through the dwelling;

(II) light switches, electrical outlets, thermostats, and other environmental controls in accessible locations;

(III) reinforcements in bathroom walls to allow later installation of grab bars; and

(IV) usable kitchens and bathrooms such that an individual in a wheelchair can maneuver about the space.

(4) Compliance with the appropriate requirements of the American National Standard for buildings and facilities providing accessibility and usability for physically handicapped people (commonly cited as "ANSI A117.1") suffices to satisfy the requirements of paragraph (3)(C)(iii).

(5) (A) If a State or unit of general local government has incorporated into its laws the requirements set forth in paragraph (3)(C), compliance with such laws shall be deemed to satisfy the requirements of that paragraph.

(B) A State or unit of general local government may review and approve newly constructed covered multifamily dwellings for the purpose of making determinations as to whether the design and construction requirements of paragraph (3)(C) are met.

(C) The Secretary shall encourage, but may not require, States and units of local government to include in their existing procedures for the review and approval of newly constructed covered multifamily dwellings, determinations as to whether the design and construction of such dwellings are consistent with paragraph (3)(C), and shall provide technical assistance to States and units of local government and other persons to implement the requirements of paragraph (3)(C).

(D) Nothing in this subchapter shall be construed to require the Secretary to review or approve the plans, designs or construction of all covered multifamily dwellings, to determine whether the design and construction of such dwellings are consistent with the requirements of paragraph 3(C).

(6) (A) Nothing in paragraph (5) shall be construed to affect the authority and responsibility of the Secretary or a State or local public agency certified pursuant to section 3610(f)(3) of this title to receive and process complaints or otherwise engage in enforcement activities under this subchapter.

(B) Determinations by a State or a unit of general local government under paragraphs (5)(A) and (B) shall not be conclusive in enforcement proceedings under this subchapter.

(7) As used in this subsection, the term "covered multifamily dwellings" means—

(A) buildings consisting of 4 or more units if such buildings have one or more elevators; and

(B) ground floor units in other buildings consisting of 4 or more units.

(8) Nothing in this subchapter shall be construed to invalidate or limit any law of a State or political subdivision of a State, or other jurisdiction in which this subchapter shall be effective, that requires dwellings to be designed and constructed in a manner that affords handicapped persons greater access than is required by this subchapter.

(9) Nothing in this subsection requires that a dwelling be made available to an individual whose tenancy would constitute a direct threat to the health or safety of other individuals or whose tenancy would result in substantial physical damage to the property of others.

(Pub. L. No. 90-284, Title VIII, § 804, 82 Stat. 83 (1968); Pub. L. No. 93-383, Title VIII, § 808(b)(1), 88 Stat. 729 (1974); Pub. L. No. 100-430, §§ 6(a)–(b)(2), (e), 15, 102 Stat. 1620, 1622, 1623, 1636 (1988))

§ 3605. Discrimination in residential real estate-related transactions

(a) In general

It shall be unlawful for any person or other entity whose business includes engaging in residential real estate-related transactions to discriminate against any person in making available such a transaction, or in the terms or conditions of such a transaction, because of race, color, religion, sex, handicap, familial status, or national origin.

(b) "Residential real estate-related transaction" defined

As used in this section, the term "residential real estate-related transaction" means any of the following:

(1) The making or purchasing of loans or providing other financial assistance—

(A) for purchasing, constructing, improving, repairing, or maintaining a dwelling; or

(B) secured by residential real estate.

(2) The selling, brokering, or appraising of residential real property.

(c) Appraisal exemption

Nothing in this subchapter prohibits a person engaged in the business of furnishing appraisals of real property to take into consideration factors other than race, color, religion, national origin, sex, handicap, or familial status.

(Pub. L. No. 90-284, Title VIII, § 805, 82 Stat. 83 (1968); Pub. L. No. 93-383, Title VIII, § 808(b)(2), 88 Stat. 729 (1974); Pub. L. No. 100-430, § 6(c), 102 Stat. 1622 (1988))

§ 3606. Discrimination in provision of brokerage services

After December 31, 1968, it shall be unlawful to deny any person access to or membership or participation in any multiple-listing service, real estate brokers' organization or other service, organization, or facility relating to the business of selling or renting dwellings, or to discriminate against him in the terms or conditions of such access, membership, or participation, on account of race, color, religion, sex, handicap, familial status, or national origin.

(Pub. L. No. 90-284, Title VIII, § 806, 82 Stat. 84 (1968); Pub. L. No. 93-383, Title VIII, § 808(b)(3), 88 Stat. 729 (1974); Pub. L. No. 100-430, § 6(b)(1), 102 Stat. 1622 (1988))

§ 3607. Exemption

(a) Religious organizations and private clubs

Nothing in this subchapter shall prohibit a religious organization, association, or society, or any nonprofit institution or organization operated, supervised or controlled by or in conjunction with a religious organization, association, or society, from limiting the sale, rental or occupancy of dwellings which it owns or operates for other than a commercial purpose to persons of the same religion, or from giving preference to such persons, unless membership in such religion is restricted on account of race, color, or national origin. Nor shall anything in this subchapter prohibit a private club not in fact open to the public, which as an incident to its primary purpose or purposes provides lodgings which it owns or operates for other than a commercial purpose, from limiting the rental or occupancy of such lodgings to its members or from giving preference to its members.

(b) Numbers of occupants; housing for older persons; persons convicted of making or distributing controlled substances; good faith defense

(1) Nothing in this subchapter limits the applicability of any reasonable local, State, or Federal restrictions regarding the maximum number of occupants permitted to occupy a dwelling. Nor does any provision in this subchapter regarding familial status apply with respect to housing for older persons.

(2) As used in this section, "housing for older persons" means housing—

   (A) provided under any State or Federal program that the Secretary determines is specifically designed and operated to assist elderly persons (as defined in the State or Federal program); or

   (B) intended for, and solely occupied by, persons 62 years of age or older; or

   (C) intended and operated for occupancy by persons 55 years of age or older, and—

   (i) at least 80 percent of the occupied units are occupied by at least one person 55 years of age or older;

   (ii) the housing facility or community publishes and adheres to policies and procedures that demonstrate the intent required under this subparagraph; and

   (iii) the housing facility or community complies with rules issued by the Secretary for verification of occupancy, which shall—

   (I) provide for verification by reliable surveys and affidavits; and

   (II) include examples of the types of policies and procedures relevant to a determination of compliance with the requirement clause (ii). Such surveys and affidavits shall be admissible in administrative and judicial proceedings for the purposes of such verification.

(3) Housing shall not fail to meet the requirements for housing for older persons by reason of:

   (A) persons residing in such housing as of Sept. 13, 1988, who do not meet the age requirements of subsections (2)(B) or (C): Provided, That new occupants of such housing meet the age requirements of subsections (2)(B) or (C); or

   (B) unoccupied units: Provided, That such units are reserved for occupancy by persons who meet the age requirements of subsections (2)(B) or (C).

(4) Nothing in this subchapter prohibits conduct against a person because such person has been convicted by any court of competent jurisdiction of the illegal manufacture or distribution of a controlled substance as defined in section 802 of Title 21.

(5) **(A)** A person shall not be held personally liable for monetary damages for a violation of this chapter if such person reasonably relied, in good faith, on the application of the exemption under this subsection relating to housing for older persons.

   (B) For the purposes of this paragraph, a person may only show good faith reliance on the application of the exemption by showing that—

   (i) such person has no actual knowledge that the facility or community is not, or will not be, eligible for such exemption; and

   (ii) the facility or community has stated formally, in writing, that the facility or community complies with the requirements for such exemption.

(Pub. L. No. 90-284, Title VIII, § 807, 82 Stat. 84 (1968); Pub. L. No. 100-430, § 6(d), 102 Stat. 1623 (1988); Pub. L. No. 104-76, §§ 2–3, 109 Stat. 787 (1995))

§ 3608. Administration

(a) Authority and responsibility

The authority and responsibility for administering this Act shall be in the Secretary of Housing and Urban Development.

(b) Assistant Secretary

The Department of Housing and Urban Development shall be provided an additional Assistant Secretary.

(c) Delegation of authority; appointment of administrative law judges; location of conciliation meetings; administrative review

The Secretary may delegate any of his functions, duties, and powers to employees of the Department of Housing and Urban Development or to boards of such employees, including functions, duties, and powers with respect to investigating, conciliating, hearing, determining, ordering, certifying, reporting, or otherwise acting as to any work, business, or matter under this subchapter. The person to whom such delegations are made with respect to hearing functions, duties, and powers shall be appointed and shall serve in the Department of Housing and Urban Development in compliance with sections 3105, 3344, 5372, and 7521 of Title 5. Insofar as possible, conciliation meetings shall be held in the cities or other localities where the discriminatory housing practices allegedly occurred. The Secretary shall by rule prescribe such rights of appeal from the decisions of his administrative law judges to other administrative law judges or to other officers in the Department, to boards of officers or to himself, as shall be appropriate and in accordance with law.

(d) Cooperation of Secretary and executive departments and agencies in administration of housing and urban development programs and activities to further fair housing purposes

All executive departments and agencies shall administer their programs and activities relating to housing and urban development (including any Federal agency having regulatory or supervisory authority over financial institutions) in a manner affirmatively to further the purposes of this subchapter and shall cooperate with the Secretary to further such purposes.

(e) Functions of Secretary

The Secretary of Housing and Urban Development shall—

   (1) make studies with respect to the nature and extent of discriminatory housing practices in representative communities, urban, suburban, and rural, throughout the United States;

   (2) publish and disseminate reports, recommendations, and information derived from such studies, including an annual report to the Congress—

   (A) specifying the nature and extent of progress made nationally in eliminating discriminatory housing practices and furthering the purposes of this subchapter, obstacles remaining to achieving equal housing opportunity, and recommendations for further legislative or executive action; and

   (B) containing tabulations of the number of instances (and the reasons therefor) in the preceding year in which—

   (i) investigations are not completed as required by section 3610(a)(1)(B) of this title;

   (ii) determinations are not made within the time specified in section 3610(g) of this title; and

(iii) hearings are not commenced or findings and conclusions are not made as required by section 3612(g) of this title;

(3) cooperate with and render technical assistance to Federal, State, local, and other public or private agencies, organizations, and institutions which are formulating or carrying on programs to prevent or eliminate discriminatory housing practices;

(4) cooperate with and render such technical and other assistance to the Community Relations Service as may be appropriate to further its activities in preventing or eliminating discriminatory housing practices;

(5) administer the programs and activities relating to housing and urban development in a manner affirmatively to further the policies of this subchapter; and

(6) annually report to the Congress, and make available to the public, data on the race, color, religion, sex, national origin, age, handicap, and family characteristics of persons and households who are applicants for, participants in, or beneficiaries or potential beneficiaries of, programs administered by the Department to the extent such characteristics are within the coverage of the provisions of law and Executive orders referred to in subsection (f) of this section which apply to such programs (and in order to develop the data to be included and made available to the public under this subsection, the Secretary shall, without regard to any other provision of law, collect such information relating to those characteristics as the Secretary determines to be necessary or appropriate).

(f) Provisions of law applicable to Department programs

The provisions of law and Executive orders to which subsection (e)(6) applies are—

(1) title VI of the Civil Rights Act of 1964 [42 U.S.C. § 2000d et seq.];

(2) this subchapter;

(3) section 794 of Title 29;

(4) the Age Discrimination Act of 1975 [42 U.S.C. § 6101 et seq.];

(5) the Equal Credit Opportunity Act [15 U.S.C. § 1691 et seq.];

(6) section 1982 of this title;

(7) section 637(a) of Title 15;

(8) section 1735f-5 of Title 12;

(9) section 5309 of this title;

(10) section 1701u of Title 12;

(11) Executive orders 11063 [42 U.S.C. § 1982 note], 11246 [42 U.S.C. § 2000e note], 11625 [15 U.S.C. § 631 note], 12250 [42 U.S.C. § 2000d-1 note], 12259 [42 U.S.C. § 3608 note; now revoked by Ex. Ord. No. 12892, Jan. 17, 1994, 59 F.R. 2939, also set out under this section], and 12432 [15 U.S.C. § 637 note]; and

(12) any other provision of law which the Secretary specifies by publication in the Federal Register for the purpose of this subsection.

(Pub. L. No. 90-284, Title VIII, § 808, 82 Stat. 84 (1968); Pub. L. No. 95-251, § 3, 92 Stat. 184 (1978); Pub. L. No. 95-454, Title VIII, § 801(a)(3)(J), 92 Stat. 1222 (1978); Pub. L. No. 100-430, § 7, 102 Stat. 1623 (1988))

§ 3608a. Collection of certain data

(a) In general

To assess the extent of compliance with Federal fair housing requirements (including the requirements established under title VI of Public Law 88-352 [42 U.S.C. § 2000d et seq.] and title VIII of Public Law 90-284 [42 U.S.C. § 3601 et seq.]), the Secretary of Agriculture shall collect, not less than annually, data on the racial and ethnic characteristics of persons eligible for, assisted, or otherwise benefiting under each community development, housing assistance, and mortgage and loan insurance and guarantee program administered by such Secretary. Such data shall be collected on a building by building basis if the Secretary determines such collection to be appropriate.

(b) Reports to Congress

The Secretary of Agriculture shall include in the annual report of such Secretary to the Congress a summary and evaluation of the data collected by such Secretary under subsection (a) of this section during the preceding year.

(Pub. L. No. 100-242, Title V, § 562, 101 Stat. 1944 (1988), as amended by Pub. L. No. 104-66, Title I, § 1071(e), 109 Stat. 720, (1995))

§ 3609. Education and conciliation; conferences and consultation; reports

Immediately after April 11, 1968, the Secretary shall commence such educational and conciliatory activities as in his judgment will further the purposes of this subchapter. He shall call conferences of persons in the housing industry and other interested parties to acquaint them with the provisions of this subchapter and his suggested means of implementing it, and shall endeavor with their advice to work out programs of voluntary compliance and of enforcement. He may pay per diem, travel, and transportation expenses for persons attending such conferences as provided in section 5703 of Title 5. He shall consult with State and local officials and other interested parties to learn the extent, if any, to which housing discrimination exists in their State or locality, and whether and how State or local enforcement programs might be utilized to combat such discrimination in connection with or in place of, the Secretary's enforcement of this subchapter. The Secretary shall issue reports on such conferences and consultations as he deems appropriate.

(Pub. L. No. 90-284, Title VIII, § 809, 82 Stat. 85 (1968))

§ 3610. Administrative enforcement; preliminary matters

(a) Complaints and answers

(1) (A) (i) An aggrieved person may, not later than one year after an alleged discriminatory housing practice has occurred or terminated, file a complaint with the Secretary alleging such discriminatory housing practice. The Secretary, on the Secretary's own initiative, may also file such a complaint.

(ii) Such complaints shall be in writing and shall contain such information and be in such form as the Secretary requires.

(iii) The Secretary may also investigate housing practices to determine whether a complaint should be brought under this section.

(B) Upon the filing of such a complaint—

(i) the Secretary shall serve notice upon the aggrieved person acknowledging such filing and advising the aggrieved person of the time limits and choice of forums provided under this subchapter;

(ii) the Secretary shall, not later than 10 days after such filing or the identification of an additional respondent under paragraph (2), serve on the respondent a notice identifying the alleged discriminatory housing practice and advising such respondent of the procedural rights and obligations of respondents under this subchapter, together with a copy of the original complaint;

(iii) each respondent may file, not later than 10 days after receipt of notice from the Secretary, an answer to such complaint; and

(iv) the Secretary shall make an investigation of the alleged discriminatory housing practice and complete such investigation within 100 days after the filing of the complaint (or, when the Secretary takes further action under subsection (f)(2) of this section with respect to a complaint, within 100 days after the commencement of such further action), unless it is impracticable to do so.

(C) If the Secretary is unable to complete the investigation within 100 days after the filing of the complaint (or, when the Secretary takes further action under subsection (f)(2) of this section with respect to a complaint, within 100 days after the commencement of such further action), the Secretary shall notify the complainant and respondent in writing of the reasons for not doing so.

(D) Complaints and answers shall be under oath or affirmation, and may be reasonably and fairly amended at any time.

(2) (A) A person who is not named as a respondent in a complaint, but who is identified as a respondent in the course of investigation, may be joined as an additional or substitute respondent upon written notice, under paragraph (1), to such person, from the Secretary.

(B) Such notice, in addition to meeting the requirements of paragraph (1), shall explain the basis for the Secretary's belief that the person to whom the notice is addressed is properly joined as a respondent.

(b) Investigative report and conciliation

(1) During the period beginning with the filing of such complaint and ending with the filing of a charge or a dismissal by the Secretary, the Secretary shall, to the extent feasible, engage in conciliation with respect to such complaint.

(2) A conciliation agreement arising out of such conciliation shall be an agreement between the respondent and the complainant, and shall be subject to approval by the Secretary.

(3) A conciliation agreement may provide for binding arbitration of the dispute arising from the complaint. Any such arbitration that results from a conciliation agreement may award appropriate relief, including monetary relief.

(4) Each conciliation agreement shall be made public unless the complainant and respondent otherwise agree and the Secretary determines that disclosure is not required to further the purposes of this subchapter.

(5) (A) At the end of each investigation under this section, the Secretary shall prepare a final investigative report containing—

(i) the names and dates of contacts with witnesses;

(ii) a summary and the dates of correspondence and other contacts with the aggrieved person and the respondent;

(iii) a summary description of other pertinent records;

(iv) a summary of witness statements; and

(v) answers to interrogatories.

(B) A final report under this paragraph may be amended if additional evidence is later discovered.

(c) Failure to comply with conciliation agreement

Whenever the Secretary has reasonable cause to believe that a respondent has breached a conciliation agreement, the Secretary shall refer the matter to the Attorney General with a recommendation that a civil action be filed under section 3614 of this title for the enforcement of such agreement.

(d) Prohibitions and requirements with respect to disclosure of information

(1) Nothing said or done in the course of conciliation under this subchapter may be made public or used as evidence in a subsequent proceeding under this subchapter without the written consent of the persons concerned.

(2) Notwithstanding paragraph (1), the Secretary shall make available to the aggrieved person and the respondent, at any time, upon request following completion of the Secretary's investigation, information derived from an investigation and any final investigative report relating to that investigation.

(e) Prompt judicial action

(1) If the Secretary concludes at any time following the filing of a complaint that prompt judicial action is necessary to carry out the purposes of this subchapter, the Secretary may authorize a civil action for appropriate temporary or preliminary relief pending final disposition of the complaint under this section. Upon receipt of such an authorization, the Attorney General shall promptly commence and maintain such an action. Any temporary restraining order or other order granting preliminary or temporary relief shall be issued in accordance with the Federal Rules of Civil Procedure. The commencement of a civil action under this subsection does not affect the initiation or continuation of administrative proceedings under this section and section 3612 of this title.

(2) Whenever the Secretary has reason to believe that a basis may exist for the commencement of proceedings against any respondent under sections 3614(a) and 3614(c) of this title or for proceedings by any governmental licensing or supervisory authorities, the Secretary shall transmit the information upon which such belief is based to the Attorney General, or to such authorities, as the case may be.

(f) Referral for State or local proceedings

(1) Whenever a complaint alleges a discriminatory housing practice—

(A) within the jurisdiction of a State or local public agency; and

(B) as to which such agency has been certified by the Secretary under this subsection;

the Secretary shall refer such complaint to that certified agency before taking any action with respect to such complaint.

(2) Except with the consent of such certified agency, the Secretary, after that referral is made, shall take no further action with respect to such complaint unless—

   (A) the certified agency has failed to commence proceedings with respect to the complaint before the end of the 30th day after the date of such referral;

   (B) the certified agency, having so commenced such proceedings, fails to carry forward such proceedings with reasonable promptness; or

   (C) the Secretary determines that the certified agency no longer qualifies for certification under this subsection with respect to the relevant jurisdiction.

(3) (A) The Secretary may certify an agency under this subsection only if the Secretary determines that—

   (i) the substantive rights protected by such agency in the jurisdiction with respect to which certification is to be made;

   (ii) the procedures followed by such agency;

   (iii) the remedies available to such agency; and

   (iv) the availability of judicial review of such agency's action;

   are substantially equivalent to those created by and under this subchapter.

   (B) Before making such certification, the Secretary shall take into account the current practices and past performance, if any, of such agency.

(4) During the period which begins on September 13, 1988, and ends 40 months after such date, each agency certified (including an agency certified for interim referrals pursuant to 24 CFR 115.11, unless such agency is subsequently denied recognition under 24 CFR 115.7) for the purposes of this subchapter on the day before such date shall for the purposes of this subsection be considered certified under this subsection with respect to those matters for which such agency was certified on that date. If the Secretary determines in an individual case that an agency has not been able to meet the certification requirements within this 40-month period due to exceptional circumstances, such as the infrequency of legislative sessions in that jurisdiction, the Secretary may extend such period by not more than 8 months.

(5) Not less frequently than every 5 years, the Secretary shall determine whether each agency certified under this subsection continues to qualify for certification. The Secretary shall take appropriate action with respect to any agency not so qualifying.

(g) Reasonable cause determination and effect

(1) The Secretary shall, within 100 days after the filing of the complaint (or, when the Secretary takes further action under subsection (f)(2) of this section with respect to a complaint, within 100 days after the commencement of such further action), determine based on the facts whether reasonable cause exists to believe that a discriminatory housing practice has occurred or is about to occur, unless it is imprac-

ticable to do so, or unless the Secretary has approved a conciliation agreement with respect to the complaint. If the Secretary is unable to make the determination within 100 days after the filing of the complaint (or, when the Secretary takes further action under subsection (f)(2) of this section with respect to a complaint, within 100 days after the commencement of such further action), the Secretary shall notify the complainant and respondent in writing of the reasons for not doing so.

(2) (A) If the Secretary determines that reasonable cause exists to believe that a discriminatory housing practice has occurred or is about to occur, the Secretary shall, except as provided in subparagraph (C), immediately issue a charge on behalf of the aggrieved person, for further proceedings under section 3612 of this title.

   (B) Such charge—

   (i) shall consist of a short and plain statement of the facts upon which the Secretary has found reasonable cause to believe that a discriminatory housing practice has occurred or is about to occur;

   (ii) shall be based on the final investigative report; and

   (iii) need not be limited to the facts or grounds alleged in the complaint filed under subsection (a) of this section.

   (C) If the Secretary determines that the matter involves the legality of any State or local zoning or other land use law or ordinance, the Secretary shall immediately refer the matter to the Attorney General for appropriate action under section 3614 of this title, instead of issuing such charge.

(3) If the Secretary determines that no reasonable cause exists to believe that a discriminatory housing practice has occurred or is about to occur, the Secretary shall promptly dismiss the complaint. The Secretary shall make public disclosure of each such dismissal.

(4) The Secretary may not issue a charge under this section regarding an alleged discriminatory housing practice after the beginning of the trial of a civil action commenced by the aggrieved party under an Act of Congress or a State law, seeking relief with respect to that discriminatory housing practice.

(h) Service of copies of charge

After the Secretary issues a charge under this section, the Secretary shall cause a copy thereof, together with information as to how to make an election under section 3612(a) of this title and the effect of such an election, to be served—

(1) on each respondent named in such charge, together with a notice of opportunity for a hearing at a time and place specified in the notice, unless that election is made; and

(2) on each aggrieved person on whose behalf the complaint was filed.

(Pub. L. No. 90-284, Title VIII, § 810, as added Pub. L. No. 100-430, § 8(2), 102 Stat. 1625 (1988))

§ 3611. Subpoenas; giving of evidence

(a) In general

The Secretary may, in accordance with this subsection, issue subpoenas and order discovery in aid of investigations and hearings under this subchapter. Such subpoenas and discovery may be ordered to the same extent and subject to the same limitations as would apply if the subpoenas or discovery were ordered or served in aid of a civil action in the United States district court for the district in which the investigation is taking place.

(b) Witness fees

Witnesses summoned by a subpoena under this subchapter shall be entitled to the same witness and mileage fees as witnesses in proceedings in United States district courts. Fees payable to a witness summoned by a subpoena issued at the request of a party shall be paid by that party or, where a party is unable to pay the fees, by the Secretary.

(c) Criminal penalties

(1) Any person who willfully fails or neglects to attend and testify or to answer any lawful inquiry or to produce records, documents, or other evidence, if it is in such person's power to do so, in obedience to the subpoena or other lawful order under subsection (a) of this section, shall be fined not more than $100,000 or imprisoned not more than one year, or both.

(2) Any person who, with intent thereby to mislead another person in any proceeding under this subchapter—

(A) makes or causes to be made any false entry or statement of fact in any report, account, record, or other document produced pursuant to subpoena or other lawful order under subsection (a) of this section;

(B) willfully neglects or fails to make or to cause to be made full, true, and correct entries in such reports, accounts, records, or other documents; or

(C) willfully mutilates, alters, or by any other means falsifies any documentary evidence;

shall be fined not more than $100,000 or imprisoned not more than one year, or both.

(Pub. L. No. 90-284, Title VIII, § 811, as added Pub. L. No. 100-430, § 8(2), 102 Stat. 1628 (1988))

§ 3612. Enforcement by Secretary

(a) Election of judicial determination

When a charge is filed under section 3610 of this title, a complainant, a respondent, or an aggrieved person on whose behalf the complaint was filed, may elect to have the claims asserted in that charge decided in a civil action under subsection (*o*) of this section in lieu of a hearing under subsection (b) of this section. The election must be made not later than 20 days after the receipt by the electing person of service under section 3610(h) of this title or, in the case of the Secretary, not later than 20 days after such service. The person making such election shall give notice of doing so to the Secretary and to all other complainants and respondents to whom the charge relates.

(b) Administrative law judge hearing in absence of election

If an election is not made under subsection (a) of this section with respect to a charge filed under section 3610 of this title, the Secretary shall provide an opportunity for a hearing on the record with respect to a charge issued under section 3610 of this title. The Secretary shall delegate the conduct of a hearing under this section to an administrative law judge appointed under section 3105 of

Title 5. The administrative law judge shall conduct the hearing at a place in the vicinity in which the discriminatory housing practice is alleged to have occurred or to be about to occur.

(c) Rights of parties

At a hearing under this section, each party may appear in person, be represented by counsel, present evidence, cross-examine witnesses, and obtain the issuance of subpoenas under section 3611 of this title. Any aggrieved person may intervene as a party in the proceeding. The Federal Rules of Evidence apply to the presentation of evidence in such hearing as they would in a civil action in a United States district court.

(d) Expedited discovery and hearing

(1) Discovery in administrative proceedings under this section shall be conducted as expeditiously and inexpensively as possible, consistent with the need of all parties to obtain relevant evidence.

(2) A hearing under this section shall be conducted as expeditiously and inexpensively as possible, consistent with the needs and rights of the parties to obtain a fair hearing and a complete record.

(3) The Secretary shall, not later than 180 days after September 13, 1988, issue rules to implement this subsection.

(e) Resolution of charge

Any resolution of a charge before a final order under this section shall require the consent of the aggrieved person on whose behalf the charge is issued.

(f) Effect of trial of civil action on administrative proceedings

An administrative law judge may not continue administrative proceedings under this section regarding any alleged discriminatory housing practice after the beginning of the trial of a civil action commenced by the aggrieved party under an Act of Congress or a State law, seeking relief with respect to that discriminatory housing practice.

(g) Hearings, findings and conclusions, and order

(1) The administrative law judge shall commence the hearing under this section no later than 120 days following the issuance of the charge, unless it is impracticable to do so. If the administrative law judge is unable to commence the hearing within 120 days after the issuance of the charge, the administrative law judge shall notify the Secretary, the aggrieved person on whose behalf the charge was filed, and the respondent, in writing of the reasons for not doing so.

(2) The administrative law judge shall make findings of fact and conclusions of law within 60 days after the end of the hearing under this section, unless it is impracticable to do so. If the administrative law judge is unable to make findings of fact and conclusions of law within such period, or any succeeding 60-day period thereafter, the administrative law judge shall notify the Secretary, the aggrieved person on whose behalf the charge was filed, and the respondent, in writing of the reasons for not doing so.

(3) If the administrative law judge finds that a respondent has engaged or is about to engage in a discriminatory housing practice, such administrative law judge shall promptly issue an order for such relief as may be appropriate, which may include actual damages suffered by the aggrieved person and injunctive or other equitable relief. Such order may, to

vindicate the public interest, assess a civil penalty against the respondent—

    (A) in an amount not exceeding $10,000 if the respondent has not been adjudged to have committed any prior discriminatory housing practice;

    (B) in an amount not exceeding $25,000 if the respondent has been adjudged to have committed one other discriminatory housing practice during the 5-year period ending on the date of the filing of this charge; and

    (C) in an amount not exceeding $50,000 if the respondent has been adjudged to have committed 2 or more discriminatory housing practices during the 7-year period ending on the date of the filing of this charge;

except that if the acts constituting the discriminatory housing practice that is the object of the charge are committed by the same natural person who has been previously adjudged to have committed acts constituting a discriminatory housing practice, then the civil penalties set forth in subparagraphs (B) and (C) may be imposed without regard to the period of time within which any subsequent discriminatory housing practice occurred.

(4) No such order shall affect any contract, sale, encumbrance, or lease consummated before the issuance of such order and involving a bona fide purchaser, encumbrancer, or tenant without actual notice of the charge filed under this title.

(5) In the case of an order with respect to a discriminatory housing practice that occurred in the course of a business subject to a licensing or regulation by a governmental agency, the Secretary shall, not later than 30 days after the date of the issuance of such order (or, if such order is judicially reviewed, 30 days after such order is in substance affirmed upon such review)—

    (A) send copies of the findings of fact, conclusions of law, and the order, to that governmental agency; and

    (B) recommend to that governmental agency appropriate disciplinary action (including, where appropriate, the suspension or revocation of the license of the respondent).

(6) In the case of an order against a respondent against whom another order was issued within the preceding 5 years under this section, the Secretary shall send a copy of each such order to the Attorney General.

(7) If the administrative law judge finds that the respondent has not engaged or is not about to engage in a discriminatory housing practice, as the case may be, such administrative law judge shall enter an order dismissing the charge. The Secretary shall make public disclosure of each such dismissal.

(h) Review by Secretary; service of final order

(1) The Secretary may review any finding, conclusion, or order issued under subsection (g) of this section. Such review shall be completed not later than 30 days after the finding, conclusion, or order is so issued; otherwise the finding, conclusion, or order becomes final.

(2) The Secretary shall cause the findings of fact and conclusions of law made with respect to any final order for relief under this section, together with a copy of such order, to be served on each aggrieved person and each respondent in the proceeding.

(i) Judicial review

(1) Any party aggrieved by a final order for relief under this section granting or denying in whole or in part the relief sought may obtain a review of such order under chapter 158 of Title 28.

(2) Notwithstanding such chapter, venue of the proceeding shall be in the judicial circuit in which the discriminatory housing practice is alleged to have occurred, and filing of the petition for review shall be not later than 30 days after the order is entered.

(j) Court enforcement of administrative order upon petition by Secretary

(1) The Secretary may petition any United States court of appeals for the circuit in which the discriminatory housing practice is alleged to have occurred or in which any respondent resides or transacts business for the enforcement of the order of the administrative law judge and for appropriate temporary relief or restraining order, by filing in such court a written petition praying that such order be enforced and for appropriate temporary relief or restraining order.

(2) The Secretary shall file in court with the petition the record in the proceeding. A copy of such petition shall be forthwith transmitted by the clerk of the court to the parties to the proceeding before the administrative law judge.

(k) Relief which may be granted

(1) Upon the filing of a petition under subsection (i) or (j) of this section, the court may—

    (A) grant to the petitioner, or any other party, such temporary relief, restraining order, or other order as the court deems just and proper;

    (B) affirm, modify, or set aside, in whole or in part, the order, or remand the order for further proceedings; and

    (C) enforce such order to the extent that such order is affirmed or modified.

(2) Any party to the proceeding before the administrative law judge may intervene in the court of appeals.

(3) No objection not made before the administrative law judge shall be considered by the court, unless the failure or neglect to urge such objection is excused because of extraordinary circumstances.

(*l*) Enforcement decree in absence of petition for review

If no petition for review is filed under subsection (i) of this section before the expiration of 45 days after the date the administrative law judge's order is entered, the administrative law judge's findings of fact and order shall be conclusive in connection with any petition for enforcement—

(1) which is filed by the Secretary under subsection (j) of this section after the end of such day; or

(2) under subsection (m) of this section.

(m) Court enforcement of administrative order upon petition of any person entitled to relief

If before the expiration of 60 days after the date the administrative law judge's order is entered, no petition for review has been filed under subsection (i) of this section, and the Secretary has not sought enforcement of the order under subsection (j) of this section, any person entitled to relief under the order may petition for a decree enforcing the order in the United States court of appeals for the circuit in which the discriminatory housing practice is alleged to have occurred.

(n) Entry of decree

The clerk of the court of appeals in which a petition for enforcement is filed under subsection (*l*) or (m) of this section shall forthwith enter a decree enforcing the order and shall transmit a copy of such decree to the Secretary, the respondent named in the petition, and to any other parties to the proceeding before the administrative law judge.

(*o*) Civil action for enforcement when election is made for such civil action

(1) If an election is made under subsection (a) of this section, the Secretary shall authorize, and not later than 30 days after the election is made the Attorney General shall commence and maintain, a civil action on behalf of the aggrieved person in a United States district court seeking relief under this subsection. Venue for such civil action shall be determined under chapter 87 of Title 28.

(2) Any aggrieved person with respect to the issues to be determined in a civil action under this subsection may intervene as of right in that civil action.

(3) In a civil action under this subsection, if the court finds that a discriminatory housing practice has occurred or is about to occur, the court may grant as relief any relief which a court could grant with respect to such discriminatory housing practice in a civil action under section 3613 of this title. Any relief so granted that would accrue to an aggrieved person in a civil action commenced by that aggrieved person under section 3613 of this title shall also accrue to that aggrieved person in a civil action under this subsection. If monetary relief is sought for the benefit of an aggrieved person who does not intervene in the civil action, the court shall not award such relief if that aggrieved person has not complied with discovery orders entered by the court.

(p) Attorney's fees

In any administrative proceeding brought under this section, or any court proceeding arising therefrom, or any civil action under this section, the administrative law judge or the court, as the case may be, in its discretion, may allow the prevailing party, other than the United States, a reasonable attorney's fee and costs. The United States shall be liable for such fees and costs to the extent provided by section 504 of Title 5 or by section 2412 of Title 28.

(Pub. L. No. 90-284, Title VIII, § 812, as added Pub. L. No. 100-430, § 8(2), 102 Stat. 1629 (1988))

§ 3613. Enforcement by private persons

(a) Civil action

(1) (A) An aggrieved person may commence a civil action in an appropriate United States district court or State court not later than 2 years after the occurrence or the termination of an alleged discriminatory housing practice, or the breach of a conciliation agreement entered into under this subchapter, whichever occurs last, to obtain appropriate relief with respect to such discriminatory housing practice or breach.

(B) The computation of such 2-year period shall not include

any time during which an administrative proceeding under this subchapter was pending with respect to a complaint or charge under this subchapter based upon such discriminatory housing practice. This subparagraph does not apply to actions arising from a breach of a conciliation agreement.

(2) An aggrieved person may commence a civil action under this subsection whether or not a complaint has been filed under section 3610(a) of this title and without regard to the status of any such complaint, but if the Secretary or a State or local agency has obtained a conciliation agreement with the consent of an aggrieved person, no action may be filed under this subsection by such aggrieved person with respect to the alleged discriminatory housing practice which forms the basis for such complaint except for the purpose of enforcing the terms of such an agreement.

(3) An aggrieved person may not commence a civil action under this subsection with respect to an alleged discriminatory housing practice which forms the basis of a charge issued by the Secretary if an administrative law judge has commenced a hearing on the record under this subchapter with respect to such charge.

(b) Appointment of attorney by court

Upon application by a person alleging a discriminatory housing practice or a person against whom such a practice is alleged, the court may—

(1) appoint an attorney for such person; or

(2) authorize the commencement or continuation of a civil action under subsection (a) of this section without the payment of fees, costs, or security, if in the opinion of the court such person is financially unable to bear the costs of such action.

(c) Relief which may be granted

(1) In a civil action under subsection (a) of this section, if the court finds that a discriminatory housing practice has occurred or is about to occur, the court may award to the plaintiff actual and punitive damages, and subject to subsection (d) of this section, may grant as relief, as the court deems appropriate, any permanent or temporary injunction, temporary restraining order, or other order (including an order enjoining the defendant from engaging in such practice or ordering such affirmative action as may be appropriate).

(2) In a civil action under subsection (a) of this section, the court, in its discretion, may allow the prevailing party, other than the United States, a reasonable attorney's fee and costs. The United States shall be liable for such fees and costs to the same extent as a private person.

(d) Effect on certain sales, encumbrances, and rentals

Relief granted under this section shall not affect any contract, sale, encumbrance, or lease consummated before the granting of such relief and involving a bona fide purchaser, encumbrancer, or tenant, without actual notice of the filing of a complaint with the Secretary or civil action under this subchapter.

(e) Intervention by Attorney General

Upon timely application, the Attorney General may intervene in such civil action, if the Attorney General certifies that the case is of general public importance. Upon such intervention the Attorney

General may obtain such relief as would be available to the Attorney General under section 3614(e) of this title in a civil action to which such section applies.

(Pub. L. No. 90-284, Title VIII, § 813, as added Pub. L. No. 100-430, § 8(2), 102 Stat. 1633 (1988))

§ 3614. Enforcement by the Attorney General

(a) Pattern or practice cases

Whenever the Attorney General has reasonable cause to believe that any person or group of persons is engaged in a pattern or practice of resistance to the full enjoyment of any of the rights granted by this subchapter, or that any group of persons has been denied any of the rights granted by this subchapter and such denial raises an issue of general public importance, the Attorney General may commence a civil action in any appropriate United States district court.

(b) On referral of discriminatory housing practice or conciliation agreement for enforcement

(1) (A) The Attorney General may commence a civil action in any appropriate United States district court for appropriate relief with respect to a discriminatory housing practice referred to the Attorney General by the Secretary under section 3610(g) of this title.

(B) A civil action under this paragraph may be commenced not later than the expiration of 18 months after the date of the occurrence or the termination of the alleged discriminatory housing practice.

(2) (A) The Attorney General may commence a civil action in any appropriate United States district court for appropriate relief with respect to breach of a conciliation agreement referred to the Attorney General by the Secretary under section 3610(c) of this title.

(B) A civil action may be commenced under this paragraph not later than the expiration of 90 days after the referral of the alleged breach under section 3610(c) of this title.

(c) Enforcement of subpoenas

The Attorney General, on behalf of the Secretary, or other party at whose request a subpoena is issued, under this subchapter, may enforce such subpoena in appropriate proceedings in the United States district court for the district in which the person to whom the subpoena was addressed resides, was served, or transacts business.

(d) Relief which may be granted in civil actions under subsections (a) and (b)

(1) In a civil action under subsection (a) or (b) of this section, the court—

(A) may award such preventive relief, including a permanent or temporary injunction, restraining order, or other order against the person responsible for a violation of this subchapter as is necessary to assure the full enjoyment of the rights granted by this subchapter;

(B) may award such other relief as the court deems appropriate, including monetary damages to persons aggrieved; and

(C) may, to vindicate the public interest, assess a civil penalty against the respondent—

(i) in an amount not exceeding $50,000, for a first violation; and

(ii) in an amount not exceeding $100,000, for any subsequent violation.

(2) In a civil action under this section, the court, in its discretion, may allow the prevailing party, other than the United States, a reasonable attorney's fee and costs. The United States shall be liable for such fees and costs to the extent provided by section 2412 of Title 28.

(e) Intervention in civil actions

Upon timely application, any person may intervene in a civil action commenced by the Attorney General under subsection (a) or (b) of this section which involves an alleged discriminatory housing practice with respect to which such person is an aggrieved person or a conciliation agreement to which such person is a party. The court may grant such appropriate relief to any such intervening party as is authorized to be granted to a plaintiff in a civil action under section 3613 of this title.

(Pub. L. No. 90-284, Title VIII, § 814, as added Pub. L. No. 100-430, § 8(2), 102 Stat. 1634 (1988))

§ 3614-1. Incentives for self-testing and self-correction[3]

(a) Privileged information

(1) Conditions for privilege

A report or result of a self-test (as that term is defined by regulation of the Secretary) shall be considered to be privileged under paragraph (2) if any person—

(A) conducts, or authorizes an independent third party to

---

3 [*Editor's Note:* The Historical and Statutory Notes to § 3614-1 provide:

Effective Date

Except as otherwise provided, section applicable to a self-test conducted before, on, or after the effective date of the regulations prescribed under subsection 2302(b)(2) of Pub. L. 104-208, set out as a note under this section, see section 2302(c) of Pub. L. 104-208, set out as a note under section 1691c-1 of Title 15, Commerce and Trade.

Issuance of regulations

Section 2302(b)(2) of Pub. L. 104-208 provided that:

(A) **In general.**—Not later than 6 months after the date of enactment of this Act [Sept. 30, 1996], in consultation with the Board and after providing notice and an opportunity for public comment, the Secretary of Housing and Urban Development shall prescribe final regulations to implement section 814A of the Fair Housing Act, as added by this section [this section].

(B) **Self-test**—

(i) **Definition.**—The regulations prescribed by the Secretary under subparagraph (A) shall include a definition of the term "self-test" for purposes of section 814A of the Fair Housing Act, as added by this section [this section].

(ii) **Requirement for self-test.**—The regulations prescribed by the Secretary under subparagraph (A) shall specify that a self-test shall be sufficiently extensive to constitute a determination of the level and effectiveness of the compliance by a person engaged

conduct, a self-test of any aspect of a residential real estate related lending transaction of that person, or any part of that transaction, in order to determine the level or effectiveness of compliance with this subchapter by that person; and

(B) has identified any possible violation of this subchapter by that person and has taken, or is taking, appropriate corrective action to address any such possible violation.

(2) Privileged self-test

If a person meets the conditions specified in subparagraphs (A) and (B) of paragraph (1) with respect to a self-test described in that paragraph, any report or results of that self-test—

(A) shall be privileged; and

(B) may not be obtained or used by any applicant, department, or agency in any—

(i) proceeding or civil action in which one or more violations of this subchapter are alleged; or

(ii) examination or investigation relating to compliance with this subchapter.

(b) Results of self-testing

(1) In general

No provision of this section may be construed to prevent an aggrieved person, complainant, department, or agency from obtaining or using a report or results of any self-test in any proceeding or civil action in which a violation of this subchapter is alleged, or in any examination or investigation of compliance with this subchapter if—

(A) the person to whom the self-test relates or any person with lawful access to the report or the results—

(i) voluntarily releases or discloses all, or any part of, the report or results to the aggrieved person, complainant, department, or agency, or to the general public; or

(ii) refers to or describes the report or results as a defense to charges of violations of this subchapter against the person to whom the self-test relates; or

(B) the report or results are sought in conjunction with an adjudication or admission of a violation of this subchapter for the sole purpose of determining an appropriate penalty or remedy.

(2) Disclosure for determination of penalty or remedy

Any report or results of a self-test that are disclosed for the purpose specified in paragraph (1)(B)—

(A) shall be used only for the particular proceeding in which the adjudication or admission referred to in paragraph (1)(B) is made; and

(B) may not be used in any other action or proceeding.

(c) Adjudication

An aggrieved person, complainant, department, or agency that challenges a privilege asserted under this section may seek a deter-

---

in residential real estate related lending activities with the Fair Housing Act [this subchapter].

(iii) Substantial similarity to certain Equal Credit Opportunity Act regulations.—The regulations prescribed under subparagraph (A) shall be substantially similar to the regulations prescribed by the Board to carry out section 704A of the Equal Credit Opportunity Act, as added by this section [15 U.S.C. § 1691c-1].]

mination of the existence and application of that privilege in—

(1) a court of competent jurisdiction; or

(2) an administrative law proceeding with appropriate jurisdiction.

(Pub. L. No. 90-284, Title VIII, § 814A, as added Pub. L. No. 104-208, Div. A, Title II, § 2302(b)(1), 110 Stat. 3009-421 (1996))

§ 3614a. Rules to implement subchapter

The Secretary may make rules (including rules for the collection, maintenance, and analysis of appropriate data) to carry out this subchapter. The Secretary shall give public notice and opportunity for comment with respect to all rules made under this section.

(Pub. L. No. 90-284, Title VIII, § 815, as added Pub. L. No. 100-430, § 8(2), 102 Stat. 1635 (1988))

§ 3615. Effect on State laws

Nothing in this subchapter shall be construed to invalidate or limit any law of a State or political subdivision of a State, or of any other jurisdiction in which this subchapter shall be effective, that grants, guarantees, or protects the same rights as are granted by this subchapter; but any law of a State, a political subdivision, or other such jurisdiction that purports to require or permit any action that would be a discriminatory housing practice under this subchapter shall to that extent be invalid.

(Pub. L. No. 90-284, Title VIII, § 815, 82 Stat. 89 (1968); renumbered § 816 by Pub. L. No. 100-430, § 8(1), 102 Stat. 1625 (1988))

§ 3616. Cooperation with State and local agencies administering fair housing laws; utilization of services and personnel; reimbursement; written agreements; publication in Federal Register

The Secretary may cooperate with State and local agencies charged with the administration of State and local fair housing laws and, with the consent of such agencies, utilize the services of such agencies and their employees and, notwithstanding any other provision of law, may reimburse such agencies and their employees for services rendered to assist him in carrying out this subchapter. In furtherance of such cooperative efforts, the Secretary may enter into written agreements with such State or local agencies. All agreements and terminations thereof shall be published in the Federal Register.

(Pub. L. No. 90-284, Title VIII, § 816, 82 Stat. 89 (1968); renumbered § 817 by Pub. L. No. 100-430, § 8(1), 102 Stat. 1625 (1988))

§ 3616a. Fair housing initiatives program

(a) In general

The Secretary of Housing and Urban Development (in this section referred to as the "Secretary") may make grants to, or (to the extent of amounts provided in appropriation Acts) enter into contracts or cooperative agreements with, State or local governments or their agencies, public or private nonprofit organizations or institutions, or other public or private entities that are formulating or carrying out programs to prevent or eliminate discriminatory housing practices, to develop, implement, carry out, or coordinate—

   (1) programs or activities designed to obtain enforcement of the rights granted by title VIII of the Act of April 11, 1968 [42 U.S.C. 3601 et seq.] (commonly referred to as the Civil Rights Act of 1968), or by State or local laws that provide rights and remedies for alleged discriminatory housing practices that are substantially equivalent to the rights and remedies provided in such title VIII, through such appropriate judicial or administrative proceedings (including informal methods of conference, conciliation, and persuasion) as are available therefor; and

   (2) education and outreach programs designed to inform the public concerning rights and obligations under the laws referred to in paragraph (1).

(b) Private enforcement initiatives

(1) In general

The Secretary shall use funds made available under this subsection to conduct, through contracts with private nonprofit fair housing enforcement organizations, investigations of violations of the rights granted under title VIII of the Civil Rights Act of 1968 [42 U.S.C. 3601 et seq.], and such enforcement activities as appropriate to remedy such violations. The Secretary may enter into multiyear contracts and take such other action as is appropriate to enhance the effectiveness of such investigations and enforcement activities.

(2) Activities

The Secretary shall use funds made available under this subsection to conduct, through contracts with private nonprofit fair housing enforcement organizations, a range of investigative and enforcement activities designed to—

   (A) carry out testing and other investigative activities in accordance with subsection (b)(1) of this section, including building the capacity for housing investigative activities in unserved or underserved areas;

   (B) discover and remedy discrimination in the public and private real estate markets and real estate-related transactions, including, but not limited to, the making or purchasing of loans or the provision of other financial assistance sales and rentals of housing and housing advertising;

   (C) carry out special projects, including the development of prototypes to respond to new or sophisticated forms of discrimination against persons protected under title VIII of the Civil Rights Act of 1968 [42 U.S.C. 3601 et seq.];

   (D) provide technical assistance to local fair housing organizations, and assist in the formation and development of new fair housing organization; and

   (E) provide funds for the costs and expenses of litigation, including expert witness fees.

(c) Funding of fair housing organizations

(1) In general

The Secretary shall use funds made available under this section to enter into contracts or cooperative agreements with qualified fair housing enforcement organizations, other private nonprofit fair housing enforcement organizations, and nonprofit groups organizing to build their capacity to provide fair housing enforcement, for the purpose of supporting the continued development or implementation of initiatives which enforce the rights granted under title VIII of the Civil Rights Act of 1968 [42 U.S.C. 3601 et seq.], as amended. Contracts or cooperative agreements may not provide more than 50 percent of the operating budget of the recipient organization for any one year.

(2) Capacity enhancement

The Secretary shall use funds made available under this section to help establish, organize, and build the capacity of fair housing enforcement organizations, particularly in those areas of the country which are currently underserved by fair housing enforcement organizations as well as those areas where large concentrations of protected classes exist. For purposes of meeting the objectives of this paragraph, the Secretary may enter into contracts or cooperative agreements with qualified fair housing enforcement organizations. The Secretary shall establish annual goals which reflect the national need for private fair housing enforcement organizations.

(d) Education and outreach

(1) In general

The Secretary, through contracts with one or more qualified fair housing enforcement organizations, other fair housing enforcement organizations, and other nonprofit organizations representing groups of persons protected under title VIII of the Civil Rights Act of 1968 [42 U.S.C. 3601 et seq.], shall establish a national education and outreach program. The national program shall be designed to provide a centralized, coordinated effort for the development and dissemination of fair housing media products, including—

   (A) public service announcements, both audio and video;

   (B) television, radio and print advertisements;

   (C) posters; and

   (D) pamphlets and brochures.

The Secretary shall designate a portion of the amounts provided in subsection (g)(4) of this section for a national program specifically for activities related to the annual national fair housing month. The Secretary shall encourage cooperation with real estate industry organizations in the national education and outreach program. The Secretary shall also encourage the dissemination of educational information and technical assistance to support compliance with the housing adaptability and accessibility guidelines contained in the Fair Housing Act Amendments of 1988.

(2) Regional and local programs

The Secretary, through contracts with fair housing enforcement organizations, other nonprofit organizations representing groups of persons protected under title VIII of the Civil Rights Act of 1968 [42 U.S.C. 3601 et seq.], State and local agencies certified by the Secretary under section 810(f) of the Fair Housing Act [42 U.S.C. 3610(f)], or other public or private entities that are formulating or carrying out programs to prevent or eliminate discriminatory housing practices, shall establish or support education and outreach programs at the regional and local levels.

(3) Community-based programs

The Secretary shall provide funding to fair housing organizations and other nonprofit organizations representing groups of persons protected under title VIII of the Civil Rights Act of 1968 [42 U.S.C. 3601 et seq.], or other public or private entities that are formulating or carrying out programs to prevent or eliminate discriminatory housing practices, to support community-based education and outreach activities, including school, church, and community presentations, conferences, and other educational activities.

(e) Program administration

(1) Not less than 30 days before providing a grant or entering into any contract or cooperative agreement to carry out activities authorized by this section, the Secretary shall submit notification of such proposed grant, contract, or cooperative agreement (including a description of the geographical distribution of such contracts) to the Committee on Banking, Housing, and Urban Affairs of the Senate and the Committee on Banking, Finance and Urban Affairs of the House of Representatives.

(2) [Repealed. Pub. L. No. 104-66, Title I, § 1071(d), 109 Stat. 720 (1995)]

(f) Regulations

(1) The Secretary shall issue such regulations as may be necessary to carry out the provisions of this section.

(2) The Secretary shall, for use during the demonstration authorized in this section, establish guidelines for testing activities funded under the private enforcement initiative of the fair housing initiatives program. The purpose of such guidelines shall be to ensure that investigations in support of fair housing enforcement efforts described in subsection (a)(1) of this section shall develop credible and objective evidence of discriminatory housing practices. Such guidelines shall apply only to activities funded under this section, shall not be construed to limit or otherwise restrict the use of facts secured through testing not funded under this section in any legal proceeding under Federal fair housing laws, and shall not be used to restrict individuals or entities, including those participating in the fair housing initiatives program, from pursuing any right or remedy guaranteed by Federal law. Not later than 6 months after the end of the demonstration period authorized in this section, the Secretary shall submit to Congress the evaluation of the Secretary of the effectiveness of such guidelines in achieving the purposes of this section.

(3) Such regulations shall include provisions governing applications for assistance under this section, and shall require each such application to contain—

(A) a description of the assisted activities proposed to be undertaken by the applicant, together with the estimated costs and schedule for completion of such activities;

(B) a description of the experience of the applicant in formulating or carrying out programs to prevent or eliminate discriminatory housing practices;

(C) available information, including studies made by or available to the applicant, indicating the nature and extent of discriminatory housing practices occurring in the general location where the applicant proposes to conduct its assisted activities, and the relationship of such activities to such practices;

(D) an estimate of such other public or private resources as may be available to assist the proposed activities;

(E) a description of proposed procedures to be used by the applicant for monitoring conduct and evaluating results of the proposed activities; and

(F) any additional information required by the Secretary.

(4) Regulations issued under this subsection shall not become effective prior to the expiration of 90 days after the Secretary transmits such regulations, in the form such regulations are intended to be published, to the Committee on Banking, Housing, and Urban Affairs of the Senate and the Committee on Banking, Finance and Urban Affairs of the House of Representatives.

(5) The Secretary shall not obligate or expend any amount under this section before the effective date of the regulations required under this subsection.

(g) Authorization of appropriations

There are authorized to be appropriated to carry out the provisions of this section, $21,000,000 for fiscal year 1993 and $26,000,000 for fiscal year 1994, of which—

(1) not less than $3,820,000 for fiscal year 1993 and $8,500,000 for fiscal year 1994 shall be for private enforcement initiatives authorized under subsection (b) of this section, divided equally between activities specified under subsection (b)(1) of this section and those specified under subsection (b)(2) of this section;

(2) not less than $2,230,000 for fiscal year 1993 and $8,500,000 for fiscal year 1994 shall be for qualified fair housing enforcement organizations authorized under subsection (c)(1) of this section;

(3) not less than $2,010,000 for fiscal year 1993 and $4,000,000 for fiscal year 1994 shall be for the creation of new fair housing enforcement organizations authorized under subsection (c)(2) of this section; and

(4) not less than $2,540,000 for fiscal year 1993 and $5,000,000 for fiscal year 1994 shall be for education and outreach programs authorized under subsection (d) of this section, to be divided equally between activities specified under subsection (d)(1) of this section and those specified under subsections (d)(2) and (d)(3) of this section.

Any amount appropriated under this section shall remain available until expended.

(h) Qualified fair housing enforcement organization

(1) The term "qualified fair housing enforcement organization" means any organization that—

(A) is organized as a private, tax-exempt, nonprofit, charitable organization;

(B) has at least 2 years experience in complaint intake, complaint investigation, testing for fair housing violations and enforcement of meritorious claims; and

(C) is engaged in all the activities listed in paragraph (1)(B) at the time of application for assistance under this section.

An organization which is not solely engaged in fair housing enforcement activities may qualify as a qualified fair housing enforcement organization, provided that the organization is actively engaged in each of the activities listed in subparagraph (B).

(2) The term "fair housing enforcement organization" means any organization that—

(A) meets the requirements specified in paragraph (1)(A);

(B) is currently engaged in the activities specified in paragraph (1)(B);

(C) upon the receipt of funds under this section will become engaged in all of the activities specified in paragraph (1)(B); and

(D) for purposes of funding under subsection (b) of this section, has at least 1 year of experience in the activities specified in paragraph (1)(B).

(i) Prohibition on use of funds

None of the funds authorized under this section may be used by the Secretary for purposes of settling claims, satisfying judgments or fulfilling court orders in any litigation action involving either the Department or housing providers funded by the Department. None of the funds authorized under this section may be used by the Department for administrative costs.

(j) Reporting requirements

Not later than 180 days after the close of each fiscal year in which assistance under this section is furnished, the Secretary shall prepare and submit to the Congress a comprehensive report which shall contain—

(1) a description of the progress made in accomplishing the objectives of this section;

(2) a summary of all the private enforcement activities carried out under this section and the use of such funds during the preceding fiscal year;

(3) a list of all fair housing enforcement organizations funded under this section during the preceding fiscal year, identified on a State-by-State basis;

(4) a summary of all education and outreach activities funded under this section and the use of such funds during the preceding fiscal year; and

(5) any findings, conclusions, or recommendations of the Secretary as a result of the funded activities.

(Pub. L. No. 100-242, Title V, Subtitle C, § 561, 101 Stat. 1942 (1988); Pub. L. No. 101-625, Title IX, Subtitle D, § 953, 104 Stat. 4419 (1990); Pub. L. No. 102-550, Title IX, Subtitle A, § 905(b), 106 Stat. 3869 (1992); Pub. L. No. 104-66, Title I, § 1071(d), 109 Stat. 720 (1995))

§ 3617. Interference, coercion, or intimidation

It shall be unlawful to coerce, intimidate, threaten, or interfere with any person in the exercise or enjoyment of, or on account of his having exercised or enjoyed, or on account of his having aided or encouraged any other person in the exercise or enjoyment of, any right granted or protected by section 3603, 3604, 3605, or 3606 of this title.

(Pub. L. No. 90-284, Title VIII, § 817, 82 Stat. 89 (1968); renumbered § 818 and amended by Pub. L. No. 100-430, §§ 8(1), 10, 102 Stat. 1625, 1635 (1988))

§ 3618. Authorization of appropriations

There are hereby authorized to be appropriated such sums as are necessary to carry out the purposes of this subchapter.

(Pub. L. No. 90-284, Title VIII, § 818, 82 Stat. 89 (1968); renumbered § 819 by Pub. L. No. 100-430, § 8(1), 102 Stat. 1625 (1988))

§ 3619. Separability of provisions

If any provision of this subchapter or the application thereof to any person or circumstances is held invalid, the remainder of the subchapter and the application of the provision to other persons not similarly situated or to other circumstances shall not be affected thereby.

(Pub. L. No. 90-284, Title VIII, § 819, 82 Stat. 89 (1968); renumbered § 820 by Pub. L. No. 100-430, § 8(1), 102 Stat. 1625 (1988))

§ 3631. Violations; penalties

Whoever, whether or not acting under color of law, by force or threat of force willfully injures, intimidates or interferes with, or attempts to injure, intimidate or interfere with—

(a) any person because of his race, color, religion, sex, handicap (as such term is defined in section 3602 of this title), familial status (as such term is defined in section 3602 of this title), or national origin and because he is or has been selling, purchasing, renting, financing, occupying, or contracting or negotiating for the sale, purchase, rental, financing or occupation of any dwelling, or applying for or participating in any service, organization, or facility relating to the business of selling or renting dwellings; or

(b) any person because he is or has been, or in order to intimidate such person or any other person or any class of persons from—

(1) participating, without discrimination on account of race, color, religion, sex, handicap (as such term is defined in section 3602 of this title), familial status (as such term is defined in section 3602 of this title), or national origin, in any of the activities, services, organizations or facilities described in subsection (a) of this section; or

(2) affording another person or class of persons opportunity or protection so to participate; or

(c) any citizen because he is or has been, or in order to discourage such citizen or any other citizen from lawfully aiding or encouraging other persons to participate, without discrimination on account of race, color, religion, sex, handicap (as such term is defined in section 3602 of this title), familial status (as such term is defined in section 3602 of this title), or national origin, in any of the activities, services, organizations or facilities described in subsection (a) of this section, or participating lawfully in speech or peaceful assembly opposing any denial of the opportunity to so participate—

shall be fined under Title 18 or imprisoned not more than one year, or both; and if bodily injury results from the acts committed in violation of this section of if such acts include the use, attempted use, or threatened use of a dangerous weapon, explosives or fire shall by fined under Title 18 or imprisoned not more than ten years, or both; and if death results from the acts committed in violation of this section of if such acts include kidnapping or an attempt to kidnap, aggravated sexual abuse or an attempt to commit aggravated sexual abuse or an attempt to kill, shall be fined under Title 18 or imprisoned for any term of years or for life, or both.

(Pub. L. No. 90-284, Title IX, § 901, 82 Stat. 89 (1968); Pub. L. No. 93-383, Title VIII, § 808(b)(4), 88 Stat. 729 (1974); Pub. L. No. 100-430, § 9, 102 Stat. 1035 (1988); Pub. L. No. 103-322, § 320103(e), 108 Stat. 2110 (1994); Pub. L. No. 104-294, Title VI, § 604(b)(15),(27), 110 Stat. 3507, 3508 (1996))

A.3 Civil Rights Acts, 42 U.S.C. §§ 1981, 1982, 1988

§ 1981. Equal rights under the law

(a) Statement of equal rights

All persons within the jurisdiction of the United States shall have the same right in every State and Territory to make and enforce contracts, to sue, be parties, give evidence, and to the full and equal benefit of all laws and proceedings for the security of persons and property as is enjoyed by white citizens, and shall be subject to like punishment, pains, penalties, taxes, licenses, and exactions of every kind, and to no other.

(b) "Make and enforce contracts" defined

For purposes of this section, the term "make and enforce contracts" includes the making, performance, modification, and termination of contracts, and the enjoyment of all benefits, privileges, terms, and conditions of the contractual relationship.

(c) Protection against impairment

The rights protected by this section are protected against impairment by nongovernmental discrimination and impairment under color of State law.

(R.S. § 1977; Pub. L. No. 102-166, Title I, § 101, 105 Stat. 1071 (1991))

§ 1982. Property rights of citizens

All citizens of the United States shall have the same right, in every State and Territory, as is enjoyed by white citizens thereof to inherit, purchase, lease, sell, hold, and convey real and personal property.

(R.S. § 1978)

§ 1988. Proceedings in vindication of civil rights

(a) Applicability of statutory and common law

The jurisdiction in civil and criminal matters conferred on the district and circuit courts by the provisions of this Title and of Title "CIVIL RIGHTS," and of Title "CRIMES," for the protection of all persons in the United States in their civil rights, and for their vindication, shall be exercised and enforced in conformity with the laws of the United States, so far as such laws are suitable to carry the same into effect; but in all cases where they are not adapted to the object, or are deficient in the provisions necessary to furnish suitable remedies and punish offenses against law, the common law, as modified and changed by the constitution and statutes of the State wherein the court having jurisdiction of such civil or criminal cause is held, so far as the same is not inconsistent with the Constitution and laws of the United States, shall be extended to and govern the said courts in the trial and disposition of the cause, and, if it is of a criminal nature, in the infliction of punishment on the party found guilty.

(b) Attorney's fees

In any action or proceeding to enforce a provision of sections 1977, 1977A, 1978, 1979, 1980, and 1981 of the Revised Statutes [42 U.S.C. §§ 1981–83, 1985, 1986], title IX of Public Law 92-318 [20 U.S.C. § 1681 et seq.], the Religious Freedom Restoration Act of 1993 [42 U.S.C. § 2000bb et seq.], the Religious Land Use and Institutionalized Persons Act of 2000, Title VI of the Civil Rights Act of 1964 [42 U.S.C. § 2000d et seq.], or section 40302 of the Violence Against Women Act of 1994, the court, in its discretion, may allow the prevailing party, other than the United States, a reasonable attorney's fee as part of the costs, except that in any action brought against a judicial officer for an act or omission taken in such officer's judicial capacity such officer shall not be held liable for any costs, including attorney's fees, unless such action was clearly in excess of such officer's jurisdiction.

(c) Expert fees

In awarding an attorney's fee under subsection (b) of this section in any action or proceeding to enforce a provision of section 1981 or 1981a of this title, the court, in its discretion, may include expert fees as part of the attorney's fee.

(R.S. § 722; Pub. L. No. 94-559, § 2, 90 Stat. 2641 (1976); Pub. L. No. 96-481, Title II, § 205(c), 94 Stat. 2330 (1980); Pub. L. No. 102-166, Title I, §§ 103, 113(a), 105 Stat. 1074, 1079 (1991); Pub. L. No. 103-322, Title IV, Subtitle C, § 40303, 108 Stat. 1942 (1994); Pub. L. No. 104-317, Title III, § 309(b), 110 Stat. 3853 (1996); Pub. L. No. 106-274, § 4(d), 114 Stat. 804 (2000))

Federal Reserve Board Regulation B (Equal Credit Opportunity)

The full text of the current Regulation B, 12 C.F.R. Part 202, is reprinted below. In 1999, the Federal Reserve Board (FRB) issued a comprehensive set of proposed revisions to Regulation B. As of the printing of this manual, however, the FRB had not issued final rules. Therefore, the version reprinted below is the version of Regulation B currently in effect. The text of the August 1999 proposed revisions to Regulation B is included on the CD-Rom accompanying this volume.

In April 2001, the FRB published an interim final rule amending Regulation B to provide for the electronic delivery of ECOA notifications. In August 2001, the FRB rescinded the October 1, 2001, deadline for compliance with the interim final rule. As of the printing of this manual, the FRB has not issued a revised final or interim rule. The text of the interim final rule on electronic delivery is included on the CD-Rom accompanying this volume.

12 C.F.R. Part 202

§ 202.1   Authority, scope and purpose.
§ 202.2   Definitions.
§ 202.3   Limited exceptions for certain classes of transactions.
§ 202.4   General rule prohibiting discrimination.
§ 202.5   Rules concerning taking of applications.
§ 202.5a   Rules on providing appraisal reports.
§ 202.6   Rules concerning evaluation of applications.
§ 202.7   Rules concerning extensions of credit.
§ 202.8   Special purpose credit programs.
§ 202.9   Notifications.
§ 202.10   Furnishing of credit information.
§ 202.11   Relation to state law.
§ 202.12   Record retention.
§ 202.13   Information for monitoring purposes.
§ 202.14   Enforcement, penalties and liabilities.
§ 202.15   Incentives for self-testing and self-correction.
Appendix A to Part 202—Federal Enforcement Agencies
Appendix B to Part 202—Model Application Forms
Appendix C to Part 202—Sample Notification Forms
Appendix D to Part 202—Issuance of Staff Interpretations

AUTHORITY: 15 U.S.C. 1691–1691f.

SOURCE: Reg. B, 50 FR 48026, Nov. 20, 1985, unless otherwise noted.

§ 202.1 Authority, scope and purpose.

(a) *Authority and scope.* This regulation is issued by the Board of Governors of the Federal Reserve System pursuant to title VII (Equal Credit Opportunity Act) of the Consumer Credit Protection Act, as amended (15 USC 1601 et seq.). Except as otherwise provided herein, the regulation applies to all persons who are creditors, as defined in § 202.2(*l*). Information collection requirements contained in this regulation have been approved by the Office of Management and Budget under the provisions of 44 USC 3501 et seq. and have been assigned OMB No. 7100-0201.

(b) *Purpose.* The purpose of this regulation is to promote the availability of credit to all creditworthy applicants without regard to race, color, religion, national origin, sex, marital status, or age (provided the applicant has the capacity to contract); to the fact that all or part of the applicant's income derives from a public assistance program; or to the fact that the applicant has in good faith exercised any right under the Consumer Credit Protection Act. The regulation prohibits creditor practices that discriminate on the basis of any of these factors. The regulation also requires creditors to notify applicants of action taken on their applications; to report credit history in the names of both spouses on an account; to retain records of credit applications; to collect information about the applicant's race and other personal characteristics in applications for certain dwelling-related loans; and to provide applicants with copies of appraisal reports used in connection with credit transactions.

[Reg. B, 50 FR 48026, Nov. 20, 1985, amended by 58 FR 65661, Dec. 16, 1993]

§ 202.2 Definitions.

For the purposes of this regulation, unless the context indicates otherwise, the following definitions apply.

(a) *Account* means an extension of credit. When employed in relation to an account, the word *use* refers only to open-end credit.

(b) *Act* means the Equal Credit Opportunity Act (title VII of the Consumer Credit Protection Act).

(c) *Adverse action.*

(1) The term means:

(i) A refusal to grant credit in substantially the amount or on substantially the terms requested in an application unless the creditor makes a counteroffer (to grant credit in a different amount or on other terms) and the applicant uses or expressly accepts the credit offered;

(ii) A termination of an account or an unfavorable change in the terms of an account that does not affect all or a substantial portion of a class of the creditor's accounts; or

(iii) A refusal to increase the amount of credit available to an applicant who has made an application for an increase.

(2) The term does not include:

(i) A change in the terms of an account expressly agreed to by an applicant.

(ii) Any action or forbearance relating to an account taken in connection with inactivity, default, or delinquency as to that account;

(iii) A refusal or failure to authorize an account transaction at a point of sale or loan, except when the refusal is a termination or an unfavorable change in the terms of an account that does not affect all or a substantial portion of a class of the creditor's accounts, or when the refusal is a denial of an application for an increase in the amount of credit available under the account;

(iv) A refusal to extend credit because applicable law prohibits the creditor from extending the credit requested; or

(v) A refusal to extend credit because the creditor does not offer the type of credit or credit plan requested.

(3) An action that falls within the definition of both paragraphs (c)(1) and (c)(2) of this section is governed by paragraph (c)(2).

(d) *Age* refers only to the age of natural persons and means the number of fully elapsed years from the date of an applicant's birth.

(e) *Applicant* means any person who requests or who has received an extension of credit from a creditor, and includes any person who is or may become contractually liable regarding an extension of credit. For purposes of § 202.7(d), the term includes guarantors, sureties, endorsers and similar parties.

(f) *Application* means an oral or written request for an extension of credit that is made in accordance with procedures established by a creditor for the type of credit requested. The term does not include the use of an account or line of credit to obtain an amount of credit that is within a previously established credit limit. A *completed application* means an application in connection with which a creditor has received all the information that the creditor regularly obtains and considers in evaluating applications for the amount and type of credit requested (including, but not limited to, credit reports, any additional information requested from the applicant, and any approvals or reports by governmental agencies or other persons that are necessary to guarantee, insure, or provide security for the credit or collateral). The creditor shall exercise reasonable diligence in obtaining such information.

(g) *Business credit** refers to extensions of credit primarily for

business or commercial (including agricultural) purposes, but excluding extensions of credit of the types described in § 202.3 (a), (b), and (d).

(h) *Consumer credit* means credit extended to a natural person primarily for personal, family, or household purposes.

(i) *Contractually liable* means expressly obligated to repay all debts arising on an account by reason of an agreement to that effect.

(j) *Credit* means the right granted by a creditor to an applicant to defer payment of a debt, incur debt and defer its payment, or purchase property or services and defer payment therefor.

(k) *Credit card* means any card, plate, coupon book, or other single credit device that may be used from time to time to obtain money, property, or services on credit.

(l) *Creditor* means a person who, in the ordinary course of business, regularly participates in the decision of whether or not to extend credit. The term includes a creditor's assignee, transferee, or subrogee who so participates. For purposes of §§ 202.4 and 202.5(a), the term also includes a person who, in the ordinary course of business, regularly refers applicants or prospective applicants to creditors, or selects or offers to select creditors to whom requests for credit may be made. A person is not a creditor regarding any violation of the act or this regulation committed by another creditor unless the person knew or had reasonable notice of the act, policy, or practice that constituted the violation before becoming involved in the credit transaction. The term does not include a person whose only participation in a credit transaction involves honoring a credit card.

(m) *Credit transaction* means every aspect of an applicant's dealings with a creditor regarding an application for credit or an existing extension of credit (including, but not limited to, information requirements; investigation procedures; standards of creditworthiness; terms of credit; furnishing of credit information; revocation, alteration, or termination of credit; and collection procedures).

(n) *Discriminate against an applicant* means to treat an applicant less favorably than other applicants.

(o) *Elderly* means age 62 or older.

(p) *Empirically derived and other credit scoring systems.*

(1) A *credit scoring system* is a system that evaluates an applicant's creditworthiness mechanically, based on key attributes of the applicant and aspects of the transaction, and that determines, alone or in conjunction with an evaluation of additional information about the applicant, whether an applicant is deemed creditworthy. To qualify as an *empirically derived, demonstrably and statistically sound, credit scoring system*, the system must be:

---

* [*Editor's note:* In 1989 the Federal Reserve Board amended § 202.2(g) to implement amendments to the ECOA contained in

the Women's Business Ownership Act. The Board's explanation of this revision, reprinted from the Supplementary Information published in the Federal Register along with the amendments, follows:

The definition of business credit previously contained in § 202.3(d)(1) has been moved to § 202.2 (Definitions), paragraph 2(g). The definition of "Board," previously contained in § 202.2(g), has been removed to avoid the need to renumber succeeding paragraphs. As used in the regulation, the term Board means the Board of Governors of the Federal Reserve System.

54 Fed. Reg. 50,482 (Dec. 7, 1989).]

(i) Based on data that are derived from an empirical comparison of sample groups or the population of creditworthy and noncreditworthy applicants who applied for credit within a reasonable preceding period of time;

(ii) Developed for the purpose of evaluating the creditworthiness of applicants with respect to the legitimate business interests of the creditor utilizing the system (including, but not limited to, minimizing bad debt losses and operating expenses in accordance with the creditor's business judgment);

(iii) Developed and validated using accepted statistical principles and methodology; and

(iv) Periodically revalidated by the use of appropriate statistical principles and methodology and adjusted as necessary to maintain predictive ability.

(2) A creditor may use an empirically derived, demonstrably and statistically sound, credit scoring system obtained from another person or may obtain credit experience from which to develop such a system. Any such system must satisfy the criteria set forth in paragraphs (p)(1) (i) through (iv) of this section; if the creditor is unable during the development process to validate the system based on its own credit experience in accordance with paragraph (p)(1) of this section, the system must be validated when sufficient credit experience becomes available. A system that fails this validity test is no longer an empirically derived, demonstrably and statistically sound, credit scoring system for that creditor.

(q) *Extend credit* and *extension of credit* mean the granting of credit in any form (including, but not limited to, credit granted in addition to any existing credit or credit limit; credit granted pursuant to an open-end credit plan; the refinancing or other renewal of credit, including the issuance of a new credit card in place of an expiring credit card or in substitution for an existing credit card; the consolidation of two or more obligations; or the continuance of existing credit without any special effort to collect at or after maturity).

(r) *Good faith* means honesty in fact in the conduct or transaction.

(s) *Inadvertent error* means a mechanical, electronic, or clerical error that a creditor demonstrates was not intentional and occurred notwithstanding the maintenance of procedures reasonably adapted to avoid such errors.

(t) *Judgmental system of evaluating applicants* means any system for evaluating the creditworthiness of an applicant other than an empirically derived, demonstrably and statistically sound, credit scoring system.

(u) *Marital status* means the state of being unmarried, married, or separated, as defined by applicable state law. The term "unmarried" includes persons who are single, divorced, or widowed.

(v) *Negative factor or value*, in relation to the age of elderly applicants, means utilizing a factor, value, or weight that is less favorable regarding elderly applicants than the creditor's experience warrants or is less favorable than the factor, value, or weight assigned to the class of applicants that are not classified as elderly and are most favored by a creditor on the basis of age.

(w) *Open-end credit* means credit extended under a plan under which a creditor may permit an applicant to make purchases or obtain loans from time to time directly from the creditor or indirectly by use of a credit card, check, or other device.

(x) *Person* means a natural person, corporation, government or governmental subdivision or agency, trust, estate, partnership, cooperative, or association.

(y) *Pertinent element of creditworthiness*, in relation to a judgmental system of evaluating applicants, means any information about applicants that a creditor obtains and considers and that has a demonstrable relationship to a determination of creditworthiness.

(z) *Prohibited basis* means race, color, religion, national origin, sex, marital status, or age (provided that the applicant has the capacity to enter into a binding contract); the fact that all or part of the applicant's income derives from any public assistance program; or the fact that the applicant has in good faith exercised any right under the Consumer Credit Protection Act or any state law upon which an exemption has been granted by the Board.

(aa) *State* means any State, the District of Columbia, the Commonwealth of Puerto Rico, or any territory or possession of the United States.

[Reg. B, 50 FR 48026, Nov. 20, 1985, amended at 54 FR 50485, Dec. 7, 1989]

§ 202.3 Limited exceptions for certain classes of transactions.**

(a) *Public utilities credit.*

** [*Editor's note:* In 1989 the Federal Reserve Board amended § 202.3(a)–(d) to implement amendments to the ECOA contained in the Women's Business Ownership Act. The Board's explanation of these revisions, reprinted from the Supplementary Information published in the Federal Register along with the amendments, follows:

In addition to business credit, Regulation B provides exceptions from certain provisions for credit extensions involving public utility services; credit extensions subject to regulation under the Securities Exchange Act; credit payable in four or fewer installments, in which no credit card is used and no finance charge is imposed ("incidental credit"); and extensions of credit to federal and state governments. In the July proposal, the Board solicited comment on the appropriateness of retaining the special rules for these classes of transactions. Except in the case of incidental credit, the Board received no unfavorable comment. The final rule retains the current exceptions in § 202.3 of the regulation for all four categories without change, except that the government credit exception has been redesignated § 202.3(d).

The Board believes that the limited exceptions remain appropriate. The exceptions for public utilities credit are minimal and relate to marital status inquiries, reporting credit information to third parties, and record retention. Public utilities credit is subject to most of the regulatory requirements including, for example, the rules governing information that may be considered in evaluating applications and the rules for notifying applicants of credit denials. Securities credit is subject to the Securities Exchange Act of 1934 which continues to impose duties upon securities brokers and dealers to ascertain certain information about business entities and individuals applying for credit, such as legal relationships and the types of ownership interest in property. Therefore, the Board believes that the exceptions from Regulation B's restrictions (on inquiries about spouses and marital status and on obtaining the signatures of guarantors and cosigners) remain appropriate. Extension of credit to governments or governmental subdivisions are subject to the general rule barring unlawful credit discrimination; the costs of compliance clearly outweigh any protections that might be afforded by applying all of the other ECOA requirements.

One commenter opposed the incidental credit exception on the ground that consumers are not receiving the full protections of the act because some retail sellers deliberately structure financing arrangements to fall within the exception. Notwithstanding this comment, the credit transactions to which the exception applies are largely incidental to some other activity (such as the providing of health care or other professional services) where the creditor extends credit as an accommodation to the consumer and is not in the business of extending credit.

Business credit exceptions

The provisions of paragraph (d) on business credit have been moved to other sections or eliminated as discussed below. Paragraph (e) on credit to governments has been redesignated paragraph (d).

Former paragraph (d)(1) containing the definition of business credit has been moved to § 202.2(g). Former paragraph (d)(2) contained exceptions for all business credit transactions relating to marital status inquiries and credit reporting; the final rule eliminates both exceptions as discussed below. The substance of the rules in paragraph (d)(3) notifications is now in § 202.9(a)(3)(ii). The substance of the rules on record retention in that paragraph is now in § 202.12(b)(5).

The final rule prohibits creditors from inquiring about the marital status of a business credit applicant for unsecured credit. The regulation permits creditors to inquire about marital status if an applicant resides in a community property state or relies on property located in such a state to repay a debt, or applies for secured credit. A few commenters expressed concern that not knowing the marital status of an applicant for unsecured business credit, particularly in the case of a sole proprietor, would adversely affect the creditor's ability to determine ownership rights in property held by the applicant. The prohibition on marital status inquiries, however, does not impair a creditor's ability to inquire about ownership rights in, or the name of any co-owner of, property relied upon by a credit applicant to satisfy a debt in the event of default. (*See generally* § 202.5(d)(1) and accompanying commentary.)

The final rule deletes an exception for business credit from § 202.10 regarding the reporting of credit information for joint accounts held by spouses. Some commenters expressed concern that eliminating the exception might lead to confusion about whether the reporting requirements apply to the business accounts of sole proprietors. Section 202.10 was designed to remedy a situation related to consumer credit accounts, where credit histories used to be reported only

(1) *Definition.* Public utilities credit refers to extensions of credit that involve public utility services provided through pipe, wire, or other connected facilities, or radio or similar transmission (including extensions of such facilities), if the charges for service, delayed payment, and any discount for prompt payment are filed with or regulated by a government unit.

(2) *Exceptions.* The following provisions of this regulation do not apply to public utilities credit:
  (i) Section 202.5(d)(1) concerning information about marital status;
  (ii) Section 202.10 relating to furnishing of credit information; and
  (iii) Section 202.12(b) relating to record retention.

(b) *Securities credit.*

(1) *Definition.* Securities credit refers to extensions of credit subject to regulation under section 7 of the Securities Exchange Act of 1934 or extensions of credit by a broker or dealer subject to regulation as a broker or dealer under the Securities Exchange Act of 1934.

(2) *Exceptions.* The following provisions of this regulation do not apply to securities credit:
  (i) Section 202.5(c) concerning information about a spouse or former spouse;
  (ii) Section 202.5(d)(1) concerning information about marital status;
  (iii) Section 202.5(d)(3) concerning information about the sex of an applicant;
  (iv) Section 202.7(b) relating to designation of name, but only to the extent necessary to prevent violation of rules regarding an account in which a broker or dealer has an interest, or rules necessitating the aggregation of accounts of spouses for the purpose of determining controlling interests, beneficial interests, beneficial ownership, or purchase limitations and restrictions;
  (v) Section 202.7(c) relating to action concerning open-end accounts, but only to the extent the action taken is on the basis of a change of name or marital status;
  (vi) Section 202.7(d) relating to the signature of a spouse or other person;
  (vii) Section 202.10 relating to furnishing of credit information; and
  (viii) Section 202.12(b) relating to record retention.

(c) *Incidental credit.*

(1) *Definition.* Incidental credit refers to extensions of consumer credit other than credit of the types described in paragraphs (a) and (b) of this section:
  (i) That are not made pursuant to the terms of a credit card account;

---

in the husband's name and, as a consequence, married women who become divorced or widowed were left without a credit history. The provision is not relevant to business applicants such as corporations or partnerships, nor is it intended to apply to individual business applicants such as sole proprietors. Consequently, as a technical matter, no specific exception is necessary. Nevertheless, to address any possible ambiguity, the Board's official staff commentary to Regulation B will make clear that the credit reporting rules apply only to consumer accounts.

54 Fed. Reg. 50,482 (Dec. 7, 1989).]

(ii) That are not subject to a finance charge (as defined in Regulation Z, 12 CFR 226.4); and

(iii) That are not payable by agreement in more than four installments.

(2) *Exceptions.* The following provisions of this regulation do not apply to incidental credit:

  (i) Section 202.5(c) concerning information about a spouse or former spouse;

  (ii) Section 202.5(d)(1) concerning information about marital status;

  (iii) Section 202.5(d)(2) concerning information about income derived from alimony, child support, or separate maintenance payments;

  (iv) Section 202.5(d)(3) concerning information about the sex of an applicant, but only to the extent necessary for medical records or similar purposes;

  (v) Section 202.7(d) relating to the signature of a spouse or other person;

  (vi) Section 202.9 relating to notifications;

  (vii) Section 202.10 relating to furnishing of credit information; and

  (viii) Section 202.12(b) relating to record retention.

(d) *Government credit.*

(1) *Definition.* Government credit refers to extensions of credit made to governments or governmental subdivisions, agencies, or instrumentalities.

(2) *Applicability of regulation.* Except for § 202.4, the general rule prohibiting discrimination on a prohibited basis, the requirements of this regulation do not apply to government credit.

[Reg. B, 50 FR 48026, Nov. 20, 1985, amended by 54 FR 50485, Dec. 7, 1989]

§ 202.4 General rule prohibiting discrimination.

A creditor shall not discriminate against an applicant on a prohibited basis regarding any aspect of a credit transaction.

§ 202.5 Rules concerning taking of applications.

(a) *Discouraging applications.* A creditor shall not make any oral or written statement, in advertising or otherwise, to applicants or prospective applicants that would discourage on a prohibited basis a reasonable person from making or pursuing an application.

(b) *General rules concerning requests for information.*

(1) Except as provided in paragraphs (c) and (d) of this section, a creditor may request any information in connection with an application.[1]

(2) *Required collection of information.* Notwithstanding paragraphs (c) and (d) of this section, a creditor shall request information for monitoring purposes as required by § 202.13 for credit secured by the applicant's dwelling. In addition, a creditor may obtain information required by a regulation, order, or agreement issued by, or entered into

with, a court or an enforcement agency (including the Attorney General of the United States or a similar state official) to monitor or enforce compliance with the act, this regulation, or other federal or state statute or regulation.

(3) *Special purpose credit.* A creditor may obtain information that is otherwise restricted to determine eligibility for a special purpose credit program, as provided in § 202.8 (c) and (d).

(c) *Information about a spouse or former spouse.*

(1) Except as permitted in this paragraph, a creditor may not request any information concerning the spouse or former spouse of an applicant.

(2) *Permissible inquiries.* A creditor may request any information concerning an applicant's spouse (or former spouse under paragraph (c)(2)(v)) that may be requested about the applicant if:

  (i) The spouse will be permitted to use the account;

  (ii) The spouse will be contractually liable on the account;

  (iii) The applicant is relying on the spouse's income as a basis for repayment of the credit requested;

  (iv) The applicant resides in a community property state or property on which the applicant is relying as a basis for repayment of the credit requested is located in such a state; or

  (v) The applicant is relying on alimony, child support, or separate maintenance payments from a spouse or former spouse as a basis for repayment of the credit requested.

(3) *Other accounts of the applicant.* A creditor may request an applicant to list any account upon which the applicant is liable and to provide the name and address in which the account is carried. A creditor may also ask the names in which an applicant has previously received credit.

(d) *Other limitations on information requests.*

(1) *Marital status.* If an applicant applies for individual unsecured credit, a creditor shall not inquire about the applicant's marital status unless the applicant resides in a community property state or is relying on property located in such a state as a basis for repayment of the credit requested. If an application is for other than individual unsecured credit, a creditor may inquire about the applicant's marital status, but shall use only the terms "married," "unmarried," and "separated." A creditor may explain that the category "unmarried" includes single, divorced, and widowed persons.

(2) *Disclosure about income from alimony, child support, or separate maintenance.* A creditor shall not inquire whether income stated in an application is derived from alimony, child support, or separate maintenance payments unless the creditor discloses to the applicant that such income need not be revealed if the applicant does not want the creditor to consider it in determining the applicant's creditworthiness.

(3) *Sex.* A creditor shall not inquire about the sex of an applicant. An applicant may be requested to designate a title on an application form (such as Ms., Miss, Mr., or Mrs.) if the form discloses that the designation of a title is optional. An application form shall otherwise use only terms that are neutral as to sex.

(4) *Childbearing, childrearing.* A creditor shall not inquire about birth control practices, intentions concerning the bear-

---

1 This paragraph does not limit or abrogate any federal or state law regarding privacy, privileged information, credit reporting limitations, or similar restrictions on obtainable information.

ing or rearing of children, or capability to bear children. A creditor may inquire about the number and ages of an applicant's dependents or about dependent-related financial obligations or expenditures, provided such information is requested without regard to sex, marital status, or any other prohibited basis.

(5) *Race, color, religion, national origin.* A creditor shall not inquire about the race, color, religion, or national origin of an applicant or any other person in connection with a credit transaction. A creditor may inquire about an applicant's permanent residence and immigration status.

(e) *Written applications.* A creditor shall take written applications for the types of credit covered by § 202.13(a), but need not take written applications for other types of credit.

§ 202.5a Rules on providing appraisal reports.

(a) *Providing appraisals.* A creditor shall provide a copy of the appraisal report used in connection with an application for credit that is to be secured by a lien on a dwelling. A creditor shall comply with either paragraph (a)(1) or (a)(2) of this section.

(1) *Routine delivery.* A creditor may routinely provide a copy of the appraisal report to an applicant (whether credit is granted or denied or the application is withdrawn).

(2) *Upon request.* A creditor that does not routinely provide appraisal reports shall provide a copy upon an applicant's written request.

(i) *Notice.* A creditor that provides appraisal reports only upon request shall notify an applicant in writing of the right to receive a copy of an appraisal report. The notice may be given at any time during the application process but no later than when the creditor provides notice of action taken under § 202.9 of this part. The notice shall specify that the applicant's request must be in writing, give the creditor's mailing address, and state the time for making request as provided in paragraph (a)(2)(ii) of this section.

(ii) *Delivery.* A creditor shall mail or deliver a copy of the appraisal report promptly (generally within 30 days) after the creditor receives an applicant's request, receives the report, or receives reimbursement from the applicant for the report, whichever is last to occur. A creditor need not provide a copy when the applicant's request is received more than 90 days after the creditor has provided notice of action taken on the application under § 202.9 of this part or 90 days after the application is withdrawn.

(b) *Credit Unions.* A creditor that is subject to the regulations of the National Credit Union Administration on making copies of appraisals available is not subject to this section.

(c) *Definitions.* For purposes of paragraph (a) of this section, the term *dwelling* means a residential structure that contains one to four units whether or not that structure is attached to real property. The term includes, but is not limited to, an individual condominium or cooperative unit, and a mobile or other manufactured home. The term *appraisal report* means the document(s) relied upon by a creditor in evaluating the value of the dwelling.

[58 FR 65657, Dec. 16. 1993]

§ 202.6 Rules concerning evaluation of applications.

(a) *General rule concerning use of information.* Except as otherwise provided in the Act and this regulation, a creditor may consider any information obtained, so long as the information is not used to discriminate against an applicant on a prohibited basis.[2]

(b) *Specific rules concerning use of information.*

(1) Except as provided in the act and this regulation, a creditor shall not take a prohibited basis into account in any system of evaluating the creditworthiness of applicants.

(2) *Age, receipt of public assistance.*

(i) Except as permitted in this paragraph (b)(2), a creditor shall not take into account an applicant's age (provided that the applicant has the capacity to enter into a binding contract) or whether an applicant's income derives from any public assistance program.

(ii) In an empirically derived, demonstrably and statistically sound, credit scoring system, a creditor may use an applicant's age as a predictive variable, provided that the age of an elderly applicant is not assigned a negative factor or value.

(iii) In a judgmental system of evaluating creditworthiness, a creditor may consider an applicant's age or whether an applicant's income derives from any public assistance program only for the purpose of determining a pertinent element of creditworthiness.

(iv) In any system of evaluating creditworthiness, a creditor may consider the age of an elderly applicant when such age is used to favor the elderly applicant in extending credit.

(3) *Childbearing, childrearing.* In evaluating creditworthiness, a creditor shall not use assumptions or aggregate statistics relating to the likelihood that any group of persons will bear or rear children or will, for that reason, receive diminished or interrupted income in the future.

(4) *Telephone listing.* A creditor shall not take into account whether there is a telephone listing in the name of an applicant for consumer credit, but may take into account whether there is a telephone in the applicant's residence.

(5) *Income.* A creditor shall not discount or exclude from consideration the income of an applicant or the spouse of an applicant because of a prohibited basis or because the income is derived from part-time employment or is an annuity, pension, or other retirement benefit; a creditor may consider the amount and probable continuance of any income in evaluating an applicant's creditworthiness. When an applicant relies on alimony, child support, or separate maintenance payments in applying for credit, the creditor shall consider such payments as income to the extent that they are likely to be consistently made.

(6) *Credit history.* To the extent that a creditor considers credit history in evaluating the creditworthiness of similarly quali-

---

2 The legislative history of the Act indicates that the Congress intended an "effects test" concept, as outlined in the employment field by the Supreme Court in the cases of *Griggs* v. *Duke Power Co.*, 401 U.S. 424 (1971), and *Albemarle Paper Co.* v. *Moody*, 422 U.S. 405 (1975), to be applicable to a creditor's determination of creditworthiness.

fied applicants for a similar type and amount of credit, in evaluating an applicant's creditworthiness a creditor shall consider:

(i) The credit history, when available, of accounts designated as accounts that the applicant and the applicant's spouse are permitted to use or for which both are contractually liable;

(ii) On the applicant's request, any information the applicant may present that tends to indicate that the credit history being considered by the creditor does not accurately reflect the applicant's creditworthiness; and

(iii) On the applicant's request, the credit history, when available, of any account reported in the name of the applicant's spouse or former spouse that the applicant can demonstrate accurately reflects the applicant's creditworthiness.

(7) *Immigration status.* A creditor may consider whether an applicant is a permanent resident of the United States, the applicant's immigration status, and any additional information that may be necessary to ascertain the creditor's rights and remedies regarding repayment.

(c) *State property laws.* A creditor's consideration or application of state property laws directly or indirectly affecting creditworthiness does not constitute unlawful discrimination for the purposes of the Act or this regulation.

§ 202.7 Rules concerning extensions of credit.

(a) *Individual accounts.* A creditor shall not refuse to grant an individual account to a creditworthy applicant on the basis of sex, marital status, or any other prohibited basis.

(b) *Designation of name.* A creditor shall not refuse to allow an applicant to open or maintain an account in a birth-given first name and a surname that is the applicant's birth-given surname, the spouse's surname, or a combined surname.

(c) *Action concerning existing open-end accounts.*

(1) *Limitations.* In the absence of evidence of the applicant's inability or unwillingness to repay, a creditor shall not take any of the following actions regarding an applicant who is contractually liable on an existing open-end account on the basis of the applicant's reaching a certain age or retiring or on the basis of a change in the applicant's name or marital status:

(i) Require a reapplication, except as provided in paragraph (c)(2) of this section;

(ii) Change the terms of the account; or

(iii) Terminate the account.

(2) *Requiring reapplication.* A creditor may require a reapplication for an open-end account on the basis of a change in the marital status of an applicant who is contractually liable if the credit granted was based in whole or in part on income of the applicant's spouse and if information available to the creditor indicates that the applicant's income may not support the amount of credit currently available.

(d) *Signature of spouse or other person.*

(1) *Rule for qualified applicant.* Except as provided in this paragraph, a creditor shall not require the signature of an applicant's spouse or other person, other than a joint applicant, on any credit instrument if the applicant qualifies

under the creditor's standards of creditworthiness for the amount and terms of the credit requested.

(2) *Unsecured credit.* If an applicant requests unsecured credit and relies in part upon property that the applicant owns jointly with another person to satisfy the creditor's standards of creditworthiness, the creditor may require the signature of the other person only on the instrument(s) necessary, or reasonably believed by the creditor to be necessary, under the law of the state in which the property is located, to enable the creditor to reach the property being relied upon in the event of the death or default of the applicant.

(3) *Unsecured credit—community property states.* If a married applicant requests unsecured credit and resides in a community property state, or if the property upon which the applicant is relying is located in such a state, a creditor may require the signature of the spouse on any instrument necessary, or reasonably believed by the creditor to be necessary, under applicable state law to make the community property available to satisfy the debt in the event of default if:

(i) Applicable state law denies the applicant power to manage or control sufficient community property to qualify for the amount of credit requested under the creditor's standards of creditworthiness; and

(ii) The applicant does not have sufficient separate property to qualify for the amount of credit requested without regard to community property.

(4) *Secured credit.* If an applicant requests secured credit, a creditor may require the signature of the applicant's spouse or other person on any instrument necessary, or reasonably believed by the creditor to be necessary, under applicable state law to make the property being offered as security available to satisfy the debt in the event of default, for example, an instrument to create a valid lien, pass clear title, waive inchoate rights or assign earnings.

(5) *Additional parties.* If, under a creditor's standards of creditworthiness, the personal liability of an additional party is necessary to support the extension of the credit requested, a creditor may request a cosigner, guarantor, or the like. The applicant's spouse may serve as an additional party, but the creditor shall not require that the spouse be the additional party.

(6) *Rights of additional parties.* A creditor shall not impose requirements upon an additional party that the creditor is prohibited from imposing upon an applicant under this section.

(e) *Insurance.* A creditor shall not refuse to extend credit and shall not terminate an account because credit life, health, accident, disability, or other credit-related insurance is not available on the basis of the applicant's age.

§ 202.8 Special purpose credit programs.

(a) *Standards for programs.* Subject to the provisions of paragraph (b) of this section, the act and this regulation permit a creditor to extend special purpose credit to applicants who meet eligibility requirements under the following types of credit programs:

(1) Any credit assistance program expressly authorized by federal or state law for the benefit of an economically disadvantaged class of persons;

(2) Any credit assistance program offered by a not-for-profit organization, as defined under section 501(c) of the Internal Revenue Code of 1954, as amended, for the benefit of its members or for the benefit of an economically disadvantaged class of persons; or

(3) Any special purpose credit program offered by a for-profit organization or in which such an organization participates to meet special social needs, if:

(i) The program is established and administered pursuant to a written plan that identifies the class of persons that the program is designed to benefit and sets forth the procedures and standards for extending credit pursuant to the program; and

(ii) The program is established and administered to extend credit to a class of persons who, under the organization's customary standards of creditworthiness, probably would not receive such credit or would receive it on less favorable terms than are ordinarily available to other applicants applying to the organization for a similar type and amount of credit.

(b) *Rules in other sections.*

(1) *General applicability.* All of the provisions of this regulation apply to each of the special purpose credit programs described in paragraph (a) of this section unless modified by this section.

(2) *Common characteristics.* A program described in paragraph (a)(2) or (a)(3) of this section qualifies as a special purpose credit program only if it was established and is administered so as not to discriminate against an applicant on any prohibited basis; however, all program participants may be required to share one or more common characteristics (for example, race, national origin, or sex) so long as the program was not established and is not administered with the purpose of evading the requirements of the act or this regulation.

(c) *Special rule concerning requests and use of information.* If participants in a special purpose credit program described in paragraph (a) of this section are required to possess one or more common characteristics (for example, race, national origin, or sex) and if the program otherwise satisfies the requirements of paragraph (a) of this section, a creditor may request and consider information regarding the common characteristic(s) in determining the applicant's eligibility for the program.

(d) *Special rule in the case of financial need.* If financial need is one of the criteria under a special purpose program described in paragraph (a) of this section, the creditor may request and consider, in determining an applicant's eligibility for the program, information regarding the applicant's martial [sic] status; alimony, child support, and separate maintenance income; and the spouse's financial resources. In addition, a creditor may obtain the signature of an applicant's spouse or other person on an application or credit instrument relating to a special purpose program if the signature is required by Federal or State law.

§ 202.9 Notifications.

(a) *Notification of action taken, ECOA notice, and statement of specific reasons.*

(1) *When notification is required.* A creditor shall notify an applicant of action taken within:

(i) 30 days after receiving a completed application concerning the creditor's approval of, counteroffer to, or adverse action on the application;

(ii) 30 days after taking adverse action on an incomplete application, unless notice is provided in accordance with paragraph (c) of this section;

(iii) 30 days after taking adverse action on an existing account; or

(iv) 90 days after notifying the applicant of a counteroffer if the applicant does not expressly accept or use the credit offered.

(2) *Content of notification when adverse action is taken.* A notification given to an applicant when adverse action is taken shall be in writing and shall contain: a statement of the action taken; the name and address of the creditor; a statement of the provisions of section 701(a) of the Act; the name and address of the Federal agency that administers compliance with respect to the creditor; and either:

(i) A statement of specific reasons for the action taken; or

(ii) A disclosure of the applicant's right to a statement of specific reasons within 30 days, if the statement is requested within 60 days of the creditor's notification. The disclosure shall include the name, address, and telephone number of the person or office from which the statement of reasons can be obtained. If the creditor chooses to provide the reasons orally, the creditor shall also disclose the applicant's right to have them confirmed in writing within 30 days of receiving a written request for confirmation from the applicant.

(3) *Notification to business credit applicants.**** For business

---

*** [*Editor's note:* In 1989 the Federal Reserve Board amended § 202.9(a)(3) to implement amendments to the ECOA contained in the Women's Business Ownership Act. The Board's explanation of this revision, reprinted from the Supplementary Information published in the Federal Register along with the amendments, follows:

Paragraph (a)(3) contains the notification requirements for business credit applicants.

Paragraph (a)(3)(i) implements section 703(a)(5) of the act, which requires creditors to inform business loan applicants, in writing, of the right to a written statement of the reasons for the denial of loan applications. These rules govern credit applications from businesses with $1 million or less in gross revenues (including applications from individuals applying for business-purpose credit), except that applications for trade similar credit (regardless of the revenue size of the business) are governed by the rules in paragraph (a)(3)(ii).

Creditors may notify business credit applicants of a credit decision orally or in writing. Notice of the credit decision must be given in accordance with the timing requirements of paragraph (a)(1)—typically within 30 days of receiving a "completed" application. Under § 202.2(f), an application is deemed to be "completed" when the creditor has received all the information it regularly obtains and considers in evaluating applications for credit (including any information requested from the applicant).

Creditors must satisfy the requirement to provide a written notice of the right to a statement of reasons in one of two ways. The creditor may follow the rule used for nonbusiness credit and give the written notice of the right to a statement of reasons after a credit denial or other adverse action is taken. And of course, as in the case of nonbusiness credit, the creditor may provide a written statement of the specific reasons for a credit denial, instead of merely giving notice of the right.

Alternatively, the creditor may give the notice to business applicants at the time of application. Notice could be given on a separate piece of paper or included on any documentation provided to the applicant, as long as the notice is given in a form the applicant may retain. The disclosure should be readily noticeable, but there are no special requirements regarding location, type size, or type face.

Whether a notice is provided at the time of application or when adverse action is taken, the notice must contain all the information required by paragraph (a)(2) except that—as noted above—creditors are permitted to give the statement of the action taken (for example, that a line of credit or a loan has been denied) orally or in writing. The information required includes the name and address of the creditor; a statement of the provisions of section 701(a) of the ECOA (the "ECOA notice"); and the name and address of the federal agency that administers compliance with respect to the creditor. Two model forms are provided in Appendix C to the regulation and are discussed below.

Oral notification for telephone applications

The Board recognizes that creditors that handle business credit applications by telephone (for example, when dealing with existing customers) might find it difficult to comply with the written notification requirements. Paragraph (a)(3)(i)(C) therefore provides that when an application for business credit is made solely by telephone, compliance with the notice requirements may be satisfied by an oral disclosure of the applicant's right to a statement of reasons for a denial of credit. In such instances, the creditor does not have to recite the information, normally required in a written notification, that is contained in the ECOA notice specified in § 202.9(b)(1).

An oral or written request for an extension of credit, if made in accordance with procedures established by a creditor for the type of credit requested, is an application under § 202.2(f). A request for an advance under an existing line of credit is not considered an "application" for credit and therefore it does not trigger the notice requirements of the regulation. *See* Regulation B, § 202.2(f) and accompanying commentary; *see also* § 202.2(c)(2).

Inquiries from potential applicants seeking credit information are not subject to the notice requirements. Such inquiries are, however, subject to

credit, a creditor shall comply with the requirements of this paragraph in the following manner:
(i) With regard to a business that had gross revenues of $1,000,000 or less in its preceding fiscal year (other than an extension of trade credit, credit incident to a factoring agreement, or other similar types of business credit), a creditor shall comply with paragraphs (a)(1) and (2) of this section, except that:
  (A) The statement of the action taken may be given orally or in writing, when adverse action is taken;
  (B) Disclosure of an applicant's right to a statement of reasons may be given at the time of application, instead of when adverse action is taken, provided the disclosure is in a form the applicant may retain and contains the information required by paragraph (a)(2)(ii) of this section and the ECOA notice specified in paragraph (b)(1) of this section;
  (C) For an application made solely by telephone, a creditor satisfies the requirements of this paragraph by an oral statement of the action taken and of the applicant's right to a statement of reasons for adverse action.
(ii) With regard to a business that had gross revenues in excess of $1,000,000 in its preceding fiscal year or an extension of trade credit, credit incident to a factoring agreement, or other similar types of business credit, a creditor shall:
  (A) Notify the applicant, orally or in writing, within a reasonable time of the action taken; and
  (B) Provide a written statement of the reasons for adverse action and the ECOA notice specified in paragraph (b)(1) of this section if the applicant makes a written request for the reasons within 60 days of being notified of the adverse action.

---

§ 202.5(a), which bars creditors from discouraging prospective applicants, on a prohibited basis, from making or pursuing an application.

The rules on notification in paragraph (a)(3)(ii), formerly part of § 202.3(d)(3), apply to credit applications by businesses with gross revenues exceeding $1 million and applications for all types of trade credit, credit incident to factoring, and similar business credit (regardless of the applicant's revenues). The Board has simplified the application of these rules for both applicants and creditors and has provided greater uniformity among the timing requirements.

Applicants for business credit covered by paragraph (a)(3)(ii) must be notified of a credit denial, orally or in writing, within a reasonable time after the creditor receives a completed application. (Notice given in accordance with the timing requirements of § 202.9(a)(1) is deemed "reasonable" in all instances.) Under the revisions, applicants have up to 60 days after a denial (the same rule as for business credit below the revenue cutoff and for nonbusiness credit) to request written reasons for the denial. This changes the previous rule, which gave business credit applicants up to 30 days after a credit denial in which to submit a written request.

54 Fed. Reg. 50,482 (Dec. 7, 1989).]

(b) *Form of ECOA notice and statement of specific reasons.*

(1) *ECOA notice.* To satisfy the disclosure requirements of paragraph (a)(2) of this section regarding section 701(a) of the Act, the creditor shall provide a notice that is substantially similar to the following:

The Federal Equal Credit Opportunity Act prohibits creditors from discriminating against credit applicants on the basis of race, color, religion, national origin, sex, marital status, age (provided the applicant has the capacity to enter into a binding contract); because all or part of the applicant's income derives from any public assistance program; or because the applicant has in good faith exercised any right under the Consumer Credit Protection Act. The Federal agency that administers compliance with this law concerning this creditor is (name and address as specified by the appropriate agency listed in Appendix A of this regulation).

(2) *Statement of specific reasons.* The statement of reasons for adverse action required by paragraph (a)(2)(i) of this section must be specific and indicate the principal reason(s) for the adverse action. Statements that the adverse action was based on the creditor's internal standards or policies or that the applicant failed to achieve the qualifying score on the creditor's credit scoring system are insufficient.

(c) *Incomplete applications.*

(1) *Notice alternatives.* Within 30 days after receiving application that is incomplete regarding matters that an applicant can complete, the creditor shall notify the applicant either:

(i) Of action taken, in accordance with paragraph (a) of this section; or

(ii) Of the incompleteness, in accordance with paragraph (c)(2) of this section.

(2) *Notice of incompleteness.* If additional information is needed from an applicant, the creditor shall send a written notice to the applicant specifying the information needed, designating a reasonable period of time for the applicant to provide the information, and informing the applicant that failure to provide the information requested will result in no further consideration being given to the application. The creditor shall have no further obligation under this section if the applicant fails to respond within the designated time period. If the applicant supplies the requested information within the designated time period, the creditor shall take action on the application and notify the applicant in accordance with paragraph (a) of this section.

(3) *Oral request for information.* At its option, a creditor may inform the applicant orally of the need for additional information; but if the application remains incomplete the creditor shall send a notice in accordance with paragraph (c)(1) of this section.

(d) *Oral notifications by small-volume creditors.* The requirements of this section (including statements of specific reasons) are satisfied by oral notifications in the case of any creditor that did not receive more than 150 applications during the preceding calendar year.

(e) *Withdrawal of approved application.* When an applicant submits an application and the parties contemplate that the applicant will inquire about its status, if the creditor approves the application and the applicant has not inquired within 30 days after applying, the creditor may treat the application as withdrawn and need not comply with paragraph (a)(1) of this section.

(f) *Multiple applicants.* When an application involves more than

one applicant, notification need only be given to one of them, but must be given to the primary applicant where one is readily apparent.

(g) *Applications submitted through a third party.* When an application is made on behalf of an applicant to more than one creditor and the applicant expressly accepts or uses credit offered by one of the creditors, notification of action taken by any of the other creditors is not required. If no credit is offered or if the applicant does not expressly accept or use any credit offered, each creditor taking adverse action must comply with this section, directly or through a third party. A notice given by a third party shall disclose the identity of each creditor on whose behalf the notice is given.

[Reg. B, 50 FR 48026, Nov. 20, 1985, amended 54 FR 50485, Dec. 7, 1989]

§ 202.10 Furnishing of credit information.

(a) *Designation of accounts.* A creditor that furnishes credit information shall designate:

(1) Any new account to reflect the participation of both spouses if the applicant's spouse is permitted to use or is contractually liable on the account (other than as a guarantor, surety, endorser, or similar party); and

(2) Any existing account to reflect such participation, within 90 days after receiving a written request to do so from one of the spouses.

(b) *Routine reports to consumer reporting agency.* If a creditor furnishes credit information to a consumer reporting agency concerning an account designated to reflect the participation of both spouses, the creditor shall furnish the information in a manner that will enable the agency to provide access to the information in the name of each spouse.

(c) *Reporting in response to inquiry.* If a creditor furnishes credit information in response to an inquiry concerning an account designated to reflect the participation of both spouses, the creditor shall furnish the information in the name of the spouse about whom the information is requested.

§ 202.11 Relation to state law.

(a) *Inconsistent state laws.* Except as otherwise provided in this section, this regulation alters, affects, or preempts only those state laws that are inconsistent with the act and this regulation and then only to the extent of the inconsistency. A state law is not inconsistent if it is more protective of an applicant.

(b) *Preempted provisions of state law.*

(1) A state law is deemed to be inconsistent with the requirements of the Act and this regulation and less protective of an applicant within the meaning of section 705(f) of the Act to the extent that the law:

(i) Requires or permits a practice or act prohibited by the Act or this regulation;

(ii) Prohibits the individual extension of consumer credit to both parties to a marriage if each spouse individually and voluntarily applies for such credit;

(iii) Prohibits inquiries or collection of data required to comply with the act or this regulation;

(iv) Prohibits asking or considering age in an empirically derived, demonstrably and statistically sound, credit scoring system to determine a pertinent element of creditworthiness, or to favor an elderly applicant; or

(v) Prohibits inquiries necessary to establish or administer a special purpose credit program as defined by § 202.8.

(2) A creditor, state, or other interested party may request the Board to determine whether a state law is inconsistent with the requirements of the Act and this regulation.

(c) *Laws on finance charges, loan ceilings.* If married applicants voluntarily apply for and obtain individual accounts with the same creditor, the accounts shall not be aggregated or otherwise combined for purposes of determining permissible finance charges or loan ceilings under any federal or state law. Permissible loan ceiling laws shall be construed to permit each spouse to become individually liable up to the amount of the loan ceilings, less the amount for which the applicant is jointly liable.

(d) *State and Federal laws not affected.* This section does not alter or annul any provision of state property laws, laws relating to the disposition of decedents' estates, or Federal or state banking regulations directed only toward insuring the solvency of financial institutions.

(e) *Exemption for state-regulated transactions.*

(1) *Applications.* A state may apply to the Board for an exemption from the requirements of the Act and this regulation for any class of credit transactions within the state. The Board will grant such an exemption if the Board determines that:

(i) The class of credit transactions is subject to state law requirements substantially similar to the Act and this regulation or that applicants are afforded greater protection under state law; and

(ii) There is adequate provision for state enforcement.

(2) *Liability and enforcement.*

(i) No exemption will extend to the civil liability provisions of section 706 or the administrative enforcement provisions of section 704 of the Act.

(ii) After an exemption has been granted, the requirements of the applicable state law (except for additional requirements not imposed by Federal law) will constitute the requirements of the Act and this regulation.

§ 202.12 Record retention.

(a) *Retention of prohibited information.* A creditor may retain in its files information that is prohibited by the Act or this regulation in evaluating applications, without violating the Act or this regulation, if the information was obtained:

(1) From any source prior to March 23, 1977;

(2) From consumer reporting agencies, an applicant, or others without the specific request of the creditor; or

(3) As required to monitor compliance with the Act and this regulation or other Federal or state statutes or regulations.

(b) *Preservation of records.*****

***

**** [*Editor's note:* In 1989 the Federal Reserve Board amended § 202.12(b) to implement amendments to the ECOA contained in the Women's Business Ownership Act. The Board's explanation of these revisions, reprinted from the Supplementary Information published in the Federal Register along with the amendments, follows:

The revisions to § 202.12(b) implement section 703(a)(5) of the act, which requires creditors to retain

(1) *Applications.* For 25 months (12 months for business credit) after the date that a creditor notifies an applicant of action taken on an application or of incompleteness, the creditor shall retain in original form or a copy thereof:

(i) Any application that it receives, any information required to be obtained concerning characteristics of the applicant to monitor compliance with the Act and this regulation or other similar law, and any other written or recorded information used in evaluating the application and not returned to the applicant at the applicant's request;

(ii) A copy of the following documents if furnished to the applicant in written form (or, if furnished orally, any notation or memorandum made by the creditor):

(A) The notification of action taken; and

(B) The statement of specific reasons for adverse action; and

(iii) Any written statement submitted by the applicant alleging a violation of the Act or this regulation.

(2) *Existing accounts.* For 25 months (12 months for business credit) after the date that a creditor notifies an applicant of adverse action regarding an existing account, the creditor shall retain as to that account, in original form or a copy thereof:

(i) Any written or recorded information concerning the adverse action; and

***

records relating to business credit applications for no less than one year. Paragraphs (b)(1) through (4) are amended to distinguish between business credit records, which must be retained for 12 months, and nonbusiness credit records, which must be retained for 25 months.

The Board had proposed in July that records relating to business credit applicants be retained for 25 months. Similarly, records relating to applications from businesses with revenues above the cutoff and applications for trade and similar credit would have been subject to a 60-day retention period in all cases and to a 25-month retention period when an applicant submitted a written request that records be retained. The Board believed the ease of compliance associated with a more uniform timing rule for all types of credit records would benefit creditors.

Many commenters supported the Board's efforts to achieve consistency in timing rules. However, commercial lenders also described the disparity in the volume of data typically obtained to evaluate consumer and business applications, and objected to the incremental costs associated with storing business records (particularly on denied loans) for 25 rather than 12 months.

The final rule provides for an overall 12-month record retention period for business credit applications. The Board believes that compliance can be monitored adequately by reviewing transactions within this time period. The rules in § 202.12(b)(4), which require the longer retention of records by creditors that are the subject of enforcement procedures and investigations, will continue to preserve records where a creditor's actions come under scrutiny.

54 Fed. Reg. 50,482 (Dec. 7, 1989).]

(ii) Any written statement submitted by the applicant alleging a violation of the act or this regulation.

(3) *Other applications.* For 25 months (12 months for business credit) after the date that a creditor receives an application for which the creditor is not required to comply with the notification requirements of § 202.9, the creditor shall retain all written or recorded information in its possession concerning the applicant, including any notation of action taken.

(4) *Enforcement proceedings and investigations.* A creditor shall retain the information specified in this section beyond 25 months (12 months for business credit) if it has actual notice that it is under investigation or is subject to an enforcement proceeding for an alleged violation of the act or this regulation by the Attorney General of the United States or by an enforcement agency charged with monitoring that creditor's compliance with the act and this regulation, or if it has been served with notice of an action filed pursuant to section 706 of the Act and § 202.14 of this regulation. The creditor shall retain the information until final disposition of the matter, unless an earlier time is allowed by order of the agency or court.

(5) *Special rule for certain business credit applications.****** With regard to a business with gross revenues in excess of $1,000,000 in its preceding fiscal year, or an extension of trade credit, credit incident to a factoring agreement or other similar types of business credit, the creditor shall retain records for at least 60 days after notifying the applicant of the action taken. If within that time period the applicant requests in writing the reasons for adverse action or that records be retained, the creditor shall retain records for 12 months.

(6) *Self-tests.* For 25 months after a self-test (as defined in

---

***** [*Editor's note:* In 1989 the Federal Reserve Board amended § 202.12(b)(5) to implement amendments to the ECOA contained in the Women's Business Ownership Act. The Board's explanation of this revision, reprinted from the Supplementary Information published in the Federal Register along with the amendments, follows:

Previously, the regulation (in § 202.3(d)(3)) required creditors to retain records for 90 days after taking action on a business credit application. If during this time an applicant made a written request to have records kept, the creditor had to retain the records for 25 months. In the revised regulation, the substance of former § 202.3(d) on record retention has been modified and moved to § 202.12(b)(5). That provision now applies only to applications from businesses with gross revenues greater than $1 million, trade credit and similar business credit applications. If a creditor receives a written request for a statement of reasons from such applicants, the creditor is required both to give the reasons and also to retain records for 12 months. This eliminates the need for rejected business credit applicants to make two distinct requests regarding the credit decision and provides uniform rules. Absent a written request from an applicant, a creditor does not have to retain records beyond the initial 60-day period.

54 Fed. Reg. 50,482 (Dec. 7, 1989).]

---

§ 202.15) has been completed, the creditor shall retain all written or recorded information about the self-test. A creditor shall retain information beyond 25 months if it has actual notice that it is under investigation or is subject to an enforcement proceeding for an alleged violation, or if it has been served with notice of a civil action. In such cases, the creditor shall retain the information until final disposition of the matter, unless an earlier time is allowed by the appropriate agency or court order.

[Reg. B, 50 FR 48026, Nov. 20, 1985, amended at 54 FR 50486, Dec. 7, 1989, and 62 FR 66419, Dec. 18, 1997]

§ 202.13 Information for monitoring purposes.

(a) *Information to be requested.* A creditor that receives an application for credit primarily for the purchase or refinancing of a dwelling occupied or to be occupied by the applicant as a principal residence, where the extension of credit will be secured by the dwelling, shall request as part of the application the following information regarding the applicant(s):

(1) Race or national origin, using the categories American Indian or Alaskan Native; Asian or Pacific Islander; Black; White; Hispanic; Other (Specify);

(2) Sex;

(3) Marital status, using the categories married, unmarried, and separated; and

(4) Age.

Dwelling means a residential structure that contains one to four units, whether or not that structure is attached to real property. The term includes, but is not limited to, an individual condominium or cooperative unit, and a mobile or other manufactured home.

(b) *Obtaining of information.* Questions regarding race or national origin, sex, marital status, and age may be listed, at the creditor's option, on the application form or on a separate form that refers to the application. The applicant(s) shall be asked but not required to supply the requested information. If the applicant(s) chooses not to provide the information or any part of it, that fact shall be noted on the form. The creditor shall then also note on the form, to the extent possible, the race or national origin and sex of the applicant(s) on the basis of visual observation or surname.

(c) *Disclosure to applicant(s).* The creditor shall inform the applicant(s) that the information regarding race or national origin, sex, marital status, and age is being requested by the Federal government for the purpose of monitoring compliance with Federal statutes that prohibit creditors from discriminating against applicants [sic] on those bases. The creditor shall also inform the applicant(s) that if the applicant(s) chooses note [sic] to provide the information, the creditor is required to note the race or national origin and sex on the basis of visual observation or surname.

(d) *Substitute monitoring program.* A monitoring program required by an agency charged with administrative enforcement under section 704 of the Act may be substituted for the requirements contained in paragraphs (a), (b), and (c).

§ 202.14 Enforcement, penalties and liabilities.

(a) *Administrative enforcement.*

(1) As set forth more fully in section 704 of the Act, adminis-

trative enforcement of the Act and this regulation regarding certain creditors is assigned to the Comptroller of the Currency, Board of Governors of the Federal Reserve System, Board of Directors of the Federal Deposit Insurance Corporation, Office of Thrift Supervision, National Credit Union Administration, Interstate Commerce Commission, Secretary of Agriculture, Farm Credit Administration, Securities and Exchange Commission, Small Business Administration, and Secretary of Transportation.

(2) Except to the extent that administrative enforcement is specifically assigned to other authorities, compliance with the requirements imposed under the act and this regulation is enforced by the Federal Trade Commission.

(b) *Penalties and liabilities.*

(1) Sections 706 (a) and (b) and 702(g) of the Act provide that any creditor that fails to comply with a requirement imposed by the Act or this regulation is subject to civil liability for actual and punitive damages in individual or class actions. Pursuant to sections 704 (b), (c), and (d) and 702(g) of the Act, violations of the Act or regulations also constitute violations of other Federal laws. Liability for punitive damages is restricted to nongovernmental entities and is limited to $10,000 in individual actions and the lesser of $500,000 or 1 percent of the creditor's net worth in class actions. Section 706(c) provides for equitable and declaratory relief and section 706(d) authorizes the awarding of costs and reasonable attorney's fees to an aggrieved applicant in a successful action.

(2) As provided in section 706(f), a civil action under the Act or this regulation may be brought in the appropriate United States district court without regard to the amount in controversy or in any other court of competent jurisdiction within two years after the date of the occurrence of the violation, or within one year after the commencement of an administrative enforcement proceeding or of a civil action brought by the Attorney General of the United States within two years after the alleged violation.

(3) If an agency responsible for administrative enforcement is unable to obtain compliance with the act or this part, it may refer the matter to the Attorney General of the United States. In addition, if the Board, the Comptroller of the Currency, the Federal Deposit Insurance Corporation, the Office of Thrift Supervision, or the National Credit Union Administration has reason to believe that one or more creditors engaged in a pattern or practice of discouraging or denying applications in violation of the act or this part, the agency shall refer the matter to the Attorney General. Furthermore, the agency may refer a matter to the Attorney General if the agency has reason to believe that one or more creditors has violated section 701(a) of the act.

(4) On referral, or whenever the Attorney General has reason to believe that one or more creditors engaged in a pattern or practice in violation of the act or this regulation, the Attorney General may bring a civil action for such relief as may be appropriate, including actual and punitive damages and injunctive relief.

(5) If the Board, the Comptroller of the Currency, the Federal Deposit Insurance Corporation, the Office of Thrift Supervision, or the National Credit Union Administration has reason to believe (as a result of a consumer complaint, conducting a consumer compliance examination, or otherwise) that a violation of the act or this part has occurred which is also a violation of the Fair Housing Act, and the matter is not referred to the Attorney General, the agency shall notify:

(i) The Secretary of Housing and Urban Development; and

(ii) The applicant that the Secretary of Housing and Urban Development has been notified and that remedies for the violation may be available under the Fair Housing Act.

(c) *Failure of compliance.* A creditor's failure to comply with §§ 202.6(b)(6), 202.9, 202.10, 202.12 or 202.13 is not a violation if it results from an inadvertent error. On discovering an error under §§ 202.9 and 202.10, the creditor shall correct it as soon as possible. If a creditor inadvertently obtains the monitoring information regarding the race or national origin and sex of the applicant in a dwelling-related transaction not overed [sic] by § 202.13, the creditor may act on and retain the application without violating the regulation.

[Reg. B, 50 FR 48026, Nov. 20, 1985, amended at 54 FR 53539, Dec. 29, 1989, 58 Fed. Reg. 65652, Dec. 16, 1993]

§ 202.15 Incentives for self-testing and self-correction.

(a) *General rules.*

(1) *Voluntary self-testing and correction.* The report or results of the self-test that a creditor voluntarily conducts (or authorizes) are privileged as provided in this section. Data collection required by law or by any governmental authority is not a voluntary self-test.

(2) *Corrective action required.* The privilege in this section applies only if the creditor has taken or is taking appropriate corrective action.

(3) *Other privileges.* The privilege created by this section does not preclude the assertion of any other privilege that may also apply.

(b) *Self-test defined.*

(1) *Definition.* A self-test is any program, practice, or study that:

(i) Is designed and used specifically to determine the extent or effectiveness of a creditor's compliance with the act or this regulation; and

(ii) Creates data or factual information that is not available and cannot be derived from loan or application files or other records related to credit transactions.

(2) *Types of information privileged.* The privilege under this section applies to the report or results of the self-test, data or factual information created by the self-test, and any analysis, opinions, and conclusions pertaining to the self-test report or results. The privilege covers workpapers or draft documents as well as final documents.

(3) *Types of information not privileged.* The privilege under this section does not apply to:

(i) Information about whether a creditor conducted a self-test, the methodology used or the scope of the self-test, the time period covered by the self-test, or the dates it was conducted; or

(ii) Loan and application files or other business records

related to credit transactions, and information derived from such files and records, even if it has been aggregated, summarized, or reorganized to facilitate analysis.

(c) *Appropriate corrective action.*

(1) *General requirement.* For the privilege in this section to apply, appropriate corrective action is required when the self-test shows that it is more likely than not that a violation occurred, even though no violation has been formally adjudicated.

(2) *Determining the scope of appropriate corrective action.* A creditor must take corrective action that is reasonably likely to remedy the cause and effect of a likely violation by:

(i) Identifying the policies or practices that are the likely cause of the violation; and

(ii) Assessing the extent and scope of any violation.

(3) *Types of relief.* Appropriate corrective action may include both prospective and remedial relief, except that to establish a privilege under this section:

(i) A creditor is not required to provide remedial relief to a tester used in a self-test;

(ii) A creditor is only required to provide remedial relief to an applicant identified by the self-test as one whose rights were more likely than not violated; and

(iii) A creditor is not required to provide remedial relief to a particular applicant if the statute of limitations applicable to the violation expired before the creditor obtained the results of the self-test or the applicant is otherwise ineligible for such relief.

(4) *No admission of violation.* Taking corrective action is not an admission that a violation occurred.

(d)(1) *Scope of privilege.* The report or results of a privileged self-test may not be obtained or used:

(i) By a government agency in any examination or investigation relating to compliance with the act or this regulation; or

(ii) By a government agency or an applicant (including a prospective applicant who alleges a violation of § 202.5(a)) in any proceeding or civil action in which a violation of the act or this regulation is alleged.

(2) *Loss of privilege.* The report or results of a self-test are not privileged under paragraph (d)(1) of this section if the creditor or a person with lawful access to the report or results):

(i) Voluntarily discloses any part of the report or results, or any other information privileged under this section, to an applicant or government agency or to the public;

(ii) Discloses any part of the report or results, or any other information privileged under this section, as a defense to charges that the creditor has violated the act or regulation; or

(iii) Fails or is unable to produce written or recorded information about the self-test that is required to be retained under § 202.12(b)(6) when the information is needed to determine whether the privilege applies. This paragraph does not limit any other penalty or remedy that may be available for a violation of § 202.12.

(3) *Limited use of privileged information.* Notwithstanding paragraph (d)(1) of this section, the self-test report or results and any other information privileged under this section may be obtained and used by an applicant or government agency solely to determine a penalty or remedy after a violation of the act or this regulation has been adjudicated or admitted. Disclosures for this limited purpose may be used only for the particular proceeding in which the adjudication or admission was made. Information disclosed under this paragraph (d)(3) remains privileged under paragraph (d)(1) of this section.

[62 FR 66412, Dec. 18, 1997, effective Jan. 30, 1998]

Appendix A to Part 202—Federal Enforcement Agencies

The following list indicates the federal agencies that enforce Regulation B for particular classes of creditors. Any questions concerning a particular creditor should be directed to its enforcement agency. Terms that are not defined in the Federal Deposit Insurance Act (12 U.S.C. 1813(s)) shall have the meaning given to them in the International Banking Act of 1978 (12 U.S.C. 3101).

National Banks and Federal Branches and Federal Agencies of Foreign Banks

Office of the Comptroller of the Currency, Customer Assistance Unit, 1301 McKinney Avenue, Suite 3710, Houston, Texas 77010.

State Member Banks, Branches and Agencies of Foreign Banks (other than federal branches, federal agencies, and insured state branches of foreign banks), Commercial Lending Companies Owned or Controlled by Foreign Banks, and Organizations Operating under Section 25 or 25A of the Federal Reserve Act

Federal Reserve Bank serving the district in which the institution is located.

Nonmember Insured Banks and Insured State Branches of Foreign Banks

Federal Deposit Insurance Corporation Regional Director for the region in which the institution is located.

Savings institutions insured under the Savings Association Insurance Fund of the FDIC and federally chartered saving banks insured under the Bank Insurance Fund of the FDIC (but not including state-chartered savings banks insured under the Bank Insurance Fund).

Office of Thrift Supervision Regional Director for the region in which the institution is located.

Federal Credit Unions

Regional office of the National Credit Union Administration serving the area in which the federal credit union is located.

Air Carriers

Assistant General Counsel for Aviation Enforcement and Proceedings, Department of Transportation, 400 Seventh Street, SW, Washington, DC 20590.

Creditors Subject to Interstate Commerce Commission

Office of Proceedings, Interstate Commerce Commission, Washington, DC 20523.

Creditors Subject to Packers and Stockyards Act

Nearest Packers and Stockyards Administration area supervisor.

Small Business Investment Companies

U.S. Small Business Administration, 1441 L Street, NW., Washington, DC 20416.

Brokers and Dealers

Securities and Exchange Commission, Washington, DC 20549.

Federal Land Banks, Federal Land Bank Associations, Federal Intermediate Credit Banks, and Production Credit Associations

Farm Credit Administration, 1501 Farm Credit Drive, McLean, Virginia 22102-5090.

Retailers, Finance Companies, and All Other Creditors Not Listed Above

FTC Regional Office for region in which the creditor operates or Federal Trade Commission, Equal Credit Opportunity, Washington, DC 20580.

[Reg. B, 50 FR 48026, Nov. 20, 1985, as amended at 54 FR 53539, Dec. 29, 1989; 56 FR 51322, Oct. 11, 1991; 57 FR 20399, May 13, 1992; 63 FR 16392, Apr. 30, 1998]

Appendix B to Part 202—Model Application Forms

This appendix contains five model credit application forms, each designated for use in a particular type of consumer credit transaction as indicated by the bracketed caption on each form. The first sample form is intended for use in open-end, unsecured transactions; the second for closed-end, secured transactions; the third for closed-end transactions, whether unsecured or secured; the fourth in transactions involving community property or occurring in community property states; and the fifth in residential mortgage transactions. The appendix also contains a model disclosure for use in complying with § 202.13 for certain dwelling-related loans. All forms contained in this appendix are models; their use by creditors is optional.

The use or modification of these forms is governed by the following instructions. A creditor may change the forms: by asking for additional information not prohibited by § 202.5; by deleting any information request; or by rearranging the format without modifying the substance of the inquiries. In any of these three instances, however, the appropriate notices regarding the optional nature of courtesy titles, the option to disclose alimony, child support, or separate maintenance, and the limitation concerning marital status inquiries must be included in the appropriate places if the items to which they relate appear on the creditor's form.

If a creditor uses an appropriate Appendix B model form, or modifies a form in accordance with the above instructions, that creditor shall be deemed to be acting in compliance with the provisions of paragraphs (c) and (d) of § 202.5 of this regulation.

[Open-end, unsecured credit]

CREDIT APPLICATION
IMPORTANT: Read these Directions before completing this Application.

Check
Appropriate
Box

☐ If you are applying for an individual account in your own name and are relying on your own income or assets and not the income or assets of another person as the basis for repayment of the credit requested, complete only Sections A and D.

☐ If you are applying for a joint account or an account that you and another person will use, complete all Sections, providing information in B about the joint applicant or user.

☐ If you are applying on an individual account, but are relying on income from alimony, child support, or separate maintenance or on the income or assets of another person as the basis for repayment of the credit requested, complete all Sections to the extent possible, providing information in B about the person on whose alimony, support, or maintenance payments or income or assets you are relying.

SECTION A—INFORMATION REGARDING APPLICANT

Full Name (Last, First, Middle): _____   Birthdate: / /

Present Street Address: _____   Years there: _____

City: _____ State: _____ Zip: _____ Telephone: _____

Social Security No.: _____ Driver's License No.: _____

Previous Street Address: _____   Years there: _____

City: _____ State: _____ Zip: _____

Present Employer: _____ Years there: _____ Telephone: _____

Position or title: _____ Name of supervisor: _____

Employer's Address: _____

Previous Employer: _____   Years there: _____

Previous Employer's Address: _____

Present net salary or commission: $ _____ per _____ No. Dependents: _____ Ages: _____

Alimony, child support, or separate maintenance income need not be revealed if you do not wish to have it considered as a basis for repaying this obligation.

Alimony, child support, separate maintenance received under: court order ☐ written agreement ☐ oral understanding ☐

Other income: $ _____ per _____ Source(s) of other income: _____

Is any income listed in this Section likely to be reduced in the next two years?
☐ Yes (Explain in detail on a separate sheet.)   No ☐

Have you ever received credit from us? _____ When? _____ Office: _____

Checking Account No.: _____ Institution and Branch: _____

Savings Account No.: _____ Institution and Branch: _____

Name of nearest relative
not living with you: _____ Telephone: _____

Relationship: _____ Address: _____

SECTION B—INFORMATION REGARDING JOINT APPLICANT, USER, OR OTHER PARTY (Use separate sheets if necessary.)

Full Name (Last, First, Middle): _____   Birthdate: / /

Relationship to Applicant (if any): _____

Present Street Address: _____   Years there: _____

City: _____ State: _____ Zip: _____ Telephone: _____

Social Security No.: _____ Driver's License No.: _____

Present Employer: _____ Years there: _____ Telephone: _____

Position or title: _____ Name of supervisor: _____

Employer's Address: _____

Previous Employer: _____   Years there: _____

Previous Employer's Address: _____

Present net salary or commission: $ _____ per _____ No. Dependents: _____ Ages: _____

Alimony, child support, or separate maintenance income need not be revealed if you do not wish to have it considered as a basis for repaying this obligation.

Alimony, child support, separate maintenance received under: court order ☐ written agreement ☐ oral understanding ☐

Other income: $ _____ per _____ Source(s) of other income: _____

Is any income listed in this Section likely to be reduced in the next two years?
☐ Yes (Explain in detail on a separate sheet.)   No ☐

Checking Account No.: _____ Institution and Branch: _____

Savings Account No.: _____ Institution and Branch: _____

Name of nearest relative not living
with Joint Applicant, User, or Other Party: _____ Telephone: _____

Relationship: _____ Address: _____

SECTION C—MARITAL STATUS
(Do not complete if this is an application for an individual account.)

Applicant: ☐ Married   ☐ Separated   ☐ Unmarried (including single, divorced, and widowed)
Other Party: ☐ Married   ☐ Separated   ☐ Unmarried (including single, divorced, and widowed)

[Open-end, unsecured credit]

SECTION D— ASSET AND DEBT INFORMATION (If Section B has been completed, this Section should be completed giving information about both the Applicant and Joint Applicant, User, or Other Person. Please mark Applicant-related information with an "A." If Section B was not completed, only give information about the Applicant in this Section.)

ASSETS OWNED (use separate sheet if necessary.)

Description of Assets	Value	Subject to Debt? Yes/No	Name(s) of Owner(s)
Cash	$		
Automobiles (Make, Model, Year)			
Cash Value of Life Insurance (Issuer, Face Value)			
Real Estate (Location, Date Acquired)			
Marketable Securities (Issuer, Type, No. of Shares)			
Other (List)			
Total Assets	$		

OUTSTANDING DEBTS (Include charge accounts, installment contracts, credit cards, rent, mortgages, etc. Use separate sheet if necessary.)

Creditor	Type of Debt or Acct. No.	Name in Which Acct. Carried	Original Debt	Present Balance	Monthly Payments	Past Due? Yes/No
1. (Landlord or Mortgage Holder)	☐ Rent Payment ☐ Mortgage		$ (Omit rent)	$ (Omit rent)	$	
2.						
3.						
4.						
5.						
6.						
Total Debts			$	$	$	

(Credit References)   Date Paid

1. $

2.

Are you a co-maker, endorser, or guarantor on any loan or contract?	Yes ☐ No ☐	If "yes" for whom?		To whom?
Are there any unsatisfied judgments against you?	Yes ☐ No ☐	Amount $	If "yes" to whom owed?	
Have you been declared bankrupt in the last 14 years?	Yes ☐ No ☐	If "yes" where?		Year

Other Obligations—(E.g., liability to pay alimony, child support, separate maintenance. Use separate sheet if necessary.)

Everything that I have stated in this application is correct to the best of my knowledge. I understand that you will retain this application whether or not it is approved. You are authorized to check my credit and employment history and to answer questions about your credit experience with me.

_____   _____   _____   _____
Applicant's Signature   Date   Other Signature   Date
                                             (Where Applicable)

[Closed-end, secured credit]

CREDIT APPLICATION

IMPORTANT: Read these Directions before completing this Application.

Check
Appropriate
Box

☐ If you are applying for individual credit in your own name and are relying on your own income or assets and not the income or assets of another person as the basis for repayment of the credit requested, complete Sections A, C, D, and E, omitting B and the second part of C.

☐ If this is an application for joint credit with another person, complete all Sections, providing information in B about the joint applicant.

☐ If you are applying for individual credit, but are relying on income from alimony, child support, or separate maintenance or on the income or assets or another person as the basis for repayment of the credit requested, complete all Sections to the extent possible, providing information in B about the person on whose alimony, support, or maintenance payments or income or assets you are relying.

Amount Requested	Payment Date Desired	Proceeds of Credit
$ _____		To be Used For _____

SECTION A—INFORMATION REGARDING APPLICANT

Full Name (Last, First, Middle): _____ Birthdate: / /

Present Street Address: _____ Years there: _____

City: _____ State: _____ Zip: _____ Telephone: _____

Social Security No.: _____ Driver's License No.: _____

Previous Street Address: _____ Years there: _____

City: _____ State: _____ Zip: _____

Present Employer: _____ Years there: _____ Telephone: _____

Position or title: _____ Name of supervisor: _____

Employer's Address: _____

Previous Employer: _____ Years there: _____

Previous Employer's Address: _____

Present net salary or commission: $ _____ per _____ No. Dependents: _____ Ages: _____

Alimony, child support, or separate maintenance income need not be revealed if you do not wish to have it considered as a basis for repaying this obligation.

Alimony, child support, separate maintenance received under: court order ☐ written agreement ☐ oral understanding ☐

Other income: $ _____ per _____ Source(s) of other income: _____

Is any income listed in this Section likely to be reduced before the credit requested is paid off?
☐ Yes (Explain in detail on a separate sheet.) No ☐

Have you ever received credit from us? _____ When? _____ Office: _____

Checking Account No.: _____ Institution and Branch: _____

Savings Account No.: _____ Institution and Branch: _____

Name of nearest relative
not living with you: _____ Telephone: _____

Relationship: _____ Address: _____

SECTION B—INFORMATION REGARDING JOINT APPLICANT, OR OTHER PARTY (Use separate sheets if necessary.)

Full Name (Last, First, Middle): _____ Birthdate: / /

Relationship to Applicant (if any): _____

Present Street Address: _____ Years there: _____

City: _____ State: _____ Zip: _____ Telephone: _____

Social Security No.: _____ Driver's License No.: _____

Present Employer: _____ Years there: _____ Telephone: _____

Position or title: _____ Name of supervisor: _____

Employer's Address: _____

Previous Employer: _____ Years there: _____

Previous Employer's Address: _____

Present net salary or commission: $ _____ per _____ No. Dependents: _____ Ages: _____

Alimony, child support, or separate maintenance income need not be revealed if you do not wish to have it considered as a basis for repaying this obligation.

Alimony, child support, separate maintenance received under: court order ☐ written agreement ☐ oral understanding ☐

Other income: $ _____ per _____ Source(s) of other income: _____

Is any income listed in this Section likely to be reduced before the credit requested is paid off?
☐ Yes (Explain in detail on a separate sheet.) No ☐

Checking Account No.: _____ Institution and Branch: _____

Savings Account No.: _____ Institution and Branch: _____

Name of nearest relative not living with
Joint Applicant or Other Party: _____

Relationship: _____ Address: _____

SECTION C—MARITAL STATUS
(Do not complete if this is an application for an individual account.)

Applicant: ☐ Married ☐ Separated ☐ Unmarried (including single, divorced, and widowed)
Other Party: ☐ Married ☐ Separated ☐ Unmarried (including single, divorced, and widowed)

[Closed-end, secured credit]

SECTION D— ASSET AND DEBT INFORMATION (If Section B has been completed, this Section should be completed giving information about both the Applicant and Joint Applicant or Other Person. Please mark Applicant-related information with an "A." If Section B was not completed, only give information about the Applicant in this Section.)

ASSETS OWNED (use separate sheet if necessary.)

Description of Assets	Value	Subject to Debt? Yes/No	Name(s) of Owner(s)
Cash	$		
Automobiles (Make, Model, Year)			
Cash Value of Life Insurance (Issuer, Face Value)			
Real Estate (Location, Date Acquired)			
Marketable Securities (Issuer, Type, No. of Shares)			
Other (List)			
Total Assets	$		

OUTSTANDING DEBTS (Include charge accounts, installment contracts, credit cards, rent, mortgages, etc. Use separate sheet if necessary.)

Creditor	Type of Debt or Acct. No.	Name in Which Acct. Carried	Original Debt	Present Balance	Monthly Payments	Past Due? Yes/No
1. (Landlord or Mortgage Holder)	☐ Rent Payment ☐ Mortgage		$ (Omit rent)	$ (Omit rent)	$	
2.						
3.						
Total Debts			$	$	$	

(Credit References)   Date Paid

1. $

2.

Are you a co-maker, endorser, or guarantor on any loan or contract?	Yes ☐ No ☐	If "yes" for whom?	To whom?
Are there any unsatisfied judgments against you?	Yes ☐ No ☐ Amount $	If "yes" to whom owed?	
Have you been declared bankrupt in the last 14 years?	Yes ☐ No ☐	If "yes" where?	Year

Other Obligations—(E.g., liability to pay alimony, child support, separate maintenance. Use separate sheet if necessary.)

SECTION E—SECURED CREDIT (Briefly describe the property to be given as security.)

and list names and addresses of all co-owners of the property:

Name   Address

If the security is real estate, give the full name of your spouse (if any): _____

     Everything that I have stated in this application is correct to the best of my knowledge. I understand that you will retain this application whether or not it is approved. You are authorized to check my credit and employment history and to answer questions about your credit experience with me.

Applicant's Signature	Date	Other Signature (Where Applicable)	Date

[Closed-end, unsecured/secured credit]

CREDIT APPLICATION
IMPORTANT: Read these Directions before completing this Application.

Check
Appropriate
Box

☐ If you are applying for individual credit in your own name and are relying on your own income or assets and not the income or assets of another person as the basis for repayment of the credit requested, complete only Sections A and D. If the requested credit is to be secured, also complete the first part of Section C and Section E.

☐ If you are applying for joint credit with another person, complete all Sections except E, providing information in B about the joint applicant. If the requested credit is to be secured, then complete Section E.

☐ If you are applying for individual credit, but are relying on income from alimony, child support, or separate maintenance or on the income or assets of another person as the basis for repayment of the credit requested, complete all Sections except E to the extent possible, providing information in B about the person on whose alimony, support, or maintenance payments or income or assets you are relying. If the requested credit is to be secured, then complete Section E.

Amount Requested   Payment Date Desired   Proceeds of Credit
$ _____   To be Used For _____

SECTION A—INFORMATION REGARDING APPLICANT

Full Name (Last, First, Middle): _____   Birthdate: / /

Present Street Address: _____
                                                                    Years there: _____

City: _____ State: _____ Zip: _____ Telephone: _____

Social Security No.: _____ Driver's License No.: _____

Previous Street Address: _____
                                                                    Years there: _____

City: _____ State: _____ Zip: _____

Present Employer: _____ Years there: _____ Telephone: _____

Position or title: _____ Name of supervisor: _____

Employer's Address: _____

Previous Employer: _____
                                                                    Years there: _____

Previous Employer's Address: _____

Present net salary or commission: $ _____ per _____ No. Dependents: _____ Ages: _____

Alimony, child support, or separate maintenance income need not be revealed if you do not wish to have it considered as a basis for repaying this obligation.

Alimony, child support, separate maintenance received under: court order ☐ written agreement ☐ oral understanding ☐

Other income: $ _____ per _____ Source(s) of other income: _____

Is any income listed in this Section likely to be reduced before the credit requested is paid off?
☐ Yes (Explain in detail on a separate sheet.)   No ☐

Have you ever received credit from us? _____ When? _____ Office: _____

Checking Account No.: _____ Institution and Branch: _____

Savings Account No.: _____ Institution and Branch: _____

Name of nearest relative
not living with you: _____
                                         Telephone: _____
Relationship: _____ Address: _____

SECTION B—INFORMATION REGARDING JOINT APPLICANT, OR OTHER PARTY (Use separate sheets if necessary.)

Full Name (Last, First, Middle): _____   Birthdate: / /

Relationship to Applicant (if any): _____

Present Street Address: _____
                                                                    Years there: _____

City: _____ State: _____ Zip: _____ Telephone: _____

Social Security No.: _____ Driver's License No.: _____

Present Employer: _____ Years there: _____ Telephone: _____

Position or title: _____ Name of supervisor: _____

Employer's Address: _____

Previous Employer: _____
                                                                    Years there: _____

Previous Employer's Address: _____

Present net salary or commission: $ _____ per _____ No. Dependents: _____ Ages: _____

Alimony, child support, or separate maintenance income need not be revealed if you do not wish to have it considered as a basis for repaying this obligation.

Alimony, child support, separate maintenance received under: court order ☐ written agreement ☐ oral understanding ☐

Other income: $ _____ per _____ Source(s) of other income: _____

Is any income listed in this Section likely to be reduced before the credit requested is paid off?
☐ Yes (Explain in detail on a separate sheet.)   No ☐

Checking Account No.: _____ Institution and Branch: _____

Savings Account No.: _____ Institution and Branch: _____

Name of nearest relative not living with
Joint Applicant or Other Party: _____
                                         Telephone: _____
Relationship: _____ Address: _____

[Closed-end, unsecured/secured credit]

SECTION C—MARITAL STATUS
(Do not complete if this is an application for individual unsecured credit.)

Applicant: ☐ Married   ☐ Separated   ☐ Unmarried (including single, divorced, and widowed)
Other Party: ☐ Married   ☐ Separated   ☐ Unmarried (including single, divorced, and widowed)

SECTION D— ASSET AND DEBT INFORMATION (If Section B has been completed, this Section should be completed giving information about both the Applicant and Joint Applicant or Other Person. Please mark Applicant-related information with an "A." If Section B was not completed, only give information about the Applicant in this Section.)

ASSETS OWNED (use separate sheet if necessary.)

Description of Assets	Value	Subject to Debt? Yes/No	Name(s) of Owner(s)
Cash	$		
Automobiles (Make, Model, Year)			
Cash Value of Life Insurance (Issuer, Face Value)			
Real Estate (Location, Date Acquired)			
Marketable Securities (Issuer, Type, No. of Shares)			
Other (List)			
Total Assets	$		

OUTSTANDING DEBTS (Include charge accounts, installment contracts, credit cards, rent, mortgages, etc. Use separate sheet if necessary.)

Creditor	Type of Debt or Acct. No.	Name in Which Acct. Carried	Original Debt	Present Balance	Monthly Payments	Past Due? Yes/No
1. (Landlord or Mortgage Holder)	☐ Rent Payment ☐ Mortgage		$ (Omit rent)	$ (Omit rent)	$	
2.						
3.						
Total Debts			$	$	$	

(Credit References)		Date Paid
1.	$	
2.		

Are you a co-maker, endorser, or guarantor on any loan or contract?	Yes ☐ No ☐	If "yes" for whom?	To whom?
Are there any unsatisfied judgments against you?	Yes ☐ No ☐ Amount $	If "yes" to whom owed?	
Have you been declared bankrupt in the last 14 years?	Yes ☐ No ☐	If "yes" where?	Year

Other Obligations—(E.g., liability to pay alimony, child support, separate maintenance. Use separate sheet if necessary.)

SECTION E—SECURED CREDIT (Complete only if credit is to be secured.) Briefly describe the property to be given as security.

and list names and addresses of all co-owners of the property:

Name	Address

If the security is real estate, give the full name of your spouse (if any): _____

Everything that I have stated in this application is correct to the best of my knowledge. I understand that you will retain this application whether or not it is approved. You are authorized to check my credit and employment history and to answer questions about your credit experience with me.

Applicant's Signature	Date	Other Signature (Where Applicable)	Date

[Community property]

CREDIT APPLICATION
IMPORTANT: Read these Directions before completing this Application.

Check Appropriate Box

☐ If you are applying for individual credit in your own name, are not married, and are not relying on alimony, child support, or separate maintenance payments or on the income or assets of another person as the basis for repayment of the credit requested, complete only Sections A and D. If the requested credit is to be secured, also complete Section E.

☐ In all other situations, complete all Sections except E, providing information in B about your spouse, a joint applicant or user, or the person on whose alimony, support, or maintenance payments or income or assets you are relying. If the requested credit is to be secured, also complete Section E.

Amount Requested   Payment Date Desired   Proceeds of Credit
$ _____   _____   To be Used For _____

SECTION A—INFORMATION REGARDING APPLICANT

Full Name (Last, First, Middle): _____   Birthdate: / /

Present Street Address: _____   Years there: _____

City: _____ State: _____ Zip: _____ Telephone: _____

Social Security No.: _____ Driver's License No.: _____

Previous Street Address: _____   Years there: _____

City: _____ State: _____ Zip: _____

Present Employer: _____ Years there: _____ Telephone: _____

Position or title: _____ Name of supervisor: _____

Employer's Address: _____

Previous Employer: _____   Years there: _____

Previous Employer's Address: _____

Present net salary or commission: $ _____ per _____ No. Dependents: _____ Ages: _____

Alimony, child support, or separate maintenance income need not be revealed if you do not wish to have it considered as a basis for repaying this obligation.

Alimony, child support, separate maintenance received under: court order ☐ written agreement ☐ oral understanding ☐

Other income: $ _____ per _____ Source(s) of other income: _____

Is any income listed in this Section likely to be reduced in the next two years or before the credit requested is paid off?
☐ Yes (Explain in detail on a separate sheet.)   No ☐

Have you ever received credit from us? _____ When? _____ Office: _____

Checking Account No.: _____ Institution and Branch: _____

Savings Account No.: _____ Institution and Branch: _____

Name of nearest relative
not living with you: _____ Telephone: _____

Relationship: _____ Address: _____

SECTION B—INFORMATION REGARDING SPOUSE, JOINT APPLICANT, USER, OR OTHER PARTY (Use separate sheets if necessary.)

Full Name (Last, First, Middle): _____   Birthdate: / /

Relationship to Applicant (if any): _____

Present Street Address: _____   Years there: _____

City: _____ State: _____ Zip: _____ Telephone: _____

Social Security No.: _____ Driver's License No.: _____

Present Employer: _____ Years there: _____ Telephone: _____

Position or title: _____ Name of supervisor: _____

Employer's Address: _____

Previous Employer: _____   Years there: _____

Previous Employer's Address: _____

Present net salary or commission: $ _____ per _____ No. Dependents: _____ Ages: _____

Alimony, child support, or separate maintenance income need not be revealed if you do not wish to have it considered as a basis for repaying this obligation.

Alimony, child support, separate maintenance received under: court order ☐ written agreement ☐ oral understanding ☐

Other income: $ _____ per _____ Source(s) of other income: _____

Is any income listed in this Section likely to be reduced in the next two years or before the credit requested is paid off?
☐ Yes (Explain in detail on a separate sheet.)   No ☐

Checking Account No.: _____ Institution and Branch: _____

Savings Account No.: _____ Institution and Branch: _____

Name of nearest relative not living with
Spouse, Joint Applicant, User, or Other Party: _____ Telephone: _____

Relationship: _____ Address: _____

[Community property]

SECTION C—MARITAL STATUS

Applicant: ☐ Married ☐ Separated ☐ Unmarried (including single, divorced, and widowed)
Other Party: ☐ Married ☐ Separated ☐ Unmarried (including single, divorced, and widowed)

SECTION D— ASSET AND DEBT INFORMATION (If Section B has been completed, this Section should be completed giving information about both the Applicant and Spouse, Joint Applicant, User, or Other Person. Please mark Applicant-related information with an "A." If Section B was not completed, only give information about the Applicant in this Section.)

ASSETS OWNED (use separate sheet if necessary.)

Description of Assets	Value	Subject to Debt? Yes/No	Name(s) of Owner(s)
Cash	$		
Automobiles (Make, Model, Year)			
Cash Value of Life Insurance (Issuer, Face Value)			
Real Estate (Location, Date Acquired)			
Marketable Securities (Issuer, Type, No. of Shares)			
Other (List)			
Total Assets	$		

OUTSTANDING DEBTS (Include charge accounts, installment contracts, credit cards, rent, mortgages, etc. Use separate sheet if necessary.)

Creditor	Type of Debt or Acct. No.	Name in Which Acct. Carried	Original Debt	Present Balance	Monthly Payments	Past Due? Yes/No
1. (Landlord or Mortgage Holder)	☐ Rent Payment ☐ Mortgage		$ (Omit rent)	$ (Omit rent)	$	
2.						
3.						
Total Debts			$	$	$	

(Credit References)		Date Paid
1.	$	
2.		

Are you a co-maker, endorser, or guarantor on any loan or contract?	Yes ☐ No ☐	If "yes" for whom?		To whom?
Are there any unsatisfied judgments against you?	Yes ☐ No ☐	Amount $	If "yes" to whom owed?	
Have you been declared bankrupt in the last 14 years?	Yes ☐ No ☐	If "yes" where?		Year

Other Obligations—(E.g., liability to pay alimony, child support, separate maintenance. Use separate sheet if necessary.)

SECTION E—SECURED CREDIT (Complete only if credit is to be secured.) Briefly describe the property to be given as security.

and list names and addresses of all co-owners of the property:

Name   Address

Everything that I have stated in this application is correct to the best of my knowledge. I understand that you will retain this application whether or not it is approved. You are authorized to check my credit and employment history and to answer questions about your credit experience with me.

Applicant's Signature	Date	Other Signature (Where Applicable)	Date

Uniform Residential Loan Application

This application is designed to be completed by the applicant(s) with the lender's assistance. Applicants should complete this form as "Borrower" or "Co-Borrower", as applicable. Co-Borrower information must also be provided (and the appropriate box checked) when ☐ the income or assets of a person other than the "Borrower" (including the Borrower's spouse) will be used as a basis for loan qualification or ☐ the income or assets of the Borrower's spouse will not be used as a basis for loan qualification, but his or her liabilities must be considered because the Borrower resides in a community property state, the security property is located in a community property state, or the Borrower is relying on other property located in a community property state as a basis for repayment of the loan.

I. TYPE OF MORTGAGE AND TERMS OF LOAN

Mortgage Applied for:	☐ VA ☐ FHA	☐ Conventional ☐ FmHA	☐ Other:	Agency Case Number	Lender Case No.

Amount $	Interest Rate %	No. of Months	Amortization Type:	☐ Fixed Rate ☐ GPM	☐ Other (explain): ☐ ARM (type):

II. PROPERTY INFORMATION AND PURPOSE OF LOAN

Subject Property Address (street, city, state, & ZIP)	No. of Units

Legal Description of Subject Property (attach description if necessary)	Year Built

Purpose of Loan	☐ Purchase ☐ Refinance	☐ Construction ☐ Construction-Permanent	☐ Other (explain):	Property will be: ☐ Primary Residence ☐ Secondary Residence ☐ Investment

Complete this line if construction or construction-permanent loan.

Year Lot Acquired	Original Cost $	Amount Existing Liens $	(a) Present Value of Lot $	(b) Cost of Improvements $	Total (a + b) $

Complete this line if this is a refinance loan.

Year Acquired	Original Cost $	Amount Existing Liens $	Purpose of Refinance	Describe Improvements ☐ made ☐ to be made Cost: $

Title will be held in what Name(s)	Manner in which Title will be held	Estate will be held in: ☐ Fee Simple ☐ Leasehold (show expiration date)

Source of Down Payment, Settlement Charges and/or Subordinate Financing (explain)	

III. BORROWER INFORMATION

Borrower	Co-Borrower
Borrower's Name (include Jr. or Sr. if applicable)	Co-Borrower's Name (include Jr. or Sr. if applicable)

Social Security Number	Home Phone (incl. area code)	Age	Yrs. School	Social Security Number	Home Phone (incl. area code)	Age	Yrs. School

☐ Married ☐ Separated ☐ Unmarried (include single, divorced, widowed)	Dependents (not listed by Co-Borrower) no. ages	☐ Married ☐ Separated ☐ Unmarried (include single, divorced, widowed)	Dependents (not listed by Borrower) no. ages

Present Address (street, city, state, ZIP) ☐ Own ☐ Rent ___ No. Yrs.	Present Address (street, city, state, ZIP) ☐ Own ☐ Rent ___ No. Yrs.

If residing at present address for less than two years, complete the following:

Former Address (street, city, state, ZIP) ☐ Own ☐ Rent ___ No. Yrs.	Former Address (street, city, state, ZIP) ☐ Own ☐ Rent ___ No. Yrs.

Former Address (street, city, state, ZIP) ☐ Own ☐ Rent ___ No. Yrs.	Former Address (street, city, state, ZIP) ☐ Own ☐ Rent ___ No. Yrs.

IV. EMPLOYMENT INFORMATION

Borrower	Co-Borrower
Name & Address of Employer ☐ Self Employed	Yrs. on this job	Name & Address of Employer ☐ Self Employed	Yrs. on this job

	Yrs. employed in this line of work/profession		Yrs. employed in this line of work/profession

Position/Title/Type of Business	Business Phone (incl. area code)	Position/Title/Type of Business	Business Phone (incl. area code)

If employed in current position for less than two years or if currently employed in more than one position, complete the following:

Name & Address of Employer ☐ Self Employed	Dates (from - to)	Name & Address of Employer ☐ Self Employed	Dates (from - to)
	Monthly Income $		Monthly Income $

Position/Title/Type of Business	Business Phone (incl. area code)	Position/Title/Type of Business	Business Phone (incl. area code)

Name & Address of Employer ☐ Self Employed	Dates (from - to)	Name & Address of Employer ☐ Self Employed	Dates (from - to)
	Monthly Income $		Monthly Income $

Position/Title/Type of Business	Business Phone (incl. area code)	Position/Title/Type of Business	Business Phone (incl. area code)

Freddie Mac Form 65 10/92   Page 1 of 4   Fannie Mae Form 1003 10/92

V. MONTHLY INCOME AND COMBINED HOUSING EXPENSE INFORMATION

Gross Monthly Income	Borrower	Co-Borrower	Total	Combined Monthly Housing Expense	Present	Proposed
Base Empl. Income *	$	$	$	Rent	$	▓▓▓
Overtime				First Mortgage (P&I)		$
Bonuses				Other Financing (P&I)		
Commissions				Hazard Insurance		
Dividends/Interest				Real Estate Taxes		
Net Rental Income				Mortgage Insurance		
Other (before completing, see the notice in "describe other income," below)				Homeowner Assn. Dues		
				Other:		
Total	$	$	$	Total	$	$

* Self Employed Borrower(s) may be required to provide additional documentation such as tax returns and financial statements.

Describe Other Income *Notice:* Alimony, child support, or separate maintenance income need not be revealed if the Borrower (B) or Co-Borrower (C) does not choose to have it considered for repaying this loan.

B/C		Monthly Amount
		$

VI. ASSETS AND LIABILITIES

This Statement and any applicable supporting schedules may be completed jointly by both married and unmarried Co-Borrowers if their assets and liabilities are sufficiently joined so that the Statement can be meaningfully and fairly presented on a combined basis; otherwise separate Statements and Schedules are required. If the Co-Borrower section was completed about a spouse, this Statement and supporting schedules must be completed about that spouse also.

Completed ☐ Jointly ☐ Not Jointly

ASSETS Description	Cash or Market Value	Liabilities and Pledged Assets...
Cash deposit toward purchase held by:	$	

Liabilities and Pledged Assets. List the creditor's name, address and account number for all outstanding debts, including automobile loans, revolving charge accounts, real estate loans, alimony, child support, stock pledges, etc. Use continuation sheet, if necessary. Indicate by (*) those liabilities which will be satisfied upon sale of real estate owned or upon refinancing of the subject property.

LIABILITIES	Monthly Payt. & Mos. Left to Pay	Unpaid Balance
Name and address of Company	$ Payt./Mos.	$

List checking and savings accounts below

Name and address of Bank, S&L, or Credit Union

Acct. no. $

(various repeated Name and address of Bank / Company sections)

Stocks & Bonds (Company name/number & description)	$
Life insurance net cash value	$
Face amount: $	
Subtotal Liquid Assets	$
Real estate owned (enter market value from schedule of real estate owned)	$
Vested interest in retirement fund	$
Net worth of business(es) owned (attach financial statement)	$
Automobiles owned (make and year)	$
Other Assets (itemize)	$

Alimony/Child Support/Separate Maintenance Payments Owed to: $

Job Related Expense (child care, union dues, etc.) $

Total Monthly Payments $

| Total Assets a. | $ | Net Worth (a minus b) $ | Total Liabilities b. | $ |

VI. ASSETS AND LIABILITIES (cont.)

Schedule of Real Estate Owned (If additional properties are owned, use continuation sheet.)

Property Address (enter S if sold, PS if pending sale or R if rental being held for income)	Type of Property	Present Market Value	Amount of Mortgages & Liens	Gross Rental Income	Mortgage Payments	Insurance, Maintenance, Taxes & Misc.	Net Rental Income
		$	$	$	$	$	$
	Totals	$	$	$	$	$	$

List any additional names under which credit has previously been received and indicate appropriate creditor name(s) and account number(s):

Alternate Name	Creditor Name	Account Number

VII. DETAILS OF TRANSACTION

a. Purchase price	$
b. Alterations, improvements, repairs	
c. Land (if acquired separately)	
d. Refinance (incl. debts to be paid off)	
e. Estimated prepaid items	
f. Estimated closing costs	
g. PMI, MIP, Funding Fee	
h. Discount (if Borrower will pay)	
i. Total costs (add items a through h)	
j. Subordinate financing	
k. Borrower's closing costs paid by Seller	
l. Other Credits (explain)	
m. Loan amount (exclude PMI, MIP, Funding Fee financed)	
n. PMI, MIP, Funding Fee financed	
o. Loan amount (add m & n)	
p. Cash from/to Borrower (subtract j, k, l & o from i)	

VIII. DECLARATIONS

If you answer "yes" to any questions a through i, please use continuation sheet for explanation.

	Borrower Yes	Borrower No	Co-Borrower Yes	Co-Borrower No
a. Are there any outstanding judgments against you?	☐	☐	☐	☐
b. Have you been declared bankrupt within the past 7 years?	☐	☐	☐	☐
c. Have you had property foreclosed upon or given title or deed in lieu thereof in the last 7 years?	☐	☐	☐	☐
d. Are you a party to a lawsuit?	☐	☐	☐	☐
e. Have you directly or indirectly been obligated on any loan which resulted in foreclosure, transfer of title in lieu of foreclosure, or judgment? (This would include such loans as home mortgage loans, SBA loans, home improvement loans, educational loans, manufactured (mobile) home loans, any mortgage, financial obligation, bond, or loan guarantee. If "Yes," provide details, including date, name and address of Lender, FHA or VA case number, if any, and reasons for the action.)	☐	☐	☐	☐
f. Are you presently delinquent or in default on any Federal debt or any other loan, mortgage, financial obligation, bond, or loan guarantee? If "Yes," give details as described in the preceding question.	☐	☐	☐	☐
g. Are you obligated to pay alimony, child support, or separate maintenance?	☐	☐	☐	☐
h. Is any part of the down payment borrowed?	☐	☐	☐	☐
i. Are you a co-maker or endorser on a note?	☐	☐	☐	☐
j. Are you a U.S. citizen?	☐	☐	☐	☐
k. Are you a permanent resident alien?	☐	☐	☐	☐
l. Do you intend to occupy the property as your primary residence? If "Yes," complete question m below.	☐	☐	☐	☐
m. Have you had an ownership interest in a property in the last three years?	☐	☐	☐	☐

(1) What type of property did you own—principal residence (PR), second home (SH), or investment property (IP)? _____

(2) How did you hold title to the home—solely by yourself (S), jointly with your spouse (SP), or jointly with another person (O)? _____

IX. ACKNOWLEDGMENT AND AGREEMENT

The undersigned specifically acknowledge(s) and agree(s) that: (1) the loan requested by this application will be secured by a first mortgage or deed of trust on the property described herein; (2) the property will not be used for any illegal or prohibited purpose or use; (3) all statements made in this application are made for the purpose of obtaining the loan indicated herein; (4) occupation of the property will be as indicated above; (5) verification or reverification of any information contained in the application may be made at any time by the Lender, its agents, successors and assigns, either directly or through a credit reporting agency, from any source named in this application, and the original copy of this application will be retained by the Lender, even if the loan is not approved; (6) the Lender, its agents, successors and assigns will rely on the information contained in the application and I/we have a continuing obligation to amend and/or supplement the information provided in this application if any of the material facts which I/we have represented herein should change prior to closing; (7) in the event my/our payments on the loan indicated in this application become delinquent, the Lender, its agents, successors and assigns, may, in addition to all their other rights and remedies, report my/our name(s) and account information to a credit reporting agency; (8) ownership of the loan may be transferred to successor or assign of the Lender without notice to me and/or the administration of the loan account may be transferred to an agent, successor or assign of the Lender with prior notice to me; (9) the Lender, its agents, successors and assigns make no representations or warranties, express or implied, to the Borrower(s) regarding the property, the condition of the property, or the value of the property.

Certification: I/We certify that the information provided in this application is true and correct as of the date set forth opposite my/our signature(s) on this application and acknowledge my/our understanding that any intentional or negligent misrepresentation(s) of the information contained in this application may result in civil liability and/or criminal penalties including, but not limited to, fine or imprisonment or both under the provisions of Title 18, United States Code, Section 1001, et seq. and liability for monetary damages to the Lender, its agents, successors and assigns, insurers and any other person who may suffer any loss due to reliance upon any misrepresentation which I/we have made on this application.

Borrower's Signature	Date	Co-Borrower's Signature	Date
X		X	

X. INFORMATION FOR GOVERNMENT MONITORING PURPOSES

The following information is requested by the Federal Government for certain types of loans related to a dwelling, in order to monitor the Lender's compliance with equal credit opportunity, fair housing and home mortgage disclosure laws. You are not required to furnish this information, but are encouraged to do so. The law provides that a Lender may neither discriminate on the basis of this information, nor on whether you choose to furnish it. However, if you choose not to furnish it, under Federal regulations this Lender is required to note race and sex on the basis of visual observation or surname. If you do not wish to furnish the above information, please check the box below. (Lender must review the above material to assure that the disclosures satisfy all requirements to which the Lender is subject under applicable state law for the particular type of loan applied for.)

BORROWER ☐ I do not wish to furnish this information

Race/National Origin: ☐ American Indian or Alaskan Native ☐ Asian or Pacific Islander ☐ White, not of Hispanic Origin ☐ Black, not of Hispanic origin ☐ Hispanic ☐ Other (specify) _____

Sex: ☐ Female ☐ Male

CO-BORROWER ☐ I do not wish to furnish this information

Race/National Origin: ☐ American Indian or Alaskan Native ☐ Asian or Pacific Islander ☐ White, not of Hispanic Origin ☐ Black, not of Hispanic origin ☐ Hispanic ☐ Other (specify) _____

Sex: ☐ Female ☐ Male

To be Completed by Interviewer

This application was taken by:
☐ face-to-face interview
☐ by mail
☐ by telephone

Interviewer's Name (print or type)	Name and Address of Interviewer's Employer
Interviewer's Signature Date	
Interviewer's Phone Number (incl. area code)	

Continuation Sheet Residential Loan Application

Use this continuation sheet if you need more space to complete the Residential Loan Application. Mark B for Borrower or C for Co-Borrower.	Borrower:	Agency Case Number:
	Co-Borrower:	Lender Case Number:

I/We fully understand that it is a Federal crime punishable by fine or imprisonment, or both, to knowingly make any false statements concerning any of the above facts as applicable under the provisions of Title 18, United States Code, Section 1001, et seq.

Borrower's Signature:	Date	Co-Borrower's Signature:	Date
X		X	

Freddie Mac Form 65   10/92   Page 4 of 4   Fannie Mae Form 1003   10/92

Appendix C to Part 202—Sample Notification Forms

This appendix contains nine sample notification forms. Forms C-1 through C-4 are intended for use in notifying an applicant that adverse action has been taken on an application or account under § 202.9(a)(1) and (2)(i) of this regulation. Form C-5 is a notice of disclosure of the right to request specific reasons for adverse action under § 202.9(a)(1) and (2)(ii). Form C-6 is designed for use in notifying an applicant, under § 202.9(c)(2), that an application is incomplete. Forms C-7 and C-8 are intended for use in connection with applications for business credit under § 202.9(a)(3). Form C-9 is designed for use in notifying an applicant of the right to receive a copy of an appraisal under § 202.5a.

Form C-1 contains the Fair Credit Reporting Act disclosure as required by sections 615(a) and (b) of that act. Forms C-2 through C-5 contain only the section 615(a) disclosure (that a creditor obtained information from a consumer reporting agency that played a part in the credit decision). A creditor must provide the 615(a) disclosure when adverse action is taken against a consumer based on information from a consumer reporting agency. A creditor must provide the section 615(b) disclosure when adverse action is taken based on information from an outside source other than a consumer reporting agency. In addition, a creditor must provide the 615(b) disclosure if the creditor obtained information from an affiliate other than information in a consumer report or other than information concerning the affiliate's own transactions or experiences with the consumer. Creditors may comply with the disclosure requirements for adverse action based on information in a consumer report obtained from an affiliate by providing *either* the 615(a) or 615(b) disclosure.

The sample forms are illustrative and may not be appropriate for all creditors. They were designed to include some of the factors that creditors most commonly consider. If a creditor chooses to use the checklist of reasons provided in one of the sample forms in this appendix and if reasons commonly used by the creditor are not provided on the form, the creditor should modify the checklist by substituting or adding other reasons. For example, if "inadequate down payment" or "no deposit relationship with us" are common reasons for taking adverse action on an application, the creditor ought to add or substitute such reasons for those presently contained on the sample forms.

If the reasons listed on the forms are not the factors actually used, a creditor will not satisfy the notice requirement by simply checking the closest identifiable factor listed. For example, some creditors consider only references from banks or other depository institutions and disregard finance company references altogether; their statement of reasons should disclose "insufficient bank references," not "insufficient credit references." Similarly, a creditor that considers bank references and other credit references as distinct factors should treat the two factors separately and disclose them as appropriate. The creditor should either add such other factors to the form or check "other" and include the appropriate explanation. The creditor need not, however, describe how or why a factor adversely affected the application. For example, the notice may say "length of residence" rather than "too short a period of residence."

A creditor may design its own notification forms or use all or a portion of the forms contained in this appendix. Proper use of Forms C-1 through C-4 will satisfy the requirements of § 202.9(a)(2)(i). Proper use of Forms C-5 and C-6 constitutes full compliance with §§ 202.9(a)(2)(ii) and 202.9(c)(2), respectively. Proper use of Forms C-7 and C-8 will satisfy the requirements of § 202.9(a)(2) (i) and (ii), respectively, for applications for business credit. Proper use of Form C-9 will satisfy the requirements of § 202.5a of this part.

Form C-1—Sample Notice of Action Taken and Statement of Reasons
Statement of Credit Denial, Termination, or Change

Date _____

Applicant's Name: _____

Applicant's Address: _____

Description of Account, Transaction, or Requested Credit:

_____

Description of Action Taken:

_____

_____

Part I—PRINCIPAL REASON(S) FOR CREDIT DENIAL, TERMINATION, OR OTHER ACTION TAKEN CONCERNING CREDIT.
This section must be completed in all instances.

_____ Credit application incomplete

_____ Insufficient number of credit references provided

_____ Unacceptable type of credit references provided

_____ Unable to verify credit references

_____ Temporary or irregular employment

_____ Unable to verify employment

_____ Length of employment

_____ Income insufficient for amount of credit requested

_____ Excessive obligations in relation to income

_____ Unable to verify income

_____ Length of residence

_____ Temporary residence

_____ Unable to verify residence

_____ No credit file

_____ Limited credit experience

_____ Poor credit performance with us

_____ Delinquent past or present credit obligations with others

_____ Garnishment, attachment, foreclosure, repossession, collection action, or judgment

_____ Bankruptcy

_____ Value or type of collateral not sufficient

_____ Other, specify:_____

Part II—DISCLOSURE OF USE OF INFORMATION OBTAINED FROM AN OUTSIDE SOURCE.

This section should be completed if the credit decision was based in whole or in part on information that has been obtained from an outside source.

_____ Our credit decision was based in whole or in part on information obtained in a report from the consumer reporting agency listed below. You have a right under the Fair Credit Reporting Act to know the information contained in your credit file at the consumer reporting agency. The reporting agency played no part in our decision and is unable to supply specific reasons why we have denied credit to you. You also have a right to a free copy of your report from the reporting agency, if you request it no later than 60 days after you receive this notice. In addition, if you find that any information contained in the report you receive is inaccurate or incomplete, you have the right to dispute the matter with the reporting agency.

Name: _____

_____

Address:_____

_____

[Toll-free] Telephone number:_____

_____ Our credit decision was based in whole or in part on information obtained from an affiliate or from an outside source other than a consumer reporting agency. Under the Fair Credit Reporting Act, you have the right to make a written request, no later than 60 days after you receive this notice, for disclosure of the nature of this information.

_____

If you have any questions regarding this notice, you should contact:

Creditor's name: _____

Creditor's address: _____

Creditor's telephone number: _____

NOTICE

The federal Equal Credit Opportunity Act prohibits creditors from discriminating against credit applicants on the basis of race, color, religion, national origin, sex, marital status, age (provided the applicant has the capacity to enter into a binding contract); because all or part of the applicant's income derives from any public assistance program; or because the applicant has in good faith exercised any right under the Consumer Credit Protection Act. The federal agency that administers compliance with this law concerning this creditor is (name and address as specified by the appropriate agency listed in appendix A).

Form C-2—Sample Notice of Action Taken and Statement of Reasons

Date_____

Dear Applicant:

Thank you for your recent application. Your request for [a loan/a credit card/an increase in your credit limit] was carefully considered, and we regret that we are unable to approve your application at this time, for the following reason(s):

Your Income:

_____ is below our minimum requirement.

_____ is insufficient to sustain payments on the amount of credit requested.

_____ could not be verified.

Your Employment:

_____ is not of sufficient length to qualify.

_____ could not be verified.

Your Credit History:

_____ of making payments on time was not satisfactory.

_____ could not be verified.

Your Application:

_____ lacks a sufficient number of credit references.

_____ lacks acceptable types of credit references.

_____ reveals that current obligations are excessive in relation to income.

Other:_____

The consumer reporting agency contacted that provided information that influenced our decision in whole or in part was [name, address and [toll-free] telephone number of the reporting agency]. The reporting agency is unable to supply specific reasons why we have denied credit to you. You do, however, have a right under the Fair Credit Reporting Act to know the information contained in your credit file. You also have a right to a free copy of your report from the reporting agency, if you request it no later than 60 days after you receive this notice. In addition, if you find that any information contained in the report you receive is inaccurate or incomplete, you have the right to dispute the matter with the reporting agency. Any questions regarding such information should be directed to [consumer reporting agency].

If you have any questions regarding this letter you should contact us at [creditor's name, address and telephone number].

NOTICE: The federal Equal Credit Opportunity Act prohibits creditors from discriminating against credit applicants on the basis of race, color, religion, national origin, sex, marital status, age (provided the applicant has the capacity to enter into a binding contract); because all or part of the applicant's income derives from any public assistance program; or because the applicant has in good faith exercised any right under the Consumer Credit Protection Act. The federal agency that administers compliance with this law concerning this creditor is (name and address as specified by the appropriate agency listed in Appendix A).

Form C-3—Sample Notice of Action Taken and Statement of Reasons (Credit Scoring)

Date_____

Dear Applicant:

Thank you for your recent application for _____ . We regret that we are unable to approve your request.

Your application was processed by a credit scoring system that assigns a numerical value to the various items of information we consider in evaluating an application. These numerical values are based upon the results of analyses of repayment histories of large numbers of customers.

The information you provided in your application did not score a sufficient number of points for approval of the application. The reasons why you did not score well compared to other applicants were:

- Insufficient bank references
- Type of occupation
- Insufficient credit experience

In evaluating your application the consumer reporting agency listed below provided us with information that in whole or in part influenced our decision. The reporting agency played no part in our decision other than providing us with credit information about you. Under the Fair Credit Reporting Act, you have a right to know the information provided to us. It can be obtained by contacting: [name, address, and [toll-free] telephone number of the consumer reporting agency]. You also have a right to a free copy of your report from the reporting agency, if you request it no later than 60 days after you receive this notice. In addition, if you find that any information contained in the report you receive is inaccurate or incomplete, you have the right to dispute the matter with the reporting agency.

If you have any questions regarding this letter, you should contact us at:

Creditor's Name: _____

Address: _____

_____

Telephone: _____

Sincerely,

NOTICE: The federal Equal Credit Opportunity Act prohibits creditors from discriminating against credit applicants on the basis of race, color, religion, national origin, sex, marital status, age (with certain limited exceptions); because all or part of the applicant's income derives from any public assistance program; or because the applicant has in good faith exercised any right under the Consumer Credit Protection Act. The federal agency that administers compliance with this law concerning this creditor is (name and address as specified by the appropriate agency listed in Appendix A).

Form C-4—Sample Notice of Action Taken, Statement of Reasons and Counteroffer

Date _____

Dear Applicant:

Thank you for your application for _____ . We are unable to offer you credit on the terms that you requested for the following reason(s): _____ .

We can, however, offer you credit on the following terms: _____ .

If this offer is acceptable to you, please notify us within [amount of time] at the following address:_____ .

Our credit decision on your application was based in whole or in part on information obtained in a report from [name, address and [toll-free] telephone number of the consumer reporting agency]. You have a right under the Fair Credit Reporting Act to know the information contained in your credit file at the consumer reporting agency. You also have a right to a free copy of your report from the reporting agency, if you request it no later than 60 days after you receive this notice. In addition, if you find that any information contained in the report you receive is inaccurate or incomplete, you have the right to dispute the matter with the reporting agency.

You should know that the federal Equal Credit Opportunity Act prohibits creditors, such as ourselves, from discriminating against credit applicants on the basis of their race, color, religion, national origin, sex, marital status, age, because they receive income from a public assistance program, or because they may have exercised their rights under the Consumer Credit Protection Act. If you believe there has been discrimination in handling your application you should contact the [name and address of the appropriate federal enforcement agency listed in Appendix A].

Sincerely,

Form C-5—Sample Disclosure of Right to Request Specific Reasons for Credit Denial

Date_____

Dear Applicant:

Thank you for applying to us for _____ .

After carefully reviewing your application, we are sorry to advise you that we cannot [open an account for you/grant a loan to you/increase your credit limit] at this time.

If you would like a statement of specific reasons why your application was denied, please contact [our credit service manager] shown below within 60 days of the date of this letter. We will provide you with the statement of reasons within 30 days after receiving your request.

Creditor's Name
Address
Telephone number

If we obtained information from a consumer reporting agency as part of our consideration of your application, its name, address, and [toll-free] telephone number is shown below. The reporting agency played no part in our decision and is unable to supply specific reasons why we have denied credit to you. You have a right to a free copy of your report from the reporting agency, if you request it no later than 60 days after you receive this notice. In addition, if you find that any information contained in the report you receive is inaccurate or incomplete, you have the right to dispute the matter with the reporting agency. You can find out about the information contained in your file (if one was used) by contacting:

> Consumer reporting agency's name
> Address
> [Toll-free] Telephone number

Sincerely,

NOTICE

The federal Equal Credit Opportunity Act prohibits creditors from discriminating against credit applicants on the basis of race, color, religion, national origin, sex, marital status, age (provided the applicant has the capacity to enter into a binding contract); because all or part of the applicant's income derives from any public assistance program; or because the applicant has in good faith exercised any right under the Consumer Credit Protection Act. The federal agency that administers compliance with this law concerning this creditor is (name and address as specified by the appropriate agency listed in Appendix A).

Form C-6—Sample Notice of Incomplete Application and Request for Additional Information

Creditor's name
Address
Telephone number

Date _____

Dear Applicant:

Thank you for your application for credit. The following information is needed to make a decision on your application: . We need to receive this information by (*date*). If we do not receive it by that date, we will regrettably be unable to give further consideration to your credit request.

Sincerely,

Form C-7—Sample Notice of Action Taken and Statement of Reasons (Business Credit)******

Creditor's name
Creditor's address

****** [*Editor's note*: In 1989 the Federal Reserve Board amended Appendix C by adding forms C-7 and C-8 to implement amendments to the ECOA contained in the Women's Business Ownership Act. In the Supplementary Information published in the Federal Register along with the amendments, the Board described Form C-7, and use of the forms in Appendix C in general, as follows:

> Form C-7 is a sample notice for giving a statement of reasons for a credit denial; the reasons for a credit denial contained in the form are illustrative only. . . .
> A creditor may design its own notices or use all or a portion of the forms contained in the appendix. Proper use of the forms will satisfy the requirements of § 202.9(a)(2)(i) and § 202.9(a)(3), respectively, for applications for business credit.

54 Fed. Reg. 50,482 (Dec. 7, 1989).]

Date _____

Dear Applicant:

Thank you for applying to us for credit. We have given your request careful consideration, and regret that we are unable to extend credit to you at this time for the following reasons:

[Insert appropriate reason, such as

Value or type of collateral not sufficient

Lack of established earnings record

Slow or past due in trade or loan payments]

Sincerely,

NOTICE: The federal Equal Credit Opportunity Act prohibits creditors from discriminating against credit applicants on the basis of race, color, religion, national origin, sex, marital status, age (provided the applicant has the capacity to enter into a binding contract); because all or part of the applicant's income derives from any public assistance program; or because the applicant has in good faith exercised any right under the Consumer Credit Protection Act. The federal agency that administers compliance with this law concerning this creditor is (name and address as specified by the appropriate agency listed in appendix A).

Form C-8—Sample Disclosure of Right to Request Specific Reasons for Credit Denial Given at Time of Application (Business Credit)*******

Creditor's name
Creditor's address

If your application for business credit is denied, you have the right to a written statement of the specific reasons for the denial. To obtain the statement, please contact [name, address and telephone number of the person or office from which the statement of reasons can be obtained] within 60 days from the date you are notified of our decision. We will send you a written statement of reasons for the denial within 30 days of receiving your request for the statement.

NOTICE: The federal Equal Credit Opportunity Act prohibits creditors from discriminating against credit applicants on the basis of race, color, religion, national origin, sex, marital status, age (provided the applicant has the capacity to enter into a binding

---

******* [*Editor's note:* In 1989 the Federal Reserve Board amended Appendix C by adding forms C-7 and C-8 to implement amendments to the ECOA contained in the Women's Business Ownership Act. In the Supplementary Information published in the Federal Register along with the amendments, the Board described Form C-8, and use of the forms in Appendix C in general, as follows:

> Form C-8 is a sample disclosure of the *right* to a statement of reasons, of the type that would be given at the time of application.
> A creditor may design its own notices or use all or a portion of the forms contained in the appendix. Proper use of the forms will satisfy the requirements of § 202.9(a)(2)(i) and § 202.9(a)(3), respectively, for applications for business credit.

54 Fed. Reg. 50,482 (Dec. 7, 1989).]

contract); because all or part of the applicant's income derives from any public assistance program; or because the applicant has in good faith exercised any right under the Consumer Credit Protection Act. The federal agency that administers compliance with this law concerning this creditor is [name and address as specified by the appropriate agency listed in appendix A].

Form C-9 Sample Disclosure of Right to Receive a Copy of an Appraisal

You have the right to a copy of the appraisal report used in connection with your application for credit. If you wish a copy, please write to us at the mailing address we have provided. We must hear from you no later than 90 days after we notify you about the action taken on your credit application or if you withdraw your application.

[In your letter, give us the following information:]

[Reg. B, 50 FR 48026, Nov. 20, 1985, amended at 54 FR 50486, Dec. 7, 1989; 58 FR 65662, Dec. 16, 1993; 63 FR 16392, Apr. 30, 1998]

Appendix D to Part 202—Issuance of Staff Interpretations

Official Staff Interpretations

Officials in the Board's Division of Consumer and Community Affairs are authorized to issue official staff interpretations of this regulation. These interpretations provide the protection afforded under section 706(e) of the Act. Except in unusual circumstances, such interpretations will not be issued separately but will be incorporated in an official commentary to the regulation, which will be amended periodically.

Requests for Issuance of Official Staff Interpretations

A request for an official staff interpretation should be in writing and addressed to the Director, Division of Consumer and Community Affairs, Board of Governors of the Federal Reserve System, Washington, D.C. 20551. The request should contain a complete statement of all relevant facts concerning the issue, including copies of all pertinent documents.

Scope of Interpretations

No staff interpretations will be issued approving creditor's forms or statements. This restriction does not apply to forms or statements whose use is required or sanctioned by a government agency.

Appendix C   Official Staff Commentary on Regulation B

FRB Official Staff Commentary, 12 C.F.R. § 202, ECO-1 to Regulation B, Dec. 16, 1985, as amended by 52 Fed. Reg. 10,733 (Apr. 3, 1987), 53 Fed. Reg. 11,044 (Apr. 5, 1988), 54 Fed. Reg. 9416 (Mar. 7, 1989), 55 Fed. Reg. 12,471 (Apr. 4, 1990), 56 Fed. Reg. 14,461 (Apr. 10, 1991) (amendments published again at 56 Fed. Reg. 16,265 (Apr. 22, 1991)), 57 Fed. Reg. 12,202 (Apr. 9, 1992), 60 Fed. Reg. 29,967 (June 5, 1995), 61 Fed. Reg. 50,948 (Sept. 30, 1996), and 62 Fed. Reg. 66,412 (Dec. 18, 1997).

The current Official Staff Commentary is reproduced below. Bracketed material in footnotes throughout the text contains additional explanatory notes from the Supplementary Information published in the Federal Register along with all amendments made through December 18, 1997, to the Official Staff Commentary text. These notes, however, are not part of the Official Staff Commentary, and are included to provide further elucidation of the Federal Reserve Board's reasoning in amending the text.

In 1999, the Federal Reserve Board (FRB) issued a comprehensive set of proposed revisions to Regulation B, including revisions to the Official Staff Commentary. As of the printing of this manual, the FRB had not issued final rules or a finalized Official Staff Commentary. The text of the August 1999 proposed revisions to the Official Staff Commentary is included on the CD-Rom accompanying this volume.

In April 2001, the FRB published an interim final rule, including revisions to the Official Staff Commentary, amending Regulation B to provide for electronic delivery of ECOA notifications. In August 2001, the FRB rescinded the October 1, 2001 deadline for compliance with the interim final rule. As of the printing of this manual, the FRB has not issued a revised final or interim rule. The text of the changes to the Official Staff Commentary made by the interim final rule on electronic delivery is included on the CD-Rom accompanying this volume.

SUPPLEMENT I TO PART 202—OFFICIAL STAFF INTERPRETATIONS

[Reg. B; ECO-1]

Following is an official staff interpretation of Regulation B issued under authority delegated by the Federal Reserve Board to officials in the Division of Consumer and Community Affairs. References are to sections of the regulation or the Equal Credit Opportunity Act (15 U.S.C. 1691 et seq.).

INTRODUCTION

1. *Official status.* Section 706(e) of the Equal Credit Opportunity Act protects a creditor from civil liability for any act done or omitted in good faith in conformity with an interpretation issued by a duly authorized official of the Federal Reserve Board. This commentary is the means by which the Division of Consumer and Community Affairs of the Federal Reserve Board issues official staff interpretations of Regulation B. Good-faith compliance with this commentary affords a creditor protection under section 706(e) of the Act.

2. *Issuance of interpretations.* Under Appendix D to the regulation, any person may request an official staff interpretation. Interpretations will be issued at the discretion of designated officials and incorporated in this commentary following publication for comment in the **Federal Register**. Except in unusual circumstances, official staff interpretations will be issued only by means of this commentary.

3. *Status of previous interpretations.* Interpretations of Regulation B previously issued by the Federal Reserve Board and its staff have been incorporated into this commentary as appropriate. All other previous Board and staff interpretations, official and unofficial, are superseded by this commentary.

4. *Footnotes.*[1] Footnotes in the regulation have the same legal effect as the text of the regulation, whether they are explanatory or illustrative in nature.

---

1   [*Editor's note:* Please note that *bracketed* material in footnotes throughout this reprint of the Official Staff Commentary has been added to provide the Federal Reserve Board's explanatory notes, which were published in the Federal Register along with amendments to the Commentary. These footnotes are *not* part of the Official Staff Commentary.]

5. *Comment designations.* The comments are designated with as much specificity as possible according to the particular regulatory provision addressed. Each comment in the commentary is identified by a number and the regulatory section or paragraph that it interprets. For example, comments to § 202.2(c) are further divided by subparagraph, such as comment 2(c)(1)(ii)-1 and comment 2(c)(2)(ii)-1.

Section 202.1—Authority, Scope, and Purpose

1(a) *Authority and scope.*

1. *Scope.* The Equal Credit Opportunity Act and Regulation B apply to all credit—commercial as well as personal—without regard to the nature or type of the credit or the creditor. If a transaction provides for the deferral of the payment of a debt, it is credit covered by Regulation B even though it may not be a credit transaction covered by Regulation Z (Truth in Lending). Further, the definition of creditor is not restricted to the party or person to whom the obligation is initially payable, as is the case under Regulation Z. Moreover, the Act and regulation apply to all methods of credit evaluation, whether performed judgmentally or by use of a credit scoring system.

2. *Foreign applicability.* Regulation B generally does not apply to lending activities that occur outside the United States. The regulation does apply to lending activities that take place within the United States (as well as the Commonwealth of Puerto Rico and any territory or possession of the United States), whether or not the applicant is a citizen.

3. *Board.*[2] The term Board, as used in this regulation, means the Board of Governors of the Federal Reserve System.

Section 202.2—Definitions

2(c) *Adverse action.*

Paragraph 2(c)(1)(i)

1. *Application for credit.*[3] A refusal to refinance or extend the term of a business or other loan is adverse action if the applicant applied in accordance with the creditor's procedures.

Paragraph 2(c)(1)(ii)

1. *Move from service area.* If a credit card issuer terminates the open-end account of a customer because the customer has moved out of the card issuer's service area, the termination is "adverse action" for purposes of the regulation unless termination on this ground was explicitly provided for in the credit agreement between the parties. In cases where termination is adverse action, notification is required under § 202.9.

2. *Termination based on credit limit.* If a creditor terminates credit accounts that have low credit limits (for example, under $400) but keeps open accounts with higher credit limits, the termination is adverse action and notification is required under § 202.9.

Paragraph 2(c)(2)(ii)

1. *Default—exercise of due-on-sale clause.* If a mortgagor sells or transfers mortgaged property without the consent of the mortgagee, and the mortgagee exercises its contractual right to accelerate the mortgage loan, the mortgagee may treat the mortgagor as being in default. An adverse action notice need not be given to the mortgagor or the transferee. (See comment 2(e)-1 for treatment of a purchaser who requests to assume the loan.)

2. *Current delinquency or default.*[4] The term adverse action does not include a creditor's termination of an account when the accountholder is currently in default or delinquent on that account. Notification in accordance with § 202.9 of the regulation generally is required, however, if the creditor's action is based on a past delinquency or default on the account.

Paragraph (2)(c)(2)(iii)

1. *Point-of-sale transactions.* Denial of credit at point of sale is not adverse action except under those circumstances specified in the regulation. For example, denial, at point of sale is not adverse action in the following situations:

- A credit cardholder presents an expired card or a card that has been reported to the card issuer as lost or stolen.
- The amount of a transaction exceeds a cash advance or credit limit.
- The circumstances (such as excessive use of a credit card in a short period of time) suggests that fraud is involved.
- The authorization facilities are not functioning.
- Billing statements have been returned to the creditor for lack of a forwarding address.

2. *Application for increase in available credit.*[5] A refusal or failure to authorize an account transaction at the point of sale or loan is not adverse action, except when the refusal is a denial of an application, submitted in accordance with the creditor's procedures, for an increase in the amount of credit.

Paragraph 2(c)(2)(v)

1. *Terms of credit versus type of credit offered.* When an applicant applies for credit and the creditor does not offer the credit terms requested by the applicant (for example, the interest rate, length of maturity, collateral, or amount of downpayment), a denial of the application for that reason is adverse action (unless the creditor makes a counteroffer that is accepted by the applicant) and the applicant is entitled to notification under § 202.9.

---

2 [*Editor's note:* "The definition of 'Board,' previously contained in § 202.2(g), is now in the commentary to § 202.1." 55 Fed. Reg. 12,471 (Apr. 4, 1990).]

3 [*Editor's note:* Added by 60 Fed. Reg. 29,967 (June 5, 1995).]

4 [*Editor's note:* "Comment 2(c)(2)(ii)-2 is added to clarify the Board's long-standing position that a notice of adverse action need not be provided in instances where a creditor takes action regarding a current delinquency or default on an account—that is, a delinquency or default that has not been cured by the time a creditor takes action on an account. Notification generally is required, however, for action based on a past delinquency or default that may have previously existed but that no longer continues." 56 Fed. Reg. 14,461 (Apr. 10, 1991).]

5 [*Editor's note:* Comment 2(c)(2)(iii)-2 added to clarify "that a denial of an application to increase available credit . . . is adverse action." 60 Fed. Reg. 29,967 (June 5, 1995).]

2(e) *Applicant.*

1. *Request to assume loan.* If a mortgagor sells or transfers the mortgaged property and the buyer makes an application to the creditor to assume the mortgage loan, the mortgagee must treat the buyer as an applicant unless its policy is not to permit assumptions.

2(f) *Application.*

1. *General.* A creditor has the latitude under the regulation to establish its own application process and to decide the type and amount of information it will require from credit applicants.

2. *Procedures established.* The term refers to the actual practices followed by a creditor for making credit decisions as well as its stated application procedures. For example, if a creditor's stated policy is to require all applications to be in writing on the creditor's application form, but the creditor also makes credit decisions based on oral requests, the creditor's establish procedures are to accept both oral and written applications.

3. *When an inquiry becomes an application.* A creditor is encouraged to provide consumers with information about loan terms. However, if in giving information to the consumer the creditor also evaluates information about the applicant, decides to decline the request, and communicates this to the applicant, the creditor has treated the inquiry as an application and must then comply with the notification requirements under § 202.9. Whether the inquiry becomes an application depends on how the creditor responds to the applicant, not on what the applicant says or asks.

4. *Examples of inquiries that are not applications.* The following examples illustrate situations in which only an inquiry has taken place:

- When a consumer calls to asks about loan terms and an employee explains the creditor's basic loan terms, such as interest rates, loan-to-value ratio, and debt-to-income ratio.
- When a consumer calls to ask about interest rates for car loans, and, in order to quote the appropriate rate, the loan officer asks for the make and sale price of the car and amount of the down-payment, then gives the consumer the rate.
- When a consumer asks about terms for a loan to purchase home and tells the loan officer her income and intended down-payment, but the loan officer only explains the creditor's loan to value ratio policy and other basic lending policies, without telling the consumer whether she qualifies for the loan.
- When a consumer calls to ask about terms for a loan to purchase vacant land and states his income, the sale price of the property to be financed, and asks whether he qualifies for a loan, and the employee responds by describing the general lending policies, explaining that he would need to look at all of the applicant's qualifications before making a decision, and offering to send an application form to the consumer.

5. *Completed application—diligence requirement.* The regulation defines a completed application in terms that give a creditor the latitude to establish its own information requirements. Nevertheless, the creditor must act with reasonable diligence to collect information needed to complete the application. For example, the creditor should request information from third parties, such as a credit report, promptly after receiving the application. If additional information is needed from the applicant, such as an address or telephone number needed to verify employment, the creditor should contact the applicant promptly. (But see comment 9(a)(1)-3, which discusses the creditor's option to deny an application on the basis of incompleteness.)

2(g) *Business credit.*

1. *Definition.*[6] The test for deciding whether a transaction qualifies as business credit is one of primary purpose. For example, an open-end credit account used for both personal and business purposes is not business credit unless the primary purpose of the account is business-related. A creditor may rely on an applicant's statement of the purpose for the credit requested.

2(j) *Credit.*

1. *General.* Regulation B covers a wider range of credit transactions than Regulation Z (Truth in Lending). For purposes of Regulation B a transaction is credit if there is a right to defer payment of a debt—regardless of whether the credit is for personal or commercial purposes, the number of installments required for repayment, or whether the transaction is subject to a finance charge.

2(l) *Creditor.*

1. *Assignees.* The term "creditor" includes all persons participating in the credit decision. This may include an assignee or a potential purchaser of the obligation who influences the credit decision by indicating whether or not it will purchase the obligation if the transaction is consummated.

2. *Referrals to creditors.* For certain purposes, the term "creditor" includes persons such as real estate brokers who do not participate in credit decisions but who regularly refer applicants to creditors or who select or offer to select creditors to whom credit requests can be made. These persons must comply with § 202.4, the general rule prohibiting discrimination, and with § 202.5(a), on discouraging applications.

2(p) *Empirically derived and other credit scoring systems.*

1. *Purpose of definition.* The definition under § 202.2(p)(1) through (iv) sets the criteria that a credit system must meet in order for the system to use age as a predictive factor. Credit systems that do not meet these criteria are judgmental systems and may consider age only for the purpose of determining a "pertinent element of credit-worthiness." (Both types of systems may favor an elderly applicant. See § 202.6(b)(2).)

2. *Periodic revalidation.*[7] The regulation does not specify how often credit scoring systems must be revalidated. To meet the

---

6 [*Editor's note:* "In the December 1989 amendments to the regulation, the definition of business credit was moved from § 202.3(d)(1) to § 202.2(g). Accordingly, comment 3(d)-1 has been redesignated comment 2(g)-1." 55 Fed. Reg. 12,471 (Apr. 4, 1990).]

7 [*Editor's note:* "The comment, as adopted, provides that creditors must periodically review their systems to ensure predictive ability, but are not required to review their systems on a continuous basis. The Board believes the required frequency

requirements for statistical soundness, the credit scoring system must be revalidated frequently enough to assure that it continues to meet recognized professional statistical standards. To ensure that predictive ability is being maintained, creditors must periodically review the performance of the system. This could be done, for example, by analyzing the loan portfolio to determine the delinquency rate for each score interval, or by analyzing population stability over time to detect deviations of recent applications from the applicant population used to validate the system. If this analysis indicates that the system no longer predicts risk with statistical soundness, the system must be adjusted as necessary to reestablish its predictive ability. A creditor is responsible for ensuring its system is validated and revalidated based on the creditor's own data when it becomes available.

3. *Pooled data scoring systems.*[8] A scoring system or the data from which to develop such a system may be obtained from either a single credit grantor or multiple credit grantors. The resulting system will qualify as an empirically derived, demonstrably and statistically sound, credit scoring system provided the criteria set forth in paragraph (p)(1) (i) through (iv) of this section are met.

4. *Effects test and disparate treatment.*[9] An empirically derived, demonstrably and statistically sound, credit scoring system may include age as a predictive factor (provided that the age of an elderly applicant is not assigned a negative factor or value). Besides age, no other prohibited basis may be used as a variable. Generally, credit scoring systems treat all applicants objectively and thus avoid problems of disparate treatment. In cases where a credit scoring system is used in conjunction with individual discretion, disparate treatment could conceivably occur in the evaluation process. In addition, neutral factors used in credit scoring systems could nonetheless be subject to challenge under the effects test. (See comment 6(a)-2 for a discussion of the effects test).

2(w) *Open-end credit.*

1. *Open-end real estate mortgages.* The term "open-end credit" does not include negotiated advances under an open-end real estate mortgage or a letter of credit.

2(z) *Prohibited basis.*

1. *Persons associated with applicant.* "Prohibited basis" as used in this regulation refers not only to certain characteristics—the race, color, religion, national origin, sex, marital status, or age—of an applicant (or officers of an applicant in the case of a corporation) but also to the characteristics of individuals with whom an applicant is affiliated or with whom the applicant associates. This means, for example, that under the general rule stated in § 202.4, a creditor may not discriminate against an applicant because of that person's personal or business dealings with members of a certain religion, because of the national origin of any persons associated with the extension of credit (such as the tenants in the apartment complex being financed), or because of the race of other residents in the neighborhood where the property offered as collateral is located.

2. *National origin.* A creditor may not refuse to grant credit because an applicant comes from a particular country but may take the applicant's immigration status into account. A creditor may also take into account any applicable law, regulation, or executive order restricting dealings with citizens (or the government) of a particular country or imposing limitations regarding credit extended for their use.

3. *Public assistance program.* Any Federal, state, or local governmental assistance program that provides a continuing, periodic income supplement, whether premised on entitlement or need, is "public assistance" for purposes of the regulation. The term includes (but is not limited to) Aid to Families with Dependent Children, food stamps, rent and mortgage supplement or assistance programs, Social Security and Supplemental Security Income, and unemployment compensation. Only physicians, hospitals, and others to whom the benefits are payable need consider Medicare and Medicaid as public assistance.

Section 202.3—Limited Exceptions for Certain Classes of Transactions

1. *Scope.* This section relieves burdens with regard to certain types of credit for which full application of the procedural requirements of the regulation is not needed. All classes of transactions remain subject to the general rule given in § 202.4, barring discrimination on a prohibited basis, and to any other provision not specifically excepted.

3(a) *Public utilities credit.*

1. *Definition.* This definition applies only to credit for the purchase of a utility service, such as electricity, gas, or telephone service. Credit provided or offered by a public utility for some other purpose—such as for financing the purchase of a gas dryer, telephone equipment, or other durable goods, or for insulation or other home improvements—is not excepted.

2. *Security deposits.* A utility company is a creditor when it supplies utility service and bills the user after the service has been provided. Thus, any credit term (such as a requirement for a security deposit) is subject to the regulation.

3. *Telephone companies.* A telephone company's credit transactions qualify for the exceptions provided in § 202.3(a)(2) only if the company is regulated by a government unit or files the charges for service, delayed payment, or any discount for prompt payment with a government unit.

3(c) *Incidental credit.*

1. *Examples.* If a service provider (such as a hospital, doctor, lawyer or retailer) allows the client or customer to defer the payment of a bill, this deferral of debt is credit for purposes of the regulation, even though there is no finance charge and no agreement for payment in installments. Because of the exceptions provided by this section, however, these particular credit extensions are excepted from compliance with certain procedural requirements as specified in the regulation.

---

depends upon a variety of factors such as changes in the local economy, and shifts in the lender's customer base. However, creditors must review their systems when evidence suggests that the systems are no longer predicting risk as intended. . . . A creditor is responsible for any system that it uses, including its revalidation, but may use a third party to perform the revalidation. In accordance with section 202.2(p)(2), if the system is developed using borrowed credit experience, the initial validation and any subsequent revalidation must be based on the creditor's own data when it becomes available." 61 Fed. Reg. 50,948 (Sept. 30, 1996).]

8 [*Editor's note:* Added by 60 Fed. Reg. 29,967 (June 5, 1995).]

9 [*Editor's note:* Added by 60 Fed. Reg. 29,967 (June 5, 1995).]

3(d) *Government credit.*

1. *Credit to governments.*[10] The exception relates to credit extended to (not by) governmental entities. For example, credit extended to a local government by a creditor in the private sector is covered by this exception, but credit extended to consumers by a federal or state housing agency does not qualify for special treatment under this category.

Section 202.4—General Rule Prohibiting Discrimination

1. *Scope of section.*[11] The general rule stated in § 202.4 covers all dealings, without exception, between an applicant and a creditor, whether or not addressed by other provisions of the regulation. Other sections of the regulation identify specific practices that the Board has decided are impermissible because they could result in credit discrimination on a basis prohibited by the act. The general rule covers, for example, application procedures, criteria used to evaluate creditworthiness, administration of accounts, and treatment of delinquent or slow accounts. Thus, whether or not specifically prohibited elsewhere in the regulation, a credit practice that treats applicants differently on a prohibited basis violates the law because it violates the general rule. Disparate treatment on a prohibited basis is illegal whether or not it results from a conscious intent to discriminate. Disparate treatment would be found, for example, where a creditor requires a minority applicant to provide greater documentation to obtain a loan than a similarly situated nonminority applicant. Disparate treatment also would be found where a creditor waives or relaxes credit standards for a nonminority applicant but not for a similarly situated minority applicant. Treating applicants differently on a prohibited basis is unlawful if the creditor lacks a legitimate nondiscriminatory reason for its action, or if the asserted reason is found to be a pretext for discrimination.

Section 202.5—Rules Concerning Taking of Applications

5(a) *Discouraging applications.*

1. *Potential applicants.* Generally, the regulation's protections apply only to persons who have requested or received an extension of credit. In keeping with the purpose of the act—to promote the availability of credit on a nondiscriminatory basis § 202.5(a) covers acts or practices directed at potential applicants. Practices prohibited by this section include:

- A statement that the applicant should not bother to apply, after the applicant states that he is retired.

- Use of words, symbols, models or other forms of communication in advertising that express, imply or suggest a discriminatory preference or a policy of exclusion in violation of the act.

- Use of interview scripts that discourage applications on a prohibited basis.

2. *Affirmative advertising.* A creditor may affirmatively solicit or encourage members of traditionally disadvantaged groups to apply for credit, especially groups that might not normally seek credit from that creditor.

5(b) *General rules concerning requests for information.*

1. *Requests for information.* This section governs the types of information that a creditor may gather. Section 202.6 governs how information may be used.

Paragraph 5(b)(2)

1. *Local laws.*[12] Information that a creditor is allowed to collect pursuant to a "state" statute or regulation includes information required by a local statute, regulation, or ordinance.

2. *Information required by Regulation C.*[13] Regulation C generally requires creditors covered by the Home Mortgage Disclosure Act (HMDA) to collect and report information about the race or national origin and sex of applicants for home improvement loans and home purchase loans, including some types of loans not covered by § 202.13. Certain creditors with assets under $30 million, though covered by HMDA, are not required to collect and report these data; but they may do so at their option under HMDA, without violating the ECOA or Regulation B.

3. *Collecting information on behalf of creditors.*[14] Loan brokers, correspondents, or other persons do not violate the ECOA or Regulation B if they collect information that they are otherwise prohibited from collecting, where the purpose of collecting the information is to provide it to a creditor that is subject to the Home Mortgage Disclosure Act or another federal or state statute or regulation requiring data collection.

---

10 [*Editor's note:* "In the December 1989 amendments to the regulation, § 202.3(e) was redesignated § 202.3(d). Accordingly, comment 3(e)-1 on governmental credit has been redesignated comment 3(d)-1." 55 Fed. Reg. 12,471 (Apr. 4, 1990).]

11 [*Editor's note:* The Board has revised the comment to clarify that treating individuals differently is not unlawful per se. However, treating individuals differently on a prohibited basis is unlawful discrimination ("disparate treatment") if there is no credible, nondiscriminatory reason that explains the difference in treatment. In the examples given, the differential treatment would constitute disparate treatment if the creditor lacked a legitimate nondiscriminatory reason for its action, or if the asserted reason was found to be a pretext for discrimination. 60 Fed. Reg. 29,967 (June 5, 1995).]

12 [*Editor's note:* "Comment 5(b)(2)-1 is added to clarify that the term 'state law,' as used in § 202.5(b)(2), includes the requirements of any political subdivision thereof. For example, a creditor may request, pursuant to a local ordinance, information required for monitoring purposes that is otherwise prohibited by § 202.5 (c) and (d)." 55 Fed. Reg. 12,471 (Apr. 4, 1990).]

13 [*Editor's note:* "Comment 5(b)(2)-2 is added to clarify that a lender subject to the Home Mortgage Disclosure Act (HMDA), but exempt (because of its asset size) from reporting data about applicant characteristics, may voluntarily collect and report the information in accordance with the requirements of HMDA and Regulation C without violating the ECOA." 55 Fed. Reg. 12,471 (Apr. 4, 1990).]

14 [*Editor's note:* "Comment 5(b)(2)-3 is added primarily to indicate that loan brokers, correspondents, or other persons do not violate the ECOA or Regulation B if they collect information about race, national origin, and sex (that they would otherwise be prohibited from collecting under the regulation) for the purpose of providing the information to a creditor subject to the Home Mortgage Disclosure Act (HMDA), 12 U.S.C. 2801–2810." 57 Fed. Reg. 12,202 (Apr. 9, 1992).]

5(d) *Other limitations on information requests.*

Paragraph 5(d)(1)

1. *Indirect disclosure of prohibited information.* The fact that certain credit-related information may indirectly disclose marital status does not bar a creditor from seeking such information. For example, the creditor may ask about:

- The applicant's obligation to pay alimony, child support, or separate maintenance.
- The source of income to be used as the basis for repaying the credit requested, which could disclose that it is the income of a spouse.
- Whether any obligation disclosed by the applicant has a co-obligor, which could disclose that the co-obligor is a spouse or former spouse.
- The ownership of assets, which could disclose the interest of a spouse.

Paragraph 5(d)(2)

1. *Disclosure about income.* The sample application forms in Appendix B to the regulation illustrate how a creditor may inform an applicant of the right not to disclose alimony, child support, or separate maintenance income.

2. *General inquiry about source of income.* Since a general inquiry about the source of income may lead an applicant to disclose alimony, child support, or separate maintenance, a creditor may not make such an inquiry on an application form without prefacing the request with the disclosure required by this paragraph.

3. *Specific inquiry about sources of income.* A creditor need not give the disclosure if the inquiry about income is specific and worded in a way that is unlikely to lead the applicant to disclose the fact that income is derived from alimony, child support or separate maintenance payments. For example, an application form that asks about specific types of income such as salary, wages, or investment income need not include the disclosure.

5(e) *Written applications.*

1. *Requirement for written applications.* The requirement of written applications for certain types of dwelling-related loans is intended to assist the federal supervisory agencies in monitoring compliance with the ECOA and the Fair Housing Act. Model application forms are provided in Appendix B to the regulation, although use of a printed form of any kind is not required. A creditor will satisfy the requirement by writing down the information that it normally considers in making a credit decision. The creditor may complete the application on behalf of an applicant and need not require the applicant to sign the application.

2. *Telephone applications.* A creditor that accepts applications by telephone for dwelling-related credit covered by section 202.13 can meet the requirements for written applications by writing down pertinent information that is provided by the applicant(s).

3. *Computerized entry.*[15] Information entered directly into and retained by a computerized system qualifies as a written application under this paragraph. (See the commentary to section

202.13(b), *Applications through electronic media* and *Applications through video.*)

Section 202.5a—Rules on Providing Appraisal Reports[16]

5a(a) *Providing appraisals.*

1. *Coverage.* This section covers applications for credit to be secured by a lien on a dwelling, as that term is defined in § 202.5a(c), whether the credit is for a business purpose (for example, a loan to start a business) or a consumer purpose (for example, a loan to finance a child's education).

2. *Renewals.* If an applicant requests that a creditor renew an existing extension of credit, and the creditor obtains a new appraisal report to evaluate the request, this section applies. This section does not apply to a renewal request if the creditor uses the appraisal report previously obtained in connection with the decision to grant credit.

5a(a)(2)(i) *Notice.*

1. *Multiple applicants.* When an application that is subject to this section involves more than one applicant, the notice about the appraisal report need only be given to one applicant, but it must be given to the primary applicant where one is readily apparent.

5a(a)(2)(ii) *Delivery.*

1. *Reimbursement.* Creditors may charge for photocopy and postage costs incurred in providing a copy of the appraisal report, unless prohibited by state or other law. If the consumer has already paid for the report—for example, as part of an application fee—the creditor may not require additional fees for the appraisal (other than photocopy and postage costs).

5a(c) *Definitions.*

1. *Appraisal reports.* Examples of appraisal reports are:

i. A report prepared by an appraiser (whether or not licensed or certified), including written comments and other documents submitted to the creditor in support of the appraiser's estimate or opinion of value.

ii. A document prepared by the creditor's staff which assigns value to the property, if a third-party appraisal report has not been used.

iii. An internal review document reflecting that the creditor's valuation is different from a valuation in a third party's appraisal report (or different from valuations that are publicly available or valuations such as manufacturers' invoices for mobile homes).

2. *Other reports.* The term "appraisal report" does not cover all documents relating to the value of the applicant's property. Examples of reports not covered are:

i. Internal documents, if a third-party appraisal report was used to establish the value of the property.

ii. Governmental agency statements of appraised value.

iii. Valuations lists that are publicly available (such as published sales prices or mortgage amounts, tax assessments, and retail price ranges) and valuations such as manufacturers' invoices for mobile homes.

---

15 [*Editor's note:* Added by 61 Fed. Reg. 50,948 (Sept. 30, 1996).]

16 [*Editor's note:* Section 202.5a was added by 60 Fed. Reg. 29,967 (June 5, 1995).]

Section 202.6—Rules Concerning Evaluation of Applications

6(a) *General rule concerning use of information.*

1. *General.* When evaluating an application for credit, a creditor generally may consider any information obtained. However, a creditor may not consider in its evaluation of creditworthiness any information that it is barred by § 202.5 from obtaining.

2. *Effects test.*[17] The effects test is a judicial doctrine that was developed in a series of employment cases decided by the Supreme Court under Title VII of the Civil Rights Act of 1964 (42 U.S.C. 2000e et seq.), and the burdens of proof for such employment cases were codified by Congress in the Civil Rights Act of 1991 (42 U.S.C. 2000e-2). Congressional intent that this doctrine apply to the credit area is documented in the Senate Report that accompanied H.R. 6516, No. 94-589, pp. 4–5; and in the House Report that accompanied H.R. 6516, No. 94-210, p. 5. The act and regulation may prohibit a creditor practice that is discriminatory in effect because it has a disproportionately negative impact on a prohibited basis, even though the creditor has no intent to discriminate and the practice appears neutral on its face, unless the creditor practice meets a legitimate business need that cannot reasonably be achieved as well by means that are less disparate in their impact. For example, requiring that applicants have incomes in excess of a certain amount to qualify for an overdraft line of credit could mean that women and minority applicants will be rejected at a higher rate than men and non-minority applicants. If there is a demonstrable relationship between the income requirement and creditworthiness for the level of credit involved, however, use of the income standard would likely be permissible.

6(b) *Specific rules concerning use of information.*

Paragraph 6(b)(1)

1. *Prohibited basis—marital status.*[18] A creditor may not use marital status as a basis for determining the applicant's creditworthiness. However, a creditor may consider an applicant's marital status for the purpose of ascertaining the creditor's rights and remedies applicable to the particular extension of credit. For example, in a secured transaction involving real property, a creditor could take into account whether state law gives the applicant's spouse an interest in the property being offered as collateral. Except to the extent necessary to determine rights and remedies for a specific credit transaction, a creditor that offers joint credit may not take the applicants' marital status into account in credit evalu-

ations. Because it is unlawful for creditors to take marital status into account, creditors are barred from applying different standards in evaluating married and unmarried applicants. In making credit decisions, creditors may not treat joint applicants differently based on the existence, the absence, or the likelihood of a marital relationship between the parties.

2. *Prohibited basis—special purpose credit.* In a special purpose credit program, a creditor may consider a prohibited basis to determine whether the applicant possesses a characteristic needed for eligibility. (See § 202.8.)

Paragraph 6(b)(2)

1. *Favoring the elderly.* Any system of evaluating creditworthiness may favor a credit applicant who is age 62 or older. A credit program that offers more favorable credit terms to applicants age 62 or older is also permissible; a program that offers more favorable credit terms to applicants at an age lower than 62 is permissible only if it meets the special-purpose credit requirements of § 202.8.

2. *Consideration of age in a credit scoring system.*[19] Age may be taken directly into account in a credit scoring system that is "demonstrably and statistically sound," as defined in section 202.2(p), with one limitation: applicants 62 years or older must be treated at least as favorably as applicants who are under 62. If age is scored by assigning points to an applicant's age category, elderly applicants must receive the same or a greater number of points as the most favored class of nonelderly applicants.

i. *Age-split scorecards.*[20] A creditor may segment the population

---

17. [*Editor's note:* "The Board recognizes that this [disparate impact] is an evolving area of law, one in which creditors and consumers alike would benefit from more specificity. However, given that the Board did not propose any amendments to this section of the commentary, the only change to the existing commentary is the addition of a reference to the Civil Rights Act of 1991, which codifies the standards used for disparate impact under Title VII. The Board will consider addressing these issues further in future commentary proposals." 60 Fed. Reg. 29,967 (June 5, 1995).]

18. [*Editor's note:* The Board revised comment 6(b)(1)-1 "to clarify that if a creditor chooses to offer joint credit, the creditor generally may not take the applicants' marital status into account in credit evaluations, except to the extent necessary for determining rights and remedies under state law." 60 Fed. Reg. 29,967 (June 5, 1995).]

19. [*Editor's note:* Amended by 61 Fed. Reg. 50,948 (Sept. 30, 1996). "The modification reflects the Board's interpretation that the ECOA and Regulation B require creditors that score age in a credit scoring system to treat elderly applicants as a class as favorably as all other classes of applicants on the basis of age. . . .

If a creditor directly scores age by assigning points to an applicant's age category, elderly applicants must receive at least the same number of points as the most favored class of non-elderly applicants. For example, if a system assigns 10 points for ages 18–20, 20 points for ages 21–27, 15 points for ages 28–39, 18 points for ages 40 to 51, and 22 points for ages 52 to 61, then applicants who are 62 and older must receive at least 22 points.

The Board believes that similarly, if a system assigns points to some other variable based on the applicant's age, applicants who are 62 and older must receive at least the same number of points as the most favored class of nonelderly applicants. For example, a system could score an applicant's type of residence based on the age of the applicant and assign points to applicants who rent their dwellings (such as 20 points for ages 18–28, 10 points for ages 29–45, and 8 points for ages 46–61). In such a system, elderly applicants who rent their dwellings must receive at least the same number of points as the most favored age class; in this example, applicants 62 and older who rent their dwellings must receive at least 20 points. This rule applies whether a creditor uses a single scorecard or more than one scorecard."]

20. [*Editor's note:* "Specifically, the Board has considered whether a creditor could segment the applicant population and develop one card for a narrow range of applicants under a certain age (sometimes called a "youth" card) and a second card for the general population. Applicants on the youth card—typically in their late twenties or younger—would be evaluated using attributes that are predictive for that age class, while applicants on

into scorecards based on the age of an applicant. In such a system, one card covers a narrow age range (for example, applicants in their twenties or younger) who are evaluated under attributes predictive for that age group. A second card covers all other applicants who are evaluated under the attributes predictive for that broad class. When a system uses a card covering a wide age range that encompasses elderly applicants, the credit scoring system does not score age. Thus, the system does not raise the issue of assigning a negative factor or value to the age of elderly applicants. But if a system segments the population by age into multiple scorecards, and includes elderly applicants in a narrower age range, the credit scoring system does score age. To comply with the act and regulation in such a case, the creditor must ensure that the system does not assign a negative factor or value to the age of elderly applicants as a class.

3. *Consideration of age in a judgmental system.* In a judgmental system, defined in § 202.2(t), a creditor may not take age directly into account in any aspect of the credit transaction. For example, the creditor may not reject an application or terminate an account because the applicant is 60 years old. But a creditor that uses a judgmental system may relate the applicant's age to other information about the applicant that the creditor considers in evaluating creditworthiness. For example:

- A creditor may consider the applicant's occupation and length of time to retirement to ascertain whether the applicant's income (including retirement income) will support the extension of credit to its maturity.
- A creditor may consider the adequacy of any security offered when the term of the credit extension exceeds the life expectancy of the applicant and the cost of realizing on the collateral

could exceed the applicant's equity. (An elderly applicant might not qualify for a 5 percent down, 30-year mortgage loan but might qualify with a larger downpayment or a shorter loan maturity.)

- A creditor may consider the applicant's age to assess the significance of the length of the applicant's employment (a young applicant may have just entered the job market) or length of time at an address (an elderly applicant may recently have retired and moved from a long-time residence).

4. *Consideration of age in a reverse mortgage.*[21] A reverse mortgage is a home-secured loan in which the borrower receives payments from the creditor, and does not become obligated to repay these amounts (other than in the case of default) until the borrower dies, moves permanently from the home or transfers title to the home, or upon a specified maturity date. Disbursements to the borrower under a reverse mortgage typically are determined by considering the value of the borrower's home, the current interest rate, and the borrower's life expectancy. A reverse mortgage program that requires borrowers to be age 62 or older is permissible under section 202.6(b)(2)(iv). In addition, under section 202.6(b)(2)(iii), a creditor may consider a borrower's age to evaluate a pertinent element of creditworthiness, such as the amount of the credit or monthly payments that the borrower will receive, or the estimated repayment date.

5. *Consideration of age in a combined system.*[22] A creditor using a credit scoring system that qualifies as "empirically derived" under § 202.2(p) may consider other factors (such as credit report or the applicant's cash flow) on a judgmental basis. Doing so will not negate the classification of the credit scoring component of the combined system as "demonstrably and statistically sound." While age could be used in the credit scoring portion, however, in the judgmental portion age may not be considered directly. It may be used only for the purpose of determining a "pertinent element of creditworthiness." (See comment 6(b)(2)-3.)

6. *Consideration of public assistance.* When considering income derived from a public assistance program, a creditor may take into account, for example:

- The length of time an applicant will likely remain eligible to receive such income.

---

the second card would be evaluated using attributes predictive for the general population. The Board believes that when a system uses a standard card for the general population with a wide age range that includes the elderly, the system does not score age. Accordingly, in this type of system, there is no issue of assigning a negative factor or value to the age of elderly applicants.

On the other hand, the Board has considered whether a creditor could segment the applicant population using scorecards with narrower age ranges. Such scorecards assign value based on characteristics predictive for that narrow age class. Unlike the use of a standard card for the general population with a wide range that includes the elderly, the Board believes that inclusion of the elderly in scorecards with narrower age ranges does score age. Since the elderly would not be evaluated using attributes for the general population, creditors may not assign a negative factor or value to the age of elderly applicants. Negative Factor or Value

Commenters suggested alternative ways that a creditor could satisfy the ECOA's requirement that a negative factor or value not be assigned to the age of elderly applicants. For example, it was suggested that creditors could be required to establish, at the time scorecards are developed, that elderly applicants as a class would not have been treated more favorably if scored using cards developed for other age categories. While the final comment does not address this issue, the Board believes one approach would be to demonstrate that no more than one-half of elderly applicants rejected under the scorecard including their age group would have been approved if scored under another card in the system." 61 Fed. Reg. 50,948 (Sept. 30, 1996).]

---

21 [*Editor's note:* "Comment 6(b)(2)-4 . . . includes a reference to default, to parallel the definition of a reverse mortgage in Regulation Z (Truth in Lending), 12 CFR 226. The comment also clarifies that a reverse mortgage program that requires applicants to be at least 62 years of age is permissible under §202.6(b)(2)(iv), which allows creditors to favor the elderly by offering products to applicants 62 and older that are not available to other customers.

The comment also clarifies that using age in a reverse mortgage transaction to determine factors such as the amount of the credit, the monthly payment that the borrower will receive, or the estimated repayment date is permissible under § 202.6(b)(2)(iii) as long as the determination is made on a case-by-case basis." 61 Fed. Reg. 50,948 (Sept. 30, 1996).]

22 [*Editor's note:* Comments 6(b)(2)-5 and -6 were renumbered by 61 Fed. Reg. 50,948 (Sept. 30, 1996). They were previously numbered comments 4 and 5.]

- Whether the applicant will continue to qualify for benefits based on the status of the applicant's dependents (such as Aid to Families with Dependent Children or Social Security payments to a minor).
- Whether the creditor can attach or garnish the income to assure payment of the debt in the event of default.

Paragraph 6(b)(5)

1. *Consideration of an individual applicant.* A creditor must evaluate income derived from part-time employment, alimony, child support, separate maintenance, retirement benefits, or public assistance (all referred to as "protected income") on an individual basis, not on the basis of aggregate statistics, and must assess its reliability or unreliability by analyzing the applicant's actual circumstances, not by analyzing statistical measures derived from a group.

2. *Payments consistently made.* In determining the likelihood of consistent payments of alimony, child support, or separate maintenance, a creditor may consider factors such as whether payments are received pursuant to a written agreement or court decree; the length of time that the payments have been received; whether the payments are regularly received by the applicant; the availability of court or other procedures to compel payment; and the creditworthiness of the payor, including the credit history of the payor when it is available to the creditor.

3. *Consideration of income.* A creditor need not consider income at all in evaluating creditworthiness. If a creditor does consider income, there are several acceptable methods, whether in a credit scoring or a judgmental system:

- A creditor may score or take into account the total sum of all income stated by the applicant without taking steps to evaluate the income.
- A creditor may evaluate each component of the applicant's income, and then score or take into account reliable income separately from income that is not reliable, or the creditor may disregard that portion of income that is not reliable before aggregating it with reliable income.
- A creditor that does not evaluate all income components for reliability must treat as reliable any component of protected income that is not evaluated.

In considering the separate components of an applicant's income, the creditor may not automatically discount or exclude from consideration any protected income. Any discounting or exclusion must be based on the applicant's actual circumstances.

4. *Part-time employment, sources of income.* A creditor may score or take into account the fact that an individual applicant has more than one source of earned income—a full-time and a part-time job or two part-time jobs. A creditor may also score or treat earned income from a secondary source differently than earned income from a primary source. However, the creditor may not score or otherwise take into account the number of sources for protected income—for example, retirement income, social security, alimony. Nor may the creditor treat negatively the fact that an applicant's only earned income is derived from a part-time job.

Paragraph 6(b)(6)

1. *Types of credit references.* A creditor may restrict the types of credit history and credit references that it will consider, provided that the restrictions are applied to all credit applicants without regard to sex, marital status, or any other prohibited basis. However, on the applicant's request, a creditor must consider credit information not reported through a credit bureau when the information relates to the same types of credit references and history that the creditor would consider if reported through a credit bureau.

Paragraph 6(b)(7)

1. *National origin— immigration status.* The applicant's immigration status and ties to the community (such as employment and continued residence in the area) could have a bearing on a creditor's ability to obtain repayment. Accordingly, the creditor may consider and differentiate, for example, between a noncitizen who is a long-time resident with permanent resident status and a noncitizen who is temporarily in this country on a student visa.

2. *National origin—citizenship.* Under the regulation a denial of credit on the ground that an applicant is not a United States citizen is nor per se discrimination based on national origin.

Section 202.7—Rules Concerning Extensions of Credit

7(a) *Individual accounts.*

1. *Open-end credit—authorized user.* A creditor may not require a creditworthy applicant seeking an individual credit account to provide additional signatures. However, the creditor may condition the designation of an authorized user by the account holder on the authorized user's becoming contractually liable for the account, as long as the creditor does not differentiate on any prohibited basis in imposing this requirement.

2. *Open-end credit—choice of authorized user.* A creditor that permits an account holder to designate an authorized user may not restrict this designation on a prohibited basis. For example, if the creditor allows the designation of spouses as authorized users, the creditor may not refuse to accept a non-spouse as an authorized user.

3. *Overdraft authority on transaction accounts.* If a transaction account (such as a checking account or NOW account) includes an overdraft line of credit, the creditor may require that all persons authorized to draw on the transaction account assume liability for any overdraft.

7(b) *Designation of name.*

1. *Single name on account.* A creditor may require that joint applicants on an account designate a single name for purposes of administering the account and that a single name be embossed on any credit card(s) issued on the account. But the creditor may not require that the name be the husband's name. (See § 202.10 for rule governing the furnishing of credit history on accounts held by spouses.)

7(c) *Action concerning existing open-end accounts.*

Paragraph 7(c)(1)

1. *Termination coincidental with marital status change.* When an account holder's marital status changes, a creditor generally may not terminate the account unless it has evidence that the account holder is unable or unwilling to repay. But the creditor may

terminate an account on which both spouses are jointly liable, even if the action coincides with a change in marital status, when one or both spouses:

- Repudiate responsibility for future charges on the joint account.
- Request separate accounts in their own names.
- Request that the joint account be closed.

2. *Updating information.* A creditor may periodically request updated information from applicants but may not use events related to a prohibited basis—such as an applicant's retirement, reaching a particular age, or change in name or marital status—to trigger such a request.

Paragraph 7(c)(2)

1. *Procedure pending reapplication.* A creditor may require a reapplication from a contractually liable party, even when there is no evidence of unwillingness or inability to repay, if (1) the credit was based on the qualifications of a person who is no longer available to support the credit and (2) the creditor has information indicating that the account holder's income by itself may be insufficient to support the credit. While a reapplication is pending, the creditor must allow the account holder full access to the account under the existing contract terms. The creditor may specify a reasonable time period within which the account holder must submit the required information.

7(d) *Signature of spouse or other person.*
1. *Qualified applicant.* The signature rules assure that qualified applicants are able to obtain credit in their own names. Thus, when an applicant requests individual credit, a creditor generally may not require the signature of another person unless the creditor has first determined that the applicant alone does not qualify for the credit requested.

2. *Unqualified applicant.* When an applicant applies for individual credit but does not alone meet a creditor's standards, the creditor may require a cosigner, guarantor or the like—but cannot require that it be the spouse. (See commentary to § 202.7(d) (5) and (6).)

Paragraph 7(d)(1)

1. *Joint applicant.* The term "joint applicant" refers to someone who applies contemporaneously with the applicant for shared or joint credit. It does not refer to someone whose signature is required by the creditor as a condition for granting the credit requested.

Paragraph 7(d)(2)[23]

1. *Jointly owned property.* If an applicant requests unsecured credit, does not own sufficient separate property, and relies on joint property to establish creditworthiness, the creditor must value the applicant's interest in the jointly owned property. A creditor may not request that a nonapplicant joint owner sign any instrument as a condition of the credit extension unless the applicant's interest does not support the amount and terms of the credit sought.

a. *Valuation of applicant's interest.* In determining the value of an applicant's interest in jointly owned property, a creditor may consider factors such as the form of ownership and the property's susceptibility to attachment, execution, severance, or partition; the value of the applicant's interest after such action; and the cost associated with the action. This determination must be based on the form of ownership prior to or at consummation, and not on the possibility of a subsequent change. For example, in determining whether a married applicant's interest in jointly owned property is sufficient to satisfy the creditor's standards of creditworthiness for individual credit, a creditor may not consider that the applicant's separate property may be transferred into tenancy by the entirety after consummation. Similarly, a creditor may not consider the possibility that the couple may divorce. Accordingly, a creditor may not require the signature of the nonapplicant spouse in these or similar circumstances.

b. *Other options to support credit.* If the applicant's interest in jointly owned property does not support the amount and terms of credit sought, the creditor may offer the applicant other options to provide additional support for the extension of credit. For example—

i. Requesting an additional party (see § 202.7(d)(5));

ii. Offering to grant the applicant's request on a secured basis (see § 202.7(d)(4)); or

iii. Asking for the signature of the joint owner on an instrument that ensures access to the property in the event of the applicant's death or default, but does not impose personal liability unless necessary under state law (e.g., a limited guarantee). A creditor may not routinely require, however, that a joint owner sign an instrument (such as a quitclaim deed) that would result in the forfeiture of the joint owner's interest in the property.

2. *Need for signature—reasonable belief.* A creditor's reasonable belief as to what instruments need to be signed by a person other than the applicant should be supported by a thorough review of pertinent statutory and decisional law or an opinion of the state attorney general.

Paragraph 7(d)(3)

1. *Residency.* In assessing the creditworthiness of a person who applies for credit in a community property state, a creditor may assume that the applicant is a resident of the state unless the applicant indicates otherwise.

---

23 [*Editor's note:* "Comment 7(d)(2)-1 addresses unsecured credit and the treatment of joint property. The comment clarifies that when determining the value of an applicant's interest in jointly owned property, a creditor must look to the actual form of ownership of the property prior to or at consummation. Several commenters asked whether in making such determinations, creditors may consider the possibility of subsequent changes to property ownership. The comment makes clear that the possibility of a subsequent change in the form of ownership may not be considered. . . . The comment retains the limitation that where, under state law, the creditor may use other instruments to reach joint property, a creditor may not routinely ask nonapplicants to sign any instrument requiring that they forfeit their interest in jointly owned property as a condition of the credit extension. . . . The comment is not intended to prevent access to jointly owned property in these circumstances [applicant's death or default], but to clarify that if state law gives a creditor access to the property by some other means—for example, through a limited guarantee—requiring nonapplicants to forfeit their interest in jointly owned property is prohibited by the regulation." 61 Fed. Reg. 50,948 (Sept. 30, 1996).]

Paragraph 7(d)(4)

1. *Creation of enforceable lien.* Some state laws require that both spouses join in executing any instrument by which real property is encumbered. If an applicant offers such property as security for credit, a creditor may require the applicant's spouse to sign the instruments necessary to create a valid security interest in the property. The creditor may not require the spouse to sign the note evidencing the credit obligation if signing only the mortgage or other security agreement is sufficient to make the property available to satisfy the debt in the event of default. However, if under state law both spouses must sign the note to create an enforceable lien, the creditor may require them to do so.

2. *Need for signature—reasonable belief.* Generally, a signature to make the secured property available will only be needed on a security agreement. A creditor's reasonable belief that, to assure access to the property, the spouse's signature is needed on an instrument that imposes personal liability should be supported by a thorough review of pertinent statutory and decisional law or an opinion of the state attorney general.

3. *Integrated instruments.* When a creditor uses an integrated instrument that combines the note and the security agreement, the spouse cannot be required to sign the integrated instrument if the signature is only needed to grant a security interest. But the spouse could be asked to sign an integrated instrument that makes clear—for example, by a legend placed next to the spouse's signature—that the spouse's signature is only to grant a security interest and that signing the instrument does not impose personal liability.

Paragraph 7(d)(5)

1. *Qualifications of additional parties.* In establishing guidelines for eligibility of guarantors, cosigners, or similar additional parties, a creditor may restrict the applicant's choice of additional parties but may not discriminate on the basis of sex, marital status or any other prohibited basis. For example, the creditor could require that the additional party live in the creditor's market area.

2. *Reliance on income of another person—individual credit.* An applicant who requests individual credit relying on the income of another person (including a spouse in a noncommunity property state) may be required to provide the signature of the other person to make the income available to pay the debt. In community property states, the signature of a spouse may be required if the applicant relies on the spouse's separate income. If the applicant relies on the spouse's future earnings that as a matter of state law cannot be characterized as community property until earned, the creditor may require the spouse's signature, but need not do so—even if it is the creditor's practice to require the signature when an applicant relies on the future earnings of a person other than a spouse. (See §202.6(c) on consideration of state property laws.)

3. *Renewals.* If the borrower's creditworthiness is reevaluated when a credit obligation is renewed, the creditor must determine whether an additional party is still warranted and, if not, release the additional party.

Paragraph 7(d)(6)[24]

1. *Guarantees.* A guarantee on an extension of credit is part of a credit transaction and therefore subject to the regulation. A creditor may require the personal guarantee of the partners, directors, or officers of a business, and the shareholders of a closely held corporation, even if the business or corporation is creditworthy. The requirement must be based on the guarantor's relationship with the business or corporation, however, and not on a prohibited basis. For example, a creditor may not require guarantees only for women-owned or minority-owned businesses. Similarly, a creditor may not require guarantees only from the married officers of a business or married shareholders of a closely held corporation.

2. *Spousal guarantees.* The rules in § 202.7(d) bar a creditor from requiring a signature of a *guarantor's spouse* just as they bar the creditor from requiring the signature of an *applicant's spouse.* For example, although a creditor may require all officers of a closely held corporation to personally guarantee a corporate loan, the creditor may not automatically require that spouses of married officers also sign the guarantee. If an evaluation of the financial circumstances of an officer indicates that an additional signature is necessary, however, the creditor may require the signature of a spouse in appropriate circumstances in accordance with § 202.7(d)(2).

7(e) *Insurance*

1. *Differences in terms.* Differences in the availability, rates, and other terms on which credit-related casualty insurance or credit life, health, accident, or disability insurance is offered or provided to an applicant does not violate Regulation B.

2. *Insurance information.* A creditor may obtain information about an applicant's age, sex, or marital status for insurance purposes. The information may only be used, however, for determining eligibility and premium rates for insurance, and not in making the credit decision.

Section 202.8—Special Purpose Credit Programs

8(a) *Standards for programs.*

1. *Determining qualified programs.* The Board does not determine whether individual programs qualify for special purpose credit status, or whether a particular program benefits an "economically disadvantaged class of persons." The agency or creditor administering or offering the loan program must make these decisions regarding the status of its program.

2. *Compliance with a program authorized by Federal or State law.* A creditor does not violate Regulation B when it complies in good faith with a regulation promulgated by a government agency implementing a special purpose credit program under § 202.8(a)(1). It is the agency's responsibility to promulgate a regulation that is consistent with Federal and State law.

3. *Expressly authorized.* Credit programs authorized by Federal or State law include programs offered pursuant to Federal, State or local statute, regulation or ordinance, or by judicial or administrative order.

4. *Creditor liability.* A refusal to grant credit to an applicant is not a violation of the act or regulation if the applicant does not meet the eligibility requirements under a special purpose credit program.

5. *Determining need.*[25] In designing a special-purpose program

---

24 [*Editor's note:* Added by 61 Fed. Reg. 50,948 (Sept. 30, 1996).]

25 [*Editor's note:* Comments 8(a)-5 and -6 were added to clarify the requirements that for-profit organizations must meet to establish special-purpose credit programs under section

under § 202.8(a), a for-profit organization must determine that the program will benefit a class of people who would otherwise be denied credit or would receive it on less favorable terms. This determination can be based on a broad analysis using the organization's own research or data from outside sources including governmental reports and studies. For example, a bank could review Home Mortgage Disclosure Act data along with demographic data for its assessment area and conclude that there is a need for a special-purpose credit program for low-income minority borrowers.

6. *Elements of the program.* The written plan must contain information that supports the need for the particular program. The plan also must either state a specific period of time for which the program will last, or contain a statement regarding when the program will be reevaluated to determine if there is a continuing need for it.

8(b) *Rules in other sections.*

1. *Applicability of rules.* A creditor that rejects an application because the applicant does not meet the eligibility requirements (common characteristic or financial need, for example) must nevertheless notify the applicant of action taken as required by 202.9.

8(c) *Special rule concerning requests and use of information.*

1. *Request of prohibited information.* This section permits a creditor to request and consider certain information that would otherwise be prohibited by §§ 202.5 and 202.6 to determine an applicant's eligibility for a particular program.

2. *Examples.* Examples of programs under which the creditor can ask for and consider information related to prohibited basis are:

- Energy conservation programs to assist the elderly, for which the creditor must consider the applicant's age.
- Programs under a Minority Enterprise Small Business Investment Corporation, for which a creditor must consider the applicant's minority status.

8(d) *Special rule in the case of financial need.*

1. *Request of prohibited information.* This section permits a creditor to request and consider certain information that would otherwise be prohibited by §§ 202.5 and 202.6, and to require signatures that would otherwise be prohibited by § 202.7(d).

2. *Examples.* Examples of programs in which financial need is a criterion are:

- Subsidized housing programs for low- to moderate-income households, for which a creditor may have to consider the applicant's receipt of alimony or child support, the spouse's or parents' income, etc.
- Student loan programs based on the family's financial need, for which a creditor may have to consider the spouse's or parents' financial resources.

3. *Student loans.* In a guaranteed student loan program, a creditor may obtain the signature of a parent as a guarantor when required by federal or state law or agency regulation, or when the student does not meet the creditor's standards of creditworthiness. (See §§ 202.7(d)(1) and (5).) The creditor may not require an

additional signature when a student has a work or credit history that satisfies the creditor's standards.

Section 202.9—Notifications

1. *Use of the term "adverse action."* The regulation does not require that a creditor use the term "adverse" in communicating to an applicant that a request for an extension of credit has not been approved. In notifying an applicant of adverse action as defined by § 202.2(c)(1), a creditor may use any words or phrases that describe the action taken on the application.

2. *Expressly withdrawn applications.* When an applicant expressly withdraws a credit application, the creditor is not required to comply with the notification requirements under § 202.9. (The creditor must, however, comply with the record retention requirements of the regulation. See § 202.12(b)(3).)

3. *When notification occurs.* Notification occurs when a creditor delivers or mails a notice to the applicant's last known address or, in the case of an oral notification, when the creditor communicates the credit decision to the applicant.

4. *Location of notice.* The notifications required under § 202.9 may appear on either or both sides of a form or letter.

5. *Prequalification and preapproval programs.*[26] Whether a creditor must provide a notice of action taken for a prequalification or preapproval request depends on the creditor's response to the request, as discussed in the commentary to section 202.2(f). For instance, a creditor may treat the request as an inquiry if the creditor provides general information such as loan terms and the maximum amount a consumer could borrow under various loan programs, explaining the process the consumer must follow to submit a mortgage application and the information the creditor will analyze in reaching a credit decision. On the other hand, a creditor has treated a request as an application, and is subject to the adverse action notice requirements of Sec. 202.9 if, after evaluating information, the creditor decides that it will not approve the request and communicates that decision to the consumer. For example, if in reviewing a request for prequalification, a creditor tells the consumer that it would not approve an application for a mortgage because of a bankruptcy in the consumer's record, the creditor has denied an application for credit.

9(a) *Notification of action taken, ECOA notice, and statement of specific reasons.*

Paragraph 9(a)(1)

1. *Timing of notice—when an application is complete.* Once a creditor has obtained all the information it normally considers in making a credit decision, the application is complete and the creditor has 30 days in which to notify the applicant of the credit decision. (See also comment 2(f)-5.)

2. *Notification of approval.* Notification of approval may be express or by implication. For example, the creditor will satisfy the notification requirement when it gives the applicant the credit card, money, property, or services requested.

3. *Incomplete application—denial for incompleteness.* When an application is incomplete regarding matters that the applicant can complete and the creditor lacks sufficient data for a credit decision, the creditor may deny the application giving as the reason for denial that the application is incomplete. The creditor has the

---

202.8(a). 60 Fed. Reg. 29,967 (June 5, 1995).]

26 [*Editor's note:* Added by 60 Fed. Reg. 29,967 (June 5, 1995).]

option, alternatively, of providing a notice of incompleteness under § 202.9(c).

4. *Incomplete application—denial for reasons other than incompleteness.* When an application is missing information but provides sufficient data for a credit decision, the creditor may evaluate the application and notify the applicant under this section as appropriate. If credit is denied, the applicant must be given the specific reasons for the credit denial (or notice of the right to receive the reasons); in this instance the incompleteness of the application cannot be given as the reason for the denial.

5. *Length of counteroffer.* Section 202.9(a)(1)(iv) does not require a creditor to hold a counteroffer open for 90 days or any other particular length of time.

6. *Counteroffer combined with adverse action notice.* A creditor that gives the applicant a combined counteroffer and adverse action notice that complies with § 202.9(a)(2) need not send a second adverse action notice if the applicant does not accept the counteroffer. A sample of a combined notice is contained in form C-4 of Appendix C to the regulation.

7. *Denial of a telephone application.* When an application is conveyed by means of telephone and adverse action is taken, the creditor must request the applicant's name and address in order to provide written notification under this section. If the applicant declines to provide that information, then the creditor has no further notification responsibility.

Paragraph 9(a)(3)[27]

1. *Coverage.* In determining the rules in this paragraph that apply to a given business credit application, a creditor may rely on the applicant's assertion about the revenue size of the business. (Applications to start a business are governed by the rules in § 202.9(a)(3)(i).) If an applicant applies for credit as a sole proprietor, the revenues of the sole proprietorship will determine which rules in the paragraph govern the application. However, if an applicant applies for business purpose credit as an individual, the rules in paragraph 9(a)(3)(i) apply unless the application is for trade or similar credit.

2. *Trade credit.* The term "trade credit" generally is limited to a financing arrangement that involves a buyer and a seller—such as a supplier who finances the sale of equipment, supplies, or inventory; it does not apply to an extension of credit by a bank or other financial institution for the financing of such items.

3. *Factoring.* Factoring refers to a purchase of accounts receivable, and thus is not subject to the act or regulation. If there is a credit extension incident to the factoring arrangement, the notification rules in § 202.9(a)(3)(ii) apply as do other relevant sections of the act and regulation.

4. *Manner of compliance.* In complying with the notice provisions of the act and regulation, creditors offering business credit may follow the rules governing consumer credit. Similarly, creditors may elect to treat all business credit the same (irrespective of revenue size) by providing notice in accordance with § 202.9 (a)(3)(i).

5. *Timing of notification.* A creditor subject to § 202.9(a)

---

27 [*Editor's note:* "Section 202.9(a)(3), added by the December 1989 amendments to the regulation, contains the rules for providing notifications on business credit applications. Comments 9(a)(3)-1 through -5 give creditors guidance in complying with this paragraph." 55 Fed. Reg. 12,471 (Apr. 4, 1990).]

(3)(ii)(A) is required to notify a business credit applicant, orally or in writing, of action taken on an application within a reasonable time of receiving a completed application. Notice provided in accordance with the timing requirements of § 202.9(a)(1) is deemed reasonable in all instances.

9(b) *Form of ECOA notice and statement specific reasons.*

Paragraph 9(b)(1)

1. *Substantially similar notice.* The ECOA notice sent with a notification of a credit denial or other adverse action will comply with the regulation if it is "substantially similar" to the notice contained in § 202.9(b)(1). For example, a creditor may add a reference to the fact that the ECOA permits age to be considered in certain scoring systems, or add a reference to a similar state statute or regulation and to a state enforcement agency.

Paragraph 9(b)(2)

1. *Number of specific reasons.* A creditor must disclose the principal reasons for denying an application or taking other adverse action. The regulation does not mandate that a specific number of reasons be disclosed, but disclosure of more than four reasons is not likely to be helpful to the applicant.

2. *Source of specific reasons.* The specific reasons disclosed under § 202.9(a)(2) and (b)(2) must relate to and accurately describe the factors actually considered or scored by a creditor.

3. *Description of reasons.* A creditor need not describe how or why a factor adversely affected an applicant. For example, the notice may say "length of residence" rather than "too short a period of residence."

4. *Credit scoring system.* If a creditor bases the denial or other adverse action on a credit scoring system, the reasons disclosed must relate only to those factors actually scored in the system. Moreover, no factor that was a principal reason for adverse action may be excluded from disclosure. The creditor must disclose the actual reasons for denial (for example, "age of automobile") even if the relationship of that factor to predicting creditworthiness may not be clear to the applicant.

5. *Credit scoring—method for selecting reasons.* The regulation does not require that any one method be used for selecting reasons for a credit denial or other adverse action that is based on a credit scoring system. Various methods will meet the requirements of the regulation. One method is to identify the factors for which the applicant's score fell furthest below the average score for each of those factors achieved by applicants whose total score was at or slightly above the minimum passing score. Another method is to identify the factors for which the applicant's score fell furthest below the average score for each of those factors achieved by all applicants. These average scores could be calculated during the development or use of the system. Any other method that produces results substantially similar to either of these methods is also acceptable under the regulation.

6. *Judgmental system.* If a creditor uses a judgmental system, the reasons for the denial or other adverse action must relate to those factors in the applicant's record actually reviewed by the person making the decision.

7. *Combined credit scoring and judgmental system.* If a creditor denies an application based on a credit evaluation system that employs both credit scoring and judgmental components, the

reasons for the denial must come from the component of the system that the applicant failed. For example, if a creditor initially credit scores an application and denies the credit request as a result of that scoring, the reasons disclosed to the applicant must relate to the factors scored in the system. If the application passes the credit scoring stage but the creditor then denies the credit request based on a judgmental assessment of the applicant's record, the reasons disclosed must relate to the factors reviewed judgmentally, even if the factors were also considered in the credit scoring component.

8. *Automatic denial.* Some credit decision methods contain features that call for automatic denial because of one or more negative factors in the applicant's record (such as the applicant's previous bad credit history with that creditor, the applicant's declaration of bankruptcy, or the fact that the applicant is a minor). When a creditor denies the credit request because of an automatic-denial factor, the creditor must disclose that specific factor.

9. *Combined ECOA-FCRA disclosures.* The ECOA requires disclosure of the principal reasons for denying or taking other adverse action on an application for an extension of credit. The Fair Credit Reporting Act requires a creditor to disclose when it has based its decision in whole or in part on information from a source other than the applicant or from its own files. Disclosing that a credit report was obtained and used to deny the application, as the FCRA requires, does not satisfy the ECOA requirement to disclose specific reasons. For example, if the applicant's credit history reveals delinquent credit obligations and the application is denied for that reason, to satisfy § 202.9(b)(2) the creditor must disclose that the application was denied because of the applicant's delinquent credit obligations. To satisfy the FCRA requirement, the credit must also disclose that a credit report was obtained and used to deny credit. Sample forms C-1 through C-5 of Appendix C of the regulation provide for the two disclosures.

9(c) Incomplete applications.

Paragraph 9(c)(2)

1. *Reapplication.* If information requested by a creditor is submitted by an applicant after the expiration of the time period designated by the creditor, the creditor may require the applicant to make a new application.

Paragraph 9(c)(3)

1. *Oral inquiries for additional information.* If the applicant fails to provide the information in response to an oral request, a creditor must send a written notice to the applicant within the 30-day period specified in § 202.9 (c)(1) and (c)(2). If the applicant does provide the information, the creditor shall take action on the application and notify the applicant in accordance with § 202.9(a).

9(g) Applications submitted through a third party.

1. *Third parties.* The notification of adverse action may be given by one of the creditors to whom an application was submitted. Alternatively, the third party may be a noncreditor.

2. *Third-party notice—enforcement agency.* If a single adverse action notice is being provided to an applicant on behalf of several creditors and they are under the jurisdiction of different federal enforcement agencies, the notice need not name each agency; disclosure of any one of them will suffice.

3. *Third-party notice—liability.* When a notice is to be provided

through a third party, a creditor is not liable for an act or omission of the third party that constitutes a violation of the regulation if the creditor accurately and in a timely manner provided the third party with the information necessary for the notification and maintains reasonable procedures adapted to prevent such violations.

Section 202.10—Furnishing of Credit Information

1. *Scope.*[28] The requirements of § 202.10 for designating and reporting credit information apply only to consumer credit transactions. Moreover, they apply only to creditors that opt to furnish credit information to credit bureaus or to other creditors; there is no requirement that a creditor furnish credit information on its accounts.

2. *Reporting on all accounts.* The requirements of § 202.10 apply only to accounts held or used by spouses. However, a creditor has the option to designate all joint accounts (or all accounts with an authorized user) to reflect the participation of both parties, whether or not the accounts are held by persons married to each other.

3. *Designating accounts.* In designating accounts and reporting credit information, a creditor need not distinguish between accounts on which the spouse is an authorized user and accounts on which the spouse is a contractually liable party.

4. *File and index systems.* The regulation does not require the creation or maintenance of separate files in the name of each participant on a joint or user account, or require any other particular system of record-keeping or indexing. It requires only that a creditor be able to report information in the name of each spouse on accounts covered by § 202.10. Thus, if a creditor receives a credit inquiry about the wife, it should be able to locate her credit file without asking the husband's name.

10(a) Designation of accounts.

1. *New parties.* When new parties who are spouses undertake a legal obligation on an account, as in the case of a mortgage loan assumption, the creditor should change the designation on the account to reflect the new parties and should furnish subsequent credit information on the account in the new names.

2. *Request to change designation of account.* A request to change the manner in which information concerning an account is furnished does not alter the legal liability of either spouse upon the account and does not require a creditor to change the name in which the account is maintained.

Section 202.11—Relation to State Law

11(a) Inconsistent state laws.

1. *Preemption determination—New York.* Effective November 11, 1988, the Board has determined that the following provisions in the state law of New York are preempted by the federal law:

---

28 [*Editor's note:* "Comment 10-1 is revised to clarify that the section applies only to consumer credit. (The rule in this section was adopted to ensure that married women are not left without credit histories if they become divorced or widowed. In the past, credit histories on joint accounts held by spouses were typically reported only in the husband's name.) The section does not apply to sole proprietors or any other business credit applicants." 55 Fed. Reg. 12,471 (Apr. 4, 1990).]

- Article 15, section 296a(1)(b)—Unlawful discriminatory practices in relation to credit on the basis of race, creed, color, national origin, age, sex, marital status, or disability. This provision is preempted to the extent that it bars taking a prohibited basis into account when establishing eligibility for certain special-purpose credit programs.
- Article 15, section 296a(1)(c)—Unlawful discriminatory practice to make any record or inquiry based on race, creed, color, national origin, age, sex, marital status, or disability. This provision is preempted to the extent that it bars a creditor from requesting and considering information regarding the particular characteristics (for example, race, national origin, or sex) required for eligibility for special-purpose credit programs.

2. *Preemption determination—Ohio.*[29] Effective July 23, 1990, the Board has determined that the following provision in the state law of Ohio is preempted by the federal law:

- Section 4112.021(B)(1)—Unlawful discriminatory practices in credit transactions. This provision is preempted to the extent that it bars asking or favorably considering the age of an elderly applicant; prohibits the consideration of age in a credit scoring system; permits without limitation the consideration of age in real estate transactions; and limits the consideration of age in special-purpose credit programs to certain government-sponsored programs identified in the state law.

Section 202.12—Record Retention

12(a) *Retention of prohibited information.*

1. *Receipt of prohibited information.* Unless the creditor specifically requested such information, a creditor does not violate this section when it receives prohibited information from a consumer reporting agency.

2. *Use of retained information.* Although a creditor may keep in its files prohibited information as provided in § 202.12(a), the creditor may use the information in evaluating credit applications only if permitted to do so by § 202.6.

12(b) *Preservation of records.*

1. *Copies.* A copy of the original record includes carbon copies, photocopies, microfilm or microfiche copies, or copies produced by any other accurate retrieval system, such as documents stored and reproduced by computer. A creditor that uses a computerized or mechanized system need not keep a written copy of a document

(for example, an adverse action notice) if it can regenerate all pertinent information in a timely manner for examination or other purposes.

2. *Computerized decisions.* A creditor that enters information items from a written application into a computerized or mechanized system and makes the credit decision mechanically, based only on the items of information entered into the system, may comply with § 202.12(b) by retaining the information actually entered. It is not required to store the complete written application, nor is it required to enter the remaining items of information into the system. If the transaction is subject to § 202.13, however, the creditor is required to enter and retain the data on personal characteristics in order to comply with the requirements of that section.

Paragraph 12(b)(3)

1. *Withdrawn and brokered applications.* In most cases, the 25-month retention period for applications runs from the date a notification is sent to the applicant granting or denying the credit requested. In certain transactions, a creditor is not obligated to provide a notice of the action taken. (See, for example, comment 9-2.) In such cases, the 25-month requirement runs from the date of application, as when:

- An application is withdrawn by the applicant.
- An application is submitted to more than one creditor on behalf of the applicant, and the application is approved by one of the other creditors.

12(b)(6) Self-tests

1. The rule requires all written or recorded information about a self-test to be retained for 25 months after a self-test has been completed. For this purpose, a self-test is completed after the creditor has obtained the results and made a determination about what corrective action, if any, is appropriate. Creditors are required to retain information about the scope of the self-test, the methodology used and time period covered by the self-test, the report or results of the self-test including any analysis or conclusions, and any corrective action taken in response to the self-test.[30]

Section 202.13—Information for Monitoring Purposes

13(a) *Information to be requested.*

1. *Natural person.* Section 202.13 applies only to applications from natural persons.

2. *Principal residence.* The requirements of § 202.13 apply only if an application relates to a dwelling that is or will be occupied by the applicant as the principal residence. A credit application related to a vacation home or a rental unit is not covered. In the case of a two- to four-unit dwelling, the application is covered if the applicant intends to occupy one of the units as a principal residence.

3. *Temporary financing.* An application for temporary financing to construct a dwelling is not subject to § 202.13. But an application for both a temporary loan to finance construction of a dwelling and a permanent mortgage loan to take effect upon the completion

---

[29] [*Editor's note:* "Comment 11(a)-2 is added to reflect a preemption determination relating to Ohio law that took effect on July 23, 1990 (55 FR 29566)." 56 Fed. Reg. 14,461 (Apr. 10, 1991).]

[30] [*Editor's note:* "The Board intends for the record retention requirement to encourage creditors to take the full measure of corrective action that is warranted in light of the self-test results." 62 Fed. Reg. 66,412 (Dec. 18, 1997).]

of construction is subject to § 202.13.

4. *New principal residence.* A person can have only one principal residence at a time. However, if a person buys or builds a new dwelling that will become that person's principal residence within a year or upon completion of construction, the new dwelling is considered the principal residence for purposes of § 202.13.

5. *Transactions not covered.* The information-collection requirements of this section apply to applications for credit primarily for the purchase or refinancing of a dwelling that is or will become the applicant's principal residence. Therefore, applications for credit secured by the applicant's principal residence but made primarily for a purpose other than the purchase or refinancing of the principal residence (such as loans for home improvement and debt consolidation) are not subject to information-collection requirements. An application for an open-end home equity line of credit is not subject to this section unless it is readily apparent to the creditor when the application is taken that the primary purpose of the line is for the purchase or refinancing of a principal dwelling.

6. *Refinancings.* A refinancing occurs when an existing obligation is satisfied and replaced by a new obligation undertaken by the same borrower. A creditor that receives an application to refinance an existing extension of credit made by that creditor for the purchase of the applicant's dwelling may request the monitoring information again but is not required to do so if it was obtained in the earlier transaction.

7. *Data collection under Regulation C.*[31] See comment 5(b)(2)-2.

13(b) *Obtaining of information.*

1. *Forms for collecting data.* A creditor may collect the information specified in § 202.13(a) either on an application form or on a separate form referring to the application.

2. *Written applications.* The regulation requires written applications for the types of credit covered by § 202.13. A creditor can satisfy this requirement by recording in writing or by means of computer the information that the applicant provides orally and that the creditor normally considers in a credit decision.

3. *Telephone, mail applications.* If an applicant does not apply in person for the credit requested, a creditor does not have to complete the monitoring information. For example:

- When a creditor accepts an application by telephone, it does not have to request the monitoring information.
- When a creditor accepts an application by mail, it does not have to make a special request to the applicant if the applicant fails to complete the monitoring information on the application form sent to the creditor.
- If it is not evident on the face of the application that it was received by mail or telephone, the creditor should indicate on the form or other application record how the application was received.

4. *Applications through electronic media.*[32] If an applicant applies through an electronic medium (for example, the Internet or a facsimile) without video capability that allows the creditor to see the applicant, the creditor may treat the application as if it were received by mail or telephone.

5. *Applications through video.* If a creditor takes an application through a medium that allows the creditor to see the applicant, the creditor treats the application as taken in person and must note the monitoring information on the basis of visual observation or surname, if the applicant chooses not to provide the information.

6. *Applications through loan-shopping services.*[33] When a creditor receives an application through an unaffiliated loan-shopping service, it does not have to request the monitoring information for purposes of the ECOA or Regulation B. Creditors subject to the Home Mortgage Disclosure Act should be aware, however, that data collection may be called for under Regulation C which generally requires creditors to report, among other things, the sex and race or national origin of an applicant on brokered applications or applications received through a correspondent.

7. *Inadvertent notation.* If a creditor inadvertently obtains the monitoring information in a dwelling related transaction not covered by § 202.13, the creditor may process and retain the application without violating the regulation.

13(c) *Disclosure to applicant(s).*

1. *Procedures for providing disclosures.* The disclosures to an applicant regarding the monitoring information may be provided in writing. Appendix B contains a sample disclosure. A creditor may devise its own disclosure so long as it is substantially similar. The creditor need not orally request the applicant to provide the monitoring information if it is requested in writing.

13(d) *Substitute monitoring program.*

1. *Substitute program.* An enforcement agency may adopt, under its established rulemaking or enforcement procedures, a program requiring creditors under its jurisdiction to collect information in addition to that required by this section.

Section 202.14—Enforcement, penalties and liabilities

14(c) *Failure of compliance.*

1. *Inadvertent errors.* Inadvertent errors include, but are not limited to, clerical mistake, calculation error, computer malfunction, and printing error. An error of legal judgment is not an inadvertent error under the regulation.

2. *Correction of error.* For inadvertent errors that occur under §§ 202.12 and 202.13, this section requires that they be corrected prospectively only.

---

31 [*Editor's note:* "A cross reference to the commentary to § 202.5(b)(2) is added as comment 13(a)-7." 55 Fed. Reg. 12,471 (Apr. 4, 1990).]

32 [*Editor's note:* Comments 13(b)-4 and -5 were added by 61 Fed. Reg. 50,948 (Sept. 30, 1996), redesignating original comments 4 and 5 as 6 and 7.]

33 [*Editor's note:* "Comment 13(b)-4 is revised to indicate that even though creditors need not obtain the monitoring information for purposes of § 202.13 of Regulation B, when receiving an application through an unaffiliated loan-shopping service, data collection may nonetheless be required for creditors subject to HMDA." 57 Fed. Reg. 12,202 (Apr. 9, 1992).]

Section 202.15
Incentives for Self-testing and Self-correction[34]

15(a) *General Rules.*

15(a)(1) *Voluntary Self-Testing and Correction.*

1. Activities required by any governmental authority are not voluntary self-tests. A governmental authority includes both administrative and judicial authorities for federal, state, and local governments.

15(a)(2) *Corrective Action Required.*

1. To qualify for the privilege, appropriate corrective action is required when the results of a self-test show that it is more likely than not that there has been a violation of the ECOA or this regulation. A self-test is also privileged when it identifies no violations.

2. In some cases, the issue of whether certain information is privileged may arise before the self-test is complete or corrective actions are fully under way. This would not necessarily prevent a creditor from asserting the privilege. In situations where the self-test is not complete, for the privilege to apply the lender must satisfy the regulation's requirements within a reasonable period of time. To assert the privilege where the self-test shows a likely violation, the rule requires, at a minimum, that the creditor establish a plan for corrective action and a method to demonstrate progress in implementing the plan. Creditors must take appropriate corrective action on a timely basis after the results of the self-test are known.

3. A creditor's determination about the type of corrective action needed, or a finding that no corrective action is required, is not conclusive in determining whether the requirements of this paragraph have been satisfied. If a creditor's claim of privilege is challenged, an assessment of the need for corrective action or the type of corrective action that is appropriate must be based on a review of the self-testing results, which may require an in camera inspection of the privileged documents.

15(a)(3) *Other privileges.*

1. A creditor may assert the privilege established under this section in addition to asserting any other privilege that may apply, such as the attorney-client privilege or the work product privilege. Self-testing data may still be privileged under this section, whether or not the creditor's assertion of another privilege is upheld.

15(b) *Self-test Defined.*

15(b)(1) *Definition.*

Paragraph 15(b)(1)(i)

1. To qualify for the privilege, a self-test must be sufficient to constitute a determination of the extent or effectiveness of the creditor's compliance with the act and Regulation B. Accordingly, a self-test is only privileged if it was designed and used for that purpose. A self-test that is designed or used to determine compliance with other laws or regulations or for other purposes is not privileged under this rule. For example, a self-test designed to evaluate employee efficiency or customers' satisfaction with the level of service provided by the creditor is not privileged even if evidence of discrimination is uncovered incidentally. If a self-test is designed for multiple purposes, only the portion designed to determine compliance with the ECOA is eligible for the privilege.

Paragraph 15(b)(1)(ii)

1. The principal attribute of self-testing is that it constitutes a voluntary undertaking by the creditor to produce new data or factual information that otherwise would not be available and could not be derived from loan or application files or other records related to credit transactions. Self-testing includes, but is not limited to, the practice of using fictitious applicants for credit (testers), either with or without the use of matched pairs. A creditor may elect to test a defined segment of its business, for example, loan applications processed by a specific branch or loan officer, or applications made for a particular type of credit or loan program. A creditor also may use other methods of generating information that is not available in loan and application files, such as surveying mortgage loan applicants. To the extent permitted by law, creditors might also develop new methods that go beyond traditional pre-application testing, such as hiring testers to submit fictitious loan applications for processing.

2. The privilege does not protect a creditor's analysis performed as part of processing or underwriting a credit application. A creditor's evaluation or analysis of its loan files, Home Mortgage Disclosure Act data, or similar types of records (such as broker or loan officer compensation records) does not produce new information about a creditor's compliance and is not a self-test for purposes of this section. Similarly, a statistical analysis of data derived from existing loan files is not privileged.

15(b)(3) *Types of Information not Privileged.*

Paragraph 15(b)(3)(i)

1. The information listed in this paragraph is not privileged and may be used to determine whether the prerequisites for the privilege have been satisfied. Accordingly, a creditor might be asked to identify the self-testing method, for example, whether pre-application testers were used or data were compiled by surveying loan applicants. Information about the scope of the self test (such as the types of credit transactions examined, or the geographic area covered by the test) also is not privileged.

Paragraph 15(b)(3)(ii)

1. Property appraisal reports, minutes of loan committee meetings or other documents reflecting the basis for a decision to approve or deny an application, loan policies or procedures, underwriting standards, and broker compensation records are examples of the types of records that are not privileged. If a creditor arranges for testers to submit loan applications for processing, the records are not related to actual credit transactions for purposes of this paragraph and may be privileged self-testing records.

15(c) *Appropriate Corrective Action.*

1. The rule only addresses what corrective actions are required for a creditor to take advantage of the privilege in this section. A creditor may still be required to take other actions or provide additional relief if a formal finding of discrimination is made.

---

[34] [*Editor's note:* Section 202.15 added by 62 Fed. Reg. 66,412 (Dec. 18, 1997), became effective January 30, 1998.]

15(c)(1) *General Requirement.*

1. Appropriate corrective action is required even though no violation has been formally adjudicated or admitted by the creditor. In determining whether it is more likely than not that a violation occurred, a creditor must treat testers as if they are actual applicants for credit. A creditor may not refuse to take appropriate corrective action under this section because the self-test used fictitious loan applicants. The fact that a tester's agreement with the creditor waives the tester's legal right to assert a violation does not eliminate the requirement for the creditor to take corrective action, although no remedial relief for the tester is required under paragraph 15(c)(3).

15(c)(2) *Determining the Scope of Appropriate Corrective Action.*

1. Whether a creditor has taken or is taking corrective action that is appropriate will be determined on a case-by-case basis. Generally, the scope of the corrective action that is needed to preserve the privilege is governed by the scope of the self-test. For example, a creditor that self-tests mortgage loans and discovers evidence of discrimination may focus its corrective actions on mortgage loans, and is not required to expand its testing to other types of loans.

2. In identifying the policies or practices that are the likely cause of the violation, a creditor might identify inadequate or improper lending policies, failure to implement established policies, employee conduct, or other causes. The extent and scope of a likely violation may be assessed by determining which areas of operations are likely to be affected by those policies and practices, for example, by determining the types of loans and stages of the application process involved and the branches or offices where the violations may have occurred.

3. Depending on the method and scope of the self-test and the results of the test, appropriate corrective action may include one or more of the following:

i. If the self-test identifies individuals whose applications were inappropriately processed, offering to extend credit if the application was improperly denied and compensating such persons for out-of-pocket costs and other compensatory damages;

ii. Correcting institutional polices or procedures that may have contributed to the likely violation, and adopting new policies as appropriate;

iii. Identifying and then training and/or disciplining the employees involved;

iv. Developing outreach programs, marketing strategies, or loan products to serve more effectively segments of the lender's markets that may have been affected by the likely discrimination; and

v. Improving audit and oversight systems to avoid a recurrence of the likely violations.

15(c)(3) *Types of Relief.*

Paragraph 15(c)(3)(ii)

1. The use of pre-application testers to identify policies and practices that illegally discriminate does not require creditors to review existing loan files for the purpose of identifying and compensating applicants who might have been adversely affected.

2. If a self-test identifies a specific applicant that was subject to discrimination on a prohibited basis, in order to qualify for the privilege in this section the creditor must provide appropriate remedial relief to that applicant; the creditor would not be required under this paragraph to identify other applicants who might also have been adversely affected.

Paragraph 15(c)(3)(iii)

1. A creditor is not required to provide remedial relief to an applicant that would not be available by law. An applicant might also be ineligible from obtaining certain types of relief due to changed circumstances. For example, a creditor is not required to offer credit to a denied applicant if the applicant no longer qualifies for the credit due to a change in financial circumstances, although some other type of relief might be appropriate.

15(d)(1) *Scope of Privilege.*

1. The privilege applies with respect to any examination, investigation or proceeding by federal, state, or local government agencies relating to compliance with the Act or this regulation. Accordingly, in a case brought under the ECOA, the privilege established under this section preempts any inconsistent laws or court rules to the extent they might require disclosure of privileged self-testing data. The privilege does not apply in other cases, for example, litigation filed solely under a state's fair lending statute. In such cases, if a court orders a creditor to disclose self-test results, the disclosure is not a voluntary disclosure or waiver of the privilege for purposes of paragraph 15(d)(2); creditors may protect the information by seeking a protective order to limit availability and use of the self-testing data and prevent dissemination beyond what is necessary in that case. Paragraph 15(d)(1) precludes a party who has obtained privileged information from using it in a case brought under the ECOA, provided the creditor has not lost the privilege through voluntarily disclosure under paragraph 15(d)(2).

15(d)(2) *Loss of Privilege.*

Paragraph 15(d)(2)(i)

1. Corrective action taken by a creditor, by itself, is not considered a voluntary disclosure of the self-test report or results. For example, a creditor does not disclose the results of a self-test merely by offering to extend credit to a denied applicant or by inviting the applicant to reapply for credit. Voluntary disclosure could occur under this paragraph, however, if the creditor disclosed the self-test results in connection with a new offer of credit.

2. Disclosure of self-testing results to an independent contractor acting as an auditor or consultant for the creditor on compliance matters does not result in loss of the privilege.

Paragraph 15(d)(2)(ii)

1. The privilege is lost if the creditor discloses privileged information, such as the results of the self-test. The privilege is not lost if the creditor merely reveals or refers to the existence of the self-test.

Paragraph 15(d)(2)(iii)

1. A creditor's claim of privilege may be challenged in a court or administrative law proceeding with appropriate jurisdiction. In resolving the issue, the presiding officer may require the creditor to produce privileged information about the self-test.

15(d)(3) *Limited Use of Privileged Information.*

1. A creditor may be required to produce privileged documents for the purpose of determining a penalty or remedy after a violation of the ECOA or Regulation B has been formally adjudicated or admitted. A creditor's compliance with this requirement does not evidence the creditor's intent to forfeit the privilege.

Appendix B—Model Application Forms

1. *FHLMC/FNMA form—residential loan application.*[35] The uniform residential loan application form (FHLMC 65/FNMA 1003) including supplemental form (FHLMC 65A/FNMA 1003A), prepared by the Federal Home Loan Mortgage Corporation and the Federal National Mortgage Association and dated May 1991 may be used by creditors without violating this regulation even though the form's listing of race or national origin categories in the "Information for Government Monitoring Purposes" section differs from the classifications currently specified in § 202.13(a)(1). The classifications used on the FNMA-FHLMC form are those required by the U.S. Office of Management and Budget for notation of race and ethnicity by federal programs in their administrative reporting and statistical activities. Creditors that are governed by the monitoring requirements of Regulation B (which limits collec-

---

35 [*Editor's note:* "Comment 1 is revised to indicate that the uniform residential loan application form dated May 1991 and prepared by the Federal Home Loan Mortgage Corporation (Freddie Mac) and the Federal National Mortgage Association (Fannie Mae) may be used by creditors without violating Regulation B—even though the monitoring information section of this form contains categories for noting an applicant's race or national origin that differ from those required by § 202.13 of the regulation. The categories on the Fannie Mae-Freddie Mac form conform to classifications specified by the U.S. Office of Management and Budget for recordkeeping, collection, and presentation of data on race and ethnicity in federal program administrative reporting and statistical activities. The comment is also revised to indicate that creditors subject to HMDA may use the form as issued, in compliance with that act and Regulation C." 57 Fed. Reg. 12,202 (Apr. 9, 1992).]

tion to applications primarily for the purchase or refinancing of the applicant's principal residence) should delete, strike, or modify the data-collection section on the form when using it for transactions not covered by § 202.13(a) to ensure that they do not collect the information. Creditors that are subject to more extensive collection requirements by a substitute monitoring program under § 202.13(d) or by the Home Mortgage Disclosure Act (HMDA) may use the form as issued, in compliance with the substitute program or HMDA.

2. *FHLMC/FNMA form—home-improvement loan application.* The home-improvement and energy loan application form (FHLMC 703/FNMA 1012), prepared by the Federal Home Loan Mortgage Corporation and the Federal National Mortgage Association and dated October 1986, complies with the requirements of the regulation for some creditors but not others because of the form's section on "Information for Government Monitoring Purposes." Creditors that are governed by § 202.13(a) of the regulation (which limits collection to applications primarily for the purchase or refinancing of the applicant's principal residence) should delete, strike, or modify the data collection section on the form when using it for transactions not covered by § 202.13(a) to assure that they do not collect the information. Creditors that are subject to more extensive collection requirements by a substitute monitoring program under § 202.13(d) may use the form as issued, in compliance with that substitute program.

Appendix C—Sample Notification Forms

Form C-9.[36] Creditors may design their own form, add to, or modify the model form to reflect their individual policies and procedures. For example, a creditor may want to add:

i. A telephone number that applicants may call to leave their name and the address to which an appraisal report should be sent.

ii. A notice of the cost the applicant will be required to pay the creditor for the appraisal or a copy of the report.

---

36 [*Editor's note:* Added by 60 Fed. Reg. 29,967 (June 5, 1995).]

HUD Fair Housing Act Regulations

Selected Fair Housing regulations from 24 C.F.R. Part 100. Reprinted are Subparts A, B, C, D, and F. Not reprinted is Subpart E, Housing for Older Persons.

PART 100—DISCRIMINATORY CONDUCT UNDER THE FAIR HOUSING ACT

Subpart A—General

Subpart B—Discriminatory Housing Practices

Subpart C—Discrimination in Residential Real Estate-Related Transactions

Subpart D—Prohibition Against Discrimination Because of Handicap

Subpart F—Interference, Coercion or Intimidation

AUTHORITY: 42 U.S.C. 3535(d), 42 U.S.C. 3600–3620

SOURCE: 54 Fed. Reg. 3283 (Jan. 23, 1989) unless otherwise noted.

PART 100—DISCRIMINATORY CONDUCT UNDER THE FAIR HOUSING ACT

Subpart A—General

§ 100.1 Authority.

This regulation is issued under the authority of the Secretary of Housing and Urban Development to administer and enforce title VIII of the Civil Rights Act of 1968, as amended by the Fair Housing Amendments Act of 1988 (the Fair Housing Act).

§ 100.5 Scope.

(a) It is the policy of the United States to provide, within constitutional limitations, for fair housing throughout the United States. No person shall be subjected to discrimination because of race, color, religion, sex, handicap, familial status, or national origin in the sale, rental, or advertising of dwellings, in the provision of brokerage services, or in the availability of residential real estate-related transactions.

(b) This part provides the Department's interpretation of the coverage of the Fair Housing Act regarding discrimination related to the sale or rental of dwellings, the provision of services in connection therewith, and the availability of residential real estate-related transactions.

(c) Nothing in this part relieves persons participating in a Federal or Federally-assisted program or activity from other requirements applicable to buildings and dwellings.

§ 100.10 Exemptions.

(a) This part does not:

(1) Prohibit a religious organization, association, or society, or any nonprofit institution or organization operated, supervised or controlled by or in conjunction with a religious organization, association, or society, from limiting the sale, rental or occupancy of dwellings which it owns or operates for other than a commercial purpose to persons of the same religion, or from giving preference to such persons, unless membership in such religion is restricted because of race, color, or national origin;

(2) Prohibit a private club, not in fact open to the public, which, incident to its primary purpose or purposes, provides lodgings which it owns or operates for other than a commercial purpose, from limiting the rental or occupancy of such lodgings to its members or from giving preference to its members;

(3) Limit the applicability of any reasonable local, State or Federal restrictions regarding the maximum number of occupants permitted to occupy a dwelling; or

(4) Prohibit conduct against a person because such person has been convicted by any court of competent jurisdiction of the illegal manufacture or distribution of a controlled substance as defined in Section 102 of the Controlled Substances Act (21 U.S.C. 802).

(b) Nothing in this part regarding discrimination based on familial status applies with respect to housing for older persons as defined in subpart E of this part.

(c) Nothing in this part, other than the prohibitions against discriminatory advertising, applies to:

(1) The sale or rental of any single family house by an owner, provided the following conditions are met:

   (i) The owner does not own or have any interest in more than three single family houses at any one time.

   (ii) The house is sold or rented without the use of a real estate broker, agent or salesperson or the facilities of any person in the business of selling or renting dwellings. If the owner selling the house does not reside in it at the time of the sale or was not the most recent resident of the house prior to such sale, the exemption in this paragraph (c)(1) of this section applies to only one such sale in any 24-month period.

(2) Rooms or units in dwellings containing living quarters occupied or intended to be occupied by no more than four families living independently of each other, if the owner actually maintains and occupies one of such living quarters as his or her residence.

§ 100.20 Definitions.

The terms Department, Fair Housing Act, and Secretary are defined in 24 CFR part 5.[1]

Aggrieved person includes any person who—

(a) Claims to have been injured by a discriminatory housing practice; or

(b) Believes that such person will be injured by a discriminatory housing practice that is about to occur.

Broker or *Agent* includes any person authorized to perform an action on behalf of another person regarding any matter related to the sale or rental of dwellings, including offers, solicitations or contracts and the administration of matters regarding such offers, solicitations or contracts or any residential real estate-related transactions.

Discriminatory housing practice means an act that is unlawful under section 804, 805, 806, or 818 of the Fair Housing Act.

Dwelling means any building, structure or portion thereof which is occupied as, or designed or intended for occupancy as, a residence by one or more families, and any vacant land which is offered for sale or lease for the construction or location thereon of any such building, structure or portion thereof.

Familial status means one or more individuals (who have not attained the age of 18 years) being domiciled with—

(a) A parent or another person having legal custody of such individual or individuals; or

(b) The designee of such parent or other person having such custody, with the written permission of such parent or other person.

The protections afforded against discrimination on the basis of familial status shall apply to any person who is pregnant or is in the process of securing legal custody of any individual who has not attained the age of 18 years.

Handicap is defined in § 100.201.

Person includes one or more individuals, corporations, partnerships, associations, labor organizations, legal representatives, mutual companies, joint-stock companies, trusts, unincorporated organizations, trustees, trustees in cases under title 11 U.S.C., receivers, and fiduciaries.

Person in the business of selling or renting dwellings means any person who:

(a) Within the preceding twelve months, has participated as principal in three or more transactions involving the sale or rental of any dwelling or any interest therein;

(b) Within the preceding twelve months, has participated as agent, other than in the sale of his or her own personal residence, in providing sales or rental facilities or sales or rental services in two or more transactions involving the sale or rental of any dwelling or any interest therein; or

(c) Is the owner of any dwelling designed or intended for occupancy by, or occupied by, five or more families.

---

1 [*Editor's Note:*

   Department means the Department of Housing and Urban Development.

   Fair Housing Act means title VIII of the Civil Rights Act of 1968, as amended by the Fair Housing Amendments Act of 1988 (42 U.S.C. 3600–3620).

   Secretary means the Secretary of the Department of Housing and Urban Development.

24 C.F.R. pt. 5.]

State means any of the several states, the District of Columbia, the Commonwealth of Puerto Rico, or any of the territories and possessions of the United States.

Subpart B—Discriminatory Housing Practices

§ 100.50 Real estate practices prohibited.

(a) This subpart provides the Department's interpretation of conduct that is unlawful housing discrimination under section 804 and section 806 of the Fair Housing Act. In general the prohibited actions are set forth under sections of this subpart which are most applicable to the discriminatory conduct described. However, an action illustrated in one section can constitute a violation under sections in the subpart. For example, the conduct described in § 100.60(b)(3) and (4) would constitute a violation of § 100.65(a) as well as § 100.60(a).

(b) It shall be unlawful to:

(1) Refuse to sell or rent a dwelling after a *bona fide* offer has been made, or to refuse to negotiate for the sale or rental of a dwelling because of race, color, religion, sex, familial status, or national origin, or to discriminate in the sale or rental of a dwelling because of handicap.

(2) Discriminate in the terms, conditions or privileges of sale or rental of a dwelling, or in the provision of services or facilities in connection with sales or rentals, because of race, color, religion, sex, handicap, familial status, or national origin.

(3) Engage in any conduct relating to the provision of housing which otherwise makes unavailable or denies dwellings to persons because of race, color, religion, sex, handicap, familial status, or national origin.

(4) Make, print or publish, or cause to be made, printed or published, any notice, statement or advertisement with respect to the sale or rental of a dwelling that indicates any preference, limitation or discrimination because of race, color, religion, sex, handicap, familial status, or national origin, or an intention to make any such preference, limitation or discrimination.

(5) Represent to any person because of race, color, religion, sex, handicap, familial status, or national origin that a dwelling is not available for sale or rental when such dwelling is in fact available.

(6) Engage in blockbusting practices in connection with the sale or rental of dwellings because of race, color, religion, sex, handicap, familial status, or national origin.

(7) Deny access to or membership or participation in, or to discriminate against any person in his or her access to or membership or participation in, any multiple-listing service, real estate brokers' association, or other service organization or facility relating to the business of selling or renting a dwelling or in the terms or conditions or membership or participation, because of race, color, religion, sex, handicap, familial status, or national origin.

(c) The application of the Fair Housing Act with respect to persons with handicaps is discussed in subpart D of this part.

§ 100.60 Unlawful refusal to sell or rent or to negotiate for the sale or rental.

(a) It shall be unlawful for a person to refuse to sell or rent a dwelling to a person who has made a *bona fide* offer, because of race, color, religion, sex, familial status, or national origin or to refuse to negotiate with a person for the sale or rental of a dwelling because of race, color, religion, sex, familial status, or national origin, or to discriminate against any person in the sale or rental of a dwelling because of handicap.

(b) Prohibited actions under this section include, but are not limited to:

(1) Failing to accept or consider a *bona fide* offer because of race, color, religion, sex, handicap, familial status, or national origin.

(2) Refusing to sell or rent a dwelling to, or to negotiate for the sale or rental of a dwelling with, any person because of race, color, religion, sex, handicap, familial status, or national origin.

(3) Imposing different sales prices or rental charges for the sale or rental of a dwelling upon any person because of race, color, religion, sex, handicap, familial status, or national origin.

(4) Using different qualification criteria or applications, or sale or rental standards or procedures, such as income standards, application requirements, application fees, credit analysis or sale or rental approval procedures or other requirements, because of race, color, religion, sex, handicap, familial status, or national origin.

(5) Evicting tenants because of their race, color, religion, sex, handicap, familial status, or national origin or because of the race, color, religion, sex, handicap, familial status, or national origin of a tenant's guest.

§ 100.65 Discrimination in terms, conditions and privileges and in services and facilities.

(a) It shall be unlawful, because of race, color, religion, sex, handicap, familial status, or national origin, to impose different terms, conditions or privileges relating to the sale or rental of a dwelling or to deny or limit services or facilities in connection with the sale or rental of a dwelling.

(b) Prohibited actions under this section include, but are not limited to:

(1) Using different provisions in leases or contracts of sale, such as those relating to rental charges, security deposits and the terms of a lease and those relating to down payment and closing requirements, because of race, color, religion, sex, handicap, familial status, or national origin.

(2) Failing or delaying maintenance or repairs of sale or rental dwellings because of race, color, religion, sex, handicap, familial status, or national origin.

(3) Failing to process an offer for the sale or rental of a dwelling or to communicate an offer accurately because of race, color, religion, sex, handicap, familial status, or national origin.

(4) Limiting the use of privileges, services or facilities associated with a dwelling because of race, color, religion, sex,

handicap, familial status, or national origin of an an [sic] owner, tenant or a person associated with him or her.

(5) Denying or limiting services or facilities in connection with the sale or rental of a dwelling, because a person failed or refused to provide sexual favors.

§ 100.70 Other prohibited sale and rental conduct.

(a) It shall be unlawful, because of race, color, religion, sex, handicap, familial status, or national origin, to restrict or attempt to restrict the choices of a person by word or conduct in connection with seeking, negotiating for, buying or renting a dwelling so as to perpetuate, or tend to perpetuate, segregated housing patterns, or to discourage or obstruct choices in a community, neighborhood or development.

(b) It shall be unlawful, because of race, color, religion, sex, handicap, familial status, or national origin, to engage in any conduct relating to the provision of housing or of services and facilities in connection therewith that otherwise makes unavailable or denies dwellings to persons.

(c) Prohibited actions under paragraph (a) of this section, which are generally referred to as unlawful steering practices, include, but are not limited to:

(1) Discouraging any person from inspecting, purchasing or renting a dwelling because of race, color, religion, sex, handicap, familial status, or national origin, or because of the race, color, religion, sex, handicap, familial status, or national origin of persons in a community, neighborhood or development.

(2) Discouraging the purchase or rental of a dwelling because of race, color, religion, sex, handicap, familial status, or national origin, by exaggerating drawbacks or failing to inform any person of desirable features of a dwelling or of a community, neighborhood, or development.

(3) Communicating to any prospective purchaser that he or she would not be comfortable or compatible with existing residents of a community, neighborhood or development because of race, color, religion, sex, handicap, familial status, or national origin.

(4) Assigning any person to a particular section of a community, neighborhood or development, or to a particular floor of a building, because of race, color, religion, sex, handicap, familial status, or national origin.

(d) Prohibited activities relating to dwellings under paragraph (b) of this section include, but are not limited to:

(1) Discharging or taking other adverse action against an employee, broker or agent because he or she refused to participate in a discriminatory housing practice.

(2) Employing codes or other devices to segregate or reject applicants, purchasers or renters, refusing to take or to show listings of dwellings in certain areas because of race, color, religion, sex, handicap, familial status, or national origin, or refusing to deal with certain brokers or agents because they or one or more of their clients are of a particular race, color, religion, sex, handicap, familial status, or national origin.

(3) Denying or delaying the processing of an application made by a purchaser or renter or refusing to approve such a person for occupancy in a cooperative or condominium dwelling

because of race, color, religion, sex, handicap, familial status, or national origin.

(4) Refusing to provide municipal services or property or hazard insurance for dwellings or providing such services or insurance differently because of race, color, religion, sex, handicap, familial status, or national origin.

§ 100.75 Discriminatory advertisements, statements and notices.

(a) It shall be unlawful to make, print or publish, or cause to be made, printed or published, any notice, statement or advertisement with respect to the sale or rental of a dwelling which indicates any preference, limitation or discrimination because of race, color, religion, sex, handicap, familial status, or national origin, or an intention to make any such preference, limitation or discrimination.

(b) The prohibitions in this section shall apply to all written or oral notices or statements by a person engaged in the sale or rental of a dwelling. Written notices and statements include any applications, flyers, brochures, deeds, signs, banners, posters, billboards or any documents used with respect to the sale or rental of a dwelling.

(c) Discriminatory notices, statements and advertisements include, but are not limited to:

(1) Using words, phrases, photographs, illustrations, symbols or forms which convey that dwellings are available or not available to a particular group of persons because of race, color, religion, sex, handicap, familial status, or national origin.

(2) Expressing to agents, brokers, employees, prospective sellers or renters or any other persons a preference for or limitation on any purchaser or renter because of race, color, religion, sex, handicap, familial status, or national origin of such persons.

(3) Selecting media or locations for advertising the sale or rental of dwellings which deny particular segments of the housing market information about housing opportunities because of race, color, religion, sex, handicap, familial status, or national origin.

(4) Refusing to publish advertising for the sale or rental of dwellings or requiring different charges or terms for such advertising because of race, color, religion, sex, handicap, familial status, or national origin.

(d) 24 CFR part 109 provides information to assist persons to advertise dwellings in a nondiscriminatory manner and describes the matters the Department will review in evaluating compliance with the Fair Housing Act and in investigating complaints alleging discriminatory housing practices involving advertising.

§ 100.80 Discriminatory representations on the availability of dwellings.

(a) It shall be unlawful, because of race, color, religion, sex, handicap, familial status, or national origin, to provide inaccurate or untrue information about the availability of dwellings for sale or rental.

(b) Prohibited actions under this section include, but are not limited to:

(1) Indicating through words or conduct that a dwelling which is available for inspection, sale, or rental has been sold or rented, because of race, color, religion, sex, handicap, familial status, or national origin.

(2) Representing that covenants or other deed, trust or lease provisions which purport to restrict the sale or rental of dwellings because of race, color, religion, sex, handicap, familial status, or national origin preclude the sale of [sic] rental of a dwelling to a person.

(3) Enforcing covenants or other deed, trust, or lease provisions which preclude the sale or rental of a dwelling to any person because of race, color, religion, sex, handicap, familial status, or national origin.

(4) Limiting information, by word or conduct, regarding suitably priced dwellings available for inspection, sale or rental, because of race, color, religion, sex, handicap, familial status, or national origin.

(5) Providing false or inaccurate information regarding the availability of a dwelling for sale or rental to any person, including testers, regardless of whether such person is actually seeking housing, because of race, color, religion, sex, handicap, familial status, or national origin.

§ 100.85 Blockbusting.

(a) It shall be unlawful, for profit, to induce or attempt to induce a person to sell or rent a dwelling by representations regarding the entry or prospective entry into the neighborhood of a person or persons of a particular race, color, religion, sex, familial status, or national origin or with a handicap.

(b) In establishing a discriminatory housing practice under this section it is not necessary that there was in fact profit as long as profit was a factor for engaging in the blockbusting activity.

(c) Prohibited actions under this section include, but are not limited to:

(1) Engaging, for profit, in conduct (including uninvited solicitations for listings) which conveys to a person that a neighborhood is undergoing or is about to undergo a change in the race, color, religion, sex, handicap, familial status, or national origin of persons residing in it, in order to encourage the person to offer a dwelling for sale or rental.

(2) Encouraging, for profit, any person to sell or rent a dwelling through assertions that the entry or prospective entry of persons of a particular race, color, religion, sex, familial status, or national origin, or with handicaps, can or will result in undesirable consequences for the project, neighborhood or community, such as a lowering of property values, an increase in criminal or antisocial behavior, or a decline in the quality of schools or other services or facilities.

§ 100.90 Discrimination in the provision of brokerage services.

(a) It shall be unlawful to deny any person access to or membership or participation in any multiple listing service, real estate brokers' organization or other service, organization, or facility relating to the business of selling or renting dwellings, or to discriminate against any person in the terms or conditions of such access, membership or participation, because of race, color, religion, sex, handicap, familial status, or national origin.

(b) Prohibited actions under this section include, but are not limited to:

(1) Setting different fees for access to or membership in a multiple listing service because of race, color, religion, sex, handicap, familial status, or national origin.

(2) Denying or limiting benefits accruing to members in a real estate brokers' organization because of race, color, religion, sex, handicap, familial status, or national origin.

(3) Imposing different standards or criteria for membership in a real estate sales or rental organization because of race, color, religion, sex, handicap, familial status, or national origin.

(4) Establishing geographic boundaries or office location or residence requirements for access to or membership or participation in any multiple listing service, real estate brokers' organization or other service, organization or facility relating to the business of selling or renting dwellings, because of race, color, religion, sex, handicap, familial status, or national origin.

Subpart C—Discrimination in Residential Real Estate-Related Transactions

§ 100.110 Discriminatory practices in residential real estate-related transactions.

(a) This subpart provides the Department's interpretation of the conduct that is unlawful housing discrimination under section 805 of the Fair Housing Act.

(b) It shall be unlawful for any person or other entity whose business includes engaging in residential real estate-related transactions to discriminate against any person in making available such a transaction, or in the terms or conditions of such a transaction, because of race, color, religion, sex, handicap, familial status, or national origin.

§ 100.115 Residential real estate-related transactions.

The term residential *real estate-related transactions* means:

(a) The making or purchasing of loans or providing other financial assistance—

(1) For purchasing, constructing, improving, repairing or maintaining a dwelling; or

(2) Secured by residential real estate; or

(b) The selling, brokering or appraising of residential real property.

§ 100.120 Discrimination in the making of loans and in the provision of other financial assistance.

(a) It shall be unlawful for any person or entity whose business includes engaging in residential real estate-related transactions to discriminate against any person in making available loans or other financial assistance for a dwelling, or which is or is to be secured by a dwelling, because of race, color, religion, sex, handicap, familial status, or national origin.

(b) Prohibited practices under this section include, but are not limited to, failing or refusing to provide to any person, in connection with a residential real estate-related transaction, information regarding the availability of loans or other financial assistance, application requirements, procedures or standards for the review and approval of loans or financial assistance, or providing information which is inaccurate or different from that provided others, because of race, color, religion, sex, handicap, familial status, or national origin.

§ 100.125 Discrimination in the purchasing of loans.

(a) It shall be unlawful for any person or entity engaged in the purchasing of loans or other debts or securities which support the purchase, construction, improvement, repair or maintenance of a dwelling, or which are secured by residential real estate, to refuse to purchase such loans, debts, or securities, or to impose different terms or conditions for such purchases, because of race, color, religion, sex, handicap, familial status, or national origin.

(b) Unlawful conduct under this section includes, but is not limited to:

(1) Purchasing loans or other debts or securities which relate to, or which are secured by dwellings in certain communities or neighborhoods but not in others because of the race, color, religion, sex, handicap, familial status, or national origin of persons in such neighborhoods or communities.

(2) Pooling or packaging loans or other debts or securities which relate to, or which are secured by, dwellings differently because of race, color, religion, sex, handicap, familial status, or national origin.

(3) Imposing or using different terms or conditions on the marketing or sale of securities issued on the basis of loans or other debts or securities which relate to, or which are secured by, dwellings because of race, color, religion, sex, handicap, familial status, or national origin.

(c) This section does not prevent consideration, in the purchasing of loans, of factors justified by business necessity, including requirements of Federal law, relating to a transaction's financial security or to protection against default or reduction of the value of the security. Thus, this provision would not preclude considerations employed in normal and prudent transactions, provided that no such factor may in any way relate to race, color, religion, sex, handicap, familial status or national origin.

§ 100.130 Discrimination in the terms and conditions for making available loans or other financial assistance.

(a) It shall be unlawful for any person or entity engaged in the making of loans or in the provision of other financial assistance relating to the purchase, construction, improvement, repair or maintenance of dwellings or which are secured by residential real estate to impose different terms or conditions for the availability of such loans or other financial assistance because of race, color, religion, sex, handicap, familial status, or national origin.

(b) Unlawful conduct under this section includes, but is not limited to:

(1) Using different policies, practices or procedures in evaluating or in determining creditworthiness of any person in connection with the provision of any loan or other financial assistance for a dwelling or for any loan or other financial assistance which is secured by residential real estate because of race, color, religion, sex, handicap, familial status, or national origin.

(2) Determining the type of loan or other financial assistance to be provided with respect to a dwelling, or fixing the amount, interest rate, duration or other terms for a loan or other financial assistance for a dwelling or which is secured by residential real estate, because of race, color, religion, sex, handicap, familial status, or national origin.

§ 100.135 Unlawful practices in the selling, brokering, or appraising of residential real property.

(a) It shall be unlawful for any person or other entity whose business includes engaging in the selling, brokering or appraising of residential real property to discriminate against any person in making available such services, or in the performance of such services, because of race, color, religion, sex, handicap, familial status, or national origin.

(b) For the purposes of this section, the term appraisal means an estimate or opinion of the value of a specified residential real property made in a business context in connection with the sale, rental, financing or refinancing of a dwelling or in connection with any activity that otherwise affects the availability of a residential real estate-related transaction, whether the appraisal is oral or written, or transmitted formally or informally. The appraisal includes all written comments and other documents submitted as support for the estimate or opinion of value.

(c) Nothing in this section prohibits a person engaged in the business of making or furnishing appraisals of residential real property from taking into consideration factors other than race, color, religion, sex, handicap, familial status, or national origin.

(d) Practices which are unlawful under this section include, but are not limited to, using an appraisal of residential real property in connection with the sale, rental, or financing of any dwelling where the person knows or reasonably should know that the appraisal improperly takes into consideration race, color, religion, sex, handicap, familial status or national origin.

§ 100.140 General rules.

(a) *Voluntary self-testing and correction.* The report or results of a self-test a lender voluntarily conducts or authorizes are privileged as provided in this subpart if the lender has taken or is taking appropriate corrective action to address likely violations identified by the self-test. Data collection required by law or any governmental authority (federal, state, or local) is not voluntary.

(b) *Other privileges.* This subpart does not abrogate any evidentiary privilege otherwise provided by law.

[62 FR 66432, Dec. 18, 1997]

§ 100.141 Definitions.

As used in this subpart:

Lender means a person who engages in a residential real estate-related lending transaction.

Residential real estate-related lending transaction means the making of a loan:

(1) For purchasing, constructing, improving, repairing, or maintaining a dwelling; or

(2) Secured by residential real estate.

Self-test means any program, practice or study a lender voluntarily conducts or authorizes which is designed and used specifically to determine the extent or effectiveness of compliance with the Fair Housing Act. The self-test must create data or factual information that is not available and cannot be derived from loan files, application files, or other residential real estate-related lending transaction records. Self-testing includes, but is not limited to, using fictitious credit applicants (testers) or conducting surveys of applicants or customers, nor is it limited to the pre-application stage of loan processing.

[62 FR 66432, Dec. 18, 1997]

§ 100.142 Types of information.

(a) The privilege under this subpart covers:

(1) The report or results of the self-test;

(2) Data or factual information created by the self-test;

(3) Workpapers, draft documents and final documents;

(4) Analyses, opinions, and conclusions if they directly result from the self-test report or results.

(b) The privilege does not cover:

(1) Information about whether a lender conducted a self-test, the methodology used or scope of the self-test, the time period covered by the self-test or the dates it was conducted;

(2) Loan files and application files, or other residential real estate-related lending transaction records (e.g., property appraisal reports, loan committee meeting minutes or other documents reflecting the basis for a decision to approve or deny a loan application, loan policies or procedures, underwriting standards, compensation records) and information or data derived from such files and records, even if such data has been aggregated, summarized or reorganized to facilitate analysis.

[62 FR 66432, Dec. 18, 1997]

§ 100.143 Appropriate corrective action.

(a) The report or results of a self-test are privileged as provided in this subpart if the lender has taken or is taking appropriate corrective action to address likely violations identified by the self-test. Appropriate corrective action is required when a self-test shows it is more likely than not that a violation occurred even though no violation was adjudicated formally.

(b) A lender must take action reasonably likely to remedy the cause and effect of the likely violation and must:

(1) Identify the policies or practices that are the likely cause of the violation, such as inadequate or improper lending poli-

cies, failure to implement established policies, employee conduct, or other causes; and

(2) Assess the extent and scope of any likely violation, by determining which areas of operation are likely to be affected by those policies and practices, such as stages of the loan application process, types of loans, or the particular branch where the likely violation has occurred. Generally, the scope of the self-test governs the scope of the appropriate corrective action.

(c) Appropriate corrective action may include both prospective and remedial relief, except that to establish a privilege under this subpart:

(1) A lender is not required to provide remedial relief to a tester in a self-test;

(2) A lender is only required to provide remedial relief to an applicant identified by the self-test as one whose rights were more likely than not violated;

(3) A lender is not required to provide remedial relief to a particular applicant if the statute of limitations applicable to the violation expired before the lender obtained the results of the self-test or the applicant is otherwise ineligible for such relief.

(d) Depending on the facts involved, appropriate corrective action may include, but is not limited to, one or more of the following:

(1) If the self-test identifies individuals whose applications were inappropriately processed, offering to extend credit if the applications were improperly denied; compensating such persons for any damages, both out-of-pocket and compensatory;

(2) Correcting any institutional policies or procedures that may have contributed to the likely violation, and adopting new policies as appropriate;

(3) Identifying, and then training and/or disciplining the employees involved;

(4) Developing outreach programs, marketing strategies, or loan products to serve more effectively the segments of the lender's market that may have been affected by the likely violation; and

(5) Improving audit and oversight systems to avoid a recurrence of the likely violations.

(e) Determination of appropriate corrective action is fact-based. Not every corrective measure listed in paragraph (d) of this section need be taken for each likely violation.

(f) Taking appropriate corrective action is not an admission by a lender that a violation occurred.

[62 FR 66432, Dec. 18, 1997]

§ 100.144 Scope of privilege.

The report or results of a self-test may not be obtained or used by an aggrieved person, complainant, department or agency in any:

(a) Proceeding or civil action in which a violation of the Fair Housing Act is alleged; or

(b) Examination or investigation relating to compliance with the Fair Housing Act.

[62 FR 66432, Dec. 18, 1997]

§ 100.145 Loss of privilege.

(a) The self-test report or results are not privileged under this subpart if the lender or person with lawful access to the report or results:

(1) Voluntarily discloses any part of the report or results or any other information privileged under this subpart to any aggrieved person, complainant, department, agency, or to the public; or

(2) Discloses the report or results or any other information privileged under this subpart as a defense to charges a lender violated the Fair Housing Act; or

(3) Fails or is unable to produce self-test records or information needed to determine whether the privilege applies.

(b) Disclosures or other actions undertaken to carry out appropriate corrective action do not cause the lender to lose the privilege.

[62 FR 66432, Dec. 18, 1997]

§ 100.146 Limited use of privileged information.

Notwithstanding Sec. 100.145, the self-test report or results may be obtained and used by an aggrieved person, applicant, department or agency solely to determine a penalty or remedy after the violation of the Fair Housing Act has been adjudicated or admitted. Disclosures for this limited purpose may be used only for the particular proceeding in which the adjudication or admission is made. Information disclosed under this section remains otherwise privileged under this subpart.

[62 FR 66432, Dec. 18, 1997]

§ 100.147 Adjudication.

An aggrieved person, complainant, department or agency that challenges a privilege asserted under Sec. 100.144 may seek a determination of the existence and application of that privilege in:

(a) A court of competent jurisdiction; or

(b) An administrative law proceeding with appropriate jurisdiction.

[62 FR 66432, Dec. 18, 1997]

§ 100.148 Effective date.

The privilege under this subpart applies to self-tests conducted both before and after January 30, 1998, except that a self-test conducted before January 30, 1998 is not privileged:

(a) If there was a court action or administrative proceeding before January 30, 1998, including the filing of a complaint alleging a violation of the Fair Housing Act with the Department or a substantially equivalent state or local agency; or

(b) If any part of the report or results were disclosed before January 30, 1998 to any aggrieved person, complainant, department or agency, or to the general public.

Subpart D—Prohibition Against Discrimination Because of Handicap

§ 100.200 Purpose.

The purpose of this subpart is to effectuate sections 6(a) and (b) and 15 of the Fair Housing Amendments Act of 1988.

§ 100.201 Definitions.

As used in this subpart:

* * *

Handicap means, with respect to a person, a physical or mental impairment which substantially limits one or more major life activities; a record of such an impairment; or being regarded as having such an impairment. This term does not include current, illegal use of or addiction to a controlled substance. For purposes of this part, an individual shall not be considered to have a handicap solely because that individual is a transvestite. As used in this definition:

(a) *Physical or mental impairment* includes:

(1) Any physiological disorder or condition, cosmetic disfigurement, or anatomical loss affecting one or more of the following body systems: Neurological; musculoskeletal; special sense organs; respiratory, including speech organs; cardiovascular; reproductive; disgestive [sic]; genito-urinary; hemic and lymphatic; skin; and endocrine; or

(2) Any mental or psychological disorder, such as mental retardation, organic brain syndrome, emotional or mental illness, and specific learning disabilities. The term *physical or mental impairment* includes, but is not limited to, such diseases and conditions as orthopedic, visual, speech and hearing impairments, cerebral palsy, autism, epilepsy, muscular dystrophy, multiple sclerosis, cancer, heart disease, diabetes, Human Immunodeficiency Virus infection, mental retardation, emotional illness, drug addiction (other than addiction caused by current, illegal use of a controlled substance) and alcoholism.

(b) *Major life activities* means functions such as caring for one's self, performing manual tasks, walking, seeing, hearing, speaking, breathing, learning and working.

(c) *Has a record of such an impairment* means has a history of, or has been misclassified as having, a mental or physical impairment that substantially limits one or more major life activities.

(d) *Is regarded as having an impairment* means:

(1) Has a physical or mental impairment that does not substantially limit one or more major life activities but that is treated by another person as constituting such a limitation;

(2) Has a physical or mental impairment that substantially limits one or more major life activities only as a result of the attitudes of other [sic] toward such impairment; or

(3) Has none of the impairments defined in paragraph (a) of this definition but is treated by another person as having such an impairment.

§ 100.202 General prohibitions against discrimination because of handicap.

(a) It shall be unlawful to discriminate in the sale or rental, or to otherwise make unavailable or deny, a dwelling to any buyer or renter because of a handicap of—

(1) That buyer or renter;

(2) A person residing in or intending to reside in that dwelling after it is so sold, rented, or made available; or

(3) Any person associated with that person.

(b) It shall be unlawful to discriminate against any person in the terms, conditions, or privileges of the sale or rental of a dwelling, or in the provision of services or facilities in connection with such dwelling, because of a handicap of—

(1) That buyer or renter;

(2) A person residing in or intending to reside in that dwelling after it is so sold, rented, or made available; or

(3) Any person associated with that person.

(c) It shall be unlawful to make an inquiry to determine whether an applicant for a dwelling, a person intending to reside in that dwelling after it is so sold, rented or made available, or any person associated with that person, has a handicap or to make inquiry as to the nature or severity of a handicap of such a person. However, this paragraph does not prohibit the following inquiries, provided these inquiries are made of all applicants, whether or not they have handicaps:

(1) Inquiry into an applicant's ability to meet the requirements of ownership or tenancy;

(2) Inquiry to determine whether an applicant is qualified for a dwelling available only to persons with handicaps or to persons with a particular type of handicap;

(3) Inquiry to determine whether an applicant for a dwelling is qualified for a priority available to persons with handicaps or to persons with a particular type of handicap;

(4) Inquiring whether an applicant for a dwelling is a current illegal abuser or addict of a controlled substance;

(5) Inquiring whether an applicant has been convicted of the illegal manufacture or distribution of a controlled substance.

(d) Nothing in this subpart requires that a dwelling be made available to an individual whose tenancy would constitute a direct threat to the health or safety of other individuals or whose tenancy would result in substantial physical damage to the property of others.

§ 100.203 Reasonable modifications of existing premises.

(a) It shall be unlawful for any person to refuse to permit, at the expense of a handicapped person, reasonable modifications of existing premises, occupied or to be occupied by a handicapped person, if the proposed modifications may be necessary to afford the handicapped person full enjoyment of the premises of a dwelling. In the case of a rental, the landlord may, where it is reasonable to do so, condition permission for a modification on the renter agreeing to restore the interior of the premises to the condition that existed before the modification, reasonable wear and tear excepted. The landlord may not increase for handicapped persons any customarily required security deposit. However, where

it is necessary in order to ensure with reasonable certainty that funds will be available to pay for the restorations at the end of the tenancy, the landlord may negotiate as part of such a restoration agreement a provision requiring that the tenant pay into an interest bearing escrow account, over a reasonable period, a reasonable amount of money not to exceed the cost of the restorations. The interest in any such account shall accrue to the benefit of the tenant.

(b) A landlord may condition permission for a modification on the renter providing a reasonable description of the proposed modifications as well as reasonable assurances that the work will be done in a workmanlike manner and that any required building permits will be obtained.

(c) The application of paragraph (a) of this section may be illustrated by the following examples:

Example (1): A tenant with a handicap asks his or her landlord for permission to install grab bars in the bathroom at his or her own expense. It is necessary to reinforce the walls with blocking between studs in order to affix the grab bars. It is unlawful for the landlord to refuse to permit the tenant, at the tenant's own expense, from making the modifications necessary to add the grab bars. However, the landlord may condition permission for the modification on the tenant agreeing to restore the bathroom to the condition that existed before the modification, reasonable wear and tear excepted. It would be reasonable for the landlord to require the tenant to remove the grab bars at the end of the tenancy. The landlord may also reasonably require that the wall to which the grab bars are to be attached be repaired and restored to its original condition, reasonable wear and tear excepted. However, it would be unreasonable for the landlord to require the tenant to remove the blocking, since the reinforced walls will not interfere in any way with the landlord's or the next tenant's use and enjoyment of the premises and may be needed by some future tenant.

Example (2): An applicant for rental housing has a child who uses a wheelchair. The bathroom door in the dwelling unit is too narrow to permit the wheelchair to pass. The applicant asks the landlord for permission to widen the doorway at the applicant's own expense. It is unlawful for the landlord to refuse to permit the applicant to make the modification. Further, the landlord may not, in usual circumstances, condition permission for the modification on the applicant paying for the doorway to be narrowed at the end of the lease because a wider doorway will not interfere with the landlord's or the next tenant's use and enjoyment of the premises.

§ 100.204 Reasonable accommodations.

(a) It shall be unlawful for any person to refuse to make reasonable accommodations in rules, policies, practices, or services, when such accommodations may be necessary to afford a handicapped person equal opportunity to use and enjoy a dwelling unit, including public and common use areas.

(b) The application of this section may be illustrated by the following examples:

Example (1): A blind applicant for rental housing wants live in a dwelling unit with a seeing eye dog. The building has a no pets policy. It is a violation of Sec. 100.204 for the owner or manager of the apartment complex to refuse to permit the applicant to live in the apartment with a seeing eye dog because, without the seeing eye dog, the blind person will not have an equal opportunity to use and enjoy a dwelling.

Example (2): Progress Gardens is a 300 unit apartment complex with 450 parking spaces which are available to tenants and guests of Progress Gardens on a first come first served basis. John applies for housing in Progress Gardens. John is mobility impaired and is unable to walk more than a short distance and therefore requests that a parking space near his unit be reserved for him so he will not have to walk very far to get to his apartment. It is a violation of Sec. 100.204 for the owner or manager of Progress Gardens to refuse to make this accommodation. Without a reserved space, John might be unable to live in Progress Gardens at all or, when he has to park in a space far from his unit, might have great difficulty getting from his car to his apartment unit. The accommodation therefore is necessary to afford John an equal opportunity to use and enjoy a dwelling. The accommodation is reasonable because it is feasible and practical under the circumstances.

§ 100.205 Design and construction requirements.

(a) Covered multifamily dwellings for first occupancy after March 13, 1991 shall be designed and constructed to have at least one building entrance on an accessible route unless it is impractical to do so because of the terrain or unusual characteristics of the site. For purposes of this section, a covered multifamily dwelling shall be deemed to be designed and constructed for first occupancy on or before March 13, 1991, if the dwelling is occupied by that date, or if the last building permit or renewal thereof for the dwelling is issued by a State, County or local government on or before June 15, 1990. The burden of establishing impracticality because of terrain or unusual site characteristics is on the person or persons who designed or constructed the housing facility.

(b) The application of paragraph (a) of this section may be illustrated by the following examples:

Example (1): A real estate developer plans to construct six covered multifamily dwelling units on a site with a hilly terrain. Because of the terrain, it will be necessary to climb a long and steep stairway in order to enter the dwellings. Since there is no practical way to provide an accessible route to any of the dwellings, one need not be provided.

Example (2): A real estate developer plans to construct a building consisting of 10 units of multifamily housing on a waterfront site that floods frequently. Because of this unusual characteristic of the site, the builder plans to construct the building on stilts. It is customary for housing in the geographic area where the site is located to be built on stilts. The housing may lawfully be constructed on the proposed site on stilts even though this means that there will be no practical way to provide an accessible route to the building entrance.

Example (3): A real estate developer plans to construct a multifamily housing facility on a particular site. The developer would like the facility to be built on the site to contain as many units as possible. Because of the configuration and terrain of the site, it is possible to construct a building with 105 units on the site provided the site does not have an accessible route leading to the building entrance. It is also possible to construct a building on the site with an accessible route leading to the building entrance. However, such a building would have no more than 100 dwelling units. The building to be constructed on the site must have a building entrance on an accessible route because it is not imprac-

tical to provide such an entrance because of the terrain or unusual characteristics of the site.

(c) All covered multifamily dwellings for first occupancy after March 13, 1991 with a building entrance on an accessible route shall be designed and constructed in such a manner that—

(1) The public and common use areas are readily accessible to and usable by handicapped persons;

(2) All the doors designed to allow passage into and within all premises are sufficiently wide to allow passage by handicapped persons in wheelchairs; and

(3) All premises within covered multifamily dwelling units contain the following features of adaptable design:

(i) An accessible route into and through the covered dwelling unit;

(ii) Light switches, electrical outlets, thermostats, and other environmental controls in accessible locations;

(iii) Reinforcements in bathroom walls to allow later installation of grab bars around the toilet, tub, shower, stall and shower seat, where such facilities are provided; and

(iv) Usable kitchens and bathrooms such that an individual in a wheelchair can maneuver about the space.

(d) The application of paragraph (c) of this section may be illustrated by the following examples:

Example (1): A developer plans to construct a 100 unit condominium apartment building with one elevator. In accordance with paragraph (a), the building has at least one accessible route leading to an accessible entrance. All 100 units are covered multifamily dwelling units and they all must be designed and constructed so that they comply with the accessibility requirements of paragraph (c) of this section.

Example (2): A developer plans to construct 30 garden apartments in a three story building. The building will not have an elevator. The building will have one accessible entrance which will be on the first floor. Since the building does not have an elevator, only the ground floor units are covered multifamily units. The ground floor is the first floor because that is the floor that has an accessible entrance. All of the dwelling units on the first floor must meet the accessibility requirements of paragraph (c) of this section and must have access to at least one of each type of public or common use area available for residents in the building.

(e) Compliance with the appropriate requirements of ANSI A117.1-1986 suffices to satisfy the requirements of paragraph (c)(3) of this section.

(f) Compliance with a duly enacted law of a State or unit of general local government that includes the requirements of paragraphs (a) and (c) of this section satisfies the requirements of paragraphs (a) and (c) of this section.

(g)(1) It is the policy of HUD to encourage States and units of general local government to include, in their existing procedures for the review and approval of newly constructed covered multifamily dwellings, determinations as to whether the design and construction of such dwellings are consistent with paragraphs (a) and (c) of this section.

(2) A State or unit of general local government may review and approve newly constructed multifamily dwellings for the purpose of making determinations as to whether the requirements of paragraphs (a) and (c) of this section are met.

(h) Determinations of compliance or noncompliance by a State or a unit of general local government under paragraph (f) or (g) of this section are not conclusive in enforcement proceedings under the Fair Housing Amendments Act.

(i) This subpart does not invalidate or limit any law of a State or political subdivision of a State that requires dwellings to be designed and constructed in a manner that affords handicapped persons greater access than is required by this subpart.

[Amended by 56 FR 11665, Mar. 20, 1991]

Subpart F—Interference, Coercion or Intimidation

§ 100.400 Prohibited interference, coercion or intimidation.

(a) This subpart provides the Department's interpretation of the conduct that is unlawful under section 818 of the Fair Housing Act.

(b) It shall be unlawful to coerce, intimidate, threaten, or interfere with any person in the exercise or enjoyment of, or on account of that person having exercised or enjoyed, or on account of that person having aided or encouraged any other person in the exercise or enjoyment of, any right granted or protected by this part.

(c) Conduct made unlawful under this section includes, but is not limited to, the following:

(1) Coercing a person, either orally, in writing, or by other means, to deny or limit the benefits provided that person in connection with the sale or rental of a dwelling or in connection with a residential real estate-related transaction because of race, color, religion, sex, handicap, familial status, or national origin.

(2) Threatening, intimidating or interfering with persons in their enjoyment of a dwelling because of the race, color, religion, sex, handicap, familial status, or national origin of such persons, or of visitors or associates of such persons.

(3) Threatening an employee or agent with dismissal or an adverse employment action, or taking such adverse employment action, for any effort to assist a person seeking access to the sale or rental of a dwelling or seeking access to any residential real estate-related transaction, because of the race, color, religion, sex, handicap, familial status, or national origin of that person or of any person associated with that person.

(4) Intimidating or threatening any person because that person is engaging in activities designed to make other persons aware of, or encouraging such other persons to exercise, rights granted or protected by this part.

(5) Retaliating against any person because that person has made a complaint, testified, assisted, or participated in any manner in a proceeding under the Fair Housing Act.

State Credit Discrimination Laws

The following is a summary of state statutes prohibiting discrimination in credit. Some statutes are similar to the federal Equal Credit Opportunity Act. Some are part of a state civil rights or human rights act, and are at least somewhat general in their application to consumer credit. As part of a general state civil rights code, there may be remedies or administrative procedures available modeled to varying degrees after those provided for in federal civil rights laws. Yet other statutes are based on the federal Fair Housing Act's provisions prohibiting discrimination in residential real estate financing, and which therefore apply only to housing financing.

Several states have more than one statute prohibiting discrimination in credit, and the scope of coverage, available remedies, and procedural rules usually vary under each statute. Advocates should therefore review all credit discrimination laws to determine which are applicable to the consumer's situation, and, if more than one is applicable, which one is most likely to provide the desired result for the consumer.

Finally, there are two caveats. First, this appendix does not include any administrative regulations which may have been promulgated pursuant to state credit discrimination statutes; practitioners must check for such regulations in their states.

Second, while we have made efforts to assure that this listing is a complete statutory survey as of this writing, it appears that the process of legislating against credit discrimination was not always done in the most orderly fashion conceivable and at times seems almost haphazard. If readers detect errors or omissions in this appendix, please let us know.

ALABAMA

Fair Housing: **Ala. Code §§ 24-8-1 to 24-8-15**
Protected Classes: Race, color, religion, sex, familial status, national origin, handicap.
Prohibited Practices: Discriminating in providing financial assistance for the purchase, construction, repair, and maintenance of a dwelling. § 24-8-6.
Scope of Coverage: Businesses involved in realty-related transactions.
Exclusions: Too numerous to list, see § 24-8-7.
Private Remedies: Permanent or temporary injunction, temporary restraining order, actual damages, punitive damages, court costs and attorney fees.
Administrative Remedies: Office of ADECA may investigate, conduct hearings and institute court proceedings to seek temporary or preliminary injunctive relief.
Statute of Limitations: Administrative complaint must be filed within 180 days of discriminatory housing practice; civil complaint must be filed within one year.

ALASKA

Civil Rights: **Alaska Stat. § 18.80.250 (Michie)** (credit transactions)
Protected Classes: Sex, physical or mental disability, marital status, changes in marital status, pregnancy, parenthood, race, religion, color or national origin.
Prohibited Practices: Discriminating in transactions involving secured or unsecured credit, housing-related credit, credit for acquisition of unimproved property, credit to a married person or disabled person, credit card in the name of the married person requesting it.
Scope of Coverage: Financial institutions or commercial institutions extending credit.
Exclusions: Doubt about person's legal capacity to contract.
Private Remedies: Individual or class action, injunction, monetary relief. § 22.10.020(i).
Administrative Remedies: Commission for Human Rights may investigate, conduct hearings, issue orders, award attorney fees to any private party, subject to judicial review.
Criminal Remedies: Any commercial or financial institution found to have willfully engaged in unlawful credit discrimination is guilty of a misdemeanor (fine of not more than $500; imprisonment for not more than 30 days, or both).
Statute of Limitations: None specified.

Civil Rights: **Alaska Stat. §§ 18.80.010 to 18.80.300 (Michie); Alaska Stat. § 18.80.240 (Michie)** (housing transactions)
Protected Classes: Sex, marital status, change in marital status, pregnancy, race, religion, color or national origin, physical or mental disability.
Prohibited Practices: Discriminating in terms, conditions, or privileges in regard to the sale, lease, or use of realty.
Scope of Coverage: Owners, lessees, managers, or others having the right to sell, lease, or rent real property.
Exclusions: "Singles only" or "married couples only" housing.
Private Remedies: Individual or class action, injunction, monetary relief. § 22.10.020(i).
Administrative Remedies: Commission for Human Rights may investigate, conduct hearings, issue orders (including damages) and attorneys fees to any private party, subject to judicial review.
Statute of Limitations: None specified.

ARIZONA

Fair Housing: **Ariz. Rev. Stat. §§ 41-1491 to 41-1491.37**
Protected Classes: Race, color, religion, sex, familial status, handicap, or national origin.
Prohibited Practices: Discriminating in providing financial assistance for the purchase, construction, repair, and maintenance of a dwelling. § 41-1491.20.

Scope of Coverage: Businesses involved in realty-related transactions.

Exclusions: Religious organizations or nonprofit entities operated by religious organizations; private club which incidentally provides lodging for its members; a dwelling which rents rooms to one sex only; housing for elderly and non-discriminatory appraisal considerations.

Private Remedies: Actual damages, punitive damages, injunction, costs, attorney fees. § 41-1491.31.

Administrative Remedies: Attorney general or civil rights division may refer to mediation, investigate, file civil action for injunctive relief, actual and punitive damages.

Statute of Limitations: Two years from the termination of the prohibited practice.

ARKANSAS

Civil Rights: **Ark. Code Ann. §§ 16-123-101 to 16-123-108 (Michie)** (credit transactions)

Protected Classes: Race, religion, national origin, gender, or any sensory, mental or physical disability.

Prohibited Practices: Interference with the right to engage in credit and other contractual transactions without discrimination. § 16-123-107(a)(4).

Private Remedies: Civil action for injunction or actual damages or both; costs and attorney fees permitted. § 16-123-107(b).

Consumer Credit: **Ark. Code Ann. §§ 4-87-101 to 4-87-105 (Michie)**

Protected Classes: Sex and marital status.

Prohibited Practices: Discriminating against equally qualified applicants of protected classes with respect to approval or denial of terms of credit.

Scope of Coverage: Consumer credit sales, consumer loans, any other extension of consumer credit, or issuance, renewal, denial or terms of any credit card.

Private Remedies: $100 to $500 statutory damages, costs and reasonable attorney fees.

Administrative Remedies: None specified.

Statute of Limitations: One year from occurrence of violation.

Miscellaneous: Class actions prohibited.

Fair Housing: **Ark. Code Ann. §§ 16-123-201 to 16-123-348 (Michie)**

Protected Classes: Religion, race, color, national origin, sex, disability, or familial status, of applicant or any person residing with applicant.

Prohibited Practices: Discrimination in the granting of financial assistance or financing in connection with a real estate transaction or in connection with the construction, maintenance, or improvement of real property, or to use any application form or keep any record or make any inquiry which indicates directly or indirectly a preference, limitation, specification or discrimination as to any protected class. § 16-123-205.

Scope of Coverage: Persons to whom application is made for financial assistance or financing, for the above purposes.

Exclusions: Application forms prescribed for the use of a lender regulated under the National Housing Act, or by a regulatory board or officer acting under the authority of the state or the United States.

Private Remedies: Civil action for injunction or actual damages or both, and costs and attorney fees permitted. § 16-123-210.

CALIFORNIA

Civil Rights: **Cal. Civ. Code §§ 51 to 52.2 (West)**

Protected Classes: Sex, race, color, religion, ancestry, national origin, disability, age, or medical condition.

Prohibited Practices: Discrimination in accommodations, advantages, facilities, privileges, or services of business establishments.

Scope of Coverage: All business establishments.

Exclusions: Qualifying senior citizens housing.

Private Remedies: Not less than $4000, and no more than three times the amount of actual damages; attorney fees.

Public Remedies: The Attorney General, district attorney, city attorney or any person aggrieved may seek a civil penalty of $25,000, an injunction, restraining order, or other order to prevent a pattern or practice of violation. The Attorney General or any district attorney or city attorney may intervene for the people of the State of California in actions seeking relief from the denial of equal protection of the laws under the Fourteenth Amendment to U.S. Constitution.

Consumer Credit: **Cal. Civ. Code § 1747.80 (West)**

Protected Classes: Race, religious creed, color, national origin, ancestry or sex.

Prohibited Practices: Refusal to issue credit card on basis of membership in a protected class.

Scope of Coverage: Credit card issuers.

Private Remedies: Actual and punitive damages; injunctive relief.

Consumer Credit: **Cal. Civ. Code §§ 1812.30 to 1812.35 (West)**

Protected Classes: Marital status (single/married).

Prohibited Practices: Offering credit on less favorable terms than to single/married counterparts. § 1812.30.

Scope of Coverage: Credit transactions generally.

Exclusions: None specified.

Private Remedies: Actual and punitive damages; injunction; reasonable attorneys fees. No class actions.

Administrative Remedies: Injunction, civil penalty.

Statute of Limitations: Two years from credit denial.

Fair Housing: **Cal. Civ. Code § 53 (West)**

Protected Classes: Race, color, creed, religion, sex, national origin, ancestry, disability.

Prohibited Practices: Provisions in written instruments relating to transfer or use of real property which purport to forbid or restrict conveyance, encumbrance, leasing or mortgaging of subject real property to member of protected class.

Scope of Coverage: Written instruments relating to real property.

Private Remedies: Declaratory action to void offending restriction or prohibition.

Miscellaneous: **Cal. Gov't Code §§ 12900–12996 (West)** (Department of Fair Employment and Housing)

Protected Classes: Race, color, religion, sex, marital status, national origin, ancestry, familial status, disability, sexual orientation and source of income.

Prohibited Practices: Discriminating or harassing in the terms, conditions or privileges relating to obtaining or using financial assistance for housing accommodations. §§ 12955 to 12989.3.

Scope of Coverage: Covers any person, bank, mortgage company or other financial institution that provides assistance for the purchase, organization or construction of any housing accommodation.

Exclusions: Discrimination on the basis of familial status does not apply to qualifying housing for older persons; religious organizations.

Private Remedies: Injunction, actual and punitive damages (not more than $10,000), costs, attorney fees.

Administrative Remedies: Order for sale or rental of the housing accommodation or like accommodation, or for provision of denied financial assistance, terms, privileges, or conditions; affirmative or prospective relief, including injunctive relief and actual damages. Civil penalty may be awarded to complainant not to exceed $10,000 for one violation, not to exceed $25,000 if respondent has been adjudged in separate accusation to have committed a prior intentional violation within prior five year period, and between $25,000 and $50,000 if two or more intentional violations within seven year period. § 12987(a)(3).

Statute of Limitations: Administrative complaint must be filed within one year (§ 12980(b)); civil complaint must be filed within the later of two years after the occurrence or termination of the alleged discriminatory practice or breach of administrative conciliation agreement. Civil action may not be commenced if administrative hearing has commenced. § 12989.1.

Miscellaneous: Cal. Health & Safety Code §§ 35800–35833 (West) (redlining)

Protected Classes: Race, color, religion, sex, marital status, national origin or ancestry.

Prohibited Practices: Redlining.

COLORADO

Consumer Credit: Colo. Rev. Stat. § 5-3-210

Protected Classes: Race, creed, religion, color, sex, marital status, national origin, or ancestry.

Prohibited Practices: Denial of credit or making terms or conditions of credit more stringent on basis of membership in a protected class.

Scope of Coverage: Consumer credit sales, consumer leases, consumer loans regulated under Title V of Colorado Uniform Consumer Credit Code (C-CCC).

Exclusions: Sellers, lessors, or lenders whose total original unpaid balances arising from consumer credit sales, leases and loans for previous calendar year are less than $1 million.

Private Remedies: Actual damages but not less than $100 nor more than $1,000 for actual and exemplary damages; costs and reasonable attorney fees. § 5-5-206.

Administrative Remedies: Administrator of C-CCC may bring administrative cease and desist proceedings or, seek injunction against violations of C-CCC, and a civil penalty for willful violations.

Statute of Limitations: None specified. (NB: The limitations for other specified C-CCC violations are either one year from the last scheduled payment of the agreement, § 5-5-202, or one year after the occurrence of the violation, § 5-5-202(5)).

Fair Housing: Colo. Rev. Stat. §§ 24-34-501 to 24-34-509

Protected Classes: Race, color, creed, religion, sex, marital status, national origin, ancestry, familial status, disability.

Prohibited Practices: To make or cause to be made any written or oral inquiry regarding membership in a protected class or to discriminate in the terms, conditions or privileges relating to the use of financial assistance for housing accommodations. § 24-34-502.

Scope of Coverage: Covers any business whose transactions include making loans for residential real estate transactions.

Private Remedies: Injunction, actual and punitive damages, costs, attorney fees.

Statute of Limitations: One year for administrative complaint; two years for private action, excluding time during which administrative proceeding is pending.

CONNECTICUT

Civil Rights: Conn. Gen. Stat. §§ 46a-66, 46a-81f, 46a-98 (credit transactions)

Protected Classes: Sex, age, race, color, religious creed, national origin, ancestry, marital status, mental retardation, learning disability, blindness, physical disability or sexual orientation (if 18 years or order).

Prohibited Practices: Discriminating against member of protected class (over eighteen years old) in any credit transaction.

Scope of Coverage: Credit transactions (including invitations to apply for credit, applications for credit, extensions of credit, or credit sales), extended by "creditors" (persons who regularly extend credit or arrange for the extension of credit for which payment of a finance charge or interest is required) in connection with loans, sale of property or services or otherwise.

Exclusions: Acts done or omitted in conformity with regulations or rulings of the Banking Commissioner, Federal Reserve Board or other government agencies with jurisdiction under the Equal Credit Opportunity Act will not result in liability.

Private Remedies: Actual damages and punitive damages not exceeding $1,000. In class action, punitive damages are recoverable up to lesser of $5,000 or 1% of creditor's net worth. § 46a-98.

Administrative Remedies: Damages resulting from the discriminatory practice. § 46a-86(d).

Statute of Limitations: Administrative complaint must be filed within 180 days after alleged act of discrimination (§ 46a-82). Civil action may be filed in lieu of (but not in addition to) administrative action within one year from the date of the alleged violation. § 46a-98.

Miscellaneous: Judicial remedy is in lieu of administrative remedy, not in addition to it.

Civil Rights: Conn. Gen. Stat. §§ 46a-51 to 46a-104; Conn. Gen. Stat. § 46a-64c(2), (7); § 46a-81e; § 46a-98a (housing transactions)

Protected Classes: Race, creed, color, national origin, ancestry, sex, marital status, age, lawful source of income, familial status, learning disability, physical or mental disability, sexual orientation.

Prohibited Practices: Discriminating against member of protected class in (i) the terms, conditions or privileges of sale or rental of a dwelling, or in providing related services or facilities, (ii) the making or purchasing of loans or providing other financial assistance for the purchase, construction, improvement, repair or maintenance of a dwelling, or which is secured by residential real estate, or (iii) the brokering, selling, or appraising of residential real property.

Scope of Coverage: Sale or rental of a dwelling; making or purchasing of loans or providing other financial assistance for purchasing, constructing, improving, repairing or maintaining a dwelling, or which is secured by residential real estate, or selling, brokering or appraising of residential real estate.

Exclusions: Certain owner-occupied dwellings; housing for older

persons; same sex accommodations with shared facilities.
Private Remedies: Injunctive relief, actual damages, attorney fees and costs. § 46a-98a.
Administrative Remedies: Actual damages, attorney fees and costs. § 46a-86(c).
Statute of Limitations: Administrative complaint must be filed within 180 days after alleged act of discrimination (§ 46a-82); civil action must be filed within one year of alleged discriminatory practice (or a breach of a conciliation agreement reached in an administrative proceeding), except that no civil action may be brought after a conciliation agreement is obtained or after commencement of an administrative hearing. § 46a-98a.

DELAWARE

Fair Housing: Del. Code Ann. tit. 6, §§ 4600–4619

Protected Classes: Race, color, national origin, religion, creed, sex, marital status, familial status, age (if eighteen or older), or handicap.
Prohibited Practices: To discriminate against any person in making available a transaction, or in the terms or conditions of any transaction, for the making, brokering or purchasing of loans, or providing other financial assistance for purchasing, constructing, improving, repairing or maintaining a dwelling, secured by residential real estate. § 4604.
Scope of Coverage: All persons who engage in residential real estate transactions, as defined above.
Private Remedies: Civil action in the county in which the discriminatory practice occurred, for actual and punitive damages, or injunction or both, costs and attorney fees in the discretion of the court. § 4613. Private person may also intervene in suit brought by Attorney General. § 4614.
Administrative Remedies: Hearing before the Delaware Human Relations Commission. (Judicial review and enforcement available.) §§ 4610–4612.
Statute of Limitations: For administrative remedy, one year after occurrence or termination of practice, or of time when practice was or reasonably should have been discovered by aggrieved person, or after breach of conciliation agreement under this chapter—whichever is later. For civil action, two years, as above. § 4613.

DISTRICT OF COLUMBIA

Civil Rights: D.C. Code Ann. §§ 2-1401.01 to 2-1403.17

Protected Classes: Race, color, religion, national origin, sex, age, marital status, personal appearance, sexual orientation, family responsibilities, disability, matriculation, political affiliation, source of income, or place of residence or business.
Prohibited Practices: To refuse to lend money, guarantee a loan, accept a deed of trust or mortgage, or otherwise refuse to make funds available for the purchase, acquisition, construction, alteration, rehabilitation, repair or maintenance of real property; to impose different conditions on such financing, or refuse to provide title or other insurance relating to the ownership or use of any interest in real property, based on the protected classes as above. To discriminate in any financial transaction involving real property on account of the location of the residence or business ("to red-line"). To make, print or publish any statement with respect to a transaction in real property, or the financing thereof, which indicates a preference, limitation or discrimination based on the protected classes. § 2-1402.21.

Private Remedies: Cause of action in any court of competent jurisdiction for damages and other appropriate remedies, including costs and attorneys fees. Aggrieved person must elect between administrative and judicial remedy. § 2-1403.16.
Administrative Remedies: Conciliation required. § 2-1403.06. If matter not resolved, hearing before Human Rights Commission. Relief includes administrative order, compensatory damages, costs and attorney fees. Judicial review and enforcement are available. §§ 2-1403.14 to 2-1403.15.
Statute of Limitations: Administrative complaint must be filed within one year of discriminatory practice or discovery thereof (§ 2-1403.04); civil actions, within two years. Filing administrative complaint precludes civil action unless complaint is dismissed on grounds of administrative convenience or withdrawn; statute tolled while complaint is pending (§ 2-1403.16).

FLORIDA

Consumer Credit: Fla. Stat. Ann. § 725.07 (West)

Protected Classes: Sex, marital status or race.
Prohibited Practices: No person can discriminate on basis of membership in protected class.
Scope of Coverage: Covers areas of loaning money, granting credit, and providing equal pay for equal services performed.
Exclusions: None specified.
Private Remedies: Compensatory and punitive damages and attorneys fees.
Administrative Remedies: None specified.
Statute of Limitations: Is that for claims founded on statutory liability, *see* Forehand v. Int'l Bus. Machines Corp., 586 F. Supp. 9 (M.D. Fla. 1984), *aff'd*, 783 F.2d 204 (11th Cir. 1986).

Fair Housing: Fla. Stat. Ann. §§ 760.22 to 760.37 (West)

Protected Classes: Race, color, national origin, sex, handicap (including AIDS, § 760.50), familial status, or religion of applicant, his/her associates or prospective owners, lessees, tenants or occupants of dwelling in relation to which the financial assistance is given.
Prohibited Practices: Denial of loans or other financial assistance or discrimination in fixing amount, interest rate, duration or other term or condition of financial assistance on a prohibited basis.
Scope of Coverage: Covers housing financing—purchase, construction, improvement, repair or maintenance of a dwelling—extended by a corporation, association, firm or enterprise which includes making real estate loans in its business; discriminating against member of protected class in making residential real estate transaction available.
Exclusions: Some specified exemptions provided for some private owners or owner-occupied dwellings; religious organizations using dwelling for other than commercial purposes; private clubs incidentally providing lodging to members; qualifying housing for older persons.
Private Remedies: Actual and punitive damages, costs and attorney fees to prevailing party. § 760.35.
Administrative Remedies: Aggrieved party may file administrative complaint; commission to seek conciliation or civil penalties.
Statute of Limitations: Administrative complaint must be filed within one year of alleged discriminatory practice. Civil action may be commenced no later than two years after alleged discriminatory practice.

GEORGIA

Consumer Credit: Ga. Code Ann. §§ 7-6-1 to 7-6-2

Protected Classes: Sex, race, religion, national origin or marital status.

Prohibited Practices: Discriminating or providing requirements which discriminate in the extending of credit or the making of loans.

Scope of Coverage: Banks, lending companies, financial institutions, retail installment seller, or person extending credit.

Private Remedies: Action for damages in court of competent jurisdiction.

Administrative Remedies: None specified.

Statute of Limitations: None specified.

Miscellaneous: Representative party actions (i.e. class actions) not allowed. Willful violation is misdemeanor with a penalty of a fine no greater than $1,000.

Fair Housing: Ga. Code Ann. §§ 8-3-200 to 8-3-223

Protected Classes: Race, color, religion, sex, disability or handicap, familial status, or national origin of person applying for housing financing or of persons associated with him in connection with such financial assistance, or prospective owners, lessees, tenants or occupants of the dwelling(s) in relation to which the financial assistance is given.

Prohibited Practices: Denial of loans or other financial assistance or discrimination in fixing amount, interest rate, duration or other terms or conditions of such credit on a prohibited basis. § 8-3-204.

Scope of Coverage: Covers real estate-related transactions—purchase, construction, improvement, appraisal, repair or maintenance of a dwelling—extended by a corporation, association, firm or enterprise which include making real estate loans in its business.

Exclusions: Some specified exemptions provided for some private owners or owner-occupied dwellings; religious organizations using dwelling for other than commercial purposes; private clubs incidentally providing lodging to members; qualifying housing for older persons.

Private Remedies: May enforce § 8-3-204 in court, though court may continue the case if conciliation efforts by administrator may result in satisfactory settlement; injunctive relief, actual damages, punitive damages, court costs and reasonable attorney fees if a prevailing plaintiff is not financially able to assume such fees.

Administrative Remedies: Aggrieved party may file administrative complaint. Attorney General also may seek injunction against pattern and practice of violation of the statute.

Statute of Limitations: One year for administrative actions and two years for civil actions.

HAWAII

Consumer Credit: Haw. Rev. Stat. §§ 477E-1 to 477E-6

Protected Classes: Marital status.

Prohibited Practices: Discrimination against any applicant with respect to any aspect of a credit transaction; aggregation of loans to determine finance charges or loan ceilings.

Scope of Coverage: Credit transactions by financial institutions, debt adjusters, extenders or arrangers of credit, assignee who participates in credit decision.

Exclusions: May inquire into marital status to determine creditor's rights and remedies; may request spousal signature to create lien or real property transaction.

Private Remedies: Actual damages, punitive damages up to $10,000 if not a class action; injunction, attorney fees.

Statute of Limitations: One year from reason to know of the violation.

Fair Housing: Haw. Rev. Stat. §§ 515-1 to 515-20

Protected Classes: Race, sex, color, religion, ancestry, marital status, familial status, disability, age, HIV infection.

Prohibited Practices: To discriminate on a prohibited basis in financial assistance in connection with a real estate transaction; to use a form of application for financial assistance or retain records or make inquiries in connection with applications for financial assistance which indicate an intent to make limitations, specifications or discrimination on a prohibited basis. § 515-5.

Scope of Coverage: Credit covered is financial assistance for sale, exchange, rental, or lease of real property or construction, rehabilitation, repair, maintenance or improvement of real property; creditors covered are "person[s] to whom application is made for [such] financial assistance."

Exclusions: Religious institutions or charitable or educational organization operated by a religious institution to give preference to members of the same religion or one sex in a real property transaction.

Private Remedies: Compensatory and punitive damages, legal and equitable relief, costs and attorney fees. § 368-17.

Administrative Remedies: Dept. of Commerce & Consumer Affairs may investigate and mediate complaints; issue cease and desist orders, order affirmative relief, actual damages ($500 for each violation unless greater damages are proven); reasonable attorney fees.

Statute of Limitations: Administrative complaint must be filed within 180 days of alleged discriminatory practice; complainant may bring civil action within ninety days of receipt of requested notice of right to sue.

IDAHO

Civil Rights: Idaho Code §§ 67-5901 to 67-5912 (Michie) (housing transactions)

Protected Classes: Race, color, religion, sex or national origin.

Prohibited Practices: Discriminating or using a form that directly or indirectly indicates an intent to make a limitation, specification or discrimination regarding real estate transaction. § 67-5909.

Scope of Coverage: Covers any person to whom an application is made for financial assistance in connection with the sale, construction, rehabilitation, repair, maintenance or improvement of real property.

Exclusions: Religious organizations.

Private Remedies: Injunction, actual and punitive damages (not more than $1000 per willful violation).

Administrative Remedies: Injunction.

Statute of Limitations: Within one year of administrative complaint.

ILLINOIS

Civil Rights: 775 Ill. Comp. Stat. §§ 5/1-101 to 5/10-103; 775 Ill. Comp. Stat. §§ 5/4-101 to 5/4-104 (credit transactions)

Protected Classes: Race, color, religion, sex, national origin, ancestry, age, marital status, handicap, or unfavorable discharge from military service. 775 Ill. Comp. Stat. §§ 5/1-102(A), 5/1-103.

Prohibited Practices: Denial or modification of services normally provided by a financial institution, denial or variation of terms of a loan; redlining; denial or variation of term of loan without considering all dependable income of each person liable for loan; refuse issuance of credit card on basis of unlawful discrimination; failure to inform credit card applicant, upon request, the reason for rejection of application; utilization of lending standards without economic basis and which constitute unlawful discrimination (i.e., discrimination on a prohibited basis).

Scope of Coverage: Loans, including loans for purchase, construction, improvement, repair or maintenance of housing accommodation, or commercial or industrial purpose loans, by financial institutions; credit cards.

Exclusions: Allows certain practices to determine creditworthiness and allow sound underwriting practices; also permits special purpose credit programs.

Private Remedies: Judicial review of agency action.

Administrative Remedies: Aggrieved party may file administrative complaint with Dept. of Human Rights. Human Rights Commission may order cease and desist, actual damages, attorney fees, extension of goods, services, privileges or advantages offered by respondent. (Articles 7A and 8A of Human Rights Act).

Statute of Limitations: Administrative complaint must be filed within 180 days.

Civil Rights: 775 Ill. Comp. Stat. §§ 5/3-101 to 5/3-106 (housing transactions)

Prohibited Classes: Race, color, religion, sex, familial status, national origin, ancestry, age, marital status, handicap, or unfavorable discharge from military service.

Prohibited Practices: Refusing to engage in a real estate transaction based on a discrimination or discriminating in making such a transaction available or altering the terms, conditions or privileges.

Scope of Coverage: Real estate transaction includes brokering, appraising and making or purchasing loans, or providing other financial assistance.

Exclusions: Certain private sales by owners of single family homes, apartment rentals in five family units in which lessor resides; private rooms; religious organizations limiting sale, rental or occupancy of dwelling owned or operated for other than a commercial purpose to persons of same religion; restriction of room rentals to single sex, persons convicted under federal law of manufacture or distribution of a controlled substance; and qualifying housing for older persons.

Private Remedies: Actual and punitive damages, injunctive relief, and attorney fees and costs.

Administrative Remedies: Recommended order for appropriate relief. § 5/8A-102.

Statute of Limitations: Administrative complaint must be filed within one year. § 5/7B-102. Civil action must be commenced within two years of termination of alleged violation (tolled while administrative proceeding is pending). § 5/10-102.

Consumer Credit: 815 Ill. Comp. Stat. §§ 140/0.01 to 140/9

Protected Classes: Race, color, religion, national origin, ancestry, age (between forty and seventy), sex, marital status, physical or mental handicap unrelated to the ability to pay or unfavorable discharge from military service.

Prohibited Practices: Denial of credit card on a prohibited basis. § 140/1a. Also prohibits requesting information regarding marital status on a credit card application except for a joint account

application or requiring reapplications for credit cards based on change in marital status unless the change causes deterioration in person's financial condition; permits cardholder to use the name he or she regularly uses, to request reasons for denial, and financial status shall be considered individually, if requested, or jointly for a married couple if requested.

Scope of Coverage: Credit card issuers.

Private Remedies: Denial of proper application on a prohibited basis and failure to inform applicant of reason for denial is a civil rights violation. 775 Ill. Comp. Stat. § 5/4-103.

Miscellaneous: Applications conforming to ECOA are deemed to be in compliance with this act.

Consumer Credit: 815 Ill. Comp. Stat. §§ 120/1 to 120/6 (Fairness in Lending Act)

Protected Classes: Geographical location of real estate, applicant's source of income (if regular and dependable), childbearing capacity of applicant or spouse.

Prohibited Practices: Denying loan or varying terms on basis of above, or use other lending standards which have no economic basis or which are discriminatory in effect. § 120/3.

Scope of Coverage: Banks, credit unions, insurance companies, mortgage banking companies or savings and loans which operate or have a place of business in Illinois.

Exclusions: Act does not preclude use of sound underwriting practices, i.e., considering the willingness and ability of borrower to pay back the loan, the market value of the real property, and diversification of the institution's investment portfolio.

Private Remedies: Action in circuit court for compensatory damages. Costs at discretion of the court.

Consumer Credit: 205 Ill. Comp. Stat. § 635/3-8 (financial regulation)

Protected Classes: Race, color, religion, national origin, age, gender or marital status.

Prohibited Practices: Refusal to grant loan, or varying terms or application procedures because of membership in protected class, or solely because of the geographic location of the proposed security.

Scope of Coverage: Residential mortgage bankers, or any person, partnership, association, corporation or other entity which engages in the business of brokering, funding, originating, servicing or purchasing residential mortgage loans.

Administrative Remedies: Commissioner of Savings and Residential Finance may ask Attorney General to sue for injunction. Commissioner may revoke, suspend or deny license, issue a reprimand, place applicant or licensee on probation and/or impose a fine of up to $10,000. § 635/4-5.

INDIANA

Civil Rights: Ind. Code § 22-9-1-1 to 22-9-1-18 (housing transactions)

Protected Classes: Race, religion, color, sex, disability, national origin, ancestry.

Prohibited Practices: Exclusion of person from equal opportunities relating to acquisition or sale of real estate, extension of credit. § 22-9-1-3.

Scope of Coverage: Individuals, corporations or other organized groups of persons.

Private Remedies: Injunction; actual damages only if lost wages,

salary, or commission. § 22-9-1-6(k).
Statute of Limitations: 180 days. § 22-9-1-3(p).

Fair Housing: **Ind. Code §§ 22-9.5-1-1 to 22-9.5-11-3**
Protected Classes: Race, color, religion, sex, disability, familial status, national origin.
Prohibited Practices: Discriminating in the making or purchasing of loans or providing other financial assistance in connection with the purchase, construction, improvement, repair, or maintenance residential real estate, or which is secured by residential real estate. § 22-9.5-5-1.
Scope of Coverage: Covers any person whose business includes engaging in residential real estate financing to sell, construct, improve, repair, maintain a dwelling.
Exclusions: Persons convicted under state or federal law of illegal manufacture or distribution of a controlled substance; religious organizations and private clubs favoring members; single family units.
Private Remedies: Injunction, actual and punitive damages, costs, attorney fees.
Administrative Remedies: Actual damages, attorney fees and court costs, and other injunctive or equitable relief.
Statute of Limitations: One year for administrative claim; one year for civil claim (excluding time that an administrative claim is pending).

IOWA

Civil Rights: **Iowa Code §§ 216.1 to 216.20; Iowa Code § 216.10** (credit transactions)
Protected Classes: Age, color, creed, national origin, race, religion, marital status, sex, physical disability, familial status.
Prohibited Practices: Refusal to loan or extend consumer credit; imposing finance charges or other terms or conditions more onerous than those regularly extended to persons of similar economic background.
Scope of Coverage: Any creditor extending consumer credit; licensed lenders under Chapter 524, 533, 534, 536 or 536A extending any credit.
Exclusions: Refusal to offer credit life or A & H insurance based on age or disability is not discriminatory if based on bona fide underwriting considerations not prohibited by Chapter 505.
Private Remedies: Administrative complaint must first be sought; judicial relief may be sought after obtaining a 120 day administrative release. District court may order same remedial action which Human Rights Commission could order. § 216.16.
Administrative Remedies: Aggrieved party may file administrative complaint. Civil Rights Commission may order *inter alia* cease and desist, actual damages (including attorneys fees), and extension of advantages, facilities, privileges and services denial due to discriminatory practices. § 216.15.
Statute of Limitations: Administrative complaint must be filed within 180 days (§ 216.15); conditions for civil actions (§ 216.16).
Miscellaneous: District court can order respondent's reasonable attorneys fees if complainant's action was frivolous. § 216.16.

Civil Rights: **Iowa Code § 216.8A (housing transactions)**
Protected Classes: Race, color, creed, sex, religion, national origin, disability, familial status.
Prohibited Practices: To discriminate against the making or purchasing of loans or providing other financial assistance in connection with a residential real estate transaction. § 216.8A(4)(b).

Scope of Coverage: Covers any person or entity whose business includes engaging in residential real estate financing for purchase, construction, improvement, repair or maintenance of residential real estate.
Private Remedies: Administrative complaint must first be sought; judicial relief may be sought after obtaining a 120 day administrative release. District court may order same remedial action which Human Rights Commission could order. § 216.16.
Administrative Remedies: Aggrieved party may file administrative complaint. Civil Rights Commission may order *inter alia* cease and desist, actual damages (including attorneys fees), and extension of advantages, facilities, privileges and services denial due to discriminatory practices. § 216.15.
Statute of Limitations: Administrative complaint must be filed within 180 days (§ 216.15); conditions for civil actions (§ 216.16).
Miscellaneous: District court can order respondent's reasonable attorneys fees if complainant's action was frivolous. § 216.16.

Consumer Credit: **Iowa Code § 537.3311**
Protected Classes: Age, color, creed, national origin, political affiliation, race, religion, sex, marital status, disability, receipt of public assistance, social security benefits, pension benefits, or exercise of rights under Iowa Consumer Credit Code (I-CCC) or other provisions of law.
Prohibited Practices: Refusal to enter into credit transaction or impose terms or conditions more onerous than those regularly extended by that creditor to consumers of similar economic background on prohibited basis.
Scope of Coverage: Consumer credit sales, consumer loans, or consumer leases as defined by I-CCC.
Exclusions: Covers only creditors as defined by I-CCC, i.e., regularly engaged in the business of making loans, leases, or selling in credit transactions of same kind. Excludes sales, loans, and leases if amount financed exceeds $25,000, certain sales of interests in land, and first liens on real property securing acquisition or construction debt.
Private Remedies: Actual damages and statutory damages not less than $100 nor more than $1,000, plus costs and attorneys fees. § 537.5201.
Administrative Remedies: Code administrator may issue cease and desist order or may seek injunctions, reformation, and actual damages which consumers or a consumer class could get.
Statute of Limitations: Open-end credit, two years after violations; closed-end credit, one year after due date of last scheduled payment. § 537.5201.
Miscellaneous: Statutory damages not available in class actions.

Miscellaneous: **Iowa Code §§ 535A.1 to 535A.9 (redlining)**
Protected Classes: Income, racial or ethnic characteristics or the age of structures in a neighborhood.
Prohibited Practices: Redlining. Classifying areas as unsuitable for mortgage loans, denying mortgage loans or varying the terms of a mortgage loan, i.e., requiring a larger down payment, or a shorter amortization period, or a higher interest rate or fees, or unreasonable underappraisal of real estate, because of the above characteristics of the geographic area.
Scope of Coverage: Banks, credit unions, insurance companies, mortgage banking companies, savings and loan associations, industrial loan companies, or any other institution or person who makes mortgage loans and operates or has a place of business in Iowa.

Exclusions: Individuals who make less than five mortgage loans a year. Does not bar the exercise of sound underwriting judgment, concerning the borrower's willingness and ability to repay, the appraised value of the property, and the diversification of the lender's portfolio.

Private Remedies: Civil action for actual damages, costs and attorney fees. § 535A.6. For bad faith noncompliance, civil penalty of up to $1000 in addition to damages. § 535A.8.

Administrative Remedies: Civil enforcement by the superintendents of banking, savings and loan associations, or credit unions, or the commissioner of insurance, depending on the kind of entity involved. Lenders must file disclosure statements regarding their loans with the Iowa Finance Authority.

KANSAS

Civil Rights: **Kan. Stat. Ann. §§ 44-1001 to 44-1044** (housing transactions)

Protected Classes: Race, religion, color, sex, national origin or ancestry of applicant, persons associated with applicant, or prospective owners, lessees, tenants or occupants of real property in relation to which financial assistance is given.

Prohibited Practices: Denial of financial assistance or making terms or conditions of credit more stringent, or keeping records or forms indicating an intent to make any preference or limitation because of membership in the protected class. § 44-1017.

Scope of Coverage: Covers housing financing—purchase, construction, improvement, repair or maintenance of real property—extended by financial institutions, persons, or firms or enterprises whose business consists in whole or in part of making real estate loans.

Exclusions: Religious organizations or nonprofit associations operated by a religion may give preference to members of their own organizations; qualifying single-family homeowners; qualifying housing for older persons. § 44-1018.

Private Remedies: De novo review; actual and punitve damages, costs and attorney fees. § 44-1021.

Administrative Remedies: Complaint must be filed within one year (§ 44-1019(a)); two years for civil actions (§ 44-1021(d)(1)).

Statute of Limitations: Aggrieved party may file administrative complaint. Civil Rights Commission may *inter alia*, issue cease and desist order, order the real estate financing, actual damages, (with $2000 limit on damages for pain, suffering and humiliation). § 44-1019.

KENTUCKY

Civil Rights: **Ky. Rev. Stat. Ann. §§ 344.010 to 344.990 (Michie); Ky. Rev. Stat. Ann. § 344.400 (Michie)** (credit transactions)

Protected Classes: Race, color, religion, national origin and sex.

Prohibited Practices: Deny credit, increase charges, fees or collateral on any credit, restrict amount or use of credit extended to any person or any related item or service, or attempt to do any of these things on a prohibited basis.

Scope of Coverage: Any credit transaction is covered, which by Ky. Rev. Stat. § 344.010(12) includes loans, retail installment sales transactions, credit cards, for both business and personal purposes, when a finance charge is imposed or repayment is provided in scheduled payments. Creditors covered by § 344.400 are "any person," defined by Ky. Rev. Stat. § 344.010(1) to include indi-

viduals, corporations, etc., but they must extend credit "in the course of the regular trade or commerce," including permitting that payment for purchases may be deferred. § 344.010(12).

Exclusions: The credit history of the individual applicant and the effect of Kentucky law on dower, curtesy, descent and distribution on a particular case may be considered.

Private Remedies: Civil action for injunctive relief, actual damages, costs, and reasonable attorney fees, in addition to other remedies authorized by the chapter. § 344.450.

Administrative Remedies: Aggrieved party may file complaint with human rights commission, which has authority to issue cease and desist orders and, *inter alia*, order that the respondent extend its services, facilities and privileges to all individuals, and payment of actual damages, including compensation for humiliation and embarrassment. §§ 344.200, 344.240.

Statute of Limitations: Administrative complaint must be filed within 180 days of alleged discriminatory practice. § 344.200(1). The limitation provision applicable to an action, commenced in the court under § 344.450 is that of Ky. Rev. Stat. § 413.120(2), currently five years. *See* Clifton v. Midway College, 702 S.W.2d 835 (Ky. 1986).

Civil Rights: **Ky. Rev. Stat. Ann. § 344.370 (Michie)** (housing transactions)

Protected Classes: Race, color, religion, national origin, sex, familial status, disability, or age of individual or present or prospective owner, tenant or occupant of the real property.

Prohibited Practices: Discriminating (a) in granting, denying, or setting terms and conditions of financial assistance or extending services in connection therewith; (b) in using forms or making or keeping records or inquiries which indicate a limitation, specification or discrimination as to race, color, religion or national origin or any intent to make such a limitation, specification, or discrimination; (c) by refusing to fully count income and expenses of both spouses, because of sex, when both spouses become or will become joint obligors in real estate transactions.

Scope of Coverage: Financial institutions, defined by Ky. Rev. Stat. § 344.010(9) as bank, banking organization, mortgage company, or insurance company or other lender to whom application is made for financial assistance for purchase, lease, acquisition, construction, rehabilitation, repair, maintenance, or improvement of real property, or any person or other entity whose business includes engaging in real estate-related transactions.

Remedies: Same as for § 344.400.

LOUISIANA

Civil Rights: **La. Rev. Stat. Ann. § 51:2255 (West)** (credit transactions)

Protected Classes: Race, creed, color, religion, national origin, disability, or sex.

Prohibited Practices: Deny credit, increase charges, fees, or collateral requirements, restrict amount or use of credit extended or impose different terms or conditions on credit or any item or service related thereto, or to attempt to do any of these things. (The credit history of the individual applicant and the application to the particular case of state law on matrimonial regimes and succession may be considered).

Scope of Coverage: Applies to "any person," including individuals (§ 51:2232(9)) in connection with "any credit transaction."

Private Remedies: Civil action for injunctive relief, actual damages, costs, and reasonable attorney fees, in addition to other remedies authorized by the chapter. § 51:2264.

Administrative Remedies: Aggrieved party may file complaint with human rights commission, which has authority to issue cease and desist orders and, *inter alia* order that the respondent extend its services, facilities and privileges to all individuals, and payment of actual damages, including compensation for humiliation and embarrassment. §§ 51:2257 to 51:2261.

Statute of Limitations: Administrative complaint must be filed within 180 days of alleged discriminatory practice. § 51:2257(A). No statute of limitation is specified for the civil action commenced in court.

Civil Rights: La. Rev. Stat. Ann. §§ 51:2231 to 51:2265 (West); La. Rev. Stat. Ann. § 51:2254 (West) (housing transactions)

Protected Classes: Race, creed, color, religion, national origin, sex, disability, or age of individual or present or prospective owner, tenant, occupant of the immovable property or persons associated with any of these.

Prohibited Practices: Discriminating (a) in granting, denying, or setting terms and conditions of financial assistance or extending services in connection therewith; (b) in using forms or making or keeping records or inquiries which indicate a limitation, specification or discrimination as to race, creed, color, religion or national origin or any intent to make such a limitation, specification, or discrimination; (c) by refusing to fully count income and expenses of both spouses, because of sex, when both spouses become or will become joint obligors in real estate transactions.

Scope of Coverage: Appears intended to cover housing financing extended by a financial institution.

Private Remedies: Civil action for injunctive relief, actual damages, costs, and reasonable attorneys fees, in addition to other remedies authorized by the chapter. § 51:2264.

Administrative Remedies: Aggrieved party may file complaint with human rights commission, which has authority to issue cease and desist orders and, *inter alia* order that the respondent extend its services, facilities and privileges to all individuals, and payment of actual damages, including compensation for humiliation and embarrassment. §§ 51:2257 to 51:2261.

Statute of Limitations: Administrative complaint must be filed within 180 days of alleged discriminatory practice. § 51:2257(A). No statute of limitation is specified for the civil action commenced in court.

Consumer Credit: La. Rev. Stat. Ann. §§ 9:3581 to 9:3583 (West)

Protected Classes: Race, color, religion, national origin, sex or marital status.

Prohibited Practices: To refuse to extend credit on a prohibited basis, to require any applicant of legal age to meet credit qualification standards not required of other similarly situated persons.

Scope of Coverage: Applies to all extensions of credit made in Louisiana between any natural person and any extender of credit.

Private Remedies: None specified. *But see* La. Rev. Stat. Ann. § 51:2255 (West).

Administrative Remedies: None specified. *But see* La. Rev. Stat. Ann. § 51:2255 (West).

Statute of Limitations: None specified. *But see* La. Rev. Stat. Ann. § 51:2255 (West).

Fair Housing: La. Rev. Stat. Ann. §§ 51:2601 to 51:2614 (West)

Protected Classes: Race, color, religion, sex, handicap, familial status, national origin.

Prohibited Practices: Discriminating in the making or purchasing of loans or other financial assistance in connection with residential real estate. § 51:2607.

Scope of Coverage: Covers any person whose business includes engaging in residential real estate financing for purchasing construction, improving, repairing, or maintaining a dwelling.

Private Remedies: Injunction, actual and punitive damages, costs, attorney fees.

Administrative Remedies: May file complaint with Attorney General who may file a civil action. Relief includes injunction, actual and punitive damages.

Statute of Limitations: One year to file complaint with Attorney General; two years to file private action.

Miscellaneous: La. Rev. Stat. § 46:2254(G), (I) (housing financing for handicapped)

Protected Classes: Handicapped persons.

Prohibited Practices: (1) *Inter alia* brokers discriminating in terms, conditions or privileges of real estate transaction or furnishing services in connection therewith on basis of handicap unrelated to otherwise qualified individual's ability to acquire, rent or maintain property, (2) financiers discriminating against otherwise qualified applicant on basis of handicap unrelated to individual's ability to acquire, rent or maintain property, or use forms or make record or inquiry which indicates limitation, specification; or discrimination based on handicap unrelated to ability to acquire, rent, or maintain property.

Scope of Coverage: Financing in connection with real estate transaction or for construction, rehabilitation, repair, maintenance or improvement of real property.

Private Remedies: Civil action for all legal remedies, including, but not limited to compensatory damages, attorneys fees and costs, and any other relief deemed appropriate. If a party filing suit under this chapter loses, the court has discretion to assess reasonable attorney fees and all court costs against him or her.

Statute of Limitations: One year from date of discriminatory act.

Miscellaneous: Complainant must send written notice to prospective defendant at least thirty days prior to filing, detailing discrimination, and both parties must make good faith effort to settle before court action.

MAINE

Civil Rights: Me. Rev. Stat. Ann. tit. 5, §§ 4595–4598 (West) (credit transactions)

Protected Classes: Age, race, color, sex, marital status, ancestry, religion, national origin.

Prohibited Practices: Refuse to extend credit on a prohibited basis. However, financial institution extending credit to married person may require both husband and wife to sign note and mortgage; may deny credit to a minor; and may consider a person's age in determining terms of credit; complying with terms and conditions of certain bona fide group insurance plans is not discriminatory.

Scope of Coverage: Applies to any extension of credit (defined as the right to defer payment of a debt or to incur debt or purchase property and services and defer payment therefor) by any "creditor" (defined as any person who regularly extends or arranges for the extension of credit for which the payment of a finance charge or interest is required.) Also, all financial institutions authorized to do business in the state must comply. Me. Rev. Stat. Ann. tit. 9-B, § 433 (West).

Private Remedies: Civil action for injunctive relief and other appropriate remedies including, but not limited to, *inter alia*, a statutory penalty of $1,000 to $3,000, depending on respondent's prior history of discrimination. Attorneys fees and costs may, in the court's discretion, be awarded to the prevailing party. Attorney fees and civil penalties may not be awarded unless complaint first filed with human rights commission, which either dismissed complaint or failed to enter into certain conciliation agreement within ninety days of finding reasonable cause. §§ 4613–4622.

Administrative Remedies: Aggrieved party may file complaint with human rights commission, which may attempt conciliation, or may itself file civil action pursuant to § 4613.

Civil Rights: Me. Rev. Stat. Ann. tit. 5, §§ 4551–4632 (West); Me. Rev. Stat. Ann. tit. 5, §§ 4581–4583 (West) (housing transactions)

Protected Classes: Race, color, sex, physical or mental disability, religion, familial status, ancestry or national origin of the applicant or of existing or prospective occupants or tenants.

Prohibited Practices: (1) Make or cause to be made inquiries concerning membership in a protected class of applicant seeking financial assistance or of existing or prospective occupants or tenants of housing accommodations which are the subject of the financing, or (2) discriminating in the granting of financial assistance or in terms, conditions or privileges relating to obtaining or using the financial assistance on a prohibited basis. §§ 4582 to 4582-A.

Scope of Coverage: "Any person" to whom application is made for loan or other financial assistance for acquisition, construction, rehabilitation, repair or maintenance of any housing accommodation (as defined by the act.).

Private Remedies: Same as for credit transactions.

Administrative Remedies: Same as for credit transactions.

Statute of Limitations: Administrative complaint must be filed within six months of alleged discriminatory act, (§ 4611). Civil action must be brought within two years of alleged discriminatory act. § 4613.

MARYLAND

Civil Rights: Md. Ann. Code art. 49B (housing transactions)

Protected Classes: Race, color, religion, creed, marital status, sex, national origin or physical or mental handicap of applicant, persons associated with him or her, or of prospective occupants, lessees, or tenants of dwellings to which financing relates (and sexual orientation, if confirmed by Nov. 2002 referendum).

Prohibited Practices: Denying loan or discriminating on a prohibited basis in setting terms or conditions of loans. Art. 49B, §§ 22, 23.

Scope of Coverage: Financial institution, etc. or other person regularly engaged in business of making mortgages or other loans for purchase, construction, improvement, or repair or maintenance of dwellings.

Exclusions: Religious organizations and private clubs favoring members. Art. 49B, § 21

Private Remedies: None specified.

Administrative Remedies: Aggrieved party may file complaint with Human Relations Commission, which has authority *inter alia*, to

issue cease and desist orders, and take affirmative action to effectuate purposes of subtitle. Commission may institute civil action to enforce compliance. Art. 49B, § 9-13.

Statute of Limitations: Administrative complaint must be filed within one year of alleged discriminatory act (art. 49B, § 27); two years for civil actions (art. 49B, § 33).

Miscellaneous: Criminal penalties for bringing malicious, unfounded complaints under subtitle art. 49B, § 12(b).

Consumer Credit: Md. Code Ann., Com. Law §§ 12-701 to 12-708 (Equal Credit Opportunity Act)

Protected Classes: Sex, marital status, race, color, religion, national origin or age.

Prohibited Practices: Discriminating on a prohibited basis with respect to any aspect of a credit transaction, including seven specifically defined prohibited practices. §§ 12-704, 12- 705.

Scope of Coverage: "Creditors," defined as persons who regularly extend, renew or continue credit (including arrangers) for personal, family or household purposes, may not discriminate against any "applicant," defined as person applying directly for an extension, renewal or continuation of credit, or indirectly by use of existing credit plan for an amount greater than previously established limit.

Private Remedies: Civil action for injunctive relief, actual damages, and, in an individual action only, up to $10,000 in punitive damages, costs and attorneys fees. In class action, total punitive damage recovery limited to lesser of $100,000 or 1% of creditor's net worth.

Administrative Remedies: Aggrieved party may file complaint with Commissioner of Consumer Credit or State Banking Commissioner, which has authority to issue cease and desist order.

Statute of Limitations: Civil action must be brought within one year of occurrence of violation.

Miscellaneous: Notice of adverse action requirements similar to federal ECOA.

Consumer Credit: Md. Code Ann., Com. Law § 12-113

Protected Classes: Race, creed, color, age, sex, marital status, handicap, or national origin; geographic area or neighborhood.

Prohibited Practices: Refusing to lend money to any person solely on a prohibited basis.

Scope of Coverage: Lenders operating under subtitle one of Title 12 (Credit Regulations) (§ 12-1019(f)) in lending money to any person.

Exclusions: Certain factors related to geographic area specifically may be the basis for a refusal to lend.

Remedies: None specified.

Consumer Credit: Md. Code Ann., Com. Law § 12-305

Protected Classes: Race, color, creed, national origin, sex, marital status, or age.

Prohibited Practices: Discriminating against any loan applicant on a prohibited basis. (Denying an application from a minor is not age discrimination).

Scope of Coverage: Licensees operating under subtitle 3 of Title 12 (§ 12-301(d)) lending to any loan applicant.

Exclusions: If conduct complies with federal ECOA, licensee is not in violation of this law.

Remedies: None specified. Violation is misdemeanor. § 12-316.

Consumer Credit: Md. Code Ann., Com. Law § 12-403.1 (secondary mortgages)

Protected Classes: Age.

Prohibited Practices: Discriminating against any applicant solely on basis of age in granting or denying loan application. (Denying application from a person under age eighteen is not age discrimination.).

Scope of Coverage: Secondary mortgage licensees (§ 12-401(b) & (c)) and lenders expressly exempt from secondary mortgage loan licensing requirements making a secondary mortgage loan (defined by § 12-401(i)), in lending to any applicant for a secondary mortgage loan.

Exclusions: "Second mortgage loan" excludes loans to bona fide corporations or commercial loans greater than $75,000.

Private Remedies: If lender violates any provision of subtitle 4 on secondary mortgage loans-credit provisions, it forfeits interest, costs or other charges with respect to the loan. § 12-413.

Consumer Credit: Md. Code Ann., Com. Law § 12-603 (retail installment sales)

Protected Class: Sex, marital status, geographic area of residence, neighborhood of residence, age.

Prohibited Practice: Refusal of credit on basis of being a member of the protected class.

Scope: Sellers or sales finance companies.

Exclusions: Buyer who is under the age of eighteen is not discriminated against solely on the basis of age.

Administrative Remedies: Aggrieved party may file complaint with Commissioner of Consumer Credit, which has the authority to order a cease and desist order. § 12-631.

Miscellaneous: Violation is a misdemeanor (fine not exceeding $100 for first offense and not exceeding $500 for any subsequent offense). § 12-636.

MASSACHUSETTS

Civil Rights: Mass. Gen. Laws ch. 151B, § 4(10) (credit transactions)

Protected Classes: Recipients of federal, state, or local public assistance, including medical assistance, or tenants receiving federal, state or local housing subsidies.

Prohibited Practices: Discriminating against any individual solely on basis of receipt of such assistance.

Scope of Coverage: Applies to any person furnishing credit, services, or renting accommodations.

Private Remedies: Persons aggrieved by practices declared unlawful by ch. 151B, § 4 may bring civil action ninety days after filing administrative complaint with Commission Against Discrimination, or sooner if a commissioner gives written assent, for damages and injunctive relief. (Temporary injunctive relief to prevent injury may be sought at any time.) Attorneys fees and costs shall be awarded unless special circumstances would render such award unjust. Ch. 151B, § 9.

Administrative Remedies: Aggrieved party may file complaint with Commission Against Discrimination, which has authority, *inter alia*, to issue cease and desist orders and to take affirmative action to effectuate purposes of chapter.

Miscellaneous: *See generally* Mass. Regs. Code tit. 804, § 7:00 (Discrimination in Credit).

Civil Rights: Mass. Gen. Laws ch. 151B, § 4(12) (credit transactions)

Protected Classes: Age sixty-two and over.

Prohibited Practices: Refusing to extend credit or charge account privileges because customer is sixty-two or over.

Scope of Coverage: Covers retail stores that provide credit or charge account privileges.

Private Remedies: Persons aggrieved by practices declared unlawful by ch. 151B, § 4 may bring civil action ninety days after filing administrative complaint with Commission Against Discrimination, or sooner if a commissioner gives written assent, for damages and injunctive relief. (Temporary injunctive relief to prevent injury may be sought at any time.) Attorneys fees and costs shall be awarded unless special circumstances would render such award unjust. Ch. 151B, § 9.

Administrative Remedies: Aggrieved party may file complaint with Commission Against Discrimination, which has authority, *inter alia*, to issue cease and desist orders and to take affirmative action to effectuate purposes of chapter.

Civil Rights: Mass. Gen. Laws ch. 151B, § 4(14) (credit transactions)

Protected Classes: Sex, sexual orientation (excluding persons whose sexual orientation involves minor children as sex object), marital status, or age.

Prohibited Practices: Denying or terminating credit or services or adversely affecting an individual's credit standing on a prohibited basis. (Certain defined conduct relating to consideration of age is specifically authorized.).

Scope of Coverage: Covers any person furnishing credit or services.

Private Remedies: Persons aggrieved by practices declared unlawful by ch. 151B, § 4 may bring civil action ninety days after filing administrative complaint with Commission Against Discrimination, or sooner if a commissioner gives written assent, for damages and injunctive relief. (Temporary injunctive relief to prevent injury may be sought at any time.) Attorneys fees and costs shall be awarded unless special circumstances would render such award unjust. Ch. 151B, § 9.

Administrative Remedies: Aggrieved party may file complaint with Commission Against Discrimination, which has authority, *inter alia*, to issue cease and desist orders and to take affirmative action to effectuate purposes of chapter.

Miscellaneous: *See generally* Mass. Regs. Code tit. 804, § 7:00 (Discrimination in Credit).

Civil Rights: Mass. Gen. Laws ch. 151B, §§ 1–10; Mass. Gen. Laws ch. 151B, § 4(3B) (housing transactions)

Protected Classes: Race, color, religion, handicap, national origin, sex, ancestry, children, sexual orientation (excluding persons whose sexual orientation involves minor children as sex object), age, or genetic information.

Prohibited Practices: Discriminating in granting a mortgage loan or in setting terms and conditions. Certain defined conduct is specifically authorized, including, *inter alia*, denying mortgage loan for duration exceeding life expectancy of applicant as determined by reference to the Individual Annuity Mortality Table.

Scope of Coverage: Persons whose business includes making mortgage loans or engaging in residential real estate-related transactions.

Private Remedies: Persons aggrieved by practices declared unlawful by ch. 151B, § 4 may bring civil action ninety days after filing administrative complaint with Commission Against Discrimination, or sooner if a commissioner gives written assent, for damages and injunctive relief. (Temporary injunctive relief to prevent injury may be sought at any time.) Attorneys fees and costs shall be awarded unless special circumstances would render such award unjust. Ch. 151B, § 9.

Administrative Remedies: Aggrieved party may file complaint with Commission Against Discrimination, which has authority, *inter alia*, to issue cease and desist orders and to take affirmative action to effectuate purposes of chapter.

Statute of Limitations: Limitation for civil action is three years after alleged discriminatory act. Administrative complaints must be filed within six months of alleged discriminatory act.

Miscellaneous: *See generally* Mass. Regs. Code tit. 804, § 7:00 (Discrimination in Credit).

MICHIGAN

Civil Rights: **Mich. Comp. Laws. §§ 37.2101 to 37.2901; Mich. Comp. Laws. § 37.2502** (housing transactions)

Protected Classes: Religion, race, color, national origin, age, sex, familial status or marital status.

Prohibited Practices: Discriminating in the terms, conditions, or privileges of a real estate transaction.

Scope of Coverage: Persons engaging in real estate transactions, or real estate brokerage or sales.

Exclusions: Qualifying multi-family units, owner-occupied accommodations and qualifying housing for senior citizens or persons 50 years of age or older.

Private Remedies: Injunctive relief, damages, attorney fees, §§ 37.2801, 37.2802.

Administrative Remedies: Injunctive relief, attorney fees, civil penalty between $10,000 and $50,000. § 37.2605.

Statute of Limitations: None specified.

Civil Rights: **Mich. Comp. Laws § 37.2504** (housing transactions)

Protected Classes: Religion, race, color, national origin, age, sex, familial status, marital status.

Prohibited Practices: Discriminating, using a form, or making records or inquiries that indicate a preference or limitation relating to the application for or the purchase of loans for residential real estate transactions.

Scope of Coverage: Covers persons whose business includes engaging in real estate transactions for acquiring, constructing, improving, repairing, or maintaining a dwelling.

Exclusions: Does not apply to applications prescribed for use of a lender regulated as a mortgagee under the national housing act.

Private Remedies: Injunction, damages, attorney fees. §§ 37.2801, 37.2802.

Administrative Remedies: Injunction, attorney fees, civil penalty between $10,000 and $50,000. § 37.2605.

Statute of Limitations: None specified. *But see* Minor v. Northville Pub. Schools, 605 F. Supp. 1185 (E.D. Mich. 1985); Kresnak v. City of Muskegon Heights, 956 F. Supp. 1327 (W.D. Mich. 1997) (three years).

Consumer Credit: **Mich. Comp. Laws §§ 493.1 to 493.25**

Protected Classes: Sex or marital status.

Prohibited Practices: Discriminating in the extension of credit on a prohibited basis. § 493.12(7).

Scope of Coverage: Applies to lenders licensed under the Regulatory Loan Act.

Private Remedies: A person making or collecting upon a loan in a prohibited manner is guilty of a misdemeanor and subject to the Credit Reform Act, §§ 445.1851–445.1864. § 493.19. Borrower may bring civil action against a regulated lender to (i) seek declaratory judgment that method, act or practice violates Credit Reform Act, (ii) obtain injunctive relief, (iii) recover $1,000 and actual damages if alleged violation involved noncredit car arrangement or $1,500 and actual damages relating to any other credit arrangement, and (iv) recover reasonable attorney fees and costs.

Consumer Credit: **Mich. Comp. Laws § 750.147a**

Protected Classes: Race, color, religion, national origin, sex, marital status or physical handicap.

Prohibited Practices: Discriminating against a member of a protected class in extending credit, granting a loan, or rating a person's creditworthiness.

Scope of Coverage: Covers any person in extending credit, granting a loan, or rating creditworthiness.

Exclusions: Non-profit corporations whose members share the same racial, religious, ethnic, marital or sexual characteristic or physical handicap and which extend credit or grant loans only to its members.

Private Remedies: Amount of $200 or damages whichever is greater. The prevailing party shall recover court costs and attorneys fees.

Administrative Remedies: None specified.

Statute of Limitations: None specified.

Miscellaneous: Class action recovery limited; criminal penalties specified.

Miscellaneous: **Mich. Comp. Laws § 37.1504** (handicapped/housing rights)

Protected Classes: Handicapped (housing financing).

Prohibited Practices: Discriminating on the basis of handicap in the making or purchasing of loans for acquiring, improving, repairing or maintaining real property, or in providing other financial assistance secured by or otherwise related to real property.

Scope of Coverage: Applies to persons to whom application is made for financial assistance in connection with real estate transaction or for repair, construction, rehabilitation, maintenance or improvement of real property.

Private Remedies: Civil action for damages, injunctive relief, and reasonable attorneys fees. § 37.1606.

Administrative Remedies: Adopts by reference administrative procedures for unfair employment practices. § 37.1605.

Miscellaneous: **Mich. Comp. Laws §§ 445.1601 to 445.1614** (redlining)

Protected Classes: Race or ethnicity.

Prohibited Practices: Denial of loan application or variation in the terms or conditions of financing residential real estate transactions based on geographic location.

Scope of Coverage: Covers credit granting institutions which include banks, savings and loan associations, unions, state housing authority, or a business entity with an in-state office making or purchasing mortgage loans.

Exclusions: Written policies or criteria uniformly applied to all neighborhoods within a particular metropolitan statistical area.

Private Remedies: $2000 in damages or actual damages plus attorney fees, whichever is greater; no class actions. § 445.1611.

Statute of Limitations: Civil action must be commenced within two years after occurrence giving rise to cause of action. § 445.1613.

MINNESOTA

Civil Rights: **Minn. Stat. Ann. § 363.03(8)** (credit transactions)
Protected Classes: Race, color, creed, religion, disability, national origin, sex, sexual orientation, marital status, recipients of public assistance.
Prohibited Practices: Discriminating in extension of credit or in requirements for obtaining credit on a prohibited basis.
Scope of Coverage: Personal or commercial credit.
Private Remedies: Civil action may be filed for injunctive relief; compensatory damages in an amount up to three times actual damages; damages for mental anguish and suffering; punitive damages of up to $8,500. The court may, in its discretion, award reasonable attorneys fees to the prevailing party. § 363.14.
Administrative Remedies: Aggrieved party may file complaint with human rights commission, which has authority to order same relief as courts may, *supra*. § 363.071(2).
Statute of Limitations: Claim must either be filed as judicial action, or filed administratively with local or state commission within one year of alleged discriminatory practice. One year period is suspended during voluntary dispute resolution process. § 363.06(3).

Civil Rights: **Minn. Stat. §§ 363.01 to 363.20; Minn. Stat. § 363.03(2)(3)** (housing transactions)
Protected Classes: Race, color, creed, religion, national origin, sex, marital status, sexual orientation, status with regard to public assistance, disability, or familial status of individual or group, or of prospective tenants or occupants of the real property.
Prohibited Practices: (a) Discriminating in real estate financing transaction in granting, withholding, modifying, renewing or setting terms and conditions of financial assistance or services connected therewith, on a prohibited basis; (b) using forms or making inquiries which indicate limitation or discrimination on a prohibited basis; (c) geographic redlining.
Scope of Coverage: Covers persons, financial institutions, lenders to whom application is made for financial assistance for purchase, acquisition, lease, rehabilitation, repair, construction, maintenance of real property.
Private Remedies: Civil action may be filed for injunctive relief; compensatory damages in an amount up to three times actual damages; damages for mental anguish and suffering; punitive damages of up to $8,500. The court may, in its discretion, award reasonable attorneys fees to the prevailing party. § 363.14.
Administrative Remedies: Aggrieved party may file complaint with human rights commission, which has authority to order same relief as courts may. § 363.071(2).

Consumer Credit: **Minn. Stat. §§ 325G.041 to 325G.042**
Protected Classes: Married women; spouses.
Prohibited Practices: Financial card issuers must issue card in current or former surname, as directed by the woman (May require that a married woman requesting a card in a former surname open a new account). Unequal treatment in evaluating credit history.
Scope of Coverage: Covers issuers of financial transaction cards, which include credit cards, courtesy cards, debit cards, etc. § 325G.02(2).
Exclusions: Telephone company credit cards.
Private Remedies: Violation of § 345G.041 declared an unfair discriminatory practice under § 363.03(8). For credit history violations, $1,000. § 325G.042(4).

MISSOURI

Civil Rights: **Mo. Rev. Stat. §§ 213.010 to 213.112** (housing transactions)
Protected Classes: Race, color, religion, national origin, ancestry, familial status, sex, or handicap of applicant, person associated with applicant in connection with the loan, or of prospective tenants, owners, lessees, or occupants of the dwelling which is the subject of the loan.
Prohibited Practices: Denying financial assistance or discriminating in setting terms or conditions of financial assistance. § 213.045.
Scope of Coverage: Covers financial institutions, corporation, firm association, etc, whose business consists in whole or in part of making commercial real estate loans, in connection with financial assistance for the purchase, construction, improvement, repair or maintenance of a dwelling.
Private Remedies: Judicial review of final agency action (§ 213.085); or civil action filed after obtaining a right to sue letter from human rights commission for injunctive relief, actual and punitive damages. Court costs and reasonable attorney fees may be awarded to prevailing party, but will be awarded to respondent only if case was without foundation. § 213.111.
Administrative Remedies: Aggrieved party may file complaint with commission on human rights, which has the authority, *inter alia*, to issue cease and desist orders, order affirmative action to implement purpose of chapter, and actual damages.
Statute of Limitations: Administrative complaint must be filed within 180 days of alleged discriminatory act. § 213.075. Court action must be brought within ninety days of commission's notification letters to the individual, but no later than two years after alleged discriminatory conduct or its reasonable discovery. § 213.011.

Consumer Credit: **Mo. Rev. Stat. §§ 314.100 to 314.115**
Protected Classes: Sex or marital status.
Prohibited Practices: Denying credit solely upon prohibited basis, except that in specified circumstances, creditor can require both spouse's signature.
Scope of Coverage: Covers any creditor and credit without limitation.
Private Remedies: Civil action may be filed for compensatory, and punitive damages not to exceed $1,000 for willful violations. § 314.105.
Statute of Limitations: One year from date credit was denied, except that time shall be tolled under certain circumstances. § 314.115.
Miscellaneous: Thirty day demand letter prior to instituting suit is required. § 314.110.

Consumer Credit: **Mo. Rev. Stat. § 408.550**
Protected Classes: Sex, marital status, age, race, religion, or exercise of rights under law.
Prohibited Practices: Denying credit on a prohibited basis, (compliance with ECOA is compliance with this act).
Scope of Coverage: Applies to creditors and transactions covered by §§ 408.015 to 408.562.
Private Remedies: Civil action may be brought for greater of $500 or actual damages, costs and attorneys fees. *See also* § 408.562.

Miscellaneous: **Mo. Rev. Stat. § 408.575** (real estate financing)
Protected Classes: Race, color, religion, national origin, handicap,

age, marital status or sex of the applicant or of race, religion, or national origin of persons living in vicinity of real estate.

Prohibited Practices: Denying real estate loan, or discriminating in any aspect of the loan transaction on a prohibited basis. Prohibition against redlining extends to age of dwelling or age of structures in immediate neighborhood.

Scope of Coverage: Covers residential real estate loans (defined as loans or refinancing of loan for acquisition, construction, repair, rehabilitation or remodeling of real estate used or intended to be used as residence by not more than four families) made by financial institutions (defined, *inter alia*, as any association or institution which operates a place of business in Missouri and makes residential real estate loans as part of its business).

Exclusions: Market factors may be considered. § 408.585.

Private Remedies: None specified, but administrative remedies are in addition to remedies "otherwise available" to any individual damaged by violation.

Administrative Remedies: Aggrieved party may file complaint with director of the appropriate regulatory agency, who can attempt conciliation and issue cease and desist order. § 408.600.

Statute of Limitations: None specified.

MONTANA

Civil Rights: **Mont. Code Ann. § 49-2-306** (credit transactions)

Protected Classes: Sex, marital status, race, creed, religion, age, physical or mental disability, color, or national origin.

Prohibited Practices: (1) "Financial institutions" cannot discriminate on a prohibited basis in terms or conditions, unless based on reasonable grounds; (2) "creditors" cannot discriminate on a prohibited basis.

Scope of Coverage: § 49-2-306(1) applies to financial institutions, defined as a commercial bank, savings bank, trust company, finance company, savings and loan association, investment company, or insurance company. § 49-2-101(13). § 49-2-306(2) applies to any creditor, defined as a person who regularly or as part of his business arranges for extension of credit for which a financial charge is required, and applies to any credit transaction, including that secured by residential real estate. § 49-2-101(5)–(7).

Exclusions: Age and mental disability may be a legitimate discriminatory criteria in credit transactions only to the extent it relates to a person's capacity to make or be bound by contract. § 49-2-403(2).

Private Remedies: Actual and punitive damages; injunctive relief; attorney fees to prevailing party. § 49-2-509.

Administrative Remedies: Damages, injunctive relief. §§ 49-2-506, 49-2-510.

Statute of Limitations: Administrative complaint must be filed within 180 days after alleged discriminatory act occurred or was discovered. (May be extended by specified period under certain limited circumstances.) § 49-2-501(2). Civil action must be filed within two years of violation. § 49-2-510(5).

Miscellaneous: This chapter provides the exclusive remedy for violations of chapter.

Civil Rights: **Mont. Code Ann. §§ 49-2-101 to 49-2-602; Mont. Code Ann. § 49-2-305(7)** (housing transactions)

Protected Classes: Sex, marital status, race, creed, religion, age, familial status, physical or mental disability, color, national origin.

Prohibited Practices: Discriminating in the making or purchasing of loans in connection with residential real estate transactions.

Scope of Coverage: Covers person or other entity whose business includes engaging in real estate transactions for purchasing, constructing, improving, repairing, or maintaining housing accommodations.

Private Remedies: Injunction, damages, attorney fees.

Administrative Remedies: Injunction, damages, civil penalty between $10,000 and $25,000. § 49-2-510.

Statute of Limitations: 180 days to file with Human Rights Commission; two years for private action (tolled during administrative proceeding).

NEBRASKA

Fair Housing: **Neb. Rev. Stat. §§ 20-301 to 20-344**

Protected Classes: Race, color, religion, sex, handicap, familial status, national origin.

Prohibited Practices: Discriminating in the making or purchasing of loans or other financial assistance in connection with residential real estate. § 20-320.

Scope of Coverage: Covers any person whose business includes engaging in residential real estate financing for purchasing, constructing, improving, repairing, or maintaining a dwelling.

Private Remedies: Injunction, actual damages, attorney fees. May file regardless of whether complaint has been filed with Commission unless a conciliation agreement has been reached. § 20-342.

Administrative Remedies: May file complaint with Commissioner who may file a civil action. Relief includes injunction, actual damages, and civil penalty of $10,000 to $50,000. § 20-337.

Statute of Limitations: One year for administrative complaint; two years for private action (tolled during administrative proceeding).

NEVADA

Consumer Credit: **Nev. Rev. Stat. §§ 598B.010 to 598B.180** (Equal Opportunity for Credit)

Protected Classes: Sex or marital status.

Prohibited Practices: Discriminating in any aspect of a credit transaction on a prohibited basis. Sets out specific guidelines for considerations in determining creditworthiness, separate accounts, and separate reporting of credit histories.

Scope of Coverage: "Creditors," those who regularly extend, renew, or continue credit or regularly arrange for such, or who participate in the decision to extend, renew, or continue credit as an assignee (credit is the right to incur debt or make purchase and defer payment or defer payment of an existing debt).

Private Remedies: Injured party may file civil action for injunction and damages (must elect between this remedy and ECOA remedies).

Administrative Remedies: Injured party may file complaint with commissioner of financial institutions, which may seek conciliation or issue cease and desist order.

Statute of Limitations: Administrative or civil action must be brought within one year.

Fair Housing: **Nev. Rev. Stat. § 207.310**

Protected Classes: Race, color, religious creed, national origin, or ancestry of the customer, or person intending to apply for loan, or person associated with the customer in connection with the loan, or prospective owners, lessees, tenants or occupants of the dwelling which is the subject of the loan, disability, familial status and sex.

Prohibited Practices: Denying or discriminating in terms or conditions of loan or other financial assistance on a prohibited basis.
Scope of Coverage: Banks, savings and loans, insurance company or person whose business consists in whole or in part of making commercial real estate loans, in relation to loans or financial assistance for the purchase, construction, improvement, or repair of a dwelling.
Private Remedies: Injunctive relief, affirmative action as is appropriate, and for actual damages for economic loss, costs, punitive damages, and reasonable attorney fees to prevailing plaintiff. § 118.120.
Statute of Limitations: One year.
Miscellaneous: Violation is a misdemeanor for first and second offenses and a gross misdemeanor for subsequent offenses.

NEW HAMPSHIRE

Civil Rights: **N.H. Rev. Stat. Ann. §§ 354-A:1 to 354-B:3** (housing transactions)
Protected Classes: Age, sex, race, color, marital status, familial status, physical or mental disability, religion, sexual orientation or national origin.
Prohibited Practices: Discrimination against protected classes in making available or varying the terms or conditions of residential real estate related transactions, including the making or purchasing of loans secured by residential real estate, or providing other financial assistance for purchasing, constructing, improving, repairing or maintaining a dwelling. §§ 354-A:9, 354-A:10.
Scope of Coverage: Any person or other entity whose business includes engaging in residential real estate transactions or the business of selling or renting dwellings or commercial structures.
Administrative Remedies: Complaint before Human Rights Commission, which may attempt conciliation, and conduct adjudicatory hearing, and issue cease and desist orders, award compensatory damages, and impose administrative fines ranging from not more than $10,000 for a first offense to not more than $50,000 for a third or subsequent offense within seven years. Judicial review and enforcement are available. § 354-A:21.
Statute of Limitations: 180 days from date of alleged discriminatory practice.
Miscellaneous: Attorney General may bring civil actions for injunctive relief; individual's right to cause of action not limited by this provision. §§ 354-B:1 to 354-B:3.

NEW JERSEY

Civil Rights: **N.J. Stat. Ann. §§ 10:5-1 to 10:5-42 (West)** (credit transactions)
Protected Classes: Race, creed, color, national origin, ancestry, familial status, marital status, sex, affectional or sexual orientation, handicap (including AIDS), genetic information, nationality of applicant or, if financing is sought for real property, of its prospective occupants or tenants.
Prohibited Practices: Discriminating in granting, extending, etc., credit or in setting conditions and terms of credit on a prohibited basis, or using forms or making records or inquiries which suggest limitations or discrimination on a prohibited basis, unless required by law to retain such information. § 10:5-12(i).
Scope of Coverage: Covers banks, banking organizations, mortgage and insurance companies or other financial institutions, lenders or credit institutions to whom application is made for *any* loan or extension of credit, *including but not limited to* financial assistance for the purchase, construction, repair, rehabilitation or maintenance of real property (emphasis added.).
Private Remedies: Complainant may file action in court without exhausting administrative remedies. § 10:5-13. Prevailing party may be awarded reasonable attorneys fees, though no award shall be made to a respondent unless the charge was brought in bad faith. § 10:5-27.1.
Administrative Remedies: Aggrieved party may file administrative complaint; agency has authority to issue cease and desist orders, and order such affirmative action as will effectuate purpose of chapter. § 10:5-17.

Miscellaneous: **N.J. Stat. Ann. § 17:16F-3 (West)** (redlining)
Protected Classes: Borrowers in specific geographical areas.
Prohibited Practices: Redlining, i.e., discriminating in acceptance or discouragement of applications, granting, withholding, extending, modifying or renewing or the fixing of terms or conditions of mortgage loan on real property located in the municipality of the lending institution simply because of location.
Scope of Coverage: Banking institutions.
Exclusions: Mortgage loans made pursuant to special public or private programs with the goal of increasing mortgages within specified geographic area.
Private Remedies: Actual damages, costs, attorneys fees.
Administrative Remedies: Commissioner of banking may issue cease and desist order; if violation continues, may assess penalty of $5000 for each offense.
Statute of Limitations: None specified.

NEW MEXICO

Civil Rights: **N.M. Stat. Ann. § 28-1-1 to 28-1-15 (Michie)** (credit transactions)
Protected Classes: Race, religion, color, national origin, ancestry, sex, spousal affiliation, or physical or mental handicap.
Prohibited Practices: (1) Considering membership in a protected class in granting, extending, modifying, renewing credit or in setting terms and conditions thereof or in extending services in connection therewith; (2) using forms or making records or inquiries which suggest limitation or discrimination on a prohibited basis. § 28-1-7(H).
Scope of Coverage: Covers any person to whom application is made for financial assistance for (1) acquisition, construction, rehabilitation, repair or maintenance of any housing accommodation or real property, or (2) any type of consumer credit, including financing for purchase of consumer good (purchased primarily for personal, family, or household purposes).
Exclusions: Exemptions to general coverage in Human Rights Act identified in § 28-1-9.
Private Remedies: Appeal of adverse administrative action is by trial de novo, including right to jury trial. Court has discretion to award actual damages and reasonable attorney fees to prevailing complaint. § 28-1-13.
Administrative Remedies: Aggrieved party may file complaint with human rights commission, which has authority to order actual damages, reasonable attorney fees if complainant was represented by private counsel, and such affirmative action as it deems necessary. §§ 28-1-10 to 28-1-13.

Statute of Limitations: Administrative complaint must be filed within 180 days after alleged occurrence.

Miscellaneous: Act has a July 1, 2006 sunset date.

NEW YORK

***Civil Rights*: N.Y. Exec. Law § 296-a (McKinney)** (credit transactions)

Protected Classes: Race, creed, color, national origin, age, sex, familial or marital status, or disability and, in cases of housing financing, of certain persons associated with applicant, or of prospective occupants or tenants of the real estate in connection with which housing is sought.

Prohibited Practices: Discriminating on a prohibited basis (1) in granting, withholding, extending, renewing, or setting terms and conditions of real property financing (residential and commercial); (2) in granting, withholding, extending, renewing, or setting terms and conditions in connection with any form of credit; (3) using forms or making inquiries or records which suggest limitation or discrimination; (4) making inquiries about childbearing or family planning; (5) refusing to consider, or discount income on a prohibited basis or because of childbearing potential; (6) discriminating against married person on basis of use of surname other than spouse's. Certain additional prohibited and permitted practices are spelled out. Notice of reasons for denial required upon request.

Scope of Coverage: Covers any creditors (person or financial institution which does business in New York and extends or arranges for the extension of credit, § 292(22)) in connection with any form of credit (defined as the right to incur debt and defer payment irrespective of whether a finance charge is imposed, § 292(20)), including housing financing.

Private Remedies: Judicial review of adverse agency action. § 298.

Administrative Remedies: In case of alleged violation by "regulated creditor" (lender licensed or supervised by banking department § 292(24)), may either file administrative complaint with superintendent of banking pursuant to § 296-a or with human rights division under § 297. Complaints concerning other creditors may be filed with the human rights division. Either agency has authority, *inter alia*, to award compensatory damages, issue cease and desist orders, and order the credit be granted.

Statute of Limitations: One year after occurrence of alleged discriminatory act.

***Civil Rights*: N.Y. Exec. Law §§ 290–301 (McKinney); N.Y. Exec. Law § 296(5)(a)–(c) (McKinney)** (housing transactions)

Protected Classes: Race, creed, color, national origin, sex, age, disability, marital status, or familial status.

Prohibited Practices: (1) Discriminating in the terms, conditions or privileges of the sale, rental or lease of a housing accommodation (constructed or to be constructed); (2) discrimination in the terms, conditions or privileges of the sale, rental or lease of land or commercial space; (3) refusal to sell, rent or lease any housing accommodation, land or commercial space.

Scope of Coverage: (1) Owner, lessee, sub-lessee, assignee, or managing agent of, or other person with right to sell, rent or lease a housing accommodation or commercial space; (2) owner, lessee, sub-lessee, or managing agent, or other person having right to sell, rent, or lease land or commercial space; (3) real estate brokers or salesmen or employees/agents thereof.

Exclusions: (1) Certain owner-occupied housing and housing ex-

clusively for persons fifty-five years of age or older; (2) & (3) sale, rental or lease of land or commercial space exclusively to persons fifty-five years of age or older.

Private Remedies: Damages and other appropriate remedies. § 297(9).

Administrative Remedies: Cease and desist order; extension of accommodation, advantages and privileges; granting the subject credit; compensatory damages; punitive damages (in housing discrimination cases only) not exceeding $10,000. § 297.

Statute of Limitations: Administrative or civil complaint must be filed within one year after alleged discriminatory practice. § 297(5). If the complaint is dismissed prior to an administrative hearing upon plaintiff's request to have election of remedies annulled, right to civil action is subject to statute of limitations from the time of filing of administrative complaint.

Miscellaneous: Civil action is precluded by filing administrative complaint, except when the division dismisses the complaint on grounds of administrative inconvenience, untimeliness, or on the grounds that the election of remedies is annulled, in which case civil action may be brought as if no administrative complaint had been filed.

***Miscellaneous*: N.Y. Banking Law § 9-f (McKinney)** (redlining)

Protected Classes: Borrowers in specific geographical areas

Prohibited Practices: Redlining, i.e., refusing to make prudent loan upon security of real property because of its geographic location if the property is located within the geographic district serviced by the banking institution.

Scope of Coverage: Banking institutions equal banks, trust companies, savings banks, savings and loans associations, credit unions, mortgage bankers and foreign banking corporations.

Private Remedies: None specified.

Administrative Remedies: Anyone denied a loan may appeal to the Superintendent of banking for review of the decision.

Statute of Limitations: None specified.

NORTH CAROLINA

***Consumer Credit*: N.C. Gen. Stat. §§ 25B-1 to 25B-4**

Protected Classes: Married and unmarried women.

Prohibited Practices: Denying credit in her own name to woman with same creditworthiness as men who would receive credit. Upon written request, credit reporting agencies must give any separate credit histories and history of joint accounts on file.

Scope of Coverage: Covers any credit, defined as obtaining money, labor or services on a deferred payment basis.

Private Remedies: Civil action may be filed for actual damages and, in the court's discretion, reasonable attorney fees.

***Consumer Credit*: N.C. Gen. Stat. §§ 53-164 to 53-191**

Protected Classes: Race, color, religion, national origin, sex or marital status.

Prohibited Practices: Denying credit or discriminating in setting terms or conditions of credit on a prohibited basis. § 53-180(d).

Scope of Coverage: Covers licensees under North Carolina Consumer Finance Act in connection with any extension of credit.

Exclusions: Certain exclusions to the Act's coverage generally are set out in § 53-191.

Private Remedies: Any loan, the making of which violates *any* provision of the Consumer Finance Act, except in limited circumstances, is void, and the creditor has no right to receive or retain

any principal or charges. § 53-166(d).
Miscellaneous: Violation is misdemeanor. § 53-166(c).

Fair Housing: **N.C. Gen. Stat. §§ 41A-1 to 41A-10**
Protected Classes: Race, color, religion, sex, national origin, handicapping condition, or familial status.
Prohibited Practices: Discrimination against protected class, in any residential real estate related transaction, including the making or purchasing of loans or providing financial assistance for purchasing, constructing, improving, repairing or maintaining a dwelling, or any transaction in which the security is residential real estate. § 41A-4(b1).
Scope of Coverage: Any person or entity whose business includes engaging in residential real estate related transactions.
Exclusions: Does not forbid lenders to inquire into financial and dependent obligations, or basing its action on income and financial abilities of any person.
Private Remedies: If conciliation (see immediately below) fails, complainant may request right to sue letter from Commission, and bring civil action for injunctive relief, actual or punitive damages, costs and attorney fees. § 41A-7.
Administrative Remedies: Complaint before Human Relations Commission. Conciliation attempt is mandatory. If conciliation fails, and neither complainant nor Commission chooses to sue, complaint may be pursued in adjudicatory hearing before Commission. Relief "as appropriate" including compensatory damages, and civil penalties. (Not more than $10,000 for first offense, not more than $25,000 for second offense within five years, not more than $50,000 for third or subsequent offense within seven years.) Judicial review of Commission actions is available.
Statute of Limitations: One year to file administrative complaint. Ten days after notice of failure of conciliation (or 130 days of Commission inaction) to request right to sue letter, one year after right to sue letter for civil action.

NORTH DAKOTA

Civil Rights: **N.D. Cent. Code §§ 14-02.4-01 to 14-02.4-23** (credit transactions)
Protected Classes: Race, color, religion, sex, national origin, age, physical or mental disability, marital status, receipt of public assistance.
Prohibited Practices: Denying credit, discriminating in setting terms or conditions on a prohibited basis (may consider credit histories and take actions permitted or required by ECOA). § 14-02.4-17.
Scope of Coverage: Covers any person acting for self or another, in connection with any credit.
Private Remedies: May bring civil action for injunctive and equitable relief, and such relief as may be appropriate. Court in its discretion may award prevailing party reasonable attorney fees.
Statute of Limitations: 300 days from alleged discriminatory act. § 14-02.4-19.

Fair Housing: **N.D. Cent. Code §§ 14-02.5-01 to 14-02.5-46**
Protected Classes: Race, color, religion, sex, national origin, age, physical or mental disability, marital status, receipt of public assistance.
Prohibited Practices: Discriminating in providing of services related to sale or rental of dwellings. § 14-02.5-02.
Scope of Coverage: Persons seeking to sell or rent dwellings.

Exclusions: Religious and private organizations favoring members (§§ 14-02.5-10, 14-02.5-11); elderly housing; persons convicted of drug-related offenses, persons of the opposite sex seeking to cohabit (§ 14-01.5-02).
Private Remedies: Actual and punitive damages, attorney fees, costs, injunctive relief. § 14-02.5-41.
Administrative Remedies: Civil penalties. § 14-02.5-32.
Statute of Limitations: One year for administrative; two years for civil action.

OHIO

Civil Rights: **Ohio Rev. Code Ann. § 4112.021 (West)** (credit transactions)
Protected Classes: Race, color, religion, age, sex, marital status, national origin, handicap, or ancestry.
Prohibited Practices: Lists eleven prohibited practices.
Scope of Coverage: Covers "creditors" (who regularly extend, renew or continue credit or arrange for such, and assignees who participate in decision to extend, renew or continue credit) in credit transactions, irrespective of whether a finance charge is imposed. Some provisions specially apply to credit reporting agencies.
Exclusions: Limited exclusions from various subsections are noted as applicable.
Private Remedies: Civil action may be filed for injunctive relief and actual and punitive damages, minimum $100, plus attorney fees. § 4112.021(D).
Administrative Remedies: May file complaint with civil rights commission, which can issue cease and desist orders and order affirmative action to effectuate purposes of act. Actual and punitive damages, attorney fees. § 4112.05.
Statute of Limitations: Six months for administrative complaint, § 4112.05(B)(1); and 180 days for civil action, § 4112.021(D).

Civil Rights: **Ohio Rev. Code Ann. §§ 4112.01 to 4112.99 (West); Ohio Rev. Code Ann. § 4112.02(H) (West)** (housing transactions)
Protected Classes: Race, color, religion, sex, ancestry, handicap, or national origin of present or prospective owner, occupant, or user of such housing.
Prohibited Practices: (1) Refusing to lend money for acquisition, construction, rehabilitation, repair or maintenance of housing; (2) discriminating in terms or conditions of such a loan; (3) refusing to consider combined income or income of either spouse in connection with mortgage credit. Specifically includes racial composition of neighborhood as an illegitimate reason for refusing credit.
Scope of Coverage: Subsection (H)(3), on refusal to lend housing financing money, applies only to persons who lend money as a principal aspect of or incident to their principal business, and not to seller-financed/owner-occupied or casual or occasional lenders. The other subsections (H)(5) and (6) do not contain this express limitation on their scope.
Exclusions: *See* Scope of Coverage, *supra*; religious or private organizations favoring members.
Private Remedies: Actual damages, reasonable attorney fees, court costs, expert witness fees, injunctive relief and punitive damages. § 4112.051.
Administrative Remedies: May file complaint with civil rights commission, which can issue cease and desist orders and order affirmative action to effectuate purposes of act. Actual and punitive damages, attorney fees. § 4112.05.
Statute of Limitations: One year for administrative or civil complaint.

OKLAHOMA

Civil Rights: **Okla. Stat. tit. 25, §§ 1451–1453** (housing transactions)

Protected Classes: Race, color, religion, gender, national origin, age, handicap, receipt of public assistance (as specified). §§ 1451–1452.

Prohibited Practices: (1) Refusing to consider income of both applicants seeking to buy or lease housing; (2) refusing to consider public assistance or court ordered alimony or child support that is verifiable as valid income; (3) discriminating in terms, conditions or privilege relating to financial assistance for purchase, repair, maintenance, etc. of housing. § 1452(A).

Scope of Coverage: Covers any person in connection with housing financing.

Exclusions: Persons convicted for drug-relate offense. Religious organizations, associations, or society or affiliated non-profit entity of sale of housing operated for other than commercial purposes to persons of same religion; private club providing incidental lodging; housing for older persons; owner-occupied single-family housing. § 1453.

Private Remedies: Actual and punitive damages, reasonable attorney fees, court costs, and injunctive relief. § 1506.3.

Administrative Remedies: Aggrieved party may file complaint with human rights commission, which has authority to, *inter alia*, actual damages, reasonable attorney fees, costs, court costs, and injunctive or equitable relief. § 1505.

Statute of Limitations: Administrative complaint must be filed within one year of alleged discriminatory act (§ 1502.2(C)); 180 day limit for complaints stating that a discriminatory practice has been committed specified by § 1502(A).

Miscellaneous: Commission order has no effect unless district court issues corresponding order. § 1505(e).

Consumer Credit: **Okla. Stat. tit. 14A, § 1-109** (Okla. Consumer Credit Code)

Protected Classes: Sex, marital status.

Prohibited Practices: Limiting or refusing to extend credit solely on a prohibited basis.

Scope of Coverage: Consumer credit sales, consumer leases, consumer loans as defined by Oklahoma Consumer Credit Code.

Private Remedies: None specified.

Administrative Remedies: Enforcement authority delegated to Administrator of Dept. of Consumer Credit.

OREGON

Civil Rights: **Or. Rev. Stat. §§ 659.010 to 659.121** (housing transactions)

Protected Classes: Race, color, religion, sex, marital status, familial status, national origin, source of income.

Prohibited Practices: Discriminating in the making or purchasing of loans or providing other financial assistance in connection with residential real estate. § 659.033.

Scope of Coverage: Covers any person or entity whose business includes engaging in residential real estate financing for purchasing, constructing, improving, repairing, or maintaining a dwelling.

Private Remedies: Compensatory damages or $200, whichever is greater, punitive damages, costs, attorneys fees. May file regardless of whether complaint has been filed with Civil Rights Commission unless a hearing has commenced. § 659.121.

Administrative Remedies: Injunction, civil penalty of up to $1000.

Statute of Limitations: Administrative complaint must be filed within one year of alleged discrimination. § 695.045. Civil action must be filed within two years of occurrence or termination of alleged discriminatory housing practice (tolled during pendency of administrative action), except that civil action may not be commenced if an administrative hearing on the record has been commenced. § 659.121(5)(b), (6).

Consumer Credit: **Or. Rev. Stat. §§ 646.861 to 646.865** (financial regulation)

Protected Classes: Persons obligated to pay child support.

Prohibited Practices: Less favorable treatment than any other credit obligation of the same amount, terms, and duration.

Private Remedies: Compensatory damages, injunction, reasonable attorneys fees, unless bona fide error or good faith conformity with laws, regulations.

PENNSYLVANIA

Civil Rights: **43 Pa. Cons. Stat. §§ 951–963** (housing transactions)

Protected Classes: Race, color, religion, creed, ancestry, national origin, sex, familial status, age, handicap or disability (including use of support animal) of applicant or prospective owner, occupant, or user of real property.

Prohibited Practices: Refusing to finance housing accommodation or commercial property; refusing to lend money or otherwise withhold financing for acquisition, construction and rehabilitation, repair, maintenance of housing accommodation or commercial property, or discriminate in terms or conditions of any such loan; or make inquiries or make or keep records containing question concerning membership in a protected class. § 955(h).

Scope of Coverage: Covers any person in connection with financing commercial real property or housing accommodation.

Exclusions: Religious institutions, charitable or educational organizations; qualifying housing for older persons; bona fide private or fraternal organizations may give preference to members of their own group if calculated to promote the aims of the group.

Private Remedies: If the commission fails to act within specified time period or dismisses the complaint, aggrieved party may bring civil action within two years of notice thereof for injunctive and any other legal and equitable relief as the court deems appropriate. § 962.

Administrative Remedies: Aggrieved party may file complaint with the human relations commission, which may, *inter alia*, order conciliation, cease and desist orders, affirmative action including but not limited to lending money on equal terms and conditions. § 959.

Statute of Limitations: Administrative complaint must be filed within 180 days of illegal discriminatory act. § 959(h).

PUERTO RICO

Fair Housing: **1 P.R. Laws Ann. § 13(e)**

Protected Classes: Politics, religion, sex, race, or color.

Prohibited Practices: Refusing to grant loan for dwelling construction.

Scope of Coverage: Natural or artificial persons engaged in business of granting loans for dwelling construction.

Private Remedies: Aggrieved party may bring civil action for actual damages, and court may award punitive damages. Tit. 1, § 14.

Miscellaneous: Violation of civil rights act is also a crime.

RHODE ISLAND

Fair Housing: **R.I. Gen. Laws §§ 34-37-1 to 34-37-9; R.I. Gen. Laws § 34-37-4(b)** (housing transactions)
Protected Classes: Race, color, religion, sex, sexual orientation, marital status, country of ancestral origin, disability, age, gender identity or expression, or familial status.
Prohibited Practices: Directly or indirectly discriminating in the terms, conditions, or privileges relating to obtaining or using any financial assistance.
Scope of Coverage: Persons to whom application is made for a loan or other form of financial assistance for the acquisition, construction, rehabilitation, repair, or maintenance of any housing accommodation.
Exclusions: Limitation by organizations, association or society, or affiliated non-profit entity, of sale of housing owned or operated for other than commercial purposes to persons of same religion; private clubs providing incidental lodging. § 34-37-4.2. Regarding gender identity or expression discrimination, three-family units in which owner resides. § 34-37-4.5.
Private Remedies: Injunction, damages, costs and attorney fees, punitive damages (§ 34-37-5(o)(3)); specifies conditions for private actions.
Administrative Remedies: Injunction, damages, costs, and attorney fees.
Statute of Limitations: Administrative complaint must be filed within one year of occurrence or termination of alleged discriminatory practice. Aggrieved party may seek right to sue in state court within specified period from filing of administrative complaint provided the commission has not secured a settlement or conciliation agreement and a hearing has not commenced. Civil action must then be filed within ninety days from grant of request for right to sue. § 34-37-5.

Fair Housing: **R.I. Gen. Laws § 34-37-4.3** (credit transactions)
Protected Classes: Sex, marital status, race or color, religion or country of ancestral origin, sexual orientation, familial status, gender identity or expression, handicap or age.
Prohibited Practices: Discriminating in granting or extending loan or credit, or in privilege or capacity to obtain credit.
Scope of Coverage: Covers financial organizations governed by tit. 19 or any other credit-granting commercial institution in conjunction with any form of loan or credit including, but not limited to, credit concerned with housing accommodations.
Exclusions: Limitation by organizations, association or society, or affiliated non-profit entity, of sale of housing owned or operated for other than commercial purposes to persons of same religion; private clubs providing incidental lodging. § 34-37-4.2. Regarding gender identity or expression discrimination, three-family units in which owner resides. § 34-37-4.5.
Private Remedies: Injunction, damages, costs and attorney fees, punitive damages. § 34-37-5(o)(3).
Administrative Remedies: Injunction, damages, costs, and attorney fees.
Statute of Limitations: Administrative complaint must be filed within one year of occurrence or termination of alleged discriminatory practice. Aggrieved party may seek right to sue in state court within specified period from filing of administrative complaint provided the commission has not secured a settlement or conciliation agreement and a hearing has not commenced. Civil action must then be filed within ninety days from grant of request for right to sue. § 34-37-5.

Fair Housing: **R.I. Gen. Laws § 34-37-5.4** (housing transactions)
Protected Classes: Race, color, religion, sex, sexual orientation, marital status, country of ancestral origin, disability, age, gender identity or expression, familial status.
Prohibited Practices: Discrimination in the making or purchasing of loans or providing other financial assistance for the purchasing, constructing, improving, repairing, or maintenance of residential real estate, in providing such assistance secured by residential real estate, or in the selling, brokering or appraising of residential real estate.
Scope of Coverage: Person or entity whose business includes making or purchasing loans or other financial assistance for purchasing, constructing, repairing, maintaining residential real estate or which is secured by same, or whose business includes selling, brokering or appraising such property.
Exclusions: Limitation by organizations, association or society, or affiliated non-profit entity, of sale of housing owned or operated for other than commercial purposes to persons of same religion; private clubs providing incidental lodging. § 34-37-4.2. Regarding gender identity or expression discrimination, three-family units in which owner resides. § 34-37-4.5.
Private Remedies: Injunction, damages, costs and attorney fees, punitive damages. § 34-37-5(o)(3).
Administrative Remedies: Injunction, damages, costs and attorneys fees. § 34-37-5.
Statute of Limitations: Administrative complaint must be filed within one year of occurrence or termination of alleged discriminatory practice. Aggrieved party may seek right to sue in state court within specified period from filing of administrative complaint provided the commission has not secured a settlement or conciliation agreement and a hearing has not commenced. Civil action must then be filed within ninety days from grant of request for right to sue. § 34-37-5.

SOUTH CAROLINA

Fair Housing: **S.C. Code Ann. §§ 31-21-10 to 31-21-150 (Law. Co-op.); S.C. Code Ann. § 31-21-40 (Law. Co-op.)**
Protected Classes: Race, color, religion, sex, familial status, national origin, or handicap.
Prohibited Practices: Refusing to sell or rent or to negotiate for the sale or rental of a dwelling; discriminating against a member of protected class in terms, conditions, or privileges of sale or rental of a dwelling, or in providing related services or facilities.
Scope of Coverage: Person or entity whose business includes making or purchasing of loans or providing other financial assistance in connection with the purchase, improvement, repair or maintenance of a dwelling or which is secured by residential real estate, or the selling, brokering or appraising of a dwelling.
Exclusions: Certain single-family homes and owner-occupied four-family units; limitation by religious organizations, associations, or society or affiliated non-profit entity of sale of housing operated for other than commercial purposes and favoring members; private club providing incidental lodging. § 31-21-70.
Private Remedies: Injunction, actual and punitive damages, costs, attorney fees.
Administrative Remedies: Injunction, actual damages, attorney fees, civil penalty.

Statute of Limitations: 180 days for administrative complaint (§ 31-21-120); one year for private action (§ 31-21-140).

Fair Housing: S.C. Code Ann. § 31-21-60 (Law. Co-op.)
Protected Classes: Race, color, religion, sex, handicap, national origin, familial status.
Prohibited Practices: To discriminate in the making or purchasing of loans or in the terms or conditions of residential real estate transactions.
Scope of Coverage: Covers any person or entity whose business includes engaging in residential real estate financing for purchase, improvement, repair, construction, or maintenance of a dwelling.
Exclusions: Certain single-family homes and owner-occupied four-family units; limitation by religious organizations, associations, or society or affiliated non-profit entity of sale of housing operated for other than commercial purposes and favoring members; private club providing incidental lodging. § 31-21-70.
Private Remedies: Injunction, actual and punitive damages, costs, attorney fees (for the prevailing party if the court determines the prevailing party cannot financially assume the fees).
Administrative Remedies: Injunction, actual damages, attorneys fees, civil penalty.
Statute of Limitations: 180 days for administrative complaint; one year for private action.

SOUTH DAKOTA

Civil Rights: S.D. Codified Laws §§ 20-13-1 to 20-13-56 (Michie); S.D. Codified Laws § 20-13-21 (Michie) (housing transactions/financing)
Protected Classes: Race, color, creed, religion, sex, ancestry, disability, national origin of applicant or prospective occupants or tenants of real property to which transaction relates.
Prohibited Practices: Discrimination against any member of a protected class in the granting, withholding, extending, modifying, renewing or in the rates, terms, conditions or privileges or the extension of services in any financial assistance relating to the purchase, lease, acquisition, construction, rehabilitation, repair or maintenance of real property.
Scope of Coverage: Any person, financial institution, lender to whom application is made for purchase, lease, acquisition, construction, rehabilitation, repair or maintenance of real property.
Private Remedies: Compensatory damages, injunctive relief, attorney fees and costs, and punitive damages.
Administrative Remedies: Cease and desist order, compensatory damages (other than pain and suffering, punitive, or consequential damages) attorney fees and allowable costs.
Statute of Limitations: Administrative complaint must be filed within 180 days of the alleged discriminatory act. § 20-13-31. Plaintiff may elect to have claims asserted in a civil action not later than twenty days after issuance of notice requiring respondent to answer administrative complain. § 20-13-35.1.
Miscellaneous: Exhaustion of administrative remedies is not required, but filing of administrative complaint is prerequisite to civil action.

Civil Rights: S.D. Codified Laws § 20-13-20 (Michie) (housing transactions)
Protected Classes: Race, color, creed, religion, sex, ancestry, disability, familial status or national origin.
Prohibited Practices: Discriminating in the terms, conditions, or

privileges of the sale, rental, lease, assignment, sublease or other transfer of real property or housing accommodation or any part, portion, or interest therein.
Scope of Coverage: Any owner of rights to housing or real property or any person acting for an owner, with or without compensation, including persons licensed as a real estate broker or salesman, attorney, auctioneer, agent, or representative by power of attorney or appointment, or any person acting under court order, deed of trust or will.
Exclusions: Certain owner-occupied duplexes; dormitory residences for unmarried students, or sororities or fraternities recognized by a public or private college or university; qualifying residences for older or disabled persons. Discrimination based upon familial status applicable only to housing accommodation. § 20-13-20.1.
Private Remedies: Compensatory damages, injunctive relief, attorney fees and costs, and punitive damages.
Administrative Remedies: Cease and desist order, compensatory damages (other than pain and suffering, punitive, or consequential damages) attorney fees and allowable costs.
Statute of Limitations: Administrative complaint must be filed within 180 days of the alleged discriminatory act. § 20-13-31. Plaintiff may elect to have claims asserted in a civil action not later than twenty days after issuance of notice requiring respondent to answer administrative complaint.

TENNESSEE

Civil Rights: Tenn. Code Ann. §§ 4-21-101 to 4-21-1004; Tenn. Code Ann. § 4-21-601 (housing transactions)
Protected Classes: Race, color, creed, religion, sex, handicap, national origin, familial status.
Prohibited Practices: Discrimination in the terms, conditions, or privileges of sale or rental of real property or housing accommodation.
Scope of Coverage: Owner or any person engaging in a real estate transaction, or a broker, salesperson, real estate operator or other employee or agent of such persons.
Exclusions: Certain owner-occupied duplexes, residences; single-sex dormitories; religious, charitable or educational institutions. § 4-21-602.
Private Remedies: Injunction, actual and punitive damages, costs, attorney fees. Filing of private action supersedes administrative action. § 4-21-311.
Administrative Remedies: Injunction, actual damages, costs, attorney fees, civil penalty between $10,000 and $50,000. § 4-21-306.
Statute of Limitations: 180 days for administrative complaint; one year for private action.
Miscellaneous: If an administrative action is filed, the human rights commission finds reasonable cause, and no conciliation agreement is reached, then either party must elect to proceed in a civil action within twenty days of receiving notice of permission to do so from the commission. § 4-21-312.

Civil Rights: Tenn. Code Ann. § 4-21-606 (housing transactions)
Protected Classes: Race, color, creed, religion, sex, handicap, national origin, familial status.
Prohibited Practices: To discriminate in the making or purchasing of loans or providing other financial assistance in connection with residential real estate transactions.

Scope of Coverage: Covers any person or entity whose business includes engaging in residential real estate financing for purchase, improvement, repair or maintenance of a dwelling.

Private Remedies: Injunction, actual and punitive damages, costs, attorneys fees. Filing of private action will supersede administrative action. § 4-21-311.

Administrative Remedies: Injunction, actual damages, costs, attorneys fees, civil penalty between $10,000 and $50,000. § 4-21-306.

Statute of Limitations: 180 days for administrative complaint; one year for private action.

Miscellaneous: If an administrative action is filed, the human rights commission finds reasonable cause, and no conciliation agreement is reached, then either party must elect to proceed in a civil action within twenty days of receiving notice of permission to do so from the commission. § 4-21-312.

Consumer Credit: Tenn. Code Ann. §§ 47-18-801 to 47-18-805

Protected Classes: Sex, handicap or marital status.

Prohibited Practices: Discriminate between equally qualified people on a prohibited basis with respect to approval, denial, or terms of credit. (Special provision relating to utility service and necessaries doctrine). §§ 47-18-802, 47-18-805.

Scope of Coverage: Covers creditors extending consumer credit and credit card issuers. (NOTE: Definition of "consumer" is limited to natural persons, but does not appear to be limited to use of credit for personal, family or household purposes. § 47-18-103(2)).

Private Remedies: Damages in individual action of $100 minimum to $1000 maximum and attorney fees. Damages in a class action are capped at $10,000. No action for UDAP damages. § 47-18-109(a)(5).

Statute of Limitations: One year from alleged discriminatory act.

Miscellaneous: Discrimination against the handicapped is also declared to be an unfair or deceptive act, except when committed by creditor or credit card issuer regulated by department of financial institutions, which has authority to investigate and dispose of complaints concerning such creditors. § 47-18-104(b)(25).

TEXAS

Consumer Credit: Tex. Fin. Code Ann. § 341.401 (Vernon)

Protected Classes: Sex, race, religion, national origin, marital status, age; income from social security or SSI; exercise of rights under the Federal Consumer Credit Protection Act.

Prohibited Practices: Denying an extension of credit, including a loan, or restricting or limiting the credit extended.

Scope of Coverage: Authorized lenders, persons licensed under Tex. Fin. Code ch. 342, banks or saving and loan institutions, or other persons involved in open-end credit car transactions (§ 301.001) or loans (ch. 342).

Private Remedies: Actual damages, punitive damages (not greater than $10,000) and court costs.

Statute of Limitations: Later of two years from occurrence of violation or four years from date of loan or retail installment transaction for closed-end credit; two years from date of occurrence for open-end credit (§ 349.402).

Miscellaneous: Claimant must choose to pursue action under this statute or under federal Consumer Credit Protection Act.

Fair Housing: Tex. Prop. Code Ann. §§ 301.001 to 301.171 (Vernon)

Protected Classes: Race, color, religion, sex, disability, national origin, familial status.

Prohibited Practices: To discriminate in the making or purchasing of loans or providing other financial assistance in connection with residential real estate transactions. § 301.026.

Scope of Coverage: Covers any person or entity whose business includes engaging in residential real estate financing for purchase, improvement, repair for maintenance of a dwelling.

Private Remedies: Injunction, actual and punitive damages, costs, attorney fees. § 301.153.

Administrative Remedies: Injunction, actual damages, costs, attorneys fees, civil penalty between $10,000 and $50,000. § 301.112.

Statute of Limitations: One year for administrative complaint (§ 301.081); two years for civil action (tolled while administrative proceeding is pending) (§ 301.151).

UTAH

Fair Housing: Utah Code Ann. §§ 57-21-1 to 57-21-14; Utah Code Ann. § 57-21-6

Protected Classes: Race, color, religion, sex, disability, national origin, familial status, source of income, association with member of protected class.

Prohibited Practices: To discriminate in the making or purchasing of loans or providing other financial assistance in connection with residential real estate transactions.

Scope of Coverage: Covers any person or entity whose business includes engaging in residential real estate financing for purchase, improvement, repair for maintenance of a dwelling.

Private Remedies: Injunction, actual and punitive damages, costs, attorney fees. § 57-21-12.

Administrative Remedies: Injunction, actual damages, costs, attorneys fees, civil penalty between $10,000 and $50,000. § 57-21-11.

Statute of Limitations: 180 days for administrative complaint (§ 57-21-9); two years for civil action (tolled while administrative proceeding is pending), except that person may not file civil action if a formal adjudicative hearing has commenced (§ 57-21-12).

Miscellaneous: Filing federal court action for relief under federal law based upon act prohibited under §§ 57-21-5, 57-21-6 bars commencement or continuation of any administrative or state court adjudicative proceeding in connection with the same claims. § 57-21-14.

Fair Housing: Utah Code Ann. § 57-21-5

Protected Classes: Race, color, religion, sex, national origin, familial status, source of income, disability, association with member of protected class.

Prohibited Practices: Discrimination against member of protected class in the terms, conditions, or privileges of the sale or rental of any dwelling or in providing related facilities or services.

Scope of Coverage: Any "person," defined as one or more individuals, corporations, limited liability companies, partnerships, associations, labor organizations, legal representatives, mutual companies, joint-stock companies, trusts, unincorporated organizations, trustees, bankruptcy trustees, receivers and fiduciaries.

Private Remedies: Injunction, actual and punitive damages, costs, attorney fees.

Administrative Remedies: Injunction, actual damages, costs, attorney fees, civil penalty between $10,000 and $15,000.

Statute of Limitations: 180 days for administrative complaint; two years for civil action (tolled while administrative proceeding is pending except that person may not file civil action if a formal adjudicatory hearing has commenced (§ 57-21-12)).

Miscellaneous: Filing federal court action for relief under federal law based upon act prohibited under §§ 57-21-5, 57-21-6 bars commencement or continuation of any administrative or state court adjudicative proceeding in connection with the same claims. § 57-21-14.

VERMONT

Consumer Credit: **Vt. Stat. Ann. tit. 8, § 10403**

Protected Classes: Race, color, religion, national origin, age, sexual orientation, sex, marital status, handicapped.

Prohibited Practices: Discrimination with respect to credit cards and personal, mortgage, and commercial loans.

Scope of Coverage: Financial institutions, licensed lenders.

Private Remedies: Punitive and actual damages; costs and attorney fees permitted.

Administrative Remedies: None specified.

Fair Housing: **Vt. Stat. Ann. tit. 9, §§ 4500–4507**

Protected Classes: Race, sex, sexual orientation, age, marital status, religious creed, color, national origin, handicap, having minor children, receipt of public assistance.

Prohibited Practices: To discriminate in the making or purchasing of loans or providing other financial assistance in connection with residential real estate transactions. § 4503(a)(6).

Scope of Coverage: Covers any person or entity whose business includes engaging in residential real estate financing for purchase, improvement, repair or maintenance of a dwelling.

Private Remedies: Injunction, actual and punitive damages, costs, attorneys fees. § 4506.

Administrative Remedies: Injunction, actual damages, costs, attorney fees, civil penalty of no more than $10,000. § 4553.

Statute of Limitations: None specified. If administrative case is not disposed of informally within six months of filing, the commission must either file action in state court or dismiss the proceedings unless all parties consent to extension. § 4554.

Miscellaneous: Initiation or completion of administrative investigation is not a prerequisite to civil action. § 4506(d).

Miscellaneous: **Vt. Stat. Ann. tit. 9, §§ 2351–2362** (motor vehicle financing)

Protected Classes: Sex, marital status, race, color, religion, national origin, age, sexual orientation, or handicapping condition (providing there is legal capacity to contract).

Prohibited Practices: Discriminating against buyer wishing to establish a motor vehicle retail installment contract on a prohibited basis. § 2362.

Scope of Coverage: Covers persons in business of selling motor vehicles in retail installment transactions. § 2351.

Private Remedies: Person not complying with *any* provision of chapter is barred from recovery of any finance charge or late charges etc., and buyer may recoup any such charges paid and attorney fees. In the case of willful violations of any provision of chapter, buyer may recover twice finance and late charges, and attorney fees. § 2361.

Miscellaneous: **Vt. Stat. Ann. tit. 9, §§ 2401–2410** (retail installment sales)

Protected Classes: Sex, marital status, race, color, religion, na-

tional origin, age, sexual orientation, or handicapping condition (providing there is legal capacity to contract).

Prohibited Practices: Discriminating against buyer wishing to establish retail installment sales contract or charge agreement. § 2410.

Scope of Coverage: Covers persons regularly and principally in business of selling goods to retail buyers in connection with such transactions. § 2401.

Private Remedies: Same as for violation of motor vehicle retail installment sales act provisions (*see above*). § 2409.

VIRGIN ISLANDS

Civil Rights: **V.I. Code Ann. §§ 61 to 75** (housing transactions)

Protected Classes: Sex, marital status, race, religion, color or national origin, creed, political affiliation.

Prohibited Practices: Discrimination in provision of services related to obtaining housing accommodations. § 64(8)(a)(ii). Discrimination in extensions, renewals, or terms of financial assistance. § 64(8)(e).

Scope of Coverage: Anyone having right to sell, rent, or lease, or agents thereof. § 64(8)(a). Financial organizations providing financial assistance in matters relating to housing, land, or commercial space. § 64(8)(e).

Exclusions: Owner-occupied two—family units.

Private Remedies: None specified.

Administrative Remedies: Commission for Human Rights may investigate, conduct hearings, and may seek penalties for misdemeanor, or initiate civil actions for injunctions and damages to aggrieved party.

Statute of Limitations: None specified.

VIRGINIA

Consumer Credit: **Va. Code Ann. §§ 59.1-21.19 to 59.1-21.28 (Michie)**

Protected Classes: Race, color, religion, national origin, sex, marital status or age (provided there is capacity to contract); public welfare recipients.

Prohibited Practices: To discriminate in regard to any aspect of a credit transaction (sets forth several prohibited and permitted practices and requires notice of decision and of right to reasons for adverse action; provisions similar to ECOA).

Scope of Coverage: Covers persons who regularly extend, continue or renew credit, who regularly arrange for such, and assignees who participate in decision to extend, renew or continue credit, with respect to credit (defined as the right to incur debt or make purchase and defer payment).

Private Remedies: Actual damages, punitive damages up to $10,000, equitable relief, costs and attorney fees. § 59.1-21.23.

Administrative Remedies: Mediation of complaint of violation. § 59.1-21.26.

Statute of Limitations: Two years from occurrence of alleged violation. § 59.1-21.23(e).

Miscellaneous: Regulations authorized by this chapter should conform to FRB's ECOA regulations, including exemptions. There is a good faith conformity with FRB regulations defense; and ECOA compliance is compliance with state act. There is an election of remedies provision as to monetary damages.

Fair Housing: **Va. Code Ann. §§ 36-96.1 to 36-96.23 (Michie); Va. Code Ann. § 36-96.4 (Michie)**

Protected Classes: Race, color, religion, national origin, sex, elderliness, familial status, handicap.

Prohibited Practices: To discriminate in the making or purchasing of loans or providing other financial assistance in connection with residential real estate transactions.

Scope of Coverage: Covers any person or entity whose business includes engaging in residential real estate financing for purchase, improvement, repair or maintenance of a dwelling.

Exclusions: Qualifying single-family housing; owner-occupied multi-family units; private membership clubs; religious or related non-profit entities owning dwelling for other than a commercial purpose; single-sex accommodations when matters of personal privacy are involved.

Private Remedies: Injunction, actual and punitive damages, costs, attorneys fees.

Administrative Remedies: Real Estate Board may refer charge to the Attorney General for civil action and court may order injunction, compensatory and punitive damages, costs, attorney fees, and a civil penalty.

Statute of Limitations: One year for administrative complaint; two years or 180 days after conclusion of administrative process for filing private action, whichever is later.

Fair Housing: Va. Code Ann. § 36-96.3 (Michie)

Protected Classes: Race, color, religion, national origin, sex, elderliness, familial status, handicap.

Prohibited Practices: Discrimination against member of protected class in the terms, conditions or privileges of sale or rental of a dwelling, or in providing related services or facilities.

Scope of Coverage: Any persons, defined as one or more individuals, corporations, partnerships, associations, labor organizations, governmental entities, legal representatives, mutual companies, joint stock companies, trust, unincorporated organizations, trustees, bankruptcy trustees, receivers and fiduciaries.

Exclusions: Drug-related offenders; Qualifying single-family housing; owner-occupied multi-family units; private membership clubs; religious or related non-profit entities owning dwelling for other than a commercial purpose; single-sex accommodations when matters of personal privacy are involved. § 36-96.2.

Private Remedies: Injunction, actual and punitive damages, costs, attorney fees. § 36-96.18.

Administrative Remedies: Real Estate Board may refer charge to the Attorney General for civil action and court may order injunction, compensatory and punitive damages, costs, attorney fees, and a civil penalty.

Statute of Limitations: One year for administrative complaint (§ 36-96.9); civil action must be commenced within later of two years or 180 days after conclusion of administrative process (§ 36-96.18).

WASHINGTON

Civil Rights: Wash. Rev. Code §§ 49.60.010 to 49.60.410; Wash. Rev. Code §§ 49.60.030(1)(d), 49.60.175, 49.60.176 (credit transactions)

Protected Classes: Race, creed, color, national origin, sex, disability (general declaration of rights in § 49.60.030) or use of trained guide dog or service dog by a disabled person; add marital status with respect to credit discrimination (§§ 49.60.175, 49.60.176).

Prohibited Practices: (1) Financial institutions cannot use a prohibited basis to determine creditworthiness (§ 49.60.175); (2) no person can deny or restrict credit, or impose different terms or conditions on credit on a prohibited basis (§ 49.60.176). Effect of community property law may be considered.

Scope of Coverage: Covers financial institutions (in the case of § 49.60.175) or any person (in the case of § 49.60.176) in connection with any credit transaction, defined broadly in § 49.60.040 to include consumer and business credit, when finance charge is imposed or provides for repayment by scheduled payments, extended in regular course of any trade or commerce.

Private Remedies: Any person injured by violation of chapter has right of action for injunctive relief, actual damages, attorney fees, or any other remedy authorized by this chapter or 42 U.S.C. §§ 2000a–2000a-6. § 49.60.030(2).

Administrative Remedies: Aggrieved party may file complaint with human rights commission, which has authority, *inter alia*, to issue cease and desist orders, order affirmative actions to effectuate purposes of chapter, award damages, except that damages for humiliation and mental suffering shall not exceed $10,000. If complaint was frivolous, unreasonable or groundless, ALJ may award reasonable attorneys fees to respondent. § 49.60.250.

Statute of Limitations: Administrative complaint must be filed within six months of alleged act of discrimination. § 49.60.230.

Miscellaneous: UDAP violation, except for those related to real estate transactions, within meaning of §§ 19.86.020 and 19.86.030, and subject to all provisions thereof, presumably including treble damages provision. § 49.60.030(3).

Civil Rights: Wash. Rev. Code § 49.60.222(j) (housing transactions)

Protected Classes: Sex, marital status, race, creed, color, national origin, families with children status, sensory, mental or physical disability.

Prohibited Practices: To discriminate in the course of negotiating, executing or financing a residential real estate transaction.

Scope of Coverage: Covers any person or entity whose business includes engaging in residential real estate financing for purchase, improvement, repair or maintenance of a dwelling

Private Remedies: Actual damages, costs and attorney fees.

Administrative Remedies: May file complaint with Human Rights Commission which may issue injunction and award damages. § 49.60.225.

Statute of Limitations: One year for administrative action. Complainant may elect to have claims decided in civil action within twenty days of service of reasonable cause finding. § 49.60.230.

Miscellaneous: Wash. Rev. Code §§ 30.04.500 to 30.04.515 (Fairness in Lending Act) (redlining)

Protected Classes: Geographic location of real estate offered as security.

Prohibited Practices: Deny or vary the terms of a loan to be secured by a single family residence, by requiring a greater down payment, a shorter amortization period, or a higher interest rate, or by deliberately underappraising the value of the security, because of the geographic location of the property, or utilizing lending standards which have no economic basis.

Scope of Coverage: Banks, trust companies, mutual savings banks, credit unions, mortgage companies, or savings and loan associations which operate or have a place of business in Washington.

Exclusions: Lender may deny on grounds of geographical area if building, remodelling, or continued habitation is prohibited or restricted by local, state or federal law or regulations. May also follow sound underwriting practices regarding borrower's ability and willingness to repay, the market value of the real estate, and the diversification of the lender's portfolio.

WEST VIRGINIA

Fair Housing: **W. Va. Code §§ 5-11A-1 to 5-11A-20; W. Va. Code § 5-11A-5**

Protected Classes: Sex, race, color, religion, blindness, handicap, familial status, ancestry, national origin.

Prohibited Practices: Discrimination against member of protected class in the terms, conditions or privileges of sale of rental of a dwelling or in providing related services or facilities.

Scope of Coverage: Sellers and renters of dwellings, excepting single-family residences. § 5-11-4.

Exclusions: Religious and private organizations favoring members; drug-related offenders; elderly housing in regard to "familial staus." § 5-11-8.

Private Remedies: Injunction, actual and punitive damages, costs, and attorney fees. § 5-11-14.

Administrative Remedies: Injunction, actual damages, and other equitable relief, costs and attorney fees. § 5-11-13.

Statute of Limitations: One year for administrative complaint (§ 5-11-11); two years for civil action (§ 5-11-14).

Fair Housing: **W. Va. Code § 5-11A-6**

Protected Classes: Sex, race, color, religion, blindness, handicap, familial status, ancestry, national origin.

Prohibited Practices: To discriminate in (i) making or purchasing of loans or providing other financial assistance which is either secured by residential real estate or used for the purchase, construction, improvement, repair or maintenance of a dwelling (§ 5-11-6); (ii) selling, brokering or appraising residential real property (§ 5-11-7).

Scope of Coverage: Covers any person or entity whose business includes engaging in residential real estate financing for purchase, improvement, repair or maintaining of a dwelling, or the selling, brokering or appraising of residential real property.

Private Remedies: Injunction, actual and punitive damages, costs and attorneys fees. § 5-11-14.

Administrative Remedies: Injunction, actual damages and other equitable relief, costs and attorney fees. § 5-11-13.

Statute of Limitations: One year for administrative complaint (§ 5-11-11); two years for private action (§ 5-11-14).

WISCONSIN

Consumer Credit: **Wis. Stat. § 138.20**

Protected Classes: Physical condition, developmental disability, sex or marital status (unless there is no legal capacity to contract).

Prohibited Practices: Discriminating in the granting or extension of credit or privilege or capacity to obtain credit. Incorporates violation of Wis. Stat. § 766.56(1) as a violation.

Scope of Coverage: Covers financial organizations, as defined in §§ 71.04(8)(a) and 71.25(10)(a) or any other credit-granting commercial institution.

Private Remedies: None specified.

Administrative Remedies: None specified (except that violator may be fined up to $1,000).

Consumer Credit: **Wis. Stat. § 224.77** (financial regulation)

Protected Classes: Sex, race, color, handicap, sexual orientation (as defined), religion, national origin, age or ancestry, lawful source of income, sex or marital status. § 224.77(1)(0).

Prohibited Practices: Unequal treatment, except in relation to housing designed to meet needs of elderly.

Scope of Coverage: Covers mortgage bankers, loan originators, or loan solicitors, as defined.

Private Remedies: May file private action for greater of actual damages (including incidental and consequential damages) or twice amount of loan origination costs but $100 minimum and $1,000 maximum per violation; reasonable costs and attorney fees. § 224.80.

Fair Housing: **Wis. Stat. § 106.50**

Protected Classes: Sex, race, color, sexual orientation (as defined), disability, religion, national origin, family status, sex, or marital status, lawful source of income, age or ancestry.

Prohibited Practices: Refusing to finance housing or discuss terms thereof, or setting different or more stringent terms or conditions for housing financing (except that terms may differ on the basis of age if reasonably related to individual applicant. § 106.50(2)(k).

Scope of Coverage: Covers "any person."

Exclusions: Qualifying housing for older persons.

Private Remedies: Civil action may be brought for injunctive relief, damages (including punitive), court costs and attorney fees to a prevailing plaintiff. § 106.50(6m).

Administrative Remedies: Economic and noneconomic damages, injunctive relief, attorney fees and costs, but not punitive damages. § 106.50(6)(h)(i).

Statute of Limitations: Administrative complaint must be filed within one year of alleged discrimination. Civil action must be filed within one year of alleged discrimination (tolled while administrative proceeding is pending).

Appendix F   Sample Pleadings

The pleadings reprinted in this appendix can also be found on the CD-Rom accompanying this volume. The CD-Rom also contains a number of additional pleadings that are not reprinted here. All pleadings in the text and on the CD-Rom are for demonstration purposes only, and must be adapted by a competent professional to fit the circumstances of a given case and the requirements of local rules and practice.

Additional pleadings available on the CD-Rom accompanying this volume are primarily from reverse redlining cases. The CD-Rom also includes expert reports from litigation challenging auto financing mark-up policies. Sample discovery requests for credit discrimination cases can be found in Appendix G, *infra*, and on the CD-Rom. Also available on the CD-Rom are pleadings from selected enforcement actions brought by the Department of Justice.

Also available from NCLC are various pleadings seeking attorney fees under various consumer protection statutes. Although primarily originating in Truth in Lending cases, these documents should be relevant to credit discrimination litigation as well:

- Attorney Fees Motion with Memorandum of Law in Settled Truth in Lending Case, Consumer Law Pleadings With Disk, Number One § 11.1 (1994);
- Attorney's Affidavit in Support of Fees in Settled TIL Case, Consumer Law Pleadings With Disk, Number One § 11.2 (1994);
- Attorney Fees Petition for Successful Appeal of TIL Decision, Consumer Law Pleading With Disk, Number One § 11.3 (1994);
- Affidavit in Support of Appellate Attorney Fees, Consumer Law Pleadings With Disk, Number One § 11.4 (1994);
- Expert's Affidavit in Case Seeking Appellate Attorney Fees, Consumer Law Pleadings With Disk, Number One § 11.5 (1994);
- Attorney Fees Materials in Repossessions and Fair Debt Collection Cases, Consumer Law Pleadings With Disk, Number 4 Ch. 4 (1998);
- Brief Requesting Attorney Fees in Repossession Civil Rights Case, Consumer Law Pleadings With Disk, Number 5 § 8.1 (1999).

F.1 Sample Complaint Alleging Denial of Home Mortgage and Discriminatory Appraisal Practices as ECOA, Fair Housing and Civil Rights Acts Violations

IN THE UNITED STATES DISTRICT COURT
FOR THE NORTHERN DISTRICT OF OHIO

```
——————————————   )
                     )
MARY AND JOHN        )
CONSUMER,            )
          Plaintiffs, )
                     )
v.                   )
                     )
HARRISON NATIONAL BANK, )
a corporation, HARRISON )
MORTGAGE COMPANY, a  )
corporation, and COLE )
& ASSOCIATES,        )
          Defendants. )
——————————————   )
```

COMPLAINT

For and in support of their complaint against defendants, plaintiffs allege and aver as follows:

1. Plaintiffs Mary and John Consumer are black citizens of the United States and of the State of Ohio, residing at 99 Oakwood Avenue, Toledo, Ohio.

2. Defendant Harrison National Bank is a corporation registered and doing business in the State of Ohio whose business consists in whole or in part in the making of real estate loans to qualified persons. Defendant Harrison National Bank is a member of the Federal Deposit Insurance Corporation (FDIC) and the Federal Savings & Loan Insurance Corporation (FSLIC).

3. Defendant Harrison Mortgage Company is a corporation registered and doing business in the State of Ohio whose business consists in whole or in part in the making of real estate loans to qualified persons. Defendant Harrison Mortgage Company is a wholly owned subsidiary of defendant Harrison National Bank, and is a member of the Federal Deposit Insurance Company (FDIC) and the Federal Savings & Loan Insurance Corporation (FSLIC).

4. Defendant Cole & Associates is, upon information and belief, a sole proprietorship or partnership with its principal place of business in Ohio, and is engaged in the business of appraising real estate.

5. On November 19, 1993 plaintiffs applied for a real estate mortgage loan from defendants Harrison National Bank and Harrison Mortgage Company for the purchase of certain real estate located at 99 Oakwood Avenue, Toledo, Ohio.

6. The terms of the real estate mortgage loan for which application was made were as follows: principal amount—$16,250; term—10 years; interest rate—10%.

7. Plaintiffs met all financial and credit requirements of defendants Harrison National Bank and Harrison Mortgage Company, and were in all respects qualified to receive a real estate mortgage loan in the amount and for the terms for which application was made.

8. Defendants Harrison National Bank and Harrison Mortgage Company received and accepted from plaintiffs $125.00 as a mortgage loan application fee, with actual or constructive knowledge of the location of the real estate located at 99 Oakwood Avenue, Toledo, Ohio.

9. As a part of its consideration of plaintiffs' mortgage loan application, defendants Harrison National Bank and Harrison Mortgage Company engaged the services of defendant Cole & Associates to prepare an appraisal of the real estate located at 99 Oakwood Avenue, Toledo, Ohio.

10. The appraisal report prepared by defendant Cole & Associates was completed on or about November 28, 1993, and consistently rated the real estate located at 99 Oakwood Avenue as "average." Average was the second highest possible rating on the scale used in the appraisal report.

11. The appraisal report prepared by defendant Cole & Associates specifically noted that the real estate located at 99 Oakwood Avenue had no physical inadequacies, needed no repairs, and had no functional obsolescence.

12. Defendant Cole & Associates appraised the property at a value of $24,500.00 using the "cost approach" method of appraisal and at a value of $22,000.00 using the "market data approach" method of appraisal. Thus, the property was appraised at substantially more than the principal amount of the mortgage loan request.

13. The racial population of the neighborhood within which the real estate at 99 Oakwood Avenue is located is over 90% black.

14. The appraisal report prepared by defendant Cole & Associates made negative comments concerning the age and condition of the neighborhood generally and of other dwellings in the neighborhood, and concluded that the location of the real estate located at 99 Oakwood Avenue and the condition of the neighborhood within which it was located might have an adverse effect on the marketability of the property.

15. On December 14, 1993 plaintiffs were notified by defendants Harrison National Bank and Harrison Mortgage Company that plaintiffs' application for a real estate mortgage loan had been denied. The stated reason for rejection of the plaintiffs' application was "Ineligible property—property lacks marketability."

16. Plaintiffs subsequently obtained a mortgage loan for the purchase of the real estate located at 99 Oakwood Avenue from another commercial mortgage lender at less favorable terms.

FIRST CLAIM FOR RELIEF

17. Plaintiffs incorporate herein the allegations contained in paragraphs 1 through 16 above.

18. Defendants Harrison National Bank and Harrison Mortgage Company with racially discriminatory intent denied the mortgage loan for which plaintiffs had applied because of the location of the real estate and/or because of the racial composition of the neighborhood within which it was located.

19. Defendants Harrison National Bank and Harrison Mortgage Company with racially discriminatory intent denied the mortgage loan for which plaintiffs had applied under pretense of using the "unmarketability" of the real estate, when in fact the appraisal report prepared by defendant Cole & Associates on the real estate located at 99 Oakwood Avenue, Toledo, indicated that the real estate was marketable.

20. The appraisal prepared by defendant Cole & Associates was racially discriminatory. It negatively described the location of the Oakwood dwelling, relied upon the physical or economic characteristics of the neighborhood in which the real estate was located, and made negative representations concerning the marketability of the real estate based upon the neighborhood in which it was located.

21. The denial of plaintiffs' mortgage loan application by defendants Harrison National Bank and Harrison Mortgage Company was based in whole or in part on the racially discriminatory appraisal prepared by defendant Cole & Associates.

22. The actions of the defendants Harrison National Bank and Harrison Mortgage Company violated the Fair Housing Act, 42 U.S.C. §§ 3601–3619.

23. As a proximate cause of the denial for racially discriminatory reasons of plaintiffs' mortgage loan application by defendants Harrison National Bank and Harrison Mortgage Company, plaintiffs have suffered compensatory damages in the form of economic loss, humiliation, embarrassment, mental anguish, inconvenience, and the deprivation of civil rights.

24. The actions of defendants Harrison National Bank and Harrison Mortgage Company were intentional and willful and warrant the imposition of punitive damages.

SECOND CLAIM FOR RELIEF

25. Plaintiffs incorporate herein the allegations contained in paragraphs 1 through 24 above.

26. The denial of plaintiffs' mortgage loan application by defendants Harrison National Bank and Harrison Mortgage Company was in violation of 42 U.S.C. § 1981.

27. As a proximate cause of the denial for racially discriminatory reasons for plaintiffs' mortgage loan application by defendants Harrison National Bank and Harrison Mortgage Company, plaintiffs have suffered compensatory damages in the from of economic loss, humiliation, embarrassment, mental anguish, inconvenience, and the deprivation of civil rights.

28. The actions of defendants Harrison National Bank and Harrison Mortgage Company were intentional and willful and warrant the imposition of punitive damages.

THIRD CLAIM FOR RELIEF

29. Plaintiffs incorporate herein the allegations contained in paragraphs 1 through 28 above.

30. The denial of plaintiffs' mortgage loan application by defendants Harrison National Bank and Harrison Mortgage Company was in violation of 42 U.S.C. § 1982.

31. As a proximate cause of the denial for racially discriminatory reasons of plaintiffs' mortgage loan application by defendants Harrison National Bank and Harrison Mortgage Company, plaintiffs have suffered compensatory damages in the form of economic loss, humiliation, embarrassment, mental anguish, inconvenience, and the deprivation of civil rights.

32. The actions of defendants Harrison National Bank and Harrison Mortgage Company were intentional and willful and warrant the imposition of punitive damages.

FOURTH CLAIM FOR RELIEF

33. Plaintiffs incorporate herein the allegations contained in paragraphs 1 through 32 above.

34. The denial of plaintiffs' mortgage loan application by defendants Harrison National Bank and Harrison Mortgage Company constitutes racial discrimination with respect to a credit transaction in violation of the Equal Credit Opportunity Act, 15 U.S.C. §§ 1691–1691f.

35. As a proximate cause of the denial for racially discriminatory reasons of plaintiffs' mortgage loan application by defendants Harrison National Bank and Harrison Mortgage Company, plaintiffs have suffered compensatory damages in the form of economic loss, humiliation, embarrassment, mental anguish, inconvenience, and the deprivation of civil rights.

36. The actions of defendants Harrison National Bank and Harrison Mortgage Company were intentional and willful and warrant the imposition of punitive damages.

FIFTH CLAIM FOR RELIEF

37. Plaintiffs incorporate herein the allegations contained in paragraphs 1 through 36 above.

38. The denial for racially discriminatory reasons of plaintiffs' mortgage loan application by defendants Harrison National Bank and Harrison Mortgage Company deprived plaintiffs of the right and benefits from these defendants' programs for extending home mortgage loans to qualified persons.

39. The conduct of defendants Harrison National Bank and Harrison Mortgage Company thereby excluded plaintiffs from participating in and receiving the benefits of programs or activities receiving federal financial assistance in violation of 42 U.S.C. § 2000d *et seq.*

40. As a proximate cause of the denial for racially discriminatory reasons of plaintiffs' mortgage loan application by defendants Harrison National Bank and Harrison Mortgage Company, plaintiffs have suffered compensatory damages in the form of economic loss, humiliation, embarrassment, mental anguish, inconvenience, and the deprivation of civil rights.

41. The actions of defendants Harrison National Bank and Harrison Mortgage Company were intentional and willful and warrant the imposition of punitive damages.

SIXTH CLAIM FOR RELIEF

42. Plaintiffs incorporate herein the allegations contained in paragraphs 1 through 41 above.

43. The preparation of a racially discriminatory appraisal report by defendant Cole & Associates violated the Fair Housing Act, 42 U.S.C. §§ 3601–3619.

44. As a proximate cause of defendant Cole & Associates' preparation of a racially discriminatory appraisal report in violation of the Fair Housing Act, plaintiffs have suffered compensatory damages in the form of economic loss, humiliation, embarrassment, mental anguish, inconvenience, and the deprivation of civil rights.

45. The actions of defendant Cole & Associates were intentional and willful and warrant the imposition of punitive damages.

SEVENTH CLAIM FOR RELIEF

46. Plaintiffs incorporate herein the allegations contained in paragraphs 1 through 45 above.

47. Defendants Harrison National Bank and Harrison Mortgage Company, and Cole & Associates intentionally conspired among themselves to deprive, either directly or indirectly, plaintiffs of

their rights to equal protection of the laws, equal privileges and immunities under the laws, and civil rights generally, all in violation of 42 U.S.C. § 1985(3).

48. As a proximate cause of the defendants' violation of 42 U.S.C. § 1985(3), plaintiffs have suffered compensatory damages in the form of economic loss, humiliation, embarrassment, mental anguish, inconvenience, and the deprivation of civil rights.

49. The actions of defendants Harrison National Bank and Harrison Mortgage Company, and Cole & Associates were intentional and willful and warrant the imposition of punitive damages.

WHEREFORE, plaintiffs pray for the following relief:

(A) A declaratory judgment that the actions of the defendants were intentionally racially discriminatory and in violation of the Fair Housing Act, the Equal Credit Opportunity Act, 42 U.S.C. § 1981, 42 U.S.C. § 1982, 42 U.S.C. § 1985(3), and 42 U.S.C. § 2000d *et seq.*; and

(B) An injunction permanently enjoining the defendants from preparing, using or relying upon racially discriminatory appraisal reports and permanently enjoining the defendants from engaging in the receipt, processing, approval or denial of applications for real estate mortgage loans; and

(C) Compensatory damages in the amount of Fifty Thousand Dollars ($50,000.00) assessed against all defendants jointly and severally; and

(D) Punitive damages in the amount of One Hundred Fifty Thousand Dollars ($150,000.00) assessed against all defendants jointly and severally; and

(E) Attorneys' fees and costs of this action; and

(F) Any other relief to which plaintiffs may be entitled in law or in equity.

JURY DEMAND

Plaintiffs hereby demand a trial by jury on all issues.

F.2 Sample Complaint Alleging ECOA Cosigner Violation

IN THE UNITED STATES DISTRICT COURT
FOR THE DISTRICT OF MASSACHUSETTS

```
——————————————————  )
MEG CONSUMER,                 )
                  Plaintiff,  )
                              )
v.                            )
                              )
FRIENDLY FINANCE CO.,         )
A Corporation,                )
                  Defendant.  )
——————————————————  )
```

COMPLAINT

COMES NOW the Plaintiff, MEG CONSUMER, by her undersigned counsel, in the above-entitled action and alleges as follows:

1. This Complaint is filed and these proceedings are instituted under the "Equal Credit Opportunity" provision of the Federal Consumer Credit Protection Act, 15 U.S.C. § 1691 *et seq.*, and

Regulation B, 12 C.F.R. 202.1 *et seq.*, to recover actual and punitive damages, declaratory relief, reasonable attorney's fees and costs of suit by reason of Defendant's violations of that Act. The jurisdiction of this Court is invoked pursuant to 15 U.S.C. § 1691e(f) of the Act.

2. Plaintiff is a natural person and is a resident and a citizen of the Commonwealth of Massachusetts and of the United States.

3. Defendant is a corporation doing business in the Commonwealth of Massachusetts and is subject to the jurisdiction of this Court. At all times relevant herein, Defendant, in the ordinary course of business, regularly extended, offered to extend or arranged for extension of credit to its consumer customers for which a finance charge was imposed.

4. Within two years prior to the filing of this action, Plaintiff entered into a credit transaction with Defendant incident to which Defendant imposed on Plaintiff a finance charge as a part of the transaction. [A copy of the disclosure statement of that transaction is attached hereto as Exhibit "A" and is made a part hereof.]

5. Defendant has violated the Equal Credit Opportunity Act and Regulation B thereunder in that:

a. Defendant required Plaintiff's husband to obtain the signature of a co-signer on this credit loan contract notwithstanding the fact that:

    i. Plaintiff's husband's application for credit was not a joint application; and

    ii. Plaintiff's husband individually qualified under Defendant's standards for creditworthiness for the amount and terms of the credit requested; and

b. Defendant required that Plaintiff MEG CONSUMER serve as the co-signer on her husband's credit instrument because of her status as his wife.

6. As a result of the aforesaid violations, Defendant is liable to Plaintiff in an amount to be proven at trial, representing Plaintiff's actual damages, punitive damages, costs of Court and reasonable attorney's fees.

WHEREFORE, Plaintiff demands judgment against Defendant as follows:

1. Declare Defendant's actions in the extension of credit to consumers in violation of the Equal Credit Opportunity Act.

2. Award Plaintiff actual damages as will be shown at trial.

3. Award Plaintiff punitive damages in an amount not greater than $10,000.00.

4. Award Plaintiff reasonable attorney's fees as provided by law, costs, and such other relief as the Court may deem just and proper.

DATED: Boston, Massachusetts:_____

Attorneys for Plaintiff

F.3 Sample Class Action Complaint Alleging ECOA Cosigner Violation

UNITED STATES DISTRICT COURT
WESTERN DISTRICT OF NEW YORK

```
_____  )
                             )
HOLLY NAMED-PLAINTIFF,       )
individually and on behalf of all  )
other persons similarly situated,  )
                  Plaintiff,  )
                             )
v.                           )  COMPLAINT
                             )
ABC FINANCIAL               )
SERVICES CO.,               )
                 Defendant.  )
_____  )
```

INTRODUCTION

1. Plaintiff brings this action on behalf of herself and a class of others similarly situated to recover for violations of the Federal Equal Credit Opportunity Act, 15 U.S.C. § 1691 *et seq.* (ECOA) and Regulation B thereunder, 12 C.F.R. § 202.1 *et seq.*

JURISDICTION

2. Jurisdiction is vested in this Court pursuant to 15 U.S.C. § 1691e(f).

PARTIES

3. Plaintiff is a natural person residing in Bison, Erie County, New York, within the Western District of New York.

4. Defendant is, on information and belief, a corporation organized under the laws of the State of New York; it does business in Bison, Erie County, New York, within the Western District of New York. It is a licensed lender subject to Article 9 of the New York Banking Law, and it regularly extends, renews or continues credit; regularly arranges for the extension, renewal or continuation of credit; regularly purchases assignments from original creditors and participates in the decision to extend, renew or continue credit.

CLASS ACTION

5. Plaintiff brings this action on behalf of a class consisting of all other persons who were made by defendant to co-sign loan agreements initiated by their spouses with defendant during the period commencing two years prior to the filing of this action, or who may be made by defendant to co-sign loan agreements initiated by their spouses with defendant in the future.

6. The class is so numerous that joinder of all members is impracticable, including, on information and belief, several hundred persons at least.

7. There are questions of law common to the class, namely whether the procedure followed by defendant of making the spouses of loan applicants co-sign loan agreements violates ECOA and Regulation B, and whether the loan forms used by defendant violate ECOA and Regulation B.

8. The claims of the representative party are typical of the claims of the class and the representative party will fairly and adequately protect the interests of the class. There is no conflict between the representative party and the members of the class and the representative party is represented by counsel employed by a federally funded Legal Services program.

9. A class action may be maintained under Rule 23(b)(2) and 23(b)(3) of the Federal Rules of Civil Procedure, since the party opposing the class has acted or refused to act on grounds generally applicable to the class, thereby making appropriate final injunctive relief or corresponding declaratory relief with respect to the class as a whole, and since the questions of law about the defendant's compliance with ECOA and Regulation B predominate over any questions affecting only individual class members and a class action is superior to other available methods of the fair and efficient adjudication of the controversy.

FACTS

10. On or about December 31, 1993, plaintiff's husband, WILSON NAMED-PLAINTIFF, and defendant entered into a consumer loan transaction.

11. This transaction was, in part, evidenced by a form entitled Loan Agreement, a true and accurate copy of which is attached hereto, marked plaintiff's Exhibit A, and incorporated herein by reference.

12. The transaction set out in paragraph 10 was also evidenced, in part, by a document purportedly making all disclosures required by the Federal Truth in Lending Act, 15 U.S.C. § 1601 *et seq.*, Regulation Z thereunder 12 C.F.R. § 226.1 *et seq.*, and the New York Banking Law to be made in connection with the particular transaction. A true and accurate copy of this document is attached hereto, marked plaintiff's Exhibit B and incorporated herein by reference.

13. Both plaintiff's Exhibits A and B contain spaces for listing information which are entitled "SPOUSE AGE" and "SPOUSE NAME," in violation of ECOA and Regulation B.

14. Plaintiff was made by defendant to co-sign the loan agreement, plaintiff's Exhibit A, thereby becoming liable to defendant for repayment of the loan.

15. Plaintiff was unemployed at the time of signing the loan agreement.

16. Under New York law, plaintiff's signature on the wage assignment of her husband and the security agreement was sufficient to secure the loan. Plaintiff's signature on the loan agreement was not necessary to secure the transaction.

17. Upon inquiring of defendant as to why she had to sign the loan agreement, plaintiff was informed that requiring a wife to co-sign a loan agreement was routine.

18. Plaintiff was at no time informed by defendant of the effect of her signature should her husband default in payment of the loan.

19. On information and belief, the form of loan agreement and policies of defendant alleged herein have been at all relevant times and still are used by defendant in all of its loan transactions.

STATEMENT OF CLAIM

20. By virtue of the foregoing, defendant has violated and is violating ECOA and Regulation B.

WHEREFORE, Plaintiff demands judgment:

1. Determining that this action is maintainable as a class action under Rule 23 of the Federal Rules of Civil Procedure.

2. Awarding the class $500,000 or one percent of defendant's net worth in punitive damages.

3. Awarding plaintiff $10,000 in punitive damages.

4. Enjoining defendant, its agents, employees and assigns from collecting or attempting to collect by any means from plaintiff any monies outstanding on the said contract of loan with plaintiff and her husband.

5. Enjoining defendant, its agents, employees and assigns from collecting or attempting to collect by any means from the members of the class any monies outstanding on the contracts of loan between defendant and the members of the class and their spouses.

6. Awarding plaintiff reasonable attorney's fees and cost of this action.

7. Awarding plaintiff and the class such other and further relief as seems just and proper.

Attorney for the Plaintiff

F.4 Sample Class Action Complaint (with Jury Demand) Alleging ECOA Adverse Action Notice Violation

IN THE UNITED STATES DISTRICT COURT
FOR THE DISTRICT OF NEW MEXICO

THERESA CREDITWORTHY, Individually and On Behalf of All Other Persons Similarly Situated, Plaintiffs, v. K COMPANY and ACE CREDIT CORPORATION, Defendants.	))))) *COMPLAINT*))) *Six (6) Person Jury*) *Demanded*)))

INTRODUCTION

This is a class action for declaratory and injunctive class relief and for declaratory and injunctive relief and actual and punitive damages as individual relief, to redress the violations by Defendants of the Equal Credit Opportunity Act, 15 U.S.C. §§ 1691, *et seq.* (hereinafter "the Act"), and Regulation B, 12 C.F.R. § 202 (hereinafter "Regulation B"), promulgated by the Board of Governors of the Federal Reserve System pursuant to Section 703 of the Act, 15 U.S.C. § 1691b.

Plaintiffs seek relief from the acts of Defendants who have utterly failed to provide to Plaintiffs any written notification of the reason(s) for their adverse credit action taken in response to credit applications submitted to K Company, which in turn submitted the applications to Ace Credit Corporation, all in attempts by Plaintiffs to purchase merchandise from K Company.

JURISDICTION

1. Jurisdiction of this Court attains pursuant to § 706(f) of the Act, 15 U.S.C. § 1691e(f).

2. This Court is authorized to grant declaratory and injunctive relief by § 706(c) of the Act, 15 U.S.C. § 1691e(c).

PARTIES

3. Plaintiff Theresa Creditworthy is a natural person who resides in Santa Fe, New Mexico.

4. Defendant K Company is a New Mexico corporation authorized to do and doing business in New Mexico as a retail seller of general merchandise in Santa Fe, New Mexico.

5. Ace Credit Corporation is a New Mexico corporation doing business in Santa Fe, New Mexico as a loan company.

CLASS ACTION

6. This action is brought as a class action pursuant to Rule 23, Federal Rules of Civil Procedure, on behalf of Mr. Burke and all other persons similarly situated, described as:

(a) all persons who, within the period beginning two years prior to the filing of this action and continuing until 30 days prior to the filing of this action, have made credit applications wherein Defendant K Company has been the arranger of credit and Defendant Ace Credit Corporation the anticipated extender of credit, adverse action has been taken in response to those applications, and no written notification as required by § 202.9(a)(2) of Regulation B has been provided to the applicants; and

(b) all persons who, from 30 days prior to the filing of this action and continuing in the future, have made or will make credit applications wherein Defendant K Company has been or will be the arranger of credit and Defendant Ace Credit Corporation the anticipated extender of credit, adverse action has or will have been taken in response to those applications, and no written notification as required by § 202.9(a)(2) of Regulation B has or will have been provided to the applicants.

7. A class action is appropriate because the class is so numerous that joinder is impracticable, there are common questions of law and fact with respect to Defendants' failure to provide the required notice, the claims of the representative party are typical of the claims of the class, and the representative party will fairly and adequately protect the interests of the class.

8. A class action pursuant to Rule 23(b)(2) is appropriate because Defendants, by their failure to provide the required notice to the class members, have and will have acted on grounds generally applicable to the class, thereby making appropriate final injunctive and declaratory relief with respect to the class as a whole.

CAUSE OF ACTION

9. On or about December 9, 1993, Plaintiff Creditworthy submitted a credit application at the K Company store in Santa Fe, New Mexico in connection with the attempted purchase by her of a wood stove.

10. Thereafter, Plaintiff telephoned the person with whom she had dealt at the K Company store and was advised by that person that her credit application had been submitted to and turned down by Ace Credit Corporation.

11. Defendants regularly extend, renew, or continue credit, arrange for the extension, renewal, or continuation of credit, or participate in the decision of whether or not to extend credit.

12. Neither defendant at any time provided Plaintiff with any written documents whatsoever in connection with the credit application or its denial.

13. Neither defendant at any time provided Plaintiff with the written notification required by § 202.9(a)(2) of Regulation B.

14. As a proximate result of Defendants' violations of the Act and Regulation B, Plaintiff has suffered actual damages of $5,000 for her embarrassment, humiliation, mental distress, and inconvenience, and Defendants are liable therefor, pursuant to § 706(a) of the Act, 15 U.S.C. § 1691e(a).

15. The acts complained of herein were done by Defendants intentionally, purposefully, and/or in reckless disregard of the rights of Plaintiff.

16. Defendants are liable to Plaintiff for statutory punitive damages of $10,000, pursuant to § 706(b) of the Act, 15 U.S.C. § 1691e(b).

17. Unless Defendants are ordered to provide to Plaintiff the written notification required by law, she will continue to suffer irreparable injury for which there is no adequate remedy at law.

18. Upon information and belief, the acts complained of herein were done by Defendants as part of a pattern and practice of failing to provide the required written notice to credit applicants regarding whom adverse action has been taken.

19. Upon information and belief, Defendants maintain no procedures designed to insure that the required written notice will be provided to the class members, or such procedures which are maintained are inadequate to insure that the required notification will be provided.

20. Regarding those class members who have already had adverse action taken on their credit applications, unless Defendants are ordered to provide to them the required written notification, they will continue to suffer irreparable injury for which there is no adequate remedy at law.

21. Regarding those class members who have as yet not had adverse action taken on their credit applications, unless Defendants are ordered by this Court to undertake to establish and maintain appropriate procedures which are adequate to insure that the required written notifications are provided, they will suffer irreparable injury for which there is no adequate remedy at law.

22. Plaintiffs are entitled to be granted reasonable attorney's fees and costs, pursuant to § 706(d) of the Act, 15 U.S.C. § 1691e(d).

JURY DEMAND

Plaintiffs hereby demand trial by a jury of six (6) persons on all issues so triable.

WHEREFORE, Plaintiffs pray that this Honorable Court grant the following relief:

1. Certify this action as a class action as alleged, and so certify it and set it for hearing on the certification issue at the earliest practicable time;

2. Declare the acts and omissions of Defendants to be violative of the Act and Regulation B;

3. Award Plaintiff actual damages of $5,000;

4. Award Plaintiff statutory punitive damages of $10,000;

5. Issue an injunction (a) ordering Defendants to provide to Plaintiff and to the class members identified in paragraph 6(a) hereof the written notification required by law and (b) ordering Defendants to establish and maintain appropriate procedures adequate to insure compliance with the Act and Regulation B;

6. Award to Plaintiff and to the class members a reasonable attorney's fee;

7. Award to Plaintiff and to the class members their costs; and

8. Grant such other and further relief as may be just and proper.

Respectfully submitted,

Attorney for Plaintiffs

F.5 Sample Complaint Alleging Discriminatory Mark-Up Practices Against Automobile Financer

A team of lawyers is responsible for litigating on behalf of consumers in this ECOA auto finance race discrimination class action. The attorneys of record include Clint Watkins, Law Office of Clint W. Watkins, 5214 Maryland Way, Suite 402, Brentwood, Tenn. 37027, (615) 376-7000, fax: (615) 376-2628, cwatkins@nashvillelaw.com ; Gil Gilmore, Gilmore Law Office, 116 Court St., P.O. Box 729, Grove Hill, Ala., (334) 275-3115, fax: (334) 275-3847, wogilmore@tds.net; Michael Terry, Terry & Gore, 209 Tenth Ave. South, Suite 310, Cummins Station, Nashville, Tenn. 37203, (615) 256-5555, fax: (615) 256-5652, tglaw@home.com; Daniel L. Berger, Seth Lesser, Darnley Stewart & Leah Guggenheimer, Bernstein Litowitz Berger & Grossmann LLP, 1285 Ave. of the Americas, New York, N.Y. 10019, (212) 554-1400, fax: (212) 554-1444, dan@BLBGLAW.com, seth@BLBGLAW.com, darnley@BLBGLAW.com & leah@BLBGLAW.com; Gary Klein, Grant & Roddy, 44 School St., Boston, Mass. 02108, (617) 248-8700, fax: (617) 248-0720, klein@grantroddy.com; Stuart Rossman, National Consumer Law Center, 18 Tremont St., Boston, Mass. 02108, (617) 523-8010, fax: (617)523-7398, srossman@nclc.org.

IN THE UNITED STATES DISTRICT COURT
FOR THE MIDDLE DISTRICT OF TENNESSEE AT
NASHVILLE

BETTY T. CASON, ROBERT F. CASON, DONALD SNEAD, WANDA SNEAD, STEPHANIE A. VAUGHN, CHAWNECY D. VAUGHN, MARY CHEATHAM and CLYDE CHEATHAM on behalf of themselves and all others similarly situated	)))))))))
Plaintiffs,	) Civil No. 3-98-0223
v.	))
NISSAN MOTOR ACCEPTANCE CORPORATION,	)))
Defendant.	))

SIXTH AMENDED CLASS ACTION COMPLAINT

NOW come the Plaintiffs, Robert F. Cason, Betty T. Cason, Donald Snead, Wanda Snead, Stephanie A. Vaughn, Chawnecy D.

Vaughn, Mary Cheatham and Clyde Cheatham on behalf of themselves and all others similarly situated, and hereby sue the defendant, stating their cause of action:

I. SHORT AND PLAIN STATEMENT

This is a class action brought by plaintiffs, on behalf of themselves and other similarly situated African-Americans, against Nissan Motor Acceptance Corporation (NMAC) under the Equal Credit Opportunity Act, 15 U.S.C § 1691, *et seq.* (ECOA) to remedy the discriminatory effects of NMAC's policy and practices in providing motor vehicle financing.

NMAC has established a specific, identifiable and uniform credit pricing system, a component of which, referred to herein as the NMAC markup policy, authorizes unchecked, subjective markup of an objective risk-based financing rate. In other words, after a finance rate acceptable to NMAC is determined by objective criteria (i.e., the individual's credit history and deal circumstances), NMAC's credit pricing policy authorizes a subjective markup of that amount. NMAC policy sets the range of markup and determines which loans are subject to markup. The effect of this credit pricing policy is a widespread discriminatory impact on African-American financing applicants, in violation of ECOA. Plaintiffs seek declaratory and injunctive relief, disgorgement and restitution of monies disparately obtained from African-Americans.

II. PARTIES

1. Plaintiffs Robert F. Cason, Betty T. Cason, Donald Snead, Wanda Snead, Stephanie A. Vaughn, Chawnecy D. Vaughn, Mary Cheatham and Clyde Cheatham are African-American adult citizens and residents of Tennessee.

2. Defendant Nissan Motor Acceptance Corporation ("NMAC") is a foreign corporation with its principal place of business at 990 W. 190th Street, Torrance, California. NMAC is a corporation organized, existing, and doing business under the laws of the State of California. NMAC is a subsidiary of Nissan Motor Corporation, USA. NMAC is the American financial arm of Nissan Company, a worldwide Japanese conglomerate.

III. JURISDICTION AND VENUE

3. This Court has jurisdiction over this action and venue is proper. Defendant transacts substantial business in Tennessee, primarily the financing of automobiles, and all or part of defendant's acts alleged in this complaint occurred in the Middle District of Tennessee.

4. This action presents a disparate impact claim based on the Equal Credit Opportunity Act (ECOA), 15 USC § 1691 et seq. This Court has original jurisdiction pursuant to 28 USC § 1331 to hear claims based upon the ECOA.

IV. TERMINOLOGY

5. The following terms, as used herein, have the following meanings:

a. **Non-recourse**—"Non-recourse" means that the assignee of a loan agreement cannot require payment by the assignor in the event of the default of the obligor. In a "non-recourse" automobile finance transaction, the finance company (NMAC) bears all the risk of default and the dealer never bears any of the risk of default. After the NMAC finance forms are completed by the customer, the dealer "assigns" the NMAC agreements to NMAC and NMAC then pays the dealer the amount financed as listed on the installment agreement. If the consumer later defaults, the dealer keeps the money it received from NMAC, owes NMAC nothing and has no responsibility regarding the default. The automobile transactions that are included in the proposed class definition are all "non-recourse" transactions.

b. **Tier**—"Tiers" are categories of risk that are assigned after evaluating many factors relative to the person and the proposed purchase. NMAC began using a tier based financing system in approximately 1990. Letter designations are used. "A" tier is the most credit worthy applicant who receives the lowest available rate. "B", "C" and "D" tier customers are progressively less credit worthy and are eligible for progressively higher rates. At different times, NMAC tiers have been referred to by names, numbers and letters. Regardless of the labels given the tiers, the concept is the same, NMAC categorizes its customers by risk and establishes an appropriate risk-related finance charge rate after considering numerous individual and deal attributes. All NMAC customers are assigned a risk tier.

c. **Buy Rate**—"Buy Rate" is the minimum interest rate required by NMAC for a particular transaction. The buy rate for a particular transaction is based on the credit risk tier the customer is assigned by NMAC. Thus, the buy rate is the minimum finance charge for a particular customer after consideration of all risk related variables pertaining to the customer's purchase. The buy rate is always set by NMAC and is never set by the dealer.

d. **Rate Sheets**—"Rate Sheets" or " Dealer Bulletins" refer to the notices that NMAC periodically sends its dealers informing the dealers of the buy rate for the different tiers. In addition to informing the dealer of the buy rate for the different tiers, the rate sheets inform the dealer how much they are allowed to markup the buy rate for each particular tier.

e. **Contract APR**—"Contract APR" (Annual Percentage Rate) is the total finance charge stated as a percentage as shown on the customer's retail installment contract.

f. **Finance Charge Markup**—"Finance Charge Markup" (Markup) is the non-risk finance charge added to the buy rate. Finance charge markup is paid by the customer to NMAC, as a component of the total finance charge (Contract APR), without the customer ever knowing that a portion of their Contract APR was markup. The term "points" is sometimes used to describe markup.

g. **Maximum Markup**—"Maximum Markup" is the maximum number of percentage points that NMAC authorizes a dealer to markup a particular transaction above the risk based buy rate. NMAC sets the dealer markup limit at various amounts depending on the tier and the particular program that the individual is financing under, such as the college graduate program (1% markup limit). In some cases, NMAC does not allow the dealer to markup the buy rate at all and in some cases it allows the dealer to markup the buy rate as much as 5 points.

h. **Dealer Participation**—"Dealer Participation" or "Dealer Commission" is that portion of the markup payable to the dealer by NMAC. During the relevant time period, the dealer has received either 75% or 77% of the markup and NMAC has kept the remainder. None of the NMAC designed forms that the customers are required to sign inform the customers of the markup policy system, or about dealer participation.

i. **NMAC Participation**—"NMAC Participation" is that portion of the markup not included in "Dealer Participation." During the relevant time period, NMAC has kept either 23% or 25% of the markup and the remainder has been paid to the dealer.

V. NMAC'S STRUCTURE

6. NMAC engages in the business of financing vehicles throughout Tennessee and the United States, through dealer/agents who serve as NMAC's credit arrangers/originators. NMAC finances more than 100,000 vehicles annually, all through its dealer arrangers/originators.

7. NMAC promotes and advertises financing expertise, and simple, flexible and convenient vehicle loans which are provided by NMAC at over 1200 Nissan dealerships nationwide.

8. Consumers in Tennessee and throughout the United States are encouraged to visit Nissan dealers to obtain NMAC vehicle financing.

9. In 1991, NMAC consolidated its retail financing operations in its Dallas, Texas processing center. Out of its central processing center, NMAC provides retail financing through approximately twelve hundred (1200) Nissan dealers in the United States.

10. NMAC does not provide automobile financing outside the United States and does not finance anything except vehicles within the United States. NMAC's retail financing system is virtually identical throughout the country.

11. NMAC's buy rates, credit risk tiers, markup limits, credit worthiness requirements, credit approval process, retail installment contract forms, approval notification form, and application forms are the same throughout the United States.

12. The only differences among states involve state usury laws, which would only be applicable to cases in which NMAC's buy rate plus NMAC's maximum markup rate exceed the state usury cap. For instance, most of NMAC's business in Arkansas is Tier A (Preferred) because of the Arkansas usury law.

13. NMAC acknowledges the virtual uniformity of its retail financing system throughout the United States. Without waiving any of the foregoing objections, there are no differences between states in the way that NMAC receives credit applications, reviews and analyzes credit applications and assigns applicants to the appropriate tier, except from time to time NMAC may choose to limit the number of retail contracts it purchases in certain States. Any differences in buy rates would be limited or qualified by any usury limitations imposed by state statute. Any differences in the number of points that can be added to the buy rate for any particular tier would be dictated by usury and other consumer finance laws in any particular state. There are no differences by state in the tier structures, dealers' discretion to charge finance rates greater than NMAC's buy rate, percentage of finance charge paid to dealers or in the way dealers are paid. (NMAC's Response to Plaintiffs' Second Set of Interrogatories, Interrogatory No. 1)

VI. NMAC'S MARKETING

14. NMAC markets its automobile retail financing services to the public under the name "*Signature*FINANCING from NMAC:" When you buy or lease with *Signature*FINANCING from Nissan Motor Acceptance Corporation (NMAC), you've made a wise choice. Because with NMAC you get a partner dedicated to one business—providing lease and loan financing for Nissan vehicles. And a company committed to one goal—

exceptional customer service. *Signature*FINANCING offers attractive rates and terms, fast response, and financing that is simple, flexible, and convenient. Only for Nissan customers and only from Nissan Motor Acceptance Corporation. (NMAC Web Page, *Signature*FINANCING from NMAC)

15. In its advertising, NMAC gives consumers two options for applying for credit. For consumers who desire to obtain NMAC's *Signature*FINANCING, they are given the option of applying directly through NMAC over the internet or they are directed to apply at NMAC dealers.

16. The customers who choose to apply directly to NMAC over the internet and who are approved, are provided a list of dealerships where they can go to complete the financing process.

17. In addition to referring customers to dealers through consumer advertising, NMAC also sends letters to existing customers with good payment records, informs them that they are pre-approved for additional NMAC financing and provides them documentation of their pre-approval to take to a NMAC dealership to consummate the new finance transaction.

18. Although there are various marketing programs used by NMAC, all of NMAC's marketing programs ultimately direct consumers to NMAC's dealers for consummation of the finance transaction.

VII. NMAC'S DEALER PROGRAM

19. The contractual relationship between NMAC and its non-recourse dealers is outlined in a one page agreement titled "RETAIL PLAN-WITHOUT RECOURSE."

20. The dealer agreement incorporates by reference dealer bulletins (rate sheets) which are used periodically to convey buy rates, markup limits, dealer participation, etc.

21. The dealer bulletins make it clear that NMAC financing must be initiated by a customer completing a NMAC credit application.

22. NMAC provides credit applications, retail Installment contracts, agreements to provide insurance, co-signer agreements, corporate/partnership resolutions and warranty disclaimers to its dealer arrangers/originators, without charge.

23. NMAC provides training to its dealers through a "dealer hotline" including training related to properly filling out NMAC required forms and, when the design of the forms changes, NMAC sends people to its dealers to reprogram the dealer's computers to work with the new forms.

24. NMAC provides training to dealers, including training regarding "basic selling techniques." One of the job duties of NMAC's sales representatives is to "Assess training needs in assigned dealerships and provide appropriate training in product knowledge and basic selling techniques to dealer personnel."

VIII. STRUCTURE OF NMAC'S CREDIT PRICING SYSTEM

A. The Dealer's Role

25. In NMAC's non-recourse retail financing program, the dealer assumes the role of a credit "arranger" or credit "originator."

26. As an arranger/originator, for customers who are not pre-approved by NMAC, NMAC's non-recourse dealers submit loan applications to NMAC via fax and NMAC faxes back the credit decision to the dealer.

27. NMAC's credit decision is analyzed and communicated back to the dealer anywhere from a nanosecond to thirty (30) minutes.

28. NMAC dealers receive a credit decision on 48% of the applications within a matter of seconds and the remaining 52% average approximately a thirty (30) minute turnaround time.

29. When NMAC is closed, NMAC dealers have the option of using "*Signature*EXPRESS," a NMAC system which grants automatic approval of transactions meeting certain specified criteria.

30. The "*Signature*EXPRESS" program grants automatic approval to credit customers who have a credit bureau credit score that meets a certain criteria and assigns those customers to a credit tier based on the same credit score.

31. Dealers are allowed to add markup to "*Signature*EXPRESS" automatic approvals in the same manner as a pre-approved customer or customers approved through the credit application process.

32. Regardless of the method in which NMAC's credit approval is obtained and the credit tier assigned, the dealer's role is the same. The dealer must comply fully with NMAC's policies and limitations and must complete the NMAC credit forms properly.

33. After obtaining credit approval from NMAC, and after NMAC assigns the credit worthiness tier and the risk-related buy rate, the dealer is then permitted to add the non-risk markup.

34. In setting the markup within the rules and limitations established by NMAC, non-recourse dealers have no reason to consider whether the vehicle is new or used, the number of months being financed, credit worthiness of the customer, occupation of the customer, income of the customer, model of the vehicle being purchased, the trade-in being made or any other risk related variable. Those factors have already been considered by NMAC, who bears the risk.

35. Once an NMAC dealer obtains the customers signature on the NMAC documents, the dealer "pays itself" for the automobile with a NMAC "sight draft" which NMAC provides to the dealer and authorizes the dealer to sign.

36. The NMAC dealer plays no role whatsoever in the process of approving or declining the customer's credit application, establishing the credit risk tier of the customer, or establishing the risk based buy rate component of the contract APR.

37. The dealer's only role in setting the terms of the credit transaction is in the imposition of the non-risk markup, which must be within the parameters authorized by NMAC.

38. The controlling mechanism regarding the imposition of markup is the agreement between the finance company and the dealership. All automobile finance companies, like NMAC, have their own rules and guidelines regarding whether a dealer is allowed to add markup and the limitations thereof.

39. NMAC's "Non-Recourse Dealer Agreement" is the same throughout the United States.

B. NMAC'S Role

40. Unlike the dealer, NMAC bears the full risk of the credit transaction. As the risk-bearer, NMAC employs a sophisticated and highly automated credit analysis process designed to categorize NMAC applicants into credit risk tiers.

41. In determining the appropriate tier, NMAC considers numerous risk related variables including credit bureau histories, payment amount, payment to income ratio, debt ratio, monthly rental obligation, monthly mortgage obligation, bankruptcies, automobile repossessions, charge-offs, foreclosures, payment histo-

ries and various other risk related attributes or variables.

42. NMAC's credit evaluation process is a proprietary credit scoring procedure that was developed utilizing a computerized regression analysis after reviewing the credit reports and two years of payment history on two hundred and thirty thousand (230,000) NMAC accounts.

43. NMAC's risk tier assignment process is an objective and automated credit scoring process.

44. NMAC touts its objective and automated tier assignment system as being "unbiased."

45. NMAC is also aware that a purely judgmental system is "more apt to be influenced by bias."

46. Despite recognizing the virtues of an objective based credit pricing system and the corresponding perils of a purely judgmental system, NMAC authorizes, provides incentives for and shares in the profits of the totally subjective markup policy.

47. If a dealer doesn't markup the buy rate, NMAC pays the dealer $100.00 to $150.00 out of the buy rate portion of the finance charge to the dealer as compensation for its role in packaging the finance transaction.

48. By providing the dealer an incentive to markup the buy rate, NMAC not only can keep for itself 23%–25% of the markup, but can keep the entire buy rate portion of the finance charge, undiminished by the dealer's $100.00–$150.00 flat rate compensation.

49. NMAC's credit pricing system empowers NMAC's dealer arrangers/originators to subjectively raise rates at will and rewards the dealer arranger/originators and NMAC for doing so.

50. NMAC, by providing a lucrative enticement to its dealers, obtains benefits from even the dealer participation component of markup which promotes dealer "referrals".

51. The markup policy destroys the objective and non-bias qualities of the automated risk tier system and results in a discriminatory credit pricing system.

52. Although NMAC has a practice of soliciting credit applications direct from the public over the internet, advertising and promoting its "attractive rates and terms" throughout the country, pre-approving existing customers for additional NMAC financing, requiring all customers to apply for credit via a NMAC credit application, and requiring all customers to execute a NMAC retail installment contract, it stringently enforces a company policy forbidding disclosure of the actual risk based rate to the customers.

53. None of the NMAC documents that finance customers are required to sign disclose the buy rate or the existence of the markup policy.

54. In 1997, Mr. and Mrs. Cason's counsel wrote NMAC and inquired as to whether any portion of the 19.49% rate was kicked back or rebated to the dealer. At the time of the inquiry, neither Mr. or Mrs. Cason nor any representative of Mr. and Mrs. Cason, knew whether or not Mr. and Mrs. Cason's 19.49% rate was equal to or in excess of NMAC's required rate. The letter asked the following questions:

1. How was the finance charge that Mr. and Ms. Cason were required to pay determined?

2. Who made the determination regarding the finance charge rate that Mr. and Ms. Cason were required to pay?

3. Is any of the finance charge that Mr. and Ms. Cason are paying being "shared" or "rebated" in any manner to any other person or entity?

4. If any of the finance charge that Mr. and Ms. Cason are paying is being "kicked back" or "rebated", or will be in the future, to

any other person or entity, please inform me what portion of the finance charge is being "kicked back" or "rebated."

55. NMAC's Legal Compliance Office responded, but refused to acknowledge that the markup policy even existed and reported that NMAC's only involvement in Mr. and Ms. Cason's transaction was as a detached after the fact purchaser of the note. "With regard to your questions concerning finance charges, the interest rate or finance charge is based on a number of factors, including credit-worthiness of the customer. NMAC does not disclose information regarding the contractual and business relationship between NMAC and authorized independent Nissan dealerships. NMAC is a financing entity only, and as such, is not privy to the negotiations between the customer and the dealer. We merely purchase, or are an assignee of, the contract. However, in any event, Mr. and Ms. Cason signed the contract agreeing to that interest rate."

56. NMAC's position regarding its involvement in automobile financing, as communicated by its Legal Compliance Office, is starkly different than the image broadcast to the public through brochures, radio, television, newspaper and various other print advertisements. NMAC presents to the world, through its world wide web site, a very involved and active image:

> Three million satisfied NMAC customers are proof positive that we not only provide the funds for their dreams, but that we're also there to answer questions, respond to inquiries, and give unsurpassed customer service. The kind of service that keeps satisfied customers coming back to NMAC again and again.

> At NMAC, we have the financing expertise you expect. We provide Nissan shoppers like you with simple, flexible and convenient loans and leases at more than 1,100 Nissan dealerships nationwide.

> So visit your Nissan dealer soon. Nissan is ready to help you turn a promising test drive into a long and very rewarding journey.

57. NMAC controls and/or influences every aspect of the dealer originated finance program by:

a. Requiring and providing specific NMAC forms to be used and training dealers regarding how to complete the NMAC required finance forms;

b. Evaluating the credit worthiness of each customer and assigning each to a credit risk tier;

c. Establishing the buy rate for each finance transaction based on the risk based tier assignment;

d. Providing a financial incentive for the dealership to add subjective non-risk charges (finance charge markup) to the risk based buy rate which rewards both the dealer and NMAC;

e. Establishing the maximum markup rate for each finance transaction;

f. Determining which loans are subject to markup;

g. Programming dealer's computers to utilize NMAC forms and training its dealers regarding "basic training techniques"; and

h. Establishing the "Dealer Participation" and "NMAC Participation" split for each transaction, which divides the markup between the dealer and NMAC.

IX. NMAC'S ECOA AWARENESS AND FAILURE TO COMPLY

58. The financial industry, including NMAC, has been put on notice for years that commission driven discretionary pricing systems in the real estate mortgage industry, like the system utilized by NMAC, produce significant discriminatory effects.

59. Unlike the real estate mortgage industry, which is required by federal law to collect race information, the automobile financing industry exploits its exemption from gathering race information for ECOA compliance monitoring purposes in order to feign ignorance of the discriminatory impact of its discretionary pricing systems.

60. NMAC has analyzed its data and confirmed the discriminatory effects of its commission driven discretionary pricing system and chosen to ignore and conceal the discriminatory impact.

61. Notice of the discriminatory effect of its commission driven discretionary pricing system, which NMAC has known for years, was distributed throughout the financing and banking industry as a result of legal proceedings by the United States Department of Justice involving similar commission driven discretionary pricing systems in the real estate mortgage industry, including:

a. *United States v. First National Bank of Vicksburg*, No. 5:94 CV 6(B)(N) (S.D. Miss. filed Jan. 21, 1994) (charging African-Americans higher interest rates);

b. *United States v. Blackpipe State Bank*, Civ. Act. No. 93-5115 (D. S.D. filed November 16, 1993) (charging American Indians higher interest rates);

c. *United States v. Huntington Mortgage Co.*, No. 1; 95 CV 2211 (N.D. Ohio filed October 18, 1995) (charging African-Americans higher fees);

d. *United States v. Security State Bank of Pecos*, No. SA 95 CA 0996 (W.D.Tex. filed October 15, 1995) (charging Hispanics higher interest rates);

e. *United States v. First National Bank of Gordon*, No. CIV-96-5035 (W.D.S.D. filed April 15, 1996) (charging American Indians higher interest rates);

f. *United States v. Fleet Mortgage Corp.*, No. 96-2279 (E.D.N.Y. filed May 7, 1996) (charging African-Americans and Hispanics higher interest rates); and

g. *United States v. Long Beach Mortgage Co.*, No. CV-96-6159 (C.D. Cal. filed Sept. 5, 1996) (charging African-Americans, Latinos, women and persons over age 55 higher interest rates).

62. Notice of the discriminatory effect of its commission driven subjective pricing was also distributed throughout the automobile financing and banking industries as a result of a plethora of articles in trade journals following the United States Department of Justice legal proceedings, including:

Two Banks To Pay Damages Following Justice Probes Into Lending Discrimination, Department of Justice Press Release 94-027 (Jan. 21, 1994).

Steve Cocheo, *Justice Department Sues Tiny South Dakota Bank for Loan Bias*, ABA Banking J., Jan. 1994, at 6.

Miles Maguire, *Blackpipe Case; Banker Charged With Bias Called Friend of the Sioux*, Reg. Compliance Watch, Apr. 18, 1994, at 1.

Steve Cocheo, *Can Banks Lend in Indian Country?*, ABA Banking J., May 1994, at 42.

Jaret Seiberg, *Maryland Thrift In Settlement with Justice Department*, Am. Banker, Aug. 23, 1994, at 1.

Holly Boss, *Chevy Chase Federal Reaches $11 Million Pact,*

Wall St.J., Aug. 23, 1994, at A2.

Michelle Singletary, *Who's Next After Chevy Chase?*, Wash. Post, Aug. 26, 1994, at B1.

Jaret Seiberg, *Industry Sees Dangerous Extension Of Bias for Discrimination Complaints,* Am. Banker, Aug. 23, 1994, at 4.

Chevy Chase Settlement, Wash. Post, Aug. 23, 1994, at A18.

Chicago Area Lender Agrees with Justice Department to Settle Lending Discrimination Claims, Department of Justice Press Release 95-306 (June 1, 1995).

Justin Fox, *Northern Trust Settles U.S. Suit by Agreeing to Pay Minorities*, Am. Banker, June 2, 1995, at 2.

Ohio Mortgage Company Agrees to Compensate African Americans Charged Higher Prices for Home Mortgages than Whites, Department of Justice Press Release 95-540 (October 18, 1995).

Kenneth R. Harney, *Lender Agrees to Settle Suit on Hidden Fees*, L.A. Times, July 7, 1996, at 1.

Ford Finance Settles in Broker Fee Litigation, Mortgage Marketplace, July 8, 1996, at 4.

Ford Files Settlement in Case Involving Broker Overages, Inside Fair Lending, Sept. 1996, at 9.

Stephen Phillips, *Lenders Likely to Review Policies*, Plain Dealer, Oct. 20, 1995, at 1C.

Edward Hulkosky, *HUD Cracks Down on High-Cost FHA Loans*, Am. Banker, Oct. 20, 1994, at 13.

Jaret Seiberg, *Huntington's Loan Bias Settlement with Justice Department Stirs Debate*, Am. Banker, Oct. 25, 1995, at 1.

Texas Banks to Pay $500,000 for Charging Hispanic Borrowers Higher Interest Rates than Equally Qualified Non-Hispanics, Department of Justice Press Release 95-541 (Oct. 18, 1995).

Justice Department Sues Nebraska Bank for Allegedly Charging Native Americans Higher Interest Rates, Department of Justice Press Release 96-165 (Apr. 15, 1996).

Nebraska Bank Nailed for Illegal Pricing, Regulatory Compliance Watch, Apr. 22, 1996, at 1.

Fleet Subsidiary To Pay $4 Million to Settle Claims that Blacks and Hispanics Were Charged Higher Loan Prices than Whites, Department of Justice Press Release 96-211 (May 7, 1996).

Kimberly Blanton, *Fleet Mortgage Settles Loan Bias Suit; Will Pay $4M to Minority Customers, End Justice Probe*, Boston Globe, May 8, 1996, at 33.

Long Beach Lender to Pay $3 Million for Allegedly Charging Higher Rates to African Americans, Hispanics, Women and the Elderly, Department of Justice Press Release 96-429 (Sept. 5, 1996).

Jaret Seiberg, *Calif. Lender Paying $4M To Settle U.S. Bias Charges*, Am. Banker, Sept. 6, 1996, at 1.

James S. Granelli, *U.S. Settles with Lender Accused of Overcharging*, L.A. Times, Sept. 6, 1996, at D1.

Kenneth Harney, *Justice Settlement Finds Not all Loan Fees Equal*, Newsday, Sept. 13, 1996, at D2.

63. NMAC does not train its staff regarding ECOA compliance related to credit pricing, does not have anyone assigned to ensure ECOA compliance related to credit pricing, does not engage in ECOA self audits, does not audit its dealer arrangers-originators, does not provide any ECOA training to its dealer arrangers-originators and does not provide any information to its dealer arrangers-originators regarding ECOA credit pricing requirements.

64. Despite clear and unequivocal notice of the unfair and discriminatory impact of a commission driven subjective pricing system, NMAC has continued its discriminatory credit pricing system and has done nothing to monitor or prevent the discriminatory impact of the system.

X. SUMMARY OF NMAC'S RETAIL FINANCE SYSTEM

65. NMAC's retail finance system, one component of which is the finance charge markup policy, can be summarized as follows:

a. Under NMAC's retail finance system, the finance charges that result from the buy rate portion of the contract APR are credit risk based charges that NMAC deems to be appropriate for the particular individual, after analyzing all individual deal and buyer variables.

b. The finance charges that result from the finance charge markup portion of the contract A.P.R. pursuant to NMAC's markup policy are totally subjective non credit risk related charges.

c. Incentives are built into the NMAC finance charge system to encourage imposition of the subjective non risk related charges. NMAC as well as NMAC's dealer's employees, management and owners profit from the imposition of subjective, non risk related charges.

d. NMAC determines the range of allowable markup and which loans are subject to markup;

e. NMAC maintains no monitoring, training or other compliance components to prevent illegal discriminatory impact, despite overwhelming recognition throughout the credit industry of the dangers associated with subjective pricing systems in a commission driven environment.

f. NMAC's finance customers pay all of their contract finance charges, including the portion resulting from the finance charge markup, directly to NMAC.

g. None of the NMAC required finance forms inform the customers that they were charged more than their eligible buy rate and do not inform them their actual contract APR was manipulated by the dealer pursuant to NMAC's markup policy.

XI. ROBERT F. AND BETTY T. CASON

66. Robert and Betty Cason are married African-Americans. Mr. Cason is a retired metro bus driver and Mrs. Cason provides care for disadvantaged children. In August, 1995, Mrs. Betty Cason went to Action Nissan in Nashville, Tennessee for the purpose of buying an automobile.

67. Action Nissan is an authorized Nissan dealer and an agent for NMAC. Action Nissan regularly advertises and sells Nissan products and is an arranger/originator of NMAC financing.

68. On or about August 25, 1995, Mr. and Mrs. Cason applied for credit with NMAC by completing a NMAC credit application which bore a prominent Nissan Motor Acceptance Corporation logo and which had been provided to Action Nissan by NMAC for purposes of assisting Action in arranging/originating consumer finance transactions on behalf of NMAC. The NMAC application which Mr. and Mrs. Cason completed was given to them by an Action Nissan employee who provided the NMAC application with the authority and approval of NMAC.

69. On or after August 25, 1995, Action Nissan faxed Mr. and Mrs. Cason's NMAC application to NMAC in accordance with the standard business practice of NMAC and its affiliated dealers.

NMAC reviewed Mr. and Mrs. Cason's application, performed a risk analysis by considering all risk related variables NMAC deemed appropriate, and determined that Mr. and Mrs. Cason were a "SPL tier" credit risk.

70. After performing its risk evaluation and determining which credit risk tier Mr. and Mrs. Cason were eligible for, NMAC faxed Action Nissan an authorization indicating that Mr. and Mrs. Cason were eligible for NMAC financing at "SPL tier".

71. By referring to NMAC's current rate sheet, Action Nissan was able to determine that Mr. and Mrs. Cason were eligible for NMAC financing at 16.49%. By referring to the same NMAC rate sheet, Action Nissan was also able to determine that NMAC had authorized Action to markup the interest rate to a maximum of 19.49% [3 points].

72. NMAC's arranger/originator, Action Nissan, also presented Mr. and Mrs. Cason with a retail installment contract which prominently bore the Nissan Motor Acceptance Corporation logo and which had been provided to Action Nissan by NMAC for purposes of assisting Action in arranging/originating NMAC consumer finance transactions.

73. The NMAC retail installment contract which Mr. and Mrs. Cason signed was given to them by an Action Nissan employee who was acting with the authority and approval of NMAC. Mr. and Mrs. Cason agreed to a price of $24,292.00, and traded a 1990 Chevrolet Blazer as down payment.

74. Mr. and Mrs. Cason were presented documents by Action Nissan which indicated they were being financed through NMAC. Mr. and Mrs. Cason agreed to a six year financing plan, which involved $20,099.06 in finance charges, and a total sales price of $50,388.67.

75. The documents presented to Mr. and Mrs. Cason represented that the financing documents were prepared by an authorized representative of NMAC, using NMAC documents, at NMAC's rate and under terms set by NMAC. For example,

a. The application that Mr. and Mrs. Cason completed in order to apply for financing bore a prominent NMAC logo.

b. The retail installment contract had the name "Nissan Motor Acceptance Corporation" and the NMAC logo imprinted in bold at the top of the retail installment contract.

c. The certificate of insurance had the name "Nissan Motor Acceptance Corporation, P.O. Box 660368, Dallas, TX 75266-0368" typed in the block labeled "Creditor".

76. The contract APR [19.49%] on the NMAC retail installment contract was actually a combination of NMAC's required risk based buy rate [16.49%] and a totally subjective finance charge markup [3%], added pursuant to NMAC's credit pricing system.

77. Instead of getting a standard and competitive rate from a large national company based on their credit risk tier, Mr. and Mrs. Cason received a significantly higher rate as a result of the undisclosed markup. In accordance with the standard method of operation employed to affect the unfair, deceptive, and discriminatory scheme, none of the various documents informed Mr. and Mrs. Cason that:

a. The rate printed on the contract titled "Nissan Motor Acceptance Corporation" was a negotiable rate, not a required rate based on NMAC's evaluation of their credit risk.

b. The 19.49% rate typed on the contract titled "Nissan Motor Acceptance Corporation" was in fact a subjective rate manipulated by Action Nissan, pursuant to NMAC's credit pricing policies and with the express approval of NMAC;

c. The 19.49% rate was not required by NMAC as a condition of financing.

d. Mr. and Mrs. Cason were eligible for financing through NMAC at 16.49 %, a rate that was 3% points lower than the 19.49% rate on the NMAC contract that was presented to Mr. and Mrs. Cason. [The difference between 16.49% and 19.49% resulted in $3,504.24 in additional finance charges.]

e. The lower risk based buy rate (16.49%) had been secretly communicated to Action Nissan by NMAC in order to disguise the non-risk related charges imposed by Action Nissan pursuant to NMAC's credit pricing policies.

f. There was an agreement between NMAC and Action Nissan that gave Action Nissan a large financial incentive to present Mr. and Mrs. Cason with a contract bearing the name of "Nissan Motor Acceptance Corporation" but with a higher rate than actually required by NMAC, or required by credit risk analysis.

78. Pursuant to the undisclosed agreement between NMAC and Action Nissan, NMAC kept 25% of the finance charge markup ($876.06—NMAC Participation) and wrote a $2,628.18 check to Action Nissan for 75% (Dealer Participation).

79. The credit pricing system employed by NMAC caused Mr. and Mrs. Cason, and other African-Americans, to pay higher markup than similarly situated white persons. The additional markup charges imposed on African-Americans were totally unrelated to credit risk factors.

XII. DONALD AND WANDA SNEAD

80. In August 2000 Donald and Wanda Snead went to Jim Johnson Nissan in Bowling Green, Kentucky for the purpose of buying an automobile. Donald and Wanda Snead are married African-Americans. Mr Snead is an educator and Mrs. Snead is employed in medical research.

81. Jim Johnson Nissan is an agent for NMAC and is authorized by NMAC to arrange/originate automobile financing transactions on behalf of NMAC.

82. Donald and Wanda Snead had previously leased a vehicle from NMAC and had been informed by NMAC that as valued customers they would be approved for financing a vehicle. At Jim Johnson Nissan, the Sneads applied for credit with NMAC.

83. Based on a comprehensive credit risk assessment, NMAC determined that the Sneads were entitled to risk-based credit at 9.75%. NMAC communicated to Jim Johnson Nissan that the Sneads were eligible to purchase the 1997 Nissan pick-up truck at a credit risk-based rate of 9.75%.

84. Pursuant to NMAC's credit pricing policy, NMAC authorized Jim Johnson Nissan to subjectively mark up the Snead's buy rate of 9.75% without disclosing either the buy rate or the markup to the Sneads. Acting pursuant to NMAC's credit pricing policy, Jim Johnson Nissan charged the Sneads a contract APR of 12.75%, adding three points of non-disclosed subjective finance charge markup. The undisclosed markup increased the Sneads' cost of credit by approximately 34%. The entire markup was paid by the Sneads to NMAC.

XIII. STEPHANIE A. VAUGHN and CHAWNECY D. VAUGHN

85. January 1996, Stephanie A. Vaughn went to Action Nissan in Nashville, Tennessee for the purpose of buying an automobile.

86. Action Nissan is an agent for NMAC and is authorized by

NMAC to arrange/originate automobile financing transactions on behalf of NMAC.

87. While at Action Nissan, Ms. Vaughn applied for credit with NMAC. Chawnecy D. Vaughn, her husband, applied as a co-buyer.

88. Based on a comprehensive credit risk assessment, NMAC determined that the Vaughns, both African-Americans, were a "Preferred Marquee" credit risk, the highest rating assigned to any NMAC customer.

89. Pursuant to NMAC's credit pricing policy, the Vaughns were entitled to a "Preferred Marquee" tier rate (8.99%), subject to the addition of a subjective markup which NMAC authorized Action Nissan to add.

90. Pursuant to NMAC's credit pricing policy, the Vaughns were charged a risk-related finance charge of $9560.63 plus a discretionary finance charge mark-up of $2115.36, for a total finance charge of $11,675.99 (10.79% APR).

91. The undisclosed markup increased the Vaughns' cost of credit by more than 22% and the entire markup was paid by the Vaughns to NMAC.

XIV. MARY AND CLYDE CHEATHAM

92. Mary and Clyde Cheatham are retired married African-Americans living on fixed incomes in Jackson, Tennessee. In February 2000, two years after this lawsuit was filed, the Cheathams agreed to purchase a 1996 Chevrolet Lumina from Carlock Nissan in Jackson, Tennessee.

93. Carlock Nissan is an agent for NMAC and is authorized by NMAC to arrange/originate automobile financing transactions on behalf of NMAC. At Carlock Nissan, the Cheathams applied for credit with NMAC. Based on a comprehensive credit risk assessment, NMAC determined that the Cheathams were in credit tier BC1 and entitled to a risk based buy rate of 9.75%. NMAC communicated the 9.75% buy rate to Carlock Nissan after a complete and objective evaluation of the Cheathams credit worthiness.

94. Pursuant to NMAC's credit pricing policy, Carlock Nissan added three points of undisclosed subjective markup to the buy rate resulting in a contract APR of 12.75%.

95. The undisclosed finance charge markup increased the Cheathams' cost of credit by approximately 33% and the entire markup was paid by the Cheathams to NMAC.

XV. 1998 ACTION NISSAN STUDY

96. In 1998, a sample of Action Nissan data confirmed the discriminatory impact of NMAC's commission driven credit pricing system. The 1998 statistical sample of data involved only transactions consummated in 1995, the same year Mr. and Mrs. Cason purchased their automobile from Action Nissan. All sampled transactions were originated in Nashville, Tennessee at Action Nissan, where Mr. and Mrs. Cason purchased their automobile.

97. The finance charge markups in the sampled transactions were not risk based charges.

98. The sampled transactions indicated that transactions involving white consumers included, on average, an undisclosed finance charge markup of $621.21 per contract.

99. The sampled transactions indicated that transactions involving African Americans included, on average, an undisclosed finance charge markup of $1,004.33 per contract. The additional

average non-risk related markup to African-Americans over and above the amount charged to white consumers, was $383.12 per contract and is not a legally justifiable disparity.

100. The sampled transactions indicated that African Americans and other minorities, on average, were charged 63% more in finance charge markup than similarly situated white persons.

XVI. THE 1999 NMAC TENNESSEE STUDY

101. In August, 1999, pursuant to a court order, NMAC produced electronic data containing all finance transactions originated by its thirty-five (35) Tennessee dealer arrangers/originators between January 1, 1995 and December 31, 1998. The court ordered data production was limited to data maintained in NMAC's active database. The data produced consisted of 12,826 finance accounts.

102. A portion of the 12,826 finance accounts were "race coded" in order to perform a statistical analysis of the incidence of finance charge markup and the mean (average) markup by race.

103. Approximately 10,000 of the accounts were "race coded" using information obtained from the Tennessee Department of Safety drivers license files, representing approximately 75% of all accounts.

104. Of the accounts that were "race coded", there were 7,605 with white primary buyers and 1,792 with African-American primary buyers.

105. The 7,605 transactions involving a white consumer as the primary buyer averaged markup of $507.94 per contract.

106. The 1,792 transactions involving an African American consumer as the primary buyer averaged markup of $969.91 per contract. The average markup charged to African Americans exceeded the average to white consumers by $461.97 per contract and is not a legally justifiable disparity.

107. African-Americans, on average, were charged 90.9% more in finance charge markup than white persons.

108. Statistical analysis of the incidence (frequency) of markup indicated African Americans are 268% more likely to experience finance charge markups than white persons. Further, analysis of this data concluded that the NMAC markup policy results in actual overages fifteen (15) standard deviations greater than the expected incidence of overages.

XVII. THE 2001 NMAC NATIONAL STUDY

109. In 2001 NMAC produced a file containing 1.1 million nationwide records of NMAC financing transactions from March 1993 to September 2000.

110. Of those transactions, 310,718 were race-coded as being black or white by CLC Compliance Technologies, Inc. through driver license data obtained from various state motor vehicles departments in the United States.

111. Plaintiffs' statistical experts analyzed the race-coded data to determine whether or not there is evidence of a disparate impact on black customers of NMAC in that they pay a higher markup than similarly situated whites.

112. The analyses found that 71.8% of black borrowers are charged a markup, as compared to 46.7% of white borrowers.

113. The incidence of a black borrower receiving a positive markup is almost three times greater (2.89) than the white incidence of receiving a markup.

114. In addition, nationally, black borrowers on average pay

more than twice the markup paid by whites: $970 versus $462, a difference of $508.

115. Black borrowers whose financing contracts are marked up are charged on average $1351 compared to $989 for whites, a difference of $362.

116. These racial disparities are highly statistically significant as the difference between the "expected" and "actual" chance of an African-American being marked up exceeds the standard deviation by 99.0 times.

117. Accounting for the fact that NMAC's markup policy permits dealers to move customers across different interest rate categories results in even larger racial disparities.

118. These findings are consistent across 33 states where sufficient data exists to draw valid statistical inferences.

119. The national statistical analysis revealed that white NMAC customers are three times more likely than blacks (27.8% v. 9.2%) to borrow at a negative markup.

120. The fact that more than half of white borrowers pay no markup at all is partially attributable to the NMAC credit pricing of special APR programs which restrict or prohibit markup in transactions that disproportionately go to white customers.

XVIII. ONE EXAMPLE

121. An egregious example of the subjective imposition of markup occurred to a young African-American couple, known herein as John and Jane Doe.

122. On July 26, 1995, John and Jane Doe financed an automobile through NMAC. The arranger/originator was a Memphis, Tennessee NMAC dealer operating under the standard non-recourse NMAC plan.

123. NMAC analyzed the credit worthiness of John and Jane Doe, which included consideration of the numerous individual and deal variables, and concluded that the appropriate risk based buy rate for John and Jane Doe was 10.9%.

124. NMAC's arranger/originator, operating within the rules and guidelines of NMAC's markup policy added a finance charge markup of 5.0 percentage points, resulting in a markup of $6,555.32.

125. Of the $6,555.32 in markup, $4,982.04 was paid to NMAC's arranger/originator (dealer participation) and the remaining $1,573.28 was kept by NMAC (NMAC participation).

126. There are thousands of examples within the NMAC data in which the markup exceeds one thousand dollars ($1,000.00).

127. Although egregious examples of markup involve both minorities and non-minorities, the negative impact of the markup policy is borne disproportionately by minorities.

XIX. EQUAL CREDIT OPPORTUNITY ACT

128. Plaintiffs incorporate herein all other allegations contained in the complaint.

129. NMAC is a creditor as defined in Regulation B, Section 202.2(l) of the Equal Credit Opportunity Act.

130. NMAC, in the ordinary course of its business, participated in every decision of whether or not to extend credit to the proposed class representatives and all prospective class members.

131. NMAC, at all times relevant to this complaint, was fully aware of the policy and practice that resulted in the discrimination described herein and, in fact, designed, controlled, implemented and profited from the discriminatory policy and practice, referred to herein as the NMAC markup policy.

132. NMAC is a creditor as defined in Regulation B, Section 202.2(l), in the capacity of a lender, in that all discriminatory actions that were taken by NMAC dealers were in accordance with the specific authority granted to the NMAC dealers by NMAC, all discriminatory actions were implemented using various forms and documents provided by NMAC to the NMAC dealers, all discriminatory actions were taken in furtherance of NMAC's goals and objectives and all discriminatory actions financially benefitted NMAC.

133. NMAC delegated to the NMAC dealers the authority to markup finance charges without regard to credit risk factors pursuant to the NMAC markup policy which resulted in unlawful discrimination.

134. All actions taken by NMAC dealers are attributable to NMAC under agency principles based on the doctrines of express authority and apparent authority.

135. NMAC is a creditor as defined in Regulation B, Section 202.2(l), in the capacity of an assignee, since NMAC, in the ordinary course of its business, participated in every decision of whether or not to extend credit to the class representatives and all class members.

136. NMAC dealer arrangers/originators are creditors as defined in Regulation B, Section 202.2(l) in that NMAC dealers, "in the ordinary course of business, regularly refers applicants or prospective applicants to creditors, or selects or offers to select creditors to whom requests for credit may be made."

137. NMAC is liable for any and all ECOA violations committed by NMAC dealers as the assignee of the NMAC dealers. All NMAC retail installment contracts, which were designed and paid for by NMAC, for all dates relevant to this lawsuit, contained the following clause as required by the Federal Trade Commission Holder Rule, 16 CFR Ch. 1, Part 433. (1-1-98) Edition: NOTICE: ANY HOLDER OF THIS CONSUMER CREDIT CONTRACT IS SUBJECT TO ALL CLAIMS AND DEFENSES WHICH THE DEBTOR COULD ASSERT AGAINST THE SELLER OF GOODS OR SERVICES OBTAINED PURSUANT HERETO OR WITH THE PROCEEDS HEREOF. RECOVERY HEREUNDER BY THE DEBTOR SHALL NOT EXCEED AMOUNTS PAID BY THE DEBTOR HEREUNDER.

138. The discriminatory charges that were charged to plaintiffs and the class members arose directly from "credit transactions" as defined in Regulation B, Section 202.2(m).

139. The discretionary charges that resulted from the NMAC markup policy were over and above the finance charge that class representatives and class members were eligible for based on their credit risk rating.

140. The average of the discretionary non-risk related charges imposed class representatives and other African-Americans pursuant to the NMAC markup policy were significantly greater than the average discretionary non-risk related charges imposed on white consumers.

141. The disparities between the terms of the credit transactions involving African Americans and the terms involving white consumers could not have occurred by chance and cannot be explained by factors unrelated to race.

142. NMAC's policies and practices, as described herein, constitute:

a. A pattern or practice of resistance to the full enjoyment of rights secured by the Equal Credit Opportunity Act, 15 U.S.C. §§ 1691-1691f; and

b. Discrimination against applicants with respect to credit transactions, on the basis of race or national origin in violation of the Equal Credit Opportunity Act, 15 U.S.C. § 1691(a)(1) and Regulation B, § 202.4.

143. Plaintiffs and prospective class members are aggrieved persons as defined in the Equal Credit Opportunity Act and have been disadvantaged as a result of NMAC's credit pricing policy.

144. Plaintiffs, on their behalf, and on behalf of all persons similarly situated, sue NMAC pursuant to the ECOA, seeking appropriate class certification, and appropriate equitable and injunctive relief.

XX. ECOA PROOF ANALYSIS—DISPARATE IMPACT

145. Plaintiffs allege that NMAC'S credit pricing policy, although facially neutral, has a disproportionately negative effect on African-Americans and other minorities.

146. Pursuant to a disparate impact analysis, the plaintiffs specifically allege:

a. The specific facially neutral NMAC practice that the plaintiffs are challenging is NMAC's markup policy, a component of NMAC's credit pricing system.

b. The disparity between the frequency and the amount of markup imposed on African Americans and that charged similarly situated white persons indicates a clear causal connection between the markup policy and the discriminatory result;

c. The disparities that exist are consistently evidenced by a statistical review of adequate, competent and relevant data sets.

d. There are no legitimate business reasons to justify NMAC's discriminatory markup policy that could not be achieved by a practice that has a far less discriminatory impact.

XXI. CLASS ACTION ALLEGATIONS

147. Plaintiffs bring this action on behalf of themselves and all other similarly situated persons. Pursuant to Rule 23 of the Federal Rules of Civil Procedure, plaintiffs seek to represent and seek certification of the following class:

Class Definition—All African-American consumers who obtained vehicle financing from NMAC in the United States pursuant to NMAC's "retail plan—without recourse," between January 1, 1990 and the date of judgement.

148. The requirements of Rule 23(a), 23(b)(2) and 23(b)(3) of the Federal Rules of Civil Procedure have been met in that:

a. **Rule 23(a)(1) Numerosity**—Plaintiffs do not know the exact size of the proposed class, since such information is in the exclusive control of defendant. Based on discovery, the nature of the commerce involved, and NMAC publications, plaintiffs believe that the proposed class members exceed 125,000. The members of the proposed class are geographically disbursed throughout the United States so that joinder of all members would be impracticable.

b. **Rule 23(a)(2) Commonality**—All of the legal and factual issues in this class action are common to each proposed class member:

(1) Whether NMAC's credit pricing policy system is a facially neutral system that has effected racial discrimination in violation of the Equal Credit Opportunity Act?

(2) Whether there are disparities between the frequency and

the amount of finance charge markup imposed on African Americans and the frequency and amount of the finance charge markup imposed on white persons of equal credit worthiness?

(3) If there is a disparity in finance charge markup, is it statistically significant enough to indicate a causal connection between the NMAC markup policy and the discriminatory result?

(4) If there is a disparity in finance charge markup, is it demonstrated by statistical evidence from an adequate, competent and relevant data set?

(5) If there is a disparity, is there a legitimate business reason to justify NMAC's markup policy that could not be achieved by a practice that has a less disparate impact?

c. **Rule 23(a)(3) Typicality**—Plaintiffs' claims are typical of the proposed class members' claims. Class representatives are (1) African-Americans who obtained vehicle financing from NMAC during the class period; and (2) were and are subject to NMAC's markup policy.

d. **Rule 23(a)(4) Adequacy of Representation**—Plaintiffs can and will fairly and adequately represent and protect the interest of the proposed class, and have no interest that conflicts with or is antagonistic to the interest of the proposed class. Plaintiffs have employed attorneys who are experienced, competent and able to adequately and vigorously pursue this class action claim. No conflict exists between plaintiffs and proposed class members because:

i. the claim of the named plaintiffs are typical of the proposed class members;

ii. all the questions of law and fact regarding the liability of the defendant are common to the proposed class, and overwhelmingly predominate over any individual issues that may exist, such that by prevailing on their own claim, plaintiffs necessarily will establish defendant's liability to all proposed class members;

iii. without the representation provided by plaintiffs, virtually no proposed class member would receive legal redress or representation for their injuries because of the small value of the individual claims and because of the burden of proving a disparate impact claim;

iv. plaintiffs and their counsel have the necessary legal support, financial and technological resources to adequately and vigorously litigate this class action, and the plaintiffs and counsel are aware of their fiduciary responsibilities to the proposed class members, and are determined to diligently discharge those duties by vigorously seeking the maximum recovery for the proposed class.

149. **Rule 23(b)(2)**—Certification is appropriate under Rule 23 of the Federal Rules of Civil Procedure because defendants have acted on grounds generally applicable to the proposed classes, thereby making appropriate final injunctive relief or corresponding declaratory relief with respect to the class as a whole. Plaintiffs seek to obtain declaratory and injunctive relief requiring NMAC to implement company policies designed to prevent the illegal discrimination described herein. The plaintiffs are requesting injunctive relief restricting or prohibiting subjective markup, requiring ECOA training of NMAC employees; requiring NMAC to provide ECOA training for its dealer arrangers/originators; and requiring ECOA monitoring to ensure an end to the discriminatory impact of the markup. If NMAC's credit pricing system is declared to be in

violation of the ECOA, any restitutionary relief could be calculated by automated and objective means and would be a part of and flow directly from the injunctive or declaratory relief . The injunctive or declaratory relief is clearly predominant.

150. **Rule 23(b)(3)**—A class action is a superior procedural vehicle for the fair and efficient adjudication of the claims asserted herein given that:

a. Common questions of law and fact overwhelmingly predominate over any individual questions that may arise, such that there would be enormous economies to the courts and the parties in litigating the common issues on a class wide instead of a repetitive individual basis. Since the plaintiffs' proof of discrimination pursuant to the ECOA claim will be based on a disparate impact analysis, the proof is the same for every class member. The proof under a disparate impact analysis is based on proving a facially neutral practice's disproportionately negative impact on minorities as compared to white persons, using relevant data and a competent statistical analysis, not based on what happened to any individual.

b. The size of a proposed class members individual restitutionary claim is too small to make individual litigation an economically viable alternative, because of the enormity of the opposition and the difficult problems in amassing statistical proof of discrimination, such that few proposed class members would have any interest in individually controlling the prosecution of separate actions;

c. Class treatment is required for optimal deterrent and compensation and for limiting the court awarded reasonable legal expenses incurred by proposed class members;

d. Despite the relatively small size of individual claims, their aggregate volume, coupled with the economies of scale inherent in litigating similar claims on a common basis, will enable this case to be litigated as a class action on a cost effective basis, especially when compared with repetitive individual litigation;

e. No unusual difficulties likely would be encountered in the management of this class in that all questions of law or fact to be litigated at the liability stage are common to the class and all restitutionary relief issues are concomitant with the liability findings which can be calculated by automated and objective means.

XXII. INJUNCTIVE RELIEF

151. Plaintiffs incorporate all other paragraphs contained in the complaint.

152. Pursuant to the Equal Credit Opportunity Act [15 USC 1691e(c)], and the inherent authority of this Court, appropriate injunctive relief should prohibit further use of the NMAC markup policy, as it presently exists; and/or require NMAC to implement a non-discriminatory dealer compensation system. Plaintiffs suggest that a non-discriminatory system should include all or some of the following:

a. Prohibition of non-risk related finance charge markup; or

b. Alternatively, restrictions limiting markup to a fixed amount for all customers;

c. Alternatively, limitation of markup to a fixed percentage;

d. Disclosure of markup to the customer;

e. ECOA training of NMAC employees;

f. ECOA training for dealer arrangers/originators;

g. Standards regarding the minimum qualifications of persons engaged in arranging/originating NMAC finance transactions;

h. Standards requiring NMAC to monitor and/or audit the racial pattern of markup;

i. Such other injunctive and/or declaratory provisions which eliminate the discriminatory effect of the markup policy and serve the purposes of ECOA.

XXIII. PRAYER FOR RELIEF

WHEREFORE, plaintiffs and the class respectfully request that this Court grant the following relief:

1. Certify this case as a class action and certify the named plaintiffs herein to be adequate class representatives and their counsel to be adequate class counsel;

2. Enter a judgment pursuant to 15 USC 1691e(c) declaring that the acts and practices of defendant complained of herein to be in violation of ECOA;

3. Pursuant to 15 USC 1691e(c), grant a permanent injunction enjoining NMAC from continuing to utilize a credit pricing policy that has a discriminatory impact on African-Americans;

4. Order NMAC, pursuant to 15 USC 1691e(c), to adopt and enforce a credit pricing policy and/or dealer compensation policy without discriminatory effect, and which comply with ECOA;

5. Order disgorgement, pursuant to 15 USC 1691e(c), of all disproportionate non-risk charges imposed on African Americans by NMAC's markup policy; and order the equitable distribution of such charges, as restitutionary relief, to all appropriate class members;

6. Award plaintiffs, pursuant to 15 USC 1691e(d), the costs of this action, including the fees and costs of experts, and reasonable attorneys' fees; and

7. Grant plaintiffs and the Class such other and further relief as this Court finds necessary and proper.

Respectfully Submitted,

Attorneys for Plaintiffs

Sample Discovery

These are sample forms and must be adapted to fit the facts of a particular case and local procedural rules. In addition, effective December 1, 1993, Rule 33(a) of the Federal Rules of Civil Procedure was amended to limit the number of interrogatories to twenty-five including subparts. This limitation may be avoided only by leave of the court with written stipulation of the parties. The reader should be aware of this amendment in cases of federal litigation, and in litigation in sate courts that similarly limit discovery. If permitted, practitioners should also consider seeking a request for admissions as an alternative or supplement to interrogatories. The consumer's attorney should plan for discovery as soon as he or she receives the case.

G.1 Interrogatories for ECOA Adverse Action Notice Violation

IN THE UNITED STATES DISTRICT COURT
FOR THE DISTRICT OF NEW MEXICO

```
————————————————  )
                                 )
THERESA CREDITWORTHY,            )
et al.,                          )
                    Plaintiffs,  )
                                 )
v.                               )
                                 )
K COMPANY, et al.,               )
                    Defendants.  )
————————————————  )
```

PLAINTIFFS' FIRST SET OF INTERROGATORIES TO DEFENDANT K COMPANY

To: K Company
[Address]

You are hereby directed to respond to the following pursuant to Rule 23, Federal Rules of Civil Procedure.

State whether each fact or piece of information supplied in response to each interrogatory is within the personal knowledge of the person responding hereto; if not, state the name, address and position of the person and the location, nature and contents, and custodian of any record from whom or which such facts or information were determined.

1. State the name, business and home address, and position of the person responding hereto on your behalf.

2. For the calendar years 1996, 1997, and 1998 state for each the number of credit applications which were received by you, either as an arranger of credit or as an anticipated extender of credit, regardless of whether said applications were ultimately approved or not.

3. State the date on which you began doing business in Santa Fe, New Mexico as alleged in the Complaint herein, the date on which you began operating from your present location in Santa Fe, New Mexico, and state the locations and the name under which you did business for operations in Santa Fe, New Mexico other than your present one.

4. For the calendar years 1996, 1997, and 1998, state the number of credit applications which you received in your Santa Fe store or office, regardless of whether you received such applications as an arranger of credit or an anticipated extender of credit, and regardless of whether the credit applications were ultimately approved.

5. For the period beginning January 1, 1996 and continuing until the present, state the procedure maintained by you to process credit applications received by you, whether as an arranger of credit or an anticipated extender of credit, detailing step by step the process used by you from its beginning to final conclusion; state whether, during the referenced period of time, these procedures have been changed, and if so, state the date on which the change occurred, the nature of the change, and the reason for the change.

6. State whether, regarding the credit applications which you receive, you attempt to provide to the applicants on whose credit applications adverse action is taken the written notification described in § 202.9(a)(2) of Regulation B; if not, describe in detail and particularly the reason(s) therefore; if so, state what procedures you maintain to ensure that such a notification is so provided, and describe in detail the contents thereof, or attach a copy thereof hereto.

7. For the period beginning two years prior to the filing of the Complaint herein and continuing until thirty days prior to the filing of the Complaint herein, state the names and addresses of all persons who have made credit applications wherein Defendant K Company has been the arranger of credit and Defendant Ace Credit Corporation the anticipated extender of credit, and adverse action has been taken in response to those applications.

8. State the names and addresses of all persons who, from thirty days prior to the filing of the Complaint herein, have made credit applications wherein Defendant K Company has been the arranger

of credit and Defendant Ace Credit Corporation the anticipated extender of credit, and adverse action has been taken in response to those applications.

9. For the persons identified in your answers to the previous two interrogatories, state whether you have retained a copy of the credit applications of those persons, the notification of action taken, and/or the statement of specific reasons for adverse action, and if so state the location of all such records, and the name, address, and position of the custodian thereof; regarding all such persons, state whether you retain any other records regarding them, and if so, identify the nature of those records and the custodian thereof. Regarding all such records, state whether you consent to the inspection and/or copying thereof by undersigned counsel at a time and place of mutual convenience; if not, state the reason(s) therefor, and if so, state the time(s) within two weeks of your filing your Answers hereto and the place within the Santa Fe or Albuquerque, New Mexico environs that you would consent to such inspection and/or copying.

10. State the time, date, and place of any contact between you or an agent, employee or representative of you and the named Plaintiff in this case, Theresa Creditworthy, the name, address and position of each such agent, employee, or representative acting on your behalf, the nature of the contact, the occasion for the contact and the contents of any conversation or remarks made during the contact; state whether there exists any record relevant or related to any such contact, and if so, state with detail and particularity the contents of the record, and the name and address of the custodian thereof, or attach a copy of all such records hereto.

11. Regarding each allegation of the Complaint herein for which you provided in your answer any response other than an unequivocal admission, state the basis on which you failed to so admit it and the steps taken by you by way of inquiry and/or investigation to confirm the truth thereof and the results of such inquiry or investigation.

12. Regarding each affirmative defense stated in your answer, state with detail and particularity the factual basis therefor and all evidence known to you or any person acting on your behalf which supports each such defense.

Respectfully submitted,

Attorney for Plaintiffs

G.2 Interrogatories for ECOA Cosigner Violation

UNITED STATES DISTRICT COURT
SOUTHERN DISTRICT OF FLORIDA

KAY SMART,	)
Plaintiff,	)
	)
v.	)
	)
FAST FINANCE	)
CORPORATION,	)
Defendant.	)

INTERROGATORIES

Pursuant to Rule 33 of the Federal Rules of Civil Procedure, the following interrogatories are addressed to defendant FAST FINANCE CORPORATION by plaintiff, KAY SMART, to be answered under oath by defendant's representative and returned within thirty (30) days.

1. Please state the name(s) and position(s) of the officer(s) or agent(s) of defendant answering each of the following interrogatories.

2. Prior to answering these interrogatories, have you made a diligent search of all books, records and papers in the custody and control of defendant, with the purpose of providing complete and accurate answers to all questions propounded? If so, please identify each such document.

3. Please describe fully the circumstances leading to the making of loan number 11290-6, including answers to the following, with respect to loan 11290-6:

  a. Describe all communications between defendant and the prospective borrower(s) from February 1, 1997 through March 30, 1998 including for each such communication:
    (1) the date(s);
    (2) the name of each employee of defendant involved;
    (3) the name of each prospective borrower involved;
    (4) the content;
    (5) the name of the person who initiated each such communication.

  b. Did the prospective borrower(s) fill out a written application(s) for the extension of credit? If so, please attach a copy(ies).

  c. Identify each person on whom credit information was sought. For each such person, please state whether a credit report was obtained. If so, please attach a copy(ies).

  d. Did Plaintiff's husband, Alfred E. Smart, alone meet defendant's standards of creditworthiness? Please explain fully:
    (1) which credit standards he met;
    (2) which credit standards he did not meet;
    (3) the source and amount of his income relied upon in making the instant extension of credit.

  e. Did Plaintiff Kay Smart, alone, meet defendant's standards of creditworthiness? Please explain fully:
    (1) which credit standards she met;
    (2) which credit standards she did not meet;
    (3) the source and amount of her income relied upon in making the instant extension of credit.

  f. Did defendant require that a cosigner or joint applicant be obtained for the loan? If so, please state:
    (1) who imposed such a requirement;
    (2) why such requirement was imposed;
    (3) the name of the particular cosigner or joint applicant required, if any.

  g. Please attach copies of the note and disclosure statement (front and back sides), chattel mortgage agreement, wage assignment, and any other documents executed in conjunction with the loan transaction.

4. Who was present at the signing of loan 11290-6 and the accompanying documents?

5. When were the credit terms of the loan transaction written on the note and accompanying documents? If March 31, 1997, state

whether prior to or subsequent to the prospective borrower(s)'s arrival at defendant's office.

6. Please describe the criteria by which defendant determines the creditworthiness of an applicant for credit, including:

   (1) copies of any written guidelines;

   (2) a description of the credit scoring system used, if any;

   (3) copies of any policy manuals or instructions provided by defendant to its employees regarding standards of credit-worthiness.

7. If a credit scoring system was used, please state the scores of plaintiff and her former husband.

8. Has defendant distributed to its offices and employees any instructions designed to insure compliance with The Equal Credit Opportunity Act and the regulations promulgated thereunder? If so, please attach copies.

9. From April 1, 1996 to the present for loans transacted in Florida, please state:

   a. The number of loans provided to joint applicants for credit;

   b. Of those loans in subpart (a), for how many loans were the joint applicants spouses?

   c. The number of loans provided to single applicants for credit;

   d. Of those loans in subpart (c), for how many loans was a cosigner required?

   e. Of those loans in subpart (d), for how may loans was the cosigner the spouse of the applicant?

Dated: March 12, 1994.

Attorneys for Plaintiff

G.3 Interrogatories for ECOA "Zip Code Redlining"

IN THE UNITED STATES DISTRICT COURT
FOR THE NORTHERN DISTRICT OF MICHIGAN

LILY APPLICANT,)
      Plaintiff,)
)
v.)
)
OPEC OIL COMPANY,)
      Defendant.)

PLAINTIFF'S FIRST SET OF INTERROGATORIES TO DEFENDANT

Comes now, Lily Applicant, plaintiff herein and pursuant to the Federal Rules of Civil Procedure and 15 U.S.C. § 1691e(i) requires the defendant to answer under oath the following interrogatories within the time and in the manner provided by law.

Note A. When used in these interrogatories, the term "Defendant" or any synonym thereof is intended to and shall embrace and include, in addition to said defendant, all employees, agents, servants, attorneys, representatives, private investigators, and others who are in possession of or may have attained information for or on behalf of defendant.

Note B. These interrogatories shall be deemed continuing so as to require supplemental answers if the defendant or the defendant's attorneys obtain further information between the time answers are served and the time of trial.

1. State the names, titles, addresses and telephone numbers of (a) the head of the credit department or division of defendant, (b) the person or persons who reviewed plaintiff's credit application, and (c) the person or persons who made the decision to deny the plaintiff's credit application.

2. In your reply dated August 20, 1998, to the plaintiff denying her credit card application, you listed as one of the principal reasons for your adverse action: "Our credit experience in your immediate geographical area." In connection with this principal reason for your adverse action, state the exact delineation of the plaintiff's "immediate geographical area" by street names, zip code area or census tract. In lieu of this, you may attach a map of the City of Shangrila outlining in red pencil said "immediate geographical area."

3. From within the plaintiff's "immediate geographical area" as delineated in response to Interrogatory 2, state the following:

   (a) the number of credit card applications received by you since March 23, 1998;

   (b) the number of credit card applications received since March 23, 1998, which you approved;

   (c) the number of credit card applications which you denied since March 23, 1998;

   (d) the date that your "credit experience" in plaintiff's "immediate geographical area" was used as a principal reason for denying credit card applications.

4. Are there any other geographical areas within the Shangrila, Michigan, metropolitan area for which your "credit experience" is used by you since March 23, 1998, as a principal reason for denial of credit card applications? If your answer is affirmative, delineate said areas in the same manner as called for in Interrogatory 2.

5. In connection with your reply to Interrogatory 4, supply the same information as to those geographical areas as provided in response to Interrogatory 3.

6. In connection with your "credit experience" in plaintiff's "immediate geographical area," state in detail what your "credit experience" has been in said area.

7. State the names and titles of the persons who participated in the decision to use plaintiff's "immediate geographical area" as a principal reason for denying credit card applications.

8. Are all credit card applications from within plaintiff's "immediate geographical area" presently denied regardless of other credit factors? If not, state in detail those factors which influence your decision to approve certain applications from within said "geographical area."

9. In your letter of August 20, 1998, denying plaintiff's credit card application, you listed as another principal reason for adverse action the plaintiff's "level of income." In connection therewith, state the following:

   (a) the level of income within the plaintiff's "immediate geographical area" which would warrant approval of a credit card application;

   (b) the level of income outside of plaintiff's "immediate geographical area" and not within a similar such area, which would warrant approval of a credit card application.

10. State the name and address of any credit reporting agency relied upon by you for credit information about the plaintiff's creditworthiness.

11. State what resources of information you relied on in reaching your decision of adverse action on plaintiff's credit application.

12. In your letter of August 20, 1998 denying plaintiff's credit card application, you listed as a principal reason for adverse action the "type of bank references." State what you mean by the term "type of bank references."

13. Did you verify any credit information on the plaintiff's credit card application by checking with the banks listed thereon? If so, what were the replies and identities of the banks?

14. Do you use any credit evaluation system or weighing system in determining whether to grant or deny credit?

15. If so, state the factors and the weight or points given to each factor in connection with your evaluation of and decision on plaintiff's application.

Attorney for Plaintiff

G.4 Request for Production of Documents in Fair Housing Case

UNITED STATES DISTRICT COURT
FOR THE NORTHERN DISTRICT OF ILLINOIS
EASTERN DIVISION

————————————)
)
RUBY HONORABLE, *et al.*,)
         Plaintiffs,)
)
v.   )
) No. 97 C 6009
EASY LIFE REAL ESTATE)
SYSTEM, INC., *et al.*,   )
         Defendants.)
————————————)

PLAINTIFFS' SECOND REQUEST FOR PRODUCTION OF DOCUMENTS TO DEFENDANTS

Plaintiffs, by and through their undersigned counsel, and pursuant to Fed. R. Civ. P. 34, request that defendants Easy Life Real Estate System, Inc., Ace Realtors, Inc., Richard Nelson and Louis Prus ("defendants") produce the following documents within 30 days of service hereof.

INSTRUCTIONS AND DEFINITIONS

Plaintiffs incorporate by reference herein the Instructions and Definitions set forth in Plaintiffs' First Set of Interrogatories to Defendants.

DOCUMENTS REQUESTED

1. All log books reflecting "REO" or "real estate owned" properties offered for sale by any of the defendants.

2. Photographs of all "REO" or "real estate owned" properties offered for sale by any of the defendants.

3. Documents reflecting comparable properties to any "REO" or "real estate owned" property offered for sale by any of the defendants.

4. Documents reflecting any estimate of the cost of repairs to make any "REO" or "real estate owned" property sellable.

5. Documents reflecting the estimated selling price of any "REO" or "real estate owned" property offered for sale by any of the defendants.

6. Documents describing the condition of the immediate area surrounding any "REO" or "real estate owned" property offered for sale by any of the defendants.

7. Documents describing your marketing plan for selling "REO" or "real estate owned" properties.

8. All Multiple Listing Service ("MLS") listings for any property offered for sale by any of the defendants.

9. Documents reflecting your policies, procedures, guidelines, rules or practices regarding retention of documents.

10. Documents reflecting your compensation plan for employees.

11. Documents reflecting your compensation plan for agents and/or brokers.

[Attorneys for Plaintiffs]

Appendix H

Consumer's Guide to Credit Discrimination Laws (Appropriate for Distribution to Clients)

H.1 Introduction

The following information was prepared by federal government regulators to inform consumers about credit discrimination laws. The information can be ordered directly from the relevant agencies. It is also available on-line at:

- Fair housing information can be downloaded from the Department of Housing and Urban Development website, http://www.hud.gov;
- Equal credit opportunity information can be downloaded from the Federal Trade Commission web site, http://www.ftc.gov;
- Rights to fair lending in home mortgages is available on the Federal Reserve Board website, http://www.federalreserve.gov.

H.2 Department of Housing and Urban Development, Fair Housing: It's Your Right

The Fair Housing Act

The Fair Housing Act prohibits discrimination in housing because of:

- Race or color
- National origin
- Religion
- Sex
- Familial status (including children under the age of 18 living with parents or legal custodians; pregnant women and people securing custody of children under 18)
- Handicap (Disability)

What Housing Is Covered?

The Fair Housing Act covers most housing. In some circumstances, the Act exempts owner-occupied buildings with no more than four units, single-family housing sold or rented without the use of a broker, and housing operated by organizations and private clubs that limit occupancy to members.

What Is Prohibited?

In the Sale and Rental of Housing: No one may take any of the following actions based on race, color, national origin, religion, sex, familial status or handicap (disability):

- Refuse to rent or sell housing
- Refuse to negotiate for housing
- Make housing unavailable
- Deny a dwelling
- Set different terms, conditions or privileges for sale or rental of a dwelling
- Provide different housing services or facilities
- Falsely deny that housing is available for inspection, sale, or rental
- For profit, persuade owners to sell or rent (blockbusting) or
- Deny anyone access to or membership in a facility or service (such as a multiple listing service) related to the sale or rental of housing.

In Mortgage Lending: No one may take any of the following actions based on race, color, national origin, religion, sex, familial status or handicap (disability):

- Refuse to make a mortgage loan
- Fail to provide information regarding loans
- Impose different terms or conditions on a loan, such as different interest rates, points, or fees
- Discriminate in appraising property
- Refuse to purchase a loan or
- Set different terms or conditions for purchasing a loan.
  In Addition: It is illegal for anyone to:
  Threaten, coerce, intimidate or interfere with anyone exercising a fair housing right or assisting others who exercise that right
- Advertise or make any statement that indicates a limitation or preference based on race, color, national origin, religion, sex, familial status, or handicap. This prohibition against discriminatory advertising applies to single-family and owner-occupied housing that is otherwise exempt from the Fair Housing Act.

Additional Protection If You Have a Disability

If you or someone associated with you:

- Have a physical or mental disability (including hearing, mobility and visual impairments, chronic alcoholism, chronic mental illness, AIDS, AIDS Related Complex and mental retardation) that substantially limits one or more major life activities

- Have a record of such a disability or
- Are regarded as having such a disability

your landlord may not:

- Refuse to let you make reasonable modifications to your dwelling or common use areas, at your expense, if necessary for the disabled person to use the housing. (Where reasonable, the landlord may permit changes only if you agree to restore the property to its original condition when you move.)
- Refuse to make reasonable accommodations in rules, policies, practices or services if necessary for the disabled person to use the housing.
  Example: A building with a "no pets" policy must allow a visually impaired tenant to keep a guide dog.
- Example: An apartment complex that offers tenants ample, unassigned parking must honor a request from a mobility-impaired tenant for a reserved space near her apartment if necessary to assure that she can have access to her apartment.
- However, housing need not be made available to a person who is a direct threat to the health or safety of others or who currently uses illegal drugs.

Requirements for New Buildings

In buildings that are ready for first occupancy after March 13, 1991, and have an elevator and four or more units:

- Public and common areas must be accessible to persons with disabilities
- Doors and hallways must be wide enough for wheelchairs
- All units must have:
  — An accessible route into and through the unit
  — Accessible light switches, electrical outlets, thermostats and other environmental controls
  — Reinforced bathroom walls to allow later installation of grab bars and
  — Kitchens and bathrooms that can be used by people in wheelchairs.

If a building with four or more units has no elevator and will be ready for first occupancy after March 13, 1991, these standards apply to ground floor units.

These requirements for new buildings do not replace any more stringent standards in State or local law.

Housing Opportunities For Families

Unless a building or community qualifies as housing for older persons, it may not discriminate based on familial status. That is, it may not discriminate against families in which one or more children under 18 live with:

- A parent
- A person who has legal custody of the child or children or
- The designee of the parent or legal custodian, with the parent or custodian's written permission.

Familial status protection also applies to pregnant women and anyone securing legal custody of a child under 18.

Exemption: Housing for older persons is exempt from the prohibition against familial status discrimination if:

- The HUD Secretary has determined that it is specifically designed for and occupied by elderly persons under a Federal, State or local government program or
- It is occupied solely by persons who are 62 or older or
- It houses at least one person who is 55 or older in at least 80 percent of the occupied units, and adheres to a policy that demonstrates an intent to house persons who are 55 or older.

A transition period permits residents on or before September 13, 1988, to continue living in the housing, regardless of their age, without interfering with the exemption.

If You Think Your Rights Have Been Violated

HUD is ready to help with any problem of housing discrimination. If you think your rights have been violated, the Housing Discrimination Complaint Form is available for you to download, complete and return, or complete online and submit, or you may write HUD a letter, or telephone the HUD Office nearest you. You have one year after an alleged violation to file a complaint with HUD, but you should file it as soon as possible.

What to Tell HUD:

- Your name and address
- The name and address of the person your complaint is against (the respondent)
- The address or other identification to the housing involved
- A short description to the alleged violation (the event that caused you to believe your rights were violated)
- The date(s) to the alleged violation

Where to Write or Call:

Send the Housing Discrimination Complaint Form or a letter to the HUD Office nearest you or you may call that office directly.

If You Are Disabled:

HUD also provides:

- A toll-free TTY phone for the hearing impaired: 1-800-927-9275.
- Interpreters
- Tapes and braille materials
- Assistance in reading and completing forms

What Happens When You File A Complaint?

HUD will notify you when it receives your complaint. Normally, HUD also will:

- Notify the alleged violator of your complaint and permit that person to submit an answer
- Investigate your complaint and determine whether there is reasonable cause to believe the Fair Housing Act has been violated
- Notify you if it cannot complete an investigation within 100 days of receiving your complaint

Conciliation

HUD will try to reach an agreement with the person your complaint is against (the respondent). A conciliation agreement must protect both you and the public interest. If an agreement is signed, HUD will take no further action on your complaint. However, if HUD has reasonable cause to believe that a conciliation agreement is breached, HUD will recommend that the Attorney General file suit.

Complaint Referrals

If HUD has determined that your State or local agency has the same fair housing powers as HUD, HUD will refer your complaint to that agency for investigation and notify you of the referral. That agency must begin work on your complaint within 30 days or HUD may take it back.

What If You Need Help Quickly?

If you need immediate help to stop a serious problem that is being caused by a Fair Housing Act violation, HUD may be able to assist you as soon as you file a complaint. HUD may authorize the Attorney General to go to court to seek temporary or preliminary relief, pending the outcome of your complaint, if:

- Irreparable harm is likely to occur without HUD's intervention
- There is substantial evidence that a violation of the Fair Housing Act occurred

Example: A builder agrees to sell a house but, after learning the buyer is black, fails to keep the agreement. The buyer files a complaint with HUD. HUD may authorize the Attorney General to go to court to prevent a sale to any other buyer until HUD investigates the complaint.

What Happens After A Complaint Investigation?

If, after investigating your complaint, HUD finds reasonable cause to believe that discrimination occurred, it will inform you. Your case will be heard in an administrative hearing within 120 days, unless you or the respondent want the case to be heard in Federal district court. Either way, there is no cost to you.

The Administrative Hearing:

If your case goes to an administrative hearing HUD attorneys will litigate the case on your behalf. You may intervene in the case and be represented by your own attorney if you wish. An Administrative Law Judge (ALA) will consider evidence from you and the respondent. If the ALA decides that discrimination occurred, the respondent can be ordered:

- To compensate you for actual damages, including humiliation, pain and suffering.
- To provide injunctive or other equitable relief, for example, to make the housing available to you.
- To pay the Federal Government a civil penalty to vindicate the public interest. The maximum penalties are $10,000 for a first violation and $50,000 for a third violation within seven years.
- To pay reasonable attorney's fees and costs.

Federal District Court

If you or the respondent choose to have your case decided in Federal District Court, the Attorney General will file a suit and litigate it on your behalf. Like the ALA, the District Court can order relief, and award actual damages, attorney's fees and costs. In addition, the court can award punitive damages.

In Addition

You May File Suit: You may file suit, at your expense, in Federal District Court or State Court within two years of an alleged violation. If you cannot afford an attorney, the Court may appoint one for you. You may bring suit even after filing a complaint, if you have not signed a conciliation agreement and an Administrative Law Judge has not started a hearing. A court may award actual and punitive damages and attorney's fees and costs.

Other Tools to Combat Housing Discrimination:

If there is noncompliance with the order of an Administrative Law Judge, HUD may seek temporary relief, enforcement of the order or a restraining order in a United States Court of Appeals.

The Attorney General may file a suit in a Federal District Court if there is reasonable cause to believe a pattern or practice of housing discrimination is occurring.

For Further Information:

The Fair Housing Act and HUD's regulations contain more detail and technical information. If you need a copy of the law or regulations, contact the HUD Office nearest you.

H.3 Federal Trade Commission, Equal Credit Opportunity

FTC FACTS for Consumers

Equal Credit Opportunity

Credit is used by millions of consumers to finance an education or a house, remodel a home, or get a small business loan.

The Equal Credit Opportunity Act (ECOA) ensures that all consumers are given an equal chance to obtain credit. This doesn't mean all consumers who apply for credit get it: Factors such as income, expenses, debt, and credit history are considerations for creditworthiness.

The law protects you when you deal with any creditor who regularly extends credit, including banks, small loan and finance companies, retail and department stores, credit card companies, and credit unions. Anyone involved in granting credit, such as real estate brokers who arrange financing, is covered by the law. Businesses applying for credit also are protected by the law.

When You Apply For Credit, A Creditor May Not...

- Discourage you from applying because of your sex, marital status, age, race, national origin, or because you receive public assistance income.

- Ask you to reveal your sex, race, national origin, or religion. A creditor may ask you to voluntarily disclose this information (except for religion) if

Facts for Consumers

you're applying for a real estate loan. This information helps federal agencies enforce anti-discrimination laws. You may be asked about your residence or immigration status.

- Ask if you're widowed or divorced. When permitted to ask marital status, a creditor may only use the terms: married, unmarried, or separated.

- Ask about your marital status if you're applying for a separate, unsecured account. A creditor may ask you to provide this information if you live in "community property" states: Arizona, California, Idaho, Louisiana, Nevada, New Mexico, Texas, and Washington. A creditor in any state may ask for this information if you apply for a joint account or one secured by property.

- Request information about your spouse, except when your spouse is applying with you; your spouse will be allowed to use the account; you are relying on your spouse's income or on alimony or child support income from a former spouse; or if you reside in a community property state.

- Inquire about your plans for having or raising children.

- Ask if you receive alimony, child support, or separate maintenance payments, *unless* you're first told that you don't have to provide this information if you won't rely on these payments to get credit. A creditor may ask if you have to pay alimony, child support, or separate maintenance payments.

When Deciding To Give You Credit, A Creditor May Not...

- Consider your sex, marital status, race, national origin, or religion.

- Consider whether you have a telephone listing in your name. A creditor *may* consider whether you have a phone.

- Consider the race of people in the neighborhood where you want to buy, refinance or improve a house with borrowed money.

- Consider your age, unless:
  - you're too young to sign contracts, generally younger than 18 years of age;
  - you're 62 or older, and the creditor will favor you because of your age;
  - it's used to determine the meaning of other factors important to creditworthiness. For example, a creditor could use your age to determine if your income might drop because you're about to retire;
  - it's used in a valid scoring system that favors applicants age 62 and older. A credit-scoring system assigns points to answers you provide to credit application questions. For example, your length of employment might be scored differently depending on your age.

When Evaluating Your Income, A Creditor May Not...

- Refuse to consider public assistance income the same way as other income.

- Discount income because of your sex or marital status. For example, a creditor cannot count a man's salary at 100 percent and a woman's at 75 percent. A creditor may not assume a woman of childbearing age will stop working to raise children.

- Discount or refuse to consider income because it comes from part-time employment or pension, annuity, or retirement benefits programs.

- Refuse to consider regular alimony, child support, or separate maintenance payments. A creditor may ask you to prove you have received this income consistently.

You Also Have The Right To...

- Have credit in your birth name (Mary Smith), your first and your spouse's last name (Mary Jones), or your first name and a combined last name (Mary Smith-Jones).

- Get credit without a cosigner, if you meet the creditor's standards.

- Have a cosigner other than your husband or wife, if one is necessary.

- Keep your own accounts after you change your name, marital status, reach a certain age, or retire, unless the creditor has evidence that you're not willing or able to pay.

- Know whether your application was accepted or rejected within 30 days of filing a complete application.

- Know why your application was rejected. The creditor must give you a notice that tells you either the specific reasons for your rejection or your right to learn the reasons if you ask within 60 days. Acceptable reasons include: "Your income was low," or "You haven't been employed long enough." Unacceptable reasons are: "You didn't meet our minimum standards," or "You didn't receive enough points on our credit-scoring system." Indefinite and vague reasons are illegal, so ask the creditor to be specific.

- Find out why you were offered less favorable terms than you applied for — unless you accept the terms. Ask for details. Examples of less favorable terms include higher finance charges or less money than you requested.

- Find out why your account was closed or why the terms of the account were made less favorable unless the account was inactive or delinquent.

A Special Note To Women

A good credit history — a record of how you paid past bills — often is necessary to get credit. Unfortunately, this hurts many married, separated, divorced, and widowed women. There are two common reasons women don't have credit histories in their own names: they lost their credit histories when they married and changed their names; or creditors reported accounts shared by married couples in the husband's name only.

If you're married, divorced, separated, or widowed, contact your local credit bureau(s) to make sure all relevant information is in a file under your own name.

If You Suspect Discrimination...

- Complain to the creditor. Make it known you're aware of the law. The creditor may find an error or reverse the decision.

- Check with your state Attorney General to see if the creditor violated state equal credit opportunity laws. Your state may decide to prosecute the creditor.

- Bring a case in federal district court. If you win, you can recover damages, including punative damages. You also can obtain compensation for attorney's fees and court costs. An attorney can advise you on how to proceed.

- Join with others and file a class action suit. You may recover punitive damages for the group of up to $500,000 or one percent of the creditor's net worth, whichever is less.

- Report violations to the appropriate government agency. If you're denied credit, the creditor must give you the name and address of the agency to contact. While some of these agencies don't resolve individual complaints, the information you provide helps them decide which companies to investigate. A list of agencies follows.

Facts for Consumers

If a retail store, department store, small loan and finance company, mortgage company, oil company, public utility, state credit union, government lending program, or travel and expense credit card company is involved, contact:
Consumer Response Center
Federal Trade Commission
600 Pennsylvania Avenue, NW
Washington, DC 20580

The FTC cannot intervene in individual disputes, but the information you provide may indicate a pattern of possible law violations that require action by the Commission.

If your complaint concerns a nationally-chartered bank (National or N.A. will be part of the name), write to:
Comptroller of the Currency
Compliance Management
Mail Stop 7-5
Washington, DC 20219

If your complaint concerns a state-chartered bank that is insured by the Federal Deposit Insurance Corporation but is not a member of the Federal Reserve System, write to:
Federal Deposit Insurance Corporation
Consumer Affairs Division
Washington, DC 20429

If your complaint concerns a federally-chartered or federally-insured savings and loan association, write to:
Office of Thrift Supervision
Consumer Affairs Program
Washington, DC 20552

If your complaint concerns a federally-chartered credit union, write to:
National Credit Union Administration
Consumer Affairs Division
Washington, DC 20456

Complaints against all kinds of creditors can be referred to:
Department of Justice
Civil Rights Division
Washington, DC 20530

For More Information

The FTC works for the consumer to prevent fraudulent, deceptive and unfair business practices in the marketplace and to provide information to help consumers spot, stop and avoid them. To file a complaint, or to get free information on any of 150 consumer topics, call toll-free, **1-877-FTC-HELP** (1-877-382-4357), or use the complaint form at www.ftc.gov. The FTC enters Internet, telemarketing, and other fraud-related complaints into **Consumer Sentinel**, a secure, online database available to hundreds of civil and criminal law enforcement agencies worldwide.

FEDERAL TRADE COMMISSION	FOR THE CONSUMER
1-877-FTC-HELP	www.ftc.gov

Federal Trade Commission
Bureau of Consumer Protection
Office of Consumer and Business Education

March 1998

H.4 Federal Reserve Board, Home Mortgages: Understanding Your Rights to Fair Lending

Understanding Your Rights to Fair Lending

Federal law protects every homebuyer looking for a mortgage loan against discrimination on the basis of race, color, national origin, religion, sex, marital status, age, receipt of public assistance funds, familial status (having children under the age of 18), handicap, or exercising your rights under other consumer credit protection laws. Lenders may not take any of these factors into account in their dealings with you.

For instance, lenders may not discourage you because of your race or national origin from applying for a mortgage loan. Whatever your color, they must offer you the same credit terms as other applicants with similar loan requests. They may not treat your application differently because of your sex or marital status or familial status. In short, they are barred from taking into account any of the factors listed here in their dealings with applicants or with potential applicants. They should:

- Willingly give you an application and other information you need on how to apply for a loan
- Willingly discuss with you the various mortgage loans they offer and give you an idea whether you can qualify for them
- Diligently act to make a decision—without undue delay— once you provide all the information asked for (including, for example, written evidence of how much you make or how much you have in savings), and once they receive other paperwork required for processing the application (such as a property appraisal)
- Not be influenced by the racial or ethnic composition of the neighborhood where the home you want to buy is located.

If you apply for a mortgage and are turned down, remember that not all institutions have the same lending standards. Shop around for another lender. But if the way you were treated suggests the possibility of unlawful discrimination, you might talk to:

Private fair housing groups

Often these groups can walk you through the mortgage process. They can also help you understand whether your experience suggests that the lender is discriminating unlawfully, and can help you decide whether to file a complaint.

Human rights agencies

These are government agencies set up by a city, county, or state government to deal with discrimination.

Attorneys

They can advise you whether the treatment you received gives you legal grounds for bringing a lawsuit against the lender. They can tell you about monetary damages and other types of relief available to individuals who can prove that illegal discrimination occurred.

Federal or state enforcement agencies

They can check the activities of mortgage lenders to make sure they complied with the laws against lending discrimination. When you write, include your name and address; name and address of the lending institu-tion you are complaining about; address of the house involved; and a short description and the date of the alleged violation.

Federal Laws Against Discrimination in Home Financing

The Fair Housing Act
prohibits discrimination in housing sales or loans on the basis of race, religion, color, national origin, sex, familial status (having children under the age of 18), or handicap.

The Equal Credit Opportunity Act prohibits discrimination in any aspect of a credit transaction on the basis of race, religion, age, color, national origin, receipt of public assistance funds, sex, marital status, or the exercise of any right under the Consumer Credit Protection Act.

Directory of Federal Agencies

The Department of Housing & Urban Developement (HUD) has primary responsibility for implementing the Fair Housing Act.

Office of Fair Housing & Equal Opportunity
Dept. of Housing and Urban Developement
Washington, DC 20410-2000
1-800-424-8590
http://www.hud.gov/complaints/housediscrim.cfm

Other federal agencies monitor compliance by particular types of lenders.

National Banks
Office of the Comptroller of the Currency
Customer Assistance Unit
1301 McKinney St.
Suite 3710
Houston, TX 77010
(800) 613-6743
www.occ.treas.gov

State Member Banks of the Federal Reserve System
Division of Consumer and Community Affairs
Mail Stop 801
Federal Reserve Board
Washington, DC 20551
(202) 452-3693
www.federalreserve.gov

Nonmember Federally Insured State Banks
Federal Deposit Insurance Corporation

Office of Compliance and Consumer Affairs
550 17th Street, N.W.
Room PA-1730, 7th Floor
Washington, DC 20429
(202) 942-3100 or
(800) 934-FDIC (934-3342)
www.fdic.gov

Savings and Loan Associations
Office of Thrift Supervision
Consumer Programs
1700 G Street, N.W., 6th Floor
Washington, DC 20552
(202) 906-6237 or
(800) 842-6929
www.ots.treas.gov

Federal Credit Unions
National Credit Union Administration
Office of Public and Congressional Affairs

1775 Duke St.
Alexandria, VA 22314
(703) 518-6330
www.ncua.gov

Other Lenders
Federal Trade Commission
Consumer Response Center
600 Pennsylvania Avenue, N.W.
Washington, DC 20580
(202) 326-3758 or
(877) FTC-HELP, toll free (877-382-4357)
www.ftc.gov

Department of Justice
Department of Justice
Civil Division
Washington, DC 20530
(202) 514-3301
www.usdoj.gov

Index

References are to sections

COSIGNERS *(Cont.)*
ECOA violations *(Cont.)*
  sample pleadings, Appx. F.2, Appx. F.3
guarantor's spouse, 5.6.8
individual credit, 5.6.2–5.6.5
information requests, 5.5.2
joint accounts, voluntary, 5.6.6
joint property reliance, 5.6.3
joint property security, 5.6.5
renewal of credit, reevaluation, 9.6
voiding obligation, 11.6.5.2

COSTS
see ATTORNEY FEES AND COSTS

COUNTERCLAIMS
defensive counterclaims, 11.7.2
statute of limitations, 11.7.2

COURTESY TITLES
see also NAMES
optional designation, 5.5.5.2.2

CREDIT
see also CREDIT ACCOUNTS; CREDIT TRANSACTIONS
applications, *see* CREDIT APPLICATIONS
arrangers of credit, *see* CREDIT ARRANGERS
defined, 2.2.2.1
denial, *see* ADVERSE ACTION
extension of credit, defined, 2.2.4.1
open-end credit, defined, 9.5.2.1
participant in decision, defined, 2.2.5.4
regularly extends credit, defined, 2.2.5.2

CREDIT ACCOUNTS
see also CREDIT CARDS; CREDIT LIMITS; CREDIT
    TRANSACTIONS
adverse action
  see also ADVERSE ACTION
  authorized users, 10.2.4.2.3
  existing accounts, 10.2.4.2.2
  new accounts, 10.2.4.2.1
applications for, *see* CREDIT APPLICATIONS
approval, notice requirements, 10.2.2
authorized users, *see* AUTHORIZED USERS
binding arbitration, *see* ARBITRATION AGREEMENTS
change in status
  creditor action, rules limiting, 9.5
  discrimination, 9.2.3
joint, *see* JOINT ACCOUNTS
name on
  see also NAMES
  courtesy titles, use, 5.5.5.2.2
  credit reporting, 9.4.2.1
  designation, 5.7
  joint accounts, 5.7
reapplications, status during, 9.5.3
refinancing, joint to individual, 5.6.6
renewal, cosigner reevaluation, 9.6
spouses
  cosignatory requirements, 5.6
  credit reporting, 9.4.2.1
  individual accounts, 5.5.5.3.1, 5.6.2–5.6.5
updated information requests, 9.5.4
use not credit application, 10.2.2

CREDIT APPLICATIONS
see also CREDIT ACCOUNTS; CREDIT TRANSACTIONS
adverse action, *see* ADVERSE ACTION
applicants
  application, necessity, 2.2.4.3
  associational protection, 3.10
  courtesy titles, 5.5.5.2.2
  defined, 2.2.4.1, 2.2.4.3, 5.5.2
  guarantors and sureties as, 2.2.4.2
  information guide, Appx. H
  multiple applicants, 10.2.10
  name designation, 5.7
  previous exercise of CCPA rights, 3.4.4.4
  seeking credit, necessity, 2.2.4.4
approved applications, notice, 10.2.2
automated underwriting systems, 6.3.2.1.3
counteroffers, 10.2.3
defined, 2.2.4.3, 10.2.4.1, 10.2.8.1
discouraging
  pre-application discrimination, 5.3
  procedures, 5.4
ECOA special requirements, 5.5.1
encouraging from minorities not discrimination, 5.3.2.1
evaluation, *see* CREDIT EVALUATION
fat file phenomenon, 5.4.3
HMDA data requirements, 4.4.5
incomplete applications, 10.2.8
  circumstances, 10.2.8.1
  creditor's duty, 10.2.8.1, 10.2.8.2
  notification, 10.2.4.1, 10.2.5, 10.2.8.2
information requests, *see* INFORMATION REQUESTS
information requirements, 5.4.4
inquiries as, 10.2.4.1, 10.2.8.1
insurance redlining, 7.3.3
investigation procedures, 5.4.4, 6.2.2.2
joint applications
  income aggregation, 6.2.2.4
  name designation, 5.7
  voluntariness, 5.6.6
multiple creditors, 10.2.11
notification requirements, *see* NOTICE OF ACTION TAKEN
online communications as, 10.2.4.1
oral applications, 5.4.2
  generally, 5.4.2.1
  home mortgage exception, 5.4.2.2
  notification requirements, 10.2.4.1
pre-application discrimination, 5.3
  marketing, 5.3.2
  pre-screening, 5.3.2.5
  treatment of applicant, 5.3.3
procedures, 5.4
  disparate levels of assistance, 5.4.3
  establishment by creditor, 10.2.8.1
  general rule, 5.4.1
  information requests, 5.4.4
  oral applications, 5.4.2
reapplications, status during, 9.5.3
record retention, 10.3.1
scores, 6.3.2.1.3
withdrawn applications, 10.2.9

CREDIT ARRANGERS
civil liability, 11.3.2
definition, 2.2.5.3.1

References are to sections

PRECEDENT
see CASE LAW

PREDATORY LENDING PRACTICES
discriminatory impact, 8.2.2
generally, 8.2.1
marketing discrimination as a force in, 5.3.2.3
reverse redlining, 8.2
   challenging, 8.3
risk-based pricing, 8.2.3

PREEMPTION
state insurance laws, 7.3.4.3
state laws by ECOA, 11.5.1.3
   age discrimination laws, 6.6.2.3

PRICE DISCRIMINATION
see also REVERSE REDLINING
differential pricing, 12.4.3.6
goods and services, 8.5
   challenging, 8.5.4
   types of discrimination, 8.5.2
markups, 8.4
overages, 8.4, 12.4.3.9
risk-based pricing, 6.4.3.2.3
   subprime market, 8.2.3
tiered-pricing, 8.4

PROMISSORY NOTES
obligations, voiding, 11.6.5.2

PROOF OF DISCRIMINATION
see also EVIDENCE
disparate impact, 4.3
   burdens of proof, 4.3.2
   ECOA standards, 4.3.2.2
   FHA standards, 4.3.2.3
   generally, 4.3.1
   prima facie case, 4.3.2.4
disparate treatment, 4.2
   burden of proof, 4.2.3.1, 4.2.3.2
   circumstantial evidence, 4.2.3
   direct evidence, 4.2.2
   generally, 4.2.1
overview, 4.1
sources of evidence, 4.4
   consumer's records, 4.4.1
   credit reporting agencies, 4.4.3
   creditor's files, 4.4.2
   ECOA monitoring data, 4.4.7
   HMDA data, 4.4.5
   non-mortgage data, 4.4.8
   other mortgage data, 4.4.6
   testers, 4.4.4

PROPERTY AND CASUALTY INSURANCE
see also INSURANCE REDLINING
credit scores, use, 6.4.3.4

PUBLIC ASSISTANCE RECIPIENTS
see also LOW-INCOME PERSONS
credit discrimination
   allowable, 6.6.3
   associational protection, application, 3.10.2
   prohibited base, 3.4.3, 6.5.2.7
   remedies, 1.1.4
credit evaluation, 6.5.2.7

information requests, restrictions, 5.5.5.5
Medicare and Medicaid recipients, status as, 2.2.2.6

PUBLIC UTILITIES
see also UTILITIES
ECOA partial exemption
   credit reporting, 9.4.1
   FRB authority, 2.2.6.4
   generally, 2.2.6.2
   record retention, 10.3.2

PUNITIVE DAMAGES
see also DAMAGES
administrative hearings, 11.6.4.2
arbitration clauses limiting, 11.4.3.4.2
civil rights cases, 11.6.4.2
class actions, 11.2.4
ECOA violations, 11.6.4.3
   actual damages, relationship, 11.6.4.3.3
   creditor's intent, 11.6.4.3.7
   creditor's resources, 11.6.4.3.5
   mandatory, 11.6.4.3.1
   noncompliance frequency and persistence, 11.6.4.3.4
   number of persons affected, 11.6.4.3.6
   other relevant factors, 11.6.4.3.8
   size limits, 11.6.4.3.2
FHA cases, 11.6.4.2
generally, 11.6.4.1
good faith defense, 11.6.4.2

RACIAL DISCRIMINATION
see also MINORITIES
auto financing, sample complaint, Appx. F.5
encouraging minority applications not, 5.3.2.1
home mortgage, sample complaint, Appx. F.1
information requests, prohibited, 5.5.5.1
prohibited bases, 3.3.1, 3.6.1

REAL ESTATE APPRAISALS
see APPRAISAL REPORTS

REAL ESTATE BROKERS
ECOA, application, 2.2.5.3.1
FHA, application, 2.3.2.3.4

REAL ESTATE TRANSACTIONS
see also RESIDENTIAL REAL ESTATE-RELATED
   TRANSACTIONS
Civil Rights Acts, scope, 2.4
discrimination, FHA overview, 1.4.1
FHA scope, 2.3.3
leases, ECOA scope, 2.2.2.2.4

RECORD RETENTION
see also CREDITORS, records; CREDIT HISTORY
business credit, 10.3.2
ECOA requirements, 4.4.7, 10.3
exempt transactions, 10.3.2
home mortgages, 5.4.2.2
inadvertent error, 10.3.6, 11.8.3.2
loan registers, access, 4.4.5
multiple creditors, 10.3.5
oral applications, 5.4.2.1
preservation, 4.4.2, 10.3.1, 10.3.4
prohibited information, 10.3.3
source of evidence, 4.4.2

RECOUPMENT CLAIMS
statute of limitations, 11.7.2

REDLINING
challenging, 7.2
  federal credit and civil rights statutes, 7.2.1
  government enforcement actions, 7.2.2
  other federal and state statutes, 7.2.3
described, 7.1
digital divide, 3.8.2
DOJ enforcement actions, 12.4.3.3
FHA application, 2.3.2.3.3
history of, 7.1
insurance, *see* INSURANCE REDLINING
reverse redlining, *see* REVERSE RELINING
sample interrogatories, Appx. G.3
statutory remedies, 1.1.4
weblining, 7.3.1

REFINANCING
joint accounts, 5.6.6

REGULATION B (FRB)
see also EQUAL CREDIT OPPORTUNITY ACT (ECOA)
electronic notification, interim final rule, 10.2.6.2.1
enforcement, 12.2.2
good faith compliance, 11.8.3.1
history, 1.3.2.3, 1.3.2.4
Official Staff Commentary, *see* OFFICIAL STAFF COMMEN-
  TARY (FRB)
partial exemptions
  business credit, 2.2.6.5
  FRB authority, 2.2.6.4
  government, credit to, 2.2.6.7
  immigration status, 3.3.3.3.1
  incidental consumer credit, 2.2.6.3
  marital status, 3.4.1
  public utilities, 2.2.6.2
  securities credit, 2.2.6.6
precedent and authority, 1.3.3.1
proposed revisions, 1.3.2.3, 1.3.3.1, 2.2.4.3, 4.4.8, 5.5.4,
  10.2.4.1, 10.3.1
text, Appx. B

REGULATIONS
ECOA, *see* REGULATION B (FRB)
FHA, *see under* FAIR HOUSING ACT

REGULATORY AGENCIES
ECOA enforcement authority, 12.2.3
fair lending enforcement policies, 12.2.4

RELIGIOUS DISCRIMINATION
information requests, prohibited, 5.5.5.1
prohibited base, 3.3.2

REMEDIES
arbitration agreements limiting, 11.4.3.4
attorney fees, *see* ATTORNEY FEES AND COSTS
credit discrimination
  available, 11.5.1.2
  selecting, 11.6
damages, *see* DAMAGES
election of remedies, 11.5.2, 11.6.7
equitable relief, *see* EQUITABLE RELIEF
FHA complaint procedure, 11.4.2.2
government enforcement, *see* GOVERNMENT ENFORCEMENT

overview of private remedies, 11.6.1
private actions, *see* LITIGATION
recoupment claims, 11.7.2
statutory remedies
  effective uses, 1.1.4
  generally, 1.1.2
  utilization, 1.1.3

RENT-TO-OWN TRANSACTIONS
ECOA scope, 2.2.2.2.5

RESIDENTIAL LEASES
see also LEASES
Civil Rights Acts, scope, 2.4
discrimination, FHA overview, 1.4.1
ECOA scope, 2.2.2.2.4
FHA scope, 2.3.3.1.1, 2.3.3.2

**RESIDENTIAL REAL ESTATE-RELATED TRANSAC-
  TIONS**
see also HOME EQUITY LOANS; HOME IMPROVEMENT
  CREDIT; HOME MORTGAGES; REAL ESTATE
  TRANSACTIONS
appraisal report, right to copy, 10.2.12
defined, 2.3.2.1
FHA overview, 1.4.1
FHA scope, 2.3.2
  arrangers and financial assisters, 2.3.2.3.1
  brokers and appraisers, 2.3.2.3.4
  creditors, 2.3.2.3
  dwelling purchase or improvement, 2.3.2.2.1
  generally, 2.3.2.1
  home equity loans, 2.3.2.2.2
  home improvement loans, 2.3.2.2.1
  home purchase loans, 2.3.2.2.1
  makers of loans, 2.3.2.3.2
  purchasers of loans, 2.3.2.3.3

RESOLUTION TRUST CORPORATION (RTC)
special defenses, 11.8.3.4

RETIREMENT INCOME
see also AGE DISCRIMINATION; ELDERLY PERSONS
credit evaluation, 6.5.2.5

REVERSE REDLINING
see also REDLINING
challenging, 8.3
defined, 8.1
DOJ enforcement actions, 12.4.3.8
remedies, 1.1.4

SALES
goods and services, *see* GOODS AND SERVICES
point of sale activity, *see* POINT OF SALE ACTIVITY
post-sale service, *see* POST-SALE SERVICE
real estate, *see* REAL ESTATE TRANSACTIONS

SAVINGS INSTITUTIONS
Community Reinvestment Act (CRA) applicability, 1.9

SECURITIES CREDIT TRANSACTIONS
ECOA partial exemptions
  cosigner rule, 5.6.1
  credit reporting, 9.4.1
  generally, 2.2.6.6
  name exemption, 5.7
  record retention, 10.3.2

SECURITY DEPOSITS
discriminatory practices, 5.8.1
injury caused by discrimination, 5.8.2

SECURITY INTERESTS
see also COLLATERAL
discriminatory practices, 5.8
joint property, signature restrictions, 5.6.5
voiding cosigner's or guarantor's obligation, 11.6.5.2

SELF-EVALUATION
agency enforcement policies, 12.2.4
statutory requirements, 1.3.2.6, 1.4.2

SELLERS
see also MERCHANTS
dwellings, FHA application, 2.3.3

SENIORS
see ELDERLY PERSONS

SEX DISCRIMINATION
see also SEXUAL ORIENTATION
courtesy titles, use, 5.5.5.2.2
familial status, relationship, 3.5.1
history, 1.3.2.1, 1.3.2.4
income sources, 6.5.2.6
information requests, restrictions, 5.5.5.2.1
names, use, 5.7
prohibited base, 3.3.4
remedies, 1.1.4

SEXUAL ORIENTATION
credit discrimination
    prohibited base, 3.7
    remedies, 1.1.4
marital status discrimination, relationship, 3.4.1

SIGNATORIES
see COSIGNERS

SPECIAL PURPOSE CREDIT PROGRAMS
ECOA compliance, 3.9.3
ECOA exception
    cosigner rule, 5.6.1
    generally, 3.9.1
    information requests, 5.5.6.4
    qualifications, 3.9.2

SPOT DELIVERY
ECOA notice violations, 10.2.3.3

SPOUSES
see also COMMUNITY PROPERTY; COSIGNERS; JOINT
        PROPERTY; MARITAL STATUS
cosignatory requirements, restrictions, 5.6
    obligation, voiding, 11.6.5.2
credit history, 6.5.3
    avoiding spouse's bad history, 6.5.3.3
    minimal, supplementing, 6.5.3.2
credit reporting, 9.4.2.1
family expense laws, 9.3
guarantors, of, signature restrictions, 5.6.8
individual credit rights, 5.6.2–5.6.5
information requests, restrictions, 5.5.5.3, 5.5.5.4
name, use, 5.7

STANDING
associational standing, 11.2.3

class actions, 11.2.4
FHA, 2.3.5, 11.2.1
    non-profit organizations, 11.2.2.3
    testers, 11.2.2.2
generally, 11.2.1
non-profit organizations, 11.2.2
testers, 11.2.2

STATE LAW
actions, limitations, 11.7.1.4
credit discrimination laws
    consumer's guide, Appx. H
    federal preemption, 6.6.2.3, 11.5.1.3
    insurance, 7.3.4.4
    overview, 1.7
    redlining, 7.2.3
    scope, 2.5, 2.6
    statute of limitations, 11.7.1.4
    summary, Appx. E
    violation as UDAP violation, 1.8
damages, *see* DAMAGES
ECOA preemption of, 11.5.1.3
    age laws, 6.6.2.3
    family expense laws, 9.3
enforcement, 12.5
NCLC manual, using, 1.2.4
overview, 1.7
prohibited bases for discrimination
    age, 3.4.2
    familial status, 3.5.1
    geographic location, 7.2.3
    handicapped status, 3.5.2
    marital status, 3.4.1
    national origin, 3.3.3
    public assistance status, 3.4.3
    race and color, 3.3.1
    religion, creed, political affiliation, 3.3.2
    sex, 3.3.4
    sexual orientation, 3.7
property laws affecting creditworthiness, 6.6.4, 9.3
redlining, challenging, 7.2.3
    insurance redlining, 7.3.4.4
remedies
    election of remedies, 11.5.2, 11.6.7
    statutory damages, 11.6.3
    UDAP, *see* UNFAIR AND DECEPTIVE ACTS AND
        PRACTICES (UDAP)
    UNIP, *see* UNFAIR INSURANCE PRACTICES (UNIP)

STATISTICS
see also MONITORING DATA
use as evidence
    census data, 4.4.6
    disparate impact, 4.3.2.4.3

STATUTE OF LIMITATIONS
affirmative actions
    advantages of various claims, 11.5.1.2
    civil rights claims, 11.7.1.3
    ECOA claims, 11.7.1.1
    FHA claims, 11.7.1.2
    state law claims, 11.7.1.4
defensive counterclaims, 11.7.2
recoupment claims, 11.7.2

References are to sections

Quick Reference to the Consumer Credit and Sales Legal Practice Series

References are to sections in *all* manuals in NCLC's Consumer Credit and Sales Legal Practice Series.

This Quick Reference pinpoints where to find specific consumer law topics analyzed in the NCLC manuals. References are to individual manual or supplement sections from the National Consumer Law Center's Consumer Credit and Sales Legal Practice Series. For more information on other volumes, see *What Your Library Should Contain* at the beginning of this volume.

This Quick Reference is a speedy means to locate key terms in the appropriate NCLC Manual. More detailed indices are found at the end of the individual NCLC volumes. The detailed contents pages at the beginning of each volume provide further elaboration once the appropriate manual is identified by use of this Quick Reference.

All pleadings and most statutory and regulatory appendices are also available from NCLC on CD-Roms that accompany the specified volume. **NCLC strongly recommends that those searching for pleadings refer to *Consumer Law Pleadings on CD-Rom*, and not to this *Quick Reference*.**

CLP2	=	Consumer Law Pleadings Number Two (1995)
CLP1	=	Consumer Law Pleadings Number One (1994)
COC	=	The Cost of Credit: Regulation and Legal Challenges (2d ed. 2000 and 2002 Supp)
CD	=	Credit Discrimination (3d ed. 2002)
FCRA	=	Fair Credit Reporting Act (4th ed. 1998 and 2001 Supp)
FDC	=	Fair Debt Collection (4th ed. 2000 and 2002 Supp)
Repo	=	Repossessions and Foreclosures (4th ed. 1999 and 2001 Supp)
Stud	=	Student Loan Law (2001)
TIL	=	Truth in Lending (4th ed. 1999 and 2001 Supp)
UDAP	=	Unfair and Deceptive Acts and Practices (5th ed. 2001 and 2002 Supp)
Warr	=	Consumer Warranty Law (2d ed. 2001 and 2002 Supp)

Abbreviations

AUS	=	Access to Utility Service (2d ed. 2001)
Auto	=	Automobile Fraud (1998 and 2001 Supp)
Arbit	=	Consumer Arbitration Agreements (2d ed. 2002)
CBPL	=	Consumer Banking and Payments Law (2d ed. 2002)
Bankr	=	Consumer Bankruptcy Law and Practice (6th ed. 2000 and 2001 Supp)
CCA	=	Consumer Class Actions: A Practical Litigation Guide (5th ed. 2002)
CLP7	=	Consumer Law Pleadings Number Seven (2001)
CLP6	=	Consumer Law Pleadings Number Six (2000)
CLP5	=	Consumer Law Pleadings Number Five (1999)
CLP4	=	Consumer Law Pleadings Number Four (1998)
CLP3	=	Consumer Law Pleadings Number Three (1997)

Abandonment of Apartment Building in Bankruptcy—Bankr § 17.8.2
Abbreviations Commonly Used by Debt Collectors—FDC App M
Abuse of Process—UDAP § 5.1.4; FDC § 10.6
Acceleration—COC §§ 5.6.2, 5.7.1; Repo § 4.1
Accessions—Repo § 3.5.3.2
Accord and Satisfaction—CBPL § 1.7.3
Account Aggregation—CBPL § 4.10
Accountants—UDAP § 5.12.8
Accrediting Agencies, Student Loans—Stud § 9.4.1.2
Accurate Information in Consumer Reports—FCRA § 9.10
Actual Damages—*See* Damages
Actuarial Rebates—COC § 5.6.3.4
Adhesion Contracts—UDAP § 5.2.3
Adjustable Rate Mortgages—TIL § 4.6.4; COC § 4.3.6
Administration of Lawsuit, Class Action—CCA Ch 13; CLP1
Admissibility of Other Bad Acts—Auto § 9.7.1.1
Advertisements as Warranties—Warr § 3.2.2.5
Advertising by Attorneys on the Internet—CLP4 Ch 10
Advertising Credit Terms—TIL §§ 5.13, 9.4
Affordability Programs, Utilities—AUS Ch 9, App F
After-Acquired Property—Repo § 3.4.5.2
Age Discrimination re Credit—CD § 3.4.2
Airline Fare Advertising—UDAP §§ 2.5, 5.4.13.1
Alteration of Checks—CBPL § 1.2
Alimony Discharged in Bankruptcy—Bankr § 14.4.3.5

References are to sections in *all* manuals in NCLC's Consumer Credit and Sales Legal Practice Series

References are to sections in *all* manuals in NCLC's Consumer Credit and Sales Legal Practice Series

References are to sections in *all* manuals in NCLC's Consumer Credit and Sales Legal Practice Series

References are to sections in *all* manuals in NCLC's Consumer Credit and Sales Legal Practice Series

About the Companion CD-Rom

CD-Rom Supersedes All Prior CD-Roms

This CD-Rom supersedes the 2001 CD accompanying *Credit Discrimination* (2d ed. 1998 and Supp.) and any other CDs and disks accompanying earlier supplements to or editions of this title. Discard the 2001 CD and any other disks. This 2002 CD-Rom contains everything found on the earlier disks and contains much additional material.

What Is on the CD-Rom

This CD-Rom features:

- Text of the ECOA, Fair Housing Act, Federal Civil Rights Acts, Community Reinvestment Act, Home Mortgage Disclosure Act, Americans with Disabilities Act, and summaries of state credit discrimination statutes;
- Regulation B, proposed changes, Interim Reg. B on electronic disclosures, Official Staff Commentary to Reg. B;
- HUD Regulations, Reg. C and Interpretations, including two 2002 amendments, technical changes, and a delayed implementation date, Reg. BB and proposed Reg. BB changes;
- 9 sample complaints;
- 7 sample discovery requests;
- 14 voir dire questions, jury instructions and other jury trial documents;
- 4 sets of class pleadings;
- 7 attorney fee documents;
- 8 other pleadings;
- 9 complaint and consent decrees in Department of Justice Cases and 2 DOJ amicus briefs;
- 3 consumer guides to credit discrimination;
- Consumer education brochures;
- The Table of Contents to this and all other NCLC manuals;
- An Index to the manual and the Quick Reference to the complete series; and
- Acrobat Reader 5.

How to Use the CD-Rom

The CD's pop-up menu quickly allows you to use the CD—just place the CD into its drive and click on the "Start (CD Home Page)" button that will pop-up in the middle of the screen. You can also access the CD by clicking on a desktop icon that you can create using the pop-up menu.[1]

All the CD-Rom's information is available in PDF (Acrobat) format, making the information:

- Highly readable (identical to the printed pages in the book);
- Easily navigated (with bookmarks, "buttons," and Internet-style forward and backward searches);
- Easy to locate with keyword searches and other quick-search techniques across the whole CD-Rom; and
- Easy to paste into a word processor.

While much of the material is also found on the CD-Rom in word processing format, we strongly recommend you use the material in PDF format, not only because it is easiest to use, contains the most features, and certain material is only available in PDF format, but also because you can easily switch back to a word processing format when preferred.

Acrobat Reader 5 comes free of charge with the CD-Rom. **We strongly recommend that new Acrobat users read the Acrobat tutorial on the Home Page. It takes two minutes and will really pay off.**

How to Find Documents in Word Processing Format

The CD-Rom presents several options to find documents in word processing format, if that is preferred to the PDF format for a certain task. One option is simply to open a document on the CD-Rom from your standard word processing program, which can be WordPerfect, Word, or any other program released since 1989. All word processing documents are in the D:\WP_Files directory—if "D" is your

---

1 Alternatively, click on the D:\Start.pdf file on "My Computer" or open that file in Acrobat—always assuming "D" is the CD-Rom drive on your computer.

CD-Rom drive.[2] Each document in that directory corresponds to an appendix in the book, and is named in the directory accordingly.

Another option is to navigate the CD in PDF format, and, when a particular document is on the screen, click on the corresponding bookmark for the "WordPerfect version of . . ." This will automatically run WordPerfect for Windows, MS Word, or *any other word processor* that is associated with the ".WPD" extension, and then open the word processing file that corresponds to the Acrobat document on the screen.[3]

Important Information Before Opening the CD-Rom Package

Before opening the CD-Rom package, please read this information. Opening the package constitutes acceptance of the following described terms. In addition, the *book* is not returnable once the seal to the *CD-Rom* has been broken.

The CD-Rom is copyrighted and all rights are reserved by the National Consumer Law Center, Inc. No copyright is claimed to the text of statutes, regulations, excerpts from court opinions, or any part of an original work prepared by a United States Government employee.

You may not commercially distribute the CD-Rom or otherwise reproduce, publish, distribute or use the disk in any manner that may infringe on any copyright or other proprietary right of the National Consumer Law Center. Nor may you otherwise transfer the disk or this agreement to any other party unless that party agrees to accept the terms and conditions of this agreement. You may use the disk on only one computer and by one user at a time.

The CD-Rom is warranted to be free of defects in materials and faulty workmanship under normal use for a period of ninety days after purchase. If a defect is discovered in the disk during this warranty period, a replacement disk can be obtained at no charge by sending the defective disk, postage

prepaid, with information identifying the purchaser, to National Consumer Law Center, Publications Department, 77 Summer Street, 10th Floor, Boston, MA 02110. After the ninety-day period, a replacement will be available on the same terms, but will also require a $15 prepayment.

The National Consumer Law Center makes no other warranty or representation, either express or implied, with respect to this disk, its quality, performance, merchantability, or fitness for a particular purpose. In no event will the National Consumer Law Center be liable for direct, indirect, special, incidental, or consequential damages arising out of the use or inability to use the disk. The exclusion of implied warranties is not effective in some states, and thus this exclusion may not apply to you.

System Requirements

Use of this CD-Rom requires a Windows-based PC with a CD-Rom drive. (MacIntosh users report success using NCLC CDs, but the CD has only been tested with Windows-based PCs.) The CD-Rom's features are optimized with Acrobat Reader 5 (2002), which is included free on this CD-Rom—you should install Acrobat Reader 5 even if you already have an earlier version of Acrobat. Much of the material on the CD-Rom can also be used with any word processor released after 1989.

One-Time Installation

When the CD-Rom is inserted in its drive, a menu will pop up automatically. (Please be patient if you have a slow CD-Rom drive; this will only take a few moments.) First, if you have not already installed Acrobat Reader 5, click on the "Install Acrobat Reader" button. Do not reboot, but then click on the "Make Shortcut Icon" button. (You need not make another shortcut icon if you already have done so for another NCLC CD.) Then reboot.

[*Note*: if the pop-up menu fails to appear, go to "My Computer," click on "D," if that is the CD-Rom drive, and then double click on "Read_Me.txt" for alternate installation and use instructions.]

---

2 The CD-Rom drive could be any letter following "D" depending on your computer's configuration.

3 For instructions on how to associate MS Word to the ".WPD" extension, go to the CD-Rom's home page and click on "Word-processing Files on CD."